To Barb, my partner and my love—
for showing me happiness that money can't buy

Vice President, Business, Economics, and UK Courseware: Donna Battista
Director of Portfolio Management: Adrienne D'Ambrosio
Senior Portfolio Manager: Kate Fernandes
Editorial Assistant: Caroline Fenn
Vice President, Product Marketing: Roxanne McCarley
Product Marketer: Kaylee Carlson
Product Marketing Assistant: Marianela Silvestri
Manager of Field Marketing, Business Publishing: Adam Goldstein
Executive Field Marketing Manager: Thomas Hayward
Vice President, Production and Digital Studio, Arts and Business: Etain O'Dea
Director of Production, Business: Jeff Holcomb
Managing Producer, Business: Alison Kalil
Content Producer: Meredith Gertz
Operations Specialist: Carol Melville
Design Lead: Kathryn Foot
Manager, Learning Tools: Brian Surette
Content Developer, Learning Tools: Sarah Peterson
Managing Producer, Digital Studio and GLP, Media Production and Development: Ashley Santora
Managing Producer, Digital Studio: Diane Lombardo
Digital Studio Producer: Melissa Honig
Digital Studio Producer: Alana Coles
Digital Content Team Lead: Noel Lotz
Digital Content Project Lead: Miguel Leonarte
Project Manager: Heidi Allgair, Cenveo® Publisher Services
Interior Design: Cenveo® Publisher Services
Cover Design: Cenveo® Publisher Services
Cover Art: Mazuryk Mykola/123RF
Printer/Binder: LSC Communications, Inc./Willard
Cover Printer: Phoenix Color/Hagerstown

Acknowledgments of third-party content appear on the appropriate page within the text or as follows:

p. 3: Quotes from TV sitcom, *How I Met Your Mother,* by Bob Saget, Twentieth Century Fox; p. 5: quote from Carl Sandburg, *The Complete Poems of Carl Sandburg,* Houghton Mifflin Harcourt, 2003; p. 14: Woody Allen quote from *The Elision Fields,* William Safire, August 13, 1989; p. 16: quotes from the movie *Arthur,* 1981, Metro Goldwyn Mayer (MGM); p. 16: quote from philosopher Arthur Schopenhauer in *The Wisdom of Life;* p. 60: quotes from "Dr. Evil," portrayed by Mike Myers in the movie *Austin Powers, International Man of Mystery;* p. 136: quote from Neil Patrick Harris as host of the 65th Emmy Awards; p. 376: Warren Buffett quote from "Omaha's Plain Dealer," *Newsweek,* April 1, 1985, p. 56; p. 386: Warren Buffett quote from Berkshire Hathaway Inc.; p. 391: Denzel Washington quote from "Rebel with Applause," *Daily Mail,* December 14, 2006, retrieved from http://www.dailymail.co.uk/home/moslive/article-421624/Rebel-Applause.html; p. 411: Warren Buffett quote from Berkshire Hathaway Inc.; p. 415: Warren Buffett quote from "Despite Setbacks, Drexel Still Calls Shots in 'Junk Bond' Revolution" by David A. Wise, *The Washington Post,* April 17, 1988; p. 434: quotes from Tracy Morgan in *30 Rock,* copyright © by NBC Universal; p. 458: Warren Buffett quote from his speech given at Harvard, 1988; p. 467: quotes from *Dilbert* comic strips, July 07, 1992 and April 17, 1995, United Features Syndicate; p. 470: quote from Paul A. Samuelson, "The Long-Term Case for Equities," *The Journal of Portfolio Management,* copyright © 1994 by Institutional Investor; p. 478: Don Philips quote from *U.S. News & World Report,* July 08, 1996; p. 507: quote from TV show *Friends* in the episode "The One with George Stephanopoulos" written by Alexa Junge.

Cataloging-in-Publication Data is available on file at the Library of Congress.

2 18

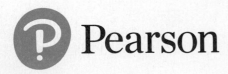

Pearson

ISBN 10: 0-13-473036-4
ISBN 13: 978-0-13-473036-3

Using proven, field-tested technology, auto-graded **Excel Projects** allow instructors to seamlessly integrate Microsoft Excel® content into their course without having to manually grade spreadsheets. Students have the opportunity to practice important **finance skills** in Excel, helping them to master key concepts and gain proficiency with the program.

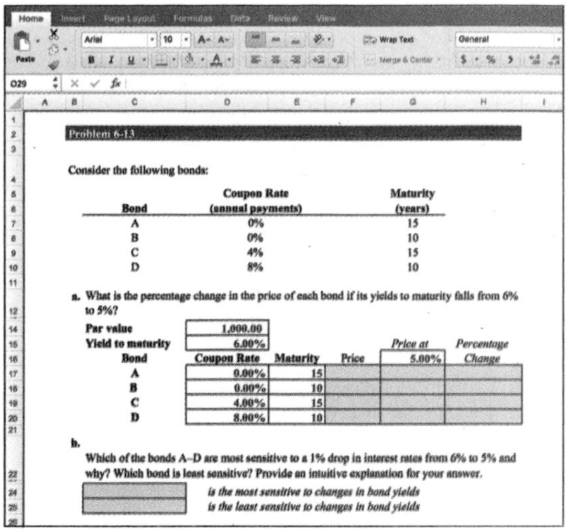

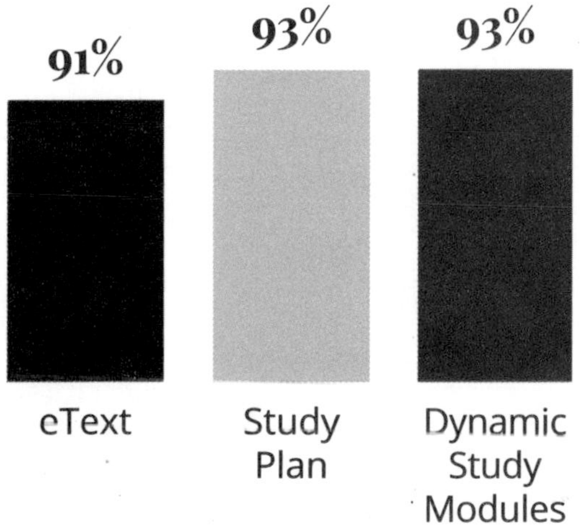

% of students who found learning tool helpful

Dynamic Study Modules help students study chapter topics effectively on their own by continuously assessing their **knowledge application** and performance in real time. These are available as graded assignments prior to class, and accessible on smartphones, tablets, and computers.

Pearson eText enhances student learning—both in and outside the classroom. Take notes, highlight, and bookmark important content, or engage with interactive lecture and example videos that bring learning to life (available with select titles). Accessible anytime, anywhere via MyLab or the app.

The **MyLab Gradebook** offers an easy way for students and instructors to view course performance. Item Analysis allows instructors to quickly see trends by analyzing details like the number of students who answered correctly/incorrectly, time on task, and median time spend on a question by question basis. And because it's correlated with the AACSB Standards, instructors can track students' progress toward outcomes that the organization has deemed important in preparing students to be **leaders.**

88%

of students would tell their instructor to keep using MyLab Finance

For additional details visit: www.pearson.com/mylab/finance

Personal Finance

Turning Money into Wealth

Eighth Edition

Arthur J. Keown

Virginia Polytechnic Institute and State University
Alumni Distinguished Professor and R.B. Pamplin Professor of Finance

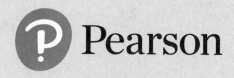

Pearson

New York, NY

The Pearson Series in Finance

Berk/DeMarzo
*Corporate Finance**
*Corporate Finance: The Core**

Berk/DeMarzo/Harford
*Fundamentals of Corporate Finance**

Brooks
*Financial Management: Core Concepts**

Copeland/Weston/Shastri
Financial Theory and Corporate Policy

Dorfman/Cather
Introduction to Risk Management and Insurance

Eakins/McNally
Corporate Finance Online

Eiteman/Stonehill/Moffett
*Multinational Business Finance**

Fabozzi
Bond Markets: Analysis and Strategies

Foerster
*Financial Management: Concepts and Applications**

Frasca
Personal Finance

Haugen
The Inefficient Stock Market: What Pays Off and Why
Modern Investment Theory

Holden
Excel Modeling in Corporate Finance
Excel Modeling in Investments

Hughes/MacDonald
International Banking: Text and Cases

Hull
Fundamentals of Futures and Options Markets
Options, Futures, and Other Derivatives

Keown
*Personal Finance: Turning Money into Wealth**

Keown/Martin/Petty
*Foundations of Finance: The Logic and Practice of Financial Management**

Madura
*Personal Finance**

McDonald
Derivatives Markets
Fundamentals of Derivatives Markets

Mishkin/Eakins
Financial Markets and Institutions

Moffett/Stonehill/Eiteman
*Fundamentals of Multinational Finance**

Pennacchi
Theory of Asset Pricing

Rejda/McNamara
Principles of Risk Management and Insurance

Smart/Gitman/Joehnk
*Fundamentals of Investing**

Solnik/McLeavey
Global Investments

Titman/Keown/Martin
*Financial Management: Principles and Applications**

Titman/Martin
Valuation: The Art and Science of Corporate Investment Decisions

Weston/Mitchell/Mulherin
Takeovers, Restructuring, and Corporate Governance

Zutter/Smart
*Principles of Managerial Finance**
*Principles of Managerial Finance—Brief Edition**

***denotes titles with** MyLab Finance.

Log onto www.pearson.com/mylab/finance to learn more.

About the Author

Arthur J. Keown is an Alumni Distinguished Professor and the R. B. Pamplin Professor of Finance at Virginia Polytechnic Institute and State University. He received his bachelor's degree from Ohio Wesleyan University, his MBA from the University of Michigan, and his doctorate from Indiana University. An award-winning teacher, he is a member of the Academy of Teaching Excellence at Virginia Tech, he has received five Certificates of Teaching Excellence, the W. E. Wine Award for Teaching Excellence, and the Alumni Teaching Excellence Award, and in 1999 he received the Outstanding Faculty Award from the State of Virginia. In 2016, he was named to be one of 10 Alumni Distinguished Professors on campus and the first and only Alumni Distinguished Professor in the Pamplin College of Business. Professor Keown is widely published in academic journals. His work has appeared in *Journal of Finance, Journal of Financial Economics, Journal of Financial and Quantitative Analysis, Journal of Financial Research, Journal of Banking and Finance, Financial Management, Journal of Portfolio Management,* and many others. Two of his books are widely used in college finance classes all over the country—*Financial Management* and *Foundations of Finance: The Logic and Practice of Financial Management.* Professor Keown is a Fellow of Decision Sciences Institute and served as Department Head for twelve years. In addition, he has served as the co-editor of both the *Journal of Financial Research* and the Financial Management Association's *Survey and Synthesis Series.* He was recently inducted into Ohio Wesleyan's Athletic Hall of Fame for wrestling. His daughter and son are both married and live in Houston, Texas, and on Jeju Island in South Korea, while he and his wife live in Blacksburg, Virginia, where he collects original art from *Mad* magazine.

Brief Contents

Contents

Preface

New to This Edition

Since the last edition of *Personal Finance: Turning Money into Wealth*, a lot has changed in the world of personal finance, and much of this is driven by the economic turmoil resulting from the recent crash of the financial markets and the worst downturn in the economy since the Great Depression. While employment has recovered, many individuals left the workforce because they were unable to find jobs; interest rates are near all-time lows and just now starting to rise; housing prices dropped and then recovered, but not evenly; consumer debt (including mortgage debt) reached $12.25 trillion, more than doubling since 2000; and student loans have continued to rise at an alarming rate and now tops $1.44 trillion, with over 11 percent of those student loan balances over 90 days delinquent or in default. While the Federal Reserve and the government have made a number of changes aimed at bringing about stability in the financial markets, the economy has had a difficult time regaining its footing. If that wasn't enough in the way of changes, the Affordable Care Act was almost dismantled, but even with the proposed legislative changes, much of it would continue to stand. As you will see, the entire book is updated to reflect the recent changes in the area of financial planning, including possible tax changes, new laws, the ever-changing investments landscape, the explosion of student loans, and credit card challenges facing graduating students, as well as other changes in the world of personal finance. In addition, when legislative changes impacting topics in this book happen, they, along with their implications for personal finance, will be made available in a companion website available at **www.pearsonhighered.com/keown/**. In short, because of these continuous and fast-paced changes occurring in the personal finance landscape, little remains exactly as it was in the previous edition. Some of the more dramatic changes to the new edition include the following revisions.

All text discussions and figures, tables, and facts have been updated to accurately reflect exciting developments in the field of finance in the last three years. Specific highlights include the following:

- **New Love & Money Feature.** Even before reading this book and taking this class you have probably realized that the way you approach personal finance has a huge impact on many different areas of your life. Certainly it will affect your ability to buy a house, your investment success, and whether or not you are able to retire early and comfortably, but it also can have just as big an impact on your love life and other personal relationships. While there is no question that money problems can cause tension in relationships, there is also no reason why it has to be this way. As you might expect, while there are some things that you simply shouldn't do when it comes to handling your money and making personal financial decisions if you want your relationships to thrive, there are also some actions you can take to keep money from sabotaging your relationships. In the Love & Money boxes, we'll not only take a look at people's attitudes towards and thinking about money and love, we'll also give you some personal finance advice aimed at helping you build better, stronger, and perhaps lasting relationships.

LOVE & MONEY

With over $1.4 trillion in student debt carried by over 40 million Americans, it seems like everyone has student debt these days. So it doesn't cause any damage to your love life, does it? Well, according to a recent TD Ameritrade survey, it does. In fact, 26 percent of those surveyed said they would be less likely to date someone with student debt. That's not as bad as we saw for credit card debt in the last chapter, but it's still substantial.

As we all know, student debt can be enormous—even reaching above $100,000. In fact, the average U.S. household with student debt owes about $49,042. It shouldn't come as any surprise that student debt can derail your love life. After all, marrying someone who owes close to $50,000 can present challenges. But why might student debt be a deal breaker? The question here is whether it was taken on as part of a bigger plan: For example, was it the only way you could realistically attend college and get that degree so that you could get the job you really aspired to, or was it simply a result of carelessness and bad financial habits? That being said, you can see why the answers to these questions are so critically important:

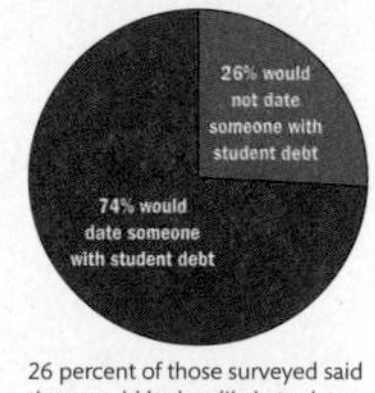

26 percent of those surveyed said they would be less likely to date someone with student debt.

Just as student loans can have a negative impact on your love life, any substantial debt can also do serious damage. NerdWallet recently polled millennials (those between 18 and 34 years old) and found that 38 percent brought auto loan debt into their new relationship, while 27 percent brought medical debt. So what's the answer? If you're bringing student or other types of debt into a relationship, what should you do?

BEHAVIORAL INSIGHTS

PRINCIPLE 9

Principle 9: Mind Games, Your Financial Personality, and Your Money While much of this book deals with saving money, much of this chapter looks at spending it—and spending it intelligently, using the smart buying process. Do you think you are a smart buyer? You are at your local mall shopping for a sweater for your dad's birthday. Ever find yourself wishing you had a calculator? How fast can you figure out what 25 percent off of $52.00 is? Would you make your "decision to purchase" faster if the seller just said "$13.00 off these sweaters today"? *Hint:* 25 percent of $52.00 is $13.00!

- **Expanded Coverage of Behavioral Finance.** Each chapter ends with a section titled "Behavioral Insights—Principle 9: Mind Games, Your Financial Personality, and Your Money." These boxes have been updated and expanded and serve not only to highlight how behavioral biases can sabotage financial well-being but also to demonstrate how an understanding of these biases can be used to avoid destructive financial behavior. In addition, we discuss how recognizing these behavioral biases can lead to better financial decisions. For example, acknowledgment of the psychological/behavioral patterns or mind games that come into play when making financial decisions may help students avoid excessive credit card and student loan debt, save more for retirement, and make better investment decisions now and in the future.
- **Increased Emphasis on the Use of the Internet and Apps for Smartphones.** This edition continues to increase emphasis on the use of apps for smartphones and the best of the Internet where appropriate. For example, the Mvelopes, Quapital, Mint.com and Level Money apps are easily installed on a smartphone and are both introduced and described when discussing budgeting, saving for your goals, and record keeping. These apps make tedious tasks easy—and, if you can imagine, fun. Apps and the best of personal finance Web sites on the Internet are also introduced when discussing credit cards, student loans, insurance, investments, and retirement planning.
- **Updated Coverage of Investments.** The Dow Jones Industiral Average has more than tripled since March 2009! This has brought about changes in basic investments and asset allocation decisions. These changes are reflected in Chapters 11 and 12. In addition, how information on investment alternatives is gathered has changed quite a bit since the previous edition – these changes are reflected in Chapter 11.
- **Updated Coverage of Bonds and the Bond Market.** While the stock market climbed dramatically since the great recession, interest rates have moved down slightly, with long-term rates reaching historical low levels. Since asset allocation decisions involve deciding how much to invest in stocks versus bonds, the impact of low interest rate on bonds is examined in Chapter 13 along with the inverse relationship between bond prices and interest rates – that is, when market interest rates rise, the value of a bond that is owned falls. This is not only examined, but the implications for asset allocation decisions are also developed and discussed.
- **Updated and Expanded Coverage of ETFs.** Chapter 14 has been retitled to "Mutual Funds and ETFs: An Easy Way to Diversify," to reflect the increased emphasis on ETFs in this chapter. Today, over $2.5 trillion is invested in ETFs, and ETFs are growing at an ever-increasing rate. Because ETFs are increasingly used as a tool for diversification by allowing investors to take an instant position in a sector or country with very low costs, they now play an increased role in the asset allocation process of investors.

Solving Teaching and Learning Challenges

Once, not that long ago, a fundamental background in financial planning and investments was not necessary for most university students. Financial instruments were not overly complex; students did not have access to numerous, high-limit credit cards which enabled them to amass significant personal debt almost effortlessly; and a college education did not involve much in the way of student loans. In addition, in an earlier age of relatively high, full-time, and stable employment, retirement planning was easy: your long-term employer basically did it for you. In such a period, financial explanations, expectations, and communications were generally straightforward, realistic, and clear. And that—by and large—has changed. Today, we are living in a world where financial instruments are increasingly complex and require a higher level of financial literacy. At an early age students are asked to make financial decisions as to how they will finance their college experience. This includes choosing between various types of student loans and even how much they will need to borrow, which will impact them for years to come. Once they graduate they will face consumer loan decisions when buying a car, furniture, appliances or even stereo equipment that involve making decisions on single-payment versus installment loans, secured versus unsecured loans, variable rate versus fixed-rate loans, as well as a decision on the maturity of the loan. Similarly, deciding on a mortgage to buy a house involves choices of not only how much to borrow, but also how to select from among the different loan structures with fixed rate, variable rate, and interest-only loans, each one having different implications for the borrower's financial future. This complexity also extends to life insurance. When the time is right to get our first life insurance policy, most of us do not seek it out—instead, someone approaches us, convinces us it's important, and then we buy it. Because insurance has a language all its own, it is often difficult to understand all of the subtle differences between one policy and another, and to know how much to buy – once again, financial literacy is the key to making good financial decisions. Finally, just 30 years ago retirement meant taking a pension from your employer and letting Social Security pick up any slack. Not anymore. Thanks to the recent drive to cut spending, employers tend not to provide pensions, and those that still do have reduced them to as little as possible. That leaves a lot of slack for Social Security, and given the unsustainability of those promised benefits from Social Security coupled with the government's drive to cut its own spending, it is likely that the Social Security system that our students see upon their retirement will not be the same one we have now, and that is also true for Medicare. Today's students will have to rely on self-directed retirement plans, 401k and IRA accounts, where they not only decide how much to save, but also how to invest that money – decisions requiring a knowledge of investing terms and tools – with the results of those decisions determining whether they have a retirement of leisure or nightmare. In effect, our students must not only know how much they will need for retirement, but they must also have a solid grounding in the terms, tools and rules of investing in order to reach their financial goals and avoid the pitfalls that might upend their financial future. The bottom line is that everyone must take responsibility for their own retirement, and the earlier that process begins, the easier it becomes.

For many students, the Personal Finance course is their initial and only exposure to personal finance, so it is important that the material is presented in a way that leaves a lasting impression. Tools, techniques, and equations are easily forgotten, but the logic and fundamental principles that drive their use, once understood, will remain and will become part of each student's "financial personality." *Personal Finance: Turning Money into Wealth*, Eighth Edition, empowers students, through the presentation of the ten fundamental principles of personal finance, to successfully make and carry out a plan for their financial future. Throughout the rest of their lives, students will have the ability to draw on these principles, which will help them effectively deal with an ever-changing financial environment.

Some of the features used to overcome teaching and learning challenges include:

- **The Ten Principles of Personal Finance.** Each chapter of the text touches back on the ten principles introduced in Chapter 1 and shows how to apply these principles to particular situations.

FIGURE 7.4 College Savings Plans Comparison

	529 College Savings Plan	529 Prepaid Tuition Plan	Coverdell Educational Savings Account
Who Owns It?	Contributor	Contributor	Contributor
What Can I Invest In?	Typically, plans provide several investment options.	Purchase units or credits at participating school.	No restrictions.
When Can It Be Used?	No age limit.	Plan may set age or grade limits.	No contributions can be made after beneficiary turns age 18, and withdrawals must be made before beneficiary turns 30. An exception is made for special needs children.
What Expenses Are Covered Besides Tuition and Fees?	Qualified education expenses for postsecondary education.	Only tuition and mandatory fees for postsecondary education are covered. Few exceptions are made.	Qualified elementary and secondary education expenses or qualified postsecondary education expenses.

- **Extensive Coverage of Student Loans and Paying for College, Covering Almost Half of Chapter 7.** This chapter, titled "Student and Consumer Loans: The Role of Planned Borrowing," gives students an in-depth look at the world of student loans to help untangle the complexities and jargon associated with them and facilitate good decision-making practices.
- **Personal Finance Worksheets.** Companion worksheets are available for this text that provide a step-by-step analysis of many of the personal finance decisions examined in the book. Instructors can assign them as homework or use them to guide students through actual decisions. Icons in the text indicate content areas, as well as cases and problems that utilize the worksheets. The worksheets are available in MyLab Finance at **http://www.pearson.com/mylab/finance** and at the Instructor's Resource Center at **http://www.pearsonhighered.com/irc**.
    - **Your Financial Plan.** This series of exercises available in MyLab Finance at **www.pearson.com/mylab/finance** utilize the worksheets and generate a very basic financial plan to explore where students are today, where they want to be in the future, and what they need to do to get there. Also included is a section on how to use a financial calculator.

CHECKLIST 13.1 Picking a Good Bond

- ☐ **Think about the effect of taxes.** Consider municipals, particularly if you're in a high tax bracket.
- ☐ **Keep the inverse relationship between interest rates and bond prices in mind.** If interest rates are very low, the only way they can go is up (which would cause bond prices to drop), so you might want to invest in shorter-term bonds.
- ☐ **If you're buying a corporate bond, avoid losers.** Look for and avoid firms that might experience major financial problems. All other firms are pretty much the same.
- ☐ **Limit yourself to bonds rated AA or above.** In this way, you minimize any worry regarding a possible default by the issuer.
- ☐ **Buy your bond when it's first issued rather than in the secondary market.** The price is generally fair, and the sales commission on a newly issued bond is paid by the issuer.
- ☐ **Avoid bonds that might get called.** Before you buy a bond, ask your broker or financial planner if the bond is likely to be called. If so, pick another one.
- ☐ **Match your bond's maturity to your investment time horizon.** In this way, you can hold the bond to maturity and avoid having to sell in the secondary market, where you don't always get a fair price.
- ☐ **Stick to large issues.** If you think you might have to sell before maturity and are buying a corporate bond, make sure you buy a bond issued by a large corporation—the secondary market is generally more active for them.
- ☐ **When in doubt, go Treasury!** If you're still unsure, it's better to be safe than sorry—buy a Treasury bond.

- **Easy-to-Follow Advice.** The proactive checklists, which appear throughout the text, serve as useful learning tools for students. These boxes identify areas of concern and propose questions to ask when buying a car, getting insurance, and investing in mutual funds, as well as performing other personal finance tasks.

LO3 Calculate the value of a bond and understand the factors that cause bond value to change.

Evaluating Bonds

Not only do you need to know bond terms and what kinds of bonds there are, but also you need to know how to evaluate them. That means understanding what a bond yield and a rating are and knowing how to read a bond quote on the Internet or in the newspaper.

Bond Ratings—A Measure of Riskiness

John Moody first began to rate bonds in 1909. Since that time, two major rating agencies—Moody's and Standard & Poor's—have provided ratings on thousands of corporate, city, and state bonds. These ratings involve a judgment about the future risk potential of a bond—specifically, its default risk, or the chance that the issuer may not be able to meet its obligation to pay interest or repay the principal sometime in the future.

- **Learning Objectives.** Each chapter opens with a set of action-oriented learning objectives. As these objectives are covered in the text, an identifying icon appears in the margin.

- **Stop and Think.** These short boxes provide students with insights as to what the material actually means—its implications and the big picture.

STOP & THINK

Look closely at the expenses and fees charged for managing a mutual fund before investing–their impact can be significant. Look, for example, at a mutual fund with an expense ratio of 1.3 percent (the average expense ratio for an actively managed equity fund–that is, a non-index mutual fund–is around 1.25 percent) versus one with an expense ratio of 0.05 percent. If you put $25,000 in both of these funds, each returning 10 percent compounded over the next 25 years, you'd end up with a not so insignificant $64,000 more in the lower-expense fund. In choosing a mutual fund, what would you look for?

- **Discussion Cases.** Each chapter closes with a set of at least two mini-cases that provide students with real-life problems that tie together the chapter topics and require a practical financial decision.

Discussion Case 1

This case is available in MyLab Finance.

Maria will be a college sophomore next year, and she is determined to have her own credit card. She will not be employed during the school year but is convinced that she can pay for credit card expenses based on her summer earnings. Maria's parents have read a number of articles about the problems of credit cards and college students, including examples of students leaving school after a downward spiral of obtaining credit cards, overspending, working to pay bills, worrying about bills, working more hours to pay bills, and eventually withdrawing from school. When Maria showed up with a handful of applications, including Visa, a Gold MasterCard, Discover, a Visa sponsored by her university, an American Express, a secured MasterCard, and a gas company card, her parents were overwhelmed. Maria admitted she didn't want them *all*. "I'm not stupid," she declared. Since Maria obviously needed to learn about credit cards, her parents agreed to cosign her application on one condition. She had to approach her choice just as she would a class project and research the following questions.

Questions

1. Assuming Maria does not really care about her parents' approval and ignores their assignment, will she be able to receive a credit card without their help? Would your answer change if Maria was a graduating senior?

- **Continuing Case of Cory and Tisha Dumont.** The book is divided into five parts, and at the end of each part, a Continuing Case provides an opportunity to synthesize and integrate the many different financial concepts presented in the book. It gives students a chance to construct financial statements, analyze a changing financial situation, calculate taxes, measure risk exposure, and develop a financial plan.

Continuing Case: Cory and Tisha Dumont

PART I: Financial Planning

The objective of the Continuing Case is to help you synthesize and integrate the various financial planning concepts you have been learning. The case will help you apply your knowledge of constructing financial statements, assessing financial data and resources, calculating taxes, measuring risk exposures, creating specific financial plans for accumulating assets, and analyzing strengths and weaknesses in financial situations.

At the end of each book part, you'll be asked to help Cory and Tisha Dumont answer their personal finance questions. By the end of the book, you'll know more about Cory and Tisha than you can imagine. Who knows—maybe you have encountered, or will encounter, the same issues that the Dumonts face. After helping the Dumonts answer their questions, perhaps you will be better equipped to achieve your own financial goals!

- **Behavioral Insights—Principle 9: Mind Games, Your Financial Personality, and Your Money.** Each chapter has a new section devoted to examining the impact of various behavioral traits and biases that we all share and that contribute to an individual's "financial personality." This exploration of patterns of thought and behavior offers insights as to why and how people sometimes make illogical or irrational personal finance decisions.

> **ACTION PLAN**
>
> **Principle 10: Just Do It!** It may seem like a long way off, but now is the time to begin saving for retirement. Here are some tips. PRINCIPLE 10
>
> ◆ **Don't procrastinate.** Remember how the time value of money works: The longer your investment time horizon is, the more your money grows. For example, if you're 22 and plan on retiring at 67, you could begin funding your Roth IRA at

◆ **Action Plan—Principle 10: Just Do It!** Each chapter ends with concise directions encouraging students to put into play the personal finance lessons learned in that chapter.

◆ **Ten Financial Life Events.** The concepts and tools in this book are all tied together in Chapter 17, the final chapter, by examining ten financial life events. Here students will gain a broad perspective on and an overview of the ways personal finance affects almost all parts of their lives. Students will clearly see that in the course of a lifetime they will experience many events that will change their goals, affect their financial resources, and create new financial obligations or opportunities. While there are many life-changing events, we focus on ten of the most common, such as getting married, having a child, and retiring. With each one, we present a comprehensive, step-by-step discussion of how to respond to it—pulling material from throughout the book and tying it all together into an action plan.

> MyLab Finance Video
>
> **Calculator Clues**
>
> **Solving for *N*—the Number of Payments**
>
> Solving for the number of payments using a financial calculator is simple. To solve for *N*, enter the known variables and solve. In this example, how many years will it take for $7,752 to grow to $20,000 at 9 percent?
>
> | | | | | | |
> |---|---|---|---|---|---|
> | Enter | | 9 | −7,752 | 0 | 20,000 |
> | | N | I/Y | PV | PMT | FV |
> | Solve for | 10.998 | | | | |
>
> The answer is 10.998, or about 11 years. You'll notice we gave the present value, $7,752, a negative sign and the future value, $20,000, a positive sign. Why? Because a calculator looks at cash flows as if it were a bank. You deposit your money in the bank (and the sign is negative because the money "leaves your hands"); then later you take your money out of the bank (and the sign is positive because the money "returns to your hands"). As a result, every problem will have a positive and a negative sign on the cash flows.

◆ **Author Videos.** Author videos help students master difficult material while ensuring that the material provides a long-lasting impact. To this end, when Calculator Clues and other mathematical topics are presented in the book, they are accompanied by videos that present the calculations in a very deliberate and intuitive way. These videos are identified in the text with MyLab Finance Video and can be accessed in **MyLab Finance** at **http://www.pearson.com/mylab/finance.**

MyLab Finance

Reach every student by pairing this text with MyLab Finance MyLab is the teaching and learning platform that empowers you to reach *every* student. By combining trusted author content with digital tools and a flexible platform, MyLab personalizes the learning experience and improves results for each student. Learn more about MyLab Finance at **http://www.pearson.com/mylab/finance**.

Deliver trusted content You deserve teaching materials that meet your own high standards for your course. That's why Pearson partners with highly respected authors to develop interactive content and course-specific resources that you can trust—and that keep your students engaged.

Empower each learner Each student learns at a different pace. Personalized learning pinpoints the precise areas where each student needs practice, giving all students the support they need—when and where they need it—to be successful.

Teach your course your way Your course is unique. So whether you'd like to build your own assignments, teach multiple sections, or set prerequisites, MyLab gives you the flexibility to easily create *your* course to fit *your* needs.

Improve student results When you teach with MyLab, student performance improves. That's why instructors have chosen MyLab for over 15 years, touching the lives of over 50 million students.

Developing Financial Life and Employability Skills

There is no question that everyone needs strong personal finance skills to thrive in today's world. This book is intended to provide you with those skills. While your newly acquired personal finance skills will help you achieve the retirement you want, they also may help you find a job and move up the ladder. A recent study conducted by the Society for Human Research Management found that 47 percent of U.S. companies run credit background checks on potential employees, and the skills acquired from this book will help you to pass that background check with flying colors. In addition, studies have shown that employees with financial problems have difficulties performing on the job. So while at first glance you may not think this book will help you get a job and then advance in your career, you're wrong. This book will do it all in a sense, help you in both your personal and professional life.

Table of Contents Overview

Personal Finance, Turning Money into Wealth provides students with a fundamental background in financial planning and investments with an emphasis on intuitive understanding of the concepts and tools so that when financial decisions have to be made in the future, the student has a strong conceptual framework from which to make those decisions.

Part 1	**Financial Planning**	
	1 The Financial Planning Process	Introduces the financial planning process; discusses its importance; describes the steps of personal financial planning; how to set your goals; how career management and education can determine your income; and how the skills acquired in this course will help you get a job and advance in it.
	2 Measuring Your Financial Health and Making a Plan	Examines the budgeting and planning process which involves measuring our wealth using a personal balance sheet; using a personal income statement to track where money comes from and where it goes; using ratios to monitor our financial health and setting up and implement a cash budget.
	3 Understanding and Appreciating the Time Value of Money	Introduces the concept of the time value of money, both providing the student with an intuitive understanding of it and the ability to move money through time with applications to personal finance.
	4 Tax Planning and Strategies	Provides an understanding of how taxes are imposed; what strategies can be used to reduce them; and what role tax planning plays in personal financial planning. In addition, while the tax documentation in this chapter was current at the time of publication, it can change at any time. To deal with any possible changes in the tax code, updates are provided at **www.pearsonhighered.com/keown**. In addition, the author-produced videos called out in this chapter (available at **www.pearson.com/mylab/finance**) and included in the etext version of the book will explain any tax changes as well as the implications of those changes.
Part 2	**Managing Your Money**	
	5 Cash or Liquid Asset Management	Examines cash management; how to automate your savings; choosing a financial institution; deciding among the various cash management alternatives; comparing rates; establishing a checking account; and how ETFs work.
	6 Using Credit Cards: The Role of Open Credit	Examines how credit cards work; the cost of credit; the different types of credit cards; determining your credit card worthiness; and how to manage your credit cards.
	7 Student and Consumer Loans: The Role of Planned Borrowing	Provides a clear understanding of your choices and costs with respect to consumer loans; how to get the best rate on your consumer loans; controlling your debt; and using student loans and paying for college.
	8 The Home and Automobile Decision	Analyzes smart buying and the home and auto decision.
Part 3	**Protecting Yourself with Insurance**	
	9 Life and Health Insurance	Demonstrates the importance of insurance; determining life insurance needs; major types of insurance coverage; the health insurance decision; how disability insurance works; and the purpose of long-term care insurance.
	10 Property and Liability Insurance	Introduces homeowner's and automobile insurance and how to file a claim and recover on a loss.

Part 4	Managing Your Investments	
	11 Investment Basics	Provides an overview of investing by examining setting goals; the intuition behind risk and return and asset allocation; efficient markets; primary and secondary markets; and finding investment information.
	12 Investing in Stocks	Introduces common stocks and how to value them along with a look at their historical risks and returns.
	13 Investing in Bonds and Other Alternatives	Describes bonds; bond valuation and yields; why bonds fluctuate in value; preferred stock and its valuation; and investing in real estate.
	14 Mutual Funds: An Easy Way to Diversify	Introduces mutual funds, ETFs, and investment trusts; the calculation of their returns; and how to select a mutual fund that is right for you.
Part 5	**Life Cycle Issues**	
	15 Retirement Planning	Develops an understanding of the challenges of retirement planning; the steps in setting up a retirement plan; the different types of retirement plans; payment choices; and how to put a plan together and monitor it.
	16 Estate Planning: Saving Your Heirs Money and Headaches	Examines the estate planning process; drafting a will; and avoiding probate.
	17 Financial Life Events—Fitting the Pieces Together	Ties things to together by examining the importance of starting to plan and save early; recognizing different financial life events with strategies to deal with them; understanding the keys to financial success; and dealing with debt in the real world.

Instructor Teaching Resources

This program comes with the following teaching resources.

Supplements available to instructors at www.pearsonhighered.com/irc	Features of the Supplement
Instructor's Manual authored by Sonya Britt of Kansas State University	• Chapter-by-chapter summaries • Chapter Context, offering insight into how the chapter integrates with the other chapters in that part and the entire text • Chapter Outlines of the concepts and terms to assist with chapter reviews • Applicable Principles, offering an explanation of the principles in the order they appear in the chapter • Suggested Projects, offering a sampling of projects that can be assigned as in-class group activities or as homework to increase the applied understanding of key concepts from the chapter • Sample solutions for all end-of-chapter questions, problems, and cases.
Test Bank authored by Brian Hart of Virginia Polytechnic Institute and State University	50 to 75 multiple-choice, true/false, short- answer, and essay questions per chapter with these annotations: • Difficulty level (1 for straight recall, 2 for some analysis, 3 for complex analysis) • Type (Multiple-choice, true/false, short-answer, essay) • Topic (The term or concept the question supports) • Learning outcome • AACSB learning standard (Ethical Understanding and Reasoning; Analytical Thinking Skills; Information Technology; Diverse and Multicultural Work; Reflective Thinking; Application of Knowledge)
Computerized TestGen	TestGen allows instructors to: • Customize, save, and generate classroom tests • Edit, add, or delete questions from the Test Item Files • Analyze test results • Organize a database of tests and student results.
PowerPoints authored by Sonya Britt of Kansas State University	Slides include all the graphs and tables from the textbook. PowerPoints meet accessibility standards for students with disabilities. Features include, but not limited to: • Keyboard and Screen Reader access • Alternative text for images • High color contrast between background and foreground colors

Acknowledgments

I gratefully acknowledge the assistance, support, and encouragement of those individuals who have contributed to *Personal Finance: Turning Money into Wealth.* Specifically, I wish to recognize the extremely helpful insights provided by many of my colleagues. For their careful comments and helpful reviews of this edition, I would like to thank:

Brenda Eichelberger, Portland State University
Christine Haririan, Bloomsburg University
Amelia Karraker, Iowa State University
Erika Lipka, Epicenter St Petersburg College
Olga McAtee, Ball State University
Tammi Metz, Mississippi State University
Ron Pearson, Bay College
Tyler Smith, Baylor University

I would also like to thank those who have provided very helpful insights in past editions. For their comments and reviews, I would like to thank:

Allen Arnold, University of Central Oklahoma
Mike Barry, Boston College
Karin Bonding, University of Virginia
Craig Bythewood, Florida Southern College
Ronald J. Cereola, James Madison University
Stephen Chambers, Johnson County Community College
Lynda S. Clark, Maple Woods Community College
Michael Collins, University of Wisconsin–Madison
Bobbie D. Corbett, Northern Virginia Community College
Charles P. Corcoran, University of Wisconsin–River Falls
Julie Cumbie, University of Central Oklahoma
Kathy J. Daruty, Los Angeles Pierce College
Howard Davidoff, Brooklyn College
Caitlin DeSoye, Bentley University and University of New Hampshire
Richard A. Deus, Sacramento City College
Yuhong Fan, Weber State University
Beverly Fuller, Portland State University
Caroline S. Fulmer, University of Alabama
Michael Gordinier, Washington University in St. Louis
Ramon Griffin, Metropolitan State College of Denver
Jack Griggs, Abilene Christian University
Carolyn M. Hair, Wake Tech. Community College
Neil D. Holden, Ohio University
Marilynn E. Hood, Texas A&M University
Joe Howell, Salt Lake Community College
Randal Ice, University of Central Oklahoma
Robert Jensen, Metropolitan Community Colleges
Ernest W. King, University of Southern Mississippi
Katherine Kocher, University of Central Oklahoma
Sophie Kong, Western Washington University
Karen Korins, University of Northern Colorado
Edward Krohn, Miami–Dade Community College

Thomas Krueger, Texas A&M University–Kingsville
Karen Lahey, University of Akron
Frances Lawrence, Louisiana State University
K. T. Magnusson, Salt Lake Community College
James E. Mallett, Stetson University
Abbas Mamoozadeh, Slippery Rock University of Pennsylvania
Robert B. McCalla, University of Wisconsin–Madison
James A. Milanese, University of North Carolina, Greensboro
Mitch Mokhtari, University of Maryland
Diann Moorman, University of Georgia
Dianne R. Morrison, University of Wisconsin–LaCrosse
James Muckell, Nyack College
Frederick H. Mull, Fort Lewis College
David W. Murphy, Madisonville Community College
David Overbye, Keller School of Management
James E. Parco, Colorado College
Eve Pentecost, University of Alabama
Oscar J. Solis, Virginia Tech
Ted Pilger, Southern Illinois University
Jack Popovich, Columbus State Community College
Robert Rencher, Liberty University
Irving E. Richards, Cuyahoga Community College
Greg Richey, California State University, San Bernardino
Bill Rives, Ohio State University
Clarence Rose, Radford University
Pat Rudolph, American University
Nick Sarantakes, Austin Community College
Daniel L. Schneid, Central Michigan University
Thomas M. Springer, Florida Atlantic University
Kevin Sullivan, Virginia Tech
James C. Thomas, Indiana University Northwest
Shafi Ullah, Broward Community College
Sam E. Veit, University of Wisconsin–Madison
Dick Verrone, University of North Carolina Wilmington
Sally Wells, Columbia College
Alex White, Virginia Tech
Martha A. Zenns, Jamestown Community College

I would like to thank a wonderful group of people at Pearson Education. I must thank the Vice President of Business Publishing, Donna Battista, who has provided leadership from the top and has kept all the parts moving. Donna has transformed the finance list at Pearson, making it the best in the industry, and in doing so has helped make this book live up to its potential. I would also like to thank Kate Fernandes, my editor, who has been great to work with. Under Kate's guidance, I believe we have produced the finest possible textbook and supplements package. Kate is truly creative, insightful, and demanding—never settling for anything but the best. I also thank Meredith Gertz, who served as the content producer on this revision. She has been great to work with, continuously offering insights and direction and often serving as a sounding board for revisions and new ideas. Meredith was fun to work with, always keeping me on task. It seemed that a day did not go by when I didn't call her for advice or help on something. In addition, I owe a debt of gratitude to Alison Kalil, managing producer—business publishing, who made this a much better book. Miguel Leonarte, who worked on MyLab Finance, also deserves a word of thanks for making MyLab Finance flow so seamlessly with the book. He has continued to refine and improve MyLab Finance, and as a result of his efforts, it has become a learning tool without equal.

I should also thank Paul Donnelly and David Cohen. Paul is a past editor and good friend, without whom this project would never have been started. Dave once served as the developmental editor and helped mold this book into a text that is fun to read. My thanks also go to Heidi Allgair of Cenveo® Publisher Services, who teamed with Pearson as project manager to oversee the book's complex production process while keeping it all on schedule and maintaining extremely high quality.

My appreciation to the people at Pearson would be incomplete without mention of the highly professional Pearson field sales staff and their managers. In my opinion, they are the best in the business, and I am honored to work with them. In particular, I must single out Bill Beville, retired national editorial advisor. He is one of the most dogged and delightful people I have ever met. Bill pursued me relentlessly until I agreed to do this book. I will always owe Bill a debt of gratitude. Bill, I'm glad you're on my side.

I also owe a great debt to Sonya Britt, an assistant professor of family studies and human services at Kansas State University and founding president of the Financial Therapy Association. In addition to preparing the PowerPoint slides and revising the Instructor's Manual, Sonya oversaw the revision of the end-of-chapter material. In doing so, she went well beyond the call of duty by refining, revising, and simplifying the end-of-chapter material and thereby greatly improving it. Her efforts made a meaningful impact on the book—strengthening it and making it more user friendly—and, as a result, she has improved the student experience. In addition, Sonya was always there to provide advice and opinions, which greatly improved this edition of the book. Moreover, she's one of the nicest and hardest-working individuals I have ever worked with. I am hoping this is a relationship that will carry on long into the future.

I must also thank Brian Hart at Virginia Tech. He not only prepared the Test Bank but also provided excellent insights into the behavioral aspects of personal finance that were incorporated into the book. In addition, Alex White at Virginia Tech provided excellent comments and help with the ethics cases.

I also express sincere gratitude to the accuracy checker, Brian Nethercutt, who meticulously reviewed the Eighth Edition textbook and the Test Bank.

Finally, I must extend my thanks to my friend and colleague Ruth Lytton. While her role on this edition was limited, her efforts in the past helped produce the outstanding cases and end-of-chapter material currently in the book. Because she is a perfectionist and an award-winning teacher, her efforts result in a pedagogy that works. When working with Ruth, I am constantly in awe of her effortless grasp of the many aspects of personal finance and of her ability to make complex concepts accessible to any student. She is truly one of the "gifted ones." Her suggestions and insights made a profound impact on the book, from start to finish, and greatly added to its value.

In past editions, Derek Klock joined Ruth in working on the case and end-of-chapter material. Derek is exceptional! If you can think of a trait you would like a coworker to have, Derek has it. On top of all that, he is one of the nicest people I have ever had the opportunity to work with.

As a final word, I express my sincere thanks to those using *Personal Finance: Turning Money into Wealth* in the classroom. I thank you for making me a part of your team.

Arthur J. Keown

PART 1 Financial Planning

It's easy to avoid thinking about financial planning—after all, sometimes just financial existence seems like a victory. The problem is that by avoiding financial planning, you are actually creating more financial problems for your future. It's just too easy to spend money without thinking—it's saving money and planning that take some thought and effort. The problem is that most of us have no background in financial planning.

Part 1: Financial Planning will begin your introduction to personal finance. We will present some of the personal finance problems you will face in the future, along with a five-step process for budgeting and planning. You will also be introduced to ten fundamental principles of personal finance in Chapter 1 that reappear throughout the book. While the tools and techniques of personal finance may change or be forgotten over time, the logic that underlies these ten principles, once understood, will become part of your "financial personality," and you will be able to draw upon these principles for the rest of your life.

In Part 1, we will focus on the first four principles:

Principle 1: The Best Protection Is Knowledge—After all, financial advice is everywhere; the hard part is differentiating between the good and bad advice, and without that ability, you're ripe for a financial disaster.

Principle 2: Nothing Happens Without a Plan—Financial planning doesn't happen without a plan, so you're going to want to begin by measuring your financial health by finding out where you stand financially, setting your goals, putting together a plan of action, and then putting that plan into play with a budget. Because without a plan, nothing will happen.

Principle 3: The Time Value of Money—In order to understand why it is so important to begin saving early, you need to understand how powerful the time value of money is. Once you understand this concept, saving becomes much more fun.

Principle 4: Taxes Affect Personal Finance Decisions—Like it or not, taxes are part of life, and as a result, your financial plan must take taxes into account.

CHAPTER 1 The Financial Planning Process

Learning Objectives

LO1	**Explain** why personal financial planning is so important.	Facing Financial Challenges
LO2	**Describe** the five basic steps of personal financial planning.	The Personal Financial Planning Process
LO3	**Set** your financial goals.	Establishing Your Financial Goals
LO4	**Explain** how career management and education can determine your income level.	Thinking About Your Career
LO5	**Identify** and explain how skills acquired in this course will help you get a job and advance in it.	Developing Skills for Your Career
LO6	**Explain** the personal finance lessons learned in the recent economic downturn.	Lessons from the Recent Economic Downturn
LO7	**List** ten principles of personal finance.	Ten Principles of Personal Finance

After nine years, the popular TV sitcom *How I Met Your Mother* came to a close. It is widely agreed that the strength of the show was that the audience could intimately relate to so many of the story lines affecting the five main characters. Marshall and Lily play a loving, but somewhat goofy, married couple. Marshall is a young lawyer and Lily a kindergarten teacher, who, along with their friends, Robin, Ted, and Barney, get into some improbable predicaments, but the financial problems they face are, unfortunately, all too realistic.

Collection Christophel/Alamy Stock Photo

Marshall has his law degree, is loaded with student loan debt, and has to decide whether to take his low-paying dream job with the nonprofit NRDC or a high-paying job with an evil law firm. It's a choice of money versus his dream, and he ends up taking the money. Meanwhile, Lily is back at their apartment with girlfriend Robin, looking over some of her new purchases. Robin asks, "How can you afford such expensive clothes?" The answer is, as you might expect, on credit, and apparently, Lily has a lot of debt. As Robin says, "Lily, you have debt the size of Mount Waddington!" "Waddington?" Lily responds. "It's the tallest mountain in Canada. It's like 4,000 meters high," Robin explains. "Meters?" Lily responds. Apparently, Lily knows about as much about meters as she does about personal finance.

Clever and improbable plot line? Not really. Unfortunately, personal financial problems are all too common. It's much easier to postpone dealing with money problems than to confront them. In fact, Lily said she was intending to take care of her credit card debt just as soon as she finished furnishing their apartment. As Robin responded, "You should be on a reality show."

How much do you know about personal finance? Hopefully more than Lily, but probably not enough. That's pretty much how it is for everyone until they've made a real effort to learn about personal finance. When did Marshall find out about Lily's credit card problems? Not until a few seasons later when they found their dream home and the loan officer informed them that their approved interest rate would be 18 percent!

Being financially secure involves more than just making money—life will be easier when you learn to balance what you make with what you spend. Unfortunately, financial planning is not something that comes naturally to most people. This text will provide you with the know-how to avoid financial pitfalls and to achieve your financial goals, whether they include a new car, a vacation home, or early retirement. In addition to providing the necessary tools and techniques for managing your personal finances, you will learn the logic behind them, allowing you to understand why they work. To make life a little easier, you will be introduced to ten basic principles that reinforce this underlying logic. If you understand these principles, you are well on your way to successful financial planning. It's just too bad Lily didn't take this class.

LO1 Explain why personal financial planning is so important.

Facing Financial Challenges

How big are the financial challenges you face? You may be gaining an appreciation for the cost of college. College tuition and fees at a private school average around $33,480 per year; and at a public school, the average in-state cost is $9,650 per year. Add to this the cost of housing and food, textbooks and computer equipment, and the "essentials"—a mini-refrigerator, a parking permit, lots of change for the laundry, a bit more cash to cover library fines, and late-night pizza money. How do most students finance the cost of college? The answer is, by borrowing.

Today, the typical grad with loans—and that's about half of all college students—will leave college with both a diploma and some $28,400 in student loans. If you add in credit card, personal, and family loans, student debt climbs to over $37,000—and many students are in far more debt than that. Take, for example, Sheri Springs-Phillips, who was written about in the *Wall Street Journal*. She's a neurology resident at Loyola University Medical Center. On her 11-year journey from the South Side of Chicago to becoming a doctor, she piled up $102,000 in debt. Although her friends think she's got it made, she worries about the $2,500 monthly loan payments that begin when she finishes her residency. Fortunately, Sheri is an exception, but just the average level of debt can be daunting. However, with a solid financial plan, even this level of debt is manageable.

Financial planning may not help you earn more, but it can help you use the money you do earn to achieve your financial goals. Say you really hope to buy a Jeep when you graduate—one with a stereo loud enough to wake the neighbors (and the dead). That's a financial goal, and a good financial plan will help you achieve it. A solid financial plan could also help you save enough to spend the summer in Europe or help you balance your budget so maybe someday you won't have a roommate. It may even help you pay off those student loans! Whatever your financial goals, the reality is this: Either you control your finances, or they control you—it's your choice.

> **STOP & THINK**
>
> Why do people *need* to make a financial plan? Because it's always easier to spend than to save. According to a survey by GoBankingRates, one in three adult Americans has nothing at all saved for retirement. On top of that, about 75 percent of all Americans over 40 are behind on saving for retirement. How do you see yourself in retirement? Now, do you think you need a plan?

Managing your finances isn't a skill you are born with. And, unfortunately, personal finance courses aren't the norm in high school, and in many families, money is not something to talk about—only to disagree on. In fact, financial problems can be a major cause of marital problems. Disagreements about money can instill a fear of finance at an early age, and a lack of financial education just makes matters worse. As a result, most people grow up feeling very uncomfortable about money. But there is nothing to be afraid of; personal financial management is a skill well worth learning.

When we first attempt to understand the subject of personal finance, we are often intimidated by the seemingly unending number of investment, insurance, and estate planning options, as well as by the fact that the subject has a language of its own. How can you make choices when you don't speak the language? Well, you can't. That's why you're reading this text and taking this course—to learn to navigate the world of money. Specifically, this text and this course will enable you to accomplish the following:

- **Manage the unplanned:** It may seem odd to plan to deal with the unexpected or unplanned. Hey, stuff happens. Unfortunately, no matter how well you plan, much of what life throws at you is unexpected. A sound financial plan will allow you to bounce back from a hard knock instead of going down for the count.
- **Accumulate wealth for special expenses:** Travel, a big wedding, college for your children, and buying a summer home are all examples of events that carry expenses

for which you'll have to plan ahead financially. Financial planning will help you map out a strategy to pay for a house by the beach or a trip around the world.

- **Save for retirement:** You may not think much about it now, but you don't want to be penniless when you're 65. A strong financial plan will help you look at the costs of retirement and develop a plan that allows you to live a life of retirement ease.
- **"Cover your assets":** A financial plan is no good if it doesn't protect what you've got. A complete financial plan will include adequate insurance at as low a cost as possible.
- **Invest intelligently:** When it comes to investing savings, arm yourself with an understanding of the basic principles of investment. And beware: There are some shady investments and investment advisors out there!
- **Minimize your payments to Uncle Sam:** Why earn money for the government? Part of financial planning is to help you legally reduce the amount of tax you have to pay on your earnings.

The Personal Financial Planning Process

LO2 Describe the five basic steps of personal financial planning.

Financial planning is an ongoing process—it changes as your financial situation and position in life change. However, there are five basic steps to personal financial planning we should examine before we continue.

Step 1: Evaluate Your Financial Health

A financial plan begins with an examination of your current financial situation. How much money do you make? How much are you spending, and what are you spending it on? To survive financially, you have to see your whole financial picture, which requires careful record keeping, especially when it comes to spending.

Keeping track of what you spend may simply be a matter of taking a few minutes each evening to enter all of the day's expenses into a book or a computer program. Is this record keeping tedious? Sure, but it will also be revealing, and it's a first step toward taking control of your financial well-being. In Chapter 2 we take a closer look at the record-keeping process.

Step 2: Define Your Financial Goals

You can't get what you want if you don't *know* what you want. The second step of the financial planning process is defining your goals, which entails writing down (or formalizing) your financial goals, attaching costs to them, and determining when the money to accomplish those goals will be needed. Unfortunately, establishing personal financial goals is something most people never actually do, perhaps because the subject is intimidating or because they have absolutely no idea how to achieve these goals. Although it is not a difficult task, it's an easy one to put off. However, only when you set goals—and analyze them and decide whether you're willing to make the financial commitment necessary to achieve them—can you reach them.

STOP & THINK

According to a recent Economic Policy Institute survey, the median family between the ages of 32 and 61 has only $5,000 saved in a retirement account, while the top 1 percent of families have a million dollars or more. That report went on to find that almost nine in ten families in the top income fifth have savings in retirement accounts, compared to fewer than one in ten families in the bottom income fifth. In addition, according to a recent Retirement Confidence Survey, retirement was the number one savings goal for Americans. It was listed 3½ times more often by those surveyed than the number two savings goal, which was a child's or grandchild's education. But even though Americans feel retirement savings are important, they don't seem to be making much progress saving. In fact, according to a recent survey by GoBankingRates, about 30 percent of those aged 55 have no retirement savings whatsoever, while 26 percent report retirement balances of less than $50,000, an amount that won't go far in retirement. Retirement is only one of many reasons why financial planning is so important. As Carl Sandburg wrote, "Nothing happens unless first a dream." Why do you think goals are so important?

Step 3: Develop a Plan of Action

The third step of the process is developing an action plan to achieve your goals. A solid personal financial plan includes an informed and controlled budget, determines your investment strategy, and reflects your unique personal goals. Although everyone's plan is a bit different, all sound financial plans include several key factors: flexibility, liquidity, protection, and minimization of taxes.

Flexibility Remember when we mentioned planning for the unplanned? That's what flexibility is all about. Your financial plan must be flexible enough to respond to changes in your life and unexpected events, such as losing your job or rear-ending the Honda in front of you. An investment plan that doesn't allow you to access your money until you retire doesn't do you much good when you suddenly get fired for using your office computer to play *The Witcher 3*, *Dead Rising 2*, or *World of Warcraft*.

Liquidity Dealing with unplanned events requires more than just flexibility. Sometimes it requires immediate access to cold, hard cash. **Liquidity** means the ability to get to your money when you need it. No one likes to think about things such as developing an illness, losing a job, or even wrecking your car. But as we said earlier, stuff happens, so you need to make sure that when it does, you have access to enough money to make it through.

Liquidity
The relative ease and speed with which you can convert noncash assets into cash. In effect, it involves having access to your money when you need it.

Protection What if the unexpected turns out to be catastrophic? Liquidity will pay the repair bill for a fender bender, but what if you are involved in a serious accident and you wind up badly injured? What if the cost of an unexpected event is a lot more than you've got? Liquidity enables you to carry on during an unexpected event, but insurance shields you from the catastrophic effect of events that would otherwise threaten your financial security. Insurance offers protection against the costliest unforeseen events, such as flood, fire, major illness, and death. However, insurance isn't free. A good financial plan includes enough insurance, at reasonable rates, to prevent financial ruin.

STOP & THINK

It's much easier to be satisfied if you think of working toward goals rather than working toward becoming "rich." That goes back to Ecclesiastes 5:10, "He that loveth silver shall not be satisfied with silver." What do you think this means?

Minimization of Taxes Finally, your financial plan must take taxes into account. Keep in mind that a chunk of your earnings goes to the government, so if you need to earn $1,000 from an investment, make sure it yields $1,000 *after taxes.* While you want to pay as little in tax as possible, your goal is not to minimize taxes per se, but to maximize the cash that is available to you after taxes have been paid.

Step 4: Implement Your Plan

Although it's important to carefully and thoughtfully develop a financial plan, it is equally important to actually stick to that plan. While you don't want to become a slave to your financial plan, you will need to track income and spending, as well as keep an eye on your long-term goals.

Remember that your financial plan is not the goal; it is the tool you use to achieve your goals. In effect, think of your financial plan not as punishment but as a road map. Your destination may change, and you may get lost or even go down a few dead ends, but if your map is good, you'll always find your way again. Remember to add new roads to your map as they are built, and be prepared to pave a few yourself to get to where you want to go. Always keep your goals in mind and keep driving toward them.

FIGURE 1.1 The Budgeting and Planning Process

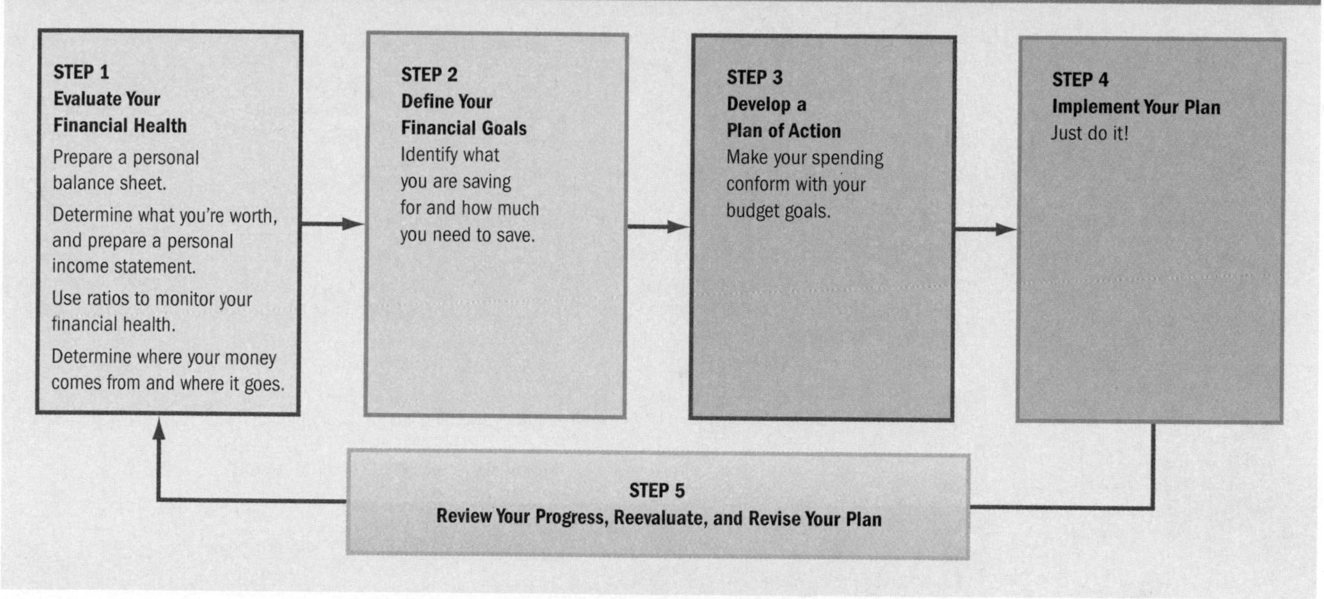

STEP 1
Evaluate Your Financial Health
Prepare a personal balance sheet.
Determine what you're worth, and prepare a personal income statement.
Use ratios to monitor your financial health.
Determine where your money comes from and where it goes.
STEP 2
Define Your Financial Goals
Identify what you are saving for and how much you need to save.
STEP 3
Develop a Plan of Action
Make your spending conform with your budget goals.
STEP 4
Implement Your Plan
Just do it!
STEP 5
Review Your Progress, Reevaluate, and Revise Your Plan

Step 5: Review Your Progress, Reevaluate, and Revise Your Plan

Let's say that on your next vacation you'd like to explore Alaska, but the only road map you have of that state is decades old. Well, to stay on course you'd better get a new map! The same is true for your financial strategy. As time passes and things change—maybe you get married or have children—you must review your progress and reexamine your plan. If necessary, you must be prepared to get a new map—to begin again and formulate a new plan.

Figure 1.1 summarizes these five basic steps to financial planning.

Establishing Your Financial Goals

LO3 Set your financial goals.

Financial goals cover three time horizons: (1) short term, (2) intermediate term, and (3) long term. Short-term goals, such as buying a television or taking a vacation, can be accomplished within a 1-year period. Intermediate-term goals may take from 1 year to 10 years to accomplish. Examples include putting aside college tuition money for your 12-year-old and accumulating enough money for a down payment on a new house. A long-term goal is one for which it takes more than 10 years to accumulate the money. Retirement is a common example of a long-term financial goal.

WORKSHEET 1

Figure 1.2 is a worksheet that lists examples of short-term, intermediate-term, and long-term goals. You can use it to determine your own objectives. In setting your goals, be as specific as possible. Rather than aiming to "save money," state the purpose of your saving efforts, such as buying a car, and determine exactly how much you want saved by what time. Also, be realistic. Your goals should reflect your financial and life situations. It's a bit unrealistic to plan for a $100,000 Porsche on an income of $15,000 a year.

Once you've set up a list of goals, you need to rank them. Prioritizing goals may make you realize that some of your goals are simply unrealistic, and you may need to reevaluate them. However, once you have your final goals in place, they become the cornerstone of your personal financial plan, serving as a guide to action and a benchmark for assessing the effectiveness of the plan.

FIGURE 1.2 Personal Financial Goals Worksheet

Goal	Priority Level	Desired Achievement Date	Anticipated Cost
Short-Term Goals (less than 1 year)			
Accumulate Emergency Funds Equal to 3 Months' Living Expenses	______	______	______
Pay Off Outstanding Bills	______	______	______
Pay Off Outstanding Credit Cards	______	______	______
Purchase Adequate Property, Health, Disability, and Liability Insurance	______	______	______
Purchase a Major Item	______	______	______
Finance a Vacation or Some Other Entertainment Item	______	______	______
Other Short-Term Goals (Specify)	______	______	______
Intermediate-Term Goals (1 to 10 years)			
Save Funds for College for an Older Child	______	______	______
Save for a Major Home Improvement	______	______	______
Save for a Down Payment on a House	______	______	______
Pay Off Outstanding Major Debt	______	______	______
Finance Very Large Items (Weddings)	______	______	______
Purchase a Vacation Home or Time-Share Unit	______	______	______
Finance a Major Vacation (Overseas)	______	______	______
Other Intermediate-Term Goals (Specify)	______	______	______
Long-Term Goals (more than 10 years)			
Save Funds for College for a Young Child	______	______	______
Purchase a Second Home for Retirement	______	______	______
Create a Retirement Fund Large Enough to Supplement Your Pension So That You Can Live at Your Current Standard	______	______	______
Take Care of Your Parents After They Retire	______	______	______
Start Your Own Business	______	______	______
Other Long-Term Goals (Specify)	______	______	______

The Life Cycle of Financial Planning

As we said earlier, people's goals change throughout their lives. Although many of these changes are due to unexpected events, the majority are based on a financial life cycle pattern. Figure 1.3 offers an example of a financial life cycle. Looking at this figure and thinking about what your own financial life cycle may look like allows you to foresee financial needs and plan ahead. Consider retirement. If you're a college student, retirement may be the furthest thing from your mind. However, if you think about your financial life cycle, you'll realize that you need to make retirement funding one of your first goals after graduation.

The first 17 or 18 years of our lives tend to involve negative income (and you thought it was only you). You can think of this as the "prenatal" stage of your financial life cycle. During this period, most people are in school and still depend on their parents to pay the bills. After high school, you may get a job, or attend college, or do both. Regardless, once your education is completed, your financial life cycle may begin in earnest. This first stage can be decades long and centers on the accumulation of wealth. For most people, this period continues through their mid-50s. During this time, goal setting, insurance, home buying, and family formation get the spotlight in terms of planning.

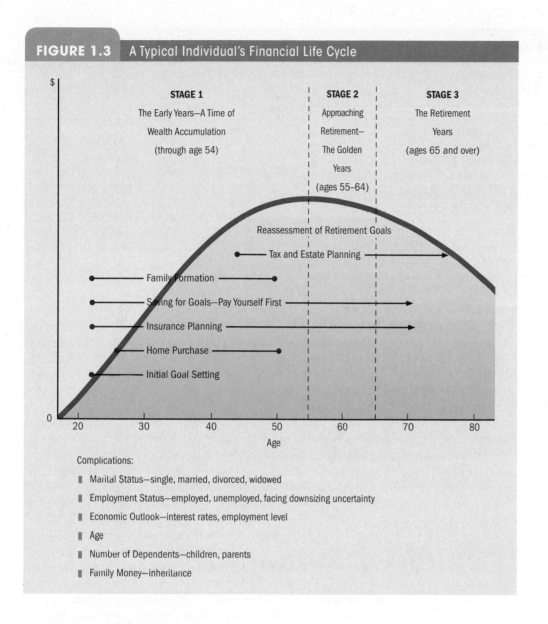

FIGURE 1.3 A Typical Individual's Financial Life Cycle

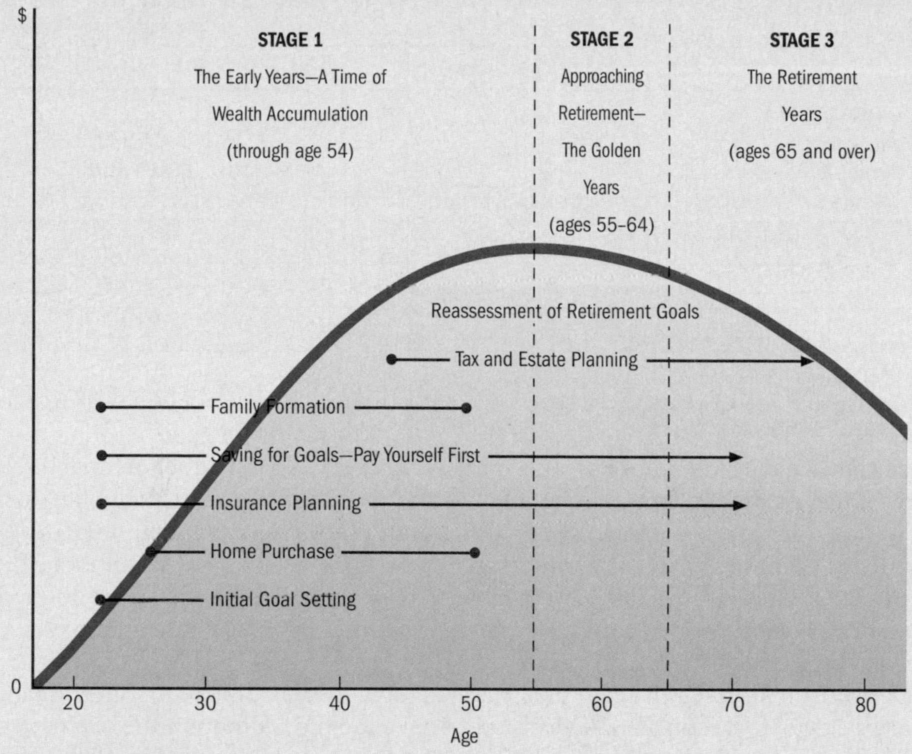

Complications:

- Marital Status—single, married, divorced, widowed
- Employment Status—employed, unemployed, facing downsizing uncertainty
- Economic Outlook—interest rates, employment level
- Age
- Number of Dependents—children, parents
- Family Money—inheritance

The second and third stages are shorter. During the second stage, which for some people may begin in their early 50s, financial goals shift to the preservation and continued growth of the wealth you have already accumulated. You may begin to think about **estate planning**—that is, planning for the passage of your wealth to your heirs. The third and final stage, retirement, often begins in the mid- to late 60s. During retirement, you are no longer saving; you are spending. However, you must still allow for some growth in your savings simply to keep **inflation** from eating them away.

Estate Planning
Planning for your eventual death and the passage of your wealth to your heirs.

Inflation
An economic condition in which rising prices reduce the purchasing power of money.

Think of the financial life cycle in terms of a family life cycle. Consider a couple who marry in their 20s or 30s, have kids shortly thereafter, spend the next 18 or 20 years raising the kids and putting them through college, and then settle down as a couple again when the kids move out to form their own families. Obviously, a typical individual's experiences don't fit everyone perfectly. Today, with more single-parent families and more young people postponing marriage, it simply isn't reasonable to refer to any family experience as typical. However, regardless of how unusual your life is, you'll be surprised at how much it has in common with a typical financial life cycle.

The early years are different for everyone. For many people, however, the biggest investment of a lifetime, purchasing a home, occurs during these early years. With a

TABLE 1.1 The Cost of Raising the Second Child in a Two-Child Family

These calculations are for the second child in a two-child family. For families with only one child, the costs of raising that child are more and can be determined by multiplying the totals by 1.27. For families with more than two children, the costs of an additional child can be determined by multiplying the totals by 0.76.

	Total Spent over 18 Years For								
Annual Income	**Annual Expenses, First 3 Years**	**Total Expenses, First 18 Years**	**Housing**	**Food**	**Transportation**	**Clothing**	**Health Care**	**Child Care and Education**	**Other[a]**
Less than $59,200	$ 9,690	$174,690	$56,880	$34,140	$24,900	$11,700	$15,120	$21,240	$10,710
$59,200-$107,400	12,680	233,610	66,240	41,400	35,490	13,260	21,720	38,040	17,460
More than $107,400	19,770	372,210	98,280	55,020	49,860	20,280	29,610	86,820	32,340

[a]Other expenses include personal-care items, entertainment, and reading material.

Source: Expenditure on Children by Families, 2015 Annual Report, U.S. Department of Agriculture, Agricultural Research Service: http://www.cnpp.usda.gov/Publications/CRC/crc2015.pdf, January 2017.

house comes a long-term borrowing commitment and your introduction to debt planning. Although the costs of owning a home may dominate your financial life during this period, you can't lose track of the rest of your plan. Therefore, you must develop a regular pattern of saving. The importance of making saving a habit cannot be overemphasized. Once you make a commitment to save, you need to ask the following questions: (1) How much can I save? (2) Is that enough? (3) Where should I invest those savings dollars?

Decisions that may not seem financial will have a major impact on your financial situation. Take, for example, the decision to have a child. Although this isn't considered primarily a financial decision, it certainly has enormous financial implications. As Table 1.1 illustrates, kids cost a lot. In fact, for a middle-income family earning $83,300 per year, the total cost of raising a second child from birth to age 18 is $233,610, and the cost of a first child would be 27 percent more, or $296,685. And the more you make, the more you spend on raising children. Those with annual incomes of more than $107,400 spend more than twice as much as those with annual incomes less than $59,200. The major differences occur in housing, child care, and education. As you look at these figures, keep in mind that they cover the costs of a child only from birth to age 18—they don't include the costs of college. Considering the $9,690 to $19,770 a year it costs to raise a child, saving to finance that child's college education is a real challenge!

You must also buy insurance to protect your assets. Initially, you may require only medical, disability, and liability insurance, but if you decide to have a family, you will need to provide for your dependents in the event of a tragedy. For families with children, adequate life insurance is essential. You will also need home, auto, and property insurance.

The second stage involves a transition from your earning years, when you will earn more than you spend, to your retirement years, when you will spend more than you earn. Exactly what happens during this transition stage and how long it lasts depends on how well you are prepared for retirement. Much of this transition involves reassessing your financial goals—including insurance protection and estate planning—to make sure you are truly prepared for retirement. As you approach retirement, you must continuously review your financial decisions, including insurance protection and estate planning. Keep in mind that this is your last opportunity to save and prepare for your retirement years, and how well you succeed at that will determine how you live during retirement.

In the last stage, during your retirement years, you'll be living off your savings. Certainly, the decision about when to retire will reflect how well you have saved. Once you retire, your financial focus is on ensuring your continued wealth, despite not having income. As always, you'll spend much of your time overseeing the management of savings and assets, but now your concern will be making sure you don't run out of money. You'll be dealing with the question of how much of your savings can you tap into each year without ever running out of money, and your investment strategy will probably become less risky because you now need to preserve rather than create wealth. In addition, your insurance concerns may include protection against the costs of an extended nursing home stay.

Finally, estate planning decisions become paramount. Things like wills, living wills, advance directives, health proxies, power of attorney, and record keeping should all be in place to help protect you, along with your assets for your heirs. These estate planning tools will help ensure that your wishes are understood and honored as you reach the end of your life. They'll also allow you to pass on your estate to whomever you want, while keeping your estate taxes at a minimum.

FACTS OF LIFE

Forty-five percent of those in the United States aged 65 and older are financially dependent on relatives, and another 30 percent live on charity. If you're like most young people, fresh out of college, you probably will have an urge to spend all that cash that you may be making for the first time in your life. Feel free to spend, as long as you manage to save for your goals, and *make sure you begin planning for your financial future now.* The key is to start the personal financial planning process early in life and make saving a habit.

Thinking About Your Career

LO4 Explain how career management and education can determine your income level.

Career planning is the process of identifying a job that you feel is important and that will lead to the lifestyle you want. When considering which career is right for you, think about the kind of work you find enjoyable and satisfying. It is also important to choose work that provides the standard of living you hope to achieve. In general, your first job isn't the one you'll spend the rest of your life doing. Most careers involve a series of positions that give you the opportunity to display your skills, that lead to a job that you find satisfying, and that allow you to balance work and your personal life. Figure 1.4 is a Job Search Worksheet that will help you manage your career.

WORKSHEET 3

Choosing a Major and a Career

The first steps in career planning are doing a self-assessment and developing an understanding of what you want. First, consider your interests, skills, values, personal traits, and desired lifestyle. What activities do you enjoy? How do you like to spend your time? What other skills do you have that might be of value in a career? Look, too, at your educational record. Which courses did you like most, and which did you like least? Which courses did you do the best in? From there, take a look at your work experience. Make a list of all the jobs you've had and all the volunteer activities you've taken part in. Think about each of these, and determine what about them you found satisfying and what not so satisfying. Why did you leave any of these situations?

Conducting an effective self-assessment means looking at many aspects of your life honestly. Once you are through, you will have a good idea of your skills and interests. Now, you can research career alternatives and identify those in which your abilities are valued. Once you've narrowed down a list of options, look at both the positive and the negative aspects of these professions. Do they offer the status and earning potential you are looking for? Are they part of a stable industry? Might they require travel or frequent relocation? Talk to people in the occupations you've targeted to learn more about what they do, as well as what they like and dislike about their jobs.

Once you've made a self-assessment, looked at career options, and talked to people in the workplace, you may be ready to decide on a career field that fits your

FIGURE 1.4 Job Search Worksheet

Notes

The Search (Complete items 1–3 on this checklist before starting your job search.)

1. **Identify Occupations**
   - List your work and life experience.
   - Review information on jobs—find out what types of jobs are hiring.
   - Identify jobs that use your talents. ____________

2. **Identify Employers**
   - Tell relatives and friends that you are job hunting—you never know who may have a lead!
   - Go to your state employment service office for assistance.
   - Use the Internet or contact employers to get company and job information. ____________

3. **Prepare Materials**
   - Write your résumé. Tailor it, if necessary, using job announcements to "fit" your skills with job requirements.
   - Write cover letters or letters of application. ____________

The Daily Effort

4. **Contact Employers**
   - Call employers directly (even if they're not advertising openings). Ask to speak to the person who would supervise you if you were hired. Make note of names.
   - Go to companies to fill out applications.

The Interview (Complete items 5–8 when you have interviews.)

5. **Prepare for Interviews**
   - Check out the Internet and learn about the company you're interviewing with.
   - Review job announcements to determine how your skills will help you do the job.
   - Assemble résumés, application forms, etc. (make sure everything is neat). ____________

6. **Go to Interviews**
   - Dress right for the interview—that, of course, will depend on the job you're applying for.
   - Go alone.
   - Be positive.
   - Thank the interviewer. ____________

7. **Evaluate Interviews**
   - Send a thank-you note to the interviewer within 24 hours of the interview.
   - Think about how you could improve the interview—remember, this may not be your last interview. ____________

8. **If You Have to Take Tests for the Job—Be Ready**
   - Find out about the test(s) you're taking.
   - Prepare for the test and brush up on job skills.
   - Relax and be confident. ____________

9. **Accept the Job!**
   - Be flexible when discussing salary (but don't sell yourself short). If you're expecting more than they offer, ask for it. The worst that can happen is that they will say no.
   - *Congratulations!* ____________

TABLE 1.2 What Majors in Different College Subjects Earn

Choice of Major	Unemployment Rate	Underemployment Rate	Median Wage Early Career	Median Wage Mid-Career
Accounting	3.3	26.5	$45,000	$70,000
Advert/Public Relations	3.0	44.0	$38,500	$61,000
Anthropology	7.0	56.2	$30,000	$50,000
Architecture	4.9	34.8	$40,000	$70,000
Business Management	4.2	60.4	$39,000	$62,000
Chemical Engineering	5.0	16.8	$70,000	$100,000
Chemistry	4.5	34.0	$38,000	$68,000
Communications	4.6	57.6	$37,000	$37,000
Elementary Education	2.0	18.6	$33,600	$42,000
Environmental Studies	5.5	53.7	$33,000	$60,000
Finance	3.8	37.2	$50,000	$80,000
Foreign Language	5.6	53.8	$32,000	$52,000
Performing Arts	6.0	65.0	$30,000	$51,000
Psychology	4.3	50.3	$31,000	$52,000

Sources: U.S. Census Bureau, American Community Survey (IPUMS); U.S. Department of Labor, O*NET. https://www.newyorkfed.org/research/college-labor-market/college-labor-market_compare-majors.html, accessed April 1, 2017.

interests and that is realistically achievable. If you are a college student who has not yet chosen a major, you will want to consider which major puts you in line for the kind of job you'd like when you graduate. You may want to talk to the people at your school's career center to find out more about how specific college majors relate to different occupations. While you want to make sure you choose a career that fits your interests, it is also good to have an idea of what that job pays when you're making this decision. Let's take a look at the average annual earnings of full-time employed college graduates with only a bachelor's degree based on their college major. As you can see from Table 1.2, the major you choose can affect how readily jobs in your field are found and how much you eventually earn. While looking at these numbers, keep in mind that these are averages—you might earn more or less than the figure given. And picking one of the "low earners" in terms of majors doesn't mean you won't be successful and earn a good wage—just look at Leslie Moonves, the president and CEO of CBS. He majored in Spanish at Bucknell. Also keep in mind that although money isn't everything, it shouldn't be ignored.

FACTS OF LIFE

If you want to scope out salaries for other jobs, try the Federal Reserve Bank of New York's Labor Market Outcomes of College Graduates by Major, https://www.newyorkfed.org/research/college-labor-market/college-labor-market_compare-majors.html

If you're still lost, you might want to try the Internet, which offers a wealth of career advice. *Occupational Outlook Handbook*, published by the U.S. Bureau of Labor Statistics, is a good source for career advice. This guide is located at **http://www.bls.gov/ooh/home.htm** and provides information on duties, education and training, pay, and outlook for hundreds of occupations. It's comprehensive, too; in fact, it looks at what it takes to get into that industry, whether there is on-the-job training, number of projected new jobs, the growth rate in jobs, and the median pay.

TABLE 1.3 Common Interview Questions

1. Tell me a little about yourself.
2. What do you know about our company and this position?
3. What are your short-term and long-term goals?
4. What are your greatest strength and your greatest weakness?
5. What is the hardest thing you have ever had to do?
6. Describe a time you worked with a difficult person, perhaps a fellow student, professor, or coworker. How did you handle it then and how would you handle it now?
7. How would you rate your performance under pressure?
8. How did you choose your major and what was your most rewarding college experience?
9. Did you participate in extracurricular activities or clubs while in school?
10. What did you like the most/least about your last job(s)?
11. What motivates you and how do you motivate others?
12. Describe a project you have worked on and your contribution.
13. Why should we hire you? What can you do for our company?
14. Are your grades a good indicator of your professional potential?
15. Is there anything else that we should know about you?

Getting a Job

Getting your first real job is a job in itself. One of the most important things to remember is to *start early*. Remember what Woody Allen once said: "Eighty-five percent of success is simply showing up." That means that if you're graduating in May, you have to put your résumé together the summer before your senior year.

Why start that early? There are three reasons. First, the beginning of fall semester is generally hectic, so if you wait until then to create your résumé, you may get delayed by a month or two. Beginning in the summer guarantees you'll be prepared to start your job search in the fall. Second, when you begin submitting your résumé before other seniors, you send a message to potential employers that you are both serious and organized—two traits employers love. Third, for many companies, the fall is the beginning of their recruiting cycle.

FACTS OF LIFE

According to a recent recruiting survey, the most common mistake that job interviewees make is talking too much.

When you are selected for an interview, the key is to be prepared. While you can't be ready for every question, there are some relatively standard questions that you should be equipped to answer. Table 1.3 lists 15 of the most common interview questions.

If possible, practice interviewing. Many colleges' career development offices provide courses or help in developing the interpersonal skills that are necessary for a good interview. Next, use the library or the Internet to find as much information as possible about the company you're interviewing with. Understand how the company makes its money, know its history and its financial status, and read up on any new developments. And be sure to make a good first impression. Dress appropriately, and get a good night's rest before your interview. Plan to arrive about 30 minutes early to guard against any unexpected delays. Display strong body language: A firm handshake, good eye contact, and straight but relaxed posture are all part of a confident image. When the interview is ended, make sure you thank the interviewer for his or her time and for giving you the opportunity to meet. Finally, when you get home, send a follow-up letter, thanking the interviewer again and reiterating your interest in the position.

Being Successful in Your Career

If you are just starting out, it is likely that you'll work for at least three or four different companies and have more than ten different jobs over the course of your working life. You may switch jobs or even careers for many reasons: You may be offered great opportunities, your personal interests may shift, or the job market in your industry may change. In this era of regular corporate restructuring, job security is not what it used to be. To protect yourself, be sure to keep your skills marketable through education and by keeping up with changing technology. To increase your value as an employee:

- Do your best work.
- Project the right image—an image aligned with the organization's values and wants.
- Gain an understanding of the power structure so that you can work within it.
- Gain visibility. Make those with power aware of your contributions.
- Take new assignments. Gain experience and an understanding of the various operations of the organization.
- Be loyal to and supportive of your boss. Remember, your boss controls your immediate future.
- Continually acquire new skills—in particular, skills that are not easy to duplicate.
- Develop a strong network of contacts in case you ever need to look for a new job.
- Pay attention to ethics because the most damaging event you, as an employee, can experience is a loss of confidence in your ethical standards. Ethical violations end careers.

The bottom line is that managing your career is an ongoing process that will end only when you finally retire.

What Determines Your Income?

What you earn does not determine how happy you are, but it does determine the standard of living you can afford. There is great variation in what different people earn at the same job with different companies, but one thing is clear: The more specialized skills and training a job requires, the higher it tends to pay.

Without question, the key differentiating factor in determining your eventual salary is how well educated you are, as Figure 1.5 shows. Right now, you may be making the best single investment you will ever make—your education. Interestingly, being married is also a trait of the wealthy. Whereas a married couple heads 70 percent of all middle-class households, that number climbs to 85 percent for wealthy households. Your financial plan must be realistic, and it must be based on your income. Let's look at some basic principles of a solid financial strategy.

STOP & THINK

A recent survey conducted by *Family Circle* magazine found that 84 percent of those surveyed felt that doing work they love was more important than making money, and 88 percent said they valued health and a happy home life above wealth. There's no reason why you shouldn't have both, provided you take what you learn in this text and this course and then put together and implement a financial plan. Are you ready to try it?

Keeping a Perspective—Money Isn't Everything

Your personal financial plan allows you to extend your financial strategy beyond the present, enabling you to achieve goals that are well off in the future. In effect, personal financial planning allows you to be realistic about your finances—to act

FIGURE 1.5 Education and Earnings

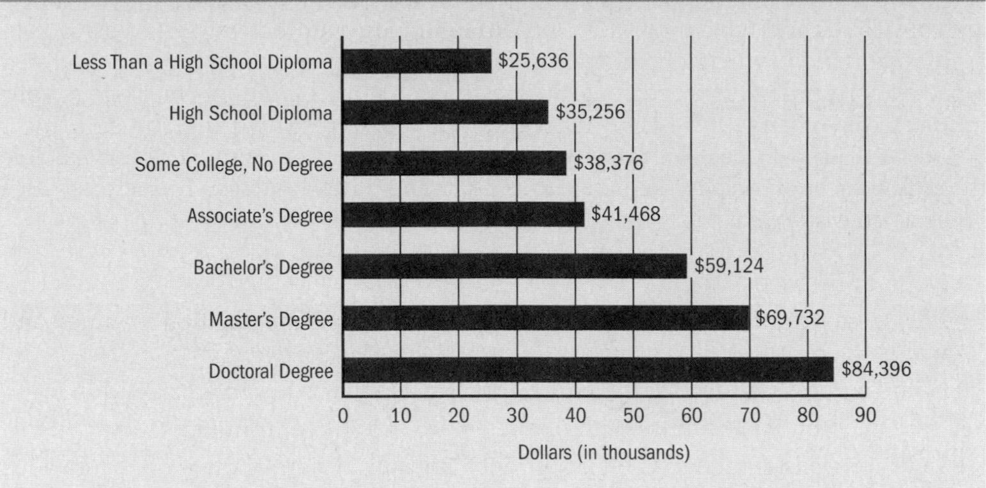

Source: Bureau of Labor Statistics, http://www.bls.gov/emp/ep_table_001.htm, accessed March 23, 2017.

your wage. Unfortunately, for some people financial goals become all-consuming. They see nothing but dollar signs and lose a healthy perspective on what is actually important in life. In the first version of the movie *Arthur*, there is an exchange between Dudley Moore and Liza Minnelli in which Moore, who plays Arthur Bach, says, "Money has screwed me up my whole life. I've always been rich, and I've never been happy." To this, Minnelli, who plays Linda Marolla (Arthur's girlfriend), replies, "Well, I've always been poor, and I've usually been happy." Arthur's mother then steps in and responds, "I've always been rich, and I've always been happy!" It's true: Money does not equal happiness. In fact, the *Wall Street Journal* reported the results of an international happiness survey and found that respondents from *Forbes*'s annual list of the 400 richest Americans scored 5.8 on the happiness scale. That's the same score reported by the Inuit of northern Greenland and the hut-dwelling Maasai of Kenya. But keep in mind that even though money doesn't necessarily bring happiness, facing college expenses or retirement without the necessary funding certainly brings anxiety. In fact, a recent survey by the American Psychological Association found that money is the leading cause of stress among Americans.

STOP & THINK

Philosopher Arthur Schopenhauer, in *The Wisdom of Life*, said that wealth is "like seawater: the more you drink, the thirstier you become." What do you think Schopenhauer meant by this?

LO5 Identify and explain how skills acquired in this course will help you get a job and advance in it.

Developing Skills for Your Career

Today it seems like most students are interested in knowing *if and how* studying personal finance will help them get and keep a good job, and even advance in that job. After all, personal finance is aimed at helping you manage and budget your money, achieve your financial goals, protect your assets, invest wisely, deal with different financial life events, and (as the title of this text says), "Turn Money into Wealth."

There is no question that what you learn in this course will help you personally, but it's important to know that it will also help you in your business career – yes, it might not seem obvious at first glance, but how you manage your personal finances will help you in the business world. Good personal finance skills will help you both to land the job you want and also to succeed in it. That may sound far-fetched, but there is plenty of research to support it. In addition, some of the skills learned in this course, like critical thinking, information technology and computing, and ethical skills, will also help you get ahead and succeed in business. Moreover, it is only through the aggregate of your educational experience that you will have the opportunity to develop the skills that employers have identified as critical to success in the workplace. Throughout this course, and specifically through this text, you'll have the opportunity to develop and practice many of those skills.

You probably don't think that your credit history could play a role in getting that job that you want, but in some cases it can. In fact, a study conducted by the Society for Human Research Management found that 47 percent of U.S. companies run credit background checks on potential employees.[1] Exactly what they are looking for is uncertain, but it is clear that they consider *how responsible you are with respect to your own personal finances* very important. Moreover, an abundance of research has shown that when employees are financially stressed, they are also distracted, and productivity suffers. Not a good scenario for promotion. So, having control over your finances may actually help you both get a job and succeed at it. Through this course, you will learn how to control your finances and manage your money responsibly.

The study of personal finance also provides students with many of the skill sets that employers seek out and value in business graduates who market themselves in virtually any discipline. The ability to bring **critical thinking** to problem-solving scenarios and make decisions or form judgments related to a particular situation or set of circumstances is an important attribute that the study of personal finance enhances. Critical thinking involves purposeful and goal-directed thinking used to define and solve problems, make decisions, and form judgments related to a particular situation or set of circumstances. This is what we do in personal finance when we, for example, look at the question "How much to save for retirement?" We develop a structured format that defines the problem, then formulate it intuitively as a mathematical model, and provide approaches to solving it that achieve our goal.

Many problems explored in personal finance, involve *saving now* to achieve a future goal (as in retirement planning) or involve *borrowing now* and repaying the loan in the future (such as taking out a student loan to further your education or a mortgage to buy a house). In effect, many of our personal finance decisions involve comparing money and cash flows that occur in different time periods. As a result, many times we will rely on Excel or financial calculators that operate similarly to Excel to solve personal finance problems that students will learn about in this text. These **information technology and computing skills** are very important to employers. Implicit in the study of personal finance is the ability to model the problem—that is, to lay out the different cash flows, as well as dates for those cash flows that reflect the true timing of those cash flows. As a result, the student learns how to model and solve personal finance problems, a real world skill that translates from your personal life to your life at work.

We will also deal with **ethical problems/issues** in personal finance. For example, we will examine something as simple as "What type of moral obligation do you have in disclosing problems your auto may have if you are selling it to another individual?" We will also look at more complex moral dilemmas. For example, "Are payday loans evil?" After all, their interest rates often go as high as 400 percent! Although they can be predatory, they can also be a useful alternative for someone who has nowhere else to turn for a loan. Many of the ethical questions we examine

---

[1]Gary Rivlin, "The Long Shadow of Bad Credit in a Job Search," *New York Times*, May 11, 2013, http://www.nytimes.com/2013/05/12/business/employers-pull-applicants-credit-reports.html

LOVE & MONEY

It might not surprise you to hear that how well you approach your own personal finances has an impact on many different areas of your life. You probably already know that it will affect your ability to buy a house, your investment success, and whether you are able to retire early and comfortably, but have you ever thought about how it might also affect your love life and other personal relationships? Yes, personal finance has a huge impact on the success, or failure, of your love life! But even though there is no question that money problems can cause tension in relationships, there is also no reason why it has to be this way. As you might expect, while there are some things that you simply shouldn't do when it comes to handling your money and making personal financial decisions if you want your relationships to thrive, there are also some actions you can take to keep money from sabotaging your relationships. In the Love & Money boxes, we'll take a look at people's attitudes toward money and love. We'll also give you some personal finance advice aimed at helping you build better, stronger, and perhaps longer-lasting relationships.

To appreciate the link between love and money, take a look at a recent Harris Poll clearly showing that finances are the biggest cause of stress in relationships!

Personal finance and money, or the mishandling thereof, can even stop a relationship before it starts; that is to say, debt can get you dumped. According to a recent TD Ameritrade survey, 44 percent of the respondents said that credit card debt would make them less likely to date a person! One reason why credit card debt may be such a social turnoff is that it may be

What Are the Main Causes of Stress in Your Relationship?

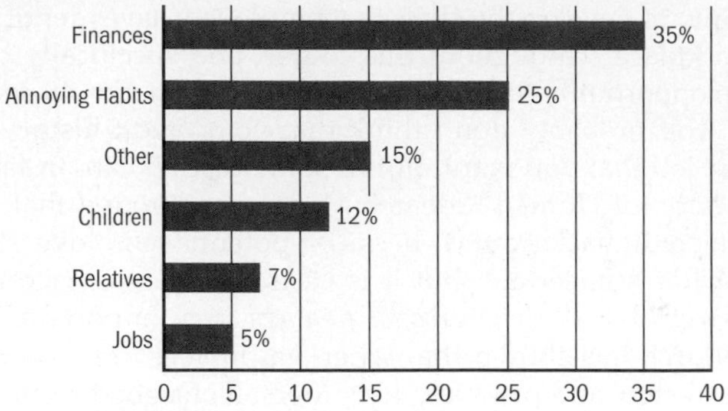

viewed as a signal of financial irresponsibility, a quality no one looks for in a potential mate. While we all know that stress can lead to arguments, additional research has found that when we argue about money, we tend to hold on to feelings of resentment longer than we do with other types of arguments. Clearly, financial fights are toxic, especially if they start early in your relationship. As a result, research finds that it may be wise to invest in financially-based premarital counseling to help avoid arguments about how money will be used in the household.[2] The bottom line here is that money and your personal finance skills and habits play a big role in determining who you might end up with and also whether or not you stay together. In the Love & Money boxes we'll give you advice to improve your odds of relationship success.

[2] Britt, S.L. & Huston, S.J. J Fam Econ Iss (2012) 33: 464. doi:10.1007/s10834-012-9304-5.

won't have easy or obvious answers, but understanding the techniques of moral reasoning and argumentation that are needed to analyze these moral and ethical issues will serve you well in your business career when you come upon an unexpected moral dilemma.

So, getting back to the question we asked earlier, perhaps you aren't a finance major and you're wondering whether or not this course will benefit you in your career. The answer is a resounding "yes," and it helps you not only in your business career, but also in your life.

LO6 Explain the personal finance lessons learned in the recent economic downturn.

Lessons from the Recent Economic Downturn

The economic downturn that started in 2008 had a painful impact on all Americans in one way or another. This pain had two root causes: first, a dramatic and swift rise in unemployment, and second, a disruption of our financial markets. Together, these two events resulted in a loss of wealth and a level of difficulty in borrowing that have not been experienced since the Great Depression. At one point, stocks had dropped in value by over 50 percent, and banks were not lending money—in short, it was a financial disaster of historic proportions. Unfortunately, no one can change the past, but this question remains: Can the lessons learned be used to change your financial future? If not, you will be destined to relive the past over and over again.

In late 2016, the Congressional Budget Office released a report on Trends in Family Wealth that looked at the impact of the recession on wealth. The results, coupled with a survey by the Pew Research center, were depressing. Family wealth plummeted as a result of the recent recession, and when asked how they had recovered from the recession in terms of household income and job situation, over half of all households responded "hardly recovered at all." When asked how their real estate value and stock market holdings had recovered, the majority of households responded that they had only "partially" recovered.

The recent recession painted a frightening picture of how vulnerable Americans are. It should also give you an idea of the deep trouble many Americans will face in retirement. As a student, retirement is generally the furthest thing from your mind—after all, you don't even have a job yet, retirement is years and years away, and you know things will work out because they always seem to. But by looking at the financial fears of those a generation ahead of you, you can get a clearer picture of what you might face in the future if you don't take action now. Moreover, when it comes to pain, we all have short memories. As we move out of the recession, and the memory of the financial pain fades, we are destined to repeat the past if we don't learn from it, falling into the old habits that brought on all the financial pain—overspending, not saving, and taking on too much debt.

What lesson can we learn from all this? First, in looking back at the recent economic downturn, it is clear that too many of us have insufficient emergency funds—one of your first financial goals should be to put together an emergency fund that is sufficient to carry you through a financial emergency. We will talk about that in the next chapter, and it will form the foundation for one of our Ten Principles of Personal Finance, which will be introduced in the next section.

What financial issues do Americans worry about the most? According to a recent Rockefeller Foundation report, without question, the answer is retirement. Over 50 percent of Americans worry about their ability to pay for retirement, with about 60 percent of those who are worried say they are "very worried." Retirement concerns outstrip employment, housing value, debt, medical costs, and health care as the area of greatest concern. For that reason, we will provide you with a strong foundation in personal finance directly related to retirement planning. Retirement may be many years away, but a comfortable and secure retirement won't come without a plan coupled with an early start.

Too much debt and health care were also identified as major concerns for Americans. Approximately 40 percent of Americans indicated that they are worried about their ability to make their debt payments. The ability both to secure adequate health insurance and to pay medical bills also showed up as a worry for about 40 percent of Americans.

Without a doubt, the economic recession of the late 2000s not only exacerbated the financial problems of most Americans but also gave us a look into the future by shedding light on the problems that will again haunt us if we do not prepare for them. Fortunately, with some financial planning, things like having sufficient emergency funds available when you need them, being able to afford a comfortable retirement and being able to retire when you want to, avoiding too much debt, and having adequate health insurance—all currently major concerns for many Americans—won't be worries for you.

LO7 List ten principles of personal finance.

Ten Principles of Personal Finance

To the first-time student of personal finance, this text may seem like a collection of tools and techniques held together solely by the binding on the book. Not so! In fact, the techniques and tools we use to teach personal financial management are all based on very straightforward logic. We can sum up this logic in ten simple principles. *Although it's not necessary to understand personal finance in order to understand these principles, it's necessary to understand these principles in order to understand personal finance.*

These principles are used throughout the text to unify and relate the topics being presented, which will help you better understand why the tools work. Let's face it, your situation and the personal finance challenges you'll face won't fit into a simple formula. You have to understand the logic behind the material in the text in order to apply it to your life.

Let's identify the ten principles that form the foundations of personal finance. Some are as much statements of common sense as they are theoretical statements. If these principles are all you remember from this course, you'll still have an excellent grasp of personal finance and, thus, a better chance of attaining wealth and achieving your financial goals. Let's take a look at the first eight principles and then the last two—the last two are separated out because they will take on special importance as we help you understand your financial personality and the behavioral aspects of personal finance and then put in place an action plan for today and as you move from college into the real world.

Principle 1: The Best Protection Is Knowledge

Finding advice on personal finance isn't hard—the hard part is differentiating between good advice and bad. The Internet, radio, television, newspapers, magazines, and even old-fashioned books are teaming up with financial gurus and guru wannabees, showering you with the latest advice on what to do with your money. While much of that advice will make someone rich, it may not be you; it may be the advice giver instead—and, even worse, that someone may be getting rich at your expense. You can turn to a professional financial planner to help you establish a lifetime financial plan, but it will be up to you to manage it. The bottom line is that you need to understand the basics of personal financial management if you are going to achieve your financial goals—it's also the only way you can protect yourself. A solid understanding of personal finance will

- Enable you to protect yourself from incompetent investment advisors.
- Provide you with an understanding of the importance of planning for your future.
- Give you the ability to make intelligent investments and take advantage of changes in the economy and interest rates.
- Allow you to extract the principles you learn here and elsewhere and apply them to your own situation.

Because financial problems in real life seldom perfectly reflect textbook problems and solutions, you must be able to abstract what you learn in order to apply it. The only way you can effectively abstract something is to understand it. As with almost everything in life, it's much easier to do it right if you understand what you're doing and why you're doing it.

And when you know what you're doing, you don't have to rely on insurance salespeople, personal financial advisors, and stockbrokers—after all, they may actually be acting in *their own* interests rather than in *your* best interests. For example, an insurance salesperson, motivated by a potential commission, may try to sell you insurance you don't need. A personal financial advisor may try to sell you financial products, such as mutual funds, that are more expensive than similar products because he or he receives a hefty commission on them.

That doesn't mean you should avoid insurance salespeople or financial planners, but you should choose them carefully. Pick a financial planner just as you pick a competent and trustworthy doctor—look for one that fits your needs and has a proven record of ethical and effective assistance to clients. If you trust your doctor—or financial planner—you have to believe he or she has your best interests at heart. Just keep your eyes open, and, of course, be aware of ulterior motives when making financial decisions.

Principle 2: Nothing Happens Without a Plan

Most people spend more time planning their summer vacation than they do planning their financial future. It's easy to avoid thinking about retirement, to avoid thinking about how you're going to pay for your children's education, and to avoid thinking about tightening your financial belt and saving money. We began this text with the statement that it is easier to spend than to save. We can go beyond even that and say that it is easier to think about how you're going to spend your money than it is to think about how you're going to save your money.

If you're like most people, you can probably spend money without thinking about it, but you can't save money without thinking about it. That's the problem. Saving isn't a natural event: It must be planned. Unfortunately, planning isn't natural either. Begin with a modest, uncomplicated financial plan. Once the discipline of saving becomes second nature, or at least accepted behavior, modify and expand your plan. The longer you put off devising a financial plan, the more difficult accomplishing goals becomes. When goals appear insurmountable, you may not even attempt to reach them.

> **STOP & THINK**
>
> All too often we utter those two words of regret, "*if only*," wistfully thinking about a "do over" in life and feeling that if we had made a different decision, then things would have turned out better for us. One of the places you least want to have that "*if only*" feeling of regret is when it comes to your finances, because "do-overs" don't happen in real life. The only way to avoid that "*if only*" feeling is with a plan.

Principle 3: The Time Value of Money

Perhaps the most important concept in personal finance is that money has a time value associated with it. Simply stated, because you can earn interest on any money you receive, money received today is worth more than money received in, say, a year. For example, if you earn $1,000 today and invest that money at 5 percent, then 1 year from today that $1,000 will be worth $1,050. If, however, 1 year from today you earn another $1,000, that will be worth just that $1,000—$50 less than the $1,000 you earned today. Although this idea is not a major surprise to most people, they simply don't grasp its importance. The importance of the time value of money is twofold. First, it allows us to understand how investments grow over time. Second, it enables us to compare dollar amounts in different time periods. If you can't do that, you'll be lost in personal finance.

In this text, we focus on ways to create and preserve wealth. To create wealth, we invest savings and allow them to grow over time. This growth is an illustration of the time value of money. In fact, much of personal finance involves efforts to move money through time. Early in your financial life cycle, you may borrow money to buy a house. In taking out that home mortgage, you are really spending money today and paying later. In saving for retirement, you are saving money today with the intention of spending it later. In each case, money is moved through time. Either

TABLE 1.4 Importance of the Interest Rate and Starting Early—Just Do It!—to Accumulate $1 Million by Age 68 Investing Your Money at 6% and 12%

Making Your Last Payment on Your 68th Birthday and Your First When You Turn:	At 6% Your Monthly Payment Would Be:	At 12% Your Monthly Payment Would Be:
20	$300	$ 33
25	413	59
30	573	108
35	806	198
40	1,151	366
50	2,582	1,320
60	8,141	6,253

you spend in today's dollars and pay back in tomorrow's dollars, or you save in today's dollars and later spend in tomorrow's dollars. Without recognizing the existence of the time value of money, it is impossible to understand **compound interest**, which allows investments to grow over time.

Compound Interest
Interest paid on interest. This occurs when interest paid on an investment is reinvested and added to the principal, thus allowing you to earn interest on the interest, as well as on the principal.

You'll also find that time is your ally. If you are 20 right now and plan on retiring at 68, you'll end up with $1 million if you begin today and save $33 at the end of each month and earn 12 percent on your investment, but you'll have to save $300 a month if you earn only 6 percent; if you begin at age 40, those figures jump to $366 a month at 12 percent and $1,151 at 6 percent; if you don't begin until age 50, you'll have to save $1,320 a month at 12 percent and $2,582 at 6 percent, as shown in Table 1.4. As you can see, it's a lot easier if you start early and earn a high return. This is all because of the time value of money.

Principle 4: Taxes Affect Personal Finance Decisions

Because taxes help to determine the realized return of an investment, they play an important role in personal finance. No investment decision should be made without first knowing the effect of taxes on the return of that investment. Thus, you must look at all your alternatives on an after-tax basis. Taxes aren't the same on all investments, so you will find that effective personal financial planning requires you to have an understanding of the tax laws and how they affect investment decisions.

Principle 5: Stuff Happens, or the Importance of Liquidity

Although much of the focus of personal financial planning is on long-term investing for lifetime goals, you must also plan for the unexpected. This means that some of your money must be available to you at any time, or *liquid*. If liquid funds are not available, an unexpected need, as a result of, say, job loss or injury, may force you to cash in a longer-term investment. You may need to act immediately, which might entail, for example, having to sell a rental property when real estate prices are low. And what if you don't have something to sell? In that case, you'll have to borrow money fast. That kind of borrowing may carry a high interest rate. It will also mean making unexpected loan repayments, which you may not be financially prepared to make. Generally, unplanned borrowing is tough to pay off; it is yet another reason to have adequate liquid funds available, and that generally means having enough liquid funds to cover 3 to 6 months of living expenses. Exactly how much is needed will be discussed in the next chapter.

Principle 6: Waste Not, Want Not—Smart Spending Matters

Managing your money involves more than just saving and investing—it also involves spending, specifically smart spending. If you're going to work hard for your money, you don't want to waste it. Unfortunately, smart spending isn't always practiced. In fact, studies suggest that over 1 in 20 of us—that's over 17 million Americans—are shopaholics; that is, they can't control their urge to shop.

When we talk about smart shopping, we will be talking about more than the four-dollar lattes, the two-pack-a-day cigarette habit, the magazines, and the 450 extra satellite channels; we'll also be talking about buying a car and a house and getting the most out of every dollar you spend.

The first step in smart buying is to differentiate want from need and understand how each purchase fits into your life. The second step is doing your homework to make sure what you get has the quality that you expect. The third step involves making a purchase and getting the best price, and the last step is maintaining your purchase.

Principle 7: Protect Yourself Against Major Catastrophes

The worst time to find out that you don't have the right amount or the right kind of insurance is just after a tragedy occurs. Just look at the flood victims in New Orleans, after Hurricane Katrina, who didn't have flood insurance. As you'll see, insurance is an unusual item to purchase. In fact, most people don't "buy" insurance; they're "sold" insurance. It's generally the insurance salesperson who initiates the sale and leads the client through the process of determining what to purchase.

What makes this process a problem is that it is extremely difficult to compare policies because of the many subtle differences they contain. Moreover, most individuals have insurance but have never read their policies. To avoid the consequences of a major tragedy, you need to buy the kind of insurance that's right for you and to know what your insurance policy really says.

The focus of insurance should be major catastrophes—those events that, although improbable, can be financially devastating. Hurricanes, floods, earthquakes, and fires are examples. These are the events that can inflict losses that you can't afford to sustain, and these are the events insurance should protect you against.

Principle 8: Risk and Return Go Hand in Hand

Why do people save money? The answer is simple: People generally save money and invest it in order to earn interest and grow their money so they will have even more money in the future. What determines how much return or interest you get on your money? Well, investors demand a *minimum return* greater than the anticipated level of inflation. Why? If inflation is expected to be 4 percent and the expected returns on the investment are only 1 percent, then the return isn't enough to cover the loss of purchasing power due to inflation. That means the investor has, in effect, lost money, and there's no sense in making an investment that loses money.

Now that you know what the minimum return is, how do you decide among investment alternatives? While all investments are risky to some degree, some are safer than others. Why would investors put their money in a risky investment when there are safer alternatives? The answer is that they won't unless they are compensated for taking that additional risk. In other words, investors demand additional expected return for taking on added risk. Notice that we refer to "expected" return rather than to "actual" return. You may have expectations and even assurances of what the returns from investing will be, but because risk exists, you can never be sure what those returns are actually going to be.

FIGURE 1.6 The Risk–Return Trade-Off

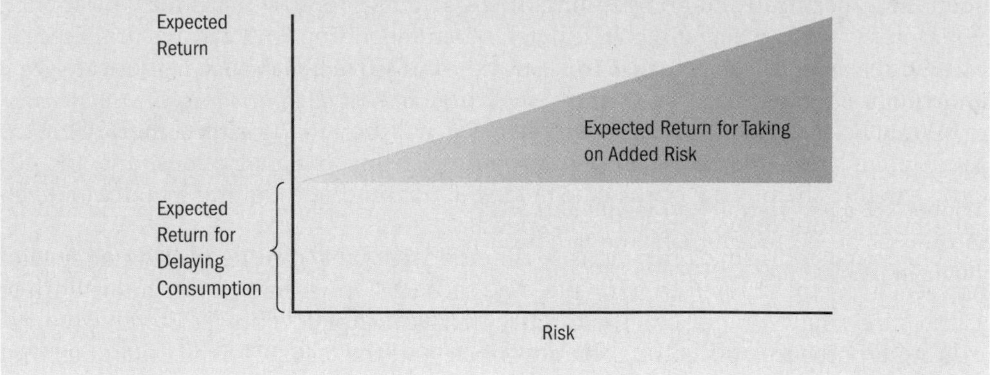

Let's face it, when it comes to investing, nothing is guaranteed in the future, and some investments have more uncertainty or risk—that is, there's a greater chance that the fat return you're expecting may not turn out. Just look at investing in government bonds versus bonds issued by Sears. In each case, you're lending money—that's what you're doing when you buy a bond, because a bond is just like a loan. The entity that issues the bond is borrowing the money and the person (you) who buys the bond is lending the money. Because there is more risk with Sears bonds—that is, there's a greater chance that Sears might not be able to pay you back—Sears bonds promise a higher rate of interest than government bonds do; otherwise, no one would buy Sears bonds. After all, you know the government will be around to pay off its loans, but Sears may not be. It's that added incentive of additional interest that convinces some investors to take on the added risk of buying a Sears bond rather than a government bond. The more risk an investment has, the higher its expected return should be. This relationship between risk and expected return is shown graphically in Figure 1.6.

Diversification
Acquisition of a variety of different investments, instead of just one, to reduce risk.

Fortunately, **diversification** lets you reduce, or "diversify away," some of your risk without affecting your expected return. The concept of diversification is illustrated by the old saying "Don't put all your eggs in one basket." When you diversify, you are spreading your money among several investments instead of putting all your money in one. Then, if one of those investments goes bust, another—you hope—goes boom to make up for the loss. In effect, diversification allows you to weather the ups and downs of investing. You don't experience the great returns, but you don't experience the great losses either—instead, you receive the average return.

BEHAVIORAL INSIGHTS

PRINCIPLE 9

Principle 9: Mind Games, Your Financial Personality, and Your Money Sure, you want to avoid financial mistakes—the problem is that a lot of those mistakes are built right into your brain. In recent years, a lot has been discovered about how our behavioral biases can lead to big financial mistakes. In effect, your mind can get in the way of good financial decision making. Take, for instance, what's called "mental accounting." Mental accounting is the tendency for people to separate money into different mental accounts, or buckets, each with a different purpose. How does this impact your personal finance decisions? It shows itself when you keep money in a savings account that pays 2 percent interest, while not paying off what you owe on a credit card that charges you 14 percent interest. It also shows up when you get your tax return, view it as "mad money," and promptly go out and spend it, while at the same time pinching pennies to save for your child's education.

This idea of mental accounts is just one of several behavioral biases and mental shortcuts that lead us unknowingly down the path to major financial mistakes. Let's look at another one of these behavioral biases, the "sunk cost effect"—once we put money into something, we become attached to it and are more likely to spend good money after bad money. For example, say you buy a very used car for $1,000, and almost immediately after you buy it, the transmission goes out. A new transmission is going to cost $1,500. This bias leads you to want to make the repair, even though the repair will cost more than the car is worth. That's because if you don't repair your car, that $1,000 you spent for it is wasted. But what's happened in the past doesn't matter; you want to base your decisions on what they're going to produce in the future. In effect, the sunk cost effect can cause you to make decisions based on the amount of money and time you have already invested in something, and the end result can be to pour good money after bad money into a car, a house, or almost anything.

> **STOP & THINK**
>
> Envy and "the comparison complex" are two behavioral traits we all have that make us focus on what others have rather than on what is important in life. Studies have shown that watching TV makes people more likely to feel that happiness is based on wealth and what you can buy, and as a result, they become less content with their lives. Have you ever felt that way? Think of an example.

Making all this harder is that everyone relates to money and financial decisions differently—and for many, it is difficult to separate out the emotions involved. In addition, some of us are more sensitive to advertising and more easily swayed to buy what we might not have intended to buy, while others take naturally to financial discipline. Unfortunately, your financial personality is tough to change. At an early age, many people seem to become "financially wired" in ways that make it hard to save, while others find it hard to spend. Our views on spending and saving and whether we have a tendency to "just not think about it" will go a long way toward determining our financial success. In fact, there are people who view money as an evil and feel uncomfortable with wealth. Recognizing your financial personality will allow you to gain control over your financial life and help you to make decisions based on choice rather than emotion and habit. Moreover, when you recognize what your financial personality is and how it impacts your decisions, you won't have to repeat the same financial mistakes for the rest of your life. Just look at Lily in the introduction to this chapter—she simply couldn't stop spending, in spite of the fact that she didn't have any money.

Throughout this text, we will try to alert you to some of the things that might be going on in your brain that you don't know about—at least those things that affect your financial decisions. If you understand these biases, you can control them, and if you recognize what your financial personality is, you can take it out of the process and avoid some of the pitfalls you'd otherwise be subject to. In fact, the last principle we will look at is based on one of these behavioral biases, and it's made tougher for some because of their financial personality.

ACTION PLAN

Principle 10: Just Do It! Each chapter will be closing with an Action Plan, and this chapter closes with the final principle, which calls you to action. Good advice is good only if you act on it.

PRINCIPLE 10

Making the commitment to actually get started may be the most difficult step in the entire personal financial planning process. In fact, people are programmed against taking on unpleasant tasks—it's one of the behavioral biases that we all have—because of a natural desire to procrastinate. If you don't believe that, just think of the last term paper you had to write—more likely than not, much of it was written the night before it was due, even though you knew, weeks before, when it would be due. However, the positive reinforcement associated with making progress toward your goals and taking control of your financial affairs generally means that once you take the first step, the following steps become much easier.

FACTS OF LIFE

Saving early can make a big difference. Say you save $50 a month at 10 percent.

Start at 25 and by 65 you'll have:	**Start at 45 and by 65 you'll have:**
$316,204	$37,968

It's much easier to save than to spend, right? No, just checking—you know the opposite is true. For most people, savings are a residual. That means that you spend what you like and save what is left, so the amount you save is simply what you earn minus what you spend. When you pay yourself first, what you spend becomes the residual. That is, you first set aside your savings, and what is left becomes the amount you can spend—that's the first step in putting your financial plan into action.

Chapter Summaries

LO1 Explain why personal financial planning is so important.

SUMMARY: Personal financial planning will enable you to (1) manage the unplanned, (2) accumulate wealth for special expenses, (3) save for retirement, (4) "cover your assets," (5) invest intelligently, and (6) minimize your payments to Uncle Sam.

LO2 Describe the five basic steps of personal financial planning.

SUMMARY: There are five basic steps to personal financial planning:

1. Evaluate your financial health.
2. Define your financial goals.
3. Develop a plan of action.
4. Implement your plan.
5. Review your progress, reevaluate, and revise your plan.

In fact, the last step in financial planning is often the first because no plan is fixed for life.

KEY TERMS

Liquidity, page 6 The relative ease and speed with which you can convert noncash assets into cash. In effect, liquidity involves having access to your money when you need it.

LO3 Set your financial goals.

SUMMARY: To reach your financial goals, you must first set them. This process involves writing down your financial goals and attaching costs to them, along with identifying when the money to accomplish those goals will be needed. Once you have set your goals, they will become the cornerstone of your personal financial plan, a guide to action, and a benchmark for evaluating the effectiveness of the plan.

Over your lifetime, your goals will change, and you will see that a general financial life cycle pattern applies to most people, even you. There are three stages in the financial life cycle: (1) the early years—a time of wealth accumulation, (2) approaching retirement—the golden years, and (3) the retirement years.

KEY TERMS

Estate Planning, page 9 Planning for your eventual death and the passage of your wealth to your heirs.

Inflation, page 9 An economic condition in which rising prices reduce the purchasing power of money.

Explain how career management and education can determine your income level. LO4

SUMMARY: In general, the better educated you are, the more you will earn. This is because the more specialized skills and training are needed for a job, the higher it tends to pay.

Identify and explain how skills acquired in this course will help you get a job and advance in it. LO5

SUMMARY: This course is not just about managing money. It also helps you develop critical thinking, quantitative reasoning, and ethical skills that you help in your personal and professional life.

Explain the personal finance lessons learned in the recent economic downturn. LO6

SUMMARY: The recent economic downturn demonstrated that too many of us have insufficient emergency funds. In addition, it showed that the financial issue that Americans worry about most is retirement. Other major problems that surfaced involved having too much debt and inadequate health insurance. A lack of financial planning left many Americans ill-prepared for the economic downturn.

List ten principles of personal finance. LO7

SUMMARY: There are ten principles on which personal financial planning is built and that motivate the techniques and tools introduced in this text.

KEY TERMS

Compound Interest, page 22 Interest paid on interest. This occurs when interest paid on an investment is reinvested and added to the principal, thus allowing you to earn interest on the interest, as well as on the principal.

Diversification, page 24 Acquisition of a variety of different investments, instead of just one, to reduce risk.

Problems and Activities

These problems are available in MyLab Finance.

1. What financial strategies should you develop as a result of studying personal financial planning? What financial problems might you avoid?

2. List the five steps in the financial planning process. For each, list an activity, or financial task, that you should accomplish in each stage of the financial life cycle.

3. Financial goals should be specific, realistic, prioritized, and anchored in time. Using these characteristics, identify five financial goals for yourself.
4. As the cornerstone of your financial plan, goals should reflect your lifestyle, serve as a guide to action, and act as a benchmark for evaluating the effectiveness of your plan. For one of the goals identified in Problem 3, explain this statement.
5. The goal of financing the cost of education is obviously important in your present stage of the financial life cycle. Explain how this goal might continue to be important in future stages.
6. For three of the questions in Table 1.3, write a concise and descriptive response. Practice your answers, and then present them to someone willing to give you suggestions for improving your responses or your delivery.
7. Explain how your financial situation is related to your career aspirations.
8. Considering the influence of finances on couple relationships, identify at least three smart financial strategies someone wanting to form a relationship and raise children should follow.
9. Explain how **Principle 5: Stuff Happens, or the Importance of Liquidity** and **Principle 7: Protect Yourself Against Major Catastrophes** may be related. What are you currently doing to protect yourself, and your financial future, from "stuff and other major catastrophes"?

Discussion Case 1

This case is available in MyLab Finance.

Jeremiah, an accountant, and Bethany just returned from their honeymoon in the Bahamas. They celebrated their marriage and Bethany's completion of her M.B.A. program. They have been encouraged by their parents to establish some personal and financial goals for their future. However, they do not know how to set or achieve these goals. They know that they would like to own their own home and have children, but those are the only goals they have considered. Jeremiah knows of a financial advisor who might be able to help with their predicament, but they don't think they can afford professional help.

Questions

1. If you were serving as the couple's financial advisor, how would you explain the five steps in the financial planning process and their importance to future financial success?

WORKSHEET 1 WORKSHEET 2

2. What financial goals (short-term, intermediate-term, and long-term) would you determine to be the most important, and which the least important, to Jeremiah and Bethany, considering their current life cycle stage? Support your answer. (*Hint:* See Worksheet 1 or Worksheet 2.)

WORKSHEET 3

3. What four common concerns should guide the development of their financial plan? How are these related to Principles 4, 5, and 7?
4. List five tips for Bethany to keep in mind when preparing for interviews. (*Hint:* Review Worksheet 3.)
5. Identify three important strategies for young professionals such as Jeremiah and Bethany to remember to ensure success in their chosen careers. Why do "ethical violations end careers"?
6. As a new couple, what information can you provide Jeremiah and Bethany about possible roadblocks? For example, what are some of the commonly reported disagreements among couples according to a recent Harris Poll?
7. Why is Principle 10 the most important principle? Why is it equally relevant to financial planning and career planning?

Discussion Case 2

This case is available in **MyLab Finance**.

Nicholas and Marita Delgados, from Rochester, Minnesota, are the proud new parents of twin daughters. This was quite a shock to them and 2-year-old Jarred. They were not prepared for twins, and this has complicated their financial plans, as well as most everything else! They had planned to pay for education costs, but now they are uncertain how to prepare for having three children in college at the same time. They love their family and truly believe that money isn't everything, but their dream to retire early and travel seems to be fading with every new expense. They need help with Step 5: Review Your Progress, Reevaluate, and Revise Your Plan. Marita has told Nicholas that she wants to attend a personal finance class at the community center, but Nicholas thinks they should seek assistance from a financial planner. As Nicholas points out, even though expenses are rising, they both have good jobs with the potential for rapid advancement and salary increases.

Questions

1. Explain to Nicholas and Marita why personal financial planning is crucial to their future. Why are Principles 1 and 2 important if they choose to seek professional advice? How might the behavioral finance biases of mental accounting and sunk costs influence their response to the professional's advice?
2. Using the information in Table 1.1, estimate the cost of raising Jarred and the twins from birth to age 18 if the Delgados' current annual income is approximately $95,000 and both parents plan to continue working full-time.
3. Explain how understanding and applying Principles 3 and 8 will be critical to funding the children's education.
4. Setting financial goals involves specifically defining the goal, determining its future cost, and pinpointing the future time when the money will be needed. Write a specific and realistic goal for funding the children's education.
5. In addition to funding the children's education, name two other short-, intermediate-, and long-term goals the Delgados should consider as they revise their financial plan.
6. With three children to consider, how might Principles 5, 6, and 7 be relevant to the Delgados' situation?

CHAPTER 2

Measuring Your Financial Health and Making a Plan

Learning Objectives

LO1	**Calculate** your level of net worth or wealth using a balance sheet.	Using a Balance Sheet to Measure Your Wealth
LO2	**Analyze** where your money comes from and where it goes using an income statement.	Using an Income Statement to Trace Your Money
LO3	**Use** ratios to identify your financial strengths and weaknesses.	Using Ratios: Financial Thermometers
LO4	**Set** up a record-keeping system to track your income and expenditures.	Record Keeping
LO5	**Implement** a financial plan or budget that will provide for the level of savings needed to achieve your goals.	Putting It All Together: Budgeting
LO6	**Decide** if a professional financial planner will play a role in your financial affairs.	Hiring a Professional

You probably have something in common with the characters on the CBS sitcom *2 Broke Girls*—that being the "broke" part. This show is about two young women (Max, a streetwise waitress and nanny, and Caroline, the sophisticated daughter of a Bernie Madoff-like criminal who finds herself disgraced and penniless after her father's arrest) starting out on their own in Brooklyn.

With a setup like this, it's no surprise that this sitcom is littered with money lessons. It shows the need for planning—after all, as Caroline has found out, if you have money, you don't want to take it for granted; it can be gone in a heartbeat. It also shows that if life deals you a financial blow, all is not lost; you can start over financially, but you do have to work at it, and you have to have a plan. As we watch Max and Caroline forge a friendship and develop a dream, we see that not having money isn't the end of life. Life can still be good, but taking financial control and attaining your goals can make it even better.

Michael Yarish/CBS Photo Archive/Getty Images

For Max and Caroline, their goal is to one day open their own cupcake shop. With each episode, we watch their many misadventures as they struggle to earn and save every penny to fulfill their dream. What are they doing to earn and save their money? In addition to their waitress jobs, they shop at the Goodwill (a definite first for Caroline), they share a one-bedroom apartment in Brooklyn (which definitely exceeds the real estate rental power of someone on a shoestring budget), they use coupons, they even open a dessert bar, and they spend their spring break housesitting at a rich customer's New York apartment. At the end of each episode, they give viewers the latest tally of their saving efforts for their cupcake business venture—which in the spring of 2017 after many ups and downs, totaled \$6,475.54.

What would help Max and Caroline reach their goal? Clearly, it is some advice about managing their money and putting together a budget. Starting out in the real world with no money, the fastest way to achieve their dream begins with keeping track of what comes in and what goes out. Remember **Principle 2: Nothing Happens Without a Plan**. Because, after all, if you don't know where your money goes, it's hard to save it. And that's the first step toward never being "1 broke girl or guy."

PRINCIPLE 2

Planning and budgeting require control—they don't come naturally. Without the ability to measure our financial health and develop a plan and budget, we will not achieve our financial goals. Showing financial restraint isn't as much fun as spending with reckless abandon, but it's a lot more fun than winding up broke

FIGURE 2.1 The Budgeting and Planning Process: Evaluating Your Financial Health and Developing a Plan of Action

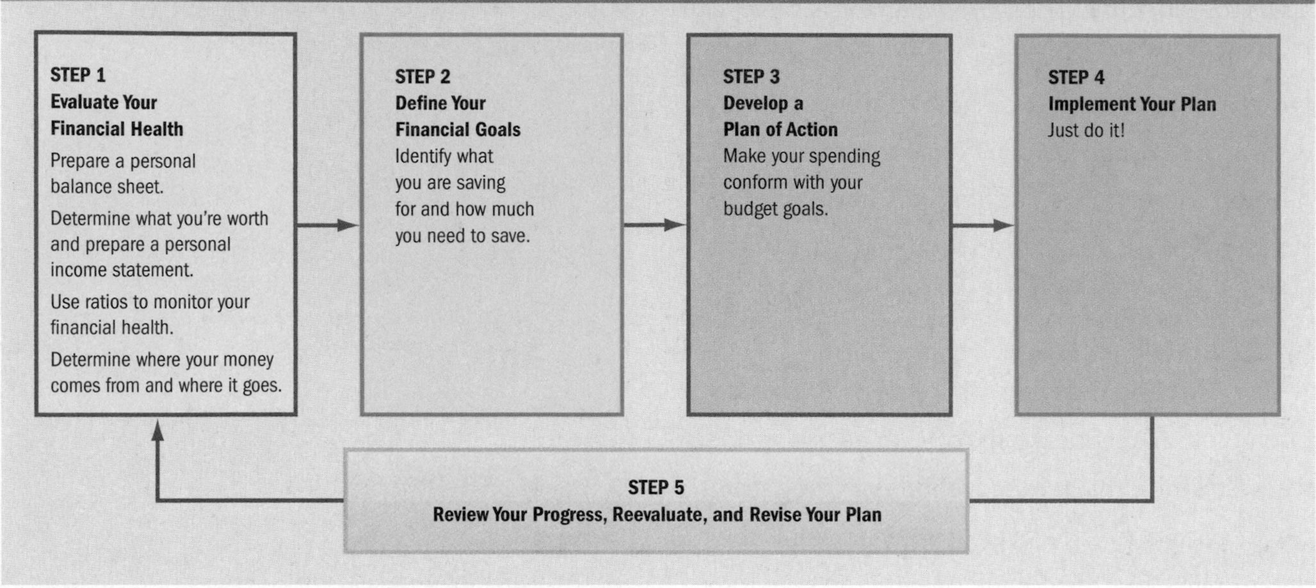
STEP 1
Evaluate Your Financial Health
Prepare a personal balance sheet.
Determine what you're worth and prepare a personal income statement.
Use ratios to monitor your financial health.
Determine where your money comes from and where it goes.
STEP 2
Define Your Financial Goals
Identify what you are saving for and how much you need to save.
STEP 3
Develop a Plan of Action
Make your spending conform with your budget goals.
STEP 4
Implement Your Plan
Just do it!
STEP 5
Review Your Progress, Reevaluate, and Revise Your Plan

and homeless. Making and sticking with a plan isn't necessarily easy, and it often involves what some people would consider sacrifices (such as getting a job over spring break instead of going down to Cancun, Mexico, Panama City, Las Vegas, or wherever to be on MTV's *Spring Break*) or just skipping that daily designer coffee. The fact is, though, that the rewards of taking financial control are worth any small sacrifices and more. After all, if you're like most people, you can probably spend money without thinking about it, but you can't save money without thinking about it—and without saving, you'll never own your own cupcake shop or achieve your own financial goal.

In this chapter, we begin the budgeting and planning process that was first outlined in Figure 1.1, specifically, working on Steps 1 and 3, as shown in Figure 2.1. We begin by measuring our wealth using a personal balance sheet and then a personal income statement to help figure out where our money came from and where it went. With this information in hand, we will use ratios to check into the status of our financial health and look at ways to keep track of all this. Finally, we will set up and implement a cash budget.

Personal Balance Sheet
A statement of your financial position on a given date. It includes the assets you own, the debt or liabilities you have incurred, and your level of wealth, which is referred to as net worth.

LO1 Calculate your level of net worth or wealth using a balance sheet.

Using a Balance Sheet to Measure Your Wealth

Before you can decide how much you need to save to reach your goals, you have to measure your financial condition—what you own and what you owe. Corporations use a balance sheet for this purpose, and so can you. A **personal balance sheet** is a statement of your financial position on a given date—a snapshot of your financial status at a particular time. It lists the **assets** you own, the debt or **liabilities** you've incurred, and your general level of wealth, which is your **net worth or equity**. Assets represent what you own. Liabilities represent your debt or what you owe. To determine your level of wealth or net worth, you subtract your level of debt or borrowing from your assets. Figure 2.2 is a sample balance sheet worksheet. We will now look at each section.

Assets
What you own.

Liabilities
What you owe; your debt or borrowing.

Net Worth or Equity
A measure of the level of your wealth. It is determined by subtracting the level of your debt or borrowing from the value of your assets.

Assets: What You Own

The first section of the balance sheet represents your assets. All your possessions are considered assets, whether or not you still owe money on them. When you estimate the value of all your assets, list them using their **fair market value**—what they could be sold for—not what they cost or what they will be worth a year from now. The fair market value can be more or less than the price you paid for a given asset, depending on what others are willing to pay for that asset now. Remember, a balance sheet is a snapshot in time, so all values must be current.

Fair Market Value
What an asset could be sold for, rather than what it cost or what it will be worth sometime in the future.

Monetary Assets There are a number of different types of assets. The first assets listed on the balance sheet are monetary assets. A monetary asset is basically a liquid asset—one that either is cash or can easily be turned into cash with little or no loss in value. Monetary assets include the cash you hold, your checking and savings account balances, and your money market funds. These are the cash and cash equivalents you use for everyday life. They also provide the necessary liquidity in case of an emergency.

FIGURE 2.2 Personal Balance Sheet

WORKSHEET 4

Assets (What You Own)		
A. Monetary Assets (bank account, etc.) (Chapter 5)		______
B. Investments (Chapters 11–15)	+	______
C. Retirement Plans (Chapter 16)	+	______
D. Housing (market value) (Chapter 8)	+	______
E. Automobiles (Chapter 8)	+	______
F. Personal Property	+	______
G. Other Assets	+	______
H. Your Total Assets (add lines A–G)	=	______
Liabilities or Debt (What You Owe)		
Current Debt		
I. Current Bills		______
J. Credit Card Debt (Chapter 6)	+	______
Long-Term Debt		
K. Housing (Chapter 8)		______
L. Automobile Loans (Chapter 8)	+	______
M. Other Debt (Chapter 7)	+	______
N. Your Total Debt (add lines I–M)	=	______
Your Net Worth		
H. Total Assets		______
N. Less: Total Debt	−	______
O. Equals: Your Net Worth	=	______

Investments The second major category of assets, investments, includes such financial assets as common stocks, mutual funds, and bonds. In general, the purpose of these assets is to accumulate wealth to satisfy a goal such as buying a house or having sufficient savings for a child's college tuition or your retirement. You can usually determine the value of your investments by checking their current price on Internet sites such as **finance.yahoo.com** or the online version of the *Wall Street Journal*, **www.wsj.com**. Your insurance policy may also be an investment asset if it has a cash surrender value. This type of insurance policy can be terminated before the insured's death, at which time the policyholder will receive the cash value of the policy. If you have this type of insurance policy, then its cash surrender value should be included as part of your investment assets. Finally, any real estate purchased for investment purposes should also appear as an asset. The common thread among all these assets is that they are not meant for use, as you would use a car or a house. Instead, they have been purchased for the purpose of generating wealth.

FACTS OF LIFE

A recent survey asked 22- to 29-year-olds what, if they could find a way to cut down on their spending, would be the first thing they would eliminate. Here are the three responses they most often made:

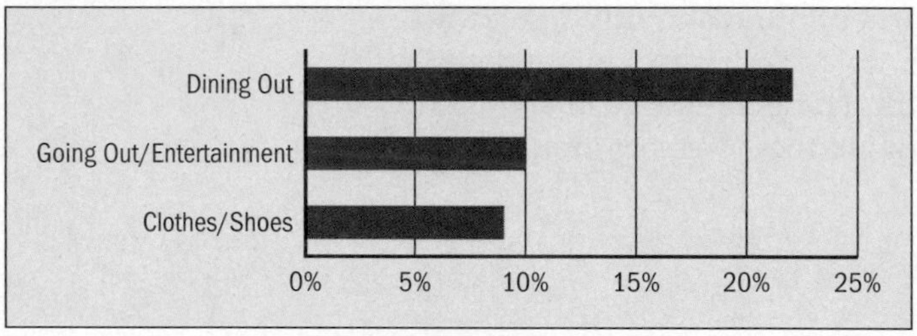

Retirement Plans These include investments made by you or your employer aimed directly at achieving your goal of saving for retirement. Retirement plans are usually in the form of IRAs, 401(k) or 403(b) plans, SEP-IRA plans, and company pension plans, which we will discuss in detail in Chapter 16. Typically, retirement plans issue quarterly statements, which list their current value.

The current value of your stake in your company's pension plan should also be included as a retirement plan asset. If you work for a company that offers a pension plan, the easiest way to value your stake in the plan is to call up your benefits office and ask how much it's worth.

Tangible Asset
A physical asset, such as a house or a car, as opposed to an investment.

Housing Your house, if you own it, constitutes another asset category. Although a house is an asset that you use—a **tangible asset**—it usually holds the majority of your savings. The value of your house recorded on the balance sheet should be its fair market value, even though at that price it may take several months for it to sell. You might consult with a real estate agent or look on **http://www.zillow.com** for help in valuing your home. Keep in mind that even if you owe money on your home, it's still yours.

Automobiles Your car, truck, motorcycle, or other vehicle also gets its own asset category. Just like your home, your vehicle is a tangible asset—one you probably use daily. However, unlike your home, your vehicle is probably worth less than you paid for it. The fair market value for vehicles almost always goes down, often starting right after you take it home from the showroom. You can find the fair market value for most vehicles in an automotive **blue book**, or try **http://www.edmunds.com**. Do not include any cars you lease as assets. If the car is leased, you don't hold title to it and, thus, don't actually own it. Likewise, a company car that you get to use but don't own wouldn't count as an asset.

Blue Book
A listing of used-car prices (by model and year manufactured), giving the average price a particular car sells for and its expected trade-in value.

Personal Property This category consists of tangible assets. Basically, personal property is all your possessions—furniture, appliances, jewelry, TVs, and so forth. In general, although you may have spent a good deal of money on these items, their fair market value will be only a fraction of the purchase amount.

Other Assets The "other" category includes anything that has not yet been accounted for. As an example, you might own part of a business, or you might have a massive collection of semivaluable (or so you think) Pez dispensers, or you might be owed money by a deadbeat friend. All of these count as assets and must appear at their fair market value on your balance sheet. Of course, if your friend is really a deadbeat, the amount owed shouldn't appear as an asset—since you'll never see it!

Summed up, these asset categories represent the total value of everything you own.

Liabilities: What You Owe

A liability is debt that you have taken on and that you must repay in the future. Most financial planners classify liabilities as current or long-term. Current liabilities are those that must be paid off within the next year, and long-term liabilities come due beyond a year's time. In listing your liabilities, be sure to include only the *unpaid* balances on those liabilities. Remember, you owe only the unpaid portion of any loan.

Current Debt In general, the current debt category consists of the total of your unpaid bills, including utility bills, past-due rent, cable TV bills, and insurance premiums that you owe. The unpaid balance on your credit cards represents a current liability because it's a debt that you should pay off within a year. Even if you have not yet received a bill for a purchase you made on credit, the amount you owe on this purchase should be included as a liability.

Long-Term Debt This category tends to consist of debt on larger assets, such as your home or car or student loan. Because of the nature of the assets it finances, long-term debt almost always involves larger amounts than does current debt. If you think about it, the very reason long-term debt covers the long term is that it involves sums too large for the average individual to be able to pay off within 1 year. The largest debt you ever take on—and, thus, the longest-term debt you ever take on—will probably be the mortgage on your home. Car loans are another major category of long-term debt. Just as a leased car is not considered an asset, the remaining lease obligation should not be considered a liability, or something that you owe. In effect, you are "renting" your car when you lease it. However, it's a very fine line between a debt obligation and a lease contract—if the lease simply can't be broken, no matter what, it may be considered debt. Keep in mind that future lease payments, future insurance payments, and future rent payments are something you may owe in the future, but they are not something you owe right now.

FACTS OF LIFE

A recent survey asked 22- to 29-year-olds whether they had worked out a monthly budget to help plan for their expenses. Their responses looked like this:

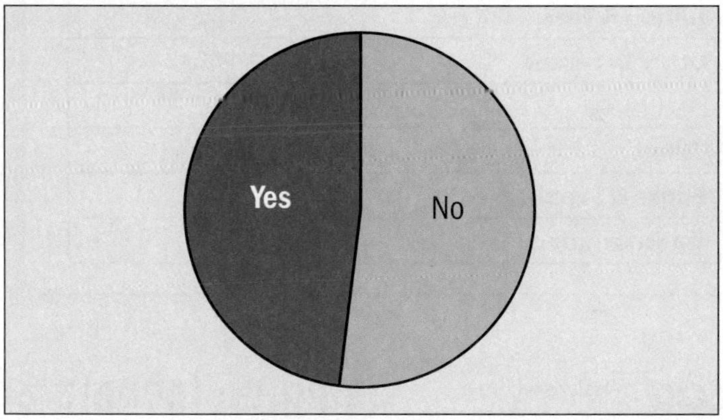

Finally, any other loans that you have outstanding should be included. For example, student loans, loans on your life insurance policy, bank loans, and installment loans are liabilities. Together, long-term debt and current liabilities represent what you owe.

Net Worth: A Measure of Your Wealth

To calculate your net worth, subtract your total debt from your total assets. This represents the level of wealth you have accumulated. If your liabilities are greater than the value of your assets, then your net worth has a negative value, and you're

Insolvent
Owing more money than one's assets are worth.

considered **insolvent**. Insolvency results from consuming more than you take in financially, and in some instances, it can lead to bankruptcy.

What is a "good" level of net worth? That depends on your goals and your place in the financial life cycle. You would expect a 25-year-old to have a considerably lower net worth than a 45-year-old. Likewise, a 45-year-old who has saved for college for three children may have a higher net worth than a 45-year-old with no children. Which one is in better financial shape? The answer doesn't necessarily depend on who has the larger net worth; rather, it is based on who has done a better job of achieving financial goals. Just to give you an idea of where most people stand, the median net worth for families where the head of the household is less than 35 is only $6,676—and rises to almost $200,000 for families where the head of the household is 60 to 69 years old. For all families, it is in the $75,000 range. Also, as you might expect, the median net worth for households where the head of the household has a college degree is over 12 times higher than for one where the head of the household does not have a high school diploma.

Your goal in financial planning is to manage your net worth or wealth in such a way that your goals are met in a timely fashion. The balance sheet enables you to measure your progress toward these goals and to monitor your financial well-being. It also allows you to detect changes in your financial well-being that might otherwise go unnoticed and correct them early on.

FACTS OF LIFE

Breakdown of Average Student Budget

Discretionary	40%
Entertainment	6.5%
Apparel & Services	6.7%
Travel & Vacation	2.7%
Other Discretionary	22%
Room & Board	26%
Tuition & Fees	19%
Other Expenses	8%
Health	1%
Other	7%
Books & Supplies	4%
Transportation	3%

Sample Balance Sheet for Larry and Louise Tate

To illustrate the construction and use of a balance sheet, we have a sample from Larry and Louise Tate, shown in Figure 2.3. Remember, a balance sheet provides a snapshot of an individual's or a family's financial worth at a given time. Because investment values fluctuate daily with the movements in the stock market, so does net worth. The balance sheet in Figure 2.3 was constructed on December 31, 2017, and reflects the value of the Tates' assets, liabilities, and net worth on that specific date.

LO2 Analyze where your money comes from and where it goes using an income statement.

Using an Income Statement to Trace Your Money

Income Statement
A statement that tells you where your money has come from and where it has gone over some period of time.

The second step in creating a personal financial plan is to trace your money. A balance sheet is like a financial snapshot: It tells you how much wealth you have accumulated as of a *certain date*. An **income statement** is more like a financial motion picture: It tells you where your money has come from and where it has gone over some *period of time*. Actually, although it's generally called an income statement, it's really an income and expenditure, or net income, statement because it looks at what you take in and subtracts from that, or "nets out," what you spend, with what is left over being the amount available for savings or investment.

An income statement can help you stay solvent by telling you whether or not you're earning more than you spend. If you're spending too much, your income statement shows exactly where your money is going, so that you can spot problem areas quickly. Of course, if you don't have a spending problem, your income statement tells you how much of your income is available for saving and for meeting

WORKSHEET 4

FIGURE 2.3 A Balance Sheet for Louise and Larry Tate, December 31, 2017

Assets (What They Own)			
MONETARY ASSETS			
A. Total Monetary Assets	**A.**	=	**3,590**
INVESTMENTS			
Mutual Funds			5,600
Individual Stocks and Bonds		+	9,500
Investment Real Estate (REITs, partnerships)		+	0
Other (life insurance—cash value, REITs, other)		+	0
B. Total Investments	**B.**	=	**15,100**
RETIREMENT PLANS			
401(k) and 403(b), SEP-IRA Plan			2,500
Company Pension		+	8,000
IRA		+	8,000
C. Total Retirement Plans	**C.**	=	**18,500**
HOUSING			
Primary Residence			170,000
Time-Shares/Condominiums and Second Home		+	70,000
D. Total Housing (market value)	**D.**	=	**240,000**
AUTOMOBILES			
E. Total Automobiles	**E.**	=	**12,000**
PERSONAL PROPERTY			
F. Total Personal Property	**F.**	=	**11,000**
OTHER ASSETS			
G. Total Other Assets	**G.**	=	**0**
TOTAL ASSETS			
H. Total Assets (add lines A–G)	**H.**	=	**300,190**
Liabilities or Debt (What They Owe)			
CURRENT BILLS			
I. Current Bills (unpaid balance)	**I.**	=	**350**
CREDIT CARD DEBT			
J. Total Credit Card Debt	**J.**	=	**1,150**
HOUSING LOANS			
First Mortgage			105,000
Second-Home Mortgage		+	52,000
Home Equity Loan		+	9,000
K. Total Housing Loans	**K.**	=	**166,000**
AUTOMOBILE LOANS			
L. Total Automobile Loans	**L.**	=	**3,000**
OTHER DEBT			
College Loans			4,000
Other Loans (installment, bank, other)		+	1,000
M. Total Other Debt	**M.**	=	**5,000**
TOTAL DEBT			
N. Total Debt (add lines I–M)	**N.**	=	**$175,500**
Net Worth			
TOTAL ASSETS			
H. Total Assets	**H.**	+	**$300,190**
LESS: TOTAL DEBT			
N. Less: Total Debt	**N.**	–	**$175,500**
EQUALS: NET WORTH			
O. Equals: Net Worth	**O.**	=	**$124,690**

Assets: This includes everything they own.

The Tates' primary investments are their home and their vacation condominium in Vail, which have market values of $170,000 and $70,000, respectively.

Adding all the assets together shows that the Tates own or have total assets of $300,190.

Liabilities: This includes everything they owe.

Just as the Tates' homes make up their primary assets, their mortgages on these homes make up their primary liabilities. Their mortgage loans total $166,000.

The Tates' total liabilities, or what they owe, equals $175,500.

We use net worth to gauge financial progress. If in future balance sheets the Tates' net worth is higher, the Tates are accumulating more wealth.

Net Worth: This is the difference between assets and liabilities and is a measure of wealth.

If the Tates sold off all their assets and paid off all their debts, they would have $124,690 in cash—that is their net worth.

WORKSHEET 5

FIGURE 2.4 A Simplified Income Statement

Your Take-Home Pay			
A. Total Income		A.	______
B. Total Income Taxes	−	B.	______
C. After-Tax Income Available for Living Expenditures or Take-Home Pay (line A minus line B)	=	C.	______
Your Living Expenses			
D. Total Housing Expenditures		D.	______
E. Total Food Expenditures	+	E.	______
F. Total Clothing and Personal Care Expenditures	+	F.	______
G. Total Transportation Expenditures	+	G.	______
H. Total Recreation Expenditures	+	H.	______
I. Total Medical Expenditures	+	I.	______
J. Total Insurance Expenditures	+	J.	______
K. Total Other Expenditures	+	K.	______
L. Total Living Expenditures (add lines D–K)	=	L.	______
Total Available for Savings and Investment			
C. After-Tax Income Available for Living Expenditures or Take-Home Pay		C.	______
L. Total Living Expenditures (add lines D–K)	−	L.	______
M. Income Available for Savings and Investment (line C minus line L)	=	M.	______

financial goals. With a good income statement, you'll never end another month wondering where all of your money went.

Personal income statements are prepared on a cash basis, meaning they're based entirely on actual cash flows. You record income only when you actually receive money, and you record expenditures only when you actually pay money out. Giving someone an IOU wouldn't appear on an income statement, but receiving a paycheck would. Buying a stereo on credit wouldn't appear on your income statement, but making a payment to the credit card company would. As a result, a personal income statement truly reflects the pattern of cash flows that you experience.

To construct an income statement, you need to record your income for the given time period and subtract from it the expenses you incurred during that period. The result tells you the amount you have available for savings. Figure 2.4 shows a general outline for an income statement.

Income: Where Your Money Comes From

For your income statement, income, or cash inflows, will include such items as wages, salary, bonuses, tips, royalties, and commissions, in addition to any other sources of income you may have. Additional sources of income might include family income, payments from the government (e.g., veterans' benefits or welfare income), retirement income, investment income, and those yearly checks you get for winning the Publishers Clearing House Sweepstakes.

Some of your income may not ever reach your pocketbook. Instead, it may be automatically invested in a voluntary retirement plan, used to pay for insurance you buy through work, or sent to the government to cover taxes. For example, if your total earnings are $50,000 and you automatically have $4,000 deducted for insurance and a retirement fund and $8,000 deducted in taxes, then your income is $50,000 even though your take-home pay is only $38,000. One good thing about having your contribution to your retirement fund automatically deducted from your salary is that it becomes automatic and you don't see it and are not tempted to spend it. In effect, you don't have to think about it and how it lowers your take-home pay. You must make sure to record the full amount of what you earned—not just the dollar value of your paycheck. Any money you receive, even if you automatically spend it (even for taxes), is considered income at the time when it is received.

Next, calculate the total amount of money you pay in federal, state, and Social Security income taxes. Then subtract your taxes from your earnings. This is your take-home pay, or the money you have available for expenditures.

Expenditures: Where Your Money Goes

Although income usually is very easy to calculate, expenditures usually are not. Why? Because many expenditures are cash transactions and do not leave a paper trail. It's hard to keep track of all the little things you spend your money on. But to create a valuable personal financial plan, you must understand where your money goes. Look at the categories of expenditures in Figure 2.4 to get an idea of the ways in which living expenses can be categorized and tracked.

Some financial planners also classify living expenses as either **variable** or **fixed expenditures**, depending on whether you have control over the expenditure. These classifications are appealing, but not all expenses fit neatly into them. For example, it's difficult to categorize car or home repairs as being either variable (you have a choice in spending this money) or fixed (you have no choice in spending this money). They may be postponable but probably not for too long.

Variable Expenditure
An expenditure over which you have control. That is, you are not obligated to make that expenditure, and it may vary from month to month.

Fixed Expenditure
An expenditure over which you have no control. You are obligated to make this expenditure, and it is generally at a constant level each month.

Where does all our money go? Turns out that what the average American household spends its money on depends on how much it earns. The more we earn, the more we spend on such things as education and entertainment. Figure 2.5 provides a breakdown of spending for households—or, as the government calls them, consumer units—with different incomes. It shows that housing is the major expenditure, with transportation and gasoline coming in second. Interestingly, but probably not a surprise, a large proportion of food expenditures occur away from home at restaurants.

Right now you may be wondering what the average or mean household income before taxes is—it turns out to be about $65,751. One thing to keep in mind with this figure is that it represents the average income, not the median or middle income. Why is that important? To calculate the average income for 100 people, you add up the incomes for all 100 and then divide that by 100. However, if that population of 100 includes some people like Warren Buffett, who make a ton of money, they raise the average income of the entire population well above what the 50th ranked person earned. Halfway between what the 50th ranked person and the 51st ranked person earned is the median of the population. You can think of that as what the "Average Joe" earns. For the United States, the median household income is less than the average income of $65,751; it's actually only about $56,516.

Also, keep in mind that the amounts in Figure 2.5 are spending averages and that they vary across the country. For example, people living in San Francisco spend quite a bit more on food because they tend to eat out more often than those who live elsewhere (better restaurants, I guess). In addition, remember that when you buy something, it actually costs more than you may think—at least in terms of how much money you must earn to buy it. For example, if you pay 28 percent of your income in federal and state taxes and you want to buy a new stereo for $720, you actually have to earn $1,000 to pay for it. The first $280 of your $1,000 earnings went to Uncle Sam, leaving you $720 for your stereo.

Preparing an Income Statement: Louise and Larry Tate

To get a better understanding of the preparation of an income statement, take a look at the one for Louise and Larry Tate in Figure 2.6. The income statement and

FIGURE 2.5 How Americans Spent Their Money in 2016

Spending on:	Low-income families: $11,890–$19,572	Middle-income families: $49,952–$62,587	High-income families: Above $144,180
Food at Home	14.6%	7.3%	5.3%
Food at Restaurants, etc.	4.9%	5.3%	5.3%
Housing	41.4%	33.5%	29.2%
Utilities	10.0%	7.9%	4.5%
Clothes & Shoes	3.2%	2.8%	4.1%
Transportation & Gasoline	13.9%	19.3%	14.4%
Health Care & Health Insurance	9.3%	8.5%	5.8%
Entertainment	5.4%	4.8%	5.4%
Education	1.4%	1.5%	4.0%
Saving for Retirement	2.6%	9.1%	16.6%

Note: Note: Because some family units spend more that their income, totals may exceed 100%.
Source: Consumer Expenditures (U.S. Department of Labor, U.S. Bureau of Labor Statistics, August 2016).

balance sheet can and should be used together. The balance sheet lets you judge your financial standing by showing your net worth, and the income statement tells you exactly how your spending and saving habits affect that net worth. If your balance sheet shows you that you're not building your net worth as much or as quickly as you'd like or that you're overspending and actually decreasing your net worth, then your income statement can help by showing you where your money is going.

FIGURE 2.6 A Personal Income Statement for Louise and Larry Tate

Take-Home Pay		
Income		
Wages and Salaries		
Wage Earner 1	$57,500	
Wage Earner 2	12,000	
= Total Wages and Salaries		69,500
+ Interest, Dividends, Royalties, Other		720
= **A. Total Income**		**$70,220**
Taxes		
Federal Income and Social Security		11,830
+ State Income		1,880
= **B. Total Income Taxes**		**$13,710**
C. After-Tax Income Available for Living Expenditures or Take-Home Pay (line A minus line B)		**$56,510**
Living Expenses		
Housing		
Rent		0
+ Mortgage Payments		19,656
+ Utilities, Maintenance, Taxes, Furniture, Other		10,820
= **D. Total Housing Expenditures**		**$30,476**
Food		
Food and Supplies		5,800
+ Restaurant Expenses		1,400
= **E. Total Food Expenditures**		**$ 7,200**
Clothing and Personal Care		
= **F. Total Clothing and Personal Care Expenditures**		**$ 2,590**
Transportation		
Automobile Loan Payments		2,588
+ Gas, Tolls, Parking, Repairs, Other		1,550
= **G. Total Transportation Expenditures**		**$ 4,138**
Recreation		
Vacation		2,000
Other Recreation		1,700
= **H. Total Recreation Expenditures**		**$ 3,700**
Medical Expenditures		
= **I. Total Medical Expenditures**		**$ 410**
Insurance Expenditures		
Health and Life		420
+ Automobile		1,260
+ Disability, Liability, Other		260
= **J. Total Insurance Expenditures**		**$ 1,940**
Other Expenditures		
Educational Expenditures (college loan payments)		1,600
+ Child Care, Other		180
= **K. Total Other Expenditures**		**$ 1,780**
L. Total Living Expenditures (add lines D–K)		**$52,234**
Total Available for Savings and Investment		
= **M. Income Available for Savings and Investment (line C minus line L)**		**$ 4,276**

Take-home pay is after-tax income—it is what you have available to spend or save.

Your income statement makes sense only if you know where your money goes. To determine your living expenses, keep a small notebook or some notepaper in your purse or wallet, and write down all your cash expenditures—do this for a month. You'll probably be surprised to see where your money went. In addition, make use of your credit card bills and cancelled checks to help you keep track.

If your take-home pay is greater than your living expenses, you can save and invest—but if your take-home pay is less than your living expenses, you've got some changes to make.

Budget
A plan for controlling cash inflows and cash outflows. Based on your goals and financial obligations, a budget limits spending in different categories.

By reviewing all your expenses and spending patterns, you can decide on specific ways to cut back on purchases and increase savings. This process of setting spending goals is referred to as setting a **budget**. As you will see later in this chapter, a smart budget includes estimates of all future expenses and helps you manage your money to meet specific financial goals.

But before you can design and implement a budget plan, you first need to analyze your balance sheet and income statement using ratios to better understand any financial shortcomings or deficiencies you discover.

LO3 Use ratios to identify your financial strengths and weaknesses.

Using Ratios: Financial Thermometers

The next step in creating your personal financial plan is to take the temperature of your finances. By themselves, the numbers in your balance sheet and income statement are helpful and informative, but they don't tell you everything you need to know about your financial well-being. You need a tool to help you glean all the meaning you can from these numbers. That tool is ratios.

Financial ratios allow you to analyze the raw data in your balance sheet and income statement and to compare them with a preset target or your own previous performance. In general, you use ratios to better understand how you're managing your financial resources. Specifically, you want answers to these questions:

1. Do I have enough liquidity to meet emergencies?
2. Can I meet my debt obligations?
3. Am I saving as much as I think I am?

Question 1: Do I Have Enough Liquidity to Meet Emergencies?

If your TV died in the middle of the playoffs or that miniseries you've been watching, would you have enough cash on hand to buy another one immediately? To judge your liquidity, you need to compare the amount of your cash and other liquid assets with the amount of debt you currently have coming due. In other words, you need to look at your balance sheet and divide your monetary assets by your current liabilities. The resultant measure of your liquidity is called the **current ratio**:

Current Ratio
A ratio aimed at determining whether you have adequate liquidity to meet emergencies; defined as monetary assets divided by current liabilities.

$$\text{current ratio} = \frac{\text{monetary assets}}{\text{current liabilities}}$$

We can see from the balance sheet for Larry and Louise Tate that their monetary assets total \$3,590 and their current liabilities (current bills and credit card debt) total \$1,500. Thus, the Tates' current ratio is:

$$\text{current ratio} = \frac{\$3{,}590}{\$1{,}500} = 2.39$$

Although there's no set rule for how large the current ratio should be, it certainly should be greater than 1.0. Most financial advisors look for a current ratio above 2.0. More important than the level of the current ratio is its trend: Is it going up, or (of more concern) is it going down? If it is going down, you have to try to find the cause. To do this, you have to see what changes have caused the ratio to decrease.

One problem with the current ratio is that people generally have a number of monthly expenses that are not considered current liabilities. For example, long-term debt payments such as mortgage payments and auto loan payments may not be considered current liabilities, but they still must be paid on a monthly basis. Therefore, it's also helpful to calculate the ratio of monetary assets to monthly living expenses, which is called the **month's living expenses covered ratio**.

Month's Living Expenses Covered Ratio
A ratio aimed at determining whether you have adequate liquidity to meet emergencies; defined as monetary assets divided by annual living expenditures divided by 12.

$$\text{months living expenses covered ratio} = \frac{\text{monetary assets}}{\text{annual living expenditures}/12}$$

As the name suggests, this ratio tells you how many months of living expenditures you can cover with your present level of monetary assets. Again, the numerator is the level of monetary assets, and the denominator is the annual living expenditures (as on line L of the income statement in Figure 2.6) divided by 12. For the Tates, this ratio would be

$$\frac{\$3{,}590}{\$52{,}234/12} = \frac{\$3{,}590}{\$4{,}353} = 0.825 \text{ month}$$

This means the Tates currently have enough cash and liquid assets on hand to cover 0.825 months of expenditures.

PRINCIPLE 8

Emergency Fund The traditional rule of thumb in personal finance is that an individual or family should have enough in the way of an **emergency fund** or rainy-day fund made up of liquid assets to cover 3 to 6 months of expenditures, in order to cover the untimely death of a television, a major car repair, or some other unexpected event. The Tates fall well short of this amount. According to a recent Money Pulse survey, 63 percent of Americans don't have enough in savings to cover an unexpected expense of $1,000! To cover an emergency, 23 percent of respondents said they would cut back spending in other categories to make ends meet, while 15 percent said they would put it on credit cards, and another 15 percent responded that they would ask for a loan from a family member or friend. The bottom line here is, if you don't have an emergency fund to cover 3 to 6 months of expenses, then you're putting your financial security at risk. Let's face it, an emergency is going to happen, it's just a matter of when.

Emergency Fund
A reserve or rainy-day fund with money set aside to be used in an emergency, when an unexpected expense is incurred or when normal income is disrupted.

Where should you invest your emergency fund? Obviously, there is a higher expected rate of return on money invested in the stock market than on money sitting in a savings account in the bank. The problem is that you may need the money as a result of a shock such as our economy underwent in 2008 and 2009. If that's the case you may have just lost your job as a result of the economic shock, and when you turn to your emergency fund for help, it may have dropped dramatically as a result of the slowdown in the economy. You want to make sure you can get the money when you need it, so a savings account is a good, though not an exciting, place to put it.

One response that many people have when thinking about an emergency fund is that it's just too much money to save, and they give up right there. When starting your emergency fund, don't think about it in terms of 3 to 6 months of expenses. Just go for $500, and then when you reach that, raise your target. But know that when it comes to an emergency fund, something is always better than nothing. Also, know that you're going to need it. According to the recent National Capability Study, there is a 60 percent probability that you'll experience some type of economic shock this year—perhaps a car dies on you or a washing machine goes bad. Once that emergency happens, don't hesitate to tap into

FACTS OF LIFE

A survey asked 22- to 29-year-olds who had finished their schooling or graduated from college the following question: When you first began living on your own after school, how would you rate your expenses?

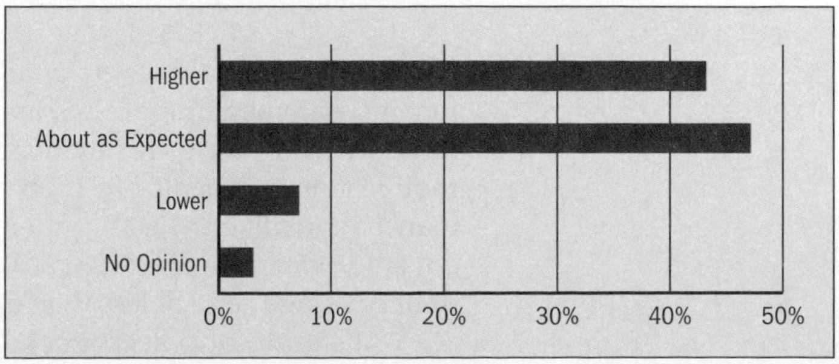

your fund. Many people turn to credit cards or payday loans rather than touch their emergency fund, but remember that this is really what it's for, and once you spend it, you can start putting it back together again. One relatively painless way of putting together an emergency fund is with an app; two great ones are Acorns or Qapital. Qapital, for example, allows you to set "rules" that trigger a deposit into your savings account. For example, you can set a rule to round up your change every time you make a purchase on a card linked to your Qapital account; this rule has saved Qapital users about $44 per month. Other possible rules include triggering a $5 saving every time you make a purchase at Starbucks, or adding a dollar to your savings every time you add a song to your Spotify playlist. The bottom line is there are a number of ways to start saving painlessly, and your job is to do it.

Regardless of how you go about putting together your emergency fund and where you invest your emergency funds, the month's living expenses covered ratio still provides a sound, easy-to-understand indication of the relative level of cash on hand. It's a better personal liquidity measure than the current ratio. You should track this ratio over time to make sure that it does not drop unexpectedly.

Question 2: Can I Meet My Debt Obligations?

A second question that ratios can answer is "Do you have the ability to meet your debt obligations?" In other words, you saw it, and you borrowed money and bought it; now can you pay for it? To answer this question, you need to look at the debt ratio and the debt coverage ratio. The **debt ratio** tells you what percentage of your assets has been financed by borrowing. This ratio can be expressed as follows:

Debt Ratio
A ratio aimed at determining whether you have the ability to meet your debt obligations; defined as total debt or liabilities divided by total assets.

$$\text{debt ratio} = \frac{\text{total debt or liabilities}}{\text{total assets}}$$

Looking at the Tates' balance sheet, we see that the level of their total debt or liabilities is $175,500 (line N of Figure 2.3), while their total assets or what they own is $300,190 (line H of Figure 2.3). Thus, their debt ratio becomes $175,500/$300,190 = 0.5846. This figure means that just over half of their assets are financed with borrowing. If you are managing your finances well, this ratio should go down as you get older.

The **long-term debt coverage ratio** relates the amount of funds available for debt repayment to the size of the debt payments. In effect, this ratio is the number of times you could make your debt payments with your current income. It focuses on long-term credit obligations such as home mortgage payments and auto loan payments. If credit card debt has reached the point where you cannot pay off the balance, it, too, represents a long-term obligation. The denominator of this ratio represents your total outstanding long-term debt payments (excluding short-term borrowing such as credit cards and bills coming due). The numerator represents the funds available to make these payments.

Long-Term Debt Coverage Ratio
A ratio aimed at determining whether you have the ability to meet your debt obligations; defined as total income available for living expenses divided by total long-term debt payments.

$$\text{long-term debt coverage ratio} = \frac{\text{total income available for living expenses}}{\text{total long-term debt payments}}$$

For the Tates, total income available for living expenses is found on line C of their income statement (Figure 2.6) and is $56,510. The only long-term debt obligations they have are their mortgage payments of $19,656 (under Housing in Figure 2.6), their automobile loan payments of $2,588 (under Transportation in Figure 2.6), and their college loan payments of $1,600 (under Other Expenditures in Figure 2.6). Thus, their debt coverage ratio is [$56,510/($19,656 + $2,588 + $1,600)] = 2.37 times. In general, a debt coverage ratio of less than approximately 2.5 should raise a caution flag.

You should also keep track of your long-term debt coverage ratio to make sure it does not creep downward. The Tates are at their limit in terms of the level of debt that they can manage comfortably. Such a low debt coverage ratio is not surprising, however, because most of their assets are tied up in housing.

Another way of looking at the debt coverage ratio is to take its inverse; that is, divide the total debt payments by the total income available for living expenses. In this case, the inverse of the Tates' debt coverage ratio is 0.43, or 43 percent, indicating that 43 percent of the Tates' total income available for living expenses goes to cover debt payments.

Question 3: Am I Saving as Much as I Think I Am?

The final question you can answer using ratios is "How much of your income are you really saving?" The answer to this question lies in the **savings ratio**, which is simply the ratio of income available for savings and investment (line M of Figure 2.6) to income available for living expenditures (line C of Figure 2.6). This ratio tells you the proportion of your after-tax income that you are saving.

Savings Ratio
A ratio aimed at determining how much you are saving; defined as income available for savings and investment divided by income available for living expenditures.

$$\text{savings ratio} = \frac{\text{income available for savings and investment}}{\text{income available for living expenditures}}$$

For the Tates, this ratio is ($4,276/$56,510) = 0.076 or 7.6 percent. This figure is in the range of what is typical in this country. Actually, for families saving for their first house, it tends to be higher, and for families that have just purchased their first house and now are experiencing large mortgage payments, it tends to be lower. Again, as with the other ratios, this ratio should be compared with past savings ratios and target savings ratios to determine whether or not the Tates are saving enough.

If you're not presently saving, then you're living above your means. The only effective way to make saving work is to pay yourself first. That is, you first set aside your savings, and what is left becomes the amount you can spend.

Record Keeping

LO4 Set up a record-keeping system to track your income and expenditures.

The fourth step in creating a personal financial plan is to keep and maintain records, for three reasons. First, without adequate records it's extremely difficult to prepare taxes. Second, a strong record-keeping system allows you to track expenses and know exactly how much you're spending and where you're spending it. In short, if you don't know where and how much you're spending, you don't have control of your finances. Third, organized record keeping makes it easier for someone else to step in during an emergency and understand your financial situation.

Record keeping really involves two steps: tracking your personal financial dealings and filing and storing your financial records in such a way that they are readily accessible. Very simply, if you don't know where financial records are, you won't be in control of your affairs.

In determining how best to track your personal financial dealings, you must keep in mind that the best system is one that you will use. For most people, this means keeping your system as simple as possible.

To begin with, credit card and check expenditures are easy to track because they leave an obvious electronic or paper trail. It's the cash expenditures that cause the most concern. Cash expenditures must be tracked as they occur; if not, they will be lost and forgotten. One way to track them is by recording them in a notebook or your checkbook register as they are made and then using these records, in addition to check and credit card transactions, to generate a monthly income statement. If you're willing to do this, that's great, but let's face it—that's pretty tedious. How can you make it easier? The simplest way to keep track of all cash expenditures is with the help of a good smartphone app, and two of the best are Mint and Level Money.

Both of these apps do an excellent job of tracking your spending history, which will lead you directly into an operating budget. Once you have a monthly budget, you can compare your annual and target budgets to determine whether or not you have any problems. Whether you do this with an app, with a computer program like Intuit's Quicken, or by hand, it's a necessary step. Remember, your budget is your best friend because the key to controlling expenditures is to keep track of them.

As we have noted, when it comes to tracking your spending and setting up a budget, Mint and Level Money are two of the best apps. Although they perform the same task, they are decidedly different. Mint provides a deeper financial planning experience, and Level Money does an excellent job of tracking expenses with minimum effort on your part.

If you want control over your personal finances, it doesn't get any better than Mint. Figure 2.7 provides an overview of Mint, which has been around since 2007. This app allows you to track cash or pending transactions and has proved to be a very intuitive tool for budgeting and managing your money. Using it, you can easily record cash you've spent or received, checks you've written, and other transactions that haven't cleared your bank yet. Mint has great graphs, which provide charting and visual displays of all of your saving and spending activity. In so doing, it pulls your financial data from all major banks and financial institutions, giving you a clear picture of your financial well-being. When you begin, Mint will even set up a starter budget for you based on up to 3 months of your spending habits. It also allows you to enter goals, and from there you can customize your budget to fit your goals. However, Mint goes much further than simply being a budgeting tool; it provides you with a powerful tool for keeping tabs on your spending, investments, and net worth using great graphs, and it helps you with development and implementation of investment strategies. As if this were not enough, Mint comes with a wealth of articles and tips on personal finance. And an accompanying a set of Mint videos will show you how to create budgets, send alerts, analyze trends, and more.

Level Money, which is outlined in Figure 2.7, provides a much simpler approach to financial planning by focusing on helping you control your spending. It works something like the gas gauge on your car—it begins each month with an estimate of your monthly income based on your financial history and then subtracts your recurring bills and daily spending. In effect, it provides you with a digital equivalent of opening your wallet and seeing what's in it—where your wallet holds all of your money regardless of where it might really be. In this way, it provides you with an easy-to-understand, real-time picture of your financial situation, helping you to stay in the black. Much of the value of this app comes from the fact that as it automatically tracks your spending history and cash flow, it reinforces your good money habits. In fact, it has been called a fitbit for personal finance because it motivates you to control your spending by insisting on awareness of your spending and your financial situation, much as the fitbit does with exercise. If your finances aren't particularly complex and you'd rather keep your effort to a minimum, give Level Money a try.

Once you've tracked your expenditures, you need to record them in an organized way similar to the income statement shown in Figure 2.4. Once again, this can be done through Mint, Level Money, or a number of other apps. If you don't have a smartphone, there are computer programs available to help you. The most popular of the personal financial management programs for the PC is Intuit's Quicken.

So how long do you have to hang on to all your financial records? The answer, of course, depends on the item. In general, items dealing with taxes must be kept for at least 6 years after the transaction takes place; some items should be kept for life. Checklist 2.1 provides a summary of where, and for how long, financial records should be kept.

FIGURE 2.7 Web-Based Financial Planning with Mint and Level Money

Web site: Mint – "the best free way to manage your money"
Address: http://www.mint.com/
Features:

- Free.
- Recommended by the *Wall Street Journal* and *Businessweek*.
- Award-winning, top-rated online finance service by PC World.
- Extremely easy to use.
- Connects securely with more than 16,000 U.S. financial institutions and automatically updates all transactions.
- Spending is automatically categorized to make it easy to see how much you're spending on food, gas, groceries, entertainment, and more.
- Has a free app available for smartphones and other electronic devices.

What can you do with Mint.com?

- View all your accounts together at the same time – from checking and savings to credit cards, retirement, and more.
- Mint automatically pulls in and categorizes your transactions daily. You only need to enter your cash transactions. All other transactions are automatically entered.
- Mint can create a budget based on your actual spending, or you can create your own. Your budget works in real time, allowing you to know how much you can spend while you're out.
- Late fees and monitor cash flow. Mint allows you to stay up-to-date with e-mail or text alerts (your choice) for budgets, fees, due dates, low balances, unusual activity, and more.
- Mint allows you to track all your expenses at a particular merchant – for example, Starbucks – to see whether you are spending more or less than usual there.
- Mint tracks all of your investments, including your brokerage and bank accounts, 401(k)s, and IRAs, keeping you up-to-date on the performance of your investments.
- Mint helps you plan for your goals – like buying a car, retirement, and buying a house – and works those goals into your budget.

Web site: Level Money – "the mobile money meter"
Address: https://levelmoney.com/
Features:

- Free.
- Extremely simple and easy to use.
- Automatically updates spendable cash as you make purchases each day, providing a simple, real-time picture of how you're doing in order to stay in the black.
- Top US banks support connections with Level Money.

What can you do with Level Money?

- Extremely simple - if you'd like some financial control without the effort, this is for you, and it's free.
- Automatically updates spendable cash as you make purchases each day.
- Automatically tracks spending history and cash flow.
- Reinforces positive habits and provides necessary insights about spending and saving.
- Calculates total income and recurring bills, calculates how much you want to save every month and subtracts that from your spendable monthly income–it then shows you how much you can spend today, this week, and this month.

WORKSHEET 6

CHECKLIST 2.1 Storing Financial Files

Home File

➔ Tax Records (may be discarded after 6 years) (Chapter 4)
- ☐ Tax returns and documentation
- ☐ Paychecks and W-2, 1099, and 5498 forms

➔ Investment Records (Chapters 11–14)
- ☐ Bank records and cancelled checks
- ☐ Safety deposit box information
- ☐ Stock, bond, mutual fund, and brokerage transactions
- ☐ Dividend records
- ☐ Any additional investment documentation

➔ Retirement and Estate Planning (Chapters 15–16)
- ☐ Copy of will
- ☐ IRA, Social Security, and pension plan documentation
- ☐ Any trusts or additional retirement documentation

➔ Personal Planning (Chapters 2, 8–10, 16)
- ☐ Personal balance sheet, budget, and income statement
- ☐ Insurance policies and documentation
- ☐ Warranties and receipts for major purchases
- ☐ Home improvement receipts
- ☐ Credit card information
- ☐ Rental agreement if renting a dwelling
- ☐ Automobile registration and title
- ☐ Powers of attorney

Safety Deposit Box Storage

➔ Investment Records (Chapters 5, 12–14)
- ☐ Listing of bank accounts and investment records

➔ Retirement and Estate Planning (Chapters 15–16)
- ☐ Copy of will and trusts
- ☐ Nondeductible IRA records

➔ Personal Planning (Chapters 6–10, 16)
- ☐ Deed, mortgage, and title insurance for home
- ☐ Personal papers (birth and death certificates, alimony, adoption/custody, divorce, military, immigration, etc.)
- ☐ Documentation of valuables (video or photos)
- ☐ Home repair/improvement receipts
- ☐ Listing of insurance policies
- ☐ Credit card information

LO5 Implement a financial plan or budget that will provide for the level of savings needed to achieve your goals.

Putting It All Together: Budgeting

Now we are ready to put our financial plan together. Chapter 1 introduced the planning cycle as a five-step process. Now that you have a better understanding of the tools involved in that process, how about a little review? Let's see how the balance sheet and income statement fit into the planning process.

The planning process begins with evaluating your financial health, which is exactly what the balance sheet and income statement are all about. Your balance sheet sums up everything you own or owe and lets you know your net worth, the basic element of financial health. Your income statement furthers your understanding by showing you where your money comes from, where it goes, and what your spending patterns are. Once you understand how much money you have coming in and how you tend to spend it, you can figure out how much you can realistically afford to save. If you don't know how much you can actually save, you can't come up with realistic financial goals, the second step of the planning process.

By providing you with information on how far you need to go to achieve a certain level of wealth and how you might realistically balance spending and saving to get there, your balance sheet and income statement not only help you set goals but also help you achieve them. Developing a plan of action to achieve your goals is the third step in the planning process, and for this, your income statement is the key.

Your income statement helps you set up a cash budget (which we examine in more detail in the next section) that allows you to manage your saving, while considering flexibility, liquidity, protection, and minimization of taxes. Once your plan is in place, you'll need to monitor your progress. Because this last step is really the same as the first, you're right back to using your balance sheet and income statement again. As you can see, without these documents, the planning process isn't nearly as effective.

STOP & THINK

What do you do if it appears that you won't reach your financial goals? You need to change either your goals or your saving pattern. Fortunately, a small change in your financial lifestyle can produce large benefits down the road. For example, if you are 22 now and you save $10 per month—that works out to about 33¢ per day—at 12 percent, by age 67 when you retire, it will have grown to over $240,000. Are there any small changes that you might make to save money?

Developing a Cash Budget

A budget is really nothing more than a plan for controlling cash inflows and outflows. The purpose of the cash budget is to keep income in line with expenditures plus savings. Your cash budget should allocate certain dollar amounts for different spending categories, based on your goals and financial obligations.

Just as with record keeping, there are two ways of putting together your cash budget: one is by hand, and that method works very well, but it's quite tedious; the other is to let an app do the work for you. The nice thing about having an app do the work is that the probability that you will meet your goals goes up dramatically! But regardless of which method you use, the process is exactly the same—the only difference is who does the work, you or the app.

To prepare a cash budget by hand, you begin with your most recent annual personal income statement. First, examine last year's total income, making any adjustments to it that you expect for the coming year. Perhaps you expect to receive a raise, plan to take a second job, or anticipate an increase in royalty payments. Based on your income level, estimate what your taxes will be. This figure provides you with an estimate of your anticipated after-tax income available for living expenditures, which is commonly called take-home pay. An app does the same thing—it bases its calculations on your income and spending patterns and then allows you to make adjustments to those numbers to reflect any changes you expect in the future.

Just as your estimate of anticipated take-home pay flows from your most recent annual personal income statement, so does your estimate of living expenses. Using last year's personal income statement, you or your app will identify recurring expenditures over which you have no control—fixed expenditures. Then you or your app will determine your variable expenses. These are the expenses that can change and over which you have complete control; you can increase or decrease them as you see fit.

If the goal is to find some free money, perhaps to save for a car or a vacation, this is the category you'll be focusing on. For example, you can generate savings just by reducing the amount you spend on food—substitute bean dip for those exotic fresh fruits as your evening snack (of course, any savings there will probably be offset by an increase in what you spend for exercise equipment this year). You must also keep in mind that when you buy on credit, you obligate yourself to future expenditures to pay off your debt. When you borrow, you are spending your future income, which limits your ability to save.

Finally, either you or your app will subtract your anticipated living expenditures from your anticipated take-home pay to determine income available for savings and investment. Then you or your app will compare your anticipated monthly savings with your target savings level, which is, as we mentioned earlier, based on a quantification of your goals. If it doesn't look as if you'll be able to fund all your goals, then you must earn more, spend less, or downsize your goals. The choice is, of course, personal; however, keep in mind that, regardless of your level of income, many people live on less than what you're earning.

How do Louise and Larry Tate develop a cash budget? First, assume that the only change in income they expect for the coming year is a $5,000 increase in wages and salaries from $69,500 to $74,500. Last year, the Tates paid approximately 20 percent in federal and state income taxes. If they pay the same percentage this year, their $5,000 raise will result in an increase in take-home pay of $4,000, with 20 percent of the raise, or $1,000, going to pay increased taxes.

The Tates' personal income statement is shown in Figure 2.6. If there are any anticipated changes in different expenditure categories, they must adjust their personal income statement—and the changes can involve increases in planned spending. A cash budget, then, does not necessarily curb spending in all areas. Instead, it allows you to decide ahead of time how much to spend where.

Assume that the Tates' target level of savings for the entire year is $6,400. If the Tates stick to this cash budget, they will exceed their target. Had this not been the case, they would have been forced to adjust their budget so that it covered their target savings. To make your annual cash budget easier to control, you should break it down into monthly budgets by simply dividing by 12.

PRINCIPLE 5

A key point to remember when budgeting is that no budget is set in stone. Remember **Principle 5: Stuff Happens**. A TV, a car, a washer—unexpected expenditures are just that, unexpected. Conversely, you may be pleasantly surprised that you wound up spending *less* than you planned. Then again, you may change your goals. You may decide that you don't want that new house; your apartment's fine for the moment. But you *do* want to buy a llama farm in Peru. Basically, the budgeting process is a dynamic one: You must continuously monitor the financial impact of change on your spending and saving habits.

Implementing the Cash Budget

Now that you've put together a cash budget and have your plan, how do you make it work? Essentially, you just put it in place and try to make a go of it for a month. At the end of the month, compare your actual expenditures in each category with your budgeted amounts. If you spent more than you budgeted, you may want to pay closer attention to expenditures in that category, or you may want to change the budgeted amount. Fortunately, if you're using Mint or Level Money, you'll have a good idea how you're doing in real time. If you end up spending more in one area than planned, you'll have to reduce spending in another area. Keep in mind that responsibility for sticking to the budget remains with you, but by examining deviations from desired spending patterns on a monthly basis, you can focus on where you need to exert additional self-control. If you'd like to try a budget template with different spending categories to use in setting up your budget, Worksheet 7, which is downloadable from the MyLab Finance Web site (**www.pearson.com/mylab/finance**), should do the trick.

WORKSHEET 7

If you still have a problem sticking to a desired budget, one possible control method is using what's generally called the envelope system. At the beginning of each month, the dollar amount of each major expenditure category is put into an envelope. To spend money in that area, simply take it out of the envelope. When the envelope is empty, you're finished spending in that area.

If your control problems are limited to a certain type of spending, you can set up envelopes just for those areas. For example, if you budgeted $120 per month for restaurant expenditures, put $120 in an envelope each month. When it is exhausted, trips to the restaurant are over for the month. This includes pizza home delivery, so no cheating! There's even a great app that will help you do this – Mvelopes. This app uses the envelope method of budgeting and applies it to the digital world, and does a pretty good job at it.

Finally, remember: If you're looking for a great mobile app coupled with a free Web-based personal financial planning Web site that allows you to keep an eye on your financial moves and track all bank accounts, credit cards, investments, and loans together, take a look at Mint. If it is a simple and effective mobile app you are looking for to control your spending, take a look at Level Money. It's also free and works as a spending meter or a gas gauge, monitoring your spending and keeping you from getting into financial trouble. See if one of them works for you. If you look back at Figure 2.7, you'll see a short description of both Mint and Level Money.

STOP & THINK

Most people spend what they earn, regardless of how much that is. It comes in and goes out. To save, you've got to change your attitude and pay yourself first. That means you won't be able to buy everything you want, and something is going to have to go. The first place to look is the *small stuff*—latte, magazines, music downloads, soda—within a day or two, most of that stuff is worthless or gone. In other words, sweat the small stuff. What have you purchased lately that might be considered "small stuff"?

LOVE & MONEY

As you probably know, communication is one of the keys to a good relationship. But did you know that honest, open communication is especially important when it comes to the topic of money? This might seem like common sense, but it is also easier said than done. If your family is like most, money is probably not something that was talked about openly when you were growing up, and that hesitancy to discuss financial matters is something that is often passed on from one generation to the next. It is also something that can lead to misunderstandings and arguments, and it is often one of the causes of divorce. But the good news is that it's also something that can be overcome.

According to a recent TD Ameritrade survey, almost 80 percent of couples surveyed who said that they discussed money at least once a week also said they were happy. When should financial discussions begin? Well before you get engaged. As you will see, money can impact your love life in some unexpected ways. In fact, in that same survey, 42 percent of respondents said that the biggest mistake they made in their relationship was "waiting too long" to discuss money. That doesn't mean this discussion will be an easy one. In fact, according to a recent Citi Card survey, almost 30 percent of respondents would like to discuss finances more often, but almost 70 percent of those who would like to discuss finances more often avoid those discussions for fear of starting an argument. That fits with the findings of a Northwestern Mutual study that found money to be a more uncomfortable discussion topic than one's own eventual death, asking adult children to move out, or sex. One reason that discussing finances and money is so tough is that you're also sharing your goals, personal feelings, and intimacies. That's not an easy thing to do, but it's important for a healthy relationship.

So how do you start a conversation about money and your finances? First, you want to pick a "happy time": some sort of positive event like a family wedding, a promotion, or even just a great weekend together. It's just too difficult to bring up money during bad times and much easier to open up when things are good. One way to do this might be to google "how to talk about money with a partner" and then simply share the article and let your partner know that it made you think that this is something you should do. (Or if you still have this text, share a "Money & Love" box or two with him or her.)

Once the conversation gets going, share your financial goals with each other, determine your net worth, and then explore a budgeting app like Mint.com with your partner. That should get you started, but before you finish, set a date in the future to continue to talk more about your finances, financial goals, and how you intend to reach them. But feel good that the toughest step, opening up a dialogue about money, is behind you. Well done!

LO6 Decide whether a professional financial planner will play a role in your financial affairs.

Hiring a Professional

The goal of this course and text is to give you the understanding, tools, and motivation to manage your own financial affairs. Sometimes, though, smart management means knowing when to ask for help. When it comes to personal financial management, there's good help to be found. You have three options available regarding working with professionals: (1) Go it alone, make your own plan, and have it checked by a professional; (2) work with a professional to come up with a plan; or (3) leave it all in the hands of a pro (though preferably not one with a bad toupee, leisure suit, and beat-up Ford Pinto). That decision need not be made until you have finished this course and have a better grasp of the process, but let's take a moment to look further at the options.

FACTS OF LIFE

A survey asked 22- to 29-year-olds how tough the financial pressures faced by their generation are compared with those faced by prior generations. Here's what they said:

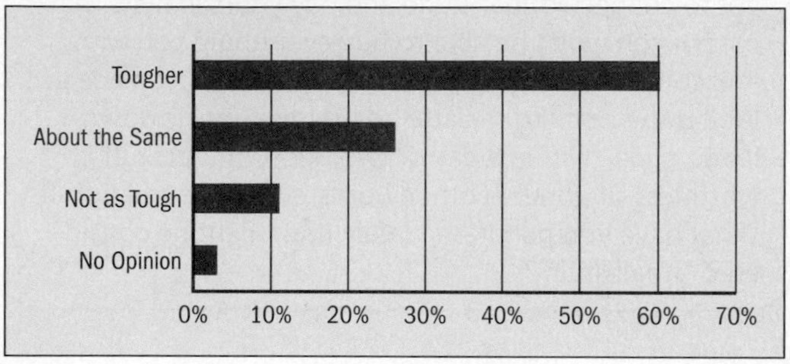

What Planners Do

For relatively simple personal financial matters, computerized financial planning programs provide basic budgeting tools and advice. However, like most standardized advice, they simply may not fit your particular situation. The more unique your situation, the greater the need for professional help.

Even if you turn over the development of your plan to a professional, however, you must understand the basics of personal financial planning in order to judge the merits of the plan and to monitor your game plan. Remember, even if you use a financial planner to put together the entire plan, you are merely receiving advice. You still bear the ultimate responsibility. This brings us back to **Principle 1: The Best Protection Is Knowledge**.

PRINCIPLE 1

It is extremely important that you find a financial planner who is competent and trustworthy. Although the overwhelming majority of financial planners are dedicated, responsible, and competent, and despite the fact that there are regulations in place meant to protect consumers, not all planners are equally qualified. Furthermore, financial planners may receive commissions on certain products, and they may talk up those more than others in order to receive this commission. Also be wary of those who promise you quick riches, and walk away from anyone using high-pressure tactics. Building wealth takes time and consistent attention.

Choosing a Professional Planner

Many financial planners are excellent at what they do. Some, however, are not so excellent. How do you choose a financial planner? The title "financial planner" is not legally defined—it just means that the individual offers comprehensive financial planning services; it says nothing about competence. It is wise to limit your search to those who have received accreditation from a professional organization:

- *A personal financial specialist* (PFS) is a certified public accountant who has passed certification tests in personal financial planning administered by the American Institute of Certified Public Accountants and has at least 3 years of personal financial planning experience.
- *A certified financial planner* (CFP) has satisfactorily completed a 10-hour, 2-day exam and has a minimum of 3 years of experience in the field.
- *A chartered financial consultant*, or ChFC, has completed coursework and ten exams administered by the American College.

After you've determined what credentials a planner has earned, consider how much experience he or she has had. Experience can teach a planner a lot about what's best for you. Also, find out whether the planner will give you advice tailored to your specific circumstances. And don't forget about referrals. Can the planner provide the names of people she or he has worked for? Do you have friends or relatives who have had good experiences with this financial planner in the past?

How Are Financial Planners Paid? Actually, there are four common ways that planners are paid:

1. *Fee-only* planners earn income only through the fees they charge, generally running from $75 to $200 per hour. They tend to work with bigger, more involved, and specialized situations. You will personally have total control of the products purchased to complete your plan, and therefore you control commission costs. However, you have to sort through a possibly overwhelming array of options and deal with several different vendors.
2. *Fee-and-commission* planners charge fees and also collect commissions on products they recommend. Fees may be lower if you choose to use some of their commissioned products, but if you're dealing with a less-than-ethical person, you could be directed toward higher-commission products. Be aware of what you're paying for.
3. *Fee offset* planners charge a fee but then reduce this fee by any commissions they earn.
4. *Commission-based* planners work on a commission basis. They can provide an analysis of your personal financial situation, offer solutions to problems, and assist you in implementing the plan. You want to make sure your planner has a wide range of financial products to choose from.

If you have trouble getting recommendations, try calling the Financial Planning Association (**http://www.fpanet.org**) at 800-322-4237 or the CFP Board of Standards (**http://www.cfp.net/search**) at 800-487-1497 or 888-237-6275 for help. Remember, you bear all the consequences of bad decisions, so you must take responsibility for choosing a good advisor.

CHECKLIST 2.2 What to Ask a Financial Planner

- ☐ How long have you been a financial planner?
- ☐ What are your credentials and professional designations?
- ☐ How do you keep up with the latest financial changes?
- ☐ Can you provide references?
- ☐ Will you show me a copy of a financial plan you made for someone with a financial situation similar to mine (with names removed to preserve confidentiality, of course)?
- ☐ Who will work with me on a regular basis? You or another member of your staff?
- ☐ Who will actually create my plan? You, a junior staffer, or a software program?
- ☐ How many financial companies do you represent?
- ☐ How are you paid—by fee or commission? How will that fee be calculated?
- ☐ Can you provide a written estimate of the services I can expect and the cost of those services?

BEHAVIORAL INSIGHTS

PRINCIPLE 9

Principle 9: Mind Games, Your Financial Personality, and Your Money Want a clearer picture of your financial situation, present and future? You need to put together a serious financial budget. If just the word *budget* makes your head spin, you are not alone.

Much of the focus of this chapter is on putting together a budget that will provide you with the level of savings necessary to meet your goals. It's hard to argue with the importance of this, but while putting a plan together is one thing, following through with it can be tough. That's because we, as humans, come with a good-sized dose of shortsightedness coupled with procrastination and inertia. It's hard to take that first step, especially when the budget choices involve trade-offs between costs and benefits that occur at different points in time—right now or off in the future. Those in the field of behavioral finance refer to this dilemma as *intertemporal choice*—the relative value people assign to two or more payoffs that occur at different periods in time.

Deep down we know things need to change— we need to put together a budget. We know we need to start saving for an emergency fund or retirement, but when push comes to shove, we tend to stand pat. Mentally, we look at things that are far off in the future in a different way than we look at things that are coming soon, and the result is that we pay much more attention to now than to tomorrow. This behavioral tendency can have an impact on all kinds of decisions that we make, including the financial ones. As a result, we end up making decisions and buying things that provide instant gratification today but result in financial obligations in the future that aren't in our budget and that we didn't really count on having to pay for. This tendency to pay more attention to the present reveals itself in all kinds of behavior. For example, let's take a look at your eating habits. If you're like most people and are given the choice between some healthy food and a yummy snack to eat this week or next week, you will most likely choose to eat the treat today and plan to eat the healthy stuff next week. Then, when the next week arrives, you'll do the same thing—and keep on postponing the healthy food far off into the future. The same thing happens with spending, and that's why it's so easy to say "Charge it" and take a trip to Cancun or buy that 60-inch TV—our brains are focused on the present as opposed to the future. It is not a marketing accident that more "big-screen" TVs are advertised and sold in the weeks before the Super Bowl.

One of the purposes of a budget is to force you to focus on the financial implications of your decisions. When you buy that new TV, you've got to build those future payments into your budget. When you sign a lease for a new apartment, you know what the monthly payments will be for the next 12–24 months into the future, and you must make sure you can afford them. Oftentimes what might not be viewed as a financial decision comes with financial implications. For example, in Chapter 1 we looked at the cost of raising a child—deciding to have a child is not a financial decision, but it is one that definitely affects your financial future. Let's look at another decision that is many times made impulsively and that carries long-run financial implications: the new puppy that, on a whim, you decide to adopt. What's the lifetime cost of a dog? According to the Humane Society, with an average lifespan of 10 to 15 years, the lifetime cost of that puppy is about $25,620.

The problem is that behaviorally we look at expenses that are far off in the future differently than we do those that are coming soon. And if you're like most people, it's pretty hard to look at a cute little puppy or kitty and see future financial responsibilities. Our brains have a hard time putting much importance on expenses 10 years out—especially when there are puppy dog eyes looking back at us.

How do you overcome this? The answer is "It isn't easy." The first step is to understand why it is important to plan and keep track of your spending by using the app Mint or Level Money. Once you've done that, you've got to make sure that you plan for the future expenses associated with anything you buy. That means you have to know what you're getting into: What are the future costs associated with charging that TV to your credit card or taking that puppy home? One of the ways to do this is with an understanding of the time value of money—a very eye-opening and important concept, which we will look at in the next chapter. Only then can you force yourself to plan out into the future and understand the financial consequences.

ACTION PLAN

PRINCIPLE 10

Principle 10: Just Do It! When you want to try to gain control of your financial life, the place to start is with a budget. And the only way to put a budget in place is to track your expenses and cash inflows. Once you've got a budget in place, the next thing you'll want to do is implement it. So here's an action plan that will help you do just that.

- If you have a smartphone and are concerned about how much work putting a budget in place will be, try the app Level Money—it's simple, it will track your expenses, and it will put you on track to develop a budget. If you are willing to put a bit more work into tracking your expenses and putting a budget together, try Mint.
- If you don't have a smartphone, keep all your receipts, or simply track all your expenditures in a little notebook.
- Once you start bringing in an income, establish an automatic savings plan that puts money in your savings plan before it gets to you.
- Set up a system for record keeping, and keep at it.

Chapter Summaries

LO1 Calculate your level of net worth or wealth using a balance sheet.

SUMMARY: A personal balance sheet is a statement of your financial position on a given date. It includes the assets you own, the debt or liabilities you have incurred, and your level of wealth. The difference between the value of your assets (what you own) and your liabilities (what you owe) is your net worth, the level of wealth that you or your family has accumulated.

KEY TERMS

Personal Balance Sheet, page 32 A statement of your financial position on a given date. It includes the assets you own, the debt or liabilities you have incurred, and your level of wealth, which is referred to as net worth.

Assets, page 33 What you own.

Liabilities, page 33 What you owe; your debt or borrowing.

Net Worth or Equity, page 33 A measure of the level of your wealth. It is determined by subtracting the level of your debt or borrowing from the value of your assets.

Fair Market Value, page 33 What an asset could be sold for, rather than what it cost or what it will be worth sometime in the future.

Tangible Asset, page 34 A physical asset, such as a house or a car, as opposed to an investment.

Blue Book, page 34 A listing of used-car prices (by model and year manufactured), giving the average price a particular car sells for and its expected trade-in value.

Insolvent, page 36 Owing more money than one's assets are worth.

LO2 Analyze where your money comes from and where it goes using an income statement.

SUMMARY: Whereas a balance sheet tells you how much wealth you have accumulated as of a *certain date*, an income statement tells you where your money has come from and where it has gone over some *period of time*. Actually, an income statement is really an income and expenditure, or net income, statement because it looks at both cash inflows and cash outflows. Once you understand where your money comes from and where it goes, you'll be able to determine whether you're saving enough to meet your goals and how you might change your expenditure patterns to meet those goals. Then you'll be able to construct a budget.

KEY TERMS

Income Statement, page 36 A statement that tells you where your money has come from and where it has gone over some period of time.

Variable Expenditure, page 39 An expenditure over which you have control. That is, you are not obligated to make that expenditure, and it may vary from month to month.

Fixed Expenditure, page 39 An expenditure over which you have no control. You are obligated to make this expenditure, and it is generally at a constant level each month.

Budget, page 42 A plan for controlling cash inflows and cash outflows. Based on your goals and financial obligations, a budget limits spending in different categories.

LO3 Use ratios to identify your financial strengths and weaknesses.

SUMMARY: Financial ratios help you to identify your financial standing. These ratios are analyzed over time to determine trends and are also compared with standards or target ratios. The purpose of using ratios is to gain a better understanding of how you are managing your financial resources.

KEY TERMS

Current Ratio, page 42 A ratio aimed at determining whether you have adequate liquidity to meet emergencies; defined as monetary assets divided by current liabilities.

Month's Living Expenses Covered Ratio, page 43 A ratio aimed at determining whether you have adequate liquidity to meet emergencies; defined as monetary assets divided by annual living expenditures divided by 12.

Emergency Fund, page 43 A reserve or rainy-day fund with money set aside to be used in an emergency, when an unexpected expense is incurred or when normal income is disrupted.

Debt Ratio, page 44 A ratio aimed at determining whether you have the ability to meet your debt obligations; defined as total debt or liabilities divided by total assets.

Long-Term Debt Coverage Ratio, page 44 A ratio aimed at determining whether you have the ability to meet your debt obligations; defined as total income available for living expenses divided by total long-term debt payments.

Savings Ratio, page 45 A ratio aimed at determining how much you are saving; defined as income available for savings and investment divided by income available for living expenditures.

LO4 Set up a record-keeping system to track your income and expenditures.

SUMMARY: To keep track of your income and expenditures and to calculate your net worth, you need a sound system of record keeping. Such a system not only helps with tax preparation but also allows you to identify how much you are spending and where you are spending it.

Implement a financial plan or budget that will provide for the level of savings needed to achieve your goals. LO5

SUMMARY: Developing a plan of action involves setting up a cash budget. The starting point for the cash budget, which is at the center of the plan of action, flows directly from the personal income statement. By comparing the income available for savings and investment with the level of savings needed to achieve your goals, you can determine whether you need to alter your current spending patterns and, if so, by how much. Once you have established a plan, it's your responsibility to stick to your budget.

Decide whether a professional financial planner will play a role in your financial affairs. LO6

SUMMARY: If you need help in financial planning, there are professional planners out there who can provide such help. You can use a professional planner simply to validate the plan you have developed, or you can hire one to put the entire plan together, from start to finish.

Problems and Activities

These problems are available in MyLab Finance.

1. Mike and Mary Jane Lee have a yearly income of $65,000 and own a house worth $90,000, two cars worth a total of $20,000, and furniture worth $10,000. The house has a mortgage of $50,000, and the cars have outstanding loans of $2,000 each. Utility bills, totaling $150 for this month, have not been paid. Calculate or use Worksheet 4 to determine their net worth, and explain what it means. How would the Lees' ages affect your assessment of their net worth? WORKSHEET 4

2. Using the preceding information, calculate the debt ratio for the Lee household.

3. Ed and Marta are paid $3,250 after taxes every month. Monthly expenses include $1,200 on housing and utilities, $550 for auto loans, $300 on food, and an average of $1,000 on clothing and other variable expenses. Calculate and interpret their savings ratio. *Hint:* Prepare an income statement or use Worksheet 5, and then compute the ratio. WORKSHEET 5

4. A rumor about "right sizing" at Ojai's engineering firm has him and his wife, Kaya, concerned about their preparation for meeting financial emergencies. Help them calculate their net worth or complete Worksheet 4, and calculate and interpret the current ratio, given the following assets and liabilities: WORKSHEET 4

Checking account	$2,000
Savings account	$4,000
Stocks	$8,000
Utility bills	$500
Credit card bills	$1,000
Auto loan	$2,600

5. Faith Brooks, a 28-year-old college graduate, never took a personal finance class. She pays her bills on time, has managed to save a little in a mutual fund, and (with the help of an inheritance) has managed a down payment on a condominium. But Faith worries about her financial situation. Given the following information, prepare Worksheet 4 and Worksheet 5. Using information from these statements, calculate the current ratio, savings ratio, month's living expenses covered ratio, debt ratio, and long-term debt coverage ratio. Interpret these financial statements and ratios for Faith. Based on your assessment, what advice would you give Faith? In addition to the following list, Faith offers these explanations: WORKSHEET 4 WORKSHEET 5

- All short-term and long-term liabilities are unpaid.
- "Other expenses, monthly" represents cash spent without a record.
- She charges all incidentals on her credit cards and pays the balances off monthly. The balances shown below represent her average monthly balances.

Visa bill	$355	Checking account	$825
Stocks	$5,500	Quarterly auto insurance (not due)	$450
MasterCard bill	$245	Inherited coin collection	$3,250
Monthly paycheck, net	$2,400	Condominium	$65,000
Annual medical expenses	$264	Food, monthly	$225
Mortgage payment, monthly	$530	Auto	$9,000
Temple Mutual Fund	$2,100	Furnishings	$5,500
401(k) retirement account	$4,500	Mortgage outstanding	$50,000
Car payment, monthly	$265	Auto loan outstanding	$4,225
Total monthly utilities	$275	Other personal property	$8,000
Savings account	$2,300	Other expenses, monthly	$150
Clothing expense, monthly	$45		

6. Your friend Dario heard about your personal finance class and asked for your help. Explain to Dario why he should establish a budget and what information he needs.

7. Dario, from the previous question, is having a hard time sticking to a budget. Explain why this might be the case, and identify strategies he can use to overcome his difficulties.

8. If the Potinsky household spends $39,000 annually on all living expenses and long-term debt, calculate the amount recommended for an emergency fund. How might household circumstances (e.g., number of wage earners in the household, available credit, and type and stability of employment) affect this decision?

9. Based on your projected salary (see information in Chapter 1 about estimating your salary through the U.S. Bureau of Labor Statistics' website - **http://www.bls.gov/ooh/home.htm)**, estimate and subtract 20 percent for taxes and benefits and another 10 percent for retirement. From the remainder, estimate and subtract the amount you plan to save annually for short-, intermediate-, and long-term goals. What you have left represents your income available for meeting all expenses. Now estimate the emergency fund you need to cover 3 to 6 months' expenses. Realistically, how long will it take you to save the needed amount?

Discussion Case 1

This case is available in MyLab Finance.

Rudabeh, 34, and Donovan, 31, want to buy their first home. Their current combined net income is $65,000, and they have two auto loans totaling $32,000. They have saved approximately $12,000 for the purchase of their home and have total assets worth $55,000, which are mostly savings for retirement. Donovan has always been cautious about spending large amounts of money, but Rudabeh really likes the idea of owning their own home although she hasn't expressed her preferences to Donovan. They do not have a budget, but they do keep track of their expenses, which amounted to $55,000 last year, including taxes. They pay off all credit card bills on a monthly basis and do not have any other debt or loans outstanding. Other than that, they do not spend a great deal of time tracking their finances.

Questions

1. What financial statements should Rudabeh and Donovan prepare to begin realizing their home purchase goal? What records should they use to compile these statements?
2. Use the worksheets, or simply calculate their net worth and income surplus. How does their net worth compare to that of other individuals younger than 35?

   WORKSHEET 4

3. Calculate and interpret their month's living expenses covered ratio and their debt ratio.
4. What other information would be necessary or helpful to develop more complete statements? Give as much detail as possible.
5. What six- to eight-step process should Rudabeh and Donovan undertake to develop a budget?
6. Why might adopting **Principle 6: Waste Not, Want Not–Smart Spending Matters** be important to Rudabeh and Donovan, given their goal of home ownership?

   WORKSHEET 6

7. What recommendations do you have for Rudabeh and Donovan regarding financial communication?

Discussion Case 2

This case is available in MyLab Finance.

Tim and Jill Taylor are retiring this year! Tim has worked for a utility company since his co-op job in college and has participated in all of the company's retirement savings plans. Jill has worked since their kids were in high school. Although they never consulted a financial planner, they have been careful to keep their insurance policies updated, to keep debt to a minimum, and to save regularly. As a result, the Taylors have a very large retirement portfolio—and now, without the restrictions of their companies' plans, lots of other investment options. Jill would like to live "the good life" for a while but also is concerned about "outliving" their money. Tim says, "I earned it, I'll spend it." Now, Tim and Jill think that consulting a professional might be a good idea to keep them on track through retirement. They haven't made too many plans, but they know they want to help pay for college costs for their grandchildren.

Questions

1. What assessments of their financial situation should Tim and Jill expect when working with a financial planner? Given their past efforts to plan their finances and control spending, will these assessments be necessary?
2. The Taylors just received statements from their companies outlining the total value of their retirement savings. How can they use this information?
3. How might a budget ensure that they will have the amount necessary to help their grandchildren?
4. Since both their income and their expenses will change, how would you suggest that they not "go overboard in living the good life" but at the same time know that they can afford some retirement luxuries?
5. Should they manage the investment portfolio themselves, or should they find a planner to manage their retirement assets and help them to develop a plan for what could be 30 years in retirement? What kind of relationship with the planner and what method of payment might work best for them?
6. Do the Taylors need to track their expenses more or less closely once they retire? Are their big expenses likely to remain the five reported by the average household?

CHAPTER 3 Understanding and Appreciating the Time Value of Money

Learning Objectives

LO1	**Explain** the mechanics of compounding.	Compound Interest and Future Values
LO2	**Understand** the power of time and the importance of the interest rate in compounding.	Compounding and the Power of Time and Interest
LO3	**Calculate** the present value of money to be received in the future.	Present Value—What's It Worth in Today's Dollars?
LO4	**Explain** what an annuity is and calculate its compound or future value.	Annuities

"Let's just do what we always do—hijack some nuclear weapons and hold the world ransom." These are the words of Dr. Evil, played by Mike Myers in the movie *Austin Powers, International Man of Mystery.* Frozen, along with his cat, Mr. Bigglesworth, in 1967 after escaping from the Electric Psychedelic Pussycat Swinger's Club in London, Dr. Evil is thawed out in 1997 and immediately resumes his evil ways.

Dr. Evil continues with his plan: "Gentlemen, it has come to my attention that a breakaway Russian republic, Ripblackastan, is about to transfer a nuclear warhead to the United Nations in a few days. Here's the plan. We get the warhead, and we hold the world ransom for ... one million dollars!"

Silence, followed by "Umm, umm, umm" from Dr. Evil's Number 2 man, played by Robert Wagner: "Don't you think we should ask for more than a million dollars? A million dollars is not exactly a lot of money these days."

"OK, then we hold the world ransom for $100 billion."

A million dollars in 1967 certainly bought more than a million dollars in 1997 did. But consider this: If Dr. Evil had taken a million dollars in 1967 and put it in the stock market, it would have accumulated to over $30.7 million when he was thawed out in 1997. However, that $30+ million wouldn't have the same purchasing power it had 30 years earlier. In fact, given the rate of inflation over that period, it would purchase only about one-fifth of what it would have purchased in 1967.

AF Archive/Alamy Stock Photo

Three decades is a long time. In 1967, the year Dr. Evil was frozen, one of the top-rated TV shows was *Bewitched*, and *The Monkees* took top honors at that year's Emmy Awards for best comedy show. The Green Bay Packers won Super Bowl I. Thirty years later, Dr. Evil woke up to those same sitcoms airing on *Nick at Night* and the Green Bay Packers winning Super Bowl XXXI. But times had changed—the world was full of personal computers, compact disks, MP3s, and cable TV.

Now, let's look into *your* future: For most of you, it will be well over 30 years before you retire. If you want to work out how much you will need for your golden years, how the heck do you look at today's dollars and come up with a dollar figure? As we saw in **Principle 3: The Time Value of Money**, a dollar received today is worth more than a dollar received in the future. For one thing, a dollar received and invested today starts earning interest sooner than a dollar received and invested at some time in the future. Remember, the **time value of money** means that we can't compare amounts of money from two different periods without adjusting for this difference in value. Clearly, if you want a firm grasp on personal finance, it's important to understand the time value of money.

PRINCIPLE 3

Time Value of Money
The concept that a dollar received today is worth more than a dollar received in the future; therefore, comparisons between amounts in different time periods cannot be made without adjustments to their values.

Just how powerful is the time value of money? Think about this: If you were to invest $1,000 at 8 percent interest for 400 years, you would end up with $23 quadrillion—approximately $5 million per person on Earth. Of course, your investments won't span 400 years—it's doubtful that you'll be cryogenically frozen like Dr. Evil and Austin Powers—but your investments will rely on the time value of money. If you manage properly, time can be the ace up your sleeve—the one that lets you pocket more than you would have imagined possible.

In personal finance, the time value of money is just as widespread as it is powerful. We're always comparing money from different periods—for example, buying a bond today and receiving interest payments in the future, borrowing money to buy a house today and paying it back over the next 30 years, or determining exactly how much to save annually to achieve a certain goal. In fact, there's very little in personal finance that doesn't have some thread of the time value of money woven through it.

LO1 Explain the mechanics of compounding.

Compound Interest and Future Values

Compound Interest
The effect of earning interest on interest, resulting from the reinvestment of interest paid on an investment's principal.

Principal
The face value of a deposit or debt instrument.

How does the time value of money turn small sums of money into extremely large sums of money? Through compound interest. **Compound interest** is basically interest paid on interest. If you take the interest you earn on an investment and reinvest it, you then start earning interest on the **principal** and the reinvested interest. In this way, the amount of interest you earn grows, or compounds.

How Compound Interest Works

Present Value (PV)
The current value—that is, the value in today's dollars—of a future sum of money.

Annual Interest Rate (*i*)
The rate charged or paid for the use of money on an annual basis.

Future Value (FV)
The value of an investment at some future point in time.

Anyone who has ever had a savings account has received compound interest. For example, suppose you place $100, which is your **present value (*PV*)**, in a savings account that pays 6 percent interest annually, which is the **annual interest rate (*i*)**. How will your savings grow? At the end of the first year, you'll have earned 6 percent, or $6, on your initial deposit of $100, giving you a total of $106 in your savings account. That $106 is the **future value (*FV*)** of your investment—that is, the value of your investment at some future point in time. The mathematical formula illustrating the payment of interest is:

Future Value or FV_1	=	Present Value or PV	×	Amount PV has increased by <u>in 1 year</u> or $(1 + i)$

$$FV_1 = PV(1+i) \tag{3.1}$$

Reinvesting
Taking money that you have earned on an investment and plowing it back into that investment.

In our example, you began with a present value of $100; then it grew by 6 percent, giving you $6 of interest; and when you add the interest you earned ($6) to what you began with ($100), you end up with $106. Assuming you leave the $6 interest payment in your savings account, which is known as **reinvesting**, what will your savings look like at the end of the second year? You begin the second year with $106, you add the interest you earned in the second year (6 percent on $106 for a total of $6.36 in interest), and you end up with $112.36.

What will your savings look like at the end of 3 years? Or 5 years? Or 10 years? Figure 3.1 illustrates how an investment of $100 would continue to grow for the first 10 years at a compound interest rate of 6 percent. Notice how the amount of interest earned annually increases each year because of compounding.

FIGURE 3.1 Compound Interest at 6 Percent over Time

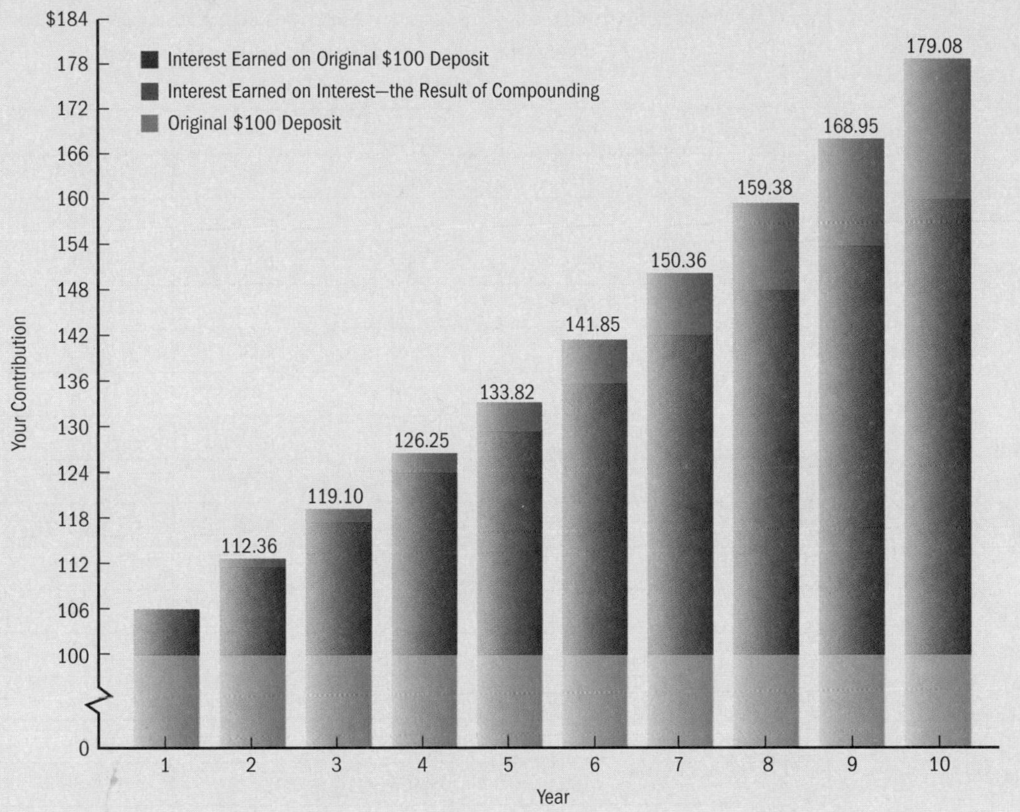

MyLab Finance Animation

Why do you earn more interest during the second year than you did during the first? Simply because you now earn interest on the sum of the original principal, or present value, *and* the interest you earned in the first year. In effect, you are now earning interest on interest, which is the concept of compound interest.

How did we determine all the future values of your investment in Figure 3.1? We took the amount we began each year with, and we let it grow by 6 percent—in effect, we just multiplied the amount we began each year with by $(1 + i)$. We can generalize the future-value equation to:

Future Value or FV_n	=	Present Value or PV	×	Amount PV has increased by **in n years** or $(1 + i)^n$

$$FV_n = PV(1 + i)^n \tag{3.2}$$

where n is equal to the number of years during which compounding occurs.

Equation (3.2) *is* the time value of money formula, and it will work for any investment that pays a fixed amount of interest, i, for the life of the investment. As we work through this chapter, sometimes we will solve for i, and other times we will solve for PV or n. Regardless, equation (3.2) is the basis for almost all of our time value calculations.

TABLE 3.1 Future Value of $1 (single amount), Future-Value Interest Factor

Instructions: Each future-value interest factor corresponds to a specific time period and interest rate. For example, to find the future-value interest factor for 5 percent and 10 years, simply move down the $i = 5\%$ column until you reach its intersection with the $n = 10$ years row: 1.629. The future value is then calculated as follows:

$$\text{future value} = \text{present value} \times \text{future-value interest factor}$$
$$\text{or } FV_n = PV\,(\text{future-value interest factor})$$

n	4%	5%	6%	7%	8%
1	1.040	1.050	1.060	1.070	1.080
2	1.082	1.102	1.124	1.145	1.166
3	1.125	1.158	1.191	1.225	1.260
4	1.170	1.216	1.262	1.311	1.360
5	1.217	1.276	1.338	1.403	1.469
6	1.265	1.340	1.419	1.501	1.587
7	1.316	1.407	1.504	1.606	1.714
8	1.369	1.477	1.594	1.718	1.851
9	1.423	1.551	1.689	1.838	1.999
10	1.480	1.629	1.791	1.967	2.159
11	1.539	1.710	1.898	2.105	2.332
20	2.191	2.653	3.207	3.870	4.661
30	3.243	4.322	5.743	7.612	10.062
40	4.801	7.040	10.285	14.974	21.724
50	7.106	11.467	18.419	29.456	46.900

The Future-Value Interest Factor

Future-Value Interest Factor
The value of $(1 + i)^n$ used as a multiplier to calculate an amount's future value.

Calculating future values by hand can be a serious chore. Luckily, you can use a calculator. Also, there are tables for the $(1 + i)^n$ part of the equation, which will now be called the **future-value interest factor** for i and n. These tables simplify your calculations by giving you the various values for combinations of i and n.

Table 3.1 is one such table (a more comprehensive version appears in Appendix A at the back of this text). Note that the amounts given in this table represent the value of $1 compounded at rate i at the end of the nth year. Thus, to calculate the future value of an initial investment, you need only determine the future-value interest factor using a calculator or a table and multiply this amount by the initial investment. In effect, you can rewrite equation (3.2) as follows:

$$\boxed{\begin{array}{c}\text{Future Value}\\ \text{or}\\ FV_n\end{array}} = \boxed{\begin{array}{c}\text{Present Value}\\ \text{or}\\ PV\end{array}} \times \boxed{\text{Future-Value Interest Factor}} \quad (3.2a)$$

Let's look at an example.

Compounded Annually
With annual compounding, the interest is received at the end of each year and then added to the original investment. Then, at the end of the second year, interest is earned on this new sum.

EXAMPLE

You receive a $1,000 academic award this year for being the best student in your personal finance course, and you place it in a savings account paying 5 percent annual interest **compounded annually**. How much will your account be worth in 10 years?

We can solve this mathematically using equation (3.2) or using the future-value interest factors in Table 3.1.

Solving Mathematically Substituting $PV = \$1{,}000$, $i = 5$ percent, and $n = 10$ years into equation (3.2), you get

$$\begin{aligned} FV_n &= PV(1 + i)^n \\ &= \$1{,}000(1 + 0.05)^{10} \\ &= \$1{,}000(1.62889) \\ &= \$1{,}628.89 \end{aligned}$$

Thus, at the end of 10 years you will have $1,628.89 in your savings account—unless, of course, you decide to add in or take out money along the way.

Solving Using the Future-Value Interest Factors In Table 3.1, at the intersection of the $n = 10$ row and the 5% column, we find a value for the future-value interest factor of 1.629. Thus:

$$\begin{aligned} \text{future value} &= \text{present value} \times \text{future-value interest factor} \\ FV_{10} &= \$1{,}000(1.629) = \$1{,}629 \end{aligned}$$

You obtain the same answer using either approach.

MyLab Finance Animation

The Rule of 72

FACTS OF LIFE

If you can earn 8 percent on your savings, then you can either spend $10,000 on a cruise today or save that money for 45 years and have $319,000 to spend during retirement.

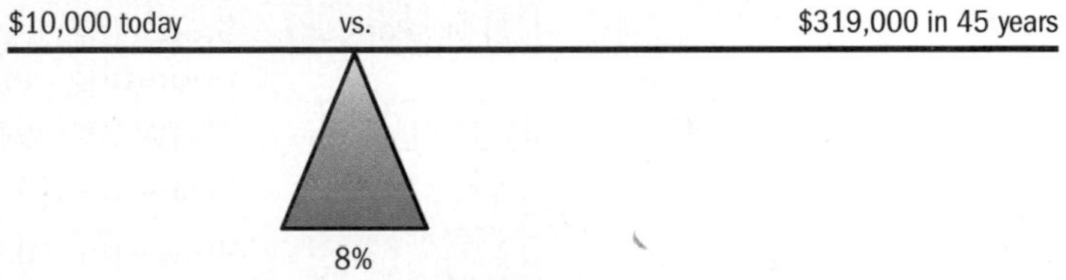

Now you know how to determine the future value of any investment. What if all you want to know is how long it will take to double your money in that investment? One simple way to approximate how long it will take for a given sum to double in value is called the **Rule of 72**. This "rule" states that you can determine how many years it will take for a given sum to double by dividing the investment's annual growth or interest rate into 72. For example, if an investment grows at an annual rate of 9 percent per year, according to the Rule of 72 it should take $72/9 = 8$ years for that sum to double.

Keep in mind that this is not a hard-and-fast rule. It is just an approximation, but it's a pretty good approximation. For example, the future-value interest factor from Table 3.1 for 9 years at 8 percent is 1.999, which is pretty close to the Rule of 72's approximation of 2.0.

Rule of 72
A helpful investment rule that states you can determine how many years it will take for a sum to double by dividing the annual growth rate into 72.

EXAMPLE

Using the Rule of 72, how long will it take to double your money if you invest it at 12 percent compounded annually?

$$\begin{aligned} \text{number of years to double} &= \frac{72}{\text{annual compound growth rate}} \\ &= \frac{72}{12} \\ &= 6 \text{ years} \end{aligned}$$

Compound Interest with Nonannual Periods

Until now we've assumed that the compounding period is always annual. Sometimes, though, financial institutions compound interest on a quarterly, daily, or even continuous basis. What happens to your investment when your compounding period

MyLab Finance Animation

FACTS OF LIFE

CNN Money recently reported that the average cost of a wedding in New York City was about $86,916. If you can earn 9 percent on your savings, your choice is whether to spend the $86,916 on a wedding or to elope, invest the $86,916, and have over $2.7 million 40 years later at retirement.

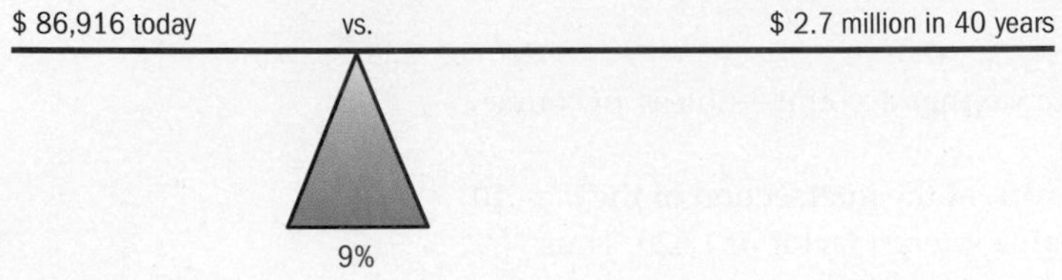

is nonannual? You earn more money faster. The sooner your interest is paid, the sooner you start earning interest on it, and the sooner you reap the benefits of compound interest.

The bottom line is that your money grows faster as the compounding period becomes shorter—for example, when it decreases from annual compounding to monthly compounding. That's because interest is earned on interest more frequently as the length of the compounding period declines.

Using an Online or Handheld Financial Calculator

Time value of money calculations can be made simple with the aid of a financial calculator. If you don't own a financial calculator, you can easily find one on the Web—there's an excellent one on the Web site that accompanies this text (**www.pearson.com/mylab/finance**). There's even a little tutorial there, and you might want to bookmark this Web site. This calculator is illustrated in Figure 3.2.

Before you try to whoop it up solving time value of money problems on your financial calculator, take note of a few keys that will prove necessary. There are five keys on a financial calculator that come into play:

N or Periods   I/Y or Rate   PV   PMT   FV

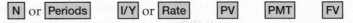

Here's what they stand for:

N or Periods	Stores (or calculates) the total number of payments or compounding periods.
I/Y or Rate	Stores (or calculates) the interest or discount rate per period.
PV	Stores (or calculates) the present value.
PMT	Stores (or calculates) the dollar amount of each annuity payment. (We talk about these payments later in the chapter; an annuity is a series of equal dollar payments for a specified number of time periods.)
FV	Stores (or calculates) the future value.

MyLab Finance Animation

FIGURE 3.2 Time Value of Money Calculator on MyLab Finance

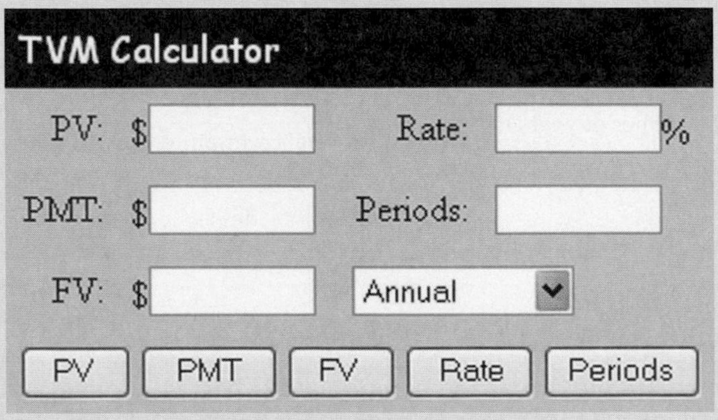

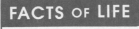

And if you're using a Texas Instruments BAII Plus calculator, here's another one you'll want to know about:

[CPT] This is the compute key on the Texas Instruments BAII Plus calculator, the calculator we use in examples in this text. If you want to compute the present value, you enter the known variables and press [CPT] [PV].

Every calculator operates a bit differently with respect to entering variables. It is a good idea to become familiar with exactly how your calculator functions.

To solve a time value of money problem using a financial calculator, all you need to do is enter the appropriate numbers for three of the four variables and then press the key of the final variable to calculate its value.

Now, let's solve an example using a financial calculator. Suppose you would like to know the rate at which $11,167 must be compounded annually for it to grow to $20,000 in 10 years. All you have to do is input the known variables and then calculate the value of the one you're looking for.

Enter	10		−11,167	0	20,000
	[N]	[I/Y]	[PV]	[PMT]	[FV]
Solve for		6.0			

Why the negative sign before the $11,167? When using a financial calculator, each problem will have at least one positive number and one negative number. In effect, a financial calculator sees money as "leaving your hands" and taking on a *negative sign* or as "returning to your hands" and taking on a *positive sign*. You'll also notice that the answer appears as 6.0 rather than 0.06. When entering interest rates, enter them as percentages rather than decimals—that is, 10 percent would be entered as 10, not 0.10.

Calculator Apps If you're looking for a calculator app, there are a few that are excellent. The first comes right from MyLab Finance and is free—just go to your app store and search for "MyLab Finance calculator" or "Pearson time value of money calculator." There are also some others that aren't free that do a great job of emulating the Texas Instruments BAII Plus Calculator—just search for "BAII Plus" and you'll find them.

Calculator Clues

Calculators are pretty easy to use. When people have problems with calculators, it is usually the result of a few common mistakes. Before you take a crack at solving a problem using a financial calculator, keep the following tips in mind:

1. Set your calculator to one payment per year. Some financial calculators use monthly payments as the default, so you will need to change the setting to annual payments.
2. Set your calculator to display at least four decimal places. Most calculators are preset to display only two decimal places. Because interest rates are so small, change your decimal setting to at least four.
3. Set your calculator to the "end" mode. Your calculator will assume cash flows occur at the end of each time period.

When you're ready to work a problem, remember:

1. Every problem will have at least one positive and one negative number.
2. You must enter a zero for any variable that isn't used in a problem, or you will have to clear the calculator before beginning a new problem. If you don't enter a value for one of the variables, your calculator won't assume that the variable is zero. Instead, your calculator will assume it carries the same number as it did during the previous problem.
3. Enter the interest rate as a percentage, not as a decimal. That means 10 percent must be entered as 10 rather than as 0.10.

LO2 Understand the power of time and the importance of the interest rate in compounding.

Compounding and the Power of Time and Interest

Manhattan Island was purchased by Peter Minuit from Native Americans in 1626 for $24 in knickknacks and jewelry. If, at the end of 1626, the Native Americans had invested their $24 at 8 percent compounded annually, it would have been worth over $303 trillion at the end of 2018, just 392 years later. That's certainly enough to buy back all of Manhattan. In fact, with $303 trillion in the bank, the $1.4 trillion to $1.7 trillion you'd have to pay to buy back all of Manhattan would seem like pocket change. The story illustrates the incredible power of time in compounding. Let's take a closer look.

The Power of Time

Why should you care about compounding? Well, the sooner you start saving for retirement and other long-term goals, the less painful the process of saving will be. Consider the tale of twin sisters who work at the Springfield DMV. Selma and Patty Bouvier decide to save for retirement, which is 35 years away. They'll both receive an 8 percent annual return on their investment over the next 35 years.

Selma invests $2,000 per year at the end of each year *only* for the first 10 years of the 35-year period—for a total of $20,000 saved. Patty doesn't start saving for 10 years and then saves $2,000 per year at the end of each year for the remaining 25 years—for a total of $50,000 saved. When they retire, Selma will have accumulated just under $200,000, while Patty will have accumulated just under $150,000, despite the fact that Selma saved for only 10 years, while Patty saved for 25 years. Figure 3.3 presents their results and illustrates the power of time in compounding.

Let's look at another example to see what this really means to you. The compound growth rate in the stock market over the 50-year period from the beginning of 1967 to the beginning of 2017 was approximately 10.09 percent. Although the rate of return on stocks has been far from constant over this period, assume for the moment that you could earn a return of 10.09 percent compounded annually on an investment in stocks. If you had invested $10,000 in stocks at the beginning of 1967 and earned 10.09 percent compounded annually, your investment would have grown to $1,222,907 by the beginning of 2017 (50 years). That would have made you one wealthy senior citizen.

Let's look at one example that illustrates the danger in just looking at the bottom-line numbers without considering the time value of money. One of today's "hot" collectibles is the Schwinn Deluxe Tornado boy's bicycle, which sold for $49.95 in 1968. In 2018, 50 years later, a Schwinn Tornado in mint condition is selling on eBay for $920.00,

FACTS OF LIFE

The power of compounding is truly amazing. Say you're 22 and intend to retire at age 65—43 years from now. If you invest $12,637 in stocks and they earn 10.7 percent compounded annually over those 43 years (that's the average return on common stocks over the past 50 years), you will accumulate $1 million by retirement—all in just 15,695 days!

FIGURE 3.3 The Power of Time in Compounding

MyLab Finance Animation

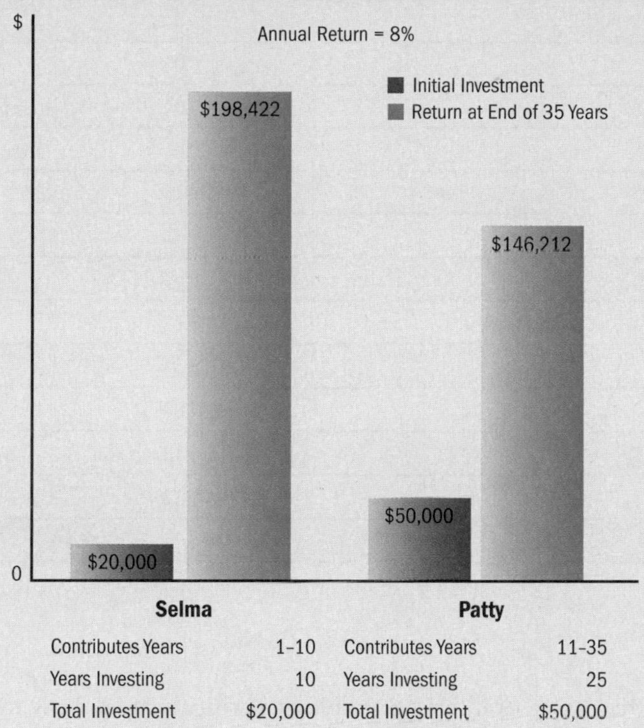

which is 18.42 times its original cost. At first glance, you might view this as a 1,842 percent return—but you'd be ignoring the time value of money. At what rate did this investment really compound? The answer is 6 percent per year, which ignores any storage costs that might have been incurred. The Schwinn may provide a great ride, but given what you just saw common stocks doing over the same period, it doesn't provide a very good return.

The Importance of the Interest Rate

It's not just time that makes money grow in value; it's also the interest rate. Most people understand that a higher interest rate earns you more money—that's why some people are willing to buy a risky bond issued by Vertis (a direct marketing firm that has experienced financial problems) paying 11 percent rather than a very safe bond issued by the government paying only 4 percent—but most people don't understand just how dramatic a difference the interest rate can make. This brings us back to **Principle 1: The Best Protection Is Knowledge**.

PRINCIPLE 1

Without an understanding of investment concepts such as the time value of money, you're a prime target for bad advice. You're also at a real disadvantage because you might not be able to take advantage of good deals and even understand basic financial principles, such as those that apply to interest rates. The bottom line is that it's much easier to do things correctly if you understand what you're doing. Let's take a closer look at interest rates.

TABLE 3.2 The Daily Double

Day	"Daily Double": 1¢ at 100% Compounded Daily Would Become
1	$0.01
2	0.02
3	0.04
4	0.08
5	0.16
6	0.32
7	0.64
8	1.28
15	163.84
20	5,242.88
25	167,772.16
30	5,368,709.12
31	10,737,418.24

Obviously, the choice of interest rate plays a critical role in how much an investment grows. But do small changes in the interest rate have much of an impact on future values? To answer this question, let's look back to Peter Minuit's purchase of Manhattan. If the Native Americans had invested their $24 at 10 percent rather than 8 percent compounded annually at the end of 1626, they would have had about $403 quadrillion by the end of 2018. That's 403 moved over 15 decimal places, or $403,000,000,000,000,000. Actually, that's enough to buy back not only Manhattan Island but also the entire world and still have plenty left over!

STOP & THINK

If you receive an inheritance of $25,000 and invest it at 6 percent (ignoring taxes) for 40 years, it will accumulate to $257,125. If you invest it at 12 percent (again ignoring taxes) over this same period, it will accumulate to $2,326,225! Almost ten times more! If the interest rate doubled, why did your investment grow almost tenfold?

Now, let's assume a lower interest rate—say, 6 percent. In that case, the $24 would have grown to a mere $199.6 billion—less than one-thousandth of what it grew to at 8 percent and only one-millionth of what it would have grown to at 10 percent. With today's real estate prices, the Native Americans might be able to buy some of Manhattan, but they would probably run into problems paying their taxes!

To illustrate the power of a high interest rate in compounding, let's look at a "daily double." A "daily double" simply means that your money doubles each day. In effect, it assumes an interest rate of 100 percent compounded on a daily basis. Let's see what can happen to a penny over a month's worth of daily doubles, assuming that the month has 31 days in it. The first day begins with 1¢, the second day it compounds to 2¢, the third day it becomes 4¢, the fourth day 8¢, the fifth day 16¢, and so forth. As shown in Table 3.2, by day 20 it would have grown to $5,242.88, and by day 31, it would have grown to over $10 million. This explains why Albert Einstein once marveled that "Compound interest is the eighth wonder of the world."

LOVE & MONEY

According to a recent LifePlan Financial Group survey, the top financial fear your spouse has and is afraid to tell you is: "I fear that we won't have enough money to retire with dignity." Obviously, the key to easing that fear is to have an understanding of how much you'll need at retirement and to have a plan to amass enough savings to get there. And, if you're going to work with a partner when saving for the future, it is of the utmost importance that you both have a firm grasp of the "time value of money." However, according to a study out of George Washington University, most Americans don't understand the concept of the time value of money—in fact, many people have never even heard the term, much less understand how it works!

Without an understanding of the time value of money and the power of compounding, it is difficult to appreciate the importance of starting to save for retirement at an early age. You can certainly see that if one partner understands this, while the other doesn't, there is the chance for conflict that can easily be avoided. In effect, not only is money power, but an understanding of the time value of money is also power, and indeed it is the key to accumulating wealth.

So what do you do if you understand the concept of the time value of money and your partner doesn't? Fortunately, while some of the calculations can be a little tricky, it is not a difficult concept to grasp, especially if you can provide some examples. A good one to use is the example from this chapter of Selma and Patty Bouvier, Marge Simpson's twin sisters, who work at the Springfield DMV. Alternatively, the power of the time value of money can also be illustrated through a story Warren Buffett tells in his 2017 HBO biography "*Becoming Warren Buffett*." It is the story of a peasant who wins a chess tournament put on by the king. The king asks the peasant what he would like as his prize. The peasant answers that he would like something for his village—specifically, that one piece of grain be placed on the first square of his chessboard, two pieces of grain on the second square, four pieces on the third, eight on the fourth, and so on. The king, thinking he was getting off easy, pledged on his word of honor that it would be done. Unfortunately for the king, by the time all 64 squares on the chessboard were filled, there were 18.5 million trillion grains of wheat on the board; the kernels were compounding at a rate of 100 percent over the 64 squares of the chessboard. That's the power of compounding and the time value of money, and that's also a lot of wheat. In fact, if each kernel of grain were one-quarter inch long, then if laid end to end, they could stretch to the sun and back 391,320 times.

The bottom line here is that you don't have to be a math genius to understand compounding. Once you do understand it, you'll find as an investor that compounding is your best friend, especially when it comes to saving and accumulating money for a large and distant goal such as retirement. But as a borrower, beware! Compounding can lay waste to your finances faster than you can imagine.

You will also want to introduce your partner to one of the many time value of money calculators online. Just google "time value of money calculator" and a bunch of them will show up. While this anxiety surrounding saving for retirement is understandable when you consider the challenges faced in achieving a financially secure retirement, with an understanding of the time value of money in hand, starting to save early is much easier to do—and that's the key. If your partner doesn't understand the concept of the time value of money and its significance, it is your obligation to correct this. Your future ability to "retire with dignity" will most certainly depend on it.

Present Value—What's It Worth in Today's Dollars?

LO3 Calculate the present value of money to be received in the future.

Up until this point, we've been moving money forward in time; that is, we know how much we have to begin with, and we are trying to determine how much that sum will grow in a certain number of years when compounded at a specific rate. We're now going to look at the reverse question: What's the value in today's dollars of a sum of money to be received in the future? That is, what's the present value?

Why is present value important to us? It lets us strip away the effects of inflation and see what future cash flows are worth in today's dollars. It also lets us compare dollar values from different periods. In later chapters, we'll use the present value to determine how much to pay for stocks and bonds.

In finding the present value of a future sum, we're moving future money back to the present. What we're doing is, in fact, nothing other than inverse compounding. When we discussed compounding, we talked about the compound interest rate and the initial investment; in determining the present value, we will talk about the **discount rate** and future value.

Discount Rate
The interest rate used to bring future dollars back to the present.

When we use the term *discount rate*, we mean the interest rate used to bring future money back to the present—that is, the interest rate used to "discount" that future money back to the present. For example, if we expect to receive a sum of money in 10 years and want to know what it would buy in today's dollars, we discount that future sum of money back to the present at the anticipated inflation rate. Other than that, the technique and the terminology remain the same, and the mathematics is simply reversed.

FACTS OF LIFE

In 2018, the cost of a new Honda Accord EX was about $24,000, and a used 2014 Honda Accord EX cost about $14,000. If you can earn 10 percent on your savings, your choice is whether to spend $24,000 on a new Honda or to save $10,000 and buy the used Honda. You could then invest the $10,000 at 10 percent and have $728,905 at retirement 45 years later.

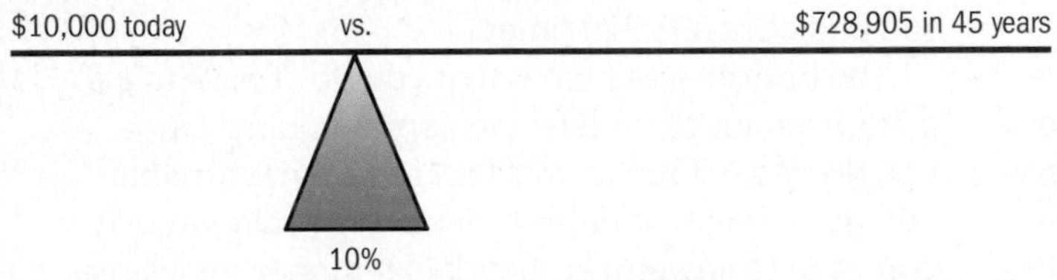

Let's return to equation (3.2), the time value of money equation. We now want to solve for present value instead of future value. To do this, we simply rearrange the terms in equation (3.2) and get

MyLab Finance Animation and Video

Present Value		Future Value at the end of n years		The inverse of the Future-Value Interest Factor
or	=	or	×	or
PV		FV_n		$\frac{1}{(1+i)^n}$

$$PV = FV_n \frac{1}{(1+i)^n} \qquad (3.3)$$

Because the mathematical procedure for determining the present value is exactly the inverse of determining the future value, the relationships among n, i, and PV are just the opposite of those we observed in future value. The present value of a future sum of money is inversely related to both the number of years until the payment will be received and the discount rate. Figure 3.4 shows this relationship graphically

Present-Value Interest Factor
The value $[1/(1+i)^n]$ used as a multiplier to calculate an amount's present value.

To help us compute present values, we once again have some handy tables. This time they calculate the $[1/(1+i)^n]$ part of the equation, which we call the **present-value interest factor** for i and n. These tables simplify the math by giving us the present-value interest factor for combinations of i and n. Appendix B (at the back of this text) presents fairly complete versions of these tables, and an abbreviated version appears in Table 3.3.

As you can see by looking at the two downward-sloping lines in the graph, the higher the interest rate is, the lower the present value of $100 received in the future will be. Also, the longer it is until you receive the $100, the smaller its present value is.

FIGURE 3.4 The Present Value of $100

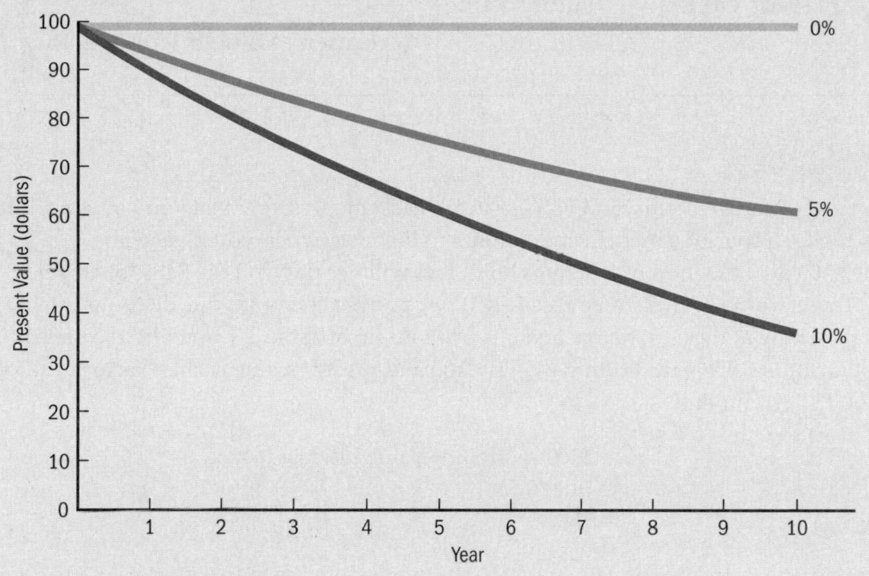

MyLab Finance Animation

A close examination of Table 3.3 shows that the values in these tables are the inverse of the values in the tables found in Appendix A and Table 3.1. Of course, this inversion makes sense because the values in Appendix A are $(1 + i)^n$ and those in Appendix B are $[1/(1 + i)^n]$. To determine the present value of a sum of money to be received at some future date, you need only determine the value of the appropriate present-value interest factor, by using a calculator or consulting the tables, and

TABLE 3.3 Present Value of $1 (single amount)

Instructions: Each present-value interest factor corresponds to a specific time period and interest rate. To find the present-value interest factor for 6 percent and 10 years, simply move down the $i = 6\%$ column until you reach its intersection with the $n = 10$ years row: 0.558. The present value is then calculated as follows:

present value = future value × present-value interest factor

n	4%	5%	6%	7%	8%
1	0.962	0.952	0.943	0.935	0.926
2	0.925	0.907	0.890	0.873	0.857
3	0.889	0.864	0.840	0.816	0.794
4	0.855	0.823	0.792	0.763	0.735
5	0.822	0.784	0.747	0.713	0.681
6	0.790	0.746	0.705	0.666	0.630
7	0.760	0.711	0.655	0.623	0.583
8	0.731	0.677	0.627	0.582	0.540
9	0.703	0.645	0.592	0.544	0.500
10	0.676	0.614	0.558	0.508	0.463
11	0.650	0.585	0.527	0.475	0.429

multiply it by the future value. In effect, you can use the new notation and rewrite equation (3.3) as follows:

$$\boxed{\begin{array}{c}\text{Present Value}\\ \text{or}\\ PV\end{array}} = \boxed{\begin{array}{c}\text{Future Value}\\ \text{or}\\ FV\end{array}} \times \boxed{\text{Present-Value Interest Factor}} \quad (3.3a)$$

EXAMPLE

You're on vacation in Florida, and you see an advertisement stating that you'll receive $100 simply for taking a tour of a model condominium. However, when you investigate, you discover that the $100 is in the form of a savings bond that will not pay you the $100 for 10 years. What is the present value of $100 to be received 10 years from today if your discount rate is 6 percent? By looking at the $n = 10$ row and $i = 6\%$ column of Table 3.3, you find the present-value interest factor is 0.558. Substituting $FV_{10} = \$100$ and present-value interest factor $= 0.558$ into equation (3.3a), you find:

$$\begin{aligned} PV &= \$100 \times \text{present-value interest factor} \\ &= \$100(0.558) \\ &= \$55.80 \end{aligned}$$

Thus, the value in today's dollars of that $100 savings bond is only $55.80. Not a bad take for touring a condo, but it's not a hundred bucks.

MyLab Finance Video

Calculator Clues

Calculating a Present Value

Note for all calculations in this chapter: If you don't have a financial calculator handy, you can use the one that is located on the Web site that accompanies this text: **www.pearson.com/mylab/finance**. Returning to the example above, we're calculating the present value of $100 to be received in 10 years, given a 6 percent interest or discount rate. For any value that does not appear in the calculations, we'll enter a value of 0.

Enter	10	6		0	100
	N	I/Y	PV	PMT	FV
Solve for			−55.84		

You'll notice that this calculator solution is slightly different from the answer we just got using the tables; that's just a matter of rounding error. You'll also notice that we get a negative value for the answer. Remember, that's because financial calculators view money just as a bank does. You deposit money in the bank (the sign is negative because the money "leaves your hands"), and later you take money out of the bank (the sign is positive because the money "returns to your hands"). Every problem with two cash flows will have one with a positive sign and one with a negative sign.

MyLab Finance Video

EXAMPLE

Let's consider the impatient son of wealthy parents who wants his inheritance NOW! He's been promised $500,000 in 40 years. Assuming the appropriate discount rate (i.e., the interest rate used to bring future money back to the present) is 6 percent, what is the present value of the $500,000? To find the present value of the estate, we need only multiply the future value, which is $500,000, times the present-value interest factor for 6 percent and 40 years. To find the present-value interest factor for 6 percent and 40 years, go to the present-value interest factor table (see Appendix B) and simply move down the $i = 6\%$ column until you reach its intersection with the $n = 40$ years row: 0.097. Thus, the present value of the estate is

$$\begin{aligned}\text{present value} &= \text{future value} \times \text{present-value interest factor}\\ &= \$500{,}000(0.097)\\ &= \$48{,}500\end{aligned}$$

The $500,000 that the son is to receive in 40 years is worth only $48,500 in today's dollars. Another way of looking at this problem is that if you deposit $48,500 in the bank today and earn 6 percent annually, then in 40 years you'll have $500,000.

Calculator Clues

Calculating a Present Value

In this example, you're solving for the present value of $500,000 to be received in 40 years, given a 6 percent interest or discount rate.

Enter	40	6		0	500,000
	N	I/Y	PV	PMT	FV
Solve for			−48,611.09		

As expected, you get a negative sign on the *PV*. Try entering a higher value for *I/Y*, and see what happens to the *PV*. Again, you'll notice a slight difference in the calculator solution due to rounding error, and the negative sign that the solution takes on.

Keep in mind that there is really only one time value of money equation. That is, equations (3.2) and (3.3) are actually identical—they simply solve for different variables. One solves for future value, the other for present value. The logic behind both equations is the same: To adjust for the time value of money, we must compare dollar values, present and future, in the same time period. Because all present values are comparable (they are all measured in dollars of the same time period), you can add and subtract the present value of inflows and outflows to determine the present value of an investment.

STOP & THINK

Why should you be interested in stripping away the effects of inflation from money you receive in the future? Because the dollar value of future money is not as important as that money's purchasing power. For example, you might be excited if you were told you would receive $1 million in 20 years. However, if you then found out that in 20 years a new car will cost $800,000, your average monthly food bill will be $15,000, and a typical month's rent on your apartment will be $30,000, you would have a different view of the $1 million. Using the time value of money to strip away the effects of inflation allows you to calculate the value of a future amount in terms of the purchasing power of today's dollars. What do you think a car will cost in 20 years?

Solving for *I/Y* and *N* Using a Financial Calculator

As you might expect, you can solve for *I/Y* and *N* using either the tables or a financial calculator. While solving for them using a financial calculator is relatively easy, solving for them using the tables is a bit more difficult, and as a result, an appendix to this chapter has been provided that explains this process.

Let's assume that BMW, the owner of MINI Cooper, has guaranteed that the price of a new MINI Cooper will always be $20,000. You'd like to buy one, but currently you have only $7,752. How many years will it take for your initial investment of $7,752 to grow to $20,000 if it is invested at 9 percent compounded annually?

In this case, we are solving for *N*, the number of years your money needs to grow. Just as in solving for *PV*, *PMT*, or *FV*, all you have to do is enter the variables you know into your financial calculator and, in this case, solve for *N*. Keep in mind that every problem will have at least one negative and one positive number, and in this problem, you'll notice that *PV* is input with a negative sign. In effect, the $7,752 is a cash outflow (the money is leaving your hands), whereas the $20,000 is money that you will receive. If you don't give one of these values a negative sign, you can't solve the problem, and if you have a TI BAII Plus calculator, you'll receive an "Error 5" message.

MyLab Finance Video

Calculator Clues

Solving for *N*–the Number of Payments

Solving for the number of payments using a financial calculator is simple. To solve for *N*, enter the known variables and solve. In this example, how many years will it take for $7,752 to grow to $20,000 at 9 percent?

	N	I/Y	PV	PMT	FV
Enter		9	−7,752	0	20,000
Solve for	10.998				

The answer is 10.998, or about 11 years. You'll notice we gave the present value, $7,752, a negative sign and the future value, $20,000, a positive sign. Why? Because a calculator looks at cash flows as if it were a bank. You deposit your money in the bank (and the sign is negative because the money "leaves your hands"); then later you take your money out of the bank (and the sign is positive because the money "returns to your hands"). As a result, every problem will have a positive and a negative sign on the cash flows.

Now let's solve for the compound annual growth rate. In 10 years, you'd really like to have $20,000 to buy a new MINI Cooper convertible, but you have only $11,167. At what rate must your $11,167 be compounded annually for it to grow to $20,000 in 10 years?

Once again you have to remember that at least one of the dollar value variables, *PV*, *PMT*, or *FV*, must take on a negative value. In this case, we will enter $11,167 as a negative value, since that money will "leave your hands" and later you will receive $20,000.

MyLab Finance Video

Calculator Clues

Solving for *I/Y*–the Rate of Return

Finding a rate of return using a financial calculator is simple. To solve for *I/Y*, enter the known variables and solve. For example, what is the growth rate of an initial investment of $11,167 that grew to $20,000 in 10 years?

	N	I/Y	PV	PMT	FV
Enter	10		−11,167	0	20,000
Solve for		6.0009			

The answer is 6.0009—about 6 percent. Just as when you solved for *N*, you gave the present value, $11,167, which was your initial investment, a negative sign, and you gave the future value, $20,000, a positive sign.

Annuity
A series of equal dollar payments coming at the end of each time period for a specified number of time periods.

LO4 Explain what an annuity is and calculate its compound or future value.

Annuities

Up to this point, we've been examining single deposits—moving them back and forth in time. Now we're going to examine annuities. Most people deal with a great number of annuities. Mortgage payments, pension funds, insurance obligations, and interest received from bonds all involve annuities. An **annuity** is a series of equal dollar payments coming at the end of each time period for a specified number of time periods (years, months, etc.). Because annuities occur frequently in finance—for example, as bond interest payments and mortgage payments—they are treated specially. Although compounding and determining the present value of an annuity can be done using equations (3.2) and (3.3), these calculations can be time-consuming, especially for larger annuities. Thus, we have modified the formulas to deal directly with annuities.

Compound Annuities

A **compound annuity** involves depositing or investing an equal sum of money at the end of each year (or time period) for a certain number of years (or time periods—e.g., months) and allowing it to grow. Perhaps you are saving money for education, a new car, or a vacation home. In each case, you'll want to know how much your savings will have grown by some point in the future.

Compound Annuity
An investment that involves depositing an equal sum of money at the end of each year for a certain number of years and allowing it to grow.

Actually, you can find the answer by using equation (3.2) and compounding each of the individual deposits to its future value. For example, if to provide for a college education, you are going to deposit $500 at the end of each year for the next 5 years in a bank where it will earn 6 percent interest, how much will you have at the end of 5 years? Compounding each of these values using equation (3.2), you find that you will have $2,818.55 at the end of 5 years.

In fact, even by saving what might seem small amounts, the power of compounding can provide you with a good deal of money in the future. In 2017, Americans ate lunch out on average twice a week, paying $11.14 per meal. If instead they took this money and invested it at only 6 percent compounded annually, in 30 years they'd have $88,448. Not only that, they might be healthier and weigh less.

As Table 3.4 shows, all we're really doing in the preceding calculation is summing up a number of future values. To simplify this process once again, there are tables providing the **future-value interest factor of an annuity** for i and n. Appendix C provides a fairly complete version of these tables, and Table 3.5 presents an abbreviated version. Using this new factor, we can calculate the future value of an annuity as follows:

Future-Value Interest Factor of an Annuity
A multiplier used to determine the future value of an annuity. The future-value interest factors for an annuity are found in Appendix C.

$$\boxed{\begin{array}{c}\text{Future Value}\\ \text{of an Annuity}\\ \text{or}\\ FV_n\end{array}} = \boxed{\begin{array}{c}\text{Annual}\\ \text{Payment}\\ \text{or}\\ PMT\end{array}} \times \boxed{\begin{array}{c}\text{Future-Value Interest Factor}\\ \text{of an Annuity}\end{array}} \quad (3.4)$$

Using the future-value interest factor of an annuity to solve our previous example involving 5 years of deposits of $500, invested at 6 percent interest, we would look

TABLE 3.4 Illustration of a 5-Year $500 Annuity Compounded at 6%

Year	0	1	2	3	4	5
Dollar deposits at end of year		500	500	500	500	500
						$500.00
						530.00
						562.00
						595.50
						631.00
Future value of the annuity						$2,818.50

TABLE 3.5 Future Value of a Series of Equal Annual Deposits (annuity), Future-Value Interest Factor of an Annuity

Instructions: Each future-value interest factor of an annuity corresponds to a specific time period (number of years) and interest rate. For example, to find the future-value interest factor of an annuity for 6 percent and 5 years, simply move down the $i = 6\%$ column until you reach its intersection with the $n = 5$ years row: 5.637. The future value is calculated as follows:

$$\text{future value} = \text{annual payment} \times \text{future-value interest factor of an annuity}$$
$$\text{or } FV_n = PMT(FVIFA_{i\%,\ n\ years})$$

n	4%	5%	6%	7%	8%
1	1.000	1.000	1.000	1.000	1.000
2	2.040	2.050	2.060	2.070	2.080
3	3.122	3.152	3.184	3.215	3.246
4	4.246	4.310	4.375	4.440	4.506
5	5.416	5.526	5.637	5.751	5.867
6	6.633	6.802	6.975	7.153	7.336
7	7.898	8.142	8.394	8.654	8.923
8	9.214	9.549	9.897	10.260	10.637
9	10.583	11.027	11.491	11.978	12.488
10	12.006	12.578	13.181	13.816	14.487
11	13.486	14.207	14.972	15.784	16.645

in the $i = 6\%$ column and $n = 5$ row and find the value of the future-value interest factor of an annuity to be 5.637. Substituting this value into equation (3.4), we get

$$\begin{aligned}\text{future value} &= \$500(5.637)\\ &= \$2,818.50\end{aligned}$$

Other than some rounding error, this is the same answer we obtained earlier. (If it weren't, I'd need to get a new job!)

Rather than asking how much you'll accumulate if you deposit an equal sum in a savings account each year, a more common question is "How much must I deposit each year to accumulate a certain amount of savings?" This question often arises when saving for large expenditures, such as retirement or a down payment on a home.

For example, you may know that you'll need $10,000 for education in 8 years. How much must you put away at the end of each year at 6 percent interest to have the college money ready? In this case, you know the values of n, i, and FV_n in equation (3.4), but you don't know the value of PMT. Substituting these example values in equation (3.4), you find:

$$\begin{aligned}\text{future value} &= \text{annual payment} \times \text{future-value interest factor of an annuity}\\ \$10,000 &= PMT(9.897)\\ \$10,000/9.897 &= PMT\\ PMT &= \$1,010.41\end{aligned}$$

STOP & THINK

If a couple goes out to dinner and a movie four times a month at $75 an outing and cuts this down to two times per month, they will save $1,800 per year. If they take this saved money and invest it at the end of each year, earning 10 percent compounded annually (ignoring taxes), in 30 years they will accumulate $296,089! What monthly expense do you think you could cut down on in order to save money?

Thus, you must invest $1,010.41 at the end of each year at 6 percent interest to accumulate $10,000 at the end of 8 years.

For a moment, let's use the future value of an annuity and think back to the discussion of the power of time. There's no question about the power of time. One way to illustrate this power is to look at how much you'd have to save each month to reach some far-off goal. Say, for example, you'd like to save up $50,000 by the time you turn 60 to use to go see a Rolling Stones concert. (There's a good chance that they'll still be on tour and that concert tickets will cost that much.)

If you can invest your money at 12 percent and start saving when you turn 21, making your last payment on your 60th birthday, you'll need to put aside only $4.25 per month. If you start at age 31, that figure will be $14.31 per month. However, if you wait until age 51, it will rise to $217.35 per month. When it comes to compounding, time is on your side.

PRINCIPLE **10**

STOP & THINK

Let's take one more look at the power of compounding. Assume you empty the change out of your pocket each day—averaging a dollar a day—and set it aside. Then, at the end of each year, you invest it ($365) at 12 percent. If you began doing this at age 18, 50 years later you would have accumulated $876,007. If you waited until you were 33 to begin your pocket-emptying ritual, you'd accumulate only $157,557. Keep in mind that between the time you were 18 and the time you turned 33, you invested only a total of $5,475. Remember **Principle 10: Just Do It!** In the world of investing, time is your best friend. Where else do you think you might be able to save a little money every day?

Calculator Clues

Future Value of an Annuity

MyLab Finance Video

At the end of each year for 50 years, you deposit $365 in an account that earns 12 percent.

Enter	50	12	0	365	
	N	I/Y	PV	PMT	FV
Solve for					−876,006.66

As expected, you get a negative sign on the *FV*. What would happen if you waited until you were 33 instead of 18 to begin? Then you'd be investing for only 35 years, so you change *N* to 35 and solve for the future value again:

Enter	35	12	0	365	
	N	I/Y	PV	PMT	FV
Solve for					−157,557.18

Present Value of an Annuity

In planning your finances, you need to examine the relative value of all your annuities. To compare them, you need to know the present value of each. Although you can find the present value of an annuity by using the present-value table in Appendix B, this process can be tedious, particularly when the annuity lasts for several years. If you wish to know what $500 received at the end of the next 5 years is worth to you, given the appropriate discount rate of 6 percent, you can separately bring each of the $500 flows back to the present at 6 percent using equation (3.3) and then add them together. Thus, the present value of this

MyLab Finance Animation

Facts of Life

Spending money involves a trade-off—spending it today, or saving it and spending the amount it grows to later. For example, when you graduate, one of your first purchases might be a car. In 2018, two of your choices would be an Audi TT for about $46,000 and a 2-year-old used Toyota Camry in great shape for about $16,000. If you saved the difference at 9 percent until you retired in 40 years, you'd have about $942,000 waiting for you!

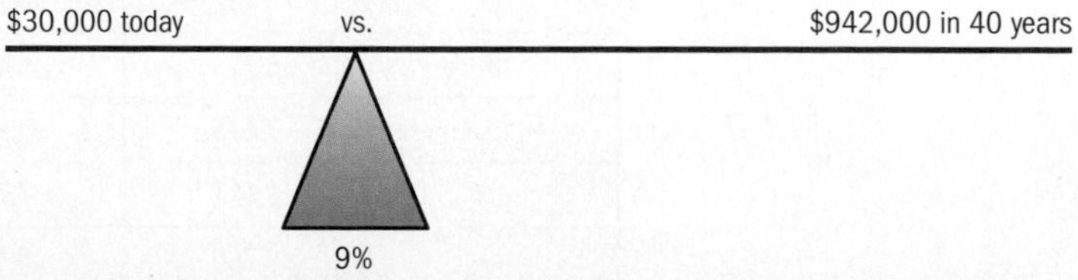

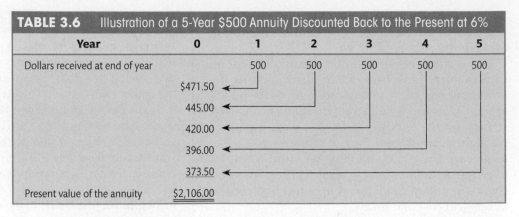

TABLE 3.6 Illustration of a 5-Year $500 Annuity Discounted Back to the Present at 6%

Year	0	1	2	3	4	5
Dollars received at end of year		500	500	500	500	500
	$471.50 ← (year 1)					
	445.00 ← (year 2)					
	420.00 ← (year 3)					
	396.00 ← (year 4)					
	373.50 ← (year 5)					
Present value of the annuity	$2,106.00					

annuity is $2,106.00. As Table 3.6 shows, all we're really doing in this calculation is adding up present values. Because annuities occur so frequently in personal finance, the process of determining the present value of an annuity has been simplified by defining the **present-value interest factor of an annuity** for i and n. The present-value interest factor of an annuity is simply the sum of the present-value interest factors for years 1 to n. Tables for values of the present-value interest factor of an annuity have once again been compiled for various combinations of i and n. Appendix D provides a fairly complete version of these tables, and Table 3.7 provides an abbreviated version.

Present-Value Interest Factor of an Annuity ($PVIFA_{i,n}$)
A multiplier used to determine the present value of an annuity. The present-value interest factors of an annuity are found in Appendix D.

Using this new factor, we can determine the present value of an annuity as follows:

$$\boxed{\begin{matrix}\text{Present Value}\\\text{of an Annuity}\\\text{or}\\PV\end{matrix}} = \boxed{\begin{matrix}\text{Annual}\\\text{Payment}\\\text{or}\\PMT\end{matrix}} \times \boxed{\begin{matrix}\text{Present-Value Interest Factor}\\\text{of an Annuity}\end{matrix}} \quad (3.5)$$

TABLE 3.7 Present Value of a Series of Annual Deposits (annuity), Present-Value Interest Factor of an Annuity

Instructions: Each present-value interest factor of an annuity corresponds to a specific time period (number of years) and interest rate. For example, to find the present-value interest factor of an annuity for 6 percent and 5 years, simply move down the $i = 6\%$ column until you reach its intersection with the $n = 5$ years row: 4.212. The future value is then calculated as follows:

present value = annual payment × present-value interest factor for an annuity

n	4%	5%	6%	7%	8%
1	0.962	0.952	0.943	0.935	0.926
2	1.886	1.859	1.833	1.808	1.783
3	2.775	2.723	2.673	2.624	2.577
4	3.630	3.546	3.465	3.387	3.312
5	4.452	4.329	4.212	4.100	3.993
6	5.242	5.076	4.917	4.767	4.623
7	6.002	5.786	5.582	5.389	5.206
8	6.733	6.463	6.210	5.971	5.747
9	7.435	7.108	6.802	6.515	6.247
10	8.111	7.722	7.360	7.024	6.710
11	8.760	8.306	7.887	7.499	7.139

Using the present-value interest factor of an annuity to solve our previous example involving \$500 received annually and discounted back to the present at 6 percent, we would look in the $i = 6\%$ column and the $n = 5$ row and find the present-value interest factor of an annuity to be 4.212. Substituting the appropriate values into equation (3.5), we find

$$\begin{aligned} \text{present value} &= \text{annual payment} \times \text{present-value interest factor of an annuity} \\ &= \$500(4.212) \\ &= \$2{,}106 \end{aligned}$$

Again, we get the same answer we did before. (We're on a roll now!) We didn't get the same answer just because we're smart. Actually, we got the same answer both times because the present-value interest factors in annuity tables are calculated by adding up the values in the present-value interest factor tables.

EXAMPLE

As part of a class action lawsuit settlement against Lee's "Press On Abs" (they caused a nasty rash), you are slated to receive \$1,000 at the end of each year for the next 10 years. What is the present value of this 10-year, \$1,000 annuity discounted back to the present at 5 percent? Substituting $n = 10$ years, $i = 5$ percent, and $PMT = \$1{,}000$ into equation (3.5), you find

$$PV = \$1{,}000 \text{ (present-value interest factor of an annuity)}$$

Determining the value for the present-value interest factor of an annuity from Table 3.7, row $n = 10$, column $i = 5\%$ and substituting it into our equation, we get

$$PV = \$1{,}000(7.722)$$
$$PV = \$7{,}722$$

Thus, the present value of this annuity is \$7,722.

Calculator Clues

MyLab Finance Video

Present Value of an Annuity

In this example, you're solving for the present value of a 10-year, \$1,000 annuity discounted back to the present at 5 percent.

Enter	10	5		1,000	0
	N	I/Y	PV	PMT	FV
Solve for			−7,721.73		

As expected, you get a negative sign on the *PV*. What happens if you enter a higher value for *I/Y*?

As with the other problems involving compounding and present-value tables, given any three of the four unknowns in equation (3.5), we can solve for the fourth. In the case of the present-value interest factor of an annuity table, we may be interested in solving for *PMT* if we know *i*, *n*, and *PV*. The financial interpretation of this action would be this: How much can be withdrawn, perhaps as a pension or to make loan payments, from an account that earns *i* percent compounded annually for each of the next *n* years if you wish to have nothing left at the end of *n* years?

How the Interest Rate and Time Work Together

Let's take one more look at how your investment will grow when you earn a higher compound return and invest for a longer time period. Rather than focusing on the math, let's just look at the results. Obviously, you have a number of choices on where to invest, so let's look at three of them—a money market or savings account that earns 0.5 percent annually, a certificate of deposit earning 2 percent annually, and stocks that earn 10 percent annually.

Here's how a single $5,000 investment grows:

	Money Market or Savings Account Earning 0.5% Annually	Certificate of Deposit Earning 2% Annually	Stocks Earning 10% Annually
Initial Investment	$5,000	$5,000	$5,000
5 years	$5,126	$5,520	$8,053
10 years	$5,256	$6,095	$12,969
15 years	$5,388	$6,729	$20,886
25 years	$5,664	$8,203	$54,174
35 years	$5,954	$9,999	$140,512
45 years	$6,258	$12,189	$364,452

Not bad at all, and as you can see, the future value increases as you increase the growth rate (*i*) and the number of years during which your money grows (*n*). You'll notice that when you go from 0.5 percent to 2 percent, the future value doubles, and when the rate is increased from 2 to 10 percent (five times higher), the future value is about 30 times more. Now let's look at what might happen if you invested $5,000 every year.

Here's how an investment of $5,000 every year grows:

	Money Market or Savings Account Earning 0.5% Annually	Certificate of Deposit Earning 2% Annually	Stocks Earning 10% Annually
Initial Investment	$5,000	$5,000	$5,000
5 years	$25,251	$26,020	$30,526
10 years	$51,140	$54,749	$79,687
15 years	$77,683	$86,467	$158,862
25 years	$132,796	$160,151	$491,735
35 years	$190,727	$249,972	$1,355,122
45 years	$251,621	$359,464	$3,594,524

Now we're talking about real money. What does all this tell you? There's amazing power in compounding, and the higher the return and the longer the time period, the more you'll end up with. It also tells you that the sooner you start saving for your financial goals, the easier they will be to achieve.

Amortized Loans

> **STOP & THINK**
>
> One of the reasons why people don't save for retirement gets back to **Principle 9: Mind Games, Your Financial Personality, and Your Money**. People tend not to save enough for retirement because retirement seems a long time away, and they think they can catch up later—it's our tendency to postpone and procrastinate that is hurting us. With an understanding of the time value of money, you can gain an understanding of why starting to save early is so important. Name two or three instances where you have procrastinated in the past.

You're not always on the receiving end of an annuity. More often, your annuity will involve paying off a loan in equal installments over time. Loans that are paid off this way, in equal periodic payments, are called **amortized loans**. Examples of amortized loans include car loans and mortgages.

Suppose you borrowed \$16,000 at 8 percent interest to buy a car and wish to repay it in four equal payments at the end of each of the next 4 years. We can use equation (3.5) to determine what the annual payments will be and solve for the value of *PMT*, the annual annuity. Again, you know three of the four values in that equation, *PV*, *i*, and *n*. *PV*, the present value of the future annuity, is \$16,000; *i*, the annual interest rate, is 8 percent; and *n*, the number of years for which the annuity will last, is 4 years. Thus, looking in the $n = 4$ row and $i = 8\%$ column of Table 3.7, you know the present-value interest factor of the annuity is 3.312. *PMT*, the annuity payment received (by the lender and paid by you) at the end of each year, is unknown. Substituting these values into equation (3.5), you find:

PRINCIPLE 9

Amortized Loan
A loan paid off in equal installments.

$$\text{present value} = \text{annual payment} \times \text{present-value interest factor of an annuity}$$
$$\$16{,}000 = PMT(3.312)$$
$$\frac{\$16{,}000}{3.312} = \frac{PMT(3.312)}{3.312}$$
$$\$4{,}831 = PMT$$

To repay the principal and interest on the outstanding loan in 4 years, the annual payments would be \$4,831. The breakdown of interest and principal payments is given in the loan amortization schedule in Figure 3.5. As you can see, the interest payment declines each year as the outstanding loan declines.

FIGURE 3.5 Loan Amortization Schedule Involving a \$16,000 Loan at 8% to Be Repaid in 4 Years

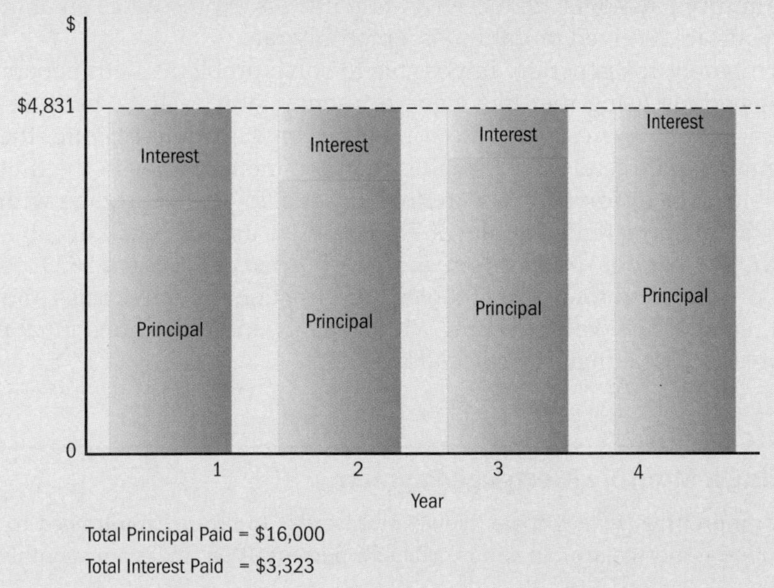

MyLab Finance Animation

MyLab Finance Video

Calculator Clues

Calculating a Loan Payment

Calculating loan payments is easy with a financial calculator. In the example above, you want to determine the loan payments on a \$16,000 loan at 8 percent that you want to pay off with four equal payments at the end of each of the next 4 years. All you need to do is plug your numbers into the calculator and solve for *PMT*. *PV* is \$16,000 because that's how much you've borrowed today, and *FV* is 0 because you will have the loan paid off after 4 years.

Enter	4	8	16,000		0
	N	I/Y	PV	PMT	FV
Solve for				−4,831	

As expected, *PMT* takes on a negative sign.

Amortized Loans with Monthly Payments Using a Financial Calculator

In our examples so far, we have assumed that only one payment is made per year and that interest is compounded annually. However, many loans—for example, auto and home loans—require monthly payments. Fortunately, dealing with monthly, as opposed to yearly, payments is easy. We simply have to make sure that our measurement of periods and interest rate is consistent; that is, if we are talking about monthly payments, then the interest rate should be expressed as the interest rate per month.

To make this adjustment, we can define a new variable, m, which is the number of times compounding occurs per year. For example, if we are talking about semiannual compounding, m is equal to 2, and if we are talking about monthly compounding, m is equal to 12. Then all we do is multiply the number of years outstanding on the loan or annuity by m, which gives us the number of times compounding occurs over the life of the loan or annuity, and this goes in your financial calculator as n, the number of periods. Then we divide the annual interest rate by m to find the interest rate per period, and this goes in your financial calculator as i.

In effect, n is the number of periods for which the annuity will last. If the annuity payments are received annually, n will be the number of years; if the payments are received monthly, n will be the number of months. If n is expressed in terms of months, then i should also be expressed in terms of the interest rate per month. Thus, if annuity payments are received annually, i is expressed as an annual rate; if the payments are received monthly, i is a monthly rate.

Unfortunately, it's generally impossible to solve problems with nonannual compounding periods using the time value of money tables. That's because when we convert an annual interest rate into a monthly or daily interest rate, the monthly or daily interest rate tends to be smaller than the interest rates in the time value of money tables. For example, if we are looking at a 15-year mortgage with monthly payments at an annual interest rate of 7 percent, we are really talking about a mortgage with 180 periods (months) at a rate of $7 \text{ percent}/12 = 0.5833$ percent per month. Unfortunately, there aren't tables with fractional interest rates and 180 periods. As a result, when we are dealing with monthly and other nonannual payments, we are forced to use a financial calculator.

MyLab Finance Video

Calculator Clues

Calculating a Monthly Mortgage Payment

You've just found the perfect home. However, in order to buy it, you'll need to take out a \$150,000, 30-year mortgage at an annual rate of 6 percent. What will your monthly mortgage payment be?

Because there are 360 monthly periods in 30 years, 360 is entered for N, and I/Y becomes 0.5 (annual interest rate of 6 percent divided by m, which is 12).

Enter	360	0.5	150,000		0
	N	I/Y	PV	PMT	FV
Solve for				−899.33	

Calculator Clues

Calculating the Present Value When Payments Are Monthly

One of the first things you'll need to decide when shopping for a house is "How much can I really afford to spend?" This will determine which houses you look at. You figure that you can afford monthly mortgage payments of $1,250 and that you can get a 30-year loan at 7.2 percent. So how big a mortgage can you afford?

We are using 360 as the number of periods, or n, because there are 30 years' worth of monthly mortgage payments and there are 360 months in 30 years. But why are we using 0.72%/12 as the value for i? Because if the annual interest rate is 7.2 percent per year, the monthly interest rate would be one-twelfth of that every month, or 7.2%/12 or 0.6 percent; remember, if n is expressed in months, then i must also be expressed as a monthly interest rate.

The easiest way to enter the interest rate here is to simply divide annual interest rate by m and then enter this number into I/Y. That way you don't have to worry about rounding error.

Enter	360	7.2 ÷ 12		1,250	0
	N	I/Y	PV	PMT	FV
Solve for			−184,152		

Perpetuities

A **perpetuity** is an annuity that continues forever. That is, every year from its establishment, this investment pays the same dollar amount and never stops paying. Determining the present value of a perpetuity is delightfully simple: You divide the payment amount by the discount rate. For example, the present value of a perpetuity that pays a constant dividend of $10 per share forever if the appropriate discount rate is 5 percent is $10/0.05 = $200. Thus, the equation representing the present value of a perpetuity is

Perpetuity An annuity that continues forever.

$$PV = PP/i \tag{3.6}$$

where

PV = the present value of the perpetuity
PP = the annual dollar amount provided by the perpetuity
i = the annual interest (or discount) rate

BEHAVIORAL INSIGHTS

PRINCIPLE 9

Principle 9: Mind Games, Your Financial Personality, and Your Money We all know how tough it is to save. There are a lot of reasons for this, one of which involves how individuals discount the future. It's not that we don't understand the importance of saving; it's just that when it comes time to save, we end up valuing current consumption more. This desire for immediate as opposed to future gains applies to all kinds of things in life. For example, you may realize that it would be great if you lost some weight—you would be healthier and feel better about yourself—so you decide to begin your diet next week. You know that by Monday you'll be able to resist that morning Starbucks hot white chocolate (with 650 calories). Both the weight loss and the Starbucks drink are in the future, so you feel pretty confident you'll be able to resist temptation. But on Monday morning, when that Starbucks drink is all you can think about and the results of weight loss are far in the future, it's likely that, in spite of your good intentions, you'll have your Starbucks.

Why is this the case? It's because many individuals don't visualize compounding and discounting calculations as they really work; instead, they discount in a "hyperbolic" fashion.[1] What does that mean? They understand that a dollar grows quickly in the short run but grows more and more slowly over time. This makes far-off goals seem less important than they should be and makes saving for those goals difficult.

How do you fix it? First, you gain an understanding of how compounding works: As the number of years and the interest rate you earn go up, so does the future value of your investment. Think of it as a "snowball effect" that happens to your money as you earn interest on your initial investment and means earning more interest on that initial amount plus the earned interest. When this happens over and over through the years, your money can really add up. This means that you want to start investing as soon as possible. Still, it's difficult. One secret of success is to pay yourself first. To make this process as painless as possible, automate it so that when your paycheck is deposited into your savings/checking account, a percentage of it is automatically transferred to a special and separate investment account—perhaps your retirement account. It is much easier to save money that you never really see! Talk to the payroll department at work, and request a "mandatory payroll deduction."

ACTION PLAN

PRINCIPLE 10

Principle 10: Just do it! There are few more important concepts than the time value of money. Putting compounding to good use will allow you to attain your goals and retire in style, whereas ignoring it may lead to something far different. Your understanding of the time value of money should help you understand why, no matter what your age, *now* is the time to start saving for retirement. So here's an action plan that puts the time value of money to good use:

- Begin saving for retirement by opening up a Roth IRA plan and, once you get a job, by maxing out your contributions to your retirement plan.
- Automate your payments to savings and retirement to help you keep disciplined.
- When accumulating money for a long-range goal such as retirement or a child's education, make sure you include the impact of inflation.
- Save your raises—when you get a raise at work, increase your savings to include that amount.
- If you're considering charging something, such as a new-generation iPhone or iPad, calculate the real cost of that purchase if it is paid out over a year or two on a credit card. You may find it's worth waiting until you've saved the funds.

[1] P. C. Fishburn & A. Rubenstein. (1982). Time preference. *International Economic Review, 23*, 677–694.

Chapter Summaries

Explain the mechanics of compounding. LO1

SUMMARY: Almost every decision in personal finance involves the techniques of compounding and exploiting the time value of money—putting aside money now to achieve some future goal. The cornerstone of the time value of money is the concept of compound interest, which is interest paid on interest.

With the time value of money, you can determine how much an investment will grow over time using the following formula:

$$FV_n = PV(1 + i)^n \quad (3.2)$$

To simplify these calculations, there are tables for the $(1 + i)^n$ part of the equation, referred to as the future-value interest factor for i and n. In effect, you can rewrite equation (3.2) as follows:

$$\text{future value} = \text{present value} \times \text{future-value interest factor} \quad (3.2a)$$

You can also use the Rule of 72 to determine how long it will take to double your invested money. This "rule" is only an approximation:

$$\text{number of years to double} = 72/\text{annual compound growth rate}$$

KEY TERMS

Time Value of Money, page 61 The concept that a dollar received today is worth more than a dollar received in the future and that, therefore, comparisons between amounts in different time periods cannot be made without adjustments to their values.

Compound Interest, page 62 The effect of earning interest on interest, resulting from the reinvestment of interest paid on an investment's principal.

Principal, page 62 The face value of the deposit or debt instrument.

Present Value (*PV*), page 62 The current value—that is, the value in today's dollars—of a future sum of money.

Annual Interest Rate (*i*), page 62 The rate charged or paid for the use of money on an annual basis.

Future Value (*FV*), page 62 The value of an investment at some future point in time.

Reinvesting, page 62 Taking money that you have earned on an investment and plowing it back into that investment.

Future-Value Interest Factor, page 64 The value of $(1 + i)^n$ used as a multiplier to calculate an amount's future value.

Compounded Annually, page 64 With annual compounding, the interest is received at the end of each year and then added to the original investment. Then, at the end of the second year, interest is earned on this new sum.

Rule of 72, page 65 A helpful investment rule that states that you can determine how many years it will take for a sum to double by dividing the annual growth rate into 72.

Understand the power of time and the importance of the interest rate in compounding. LO2

SUMMARY: It is important to understand the role of the interest rate in determining how large an investment grows. Together, time and the interest rate determine how much you will need to save in order to achieve your goals. You can increase your future value by increasing either the interest rate or the number of years for which your money is compounded.

LO3 Calculate the present value of money to be received in the future.

SUMMARY: Many times we want to solve for present value instead of future value. We use the following formula to do this:

$$\text{Present Value or } PV = \text{Future Value or } FV_n \times \text{Present-Value Interest Factor} \quad (3.3a)$$

KEY TERMS

Discount Rate, page 72 The interest rate used to bring future dollars back to the present.

Present-Value Interest Factor, page 72 The value $[1/(1+i)^n]$ used as a multiplier to calculate an amount's present value.

LO4 Explain what an annuity is and calculate its compound or future value.

SUMMARY: An annuity is a series of equal annual dollar payments coming at the end of each year for a specified number of years. Because annuities occur frequently in finance—for example, as bond interest payments and mortgage payments—they receive special treatment. A compound annuity involves depositing or investing an equal sum of money at the end of each year for a certain number of years and allowing it to grow.

$$\text{Future Value of an Annuity or } FV_n = \text{Annual Payment or } PMT \times \text{Future-Value Interest Factor of an Annuity} \quad (3.4)$$

To find the present value of an annuity, we use the following formula:

$$\text{Present Value of an Annuity or } PV = \text{Annual Payment or } PMT \times \text{Present-Value Interest Factor of an Annuity} \quad (3.5)$$

Many times annuities involve paying off a loan in equal installments over time. Loans that are paid off this way, in equal periodic payments, are called amortized loans. Examples of amortized loans include car loans and mortgages.

KEY TERMS

Annuity, page 76 A series of equal dollar payments coming at the end of each time period for a specified number of time periods.

Compound Annuity, page 77 An investment that involves depositing an equal sum of money at the end of each year for a certain number of years and allowing it to grow.

Future-Value Interest Factor of an Annuity, page 77 A multiplier used to determine the future value of an annuity. The future-value interest factors of an annuity are found in Appendix C.

Present-Value Interest Factor of an Annuity ($PVIFA_{i,n}$), page 80 A multiplier used to determine the present value of an annuity. The present-value interest factors of an annuity are found in Appendix D.

Amortized Loan, page 83 A loan paid off in equal installments.

Perpetuity, page 85 An annuity that continues forever.

Problems and Activities

These problems are available in MyLab Finance.

1. Your mother just received a $250,000 inheritance. If she invests her money in a diversified equity portfolio returning 8 percent per year, approximately how long will it take her to become a millionaire?
2. Linda Baer has already saved $6,500 to buy a used vehicle. Ignoring taxes and assuming her money is invested in a money market account earning 3 percent compounded annually, how long will it take to buy a car that costs $9,000?
3. Paul just graduated from college and landed his first "real" job, which pays $33,000 a year. In 10 years, what will he need to earn to maintain the same purchasing power if inflation averages 3 percent?
4. Anthony and Michelle Constantino just got married and received $30,000 in cash gifts for their wedding. How much will they have on their 25th anniversary if they place half of this money in a fixed-rate investment earning 7 percent compounded annually? Would the future value be larger or smaller if the compounding period were 6 months? How much more or less would they have earned with this shorter compounding period?
5. Calculate the future value of $5,000 earning 5 percent after 1 year, assuming annual compounding. Now, calculate the future value of $5,000 earning 5 percent after 20 years.
6. Ahmed just turned 22 and wants to have $10,283 saved in 8 years, by his 30th birthday. Assuming no additional deposits, if he currently has $6,000 in an intermediate-term bond fund earning a 5 percent yield, will he reach his goal? If not, what rate of return is required to meet his goal?
7. If another *Austin Powers* movie had been released in 2018 and Dr. Evil, now armed with a financial calculator, wants to hold the Earth ransom for $10,000,000, what inflation rate would Dr. Evil use to make his ransom equivalent to $1 million in 1967? (*Hint:* Inflation is compounded on an annual basis.)
8. When Derek was a small child, his grandfather established a trust fund for him to receive $20,000 on his 35th birthday. Derek just turned 23. What is the value of his trust today if the trust fund earned 7 percent interest? If he had to wait until age 40 to receive the money, what would be the present value of the $20,000 to be received in 17 years?
9. You and 11 coworkers have just won $12 million ($1 million each) from the state lottery. Assuming that you each receive your share over 20 years and that the state lottery earns a 4 percent return on its funds, what is the present value of your prize before taxes if you request the "up-front cash" option?
10. Richard is 65 years old and about to retire. He has $500,000 saved to supplement his pension and Social Security and would like to withdraw it in equal annual dollar amounts so that nothing is left after 15 years. How much does he have to withdraw each year if he earns 5 percent on his money?
11. Assume you are 25 and earn $35,000 per year, never expect to receive a raise, and plan to retire at age 55. If you invest 5 percent of your salary in a 401(k) plan returning 10 percent annually, and the company provides a $0.50 per $1.00 match on your contributions up to 3 percent of your salary, what is the estimated future value of your 401(k) account? Once you retire, how much can you withdraw monthly if you want to deplete your account over 30 years?
12. Shaylea, age 22, just started working full-time and plans to deposit $5,000 annually into an IRA earning 8 percent interest compounded annually. How much will she have in 20 years, in 30 years, and in 40 years? If she changed her investment period and instead invested $417 monthly, and the investment also changed to monthly

compounding, how much would she have after the same three time periods? Comment on the differences over time.

13. Your grandmother just gave you $6,000. You'd like to see what it might grow to if you invest it.

a. Calculate the future value of $6,000, given that it will be invested for 5 years at an annual interest rate of 6 percent.

b. Recalculate part (a) using a compounding period that is semiannual (every 6 months).

c. Now let's look at what might happen if you can invest the money at a 10 percent rate rather than a 5 percent rate. Recalculate parts (a) and (b) for a 10 percent annual interest rate.

d. Now let's see what might happen if you invest the money for 12 years rather than 5 years. Recalculate part (a) using a time horizon of 12 years (the annual interest rate is still 6 percent).

14. If you deposit $3,500 today into an account earning an 8 percent annual rate of return, what will your account be worth in 35 years (assuming no further deposits)? In 40 years?

15. Sarah Wiggum would like to make a single investment and have $2 million at the time of her retirement in 35 years. She has found a mutual fund that will earn 4 percent annually. How much will Sarah have to invest today? If Sarah invests that amount and could earn a 14 percent annual return, how soon could she retire, assuming she is still going to retire when she has $2 million?

16. Kirk Van Houten, who has been married for 23 years, would like to buy his wife an expensive diamond ring with a platinum setting on their 30-year wedding anniversary. Assume that the cost of the ring will be $12,000 in 7 years. Kirk currently has $4,510 to invest. What annual rate of return must Kirk earn on his investment to accumulate enough money to pay for the ring?

17. Seven years ago, Lance Murdock purchased a wooden statue of a Conquistador for $7,600 to put in his home office. Lance has recently married, and his home office is being converted into a sewing room. His new wife, who has far better taste than Lance, thinks the Conquistador is hideous and must go immediately. Lance decides to sell it on eBay and only receives $5,200 for it, so he takes a loss on the investment. What is his rate of return—that is, the value of i?

18. You are offered $100,000 today or $300,000 in 13 years. Assuming that you can earn 8 percent on your money, which should you choose?

19. In March 1963, Ironman was first introduced in issue number 39 of *Tales of Suspense*. The original price for that issue was 12 cents. By March 2018, 55 years later, the value of this comic book had risen to $6,200. What annual rate of interest would you have earned if you had bought the comic in 1963 and sold it in 2018 (55 years later)?

20. You are graduating from college at the end of this semester and have decided to invest $5,000 at the end of each year into a Roth IRA (a retirement investment account that grows tax free and is not taxed when it is liquidated) for the next 45 years. If you earn 8 percent compounded annually on your investment of $5,000 at the end of each year, how much will you have when you retire in 45 years? How much will you have if you wait 10 years before beginning to save and make only 35 payments into your retirement account?

21. To pay for your education, you've taken out $25,000 in student loans. If you make monthly payments over 15 years at 7 percent compounded monthly, how much are your monthly student loan payments?

22. How long will it take to pay off a loan of $50,000 at an annual rate of 6 percent compounded monthly if you make monthly payments of $600 (round up)?

23. You've just bought a new flat-screen TV for $3,000, and the store you bought it from offers to let you finance the entire purchase at an annual rate of 14 percent compounded monthly. If you take the financing and make monthly payments of $100, how long will it take to pay the loan off? How much will you pay in interest over the life of the loan? (That is, what is the difference between the total of all your payments and the amount of your payments that went toward your principal of $3,000?)

24. Chris Griffin has a $5,000 debt balance on his Visa card that charges 18.9 percent compounded monthly, and his minimum monthly payment is 3 percent of his debt balance, which is $150. How many months (round up) will it take Chris to pay off his credit card debt if he pays the current minimum payment of $150 at the end of each month? If Chris makes monthly payments of $200 at the end of each month, how long will it take him to pay off his credit card debt? (Round up.)

Discussion Case 1

This case is available in **MyLab Finance**.

Jinhee Ju, 27, just received a promotion at work that increased her annual salary to $37,000. She is eligible to participate in her employer's 401(k) plan, in which the employer matches dollar-for-dollar workers' contributions up to 5 percent of salary. However, Jinhee wants to buy a new $25,000 car in 3 years, and she wants to save enough money to make a $7,000 down payment on the car and finance the balance.

Also in her plans is a wedding. Jinhee and her boyfriend, Paul, have set a wedding date 2 years in the future, after he finishes medical school. Paul will have $100,000 of student loans to repay after graduation. But both Jinhee and Paul want to buy a home of their own as soon as possible. This might be possible because at age 30, Jinhee will be eligible to access a $50,000 trust fund left to her as an inheritance by her late grandfather. Her trust fund is invested in 7 percent government bonds.

Questions

1. Justify Jinhee's participation in her employer's 401(k) plan using the time value of money concepts.

2. Calculate the amount that Jinhee needs to save each year for the down payment on a new car, assuming she can earn 6 percent on her savings. Calculate how much she will need to save on a monthly basis, assuming monthly compounding. For each scenario, how much of her down payment will come from interest earned?

3. What will be the value of Jinhee's trust fund at age 60, assuming she takes possession of half of the money at age 30 for a house down payment and leaves the other half of the money untouched where it is currently invested?

4. What is Paul's annual payment if he wants to repay his student loans completely within 10 years and he pays a 5 percent interest rate? How much more or less would Paul pay if the loans compounded interest on a monthly basis and Paul also paid the loans on a monthly basis?

5. List at least three actions that Jinhee and Paul could take to make the time value of money work in their favor.

Discussion Case 2

This case is available in **MyLab Finance**.

Doug Klock, 56, just retired after 31 years of teaching. He is a husband and father of three children, two of whom are still dependent. He received a $150,000 lump-sum retirement bonus and will receive $2,800 per month from his retirement annuity. He has saved $150,000 in a 403(b) retirement plan and another $100,000 in other accounts. His 403(b) plan is invested in mutual funds, but most of his other investments are in bank accounts earning 2 or 3 percent annually. Doug has asked your advice in deciding where to invest his lump-sum bonus and other accounts now that he has retired. He also wants to know how much he can withdraw per month, considering he has two children in college and a nonworking spouse. His current monthly expenses total $5,800. He does not intend to begin receiving Social Security until age 67, and his monthly benefit will amount to $1,550. He has grown accustomed to some risk but wants most of his money in FDIC-insured accounts.

Questions

1. Assuming Doug has another account set aside for emergencies, how much can he withdraw on a monthly basis to supplement his retirement annuity if his investments return 5 percent annually and he expects to live 30 more years?
2. Ignoring his Social Security benefit, is the amount determined in Question 1 sufficient to meet his current monthly expenses? If not, how long will his retirement last if his current expenses remain at $5,800 per month? How long will it last if his expenses are reduced to $4,500 per month? (*Hint:* Use the information in the appendix to this chapter to solve this problem.)
3. If he withdraws $3,000 per month, how much will he have in 11 years when he turns 67? If he begins to receive Social Security payments of $1,550 at age 67, for how many years can he continue to withdraw $1,450 per month from his investments?
4. If the inflation rate averages 3 percent during Doug's retirement, how old will he be when prices have doubled from current levels? How much will a soda cost when Doug dies if he lives the full 30 years and the soda costs $1 today?

Appendix

Crunchin' the Numbers—Advanced Topics in Time Value of Money Using the Tables

Solving for *I/Y* and *N* Using the Tables

As you might expect, you can solve for *I/Y* and *N* using the tables or a calculator, as illustrated earlier in this chapter. With the tables, you first find the table value you're looking for, and then you see what column (if you're solving for *I/Y*) or row (if you're solving for *N*) it is in. Take a look at the examples that follow.

Let's assume that Chrysler has guaranteed that the price of a new Jeep will always be $20,000. You'd like to buy one, but currently you have only $10,805. How many years will it take for your initial investment of $10,805 to grow to $20,000 if it is invested at 8 percent compounded annually? You can use equation (3.2a) to solve this problem. Substituting the known values in equation (3.2a), you find

$$\text{future value} = \text{present value} \times \text{future-value interest factor}$$
$$\$20{,}000 = \$10{,}805 \times \text{future-value interest factor}$$
$$\frac{\$20{,}000}{\$10{,}805} = \frac{\$10{,}805 \times \text{future-value interest factor}}{\$10{,}805}$$
$$1.851 = \text{future-value interest factor}$$

Thus, you're looking for a value of 1.851 in the future-value interest factor tables, and you know it must be in the $i = 8\%$ column. To finish solving the problem, look down the $i = 8\%$ column for the value closest to 1.851. You'll find that it occurs in the $n = 8$ row. Thus, it will take 8 years for an initial investment of $10,805 to grow to $20,000 if it is invested at 8 percent compounded annually.

Now let's solve for the compound annual growth rate. In 10 years, you'd really like to have $20,000 to buy a new Jeep, but you have only $11,167. At what rate must your $11,167 be compounded annually for it to grow to $20,000 in 10 years? Substituting the known variables into equation (3.4a), you get

$$\text{future value} = \text{present value} \times \text{future-value interest factor}$$
$$\$20{,}000 = \$11{,}167 \times \text{future-value interest factor}$$
$$\frac{\$20{,}000}{\$11{,}167} = \frac{\$11{,}167 \times \text{future-value interest factor}}{\$11{,}167}$$
$$1.791 = \text{future-value interest factor}$$

You look in the $n = 10$ row of the future-value interest factor tables for a value of 1.791, and you find it in the $i = 6\%$ column. Thus, if you want your initial investment of $11,167 to grow to $20,000 in 10 years, you must invest it at 6 percent.

CHAPTER 4

Tax Planning and Strategies*

Learning Objectives

LO1	**Identify** and understand the major federal income tax features that affect all taxpayers.	**The Federal Income Tax Structure**
LO2	**Describe** other taxes that you must pay.	**Other Taxes**
LO3	**Understand** what is taxable income and how taxes are determined.	**Calculating Your Taxes**
LO4	**Choose** the tax form that's right for you, file, and survive an audit if necessary.	**Other Filing Considerations**
LO5	**Calculate** your income taxes.	**Model Taxpayers: The Taylors File Their Federal Tax Return**
LO6	**Minimize** your taxes.	**Tax Strategies to Lower Your Taxes**

One recurring survey question on the long-running, popular television game show *Family Feud* is "Can you name something that occurs just once a year?" The answers usually include "birthday," "anniversary," and "New Year's Eve," but the number one answer is always "taxes." Even when it comes to TV shows, taxes are a hot topic. For example, "The Trouble with Trillions" episode of *The Simpsons* begins with the family watching the 11 o'clock news on April 14. Kent Brockman, the local anchorman for Channel 6, is reporting from the Springfield Post Office, showing the frantic scene as taxpayers mail off their returns "just in time!" Homer proudly chimes in that he's got it all under control because he paid his taxes over a year ago.

*Tax documentation in this chapter was current at the time of publication. However, due to the changing nature of tax legislation, this information is often updated. Please visit www.pearsonhighered.com/keown for updates made to this chapter. In addition, the author-produced videos called out in this chapter (available at www.pearson.com/mylab/finance) and included in the etext version of the book will explain any tax changes as well as the implications of those changes.

A shocked Lisa informs him that you have to pay taxes every year! Panic sets in, and Homer begins to frantically put together his return, shouting "Marge, how many kids do we have? No time to count, I'll just estimate—nine. If anyone asks, you need 24-hour nursing care, Lisa is a clergyman, Maggie is really seven people, and Bart was wounded in Vietnam."

"Cool!" replies Bart.

It isn't only cartoon characters that have trouble with the Internal Revenue Service. In 2012, it was reported that Olympic gold medal skier Lindsey Vonn and her estranged husband, Thomas, owed $1,705,437 in taxes from 2010. Lindsey was able to settle the issue as soon as she found out about it, posting on Facebook "This is an important lesson for me. Not being in control of my finances and relying on someone else [referring to ex-husband, Thomas] who you believed had your best interest at heart was a mistake."

AF Archive/Alamy Stock Photo

Lindsey is not the only prominent athlete or celebrity to run into financial trouble regarding taxes. Nicholas Cage, Ja Rule, Al Pacino, Snoop Dogg, Lauryn Hill, Plaxico Burress, and Lil' Kim have all had tax troubles—and the list goes on and on. Most of them reported that they seemed to lose track of their finances and depended on managers to take care of them and have their backs.

Let's take a look at Willie Nelson. He has made millions of dollars and spent millions of dollars, and for quite some time, he ignored his taxes entirely. That lack of attention finally caught up with him in 1990, when the IRS sent him a bill for $32 million. Yikes! But as Willie said, "Thirty-two million ain't much if you say it fast." How did Willie manage to run up such a tax bill? On bad advice. He got involved in a number of tax shelters (investments aimed at lowering your taxes) that were disallowed by the IRS because they were such blatant tax-avoidance schemes. Eventually, Willie and the IRS settled on a $9 million payment, and Willie sued the accounting firm of Price Waterhouse, claiming it had mismanaged his finances. By 1995, Willie had paid back the government, but to do it, he had to auction off nearly all of his possessions—leaving him with his long hair and beard, headband, worn blue jeans, guitar, and little else.

Mention the IRS and most people cringe. Few of us relish the thought of tax planning because taxes are unavoidable, too high, and determined by a tax code that is close to incomprehensible. However, like it or not, taxes are a fact of life, and they have a dramatic impact on many aspects of your finances—in particular, your investment choices.

PRINCIPLE 4

Most of the financial decisions that you make are affected in one way or another by taxes—that's **Principle 4: Taxes Affect Personal Finance Decisions**. Given that the average American pays over $10,000 annually in taxes, limiting Uncle Sam's cut of your income is important. Remember, what you pay in April each year is based on income, expenses, and tax-planning decisions from the previous year. If you don't understand the tax system, you're probably paying more than you have to. The primary purpose of this chapter is not to teach you all the ins and outs of filing your own return but rather to help you understand how taxes are imposed, what strategies can be used to reduce them, and what role tax planning plays in personal financial planning. With proper tax planning, you will be able to achieve your financial goals, and you will avoid wasting money in tax payments, as well as looking at your tax bill and saying "D'oh!"

Progressive or Graduated Tax
A tax system in which tax rates increase for higher incomes.

Tax Brackets
Income ranges in which the same marginal tax rates apply. For example, an individual might fall into the 15 percent or 28 percent marginal tax bracket.

Personal Exemption
An IRS-allowed reduction in your income before you compute your taxes. You are given one exemption for yourself, one for your spouse, and one for each dependent.

The Federal Income Tax Structure

LO1 Identify and understand the major federal income tax features that affect all taxpayers.

The starting point for tax planning begins with looking at the overall structure of the income tax. At present, the federal tax code is under assault, with President Trump promising major changes. Exactly when or if this will happen is a good question, but even with the proposed changes, the essence of our tax code will most likely remain the same. This means that if you can develop an intuitive understanding of how taxes work, you'll be able to quickly understand the effect of those changes. However, if and when any legislative changes to the tax code occur, updates, including the personal finance implications, will be provided on the companion website (http://pearsonhighered.com/keown). Our present tax structure is a **progressive or graduated tax**, meaning that increased income is taxed at increasing rates, and that will remain even under the proposed tax changes. This system is based on the idea that those who earn more can afford to pay a higher percentage of their income in taxes. This is why people who earn different incomes fall into different **tax brackets**.

However, not all income is taxed. Some income is tax free because of **personal exemptions**, and other income is shielded by **deductions**—either **itemized deductions** or **standard deductions**. Your **taxable income** is a function of three numbers—**adjusted gross income (AGI)**, deductions, and exemptions. From there, the tax rates determine how much of the difference between income and deductions will be taken away in taxes. Table 4.1 provides the 2017 federal income tax rates for two of several different classifications of taxpayers.

To better understand what the rates in Table 4.1 actually mean, let's see what you might have paid in taxes in 2017 if you were married with three children, had

Deductions
Expenses that reduce taxable income.

Itemized Deductions
Deductions calculated using Schedule A. The allowable deductions are added up and then subtracted from adjusted gross income.

Standard Deduction
A set deduction allowed by the IRS, regardless of what a taxpayer's expenses actually were.

Taxable Income
Income subject to taxes.

Adjusted Gross Income (AGI)
Your taxable income from all sources minus specific adjustments (for example, IRA contributions, student loan interest payments, and alimony paid by you) but before deducting your standard or itemized deductions.

MyLab Finance Video

TABLE 4.1 Tax Rates and Brackets for Tax Year 2017

Tax Bracket	If Taxable Income Is:	The Tax Is:
Single Filers		
10%	Not over $9,325	10% of taxable income
15%	$9,325–$37,950	$932.50 + 15% of excess over $9,325
25%	$37,950–$91,900	$5,226.25 + 25% of excess over $37,950
28%	$91,900–$191,650	$18,713.75 + 28% of excess over $91,900
33%	$191,650–$416,700	$46,643.75 + 33% of excess over $191,650
35%	$416,700–$418,400	$120,910.25 + 35% of excess over $416,700
39.6%	Over $418,400	$121,505.25 + 39.6% of excess over $418,400
Married Filing Joint Returns and Surviving Spouses		
Tax Bracket	**If Taxable Income Is:**	**The Tax Is:**
10%	Not over $18,650	10% of taxable income
15%	$18,650–$75,900	$1,865 + 15% of excess over $18,650
25%	$75,900–$153,100	$10,452.50 + 25% of excess over $75,900
28%	$153,100–$233,350	$29,752.50 + 28% of excess over $153,100
33%	$233,350–$416,700	$52,222.50 + 33% of excess over $233,350
35%	$416,700–$470,700	$112,728 + 35% of excess over $416,700
39.6%	Over $470,700	$131,628 + 39.6% of excess over $470,700

a combined income of $70,000, and were filing a joint return. First, we'll determine your adjusted gross income, which from now on we'll call your AGI. The $70,000 is your gross income, and from that, you subtract certain adjustments allowed by law to arrive at your AGI. For example, let's say you made a $2,000 deductible IRA contribution and paid $900 interest on a student loan. You subtract these figures from $70,000 to find your AGI of $67,100. Remember, however, that your total income of $70,000 isn't taxed, nor is your AGI of $67,100; *only the difference between your AGI and your exemptions and deductions is taxed.*

Next, you subtract personal exemptions and deductions. To begin with, you receive one exemption for each family member you claim on your tax return—one for you, your spouse, and each of your three children. Each exemption allows you to subtract $4,050 from your income, resulting in a total reduction of $20,250. Next, you need to subtract either the standard deduction or your itemized deductions, both of which we'll talk about in detail later in this chapter. Let's assume you use the standard deduction because it's higher than your itemized deductions are. For the 2017 tax year, that gives you a deduction of $12,700. The minimum level of exemptions and deductions that you have is $20,250 + $12,700 = $32,950. Subtracting these from your AGI of $67,100 leaves taxable income of $34,150.

Your deductions have brought you to the 15 percent tax bracket. Does that mean you have

STOP & THINK

It was the Massachusetts Bay Colony that first imposed income taxes in the New World in 1643. Even though taxes have been around for hundreds of years, it doesn't mean you pay more than your fair share. Do you think you have a patriotic duty to pay extra taxes? Answer: No. As Judge Learned Hand of the U.S. Court of Appeals said, "Anyone may so arrange his affairs that his taxes shall be as low as possible; he is not bound to choose that pattern which will best pay the treasury; there is not even a patriotic duty to increase one's taxes." What "tax breaks" have you taken or do you expect to take in the future?

to pay 15 percent of your taxable income of $34,150 in taxes? No. Remember, tax rates are graduated, which means that income is taxed at increasing rates. It means that the last dollars you earned are taxed at 15 percent. As Table 4.1 shows, the first $18,650 of taxable income are taxed at 10 percent, and the next $15,500 (income from $18,650 to $34,150) are taxed at 15 percent, resulting in a total tax bill before tax credits of $4,190.00.[1]

Taxable Income: $34,150	×	Tax Rate	=	Taxes Paid
$0 to $18,650 ($18,650)	×	10%	=	$1,865
$18,650 to $34,150 ($15,500)	×	15%	=	$2,325
		Total taxes before credits	=	$4,190

Marginal Versus Average Rates

Let's take another look at the tax rates you paid in the previous example. There are two ways we measure your tax rate: We measure the average tax rate, which relates taxes to total income, and we measure the marginal tax rate, which looks at the percentage of the next dollar earned that will go toward taxes. You paid taxes of $4,190 on taxable income of $34,150, so your average tax rate on *taxable income* was about 12.3 percent. Your average tax rate on your *overall* income of $70,000 was $4,190/$70,000, or about 6.0 percent. The term *average tax rate* refers to this latter figure—the average amount of your total income taken away in taxes.

While it's good to know what percentage of your taxable income and what percentage of your overall income go toward taxes, it's even more important to know what percentage of the next dollar you earn will go toward paying taxes. Why? Because it is the tax rate that you pay on the next dollar of earning that is important in making financial decisions. For example, if you were looking at an additional part-time job that would produce $1,500 per year in income, you would be concerned with how much in taxes you'd pay on that $1,500. The tax rate that is important in making this decision is your **marginal tax rate or marginal tax bracket**, which is the percentage of the last dollar you made that goes to taxes or the tax bracket that your taxable income falls into. If your taxable income is $34,150, and $34,150 falls in the 15 percent tax bracket, then 15 percent is your marginal tax rate. If you earn $1,500 on that part-time job, it is your marginal tax rate that determines how much of that money you have left to spend.

Marginal Tax Rate or Marginal Tax Bracket
The percentage of the last dollar you earn that goes toward taxes.

In addition, if you are in the 15 percent marginal tax bracket and have a choice of investing in tax-free bonds that earn 7 percent or taxable bonds that earn 8 percent, your marginal tax rate can help you determine which is the better investment. Even though your average tax rate may be only 6.0 percent, assuming this additional income does not push you into a new tax bracket, it will be taxed at your current marginal tax rate, which, in this example, is 15 percent. To make a fair comparison, you must look at your after-tax returns. The tax-free bond would still return 7 percent after taxes, but the 8 percent bond would have 15 percent of its returns confiscated for taxes, resulting in a return of $8\% \times (1 - 0.15) = 6.85\%$.

[1]As we will see shortly, this amount drops even more because of the child tax credit, which in 2017 provided qualifying families with a tax credit of $1,000 for each child under age 17 as of the close of each year. This tax credit offsets taxes owed on a dollar-for-dollar basis. That is, if you owe $5,000 in taxes and have a $1,000 tax credit, you need to write the IRS a check for only $4,000. Also, you'll notice that if you use the tax tables, you get a slightly different number. That's because the tax tables calculate an "average" rate over each $50 range.

FIGURE 4.1 Historical Top Marginal Income Tax Rate

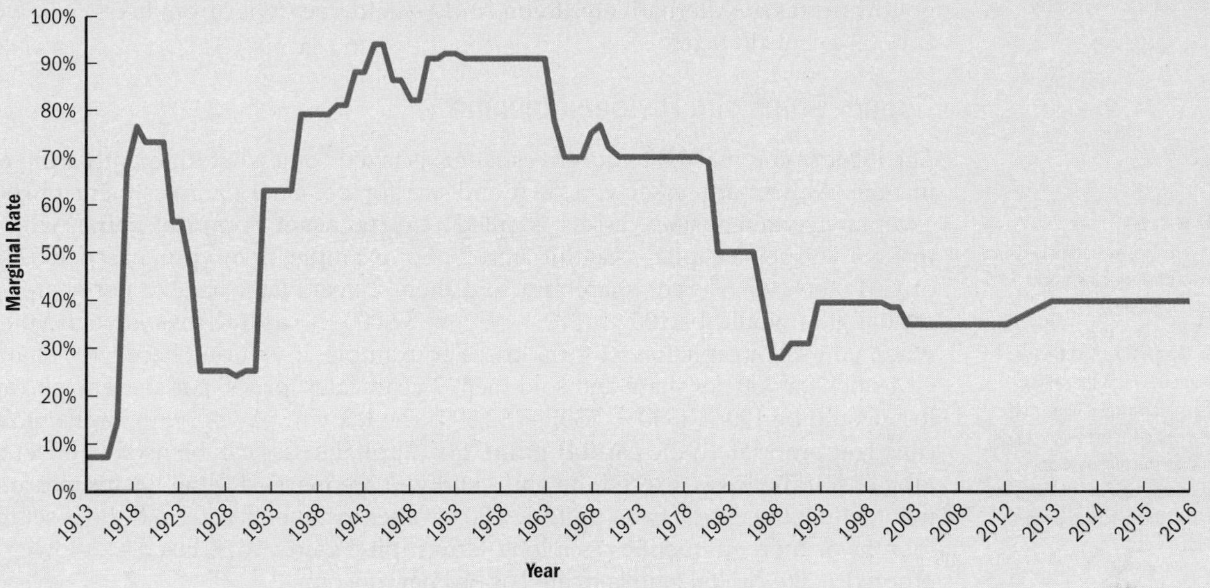

Your marginal tax rate also becomes important when you're considering investing in a **tax-deferred** retirement plan. The government allows tax deductions for the funds you contribute to this kind of retirement plan. So if you are in the 15-percent marginal tax bracket and you contribute $1,000 to a tax-deferred retirement plan, you lower your taxes by $150 (0.150 × $1,000). This reduction allows you to invest the entire $1,000 rather than only $850—that is, $1,000 less $150 in taxes.

Tax-Deferred
Income on which the payment of taxes is postponed until some future date.

As you can see from Table 4.1, once you earn enough to pay taxes—that is, have income beyond the personal exemption and standard deduction levels—there are seven different marginal tax rates ranging from 10 percent to 39.6 percent. However, whenever Congress wishes, it can change the tax rates and the tax code. As you can see in Figure 4.1, back in 1964 the top marginal rate was 91 percent, and in 1981, it was still at 70 percent. Needless to say, changes in the marginal tax rates have a major impact on investment strategies, so you need to keep a close eye on tax law changes.

Effective Marginal Tax Rate

Federal income taxes are not the only income-based taxes you pay. Many states impose state income taxes, some cities impose city or local taxes, and there are also Social Security taxes. Each of these taxes is imposed at a different rate. As a result of these taxes, your effective marginal tax rate—the tax rate you pay when all income tax rates are combined—is greater than the marginal tax rate on your federal income taxes.

To determine your effective marginal tax rate, you need to add up the rates of the different taxes you pay on income. Let's assume you have a marginal federal tax rate of 25 percent, a state income tax rate of 4.75 percent, and a city income tax rate

STOP & THINK

You really should know what your effective marginal tax rate is. It not only tells you how much more you'll have to pay in taxes on any additional income (the bad news) but also tells you how any additional deductions will reduce your taxes (the good news). What is your effective marginal tax rate?

of 2 percent. The tax for Social Security and Medicare is 7.65 percent, so your total effective marginal tax rate is 39.4 percent (25% + 4.75% + 2% + 7.65%). That means that if you were to receive one more dollar of income, 39.4 cents of that dollar would go toward taxes. Alternatively, if you could shield one dollar from taxes, you would save 39.4 cents in taxes.

Capital Gains and Dividend Income

Capital Asset
An asset you own, except for certain business assets, including stocks, bonds, and real estate.

Capital Gain/Capital Loss
The amount by which the selling price of a capital asset differs from its purchase price. If the selling price is higher than the purchase price, a capital gain results; if the selling price is lower than the purchase price, a capital loss results.

Capital Gains Tax
The tax you pay on your realized capital gains.

The income you make on your investments is taxed somewhat differently from other income. Almost any asset you own and use for personal or investment purposes, except for certain business assets, is called a **capital asset**. A **capital gain** is what you make if you sell a capital asset for a profit. For example, if you purchased 100 shares of GM stock for $50 per share and sold them 2 years later for $70 per share, your capital gain would be 100 × ($70 − $50) = $2,000. A **capital loss** is what you lose when you sell a capital asset for a loss. For example, if you purchased 100 shares of GM stock for $50 per share and sold them 2 years later for $30 per share, your capital loss would be 100 × ($50 − $30) = $2,000. The tax you pay on your capital gains is called, appropriately, the **capital gains tax**. Capital losses can be used to offset capital gains. If the losses exceed the gains and you are married filing a joint return, you may deduct the excess from up to $3,000 of other income. If you hold the asset for 12 months or more, it qualifies as a long-term capital gain and is taxed at a lower rate; otherwise, the capital gain is treated as ordinary income.

The tax laws provide a lower tax rate on both the long-term capital gains and the dividends received by individuals from most domestic corporations and many foreign companies.[2] Although the long-term capital gains tax applies to profits from the sale of stocks, bonds, and most other investments, it doesn't apply to gains from the sale of collectibles like coins or art—they are taxed at a maximum 28 percent rate. In addition, real estate investments don't necessarily receive the full benefit of the cut.

FACTS OF LIFE

Our present income tax system first appeared in 1913. That was the year the zipper was invented and Cracker Jacks first put toys in boxes. Back then the first $3,000 of income for an individual or $4,000 of income for a married couple were tax free; then the rate started at 1 percent. Although a break on the first $3,000 or $4,000 may not sound like much now, back in 1913 it was quite a bit. In fact, only 1 percent of the population had to pay income taxes.

How much do capital gains or dividend income save you? That depends on your tax bracket. If you were in the 35 percent tax bracket and had long-term capital gains or dividend income of $50,000, you would have paid only $7,500 in taxes. If this $50,000 of income had been from wages, you would have paid $17,500, or more than twice what you would have paid on long-term capital gains or dividend income.

Just as valuable as the tax break on capital gains income is the fact that you do not have to claim it—and therefore pay taxes on it—until you sell the asset. That is, you can decide when you want to claim your capital gains. For example, at the end of 1994 you may have invested $17,000 in Berkshire Hathaway stock, only to see it grow in value, reaching $250,000 by mid-2017. Although you've "made" $233,000 on your investment, you don't have to pay any taxes on this gain. You pay taxes only when you sell the stock and realize the gain. In effect, you can postpone your capital gains taxes. As long as you can earn interest on money you don't pay out in taxes, it's better to postpone paying taxes for as long as possible—that's what we learned in **Principle 3: The Time Value of Money**. Because the maximum tax rate on long-term capital gains is lower than the ordinary tax rate and you

PRINCIPLE 3

[2]For dividend income to qualify for the reduced rate, the stock issuing the dividend must be held for more than 61 days during the 120-day period beginning 60 days before the ex-dividend date (that is, when the stock sells without the dividend).

have the ability to postpone that tax liability, capital gains income is preferable to ordinary income.

Long-Term Capital Gains on Homes For most homeowners, there are no capital gains taxes on the sale of their homes. There is an exemption from taxation for gains of up to $500,000 for couples filing jointly or $250,000 for those filing single on the sale of a principal residence. To be eligible for the complete exemption, the home must be your principal residence, and you must have occupied it for at least 2 years during the 5 years before the sale. You are eligible for this exemption once every 2 years.

Filing Status While Table 4.1 shows only two of the four different filing statuses, you can see that filing status plays a major role in determining what you pay in the way of taxes. But you may not have much of a choice in deciding your filing status. Filing status is somewhat akin to marital status. But as is always the case with taxes, it's not that simple. Let's look at the different classifications.

Single You are single at the end of the year and do not have any dependent children.

Married Filing Jointly and Surviving Spouses You file a joint return with your spouse, combining incomes and deductions into a single return. If your spouse dies, you can still qualify for this status for up to 2 years after the year in which your spouse died if you have a dependent child living with you, you pay more than half the cost of keeping up your home, and you are not remarried. Of course, if you remarry, you can file a joint return with your new spouse.

Married Filing Separately Married couples also have the choice of filing separately. It is hard to say ahead of time whether you will do better filing jointly or separately—the best idea is to figure your taxes both ways and, of course, go with the lower number. This status is often used when a couple is separated or in the process of getting a divorce.

Head of Household Head of household status applies to someone who is unmarried and has at least one child or relative living with him or her. The advantage of this status is that your tax rate will be lower and your standard deduction higher than if you had filed with single status. To qualify for head of household status, you must be unmarried on the last day of the tax year, have paid more than half the cost of keeping up your home, and have had a child or dependent live with you for at least half of the year.

Cost-of-Living Increases in Tax Brackets, Exemptions, and Deductions

Since 1985, tax brackets have changed annually to reflect increases in the cost of living (inflation). In addition, the standard deductions and personal exemptions are increased to reflect the increased cost of living.

The purpose of these adjustments is to make sure your tax payments don't go up just because you've received a cost-of-living increase in your wages. In the past, taxpayers' incomes rose during periods of high inflation, but their purchasing power didn't. As a result, rising incomes that only kept pace with inflation nudged taxpayers into higher tax brackets. In effect, taxpayers paid more taxes, while the real value of their wages remained constant.

The tax increase caused by inflation is referred to as **bracket creep**. For those whose earnings remain the same each year, the inflation adjustment of tax brackets actually results in lower taxes. Of course, if your earnings don't increase to keep pace with inflation, you're worse off with each passing year and probably deserve a reduced tax bill!

Bracket Creep
The movement into a higher tax bracket when wages are increased as a result of inflation.

Paying Your Income Taxes

Taxes are collected on a pay-as-you-go basis. Most taxes—about 70 percent of individual income taxes—are collected through withholding from wages. The idea behind withholding is to collect taxes gradually so that when your taxes are due in the spring, you won't feel the pain of paying in one lump sum. Also, without withholding, too many people would spend the money they should be saving for taxes. These withholdings also cover Social Security and state and local taxes. Other ways in which taxes are collected include quarterly estimated taxes sent to the IRS, payments with the tax return, and withholding from stock dividends, retirement funds, and prizes or gambling winnings.

STOP & THINK

"Isn't this exciting! I earned this. I wiped tables for it, I steamed milk for it, and it's [*opening her paycheck*] not worth it! Who's FICA? Why is he getting my money?" This is the response of Rachel Green on the TV show *Friends* upon seeing her first Central Perk paycheck on the episode "The One with George Stephanopoulos." Your first paycheck can be a real shock. Federal, state, and local taxes, in addition to FICA, a contribution to your firm's hospitalization plan, and retirement savings, take a real bite out of your paycheck. Financial planning is all the more important if you're to make the best use of what's left. Are you surprised by how large FICA taxes are?

You do have some control over how much is deducted for taxes from your wages. Your withholdings are determined by your income level and by the information you provide on your W-4 form. The W-4 form shows marital status, the number of exemptions you wish to claim (remember, you get one for yourself, one for your spouse, and one for each dependent), and any additional withholding you would like. Most people fill out their W-4 when they begin employment and never make changes to it. However, if you find you're paying too much in taxes at tax time or your refund is too large, revising your W-4 to make appropriate adjustments might not be a bad idea.

LO2 Describe other taxes that you must pay.

Other Taxes

Other Income-Based Taxes

Social Security
A federal program that provides disability and retirement benefits based on years worked, amount paid into the plan, and retirement age.

Medicare
The federal government's insurance program to provide medical benefits to those over 65.

Social Security or FICA **Social Security** is a mandatory insurance program administered by the government that provides for you and your family in the event of death, disability, health problems, or retirement. To pay for these benefits, both you and your employer pay into the system. Each typically pays 7.65 percent of your gross salary. This deduction appears on your pay slip as "FICA," which stands for the Federal Insurance Contributions Act. These funds actually go to both Social Security and **Medicare**, which is a government health-care insurance program. Interestingly, most Americans pay more in these "payroll taxes" than they do in federal income taxes.

STOP & THINK

Unfortunately, the Social Security system is feeling financial strains because there are more people receiving benefits than ever before and that number is only going to grow. Forty years ago, 16 workers contributed for every Social Security recipient. Today, the ratio is down to 3 workers for every recipient, and in another 40 years, it will be down to 2 workers for every recipient. What types of changes in the Social Security system do you expect by the time you are ready to receive benefits?

The FICA tax is typically deducted from your salary at 7.65 percent (6.20 percent for Social Security and 1.45 percent for Medicare) until your salary reaches a point ($127,200 in 2017) where it is no longer taxed the 6.20 percent for Social Security. Medicare, however, keeps on taxing after the Social Security cap has been reached, taking an additional 1.45 percent of your total salary from both you and your employer. If you are self-employed, you have to pay both the employer and the employee portions of FICA, for a total rate of 15.3 percent. However, if you're self-employed, half of your contribution is tax deductible.[3] In addition, for 2017 the Affordable Care Act required those who can afford health insurance but who choose not to buy it to pay a "fee" or penalty of the *higher* of 2.5 percent of your household income *or* $695 per adult and $347.50 per child under 18 with a maximum of $2,085—but, as with the current tax code, the future of this fee or penalty and the Affordable Care Act is in question under President Trump.

State and Local Income Taxes As we said earlier, most individuals also face state and, in some cases, local income taxes. Most states impose some type of income tax, though the level varies greatly from state to state. Local income taxes are relatively uncommon and are generally confined to large cities. New York City, for example, imposes an income tax.

Non-Income-Based Taxes

In addition to paying federal income taxes, Social Security taxes, and state and local taxes, you face excise taxes, sales taxes, property taxes, and gift and estate taxes.

Excise taxes are taxes imposed on specific purchases, such as alcoholic beverages, cigarettes, gasoline, telephone service, jewelry, and air travel. Often such taxes are aimed at reducing consumption of the items being taxed. For example, liquor and tobacco taxes are referred to as "sin taxes."

Most local taxes take the form of property taxes on real estate and personal property, such as automobiles and boats. The level of property taxes is based on the assessed value of real estate or other property.

Some states and localities also impose sales taxes on certain purchases. These taxes can range up to 8.875 percent (in New York) and in general cover most sales, with the exception of food and drugs. Because these tax rates are fixed—everyone in New York pays the 8.875 percent sales tax—lower-income individuals pay a higher *percentage* of their income in sales taxes than higher-income people do. Unfortunately, these taxes are quite difficult to avoid.

Gift and estate taxes are imposed when you transfer wealth to another person, either when you die, in the case of estate taxes, or while you're alive, in the case of gift taxes. For 2017, the tax code allowed an estate valued at up to $5.49 million to be transferred tax free to any heir. If the estate is valued at more than $5.49 million, the amount over $5.49 million is taxed at 40 percent. Also, spouses may combine their $5.49 million tax-free transfer amounts and pass on assets free of estate tax on a taxable estate of up to $10.98 million at the death of the second spouse, provided they didn't use up some of their $5.49 million tax-free transfer by gifting large amounts during their lifetimes. The U.S. Tax Code also allows for an unlimited marital deduction for gift and estate tax purposes. This means that when a husband or wife dies, the estate, regardless of size, can be transferred to the survivor tax free.

Calculating Your Taxes

LO3 Understand what is taxable income and how taxes are determined.

Must everyone file a tax return? Not everyone is required to file an income tax return each year. Generally, if your total income for the year doesn't exceed the standard deduction plus one *exemption* and you aren't a **dependent** of another taxpayer, then

Dependent
A person you support financially.

[3]Individuals with a high income ($250,000 for married couples filing jointly, $125,000 for married couples filing separately, and $200,000 for those filing single) pay an additional 0.9 percent in Medicare taxes. This additional 0.9 percent tax was added by the Affordable Care Act, and President Trump has proposed eliminating it. Depending on the amount of taxable wages, the combined Social Security and Medicare employee tax rate in 2017 ranged from 7.65 percent (6.20% + 1.45%) to 8.55 percent (6.2% + 1.45% + 0.9% on Medicare wages in excess of $200,000 for high-income earners). For self-employed high-income earners, their rate rose to 16.2 percent.

you don't need to file a federal tax return. If you think you don't need to file, calculate your taxes anyway because you may be owed a refund, which you won't receive unless you file a tax return.

Step 1: Determining Gross or Total Income

Total or Gross Income
The sum of all your taxable income from all sources.

Active Income
Income that comes from wages or a business.

Portfolio or Investment Income
Income that comes from securities.

Passive Income
Income that comes from activities in which the taxpayer does not actively participate.

When you file a tax return, the first step in calculating your taxes is determining your total income. **Total or gross income** is the sum of all taxable income from all sources. Actually, the IRS defines three different types of income—**active income** (from wages, salaries, and tips or from a business), **portfolio or investment income** (from securities, including dividends and interest), and **passive income** (from activities in which the taxpayer does not actively participate, such as rental income and royalties). Generally, your wages are reported to you on a W-2 form, while interest and dividends are reported on a Form 1099. Total income also includes alimony, business income, capital gains, taxable IRA distributions, pensions and annuities, rental income, royalties, farm income, unemployment compensation, and taxable Social Security benefits. In short, whatever you receive in taxable income is summed to make up your total or gross income:

$$\text{Gross Income} = \text{Sum of Taxable Income from All Sources}$$

FACTS OF LIFE

Where's the highest tax rate you face? It's probably in your state lottery. It's not really a tax in the normal sense, but if you look at the state's "cut" as a percentage of the value of lottery tickets (prize money plus administrative cost), it runs, on average across the United States, over 40 percent, varying from state to state. For example, Delaware's rate is about 47 percent. And that doesn't include the state and federal taxes on any winnings!

Although this calculation is relatively straightforward, it's harder than it looks because of the IRS and its lovely little rules.

Remember that not all income is taxable, so not all income is included in total income. The main source of tax-exempt income is interest on state and local debt. Other sources include gifts, inheritances, earnings on your IRA, federal income tax refunds, child support payments, welfare benefits, and foreign income incurred by U.S. citizens living and working abroad.

Step 2: Calculating Adjusted Gross Income

Adjusted Gross Income (AGI)
Your taxable income from all sources minus specific adjustments (for example, IRA contributions, student loan interest payments, and alimony paid by you) but before deducting your standard or itemized deductions.

Adjusted gross income (AGI) is gross income less allowable adjustments. Adjustments to gross income include payments set aside for retirement, some moving expenses, and alimony payments. In effect, the IRS allows you to reduce your taxable income when you incur specific expenses or when you contribute to certain retirement plans. The advantage of these deductions is that they lower your taxes, allowing you to invest or spend (but hopefully invest) money that you would otherwise send to Uncle Sam.

A list of the adjustments is found on Form 1040, page 1. Some of the adjustments that the IRS allows include

IRA
A tax-advantaged retirement account. The contribution may or may not be tax deductible, depending on the individual's income level and whether he or she, or his or her spouse, is covered by a company retirement plan.

- Contributions to qualified retirement accounts—for example, **IRAs** and 401(k) and 403(b) plans.
- Interest paid on student loans.
- Moving expenses.
- Half of the Social Security and Medicare taxes for self-employed filers.
- Alimony payments.
- Health savings accounts.
- Unreimbursed educator expenses for kindergarten through grade 12 teachers.

Because adjustments to income reduce your taxes, it's important to understand these adjustments and take advantage of them. After adding up all your adjustments to income, you subtract this amount from total income to arrive at your AGI:

Gross Income = Sum of Taxable Income from All Sources

Less

Adjustments to Gross Income: Tax-Deductible Expenses and Retirement Contributions (traditional IRAs, 401(k) and 403(b) plans, moving expenses, and so on)

Equals

AGI

Step 3: Subtracting Deductions

MyLab Finance Video

Once you know your AGI, the next step is to subtract your deductions. You have your choice of taking the standard deduction or itemizing, whichever benefits you the most. Obviously, taking the largest possible deduction is important. For example, if you're in the 33 percent marginal tax bracket and you're able to take an additional \$5,000 in deductions, you've actually reduced your tax bill by $\$5{,}000 \times 0.33 = \$1{,}650$. That's \$1,650 that you can spend on Domino's pizza or invest for retirement—whichever seems more important.

What's the difference between standardized and itemized deductions? On the simplest level, one is calculated for you, and the other you have to calculate yourself. Of course, the answer's really more complicated than that. Let's start by taking a look at the deductions you have to calculate yourself—itemized deductions.

Itemized Deductions The IRS has decided that you shouldn't be taxed on income that's used to pay for certain expenses. These are considered deductible expenses. Itemizing is simply listing all the deductions you're allowed to take. Of course, it's your responsibility to determine and document these deductible expenses.[4]

For most of us, which expenses count as deductible? Let's look at the most common ones.

- **Medical and Dental Expenses.** Medical and dental expenses are deductible only to the extent that they exceed 10 percent of your AGI.[5] For an individual with an AGI of \$60,000, only those medical and dental expenses in excess of \$6,000 (which is 10 percent of \$60,000) are deductible. The definition of what's considered a medical or dental expense is quite broad and includes medical treatment, hospital care, prescription drugs, and health insurance.

FACTS OF LIFE

As has been noted, President Trump has proposed major changes to the tax code including the elimination of many deductions. One deduction that isn't likely to be eliminated, but may be cappped, is the mortgage interest deduction, but also proposed is a doubling of the standard deduction which would make it more likely that taxpayers will choose the standard deduction instead of itemizing, thereby making the mortgage deduction irrelevant. In fact, Zillow has estimated that a homeowner buying a home today would need to purchase a home worth \$801,000 or more in order for there to be value in taking advantage of the mortgage interest deduction. The end result would be that owning a home would become more expensive because it won't come with a tax break (which is often cited as a reason for buying a home). But keep in mind, that's only the "proposed" tax change, if and when it becomes law, it will no doubt be very different.

---

[4]The amount of itemized deductions and personal exemptions you can take is phased out for higher-income taxpayers. For tax year 2017, the limitation for itemized deductions on individual returns began at \$261,500 (\$313,800 for married couples filing jointly). These limitations are indexed for inflation.

[5]Until the end of 2016, the threshold for itemized deductions for medical expenses for individuals age 65 and older and their spouses was 7.5% rather than 10%; beginning in 2017 the 10 percent threshold applied to all taxpayers.

- **Tax Expenses.** Some, but not all, tax expenses are deductible. Although the biggest chunk of taxes you pay—federal and Social Security taxes—are not tax deductible, state and local income taxes, along with real estate taxes, are deductible. In addition, any county or city income taxes are tax deductible. Some states impose a personal property tax—generally a tax on automobiles—which is also tax deductible.
- **Home Mortgage and Investment Interest Payments.** Several types of interest are tax deductible. Interest that you pay on your home mortgage is deductible. Interest on **home equity loans** is also deductible up to $1,000,000 (the limit is $500,000 in mortgage debt if married and filing separately). The last type of tax-deductible interest is investment interest, or interest on money borrowed to invest. The maximum deduction on investment interest is limited to the amount of investment income that you earn. Why does the IRS let you deduct these interest payments? Because the government wants to make it easier for you to buy a house and make investments to help the overall economy. By making home interest payments tax deductible, the government is, in effect, subsidizing your purchase of a home.

Home Equity Loan
A loan that uses your home as collateral—that is, a loan that is secured by your home. If you default, the lender can take possession of your home to recapture money lost on the loan.

- **Gifts to Charity.** Charitable gifts to qualified organizations are tax deductible. If you're in the 25 percent tax bracket and you give $1,000 to a charitable organization, it really only costs you $750 because you've given away $1,000 and as a result lowered your taxes by $250 (0.25 × $1,000). Generally, you are allowed to deduct up to 50 percent of your AGI. In effect, Congress is encouraging you to make charitable gifts. The only requirement for this deduction is that the gift go to a qualified organization and that if you make a single gift of more than $250, you show a receipt for that gift (a cancelled check won't do). Of course, regardless of the size of the gift, you must make sure that you maintain good records. If you can't keep track of your donations, how can you deduct them?
- **Casualty and Theft Loss.** Although you're able to deduct casualty and theft losses, this deduction is rather limited and is of value only to those who suffer huge losses or have very low earnings. The reason for its limited usefulness is that (1) for tax purposes, the first $100 of losses is excluded and (2) you can deduct the remaining losses only to the extent that they exceed 10 percent of your AGI.
- **Miscellaneous Deductibles.** These deductions include unreimbursed job-related expenses, tax preparation expenses, and investment-related expenses. The problem with these expenses is that they are deductible only to the extent that they are in excess of 2 percent of your AGI. In general, this percentage is a tough hurdle to pass, and as a result, most taxpayers are not able to benefit from miscellaneous deductions.

The Standard Deduction The alternative to itemizing deductions is taking the standard deduction. Basically, the standard deduction is the government's best estimate of what the average person would be able to deduct by itemizing. In other words, with the standard deduction, the government has done the computation for you already. You don't need to figure out your expenses and provide receipts or justification. Unlike itemized deductions, which are limited for higher AGI levels, the standard deduction remains the same, regardless of income level. In fact, the level of the standard deduction increases every year to keep up with inflation. Figure 4.2 provides the standard deductions for 2016 and 2017. Note that additional standard deductions are given to persons who are elderly and persons who are blind.

The Choice: Itemizing Deductions or Taking the Standard Deduction The decision whether to take the standard deduction or itemize may not be particularly difficult if one provides a greater deduction than the other. The choice becomes much more difficult, and also more interesting, when they are close in value. In that case, it may be best to bunch your deductions and alternate each year between taking the standard deduction and itemizing.

FIGURE 4.2 Standard Deduction Amounts

Filing Status	**2016**	**2017**
Single	$6,300	$6,350
Married Filing Jointly or Surviving Spouse	$12,600	$12,700
Head of Household	$9,300	$9,350
Married Filing Separately	$6,300	$6,350

Additional Standard Deductions for Persons Who Are Elderly or Blind: For a taxpayer (and spouse) who is elderly (age 65 or over) or blind, there is an additional deduction allowed.

In effect, you try to avoid incurring deductible expenses in years that you don't itemize. If possible, you postpone them to years when you do itemize and therefore get credit for them. For example, you might make 13 monthly mortgage payments in the year you itemize and only 11 in the year you take the standard deduction. There's no question that taking the standard deduction is easier than itemizing, but don't choose to take the standard deduction just because it's simpler—you don't want laziness to cost you money.

Step 4: Claiming Your Exemptions

Once you've subtracted the deductions from the AGI, you're ready to subtract the exemptions. An **exemption** is a deduction that you can make on your return for each person supported by the income on your tax return. The government provides these exemptions so that everyone will have a little bit of untaxed money to spend on necessities. In effect, each exemption allowed you to lower your taxable income by $4,050 for the 2016 and 2017 tax years.[6] Thus, if you were in the 28 percent marginal tax bracket, each exemption you took in 2016 or 2017 lowered your taxes by $1,134 (that is, $4,050 × 0.28).[7]

Exemption
A deduction you can take on your return for each person supported by the income listed on your tax return.

There are two types of exemptions—personal and dependency. You receive a personal exemption for yourself, regardless of your filing status, or for yourself and your spouse if filing a joint return, no questions asked. However, qualifying for a dependency exemption is more difficult. To qualify:

- Dependents must pass a relationship or household member test. If they're related to you as children, grandchildren, stepchildren, siblings, parents, grandparents, stepparents, uncles, aunts, nieces, nephews, or in-laws, they're considered to have a qualifying relationship. In fact, almost any relationship short of being a cousin qualifies under the IRS. If they're not related to you, then they must have lived with you over the entire tax year.
- The individual being claimed as a dependent generally can't earn more than the exemption amount. However, this income test does not apply to your children under the age of 19 or to your children under the age of 24 who are full-time students.

[6]Exemptions, like standard deductions, are raised each year to match inflation rates; for example, the personal exemption was $4,000 in 2013 and rose to $4,050 in 2016 and 2017.
[7]Just as with itemized deductions, there is a phase-out for personal exemptions for high-income taxpayers. For tax year 2016, this phase-out began for individuals with AGI of $259,400 ($261,500 for tax year 2017) and for married couples filing jointly with AGI of $311,300 ($313,800 for tax year 2017). For tax year 2016, the personal exemption phase-out was complete at $381,900 ($384,800 for tax year 2017) for individual taxpayers and $433,800 ($436,300 for tax year 2017) for married couples filing jointly.

- You must provide more than half of the dependent's support.
- The dependent must be a U.S. citizen, resident, or national or a resident of either Mexico or Canada.

Step 5: Calculating Your Taxable Income and, from That, Calculating Your Base Income Tax

Now that you've subtracted your deductions and exemptions from your AGI, you know your taxable income, which is the amount your taxes are based on. Figure 4.3

FIGURE 4.3 Calculating Your Taxes

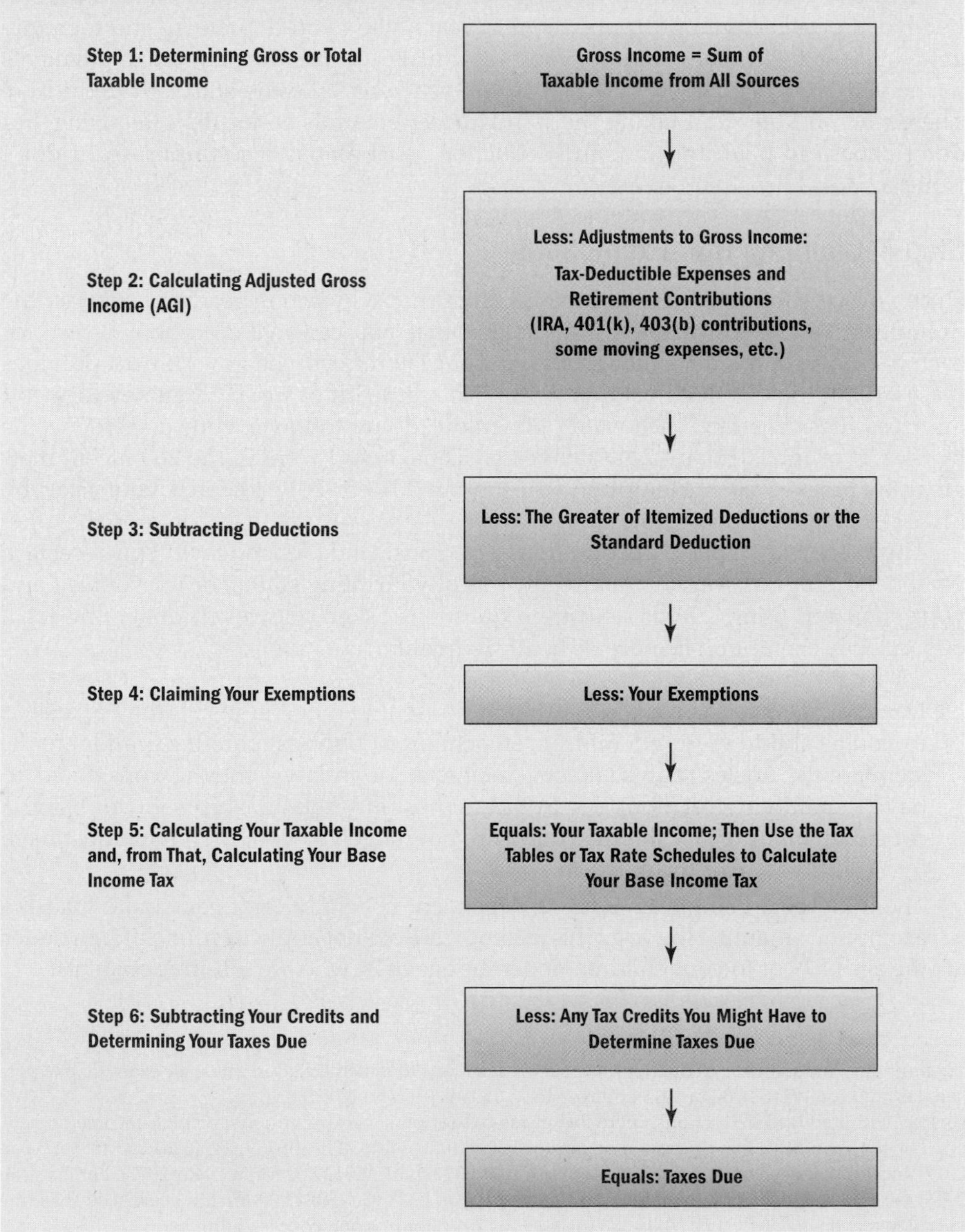
Step 1: Determining Gross or Total Taxable Income
Gross Income = Sum of Taxable Income from All Sources
Step 2: Calculating Adjusted Gross Income (AGI)
Less: Adjustments to Gross Income:
Tax-Deductible Expenses and Retirement Contributions (IRA, 401(k), 403(b) contributions, some moving expenses, etc.)
Step 3: Subtracting Deductions
Less: The Greater of Itemized Deductions or the Standard Deduction
Step 4: Claiming Your Exemptions
Less: Your Exemptions
Step 5: Calculating Your Taxable Income and, from That, Calculating Your Base Income Tax
Equals: Your Taxable Income; Then Use the Tax Tables or Tax Rate Schedules to Calculate Your Base Income Tax
Step 6: Subtracting Your Credits and Determining Your Taxes Due
Less: Any Tax Credits You Might Have to Determine Taxes Due
Equals: Taxes Due

FIGURE 4.4 Determining Your Taxes Using the 2016 Tax Tables

Assuming you are married filing jointly with taxable income of $48,023, your taxes are $6,276.

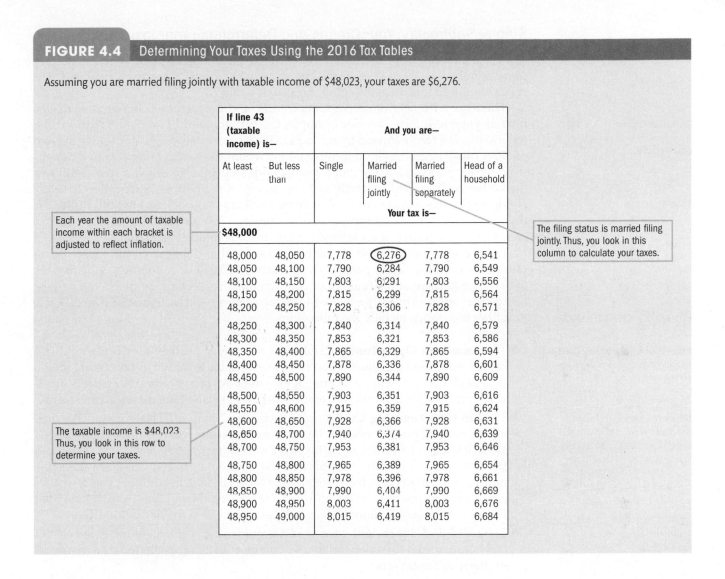

Each year the amount of taxable income within each bracket is adjusted to reflect inflation.

The taxable income is $48,023. Thus, you look in this row to determine your taxes.

The filing status is married filing jointly. Thus, you look in this column to calculate your taxes.

If line 43 (taxable income) is—		And you are—			
At least	But less than	Single	Married filing jointly	Married filing separately	Head of a household
		Your tax is—			
$48,000					
48,000	48,050	7,778	6,276	7,778	6,541
48,050	48,100	7,790	6,284	7,790	6,549
48,100	48,150	7,803	6,291	7,803	6,556
48,150	48,200	7,815	6,299	7,815	6,564
48,200	48,250	7,828	6,306	7,828	6,571
48,250	48,300	7,840	6,314	7,840	6,579
48,300	48,350	7,853	6,321	7,853	6,586
48,350	48,400	7,865	6,329	7,865	6,594
48,400	48,450	7,878	6,336	7,878	6,601
48,450	48,500	7,890	6,344	7,890	6,609
48,500	48,550	7,903	6,351	7,903	6,616
48,550	48,600	7,915	6,359	7,915	6,624
48,600	48,650	7,928	6,366	7,928	6,631
48,650	48,700	7,940	6,374	7,940	6,639
48,700	48,750	7,953	6,381	7,953	6,646
48,750	48,800	7,965	6,389	7,965	6,654
48,800	48,850	7,978	6,396	7,978	6,661
48,850	48,900	7,990	6,404	7,990	6,669
48,900	48,950	8,003	6,411	8,003	6,676
48,950	49,000	8,015	6,419	8,015	6,684

shows these calculations. For most taxpayers, once you've determined your taxable income, your income tax can be determined directly using the tax tables found in the middle of your federal income tax instructions booklet. The intersection of your taxable income and your filing status determines your taxes due, as shown in Figure 4.4 using the 2016 tax tables.

If your taxable income is greater than $100,000, you must determine your taxes using the rate schedules because the tax tables don't go that high. The tax rate schedules are found at the end of your federal income tax instructions booklet and were provided earlier in Table 4.1.

There's also an alternative minimum tax (AMT) that's aimed at preventing the very wealthy from using tax breaks to the extent that they pay little or nothing. This tax is aimed at the very wealthy, and since 2013, the AMT brackets have been annually adjusted for inflation. It is estimated that about 4 million taxpayers will have paid on average over $6,000 in AMT in 2016. The AMT applies different rules in calculating taxable income and then applies a 26 percent and a 28 percent tax rate to all income. The future of the AMT is in doubt, as it has been targeted for elimination by President Trump.

Step 6: Subtracting Your Credits and Determining Your Taxes Due

Tax credits reduce your taxes in a direct dollar-for-dollar manner. Whereas deductions merely lower the taxable income from which your taxes are calculated, tax credits are used to reduce the actual taxes that you pay.

Child Tax Credit
A tax credit given for each qualifying child under 17.

There are a number of different tax credits, and they tend to phase out or disappear as your AGI increases. For example, for 2016 the **child tax credit** reduced the federal income tax you owed by up to $1,000 for each qualifying child under the age of 17. A qualifying child is an individual for whom the taxpayer can claim a dependency exemption and is the child, grandchild, stepchild, or eligible foster child of the taxpayer. This child tax credit is given on top of the personal exemption for each child. Again, this is a tax credit, which means it cuts your federal tax bill dollar for dollar. Thus, a family with three children under 17 saves $3,000 in taxes. This tax credit can even become a tax refund for low-income families who don't pay taxes.

However, at the high end of the income scale, this child tax credit begins being phased out after a single parent's AGI reaches $75,000 or a couple's AGI reaches $110,000, regardless of the number of children they have. Once the phase-out begins, the credit is reduced by $50 for every $1,000 the single parent earns in AGI over $75,000.

Other tax credits include the following:

MyLab Finance Video

American Opportunity Credit
A tax credit of up to $2,500 per year per student.

Lifetime Learning Credit
A tax credit for all years of college or graduate school. It also applies to working adults taking classes to improve their work skills.

Child and Dependent Care Credit
A tax credit that offsets your taxes in a direct dollar-for-dollar manner for child and dependent care expenses.

Earned Income Credit
A tax credit available to low-income taxpayers that effectively serves as a negative income tax.

Health-Care Premium Credit
A tax credit available to low-income taxpayers who purchased coverage through the Health Insurance Marketplace.

- The **American Opportunity Credit** is a refundable tax credit for undergraduate college education expenses. This credit provides up to $2,500 in tax credits on the first $4,000 of qualifying educational expenses. At present, the tax credit is available only through 2017 unless Congress decides to extend the credit to other years.[8]
- The **Lifetime Learning Credit** provides tax credits up to $2,000 for students during all years of postsecondary education and for courses to acquire or improve job skills; it is also phased out as the taxpayer's earnings rise. While you can claim both the American Opportunity Credit and the Lifetime Learning Credit on the same return, you cannot claim them both for the same student. In addition, you can claim either in the same year that you receive a tax-free distribution from a Coverdell Education Savings Account (Coverdell ESA), also called the Education IRA.
- The **child and dependent care credit** provides a credit to help offset the cost of child care or care for a dependent of any age who is incapacitated due to mental or physical limitations.
- The **earned income credit**, which is available to low-income taxpayers, effectively serves as a negative income tax. With the child and dependent care credit, you can't get a credit for more than you owed in taxes, but with the earned income credit, you can actually get a credit for more than you paid in taxes. In other words, you can pay no taxes and get money back from the IRS. Just as with other tax credits, the earned income credit is phased out for those with higher income levels.
- Under the Affordable Care Act, also often referred to as ObamaCare, a **health-care premium credit** is available to low-income taxpayers who purchased coverage through the Health Insurance Marketplace. It is available only to taxpayers with household incomes between 100% and 400% of the federal poverty level, which for the 2016 tax year was $11,770 to $47,080 for singles and $24,250 to $97,000 for a family of four. Not everyone qualifies—those eligible for Medicare or other federal insurance don't qualify. Nor do those who can get affordable insurance through their work. If you are eligible for the credit, you can choose to either get it now by having some or all of the estimated credit paid in advance directly to your insurance company to lower what you pay out-of-pocket for

[8] This credit is reduced for individuals with AGIs beginning at $80,000 and totally phased out at $90,000. For married filing jointly, the credit is phased out between $160,000 and $180,000.

your monthly premiums or get it later by taking the credit when you file your tax return. As you probably know, the Affordable Care Act has been under siege in Congress, but as of now, it is still intact. However, you should not count on this credit before checking its status because it may disappear or be changed by the time you want to use it.

- The **adoption credit** allows for a tax credit for the qualifying cost of adopting a child under the age of 18 or someone who is physically or mentally incapable of self-care.

Adoption Credit
A tax credit of up to $13,570 for 2017 available for qualifying costs of adopting a child.

In addition, these taxpayers are eligible for additional tax credits:

- Totally disabled taxpayers and those over 65 with low incomes
- Taxpayers who pay income tax to another country
- Those who overpay Social Security taxes because they work more than one job

Although there are not nearly the number of tax credits that there once were, it behooves you to be aware of what qualifies for a tax credit and to take advantage of any credit you qualify for. Once again, *tax credits are subtracted directly from taxes due on a dollar-for-dollar basis.* Your total income tax becomes your base income tax less your tax credits:

Base Income Tax (from tax tables or tax rate calculations)
Less
Tax Credits
Equals
Total Income Tax Due

Other Filing Considerations

LO4 Choose the tax form that's right for you, file, and survive an audit if necessary.

Before you file, you'll have to pick a form and decide if you want to file electronically or not. You'll also want to know how to file an amended return, what to do if you can't make the tax deadline, and where to get help. Fortunately, April 15 comes only once a year.

Choosing a Tax Form

A key to calculating your taxes is deciding which Form 1040 to use: 1040EZ, 1040A, or 1040. If the IRS has sent you material, it's already made a guess as to what form you'll need and has included it. Still, you have the option of choosing a different form if you prefer.

Form 1040EZ is aimed at those who have no dependents, whose taxable income is less than $100,000 per year, and who don't itemize. As its name implies, it is an "easy" form to fill out. Form 1040EZ consists of only 12 lines of information, and the instructions fit on the back of the form. In fact, it can even be filled out over the telephone. Checklist 4.1 provides some of the basic requirements you must meet in order to use Form 1040EZ.

Slightly less "EZ" than Form 1040EZ, but still not too complicated, is Form 1040A, the original easy form. Although it still limits total taxable income to $100,000, this income can come from interest, dividends, Social Security benefits, pensions and annuities, scholarships, IRA distributions, and unemployment compensation.

CHECKLIST 4.1 You Might Be Able to Use Form 1040EZ If . . .

- ☐ Your filing status is either single or married filing jointly.
- ☐ You don't itemize deductions.
- ☐ Your taxable income is below $100,000.
- ☐ You are under age 65.
- ☐ Your taxable interest income is less than $1,500.
- ☐ You have no dependents.
- ☐ You aren't making a deductible contribution to an IRA or a deduction for student loan interest.
- ☐ You don't have alimony, taxable pension benefits, or Social Security benefits to report.

CHECKLIST 4.2 You Might Be Able to Use Form 1040A If . . .

- ☐ You don't itemize deductions.
- ☐ Your taxable income is below $100,000.
- ☐ You have capital gain distributions but no other capital gains or losses.
- ☐ Your only tax credits are child, education, earned income, child and dependent care expenses, elderly, and retirement savings contribution tax credits.
- ☐ Your only deductions are IRA contribution or student loan interest deductions.
- ☐ Your income is limited to wages, salaries, tips, and the like; interest; dividends; capital gain distributions; IRA distributions; pensions and annuities; unemployment compensation; and Social Security benefits.

In effect, it allows for a much broader range of income sources than is allowed on Form 1040EZ. Form 1040A also allows for dependents and deductible contributions to an IRA. Checklist 4.2 provides some of the basic requirements you must meet in order to use Form 1040A.

Form 1040, also called the 1040 long form, is used by everyone else—about 60 percent of all taxpayers—and throws "easy" right out the door. It's longer because it allows for the many complications that can make filing taxes a frustrating experience. On the bright side, though, the 1040 long form allows for the opportunity to avoid paying more in the way of taxes than is legally required. That is, it allows for itemized deductions and adjustments to income that can result in lower taxes. Obviously, your choice of a tax form should not be based on what's easiest to fill out. It should be based on what's financially advantageous to you.

Schedules
Attachments to Form 1040 on which you provide additional information.

Along with Form 1040, there are a number of **schedules**. A schedule is an attachment to Form 1040 on which you provide information regarding income and expenses that flow through to Form 1040. Some of the more common schedules are listed in Table 4.2. If you need an IRS schedule or form, the easiest way to get it is to

TABLE 4.2 Common Schedules Used with Form 1040

Schedule A: Itemized Deductions	Schedule EIC: Earned Income Credit
Schedule B: Interest and Dividend Income	Schedule F: Profit or Loss from Farming
Schedule C: Profit or Loss from Business	Schedule H: Household Employment Taxes
Schedule D: Capital Gains and Losses	Schedule R: Credit for the Elderly or the Disabled
Schedule E: Supplemental Income and Loss	Schedule SE: Self-Employment Tax

download it off the IRS Web site at **http://www.irs.gov**; you can also call 800-TAX-FORM, and the IRS will send it directly to you.

Electronic Filing

While you may not have a choice on paying your taxes, you do have a choice on how to file your tax return. You can file by mail or you can e-file—that is, file your return electronically. In fact, about 91 percent of all tax returns used e-file in 2016. The benefits of filing electronically include

- Faster refunds: Direct deposit can speed refunds to e-filers in as few as 10 days.
- More accurate returns: IRS computers quickly and automatically check for errors or other missing information, making e-filed returns more accurate and reducing the chance of receiving an error letter from the IRS.
- Quick electronic confirmation: Computer e-filers receive an acknowledgment that the IRS has received their returns.
- Reduced paperwork with electronic signatures: There is nothing to mail to the IRS.

Free File For the 2016 tax year, taxpayers with an AGI of $64,000 or less were eligible to use Free File. Free File is set up so that 70 percent of U.S. taxpayers are eligible to use it. New and repeat users must access Free File only through the IRS Web site; otherwise, the e-file provider might charge them a fee. So be sure to go to **http://www.irs.gov/efile** to obtain additional information and access Free File.

Filing Late and Amending Returns

Although most returns are filed by April 15, sometimes taxpayers can't make the deadline. In addition, if you discover an error in a prior year's return, you can file an amended return.

Filing Late If you're unable to file by April 15, you can request a filing extension from the IRS. You must file Form 4868, Application for Automatic Extension of Time to File U.S. Individual Income Tax Return. If you request a filing extension, the extension is automatic—no questions asked. This extension gives you an additional 6 months to file your return.

As you might expect, a filing extension is a fairly popular request, with over 12 million taxpayers asking for one each year. However, the IRS isn't about to let you off the hook for taxes you owe. In addition to filling out the extension request form, you're asked to enclose a check for any estimated taxes you owe. If you don't enclose a check, you'll be charged interest on the taxes you owe. Moreover, if the amount due is more than 10 percent of your tax bill, you'll be charged a late penalty of $\frac{1}{2}$ percent per month.

Amending Returns It's not unusual for someone to make a mistake on a tax return or to realize later that a deduction was omitted. To amend your return, use Form 1040X, Amended U.S. Individual Income Tax Return. In fact, you can even amend an amended tax return.

There are some limitations on the use of an amended return. For example, there is a limit on how far back you can go: You can't file an amended return more than 3 years after the original tax due date for the return you are amending. Finally, if you file an amended federal return, make sure you also amend your state and local returns.

Being Audited

Audit
An examination of your tax return by the IRS.

In 2016, the IRS audited about 0.8 percent of all tax returns, or 1 in every 120 households, and in 2017, with cuts to the IRS, that fell to about 0.7 percent, or 1 in every 143 households. What might bring on an **audit**? Unfortunately, you may just have bad luck—the IRS randomly selects a large number of returns each year. You may also be audited because you were audited in the past, particularly if the IRS found some error in your return. In this case, the IRS is merely checking to make sure the error doesn't occur again. You may have been selected because you earn a lot of money. If your itemized deductions are much higher than those of other taxpayers with similar income, your odds of being audited rise even further. In addition, your odds of being audited go up significantly if your return contains a Schedule C for self-employment income. If your expenses on Schedule C amount to more than one-third of your Schedule C income, the odds of an audit rise again.

No one wants to be audited, but unless you've been cheating on your taxes, it's nothing to worry about. Audits come in different forms. Some only ask for additional information and can be handled through the mail. Others require you to meet face-to-face with an IRS representative. In either case, you're given several weeks to prepare your response.

The first step in preparing for an audit is to reexamine the areas in which the IRS has questions. You should gather all supporting data you have—cancelled checks, receipts, records—and then try to anticipate any questions the IRS might have and formulate responses to them. The key to winning an audit is good records. If you need help, you can hire a tax accountant or attorney. In fact, this agent can go to the audit in your place, provided you sign a power of attorney form.

If you're not satisfied with the outcome of the audit, you have the right to appeal. The first step is to see the auditor. Present your argument, and see if you can win the appeal with additional information. If you are still not satisfied with the results, you turn to your auditor's manager. If you are still not satisfied, you can file a formal appeal and even go to tax court if necessary.

Unfortunately, an appeal does not guarantee satisfaction. The important point is that you have the right to receive credit for any and all legal deductions, and you should not let fear of being audited interfere with paying the minimum amount of income taxes, provided you do it legally.

Help in Preparing Taxes

Sometimes preparing your taxes is more than you can handle by yourself. The first place to look for help is the IRS. While that may seem akin to consorting with the enemy, the IRS is a good place to start. Information from the IRS is provided by knowledgeable persons, and it's cheap—in fact, it's free. In addition to the instructions provided with your income tax form, the IRS has a number of booklets that can be extremely helpful. One of the more informative is IRS Publication 17, *Your Federal Income Tax*, which gives detailed, step-by-step instructions to aid you in filing your taxes and is available at **http://www.irs.gov/pub/irs-pdf/p17.pdf**.

The IRS also provides a phone service, a toll-free "hotline" for tax questions. Although the IRS won't accept any liability for incorrect advice, representatives are generally correct. Moreover, using the IRS hotline as a reference can save you both time and money in getting that answer. The major problem with using the hotline is that it's often busy. The closer you get to April 15, the more difficult it is to connect. The IRS also provides a walk-in service in most areas, where you can meet directly with an IRS employee. Once again, the closer it is to April 15, the harder it is to get an appointment.

Probably the easiest way to file is through Free File, and if your return is too complicated for that, there is Intuit's TurboTax or TaxCut by H&R Block Financial. Your final option in preparing your taxes is to hire a tax specialist. Although going to a specialist sounds safe, remember that tax specialists are not licensed or tested—anyone can declare himself or herself to be a tax specialist. There are some rules governing tax specialists, but there's no penalty imposed on your advisor if you pay too much in taxes.

Tax specialists can be divided into those with a national affiliation, such as H&R Block, and independent tax specialists. One advantage of the national affiliation is that employees generally get standardized training, keeping them current with the latest IRS changes and rulings. With independent tax specialists, there's much more variability in terms of their training and the quality of their work.

If you decide to use a tax specialist, you should make sure you avoid the April rush. Because of the volume of tax work that's done near the filing deadline, last-minute returns may not get the attention they deserve. In addition, make sure you get references and inquire about the specialist's background and experience. If your tax specialist does not begin with an extensive interview in which your financial affairs are fully probed, you probably won't get your money's worth.

FACTS OF LIFE

Phishing scams often take the form of an e-mail that appears to come from a legitimate source. Some scam e-mails falsely claim to come from the IRS. For example, one phishing scam involved a bogus e-mail telling recipients they were being penalized $10,000 for failing to file on time. Keep in mind that the IRS never uses e-mail to contact taxpayers about their tax issues.

Model Taxpayers: The Taylors File Their Federal Tax Return

LO5 Calculate your income taxes.

Let's take a look at the various steps in calculating 2016 taxes using Form 1040.[9] We'll use the Taylors as an example. Chuck and Dianne Taylor have two children: Lindsey, who's 4, and Kathleen, who's 6. Chuck is a repairman for Burlington Industries, where he earned $51,900 in 2016, and Dianne works part-time at a coffee shop, where she earned $6,250 in 2016. On Chuck's and Dianne's wages and salaries, there was a total of $4,750 in federal tax withheld.

In addition, in 2016 the Taylors received interest income of $760, $755 in capital gains on stock they held for less than 12 months and then sold,[10] and a gift of $10,000 from Chuck's parents. Chuck also contributed $1,668 to his traditional IRA, which is a tax-deferred retirement plan.

The Taylors had another, more interesting source of income: They were winners on *The Price Is Right*. Dianne won a 2016 Honda Civic just by telling Drew Carey the third number in its price. A stunned Dianne Taylor stood on the stage of the CBS studio in Burbank, California, hearing the announcer say, "That's right, Dianne, this brand-new Honda Accord comes fully equipped with air, rearview camera, automatic windows, and California emission controls. You'll enjoy making heads turn as you drive down the street in this, your new car!" What she didn't hear is that she would have to pay taxes on her prize. What she's taxed on is the fair market price of the car, which is interpreted as what she could realize on an immediate resale. In this case, that amount was $20,500, and it became part of the Taylors' taxable income.

Because the Taylors had income from a prize (which must be listed on Form 1040 under "Other income"), they had no choice but to use the 1040 long form. The first step they had to take was to get organized, which means gathering together a copy of last year's return along with all of this year's tax-related information: salary, taxes withheld, mortgage payments, the market price of the car Dianne won, medical expenses, and so on. Fortunately, over the past year the Taylors set aside all their tax-related materials in a folder in Dianne's desk.

---

[9]Updated tax forms are available at **http://irs.gov**.

[10]Since the capital gains were realized on stock held for less than 12 months, the entire gain is taxable as ordinary income.

FIGURE 4.5 2016 Federal Income Tax Return for the Taylors, Using Form 1040*

Take the time to set up a good tax record-keeping system. Once it's set up, use it!

Married people generally file as married filing jointly (in general, it saves money over filing separately), but for those with widely divergent levels of income and deductions, it might be better to use the married filing separately status.

If you work for yourself, report your income on Schedule C.

If you put money into an IRA or tax-deferred retirement plan and you haven't yet paid taxes on that money, you will have to pay taxes on it when you withdraw it at retirement.

Form **1040** Department of the Treasury—Internal Revenue Service (99) **U.S. Individual Income Tax Return** **2016** OMB No. 1545-0074 IRS Use Only—Do not write or staple in this space.

For the year Jan. 1–Dec. 31, 2016, or other tax year beginning , 2016, ending , 20 — See separate instructions.

Your first name and initial	Last name	Your social security number
Chuck B.	**Taylor**	**111-11-1111**
If a joint return, spouse's first name and initial	Last name	Spouse's social security number
Dianne P.	**Taylor**	**222-22-2222**
Home address (number and street). If you have a P.O. box, see instructions. **1969 Yellow Jacket Dr.**	Apt. no.	▲ Make sure the SSN(s) above and on line 6c are correct.
City, town or post office, state, and ZIP code. If you have a foreign address, also complete spaces below (see instructions). **Ross, GA 12345**		**Presidential Election Campaign**
Foreign country name	Foreign province/state/county / Foreign postal code	Check here if you, or your spouse if filing jointly, want $3 to go to this fund. Checking a box below will not change your tax or refund. ☑ You ☑ Spouse

Filing Status

Check only one box.

1 ☐ Single
2 ☑ Married filing jointly (even if only one had income)
3 ☐ Married filing separately. Enter spouse's SSN above and full name here. ▶
4 ☐ Head of household (with qualifying person). (See instructions.) If the qualifying person is a child but not your dependent, enter this child's name here. ▶
5 ☐ Qualifying widow(er) with dependent child

Exemptions

6a ☑ **Yourself.** If someone can claim you as a dependent, **do not** check box 6a — Boxes checked on 6a and 6b: 2
b ☑ **Spouse**
c **Dependents:**

(1) First name Last name	(2) Dependent's social security number	(3) Dependent's relationship to you	(4) ✓ if child under age 17 qualifying for child tax credit (see instructions)
Kathleen Taylor	333-33-3333	daughter	☑
Lindsay Taylor	444-44-4444	daughter	☑
			☐
			☐

If more than four dependents, see instructions and check here ▶ ☐

No. of children on 6c who: • lived with you 2 • did not live with you due to divorce or separation (see instructions) Dependents on 6c not entered above

d Total number of exemptions claimed — Add numbers on lines above ▶ **4**

Income

Attach Form(s) W-2 here. Also attach Forms W-2G and 1099-R if tax was withheld.

If you did not get a W-2, see instructions.

7	Wages, salaries, tips, etc. Attach Form(s) W-2	7	58,150
8a	**Taxable** interest. Attach Schedule B if required	8a	760
b	**Tax-exempt** interest. **Do not** include on line 8a — 8b		
9a	Ordinary dividends. Attach Schedule B if required	9a	
b	Qualified dividends — 9b		
10	Taxable refunds, credits, or offsets of state and local income taxes	10	
11	Alimony received	11	
12	Business income or (loss). Attach Schedule C or C-EZ	12	
13	Capital gain or (loss). Attach Schedule D if required. If not required, check here ▶ ☐	13	755
14	Other gains or (losses). Attach Form 4797	14	
15a	IRA distributions 15a — b Taxable amount	15b	
16a	Pensions and annuities 16a — b Taxable amount	16b	
17	Rental real estate, royalties, partnerships, S corporations, trusts, etc. Attach Schedule E	17	
18	Farm income or (loss). Attach Schedule F	18	
19	Unemployment compensation	19	
20a	Social security benefits 20a — b Taxable amount	20b	
21	Other income. List type and amount	21	20,500
22	Combine the amounts in the far right column for lines 7 through 21. This is your **total income** ▶	22	80,165

Adjusted Gross Income

23	Educator expenses	23			
24	Certain business expenses of reservists, performing artists, and fee-basis government officials. Attach Form 2106 or 2106-EZ	24			
25	Health savings account deduction. Attach Form 8889	25			
26	Moving expenses. Attach Form 3903	26			
27	Deductible part of self-employment tax. Attach Schedule SE	27			
28	Self-employed SEP, SIMPLE, and qualified plans	28			
29	Self-employed health insurance deduction	29			
30	Penalty on early withdrawal of savings	30			
31a	Alimony paid b Recipient's SSN ▶	31a			
32	IRA deduction	32	1,668		
33	Student loan interest deduction	33			
34	Tuition and fees. Attach Form 8917	34			
35	Domestic production activities deduction. Attach Form 8903	35			
36	Add lines 23 through 35			36	1,668
37	Subtract line 36 from line 22. This is your **adjusted gross income** ▶			37	78,497

For Disclosure, Privacy Act, and Paperwork Reduction Act Notice, see separate instructions. Cat. No. 11320B Form **1040** (2016)

One of the first questions asked on Form 1040 is filing status. The best way to determine that is to calculate your taxes filing both jointly and separately and then use the status that gives you the lowest number. For now, let's assume that filing a joint return is the better option for the Taylors. The Taylors claimed a total of four exemptions—one each for Chuck, Dianne, Kathleen, and Lindsey. Figure 4.5 shows the Taylors' 2016 Form 1040. We'll use this figure as a reference as we examine how the Taylors calculated their taxes. All line references correspond to the numbered lines shown on Form 1040.

FIGURE 4.5 2016 Federal Income Tax Return for the Taylors, Using Form 1040 (*continued*)

Before sitting down to do your taxes, gather up everything you will need, including any tax-related business expenses from the previous year.

If you pay for child or dependent care while you are working, you may be entitled to a tax credit.

Form 1040 (2016) Page **2**

Tax and Credits	38	Amount from line 37 (adjusted gross income)	38	78,497
	39a	Check if: ☐ **You** were born before January 2, 1952, ☐ Blind. ☐ **Spouse** was born before January 2, 1952, ☐ Blind. } **Total boxes checked** ▶ 39a ☐		
	b	If your spouse itemizes on a separate return or you were a dual-status alien, check here ▶ 39b ☐		
Standard Deduction for— • People who check any box on line 39a or 39b **or** who can be claimed as a dependent, see instructions. • All others: Single or Married filing separately, $6,300 Married filing jointly or Qualifying widow(er), $12,600 Head of household, $9,300	40	**Itemized deductions** (from Schedule A) **or** your **standard deduction** (see left margin)	40	14,274
	41	Subtract line 40 from line 38	41	64,223
	42	**Exemptions.** If line 38 is $155,650 or less, multiply $4,050 by the number on line 6d. Otherwise, see instructions	42	16,200
	43	**Taxable income.** Subtract line 42 from line 41. If line 42 is more than line 41, enter -0-	43	48,023
	44	**Tax** (see instructions). Check if any from: **a** ☐ Form(s) 8814 **b** ☐ Form 4972 **c** ☐	44	6,276
	45	**Alternative minimum tax** (see instructions). Attach Form 6251	45	
	46	Excess advance premium tax credit repayment. Attach Form 8962	46	
	47	Add lines 44, 45, and 46 ▶	47	
	48	Foreign tax credit. Attach Form 1116 if required — 48		
	49	Credit for child and dependent care expenses. Attach Form 2441 — 49		
	50	Education credits from Form 8863, line 19 — 50		
	51	Retirement savings contributions credit. Attach Form 8880 — 51		
	52	Child tax credit. Attach Schedule 8812, if required — 52: 2,000		
	53	Residential energy credits. Attach Form 5695 — 53		
	54	Other credits from Form: **a** ☐ 3800 **b** ☐ 8801 **c** ☐ — 54		
	55	Add lines 48 through 54. These are your **total credits**	55	2,000
	56	Subtract line 55 from line 47. If line 55 is more than line 47, enter -0- ▶	56	4,276
Other Taxes	57	Self-employment tax. Attach Schedule SE	57	
	58	Unreported social security and Medicare tax from Form: **a** ☐ 4137 **b** ☐ 8919	58	
	59	Additional tax on IRAs, other qualified retirement plans, etc. Attach Form 5329 if required	59	
	60a	Household employment taxes from Schedule H	60a	
	b	First-time homebuyer credit repayment. Attach Form 5405 if required	60b	
	61	Health care: individual responsibility (see instructions) Full-year coverage ☐	61	
	62	Taxes from: **a** ☐ Form 8959 **b** ☐ Form 8960 **c** ☐ Instructions; enter code(s)	62	
	63	Add lines 56 through 62. This is your **total tax** ▶	63	4,276
Payments	64	Federal income tax withheld from Forms W-2 and 1099 — 64: 4,750		
	65	2016 estimated tax payments and amount applied from 2015 return — 65		
If you have a qualifying child, attach Schedule EIC.	66a	**Earned income credit (EIC)** — 66a		
	b	Nontaxable combat pay election — 66b		
	67	Additional child tax credit. Attach Schedule 8812 — 67		
	68	American opportunity credit from Form 8863, line 8 — 68		
	69	Net premium tax credit. Attach Form 8962 — 69		
	70	Amount paid with request for extension to file — 70		
	71	Excess social security and tier 1 RRTA tax withheld — 71		
	72	Credit for federal tax on fuels. Attach Form 4136 — 72		
	73	Credits from Form: **a** ☐ 2439 **b** ☐ Reserved **c** ☐ 8885 **d** ☐ — 73		
	74	Add lines 64, 65, 66a, and 67 through 73. These are your **total payments** ▶	74	4,750
Refund	75	If line 74 is more than line 63, subtract line 63 from line 74. This is the amount you **overpaid**	75	474
	76a	Amount of line 75 you want **refunded to you.** If Form 8888 is attached, check here ▶ ☐	76a	474
Direct deposit? See instructions.	▶ b	Routing number ▶ c Type: ☐ Checking ☐ Savings		
	▶ d	Account number		
	77	Amount of line 75 you want **applied to your 2017 estimated tax** ▶ 77		
Amount You Owe	78	**Amount you owe.** Subtract line 74 from line 63. For details on how to pay, see instructions ▶	78	
	79	Estimated tax penalty (see instructions) — 79		

Third Party Designee Do you want to allow another person to discuss this return with the IRS (see instructions)? ☐ **Yes.** Complete below. ☐ **No**
Designee's name ▶ Phone no. ▶ Personal identification number (PIN) ▶

Sign Here Under penalties of perjury, I declare that I have examined this return and accompanying schedules and statements, and to the best of my knowledge and belief, they are true, correct, and accurately list all amounts and sources of income I received during the tax year. Declaration of preparer (other than taxpayer) is based on all information of which preparer has any knowledge.

Joint return? See instructions. Keep a copy for your records.

Your signature	Date	Your occupation	Daytime phone number
		Repairman	**555-555-5555**
Spouse's signature. If a joint return, **both** must sign.	Date	Spouse's occupation	If the IRS sent you an Identity Protection PIN, enter it here (see inst.)
		Barista	

Paid Preparer Use Only

Print/Type preparer's name	Preparer's signature	Date	Check ☐ if self-employed	PTIN
Firm's name ▶			Firm's EIN ▶	
Firm's address ▶			Phone no.	

www.irs.gov/form1040 Form **1040** (2016)

*Updated tax forms are available at **http://irs.gov**.

Determining Gross or Total Income (line 22)

Remember, gross or total income is the sum of all your taxable income from all sources. For the Taylors, it includes Chuck's and Dianne's wages and salaries of $51,900 + 6,250 = $58,150 (line 7). It also includes taxable interest income of $760 (line 8a) and $755 in capital gains (line 13). In addition, line 21, other income, includes $20,500, the fair market value of the car Dianne won on *The Price Is Right.* All this taxable income is summed to make up total income (line 22):

Chuck's and Dianne's salaries and wages (line 7)	$58,150
Taxable interest income (line 8a)	760
Capital gains (line 13)	755
Other income (line 21)	20,500
Total income (line 22)	$80,165

Notice that the $10,000 gift from Chuck's parents does not appear as income. This is because gifts are not considered taxable income. Other common sources of income that would not be taxed include interest on state and local debt.

Subtracting Adjustments to Gross or Total Income and Calculating Adjusted Gross Income (line 37)

For the Taylors, the only adjustment to total income was Chuck's IRA deduction of $1,668. Thus, the total adjustment made in calculating the Taylors' AGI was $1,668. Subtracting this adjustment from total income gave the Taylors an AGI of $78,497.

Subtracting Deductions (line 40)

The Taylors had their choice of taking the standard deduction, which for 2016 was $12,600, or itemizing their deductions. The Taylors' itemized deductions amounted to $14,274, primarily as a result of interest paid on their home mortgage. Figure 4.6 shows the Taylors' deductions. In addition to home mortgage interest payments of $11,079, they paid $2,543 in state and local income taxes and real estate taxes and made tax-deductible charitable contributions of $652, for a total of $14,274 in deductions. The Taylors were unable to deduct any medical or miscellaneous expenses because neither of these exceeded the AGI limitations set by the IRS. Because the total of the itemized deductions exceeded the standard deduction, they chose to itemize. The itemized deduction of $14,274 was entered in line 40 on Form 1040. Subtracting this amount from their AGI reduced their taxable income to $64,223 (line 41).

Claiming Exemptions (line 42)

The Taylors qualified for four exemptions, with the 2016 exemption amount being $4,050. Thus, the level of total exemptions entered on line 42 was $4 \times 4{,}050 = \$16{,}200$. Subtracting this amount further reduced their taxable income to $\$64{,}223 - \$16{,}200 = \$48{,}023$ (line 43).

Calculating Total Tax (line 63)

For the Taylors, their base income tax could be calculated directly from the tax tables provided in the federal instructions booklet. Their tax came out to $6,276, which is shown in Figure 4.4 and was entered on line 44. Because the Taylors hade dependent children under the age of 17, they qualified for the child tax credit. Remember, a tax credit is subtracted directly from taxes owed. The child tax credit for tax year 2016 was $1,000 per dependent child, so the Taylors received a $2,000 child tax credit. This amount was entered on line 52. Because the total credits entered on line 55 were $2,000, line 56 became $4,276.

During 2016, the Taylors had $4,750 in federal income tax withheld; thus, total tax payments of $4,750 appeared in line 74. Because they owed ($4,276) less than they paid ($4,750), they received a refund of the difference of $474 from the IRS.

FIGURE 4.6 Schedule A from the Taylors' 2016 Federal Income Tax Return*

Only those medical expenses that exceed 10% of your adjusted gross income are tax deductible.

The state, local, personal property, real estate, and foreign income taxes you paid are tax deductible.

Charitable contributions are deductible. However, if you make noncash contributions of clothing, goods, or property, they must be listed on Form 8283 if they exceed $500.

Only if total job-related and other expenses exceed 2% of your adjusted gross income are they tax deductible.

SCHEDULE A (Form 1040)
Department of the Treasury Internal Revenue Service (99)

Itemized Deductions

► Information about Schedule A and its separate instructions is at *www.irs.gov/schedulea*.
► Attach to Form 1040.

OMB No. 1545-0074
2016
Attachment Sequence No. 07

Name(s) shown on Form 1040: **Chuck and Dianne Taylor**
Your social security number: 111 11 1111

Medical and Dental Expenses		**Caution.** Do not include expenses reimbursed or paid by others.				
	1	Medical and dental expenses (see instructions)	1	349		
	2	Enter amount from Form 1040, line 38	2			
	3	Multiply line 2 by 10% (.10). But if either you or your spouse was born before January 2, 1952, multiply line 2 by 7.5% (.075) instead	3	7,850		
	4	Subtract line 3 from line 1. If line 3 is more than line 1, enter -0-			4	0
Taxes You Paid	5	State and local **(check only one box):** a ☐ Income taxes, **or** b ☐ General sales taxes	5	2,217		
	6	Real estate taxes (see instructions)	6	326		
	7	Personal property taxes	7			
	8	Other taxes. List type and amount ►	8			
	9	Add lines 5 through 8			9	2,543
Interest You Paid	10	Home mortgage interest and points reported to you on Form 1098	10	11,079		
Note. Your mortgage interest deduction may be limited (see instructions).	11	Home mortgage interest not reported to you on Form 1098. If paid to the person from whom you bought the home, see instructions and show that person's name, identifying no., and address ►	11			
	12	Points not reported to you on Form 1098. See instructions for special rules	12			
	13	Mortgage insurance premiums (see instructions)	13			
	14	Investment interest. Attach Form 4952 if required. (See instructions.)	14			
	15	Add lines 10 through 14			15	11,079
Gifts to Charity	16	Gifts by cash or check. If you made any gift of $250 or more, see instructions	16	652		
If you made a gift and got a benefit for it, see instructions.	17	Other than by cash or check. If any gift of $250 or more, see instructions. You **must** attach Form 8283 if over $500	17			
	18	Carryover from prior year	18			
	19	Add lines 16 through 18			19	652
Casualty and Theft Losses	20	Casualty or theft loss(es). Attach Form 4684. (See instructions.)			20	0
Job Expenses and Certain Miscellaneous Deductions	21	Unreimbursed employee expenses—job travel, union dues, job education, etc. Attach Form 2106 or 2106-EZ if required. (See instructions.) ►	21			
	22	Tax preparation fees	22			
	23	Other expenses—investment, safe deposit box, etc. List type and amount ►	23	50		
	24	Add lines 21 through 23	24	50		
	25	Enter amount from Form 1040, line 38 [25] 78,497				
	26	Multiply line 25 by 2% (0.02)	26	1,570		
	27	Subtract line 26 from line 24. If line 26 is more than line 24, enter -0-			27	0
Other Miscellaneous Deductions	28	Other—from list in instructions. List type and amount ►			28	0
Total Itemized Deductions	29	Is Form 1040, line 38, over $150,000? ☐ **No.** Your deduction is not limited. Add the amounts in the far right column for lines 4 through 28. Also, enter this amount on Form 1040, line 40. ☐ **Yes.** Your deduction may be limited. See the Itemized Deductions Worksheet in the instructions to figure the amount to enter.			29	14,274
	30	If you elect to itemize deductions even though they are less than your standard deduction, check here ► ☐				

For Paperwork Reduction Act Notice, see Form 1040 instructions. Cat. No. 17145C **Schedule A (Form 1040) 2016**

*Updated tax forms are available at **http://irs.gov**.

Tax Strategies to Lower Your Taxes

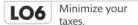

LO6 Minimize your taxes.

So far we've looked only at preparing your taxes. We now turn to the very important topic of tax planning strategies. Although a tax specialist can help you identify deductions you might otherwise miss, once you begin to prepare your taxes it's probably too late for any strategy that will result in reduced taxes. Tax planning, in general, must be done well ahead of time.

Few people do their tax planning alone. Instead, they consult a certified public accountant (CPA) or even a tax attorney. However, before you see a specialist, you should have a good understanding of how the tax code works so that you can work with a specialist to map out a strategy that suits your needs.

The basic reason for tax planning is to minimize unnecessary tax payments. While the IRS has closed a number of tax loopholes in recent years, there still are many strategies that make sense. Tax strategies should be methods of supplementing a sound investment strategy rather than the focal point of investing.

Keep in mind that Congress and the IRS are continuously tinkering with the tax laws. Your strategy should be to supplement a solid investment strategy with tax considerations.

There are five general tax strategies you can use:

- Maximize deductions.
- Look to capital gains and dividend income.
- Shift income to family members in lower tax brackets.
- Receive tax-exempt income.
- Defer taxes to the future.

Each of these strategies is aimed at avoiding unnecessary taxes, not evading taxes by, for example, overstating deductions or not reporting all your income. It's certainly illegal and unwise to evade taxes, but it's foolish to pay more than your fair share.

Maximize Deductions

Strategies for maximizing deductions center on three different tactics: (1) using tax-deferred retirement programs to reduce taxes, (2) using your home as a tax shelter, and (3) shifting and bunching deductions. Each of these three tactics has the same goal: to reduce taxable income to its minimum level.

Using Tax-Deferred Retirement Programs To encourage retirement savings, the government allows several different types of tax-deferred retirement programs. The advantage of these plans is that you (1) don't pay taxes on the money you invest and (2) don't pay taxes on the interest earned by your retirement account. Let's look at the difference that results from putting your savings in a tax-deferred retirement plan instead of in a normal savings account, both earning a 10 percent return. Let's also assume that you are in the 25 percent marginal tax bracket.

STOP & THINK

It's hard to overstress how valuable tax-deferred retirement plans actually are. Not only do they reduce taxable income, but also the contributions grow tax deferred, and many companies match part of your contribution, putting in 50 cents for each dollar that you contribute. Why do you think the government offers tax-deferred retirement plans?

If you took $1,000 of your taxable earnings and decided to invest without using a tax-deferred retirement plan earning 10 percent, you would first pay $250 in taxes, leaving you with only $750 to invest. During the first year, you would earn $75 in interest and pay $18.75 in taxes, leaving you with $56.25 of interest after taxes. At the end of the year, you would have $806.25 saved. If you let this amount grow at 10 percent before taxes for 25 years, it would accumulate to a total of $4,573.75.

Now, let's look at what would happen if you put your money in a tax-deferred account, also earning 10 percent. First, you wouldn't pay taxes on the $1,000 because taxes aren't assessed until you withdraw the money from this account. Thus, you would earn 10 percent interest on $1,000 for a total of $100 interest. In addition, because this is a tax-deferred account, you wouldn't pay taxes on any of this interest, giving you a total of $1,100 after the year. If you left this amount in the tax-deferred account for 25 years, you would have accumulated $10,834.

Of course, you eventually would have to pay taxes on this amount, but even after paying 25 percent taxes on $10,834, you would still have about $8,126.03. Why is the difference between the investments so great? Because you've been able to earn interest on money that would have otherwise already been collected by the IRS.

Using Your Home as a Tax Shelter The tax benefits associated with owning a home are twofold. First, mortgage interest payments are tax deductible and, as such, reduce your taxes. Second, when you eventually sell your house, you are exempt from paying taxes on gains of up to $500,000 for couples filing jointly and $250,000 for those filing singly on the sale of a principal residence.

Just how valuable is the deductibility of your home mortgage interest payments? That depends on several factors. For those in the highest tax brackets, the tax deductibility is much more valuable than it is for those in the lowest bracket. However, if you earn too much, this deduction begins to lose value because of the phase-out of itemized deductions discussed earlier. In addition, if you do not itemize deductions, the tax deductibility of mortgage interest payments is of no value. Moreover, if you had taken the standard deduction without them and now itemize with them, they would reduce your taxable income only by the difference between the standard deduction and your itemized deductions.

The amount that this reduction in taxable income reduces your taxes is equal to their value. In effect, the tax deductibility of mortgage interest payments reduces the cost of your mortgage by (1 – marginal tax rate). Thus, the after-tax cost of a home mortgage can be determined as follows:

$$\text{after-tax cost of mortgage interest} = \frac{\text{before-tax cost of}}{\text{mortgage interest}} \times (1 - \text{marginal tax rate})$$

MyLab Finance Video

In short, the value of the tax deductibility of mortgage interest payments depends on your marginal tax bracket and whether or not you itemize deductions.

In addition, by using your home as collateral, you can take out a home equity loan and deduct your interest payments. This deduction lowers the cost of borrowing and could end up being the least expensive way of raising money.

Shifting and Bunching Deductions When we discussed itemizing versus taking the standard deduction, we presented the concept of shifting and bunching deductions. The decision whether to take the standard deduction or itemize becomes difficult when they are close in value. The concept of shifting and bunching deductions involves trying to avoid incurring deductible expenses in years that you don't itemize. Instead, you postpone them to years when you do itemize and therefore get credit for them.

Look to Capital Gains and Dividend Income

Recall from our earlier discussion that capital gain refers to the amount by which the selling price of a capital asset—that is, an asset being kept for investment purposes such as stocks, bonds, or real estate—exceeds its purchase price. The example we used was the purchase of 100 shares of GM stock for $50 per share and the sale 2 years later of those same shares of GM stock for $70 per share. In this case, your capital gains would be 100 × ($70−$50) = $2,000.

If you hold an asset for a year or more, the gain is taxed at a rate of 15 percent for taxpayers who are in the 25, 28, 33, and 35 percent marginal tax brackets, and there is no tax for taxpayers in the 10 and 15 percent brackets. However, for those in the 39.6 percent marginal tax bracket, there is a 20 percent tax. Thus, if you were in the 35 percent marginal tax bracket, you'd pay less than half your ordinary tax rate, and if you were in the 39.6 percent tax bracket, it would be about half your normal rate.

The other benefit from capital gains is the fact that you don't have to claim it—and therefore pay taxes on it—until you sell the asset. In effect, you can postpone paying taxes by not selling the asset. Without question, if you have to pay taxes, it's better to pay 10 years from now than today—that way you can hold onto your money longer and, while you're holding onto it, earn a return on it. In addition to getting a tax break on capital gains, you get a tax break on dividend income. Qualified dividends from domestic corporations and qualified foreign corporations are taxed at the same low rates as long-term capital gains.

Shift Income to Family Members in Lower Tax Brackets

Income shifting involves transferring income from family members in high tax brackets to those in lower tax brackets. This process can be complex and involve lawyers and the establishment of **trusts**. A less complicated kind of income shifting involves a relatively simple idea—gifts. You're allowed to give $14,000 per year tax free to as many different people as you like.[11] One of the nice things about annual gifts of less than $14,000 is that the person receiving the gift doesn't pay any taxes either. On annual gifts of $14,000 or less, neither the person who gives nor the person who receives pays any taxes. Best of all, every year you get another gift exclusion that allows you to give $14,000 tax free to as many different people as you like.

Trust
A fiduciary agreement in which one individual holds property for the benefit of another person.

FACTS OF LIFE

According to a *Wall Street Journal* survey, two-fifths of tax-filing adults don't do anything to minimize their taxes.

Receive Tax-Exempt Income

Interest paid on state and local government debt is tax exempt for federal income tax purposes. This means that if you buy a bond issued by a state or city (a municipal bond), you can collect the interest and not have to pay any taxes on it. For example, California's Foothill/Eastern Transportation Agency issued about $2.2 billion in bonds set to mature in 2053. The equivalent taxable yield on a municipal bond is calculated as follows:

MyLab Finance Video

$$\text{equivalent taxable yield} = \frac{\text{tax-free yield on the municipal bond}}{(1 - \text{investor's marginal tax bracket})}$$

Thus, if you're in the 28 percent marginal tax bracket, the equivalent taxable yield on a 6 percent municipal bond would be 6% ÷ 72% = 8.33 percent. In effect, this means that on an after-tax basis, a taxable bond yielding 8.33 percent and a municipal bond yielding 6 percent are equivalent. The higher your marginal tax bracket, the more beneficial tax-free income is.

Defer Taxes to the Future

As we've already seen, tax-deferred retirement programs such as traditional IRAs, SIMPLE IRAs, **401(k) plans**, and 403(b) plans allow you to defer taxes to the future rather than paying those taxes today. Roth IRAs allow taxes to be paid on the contribution and never again. The idea is to allow you to earn interest on money that would have otherwise already been collected by the IRS.

401(k) Plan
A tax-deferred retirement plan.

This concept also applies to capital gains because you can postpone capital gains taxes until you sell the asset. If you don't recognize all these terms, don't worry. We'll discuss them in depth later in the book. For now, the important point is that saving on a tax-deferred basis has real benefits.

[11] Based on tax year 2017.

BEHAVIORAL INSIGHTS

PRINCIPLE 9

Principle 9: Mind Games, Your Financial Personality, and Your Money How many times have you heard someone say, "I can't wait until my tax refund gets here!" Do you think that they are excited because they will be able to put some extra money toward paying down their debt? Or do you think they might be planning a weekend getaway? A new pair of boots? Closer-to-the-stage concert tickets?

The behavioral finance concept of mental accounting, where individuals separate their money into different accounts or buckets, has an impact on an individual's financial well-being in many different ways. And it is a fact that every year around April millions of Americans receive a tax refund and immediately put that money into a "mental bucket" and treat it as if it is different from the rest of their money. It is viewed as "found" or "free" money. In fact, for many, it is viewed the same way lottery winnings are viewed. As a result, many times this money is *not* used to pay down credit card debt or put into an emergency fund but spent in an urgent trip to Best Buy or on vacations.

You must realize that you aren't the only one excited about your tax refund. This is a slow time of year at the local mall, and marketers are well aware that millions of Americans are receiving checks in the mail! Everyone is having a "sale"—department stores, restaurants, bars, and even airlines and hotels. So keep in mind, especially if you are someone who puts tax refund dollars into a special "mental bucket," that there will be plenty of temptations out there.

If you do receive a tax refund, remember that it is simply the return of money you earned and had given to Uncle Sam—in effect, it's *your hard-earned money*. Studies have shown that we'll spend a $50 bonus from our job more easily than we'll spend $50 that we are told we earned as salary that was mistakenly withheld. Make sure you treat your tax refund as your "money earned" and spend it in line with your financial goals. You won't be sorry.

ACTION PLAN

PRINCIPLE 10

Principle 10: Just Do It! As Homer Simpson found out in the introduction to this chapter, taxes happen every year, and they're a lot easier to file if you give yourself a bit of lead time. So here are some tips to help make it all a bit easier.

- **Make your withholding match up with your income.** Sign up for enough in the way of withholding that you don't have to pay additional taxes in April. But if you got a refund last year, set a deadline to change your W-4. About the worst investment, besides burying your money in the backyard, is giving the U.S. government an interest-free loan of your earnings for the year. Think about it: A $3,000 refund adds up to about $250 in extra taxes each month—that could go a long way toward making a car payment or paying down your student debt.
- **Make it easy on yourself—use tax software.** Use TurboTax or TaxCut software, and when you use it the following year, all your personal information will be automatically loaded.
- **Keep track of your deductions.** If you itemize deductions and don't use accounting software, circle any deductible items in your check register or on hard copies of your credit/debit card statements. At the end of the year, check off each circled item as you list it, and make sure you have receipts where needed.

- **Know your cost basis.** One of the most time-consuming tasks in tax preparation is determining the cost basis of investments that were liquidated during the year. If you don't have records of the original purchase and intervening transactions, you are at the mercy of a brokerage house or investment company to provide the documentation. Prepare a folder when you first set up a stock or a mutual fund account, and keep every statement. Just a little organization can save time and ensure that the proper amount of tax is paid.

Chapter Summaries

LO1 Identify and understand the major federal income tax features that affect all taxpayers.

SUMMARY: Your taxable income is a function of three numbers—adjusted gross income (AGI), deductions, and exemptions. From there, the tax rates determine how much of the difference between income and deductions will be taken away in taxes. A capital gain is the amount by which the selling price of a capital asset—that is, an asset being kept for investment purposes such as stocks or bonds—exceeds its purchase price. Net long-term capital gains less any net short-term capital losses are taxed at a lower maximum rate than ordinary income (short-term gains are treated as ordinary income). In addition to income taxes, you must pay Social Security and Medicare taxes.

KEY TERMS

Progressive or Graduated Tax, page 96 A tax system in which tax rates increase for higher incomes.

Tax Brackets, page 96 Income ranges in which the same marginal tax rates apply. For example, an individual might fall into the 15 percent or 28 percent marginal tax bracket.

Personal Exemption, page 96 An IRS-allowed reduction in your income before you compute your taxes. You are given one exemption for yourself, one for your spouse, and one for each dependent.

Deductions, page 96 Expenses that reduce taxable income.

Itemized Deductions, page 96 Deductions calculated using Schedule A. The allowable deductions are added up and then subtracted from adjusted gross income.

Standard Deduction, page 96 A set deduction allowed by the IRS, regardless of what a taxpayer's expenses actually were.

Taxable Income, page 96 Income subject to taxes.

Adjusted Gross Income (AGI), page 96 Your taxable income from all sources minus specific adjustments (for example, IRA contributions, student loan interest payments, and alimony paid by you) but before deducting your standard or itemized deductions.

Marginal Tax Rate or Marginal Tax Bracket, page 98 The percentage of the last dollar you earn that goes toward taxes.

Tax-Deferred, page 99 Income on which the payment of taxes is postponed until some future date.

Capital Asset, page 100 Almost any asset you own, except for certain business assets, including stocks, bonds, and real estate.

Capital Gain/Capital Loss, page 100 The amount by which the selling price of a capital asset differs from its purchase price. If the selling price is higher than the purchase price, a capital gain results; if the selling price is lower than the purchase price, a capital loss results.

Capital Gains Tax, page 100 The tax you pay on your realized capital gains.

Bracket Creep, page 101 The movement into a higher tax bracket when wages are increased as a result of inflation.

Describe other taxes that you must pay. LO2

SUMMARY: In addition to federal income taxes and Social Security and Medicare taxes, you must pay state and local taxes, excise taxes, sales taxes, property taxes, and gift and estate taxes.

KEY TERMS

Social Security, page 102 A federal program that provides disability and retirement benefits based on years worked, amount paid into the plan, and retirement age.

Medicare, page 102 The federal government's insurance program to provide medical benefits to those over 65.

Understand what is taxable income and how taxes are determined. LO3

SUMMARY: To calculate your taxes, you must first determine your total income by summing up your taxable income from all sources. From this amount, adjustments that center on tax-deductible expenses and retirement contributions are subtracted, with the result being AGI. From AGI, the deductions (the greater of either the itemized deductions or the standard deduction) and the exemptions are subtracted, with the end result being taxable income.

KEY TERMS

Dependent, page 103 A person you support financially.

Total or Gross Income, page 104 The sum of all your taxable income from all sources.

Active Income, page 104 Income that comes from wages or a business.

Portfolio or Investment Income, page 104 Income that comes from securities.

Passive Income, page 104 Income that comes from activities in which the taxpayer does not actively participate.

Adjusted Gross Income (AGI), page 104 Your taxable income from all sources minus specific adjustments (for example, IRA contributions, student loan interest payments, and alimony paid by you) but before deducting your standard or itemized deductions.

IRA, page 104 A tax-advantaged retirement account. The contribution may or may not be tax deductible, depending on the individual's income level and whether he or she, or his or her spouse, is covered by a company retirement plan.

Home Equity Loan, page 106 A loan that uses your home as collateral—that is, a loan that is secured by your home. If you default, the lender can take possession of your home to recapture money lost on the loan.

Exemption, page 107 A deduction you can take on your return for each person supported by the income listed on your tax return.

Child Tax Credit, page 110 A tax credit given for each qualifying child under 17.

American Opportunity Credit, page 110 A tax credit of up to $2,500 per year per student.

Lifetime Learning Credit, page 110 A tax credit for all years of college or graduate school. It also applies to working adults taking classes to improve their work skills.

Child and Dependent Care Credit, page 110 A tax credit that offsets your taxes in a direct dollar-for-dollar manner for child and dependent care expenses.

Earned Income Credit, page 110 A tax credit available to low-income taxpayers that effectively serves as a negative income tax.

Health-Care Premium Credit, page 110 A tax credit available to low-income taxpayers who purchased coverage through the Health Insurance Marketplace.

Adoption Credit, page 111 A tax credit of up to $13,570 for 2017 available for qualifying costs of adopting a child.

LO4 Choose the tax form that's right for you, file, and survive an audit if necessary.

SUMMARY: It is important to understand who must file tax returns, when they must file, what forms to use, what electronic filing is, and what information is needed to prepare a tax return. Those unable to file by April 15 can request a filing extension from the IRS. In addition, those who discover an error in a prior year's return can file an amended return.

Audits can happen to anyone but are more likely to happen to those who have higher incomes or who are self-employed. The first step in preparing for an audit is to reexamine the areas in which the IRS has questions. Taxpayers who are not satisfied with the outcome of their audit have the right to appeal.

KEY TERMS

Schedules, page 112 Attachments to Form 1040 on which you provide additional information.

Audit, page 114 An examination of your tax return by the IRS.

LO5 Calculate your income taxes.

SUMMARY: For help in filing a tax return, the first place to look is the IRS. Tax specialists are people trained—to one degree or another—to help others plan for taxes and prepare their tax returns.

LO6 Minimize your taxes.

SUMMARY: Five general tax strategies can be used to keep tax bills to a minimum:

- Maximize deductions.
- Look to capital gains and dividend income.
- Shift income to family members in lower tax brackets.
- Receive tax-exempt income.
- Defer taxes to the future.

KEY TERMS

Trust, page 122 A fiduciary agreement in which one individual holds property for the benefit of another person.

401(k) Plan, page 122 A tax-deferred retirement plan.

Problems and Activities

These problems are available in MyLab Finance.

1. The Lees, a family of two adults and two dependent children under age 16, had a gross annual income of $68,000 for 2017. Determine their standard deduction, exemption, and child tax credit amounts, as well as their marginal and average tax rates, assuming their filing status is married filing jointly.
2. Consider three investors who need to partially liquidate investments to raise cash. In this case, all investments have been held for 3 or more years. Investor A waited for a $1,500 qualified dividend distribution from her mutual fund, and Investor B received $1,500 in interest income from a certificate of deposit. However, because investor C could not wait for a distribution, he decided to sell $1,500 of appreciated stock shares. Assuming no commissions, no sales charges, and no state income tax and a 25 percent federal marginal tax bracket, which investment will provide the greatest after-tax amount?

3. Sukeeta, a young mother, is preparing to file her 2017 income tax return. Her husband, who was tragically killed in a boating accident in the summer of 2017, always handled the tax filing. Assuming she does not itemize deductions, which filing status should she use? Why? Does she have a choice of status? Which tax form should she use?

4. A couple with three dependent children has an annual AGI of $238,500. Calculate the total dollar amount of personal exemptions that they can claim for the 2017 tax year.

5. Bee and Barney Mayberry have $71,500 in gross income and enough allowable deductions to itemize. Determine the best income tax form for them to use if they are filing jointly. Explain the major reason they can't use the other forms.

6. Calculate the total 2017 tax liability for a surviving spouse with one dependent child with a gross income of $46,250, no salary reductions for employer-provided benefits, and no itemized deductions.

7. Using the married filing jointly status and their income and expense statement below, calculate the 2014 tax liability for Shameka and Curtis Williams. First, use the standard deduction, and then use itemized deductions.

Income	
Earned income	$53,000
Interest income	$2,100
Expenses	
Home mortgage interest	$7,900
Real estate and state income taxes	$5,850
Miscellaneous deductions	$800

Briefly explain to the Williamses which method they should use and why.

8. Calculate the 2017 total tax for Gordon Geist, a single taxpayer with no dependents and no itemized deductions. He has an active income of $40,000, a short-term capital gain income of $4,000 from the sale of stock, and $7,800 from book royalties. What is Gordon's average tax rate?

9. Aliza Grajek is a self-employed nurse with 2017 gross income of $68,000 and taxable annual income (federal and state) of $55,000 after adjustments, exemptions, and deductions. Calculate her total 2017 income tax liability, including federal and FICA taxes.

10. Mrs. Hubbard, a mother of two, has been selected for an audit. Advise her on what to do to prepare for the audit and what to do if the audit does not turn out favorably.

11. Harry and Harriet Potter are in their golden years. Discuss the best tax reduction method for them to use in reducing their estate taxes.

Discussion Case 1

This case is available in **MyLab Finance**.

Holly and Zachary Neal, from Dublin, Virginia, are preparing to file their 2017 income taxes. Their children are grown; however, Holly's mother, Martha, has moved in with them, so Holly is no longer working. Martha is dependent on their income for support except for her $536 monthly Social Security benefit.

Zachary works for a software company and earns enough to keep their heads above water; however, he had to discontinue participation in his retirement plan so they could pay the bills.

Holly is taking this opportunity to work toward her master's degree. They know they will file jointly but need your help preparing their federal tax return. They have gathered all of the appropriate records, as follows:

1099-DIV, Capital Gains, short-term	$900
Zachary's W-2, Wage and Tax Statement	$54,500
Gambling winnings	$1,500
Inheritance	$35,000
Holly's and Zachary's aggregate traditional IRA contribution	$5,000
Martha's unreimbursed medical expenses	$5,100
Holly's and Zachary's unreimbursed medical expenses	$1,700
Martha's total living expenses, excluding medical	$13,000
State taxes withheld and owed	$2,280
Mortgage interest expense	$6,000
Holly's student loan interest payments	$590
Holly's education expense	$5,450

Questions

1. Are Martha's unreimbursed medical expenses deductible on the Neals' tax return? Why or why not?
2. Is Martha required to file a tax return? Why or why not?
3. What tax advantage(s), attributable to Holly's education expenses, can the Neals include on their return?
4. How much of the total medical expenses will the Neals be able to deduct on their taxes?
5. Can the Neals' IRA contributions be deducted on their tax return? If so, to what extent?
6. Would the Neals benefit from itemizing their deductions? Why?
7. Calculate the Neals' total 2017 tax liability using the method most advantageous to them.
8. Should Zachary have his employer adjust his federal tax withholding amount? Why or why not?

Discussion Case 2

This case is available in **MyLab Finance**.

Austin and Anya Gould are a middle-aged couple with two children—Rusty, age 13, and Sam, age 11—whom they adopted this year. They also bought a new home in the area to give the children a yard in which to play. The Goulds have an extensive retirement portfolio invested primarily in growth-oriented mutual funds. Their annual investment income is only $500, none of which is attributable to capital gains. Austin works in the banking industry and receives an annual income of $32,500. Anya, who owns the only travel agency in town, makes about $40,000 a year.

The Goulds give extensively to charities. They also have tax deductions from their mortgage interest expense, business expenses, tax expenses, and unreimbursed medical expenses, as follows:

Health insurance (provided by Anya)	$2,200
Rusty's braces	$1,500
Mortgage interest expense	$7,200
Real estate taxes	$900
Investment and tax planning expenses	$1,450

Other medical expenses	$3,600
Charitable contributions	$3,500
Moving expenses	$3,000
Austin's unreimbursed business expenses	$2,300
Qualified adoption expenses	$6,700
State taxes withheld and owed	$4,000

Remember that Anya has some special tax expense deductions because she is self-employed. Be sure to include them when estimating their 2017 taxes.

Questions

1. Calculate Anya's Social Security and Medicare taxes. Calculate how much of these taxes are deductible.
2. Calculate the Goulds' total income and adjusted gross income for the year.
3. Are the moving expenses deductible? Why or why not?
4. Should the Goulds take the standard deduction or should they itemize? What is the amount of their deduction?
5. What tax form will the Goulds use? Why?
6. What credits might the Goulds use to reduce their tax liability?

Continuing Case: Cory and Tisha Dumont

PART I: Financial Planning

The objective of the Continuing Case is to help you synthesize and integrate the various financial planning concepts you have been learning. The case will help you apply your knowledge of constructing financial statements, assessing financial data and resources, calculating taxes, measuring risk exposures, creating specific financial plans for accumulating assets, and analyzing strengths and weaknesses in financial situations.

At the end of each book part, you'll be asked to help Cory and Tisha Dumont answer their personal finance questions. By the end of the book, you'll know more about Cory and Tisha than you can imagine. Who knows—maybe you have encountered, or will encounter, the same issues that the Dumonts face. After helping the Dumonts answer their questions, perhaps you will be better equipped to achieve your own financial goals!

Background

Cory and Tisha Dumont recently read an article on personal financial planning in *Money*. The article discussed common financial dilemmas that families face throughout the life cycle. After reading the article, Cory and Tisha realized they have a lot to learn. They are considering enrolling in a personal finance course at their local university but feel they need more urgent help right now. Based on record-keeping suggestions in the *Money* article, Cory and Tisha have put together the following information to help you answer their personal finance questions.

1. *Family:* Cory and Tisha met in college when they were in their early 20s. They continued to date after graduation, and 6 years ago they got married. Cory is 31 years old. Tisha is 30 years old. Their son, Chad, just turned 4 years old, and their daughter, Haley, is 2 years old. They also have a very fat tabby cat named Ms. Cat.
2. *Employment:* Cory works as a store manager and makes $45,000 a year. Tisha works as an accountant and earns $53,000 a year.

3. *Housing:* The Dumonts currently rent a three-bedroom townhome for $2,000 per month, but they hope to buy a house. Tisha indicated that she would like to purchase a home within the next 3 to 5 years. The Dumonts are well on their way to achieving their goal. They opted for a small wedding and applied all gifts and family contributions to a market index mutual fund for their "dream" house. When they last checked, the fund account had a balance of $13,000.

Financial Concerns

1. *Taxes:* Cory and Tisha have been surprised at the amount of federal, state, Social Security, and Medicare taxes withheld from their pay. They aren't sure if the tax calculations are correct.
2. *Insurance:* They are unsure about the amount of automobile, home, health, and life insurance they need. Up until this point, they have always chosen the lowest premiums without much regard to coverage. They were a little amazed to learn recently that the cash value of Tisha's life insurance policy is only $1,800, although they have paid annual premiums of $720 for several years.
3. *Credit and cash management:* Cory and Tisha are curious about the use of credit. It seems they receive new credit card offers each week that promise a low interest rate and other bonuses. They aren't sure if they should be taking advantage of these offers or keeping their current credit cards. They are often surprised by the amount charged on their monthly credit card statements, and although they make a $100 payment each month, their combined account balances always seem to hover around $1,300. It is common for them to withdraw money from bank ATMs to cover daily expenses, and they usually carry about $100 in cash between them. Even so, it seems they often rely on their credit cards to make ends meet.
4. *Savings:* Cory and Tisha were intrigued by one of the recommendations made in the *Money* article: "Pay yourself first." In fact, it was this statement that prompted the Dumonts to review their finances. They like the concept but are unsure of how to go about implementing such a goal. They currently have a savings account balance of $2,500 that earns 3 percent in annual interest. The bank where they have their checking account requires them to keep a minimum balance of $1,000 in order to earn annual interest of 0.75 percent. Their current checking account balance is $1,800.
5. *College savings:* Cory and Tisha are concerned about college expenses for Chad and Haley, as they have experienced the impact of long-term student loan payments on their own financial situation.
6. *Retirement savings:* Cory and Tisha both know that they participate in a "qualified retirement plan" at work, but they don't know exactly what that means. When you asked for more information, they showed you their statements online, which indicated a current balance of $21,760 in Cory's 401(k) and $19,680 in Tisha's 401(k). They do not currently have an IRA or access to profit-sharing plans. A recent statement from Cory's former employer indicated a value of $2,500 in retirement funds that he left with that company.
7. *Risk:* Cory is quick to point out that he doesn't like financial surprises. Tisha, on the other hand, indicated that she is willing to take financial risks when she thinks the returns are worthwhile.
8. *Estate planning issues:* The Dumonts do not have a will or any other estate planning documents.
9. *Recreation and health:* Cory and Tisha enjoy bicycling and hiking with Chad and Haley. They also enjoy playing golf and have considered joining a golf club that charges a $250 monthly fee. The Dumonts are in good health, although they think that Chad will need glasses and braces in the next few years.

Additional Information

Other Estimated Annual Expenditures:

Food (at home and dining out)	$6,900
Clothing	$3,300
Auto insurance	$2,200
Transportation (use, maintenance, licensing)	$2,400
Dental and health care	$850
Life insurance for Tisha	$720
Medical insurance (pretax employer deduction for a family plan, Tisha)	$3,200
401(k) retirement contribution (pretax employer deduction, Cory)	$2,250
401(k) retirement contribution (pretax employer deduction, Tisha)	$2,650
Renter's insurance	$600
Utilities (electricity, water/sewer, cable/Internet)	$3,900
Entertainment	$2,400
Telecommunications (cell phones)	$1,800
Taxes (federal, state, Medicare, Social Security, employer deduction)	$22,000
Property taxes (auto)	$695
Charitable donations	$2,400
Day care	$10,000
Savings	$1,200
Miscellaneous	$2,400

Other Assets:

- Automobile No. 1

  2-year-old, midsize SUV with a fair market value (FMV) of $14,800

  Amount owed: $12,925 (36 months remaining on the loan)

  Monthly payment: $405
- Automobile No. 2

  4-year-old, 2-door coupe with an FMV of $7,800

  Amount owed: $0
- Household furniture, electronics, and other personal property worth approximately $12,000
- Antique jewelry

  Tisha received this as an inheritance from her grandmother and said that she would never part with it. The jewelry has an estimated value of $19,700.
- When Tisha turned 21, her father gave her 100 shares of the Great Basin Balanced Mutual Fund worth $1,000. Today, the fund is worth $2,300.

Other Consumer Debt:

- Credit card debt (Visa, MasterCard, Discover, American Express, and several store cards)

  $1,300 revolving outstanding balance

  $50 minimum monthly payments (approximate)

  $100 actual monthly payments
- Student loan debt (for Cory)

  $8,200 balance

  $196 monthly payment (48 months remaining on the loan)

  $652 interest payment for 2007

- Furniture company loan
  $5,300 balance
  $210 monthly payment (30 months remaining on the loan)

Questions

WORKSHEET 1

WORKSHEET 5

WORKSHEET 4

1. Identify the stage of the life cycle that best describes Cory and Tisha today. What important financial planning issues characterize this stage?
2. Based on the issues identified in Question 1 and your knowledge of the Dumont household, help Cory and Tisha complete Worksheet 1 to identify their short-term, intermediate-term, and long-term financial goals.
3. Complete a simplified income statement for the Dumonts. (*Hints:* Data are presented both as background material and as listed annual expenses. Use Worksheet 5 as a guide.)
4. Develop a balance sheet for the Dumonts (see Worksheet 4). Do they have a positive or negative net worth?
5. Using information from the income and expense statements and the balance sheet, calculate the following ratios:
   a. Current ratio
   b. Month's living expenses covered ratio
   c. Debt ratio
   d. Long-term debt coverage ratio
   e. Savings ratio
6. Use the information provided by the ratio analysis to assess the Dumonts' financial health. (*Hint*: Use the recommended ratio limits provided in Chapter 2 as guidelines for measuring the Dumonts' financial flexibility and liquidity.) What recommendations would you make to improve their financial health?
7. Do the Dumonts have an emergency fund? Should they? How much would you recommend that they have in an emergency fund?
8. According to the *Money* article that Cory and Tisha read, they can expect to pay about $100,000 in tuition and related college expenses when Chad enters college and even more for Haley. The Dumonts hope that Chad will receive academic scholarships that will reduce their total college costs to about $40,000. Assuming that the Dumonts start a college savings program today and manage to earn 7 percent a year, ignoring taxes, until Chad is 18, how much will they need to save each year? How much will the Dumonts need to save each year if Chad does not receive scholarships? See Chapter 3.
9. How much will the Dumonts need to save each year to accumulate $40,000 for Haley to attend college if they can earn 7 percent on their savings? Assuming that the Dumonts need to accumulate $110,000 to fund all of Haley's college expenses, how much do they need to? See Chapter 3.
10. How much will Tisha's Great Basin Balanced Mutual Fund shares (currently valued at $2,300) be worth when Chad enters college, assuming the fund returns 7 percent after taxes on an annualized basis? How much will the shares be worth when Haley turns 18 years old? What will be the value of the shares when Tisha retires at age 67, assuming a 9 percent after-tax return and no deductions from the account? What has been the actual annualized rate of return for the fund since Tisha received it as a gift? See Chapter 3.
11. Recall that the Dumonts set up a savings fund for a future down payment with gifts and contributions from their wedding. How much will this market index

fund valued at $13,000 be worth in 3, 5, and 7 years if they can earn a current rate of return of 6 percent? How much will the fund be worth in 3, 5, and 7 years if they can obtain an 8 percent rate of return? See Chapter 3.

12. Assuming an 8 percent return for the current year from their market index fund valued at $13,000 and a 15 percent federal marginal tax rate, how much will the Dumonts pay in taxes on their investment, either from their savings or from current income, this year? By how much, after taxes, will their account grow this year? See Chapters 3 and 4.

13. Assuming that Cory does nothing with his 401(k) retirement account from his former employer and that the account grows at a rate of 5 percent annually, how much will Cory have when he retires at 67? If, instead, Cory takes control of the money and invests it in a tax-deferred IRA earning 10 percent annually, how much will he have at age 67? See Chapter 3.

14. Using the income and expense estimates provided by Tisha, calculate the Dumonts' taxable income using the 2017 tax information provided in the text. (*Note*: Ignore unearned taxable income from savings and investments.)

a. Do the Dumonts have enough tax-deductible expenses to itemize deductions?

b. Explain the tax ramifications of Cory's student loan interest, estimated to be $652 for 2017.

c. How much Social Security and Medicare taxes are withheld from Cory's and Tisha's income?

d. What is the Dumonts' total federal income tax liability?

e. Do the Dumonts qualify for the child tax credit? If so, how will it affect their federal income tax liability? How will a payment or refund be determined?

15. Based on the total Social Security tax, Medicare tax, and federal income tax liabilities calculated above, how close did Tisha come in estimating their tax liability? How does the difference between the estimated and actual tax liabilities change their financial situation? What recommendations would you make?

16. Calculate and interpret for Cory and Tisha the differences among their marginal tax rate, average tax rate, and effective marginal tax rate. How might these rates change with life events, such as salary increases or the purchase of their home?

PART 2 Managing Your Money

Now that you have an understanding of the financial planning process, it is time to turn to managing your money. This involves making sure not only that you have adequate liquidity but also that your borrowing habits don't keep you from meeting your personal financial goals and that when you spend money, you do it wisely.

Part 2 begins with an examination of cash and liquidity management with the goal of understanding how to manage your liquid funds effectively. We will then take a look at student loans and the use of credit cards and consumer loans. As you may already know, there may not be more dangerous treats to your financial well-being than student loans and credit cards. We will also look at what determines your credit score and how to keep it in good shape. Finally, we will look at smart ways to spend your money, specifically focusing on two of the biggest purchases you will ever make—your car and your home.

In Part 2, we will concentrate on Principles 5 and 6:

Principle 5: Stuff Happens, or the Importance of Liquidity—While much of personal financial planning focuses on achieving lifetime goals, it is impossible to reach those goals if you aren't prepared for the unexpected, such as the untimely death of a car, the loss of a job, or an injury.

Principle 6: Waste Not, Want Not—Smart Spending Matters—Planning your personal finances and managing your money involve more than just saving and investing; they also involve spending—specifically, smart spending. Money isn't easy to come by, so you don't want to waste it.

In addition, we will touch on these principles:

Principle 1: The Best Protection Is Knowledge

Principle 3: The Time Value of Money

Principle 8: Risk and Return Go Hand in Hand

Principle 9: Mind Games, Your Financial Personality, and Your Money

Principle 10: Just Do It!

CHAPTER 5 Cash or Liquid Asset Management

Learning Objectives

LO1	**Manage** your cash and understand why you need liquid assets.	**Managing Liquid Assets**
LO2	**Automate** your savings.	**Automating Savings: Pay Yourself First**
LO3	**Choose** from among the different types of financial institutions that provide cash management services.	**Financial Institutions**
LO4	**Compare** the various cash management alternatives.	**Cash Management Alternatives**
LO5	**Compare** rates on the different liquid investment alternatives.	**Comparing Cash Management Alternatives**
LO6	**Establish** and use a checking account.	**Establishing and Using a Checking Account**
LO7	**Transfer** funds electronically and understand how electronic funds transfers (EFTs) work.	**Electronic Funds Transfers**

"I love television, because it's more than entertainment; it's education!" Those are the words of Neil Patrick Harris (Barney Stinson in *How I Met Your Mother*), host of the 65th Emmy Awards, and some of those educational lessons involve personal finance.

There are times when you need money quickly: The car you depend on to get to school and work needs new brakes (that could easily cost between

$300 and $500); the water heater springs a leak (you will need to come up with $1,200 or settle on cold showers); and if you are Haley Dunphy, the eldest daughter of Claire and Phil of *Modern Family*, something might have "just gone wrong," and you desperately need $900. So where do you go when you need money quickly? For Haley, the answer is to your siblings. After being turned down by sister Alex, Haley tries Luke, her younger brother, and much to her surprise, he has quite a stash of money—"I've saved $1,217. It wasn't even hard." He's been skimming money from his parents for years, getting lunch money from both his father and his mother, and of course, he's taken good care of it.

Eric Liebowitz/Disney ABC Television Group/Getty Images

To Haley's pleas for $900, Luke responds, "Look, I'd love to help you out, but I'm not very liquid right now. It's in a block of ice. I got the idea when I heard about rich guys with frozen assets." Since he's "not very liquid right now," he is physically unable to help Haley out.

We all need to keep something set aside in the way of liquid assets. We all need an emergency fund—which you won't really appreciate until you have to use it. Planning for the unexpected—that's the whole idea behind **Principle 5: Stuff Happens, or the Importance of Liquidity**.

PRINCIPLE 5

Unless you're a psychic, you can't predict the unexpected (it wouldn't be unexpected then, would it?), but you can prepare for it. An emergency fund forms the foundation of your financial plan; it gives you an "out" when there is a financial crisis. It can keep you from having to take on debt. Living without an emergency fund is like walking on a high wire without a safety net—it's just something that smart people don't do. You've got to plan for the unexpected, and as many people recently learned the hard way, as our economy took a dip and people were laid off, had hours cut, or even lost their jobs, the unexpected sometimes happens. That's why one of your first tasks as you start taking responsibility for your financial life is to establish an emergency fund. After all, don't risk financial ruin due to an unforeseen expense—like for Haley, "something might just go wrong." In Haley's case, it was the result of a series of bad decisions: collecting $900 from her friends with the promise of getting everyone a fake ID and then giving the money to a scammer. In the end, it all works out—after all, it's a comedy—and her family comes to her rescue.

Having an emergency fund available is part of good personal financial management, and in this chapter, we discuss how to effectively manage the liquid funds that make up your emergency fund. After all, when you think about it, an emergency fund really is a good idea—you just want to make sure it isn't frozen.

LO1 Manage your cash and understand why you need liquid assets.

Managing Liquid Assets

Cash Management
The management of cash and near cash (liquid) assets.

Liquid Assets
Cash and investments that can easily be converted into cash, such as checking accounts, money market funds, and certificates of deposit (CDs).

Cash management is deciding how much to keep in liquid assets and where to keep it. Thirty years ago cash management meant putting your cash in a checking or savings account at a local bank. All banks were pretty much the same, and their services were limited. Today, the situation is very different: Sparked by less regulation and increased competition, banks and other financial institutions offer an array of account types and investments. To understand the underlying logic of modern cash management and, thus, learn how to manage your **liquid assets**, you need to understand the differences in financial institutions, their products, and their services.

Cash management means not only making choices among all the alternatives but also maintaining and managing the results of those choices. Why do you need to keep some of your money in liquid assets? So you can pay your bills and your other normal living expenses, as well as having money to cover unexpected expenses, without having to dip into your long-term investments—that is, so you aren't forced to sell stocks or real estate when you don't want to.

FACTS OF LIFE

One problem with carrying cash is that it's easy to spend and many times you can't even recall where you spent it. According to a recent survey, every year about $2,340 in cash "disappears" from Americans' wallets—they simply lose track of that much spending.

One way to think of liquid assets is as a reservoir, with money moving in as wages are received and moving out as living expenses are paid. In effect, money moves in and out, and an adequate level of liquid assets keeps this reservoir from running dry. Hey, you don't want your liquid assets to evaporate!

PRINCIPLE 8

Just as with everything else in personal finance, there are risk–return trade-offs associated with keeping money in the form of liquid assets—it's **Principle 8: Risk and Return Go Hand in Hand** in action. Because liquid assets can be turned into cash quickly and with no loss, they have little risk associated with them. However, because they have little risk, they don't provide a high return. Simply put, liquid assets are characterized by low risk and low expected return. It's really the low risk that's important in cash management.

There's another type of risk associated with keeping liquid assets: The more cash you have, the more you're tempted to spend. Remember your cash budget from Chapter 2? Well, the easiest way to blow your budget is by walking around a mall with your debit card in your wallet or a pocketful of cash. Don't worry, though—even if you lack self-restraint, cash management can help. You see, cash management doesn't just involve deciding where to keep your cash; it also involves managing your money and staying on your budget.

LO2 Automate your savings.

Automating Savings: Pay Yourself First

PRINCIPLE 10

You can easily use cash management alternatives to automate your savings by having income automatically deducted from your paycheck and placed into savings. It all boils down to paying yourself first. As **Principle 10: Just Do It!** points out, if you don't start, it won't happen. Automating your savings is a great way to make saving less of a chore, and you're less likely to spend money if it never becomes part of your liquid assets reservoir. If you have some of your income automatically deducted from your paycheck and placed in savings, you can learn to live within your budget.

Moreover, as you know from **Principle 3: The Time Value of Money**, the earlier you start, the easier it is to achieve your goals. Don't put off financial discipline until you're "making more money"—start today.

PRINCIPLE 3

Many cash management alternatives lend themselves well to an automated deposit program, and we'll take a look at several of them in this chapter. The advantage of the automated payroll deduction plan is that not only is the money withdrawn from your pay before you get a chance to think about spending it, but also it's immediately deposited in an account to earn interest. Thus, your money is immediately put to work.

If you're looking for a little help in making all this work, take a look at the apps Qapital and Digit. Both of these apps use mobile technology to make saving for goals not only automatic and easy but also relatively painless. For example, with Qapital you can set up a saving rule that tells the app to save $4 every time you buy a latte. That kind of rule can both help you save and, since it essentially doubles the price of a latte, help you cut down on those daily extravagances that you probably don't need.

Financial Institutions

LO3 Choose from among the different types of financial institutions that provide cash management services.

Before we examine the different types of liquid asset accounts, let's take a look at the financial institutions that offer them. As we mentioned earlier, the differences between a traditional bank and other types of financial institutions have narrowed dramatically in the last few decades. Although it's sometimes difficult to differentiate between types of financial institutions, they can be categorized as **deposit-type financial institutions**, which are commonly referred to as "banks," or **nondeposit-type financial institutions**, such as mutual funds and stockbrokerage firms. But as you'll see, the distinction between these institutions can be a bit arbitrary.

Deposit-Type Financial Institutions
Financial institutions that provide traditional checking and savings accounts. Commonly referred to as "banks."

Nondeposit-Type Financial Institutions
Financial institutions, such as mutual funds and stockbrokerage firms, that don't provide checking and savings accounts.

"Banks" or Deposit-Type Financial Institutions

Financial institutions that provide traditional checking and savings accounts are commonly called "banks" or deposit-type financial institutions. Technically, many of these institutions aren't actually banks but are, in fact, other types of financial institutions that act very similarly to banks. Table 5.1 provides a summary of the different deposit-type financial institutions.

Nondeposit-Type Financial Institutions

Today, mutual fund companies, stockbrokerage firms, insurance companies, and some other firms have moved into what used to be banking territory and have begun offering services that look an awful lot like those offered by banks. For example, you can have a checking account with Merrill Lynch and a home mortgage with General Electric. This banking competition from outside the traditional banking industry is a relatively recent occurrence, with its roots in the deregulation of the 1980s. However, the competition has been a two-way street. While the deregulation has allowed brokerage firms to offer traditional banking services, it has also let banks offer services traditionally found only at investment companies. Table 5.2 provides a summary of different nondeposit-type financial institutions.

TABLE 5.1 "Banks" or Deposit-Type Financial Institutions

Commercial Banks	These offer the widest variety of financial services, including checking and savings accounts, credit cards, safety-deposit boxes, financial consulting, and all types of lending services. They also dominate in terms of the dollar value of the assets they hold, and they have more branch offices or locations than any other type of financial institution. In addition, they tend to have neighborhood locations, which allow for personal relationships.
Savings and Loan Associations (S&Ls or "thrifts")	S&Ls were originally established to provide mortgage loans to depositors; today, services offered by S&Ls and commercial banks have become very similar, with both offering almost identical savings alternatives. However, S&L accounts often earn one-quarter percent more interest than savings accounts at competing commercial banks.
Savings Banks	Savings banks are close cousins to S&Ls and are generally found in the northeastern United States. Their primary purpose historically has been to provide mortgage funding to their depositors.
Credit Unions	Credit unions are established by a wide variety of organizations such as churches, universities, trade unions, and corporations. They are open only to members of that organization and are quite similar to commercial banks and S&Ls. Because of their tax-exempt status as not-for-profit organizations, they are generally more efficient, often pay higher interest rates, have lower fees, and have more favorable loan rates than commercial banks.

Online and Mobile Banking

Online and Mobile Banking
The ability to perform banking operations through your personal computer, mobile phone, or other online device.

Online and mobile banking—the ability to access your accounts and conduct business transactions through the Internet, a mobile phone, or some other online device—is a service offered by banks, S&Ls, credit unions, and other financial institutions. With online and mobile banking, you may be able to:

- Access your accounts at any time of day.
- Check your balances and see when checks have cleared and when deposits have been made.
- Transfer funds between accounts.
- Download your financial information directly into your personal finance or tax software.
- Pay bills and receive payments online.

Online and mobile banking also allows you to choose an Internet-only bank if you wish. An Internet-only bank is one that does not have physical branches, and as

TABLE 5.2 Nondeposit-Type Financial Institutions

Mutual Funds	A mutual fund is an investment fund that raises money from investors, pools that money, and invests it in a collection of stocks and/or bonds that is managed by a professional investment manager. Mutual funds earn dividends on stocks and interest on bonds, and they pay out this income to the fund owners in distributions.
Stockbrokerage Firms	Stockbrokerage firms that have traditionally dealt only with investments such as stocks (hence, their name) have recently introduced a wide variety of cash management tools, including financial counseling, credit cards, and their own money market mutual funds (which we'll talk about later). In effect, they've entered into direct competition with traditional banks.

TABLE 5.3 Online and Mobile Banking

Advantages of Online and Mobile Banking
• **Personal financial management support:** You can import data into a personal finance program such as Mint.com, Quicken, or TurboTax. • **Convenience:** You can view and track your accounts, pay bills, and view up-to-the-minute credit card activity anytime, from anywhere. • **Efficiency:** You can access and manage all of your bank accounts, including individual retirement accounts, CDs, and even securities, from one secure site and transfer funds between your checking and savings accounts or to another customer's account. • **Effectiveness:** Many online and mobile banking sites provide stock quotes, rate alerts, and personal financial management support that allows you to import data into a personal finance program such as Mint.com.
Disadvantages of Online and Mobile Banking
• **Start-up time:** It takes time and some effort to register for your bank's online and mobile program. If you are setting up an account together with a spouse, you may have to sign a durable power of attorney before the bank will display all of your holdings together. • **Adapting to online and mobile banking:** Banking sites can be difficult to navigate at first, so expect to spend some time working through the tutorial. In addition, these sites periodically change, which may require reentering data. • **Feeling comfortable:** Many people just don't feel comfortable banking online, and regardless of how comfortable you feel, you should always print the transaction receipt and keep it with your bank records until it shows up on your bank statement. • **Customer service:** The potential for poor customer service is a downside to online and mobile banking.

a result, you can access it only through the Internet. Because of the cost savings that Internet-only banks experience, many times they provide higher interest rates and lower fees than traditional banks. Table 5.3 lists the advantages and disadvantages of online banking.

> **FACTS OF LIFE**
>
> According to a late 2016 Gallup poll, individuals are almost evenly split between brick-and-mortar branch offices offering telephone contact (47%) and Web site or mobile apps (50%) as the preferred method for interacting with financial institutions, with younger Americans having a preference for Web site or mobile apps.

What to Look for in a Financial Institution

So how do you choose among all these alternatives? Well, in order to know, you need answers to these questions:

- Which financial institution offers the kind of services you want and need? Let's say you want to open a checking account and a money market account and you need a $5,000 home equity loan. Look to institutions that offer these products.
- Is your investment safe? Is your investment insured? Is this financial institution sound?
- What are all the costs and returns associated with the services you want? Find out whether there are minimum deposit requirements or hidden fees. Look for the lowest costs and highest returns.

Once you've answered these questions, look at the personal service offered. You want a financial institution that will work for you—one where you can talk to and get to know the manager. The more personal the relationship you have with your financial institution, the more you'll be able to adapt its services to your needs, and the better you'll feel about your investment. Also consider convenience. You want an institution with a convenient location and convenient hours.

Finally, there's no reason why you should limit yourself to one institution. In fact, financial institutions have different strengths and offer different services at different costs. Feel free to mix and match to take advantage of their different strengths and rates and to get the best and most appropriate services you can.

LO4 Compare the various cash management alternatives.

Cash Management Alternatives

Now that we know what kinds of financial institutions exist, let's take a look at the cash management alternatives they offer.

Checking Accounts

A checking account is a federally protected account in which you deposit your liquid funds so you can withdraw them quickly and easily by means of a written check or debit card.

Advantages:
Liquid
Safe—federally insured
Low minimum balance
Convenient

Many people use checking accounts as a convenient way of paying bills, which is so much better than carrying around a wad of cash or, worse yet, putting that cash in the mail! Checking accounts are easy to open, often requiring a low minimum balance. In deciding among the available types of checking accounts, it may seem as though there are countless choices, but really there are just two basic types: interest bearing and non-interest bearing. A non-interest-bearing checking account is actually a **demand deposit account**. Usually, with a demand deposit account the customer pays for the checking privilege by maintaining a minimum balance or being charged per check.

Demand Deposit Account A type of checking account that pays no interest on your balance.

As you can guess from the name, an interest-bearing checking account pays interest. Another name for an interest-bearing checking account is a **NOW (negotiable order of withdrawal) account**. NOW accounts are simply checking accounts on which you earn interest on your balance.

NOW (Negotiable Order of Withdrawal) Account A checking account that pays interest on your balance.

Everyone knows that an account that pays interest is more desirable from a financial standpoint than an account that doesn't pay interest, right? Not necessarily.

Disadvantages:
Opportunity cost —minimum balance required
Monthly fee charged if monthly balance is not met
Interest bearing accounts pay less than some other alternatives and non-interest-bearing accounts do not pay interest

Receiving interest on your "money in waiting" is good, but read the fine print. If you must maintain a minimum balance and you happen to dip below it, you might not earn any interest for that month, and you might even have to pay a penalty in addition to your monthly fee.

The monthly fee, of course, represents a cost, but so does the minimum balance, which forces you to hold more money in your checking account than you otherwise would. This is called the forced balance, and it represents what we call the opportunity cost, or the cost of something in terms of the opportunity you forgo to have it. In this case, you could use that minimum balance to pay down your school loan or to take a trip to the Bahamas.

Even though an interest-bearing checking account pays interest, it generally pays less than other cash management alternatives, which we will discuss shortly. Given this and the additional costs, an interest-bearing checking account is not always preferable.

Because a checking account is one of the most important liquid assets you'll ever have, we take a much closer look at the mechanics of opening one later in this chapter.

Savings Accounts

A **savings account** allows you to keep your money in a safe, federally insured financial institution while it earns a guaranteed fixed return or interest.

Savings Account
A time deposit account that pays interest.

Advantages:

Liquid
Safe—federally insured
Earns higher interest than a checking account

A savings account is extremely liquid and gives you relatively quick access to your money. It is also very easy to set up and maintain your account. In the past, withdrawals and other transactions would have been registered in a passbook, which is why many savings accounts used to be called "passbook" accounts. Today, although passbook accounts still exist, statement accounts—where the customer receives a monthly statement of the account's balance and activities—are replacing passbook accounts as the dominant type of savings account.

Disadvantages:

Minimum holding time and/or balance
Charges/fees
Low interest rate

A savings account is also called a time deposit because you may be required to keep your money deposited for a minimum time period before you can withdraw it. There may be charges if your account dips below a certain balance, and there may even be fees charged for inquiries on an account balance. Because savings accounts are extremely liquid, they don't have a high yield.

Money Market Deposit Accounts

A **money market deposit account (MMDA)** is an alternative to the savings accounts offered by commercial banks. It works about the same way a savings account works—you deposit your money in a bank and have access to it through an ATM or by writing a limited number of checks.

Money Market Deposit Account (MMDA)
A bank account that pays a rate of interest that varies with the current market rate of interest.

Advantages:

Safe—federally insured
Earns interest
Check-writing privileges

With an MMDA, you receive a rate of interest that varies with the current market rate of interest, but it is not a guaranteed fixed rate. The primary advantage of an MMDA over a savings account is that although this rate fluctuates on a weekly basis, it is, in general, higher than the fixed rate paid on savings accounts. In addition, some MMDAs offer a limited check-writing service, generally five or six checks per month.

STOP & THINK

You shouldn't be enticed to put your savings in an MMDA just because it pays a bit more than a standard savings account. You must also look carefully at the minimum required balance. Many times, this minimum balance forces you to keep more in the MMDA than you would otherwise. If you have an MMDA, what is the minimum balance?

Disadvantages:

High minimum balance/penalties
Interest rates below alternatives

When comparing an MMDA to a typical savings account, you might find that it generally requires a higher minimum balance, sometimes as much as $1,000, and imposes penalties if your balance drops below this level. When compared to other investment alternatives such as CDs and mutual funds, which we will look at next, it sometimes pays less interest and suffers from its relative return in addition to the minimum balance required.

Therefore, when considering investing funds in an MMDA, compare all the associated costs with the return, and then compare it to other investment alternatives.

Certificates of Deposit

Certificate of Deposit (CD)
A savings alternative that pays a fixed rate of interest while keeping your funds on deposit for a set period of time that can range from 30 days to several years.

A **certificate of deposit (CD)** is a savings alternative paying a fixed rate of interest while keeping your funds on deposit for a set period of time, which can range from 30 days to several years.

Advantages:

Safe—federally insured
Fixed interest rate (beneficial if interest rates drop)
Convenient—buy through payroll deduction plan

CDs are a good place to hold your money until you want to do something else with it. The longer the time period for which the funds are tied up in the CD, the higher the interest rate paid on the CD. The interest rate is usually fixed, so even if interest rates drop, you still receive the promised rate—unfortunately, that rate has been very low recently, with 1- and 2-year CD rates averaging between 1 and 2 percent in 2017. In addition, the rate your CD earns depends on its size; the larger the deposit in the CD, the higher the interest rate. CDs are for money that you have in hand now and want to keep safe. They are generally considered liquid assets because their maturity lengths are fairly short. Maybe you have money now from your summer job with College Pro Painters that you plan to use for *next* year's tuition. A CD will hold that money out of temptation's way and return more than will a general savings account.

Disadvantages:

Penalty for early withdrawal
Fixed interest rate (bad if interest rates rise)
Minimum deposit required

With a CD, one of the trade-offs is loss of liquidity versus higher return. If you need your money before the CD matures or comes due, you may face an early withdrawal penalty. Knowing how much money you will receive at maturity is generally a good thing, but if you lock in a low rate, as you would have in 2017, and then interest rates rise, the interest you receive on your CD stays fixed at its lower rate.

The rate you can earn on a CD varies from bank to bank and between banks and other institutions that offer them, such as brokerage firms. To research rates offered by institutions both inside and outside your local area, try BankRate.com (**http://www.bankrate.com**), where you can find the best rates in the country. Purchasing a CD from a financial institution in another geographic region usually entails simply wiring or mailing your funds to the target bank, and sometimes your local bank will match those rates found elsewhere.

Money Market Mutual Funds

Money Market Mutual Fund (MMMF)
A mutual fund that invests in short-term (generally with a maturity of less than 90 days) notes of very high denomination.

Money market mutual funds (MMMFs) provide an interesting alternative to traditional liquid investments offered by financial institutions. Investors in MMMFs receive interest on a pool of investments less an administrative fee. An MMMF draws together the savings of many individuals and invests those funds in very large, creditworthy debt issued by the government or by large corporations.

Advantages:

Relatively high interest rates
Check-writing privileges
Limited risk due to short maturity of investments
Convenient—buy through payroll deduction plan

By pooling investments, investors can purchase higher-priced investments and, thus, earn a higher rate of return than they could get individually. MMMFs almost always have a higher yield than do bank money market deposit accounts or traditional savings accounts.

The interest rate earned on an MMMF varies daily as interest rates change. Exactly how much more they yield than MMDAs depends, of course, on the level of interest rates—which in 2017, although rising, were quite low, averaging less than 1 percent. One nice feature of MMMFs is that they allow limited check-writing privileges, although there's generally a minimum amount for which the check must be written. However, in an attempt to lure funds away from bank checking accounts, many MMMFs have lifted limits on both the number of checks written and the check amounts.

Disadvantages:

Administrative fees
Minimum initial investment
Not federally insured
Minimum check amount (maybe)

For most MMMFs, there is a minimum initial investment of between \$500 and \$2,000, after which there may be a minimum level for subsequent deposits. Remember, too, that they carry administrative costs. Although MMMFs are not perfect substitutes for checking accounts, they do provide an attractive place to put excess funds awaiting more permanent investment.

FACTS OF LIFE

According to a recent survey, 48 percent of Americans suffer from "mystery spending"—that is, they can't identify where they spend cash. Seven percent of those surveyed said they lose track of \$100 or more each month.

Asset Management Accounts

Asset management accounts are comprehensive financial services packages offered by brokerage firms and, recently, by some investment banking institutions. Such a package can include banking services, such as a checking account, credit card, debit card, MMMF, loans, and automatic payment of any fixed debt such as mortgages, and brokerage services, such as buying and selling stocks or bonds and setting up a system for the direct payment of interest, dividends, and proceeds from security sales into the MMMF.

Asset Management Account
A comprehensive financial services package offered by a brokerage firm, which can include a checking account, credit and debit cards, MMMF, loans, automatic payment of fixed payments such as mortgages, brokerage services (buying and selling stocks or bonds), and a system for the direct payment of interest, dividends, and proceeds from security sales into the MMMF.

Advantages:

Monthly summary statements
Automatic coordination of money management
Unlimited check writing
Relatively high return

The parent brokerage firm provides the customer with a monthly statement summarizing all financial activities. The major advantage of an asset management account is that it automatically coordinates the flow of funds into and out of your MMMF. The parent brokerage firm does this with a computer program that "sweeps" funds into and out of the MMMF.

Disadvantages:

Costly—monthly/quarterly fees and commissions
Minimum initial investment
Not federally insured

In addition to monthly, quarterly, or annual service charges of $50 to $125, there is generally a rather large minimum balance required, ranging upward of $10,000 in stocks and cash. Also, brokerage firms charge commissions on any stock transactions they perform. Thus, although the benefits of an asset management account may be great, they come with a fairly steep price *and no guarantee of return*. In short, although these accounts are an interesting alternative cash management tool, you must weigh the service charge, the high minimum balance, and the relatively high commissions on any stock sales against their returns in making your decision.

U.S. Treasury Bills, or T-Bills

U.S. Treasury Bill or T-Bill
A short-term note of debt issued by the federal government, with a maturity ranging from a few days to 12 months.

U.S. Treasury bills, or T-bills, are short-term notes of debt issued by the federal government, with maturities ranging from a few days to 12 months.

Advantages:

Risk-free—issued by the U.S. Treasury
Exempt from state and local taxes
Federal taxes vary with current rates

Denomination
The face value or amount that's returned to the debtholder at maturity. It's also referred to as the debt's par value.

The minimum **denomination**, or face value, is $1,000. When you purchase a T-bill, you don't receive any interest payment. Instead, your interest comes in the form of appreciation. That is, you pay less than its face value, and when the T-bill matures, you receive its full face value.

With a T-bill, when you need cash, all you do is sell the T-bill through a broker. While this is easy, it is less convenient than going to an ATM or writing a check. T-bills are also extremely safe, having been issued by the federal government. In terms of returns, the interest rates carried on T-bills are similar to those on MMMFs; that is, in 2017 they were quite low, with 12-month rates around 1 percent. In addition, your return, although subject to federal taxes, isn't subject to state or local taxes.

Disadvantage:

Low rate of return because they are risk free

The only negative associated with T-bills is the fact that you won't get a great return because they are exceptionally safe. Generally, CDs and MMMFs will give you a higher rate of interest.

U.S. Savings Bonds

U.S. Savings Bond
A type of security that's actually a loan on which you receive interest, generally every 6 months for the life of the bond. When the bond matures, or comes due, you get back your investment, or "loan." What you get back at maturity is usually the face value of the loan, although the amount you get could be more or less than what you paid for the bond originally.

U.S. Savings Bonds are safe, low-risk savings products issued by the U.S. Treasury. When you buy them, you are making a loan to the federal government. They offer a safe place for your money.

Advantages:

Safe—issued by the U.S. Treasury
Affordable—available in low denominations
Taxes—no state or local taxes; exempt from federal taxes if used for education
Convenient—buy through payroll deduction plan, online, or at most financial institutions
Redeem at any bank
No sales commissions or fees

Series EE and Series I bonds are safe investment vehicles because they are backed by the federal government. They can be purchased for as little as $25, as much as $10,000, or anything in between; for example, you can purchase a Series EE bond for $123.45 if you like. Interest is added to the bond monthly and paid when you cash it in. Savings Bonds have a 12-month minimum holding period (neither series can be cashed in during the first year), and a penalty of the last 3 months' accumulated interest is charged if they are redeemed within 5 years of issue (after that time, there is no penalty). They are exempt from local and state taxes, as well as from federal taxes if they are used for educational purposes. Savings Bonds can be purchased quite easily through **http://www.TreasuryDirect.gov** and never have any commissions or fees.

STOP & THINK

As we saw in the recent economic downturn, one of the mistakes many people made was not having a large enough emergency fund. On the other hand, another common mistake many people make is keeping too much in very liquid assets. They view investments in CDs and MMMFs as "safe." In reality, they're not safe in the sense that they'll have a difficult time keeping pace with inflation, let alone growing in terms of purchasing power. In short, just as too little in liquid assets is dangerous and can be costly when an emergency occurs, too much in liquid assets is dangerous in that you may tie up too much of your savings in low-return investments. As a result, you may not be able to achieve your future goals like retirement. Striking a balance is the key. Why is striking a balance between liquidity and returns so important?

There are a number of differences between EE and I bonds. One difference is that EE bonds pay a fixed interest rate, whereas I bonds grow with inflation-indexed earnings for up to 30 years. They usually increase in value every month, and their interest is compounded semiannually. The I bond earnings rate is set by a combining two separate rates: A fixed rate of return and a semiannual inflation rate are combined to determine the bond's earnings rate for the next 6 months. The only certainty with I bonds is that they will not fall below the most recent redemption value during any 6-month period.

To get the current rates on Series EE and Series I bonds, you can call 800-US-BONDS or check the Web site at **http://www.savingsbond.gov**.

Disadvantages:

Low liquidity—must hold for 12 months; penalty if redeemed before 5 years
Long maturity
Interest compounds only semiannually
Limits on how many you can buy per year
Other investments may earn more

Both Series EE and Series I bonds have features that can make them an attractive investment alternative. But how do they stack up against the other cash management alternatives? In terms of safety, not bad; but in terms of liquidity, not that good. Remember, if you cash them in before maturity, you may receive a reduced return. However, if you're using them to save money for a long-term goal such as your child's college tuition, liquidity is not so important. After all, the money is for college, not for emergencies!

Comparing Cash Management Alternatives

LO5 Compare rates on the different liquid investment alternatives.

Now that you know what cash management alternatives are available to you, how do you compare them to determine what's best for you? First, you consider service and convenience, but then to decide between them, you need to (1) examine returns using comparable interest rates, (2) take into account their tax status, and (3) consider their safety or risk. Table 5.4 provides a summary comparison of the different types of cash management alternatives that we have looked at in this chapter.

TABLE 5.4 Different Cash Management Alternatives

Cash Management Technique	Advantages	Disadvantages
Checking or Demand Deposit Accounts	Liquid Safe—federally insured Low minimum balance Convenient	Minimum balance required Monthly fee Opportunity cost Pays less than some other alternatives for your money
Savings or Time Deposit Accounts	Liquid Safe—federally insured Earns higher interest than a checking account	Minimum holding time and/or balance Charges/fees Low interest rate
Money Market Deposit Accounts	Safe—federally insured Earns interest Check-writing privileges	High minimum balance/penalties Interest rates below alternatives
Certificates of Deposit	Safe—federally insured Fixed interest rate (beneficial if interest rates drop) Convenient—buy through payroll deduction plan	Penalty for early withdrawal Fixed interest rate (bad if interest rates rise) Minimum deposit required
Money Market Mutual Funds	Relatively high interest rates Check-writing privileges Limited risk due to short maturity of investments Convenient—buy through payroll deduction plan	Administrative fees Minimum initial investment Not federally insured Minimum check amount (maybe)
Asset Management Accounts	Monthly summary statements Automatic coordination of money management Unlimited check writing Relatively high return	Costly—monthly/quarterly fees and commissions Minimum initial investment Not federally insured
U.S. Treasury Bills, or T-Bills	Risk-free—issued by the U.S. Treasury Exempt from state and local taxes Federal taxes vary with current rates	Low rate of return because they are risk free
U.S. Savings Bonds	Safe—issued by the U.S. Treasury Affordable—available in low denominations Taxes—no state or local taxes; exempt from federal taxes if used for education Convenient—buy through payroll deduction plan, online, or at most financial institutions Redeem at any bank No sales commissions or fees	Low liquidity—must hold for 12 months; penalty if redeemed before 5 years Long maturity Interest compounds only semiannually Limits on how many you can buy per year Other investments may earn more

Comparable Interest Rates

To make intelligent decisions on where to invest your money, you need to compare interest rates. Unfortunately, comparing interest rates is difficult because some rates are quoted as compounded annually and others are quoted as compounded quarterly or even daily. The only way to logically compare interest rates is to convert them to some common compounding period. That's what the **annual percentage yield (APY)**, also referred to as the equivalent annual rate (EAR), is all about.

Annual Percentage Yield (APY) The amount you earn on an investment in one year, expressed as a percentage. The APY formula converts interest rates compounded for different periods into comparable annual rates, allowing you to easily compare interest rates.

The Truth in Savings Act of 1993 requires financial institutions to report the rate of interest using the APY so that it's easier for the consumer to make comparisons. The APY formula converts interest rates compounded for different periods into comparable annual rates, allowing you to easily compare interest rates. However, make sure that you're comparing APYs and not "quoted rates," which may assume different compounding periods.

Once you understand differences in rates, make sure you understand the method used to determine the account balance on which interest will be paid. Is it your actual balance, your lowest monthly balance, or what? The method that's the best for you, the saver, bases interest on your money from the day you deposit it until the day you withdraw it. Fortunately, this is the method most institutions use, but it's still good to make sure.

STOP & THINK

The idea behind cash management is to keep money, but not too much, set aside in case there is an emergency. The more you keep set aside, the safer you are, but the money you set aside will be lucky to keep pace with inflation. For example, in 2017 the Vanguard Prime Money Market Fund earned 0.45%, and if you were in the 30 percent marginal tax bracket, your after-tax return would have been $0.45\%(1 - 0.30) = 0.315\%$. If inflation was 2 percent, your real return, which is what you would have earned after inflation, would have been $0.315\% - 2.0\% = -1.685\%$. Should you be more concerned with your before- or after-tax real return?

Tax Considerations

As we saw in Chapter 4, taxes can affect the real rate of return on investments. In comparing the returns on cash management investment alternatives, you must also make sure that the rates you compare are all on the same tax basis—that is, that they are all either before- or after-tax calculations. On some investments, part of the return is taxable and part is tax exempt, making these calculations a bit tricky.

As you recall from Chapter 4, calculation of the after-tax return begins with a determination of your marginal tax bracket, the tax rate at which any additional income you receive will be taxed. This marginal tax rate combines the federal and state tax rates that you pay on the investment that you're considering. The **after-tax return** can then be determined as follows:

After-Tax Return
The actual return you earn on taxable investments once taxes have been paid. It is equal to taxable return × (1 − marginal tax rate) + nontaxable return].

$$\text{after-tax return} = \text{taxable return} \times (1 - \text{marginal tax rate}) + \text{nontaxable return}$$

Here's an example: Assume you're considering two MMMFs. For illustrative purposes, let's assume the interest rates on these MMMFs are much higher than they actually were in 2017. Let's assume that Fund A is tax exempt and pays 5 percent and Fund B is taxable and pays 6.5 percent. Further assume that your top tax bracket is 25 percent and you live in a state that doesn't impose income taxes. Which of these two alternatives is better? To compare them, you must put both on an after-tax basis:

MyLab Finance Video

$$\text{Fund A's after-tax return} = 5\%$$

(Remember, its a tax-exempt fund, so its all nontaxable.)

$$\text{Fund B's after-tax return given a 25\% marginal tax bracket} = 6.5\% \times (1 - 0.25) = 4.875\%$$

Thus, given your marginal tax bracket, Fund A, which provides a tax-exempt return of 5 percent, is the better of the two alternatives.

Keep in mind that although Fund A may be the better alternative for you, it's not the best alternative for everyone. For example, the after-tax return on Fund B for a person with a marginal tax rate of 10 percent is:

$$\text{Fund B's after-tax return given a 10\% marginal tax bracket}$$
$$= 6.5\% \times (1 - 0.10) = 5.85\%$$

Thus, the higher your marginal tax bracket, the more you benefit from a tax-exempt investment.

In calculating the after-tax return, keep in mind that you are interested in the return after *both* federal and state taxes are subtracted. When calculating the after-tax return on a Treasury bond, which is taxed at the federal but not the state level, you must adjust for federal taxes. Likewise, when calculating the after-tax return on a municipal bond that is tax exempt at the federal but not the state level, you must adjust for state taxes, but keep in mind that this feature is one that could change as the tax laws evolve.

Safety

You might think that any deposit in any financial institution is safe. Not so. Some banks and S&Ls take more risk than they should. Sometimes that risk catches up with them, and it's your money that's lost. However, some deposits at financial institutions are insured, and some cash management alternatives are safer than others. To understand how safe your investments are, it's necessary to understand how federal insurance works and how MMMFs operate.

Federal Deposit Insurance Corporation (FDIC)
The federal agency that insures deposits at commercial banks and S&Ls.

National Credit Union Association
The federal agency that insures accounts at credit unions.

Federal Deposit Insurance Although most liquid investments are quite safe, federal deposit insurance eliminates any questions and worries you might have about safety. The **Federal Deposit Insurance Corporation (FDIC)** insures deposits at commercial banks and S&Ls, and the **National Credit Union Association** insures accounts at credit unions. These are federal agencies established to protect you against failures involving financial institutions.

Today, if your account is with a federally insured institution, it's insured for up to $250,000 per depositor (not per account). For example, you may have $190,000 in a savings account and $80,000 in a checking account, both in your name at the same institution. Your combined money ($270,000) is insured for only $250,000. However, if one of these accounts is held in your name and one in your spouse's name or if the accounts are in different ownership categories (single accounts, joint accounts, directed retirement accounts, or revocable trust accounts), both are fully insured. If you want more coverage, you can simply spread your accounts among different federally insured banks, and each account at each separate bank receives the $250,000 insurance. This insurance guarantees that you'll get back your money, up to the insured limit, if the financial institution goes bust.

Money Market Mutual Funds Although funds in MMMFs aren't insured, they're invested in a diversified portfolio of government bonds guaranteed by the government and short-term corporate bonds that are virtually risk free. Investment in an MMMF is safe because it is well diversified and investments are limited to very short-term government and corporate debt. Because it takes time for a corporation's problems to become so severe that it defaults on its debt, it's relatively easy to predict whether debt is risky if it has only a 90-day maturity.

Thus, MMMFs are essentially risk free. The only risk they might have would be associated with possible criminal activity on the part of the fund managers. This risk is eliminated through effective monitoring of the fund's activities, which occurs in the larger funds. Investing in a large, high-quality MMMF is largely risk free.

FACTS OF LIFE

American men under the age of 34 are the biggest "mystery spenders"; that is, they can't identify where they spend cash. Their cash mystery spending averages $59 per week, or $3,078 per year, with more than half of them saying their cash tends to disappear most often during a night out.

LO6 Establish and use a checking account.

Establishing and Using a Checking Account

There are a lot of alternatives available for cash management, but it would be almost impossible to function in today's economy without a checking account. Most people write checks to cover the rent, utility bills, and tuition. Carrying cash to cover these sizable bills would be too dangerous—checks are convenient and simple. In fact, each year approximately 60 billion checks are written.

Let's look at how to open and maintain a checking account. Keep in mind that checking accounts can be set up at all types of financial institutions, not just commercial banks.

Choosing a Financial Institution

The first step in opening a checking account is choosing a financial institution. In deciding where to open a checking account, you should consider the three Cs—cost, convenience, and consideration—in addition to the safety of the financial institution. Remember, when opening a checking account, you're also forming a financial relationship with the institution. Thus, you should consider not only cost but also convenience and how comfortable you are with the manager and employees. Checklist 5.1 provides some specific items that make up the three Cs.

The Cost Factor The cost of the account is probably the basic factor in determining what type of account to open and where to open it. If you maintain the required minimum balance, some financial institutions provide you with free checking privileges. This minimum balance can vary dramatically, going all the way up to $10,000. If the minimum isn't maintained, one of a number of alternative fee structures will be imposed. Let's take a moment to examine the fee arrangements for checking accounts.

Monthly Fee With a monthly fee arrangement, you pay a set fee, regardless of your average balance and how many checks you write.

Minimum Balance Under a minimum balance arrangement, your monthly fee depends upon how much cash you maintain in your account. If your average balance exceeds a set level, the monthly fee is waived; if not, you pay the monthly fee. Even if the fee is waived, you still pay the opportunity cost of having your funds tied up in the minimum balance, where they either do not earn interest or earn it at a very low rate.

Charge per Check At some financial institutions, in addition to paying a small fixed monthly fee, there is a charge per check. The trade-off here is that if you don't use many checks, the total cost of this type of account may be considerably less than that of an account with a higher monthly fee and no per-check charge.

Balance-Dependent Scaled Fees Under balance-dependent scaled fees, the fee declines depending on the average balance held. That is, for accounts with small average balances, there is a relatively high monthly fee. However, for accounts with

CHECKLIST 5.1 The Three Cs of Choosing a Financial Institution

Cost
- ☐ Fees
- ☐ Rates
- ☐ Minimum balances
- ☐ Per-check charges

Convenience
- ☐ Location
- ☐ Access to ATMs
- ☐ Availability of safety-deposit boxes
- ☐ Availability of direct deposit services
- ☐ Availability of overdraft protection

Consideration
- ☐ Personal attention provided
- ☐ Financial advice that you are comfortable accessing

Safety—The Final Consideration
- ☐ Federal deposit insurance

Direct Deposit
The depositing of payments, such as payroll checks, directly into your checking account. This is done electronically.

Safety-Deposit Box
A storage unit at a bank or other financial institution in which valuables and important documents are stored for safekeeping.

Overdraft Protection
The provision of an automatic loan to your checking account whenever sufficient funds are not available to cover checks that have been written against the account.

larger average balances, the monthly fee declines, and eventually, it is eliminated for accounts with very large average balances.

The Convenience Factor In addition to low cost, your financial institution should offer services that make it easy to use. Obviously, you want an institution located near your home—the closer you are to the bank and the more ATMs the bank offers, the easier it is to make financial transactions. In addition, safety-deposit boxes, **direct deposit** services, and overdraft protection are other conveniences.

Safety-Deposit Boxes **Safety-deposit boxes** serve as important storage places for financial documents and valuables. Depending on the type of account you have, safety-deposit boxes can be free or cost as little as $25 to $50 per year, with the costs varying by location and increasing as the size of the box increases.

Overdraft Protection **Overdraft protection** is an automatic loan made to your checking account or your bank credit card whenever your account doesn't contain enough cash to cover the checks that you've written against it. Checks drawn against a checking account or credit card with overdraft protection will not bounce. Given the charges for bounced checks and the hassle of dealing with them, you probably want some type of protection—but remember, this is considered a loan with added fees! Is this a good idea when it comes to your debit card? Probably not—so don't "opt in" to debit card overdraft protection. The reason for this is that your bank or credit union can't charge you a fee for an overdraft with your debit card or at an ATM unless you opt in to overdraft coverage for these transactions. Instead, if you don't have that money to spend, your ATM request for money will simply be declined. Table 5.5 provides some more ideas on how to limit your overdraft fees.

FACTS OF LIFE

Overdraft fees are huge—in 2015, totaling $11.6 billion in revenue and accounting for 8% of reporting banks' net income! Moreover, according to a 2015 study from the Pew Charitable Trusts, about half of banks maximize potential overdraft fees by changing the order in which checks and transactions are processed, going from the largest to smallest. Here's how it works. Let's say you have $800 in your checking account and write one check for $800 and eight checks for $100. If the bank processes the $800 check first, all eight $100 checks will bounce, resulting in eight overdraft fees. On the other hand, if the bank processes the eight $100 checks first, then only the $800 check will end up with an overdraft fee. The bottom line here is this: While overdraft protection is great, you don't want to rely on it; instead, keep track of how much money is in your account and don't bounce checks!

TABLE 5.5 How You Can Reduce or Eliminate Overdraft Fees

- **You can opt out of overdraft protection programs anytime.** This means that your debit or ATM card may be declined if you don't have enough money in your account to cover a purchase or ATM withdrawal. However, it also means you won't be charged for these transactions.
- **Link your checking account to a savings account.** If you overdraw your checking account, your bank will take money from your linked savings account to cover the difference. You may be charged a transfer fee when this happens, but it's usually much lower than the fee for an overdraft.
- **Ask your financial institution if you're eligible for a line of credit or linked credit card to cover overdrafts.** You may have to pay a fee when the credit line is tapped, and you will owe interest on the amount you borrowed, but this is still a much cheaper way to cover a brief cash shortfall.
- **Track your balance as carefully as you can, and sign up for low-balance alerts to let you know when you're at risk of overdrawing your account.** If you have regular electronic transfers, such as rent, mortgage payments, or utility bills, make sure you know how much they are and on what day they occur. You also need to know when the funds you have deposited become available for your use.
- **Shop around for a different account.** Get a copy of your bank or credit union's list of account fees, or ask about them, and then compare them with account fees at other banks or credit unions. Assess your habits honestly, and consider penalty fees, such as overdraft and non-sufficient funds charges, as well as monthly maintenance, ATM surcharge, and other service fees. When comparing banks or credit unions, also consider factors such as the hours of operation, locations, access to public transportation, available products and services, and reputation for customer service.

Source: Consumer advisory: You've got options when it comes to overdraft by Dan Rutherford, APR 28, 2015. Published by Consumer Financial Protection Bureau. http://www.consumerfinance.gov/about-us/blog/consumer-advisory-youve-got-options-when-it-comes-to-overdraft/, accessed December 14, 2016.

Another convenience is the ability to **stop payment** on a check. If you want to cancel a check you've already written, you can go online or call your financial institution and ask that payment on this check be stopped. You'll generally have to follow up with a written authorization, and the service involves a cost of between $5 and $20.

Stop Payment
An order you can give your financial institution to stop payment on a check you've written.

The Consideration Factor In choosing a financial institution, you want one that gives personal attention. If you have a problem, you want to feel comfortable in approaching a teller with it. And in case you need financial advice, you want a knowledgeable, approachable person at your branch. Although ATMs are extremely convenient, they don't answer questions, correct whatever's wrong, or work with you when you need a loan.

Balancing Your Checking Account

Anyone who's ever tried to build anything with blocks knows that unbalanced objects tend to fall over. Checking accounts can be the same way. If the records you keep in your check register produce the same numbers that appear in your statement or online, your checking account is balanced. If not, well, you'd better hope that you have overdraft protection. Although it's not essential that your checking account be perfectly balanced at all times, you're a lot less likely to accidentally bounce a check if your account is balanced.

The basics of balancing a checkbook are relatively simple. First, keep track of every transaction—every check you write, every deposit, every ATM transaction—and enter it in your check register. Obviously, if you don't keep track of the checks you've written and the ATM withdrawals you've made, you can't balance your checkbook. Then, when your monthly statement arrives, compare it to your check register to make sure that no mistakes have been made. Your checks clear electronically, which means fast, and you will receive an electronic image of your cancelled check or simply a notation of it in your checking account statement. This means that when you write a check, you have to make sure you have enough money in your account to cover that check on the day you write it, not on the day you *think* it will clear your bank. If you've received interest on your account or incurred any bank charges, enter them. Then reconcile your register balance with the statement balance.

By reconciling your register balance with the monthly statement you receive from the bank, you can locate any errors you or the bank has made. Figures 5.1 and 5.2 show you how to balance a checking account. Many banks provide a reconciliation form on the back of the monthly statement. To determine your balance, begin with the ending statement balance shown on your monthly statement. To this, you add any deposits or credits you've made since the statement date. Then you subtract any outstanding checks or debits issued by you but not yet paid as of the date of the statement. The difference should be the ending balance on your current statement. If this number doesn't agree with the account register balance, check your math, and make sure that all transactions are correct and entered into your register.

Other Types of Checks

If the price of something you wish to purchase is very large or you are buying abroad, a personal check isn't an acceptable form of payment. After all, what guarantee do sellers have that you've got enough money in your account to cover the check? In that case, you can guarantee payment through the use of a cashier's check, a certified check, a money order, or a traveler's check.

Cashier's Check A **cashier's check** is a check drawn on the bank's or financial institution's account. People with no checking account can use these checks. Because it's

Cashier's Check
A check drawn on a bank's or financial institution's account.

FIGURE 5.1 Worksheet for Balancing Your Checking Account

1. Record in your check register all items that appear on the monthly statement received from the bank that have not previously been entered—for example, cash withdrawals from an ATM, automatic transfers, service charges, and any other transactions.
2. In your checking account register, check off any deposits or credits and checks or debits shown on the monthly statement.
3. In Section A: Deposits and Credits below, list any deposits that have been made since the date of the statement.

Section A: Deposits and Credits

Date	**Amount**
1.	
2.	
3.	
4.	
5.	
Total Amount:	________

Section B: Outstanding Checks and Debits

Check Number	**Amount**
1.	
2.	
3.	
4.	
5.	
Total Amount:	________

4. In Section B: Outstanding Checks and Debits above, list any checks and debits issued by you that have not yet been reported on your account statement.
5. Write in the ending statement balance provided in the monthly statement that you received from your bank. .... ________
6. Write in the total amount of the deposits and credits you have made since the statement date (total of Section A above). .... + ________
7. Total the amounts in lines 5 and 6. .... = ________
8. Write in the total amounts of outstanding checks and debits (total of Section B above). .... – ________
9. Subtract the amount in line 8 from the amount in line 7. This is your **adjusted statement balance.** .... = ________

If your adjusted statement balance as calculated above does not agree with your account register balance:

A. Review last month's reconcilement to make sure any differences were corrected.
B. Check to make sure that all deposits, interest earned, and service charges shown on the monthly statement from your bank are included in your account register.
C. Check your addition and subtraction in both your account register and in this month's checking account balance reconcilement above.

FIGURE 5.2 Balancing Your Checking Account

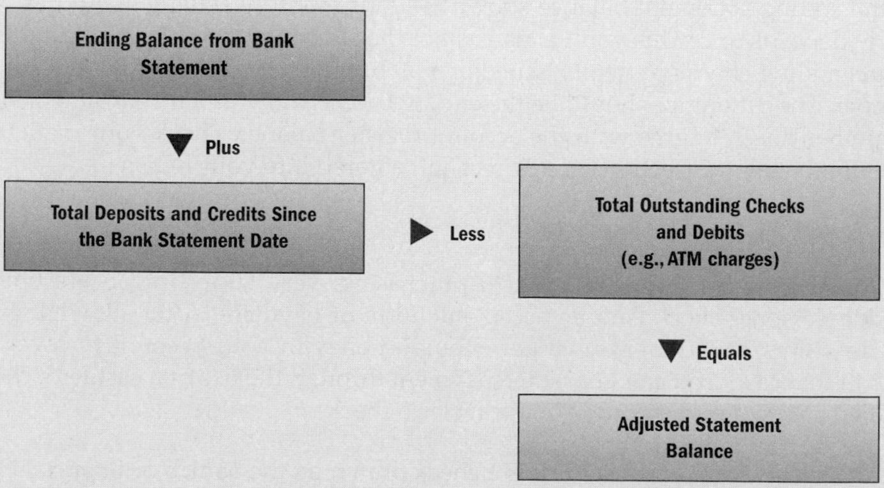

really a check from a bank, it can bounce only if the bank doesn't have funds to cover it—which isn't too likely. A cashier's check usually costs you a fee of around $10, as well as the amount of the check. The bank then writes a check from its own account to a specific payee.

LOVE & MONEY

Once you are living together with someone in a permanent relationship, one of the first money decisions you'll be faced with is how to handle your basic finances—more specifically, how to pay the everyday joint bills. And that raises the checkbook question: Should all earnings be merged into one account, or should you have two or three accounts, one for each of you along with a joint account?

According to a recent TD Ameritrade survey, over half of couples (58%) have at least one bank account that they share with their partner, while 24 percent have only separate accounts. Looking at those respondents in the 18–32 age group, the share of couples who have only separate accounts climbs to 32 percent. Unfortunately, there isn't one way of combining a couple's money that is necessarily right for everyone, but regardless of how you approach this question, you'll need to find a way to share and keep track of all of your financial information.

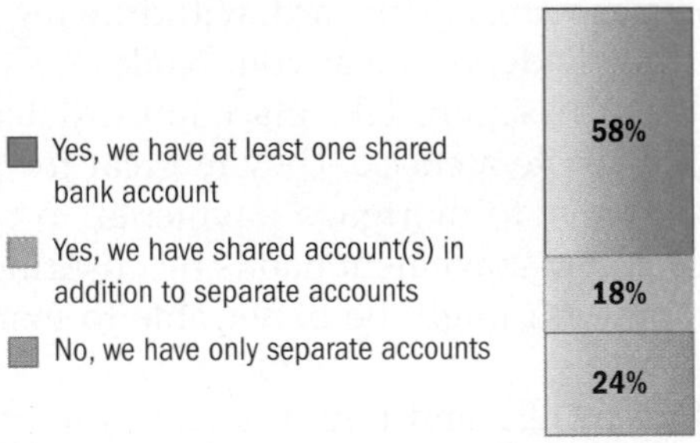

How you decide to handle your finances is totally up to you as a couple, but the bottom line is that whatever you do, you've got to be in agreement and make sure you are both on the same page. So where should you start? The argument for each of you having a small amount of money that you have separate control over coupled with a primary or joint account that you share is that such a setup may not only help to avoid conflicts when the partners have different likes and dislikes but also put more meaning into gift giving—adding a bit of self-sacrifice to any gift, as it would come out of your smaller, separate account. Also, giving each partner some separate money that he or she alone controls may help keep one partner from dominating the relationship financially. Under this arrangement, the joint account would be used for everyday items that are fundamental and shared like rent, insurance, utilities, taxes, food, and savings, and the smaller separate accounts would be used for personal spending.

On the other hand, some argue that combining all finances into one account may help you work together as a financial team and be more open with each other about how you are spending money. But keep in mind when making this decision that research has found couples are happiest when they have some discretionary money in addition to having a joint account for essentials.

Regardless of which approach you take, it will be successful only if you work together when creating your budget and funding your accounts, and that involves having "How should we handle our money?" conversations. You should have them early and often to make sure you are still on the same page, especially as life circumstances change with, for example, the loss of a job, a return to school, the purchase of a house, or the arrival of a baby. And if you decide to go with a joint account, while one person may manage that account, you both need to set aside a block of time to go over your monthly statements to understand where the money is going. Along with all of this, you will also want to make sure that you are saving for your financial goals, both short- and long-term; that you both understand their importance; and that you make their funding automatic.

While this doesn't sound too difficult, money discussions can be very emotional and can sometimes feel very personal. Remember that studies have shown that arguments about money are by far the top predictor of divorce![1] It's not usually the lack of adequate amounts of money but the lack of the ability to talk about it—especially if you are not on the same page!

[1] J. Dew, S. Britt, and S. Huston, "Examining the Relationship Between Financial Issues and Divorce," *Family Relations* 61, no. 4 (2012): 615–628.

Certified Check
A personal check that's been certified as being good by the financial institution on which it's drawn.

Certified Check A **certified check** is a personal check that has been certified as being good by the financial institution on which it's drawn. To certify a check, the bank first makes sure there are sufficient funds in the individual's account to cover the check. The bank then immediately freezes funds equal to the amount of the check and certifies the check. The cost for this service generally runs around $10 per certified check.

Money Order
A check similar to a cashier's check except that it is generally issued by the U.S. Postal Service or some other nonbanking institution.

Money Order A **money order** is a variation of the cashier's check, except that the U.S. Postal Service or one of many other nonbanking institutions generally issues it. For example, money orders can be purchased at many 7-Eleven stores! The fee associated with a money order generally varies, depending on the size of the money order.

Traveler's Checks
Checks issued by large financial institutions, such as Citibank, Visa, and American Express, that are sold through local banking institutions and are similar to cashier's checks except that they don't specify a specific payee and they come in specific denominations ($20, $50, and $100).

Traveler's Checks **Traveler's checks** are similar to cashier's checks except that they don't name a specific payee and they come in specific denominations ($20, $50, and $100). They're issued by large financial institutions, such as Citibank, Visa, and American Express, and are sold through local banking institutions. The advantage of traveler's checks is that they're accepted almost anywhere in the world because they are viewed as riskless checks. Also, if lost or stolen, they're generally replaced quickly, without charge. The cost to purchase traveler's checks is generally 1 percent. Thus, $500 worth of traveler's checks would carry a $5 purchase fee. However, given the increased acceptance of credit and debt cards coupled with the availability of ATMs across the world, the use of traveler's checks has dropped sharply.

LO7 Transfer funds electronically and understand how electronic funds transfers (EFTs) work.

Electronic Funds Transfers

Electronic Funds Transfer (EFT)
Any financial transaction that takes place electronically.

Electronic funds transfer (EFT), which refers to any financial transaction that takes place electronically, is the most rapidly changing area of cash management today. With an EFT, funds move between accounts instantly and without paper. Examples of EFTs are paying for groceries with a debit card, withdrawing cash from an ATM, and having your paycheck directly deposited at your bank.

The advantages of EFTs are that the transactions take place immediately and the consumer doesn't have to carry cash or write a check. They're great for paying all kinds of charges from insurance premiums, to mortgage payments, to phone and utility bills. EFTs can tighten up your cash management habits by ensuring that you never have to carry cash. It's ironic, but you might be better able to manage your cash by not using cash.

To give you a better understanding of EFT and how it affects you, we discuss ATMs, debit cards, and smart cards in the following sections. You'll notice that there's no mention of credit cards here. Why? Because credit cards don't involve the electronic transfer of money—they involve the electronic *borrowing* of money. Don't worry—we deal with them in detail in the next chapter.

Automated Teller Machines

Automated Teller Machine (ATM) or Cash Machine
A machine found at most financial institutions that can be used to make withdrawals, deposits, transfers, and account inquiries.

An **automated teller machine (ATM) or cash machine** provides cash instantly and can be accessed through a credit or debit card. If you use a credit card to access the ATM, then the cash is "borrowed" from the line of credit you have with the financial institution that issued your credit card. Because these funds are borrowed, you begin paying usually very high interest on them immediately. You can also use the ATM to access funds held in an account—for example, you can withdraw funds from your checking account using a debit card.

The obvious appeal of ATMs is their convenience. ATMs never close and are available in many parts of the world. To use an ATM, you insert or swipe your card; punch in your **personal identification number,** or **PIN**, which is a four- to seven-digit number assigned to your account; and indicate how much cash you'd like. Easy, right? But as with everything else in finance, there's a cost to convenience. In the case of ATMs, most banks charge an access fee for any transaction. If you're using an ATM not owned by the bank that issued your card, your bank may charge you up to $3 per transaction. The bank that owns the ATM can also charge you up to $2 for using its machine. At a grand total of up to $5 per transaction, using an ATM can be quite expensive.

Personal Identification Number (PIN)
A four- to seven-digit personal identification number assigned to your account.

The big problem with an ATM transaction is crime. Since most people who walk away from an ATM have money on them, ATMs tend to attract criminals. This doesn't mean that you shouldn't use them, but you should be careful. Don't use them late at night, don't use them in isolated areas, don't be the only person at the ATM, and don't drive up to an ATM in an unlocked car.

In addition, take care that no one has access to your PIN. Although your liability for unauthorized transactions on an ATM is only $50 if you notify the bank immediately, it jumps to $500 if a delay of 2 days in reporting occurs and becomes unlimited if the delay exceeds 60 days. You should choose a PIN different from your birthday, Social Security number, street address, or any other number a criminal might logically guess. Checklist 5.2 provides a number of steps to follow to ensure ATM security.

Debit Cards

A **debit card** is something of a cross between a credit card and a checking account. It's like a credit card in that it's a plastic card you can use instead of cash, but it works more like a checking account. When you write a check, you're spending money that you have in your checking account. Unless you have overdraft protection, you can't write a check for more than what is in your account. A debit card is linked to an account, and when you use it, you're spending the money in that account. It's kind of like writing an electronic check, only there's no paper involved and the check gets "cashed" instantly. When the money in your account runs out, you can't use your debit card again until you make another deposit.

Debit Card
A card that allows you to access the money in your accounts electronically.

CHECKLIST 5.2 ATM Security

Keep Your Card Secure

- ☐ Treat your ATM card like cash. Always keep your card in a safe place.
- ☐ Keep your PIN a secret. Memorize your code. Never write it on your card or store it with the card. Never tell your code to anyone. And never let someone else enter your code for you.
- ☐ Report a lost or stolen card at once.
- ☐ Check your receipts against your monthly statement to guard against ATM fraud.

Security at ATMs

- ☐ Always observe your surroundings before conducting an ATM transaction.
- ☐ If an ATM is obstructed from view or poorly lit, go to another ATM.
- ☐ If you are using a walk-up ATM, take a companion along if possible—especially at night.
- ☐ Minimize time spent at the ATM by having your card out and ready to use.
- ☐ If you see anyone or anything suspicious while conducting a transaction, cancel your transaction and leave.
- ☐ If you are followed after making an ATM transaction, go immediately to a heavily populated, well-lighted area, and call the police.
- ☐ If you are at a drive-up ATM, keep your engine running, the doors locked, and the windows up at all times when waiting in line. Before rolling down the window to use the ATM, check the entire area for anything or anyone suspicious.

Debit cards, like credit cards, allow you to avoid carrying cash, but they make it impossible to rack up a big credit card balance. With a debit card, you're spending your own money as opposed to borrowing money. You probably have a debit card now: Your ATM card is actually a type of debit card in that it gives you access to your checking account, but many ATM cards do even more. They also give you access to your savings account and allow you to transfer money between your different accounts.

While you can keep using your debit card as long as you have money in your account, card "blocking" can leave some of your money inaccessible. Card blocking occurs when you use a debit card (or credit card) to check into a hotel or rent a car and the anticipated expenses are blocked—in effect, placing a hold on the money. For example, if you check into a $100-a-day hotel for 4 days, the hotel will likely block $400 on your debit (or credit) card. If you pay your bill when you check out using the same card, the block will be lifted in a day or two. However, if you use another card to pay the bill, it is likely that the $400 block will remain on your account for up to 15 days. If you don't have a big balance, this can be a problem. To avoid it, use the same card to pay the bill that you used at the beginning of the transaction. In addition, blocking policies vary quite a bit from one card issuer to another, so you might want to shop around and ask what the blocking policies are when you're looking for a new card.

Smart Cards

Smart Card
Similar to a debit card, but this card actually magnetically stores its own accounts. Funds are transferred into the card, which is then used the same way you'd use a debit card. When the funds run out, the card is useless until more funds are magnetically transferred in.

Smart cards, sometimes called memory cards or electronic wallets, are a variation on debit cards, but instead of withdrawing funds from a designated account with a bank, you withdraw them from an account that's actually stored magnetically in the smart card. In fact, your smart card may include more than just money; it may include your ID—perhaps a driver's license or your student ID—along with insurance information, medical history, or any other type of information that would be handy to have. At Virginia Tech, the student ID, called the Hokie Passport, also serves as a smart card and can be used at dining services, vending machines, and many merchants in town; similarly, James Madison University's smart card is called the JAC card and works just like the one at Virginia Tech. In fact, smart cards have become very common at colleges and universities.

The advantages to the issuing agency are that it receives use of the funds in the smart cards before the transactions are completed and smart cards can reduce paperwork considerably. The advantages to the user are that smart cards are convenient and reduce the need to carry cash.

Prepaid Debit or Gift Cards

If you've made a purchase with a merchant gift card, placed phone calls with a prepaid telephone card, or bought something using a prepaid debit card, you've used a prepaid debit or gift card. There are actually two different types of gift or stored-value cards: The first is the single-purpose or "closed-loop" card, which can be used only at one store for one purpose; the second is the multipurpose or "open-loop" card, which can be used all over, just like a credit card. This type of card is becoming more and more common. Many employees receive their paychecks on a stored-value card, with more than 1,000 companies, including Walmart, FedEx, McDonald's, U-Haul, UPS, Coca-Cola, and Denny's offering to pay employees with Visa Payroll cards, which are a form of stored-value cards, instead of checks.

Beware, however, because stored-value cards come with a wide range of features and fee structures. For example, many have activation fees, maintenance fees, and ATM transaction fees. On top of these common fees, some also have reload fees, transaction limit fees, inactivity fees, dispute fees, and money transfer fees.

Fixing Mistakes—Theirs, Not Yours

How can errors occur in EFTs? Sometimes they're human errors, and sometimes they're computer errors. The first step in dealing with errors is to avoid letting them occur. You may not have much control with computer errors, but you can avoid human errors.

Perhaps the most common human error involves deposits, with most problems stemming from cash deposits made directly into an ATM. To avoid this type of error, never deposit cash in an ATM. If an error occurs and you aren't credited for what you deposited, it's very difficult to prove that you're right.

If an error does occur, report it immediately. Call the bank, and if it's closed, try to leave a message. By law, you must write to the bank within 60 days of receiving your statement. If you can't settle the dispute with the bank, there's an online complaint form on the Federal Reserve Board's Division of Consumer and Community Affairs Web site.

BEHAVIORAL INSIGHTS

PRINCIPLE 9

Principle 9: Mind Games, Your Financial Personality, and Your Money It's tough saving for anything, let alone an emergency fund. After all, you're saving for something you don't expect or want to happen—some unknown emergency. Wouldn't it be simpler to avoid an emergency in the first place? The problem is that emergencies tend to be things you don't have control over, and when they happen, they can be catastrophic to your budget, your savings, and your ability to pay down your debt. Still, there always seems to be something more enjoyable or interesting to do with your money than to save it for an unforeseen future event.

You are not the only one who has difficulty saving for something "that you don't want to happen sometime in your future." The problem you are facing comes from what behavioral finance calls "temporal myopia," meaning that when people are uncertain about the future, they tend to discount it dramatically—and in the extreme comes the phrase "Eat, drink, and be merry, for tomorrow we may die." It also explains why, even though we know we need to exercise, it's so easy to turn the alarm off, skip that morning run, and get an extra hour of sleep.

A typical example of temporal myopia comes from a study where a group of people are asked to make this choice: Would you want \$100 now or \$120 one month from now? Most people make the "intertemporal" choice of \$100 right now even though making an extra \$20 in one month would be a very good yield. Interestingly, when the same group is asked to choose between \$100 in 12 months and \$120 in 13 months, their strategy is reversed, and they choose the \$120 in 13 months. Why is this? Behavioral finance tells us that because the immediate reward is off the table and both rewards are placed in the future, we behave more rationally. Our appetite for immediate reward is very powerful and interferes with our decision making.

So if you know you need to save for an emergency fund, or for any other goal, how can you make it happen? One way is to remove the decision by precommitting—commit to having money taken directly out of your monthly paycheck and put into a separate emergency fund bank account. If you've already got that emergency fund up and running but want to get into better physical shape, purchasing an annual gym membership is a good way of precommitting. That way you've taken away the cost of going to the gym, and your guilt over wasting that money may inspire you to go work out.

ACTION PLAN

PRINCIPLE 10

Principle 10: Just Do It! If you're having a hard time handling your cash, it's hard to make much progress in terms of your financial plan. Here are some tips that will help you start to manage your cash, paving the way to more financial control.

- **Create an emergency fund before you have an emergency.** Having cash on hand when you need it can help save your financial plan and budget.
- **Be careful when you bank online.** Make sure you use a strong password and a secure network, and never pay bills from public wi-fi hotspots.
- **Pay your bills online.** You'll find that by paying your monthly bills online, it becomes easier to stay on top of your money as it goes in and out because transactions are tracked for you. Also, set up e-mail alerts to remind you of when to make monetary transfers.
- **If possible, have your bills automatically paid.** Use automatic withdrawal to pay your bills so they are never late. If you do automate bill payment, make sure you take the time to *read your bills*—you must know where your money is going, and you must know exactly how much money is being withdrawn.
- **Use online alerts to your advantage.** Many banks will help you avoid fees by setting up alerts to let you know when your credit card bill is due and when your credit card balance reaches a limit that you set. These alerts will be sent to your mobile phone or e-mail address and will provide you with peace of mind, protect your credit score, and save you money. In addition, many banks will send you alerts when your mortgage payment is due and when activity occurs on your credit card and will track your ATM withdrawals and debit card purchases.

Chapter Summaries

LO1 Manage your cash and understand why you need liquid assets.

SUMMARY: Cash management is the control of your cash and liquid assets. Liquid assets allow you to invest your money while still keeping it available to pay bills or to cover an emergency. Although liquid asset investments are low risk and provide you with emergency funds, they don't provide you with a very good return. The basic idea behind cash management is balancing the risk of not having enough in the way of liquid assets with the potential for greater return on other investments.

KEY TERMS

Cash Management, page 138 The management of cash and near cash (liquid) assets.

Liquid Assets, page 138 Cash and investments that can easily be converted into cash, such as checking accounts, money market funds, and certificates of deposit (CDs).

Automate your savings.

LO2

SUMMARY: The key to meeting long-term goals is to make saving a part of your everyday life. Having some of your income automatically placed in savings forces you to learn to live at your take-home salary level.

Choose from among the different types of financial institutions that provide cash management services.

LO3

SUMMARY: In recent years, there have been many changes in the field of cash management, and nowhere is this more evident than in financial institutions themselves. Industry changes and increased competition have resulted in a vast reshaping of many institutions. However, we can still divide them into deposit-type institutions (banks) and nondeposit-type institutions. Recently, nondeposit institutions have been offering traditional banking services, resulting in more choices than ever for managing cash.

KEY TERMS

Deposit-Type Financial Institutions, page 139 Financial institutions that provide traditional checking and savings accounts. Commonly referred to as "banks."

Nondeposit-Type Financial Institutions, page 139 Financial institutions, such as mutual funds and stockbrokerage firms, that don't provide checking and savings accounts.

Online and Mobile Banking, page 140 The ability to perform banking operations through your personal computer, mobile phone, or other online device.

Compare the various cash management alternatives.

LO4

SUMMARY: Given the number of different financial institutions vying for your liquid funds, it's no surprise that there is a variety of different cash management alternatives. These include checking accounts, savings accounts, money market deposit accounts, certificates of deposit, money market mutual funds, asset management accounts, T-bills, and savings bonds.

KEY TERMS

Demand Deposit Account, page 142 A type of checking account that pays no interest on your balance.

NOW (Negotiable Order of Withdrawal) Account, page 142 A checking account that pays interest on your balance.

Savings Account, page 143 A time deposit account that pays interest.

Money Market Deposit Account (MMDA), page 143 A bank account that pays a rate of interest that varies with the current market rate of interest.

Certificate of Deposit (CD), page 144 A savings alternative that pays a fixed rate of interest while keeping your funds on deposit for a set period of time that can range from 30 days to several years.

Money Market Mutual Fund (MMMF), page 144 A mutual funds that invests in short-term (generally with a maturity of less than 90 days) notes of very high denomination.

Asset Management Account, page 145 A comprehensive financial services package offered by a brokerage firm, which can include a checking account, credit and debit cards, MMMF, loans, automatic payment of fixed payments such as mortgages, brokerage services (buying and selling stocks or bonds), and a system for the direct payment of interest, dividends, and proceeds from security sales into the MMMF.

U.S. Treasury Bill or T-Bill, page 146 A short-term note of debt issued by the federal government with a maturity ranging from a few days to 12 months.

Denomination, page 146 The face value or amount that's returned to the debtholder at maturity. It's also referred to as the debt's par value.

U.S. Savings Bond, page 146 A type of security that's actually a loan on which you receive interest, generally every 6 months for the life of the bond. When the bond matures, or comes due, you get back your investment, or "loan." What you get back at maturity is usually the face value of the loan, although the amount you get could be more or less than what you paid for the bond originally.

LO5 Compare rates on the different liquid investment alternatives.

SUMMARY: When comparing different liquid investment alternatives, you must look not only at what their return is but also at how safe they are. In addition, you must remember that the only valid rate comparisons are ones that use similar compounding methods (annual, semiannual, and so on) and have similar tax treatment.

KEY TERMS

Annual Percentage Yield (APY), page 148 The amount you earn on an investment in one year, expressed as a percentage. The APY formula converts interest rates compounded for different periods into comparable annual rates, allowing you to easily compare interest rates.

After-Tax Return, page 149 The actual return you earn on taxable investments once taxes have been paid. It is equal to taxable return × (1 − marginal tax rate) + nontaxable return.

Federal Deposit Insurance Corporation (FDIC), page 150 The federal agency that insures deposits at commercial banks and S&Ls.

National Credit Union Association, page 150 The federal agency that insures accounts at credit unions.

LO6 Establish and use a checking account.

SUMMARY: Your checking account is your most essential cash management tool. When deciding where to open a checking account, you should give consideration to the three Cs: cost, convenience, and consideration. You should also keep an eye out for safety: Are your funds federally insured?

KEY TERMS

Direct Deposit, page 152 The depositing of payments, such as payroll checks, directly into your checking account. This is done electronically.

Safety-Deposit Box, page 152 A storage unit at a bank or other financial institution in which valuables and important documents are stored for safekeeping.

Overdraft Protection, page 152 The provision of an automatic loan to your checking account whenever sufficient funds are not available to cover checks that have been written against the account.

Stop Payment, page 153 An order you can give your financial institution to stop payment on a check you've written.

Cashier's Check, page 153 A check drawn on a bank's or financial institution's account.

Certified Check, page 156 A personal check that's been certified as being good by the financial institution on which it's drawn.

Money Order, page 156 A check similar to a cashier's check except that it is generally issued by the U.S. Postal Service or some other nonbanking institution.

Traveler's Checks, page 156 Checks issued by large financial institutions, such as Citibank, Visa, and American Express, that are sold through local banking institutions and are similar to cashier's checks except that they don't specify a specific payee and they come in specific denominations ($20, $50, and $100).

Transfer funds electronically and understand how electronic funds transfers (EFTs) work. LO7

SUMMARY: *Electronic funds transfer* refers to any financial transaction that takes place electronically—for example, paying for dinner with a debit card or having your paycheck deposited directly. The advantage of an electronic funds transfer is that the transaction takes place immediately and the consumer does not have to carry cash or write a check.

KEY TERMS

Electronic Funds Transfer (EFT), page 156 Any financial transaction that takes place electronically.

Automated Teller Machine (ATM) or Cash Machine, page 156 A machine found at most financial institutions that can be used to make withdrawals, deposits, transfers, and account inquiries.

Personal Identification Number (PIN), page 157 A four- to seven-digit personal identification number assigned to your account.

Debit Card, page 157 A card that allows you to access the money in your accounts electronically.

Smart Card, page 158 Similar to a debit card, but this card actually magnetically stores its own accounts. Funds are transferred into the card, which is then used the same way you'd use a debit card. When the funds run out, the card is useless until more funds are magnetically transferred in.

Problems and Activities

These problems are available in MyLab Finance.

1. Name three characteristics of liquid assets. What are the disadvantages of having too much or too little money held as liquid assets?
2. Use Worksheet 1 to list three short-term goals and/or expenses for which a savings account, money market mutual fund, or other liquid assets vehicle would be the appropriate place for your money. WORKSHEET 1
3. What is the primary advantage of automating your savings?
4. After reading the new account insert in his monthly statement, Tony Mercadante determined that the FDIC considers a joint account as a separate depositor. He and his wife, Cynthia, have three accounts at ABC Bank & Trust, one joint account with a balance of $60,000 and two individual accounts—his has a $150,000 balance, and hers has a $254,000 balance. What amounts of FDIC coverage do they each have?
5. Your friend Ed has a money market mutual fund account, automatic deposit of his paycheck into an interest-bearing checking account at the company credit union, and a CD from the local branch of a bank that advertises "coast-to-coast" banking. What is the benefit of "mixing and matching" financial institutions and their services?
6. Calculate the percentage return on a 1-year Treasury bill with a face value of $10,000 if you pay $9,800 to purchase it and receive its full face value at maturity.
7. Calculate the after-tax return of a 4.65 percent, 20-year, A-rated corporate bond for an investor in the 10 percent marginal tax bracket. Compare this yield to that of a 3.25 percent, 20-year, A-rated, tax-exempt municipal bond, and explain which alternative is better. Repeat the calculations and comparison for an investor in the 25 percent marginal tax bracket.

8. Assuming a 1-year money market account investment at 1.5 percent (APY), a 2.5 percent inflation rate, a 25 percent marginal tax bracket, and a constant $50,000 balance, calculate the after-tax rate of return, the real rate of return, and the total monetary return. What are the implications of this result for cash management decisions?
9. What are the primary advantages and disadvantages of an Internet-only bank?

Discussion Case 1

This case is available in **MyLab Finance**.

Shu Chang, 22, has just moved to Denver to begin her first professional job. She is concerned about her finances; specifically, she wants to save for "a rainy day" and a new car purchase in 2 years. Shu's new job pays $30,500, of which she keeps $24,000 after taxes. Her monthly expenses total $1,600. Shu's new employer offers a 401(k) plan and matches employees' contributions up to 6 percent of their salary. The employer also provides a credit union and a U.S. Savings Bond purchase program. Shu also just inherited $5,000.

Shu's older brother, Wen, has urged Shu to start saving from "day one" on the job. Wen has lost a job twice in the last 5 years through company downsizing and now keeps $35,000 in a 2 percent money market mutual fund in case it happens again. Wen's annual take-home pay is $48,000.

Shu has started shopping around for accounts to hold her liquid assets. She'd like to earn the highest rate possible and avoid paying fees for falling below a specified minimum balance. She plans to open two accounts: one for paying monthly bills and another for short-term savings.

Questions

1. Name at least three ways that Shu could automate her asset management. Suggest at least one option for each of retirement savings, general savings, and general convenience.
2. What major factors should Shu consider when selecting a checking and/or savings account?
3. Why does Shu need an emergency fund? Assuming she wants to follow her brother's lead, how much emergency savings should she try to set aside? What type of account would you recommend for her emergency fund?
4. Comment on Wen's use of liquid assets. How is his savings philosophy both risky and conservative? What is the real after-tax rate of return, assuming a 3 percent inflation rate and a 25 percent marginal tax bracket?
5. Shu has narrowed her "savings" account choices to a standard checking account paying 0.25 percent, a money market deposit account paying 1 percent, and a money market mutual fund earning 1.75 percent. Which liquid asset vehicle would you recommend for paying monthly expenses, and which would you recommend for saving for the car down payment? Explain the advantages and disadvantages associated with each choice.
6. Shu has heard that some local auto dealerships may require a cashier's check for the down payment. Why is a cashier's check preferable to a certified check?

Discussion Case 2

This case is available in **MyLab Finance**.

Jarod Douglas Jones is a young professional just getting started in the world. He has been having some difficulty getting his checkbook to match his bank statement. Last month all he had to do was subtract the service charge from his checkbook register and the amounts matched. This month is different. He would like your help reconciling the problem. Help him find his mistake(s) and learn the procedures for balancing his checkbook each month.

Hint: Use Figure 5.1 or Worksheet 8.

WORKSHEET 8

Big USA Bank

Summary		
Beginning balance	6/27	$1,964.17
Total deposits		$2,823.46
Total withdrawals		$2,982.74
Service charge		$4.50
ATM fees		$3.00
Ending balance	7/29	$1,797.39
Deposits and Electronic Credits		
Automatic payroll	6/30	$1,161.73
Automatic payroll	7/15	$1,161.73
Branch deposit	7/23	$500.00
Withdrawals and Electronic Debits		
Auto insurance	7/1	$70.50
Visa–Check 1074	7/5	$45.20
Big Al's All U-Care-To-Eat	7/7	$39.00
ATM	7/10	$30.00
A Cut Above Hair Salon	7/19	$23.00
ATM	7/21	$50.00
Checks		
1071	7/01	$30.00
1072	7/03	$50.00
1073	7/08	$100.00
1074	7/06	See above
1075	7/09	$147.11
1076	7/16	$69.75
1077	7/10	$27.81
1078	7/12	$302.20
1080*	7/20	$350.00
1081	7/21	$20.50
1082	7/22	$1,599.11
1084*	7/23	$28.56

*Break in Sequence

Date	Number	Payee/Description	Credit	Debit	Balance
					$2,005.98
24-Jun	1070	Dinner out		$41.81	($41.81)
					$1,964.17
26-Jun	1071	Cash		$30.00	($30.00)
					$1,934.17
29-Jun	1072	Video game		$50.00	($50.00)
					$1,884.17
30-Jun		Payroll	$1,161.73		$1,161.73
					$3,045.90
1-Jul		Auto insurance		$70.50	($70.50)
					$2,975.40
1-Jul	1073	Cash		$100.00	($100.00)
					$2,875.40
3-Jul	1074	Visa		$45.20	($45.20)
					$2,830.20
3-Jul	1075	Store card		$147.11	($147.11)
					$2,683.09
8-Jul	1076	Gas card		$69.75	($69.75)
					$2,623.34
8-Jul	1077	Cell phone		$27.81	($27.81)
					$2,595.53
9-Jul	1078	Owed to parents		$302.20	($320.20)
					$2,275.33
12-Jul	1079	Dinner out		$37.87	($37.87)
					$2,237.46
15-Jul		Payroll	$1,161.73		$1,161.73
					$3,399.19
15-Jul	1080	Auto payment		$350.00	($350.00)
					$3,049.19
15-Jul	1081	MasterCard		$20.50	($20.50)
					$3,028.69
18-Jul	1082	Discover Card		$1,599.11	($1,599.11)
					$1,429.58
18-Jul	1083	Cash		$125.00	($125.00)
					$1,304.58
19-Jul		Haircut		$23.00	($23.00)
					$1,281.58

Date	Number	Payee/Description	Credit	Debit	Balance
23-Jul	1084	Cell phone		$28.56	($28.56)
					$1,253.02
23-Jul		Gift	$500.00		$500.00
					$1,753.02
21-Jul		ATM withdrawal		$51.50	($51.50)
					$1,701.52
28-Jul	1085	Cheap Food Store		$47.25	($47.25)
					$1,654.27
29-Jul	1086	Sears		$9.16	($9.16)
					$1,645.11

CHAPTER 6

Using Credit Cards: The Role of Open Credit

Learning Objectives

LO1	**Know** how credit cards work.	**A First Look at Credit Cards and Open Credit**
LO2	**Understand** the costs of credit.	**The Pros and Cons of Credit Cards**
LO3	**Describe** the different types of credit cards.	**Choosing a Source of Open Credit**
LO4	**Know** what determines your credit card worthiness and how to secure a credit card.	**Getting a Credit Card**
LO5	**Manage** your credit cards and open credit.	**Controlling and Managing Your Credit Cards and Open Credit**

We've all said those three little words, and lived to regret it ... "just charge it." Credit cards are easy to get and, for many of us, much too easy to use. How tough is it to get one? You probably know by now—not tough at all. In fact, about two-thirds of all college freshmen have credit cards, and by their senior year, over 90 percent of all students have at least one.

Be it in real life or in TV land, you can find countless stories revolving around the perils of plastic. And if you want a credit card, you can surely get one—after all, students are prime customers for credit card companies. In the world of TV, even Bart Simpson got one. It all happened after complaining that he never gets any mail. Marge gave him the family's junk mail, and one piece of that junk mail was a credit card application. It didn't take Bart long to fill it out—giving his occupation as a "butt doctor," his income as "whatever I find I keep," and his name as "Santa's Little Helper," which also happens to be the name of Bart's dog on TV. That's all it took—and in real life, it doesn't take much more. Then 6 to 8 weeks later it arrives—a credit card issued by the Money Bank to Santos L. Helper. As you can imagine, things get a bit out of control from there, as Bart goes on a spending spree, ordering gifts for all the family from the "Covet House" catalog—a Vancouver smoked salmon and a radio-frying pan for Marge, a golf shirt with corporate logo for Homer, "Trucker's Choice Stay-Alert Capsules" for Lisa, and all kinds of stuff for himself, including a "limited edition" Collie.

Photo 12/Alamy Stock Photo

Debt isn't a bad thing; in fact, some debt is good. But it's dangerous—it's easy to take on more debt than you should. And the most dangerous debt is right in your pocket—your credit card. Still, it's a necessity in today's world.

If you've ever had to make hotel reservations or buy concert tickets over the phone or on the Internet, you understand that in today's economy you really need to have a credit card. And almost everyone has one. In fact, Americans hold more than 1.5 billion credit cards of all types—that's over four and a half cards for each man, woman, and child; almost half of these are Visas and MasterCards, with the remainder being department store, oil company, and other merchants' charge cards. There's just no denying that having and using credit cards has become part of our financial culture.

You can't beat them for convenience, but if you're not careful, credit cards will cost you. They can be mighty expensive; some charge over 20 percent interest on unpaid balances. Because most people don't consider these interest charges when they're buying whatever it is they've just got to have, bank credit card debt (excluding store and gas credit cards) in the United States is estimated to be around $747 billion. In 2017, the average U.S. household had credit card debt of $5,700, but many households don't carry any credit card debt at all, so if you just look at the indebted households, the average balance rises to $16,048. If the interest rate on the $747 billion that Americans owed was 20 percent, Americans were paying almost $150 billion each year in credit card charges. Unless you want to be one of the people paying a share of that $150 billion, you need to manage your credit cards wisely.

LO1 Know how credit cards work.

A First Look at Credit Cards and Open Credit

Credit
Receiving cash, goods, or services with an obligation to pay later.

Consumer Credit
Credit purchases for personal needs other than for home mortgages—this can include anything from an auto loan to credit card debt.

Open Credit or Revolving Credit
A line of credit that you can use and then pay back at whatever pace you like so long as you pay a minimum amount each month, paying interest on the unpaid balance.

Credit involves receiving cash, goods, or services with an obligation to pay later. In shopper's language, "Charge it," "Put it on my account," and "I'll pay for it with plastic" are all opening lines to the use of credit. Credit purchases made for personal needs other than for home mortgages are referred to collectively as **consumer credit**—this can include anything from an auto loan to credit card debt.

Open credit or revolving credit is a line of consumer credit extended before you make a purchase. Once you use open credit, you can pay back your debt at whatever pace you like so long as you pay a specified minimum amount each month. Today, most open credit comes in the form of credit card purchases, but open credit is actually any type of charge or credit account because with a charge or credit account you've been extended a line of credit before you make a purchase. Examples of open credit range from the charge account you have at a local hardware store, to an Exxon charge card, to a credit account you have with your broker, to your Elvis Presley Visa card. However, credit cards dominate, which isn't that surprising, given that there are around 7,000 different kinds of Visas, MasterCards, and other cards to choose from. Because of the predominance of credit cards, most of our discussion focuses on them, but the same basic principles apply to all credit and charge accounts.

When buying on credit, you can charge whatever you want as long as you stay under the credit limit. Each month you'll receive a statement that shows both the outstanding balance on your account and the minimum payment due. You can then pay anywhere between the minimum payment and the balance. Any unpaid balance plus interest on that unpaid balance carries over and becomes part of next month's outstanding balance. As long as you pay the minimum amount every month, the credit issuer will continue to extend to you a credit limit or line of credit, which is a preapproved amount of credit given in advance of any purchase.

As you probably already know, the higher the balance you maintain on your credit lines, the higher your costs will be. But other factors, too, determine your costs. The following sections discuss the basic factors that affect the costs of credit cards and other forms of open credit, including the interest rate, the balance calculation method, the cost of cash advances, the grace period, the annual fee, and other additional or penalty fees.

Interest Rates

Annual Percentage Rate (APR)
The true simple interest rate paid over the life of the loan. It's a reasonable approximation of the true cost of borrowing, and the Truth in Lending Act requires that all consumer loan agreements disclose the APR in bold print.

The main factor that determines the cost of a line of credit is the **annual percentage rate (APR)**, which is the true simple interest rate paid over the life of the loan. It takes most of the costs into account, including interest on the balance, the loan processing fee, and the document preparation fee, but it only sometimes includes the loan application fee and normally does not include the cost of credit reports. The importance of the APR is that while there can be differences in what's included in it, it's calculated the same way by all lenders, and the federal Truth in Lending Act requires that all consumer loan agreements disclose the APR in bold print. As a result, it's a good place to start to compare competing lines of credit.

Some credit cards have fixed APRs, and some have variable APRs. With a variable-rate credit card, the rate you pay is tied to another interest rate. For example, many credit cards are tied to the prime rate of interest, which is the rate banks charge their best customers. Variable-APR credit cards typically charge the prime rate plus a percentage. So if the interest rate that variable-rate credit cards charge varies, then the interest rate that fixed-rate cards charge is fixed and *doesn't* vary, right? No! The interest rate a fixed-rate credit card charges may indeed change. All the credit card company needs to do is to inform you in writing at least 45 days before changing its rates.

APRs vary dramatically from one credit account to another. In 2017, when the national average APR on standard variable-rate credit cards was over 16.0 percent, Citibank had credit cards with rates from about 12.5 percent all the way up to 29.99 percent! Rates not only vary from one credit account to another but also can vary over time on the same card. Some rates stay fixed, but others change based on the cardholder's payment history along with market factors—for example, when interest rates in general change.

PRINCIPLE 9

STOP & THINK

Remember **Principle 9: Mind Games, Your Financial Personality, and Your Money**? It's much easier to spend money if you don't have to think about it. As a result, people tend to spend more and make additional purchases if they can get through lines faster and swipe their card. Don't just do it because it's there and it's easy–take control of your own financial life. The graph below looks at undergraduates and the surprise they have experienced when opening their credit card bills. Has that happened to you? If so, why do you think that's the case?

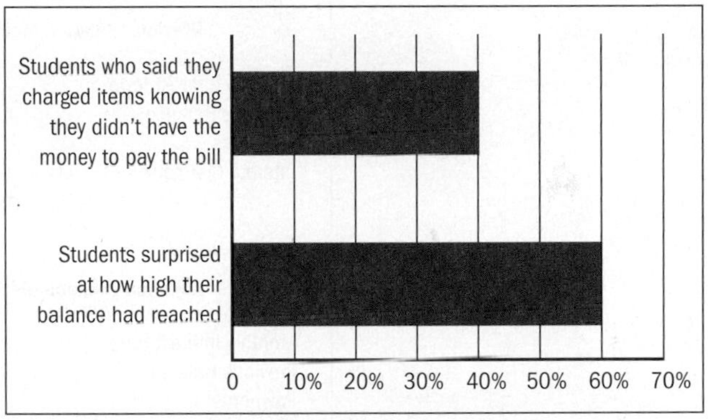

Some credit cards also offer low introductory rates called "teaser rates." These initial rates, which last 6 months to a year, can run as low as 0 percent but can jump to 17 to 18 percent after the introductory period is over. About two-thirds of the credit card offers sent out in the mail each year have some type of teaser rate.

Also keep in mind that most credit accounts compound interest—that is, you end up paying interest on interest. So if your credit card compounds interest on a monthly basis and you carry a balance, you could end up paying a rate of 21.7 percent on a credit card with a 19.8 percent APR. Think about what that does to the real cost of your Starbucks!

Calculating the Balance Owed

Once you know your APR, it's easy to calculate the cost of your credit account. You simply multiply your APR by your outstanding balance. That's easy enough, right? Wrong. The **method of determining the balance (or balance calculation method)** varies from one credit account to another. Before we get into the nitty gritty of the different ways that balances are calculated, remember this: If you don't carry a balance—if you pay off your outstanding balance each month—there is no unpaid balance and therefore no interest charge! Paying off your balance each month will make selecting a credit card easier (because you won't have to be concerned with interest rates) and will almost certainly make you richer—seriously. Unfortunately, not everyone does; in fact, according to the Federal Reserve Survey of Consumer Finances, 71 percent of cardholders ages 25 to 34 don't pay off their credit cards every month—they're still making someone rich but, unfortunately, not themselves.

Method of Determining the Balance (or Balance Calculation Method)
The method by which a credit card balance is determined. The finance charges are then based on the level of this balance.

The three primary methods used to determine interest charges on an unpaid credit balance are (1) the average daily balance method, (2) the previous balance method, and (3) the adjusted balance method.

- **Average daily balance method:** Your average daily balance is calculated by adding up your daily balances during the billing period and dividing this sum by the number of billing period days. Interest payments are based on this balance. The Bankcard Holders Association of America reports this method is used by about 95 percent of all bank card issuers.
- **Previous balance method:** Interest payments are charged against what you owed at the end of the previous billing period. There is no credit given for current month's payments. This method is relatively simple, but it's also expensive.

Average Daily Balance Method
A method of calculating the balance on which interest is paid by summing the outstanding balances owed each day during the billing period and dividing by the number of days in the period.

Previous Balance Method
A method of calculating interest payments on outstanding credit using the balance at the end of the previous billing period.

FIGURE 6.1 Calculation of Interest on Outstanding Balances

Example: Your credit card's annual interest rate is 18 percent, and you begin the month with a previous balance of $1,000. In addition, your payments against your credit card balance this month are $900, which are made on the 15th of the month. You make no additional purchases during the month.

Calculate your average daily balance by summing the daily balances and dividing by the number of days in the period.

Average Daily Balance Method

Monthly Interest Rate	1.5%
Sum of All Daily Balances During the Billing Period	$16,500
Days in Billing Period	30 days
Average Daily Balance	$550
Interest Charged	$8.25 ($550 × 1.5%)

Under the previous balance method, interest payments are charged against the balance at the end of the previous billing period. In effect, interest is charged on the entire closing balance, regardless of whether or not payments and returns are made. Thus, regardless of the size of any partial credit repayment during the month, you will still pay interest on the total unpaid balance you had at the end of the previous billing period.

Previous Balance Method

Monthly Interest Rate	1.5%
Previous Balance	$1,000
Payments	$900
Interest Charged	$15.00 ($1,000 × 1.5%)

The adjusted balance method is a favorable variation of the previous balance method in which interest payments are charged against the balance at the end of the previous billing period less any payments and returns made. Because interest is not charged on payments, this method results in lower interest charges than does the previous balance method.

Adjusted Balance Method

Monthly Interest Rate	1.5%
Previous Balance	$1,000
Payments	$900
Interest Charged	$1.50 ($100 × 1.5%)

Adjusted Balance Method
A method of calculating interest payments on outstanding credit in which interest payments are charged against the balance at the end of the previous billing period less any payments and returns made.

- **Adjusted balance method:** Interest is charged against the previous month's balance only after any payments have been subtracted. Because interest isn't charged on payments, this method results in lower interest charges than the previous balance method.

An example of interest calculations using these three methods is given in Figure 6.1.

To say the least, calculating the charges on your balance is extremely confusing. There's one surefire way around this problem: Pay off your balance every month.

Buying Money: The Cash Advance

Many credit cards allow you to get cash advances at ATMs. In effect, you're taking out a loan when you get a cash advance—and it's an extremely expensive way to borrow money. When you purchase an item with a credit card, interest is not charged until after the date the payment is due if you pay off your balance in full each month; however, when you withdraw cash from an ATM using your credit card, you begin paying interest *immediately*. Also, many credit cards charge a higher interest rate on cash advances than they do on normal purchases.

FACTS OF LIFE

Of the 3.8 credit cards held by the average adopter, 2 cards earned rewards, and 1.8 cards did not.

In addition, cash advances generally carry an up-front fee of 2 to 4 percent of the amount advanced. Finally, many cards require you to pay down the balance for purchases before you pay down the higher-interest-rate cash advance balance. Keep in mind that although you can give yourself a big, fat, immediate cash loan using your credit card, that loan comes with some big, fat, immediate charges.

Grace Period

Typically, the lender allows you a **grace period** before charging interest on an outstanding balance if you pay off your balance in full each month. For most credit cards, there's a 21- to 25-day grace period from the date of the bill. Once the grace period has passed, you're charged the APR on the balance as determined by the credit card issuer.

Grace Period
The length of time given to make a payment before interest is charged against the outstanding balance on a credit card.

As a result of the grace period, finance charges might not be assessed against credit card purchases for almost 2 months. For example, if the credit card issuer mails out bills on the first of the month, a purchase made on the second of the month would not appear until the next month's bill and would not have to be paid until the end of the grace period—21 to 25 days after that—a total of almost 2 months. Although most credit cards allow a grace period on normal purchases, it's a general rule that with cash advances there is no grace period, meaning that finance charges are assessed against the cash advance from the date it is received.

Beware! Some credit cards don't have a grace period—that is, you start paying interest when you make the purchase. If your credit card doesn't provide for a grace period, that means you pay a finance charge on every purchase you make with your credit card! Read the fine print!

The most confusing aspect of grace periods is this: With most credit cards, if you don't completely pay off all your previous month's borrowing, then the grace period doesn't apply, and you begin paying interest immediately on new purchases. In fact, the size of your unpaid balance doesn't matter—it could be only one penny. The result is the same: On most credit cards, the grace period is cancelled if you carry an unpaid balance from the previous month.

Annual Fee

Some credit card issuers also impose an **annual fee** for the privilege of using their card. Typically, the charge ranges from $10 to $100, but the American Express Centurion Card charges a $2,500 annual fee—and there's also a $7,500 initiation fee for the first year. These fees add up quickly if you have several cards. However, over 70 percent of the 25 biggest credit card issuers don't charge an annual fee, and others don't charge one as long as you use their card at least once per year.

Annual Fee
A fixed annual charge imposed by a credit card issuer.

How do these card issuers make money? Well, there's the rate of interest they charge on outstanding balances, plus they charge a fee to the merchants that accept their card. Typically, when you charge a purchase against your credit card, the merchant pays a percentage of the sale, called the **merchant's discount fee**, to the credit card issuer. This fee averages between 1 and 3 percent (and in some cases up to 10 percent) of the amount charged if the card is swiped and about a half a percent more for online transactions.

Merchant's Discount Fee
The percentage of the sale that the merchant pays to the credit card issuer.

Additional Fees

If credit card issuers make money from merchant discount fees every time you use their cards, you'd think that paying your annual fee and the sometimes exorbitant interest on your balance would be enough to keep them happy. Of course, you'd be wrong. There are still plenty of additional and penalty fees.

Cash Advance Fee
A charge for making a cash advance, paid as either a fixed amount or a percentage of the cash advance.

First, there's a **cash advance fee**, which we talked about earlier. It is either a fixed amount—for example, $5 per transaction—or a percentage—usually around 3 percent—of the cash advance. Remember, that's on top of the interest you are charged from the date of the advance. Remember, too, that some credit card issuers charge a higher interest rate on cash advances than they do on normal charges to the card. Bottom line? A small cash advance can wind up being a big financial setback.

Late Fee
A fee imposed as a result of not paying your credit card bill on time.

Another fee you might get stuck paying is a **late fee**, which results from not paying your credit card bill on time. As a result of 2009's CARD Act, credit card late fees are capped at $25 for occasional late payments; however, if the cardholder is late more than once in a 6-month period, the fees can be higher. By "on time," the credit card company may mean more than just a specific date; it may also mean a specific time—say, 1 P.M. On top of the late fee, you might also get hit with an **over-the-limit fee** for charging more than your credit limit allows.

Over-the-Limit Fee
A fee imposed whenever you go over your credit limit.

Penalty Rate
The rate you pay if you don't make your minimum payments on time.

Finally, there are **penalty rates**. This is the interest rate you pay on your balance if you don't make your minimum payments on time. For example, the rate you pay on your balance could rise by 10 percent or more if you don't make your minimum payment on time. Considering that if you don't make your minimum payment on time, you will also be paying a late fee, it is clear that to avoid being crushed by credit card costs, you should always make your minimum payment by the date the payment is due!

Lastly, watch closely for changes in policies and rates. These are usually announced via "bill stuffers"—notices enclosed with your bill. Be alert for the words "Important Notice of Change in Terms," which may signal a higher interest rate, a bigger late fee, or a shorter grace period.

When choosing a credit card, the bottom line is this: Beware! Before you sign up for that Lady-GagaUltraTitanium card with a $100,000 line of credit and an introductory 0.0 percent APR, read the fine print.

STOP & THINK

If you pay only your minimum balance, you might be paying for a long time. If you have a balance of $3,900 on a card with an 18 percent APR and you pay only the minimum amount required by some cards each month, paying off your bill will take 35 years. Moreover, you'll end up paying $10,096 in interest in addition to the principal of $3,900. What to do? Answer: Avoid carrying a balance; pay off your credit card balance each month. If you do carry a balance, pay it off as quickly as possible. If you've ever carried a balance, what's the highest it's been?

LO2 Understand the costs of credit.

The Pros and Cons of Credit Cards

Now that you know how expensive credit can be, why would you ever want to use it? Well, there are some good reasons. Let's take a look at these advantages and then the disadvantages.

The Advantages of Credit Cards

Without question, it would be difficult to function in society today without some kind of credit card or open credit. Simple tasks such as making hotel reservations would be nearly impossible without a credit card. Credit cards can be used as identification when cashing checks, for gym memberships, and almost anywhere else multiple pieces of identification are needed. And using credit extends your shopping opportunities—it's nearly impossible to make a purchase over the phone or on the Internet without a credit card.

Consider, too, that it's more convenient to purchase items with credit cards. Not only do you receive an itemized billing of exactly how much you spent and where you spent it, but also you reduce the risk of theft associated with carrying around large amounts of cash. Open credit also is a source of temporary emergency funds. If you have enough open credit to cover emergency expenses, you don't need to keep as much in liquid emergency funds. Credit, then, frees you to put your money into higher-yielding investments.

By purchasing an item on credit, you get to use it before you actually pay for it. Thus, when you buy some new lululemon pants or an Adele CD and charge it, you can wear the pants or play the CD as much as you like in spite of the fact that you won't really pay for it until you pay your next credit card bill. And by using a single credit card to make purchases from a variety of sources, you consolidate your bills. You can also use credit to consolidate your debt. Many individuals with numerous outstanding bills transfer all these debts to a single credit card in an effort to get better control over their borrowing.

If the price of an item that you intend to purchase is about to go up, buying the item on credit today lets you pay less than you'd have to pay tomorrow. In addition, if you pay your full credit card balance each month, a credit card allows you to earn interest from the date of purchase until the payment date on money you would not have if you paid cash.

Many cards offer "free" extended product warranties and travel insurance. Some offer frequent flier miles on your favorite airline or credit toward the purchase of anything from Shell gasoline and GM cars to toys at Toys "R" Us and even blackjack and card-counting lessons from a professional player. These benefits, while valuable, may not actually be free—the cards that offer them are likely to carry an annual fee.

The Drawbacks of Credit Cards

Although credit cards are indispensable in today's economy, they've also caused enormous problems for many individuals. There are many reasons to be wary of credit cards and open credit. While there are more advantages to credit cards than there are disadvantages, the disadvantages are significant.

First, it's simply too easy to spend money with a credit card because it seems as if you haven't really spent money. Moreover, it's too easy to lose track of exactly how much you've spent because what you've charged doesn't appear until your monthly statement shows up. If you've overspent, your only recourse may be to pay off your purchases over time, paying hefty amounts of interest and spending much more than you'd bargained for.

It's not just that you pay interest on an unpaid credit card balance; it's the high rate of interest you pay that makes credit card borrowing so unappealing. For example, in 2017 the average 15-year fixed-rate home mortgage charged 3.49 percent, the average home equity line of credit charged 5.22 percent, and the average credit card charged 16.31 percent. At the same time, 1-year CDs paid less than 1 percent. Banks are effectively borrowing money at 1 percent and lending it out—by issuing credit cards—at over 16 percent. That's quite a tidy profit, and it explains why you keep getting credit card applications in the mail.

Any time you use a credit card, you're obligating future income. That is, in the future you'll have less budget flexibility because a portion of your take-home pay will have to be used to pay off credit card expenditures plus any interest on your unpaid balance. If you don't control your spending, you can wind up with some heavy budgetary problems as a larger and larger portion of your income goes toward paying off past debt and interest owed. If this problem sounds familiar, look no further than our national debt.

Just how well do undergraduates do at paying off their credit card bills? Not that well at all, according to a study by Nellie Mae. As shown in Figure 6.2, only 17 percent of undergraduates pay off their credit cards each month, while 38 percent make more than the minimum payment but always carry a balance on their credit cards.

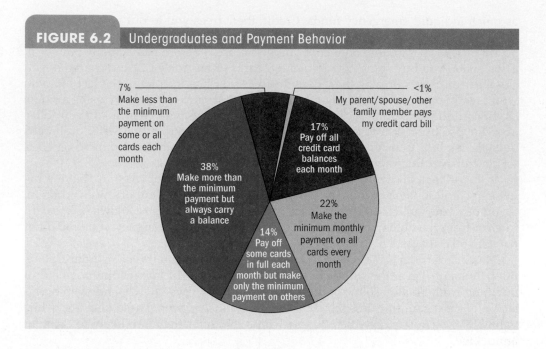

FIGURE 6.2 Undergraduates and Payment Behavior

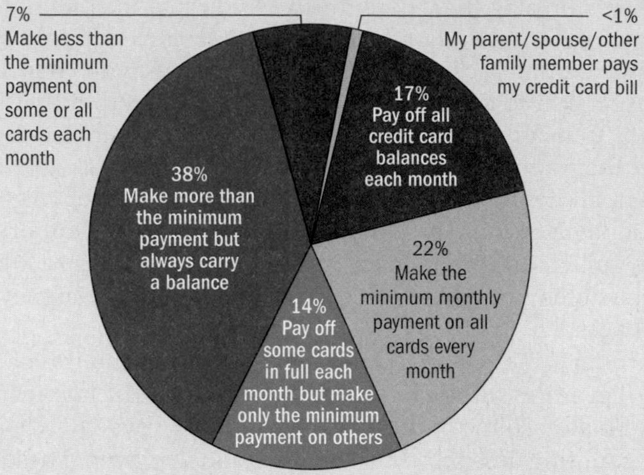

What the CARD Act Means for You

With the passage of the Credit Card Accountability, Responsibility, and Disclosure (CARD) Act of 2009 came sweeping reform, resulting in new credit card rules. Let's take a look at them.[1]

1. **Notification of rate increase.** Your credit card company must send you a notice 45 days before they can:
   - Increase your interest rate,
   - Change certain fees (such as annual fees, cash advance fees, and late fees), or
   - Make other significant changes to the terms of your card.

   The company does *not* have to send you a 45-day advance notice if:
   - You have a variable interest rate tied to an index and that rate goes up,
   - Your introductory rate expires and reverts to the previously disclosed "go-to" rate, or
   - Your rate increases because you haven't made your payments as agreed.
2. **Notification of schedule for payoff.** Your credit card company has to tell you how long it will take to pay off your balance and how much you will need to pay each month in order to pay off your balance in 3 years. This should appear on your statement each month.
3. **No interest rate increases for the first year.** Your credit card company cannot increase your rate for the first 12 months after you open an account unless:
   - Your card has a variable interest rate tied to an index and the index goes up,
   - Your card's introductory rate expires and your rate reverts to the "go-to" rate the company disclosed when you got the card, or
   - You are more than 60 days late in paying your bill.

[1] *Source:* Consumer Financial Protection Bureau, **http://files.consumerfinance.gov/f/201309_cfpb_card-act-report**.pdf, accessed April 1, 2017.

4. **Increased rates apply only to new charges.**
5. **Restrictions on over-the-limit transactions.**
6. **Caps on high-fee cards.** Card fees cannot total more than 25 percent of the initial credit limit.
7. **Protections for underage consumers.**
8. **Standard payment dates and times.**
9. **Payments directed to highest-interest balances first.** If you make more than the minimum payment on your credit card bill, your credit card company must in general apply the excess amount to the balance with the highest interest rate.
10. **Fee limits.** Your credit card company cannot charge you a fee of more than $25 unless:
    - One of your last six payments was late, in which case your fee may be up to $35, or
    - It can show that the costs resulting from late payments justify a higher fee.

    In addition, your credit card company cannot charge a late payment fee that is greater than your minimum payment. Similarly, if you exceed your credit limit by $5, you can't be charged an over-the-limit fee of more than $5.
11. **No inactivity fees.**

Choosing a Source of Open Credit

LO3 Describe the different types of credit cards.

There are several different types of open credit available today, including some credit card variations along with the traditional charge account. Let's take a look at these options and discuss how to choose which one is best for you.

Bank Credit Cards

Bank Credit Card
A credit card issued by a bank or large corporation, generally as a Visa or MasterCard.

Most credit card purchases are made on bank credit cards. A **bank credit card** is a credit card issued by a bank or large corporation; for example, AT&T and Quicken both issue credit cards, generally as a Visa or MasterCard. Visa and MasterCard don't actually issue cards themselves; rather, they act as franchise organizations that provide credit authorization systems, accounting-statement record keeping, and advertising services and allow banks and large corporations to issue the cards with the Visa or MasterCard name. Within certain broad limits, banks can establish their own policies with respect to interest, grace periods, fees, and services, so there are dramatic differences among bank credit cards.

Visa and MasterCard are so popular because they provide an efficient system of credit authorization. Being able to check a customer's credit at the time of purchase provides merchants with an assurance that there is no problem with the credit card or line of credit. It has led to the wide acceptance of these bank credit cards both in the United States and abroad. Today, there are over 7,000 to choose from.

Many bank cards offer benefits such as rental-car damage coverage, extended warranties, and travel accident insurance, as well as frequent flier miles and rebates of all kinds. Generally, bank cards that provide rebates are "co-branded" or "rebate cards." They have a "brand name" listed on the card, such as Marriott Resorts or Disney, and provide rebates and discounts on Marriott Resorts, airline tickets, and Disney vacations.

In addition, many bank cards come with reward programs in which you earn points that may be redeemed for travel, merchandise, and cash rebates. But once again, the terms on reward cards can vary dramatically. To check for rewards programs and compare annual fees and interest rates, visit **http://www.bankrate.com**. Obviously,

STOP & THINK

Even if you're "preapproved" for a card at a certain interest rate with a specific fee structure, it doesn't mean that that's the card you'll actually get. After the credit card company reviews your credit history and the facts you disclose in the application, you may be sent a card with less-favorable terms than the one originally offered to you. Would you activate the new card before you looked closely at the terms? Do you think this practice is ethical? Why or why not?

reward programs are great as long as you pay off your credit card every month. But you don't want the potential for airline miles or bonus points to cause you to charge more than you would otherwise. You want to make sure the benefits are worth more than the card's costs, including the annual fee.

The one card that is a bit different is the Discover card. Although Visa and MasterCard license their services to the banks that in turn issue the credit cards, the Discover card is issued by a single bank. It also contains some unusual features: It carries no annual fee, provides a free monthly credit score, and returns to cardholders a small percentage of their annual purchases.

Bank Credit Card Variations

There are several different card classes of bank credit cards. A card class refers to the credit level of the cardholder. At the low end is the standard card, with credit limits from $500 to $3,000. Above that are Gold cards, such as the Visa Gold card, which offer a bigger line of credit—generally, $5,000 and up—and provide extra perks or incentives. Finally, there are **premium or prestige credit cards**, which offer extremely high credit limits and benefits beyond a standard credit card, including things like emergency medical and legal services, travel insurance and services, rebates, and warranties on new purchases. In addition, Visa and MasterCard even offer Black cards, with higher credit limits and even more benefits.

Premium or Prestige Credit Card
A bank credit card that offers credit limits as high as $100,000 or more in addition to numerous added perks, including emergency medical and legal services, travel services, rebates, and insurance on new purchases.

Another variation of the bank credit card is the **affinity card**, which is a credit card issued in conjunction with a specific charity or organization, such as the Sierra Club, Mothers Against Drunk Driving (MADD), the National Rifle Association (NRA), and many colleges and universities. The card bears the sponsoring group's name, logo, or picture. These cards send a portion of their annual fee or a percentage of the purchases back to the sponsoring organization.

Affinity Card
A credit card issued in conjunction with a specific charity or organization. It carries the sponsoring group's name and/or picture on the credit card itself and sends a portion of the annual fee or a percentage of the purchases back to the sponsoring organization.

Although the fees and annual interest rates on affinity cards vary from card to card, in general affinity cards are expensive. Annual fees start at $20 and increase to $200 or more, and their interest rates tend to be higher than those of most bank cards. Still, many individuals use them, seeing them as an easy way to support their favorite charity or organization. Actually, it can be an expensive way to make charitable donations, particularly if you ever maintain an unpaid balance. Also, a large part of your charitable donation actually gets "donated" to the issuing bank, and you can't take a tax deduction for that donation!

The final variation on the bank credit card is the **secured credit card**. A secured credit card is a regular bank credit card backed by the pledge of some collateralized asset. If you can't pay what you've charged to your credit card, the issuing bank has a specific asset it can lay claim to. For example, your credit card may be linked to a CD you hold in the issuing bank. If you can't pay off your charges, it's so long, CD. For the bank, no customer is a bad risk if he or she is able to put up collateral. But what's the benefit to you? Why would you want a secured credit card? Well, you may not have a choice. If you're a bad credit risk, it may be the only credit card you can get.

Secured Credit Card
A credit card backed by the pledge of some collateralized asset.

Travel and Entertainment Cards

Travel and entertainment (T&E) cards, such as the American Express Corporate card, were initially aimed at providing business customers with a means of paying for travel, business entertainment, and other business expenses, while keeping these charges separate from personal expenditures. Over time, however, T&E cards have come to be used similarly to traditional bank credit cards. The major difference

Travel and Entertainment (T&E) Card
A credit card initially meant for business customers to allow them to pay for travel and entertainment expenses, keeping them separate from their other expenditures.

between T&E cards and bank credit cards is that T&E cards *do not* offer revolving credit and require full payment of the balance each month. Aside from the prestige that they may afford holders, their only advantage is their interest-free grace period.

The issuer's only income from these cards is the annual fee, which can run as high as $2,500 per year, and the merchant's discount fee on each purchase. The three primary issuers of T&E cards are American Express, Diners Club, and Carte Blanche, with American Express dominating this market. There are also T&E premium or prestige cards.

Single-Purpose Cards

A **single-purpose card** is a credit card that can be used only at a specific company. For example, a Texaco credit card can be used to charge purchases only at a Texaco service station. These companies issue their own cards and avoid merchant's discount fees. The terms associated with single-purpose cards vary dramatically from card to card: Some allow for revolving credit, while others do not; some provide a discount when used; and in general, they don't charge annual fees.

Single-Purpose Card
A credit card that can be used only at a specific company.

Traditional Charge Accounts

A **traditional charge account** is a charge account offered by a business. For example, phone and utility companies and even doctors and dentists provide services and bill you later, usually giving you a grace period to pay up. This payment system is a type of open credit account—one in which no cards are involved. After you receive your monthly bill, you're expected to pay it in full. If payment is not received by the due date, an interest penalty is generally tacked on.

Traditional Charge Account
A charge account, as opposed to a credit card, that can be used to make purchases only at the issuing company.

The major advantage of a charge account is convenience. Just think how tedious it would be to have to pay for each long-distance phone call or to pay for your electricity on a daily basis. In addition, there's the benefit of an interest-free grace period and the use of services before having to pay for them. For the billing company, a traditional charge account is primarily a matter of convenience—it's just an easy and efficient way to collect bills.

The Choice: What's Best for You

In evaluating the many kinds of credit cards available, you'll find that different cards have different strong points. Some cards have low fees and extended grace periods but high interest rates. Although this may be the best combination for some, it may be the worst for others. You have to understand how you're going to use the card before you can decide which one to choose. Most individuals use credit cards for convenience, for credit, or both.

A *credit user* generally carries an unpaid balance from month to month. Most credit users don't use the grace period, and the annual fee pales relative to the amount of interest they pay annually. If you're a credit user, the most important decision factor is the APR, or interest rate on the unpaid balance, because it will be the largest credit expense you face. Should the issuing bank's location be a concern in choosing a credit card? No: Regardless of where your credit card issuer is located, your card works essentially the same. A credit user should search as far and wide as necessary to get the card with the lowest possible interest rate.

For a *convenience user*—someone who pays off the credit card balance each month—the interest rate is irrelevant. Convenience users should look for a credit card with a low annual fee and an interest-free grace period. The interest-free grace period is especially important because it allows convenience users to pay off their balance each month without incurring any interest payments. Beyond a low annual fee and an interest-free grace period, a convenience user might consider a card that carries benefits, such as a Marriott credit card or one with frequent flier miles.

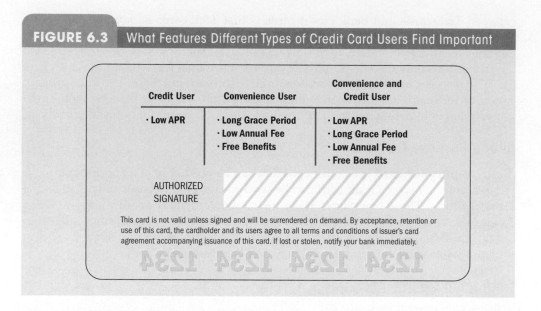

FIGURE 6.3 What Features Different Types of Credit Card Users Find Important

Credit User	Convenience User	Convenience and Credit User
· Low APR	· Long Grace Period · Low Annual Fee · Free Benefits	· Low APR · Long Grace Period · Low Annual Fee · Free Benefits

AUTHORIZED SIGNATURE

This card is not valid unless signed and will be surrendered on demand. By acceptance, retention or use of this card, the cardholder and its users agree to all terms and conditions of issuer's card agreement accompanying issuance of this card. If lost or stolen, notify your bank immediately.

A *convenience and credit user* is someone who generally, but not always, pays off all of the balance. For this type of credit user, the ideal card is one with an interest-free grace period, a low interest rate on the unpaid balance, and no annual fee. Unfortunately, finding all of this in one card is next to impossible. Convenience and credit users therefore must simply look for the combination of features they think will result in the lowest total cost, considering both the interest rate and the annual fee. Figure 6.3 shows what features different types of credit card users find important.

LO4 Know what determines your credit card worthiness and how to secure a credit card.

Getting a Credit Card

For a college student today, getting a credit card is generally not a problem. Credit card issuers see college students as excellent prospects. They may not be earning much now, but their future earning prospects are bright. Also, some lenders try to ensure themselves of payment by requiring parents to cosign on the credit cards; others simply assume that the student's parents will step in if there are problems paying off any debt. Credit card issuers used to set up shop near large campuses and offer free gifts—anything from free or discounted flights to free Frisbees—for those who applied. Fortunately, the CARD Act has toned down the actions of credit card issuers by banning offers of freebies (pizzas and T-shirts, for example) if students sign up for credit cards on or near campus (where "near campus" is defined as within 1,000 feet) or at college-sponsored events. In addition, credit card issuers are now banned from issuing credit cards to persons under 21 unless they can show proof that they can repay the credit card loans independently or someone over 21 cosigns on the account with them. But once you're 21, you're fair game. And there are plenty of credit card offers to go around. In fact, credit card companies send out a whopping 6 billion credit card offers annually, or roughly 60 per U.S. household! As for the average college student, prior to the new law they received about eight solicitations a year.

For a student, getting a credit card is an excellent idea. First, it can be used for emergency funds while away from home. Second, by using a credit card prudently, a student can build up a solid credit history. Is your credit history important? Well, yes, if you ever want to do such things as buy a house, rent an apartment, or get a job.

The first step in obtaining a credit card is applying. The application focuses on factors that determine your creditworthiness, or your ability and willingness to repay any charges incurred. Sometimes the lender may insist on an interview. You've absolutely got to be honest and consistent in the application process. If your answers are inconsistent or don't conform to what the lender has found out independently, your application will be turned down. Let's find out what makes you creditworthy.

FACTS OF LIFE

Cosigning anything isn't a great idea. According to a recent GOBankingRates survey, 38 percent of cosigners had to pay some or all of the entire bill because the primary borrower didn't pay. Before cosigning for anything, think about the possible consequences.

Credit Evaluation: The Five Cs of Credit

In determining what makes an individual creditworthy, most lenders refer to the "five Cs" of credit: character, capacity, capital, collateral, and conditions. *Character* refers to your sense of responsibility with respect to debt payment. Have you established a record of timely repayment of past debts, such as student loans? Keep in mind that exhibiting good character involves not overextending yourself with respect to credit—that is, not taking on too much debt, given your income level. In assessing your character, lenders also look at how long you've lived at one address and how long you've held your current job. In effect, stability often passes for character.

Capacity and *capital* work together in determining your ability to repay any credit card charges. In assessing your *capacity*, lenders look to both your current income level and your current level of borrowing—that is, lenders are concerned with your level of nonobligated income. Most financial advisors suggest that your total debt payments, including mortgage payments, should account for less than 36 percent of your gross pay.

Capital refers to the size of your financial holdings or investment portfolio. Obviously, the more you have in savings, the more creditworthy you are. By looking at your capital, lenders want to know whether your income is sufficient to provide for the debt you've already incurred. The larger your nonobligated annual income (capacity) and the value of your investment portfolio (capital), the more creditworthy you are.

Collateral refers to assets or property offered as security to obtain credit. If you were to default on a loan, the collateral—perhaps a car or a piece of land—would be sold, and the proceeds from the sale would go to repay the debt. The more your collateral is worth, the more creditworthy you are.

The last of the five Cs is *conditions*. Conditions refers to the impact the current economic environment may have on your ability to repay any borrowing. You may appear to be strong in all other aspects, but if you're laid off because of a downswing in the economy, you might not be able to meet your obligations.

The Key to Getting Credit: Your Credit Score Credit card issuers verify the information you put down on your application and get information about your character and financial situation through a credit report supplied from a credit bureau. A **credit bureau** is a private organization that maintains credit information on individuals, which it allows subscribers to access for a fee. There are three primary credit bureaus: Experian, TransUnion, and Equifax Credit Information Services. These credit bureaus put together a credit report on you and assign you a credit score based on their evaluation of your creditworthiness.

Credit Bureau
A company that gathers information on consumers' financial history, including how quickly they have paid bills and whether they have been delinquent on bills in the past. The company summarizes this information and sells it to customers.

Your credit report contains only information regarding your financial situation and dealings. It contains no information about your personal lifestyle. Also, a credit bureau doesn't make credit decisions: It merely supplies data that banks, savings and loan associations, department stores, or other creditors use to make credit decisions. But make no mistake: Your credit information not only plays a big role in whether you get that loan but also helps determine how high your interest rate will be.

Credit Scoring
The numerical evaluation or "scoring" of credit applicants based on their credit history.

Determining Creditworthiness Once your credit information has been assembled, it is translated into a three-digit number—your credit score—which measures your creditworthiness. Although some lenders look at each application individually and make a judgment call, it's more common that your credit application will be evaluated using credit scoring. **Credit scoring** involves the numerical evaluation or "scoring" of applicants. This score is then evaluated according to a predetermined standard. If your score is at or above the acceptance standard, you are approved for credit. Credit scoring is efficient and relatively inexpensive for the lender. Its benefit to the borrower is that because it reduces the lender's uncertainty, the lender is more often able to make credit available to good-risk customers at lower interest rates. However, credit scoring is not a flawless method of evaluating creditworthiness.

Your Credit Score

Your credit score has an enormous effect on your financial life, influencing everything from the rate you pay on your credit cards, to the size of your credit line, to your insurance rates, to your mortgage rate, to the amount of junk mail you receive asking you to take on one more credit card. In short, when it comes to lending money, you'll be evaluated by your credit score. With a strong credit score, you'll also be paying a much lower interest rate on any money you borrow.

How Your Credit Score Is Computed—FICO and VantageScore There are two primary credit scoring systems—FICO and VantageScore—with FICO being the dominant one. Although FICO scores go by a number of different names depending on which credit bureau is calculating the credit score, they are all calculated using models developed by the Fair Isaac Corporation. VantageScore is an alternative to FICO scores and is aimed at helping lenders better evaluate those with poor, or subprime, credit. In fact, VantageScore gives lenders access to 30–35 million creditworthy consumers who would have been invisible under the alternative credit scoring models. FICO and VantageScore both begin with the information on your credit report and use this information to calculate a score that can run from 300 all the way to 850. Figure 6.4 provides the distribution of the percentages of the population with

FIGURE 6.4 National Distribution of FICO Scores

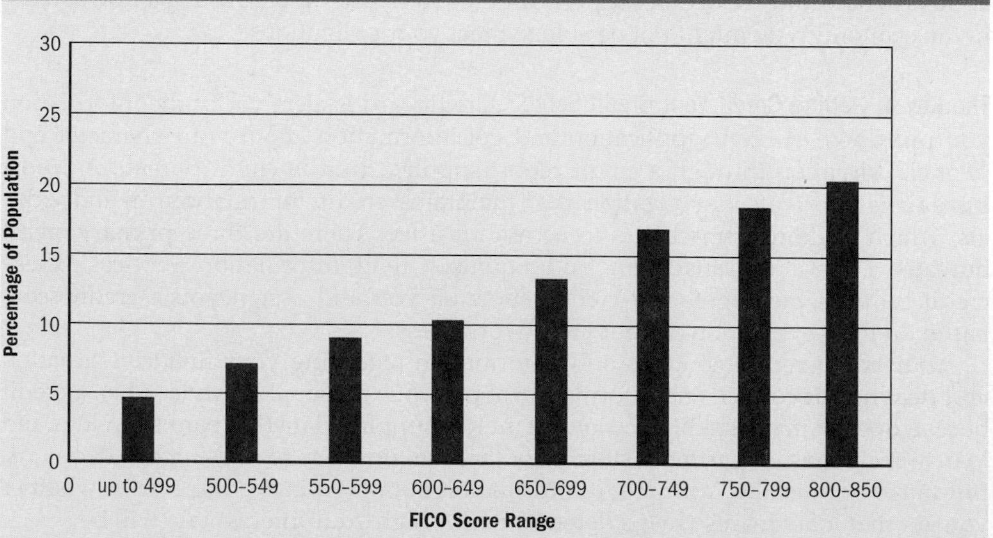

Source: FICO Score Distribution, FICO. http://www.fico.com/en/blogs/risk-compliance/us-credit-quality-rising-the-beat-goes-on/, accessed, March 27, 2017.

different FICO scores. There are a number of innovations incorporated into VantageScore: Debt collections that have been paid off are not considered, and negative credit history caused by natural disasters like tornadoes and hurricanes is ignored. If you're interested, you can get an estimate of what your credit score is online at **http://www.myfico.com/ficocreditscoreestimator**. You'll also find that your credit score may vary from credit bureau to credit bureau; while the different credit bureaus may be using the same credit scoring model to come up with a score, they may have different credit data in your file or use slightly different calculation methods. These FICO and VantageScore scores are then provided to lenders by the different credit bureaus.

What's a good credit score? In April of 2017, the average credit score nationwide reached 700, which is its highest level since 2005, but to get the best mortgage rate you'll need a score of 760 or higher and a score of around 620 oftentimes serving as a cutoff point for receiving credit for many lenders. In effect, a good credit score doesn't just mean that you'll get a loan; it also means that you'll be paying less for it. For example, a person with a 760 score will be offered an interest rate about 1.569 percent less than that offered to a person with a 639 score. Table 6.1 gives representative rates for different FICO scores along with what the monthly interest payments would be on a $300,000, 30-year fixed mortgage loan and a $25,000, 36-month auto loan in April 2017.

While a low FICO score will cost you quite a bit when it comes time to get a mortgage loan, it costs even more when you look at its impact on your credit card rate. It's not unusual for a low FICO score to result in a credit card rate that is twice the rate paid by those with a high FICO score.

It is important to note that your credit score is not the only factor that lenders use in determining whether or not you get credit. For example, in the decision whether or not to give you a mortgage loan, the lending agency will look at your employment history, the type of job you have, the value of the property relative to the value of the loan, and the total amount of debt you currently have. In addition, you should know that the lending agency can't even calculate a FICO score for you unless you

STOP & THINK

Forbes recently reported that there may be some new items coming to your credit score. Apparently, Fair Isaac, the folks that calculate your FICO score, are looking at new strategies to measure your creditworthiness using information offered on social networking sites like Facebook. One possibility is for them to scan how many times the word *wasted* comes up in your social media updates. Since responsibility is an indicator of how likely you are to repay your debts, this addition adds predictive value. As we will see in the insurance chapter, credit scores are also used to determine insurance rates. Again, responsible behavior goes a long way in determining the likelihood of a claim on an auto or a homeowners policy. This is just one more reason why you might want to clean up your social media records.

TABLE 6.1 Representative Rates and Monthly Payments for Different FICO Scores

30-Year Fixed Mortgage			36-Month Auto Loan		
FICO Score	**APR**	**Monthly Payment**	**FICO Score**	**APR**	**Monthly Payment**
760–850	3.831%	$1,403	720–850	3.466%	$732
700–759	4.053%	$1,441	690–719	4.482%	$743
680–699	4.23%	$1,472	660–689	6.895%	$771
660–679	4.444%	$1,510	620–659	9.589%	$802
640–659	4.874%	$1,587	590–619	13.902%	$853
620–639	5.42%	$1,688	500–589	15.138%	$868
Mortgage loan amount: $300,000			Auto loan amount: $25,000		

have had at least one credit account open for at least 6 months and have used that credit card in that time. In effect, if you haven't been using credit over the past 6 months, the lending agency can't calculate your FICO score. Before looking at how your credit score is calculated, let's take a look at what is in your credit report.

What's in Your Credit Report While each credit reporting agency uses a different format, all credit reports contain the same basic information. In your credit report, you'll find:

- **Identifying Information:** This includes your name, address, Social Security number, date of birth, and employment information; this information is used to identify you and is not used in determining your credit score.
- **Trade Lines or Credit Accounts:** Lenders report on each account you have established with them. This information includes the type of account (credit cards, student loans, auto loan, mortgage, etc.), along with creditor and account number, balance, date opened, payment history, and current status (such as "OK," "Closed by customer," or "30 days late payment").
- **Inquiries:** When you apply for a loan, you authorize your lender to ask for a copy of your credit report. This results in inquiries appearing on your credit report. Everyone who accessed your credit report within the last 2 years appears in this list in this section of your credit report. Your credit report also lists both "voluntary" inquiries, spurred by your own requests for credit, and "involuntary" inquiries, such as when lenders order your report so as to make you a preapproved credit offer in the mail.
- **Public Record and Collection Items:** Your credit report also includes public record information collected from state and county courts and information on non-loan-related items from collection agencies, excluding tax lien and civil judgment data. Public record information includes bankruptcies, foreclosures, lawsuits, wage attachments, and non-tax liens.

The Factors That Determine Your Credit Score Now let's look at the five factors that determine your credit score, with Figure 6.5 illustrating this breakdown.

1. **Your Payment History (35 percent of your score):** Your payment history is very important. Do not skip any payments. Try to always pay at least the minimum due.

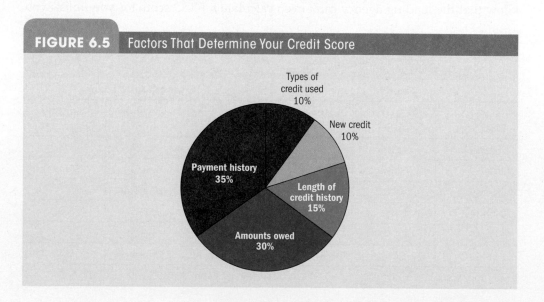

FIGURE 6.5 Factors That Determine Your Credit Score

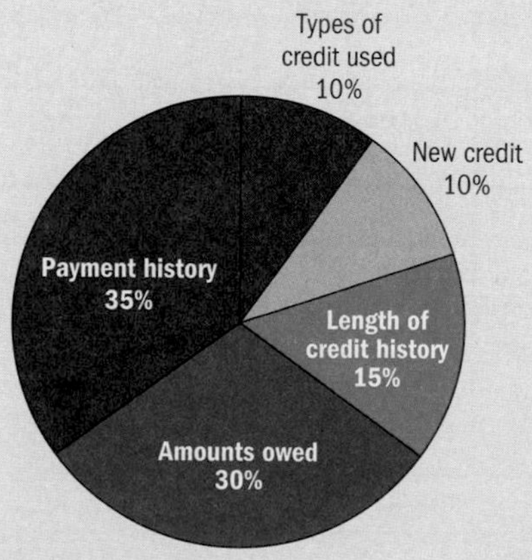

A lender that is considering extending credit to you wants to know how you've handled your credit payments in the past. Can you repay money that is lent to you?

2. **The Amount You Owe (30 percent of your score):** How much do you owe on your credit cards, your mortgage, your car loans, and any other outstanding debt? What is your total available credit? The lower the debt-to-credit ratio, the better.
3. **Length of Credit History (15 percent of your score):** The longer your credit accounts have been open and the longer you have had accounts with the same creditors, the higher your credit score will be. A short history is fine as long as payments have been on time and there is not too much debt.
4. **Types of Credit Used (10 percent of your score):** The wider the variety of credit that you have, the better. If you have several different types of credit outstanding—for example, credit cards, retail accounts, installment loans, an auto loan, and a mortgage loan—that is seen as an indication that you know how to handle your money.
5. **New Credit (10 percent of your score):** If you have recently made a lot of applications for credit, you will lose points on your FICO score. This is because individuals who are moving toward bankruptcy generally take one last grasp at credit, hoping it will keep them afloat.

Monitoring Your Credit Score It's important to monitor your credit score. First, you must ensure that there are no errors in your credit report, since that's what is used to calculate your credit score. To do this, you'll need to get a copy of your credit report annually. Some experts recommend getting a copy every few months to monitor for identity theft. The Fair and Accurate Credit Transactions (FACT) Act allows you to request one free copy of your credit report each year from the three major credit bureaus: Experian, Equifax, and TransUnion. If you'd like more information on how to request your report, log in to **www.annualcreditreport.com**. Take care to ensure that you reach the FACT Act–supported site, as imposter Web sites are on the rise. Table 6.2 provides additional information on the FACT Act.

If you've already used up your one free report from each of the three credit bureaus this year and would like another, you can either order online (**http://www.MyFico.com**) or contact the credit bureaus directly. Once you have your credit report, you should make sure that the information in it is correct. Look at all the

TABLE 6.2 The Fair and Accurate Credit Transactions Act
The Fair and Accurate Credit Transactions (FACT) Act was signed in 2003, with many of its provisions becoming active in 2004 and 2005. It provides:
Protection Against Identity Theft
• You can now request one free copy of your credit report each year from each of the three major credit bureaus: Experian, Equifax, and TransUnion. You can get information about the availability of credit reports by logging in to **http://www.annualcreditreport.com** or calling 1-877-322-8228. It may be safer to call for your credit report using the toll-free number because of all the imposter Web sites—and there are plenty of them! • With just one phone call to a single credit bureau, you can place a fraud alert on your credit record and improve the security of your credit rating. • Once you've placed a fraud alert on your credit record, anyone who uses your credit report is required to take additional measures to confirm your identity before opening an account. • Only the last five digits of your credit card number will be printed on electronic receipts.
Standards for Information Sharing and Credit Reporting
• Federal law governing credit reporting will override inconsistent state laws. • New limits are imposed on the sharing of medical information and the use of customer information among affiliated companies.

credit accounts listed, and make sure that they are yours and that they are correct. Do mistakes appear often in credit reports? The National Association of Public Interest Research Groups says that 79 percent of the credit reports it surveyed contained either serious errors or other mistakes of some kind. Moreover, it found that 25 percent of the credit reports it surveyed contained errors that were significant enough to result in the denial of credit—errors such as false delinquencies and accounts that did not belong to the consumer.

Consumer Credit Rights

The easiest way to resolve a credit complaint is to take it directly to the creditor. However, if that doesn't work, there are a number of federal laws aimed at protecting you if you have a complaint about credit.

The Credit Bureau and Your Rights Because your credit report is so important, Congress passed the Fair and Accurate Credit Transactions (FACT) Act in 2003, which we discussed earlier. This act allows you to request one free copy of your credit report each year from the three major credit bureaus: Experian, Equifax, and TransUnion.

If the information in your file isn't accurate or complete, contact the credit bureaus; their contact information is given in Table 6.3. They must investigate any errors you point out and make corrections. For example, your file may inadvertently contain information about someone with a name very similar to yours, or it may contain incorrect or incomplete credit information, perhaps listing accounts that are closed or that you never had. If there are any mistakes, you should notify the credit bureau so it can investigate and make the corrections.

If the credit bureau investigates and determines that the information in your report is accurate, you have the right to have a statement in your file presenting your view of the issue. This statement gives you the chance to dispute the accuracy of information in your file. In any case, if you do find inaccuracies, point them out immediately.

The Fair Credit Reporting Act (FCRA) limits the length of time damaging information can remain in your file. Bankruptcy information can remain in your file for only 10 years, and other negative information must be removed from your file after 7 years.

The FCRA also limits access to your credit file to those who have a legitimate right to view it, such as a financial institution considering extending you credit, an employer, or a company doing business with you. You also have the right to know who has seen your credit report.

If Your Credit Card Application Is Rejected If your credit card application is rejected, you have two choices. First, you can apply for a card with another financial

TABLE 6.3 National Credit Bureaus

	Equifax Credit Information Services http://www.equifax.com	Experian (formerly TRW) http://www.experian.com	TransUnion http://www.tuc.com
To Report Fraud	888-766-0008	888-397-3742	800-680-7289
To Dispute Something in Your Report	P.O. Box 740256 Atlanta, GA 30348 866-349-5191	P.O. Box 4500 Allen, TX 75013 888-397-3742	2 Baldwin Place P.O. Box 1000 Chester, PA 19016 800-916-8800

TABLE 6.4 Major Provisions of Consumer Credit Laws

Truth in Lending Act of 1968: Requires lenders to disclose the true cost of consumer credit, explaining all charges, terms, and conditions involved. It requires that consumers be provided with the total finance charge and annual percentage rate on the loan.
Truth in Lending Act (amended 1971): Prohibits lenders from sending unauthorized credit cards and limits cardholders' liability to $50 for unauthorized use.
Fair Credit Billing Act of 1975: Sets procedures for correcting billing errors on open credit accounts. It also allows consumers to withhold payment for defective goods purchased with a credit card. In addition, it sets limits on the time some information can be kept in consumers' credit files.
Equal Credit Opportunity Act of 1975: Prohibits credit discrimination on the basis of sex and marital status. It also requires lenders to provide a written statement explaining any adverse action taken.
Equal Credit Opportunity Act (amended 1977): Prohibits credit discrimination based on race, national origin, religion, age, or receipt of public assistance.
Fair Debt Collection Practices Act of 1978: Prohibits unfair, abusive, and deceptive practices by debt collectors and establishes procedures for debt collection.
Truth in Lending Act (amended 1982): Requires installment credit contracts to be written in plain English.
Fair Credit Reporting Reform Act of 1996 (updated version of the Fair Credit Reporting Act of 1971): Requires that consumers be provided with the name of any credit agency supplying a credit report that leads to the denial of credit. It gives consumers the right to know what is in their credit reports and challenge incorrect information. It also requires that employers get written permission from current or prospective employees before reviewing their credit files. In addition, it allows consumers to sue creditors if reporting errors are not corrected.
Fair and Accurate Credit Transactions (FACT) Act of 2003: It allows consumers to request one free copy of their credit report each year from the three major credit bureaus.
Credit Card Accountability, Responsibility, and Disclosure (CARD) Act of 2009: Bans unfair rate increases by banning retroactive rate increases and providing first-year protection; prevents unfair fee traps (for example, late-fee traps); requires cardholders to opt in to over-the-limit fees, restrains unfair subprime fees, and limits fees on gift and stored-value cards; requires plain sight and plain language disclosures; adds new accountability measures for regulators; and provides new protections for college students and young adults, including a requirement that card issuers and universities disclose agreements with respect to the marketing or distribution of credit cards to students.
Dodd-Frank Wall Street Reform and Consumer Protection Act (Dodd-Frank Act) of 2010: Creates the Consumer Financial Protection Bureau (CFPB) with the purpose of educating consumers, enforcing federal consumer laws, and gathering and analyzing information that will help consumers gain a better understanding of financial questions that they face.

institution. Getting rejected at one bank doesn't necessarily mean you'll get rejected at another. Second, find out why you've been rejected. Set up an appointment with the credit card manager, and find out what caused your rejection. Once you know the reason, address the problem. You might have to correct inaccurate information on your credit report, or you might have to change how you do things.

Resolving Billing Errors Your credit card statement may contain a math error, it may include billing for an item you never received, it may include double billing for an item you purchased—the possible errors are many. Fortunately, the Fair Credit Billing Act (FCBA) provides a procedure for correcting billing errors. Under the FCBA, you're allowed to withhold payment for the item in question while you petition the card issuer to investigate the matter. Table 6.4 provides a summary of the major laws governing consumer credit.

FACTS OF LIFE

Graduate school is expensive. According to a study of graduate students by Nellie Mae, whereas 93 percent of the graduate student survey respondents make at least the required minimum monthly credit card payments, only 20 percent said they pay off their cards in full each month.

To begin an investigation of a billing problem, the FCBA requires that you notify your card issuer *in writing within 60 days* of the statement date. In your inquiry, you must include your name, address, and account number in addition to a description of the error, including its date, the dollar amount of the billing error, and the reason you feel it's in error. You should also note in your letter that you're making this billing inquiry under the FCBA.

This letter should then be sent to the "billing inquiry" or "billing error" address given on your credit card bill. Because most bill payments are handled automatically, enclosing your complaint with your payment will likely ensure that it'll be lost forever. Moreover, the FCBA requires that an address to which billing questions should be directed be included on your statement. Make sure you keep a copy of your letter for future reference.

Within 30 days, you should receive notice that an investigation of your complaint has been initiated. The card issuer has 90 days or two billing cycles to complete the investigation. On completion of the investigation, either your account will be credited the disputed amount, or you'll receive an explanation from the card issuer as to why it feels your complaint isn't legitimate.

You can continue to dispute your billing charges by notifying the card issuer within your grace period, but the process of correcting it becomes more complicated. If you don't pay, you can be reported delinquent to the credit bureaus, and you risk the chance of being sued by the card issuer and having your credit rating go down the tubes. Still, if you feel the bank isn't handling your inquiry in an appropriate manner, contact the regulatory agency that oversees the card. Alternatively, you could contact an attorney or consider filing a claim in small claims court.

The Consumer Financial Protection Bureau The Consumer Financial Protection Bureau (CFPB) provides a single location for financial protection and oversight—and its job is to help consumers make better decisions. For example, when you shop for a financial product, be it a home loan, a credit card, or a student loan, how do you know it's the best deal? You can wade through all the advertising and page after page of fine print, but once you've done that, it is still difficult to make side-by-side comparisons, and it is all too easy to end up with a deal that doesn't work for you and your family. As we saw in the recent financial crisis, this has real-life consequences—for you and for the whole economy. We saw consumers take on more and more dangerous loans, including millions of risky and unaffordable mortgages, and we know how all that turned out. What was our government doing during all this? Many government agencies supervised different parts of the system, and these parts did not interact. As a result, it was nearly impossible for people to hold any one agency accountable.

To remedy this, the CFPB was created and given the oversight authority to make sure that consumer financial markets work. Its job is to make credit products and other consumer financial services easier to understand by making sure that prices are clear up front and risks are easy to see. The CFPB also cut down on the fine print and made the prices and risks clear for mortgages, credit cards, and other kinds of financial products and services. This way it will be easier to do some comparison shopping and choose the products that are the best for you and your situation.

Identity Theft

Identity Theft
The use of your name, address, Social Security number, bank or credit card account number, or other identifying information by someone other than you without your knowledge to commit fraud or other crimes.

Identity theft occurs when someone uses your name, address, Social Security number, bank or credit card account number, or other identifying information without your knowledge to commit fraud or other crimes.

In general, identity fraud tends to be a "low-tech" crime. Typically, personal identifying information is stolen from a person's purse or wallet or from his or her mail or trash. Sometimes it is garnered from a change of address form the thieves filled out to divert your mail. Less often, it is obtained from hacking into a computer or is a result of "pretexting," which involves getting your personal information under false pretenses. For example, pretexters may call you on the telephone, claiming to be from a survey firm and wanting to ask you a few questions, or they may send you an e-mail, claiming to be from eBay or Citibank and stating that unless you respond to the e-mail and provide personal information, your account will be closed.

Once identity thieves have the information they need, they can go on a spending spree with your credit card, open new credit cards, take out loans, and even establish phone service in your name—in short, these thieves can make your life miserable. Granted, you aren't liable for these charges, but getting things straightened out can be a royal pain.

How Do You Know If You're a Victim of Identity Theft? The following are signs that identity theft may have happened to you:

- You receive a credit card that you didn't apply for.
- You are denied credit, or you are offered less-than-favorable credit terms, such as a high interest rate, for no apparent reason.
- You receive calls or letters from debt collectors or businesses about merchandise or services you didn't buy.
- You fail to receive bills or other mail.

If you think your identity has been stolen, here's what to do:

STEP 1: Contact the fraud department of any one of the three major credit bureaus to place a fraud alert on your credit file.

STEP 2: Close the accounts that you know or that you believe have been tampered with or opened fraudulently.

STEP 3: File a police report.

STEP 4: File a complaint with the Federal Trade Commission at the government's consumer information Web site (**http://www.consumer.gov**).

Controlling and Managing Your Credit Cards and Open Credit

LO5 Manage your credit cards and open credit.

The first step in managing your credit is knowing what you have charged. It's far too easy to charge a pizza here, a gas fill-up there, and so forth until all control is lost. Remember, a lot of personal finance is about control. If you don't keep track of what you spend, it's hard to control what you spend.

Reducing Your Balance

In addition to knowing exactly what the interest charge is on your credit card, it's important to understand how long it takes to pay off debt if you don't make meaningful payments—that is, payments well above the required minimum monthly payment. First, most credit cards require that you pay about 4 percent of your outstanding balance monthly. This means that if you're paying 18 percent interest on that balance, you're getting almost nowhere.

To get an idea of how long it takes to get rid of credit card debt, let's look at an example. Keep in mind that your credit card interest rate, as well as your beginning

TABLE 6.5 How Long It Can Take to Eliminate Credit Card Debt

Each Month Pay This Percentage of the Initial Outstanding Balance	Annual Credit Card Interest Rate			
	9%	12%	15%	18%
4%	28 months	29 months	30 months	32 months
5%	22 months	22 months	23 months	24 months
10%	10 months	11 months	11 months	11 months
15%	7 months	7 months	7 months	7 months

1. **Step 1:** Find the row that corresponds to the percentage of your initial balance that you intend to pay off each month. If you have an initial outstanding balance of $5,000 and you intend to pay off $200 each month, you will be paying off $200/$5,000 = 4 percent each month. Thus, you should look in the 4% row.
2. **Step 2:** Find the column that corresponds to the annual percentage that you pay on your credit card. If your credit card charges 15 percent interest, look in the 15% column.
3. **Step 3:** The intersection of the payments row and the credit card interest column shows how many months it will take to pay off your initial balance. If you pay off 4 percent of your initial balance each month and the card charges 15 percent interest, it will take 30 months to pay off your initial balance.

If you pay off only 2 percent of your initial balance per month and the credit card interest rate is 15 percent, it will take 79 months, or over 6½ years, to pay off your credit card debt. Keep in mind that this time frame assumes you don't charge anything more on your card. If you have a substantial balance and keep charging, you may never get out of debt.

balance and the amount you pay off each month, plays a role in determining how long it takes to eliminate your debt. If your initial balance is $3,000 and you pay off 4 percent each month, you'll be paying $120 a month. Table 6.5 shows you how to calculate how long it will take to pay off your balance. Simply find the intersection of the percentage of your initial balance that you are paying off and the interest rate on your credit card.

Protecting Against Fraud

What happens if your credit card is stolen? If you report the loss before any fraudulent charges occur, you owe nothing. However, if charges are made before you report the card missing, your liability is limited to $50 per card. (This liability limit makes credit card insurance unnecessary.) Still, it is the inconvenience associated with the loss of your credit card that makes it important to guard against fraud.

Most steps to guard against credit card fraud are obvious. First, save all your credit card receipts, and compare them against your credit card bill to make sure there are no false charges. After you've compared them with your billings, destroy these receipts because they contain your credit card number.

Second, do not give out your credit card number over the telephone unless you're purchasing an item, you initiated the sale, and the telephone you're using is a private landline. A thief can easily eavesdrop on a conversation taking place at a public phone, and cell phones are not as secure as landlines. Finally, never leave a store without your card. One way of ensuring you never leave your card behind is to hold your wallet in your hand until you receive your credit card back. Table 6.6 provides some tips on avoiding identity theft.

Trouble Signs in Credit Card Spending

The next step in controlling credit card borrowing is to examine your credit card habits and determine whether you have a problem. Although there's no simple

TABLE 6.6 How to Prevent Identity Theft
• In a safe place at home, keep a detailed list of all your credit and debit cards and other accounts, including the 24-hour customer service phone number for each. This information will help you cancel your accounts quickly and minimize the danger to your finances.
• Don't carry documents that include your Social Security number or any PINs, passwords, or access codes for bank or credit cards.
• Keep your birth certificate, passport, and Social Security card in a fireproof strongbox in your home or in a safety-deposit box. If you lose your driver's license, these will be your only official forms of identification.
• Check your credit reports with the three national credit bureaus—TransUnion, Experian, and Equifax—for suspicious activity at least once a year. Federal law entitles you to a free annual report; to get it, call 877-322-8228 or complete the Annual Credit Report Request Form and mail it to Annual Credit Report Request Service, P.O. Box 105281, Atlanta, GA 30348-5281.

formula for highlighting problems, many financial planners use a credit card habits quiz that forces you to look at your behavior and recognize any weaknesses you might have.

Checklist 6.1 provides sample questions that are used in a credit card habits quiz. The questions are intended to make you think about and reevaluate your credit card habits. If you answer "yes" to any question, you may have a problem.

If You Can't Pay Your Credit Card Bills

Once you've gotten into trouble through the overuse of credit cards, getting out is a real hassle. The first step is, of course, putting in place a budget that brings in more money than you spend. This involves self-control—making sure you *act your wage*. Within this budget, paying off your credit card must come off the top—that is, before you get a chance to spend any money at all, you take care of your planned contribution toward paying off your credit card debt. Along with this remedy, there are other options you might consider. First, you should make sure you have the least expensive credit card possible, given your habits. You should have a credit card that fits your usage habits.

You might also consider using savings to pay off current credit card debt. If it has to happen at all, it should happen only once—when you are reevaluating spending

CHECKLIST 6.1 The Credit Card Habits Quiz

If you answer "yes" to any of these questions, you may have problems controlling your credit card spending.

- ☐ Do you make only the minimum payment on your credit card each month?
- ☐ Have you reached your spending limit on one or more credit cards?
- ☐ When out to dinner with a group of friends, do you pay the entire bill with your credit card and have them reimburse you for their share with cash?
- ☐ Do you wait for your monthly bill to determine how much you have charged on your credit card rather than keeping track of all your credit card spending as it occurs?
- ☐ Do you get cash advances because you do not have enough money in your checking account?
- ☐ Have you been turned down for credit or had one of your credit cards cancelled?
- ☐ Have you used some of your savings to pay off credit card bills?
- ☐ Do you know how much of your credit card bill is from interest?
- ☐ Does your stomach start churning when you get your credit card bill?

LOVE & MONEY

No one likes credit card debt, and that's a fact that comes through loud and clear in the world of dating. A 2016 TD Ameritrade survey found that 44 percent of the respondents said that credit card debt would make them less likely to date someone.

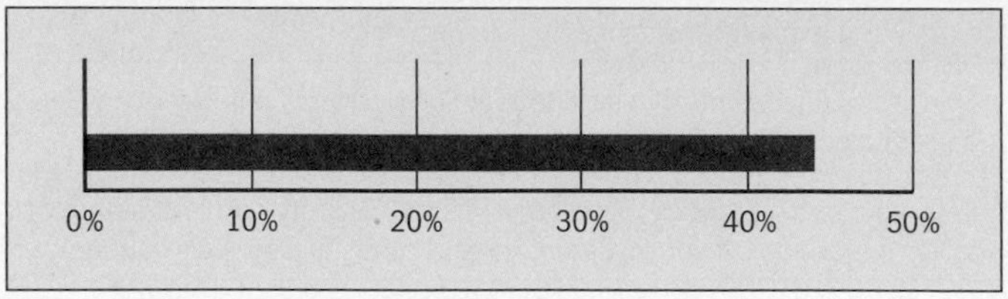

Forty-four percent said credit card debt would make them less likely to date a person.

Why do you think this is the case? One possible explanation is that credit card debt could be a sign of irresponsible spending, and that can spell all kinds of problems. After all, the authors of "Examining the Relationship Between Financial Issues and Divorce"[2] found that arguments about money are the top predictor of divorce—not in-laws, children, or sex but money—and that holds true for both men and women.

So what do you do if you are the one with the debt? Changing your financial habits isn't an easy thing to do, but if you do have a spending problem, face up to it, and fix it as soon as possible. Getting back to ground level may involve some sacrifice, but if it almost doubles your dating pool, it might be worth it. Moreover, you'll feel much better about yourself if you've got control over your credit card.

What if you find out that you're dating someone with major credit card debt? The real question here is "Does he or she have a plan to deal with the debt—that is, to undo it?" You most likely want a partner who is financially responsible because, after all, you're going to have to work with that person to make a financial future, and bad financial habits are an equal-opportunity marriage destroyer—for many, the strain they put on a relationship is too much to handle. Once a relationship begins to get serious, you will probably have at least some idea about your partner's spending habits and how they compare and contrast with yours. Knowing that money will be an ever-present partner in your life, the money conversation must be a priority.

If you are the one with the debt: Come clean. Accept the responsibility that it is your debt to pay. Reveal how it happened and how much there is. Talk about your plan to pay it off—make it a plan that you can both stick to. Make it a priority.

If you are the one who is finding out about your partner's debt: Get the details. Try not to judge. Listen to the payoff plan. When appropriate, ask about your partner's salary, savings, debt payment options, and even credit scores and credit history. Cooperate in making a plan to encourage your partner in his or her payoff plan, *or* become a willing participant in helping to pay off the debt. The key is to keep an honest dialogue going, work things out together, and have a plan and stick with it.

[2] J. Dew, S. Britt, and S. Huston, "Examining the Relationship Between Financial Issues and Divorce," *Family Relations* 61, no. 4 (2012): 615–628.

behavior and making a permanent change in the way you use credit cards. Using savings may be a good *one-time solution* because the interest rate on the unpaid balance on an average credit card is approximately 16 percent. If you're only earning 4 percent after taxes on your savings, then by using savings to pay off credit card borrowing, you'll save 12 percent. However, this won't help you if you don't change your credit card habits. Another alternative that you might consider to lower the cost of your outstanding debt is to use a secured loan or a home equity loan to pay off your high-cost credit card debt.We'll look at consumer loans and debt of this type in Chapter 7.

Also, don't be hesitant about contacting your card company and asking for help. According to a 2017 **CreditCards.com** survey, 69 percent of those who asked for a lower interest rate got one. Also, 87 percent of those who asked for a late payment fee waiver also got that. The point here is you've got to take the offensive—you've got to ask, after all, you've got nothing to lose.

BEHAVIORAL INSIGHTS

PRINCIPLE 9

Principle 9: Mind Games, Your Financial Personality, and Your Money When is a dollar a dollar? Are all dollars really created equal? Think these questions are easy to answer? You might be surprised.

Have you heard the joke about the "honeymooners in Las Vegas"? It goes something like this: The newlyweds went to Las Vegas on their honeymoon, and three days into their weeklong adventure they had already lost the $1,000 they brought with them to gamble. Just as the new groom was getting ready for bed, he found one last $10 chip in his pocket and decided to go down to the tables and bet it. Much to his amazement he simply couldn't lose, and within an hour, he was up to $5 million, winning every time the roulette wheel spun. As he got ready to head back up to the room, he decided to place one last bet, wagering all his money at the roulette wheel—and he lost everything. He returned to their room, and as he was getting into bed, his wife asked him where he had been—he replied that he was downstairs gambling; she asked how he did, and he replied, "I lost $10." All money, whether you earn it through hard work or you win it gambling, buys the same amount of stuff at Best Buy. But people tend to put money into different "buckets" or "accounts."

Welcome to the world of "mental accounting," where people have the tendency to value some dollars less than other dollars and have no trouble wasting them—like money won and then lost gambling. Do you find yourself categorizing and handling money differently depending on where it came from, how it is kept, and how you did or plan to spend it?

It turns out that the concept of mental accounting and your credit card are a dangerous mix. A credit card makes it easy to create a special account or "money bucket" where you save that unexpected "extra money" for a Las Vegas vacation while you're still purchasing necessities with your credit card, as well as carrying credit card debt. It makes no sense to put money aside in a bank account for your vacation trip and have it earn less than half a percent while you're paying close to 20 percent on your unpaid credit card balance. In this instance, the vacation fund money is being treated differently from the money that you would use to pay down your credit card debt.

Behavioral finance research has found another place where people make mistakes with credit cards, and it's probably not a surprise to you. Studies show that most people find it much easier to charge something than to pay for it with cash. In fact, there is a famous study where researchers auction off tickets to a Celtics game: Half the participants are told that if they win, they have to pay for the tickets the next day in cash, and the other half are told that they can charge it. Either way, the participants are bidding on the same tickets. What happens? Those who can pay with their credit card bid, on average, twice what those who have to pay in cash bid. When you're "charging it," there is this vague feeling that you aren't really spending your dollars. With cash, it can be painful to realize you just spent $45 on a nice steak dinner as you pull those dollars out of your wallet and lay them on the table. What's happening? Again, mental accounting, where you view money coming from a credit card differently than money in the form of dollar bills.

PRINCIPLE 1

But mental accounting isn't all bad. When you have a good understanding of money and how it works—which is the goal of this book and **Principle 1: Knowledge Is the Best Protection**—you will be able to create money buckets for your emergency fund, your retirement savings, and the fund for your children's education. And studies have shown that when you feel your savings are going toward a specific goal, you tend to save more. With a conscious understanding of how mental accounting works, you should be able to take that birthday money, your overtime bonus pay, and even your tax refund and use it to pay down your debt or save in a manner that enhances your financial future.

Behavioral finance has also uncovered something interesting with respect to credit scores. According to a 2016 study by CardRatings.com, while men tend to overestimate their credit score, women tend to underestimate theirs. This finding tends to hold regardless of whether they actually have a good or a poor credit score, and it is consistent with other findings in behavioral finance that men are more confident than women with respect to money. What makes this so interesting is that according to a December 2015 study by Experian, women tend to have slightly better credit scores than men. Rather than just estimating your credit score, regardless of your gender, you should know what it is, and if it needs repair, go at it!

The next section is your action plan, which puts **Principle 10: Just Do It!** into play. Inertia is another behavioral finance trait—don't fall prey to it. Take what's given in the next section, and go at it.

ACTION PLAN

PRINCIPLE 10

Principle 10: Just Do It! This is the time to make smart use of your credit card and begin building up your credit score so that you can borrow at a low interest rate later in life. So here's an action plan that will help you do just that.

- Get a credit card, and *always* make payments on time.
- Use your credit card regularly, but spend only what you can afford, and keep credit card debt low.
- Stay under your credit limit—make it a goal to stay at least 30 percent below your total credit limit.
- Don't take out cash advances.
- Keep your credit card accounts open for as long as possible.
- Never open a lot of new accounts all at once—you want the average age of your accounts to be long.
- Don't shy away from installment loans—they will raise your score.
- Be on the alert—check your credit report regularly for errors, and check your credit card account for any suspicious or unusual activity.

Chapter Summaries

Know how credit cards work. LO1

SUMMARY: Open credit is a running line of credit that you can use to make charges up to a certain point as long as you pay off a minimum amount of your debt each month. The main form of open credit is the credit card, which has become an essential part of our personal finances.

KEY TERMS

Credit, page 170 Receiving cash, goods, or services with an obligation to pay later.

Consumer Credit, page 170 Credit purchases for personal needs other than for home mortgages—this can include anything from an auto loan to credit card debt.

Open Credit or Revolving Credit, page 170 A line of credit that you can use and then pay back at whatever pace you like so long as you pay a minimum amount each month, paying interest on the unpaid balance.

Annual Percentage Rate (APR), page 170 The true simple interest rate paid over the life of the loan. It's a reasonable approximation of the true cost of borrowing, and the Truth in Lending Act requires that all consumer loan agreements disclose the APR in bold print.

Method of Determining the Balance (or Balance Calculation Method), page 171 The method by which a credit card balance is determined. The finance charges are then based on the level of this balance.

Average Daily Balance Method, page 171 A method of calculating the balance on which interest is paid by summing the outstanding balances owed each day during the billing period and dividing by the number of days in the period.

Previous Balance Method, page 171 A method of calculating interest payments on outstanding credit using the balance at the end of the previous billing period.

Adjusted Balance Method, page 172 A method of calculating interest payments on outstanding credit in which interest payments are charged against the balance at the end of the previous billing period less any payments and returns made.

Grace Period, page 173 The length of time given to make a payment before interest is charged against the outstanding balance on a credit card.

Annual Fee, page 173 A fixed annual charge imposed by a credit card issuer.

Merchant's Discount Fee, page 173 The percentage of the sale that the merchant pays to the credit card issuer.

Cash Advance Fee, page 174 A charge for making a cash advance, paid as either a fixed amount or a percentage of the cash advance.

Late Fee, page 174 A fee imposed as a result of not paying your credit card bill on time.

Over-the-Limit Fee, page 174 A fee imposed whenever you go over your credit limit.

Penalty Rate, page 174 The rate you pay if you don't make your minimum payments on time.

Understand the costs of credit. LO2

SUMMARY: Basic factors that affect the cost of open credit are the interest rate, the balance calculation method, the cost of cash advances, the grace period, the annual fee, and other additional or penalty fees, including the over-the-limit fee and penalty rates. The advantages of using credit cards or open credit include (1) convenience or ease of shopping, (2) emergency use, (3) the ability to consume before you pay, (4) consolidation of bills, (5) the ability to buy in anticipation of price increases, (6) a source of interest-free credit, (7) the ability to make reservations, (8) a form of identification, and (9) a possible source of free benefits.

The reasons you should be wary of credit cards and open credit are that it's possible to lose control of spending, they are expensive, and you'll have less income to spend in the future.

LO3 Describe the different types of credit cards.

SUMMARY: There are many choices of open credit lines, including different types of credit cards, as well as charge accounts. There are three basic types of credit cards: bank credit cards, travel and entertainment cards, and single-purpose cards.

KEY TERMS

Bank Credit Card, page 177 A credit card issued by a bank or large corporation, generally as a Visa or MasterCard.

Premium or Prestige Credit Card, page 178 A bank credit card that offers credit limits as high as $100,000 or more in addition to numerous added perks, including emergency medical and legal services, travel services, rebates, and insurance on new purchases.

Affinity Card, page 178 A credit card issued in conjunction with a specific charity or organization. It carries the sponsoring group's name and/or picture on the credit card itself and sends a portion of the annual fee or a percentage of the purchases back to the sponsoring organization.

Secured Credit Card, page 178 A credit card backed by the pledge of some collateralized asset.

Travel and Entertainment (T&E) Card, page 178 A credit card initially meant for business customers to allow them to pay for travel and entertainment expenses, keeping them separate from their other expenditures.

Single-Purpose Card, page 179 A credit card that can be used only at a specific company.

Traditional Charge Account, page 179 A charge account, as opposed to a credit card, that can be used to make purchases only at the issuing company.

LO4 Know what determines your credit card worthiness and how to secure a credit card.

SUMMARY: In determining what makes an individual creditworthy, most lenders refer to the "five Cs" of credit—character, capacity, capital, collateral, and conditions. The credit card issuer verifies the information you put down on your application against your credit report from a credit bureau. A credit bureau is a private organization that maintains credit information on individuals. The three national credit bureaus are Experian, TransUnion, and Equifax Credit Information Services. Under the Fair Credit Reporting Act (FCRA) passed by Congress in 1971 (and subsequently amended to help ensure that credit reports are accurate), you have the right to view your credit report.

KEY TERMS

Credit Bureau, page 181 A company that gathers information on consumers' financial history, including how quickly they have paid bills and whether they have been delinquent on bills in the past. The company summarizes this information and sells it to customers.

Credit Scoring, page 182 The numerical evaluation or "scoring" of credit applicants based on their credit history.

Identity Theft, page 188 The use of your name, address, Social Security number, bank or credit card account number, or other identifying information by someone other than you without your knowledge to commit fraud or other crimes.

LO5 Manage your credit cards and open credit.

SUMMARY: Different credit cards charge different annual percentage rates (APRs), and they also calculate the finance charges imposed in different ways. It is important to know how the unpaid balance is calculated. To control credit card use, focus on controlling credit card spending and look for signs of trouble.

Problems and Activities

These problems are available in MyLab Finance.

1. Paying a $30 annual fee for the privilege of using a credit card can be thought of as adding $2.50 to your monthly bill. What other card features and fees affect the cost of credit?
2. Ted and Tiffany are meeting Mitch and Amber at the Green Turtle Club later in the evening. Wanting to set some limits on what could be an expensive evening, Ted stops at the ATM and uses his credit card to get a cash advance. When the two couples meet for dinner, Tiffany tells Amber that she is going to splurge and get lobster because Ted is rolling in cash. Mitch overhears this and begins to laugh at Ted for making such a financial blunder. Ted argues that Mitch is blind to the convenience and control offered by cash advances, as research shows that people tend to spend more when using credit cards. Tiffany and Amber ask you to determine who is right, but you must thoroughly defend your answer to settle the argument.
3. In the previous question, what are the possible consequences of Tiffany learning of Ted's credit card debt?
4. Credit card issuers often use credit bureau data to "preselect" consumers who will be sent marketing materials and application forms. Describe the profile of a consumer who might be sent an application for a bank credit card, a premium or prestige credit card, an affinity credit card, and a secured credit card.
5. With only a part-time job and the need for a professional wardrobe, Rachel quickly maxed out her credit card the summer after graduation. With her first full-time paycheck in August, she vowed to pay $240 each month toward paying down her $8,000 outstanding balance and to not use the card. The card has an annual interest rate of 18 percent. How long will it take Rachel to pay for her wardrobe? Should she shop for a new card? Why or why not?
6. Consumer credit laws have been implemented over the years to protect consumers against creditor abuses. Match the following consumer credit issues with the appropriate consumer credit law:
   - Controls debt collection procedures and practice
   - Prohibits credit discrimination because of race, age, or national origin
   - Establishes the APR and requires the disclosure of all credit-related costs
   - Requires credit contracts to be written in plain English
   - Requires a "rejection letter" or written explanation of any adverse action taken
   - Limits marketing of credit cards to the mailing of application packets and prohibits the mailing of unrequested credit cards
   - Allows payment for defective goods purchased with a credit card to be legally withheld
   - Limits fraudulent card use to $50 payment by the cardholder
   - Ensures that divorced individuals can receive credit
   - Provides annual access to one free credit report from each of the major credit bureaus
   - Reduces credit card late fees to $25
   - Limits the issuance of credit cards to consumers under age 21
   - Requires clear and simple disclosures related to international money transfers
7. Javier is currently paying $1,200 in interest on his credit cards annually. If, instead of paying interest, he saved this amount every year, how much would he accumulate in a tax-deferred account earning 8 percent over 10, 15, and 20 years?

Discussion Case 1

This case is available in **MyLab Finance**.

Maria will be a college sophomore next year, and she is determined to have her own credit card. She will not be employed during the school year but is convinced that she can pay for credit card expenses based on her summer earnings. Maria's parents have read a number of articles about the problems of credit cards and college students, including examples of students leaving school after a downward spiral of obtaining credit cards, overspending, working to pay bills, worrying about bills, working more hours to pay bills, and eventually withdrawing from school. When Maria showed up with a handful of applications, including Visa, a Gold MasterCard, Discover, a Visa sponsored by her university, an American Express, a secured MasterCard, and a gas company card, her parents were overwhelmed. Maria admitted she didn't want them *all*. "I'm not stupid," she declared. Since Maria obviously needed to learn about credit cards, her parents agreed to cosign her application on one condition. She had to approach her choice just as she would a class project and research the following questions.

Questions

1. Assuming Maria does not really care about her parents' approval and ignores their assignment, will she be able to receive a credit card without their help? Would your answer change if Maria was a graduating senior?
2. Why would an unemployed college student need a credit card? What are the advantages of having a credit card? What are the disadvantages?
3. Should Maria have more than one card? What is the recommended number of credit cards for the average consumer?
4. Shopping for credit can be compared to shopping for any other consumer product—consider the product's cost, features, advantages, and disadvantages. In other words, does the product meet the user's needs? Help Maria compare her credit choices, given the applications she has collected.
5. Based on the analysis in Question 4, what class(es) of credit cards, if any, should Maria seriously consider? What other products, if any, might she consider applying for?
6. List and summarize the basic factors that affect credit card costs. Rank these factors in terms of importance and relevance based on Maria's situation.
7. While comparing the applications she had collected, Maria was thrilled to receive a "preapproved" offer for a standard card. What precautions should Maria be alert to when considering this offer?
8. If Maria uses her card only for her books this fall and next fall, how will these purchases affect her monthly payments if she still wants to eliminate her balance and be debt free in 24 months? (Assume that her book purchases are for $600 and are 3 months and 15 months away.)
9. To avoid credit abuse problems, what are the most important rules for Maria to follow when using a credit card?
10. How might Maria's credit card use impact her future job search? What should she do to avoid any problems?
11. To avoid credit card fraud or identity theft problems, what are the most important rules for Maria to follow when using a credit card?

Discussion Case 2

This case is available in **MyLab Finance**.

Garth was amazed to hear that his friend Lindsey always pays off her credit card balance each month. Garth just assumed that everyone used credit cards the same way—buy now, pay later—only in his case, months later. He buys almost everything he needs or wants, including clothes, food, and entertainment, with his card. When Lindsey asked him about the balance calculation method, APR, grace period, and other fees and features of his card, Garth was clueless. He reasoned that his credit card was a safe and convenient way to shop and that it allowed him to buy expensive items by paying minimum monthly payments. Overall, Garth thought of himself as a responsible credit user, despite the fact that he had been late making a few monthly payments and, once or twice, had gone over his credit limit. He also uses his card regularly to obtain cash advances. After hearing all of this, Lindsey is worried about her friend. She has come to you for help in answering the following questions.

Questions

1. What type of credit user is Garth? Based on your answer, what is the number one factor that should influence Garth's choice of a credit card?
2. Lindsey insisted that Garth request a free credit report. List and briefly explain the information that Lindsey will need to help Garth decipher his report.
3. Nathaniel, another friend, suggested that Garth should obtain a secured credit card or, better yet, a Titanium card. Do you agree? Why or why not?
4. Based on what you know about Garth, what kind of additional fees and penalties is he most likely to encounter? What is the impact of these fees and penalties on Garth?
5. Explain the differences in credit card interest rates described as fixed, variable, teaser, and penalty rates. How do these different rates affect the cost of using a credit card?
6. What factors should Garth consider if he decides to transfer his current card balance to another card?
7. Much to Garth's surprise, his last credit card application was rejected. What actions, if any, should he take? Why should he be concerned about this rejection if he still has his other cards?
8. Use Table 6.5 to determine how many months Garth will need to pay off a $3,000 outstanding balance if he pays $150 per month with an APR of 15 percent and he does not make any additional purchases. Tell Garth how much his monthly payment needs to be in order to eliminate his debt in 11 months, assuming no additional purchases.
9. After Lindsey's crash course on credit education, Garth decided to discipline himself by closing a couple of his older accounts. Is this a good strategy?
10. What advice would you give Garth if he has trouble paying his credit card bill in the future?

CHAPTER 7 Student and Consumer Loans: The Role of Planned Borrowing

Learning Objectives

LO1	**Understand** the various consumer loans.	**Consumer Loans—Your Choices**
LO2	**Calculate** the cost of a consumer loan.	**Cost and Early Payment of Consumer Loans**
LO3	**Pick** an appropriate source for your loan.	**Getting the Best Rate on Your Consumer Loans**
LO4	**Control** your debt.	**Controlling Your Use of Debt**
LO5	**Understand** the alternatives for financing your college education.	**Student Loans and Paying for College**

G*lee*, a television show focusing on the members of "New Directions," the glee club at William McKinley High School, and their teachers, while clearly fictional, seemed to continuously confront many of the most difficult "real-life" issues facing high school students today. As the series progressed, we watched as some of the senior members of the glee club graduate and head to college. Quinn went to Yale, while Kurt, Blaine, and Rachel all went to the "New York Academy of the Dramatic Arts" (NYADA), which, while being the number one school in the nation for musical theater, is fictional—but it does sound a bit like Julliard. In addition, we saw Sue Sylvester (PE teacher turned high school principal) hook Santana up with a scholarship to "the nation's top cheerleading program," at the University of Louisville.

Episode after episode it seemed like there wasn't a real-life issue that Glee hadn't tackled, but there is one, and it's one of the biggest—student loans and

Adam Rose/Fox/Everett Collection

paying for college. It's great that Quinn got into Yale, but how is she going to handle the $58,000 a year it costs? Unfortunately for Santana, Louisville doesn't give cheerleading scholarships. And while NYADA may not exist, it is—much like its real-world counterpart, Julliard—very competitive and accepts around 20 students per year. And with Julliard costing between $50,000 and $60,000 per year, it's a safe bet the same would go for NYADA. Paying off their student loans after graduation may be a challenge—after all, the median earnings of a drama and theater arts major are only about $40,000.

While the fictional land of *Glee* may not be taking on the challenges of paying for college, Jane Lynch, the actor who played Sue Sylvester, is going after it. She recently announced the formation of the National College Finance Center, a non-profit Web site that she helped launch with the mission of "providing students and their families with unbiased information on financing their college educations." Why would she do this? As with most of us, when something starts to affect us personally, it opens our eyes—Jane has nieces and nephews who recently graduated from college and are strapped with terrific amounts of college debt. Seeing firsthand the far-reaching effects this debt has had on her family, she was eager to step in and promote a Web site that could give both families and students easy access to much-needed information at the start of their college careers.

When Jane appeared on MSNBC's *Morning Joe*, host Mika Brzezinski praised her for taking this step in promoting access to this important information. With one daughter in college and another soon to be, Mika, too, has been involved firsthand in the process of applying, accepting, and meeting head on the dizzying challenges that 18-year-olds face as they enter the world of higher education. Although Mika's children might not be strapped with massive student loans, she has witnessed and reported on the easy access to student loans and the far-reaching consequences that could result from graduating with high debt, fewer employment possibilities, and lower wages.

The average student loan debt balance for those under 30 is a whopping $30,156, according to new numbers from the Federal Reserve. Jane Lynch definitely finds this an "ungleeful" situation.

LO1 Understand the various consumer loans.

Consumer Loans—Your Choices

Consumer Loan
A loan involving a formal contract that details exactly how much you're borrowing and when and how you're going to pay it back.

In Chapter 6, we examined credit cards and other sources of open credit. We now turn our attention to **consumer loans** and then move on to student loans. You can think of consumer loans as the next step up in debt. They're stricter and more formal than credit cards and other open credit. Instead of giving you a limited, borrow-when-you-want open line of credit, they involve formal contracts detailing exactly how much you're borrowing and exactly when and how you're going to pay it back. Open credit is for making convenience purchases—tonight's dinner or the latest *Guardians of the Galaxy* DVD. Consumer loans are usually used for bigger purchases. With consumer loans, you can borrow more and pay it back at a slower pace than you can with open credit, but you have to lock yourself into a set repayment schedule. Because it forces you to plan your purchase and your repayment, consumer loans are sometimes called "planned borrowing."

It would be ideal to have enough cash on hand to buy everything you need or want. Hey, no one likes owing someone else money. However, sometimes purchases are too big or the timing is such that you have to borrow money to finance a particular goal and pay for it later. Consumer loans allow you to do just that. However, consumer loans carry a price. While they let you consume more now, they create a financial obligation that can be a burden later. Not all consumer loans look the same. They can range from unsecured, fixed-rate, single-payment loans to secured, variable-rate, installment loans. What does all that mean? Let's take a look at the characteristics and associated terminology of consumer loans, the loan contract, and the special types of consumer loans.

First Decision: Single-Payment Versus Installment Loans

Single-Payment or Balloon Loan
A loan that is paid back in a single lump-sum payment at maturity, or the due date of the loan, which is usually specified in the loan contract. At that date, you pay back the amount you borrowed plus all interest charges.

Bridge or Interim Loan
A short-term loan that provides funding until a longer-term source can be secured or until additional financing is found.

Installment Loan
A loan that calls for repayment of both the interest and the principal at regular intervals, with the payment levels set in such a way that the loan expires at a preset date.

Loan Amortization
The repayment of a loan using equal monthly payments that cover a portion of the principal and the interest on the declining balance. The amount of the monthly payment going toward the interest starts off large and steadily declines, while the amount going toward the principal starts off small and steadily increases.

Consumer loans can be either single-payment loans or installment loans. A **single-payment or balloon loan** is a loan that's paid back in a single lump-sum payment at maturity, or the due date of the loan, which is usually specified in the loan contract. At that date, you pay back the amount you borrowed plus all interest charges. Single-payment loans generally have a relatively short maturity of less than 1 year. Needless to say, paying off a loan of this kind is generally quite difficult unless you have access to a large amount of money when it matures. As a result, they're generally used as **bridge or interim loans**, providing short-term funding until longer-term or additional financing is found. Bridge loans might be used in financing the building of a house, with the mortgage loan used to pay off the bridge loan and provide more permanent funding.

An **installment loan** calls for repayment of both interest and principal at regular intervals, with the payment levels set so that the loan expires at a preset date. The amount of the monthly payment going toward the interest starts off large and steadily decreases, while the amount going toward the principal starts off small and steadily increases. In effect, as you pay off more of the loan each month, your interest expenses decline, and your principal payments increase. This process is commonly referred to as **loan amortization**. Installment loans are very common and are used to finance cars, appliances, and other big-ticket items.

Second Decision: Secured Versus Unsecured Loans

Secured Loan
A loan that's guaranteed by a specific asset.

Consumer loans are either secured or unsecured. A **secured loan** is guaranteed by a specific asset. If you can't meet the loan payments, that asset can be seized and sold to cover the amount due. Many times the asset purchased with the funds from the loan is used for security. For example, if you borrow money to buy a car, that car is generally used as collateral for the loan. If you don't make your car payment, your car may be repossessed.

Repossessed collateral, though, may or may not cover what you owe. That is, after the collateral is repossessed, you could still owe money. For example, if you owed $40,000 on your house, but the bank could get only $35,000 for it, you'd still owe another $5,000. That means you'd have your home repossessed and still owe money on it! Other assets commonly used as security for a loan are certificates of deposit (CDs), stocks, jewelry, land, and bank accounts. Securities reduce lender risk, so lenders charge a lower rate on a secured loan than they do on a comparable unsecured loan.

An **unsecured loan** requires no collateral. In general, larger unsecured loans are given only to borrowers with excellent credit histories because the only security the lender has is the individual's promise to pay. The big disadvantage of unsecured loans is that they're quite expensive.

Unsecured Loan
A loan that's not guaranteed by a specific asset.

Third Decision: Variable-Rate Versus Fixed-Rate Loans

The interest payments associated with a consumer loan can be either fixed or variable. A **fixed-interest-rate loan** maintains a single interest rate for the duration of the loan. Regardless of whether market interest rates swing up or down, the interest rate you pay remains fixed. The vast majority of consumer loans have fixed rates.

Fixed-Interest-Rate Loan
A loan with an interest rate that stays fixed for the duration of the loan.

A **variable- or adjustable-interest-rate loan** is tied to a market interest rate, such as the prime rate or the 6-month Treasury bill rate. The interest rate you pay varies as that market rate changes. The **prime rate** is the interest rate banks charge to their most creditworthy customers. Most consumer loans are set above the prime rate or the Treasury bill rate. For example, your loan might be set at 4 percent over prime. In this case, if the prime rate is 3.5 percent at the moment, the rate you pay on your variable-rate loan is 7.5 percent. If the prime jumps to 7 percent, your rate changes to 11 percent.

Variable- or Adjustable-Interest-Rate Loan
A loan in which the interest rate does not stay fixed but varies based on the market interest rate.

Prime Rate
The interest rate banks charge to their most creditworthy, or "prime," customers.

Not all variable-rate loans are the same. For example, rates may be adjusted at different, but fixed, intervals. Some loans adjust every month, others every year. The less frequently the loan adjusts, the less you have to worry about rate changes. You should also know the volatility of the interest rate to which the loan is pegged. In general, short-term market rates tend to change more than long-term market rates. Therefore, variable-rate loans tied to the 6-month Treasury bill rate expose you to more risk of rate changes than do loans tied to the 20-year Treasury bond rate.

Of course, variable-rate loans usually have rate caps that prevent interest rates from varying too much. The periodic cap limits the maximum the interest rate can jump during one adjustment. The lifetime cap limits the amount that the interest rate can jump over the life of the loan. The larger the fluctuations allowed by the caps, the greater the risk. The bottom line on a variable-interest-rate loan is that if interest rates drop, you win, and if interest rates rise, you lose.

FACTS OF LIFE

Anyone can rack up debt. In 1999, Elton John secured a $40 million loan from a London bank to consolidate and pay off the debts he had accumulated while racking up as much as $400,000 a week in credit card bills.

So which is better, a fixed-rate loan or a variable-rate loan? Neither one necessarily. The choice between a variable- and a fixed-rate loan is another example of **Principle 8: Risk and Return Go Hand in Hand**. With a variable-rate loan, the borrower bears the risk that interest rates will go up and the payments will increase accordingly. With a fixed-rate loan, the lender bears the risk that interest rates will go up and—because the interest rate of the loan is fixed—that they will lose interest income. Because the lender bears more risk, fixed-rate loans generally cost more than variable-rate loans.

PRINCIPLE 8

An alternative to a fixed- or variable-rate loan is a convertible loan. A **convertible loan** is a variable-rate loan that can be converted into a fixed-rate loan at the

Convertible Loan
A variable-rate loan that can be converted into a fixed-rate loan at the borrower's option at specified dates in the future.

borrower's option at specified dates in the future. Although convertible loans are much less common than variable- or fixed-rate loans, they do offer the advantage of the lower cost of a variable-rate loan, along with the ability to lock into the savings of a fixed-rate loan.

Fourth Decision: The Loan's Maturity—Shorter- Versus Longer-Term Loans

With a shorter-term loan, the monthly payments are larger because you are paying off more of the amount that you've borrowed each month. For example, if you borrow $10,000 at 8 percent, with a 3-year loan, your monthly payments are $313, but if the loan is for 10 years rather than 3 years, the payments drop to $121 per month. However, even though your monthly interest payments are smaller with the 10-year loan, the total amount of interest you pay over the life of the loan is more.

Still, agreeing to a shorter-term loan often results in a lower interest rate on your loan. Why is that the case? Lenders generally charge a lower interest rate on shorter-term loans because the shorter the term, the lower the probability that you will experience a financial disaster such as the loss of your job or a medical emergency.

Understand the Terms of the Loan: The Loan Contract

The loan contract spells out all the conditions of the loan in exhaustive detail. If the item being purchased is to be used as collateral for the loan, then the contract will contain a **security agreement** saying so. The security agreement identifies whether the lender or borrower retains control over the item being purchased. The formal agreement stating the payment schedule and the rights of both lender and borrower in the case of **default** is outlined in the **note**.

Security Agreement
An agreement that identifies whether the lender or borrower retains control over the item being purchased.

Default
The failure of a borrower to make a scheduled interest or principal payment.

Note
The formal document that outlines the legal obligations of both the lender and the borrower.

The note is standard on all loans, and the security agreement is standard on secured loans. Other clauses that sometimes appear in a loan contract include an insurance agreement clause, an acceleration clause, a deficiency payment clause, and a recourse clause. An example of an installment purchase contract is given in Figure 7.1.

Insurance Agreement Clause With an **insurance agreement clause**, you're required to purchase credit life insurance to pay off the loan in the event of your death. For you, credit life insurance adds nothing to the loan other than cost. It's really the lender who benefits. If an insurance agreement clause is included, its cost should justifiably be included as a cost of the loan.

Insurance Agreement Clause
A loan requirement that a borrower purchase credit life insurance that will pay off the loan in the event of the borrower's death.

Acceleration Clause An **acceleration clause** states that if you miss one payment, the entire loan comes due immediately. If at that time you can't pay off the entire loan, the collateral will be repossessed and sold to pay off the balance due. Acceleration clauses are standard in most loans. However, lenders usually won't immediately invoke the acceleration clause but instead will allow you a chance to make good on the overdue payments.

Acceleration Clause
A loan requirement stating that if the borrower misses one payment, the entire loan comes due immediately.

Deficiency Payments Clause A **deficiency payments clause** states that if you default on a secured loan, not only can the lender repossess whatever is secured, but also if the sale of that asset doesn't cover what you owe, you can be billed for the difference.

Deficiency Payments Clause
A loan requirement stating that if you default on a secured loan, not only can the lender repossess whatever is secured, but also, if the sale of that asset doesn't cover what is owed, you can be billed for the difference.

To make sense out of this clause, let's say you missed some car payments and had your car repossessed. If you owed a balance of $10,000 and the car was sold at auction by the lender for only $9,000, you'd still owe $1,000. In addition, under the deficiency payments clause you would also be responsible for collection costs of, say, $150; selling costs of perhaps another $150; and attorney fees of, say, $100. As a result, you'd not only lose your car but also be billed for $1,400 ($1,000 + $150 + $150 + $100).

FIGURE 7.1 An Installment Purchase Contract

Keep in mind when signing an installment purchase contract that the loan you are taking out is a product, just like a television or an automobile. You should make sure that it's something you can afford and that you understand what you're signing.

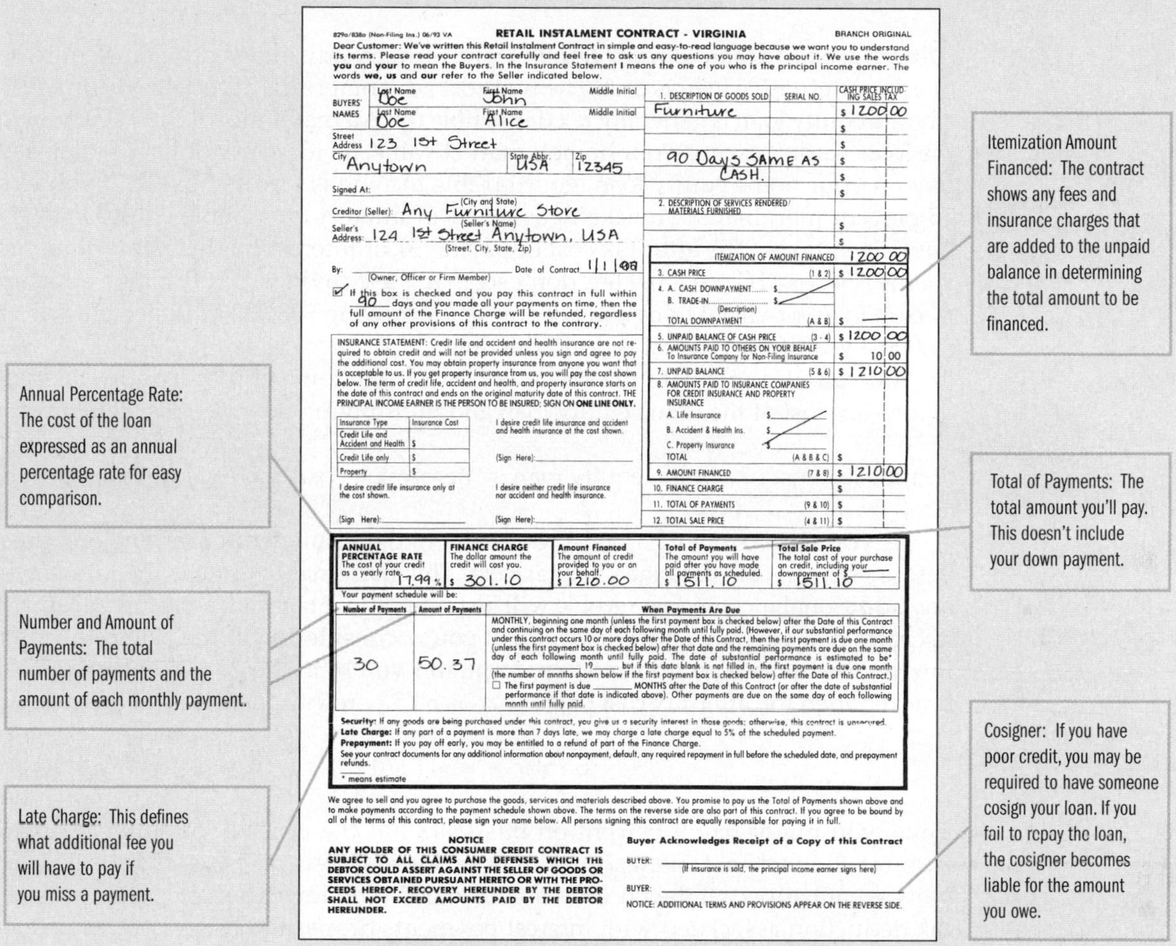

829a/838a (Non-Filing Ins.) 06/93 VA **RETAIL INSTALMENT CONTRACT - VIRGINIA** BRANCH ORIGINAL

Dear Customer: We've written this Retail Instalment Contract in simple and easy-to-read language because we want you to understand its terms. Please read your contract carefully and feel free to ask us any questions you may have about it. We use the words **you** and **your** to mean the Buyers. In the Insurance Statement **I** means the one of you who is the principal income earner. The words **we, us** and **our** refer to the Seller indicated below.

BUYERS' NAMES: Last Name Doe, First Name John, Middle Initial; Last Name Doe, First Name Alice, Middle Initial

Street Address 123 1st Street

City Anytown State Abbr. USA Zip 12345

Signed At: (City and State)

Creditor (Seller): Any Furniture Store (Seller's Name)

Seller's Address: 124 1st Street Anytown, USA (Street, City, State, Zip)

By: (Owner, Officer or Firm Member) Date of Contract 1/1/[illegible]

☑ If this box is checked and you pay this contract in full within 90 days and you made all your payments on time, then the full amount of the Finance Charge will be refunded, regardless of any other provisions of this contract to the contrary.

1. DESCRIPTION OF GOODS SOLD	SERIAL NO.	CASH PRICE INCLUDING SALES TAX
Furniture		$ 1200.00
		$
		$
90 Days SAME AS CASH.		$
		$
		$
2. DESCRIPTION OF SERVICES RENDERED/ MATERIALS FURNISHED		
		$
		$

ITEMIZATION OF AMOUNT FINANCED		1200.00
3. CASH PRICE	(1 & 2)	$ 1200.00
4. A. CASH DOWNPAYMENT $ B. TRADE-IN $ (Description)		
TOTAL DOWNPAYMENT	(A & B)	$ —
5. UNPAID BALANCE OF CASH PRICE	(3 - 4)	$ 1200.00
6. AMOUNTS PAID TO OTHERS ON YOUR BEHALF To Insurance Company for Non-Filing Insurance		$ 10.00
7. UNPAID BALANCE	(5 & 6)	$ 1210.00
8. AMOUNTS PAID TO INSURANCE COMPANIES FOR CREDIT INSURANCE AND PROPERTY INSURANCE A. Life Insurance $ B. Accident & Health Ins. $ C. Property Insurance $		
TOTAL	(A & B & C)	$
9. AMOUNT FINANCED	(7 & 8)	$ 1210.00
10. FINANCE CHARGE		$
11. TOTAL OF PAYMENTS	(9 & 10)	$
12. TOTAL SALE PRICE	(4 & 11)	$

INSURANCE STATEMENT: Credit life and accident and health insurance are not required to obtain credit and will not be provided unless you sign and agree to pay the additional cost. You may obtain property insurance from anyone you want that is acceptable to us. If you get property insurance from us, you will pay the cost shown below. The term of credit life, accident and health, and property insurance starts on the date of this contract and ends on the original maturity date of this contract. THE PRINCIPAL INCOME EARNER IS THE PERSON TO BE INSURED; SIGN ON **ONE LINE ONLY.**

Insurance Type	Insurance Cost
Credit Life and Accident and Health	$
Credit Life only	$
Property	$

I desire credit life insurance and accident and health insurance at the cost shown. (Sign Here):

I desire credit life insurance only at the cost shown. (Sign Here):

I desire neither credit life insurance nor accident and health insurance. (Sign Here):

ANNUAL PERCENTAGE RATE The cost of your credit as a yearly rate.	FINANCE CHARGE The dollar amount the credit will cost you.	Amount Financed The amount of credit provided to you or on your behalf.	Total of Payments The amount you will have paid after you have made all payments as scheduled.	Total Sale Price The total cost of your purchase on credit, including your downpayment of $ —
17.99 %	$ 301.10	$ 1210.00	$ 1511.10	$ 1511.10

Your payment schedule will be:

Number of Payments	Amount of Payments	When Payments Are Due
30	50.37	MONTHLY, beginning one month (unless the first payment box is checked below) after the Date of this Contract and continuing on the same day of each following month until fully paid. (However, if our substantial performance under this contract occurs 10 or more days after the Date of this Contract, then the first payment is due one month (unless the first payment box is checked below) after that date and the remaining payments are due on the same day of each following month until fully paid. The date of substantial performance is estimated to be* ________, 19____, but if this date blank is not filled in, the first payment is due one month (the number of months shown below if the first payment box is checked below) after the Date of this Contract.) ☐ The first payment is due ______ MONTHS after the Date of this Contract (or after the date of substantial performance if that date is indicated above). Other payments are due on the same day of each following month until fully paid.

Security: If any goods are being purchased under this contract, you give us a security interest in those goods; otherwise, this contract is unsecured.
Late Charge: If any part of a payment is more than 7 days late, we may charge a late charge equal to 5% of the scheduled payment.
Prepayment: If you pay off early, you may be entitled to a refund of part of the Finance Charge.
See your contract documents for any additional information about nonpayment, default, any required repayment in full before the scheduled date, and prepayment refunds.

* means estimate

We agree to sell and you agree to purchase the goods, services and materials described above. You promise to pay us the Total of Payments shown above and to make payments according to the payment schedule shown above. The terms on the reverse side are also part of this contract. If you agree to be bound by all of the terms of this contract, please sign your name below. All persons signing this contract are equally responsible for paying it in full.

NOTICE
ANY HOLDER OF THIS CONSUMER CREDIT CONTRACT IS SUBJECT TO ALL CLAIMS AND DEFENSES WHICH THE DEBTOR COULD ASSERT AGAINST THE SELLER OF GOODS OR SERVICES OBTAINED PURSUANT HERETO OR WITH THE PROCEEDS HEREOF. RECOVERY HEREUNDER BY THE DEBTOR SHALL NOT EXCEED AMOUNTS PAID BY THE DEBTOR HEREUNDER.

Buyer Acknowledges Receipt of a Copy of this Contract
BUYER: ________ (If insurance is sold, the principal income earner signs here)
BUYER: ________
NOTICE: ADDITIONAL TERMS AND PROVISIONS APPEAR ON THE REVERSE SIDE.

Itemization Amount Financed: The contract shows any fees and insurance charges that are added to the unpaid balance in determining the total amount to be financed.
Annual Percentage Rate: The cost of the loan expressed as an annual percentage rate for easy comparison.
Total of Payments: The total amount you'll pay. This doesn't include your down payment.
Number and Amount of Payments: The total number of payments and the amount of each monthly payment.
Cosigner: If you have poor credit, you may be required to have someone cosign your loan. If you fail to repay the loan, the cosigner becomes liable for the amount you owe.
Late Charge: This defines what additional fee you will have to pay if you miss a payment.

Recourse Clause A **recourse clause** defines what actions a lender can take to claim money from you in case you default. The recourse clause may allow the lender to attach your wages, which means that a certain portion of your salary goes directly to the lender to pay off your debt.

Recourse Clause
A clause in a loan contract defining what actions a lender can take to claim money from a borrower in the case of default.

Special Types of Consumer Loans

Although consumer loans are used for almost anything, several special-purpose consumer loans deserve close attention. It's important to look at these loans not only because they are extremely common but also because they include unique advantages and disadvantages you should be aware of.

Home Equity Loans A **home equity loan or second mortgage** is special type of secured loan that uses the built-up equity in your home as collateral against the loan. Generally, you can borrow from 50 to 85 percent of your equity—that is, your home

Home Equity Loan or Second Mortgage
A loan that uses a borrower's built-up equity in his or her home as collateral against the loan.

value minus your first mortgage balance. For example, if you own a home with a market value of $200,000 and have an outstanding balance on your first mortgage of $80,000, your home equity is $120,000. With this much equity, you can get a home equity loan of between $60,000 and $102,000 (0.50 × $120,000, and 0.85 × $120,000, respectively). In this case, your home is security on a loan that can be used for any purpose (it needn't be home related).

Advantages of Home Equity Loans The primary advantage of a home equity loan over an alternative loan is cost. The first cost advantage arises because the interest on a home equity loan is generally tax deductible up to a maximum of $100,000, provided the loan doesn't exceed your home's market value. So for every dollar of interest you pay on your home equity loan, your taxable income is lowered by $1. If you're in a 25 percent marginal tax bracket, paying $1 of interest on a home equity loan saves you 25¢ in taxes. The after-tax cost of paying $1 of interest on this home equity loan is only 75¢, or $1(1 − 0.25). Hey, don't scoff at a 25¢ savings. That change adds up: A person in a 25 percent marginal tax bracket borrowing $33,333 at 12 percent will save $1,000 a year if the interest is tax deductible.

You can also calculate the after-tax cost of the home equity loan by taking the before-tax cost of the home equity loan and multiplying it by (1 − marginal tax rate):

$$\text{after-tax cost of a home equity loan} = \text{before-tax cost} \times (1 - \text{marginal tax rate})$$

As you recall from Chapter 4, you have to determine your marginal tax bracket before you can calculate the after-tax cost. This marginal tax rate is the rate at which any additional income you receive will be taxed, and it combines the federal and state tax rates that you pay on the investment you're considering. If the before-tax interest rate on the home equity loan is 9 percent and you're in the 25 percent marginal tax bracket, then the after-tax cost of the loan is 6.75 percent, calculated as follows:

$$6.75\% = 9\%(1 - 0.25)$$

Thus, you might pay 9 percent on this loan, but the cost to you, after taking into account the fact that interest on this loan lowers your taxes, is only 6.75 percent. Now what happens if the tax rates are lowered? With lower tax rates, the value of the tax deduction associated with interest payments drops, and as a result, the after-tax cost of home equity loans increases.

The second cost advantage of home equity loans is that they generally carry a lower interest rate than do other consumer loans. Because home equity loans are secured loans, lenders consider them less risky and charge a lower interest rate on them.

Disadvantages and Dangers of Home Equity Loans The major disadvantage of a home equity loan is that it puts your home at risk. When you decide on a home equity loan, use caution and make sure that you aren't taking on more debt than you can support.

The use of a home equity loan also limits future financing flexibility. Although it's an excellent source of emergency funding, you can have only one home equity loan outstanding at a time. And don't forget that any borrowing places an obligation on future earnings and reduces future disposable income.

In the mid-2000s, before the housing bust, many people believed that real estate could only go up in value—constantly appreciating in price. In hindsight, it's pretty clear that's not always the case, and when it goes down, it can go a long way down. Much of the sales pitch of home equity loans was that they were an easy way to capture some of the price appreciation in your home. The problem was that the price appreciation might not be around for long if housing prices dropped.

Prior to the 1980s, home equity loans were referred to as "second mortgages," which gave consumers the feeling that they were taking on more debt than they should—as a result, second mortgages weren't that popular. In order to make them more appealing, second mortgages became home equity loans, and their popularity soared—after all, it was the home owner's equity, so why not tap into it? In fact, one advertisement declared, "Now, when the value of your home goes up, you can take credit for it."[1] The end result was that many consumers used their homes as an ATM machine, and when the housing crash came, they lost their homes.

Automobile Loans An **automobile loan** is a secured loan made specifically for the purchase of an automobile, with the automobile being purchased used as the collateral. These loans are generally short-term, often only 24, 36, or 48 months, although they can be as long as 5 or 6 years. In recent years, automobile loans have been used as a marketing tool to sell cars. For example, in 2017, while the national average auto loan rate was about 3.00 percent, Toyota and Nissan were offering a 0.0 percent rate on many of their new cars. The rate on auto loans is also quite low because lenders know that if you don't pay, they'll repossess your car and sell it to someone else to pay off the loan.

Automobile Loan
A loan made specifically for the purchase of an automobile, which uses the automobile as collateral against the loan.

Cost and Early Payment of Consumer Loans

LO2 Calculate the cost of a consumer loan.

Before deciding whether to borrow money, you should know exactly what the loan costs and what flexibility you have in terms of paying it off early. Fortunately, this information is readily available. In fact, under the Truth in Lending Act, you must be informed in writing of the total finance charges and the annual percentage rate of the loan before you sign a loan agreement.

The finance charges include all the costs associated with the loan—for example, interest payments, loan-processing fees, fees for a credit check, and any required insurance fees. The **annual percentage rate, or APR**, is the simple percentage cost of all finance charges over the life of the loan on an annual basis. Keep in mind that this includes noninterest finance charges.

Annual Percentage Rate or APR
The true simple interest rate paid over the life of a loan. It's a reasonable approximation for the true cost of borrowing, and the Truth in Lending Act requires that all consumer loan agreements disclose the APR in bold print.

As noted earlier, consumer loans fall into two categories: (1) single-payment or balloon loans and (2) installment loans.

Cost of Single-Payment Loans

The Truth in Lending Act requires lenders to provide you with the finance charges and APR associated with a loan, but it's a good idea to be familiar with the two different ways loans are made—one that removes interest at the beginning (the discount method) and one that doesn't (the simple interest method). The APR and finance charges are given to you in the form of a **loan disclosure statement** similar to the one shown in Figure 7.2.

Loan Disclosure Statement
A statement that provides the APR and interest charges associated with a loan.

Simple Interest Method Interest under the simple interest loan method is calculated as follows:

$$\text{interest} = \text{principal} \times \text{interest rate} \times \text{time}$$

The principal is the amount borrowed, the interest rate is exactly what you think it is, and the time is the period over which the funds are borrowed. For example, if

[1] Louise Story, "Home Equity Frenzy Was a Bank Ad Come True," *New York Times*, August 14, 2008.

FIGURE 7.2 A Loan Disclosure Statement

A loan disclosure statement is required by the Truth in Lending Act and provides the APR, the finance charges, and the total of payments associated with the loan.

Annual Percentage Rate: The annual percentage rate, or APR, is the true simple interest rate paid over the life of the loan. It is calculated by dividing the average annual finance charge by the average loan balance outstanding.

Finance Charge: The finance charge includes all the costs associated with the loan—for example, interest payments, loan-processing fees, fees for a credit check, and any required insurance fees.

Amount Financed: This is the amount you are borrowing, or the principal.

Total of Payments: This is the sum of your finance charge and the amount that you are borrowing.

ANNUAL PERCENTAGE RATE The cost of my credit as a yearly rate.	FINANCE CHARGE The dollar amount the credit will cost me.	**Amount Financed.** The amount of credit provided to me or on my behalf.	**Total of Payments.** The amount I will have paid after I have made all payments as scheduled.

I have the right to receive at this time an itemization of the Amount Financed: (________) I want an itemization. (________) I do not want an itemization.
(Initials) (Initials)

My payment schedule will be:

No. of Payments	Payment Amount	Frequency	Due Date	No. of Payments	Payment Amount	Frequency	Due Date

Variable Rate.
If my loan, as indicated above, has a variable rate, my interest rate may increase during the term of my loan based on movement of the WSJ Prime Rate. My interest rate will not increase more than once each month. If my loan is secured by a principal dwelling for a term greater than one year, disclosures about the variable rate have been provided to me earlier.

___ If indicated, my loan has multiple payments for a term of more than 60 months. Any increase in my interest rate will increase the number of payments and may increase the payment amounts. If my loan were for $10,000 for 144 months at 12% and the interest rate increased to 12.50% in three months, my regular payment would increase by $7.30 beginning with my Sixty-First payment.

___ MAXIMUM RATE. If indicated, the maximum interest rate will not exceed:

___ If indicated, my loan has multiple payments for a term of 60 months or less. Any increase in my interest rate will increase the number of payments. If my loan were for $10,000 for 60 months at 12% and the interest rate increased to 12.50% in three months I would have to make one additional payment of $196.56.

___ If indicated, my loan has a single payment. Any increase in my interest rate will increase the amount due at maturity. If my loan were for $10,000 at 12% for 90 days, and my interest rate increased to 12.25% in 20 days, then my final payment would increase by $4.80.

Security. I am giving a security interest in:

___ the goods or property being purchased. ___ other (describe):

Collateral securing other loans with you may also secure this loan, except my principal dwelling or household goods.

Filing Fees. **Prepayment.** If I pay off early, I may have to pay a penalty and I will not be entitled to a refund of part of any prepaid finance charge.

Late charges. If you receive any payment 8 days or more after the due date, I agree to pay you a late charge of 5% of my payment.

___ If indicated, this loan is for the purchase of property used as my principal dwelling and someone buying my principal dwelling cannot assume the remainder of my loan on the original terms.

___ If indicated, the Annual Percentage Rate does not take into account my required deposit.

I may see my contract documents for any additional information about nonpayment, default, any required repayment in full before the scheduled due date, and prepayment refunds and penalties.

I understand that credit life and credit disability insurance are not required to get this loan. **You will not provide it unless I sign the NOTICE OF PROPOSED GROUP CREDIT INSURANCE form and agree to pay the cost.** If I want any of these insurance coverages, I must be sure that the insurance coverage I want is indicated, that the amount of the premium is filled in, and that I have signed below. If I request credit life insurance or credit disability insurance, I have the right to rescind the insurance policy or certificate of insurance by giving written notice to the insurance company within 15 days from the date I received the policy or certificate. The term of any insurance I request is for the stated term of this loan unless shown otherwise.

INSURED #1	INSURED #2	TYPE	PREMIUM
___	___	Credit Life	
___		Credit Disability	

If this loan is secured, I may obtain property insurance from any insurer I choose.

I request coverage(s) checked for the premiums shown above ______________________
Signature of Insured #1 (Life only or Life and Disability)

I request coverage(s) checked for the premiums shown above ______________________
Signature of Insured #2 (Life only)

$10,000 is borrowed for 6 months at an annual rate of 12 percent, the interest charges are $600, calculated as follows:

$$\$600 = \$10,000 \times 0.12 \times \frac{1}{2}$$

Note that the value for time is ½ because the money is borrowed for half of a year. If we're talking about single-payment loans, both the interest and the principal are due at maturity. Thus, in the loan we've just described, you receive $10,000 when you take out the loan, and 6 months later you repay $10,600.

For single-payment loans, the stated interest rate and the APR are always the same if there are no noninterest finance charges. The APR can be calculated as follows:

$$\text{APR} = \frac{\text{average annual finance charges}}{\text{average loan balance outstanding}}$$

In this case:

$$\text{APR} = \frac{(\$600/0.5)}{\$10,000} = \frac{\$1,200}{\$10,000} = 0.12, \text{ or } 12\%$$

Notice that the annual finance charges are equal to the total finance charges divided by the number of periods the loan continues. In this case, it's a 6-month loan, and because we paid $600 to have the loan for 6 months, we'd have had to pay $1,200 if the loan was outstanding for a full year. Therefore, the annual finance charges are $1,200. Keep in mind that if there had been noninterest finance charges, they would have been included as part of the annual finance charges.

FACTS OF LIFE

The average law school grad leaves school with more than $140,000 in loans, whereas the average med student owes almost $162,000 at graduation.

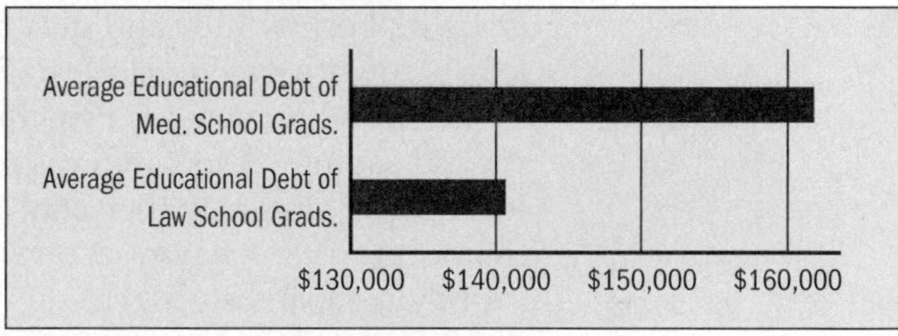

Discount Method With a discount method single-payment loan, the entire interest charge is subtracted from the loan principal before you receive the money, and at maturity, you repay the principal. For example, if you borrow $10,000 for 1 year and the interest rate is 11 percent, your finance charge is $1,100($10,000 × 0.11). Under the discount method, you receive only $8,900 ($10,000 less the interest of $1,100), and in 1 year, you have to repay the entire principal of $10,000. In effect, you really have a loan of only $8,900 because the interest is prepaid. The APR for this example is 12.36 percent, calculated as follows:

$$\text{APR} = \frac{\$1,100}{\$8,900} = 0.1236, \text{ or } 12.36\%$$

Again, you'll notice that we have assumed there are no noninterest finance charges. Returning to our earlier example, if $10,000 is loaned at 12 percent for 6 months using the discount method, the APR is 13.64 percent, calculated as follows:

$$\text{APR} = \frac{(\$600/0.5)}{\$8,800} = \frac{\$1,200}{\$8,800} = 0.1364, \text{ or } 13.64\%$$

Notice that the APR is larger when money is loaned under the discount method than when it is loaned under the simple interest method. Why? Because with the discount method, interest is taken out before you receive the loan, so you actually receive less than the stated principal of the loan.

Payday Loans—A Dangerous Kind of Single-Payment Loan

FACTS OF LIFE

Here's a true story: Sandra Harris, an accounting technician, from Wilmington, North Carolina, found herself in a cash crunch after her husband had lost his job as an executive chef. Her car insurance was due, and she didn't have the money, so she turned to Payday Loans Direct, paid the $50 fee for a $200 loan, and was able to pay her insurance bill on time. When the loan came due, she was ready to pay it off, but instead she renewed it, and then renewed it again, and raised it, and took out more payday loans. At the end of 6 months, she was paying over $600 per month in fees, none of which applied to her debt, and paid a total $8,000 in fees for six payday loans. As with many payday loans, this one came with a sad ending, as she was evicted and her car was repossessed.

Be wary of "payday loans." Payday loans, generally given by check-cashing companies, are aimed at people who have jobs and checking accounts but who need some money (usually $100 to $500) to tide them over for 1 or 2 weeks, or until their next "payday." For some borrowers, it is a loan of last resort. They are desperate borrowers that simply don't have another choice—and for them, it's still a bad choice. Payday lenders are everywhere; in fact, there are more payday lenders than there are McDonald's and Starbucks locations. Lately, these loans have even surfaced on college campuses where students may not even have a job or a paycheck, just an allowance from home. The cost on these loans comes in the form of a fee, which generally runs from $15 to $30 for the 1- or 2-week loan.

The loans work like this: You need $100 to cover you until your next paycheck or money from home. So you go to a payday lender and borrow $100. The payday lender gets a check from you for $115 drawn on your empty bank account. Then 2 weeks later, when you get paid or you get that check from home, the lender either cashes the check or lets you "flip" the loan (pay another fee to renew the loan for another 2 weeks). If you annualized the interest rate, you'd find that you're borrowing at an interest rate of close to 400 percent. Even worse, if your fee is $30 (that is, if you borrow $100 and give the payday lender a check for $130 to cover your $100 loan), you are paying close to 800 percent interest. Not a very wise way to borrow money, is it? Remember **Principle 1: The Best Protection Is Knowledge**, along with the old saying "A fool and his money are soon parted." On HBO's *Last Week Tonight*, John Oliver put it another way: "Basically, payday loans are the Lay's potato chips of finance. You can't have just one, and they're terrible for you."[2]

PRINCIPLE 1

Payday loans are awful—if you're thinking about getting one, "just say no." They don't benefit borrowers but instead trap them in a cycle of borrowing. How bad are they? Just look to Table 7.1 for an answer.

Certainly, there have been attempts to eliminate these loans In 2006, Congress acted to protect military families by prohibiting payday and title lenders from charging higher than 36 percent APR, but this just protected men and women in the service. On a broader front, 17 states and the District of Columbia have enacted strong payday loan laws. For example, in Georgia payday lending is explicitly prohibited and a violation of racketeering laws, while in New York and New Jersey payday lending is

TABLE 7.1 Payday Loans by the Numbers

$15 per $100 borrowed: Median fees on a typical 14-day loan
$350: Median size of a payday loan
391 percent: Annual percentage rate (APR) yields on typical $15 per $100, 14-day payday loans
199 days: Median number of days borrowers are indebted annually
$458: Median fees incurred by a payday loan consumer

Source: Consumer Financial Protection Bureau, "Consumer Financial Protection Bureau Study Finds Debt Trap Concerns with Payday and Deposit Advance Loans," http://files.consumerfinance.gov/f/201304_cfpb_payday-factsheet.pdf, accessed July 9, 2017.

[2]Last Week Tonight with John Oliver, HBO, Episode 14, August 10, 2014.

prohibited through their criminal usury statutes, limiting annual interest on loans to 25 percent and 30 percent, respectively. On the other hand, payday loans are legal in the other 33 states. Further, even where there are payday loan laws, payday lenders find ways around them. The way this industry has been able to rise up after legislative attempts to curb it caused John Oliver on HBO's *Last Week Tonight* to say that trying to defeat this industry is like "legislative Whack-A-Mole." He added that "just when you think you've squashed them, they pop up somewhere else, wearing a completely different outfit."[3] One method they have used to avoid legislation is to operate through the Internet, and today over 21 percent of all payday loans take place over the Internet. You would think this would still be illegal, but to circumvent these laws, a number of payday lenders have partnered with American Indian tribes, and as arms of American Indian tribes, they are protected from enforcement action. The result is that if there isn't a payday lender tempting you around the corner, there is one looking for you online.

Cost of Installment Loans

With an installment loan, repayment of both the interest and the principal occurs at regular intervals, with payment levels set so that the loan expires at a preset date. Installment loans use either the simple interest or the add-on method to determine what the payments will be.

MyLab Finance Video

Simple Interest Method The simple interest method is the most common method of calculating payments on an installment loan. Recall that the monthly payments on an installment loan remain the same each month, but the portion of your monthly payment that goes toward the interest declines each month, while the portion going toward the principal increases. In effect, you pay interest only on the unpaid balance of the loan, which declines as it's gradually paid off.

We can determine your monthly payment on an installment loan using either a financial calculator (using the present value of an annuity calculation to determine *PMT*, the payment) or financial tables. The trick here, as you learned in Chapter 3, is to input the number of months in *N* and convert the annual interest rate into a monthly interest rate. To convert the annual interest rate into its monthly equivalent, we simply divide the annual interest rate by 12. Let's look at the example of a 12-month installment loan for $5,000 at 14 percent.

Calculator Clues

Since the example loan is one with 12 monthly payments, *N* is expressed as the number of months, which is 12, and *I/Y* becomes the interest rate per month. To calculate the interest rate per month, we simply divide the annual rate by 12, which is 14/12. Once you've input the values, you solve for *PMT* by entering CPT PMT:

Enter	12	14/12	5,000		0
	N	I/Y	PV	PMT	FV
Solve for				−448.94	

The answer in the output row is shown as a negative number. Remember, with a financial calculator, each problem will have two cash flows, and one will be a positive number and one a negative number. The idea is that you borrow money from the bank (a positive number because "you receive the money") and at some other point in time you pay the money back to the bank (a negative number because "you pay it back").

Thus, a 12-month installment loan of $5,000 at 14 percent interest would result in monthly payments of $448.94.

[3]Ibid.

TABLE 7.2 Monthly Installment Loan Tables ($1,000 loan with interest payments compounded monthly)

	Loan Maturity (in months)				
Interest	**6**	**12**	**18**	**24**	**30**
13.00%	173.04	89.32	61.45	47.54	39.22
13.25%	173.17	89.43	61.56	47.66	39.34
13.50%	173.29	89.55	61.68	47.78	39.46
13.75%	173.41	89.67	61.80	47.89	39.58
14.00%	173.54	**89.79**	61.92	48.01	39.70
14.25%	173.66	89.90	62.03	48.13	39.82
14.50%	173.79	90.02	62.15	48.25	39.94
14.75%	173.91	90.14	62.27	48.37	40.06
15.00%	174.03	90.26	62.38	48.49	40.18

Example: Determine the monthly payment on a 12-month, 14% installment loan for $5,000.

Step 1: Looking at the intersection of the 14% row and the 12-month column, we find that the monthly payment on a similar $1,000 installment loan is $89.79.

Step 2: To determine the monthly payment on a $5,000 loan, we need only multiply $89.79 by 5 because this loan is for $5,000 rather than $1,000.

We can also determine the monthly payment using installment loan tables, which appear in Appendix E in the back of the book and in an abbreviated form in Table 7.2. Looking at the intersection of the 14% row and the 12-month column, we find that the monthly payment on a similar $1,000 installment loan is $89.79. To determine the monthly payment on a $5,000 loan, we need only multiply this amount by 5 because this loan is for $5,000, not $1,000. Thus, using the tables we find that the monthly payment is $448.95 (the difference between this and what we determined using a calculator, $448.94, is simply a rounding error). Remember, your loan payments remain constant, and as you pay off more of the loan each month, your interest expenses decline. Therefore, your principal payment increases, as shown in Table 7.3.

TABLE 7.3 Illustration of a 12-Month Installment Loan for $5,000 at 14%

Month	Starting Balance	Total Monthly Payment	Interest Monthly Payment	Principal Monthly Payment	Ending Balance
1	$5,000.00	$448.94	$58.33	$390.61	$4,609.39
2	4,609.39	448.94	53.78	395.16	4,214.23
3	4,214.23	448.94	49.17	399.77	3,814.46
4	3,814.46	448.94	44.50	404.44	3,410.02
5	3,410.02	448.94	39.78	409.16	3,000.86
6	3,000.86	448.94	35.01	413.93	2,586.93
7	2,586.93	448.94	30.18	418.76	2,168.17
8	2,168.17	448.94	25.30	423.64	1,744.53
9	1,744.53	448.94	20.35	428.59	1,315.94
10	1,315.94	448.94	15.35	433.59	882.35
11	882.35	448.94	10.29	438.65	443.70
12	443.70	448.94	5.18	443.76	0.00*
Total		$5,387.28	$387.22	$5,000.06	

*Actually, you've overpaid by 6¢

Because you're paying interest only on the unpaid balance, if there are no noninterest finance charges, the stated interest rate is equal to the APR. In effect, there's no trickery here; you just pay interest on what you owe.

Add-On Method With an add-on interest installment loan, interest charges are calculated using the original balance. These charges are then added to the loan, and this amount is paid off over the life of the loan. Loans using the add-on method can be quite costly and, in general, should be avoided. Look back at our example of a 12-month, \$5,000 loan at 14 percent. You'd first calculate the total interest payments to be \$700, as follows:

$$\text{interest} = \text{principal} \times \text{interest rate} \times \text{time}$$

$$\text{interest} = \$5{,}000 \times 0.14 \times 1 = \$700$$

You'd then add this interest payment to the principal to determine your total repayment amount. To determine your monthly payment, just divide this figure by the number of months over which the loan is to be repaid. In this case, the loan is to be repaid over 12 months; thus, the monthly payment is \$475.

$$\frac{\$700 + \$5{,}000}{12} = \$475$$

This results in an APR of close to 25 percent, as shown in Table 7.4. As you can see, there's a very big difference between the stated interest rate, which is 14 percent, and the APR. In fact, the add-on method generally results in an APR of close to twice the level of the stated interest rate. That's because you're paying interest on the original principal over the entire life of the loan.

Even though the amount of outstanding principal keeps decreasing as you pay back the loan, you still pay interest on the amount you originally borrowed. That's

TABLE 7.4 Calculating the APR for an Add-On Loan

Situation	You are considering a 12-month add-on loan for \$5,000 at 14% with a total finance charge of \$700. This loan has 12 monthly payments of \$475. What is the loan's APR?
Solution	Use the N-ratio method to approximate the loan's APR. The N-ratio method approximates an add-on loan's APR using the following formula: $$APR = \frac{M \times (95N + 9) \times F}{12N \times (N + 1) \times (4P + F)}$$ where M = number of payments in a year N = number of payments over the life of the loan F = total finance charge P = loan principal (amount borrowed) In this example, $M = 12$, $N = 12$, $F = \$700$, *and* $P = \$5{,}000$. Substituting these numbers into the N-ratio method's approximation formula, you get $$APR = \frac{12 \times [(95 \times 12) + 9] \times \$700}{(12 \times 12) \times (12 + 1) \times [(4 \times \$5{,}000) + \$700]}$$ $$= \frac{12 \times 1{,}149 \times \$700}{144 \times 13 \times \$20{,}700}$$ $$= \frac{\$9{,}651{,}600}{\$38{,}750{,}400}$$ $$= 0.2491, \text{ or } 24.91\%$$ Thus, the APR on this 12-month, 14% add-on loan is actually 24.91%.

why there is such a big difference between the advertised rate of 14 percent and the actual APR of close to 25 percent in the example. Fortunately, the Truth in Lending Act requires lenders to disclose the loan's APR, thereby giving you a more accurate read on the cost of the loan, regardless of the method used to calculate interest payments.

N-Ratio Method
A method of approximating the APR.

The calculation of the APR for add-on loans is extremely complicated. However, an approximation can be calculated using the **N-ratio method**, which is shown in Table 7.4.

Early Payment of an Add-On Loan

With an installment loan, if you decide to pay off your loan before its maturity, you must first determine how much principal you still owe. Under the simple interest method, interest is paid only on the remaining balance or principal, and it's relatively easy to figure out how much principal remains to be paid.

If you want to repay an add-on interest installment loan early, things get a little tougher. There is usually a provision in the loan contract for calculating the unpaid principal and the amount of interest that you would no longer owe if the loan was repaid early. The most common method for determining how much interest you have paid on an add-on interest installment loan is the **rule of 78s or the sum of the year's digits**.

Rule of 78s or Sum of the Year's Digits
A rule to determine what proportion of each loan payment goes toward paying the interest and what proportion goes toward paying the principal.

The rule of 78s determines what proportion of each payment goes toward paying the principal. Table 7.5 looks at our earlier example of a 12-month, $5,000 loan at 14 percent. According to the rule of 78s, more interest is paid in the early periods because you owe more money in the early periods, since the loan hasn't been paid down yet. In the example in Table 7.5, in the first month it is assumed that 12/78 of the total interest is paid, while in the last month, only 1/78 of the total interest is paid.

TABLE 7.5 Early Payoff of an Add-On Loan—The Rule of 78s

Situation	You have a 12-month add-on loan for $5,000 at 14%. You have been paying $475 a month for the past 6 months. You would like to pay off this loan. How much do you still owe?
Solution	Use the rule of 78s to determine what you still owe. **Step 1: Sum up all the months' digits.** First, number each month in descending order down to 1: that is, if it is a 12-month loan, the first month would be assigned 12, the second month 11, and so forth. Then add up all these numbers. One shortcut is to calculate the sum of the months' digits using the following formula: $\text{sum of digits} = \left(\frac{N}{2}\right) \times (N + 1)$ where N is the number of months in the original loan. $\text{sum of digits} = \left(\frac{12}{2}\right) \times (12 + 1) = 78$ **Step 2: Sum the remaining months' digits.** Now, you sum the numbers of the remaining months: $6 + 5 + 4 + 3 + 2 + 1 = 21$ **Step 3: Determine the portion of the interest that will be avoided if the loan is repaid early.** Divide the result in Step 2 by the result in Step 1. $\text{portion of interest avoided} = \frac{21}{78}$ **Step 4: Determine the dollar interest charge avoided by an early payment.** Multiply the result in Step 3 times the total dollar interest charge on the loan to determine how much interest will be avoided by an early payment. Total dollar interest is 0.14 × $5,000 × 1. Thus, the dollar interest charge avoided by an early repayment is $\left(\frac{21}{78}\right) \times (0.14 \times \$5{,}000 \times 1 \text{ year}) = \$188.46$ **Step 5: Calculate the payoff for the loan.** Subtract the result from Step 4 (the interest charges avoided) from total amount due to the lender for the remaining payments. In this case, there are six payments of $475 for a total of $2,850 (6 × $475 = $2,850). Subtracting $188.46 from this amount yields $2,661.54.

What is the bottom line with respect to add-on loans? First, they are very expensive and should be avoided if at all possible. Moreover, if you decide to pay off your loan early, you could be in for a surprise—there may be a penalty imposed on an early payoff. In fact, it's not uncommon for lenders to keep 20 percent of your prepaid interest as a prepayment penalty. In addition, most add-on loans of a year or less don't allow for any rebate of prepaid interest if you decide to pay the loan off early.

STOP & THINK

In ancient India and Nepal, creditors would "fast on" debtors to collect what was owed them. This involved the creditor sitting at the debtor's front door and fasting until the debt was collected. If the creditor died of starvation, the locals would drag the debtor from his house and beat him to death. Do you think this was an effective approach? Why or why not?

Getting the Best Rate on Your Consumer Loans

LO3 Pick an appropriate source for your loan.

You should approach applying for a consumer loan in the same way you approach any other consumer purchase. Shop around for the best deal, and be prepared to negotiate. Remember, you're the customer.

Where should you shop for a loan? Well, that depends. There's no one perfect lender for everyone. Table 7.6 lists a number of possible credit sources, along with

TABLE 7.6 Possible Sources of Credit

Lenders	Types of Loans	Advantages	Limitations
Commercial banks	Home mortgage Home improvement Education Personal Auto, mobile home	Widely available Financial counseling may be offered	Generally competitive Do not take credit risks Primarily larger loans
Savings and loan associations	Home mortgage Home improvement Education* Personal* Auto, mobile home*	Low costs May provide financial counseling	Selective in lending, only lend to good risks
Credit unions	Home mortgage Home improvement Education Personal Auto, mobile home	Easy to arrange for member in good standing Lowest rates Excellent service	Lend to members only
Sales financing companies (financing where you made the purchase)	Auto Appliance (major) Boat Mobile home	Very convenient Good terms during special promotions Easy to get Processed quickly	High rates Because loan is secured, defaulting can mean loss of item and payments already made
Small loan companies (personal finance companies)	Auto Personal	Easy to get Good credit rating not required Processed quickly	High rates Cosigner often required Maximum size limited by law
Insurance companies	General-purpose loans	Easy to arrange low rates Can borrow up to 95% of a life insurance policy's surrender value No obligation to repay	Outstanding loan and accumulated interest reduce payment to survivors Policy ownership is required
Brokerage firms	Margin account General-purpose loans, using investments as security	Easy to arrange Little delay in getting money Flexible repayment	Changing value of investments can require payment of additional security Margin requirements can change

*In some states only.

the types of loans they make and the advantages and limitations of borrowing from those institutions. Let's take a look at some, starting with the least expensive sources.

Inexpensive Sources

In general, the least expensive source of funds is your family. You don't usually pay the market rate on a family loan; instead, you may pay what your family members would have earned had they kept this money in a savings account. The obvious downside to a family loan is that if you can't repay it, your family suffers. Also, many people feel uncomfortable borrowing money from their families.

Home equity loans and other types of secured loans are also relatively inexpensive because the lending agency has an asset to claim if you can't pay up. The downside of loans of this type is that while assets are tied up as collateral, you can't take out additional first loans on them, so you lose some financing flexibility. Also, if you can't make your payments, you lose your assets. Where do you look for home equity loans? Almost all lending agencies offer them.

Insurance companies that lend on the cash value of life insurance policies also offer relatively low rates. Their rates are low because they're really not taking on any risk—you're borrowing against the cash value of an insurance policy you have with them.

> **STOP & THINK**
>
> When your borrowing isn't tax deductible, which is the case when it's not your mortgage or a home equity loan, the cost of borrowing is actually higher than it appears. If you're in the 30 percent marginal tax bracket, in order to pay $70 of interest you must actually earn $100, with Uncle Sam taking the first $30 out for taxes and leaving you $70 for your interest payment. Given your marginal tax rate, how much would you need to earn to pay $70 of interest if your borrowing wasn't tax deductible? But keep in mind, all this may change because the interest deduction on home equity loans is a target under the changes proposed to the tax code.

More Expensive Sources

Credit unions, savings and loan associations, and commercial banks are also good sources of funds. The precise cost of borrowing from each of these institutions depends on whether the loan is secured or unsecured, what the length of the loan is, and whether the loan has a variable or a fixed interest rate. More important is the fact that the same loan may have a significantly different interest rate from one lender to another. Remember, you've got to shop around for your loan. Although these three sources offer loans that are quite similar in nature, credit unions generally offer the most favorable terms.

Most Expensive Sources

In general, financing from retail stores on purchases you make in them is quite expensive. Borrowing from a finance company or small loan company is also extremely expensive. Unfortunately, to borrow from other sources, you generally need a solid credit rating. In effect, those who are in the most desperate financial shape generally have to pay the most for credit, which in turn keeps them in desperate financial shape.

Keys to Getting the Best Rate

PRINCIPLE 8

How do you get the most favorable interest rate on a loan? The primary key is a strong credit rating. The other keys to securing a favorable rate all involve **Principle 8: Risk and Return Go Hand in Hand**. To get a low rate, the loan must be relatively risk free to the lender. Other than improving your credit rating, there are four ways to reduce the lender's risk. First, use a variable-rate loan. With a

4 key ideas. →

variable-rate loan you, rather than your bank, will suffer if interest rates rise. A variable-rate loan allows a lender to charge you an interest rate that goes up and down with market interest rates, so the lender then gives you a lower interest rate. If you can't afford the payments if interest rates rise, stay away from variable-rate loans. Second, keep the length, or term, of the loan as short as possible. Interest rates decrease as the length of the loan decreases. As we mentioned earlier, the shorter the term, the lower the probability that you will experience a financial disaster before you pay off your loan and the less risk that you will default. Third, provide collateral for the loan. Secured loans are less risky because the lender has an asset designated as collateral in the event of default by the borrower. Finally, put a large down payment toward anything you finance. The larger your down payment, the less you have to borrow and the larger your ownership stake in the asset you are financing. Having a large ownership stake in something is seen as increasing the borrower's desire to pay off the loan.

Should You Borrow or Pay Cash?

In any debt decision, control and planning are the key words. Overriding all your personal finance decisions is the act of setting a budget, living within that budget, and understanding the consequences of your actions.

Debt is, in general, quite expensive. Before you borrow to spend, STOP! Remember, not only does your purchase cost more because of the interest on your loans, but also making indebtedness a permanent feature in your financial portfolio tends to impair your future financial flexibility.

Don't borrow to spend if you can avoid it. Decide whether or not you really need to buy that new item. Does it fit into your personal financial planning program? If the answer is no, the process stops there. If the answer is yes, the question becomes whether or not to borrow. In deciding to use cash rather than credit, you must be sure that using cash doesn't materially affect your goal of having sufficient liquidity to carry you through a financial emergency. The answer to this question may leave you with no choice but to borrow. Then you have to ask whether the cost of borrowing to purchase the item is greater or less than what you are earning on your savings. Sometimes the interest rate you will be charged on the funds you borrow is so low that you are better off borrowing at that low rate than using your savings. For example, if Ford is offering 0.1 percent financing on a new car, you might be better off keeping your money in a money market account where it is earning 1 percent and borrowing the money for the car at 0.1 percent from Ford. On the other hand, if Ford is offering 5 percent financing and you are earning only 1 percent on your savings, you are better off using your savings. In short, if the benefits outweigh the costs, borrowing makes sense.

Controlling Your Use of Debt

LO4 Control your debt.

The first step in controlling debt is to determine how much debt you can comfortably handle. The debt level with which you're comfortable and which you may need changes as you pass through different stages of the financial life cycle. Early on, housing and family demands coupled with a relatively low income level make it natural for individuals to build up debt. In later years, as income rises, debt as a portion of income tends to decline.

The bottom line is that you must use your common sense in analyzing your commitments. However, there are several measures that you can use to control your commitments. They include the debt limit ratio and the debt resolution rule.

Debt Limit Ratio

The debt limit ratio is a measure of the percentage of your take-home pay or income taken up by nonmortgage debt payments.

$$\text{debt limit ratio} = \frac{\text{total monthly nonmortgage debt payments}}{\text{total monthly take-home pay}}$$

An individual's total debt can be divided into consumer debt and mortgage debt. Mortgage payments aren't included in the debt limit ratio because this ratio measures your commitment to consumer credit, which tends to be a more expensive type of debt. In order to maintain a reasonable degree of flexibility, ideally you should strive to keep this ratio below 15 percent. At that debt level, you still have a borrowing reserve for emergencies and the unexpected. That is, because of your low level of debt commitment, you should easily be able to secure additional borrowing without stretching your debt commitment to an uncomfortable level.

Once this ratio reaches 20 percent, most financial planners would advise you to limit the use of any additional consumer debt. One problem when consumer debt payments reach this level is the lack of access to additional debt in an emergency. The importance of maintaining an adequate degree of financial flexibility can't be overemphasized. Obviously, as this ratio increases, your future financial flexibility declines.

Many lenders use what is called the 28/36 rule in evaluating mortgage applicants. That is, if your total projected monthly mortgage payment (including insurance and real estate taxes) falls below 28 percent of your gross monthly income and your total monthly debt payments—including this mortgage payment plus any consumer credit payments—fall below 36 percent, you're considered a good credit risk. If you don't meet this minimum standard, you may be required to come up with a larger down payment, or you may simply be rejected.

Debt Resolution Rule

The debt resolution rule is used by financial planners to help control debt obligations, excluding borrowing associated with education and home financing, by forcing you to repay all your outstanding debt obligations every four years. The logic behind this rule is that consumer credit should be short-term in nature. If it lasts over four years, it's not short-term. Unfortunately, it's all too easy to rely on consumer credit as a long-term source of funding. Given its relative costs, this type of funding should be used sparingly.

Controlling Consumer Debt

The key to controlling consumer debt is to make sure it fits with your financial goals and the budget you've developed to achieve these goals. This process is discussed in Chapter 2. What we're talking about here is control. As you know, control is a major issue in personal finance.

The inspiration for financial discipline comes with an understanding of how costly and potentially painful the alternative is. It's easy to walk out of college with a lot of consumer debt. However, keep in mind the cost of borrowing and how it limits your future financial flexibility.

What might tip you off that you might be in financial trouble? In the previous chapter, we looked at some signs that you might have problems with your credit cards; now let's take a look at Checklist 7.1 for some clues that you might be in financial trouble.

CHECKLIST 7.1 Financial Danger Quiz

If you answer "yes" to any of these questions, you might be in financial trouble.

- ☐ Do you have little or no savings?
- ☐ Do you know what to expect when you get your bank or credit card statement?
- ☐ Have you been turned down for a loan?
- ☐ Do you carry credit card debt from month to month?
- ☐ Do your fixed expenses seem to eat up most or all of your income?
- ☐ Do you have insufficient health insurance?
- ☐ Do you live without a budget?
- ☐ Are you borrowing from one lender to pay another?
- ☐ Are you uncertain about the kind of mortgage you have?
- ☐ Have you ever taken out a payday loan?
- ☐ Do creditors call you about payments?
- ☐ Are you uncertain about the total amount of your debts?
- ☐ Have you had more than one check returned because of insufficient funds?
- ☐ Does the trip to the mailbox terrify you because you aren't sure what you'll find in the way of bills?
- ☐ Are your debts impacting your home life?
- ☐ Do you find your financial problems seem overwhelming?

What to Do If You Can't Pay Your Bills

Once you have gotten into trouble through the overuse of credit, getting out becomes a difficult and painful task. The first step is, of course, putting in place a budget that brings in more money than goes out. The second step involves self-control in the use of credit.

Go to Your Creditor The first place to go if you can't pay a bill is to your creditor. If you owe money to a bank, go there first. The bank may be willing to restructure the loan.

Go to a Credit Counselor If your creditors are unable or unwilling to help you resolve your dilemma, consider seeking help from a **credit or debt counselor**, a trained professional specializing in developing personal budgets and debt repayment programs. A credit counselor helps you organize your finances and develop a workable plan to pay off your debts. However, you must be careful when choosing a credit or debt counselor. One good place to find a reliable credit counselor is the Consumer Credit Counseling Service (800-388-2227 or on the Web at **http://www.nfcc.org**), which is a nonprofit agency affiliated with the National Foundation for Consumer Credit. Before you sign on with a credit counselor, make sure you investigate his or her qualifications by checking with your local Better Business Bureau and state consumer protection office to see if there have been any complaints registered against him or her.

Credit or Debt Counselor
A trained professional specializing in developing personal budgets and debt repayment programs.

Other Options In addition, there are other options, which we looked at in Chapter 6, that you might consider. First, you should make sure you're borrowing as inexpensively as possible. Small loan companies sometimes charge as much as 40 percent on loans. Avoid them, and see if there's a cheaper way to get the funds you need.

A second option to consider is using savings to pay off current debt. You shouldn't do so more than once—only when reevaluating and changing your spending and credit use patterns. If you are earning only 4 percent after taxes on your savings, then using savings to pay off consumer debt at

FACTS OF LIFE

There are now over 22,000 payday loan shops in the United States.

10 or 12 percent may be a good idea. However, your borrowing should be controlled in such a way that it doesn't get out of hand and doesn't warrant this remedy on a regular basis. This is an emergency measure to be taken only in an extreme situation.

Another alternative is to use a debt consolidation loan—rolling multiple debts into a single loan, hopefully with a lower interest rate—to stretch out and lower your payments. A **debt consolidation loan** won't eliminate your debt problems; it merely restructures the payments associated with paying off your current debt. Before you sign on with a debt consolidation company, make sure that you know what you're getting into and that this is a company you want to work with—check it out with the Better Business Bureau and the state consumer protection office. Again, this isn't the optimum solution. The best solution is to take control of your borrowing from the onset.

Debt Consolidation Loan
A loan used to pay off all your current debts.

Bankruptcy as the Last Resort A final alternative in the most extreme case of debt is personal **bankruptcy**. This is not a step to be taken lightly. It doesn't wipe out all your obligations—for example, student loans, alimony, and tax liabilities remain—but it relieves some of the financial pressure.

Bankruptcy
The inability to pay off your debts.

What are some of the leading causes of bankruptcy?

- **Major illness**: This generally comes with major costs and possible job loss.
- **Credit**: Easy availability of credit leads to living beyond your means.
- **Divorce**: It's expensive, what with lawyers, child support, alimony, and splitting up assets.
- **Job loss**: Bills continue even with no income! Savings can be wiped out.

There are several types of bankruptcy, and the two most commonly used types are Chapter 13, the wage earner's plan, and Chapter 7, straight bankruptcy.

Chapter 13: The Wage Earner's Plan To file for Chapter 13 bankruptcy, you must have a regular income, secured debts of less than $1,184,200, and unsecured debts of less than $394,725 (these limits are adjusted each year for inflation; the figures shown here are from March 2017). Under Chapter 13, you design a plan that will allow you to repay the majority of your debts, whereas under Chapter 7 bankruptcy, most of your debts are discharged. The repayment schedule under Chapter 13 is designed so that you can continue to cover normal living expenses while still meeting the repayment obligation. You maintain title to and possession of your assets and, other than following the new debt repayment schedule, continue on with life as before. For your creditors, it means a controlled repayment of debt obligations with the court's supervision. For you, it may mean relief from the harassment of bill collectors and the pressure of never knowing how future obligations will be met.

Bankruptcy happens to all kinds of good people, and it can provide breathing room to start over when there's no hope. Burt Reynolds, Kim Basinger, Toni Braxton, Marion "Suge" Knight, and Mike Tyson all have filed for bankruptcy. Even 50 Cent, once one of the five richest hip-hop artists in the world with a net worth at around $155 million, filed for bankruptcy in 2015 as a result of

STOP & THINK

Debt consolidation loans are very appealing because they offer hope to those who can't keep up with their current payment schedules. Before taking out a debt consolidation loan, however, keep in mind that you may be paying a higher interest rate on the consolidation loan than you are on your current debt. If the problems that led you into this dilemma in the first place aren't solved, do you think a debt consolidation loan will result in a permanent solution? What will you need to do to solve your debt problems?

FACTS OF LIFE

Bankruptcies went up dramatically in the last century. Before then, people didn't live as long, and when they did get sick, they died–in effect, death kept them out of financial trouble. Today, medicine can do wonders, but it can also put you in a financial predicament that is hard to recover from.

bad investments and a big lawsuit. By 2017 he was able to clear his debts and was discharged from bankruptcy.

Chapter 7: Straight Bankruptcy Chapter 7 bankruptcy, or straight bankruptcy, is a more severe type of bankruptcy. Under Chapter 7, the individual who doesn't have any possibility of repaying debts is given the opportunity to eliminate them and begin again. Exactly what assets one can keep varies from state to state, but the home equity exemption is limited to $125,000 if the property was acquired within the previous $3\frac{1}{3}$ years.

To qualify for Chapter 7 bankruptcy, as opposed to Chapter 13, you must pass a "means test," which determines if your disposable income is lower than your "qualified" monthly expenses, and you must own little property other than basic necessities. The means test attempts to determine if you are earning enough to be able to pay off at least some of your debt. If you make more than the median income in your state, have more than $100 a month of disposable income, or have enough disposable income to repay at least 25 percent of your debt over 5 years, then you may have to do a Chapter 13 bankruptcy. In addition, within 6 months of when you can file for bankruptcy, you must complete a credit counseling course, the purpose of which is to inform consumers of the consequences of bankruptcy. Then, before any debts are discharged, you must also take a course in personal financial management.

The bottom line is that while you will not lose everything, you will have to sell a good portion of your assets in order to satisfy Chapter 7 requirements. Most of your debts will be wiped out, but some will remain, such as child support, alimony, student loans, and taxes. A trustee arranges to collect and sell all of your nonexempt property, with the proceeds divided among the creditors. In short, the courts confiscate and sell most of your assets to pay off creditors and, in return, eliminate most of your debts. Needless to say, Chapter 7 bankruptcy is a drastic step and should be taken only after consultation with a financial advisor and your lawyer.

Student Loans and Paying for College

LO5 Understand the alternatives for financing your college education.

If you are reading this, you are probably already enrolled in college, and chances are you have already had to look into taking out a loan. Since this is an issue for you, or could be if your financial circumstances change, this section will be presented as if you are a "first timer" in the market for a **student loan**, an area that is growing by leaps and bounds. Remember **Principle 1: The Best Protection Is Knowledge**—it is never too late to understand the long-term implications of student loans.

Student Loan
A loan with a low, federally subsidized interest rate given to students based on financial need.

PRINCIPLE 1

You probably already know how expensive college is—it's a lesson that most people learn from experience. If you have kids or think about having them, you will face the question of how you're going to afford your children's education. So whether it's for you or for your future children, it's going to be a challenge to make it through all this without a trip to the poorhouse along the way. After all, many private schools cost upward of $50,000 (and more) a year, and with college costs rising at 5 percent a year, in the words of Mick Jagger, "What can a poor boy do?"

So how do you finance your college education without mortgaging your future? To answer this question, you need to understand what the alternatives are among the many choices that are facing you:

- Understand the consequences of your choice of school and of your major course of study,
- Understand what costs are (including tuition and living expenses) and what you need to do to borrow less and borrow smarter,

FIGURE 7.3 Earnings and Unemployment Rates by Educational Attainment, 2015

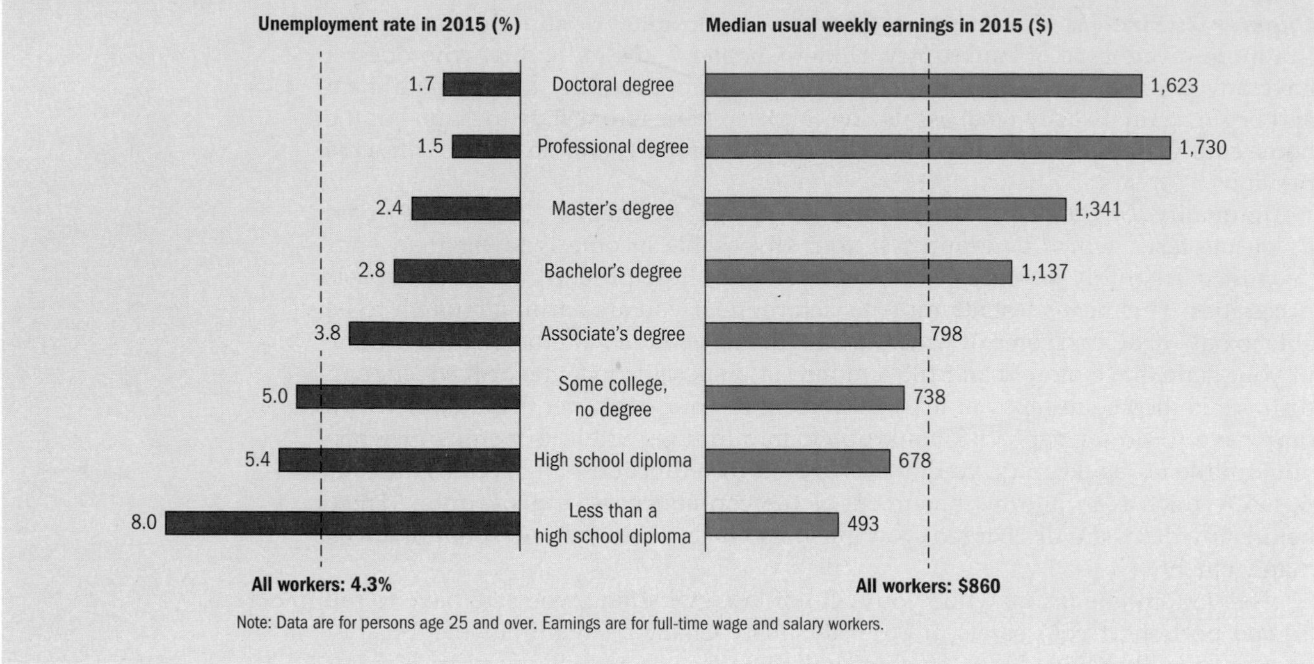

Source: Bureau of Labor Statistics, http://www.bls.gov/emp/ep_chart_001.htm, accessed April 6, 2017.

- Manage your money well while on campus, and
- Repay your loans eventually without sacrificing your financial goals.

Before we jump in and make sense out of college loans and paying for college, let's take a step back and look at what we're trying to do. There is no question that going to college *can* be a good investment—the problem is that this isn't always the case. College graduates don't earn more money simply because they passed enough classes to earn a degree. They earn more money because they are more productive and often have a drive or ambition that translates well in the real world. They may have a skill set that is in demand and hard to replicate, or they may have critical thinking skills that allow them to be more productive. What does all that mean? It means that when you see a graph like the one in Figure 7.3, you have to take it with a grain of salt. Some of the individuals who went on to higher education would have done very well even if they hadn't gone to college—they were that bright and talented. And then there are those who left college and made it big—think Steve Jobs, Mark Zuckerburg, or Lady Gaga. In addition, these data are based on individuals who went to college in the past, when college wasn't all that common. After all, back in 1980 only about 16 percent of adults 25 and older were college grads, and by 1990, that number had risen only to a bit over 21 percent. What's it going to be like in the future? Today, about 66 percent of high school graduates choose to attend college. The bottom line is that in the future, your future, the competition is going to be better educated.

So Many Choices—Schools and Majors

The first big decision you will make regarding college is where to go. Costs can vary dramatically among schools. In 2017, the total cost for 1 year at a public 4-year university was $24,610 for an in-state student; for an out-of-state student, it climbed to

$38,890; and for a student at a private 4-year university, it came in at $49,320. Keep in mind that this is only the average—for example, New York University runs around $77,000 a year.

What all this means is that you need to pick your college carefully, making sure that it's the right choice for you both educationally and financially, so that you don't face costs that you simply can't afford. Keep in mind that oftentimes in-state schools and community colleges cost less than out-of-state schools. Also, getting an idea as to what your future income might be should play a role in determining how much you should borrow. As you know, starting salaries vary dramatically depending on your career path, so if you have to borrow money, you need to think about how your student loan will impact your future. After all, you want to make sure that your student loan payments will be manageable and will take away only a small portion of your starting salary once you graduate.

It is also important for you to understand that not all college majors pay off in the same way. As we saw in Chapter 1, while you want to pick a major that takes advantage of your interests, skills, values, personal traits, and desired lifestyle, you also want to be aware of the kinds of jobs that a particular major opens up and the salaries and job security inherent in those jobs. Make sure you understand the positive and negative aspects of the professions your major might lead you into. Do they offer the status and earning potential you are looking for? Are they part of a stable industry? Might they require travel or frequent relocation? And through all of this, keep in mind that the major you pick will lead you into your career.

While earning potential isn't the only issue a student should consider when selecting a major, it is an important one. As you saw in Chapter 1, the returns your college degree provides depend on the major—in fact, according to a recent study, the highest-earning major earns 314 percent more than the lowest-earning major.[4]

Borrowing Less and Borrowing Smarter

Want to make it through college while avoiding the poorhouse? Keep the costs down. This means comparing financial aid packages and college costs. Fortunately, the U.S. Department of Education offers a Financial Aid Shopping Sheet (**http://collegecost.ed.gov/shopping_sheet.pdf**), and the Consumer Financial Protection Bureau has an online Compare College Costs and Financial Aid Offers worksheet, providing links to costs at different schools, including tuition, fees, estimated student expenses, average financial aid, retention and graduation rates, and net price.

One way to make the college of your dreams affordable is through grants, loans, and work-study funding. To apply for this aid, you need to fill out a Free Application for Student Aid, or FAFSA, which becomes available on October 1 for the upcoming academic year. Remember to report the income from tax returns dated two years prior to your enrollment. This form is then sent to the colleges you've selected and is used to determine how much aid you will receive. Shortly after you fill out this form, you will receive your Student Aid Report, or SAR, which summarizes all the information you submitted on your FAFSA. Check it carefully, correct any mistakes that you find, and make sure to list any "special circumstances." Perhaps your parents are supporting your grandparents—make sure you let the colleges know because this could affect the amount of aid you are offered. The SAR will provide you with your Expected Family Contribution, or EFC, which in turn is used to determine your eligibility for federal student aid—it doesn't mean your family has to contribute that amount.

---

[4]Georgetown University, Center on Education and the Workforce, "What's It Worth? The Economic Value of College Majors," https://cew.georgetown.edu/cew-reports/whats-it-worth-the-economic-value-of-college-majors/, accessed April 6, 2017.

Once you are accepted by a college, the kind and amount of aid offered will be in your award letter. Hopefully, this will result in a grant or work-study money, both of which are great because you *won't have to pay them back*. Unfortunately, there is no mandatory format for this letter, so it is crucial that you read it very carefully and understand

- The difference between free aid (grants) and loans (must be repaid);
- The cost of attending a particular school that remains after free aid is used—aid and tuition usually do not remain the same year after year, as tuition rises and interest rates on additional loans may rise; and
- Miscellaneous costs—dorm and food plans, the cost of living in that town/city, and travel back and forth to home.

When the new FAFSA becomes available in October for the upcoming academic year, fill it out for free on the FAFSA Web site (**http://fafsa.ed.gov**). Remember to complete one of these every year you're in school because you must reapply for student loans each year. Keep in mind that every state has its own deadline, so it is a good idea to complete the form as soon as it is available. The earlier you apply for student aid, the more you could receive, as college and state funding can be granted on a first-come, first-served basis. You are responsible for knowing these deadlines!

Be sure you look into any state and local grants and scholarships that might be available. The U.S. Department of Education has a listing of state grants that you should check out. In addition, there are a number of free scholarship search options available. Service members, veterans, and their families may be eligible for GI Bill benefits and/or military tuition assistance. There are also two federal tax credits available to help offset your costs: the American Opportunity Credit, allowing you to claim $2,500/year for the first four years, and the Lifetime Learning Credit, allowing you to claim $2,000/per year for college costs (tuition and fees). You cannot double-dip expenses, though. To claim either credit, you must have separate expenses that have not been covered by a scholarship or grant. You *can* claim the credit if you used student loans to pay the expenses. So even if you wouldn't normally file a tax return because of your income level, make sure you do, or you will miss out on these tax credits. But be aware that proposed changes in the tax laws include an elimination of the Lifetime Learning Credit.

One thing to keep in mind is that you're not just paying for 1 year of school. About half of all colleges practice "front loading of grants," which means that your grants as a freshman will be more generous than your grants as a sophomore, junior, or senior. If you need more money than that provided by grants, work-study funding, and cost-cutting measures (for example, taking on another roommate), then you'll have to borrow money. Borrowing money by taking out a loan means that this money will have to be repaid for the first 10 years or more after you graduate.

As you may already know from talking to friends and relatives, about two-thirds of all undergraduates use loans to help pay for their education. How much did they borrow? The average student debt, including money borrowed by the student's parents for education expenses, is over $29,000, and according to a recent Fidelity survey, total debt—including credit card debt and personal and family loans—runs over $35,000. It's a bit lower for students who go to public colleges and higher for those who go to private colleges—but it's a lot either way.

Just so you don't feel alone, let's ask, "How much student debt is there?" Well, the Consumer Financial Protection Bureau estimates that outstanding student loan debt—both private student loans and government student loans—is over $1.4 trillion and that student loans guaranteed or held by the federal government are over $1 trillion, actually exceeding the total amount of credit card debt. And we all know how much credit card debt there is—lots! So while it seems normal to borrow for your college education, keep in mind that the more you borrow, the more you have to repay—but if you do need to borrow money, what are your choices?

Paying for Your College Education

Paying for your college education includes saving money, cutting all possible costs, being realistic about your choices, and, finally, borrowing money.

Saving for College If you are currently in college and need help paying for school, this might be a little late to help you—but if you are thinking about your children's future education, this is a must-read. With that in mind, it is important to get your priorities—as far as your financial plan goes—in order. First, pay down your debt and max out your retirement contributions before setting aside money for a child's future college expenses. Why? Because your child can always apply for financial help for school, but you can't get help for your debt or retirement.

A **529 plan** is a tax-advantaged savings plan designed to encourage saving for future college costs, and it comes in two forms: prepaid tuition plans and college savings plans. All states sponsor at least one type of 529 plan. Investment options, tax advantages, how it can be used, and fees can vary between states and plans.

529 Plan
A tax-advantaged savings plan designed to encourage saving for future college costs that comes in two forms: prepaid tuition plans and college savings plans.

Prepaid tuition plans generally allow college savers to purchase units or credits at participating colleges and universities for future tuition and, in some cases, room and board. Most prepaid tuition plans are sponsored by state governments and have residency requirements. Many state governments guarantee investments in prepaid tuition plans that they sponsor.

Prepaid Tuition Plan
A college saving plan that allows for the purchase of units or credits at participating colleges and universities for future tuition.

College savings plans generally permit a college saver (the prospective student or a parent or grandparent) to establish an account for the purpose of paying for future eligible college expenses like tuition, books, and room and board. Withdrawals from college savings plans can generally be used at any college or university.

College Savings Plan
A plan that allows a college saver (the prospective student or a parent or grandparent) to establish an account for the purpose of paying for future eligible college expenses.

Among the biggest advantages of 529 plans over other college savings options are the tax advantages they offer. Earnings grow tax deferred, and withdrawals are tax free when used for qualified education expenses. Also, anyone can contribute to a 529 plan, as there are no income limitations. For most wealthy families, 529 plans are one of the few available tax-advantaged college savings options.

A **Coverdell Education Savings Account (ESA)** allows you to make an annual nondeductible contribution of up to $2,000 per year/per person to a specially designated investment trust account. There are contributor income limitations. The account will grow free of federal income tax with tax-free withdrawals. Its main advantage is that it can be used for elementary and secondary as well as higher education purposes. However, contributions stop when the student becomes 18 and must be used by age 30. Any "leftover money" will be charged a penalty as well as taxes.

Coverdell Education Savings Account (ESA)
A savings account that allows you to make an annual nondeductible contribution of up to $2,000 per year/per person to a specially designated investment trust account.

The two 529 plans and the Coverdell ESA are only three of several ways to save for college. It is important to note that they are tax-advantaged saving. Figure 7.4 compares the three most popular savings plans.

Borrowing Money—Federal Student Loans and Private Loans Need a student loan? There are essentially two choices: federal student loans and private loans. Without question, for most borrowers, federal student loans, which are funded by the government, are the better choice. Once you begin paying back your federal loans, the interest rate will be fixed—this is important because it lets you know exactly how much your payments will be after graduation.

Federal student loans are funded by the federal government, and the U.S. Department of Education is your lender. The Federal Perkins Loan Program is offered for those with exceptional need, and four types of Direct Loans are available:

Federal Student Loans
Loans that are funded by the federal government with the U.S. Department of Education as your lender.

FIGURE 7.4 College Savings Plans Comparison

	529 College Savings Plan	529 Prepaid Tuition Plan	Coverdell Educational Savings Account
Who Owns It?	Contributor	Contributor	Contributor
What Can I Invest In?	Typically, plans provide several investment options.	Purchase units or credits at participating school.	No restrictions.
When Can It Be Used?	No age limit.	Plan may set age or grade limits.	No contributions can be made after beneficiary turns age 18, and withdrawals must be made before beneficiary turns 30. An exception is made for special needs children.
What Expenses Are Covered Besides Tuition and Fees?	Qualified education expenses for postsecondary education.	Only tuition and mandatory fees for postsecondary education are covered. Few exceptions are made.	Qualified elementary and secondary education expenses or qualified postsecondary education expenses.
How Much Can I Contribute?	Varies from plan to plan. Majority of plans permit total contributions in excess of $250,000 per beneficiary.	Fixed by terms of contract you purchase.	Contributor: $2,000 per beneficiary per year. Beneficiary: $2,000, does not matter how many ESAs are set up.
Federal Tax Advantages	Earnings grow tax deferred and are tax free if used for qualified education expenses.	Earnings grow tax deferred and are tax free if used for qualified education expenses.	Earnings grow tax deferred and are tax free if used for qualified education expenses.
State Tax Advantages	Vary from state to state, but some states provide tax deduction for contributions, tax-free earnings growth, and tax-free withdrawals for qualified education expenses.	Vary from state to state, but some states provide tax deduction for contributions, tax-free earnings growth, and tax-free withdrawals for qualified education expenses.	None
Income Phase-Out	None	None	Single filers: $95,000–$110,000 Joint filers: $190,000–$220,000
What Are Penalties for "Other Use"?	Earnings are taxed as ordinary income and may be subject to 10 percent penalty.	Earnings are taxed as ordinary income and may be subject to 10 percent penalty.	Withdrawals that exceed the beneficiary's education expenses for the year may be taxable.

Source: Smart Saving for College–Better Buy Degrees. Copyright © 2016 FINRA. Reprinted with permission from FINRA.

Federal Perkins Loan Program
A school-based loan program for undergraduate and graduate students who have exceptional financial need.

Direct Subsidized Loans
Subsidized student loans made only to undergraduates who establish financial need.

- The **Federal Perkins Loan Program** is a school-based loan program for undergraduate and graduate students who have exceptional financial need.
- **Direct Subsidized Loans** are made only to undergraduates who establish financial need. The government pays the interest on this loan while the student is still in school and during the 6-month grace period following graduation before the student starts loan repayment.
- **Direct Unsubsidized Loans** are made to undergraduate, graduate, and professional students. It is not necessary to establish financial need. If a student chooses

not to pay interest while in school or during the grace period after graduation, the interest accumulates and is added to the principal of the student's loan.

- **Direct PLUS Loans** are made only to graduate or professional students, and **Direct PLUSParent Loans** are made to the parents of dependent undergraduate students. A credit check is required, interest begins accruing immediately, and payments are deferred for 6 months.
- **Direct Consolidation Loans** allow students to combine all of their eligible federal student loans into one loan.

Direct Unsubsidized Loans Unsubsidized student loans made to undergraduate, graduate, and professional students.

Direct PLUS Loans Student loans made only to graduate or professional students.

Direct PLUSParent Loans Student loans made to the parents of dependent undergraduate students.

Direct Consolidation Loans Loans that allow students to combine all of their eligible federal student loans into one loan.

As mentioned, with federal loans, the interest rate *is fixed over the life of the loan*, but every year on July 1 the interest rate on *new loans* changes. The rate is pegged to the interest rate on 10-year Treasury notes plus an add-on:[5]

$$\text{federal loan rate} = \text{10-year Treasury note rate} + \text{add-on}$$

For example, for the 2017–2018 loan year, the rate on 10-year Treasury notes was 2.40 percent, and the add-ons set by the government were 2.05 percent for Direct Subsidized and Direct Unsubsidized Undergraduate Loans, 3.60 percent for Direct Unsubsidized Graduate Loans, and 4.60 percent for Direct PLUS Loans. Thus, for 2017–2018, the rates on new loans were

- Direct Subsidized and Unsubsidized Undergraduate Loans = 2.40% + 2.05% = 4.45%
- Direct Unsubsidized Graduate Loans = 2.40% + 3.60% = 6.00%
- Direct PLUS Loans = 2.40% + 4.60% = 7.00%

Keep in mind that every year the interest rate on *new loans* changes. For 2017–2018, the interest rate on Direct Subsidized and Unsubsidized Undergraduate Loans was 4.45%, but as interest rates on 10-year Treasury notes go up, so will the student loan rates. This is something you should be aware of because most students take out loans every year. Fortunately, there is a cap on these interest rates—that is, the rates cannot go above certain interest rates, with Direct Subsidized and Unsubsidized Undergraduate Loans capped at 8.25 percent, Direct Unsubsidized Graduate Loans capped at 9.50 percent, and Direct PLUS Loans capped at 10.50 percent. With interest rates at relatively low levels, there is a good chance that student loan rates may continue to rise in the future, but at least the cap will keep them from climbing too high. Table 7.7 provides an overview of the federal loan alternatives.

Private student loans are meant to provide you with funds only after you have exhausted all federal financial aid. Private loans are usually offered by commercial banks and credit unions. There are many options for private loans, and it is essential that you read the fine print and understand the terms of the loan. The interest rates on these loans are often variable, which means your interest rates and payments could go up over time—not a good thing. In addition, private loans can be more expensive—in fact, over the past few years some have come with rates as high as 16 percent—also not a good thing. On top of this, they generally don't provide the options to reduce or postpone payments—a benefit that comes with government loans. The bottom line is that federal student loans are a better deal than private student loans, so you want to explore them first—and if you're still short of money, try cutting costs in any way possible.

Private Student Loans Student loans used after you have exhausted all federal financial aid. Private loans are usually offered by commercial banks and credit unions.

[5]Bipartisan Student Loan Certainty Act of 2013.

TABLE 7.7 Federal Student Loan Comparisons

Federal Student Loan Program/Type of Loan	Program Details (interest subject to change yearly)	Annual Award Limits (subject to change yearly)
Federal Perkins Loan Program	• For undergraduate, graduate, and professional students • Interest = 5%; no loan fees; 9-month grace period after graduation • Funds depend on student's exceptional financial need and availability of funds at the college • The college is the lender	• Undergraduate students: up to $5,500/yr • Graduate and professional degree students: up to $8,000/yr
Direct Subsidized (Stafford Loan)	• For undergraduate students with need • Borrower is *not* charged interest while in college and during grace and deferment periods • Interest = 4.45%* • The U.S. Department of Education is the lender	• Annual subsidized limits: 1st year = $3,500 2nd year = $4,500 3rd & 4th years = $5,500
Direct Unsubsidized (Stafford Loan)	• For undergraduate and graduate students • Interest: Borrower responsible • Undergrad = 4.45%* • Graduate = 6.00%* • The U.S. Department of Education is the lender	• Dependent undergrads, $2,000 unsubsidized in addition to subsidized limits • Independent undergrads, $6,000 to $7,000 depending on year in addition to subsidized limits
Direct PLUS PLUSParent, and GraduatePLUS Loan	• PLUSParent for parent(s) of dependent students and GraduatePLUS for graduate and professional students • Interest = 7.00%* • Credit check required • The U.S. Department of Education is the lender	• Maximum amount is cost of attendance minus any other financial aid the student receives
Direct Consolidation Loan	• All federal student loans can combine except PLUSParent • Interest = fixed, based on weighted average rates of combined loans • Once loans are combined, they cannot be removed • Combine during grace period	• Total of all federal loans • Private loans cannot be included

Note: For additional information on federal student aid, visit http://www.studentaid.ed.gov.
*Interest rates for loans issued in 2017-2018.

FACTS OF LIFE

A recent academic paper out of the University of North Carolina at Greensboro found that each $10,000 in additional student debt decreases the borrower's long-term probability of marriage by 7 percentage points.

Suppose you have maxed out federal financial aid avenues and reviewed "other alternatives" such as making sure the school you picked makes sense for you financially, exploring the possibility of part-time employment, and cutting all costs possible. If you still need money, a private loan is the answer, but your first stop should be your school's financial aid office. The financial aid office "is your friend"—the people who work there have considerable knowledge and experience and can help you succeed on your educational journey. They will actively assist you in seeking and securing financial resources. There you will get a form certifying that you need additional aid to cover your college costs. This form is required by most lenders. Your financial aid office may have some advice on where to look—and what you want to be looking for is the lowest interest rate coupled with flexibility in the event that you experience trouble making payments. You will probably have to have a cosigner on your loan—in fact, in 2016 nearly 94 percent of all private student loans required one. Since your cosigner will be making payments if you can't or don't, your cosigner will likely be a parent or other relative, and you'll want to line that person up ahead of time. One thing to consider is a loan that offers a

TABLE 7.8 Federal Versus Private Student Loans

	Federal Loans	Private Loans
What You Need to Know	Take advantage of federal loan options before seeking private loans. Federal student loans almost always cost less and are easier to repay.	Private loans are generally more costly than federal loans and offer little flexibility if you are having trouble making your payments.
Benefits	Many federal student loans are subsidized and have fixed interest rates. Most students are eligible, and repayment terms are flexible.	You can borrow larger amounts. If you shop around and have a good credit rating, you may be able to find low interest rates.
Risks	The amount of money you can borrow is limited, and a portion of your wages and tax refunds could be taken by the government if you neglect repayment responsibilities.	Your interest rate and monthly payment could change with little warning, and you have fewer options for when and how much you repay.
How to Repay	6-month grace period for undergraduates. Flexible monthly payments based on income or financial hardship, and possible debt forgiveness for teaching, military service, and other public service work.	6-month grace period for most loans. Very limited flexibility for those with financial need or hardship. Currently, there is no forgiveness for private student loans.
Interest Rates	Rates are fixed once you have the loan. The rates for new loans change annually and are tied to the 10-year Treasury note rate. The Direct Subsidized and Perkins Loans have no interest while you're in school.	Rates are often variable and can change over time. They depend on your credit rating and other factors. You are charged interest while you are in school.
Who Is Eligible	Almost everyone is eligible for federal loans; those with exceptional need qualify for lowest rates.	Lenders decide eligibility based on your credit rating and other factors, and you will likely need a cosigner.
Loan Limits	Vary with the type of loan but cannot exceed your college costs. Generally, undergraduates can max out at $5,500-$12,000 per year; graduates at $8,000-$20,500 per year.	Vary depending on your credit rating and other factors, but generally you should not borrow more than your college costs.

Source: Adapted from Consumer Financial Protection Bureau, http://www.consumerfinance.gov/paying-for-college/choose-a-student-loan/#o1, accessed July 9, 2017.

"cosigner release" after a certain number of on-time payments. Table 7.8 provides a more detailed comparison of federal and private loans, looking at repayment, interest rates, who is eligible, and loan limits.

Compare Financial Aid and College Costs Once you have an idea of what your aid offers and funding alternatives are at the different schools you're considering, the next step is to carefully compare them. If you are considering one of the more than 2,000 colleges and universities that use the U.S. Department of Education's Financial Aid Shopping Sheet, you'll get a standardized letter that makes comparing different financial aid packages easier and allows for informed decisions with respect to your choice of college. If not, go to the Consumer Financial Protection Bureau Web site, and look at its page titled "Compare College Costs and Financial Aid Offers." It allows you to input costs and aid in a way that makes comparisons relatively easy. Also remember that the financial aid office is an invaluable source of information.

Manage Your Money Responsibly

Once you've made your loan decision, you have to make sure you have a landing place for any money that you might be receiving. We discussed your banking alternatives in Chapter 5, and the same advantages and disadvantages discussed there apply here as to the different bank account options. If you don't already have a bank account, make sure you get one set up as soon as possible. This will allow you to sign up for direct deposit with your school, and you'll generally get your money faster with direct deposit. As we discussed in Chapter 5, look into whether the bank charges monthly fees, out-of-network ATM fees, overdraft fees, debit card use fees, or service fees for paying bills online. Will direct deposit help avoid some of these fees? In other words, make sure you hang onto as much of the money you receive as possible.

Repaying Your Loans

You have taken out your loan(s) and have spent (or are still spending) the money on getting your higher education—congratulations! But now it's time to pay up. Getting the money was nice and helpful, but paying it back is serious business.

Repayment Plans There are basically four types of repayment plans with several choices that affect the length of time you pay, monthly payment amount, interest paid, and possible forgiveness; these include

- *Standard Repayment* (10-year term; you pay the lowest amount of interest): this is the automatic repayment plan unless you choose another plan.
- *Extended Repayment* (10- to 30-year term): additional number of payments and additional interest paid.
- *Income-Based Repayment:* based on a percentage of discretionary income, not the amount owed; yields low monthly payment but additional interest paid; 25-year term of payments before loan forgiveness.
- *Graduated Repayment:* starts low and monthly payment increases every 2 years; yields low monthly payment but additional interest paid; 25- to 30-year term of payments before loan forgiveness.

Deferment
The ability to postpone your student loan payments for up to 3 years while you are enrolled at least half-time in school, are unemployed, or meet hardship standards.

Forbearance
The ability to stop making student loan payments temporarily for a qualified reason such as illness, financial hardship, or service in a medical or dental internship or residency.

Deferment If you are enrolled at least half-time in school, are unemployed, or meet hardship standards, you can postpone payment on a loan for up to 3 years. Interest does not accrue if the loan is subsidized.

Forbearance You can stop making payments temporarily for a qualified reason such as illness, financial hardship, or service in a medical or dental internship or residency. Interest continues to accrue during the nonpayment time.

The world of college debt is constantly evolving. Rules regarding federal and private student loans and interest are sure to change as you navigate the yearly process of researching, obtaining, and, finally, taking the critical step of repaying those loans. It will be your responsibility to stay on top of this information. You will have help! As soon as your loan is paid out to you or your school by the U.S. Department of Education, you will be assigned a *loan servicer* to help you manage the repayment of your federal student loan(s)—*for free*. Do not pay anyone to do this. You should keep all paperwork from and contact information for your servicer, let your servicer know your current contact information (updating it whenever you move), and contact your servicer when you have questions or need help regarding repayment plans, setting up automatic payments, consolidation advice, and so forth. Basically, your servicer is your go-to resource throughout the repayment process. Remember that you can call your servicer, but an even better idea is to send your questions through your servicer's messaging system. This gives you a paper trail of your questions and his or her answers! Fortunately, the U.S. Department of Education has very good and up-to-date Web sites that should answer most of your questions, and remember to use the financial aid office at your school—the people who work there are the experts in this area, and they have your best interest at heart.

LOVE & MONEY

With over $1.4 trillion in student debt carried by over 40 million Americans, it seems like everyone has student debt these days. So it doesn't cause any damage to your love life, does it? Well, according to a recent TD Ameritrade survey, it does. In fact, 26 percent of those surveyed said they would be less likely to date someone with student debt. That's not as bad as we saw for credit card debt in the last chapter, but it's still substantial.

As we all know, student debt can be enormous—even reaching above $100,000. In fact, the average U.S. household with student debt owes about $49,042. It shouldn't come as any surprise that student debt can derail your love life. After all, marrying someone who owes close to $50,000 can present challenges. But why might student debt be a deal breaker? The question here is whether it was taken on as part of a bigger plan: For example, was it the only way you could realistically attend college and get that degree so that you could get the job you really aspired to, or was it simply a result of carelessness and bad financial habits? That being said, you can see why the answers to these questions are so critically important:

- Is there a plan to pay the loan off?
- Does "extra money" go toward the loan, or is it spent on the fun activity of the day?
- If the debt was the result of bad financial habits, are those habits a thing of the past?

If there is a plan, there is a good chance that the person is responsible and financially committed—the kind of person that won't drag you into financial problems in the future.

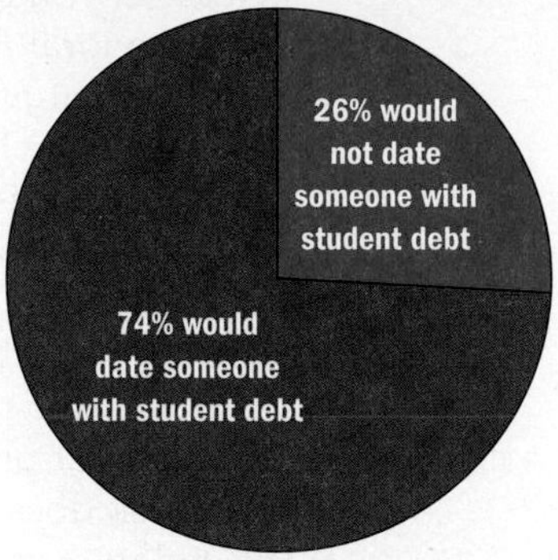

26 percent of those surveyed said they would be less likely to date someone with student debt.

Just as student loans can have a negative impact on your love life, any substantial debt can also do serious damage. NerdWallet recently polled millennials (those between 18 and 34 years old) and found that 38 percent brought auto loan debt into their new relationship, while 27 percent brought medical debt. So what's the answer? If you're bringing student or other types of debt into a relationship, what should you do? And if it's your partner with the debt, how can you make things work? The key is openness and honesty. Once the relationship gets serious, it's time to bring everything to the table. Each partner should be aware of where the other partner stands with respect to debt and money. After that, you need to put together a plan for dealing with the debt and align your financial goals. While you may not have the amount of financial flexibility a debt-free relationship has, there is a good deal of satisfaction in setting realistic goals and working toward them as a couple.

BEHAVIORAL INSIGHTS

PRINCIPLE 9

Principle 9: Mind Games, Your Financial Personality, and Your Money Try this little experiment: Write down on a piece of paper six things you own that are in your current home. Make two copies of the paper. On one copy, write down how much you would have to be paid to sell each item. On the second page, write down how much you would be willing to pay for each item if you found it at the local thrift shop. Really, try this and we will talk about it later.

In this chapter, we have looked into various types of loans and debt, and you know that there is no question that spending too much can lead to too much debt. So how do you control your spending? One way to do this is to understand how marketers get you to purchase more than you really want.

Behavioral finance tells us that one very successful marketing trick involves the "endowment effect," which describes the fact that people put more value on things that they own. To exploit this behavioral trait, marketers offer trial periods and money-back guarantees. "Take it home and try it in your house—see if you like it, and then if you do, you can buy it—but no pressure from us." But once that product, whether it is a new TV, furniture, a rug, or something else, is in your home, the endowment effect kicks in—and the endowment effect increases the value of that product to you.

The endowment effect is also quite successfully used by sellers on eBay. To raise the eventual price of an item, the seller will open the bidding at a very low price. What this does is increase the number of bidders, and when you are a high bidder, the endowment effect kicks in. Because you are a high bidder at some point, the item you are bidding on feels like it is already yours—and that raises its value to you.

Let's revisit the little exercise proposed at the start. If you are like most people, you will find that the prices on the first page—what you would have to be paid to sell the things you already have in your home—are much higher than those on the second page—what you would pay for the items if found in a thrift shop—because ownership in and of itself seems to add value to your objects. The endowment effect demonstrates that we tend to fall in love with what we own and become resistant to change.

How do you combat the endowment effect? It's not easy, but if you understand how marketers are "playing" you, it becomes easier to avoid being played. So when you get the chance to "try it at home, risk free for two weeks" or when you enter that bid on eBay, be aware of what you've just done. Decide if you really want this product or if it is your emotions at work.

A final thought, taking us back into the world of student loans, concerns *choice*. Behavioral research has demonstrated that too many choices can be demotivating. The student loan landscape is filled with so many choices that it often leads to cognitive overload. What type of loan should I go for? What repayment plan is best for me? What will my future income be? And while plans may seem similar on the surface, they may actually be quite different. Studies have found that this choice-loaded landscape leads many students to just choose whatever a friend has chosen and often take on more debt than they need to—spending the money on so much more than just their tuition, books, and traditional educational expenses. It's money; they have it, they spend it, and they just apply for more. Studies have shown that help from an expert—like someone in the financial aid office—will narrow the choices and lead you to more responsible borrowing.

ACTION PLAN

PRINCIPLE 10

Principle 10: Just Do It! If you're like most students, you're going to graduate with student loans. It doesn't matter what their size is; you aren't going to like them. And what you're going to want to do is to control them rather than letting them control you. Here are a number of tips that will make your life with student loans as good as possible.

- **Mind your loans.** Make sure you know the details of your student loans: who the lender is (usually a *loan servicer* collects the payments on your loans) and what the balance and the repayment status are for all of your student loans. Make a file folder for each loan and a master checklist of all info as a quick reference.

- **Watch your grace period closely—and don't miss your first payment.** Your grace period determines when you have to begin paying back your loan. For Direct (Stafford) Loans, it's 6 months, but it's 9 months for Perkins Loans. For private student loans, the grace period can vary. This is really important! So if you don't know this, look at the paperwork that came with your loan, or contact your lender or loan servicer. Now is the time to set up automatic payments through your bank.
- **Keep connected.** If you move or change your e-mail address, keep your lender or loan servicer posted; it's your responsibility. You'll also want to make sure you read what they send you. It's not junk mail; it's mail from your lender.
- **Know your repayment choices, and pick the one that fits you.** The default repayment scheme is the standard 10-year repayment plan. But there are other options. If you have other debt, look at the interest rate on it, and make sure you are paying off the debt with the highest interest rate first.
- **If you have problems, deal with them.** As you know from **Principle 7: Stuff Happens**, you can lose a job, get sick, or experience some other unexpected financial problem. Remember, there are federal loan deferments and forbearance. But keep in mind that interest accrues during forbearance. If your job after graduation doesn't pay enough for you to pay off your student loans, you should check out income-based repayment. The bottom line is that if you have problems, it's your responsibility to deal with them. Don't ignore them—they won't go away. Don't just stop paying—default kicks in on federal loans after 9 months of nonpayment. And that's a place you don't want to go: your total loan balance becomes due, your credit score is trashed, what you owe will increase dramatically, and to top it off, the government can garnish your wages and seize your tax refunds if you defaulted on a federal loan.

PRINCIPLE 7

- **Go after your most expensive loan first.** If you are paying off several loans ahead of schedule, go after the one with the highest interest rate first. If you have private student loans, it will be them. They have higher interest rates and less flexibility, so go after them first.
- **To consolidate or not to consolidate?** Loan consolidation will allow you to simplify monthly payments by rolling multiple loans into one loan. This must be done while at least one of the loans is still in its grace period. There isn't an interest rate break, but you will have a single monthly payment for your new federal Direct Consolidation Loan. If you're considering consolidating private loans into a private consolidation loan, look at the interest rate—it may or may not be a good idea. One thing is for sure—never consolidate federal loans into a private student loan: You'll lose all the repayment options and borrower benefits; things like unemployment deferments and loan forgiveness programs will be gone!
- **If it's available, seek loan forgiveness.** If you work full-time in a public service job, you may qualify for public service loan forgiveness. Just google public service loan forgiveness, and you'll find all the information you need.

Chapter Summaries

Understand the various consumer loans. LO1

SUMMARY: A single-payment loan is a loan that's paid back in a single lump-sum payment at maturity. In general, these loans have a stated maturity date. An installment loan calls for repayment of both interest and principal at regular intervals, with the payment levels set in such a way that the loan expires at a preset date.

Consumer loans are either secured or unsecured. A secured loan is a loan that is guaranteed by a specific asset. With an unsecured loan, no collateral is required.

With a fixed-interest-rate loan, the interest rate is fixed for the duration of the loan, but with a variable-interest-rate loan, the interest rate is tied to a market interest rate and periodically adjusts to reflect movements in that market interest rate. A home equity loan, or second mortgage, is a loan that uses a borrower's built-up equity in his or her home as collateral against the loan.

KEY TERMS

Consumer Loan, page 202 A loan involving a formal contract that details exactly how much you're borrowing and when and how you're going to pay it back.

Single-Payment or Balloon Loan, page 202 A loan that is paid back in a single lump-sum payment at maturity or the due date of the loan, which is usually specified in the loan contract. At that date, you pay back the amount you borrowed plus all interest charges.

Bridge or Interim Loan, page 202 A short-term loan that provides funding until a longer-term source can be secured or until additional financing is found.

Installment Loan, page 202 A loan that calls for repayment of both the interest and the principal at regular intervals, with the payment levels set in such a way that the loan expires at a preset date.

Loan Amortization, page 202 The repayment of a loan using equal monthly payments that cover a portion of the principal and the interest on the declining balance. The amount of the monthly payment going toward the interest starts off large and steadily declines, while the amount going toward the principal starts off small and steadily increases.

Secured Loan, page 202 A loan that's guaranteed by a specific asset.

Unsecured Loan, page 203 A loan that's not guaranteed by a specific asset.

Fixed-Interest-Rate Loan, page 203 A loan with an interest rate that stays fixed for the duration of the loan.

Variable- or Adjustable-Interest-Rate Loan, page 203 A loan in which the interest rate does not stay fixed but varies based on the market interest rate.

Prime Rate, page 203 The interest rate banks charge to their most creditworthy, or "prime," customers.

Convertible Loan, page 203 A variable-rate loan that can be converted into a fixed-rate loan at the borrower's option at specified dates in the future.

Security Agreement, page 204 An agreement that identifies whether the lender or borrower retains control over the item being purchased.

Default, page 204 The failure of a borrower to make a scheduled interest or principal payment.

Note, page 204 The formal document that outlines the legal obligations of both the lender and the borrower.

Insurance Agreement Clause, page 204 A loan requirement that a borrower purchase credit life insurance that will pay off the loan in the event of the borrower's death.

Acceleration Clause, page 204 A loan requirement stating that if the borrower misses one payment, the entire loan comes due immediately.

Deficiency Payments Clause, page 204 A loan requirement stating that if you default on a secured loan, not only can the lender repossess whatever is secured, but also, if the sale of that asset doesn't cover what is owed, you can be billed for the difference.

Recourse Clause, page 205 A clause in a loan contract defining what actions a lender can take to claim money from a borrower in the case of default.

Home Equity Loan or Second Mortgage, page 205 A loan that uses a borrower's built-up equity in his or her home as collateral against the loan.

Automobile Loan, page 207 A loan made specifically for the purchase of an automobile, which uses the automobile as collateral against the loan.

Calculate the cost of a consumer loan. LO2

SUMMARY: It's important to know exactly what a loan costs. The finance charges include all the costs associated with the loan—interest payments, loan-processing fees, fees for a credit check, and any required insurance fees. The APR is the simple percentage cost of the credit paid over the life of the loan on an annual basis.

KEY TERMS

Annual Percentage Rate or APR, page 207 The true simple interest rate paid over the life of a loan. It's a reasonable approximation for the true cost of borrowing, and the Truth in Lending Act requires that all consumer loan agreements disclose the APR in bold print.

Loan Disclosure Statement, page 207 A statement that provides the APR and interest charges associated with a loan.

***N*-Ratio Method, page 214** A method of approximating the APR.

Rule of 78s or Sum of the Year's Digits, page 214 A rule to determine what proportion of each loan payment goes toward paying the interest and what proportion goes toward paying the principal.

Pick an appropriate source for your loan. LO3

SUMMARY: There are numerous sources of consumer loans, which vary dramatically in terms of cost, including family, insurance companies, credit unions, savings and loan associations, commercial banks, small loan companies, retail stores, and credit cards.

The key to getting a favorable rate on a loan, or even qualifying for a loan in the first place, is a strong credit rating. In addition, there are four other ways that you can reduce the lender's risk and thereby secure a favorable rate: (1) use a variable-rate loan, (2) keep the term of the loan as short as possible, (3) provide collateral for the loan, and (4) make a large down payment toward the item being financed.

Control your debt. LO4

SUMMARY: Before borrowing, you must make sure that borrowing fits within your financial plan, including living within your budget, and that you understand all the consequences of your actions. You must also determine how much debt you can afford. Not only should you use your common sense in analyzing your debt commitments, but also you should measure the severity of your credit commitments using the ratio of the non-mortgage debt service to take-home pay and the debt resolution rule.

KEY TERMS

Credit or Debt Counselor, page 219 A trained professional specializing in developing personal budgets and debt repayment programs.

Debt Consolidation Loan, page 220 A loan used to pay off all your current debts.

Bankruptcy, page 220 The inability to pay off your debts.

Understand the alternatives for financing your college education. LO5

SUMMARY: In funding your college education, you'll want to understand the importance of your school and major, know what the costs are, manage your money well, and repay your loans without sacrificing your financial goals. In terms of saving for college, you'll want to make the most of tax-advantaged savings alternatives like 529 plans and Coverdell Educational Savings Accounts (ESAs). If you have to borrow money, federal student loans will most likely be the better choice.

KEY TERMS

Student Loan, page 221 A loan with a low, federally subsidized interest rate given to students based on financial need.

529 Plan, page 225 A tax-advantaged savings plan designed to encourage saving for future college costs that comes in two forms: prepaid tuition plans and college savings plans.

Prepaid Tuition Plan, page 225 A college saving plan that allows for the purchase of units or credits at participating colleges and universities for future tuition.

College Savings Plan, page 225 A plan that allows a college saver (the prospective student or a parent or grandparent) to establish an account for the purpose of paying for future eligible college expenses.

Coverdell Education Savings Account (ESA), page 225 A savings account that allows you to make an annual nondeductible contribution of up to $2,000 per year/per person to a specially designated investment trust account.

Federal Student Loans, page 225 Loans that are funded by the federal government with the U.S. Department of Education as your lender.

Federal Perkins Loan Program, page 226 A school-based loan program for undergraduate and graduate students who have exceptional financial need.

Direct Subsidized Loans, page 226 Subsidized student loans made only to undergraduates who establish financial need.

Direct Unsubsidized Loans, page 226 Unsubsidized student loans made to undergraduate, graduate, and professional students.

Direct PLUS Loans, page 227 Student loans made only to graduate or professional students.

Direct PLUSParent Loans, page 227 Student loans made to the parents of dependent undergraduate students.

Direct Consolidation Loans, page 227 Loans that allow students to combine all of their eligible federal student loans into one loan.

Private Student Loans, page 227 Student loans used after you have exhausted all federal financial aid. Private loans are usually offered by commercial banks and credit unions.

Deferment, page 230 The ability to postpone your student loan payments for up to 3 years while you are enrolled at least half-time in school, are unemployed, or meet hardship standards.

Forbearance, page 230 The ability to stop making student loan payments temporarily for a qualified reason such as illness, financial hardship, or service in a medical or dental internship or residency.

Problems and Activities

These problems are available in MyLab Finance.

1. Shirley, a recent college graduate, excitedly described to her older sister the $1,500 sofa, chair, and tables she found today. However, when asked, she could not tell her sister which interest calculation method was to be used on her credit-based purchase. Calculate the monthly payments and total cost for a bank loan assuming a 1-year repayment period and 14 percent interest. Now, assume the store uses the add-on method of interest calculation. Calculate the monthly payment and total cost with a 1-year repayment period and 12 percent interest. Explain why the bank payment and total cost are lower even though the stated interest rate is higher.

2. Using the information on the two loans described in Problem 2, how much interest will Shirley "save" or be rebated if she can repay the loans after 6 months?

3. Which results in a lower total interest charge, borrowing $1,000 to be repaid 12 months later as a single-payment loan or borrowing $1,000 to be repaid as a

12-month installment loan? Assume a simple interest method of calculation at 12 percent interest. Defend your answer.

4. Consumers should comparison shop for credit just as they would for any other consumer good or service. How might a consumer's stage of the financial life cycle, income, net worth, or credit score affect the availability of loan sources and the associated cost of the loans offered?

5. Name two advantages and two disadvantages of secured loans versus unsecured loans.

6. You just took out a variable-interest-rate consumer loan set at 3 percent over prime. After 1 year, your rate jumps to 4 percent over prime. Treasury bills are currently paying 2 percent. What is the new interest rate on your consumer loan?

7. Antonio would like to replace his golf clubs with a custom-measured set. A local sporting goods megastore is advertising custom clubs for $800, including a new bag. In-store financing is available at 2 percent, or he can choose not to renew his $500 certificate of deposit (CD), which just matured. The advertised CD renewal rate is 2 percent. Antonio knows the in-store financing costs will not affect his taxes, but he knows he'll pay taxes (25% federal taxes and 5.75% state taxes) on the CD interest earnings. Should he cash in the CD or use the in-store financing? Why?

8. Noel and Herman need to replace Noel's car. But with the furniture and appliance payments, the credit card bills, and Herman's car payment, they are uncertain if they can afford another payment. The auto-financing representative has asked, "What size payments are you thinking of?" Current payments (excluding the potential cost of Noel's car) total $475 of their $3,250 combined monthly take-home pay. Calculate the debt limit ratio to help them decide about the car purchase and answer the question "What size payments are you thinking of?" by first assuming a 15 percent limit and then "stretching" it to a 20 percent limit.

9. Noel and Herman are now trying to decide between a 48-month and a 60-month car loan. If the loan is for $10,000 at 6 percent, what is the difference in the monthly payments?

10. What is the total amount Bae will have to repay for his $25,000 student loan if the interest rate is 6 percent over 10 years? What is the total amount he would have to repay if the $25,000 was a grant instead of a loan?

11. Assuming you meet the income and other qualifications, what is the maximum amount of educational tax credits you can claim for 4 years of school at your state university? (*Hint:* See the section about the American Opportunity Credit and the Lifetime Learning Credit.)

12. Liam just graduated from his state university with $29,000 in student loan debt. He is curious what his monthly payments will be if he repays over the standard 10 years at 5 percent. Liam also has an emergency fund that pays 3 percent. Should he use some of that money to repay his student loans early? Why?

13. Noah took out $20,000 in private student loans at 16 percent APR. His cousin Ava took out the same amount of student loans, but she got a federal student loan with an APR of 4.66 percent. What is the difference in the amounts Noah and Ava will pay for their student loans (over 10 years), assuming the interest starts accumulating on the same day?

Discussion Case 1

This case is available in **MyLab Finance.**

Karou is considering different options for financing the $12,000 balance on her planned new car purchase. The cheapest advertised rate among the local banks is 7 percent for a 48-month car loan. The current rate on her revolving home equity line is 8.5 percent. Karou is in the 25 percent federal tax bracket and the 5.75 percent state tax bracket.

Questions

1. Calculate Karou's monthly car payment using your financial calculator. Compare the payment amount if she uses the 48-month car loan through her local bank versus her home equity line of credit. Assume both loans will amortize over 48 months, and use the simple interest method.
2. What are Karou's income tax savings over the life of the loan if she chooses to use her home equity line of credit to finance the purchase of her new car?
3. Which loan offers the lower payment? Which loan has the lower after-tax cost? Use this information to determine which loan she should choose.
4. In a discussion with her father about financing her new car, Karou was surprised to hear that he once financed a car with the add-on method of interest calculation. He planned to repay the $2,000 loan within 1 year but was able to do so after 9 months because of a bonus he earned at work. The interest rate was 5 percent. Calculate the monthly payments, as well as the final payment to pay off the loan. How much interest was "saved," or rebated, using this method of financing and the rule of 78s?
5. Assume Karou's father could finance $2,000 today at 5 percent using the simple interest method of calculation. How much would the payments be? Calculate the final payment to pay off the loan after 9 months. How much interest was "saved"?
6. Considering the information in Questions 4 and 5, calculate the difference in finance charges, assuming neither loan was paid off early.
7. Assuming Karou did not have access to a home equity line, what factors might she consider to reduce the lender's risk and therefore "buy" herself a lower-cost loan? (*Hint:* Consider **Principle 8: Risk and Return Go Hand in Hand**.)

PRINCIPLE 8

8. What is the collateral for each of the loans Karou is considering? If the bank repossessed her car, would she still have to repay her loan?

Discussion Case 2

This case is available in **MyLab Finance.**

You work in your college's financial aid office, and Mary Lou Hennings, a junior, has come to you for advice. She just found out that her father has been "downsized" from his job. To ensure that she has sufficient funding for her senior year, she needs to apply for a loan to help with expenses. She has a part-time job with take-home pay of $375 per month. She expects her annual net earnings to be approximately $30,000 after graduation, and she plans to continue living at home for another year or two. Her parents have told her she can use up to $10,000 of their home equity line of credit; however, she is not sure she wants to do that. She does not have any debt except for 3 more years of monthly auto payments of $189. She is worried about trying to pay for an additional loan while still in school, although her dad is convinced he will find another job soon and be able to make the payments.

Questions

1. Explain the difference between a Direct Subsidized Loan and a Direct Unsubsidized Loan to Mary Lou.
2. What types of student loans are available to Mary Lou, and what lending limits apply? When would repayment of the loans begin?
3. Assume her student loan will have an interest rate of 7 percent and her parents' home equity line has a rate of 9.25 percent. If both loans have a 10-year maturity, what will her monthly payment be for each on a loan of $5,000, ignoring any possible deferments?
4. Explain the tax consequences of the two options, assuming Mary Lou is in the 10 percent marginal federal tax bracket and her parents are in the 25 percent tax bracket. No state income tax is assessed.
5. Using her current income, calculate her debt limit ratio for the most expensive school loan and her auto loan during school. Using her projected income, calculate her debt limit ratio for the loans after graduation.
6. What are the advantages and disadvantages of loan consolidation? What factors should Mary Lou consider when contemplating consolidation?
7. If Mary Lou suffers financially and has to file for bankruptcy, will her student loan debt be forgiven?
8. Considering all available information, which loan would you suggest to Mary Lou? Why? Are there other options for financing her education?

CHAPTER 8 The Home and Automobile Decision

Learning Objectives

LO1	**Make** good buying decisions.	**Smart Buying**
LO2	**Choose** a vehicle that suits your needs and budget.	**Smart Buying in Action: Buying a Vehicle**
LO3	**Choose** housing that meets your needs.	**Smart Buying in Action: Housing**
LO4	**Decide** whether to rent or buy housing.	**Renting Versus Buying**
LO5	**Calculate** the costs of buying a home.	**Determining What You Can Afford**
LO6	**Get** the most out of your mortgage.	**Financing the Purchase—The Mortgage**

It looks realistic enough. Phil and Claire Dunphy from *Modern Family* live in a cute Brentwood, California, home in the suburbs of Los Angeles with four bedrooms, five baths, a picket fence around the front yard, and three challenging kids. What might something like that cost? The answer is probably in the $2.6 million range. If they borrowed $2.5 million for the house using a 20-year mortgage, what would their monthly mortgage payments be? Probably close to $16,000 per month, which adds up to around $192,000 over a year—and that doesn't include insurance or taxes. While Claire has taken over for her dad and is probably doing quite well, making those mortgage payments might be tough for Phil, a real estate salesman, given the fact that the median pay for a real estate broker is $41,990.

How about Dre and Bow Johnson on *Black-ish*? Dre is in advertising and Bow is an anesthesiologist. The average salary for an anesthesiologist is about $270,000, and someone in advertising might make about $80,000, so together they have a

Ron Tom/Disney ABC Television Group/Getty Images

pretty good income. But the house they live in, or at least the one that is shown on TV, is located in Sherman Oaks and would cost about $3.2 million. If they borrowed $3 million with a 20-year mortgage at 4.5 percent, they would have mortgage payments of about $19,000 per month. That's $228,000 a year, and it doesn't include taxes or insurance! Again, possible—but probably not particularly realistic. *But* not everything on TV is unrealistic. Leslie Knope (*Parks and Recreation*) has a cute four-bedroom house in Pawnee, Indiana. It probably sells for about $175,000—and if she put $50,000 down, her monthly mortgage payments on a 20-year mortgage at 6 percent would be under $900. When you choose a house or a place to rent, you'll want to make sure that it fits your housing needs and, maybe even more important, that it fits your budget.

What would make a home "perfect" for you? As you might imagine—or perhaps already know—buying a house isn't just a financial decision; it's also a personal and emotional one, so it has to fit both your lifestyle and your wallet. For most people, buying a home is the single biggest investment they'll ever make, which is why it's so important to understand all the complexities and financial implications of this purchase. It is essential that you get it right.

Buying a car is another major purchasing decision. Although a car isn't considered an investment, it is an expenditure—and a huge one at that. In either case, when buying a house or a car, you're probably going to need a loan and are thus committing a large portion of your future earnings over a long period of time. Because both of these purchases have a dramatic impact on your personal finances, you need to consider each carefully. Fortunately, there is a lot of advice out there—we will walk through the steps of "smart buying."

Smart Buying

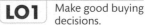

LO1 Make good buying decisions.

In this chapter, we talk about spending money rather than saving it. Just as you work hard to save money, you should also work hard when spending it, taking the time to make well-thought-out and well-researched buying decisions. To help you do this, we'll look at four steps in a smart buying process. You can apply this process to any major purchasing decision. It is a way to place some control on your purchasing, a way to ensure that your final selection is not only the best product for the best price but also a product that you need at a cost that fits your budget. One of the big benefits of this approach is that it eliminates impulse buying, a sure budget blower if there ever was one.

Let's look at each of the four steps to smart buying in general. Then we'll apply these steps, first to an automobile purchase and then to a home purchase.

Step 1: Differentiate Want from Need

Even before deciding to make a purchase, smart buying requires that you separate your wants from your needs. This doesn't mean that you can never buy anything just because you want it; it just means that you need to recognize such a purchase for what it is and make sure you can afford it. For most of us, "want" purchases often carry a trade-off. A new iPod, for example, may mean sacrificing other material wants—such as forgoing your daily latte for the next 6 months. Steve Martin and Amy Poehler are featured in a *Saturday Night Live* skit about an in-debt married couple approached by a salesperson trying to sell a financial guide titled *Don't Buy Stuff You Cannot Afford*. Amy asks the salesperson, "What if I want something, but I don't have any money?" "You don't buy it," the salesperson replies. Simple, but it works. Carl Richards, who writes the weekly Sketch Guy column in the *New York Times*, advocates a 72-hour purchase pause. That is, take 3 days to reflect on a potential purchase, and if it still seems to make sense 3 days later, go ahead with it—in other words, eliminate impulse shopping. The important thing to determine before buying a "want" is whether the purchase will interfere with your ability to pay for your needs. It's one thing to give up Starbucks; it's another to not be able to pay your rent!

Step 2: Do Your Homework

After deciding to make a purchase, make sure you do it wisely. Let's say you are in the market for a new HDTV. The first thing you need to know is how much you can afford to spend. After you determine what your budget will allow, take time to research the details. What is the price range for HDTVs? What are the differences in quality? What are the features of each brand?

Do some comparison shopping. For many purchases, you can start your research with *Consumer Reports*, a publication that provides unbiased ratings and recommendations for a host of products and services. It's available at your library or bookstore. In terms of great apps, RedLaser is one that will save you money on the spot and let you know if you're getting a good deal or not. Simply scan the product's bar code, and it will alert you to lower prices online or at nearby stores. Another informative guide on smart buying, the *Consumer Action Handbook*, is downloadable from the Internet at **https://www.usa.gov/handbook**.

Step 3: Make Your Purchase

When you're ready to make your purchase, it is sometimes just a matter of going to the cheapest source and buying the product. However, with some products, such as a car, there may be negotiation involved. In purchases that require haggling, you increase your chances of getting the best deal possible by first doing all the research you can. One key to negotiating a good price is knowing the markup on the product—the price the dealer adds on above what he or she paid for the product. (This is part of Step 2: Do Your Homework.) Knowing the markup gives you an idea of how much room there is for negotiation. You also want to make sure that you're dealing with someone who has the authority to lower the price. And be sure to consider the various financing alternatives, determining not only which is the best deal but also which alternative best fits your monthly budget. Checklist 8.1 gives some tips on smart buying.

CHECKLIST 8.1 Before You Buy

- ☐ Before you buy, know exactly what you want and what you can afford.
- ☐ Do your research. Check the internet for ratings and reviews, ask family, friends, and others you trust for advice based on their experience. Gather information about the seller and the item or service you are purchasing.
- ☐ Never buy on impulse or if you feel pressure to buy; this includes donating to charity.
- ☐ Before you buy, know what the seller's refund, return, and cancellation policies are.
- ☐ Make sure you read the contract before you sign it and don't sign it if you don't understand it, or if there are any blank spaces in it.
- ☐ With high-pressure sales tactics the best thing to do is to walk out. Never allow yourself to feel forced or pressured into buying something.
- ☐ Never do business over the telephone with companies you do not know.
- ☐ Never rely on a salesperson's verbal promises. Get everything in writing.

Source: U.S. Office of Consumer Affairs, Consumer's Resource Handbook, 2017.

Step 4: Maintain Your Purchase

Smart buying means getting the best product or service at the best price with financing that's right for you. Smart buying also means maintaining your purchase after the deal is done, which includes physically maintaining what you've bought, as well as resolving any complaints or issues about the purchase or the product. If you have a problem, the first thing to do is contact the seller. If that doesn't do it, contact the headquarters of the company that made or sold the product. Most large companies have a toll-free 800 number, which you can find on the product's instructions or on the company's Web site.

You can also write to the company. Make sure to address your letter to the consumer office or the company president. In your correspondence, describe the problem, what you've done so far to try to resolve it, and what action you'd like taken. Do you want your money back, or do you want the product exchanged? Keep in mind that your problem may not be resolved immediately. When dealing with a company directly, keep notes, including the name of the person with whom you spoke, the date, and what was done. Save copies of all letters to and from the company.

If your problem still isn't resolved, it's time to work through such organizations as the Better Business Bureau, along with other local, state, and federal organizations that might provide help. Checklist 8.2 gives some tips on making a complaint, while Figure 8.1 provides a sample complaint letter.

CHECKLIST 8.2 Making a Complaint

- ☐ **A written letter or an email are the best approach.** You will have a record of your communication with the company. Our sample letter can help you prepare a written complaint.
- ☐ **Be brief and to the point.** Make sure you include a description of what you bought, serial or model numbers, the name and location of the seller, and when you made the purchase.
- ☐ **State exactly what you want done** about the problem. Be reasonable, after all, you want a solution.
- ☐ **Don't write an angry, sarcastic, or threatening letter.**
- ☐ **Provide your name, and contact information.** If an account is involved, be sure to include the account number.
- ☐ **Keep records**; include the dates along with the name of the person with whom you spoke and what was done, if anything. If you're using the company's online complaint form, take a screenshot before you "submit."

Source: U.S. Office of Consumer Affairs, Consumer's Resource Handbook, 2017.

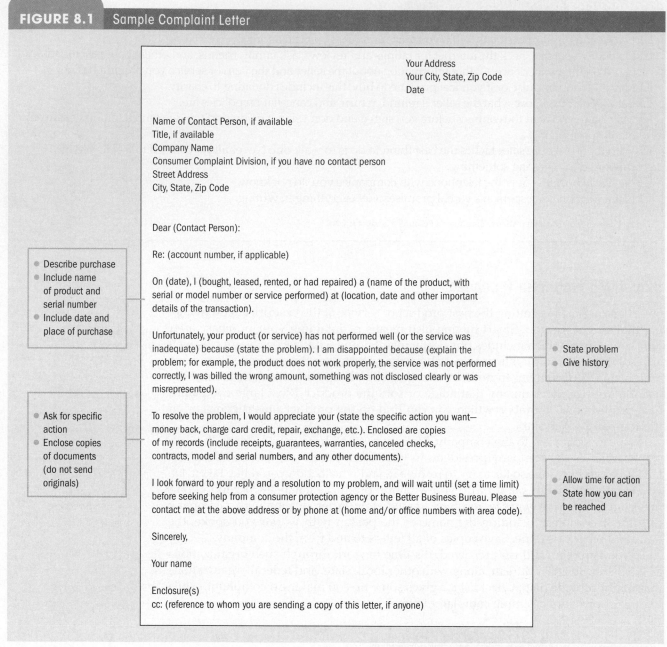

FIGURE 8.1 Sample Complaint Letter

Your Address
Your City, State, Zip Code
Date

Name of Contact Person, if available
Title, if available
Company Name
Consumer Complaint Division, if you have no contact person
Street Address
City, State, Zip Code

Dear (Contact Person):

Re: (account number, if applicable)

On (date), I (bought, leased, rented, or had repaired) a (name of the product, with serial or model number or service performed) at (location, date and other important details of the transaction).

- Describe purchase
- Include name of product and serial number
- Include date and place of purchase

Unfortunately, your product (or service) has not performed well (or the service was inadequate) because (state the problem). I am disappointed because (explain the problem; for example, the product does not work properly, the service was not performed correctly, I was billed the wrong amount, something was not disclosed clearly or was misrepresented).

- State problem
- Give history

To resolve the problem, I would appreciate your (state the specific action you want—money back, charge card credit, repair, exchange, etc.). Enclosed are copies of my records (include receipts, guarantees, warranties, canceled checks, contracts, model and serial numbers, and any other documents).

- Ask for specific action
- Enclose copies of documents (do not send originals)

I look forward to your reply and a resolution to my problem, and will wait until (set a time limit) before seeking help from a consumer protection agency or the Better Business Bureau. Please contact me at the above address or by phone at (home and/or office numbers with area code).

- Allow time for action
- State how you can be reached

Sincerely,

Your name

Enclosure(s)
cc: (reference to whom you are sending a copy of this letter, if anyone)

Source: U.S. General Services Administration, *Consumer Action Handbook*, 2017.

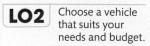

LO2 Choose a vehicle that suits your needs and budget.

Smart Buying in Action: Buying a Vehicle

Next to buying a house, your vehicle is probably your largest investment. Although there are major differences between buying a stereo and a car or truck—the price, for one thing—the process is essentially the same.

Ten years ago the only decision to be made when purchasing a new car was whether to buy a new one or a used one. Today, you can also consider leasing—in fact, in 2009 only about 16 percent of all new cars were leased, but by 2017, this

LOVE & MONEY

The first step in the smart buying process introduced earlier in this chapter involves differentiating want from need, and it implies a real level of control. It means you can't spend frivolously and you have to think through purchases and buy only what you can afford. While the absence of "smart buying" can do serious damage to your finances, the damage it does to your love life can be even more harmful. As you should know by now, money is the number one source of friction for couples, and uncontrolled spending is a true hot button.

A recent *Money* magazine survey of couples found that their partner's spending habits were the number one reason for arguments about money.

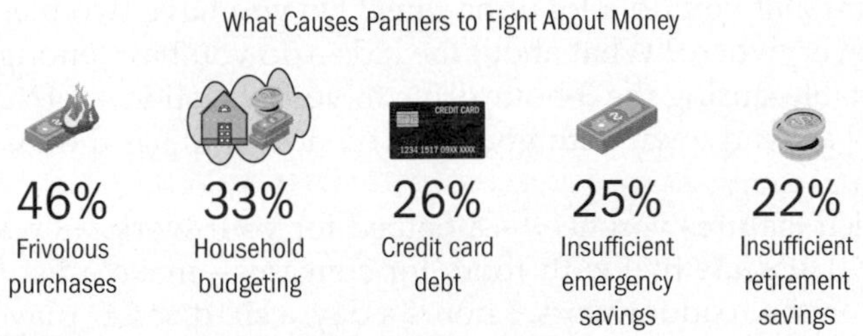

To really understand the friction that frivolous purchases cause in a relationship, you need to keep in mind that partners argue about money more than they do about children, in-laws, household chores, lack of quality time together, meals, and even sex. And when asked who has the bad spending habits, both men and women point to their partner.

One of the causes of all this is that people often marry their money opposites. That is, a saver many fall in love with a spender, drawn to his or her spontaneous personality. Alternatively, a spender may be attracted to the financial security that a saver provides. In fact, a recent SunTrust survey found that 37 percent of respondents identified both themselves and their partner as "savers" and 15 percent said they are both "spenders." However, the remaining 47 percent said that they and their partner do not share the same spending habits. Given that fact, it is not unexpected that spending habits bring on arguments.

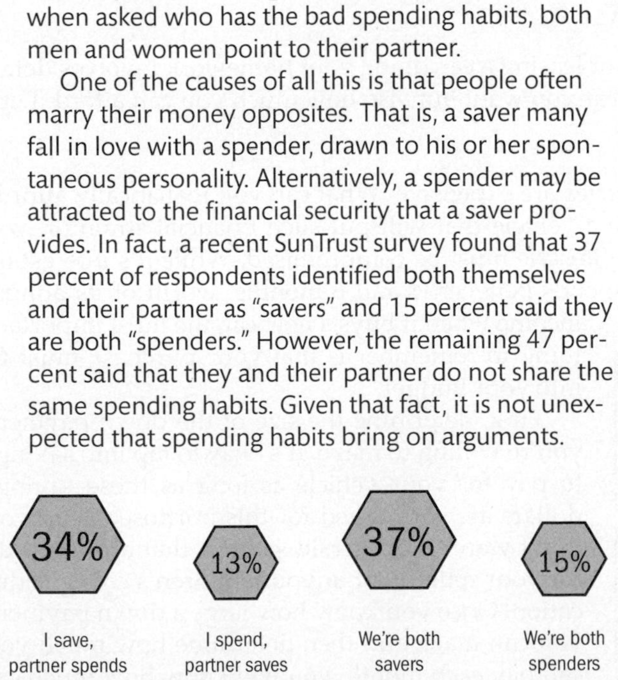

On top of all this, both men and women feel that they are more concerned with money matters than their partner.

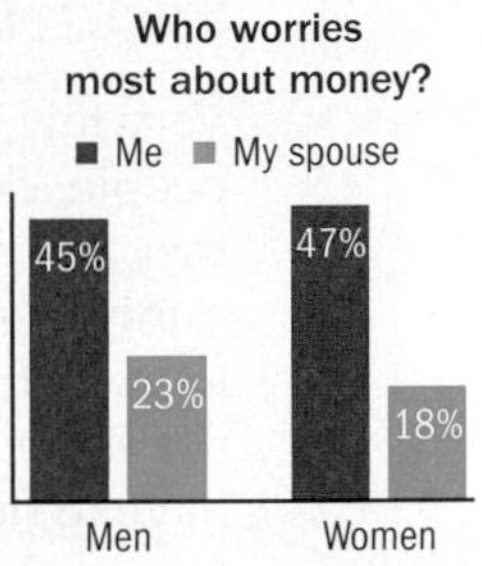

The SunTrust survey also found that 36 percent of those in a serious relationship don't seek their spouse's or partner's advice before making a purchase, no matter the amount. Would this matter to you? Does it depend on how much was spent? An Experian survey of 1,000 newlyweds in May 2016 found that on average they would spend more than $800 without telling their spouse, with men spending more, about $1,259, and women averaging $383 before they felt they should "tell." About 16 percent (mostly men) said that "unknown to their spouse" they have a "secret financial account." It should be clear that all this makes things ripe for an argument. However, regardless of the reasons that draw unlike financial personalities together and regardless of why one partner is more concerned about money matters than the other, the arguments spawned from spending must be dealt with and should be approached by examining your goals and your progress toward them as a couple. Probably, the most important question is "Will these spending habits keep us from achieving our financial goals?" If they won't, then they aren't too much of a problem, but if they will, then they need to be discussed and dealt with. This is also where a little discretionary spending money may help by providing a limit on spontaneous spending while giving each partner a bit of spending autonomy.

Combining your life and your finances with a spouse or partner also means combining your spending. When you think about the fact that the word *spending* is often followed by the word *habits*, you might more clearly understand the need for a well-thought-out and -discussed smart buying plan.

number had risen to around 28 percent. What brought on this new method of vehicle financing? Sticker shock. Today, the cost of a new vehicle is beyond the financial means of many Americans. Leasing, which is becoming increasingly popular, offers an affordable alternative. In effect, leasing is renting a vehicle for an extended period, with a small or no down payment and low monthly payments. To understand the process of purchasing or leasing a vehicle, we'll follow the basic smart buying process, adapting it to fit the vehicle decision.

Step 1: Differentiate Want from Need

Very few decisions pit needs against wants as directly as which car to buy. For most people, choosing a car is more than deciding what best suits their lifestyle and what they can afford; people want a car that reflects who they are. A new Dodge Caravan minivan may be the most practical choice for you, your husband, and your three kids, but you may still really *want* a MINI Cooper convertible, which costs about the same. In making this decision, as with any major purchase decision, you'll first have to decide which features and qualities you need and which features and qualities you just want. The facts of your life will dictate many of the features that you need. Does your work require that you do a lot of hauling? Do you have two black labs that you take with you everywhere? What about the kids—do you have enough room for them to be comfortable during the 3-hour drive to your vacation spot? Or do you need a car just to tool around town with your best friend? (If this is the case, buy the MINI Cooper.)

After you determine which features you need—a flatbed for your work, a "way back" for the dogs, or a car that seats five with room for suitcases—make a list of features you want. If you're on the road for work 3 hours a day, a six-disc CD player may seem vital to you. Or you may really crave a DVD player for your car, knowing that if the kids can watch *Frozen* over and over on the long drive to Grandma's, you'll get a bit more peace and quiet.

Now that you have a list of what you need and what you want, how do you know what you can afford? Let's find out.

Step 2: Do Your Homework

When considering purchasing or leasing a car, doing your homework involves determining not only what kind of car you want but also how much you can afford. Let's look at the issue of money first.

PRINCIPLE 9

How Much Can You Afford? Vehicles are expensive. What can you realistically afford? It makes no sense to purchase a vehicle that will put such financial strain on you that either other goals or your lifestyle must be compromised. While it's interesting to note that a typical family spends between 4 and 6 months' worth of its annual income when it buys a new car, the most important thing to remember is that your purchase must fit into your budget.

First, determine the size of the down payment you're willing to make. It's okay to tap into savings to pay for your vehicle as long as those savings dollars are earmarked for this purpose. What you don't want to do is raid savings that are set aside for your retirement or your children's college education. Once you know how large a down payment you can make and then determine how much you can pay each month, you will know how much car you can buy.

STOP & THINK

When setting a price for a car or home, sellers often take advantage of **Principle 9: Mind Games, Your Financial Personality, and Your Money**. Buyers tend to focus on the first digit of a price, so to the buyer $6,999 seems quite a bit cheaper than $7,000. That's because we read the numbers from left to right and the impression of whether the price is high or low is based on the first thing a buyer sees. What are some examples of pricing that rely on this mental trait?

Once you find that car, how do you know whether you can afford it? How do you determine the monthly payment? First, call up your local bank and credit union to ask about auto loan rates. You can then determine what your monthly payment will be by using the same techniques learned in Chapters 3 and 7 when we looked at installment loans because auto loans are installment loans for a vehicle. Remember, you can determine your monthly payment on an installment or auto loan using either a financial calculator (using the present value of an annuity calculation to determine *PMT*, the payment) or the installment loan tables that appear in Appendix E .

The trick here, as you learned in Chapter 3, is to input the number of months in *N* and convert the annual interest rate to a monthly interest rate. To convert the annual interest rate to its monthly equivalent, we simply divide the annual interest rate by 12. Here's an example.

Calculator Clues

MyLab Finance Video

Let's look at a 36-month installment loan for $15,000 at 10 percent. Since the payments are monthly, *N* is expressed as the number of months, which is 36, and *I/Y* becomes the interest rate per month, which is the annual rate (10 percent) divided by 12, or 10/12. Once you've input the values, you solve for *PMT* by entering [CPT] [PMT]:

Enter	36	10/12	15,000		0
	N	I/Y	PV	PMT	FV
Solve for				−484.01	

Notice that the answer in the output row is shown as a negative number. Remember, with a financial calculator, each problem has two cash flows—a positive and a negative: the positive because you "receive money from the bank" and the negative because you "pay the money back."

The answer as shown in the output row is −$484.01. Thus, a 36-month installment loan of $15,000 at 10 percent results in monthly payments of $484.01.

Using the installment loan tables that appear in Appendix E and in an abbreviated form in Table 7.3 is just as easy as using a financial calculator. Looking in the interest row and the 36-month column, we find that the monthly payment on a similar $1,000 installment loan would be $32.27. To determine the monthly payment on a $15,000 loan, we need only multiply this amount by 15. Using the tables, we find that the monthly payments are $484.05.

So if you buy a vehicle and finance $15,000 of its price over 36 months, your monthly payment will be approximately $484. Can you come up with this much every month for 3 years? Only you can decide. If in order to make that kind of monthly payment you will have to change your lifestyle considerably, perhaps it's time to think about a different, more affordable vehicle. Or you might investigate a used vehicle of the same model.

Today, with all the formerly leased vehicles coming back on the market as used vehicles, a reasonable alternative to help you align what you want with what you can afford may be a used vehicle. In general, a used vehicle costs less and requires less in the way of a down payment. In fact, the savings from buying a used vehicle instead of a new vehicle every 3 years have been estimated to be between $1,500 and $2,000 per year. Moreover, a used vehicle tends to decline in value much more slowly than a new vehicle. The downside of purchasing a used vehicle is that it is more likely to have mechanical problems and may not be under warranty.

STOP & THINK

When selling your car, take advantage of **Principle 9: Mind Games, Your Financial Personality, and Your Money**, and get the best price possible. If your car has a favorable book value, tell the potential buyer what it is. In doing so, you can affect what the buyer thinks the car is actually worth. If you saw the book value of a car you were considering, how would it impact what you thought the car was worth?

Which Vehicle Is Right for You? Now, let's turn to the decision of what vehicle is best for you. Start by comparison shopping, which means looking at the choices and trading off the price against product attributes and quality. Use all resources available to do your comparison shopping—read magazines, go on the Web, and take the time to visit several auto dealers in person. Remember, buying a vehicle is a personal decision. Every vehicle drives a bit differently, and your choice should fit you financially as well as physically, so be sure to take any vehicle you're considering for a test drive before you purchase it.

PRINCIPLE 9

Also make sure you consider differences in operating and insurance costs. For example, due to increased repairs, a used vehicle generally costs more to operate than a new vehicle. You'll also want to consider the vehicle's warranty—the better the warranty, the lower the future costs. In addition, insurance costs on different cars vary dramatically. That Mercedes SL65 AMG roadster is going to have much more expensive insurance, about $3,500, than a Ford Taurus, at only $1,270.

Step 3: Make Your Purchase

Once you've decided what vehicle is best for you, the next hurdle is getting it for a fair price. To determine a fair price, you must first know what the dealer cost or invoice price is. This is a relatively easy number to come by. It can be found in the *Edmunds Car Buying Guide*, which is available at most libraries and bookstores and on the Internet at the Edmunds site, **http://www.edmunds.com**, or at the Kelley Blue Book site, **http://www.kbb.com**, which provides the manufacturer's suggested retail price, the dealer's invoice price, any rebates and financing incentives, projected resale values, and insurance premium information, along with reviews and evaluations.

Holdback
In auto sales, an amount of money, generally in the 2 to 3 percent range, that the manufacturer gives the dealer after the sale of an automobile.

The factory invoice price is important in determining how much the dealer pays for the car, but it isn't the whole story because when most cars are sold, the dealer receives a **holdback** from the manufacturer, which amounts to 2 to 3 percent of the price of the vehicle. For example, in 2017 a new Ford Explorer had a sticker price of $31,600, and the dealer cost or invoice price was $29,783, so the markup appears to be only 6.1 percent. However, if the dealer sold that Explorer, he or she would receive a 3 percent holdback amounting to $948. Including the holdback, the markup would actually be 9.6 percent. In addition, Ford was offering a $1,000 rebate, so you'd actually pay even less—and that rebate "from Ford" does not impact what your dealer receives. So keep in mind that the average markup on a new vehicle is just over 6 percent, the holdback is 2–3 percent, and there might be a rebate from the manufacturer or some dealer incentives that can affect the actual price you pay. Edmunds suggests you not try to negotiate for the holdback, but in bargaining, if the dealer says it is not making money on the deal, that would be a good time to mention the holdback. But just knowing about this incentive should help you as you negotiate a price that's close to the actual invoice price of the car.

Now you're ready to approach several dealers and get quotes on the vehicle you want. You want to be prepared when you're ready to negotiate. Checklist 8.3 provides a list of buying tips.

In general, you shouldn't have to pay more than $100 to $500 after rebates over the invoice price on the vehicle if it's American-made and a bit more over invoice for a foreign-built vehicle. However, what you pay depends on the demand for the car and the size of the holdback from the manufacturer to the dealer. Getting quotes is the best way to determine what a good price is.

CHECKLIST 8.3 Tips on Buying a New Vehicle

- ☐ Understand what you need and what you can afford. Read reviews and consult Consumer Reports (**http://www.consumerreports.org**).
- ☐ Know what the dealer has paid. You can order this information for a small fee from consumer publications you can find at your local library or get it for free on the Internet at the Kelley Blue Book site (**http://www.kbb.com**). From there, negotiate from the dealer's cost up, not from the sticker price down.
- ☐ Know if the manufacturer is offering rebates. You can find this information here: **http://www.carsdirect.com** and **http://www.autopedia.com/html/Rebate.html**.
- ☐ Get several quotes and make sure you know whether the prices quoted are the prices before or after the rebates are deducted. Consumer Reports also has a buying service you can get a quote from **http://www.consumerreports.org/buying-a-car/build-and-buy-car-buying-service/**
- ☐ If you're financing your car, compare financing from different sources (e.g., banks, credit unions, and other dealers) before you sign the contract.
- ☐ Beware of adding expensive extras you probably don't need to your purchase (e.g., credit insurance, service contracts, or rustproofing).
- ☐ Be sure to inspect and test-drive the vehicle you plan to buy, and do not take possession of the car until the whole deal, including financing, is finalized.
- ☐ Take your time—leave your checkbook at home, and don't buy because the salesperson is pressuring you to make a decision.
- ☐ Don't be afraid to leave without buying. Car salesmen are awfully good at selling cars and don't want you to leave. Also, it's not uncommon to get the best deal when you're in your car ready to leave.
- ☐ The end of the month is the best time to buy a car: This is when dealers are trying to meet quotas, so they may be willing to take less now than at other times of the month.

Source: U.S. Office of Consumer Affairs, Consumer's Resource Handbook, 2016.

CHECKLIST 8.4 Buying a Used Vehicle

- ☐ Check out the Consumer Reports Used Car Buying Guide **http://www.consumerreports.org/cro/cars/used-cars/buying-advice/index.htm** along with the Kelley Blue Book **https://www.kbb.com** or NDAD Guide **http://www.nadaguides.com** to determine the fair price.
- ☐ Negotiate!
- ☐ Make sure to shop during daylight hours so that you can thoroughly inspect the car and take a test drive. Don't forget to check all the lights, air-conditioner, heater, and other parts of the electrical system.
- ☐ Before you buy the car, get it inspected by an independent mechanic of your choice.
- ☐ Make sure to ask questions about the previous ownership and mechanical history of the car. If possible, contact the former owner to find out if the car was in an accident or had any other problems.
- ☐ Never sign anything that you don't understand. Read all the documents carefully. Negotiate the changes you want and get them written into the contract.

Source: U.S. Office of Consumer Affairs, Consumer's Resource Handbook, 2016.

If you're considering a used car, the negotiating process is a bit more complicated. Again, when you find the car you want, you must determine a fair price. Used-car prices can be found in the *National Automobile Dealers Association (NADA) Official Used Car Guide* and in *Edmunds Used Car Prices*, both of which are generally available at local libraries, or at the Kelley Blue Book site, **http://www.kbb.com**. Checklist 8.4 provides a list of things to consider when purchasing a pre-owned vehicle.

Financing Alternatives In general, the cheapest way to buy a car is with cash. Unfortunately, the high price of a new car or truck often makes this an unrealistic alternative. While most auto dealerships offer financing on both new and pre-owned vehicles, it's vital to investigate all the financing options before you buy. Check out the alternatives offered by your bank and your credit union. Investigate the possibility of a home equity loan and its tax advantages, but keep in mind, this may change in the future. When you're negotiating the price of a new vehicle, keep the question of financing out of the negotiations; retain the flexibility to borrow money where it's cheapest. Remember, though, that the auto dealer may offer the best deal in financing. In Chapter 7, we noted that an auto loan is simply a short-term secured loan made to finance the purchase of a vehicle, with that vehicle serving as the collateral for the loan. Often automakers offer very low-cost loans, even down to 0.0 percent, as a marketing tool, sometimes to sell models that are not in high demand.

As you might expect, the shorter the term you borrow for, the higher the monthly payments. For example, if you borrow $15,000 at 4.5 percent for 24 months, your monthly payment is $654.72, but if your payments are spread out over 48 months, they drop to $342.05.

And don't forget about the option to lease. Leasing usually appeals to those who are financially stable, prefer to get a new vehicle every few years, drive less than 15,000 miles annually, and would rather not put up with the hassle of trade-in and maintenance. It's also popular with those who have good credit but don't have the up-front money needed to buy a new vehicle.

Checklist 8.5 provides a brief profile of those who might want to give leasing serious consideration. It covers a lot of people. In fact, almost one-third of all new vehicles are leased instead of purchased, and this figure rises to over 50 percent for the more expensive models. However, because leasing is so different from buying, many people don't fully understand the process.

There are two basic types of leases: closed-end leases and open-end leases. About 80 percent of all new vehicle leases are **closed-end leases or walk-away leases**, in which you return the vehicle at the end of the lease and literally walk away from any further responsibilities. You just need to bring the vehicle back in good condition with normal wear and tear, and the vehicle dealer assumes the responsibility for reselling the vehicle. Many closed-end leases also contain a **purchase option**, which allows you to buy the vehicle at the end of the lease for its residual value or a fixed price specified in the lease.

With an **open-end lease**, when the lease expires, the current market value of the vehicle is compared to what the value of the vehicle was estimated to be as specified in the lease contract. If the vehicle is worth less at the end of the lease than was estimated originally, the open-end lease requires you to pay the difference. That

Closed-End Lease or Walk-Away Lease
A vehicle lease in which you return the vehicle at the end of the lease and literally walk away from any further responsibilities. You just need to bring the vehicle back in good condition with normal wear and tear, and the vehicle dealer assumes the responsibility for reselling the vehicle.

Purchase Option
A vehicle lease option that allows you to buy the vehicle at the end of the lease for either its residual value or a fixed price that is specified in the lease.

Open-End Lease
A vehicle lease stating that when the lease expires, the current market value of the vehicle will be compared to its residual value, as specified in the lease.

CHECKLIST 8.5 Leasing May Make Sense If . . .

- ☐ The lease under consideration is a closed-end, not an open-end, lease.
- ☐ You are financially stable.
- ☐ It is important to you that you have a new car every 2 to 4 years.
- ☐ You do not drive over 15,000 miles annually.
- ☐ You take good care of your car, and it ages with only normal wear and tear.
- ☐ You are not bothered by the thought of monthly payments that never end.
- ☐ You use your vehicle for business travel.
- ☐ You do not modify your car (e.g., add superchargers or after-market suspension components).
- ☐ The manufacturer of the vehicle you are interested in is offering very low-priced leasing options.

difference can mean an awful lot of money to you; without question, you don't want an open-end lease.

Exactly how is the cost of your lease determined? Whether you have a walk-away lease or an open-end lease, the amount you pay for the lease is determined by two factors. The first is how much the value of the vehicle you're leasing is expected to decline while you're leasing it. For example, if you take out a 2-year lease on a vehicle that is worth $25,000 new and is expected to drop in value to $16,000 after 2 years, you will pay the difference ($25,000 − $16,000 = $9,000) plus finance charges. In addition to the depreciation charge, there's a rent charge, which is actually the finance charge built into the lease and is like the total interest charged on a loan. Your monthly lease payment depends on the following criteria:

- The agreed-on price of the vehicle
- Any other up-front fees, such as taxes, insurance, or service contracts
- Your down payment plus any trade-in allowance or rebate
- The value of the vehicle at the end of the lease
- The rent or finance charges
- The length of the lease

Because of all the difficulties consumers have had in evaluating vehicle leases, the Federal Reserve Board requires dealers and other leasing companies to provide customers with a leasing worksheet explaining the charges. A copy of such a worksheet is provided in Figure 8.2.

Keys to getting a good lease include the following:

- Negotiate a fair, agreed-on value for the car before you sign the lease.
  - Don't express your interest in leasing until you negotiate the vehicle's price.
- Down payment—try to keep to a minimum.
- Warranty—make sure it covers the entire lease period for all major repairs.
  - Define "normal wear and tear."
- Termination fee (for ending the lease early)—know what it is!
  - Have insurance protection to cover an early termination policy in case of an accident.
- Depreciation factor—since the lease payment is based on what the vehicle is worth at the end of the lease, you might pay less on a more expensive car that depreciates slowly.
- Rent or finance charge—you want the lowest possible. You can find a listing of subsidized leases on the Edmunds Web site.

PRINCIPLE 9

To determine whether it's better to lease or to buy, you simply need to compare the costs of each over the *same* time frame. That is, you need to compare a 2-year lease with buying and financing a vehicle over 2 years. In addition, as the market for leasing previously leased, 2-year-old vehicles expands, there may be new opportunities, provided you understand the mechanics of leasing.

Figure 8.3 provides a comparative analysis for a lease-versus-purchase decision. In this figure, the cost of purchasing is $13,504.32, whereas the cost of leasing is $14,328.42. Thus, it's cheaper to purchase the Lexus in this example than it is to lease it.

STOP & THINK

What's in a price? The answer is quite a bit, and that's because of **Principle 9: Mind Games, Your Financial Personality, and Your Money**. You'll find that the price you set for your car or house will impact the price a buyer is willing to pay. When you set a high price, buyers use that information when they determine how much they think the car or house is actually worth. However, if you set the price ridiculously high, the impact of the price will be much less than if you set a high but realistic price.

FIGURE 8.2 Federal Consumer Leasing Act Lease Disclosure Form

Be very wary of any "other charges." If there are any, ask about them and check with other dealers to see if they impose similar charges.

The gross capitalized cost is the negotiated "selling price." It should be less than the manufacturer's suggested retail price.

The residual value is the projected market value of the car at the end of the lease. This is negotiated. The difference between this value and the gross capitalized cost (less any down payment, trade-in, rebate, or noncash credit) is what you're charged for over the lease period.

While it's difficult to define, normal wear and tear generally refers to normal dings, dents, small scratches, stone chips, and tire wear over the period of the lease. Excessive wear and use would refer to missing parts; damaged body panels; cuts, tears, and burns in the upholstery; broken glass; and other damage beyond what might be expected. Because it's so difficult to define, you should insist that it be defined in the lease contract.

Date ____________

Lessor(s) ____________ **Lessee(s)** ____________

Amount Due at Lease Signing (Itemized below)*	**Monthly Payments**	**Other Charges** (not part of your monthly payment)	**Total of Payments** (The amount you will have paid by the end of the lease)
$ ________	Your first monthly payment of $ ______ is due on ______, followed by ______ payments of $ ______ due on the ______ of each month. The total of your monthly payments is $ ______.	Disposition fee (if you do not purchase the vehicle) $ ______ [Annual tax] ______ $ ______ Total $ ______	$ ________

Itemization of Amount Due at Lease Signing

Amount Due at Lease Signing:		**How the Amount Due at Lease Signing will be paid:**	
Capitalized cost reduction	$ ______	Net trade-in allowance	$ ______
First monthly payment	______	Rebates and noncash credits	______
Refundable security deposit	______	Amount to be paid in cash	______
Title fees	______		
Registration fees	______		
______	______		
Total	$ ______	Total	$ ______

Your monthly payment is determined as shown below:

Gross capitalized cost. The agreed upon value of the vehicle ($ ______) and any items you pay over the lease term (such as service contracts, insurance, and any outstanding prior loan or lease balance) .... $ ______

If you want an itemization of this amount, please check this box. ☐

Capitalized cost reduction. The amount of any net trade-in allowance, rebate, noncash credit, or cash you pay that reduces the gross capitalized cost	–	______
Adjusted capitalized cost. The amount used in calculating your base monthly payment	=	______
Residual value. The value of the vehicle at the end of the lease used in calculating your base monthly payment	–	______
Depreciation and any amortized amounts. The amount charged for the vehicle's decline in value through normal use and for other items paid over the lease term	=	______
Rent charge. The amount charged in addition to the depreciation and any amortized amounts	+	______
Total of base monthly payments. The depreciation and any amortized amounts plus the rent charge	=	______
Lease term. The number of months in your lease	÷	______
Base monthly payment	=	______
Monthly sales/use tax	+	______
______	+	______
Total monthly payment	=$	______

Early Termination. You may have to pay a substantial charge if you end this lease early. The charge may be up to several thousand dollars. The actual charge will depend on when the lease is terminated. The earlier you end the lease, the greater this charge is likely to be.

Excessive Wear and Use. You may be charged for excessive wear based on our standards for normal use [and for mileage in excess of ______ miles per year at the rate of ______ per mile].

Purchase Option at End of Lease Term. [You have an option to purchase the vehicle at the end of the lease term for $ ______ [and a purchase option fee of $ ______].] [You do not have an option to purchase the vehicle at the end of the lease term.]

Other Important Terms. See your lease documents for additional information on early termination, purchase options and maintenance responsibilities, warranties, late and default charges, insurance, and any security interest, if applicable.

Step 4: Maintain Your Purchase

Given the size of the investment you make in a vehicle, it only makes sense to keep the vehicle in the best running order possible. The place to start is by reading the owner's manual and following its regular maintenance instructions. Set up a "car file" for all car-related paperwork—warranties, insurance information, maintenance records, recalls, repairs, and so on.

FIGURE 8.3 Worksheet for the Lease-Versus-Purchase Decision

ASSUMPTIONS: Lexus IS-250—2 years

Purchase	**Lease**
Price = $34,000	Capitalized cost = $34,000
Down payment = $6,800*	Capitalized cost reduction = $2,950*
2-year loan for $27,500 at 8% = monthly payment of $1,230.18	Monthly lease payments = $459.83
	Security deposit = $475
5% opportunity cost of down payment	5% opportunity cost of down payment

Expected market value of car at the end of 2 years = $23,500. (This value is subtracted in the "Purchase" situation and is used to negotiate the monthly lease payment in the "Lease" situation.)

COST OF PURCHASING

		Your Numbers
a. Agreed-upon purchase price	$34,000	
b. Down payment	$6,800	
c. Total loan payments (monthly loan payment of $1,230.18 × 24 months)	$29,524.32	
d. Opportunity cost on down payment (5% opportunity cost × 2 years × line b)	$680	
e. Less: Expected market value of the car at the end of the loan	–$23,500	
f. **Total cost of purchasing (lines b + c + d – e)**	**$13,504.32**	

COST OF LEASING

		Your Numbers
g. Down payment (capitalized cost reduction) of $2,950 plus security deposit of $475	$3,425	
h. Total lease payments (monthly lease payments of $459.83 × 24 months)	$11,035.92	
i. Opportunity cost of total initial payment (5% opportunity cost × 2 years × line g)	$342.50	
j. Any end-of-lease charges (perhaps for excess miles), if applicable	$0	
k. Less: Refund of security deposit	–$475.00	
l. **Total cost of leasing (lines g + h + i + j – k)**	**$14,328.42**	

*We ignore taxes, title, and registration in this example because they are generally the same whether you lease or purchase the car.

And don't ignore signs of trouble. You drive your car every day, and you know how it feels and sounds. Listen for unusual sounds; look for drips, leaks, smoke, and warning lights; and pay attention to gauge readings. Also, watch for any changes in acceleration, engine performance, gas mileage, or fluid levels. If you notice any changes in your car's performance, take it for servicing as soon as possible, and be prepared to describe the symptoms accurately.

With a new car purchase, and with some pre-owned purchases, your first line of protection is the warranty, which provides coverage for the basic parts against manufacturer's defects for a set period of time or miles. In addition, corrosion coverage is provided, along with coverage of the engine, transmission, and power train. For most cars, this coverage extends through the first 3 to 5 years of ownership or 36,000 miles, whichever comes first. Also, most warranties extend coverage on the power train, many times up to 5 years or 100,000 miles.

It's a good idea to choose a repair facility before you need one. To find the best, ask friends and associates for recommendations. Even in this high-tech era, old-fashioned word-of-mouth recommendations are still most valuable. At the repair shop, look for evidence of qualified technicians, such as trade school diplomas, certificates of advanced course work, and ASE certifications (that is, certification by the National Institute for Automotive Service Excellence)—a national standard of technician competence. If the service was not all you expected, don't rush to another shop. Discuss the problem with the manager or owner. Give the business a chance to resolve the problem. Reputable shops value customer feedback and will make a sincere effort to keep your business.

But what happens if a repair shop or the dealer just can't fix your problems? The answer is *lemon laws*. All states and the District of Columbia provide for a refund if the manufacturer can't seem to fix your problem. Generally, these laws require that you make at least four attempts to fix the problem and that your car be out of service for at least 30 days during the first year after purchase or the first 12,000 miles. If that's the case, you're entitled to a refund on your purchase.

LO3 Choose housing that meets your needs.

Smart Buying in Action: Housing

Why is owning our own home so important to so many of us? Well, it's part of the American dream. At least in the United States, many people equate owning their own home with financial success: You've made it, at least in part, if you own your own home. Also it's just kind of neat to own something large enough to walk around in.

Buying something as large as a house takes a lot of money. In fact, as you saw in Figure 2.5, a middle-income family spends about a third of their income on housing. Home ownership is also an investment—the biggest investment you're likely to make. So it's important that you approach buying a house not only as the attainment of your dream but also as the investment that it is. If you don't, your dream could quickly become a nightmare.

How do you go about making a smart housing decision? You use the smart buying approach. Let's take a closer look at the process when it's applied to buying a home.

Your Housing Options

For most people, lifestyle is a major player in their housing choice. Kids, schools, pets, privacy, sociability, space, and other lifestyle concerns tend to point people toward one type of housing or another. The needs-versus-wants issue also plays a major role. Many people would like to live in a mansion, but that kind of housing just doesn't fit into many monthly budgets. Together, your lifestyle, wants, and needs, constrained by your monthly budget, provide focus on a realistic housing alternative for you.

You know what kind of lifestyle you have, but you might not know what type of housing will best suit it. In fact, you might not even know what types of housing are available. Let's take a minute to examine the basic choices.

Houses A house is the popular choice for most individuals because it offers space and privacy. It also offers greater control over style, decoration, and home improvement. If you want your home to build equity or wealth, buying a house may be a good choice. However, home ownership carries with it more work than do other housing choices. If you own the house, you're responsible for maintenance, repair, and renovations.

Cooperative (Co-op)
An apartment building or group of apartments owned by a corporation in which the residents of the building are the stockholders.

Cooperatives and Condominiums A **cooperative (co-op)** is an apartment building or group of apartments owned by a corporation in which the residents of the building are the stockholders. The residents buy stock in the corporation, which in turn gives them the right to occupy a unit in the building. Although the residents don't own their units, they do have a right to occupy their units for as long as they own stock in the cooperative. One problem with co-ops is that you may have a tough time getting a mortgage because many banks and other financial institutions may be uncomfortable using the stock as collateral. In addition to purchasing stock in the corporation, shareholders have to pay a monthly **homeowner's fee** to the cooperative corporation, which in turn is responsible for paying taxes and maintaining the building and grounds.

Homeowner's Fee
A monthly fee paid by shareholders to the cooperative corporation for paying property taxes and maintaining the building and grounds.

Whether or not a co-op is for you depends on your lifestyle. If you're looking for an affordable, low-maintenance situation with a good helping of shared amenities such as swimming pools, tennis courts, health centers, and security guards, a co-op may be a good alternative. However, if you're more interested in privacy and control over style and decoration, a co-op may be a poor choice. In addition, co-ops generally have less potential than houses for capital appreciation, and they can be difficult to sell.

A **condominium (condo)** is a type of apartment or apartment complex that allows for individual ownership of the dwelling units but joint ownership of the land, common areas, and facilities, including swimming pools, tennis courts, health facilities, parking lots, and grounds. In effect, you pay for and own your apartment, and you have a proportionate share of the land and common areas. As with a co-op, you still have to pay a maintenance fee, which generally covers interest, taxes, groundskeeping, water, and utilities.

Condominium (Condo)
A type of apartment building or apartment complex that allows for the individual ownership of the apartment units but joint ownership of the land, common areas, and facilities.

The forms that condos take can vary greatly—from apartment buildings or townhouses to office buildings or high-rises on the oceanfront. The advantages and disadvantages of living in a condo are similar to those of living in a co-op. However, condos allow for the direct ownership of a specific unit, not just shares in a corporation.

Apartments and Other Rental Housing These types of housing appeal to those who are interested in an affordable, low-maintenance situation with little financial commitment and who want to be able to move with minimum inconvenience. This description often fits young, single people, since when they start out they may not have the funds available to buy a home or may not yet be committed to a geographical area. For others, rental housing may simply be a lifestyle decision. You may want limited upkeep and no long-term commitment, or you may want to be free to change to a job that may take you away from the area. Most of us, at some point, live in rental housing. The downside of apartment life generally involves a lack of choice. For example, you may not be allowed to have a pet, or you may have limited ability to remodel the apartment to fit your taste.

FACTS OF LIFE

House sizes have increased, while family sizes have decreased:

1970, Median Single-Family Home	2017, Median Single-Family Home
1,385 square feet	2,467 square feet
3.14 people	2.6 people

Step 1: Differentiate Want from Need

Just as with any other major buying decision, the first step in purchasing housing is to determine what it is you want versus what it is you need. Begin by determining what is most important to you about a new home. Is the quality of the schools that your children will attend top priority? Or is it more important that you're free to take that big promotion when it comes your way—the one that will require you to move across the country? You also need to examine your budget and determine how much you can and are willing to spend on housing costs.

Generally, house hunting or apartment shopping is exciting, although it may also be exhausting, frustrating, and confusing. One way to make the experience as pleasant as possible is to know as much as you can about what you want before you begin to look. First, consider location. Life in the country is a lot different from life in the suburbs, which is a lot different from life in the city. Also keep in mind that research has shown that, for many people, commuting is the unhappiest time of their day—so consider your commute to work when choosing a location. Determine what's most important to you: solitude, community, commute, or the action that city life promises? Once you're convinced which setting suits you, consider the neighborhood. Is it safe? Is it convenient to your job, to shopping, to schools? And what about the schools? How does the school district in the neighborhood you're considering compare to other districts in the state and across the country?

Step 2: Do Your Homework

When you first consider buying a home, you must—as with any major purchase—do your homework. Your homework regarding home ownership is twofold. First, you must investigate the potential home and all that goes with it—the neighborhood, the lifestyle of the community, and the degree to which the home fits your needs. The second part of your homework includes understanding how much you can afford to pay for a home. Let's first talk about how to find the kind of neighborhood and the community lifestyle that best suit you.

How do you get information about a neighborhood/community? Without question, start with the Internet—and you should visit more than one Web site. There are some great Web sites for this information, and one of the best is Neighborhood Scout (**http://www.neighborhoodscout.com**). Unfortunately, Neighborhood Scout is a bit expensive, running about $40 for a 1-month subscription, but it provides a wealth of information on schools, home appreciation rates by neighborhood, and crime rates. Considering the amount you will invest in a new home, this may be information you will want/need to have. Another great Web site is Homefair.com (**http://www.homefair.com**), which is free. This Web site provides cost-of-living comparisons between cities, city reports, crime statistics, and school reports, along with information on choosing the right school for your children.

But, of course, one of the biggest elements in deciding where to live is money. How do you even know what buying a home costs? Let's get to work on answering this important question.

To make a sound decision as to what to buy, where to buy, or whether to buy at all, you need to understand the costs that come with home ownership. These costs can be divided into (1) one-time, or initial, costs; (2) recurring costs; and (3) maintenance and operating costs. Let's look at each of them.

One-Time Costs Houses cost a lot of money! As a result, almost no one can afford to pay for a house all at once. For anyone who can, the entire price of the house is a one-time cost. For the rest of us, there are several one-time, or nonrecurring costs. Let's start by looking at the **down payment**, which is the up-front money due at the time of the sale when buying a home.

Down Payment
The amount of money outside of or not covered by mortgage funds that the home buyer puts down on a home at the time of sale.

The down payment is the buyer's equity, or ownership share, in the house, and lenders like to see a large down payment. Why? Because if a borrower stops payment on a loan, he or she loses the title to the house as well as the equity. The more equity—that is, the larger the down payment—the more the borrower stands to lose by not paying, and thus the more likely the borrower is to keep up with the loan payments.

Your down payment will vary according to the type of financing you receive. For traditional mortgage loans, the typical down payment is 20 percent. Thus, for a $150,000 home, a typical down payment is $30,000. Needless to say, that's an awful lot of money. Fortunately, for those who cannot come up with a 20 percent down payment, there are alternatives. For example, you can buy private mortgage insurance, which is insurance that covers the lender if you default. This will allow you to pay as little as 5 percent down.

Another one-time expense for home buyers is **closing or settlement costs**. Although they vary quite a bit from house to house, depending on the size of the loan, the local costs, and the loan arrangements made, they typically range from 3 to 7 percent of the cost of the house.

Closing or Settlement Costs
Expenses associated with finalizing the transfer of ownership of the house.

Several of the more important components of closing costs include

- **Points or discount points:** Points are a one-time additional interest charge by the lender, due at closing—that is, when the sale is final. Each point is equal to 1 percent of the mortgage loan. Thus, if you get a $120,000 loan with two points, the two points total $2,400, or $1,200 each. Lenders use these points to raise the effective cost of the loan, but points can also be used as a bargaining chip. Many times you'll see trade-offs between interest rates and points—you can get a lower rate with high points or a higher rate with no points.

  The longer you plan on staying in a home, the more important a low interest rate is. You pay points only once, at closing, but you pay interest over the life of the loan. If you're planning on staying in your home for a long time, you might be better off taking a few points to get a lower rate. If you don't expect to be there too long, it's important to keep the points you pay to a minimum. The only virtue of points is that they're tax deductible when associated with financing the purchase of a home.

Points or Discount Points
Charges used to raise the effective cost of the mortgage loan, which must be paid in full at the time of the closing.

- **Loan origination fee:** A loan origination fee is generally one point, or 1 percent of the loan amount. Its purpose is to compensate the lender for the cost of reviewing and finalizing the loan. Unfortunately, because it's not considered an interest payment, it's not tax deductible.
- **Loan application fee:** The loan application fee, also paid to the lender, is generally in the $200 to $300 range and covers some of the processing costs associated with the loan.
- **Appraisal fee:** An appraisal is an estimate of what your home and property are worth. Lenders require an appraisal before a mortgage loan is approved so they can be sure that they aren't lending you more money than the value of the property. Although the costs for an appraisal vary depending on the size and location of the house, an appraisal fee usually runs between $200 and $300.
- **Other fees and costs:** There are many other fees and charges you'll pay when buying a home. For example, a **title search** fee is paid to an attorney for searching public land records to make sure the person selling you the property really owns it. Title insurance must be purchased to protect you against challenges to the title, perhaps due to a forged deed. There's also an attorney's fee for work on the sales contract, a notary fee, a fee for recording the deed at the courthouse, the cost of your credit report, and the cost of termite and radon inspections to make sure the house is in good shape.

Loan Origination Fee
A fee of generally one point, or 1 percent of the loan amount. Its purpose is to compensate the lender for the cost of reviewing and finalizing the loan.

Loan Application Fee
A fee, generally in the $200 to $300 range, that is meant to defer some of the processing costs associated with the loan.

Appraisal Fee
A fee for an appraisal of the house, which is generally required before a mortgage loan is approved. Although the cost varies depending on the size and location of the house, it can easily run between $200 and $300.

Title Search
An investigation of the public land records to determine the legal ownership rights to property or a home.

Figure 8.4 gives a summary of typical one-time costs on a $120,000 mortgage loan—buying a $150,000 house with 20 percent down. You'll notice in this example that one-time costs amount to almost 24 percent of the cost of the house. Keep in mind that the law requires that the annual percentage rate (APR) on a mortgage be disclosed to the borrower. Although points must be included in the calculations, the fees for the loan application, the appraisal, and the credit check are not. In addition, the lender can change the APR by as much as one-eighth of a percent before settlement without notifying the buyer.

Recurring Costs The primary recurring cost—one you will pay again and again—is the monthly mortgage payment, the size of which depends on how much you

FIGURE 8.4 Estimated Initial Costs of Buying a Home: The Down Payment, Points, and Closing Costs on the Purchase of a $150,000 House, Borrowing $120,000, with 20% Down at a Rate of 4.5% with 2 Points

Down Payment	$30,000
Points	2,400
Loan Origination Fee	1,200
Loan Application Fee	300
Appraisal Fee	300
Title Search Fee	200
Title Insurance	500
Attorney's Fee	400
Recording Fee	20
Credit Report	50
Termite and Radon Inspection Fee	150
Notary Fee	50
Total Initial Costs	**$35,570**

borrow, at what interest rate, and for how long. Basically, the higher the interest rate and the shorter the length of the loan, the higher your monthly payments will be.

MyLab Finance Video

Table 8.1 shows the level of monthly payments required to repay a $10,000 loan at various combinations of interest rates and maturities. From Table 8.1, you can see that on a $10,000, 15-year mortgage loan at 4.5 percent, the monthly payments will be $76.50. If you increase the maturity to 30 years, though, the monthly payments will drop to $50.67. Thus, if you are considering a $130,000, 15-year mortgage loan at 4.5 percent, the payments will be $994.50 ($130,000 / $10,000 × $76.50 = $994.50). Similarly, the monthly payments on a $130,000, 30-year mortgage loan at 4.5 percent will be $658.71 ($130,000 / $10,000 × $50.67 = $658.71).

PITI
An acronym standing for the total of your monthly principal, interest, taxes, and insurance.

Escrow Account
A reserve account in which funds are deposited, generally on a monthly basis, and accumulate over time until they are drawn out to pay for property taxes and insurance premiums.

The monthly mortgage payment, the primary recurring cost, is actually made up of four costs, generally referred to as **PITI**, which stands for principal, interest, taxes, and insurance. In addition to paying off the loan principal and interest charges, you also need to pay property taxes and insurance premiums. These monthly property tax and insurance payments are generally made along with your loan principal and interest payments and are held for you in a special reserve account, called an **escrow account**. Funds accumulate over time until they are drawn out to pay property taxes and insurance premiums.

The logic behind an escrow account is this: Paying your insurance and taxes regularly, in small amounts, is less painful than paying them in one large, annual lump sum. Lenders often use the total PITI level to measure an individual's financial capacity. As a rule of thumb, your PITI costs shouldn't exceed 28 percent of your pretax monthly income.

STOP & THINK

Remodeling is not as good an investment as purchasing the house in the first place. A recent survey showed that you can expect to recoup 95 percent of the cost of kitchen remodeling, 83 percent of a family room addition, 77 percent of a bathroom remodeling, and 72 percent from the addition of a deck. This means that if you remodel your bathroom, you'll lose 23 percent—without question, a bad investment. What rooms have you or your parents remodeled?

Maintenance and Operating Costs Whether the house you buy is old or new, big or small, in the country or in the city, you'll have maintenance and operating costs. Examples of these costs are roof

TABLE 8.1 Monthly Mortgage Payments Required to Repay a $10,000 Loan with Different Interest Rates and Different Maturities

	Loan Maturity					
Rate of Interest (%)	**10 Years**	**15 Years**	**20 Years**	**25 Years**	**30 Years**	**40 Years**
3.5	$98.89	$71.49	$58.00	$50.06	$44.90	$38.74
4.0	101.25	73.97	60.60	52.78	47.74	41.79
4.5	103.64	76.50	63.26	55.58	50.67	44.96
5.0	106.07	79.08	66.00	58.46	53.68	48.22
5.5	108.53	81.71	68.79	61.41	56.79	51.58
6.0	111.02	84.39	71.64	64.43	59.96	50.22
6.5	113.55	87.11	74.56	67.52	63.21	58.55
7.0	116.11	89.88	77.53	70.68	66.53	62.14
7.5	118.71	92.71	80.56	73.90	69.93	65.81
8.0	121.33	95.57	83.65	77.19	73.38	69.53
8.5	123.99	98.48	86.79	80.53	76.90	73.31
9.0	126.68	101.43	89.98	83.92	80.47	77.14
9.5	129.40	104.43	93.22	87.37	84.09	81.01
10.0	132.16	107.47	96.51	90.88	87.76	84.91
10.5	134.94	110.54	99.84	94.42	91.48	88.86
11.0	137.76	113.66	103.22	98.02	95.24	92.83

Calculating monthly payments on a loan:

Step 1: Divide the amount borrowed by $10,000. For example, for a $100,000 loan, the Step 1 value would be $100,000/$10,000 = 10.

Step 2: Find the monthly payment for a $10,000 loan at the appropriate interest rate and maturity in the table above. For a 15-year mortgage at 9%, the value would be $101.43.

Step 3: Multiply the Step 1 value by the Step 2 value. In the example, this is 10 × $101.43 = $1,014.30.

repairs, new appliances, and landscaping. Don't forget to plan for these expenses when buying a home. Even home buyers who budget for maintenance and operating costs are still often shocked by their first repair bill or the cost of a Japanese maple sapling!

Renting Versus Buying

LO4 Decide whether to rent or buy housing.

For most people, the rent-versus-buy decision is based not on finances but on lifestyle. Perhaps you want to rent an apartment because you want the freedom to be able to take a promotion that comes your way, or you may want to buy a house because you want to live in a particular neighborhood. Let's examine Figure 8.5, which provides a listing of advantages to both renting and buying. As you can see, many of the reasons for renting center on flexibility—both financial flexibility, because renting generally involves lower monthly payments, and lifestyle flexibility, because you can avoid the responsibilities associated with ownership.

Although the rent-or-buy decision is usually less about money than about life choices, before making this decision it's a good idea to understand its financial implications. First, compare the costs associated with each alternative. Interestingly, the results that you get often depend mainly on how long you're planning to live in

FIGURE 8.5 Renting Versus Buying

Renting		Buying
• Mobility; can relocate without incurring real estate selling costs • No down payment required • May involve a lower monthly cash flow—you pay only rent; a homeowner pays the mortgage, taxes, insurance, and upkeep • Avoids the risk of falling housing prices • Many times extensive amenities such as swimming pools, tennis courts, and health clubs are provided • No home repair and maintenance • No groundskeeping • No property taxes • You are immune to losses due to housing price depreciation	VS.	• Allows you to build up equity over time • Possibility of property's appreciation • Allows for a good deal of personal freedom to remodel, landscape, and redecorate to suit your taste • Significant tax advantages, including deduction of interest and property taxes • No chance of rent rising over time • Your home is a potential source of cash in the form of home equity loans

the place. Why? Well, when you buy a house or apartment, you experience a lot of up-front, one-time costs. However, the major financial advantages—price appreciation and tax benefits—occur gradually over time, taking a number of years of price appreciation and tax benefits to offset those initial up-front costs. With renting, you don't have those large, one-time costs—in fact, you generally just have a security deposit that you get back when you move out.

Figure 8.6 presents the financial aspects of the rent-versus-buy decision.[1] In the example, the alternatives compared are renting an apartment for $900 per month and buying a house for $100,000 with 20 percent down and a 30-year mortgage at 8 percent, which includes monthly payments of $587.01 (calculated using a financial calculator; if calculated using Table 8.1, the monthly payment is $587.04, with the difference due to a rounding error). You'll notice that in this example we've ignored the time value of money to simplify the analysis.

The primary cost of renting is the rent itself. The total cost of renting for 7 years is simply seven times the cost of renting for 1 year, although rent will probably increase over those 7 years. Other costs of renting include renter's insurance and the opportunity cost of lost interest due to having funds tied up in the security deposit.

The costs of buying are more complex. Although we have discussed most of the costs associated with owning a home, one cost we haven't looked at yet is the opportunity cost of having money tied up in a down payment. Because the money used for your down payment can no longer be invested to earn a profit, you should consider the after-tax return you'd have earned on this money as a cost of buying. Another cost of ownership comes when you may eventually sell—that's the one-time selling cost resulting from the sales commission to a real estate broker.

Notice that the down payment itself isn't a cost; only the opportunity cost represents a cost. That's because you still have that money; it's still yours. In fact, it's your equity in your house or apartment.

These costs are partially offset by the benefits of ownership, which include the accumulation of equity resulting from a portion of the mortgage payment going toward the loan principal and the appreciation in the value of the home. Further,

[1]The detailed calculations for Figure 8.6 are provided in the appendix to this chapter.

FIGURE 8.6 Worksheet for the Rent-Versus-Buy Decision

ASSUMPTIONS: Buying option: $20,000 down and an $80,000, 30-year mortgage at 8%. Rental option: $900 per month. Time frames: 1 year and 7 years; 28% marginal tax rate; after-tax rate of return = 5%; house appreciates in value at 3% per year; sales commission is 5% of the price of the house; closing costs = $5,000, which includes 2 points.

	1 Year	7 Years
COST OF RENTING		
a. Total rent payments	a. $10,800	a. $75,600
b. Total renter's insurance payments	+ b. $250	+ b. $1,750
c. Interest lost as a result of making a security deposit (security deposit times after-tax interest rate)	+ c. $90	+ c. $630
d. **Total cost of renting (lines a + b + c)**	= d. $11,140	= d. $77,980
COST OF BUYING		
e. Total mortgage payments	e. $7,044	e. $49,309
f. Property taxes (annual)	+ f. $2,200	+ f. $15,400
g. Homeowner's insurance (annual)	+ g. $600	+ g. $4,200
h. Maintenance, repairs, and any additional utilities	+ h. $500	+ h. $3,500
i. After-tax cost of interest lost due to down payment	+ i. $1,000	+ i. $7,000
j. Closing costs	+ j. $5,000	+ j. $5,000
k. Less: mortgage payments going toward principal	− k. $668	− k. $6,018
l. Less: home appreciation less sales commission when sold	− l. −$2,150*	− l. $14,950
m. **Equals: cost of buying a home for those who don't itemize (lines e + f + g + h + i + j − k − l)**	=m. $17,826	=m. $63,441
Additional savings to home buyers who itemize		
n. Less tax savings from deductibility of interest payments	− n. $1,785	− n. $12,121
o. Less tax savings from deductibility of property taxes	− o. $616	− o. $4,312
p. Less tax savings from deductibility of points	− p. $448	− p. $448
q. **Total cost of buying a home to those who itemize (line m minus lines n through p)**	= q. $14,977	= q. $46,560
Advantage of buying to those who *do not itemize* = Total cost of renting − total cost of buying for those who *do not itemize*: if negative, rent; if positive, buy (line d − line m)	−$6,686	+$14,539
Advantage of buying to those who *itemize* = Total cost of renting − total cost of buying for those who *itemize:* if negative, rent; if positive, buy (line d − line q)	−$3,837	+$31,420

*Note: If you own the home for only 1 year, the value here is negative, meaning the sales commission is greater than the appreciation in home value. Thus, this is an additional cost, not a savings, and we are subtracting a negative—in effect, adding the $2,150 to the cost of buying the house.

substantial savings are available to those who itemize their tax deductions. These savings result from the tax deductibility of the interest portion of mortgage payments, property taxes, and any points paid in the closing costs. If you don't itemize your deductions, you don't reap the tax benefits from these deductions.

Look at Figure 8.6 and notice two major points. First, buying a home generally isn't financially desirable if you don't intend to stay in it for more than 2 or 3 years. The longer you stay in the home, the more it hopefully appreciates in value, and the more financially advantageous buying (and selling) is. Second, the benefits of buying instead of renting are substantially greater for those who itemize their tax deductions than for those who don't itemize. In fact, the advantage of buying over renting is more than twice as large for those who itemize ($31,420.00) as for those who don't itemize ($14,539.00) when looking at the 7-year time frame.

For many people, buying a home is a good means of "forced savings." Because some of your mortgage payment goes toward paying off the loan principal, a mortgage forces you to save in a sense. Although you're really buying something rather than saving, you are buying something that not only doesn't get "used up" but also may appreciate in value over time.

Even after all this, a house may not be for you when you graduate—owning a home may not be simply a financial decision. That's because when you graduate from college, your life may be filled with unknowns. You may have a job, but you may decide it's not for you, or you may get transferred. Until you find some stability in your life, a house may not fit your lifestyle because a house limits your flexibility.

LO5 Calculate the costs of buying a home.

Determining What You Can Afford

We've looked at all the costs associated with buying a home and compared the advantages of renting versus buying. Let's say you decide to buy a home. Before you begin your house hunt in earnest, you have to answer one question: How much can I afford to spend? But in order to do that, you must first answer three others: (1) What is the maximum amount that a bank will lend me? (2) Should I borrow up to this maximum? (3) How big a down payment can I afford? An answer that will be largely determined by your savings.

Let's look at the first question. Regardless of what you think you can afford, banks and other lenders impose a maximum amount that they want to lend you based on your income and current debt levels. Specifically, they look at three things: (1) your financial history, (2) your ability to pay, and (3) the appraised value of the home you are interested in buying.

Financial History In evaluating your financial history, lenders generally focus on the steadiness of your income, your credit report, and your FICO credit score. If you're self-employed, you may have to provide proof that you've maintained steady income for the past several years. It's wise to check out your FICO score and get a copy of your credit report several months before applying for a loan to allow time for the correction of any errors that may appear on it. If a lender doesn't like the look of your financial history, you'll have a tough time obtaining a mortgage.

Calculating Your Mortgage Limit The maximum loan you'll qualify for is determined by the financial picture that develops as the lender reviews the following three measures of your ability to pay. The lowest amount wins. Figure 8.7 shows the basic methods lenders use to determine how much they'll loan you.

Method 1—Ability to Pay—PITI to Monthly Gross Income Lenders generally measure your ability to pay through the use of ratios. In particular, they look at the percentage of your income that goes to housing costs. The lenders tend to look at the ratio of your PITI to your monthly gross income. In general, lenders would like to see this ratio at a maximum of 28 percent.

Method 2—Ability to Pay—PITI Plus Other Debt Payments to Monthly Gross Income Lenders also look at the ratio of your PITI plus any other debt payments that will take over 10 months to pay off compared to your monthly gross income. This ratio is used to account for the fact that many individuals have a sizable amount of outstanding debt, including student loans, car loans, and credit card debt. In general, lenders would like to see this ratio at a maximum of 36 percent. Note that different lenders may calculate these and other ratios a bit differently. They may also have different acceptable maximums.

Method 3—Appraised Home Value Regardless of your financial history and ability-to-=pay ratios, most lenders limit mortgage loans to 80 percent of the appraised

FIGURE 8.7 Worksheet for Calculating the Maximum Mortgage Loan for Which You Qualify

ASSUMPTIONS: Annual gross income = $65,000
Estimated monthly real estate taxes and insurance = $200
Anticipated interest rate on the mortgage loan = 8%
Mortgage maturity = 30 years
Current nonmortgage debt payments = $400
Funds available for down payment and closing costs = $56,000
Closing costs are estimated to be $10,000
Minimum acceptable down payment = 20%

METHOD 1—The Ability to Pay PITI Ratio (PI = Principal and Interest, TI = Taxes and Insurance)

(Lenders limit your monthly housing costs, as measured by PITI, to 28% of your gross monthly income.)

			Your Numbers
a. Monthly income (annual income divided by 12)		$5,417	______
b. Times 28% ($5,417 × 0.28) = PITI limit	× 0.28 =	$1,517	______
c. Less: estimated monthly real estate taxes and insurance payments of $200 per month (TI)	−	$200	______
d. Equals your **maximum monthly mortgage payment** (PI)	=	$1,317	______
Steps to determine the **maximum mortgage loan level:**			
STEP 1: Using Table 8.1, determine monthly mortgage payment with a 30-year maturity and an 8% interest rate	=	$73.38	______
STEP 2: Divide the maximum monthly mortgage payment (line d) by the monthly mortgage payment (Step 1) and multiply by the amount of the mortgage ($10,000) ($1,317/$73.78) × $10,000	=	$179,477	______

METHOD 2—The Ability to Pay PITI Plus Other Fixed Monthly Payments Ratio

(Lenders use 36% of your total current monthly fixed payments to determine the amount of your loan.)

			Your Numbers
e. Monthly income (annual income divided by 12)		$5,417	______
f. Times 36% ($5,417 × 0.36) = PITI limit	× 0.36 =	$1,950	______
g. Less current nonmortgage debt payments	−	$400	______
h. Less estimated monthly real estate tax and insurance payments of $200 per month (TI)	−	$200	______
i. Equals your **maximum monthly mortgage payment** (PI)	=	$1,350	______
Steps to determine the **maximum mortgage loan level:**			
STEP 1: Using Table 8.1, determine monthly mortgage payment with a 30-year maturity and an 8% interest rate	=	$73.38	______
STEP 2: Divide the maximum monthly mortgage payment (line i) by the monthly mortgage payment (Step 1) and multiply by the amount of the mortgage ($10,000) ($1,350/$73.78) × $10,000	=	$183,974	______

METHOD 3—The "80 Percent of the Appraised Value of the House" Rule

(You pay 20% of the appraised value and can borrow 80% of the appraised value of the house.)

j. Funds available for down payment and closing costs		$56,000	______
k. Less closing costs	−	$10,000	______
l. Equals funds available for the down payment (the 20%)	=	$46,000	______
m. Times 4 equals the maximum mortgage level (the 80%)	× 4.0 =	$184,000	______
Conclusion: maximum mortgage level for which you will qualify (the lowest of the amounts using Methods 1, 2, and 3):	=	$179,477	______

value of the house. This limitation protects lenders by forcing the borrower to put up a substantial down payment. Lenders assume that the larger a borrower's down payment, the less likely he or she will default on the loan.

If a borrower does default, the lender assumes possession of the home, and the 80 percent limitation protects the lender in another way. The lender will sell the home to recoup its losses on the loan, and with the 80 percent rule in effect, the asking price of the home could fall by a full 20 percent—the same amount the borrower initially had to pay out—and the lender would still be able to recover the full amount it loaned out.

How Much Should You Borrow? Although a bank may be willing to lend you $150,000, you might not want to borrow that much. Taking on a mortgage means a large commitment of future earnings. Before deciding how much to borrow, look at your overall financial plan. Will a $150,000 mortgage keep you from meeting your other goals—in particular, your retirement goals? Moreover, will it put such a strain on your monthly budget that you can no longer maintain the lifestyle you want? Don't let your mortgage payments, or any other debt payments, control your life. Only you can decide just how much you're interested in borrowing. Just because a bank will loan you $150K doesn't mean you have to borrow that much! Look at your own financial situation, monthly budget, goals, and lifestyle, and decide for yourself how much you want to take on.

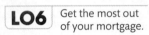

LO6 Get the most out of your mortgage.

Financing the Purchase—The Mortgage

Just as a home is the biggest purchase you will likely ever make, a mortgage is the biggest loan you will likely ever take on. To say the least, not all mortgages are the same. In fact, whether or not you can afford to buy a house depends not only on how much the house costs but also on the specifics of the mortgage, such as how long it lasts, whether the interest rate changes over time, and whether the loan is insured by the government. Let's take a closer look at mortgages, where you get them, and how they work.

Sources of Mortgages

Savings and loan associations (S&Ls) and commercial banks are the primary sources of mortgage loans, but they certainly aren't the only sources. Other traditional lenders, such as credit unions and mutual savings banks, offer mortgage loans, as do specialized lenders, such as mortgage bankers and mortgage brokers.

Mortgage Banker
Someone who originates mortgage loans with funds from other investors, such as pension funds and insurance companies, and services the monthly payments.

Mortgage bankers originate mortgage loans; sell them to banks, pension funds, and insurance companies; and service or collect the monthly payments. Their only business is making mortgage loans, and in general, they deal only in fixed-rate mortgage loans. There's really no advantage or disadvantage to using a mortgage banker instead of a traditional source of mortgage loans, such as an S&L. Hey, if the mortgage banker's got the most favorable rate or the best deal, go for it.

Mortgage Broker
A middleman who, for a fee, secures mortgage loans for borrowers but doesn't actually make those mortgage loans. A mortgage broker will find the best loan available for the borrower.

Mortgage brokers are the middlemen whose job it is to place mortgage loans with lenders for a fee but not to originate those loans. The advantage of using mortgage brokers is that they do the comparison shopping for you. That is, they work with a number of lenders and choose the best terms and rates available.

Conventional and Government-Backed Mortgages

Conventional Mortgage Loan
A loan from a bank or an S&L that is secured by the property being purchased.

Once you find the right lender and get your mortgage, it can be categorized as conventional or government-backed. **Conventional mortgage loans** are simply loans from a bank or an S&L secured by the property being purchased. If you default on a mortgage loan, the lender seizes the property, sells it, and recovers the funds owed.

With **government-backed mortgage loans**, the traditional lender still makes the loan, but the government insures it. Veterans Administration (VA) and Federal Housing Administration (FHA) loans are the two primary types of government-backed loans and have accounted for an increasing percentage of new mortgages in recent years. Not every U.S. citizen one qualifies for an FHA loan, you must have a minimum FICO score of 580 and the minimum down payment is 3.5 percent – there are other restrictions, but those are the two primary ones. Traditionally, FHA and VA loans have been a favorite for first-time buyers who do not have the 10- or 20-percent down payment traditionally required for other mortgages. However, during the housing bubble of the mid-2000s, they fell out of favor as private lenders entered the housing market with low- and no-down-payment mortgages for applicants with almost no income.

Government-Backed Mortgage Loan
A mortgage loan made by a traditional lender but insured by the government.

The FHA and VA programs are quite similar, and they both share the same basic advantages and disadvantages. The primary advantages of VA and FHA loans include the following:

- An interest rate 0.5 to 1 percentage point below that of conventional mortgage loans
- A down payment as low as 3.5 percent required on FHA loans and no down payment required on VA loans
- Less strict financial requirements

The primary disadvantages of VA and FHA loans include the following:

- Increased paperwork required to qualify for the loan
- Higher costs due to mortgage insurance premiums required with FHA loans; guarantee fees required with VA loans
- Limits on the amount of funding that can be obtained

Although the FHA guarantees the entire loan, it doesn't assume all the costs for the required mortgage insurance. In fact, with an FHA loan you're expected to pay for a portion of the cost. However, because FHA loans are guaranteed, the interest rate charged on them is generally below the rate charged on conventional loans, so you can still wind up saving money.

Access to VA mortgages is much more limited: Only veterans and their unmarried surviving spouses are eligible for them. In addition, FHA loans can be either fixed- or variable-rate loans, but VA loans must be fixed-rate loans, with the rate generally being between 0.5 and 1 percentage point below that of conventional loans. VA loans don't require anything in the way of a down payment, but they do require a VA funding fee payable at closing.

Fixed-Rate Mortgages

Although conventional and government-backed are broad classifications for mortgages, there are also more refined classifications, such as fixed versus variable rate. A fixed-rate mortgage is one on which the monthly payment doesn't change, regardless of what happens to market interest rates. If the mortgage interest rate is low when you are getting your loan, a fixed-rate mortgage allows you to lock in that low rate for the rest of the loan. The term or length of fixed-rate mortgages is generally either 15 or 30 years, with 30-year fixed-rate mortgage loans being the most popular. Many mortgages also come with assumability and prepayment privileges.

An **assumable loan** is one that can be transferred to a new buyer, who simply assumes or takes over the mortgage obligations. As a result, the new buyer doesn't incur the costs of obtaining a new loan. Moreover, if the interest rate has gone up since the original assumable mortgage was taken out, the buyer can assume the

Assumable Loan
A mortgage loan that can be transferred to a new buyer, who simply assumes or takes over the mortgage obligations. Such a mortgage saves the new buyer the costs of obtaining a new mortgage loan.

mortgage at the lower rate. For example, if the mortgage was originally issued at 4.25 percent and the rate has now gone up to 7 percent, the buyer can assume the mortgage at 4.25 percent. These advantages make it easier to sell a home with an assumable mortgage, particularly when the interest rate has gone up since the mortgage was issued. The assumability privilege is common to all FHA loans and is also common to many conventional mortgage loans.

Prepayment Privilege
A clause in a mortgage allowing the borrower to make early cash payments that are applied toward the principal.

The **prepayment privilege** allows the borrower to make early cash payments that are applied toward the principal, thus reducing the amount of interest due, or, if interest rates fall, to simply refinance. Many mortgages restrict prepayment by limiting the amount that can be prepaid or charging a penalty for prepayment.

Adjustable-Rate Mortgages

Adjustable-Rate Mortgage (ARM)
A mortgage in which the interest rate charged fluctuates with the level of current interest rates. The loan fluctuates, or is adjusted, at set intervals (say, every year) and only within set limits.

With an **adjustable-rate mortgage (ARM)**, the interest rate fluctuates according to the level of current market interest rates within limits and at specific intervals. From the lender's point of view, ARMs are wonderful because they allow for a match between the rate the lender pays on savings accounts to fund the loan and the income from the loan. Because lenders like ARMs so much, they generally charge a lower rate of interest on them—that's the appeal of ARMs to borrowers.

From the borrower's perspective, you're better off with an ARM if interest rates drop because your interest rate drops accordingly and you won't have to refinance, which costs money. On the other hand, if interest rates rise, you're better off with a fixed-rate loan because you will have locked in a low rate.

To understand ARMs, you must understand the terminology surrounding them, including the initial rate, index, margin, adjustment interval, rate cap, payment cap, and negative amortization.

Initial Rate
The initial rate charged on an ARM, sometimes called the teaser rate. This rate holds only for a short period, usually between 3 and 24 months, before being adjusted, at which point it generally rises.

Initial Rate The **initial rate** is sometimes called the teaser rate for a reason. This rate holds only for a short period, usually between 3 and 24 months. In some cases, it's set deceptively low. Once the rate is allowed to move up and down, or float, it generally rises. In evaluating the cost of the ARM, you should focus on the ARM's real rate—that is, what the rate would be today if it wasn't for the teaser rate.

Interest Rate Index The rate on an ARM is tied to an interest rate index that's not controlled by the lender. As that interest rate index rises and falls, so does the ARM rate. The following are some of the more common indexes:

- The rate on 6- or 12-month U.S. Treasury securities
- The Federal Housing Finance Board's National Average Contract Mortgage rate, which is the national average mortgage loan rate
- The average cost of funds as measured by either the average rate paid on CDs or the 11th Federal Home Loan Bank District Cost of Funds

Which index is the best is debatable. However, stable indexes are better because they won't produce radical rate shifts. When shopping for an ARM, be sure to ask for some historical data on the index from your lender.

Margin Your ARM may be set at the 6-month U.S. Treasury bill rate plus a 2 percent margin. The margin is the amount added to the index rate to obtain the rate at which the ARM is set. Thus:

$$\text{ARM rate} = \text{index rate} + \text{margin}$$

If the index rate is 2.0 percent and the margin is 2.5 percent, then the ARM rate is 4.5 percent.

Adjustment Interval The adjustment interval defines how frequently the rate on the ARM will be reset. One year is the most common adjustment period, although some ARMs have adjustment intervals as short as 3 months and some as long as 7 years.

An adjustment interval of 1 year means that every year—generally on the anniversary of the loan—the rate on the ARM is reset to the index rate plus the margin. In general, it's better to have a longer adjustment interval because the shorter the adjustment interval, the more volatile the mortgage payments.

Rate Cap The rate cap limits how much the interest rate on an ARM can change. Most ARMs have both periodic caps and lifetime caps. A *periodic cap* limits the amount by which the interest rate can change during any adjustment. Normally, the ARM rate will go up 3 percent if the index goes up 3 percent. However, if the periodic cap is 2 percent and the index rate increases by 3 percent, the rate on the ARM will still increase only by 2 percent. Most conventional ARM loans have periodic caps of 2 percent. FHA loans have 1 percent periodic caps.

The *lifetime cap* limits the amount by which the interest rate can change during the life of the ARM. Thus, for an ARM with an initial rate of 6 percent and a lifetime cap of 5 percent, the highest and lowest this ARM can go are 11 percent and 1 percent, respectively. Borrowers love lifetime caps because they limit the ARM rate to a specific range. In evaluating a lifetime cap, be sure that you know whether the cap is linked to the initial or the real rate.

Payment Cap A payment cap sets a dollar limit on how much your monthly payment can increase during any adjustment period. A payment cap limits the change in the monthly mortgage payment, but it doesn't limit changes in the interest rate being charged on the borrowed money. If the payments are capped and the interest rate isn't capped, when interest rates go up, more of your mortgage payment could end up going toward interest and not principal.

In fact, if interest rates keep going up, it's possible that the monthly payment amount will be too small to even cover the interest due and you will end up owing more than you borrowed. In this case, **negative amortization** occurs. When this happens, the unpaid interest is added to the unpaid balance on the loan. In effect, the size of the mortgage balance can grow over time, and you can end up owing more than the original amount of the loan. You pay interest on your unpaid interest, and the term of the loan can drag out. Because negative amortization is something to avoid and can occur only when there's a payment cap but not an interest rate cap, you should avoid mortgages with payment but not interest rate caps.

Negative Amortization
A situation in which the monthly payments are less than the interest that's due on the loan. As a result, the unpaid interest is added to the principal, and you end up owing more at the end of the month than you did at the beginning of the month.

ARM Innovations Over the years, several variations of the standard ARM have been introduced:

- **Convertible ARM:** Offers the borrower the option to convert the ARM loan to a fixed-rate loan before a designated time. There is a nominal fee involved.
- **Reduction-Option ARM:** Offers the borrower a one-time opportunity to adjust the interest rate on the loan. This offer generally occurs in years 2 through 6, and you choose if and when you will use it.
- **Two-Step ARM:** Combines the aspects of fixed-rate and adjustable-rate mortgages. It starts off with a lower rate than the current market fixed-rate loan, and after a certain period, the interest rate changes and remains at the current market rate for the life of the loan. The two most common types of two-step mortgages are the 5/25 and 7/23, offering the lower interest rate for the first 5 or 7 years and then adjusting the rate for the remaining 25 or 23 years.

Adjustable-Rate Versus Fixed-Rate Mortgages

For the homebuyer, the primary advantage of an ARM is that the initial rate charged is lower than that on fixed-rate loans. Initial ARM rates are lower because the borrower assumes the risk that interest rates will rise. Thus, the rate gap between 1-year adjustable-rate mortgages and 30-year fixed-rate mortgages is generally between 0.5 and 2 percent. For example, in mid-2017, the rate gap was less than 1 percent.

One commonly stated advantage of this low initial rate is that you may qualify for a larger loan because your monthly payment, PITI, is lower. However, if interest rates rise, pushing your monthly ARM payment upward, you may find yourself overcommitted.

Don't choose an ARM in the hope that interest rates will fall and your payments will be lower. Predicting future interest rates certainly isn't something on which you want to gamble your house and financial future. You can be sure that interest rates will never fall below zero (which would mean that lenders would owe *you* money!), but you can never be sure just how high they'll rise. If you have a lifetime cap on your mortgage, you know just how high your rates can rise, but this knowledge doesn't help if you're hoping never to have to pay that much. In short, if you can't afford the maximum payment you might have to make on an ARM if interest rates should rise, you probably shouldn't take it on.

In general, a fixed-rate mortgage is better than an adjustable-rate mortgage. With a fixed-rate mortgage, you know your payments and, as a result, can plan for them in advance. Don't forget that the basis of personal financial management is control and planning, and a fixed-rate mortgage allows for both. ARMs allow for neither. If you don't like financial risk and have difficulty handling financial stress, ARMs are dangerous.

Still, if you intend to stay in the house only a few years or if current interest rates are extremely high, you may want to consider an ARM. Remember, much of the advantage of an ARM comes in the early years when you're guaranteed a low rate.

Specialty Mortgage Options

Most of the alternative mortgage options serve the same purpose: to keep the initial mortgage payments as low as possible to make buying a house more affordable to first-time and cash-strapped buyers. Unfortunately, keeping the payments down in the early years generally means larger payments in the later years or some other concession.

Balloon Payment Mortgage
A mortgage with relatively small monthly payments for several years (generally 5 or 7 years), after which the loan must be paid off in one large balloon payment.

Balloon Payment Mortgages With a **balloon payment mortgage**, you make relatively small monthly payments for several years (generally 5 or 7 years), after which the loan comes due and you must pay it off in one large payment. Exactly how large the initial payments are varies. In some cases, the initial mortgage payments are only large enough to cover the interest on the loan, and in other cases, the payments may be equivalent to the loan's amortized value over 30 years. However, what balloon payment mortgage loans all have in common is that the payments are constant for a few years and then the loan comes due and is paid off with a very large, final payment.

Some traditional lenders don't offer balloon payment mortgages. In fact, most of these mortgages are offered by the sellers themselves, who are anxious to sell the house but don't need the funds from the sale immediately. Watch out for balloon mortgages because they come with serious potential problems. For many individuals, coming up with the final balloon payment is difficult at best. It generally means having to take out a new mortgage just to pay off the old one. If interest rates have risen, the home owner will be forced to refinance at a higher rate.

In addition, when the balloon payment comes due, the home owner may have very little in the way of equity in the home if the monthly payments have included only interest. In fact, if the market value of the home has declined, the balloon payment that's due could be more than the house is worth.

STOP & THINK

When setting a price for your home, take advantage of **Principle 9: Mind Games, Your Financial Personality, and Your Money**, and use it to send a message to a potential buyer. If you think your house will fetch \$498,000, a round figure such as \$500,000 sends buyers the message of quality, while a precise figure such as \$495,765 sends the message that the house is a bargain and that you've given the price a lot of thought. Mentally, if you're trying to give the impression of prestige, use a round number; if you're trying to give the impression of a bargain, use a precise number. Do you think you, as a buyer, might react this way?

Graduated Payment Mortgages With a **graduated payment mortgage**, the payments are set in advance in such a way that they rise steadily for a specified period of time, generally 5 to 10 years, and then level off. The selling point behind graduated payment mortgages is that the initial payments are relatively low, so you'll be able to afford a house sooner. The assumption is that, as your earning power increases over time, you'll be able to afford the rising payments. In effect, you're assuming that your income will grow into the level of the future payments. Unfortunately, you might be assuming incorrectly, and you might be putting an obligation on your future income that you can't handle.

PRINCIPLE 9

Graduated Payment Mortgage
A mortgage in which payments are arranged so they steadily rise for a specified period of time, generally 5 to 10 years, and then level off.

Growing Equity Mortgages A **growing equity mortgage** is designed to let the home buyer pay off the mortgage early, which is done by paying a little extra each year. It doesn't really help the cash-strapped buyer. Payments on a growing equity mortgage begin at the same level as on a conventional 30-year fixed-rate mortgage. Each year the payments increase, and this increase goes toward paying off the principal.

With a growing equity mortgage, you know how your payments are going to increase ahead of time. Generally, they increase by between 2 and 9 percent each year. The result is that a 30-year mortgage is paid off in less than 20 years. While a growing equity mortgage forces a disciplined prepayment of your mortgage, there is no advantage, and there is less flexibility, over a fixed-rate mortgage loan with a prepayment clause.

Growing Equity Mortgage
A conventional 30-year mortgage in which prepayment is automatic and planned for. Payments begin at the same level as those for a 30-year fixed-rate mortgage and then rise annually—generally increasing at between 2 and 9 percent per year—allowing the mortgage to be paid off early.

Shared Appreciation Mortgages With a **shared appreciation mortgage**, the borrower receives a below-market interest rate. In return, the lender receives a portion of the future appreciation (usually between 30 and 50 percent) in the value of the home. Thus, if you purchase a \$100,000 home with a shared appreciation mortgage that promises the lender 50 percent of any price appreciation and 10 years later you sell the home for \$180,000, the lender will receive one-half of the \$80,000 price appreciation. Generally, mortgages of this type are issued not by traditional mortgage lenders but by family members or investors.

Shared Appreciation Mortgage
A mortgage in which the borrower receives a below-market interest rate in return for which the lender receives a portion of the future appreciation (generally between 30 and 50 percent) in the value of the home.

Interest-Only Mortgages This term can be a bit misleading, since there's no such thing as an interest-only mortgage; eventually, you have to pay the loan principal as well. An **interest-only mortgage** is actually a combination of an interest-only payment scheme for an initial set period and a traditional mortgage payment. As a result, you make only interest payments for an initial set period, after which you make both interest and principal payments. Once the interest-only period ends, your monthly payments are adjusted upward to reflect full amortization over the remaining years of the loan.

Interest-Only Mortgage
A mortgage with interest-only payments for an initial set period (e.g., for 5 years on a 30-year loan); after this period, the borrower pays interest and principal with payments adjusted upward to reflect full amortization over the remaining years of the loan.

Option Payment ARM Mortgages With an option payment ARM mortgage, you have the option of making different types of mortgage payments each month. Your options might include:

- An amount less than the interest due on the loan
- Interest only on the loan
- The payment amount that would be required on a 15- or 30-year fixed-rate loan

Risks Associated with Specialty Mortgages Because specialty mortgages are adjustable-rate loans, there can be a big jump in monthly payments if interest rates rise, and with some types of specialty mortgages, the amount you owe can actually climb over time. As such, you should think twice before taking on a specialty mortgage. Be sure to read the fine print. Make sure you know exactly how much your monthly payment could increase, when this might happen, and whether you could afford it. You should also look very closely at any penalties that you might incur if you try to refinance your mortgage.

A Word of Warning: Beware of Subprime Mortgages and Predatory Lending

"Bad Credit, No Problem!" With that come-on, lenders have targeted subprime borrowers, and unscrupulous lenders have used it as a lead-in to abusive lending practices, often referred to as predatory lending. Subprime, or nonprime, mortgages are simply mortgages, 80 percent of which are ARMs, taken out by borrowers with low credit scores. Although there is nothing wrong with individuals with less-than-perfect credit borrowing to buy a house, in recent years this market has been flooded with predatory lenders who have taken advantage of these borrowers, steering them into high-cost loans that they have little chance of paying off when they could have qualified for lower cost, more affordable financing.

PRINCIPLE 1

How do you avoid predatory lending? The answer is with knowledge—just think back to **Principle 1: The Best Protection Is Knowledge**. Take a look at some common predatory mortgage lending practices shown in Figure 8.8.

FIGURE 8.8 Common Predatory Mortgage Lending Practices

Common Predatory Mortgage Lending Practices

- **Steering** Charging high interest rates (9 to 20 percent) on subprime mortgages for borrowers who have good enough credit to qualify for prime-rate loans.
- **Excessive Points and Broker Fees** These are costs not directly reflected in interest rates. With predatory loans, these fees can be over 5 percent.
- **Not Considering the Borrower's Ability to Pay** Predatory mortgage lenders often loan more than the borrower can afford to repay. In fact, predatory mortgage lenders have been known to encourage borrowers to lie about their income to borrow more than they can afford.
- **Yield-Spread Premiums or Kickbacks to Brokers** With many predatory mortgages, the mortgage broker gets a kickback from the lender for delivering loans with excessively high interest rates.
- **Balloon Loans** Loans with an unreasonably high payment due at the end of or during the loan's term. In many cases, the balloon payment is hidden and is almost the size of the original loan. The end result is that these loans force foreclosure or refinancing.
- **Loan Flipping** With predatory mortgage lending, lenders may "flip" a loan by unnecessarily refinancing it with no benefit to the borrower.
- **Prepayment Penalties** Excessive fees that the borrower must pay if the loan is paid off early or refinanced. The purpose of these prepayment penalties is to lock the borrower into the high-interest loan.
- **Upward Only Adjustable Rate Mortgages (ARMs)** These are ARMs that adjust only upward, with the borrower's interest rate and monthly payment climbing as often as every 6 months.
- **Bait and Switch Costs** The cost or loan terms at closing are not what the borrower agreed to.

Mortgage Decisions: Length or Term of the Loan

Another decision faced by home buyers is whether to go for a 15- or 30-year maturity on their mortgage. Three things to consider when making this decision are (1) prepayment opportunities, (2) the size of the monthly payments, and (3) the interest rate.

If you secure a 30-year mortgage with a prepayment privilege, you can easily pay it off in 15 years by making additional payments every month. Why not just take out a 15-year loan if you're planning on paying it off within 15 years anyway?

With a 30-year loan, you aren't locked into paying the higher monthly rates of a 15-year loan, and you have the flexibility of being able to skip making your additional payments and pay a much lower amount per month if an emergency arises. Thus, at first glance, for those with financial discipline, the 30-year mortgage is preferable. However, there is one additional variable that needs to be added into the equation: the interest rate.

In general, the interest rate on 15-year mortgages is lower than the rate on 30-year mortgages. For example, in 2017 the average rate on a 30-year fixed-rate mortgage was 4.25 percent, and the average rate on a 15-year fixed-rate mortgage was 3.40 percent. Interest also comes into play when you consider your overall payments. A longer term means you pay interest over a longer period. For example, let's look at a 30-year, 5 percent fixed-rate mortgage for $100,000. The monthly payments on such a mortgage are $536.82.

Figure 8.9 illustrates the portion of each payment that goes toward the principal on a 30-year, 5 percent fixed-rate mortgage. As you can see, initially a small portion of the monthly payment goes toward repaying the loan's principal. The result is that over the life of a longer-term mortgage, total interest payments are much larger.

Table 8.2 shows the impact of the loan term on total interest paid. Keep in mind that these calculations are for a 5 percent mortgage. If the mortgage rate is higher, the total interest payments for the longer-term loan will be proportionately greater. In effect, as interest rates increase, this relationship becomes even more dramatic. Also, keep in mind that this relationship is amplified by the fact that you would pay a lower interest rate on the shorter-term mortgage.

FIGURE 8.9 The Portion of Each Payment That Goes Toward the Principal and Interest on a 30-Year, 5% Fixed-Rate Mortgage for $100,000

MyLab Finance Animation

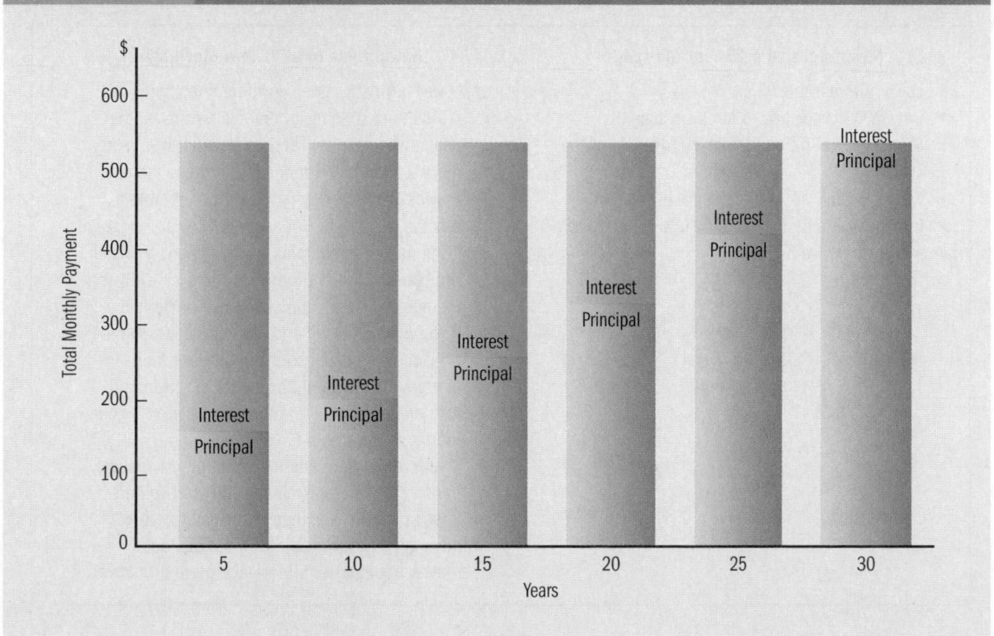

TABLE 8.2 Impact of the Loan Term on the Total Interest Paid and Monthly Payment for a $100,000 Fixed-Rate Mortgage at 5%

Length of Mortgage Loan	Monthly Payment	Total Interest
10 years	$1,060.66	$27,278.62
15 years	790.80	$42,342.85
20 years	659.96	$58,389.36
30 years	536.82	$93,255.78

Unfortunately, the total level of interest paid doesn't tell the whole story. There are two other complications: the time value of money and the effect of taxes. Remember, with a longer-term mortgage, your payments are lower but are stretched out longer. As a result, you're paying back your loan with future dollars that are worth less because of inflation.

In other words, when you make the smaller 30-year payment, you can take the difference in payments and invest it until the end of the 30-year period. Of course, with a 15-year mortgage, when the 15-year period ends, you can invest the amount you were paying each month until the end of the 30-year period. Exactly what you have at the end of 30 years depends on what assumptions you make about what you could earn on these investments. Also, don't forget that interest on home mortgages is tax deductible and lowers taxes. As a result, the tax effect favors the longer-term mortgage. But keep in mind that this may change with changes to the tax code, with a possibility that there will be a reduction in the amount of interest that can be deducted possibly limited to mortgages of $500,000 or less.

Figure 8.10 provides a listing of some of the advantages of 15- and 30-year mortgages. When deciding on a term length for your mortgage, make sure you weigh all these factors. You've also got to make sure that what you do fits into your grand

FIGURE 8.10 Comparing a Shorter- Versus a Longer-Term Loan

Advantages to a 15-Year Mortgage

- Lower interest rate.
- Provides a discipline to force savings.
- Saves quite a bit of interest over the life of the mortgage.
- Equity is built up at a faster pace.
- Increased equity may allow you to trade up to a more expensive house.

Advantages to a 30-Year Mortgage

- Lower payments give you more financial flexibility—if a financial emergency arises, the payments are lower, and as a result, you have more uncommitted money to address the emergency.
- Provides affordability—you may not be able to buy the house you want with a 15-year mortgage.
- If the mortgage contains a prepayment provision, you can mimic the payment pattern on a 15-year mortgage while maintaining financial flexibility.
- If you are borrowing on credit cards, which are a much more expensive form of debt than mortgages, you would be better off paying off your credit card debt before you take on higher mortgage payments.
- If your investment alternative earns returns well above the mortgage interest rate and you are a disciplined saver, that, along with the tax advantage associated with mortgage debt, makes a longer-term mortgage more attractive.

financial plan. You certainly don't want to be making extra payments to pay off a 5 percent mortgage while you're borrowing money on your credit card at 18 or 20 percent. Also, don't let repaying your mortgage get in the way of your other financial goals.

Coming Up with the Down Payment

For many people, especially those buying their first home, the real challenge is getting together a down payment. The most obvious and best way of coming up with a down payment is to save. If owning a home is one of your financial goals, saving for it should have a place in your financial budget. For most home buyers, saving enough for a down payment takes a few years.

In addition to saving, many first-time home buyers rely on gifts and funds from parents or relatives. In fact, approximately 30 percent of all first-time home buyers receive some financial aid from parents or relatives. But for conventional loans—that is, loans that are not federally backed—at least 5 percent of the closing costs have to come from the home buyer rather than from gifts. Actually, most lenders require a "gift letter" stating that any funds contributed by relatives don't have to be repaid.

If you're having trouble raising enough money for a down payment, you might consider trying to reduce the size of the down payment you need. Federally backed loans—Federal Housing Administration (FHA), Department of Veteran Affairs (VA), and Farmers Home Administration (FmHA) loans—don't require as large a down payment as conventional loans. In fact, the FHA allows a minimum down payment of as little as 5 percent on older homes and 10 percent on new homes.

If all else fails, consider **private mortgage insurance**. This type of insurance protects the lender in the event that the borrower is unable to make the mortgage payments. It is paid for by the borrower and generally runs from 0.3 to 1.5 percent of the loan amount, depending on the down payment level. With private mortgage insurance, many lenders will allow you to borrow more than 80 percent of the appraised value of the home.

Private Mortgage Insurance
Insurance that protects the lender in the event that the borrower is unable to make the mortgage payments.

A final source of funds for your down payment is your individual retirement account (IRA). First-time home buyers can withdraw up to $10,000 from their IRAs without penalty before age 59½. While this is a possible source, it's also one that you should try to avoid. Remember, taking money out of your IRA is just trading off one goal (financial security at retirement) for another (home ownership). The problem is that your IRA grows tax free, and once you take the money out, you can't get it back in. Moreover, if it is a traditional (as opposed to a Roth) IRA, you will have to pay income tax on the distribution. This means that if you are in the 25 percent marginal tax bracket, you'll withdraw $10,000 and pay $2,500 in taxes on the withdrawal, leaving you with $7,500 for your down payment.

Prequalifying

Although your ability to pay, in addition to the level of funds you have available for a down payment, should give you a realistic idea of how large a mortgage loan you'll qualify for, it's a good idea to have this amount confirmed by seeing a lender and prequalifying for a loan. To do this, ask a lender to determine how large a mortgage loan it will give you and provide you with a letter stating its willingness to lend you this sum. Prequalification lessens the uncertainty surrounding what you can and can't spend, making you a more attractive buyer to potential sellers.

Step 3: Make Your Purchase

Just as with any other major purchase, buying a home involves comparison shopping with an eye on price, product attributes (in this case, location, schools, number of rooms, and so forth), and quality (in this case, the quality of the house or apartment). Finding the right house or apartment is both involved and important. Our discussion of the search process focuses primarily on buying a house, but the same search principles apply to buying a condo or renting an apartment.

Once you know what you're looking for, it's time to start looking. Most home buyers enlist the aid of a real estate agent. These agents can provide buyers with a lot of help in searching for homes and deciding on good neighborhoods, but you should note that the traditional real estate agent is really working for the seller: It's the seller who pays the real estate agent's commission. As a result, your best interests and the agent's best interests may be in conflict. Thus, although the agent may be your friend, you should make your own decisions based on a thorough understanding of the alternatives. Differentiating between advice and a sales pitch and protecting yourself with knowledge relate to **Principle 1: The Best Protection Is Knowledge**. The traditional real estate agent has a bit of a conflict of interest, and it's the buyer's interests that lose out. In addition, real estate agents can sell only listed property—that is, property on which a real estate firm has a contract to sell.

PRINCIPLE 1

FACTS OF LIFE

The number of individuals selling their homes without the help of a realtor had been steadily rising up until the housing crash, but it has dropped since then as sellers have looked for all the help they can get in selling their homes.

19% of sellers sold their homes without a realtor in 1997.
20% of sellers sold their homes without a realtor in 2006.
13% of sellers sold their homes without a realtor in 2016.

Although this conflict of interest doesn't negate the benefits of using a real estate agent, you should definitely take some precautions. For example, you should never let your agent know your top price. If you tell the agent your top price, he or she may share that information with the seller, in which case your negotiating power will go out the window. You should also let the broker know that you intend to stay within your budget. If you don't get a particular house because it's more than you're able or willing to pay, let it go. There are always others.

Independent or Exclusive Buyer-Broker
A real estate agent hired by the prospective home buyer who exclusively represents the home buyer. Such brokers are obligated to get the buyer the best possible deal and, in general, are paid by splitting the commission with the seller's agent.

An alternative to the traditional real estate agent is the **independent or exclusive buyer-broker**. This type of broker is a real estate agent who is hired by the prospective buyer, represents the buyer exclusively, and is obligated to get the buyer the best possible deal. In general, the broker is paid by splitting the commission with the seller's agent. Buyer-brokers aren't limited in their search to properties that have been listed through real estate firms. They show both unlisted homes—that is, homes being sold directly by the owner—and listed homes.

Moreover, because buyer-brokers work for the buyer, they tend to be more objective and critical in examining a house. Although exclusive buyer-brokers have gained popularity, they still aren't that common in many areas of the country. If you're interested in using a buyer-broker and can't find one, you can obtain a referral from the National Association of Exclusive Buyer Agents at **http://www.naeba.org/**.

There is also a wealth of information on the Internet to help with selecting a home and making the purchase. One of the first places to explore is the U.S. Department of Housing and Urban Development's Buying a Home Web site at **http://www.hud.gov/buying/index.cfm**. It has information on your rights as a home buyer, how much mortgage you can afford, finding a real estate broker, shopping for a home, building a home, and more. Another great source of information on the Web is **Homefair.com** at **http://www.homefair.com/**, which provides information on picking the right city, school reports, finding an apartment, finding a home, and organizing your move. Also take a look at Checklist 8.6.

Real Estate Short Sale
A sale of property where the proceeds from the sale fall short of the balance owed on the property.

What about short sales? A **real estate short sale** occurs when the proceeds from the sale of the property fall short of the balance owed on the property. First, let's try to gain an understanding of why a short sale might occur. Let's assume that you aren't able to make your mortgage payments, but because real estate is in a slump, your house is now worth less than the amount you still owe the bank. For example, you still owe $250,000 on the house you bought 2 years ago for $350,000, but the house is now valued at $175,000. If it goes into foreclosure, you'll not only lose your home but also have difficulty buying another house for years to come because of a poor credit

CHECKLIST 8.6 A Housing Checklist for Buyers and Sellers

If you're selling your house and decide to work with a realtor:

- ☐ Look for a realtor that works full-time and has at least 3 years' experience. Ask how many transactions the realtor made during the previous year and the year before that—a good realtor sells at least 30 homes per year.
- ☐ Make sure that there is an "out clause" in the contract, which allows you to terminate the contact whenever you want—you don't want to lock in a bad agent for 6 months.
- ☐ Pick a realtor who works and lives in your area.

If you're buying a house:

- ☐ When you're deciding what you can afford, remember, those numbers are meant as a ceiling, not a floor.
- ☐ If at all possible, try to avoid the need for private mortgage insurance by putting down at least 20 percent of a home's cost.
- ☐ When you're looking at what to borrow, borrow what you need, not what you can. Many times lenders will offer you the maximum you can borrow—just go for what you need.
- ☐ Understand how your real estate agent is being compensated. Generally, it is through a commission, which means the more you pay, the more they make.

record. Your bank would like to move the property because it's not receiving any mortgage payments, and it would also like to avoid foreclosure, which is costly for banks. Through a short sale, your house is sold for less than you still owe, but since there is no foreclosure, there is less damage to your credit standing. In general, the bank loses the difference between what is owed and what it receives from the sale of the house. How common are short sales? As a result of the housing crash, they are quite common. In fact, in 2013 about 16 percent of all real estate transactions were short sales, although by 2016, that proportion had dropped to only 3 percent.

When you find a house you like, you need to have it inspected. The house might be falling apart. Hey, it might even be haunted! A good home should be structurally sound, and its heating, air-conditioning, plumbing, and electrical systems should be free from problems. Unfortunately, very few home buyers are truly qualified to inspect and evaluate these aspects of a home. If you're not one of the lucky few, you should enlist the aid of a professional building inspector. You should be able to get the name of an inspector from your real estate agent or the local chamber of commerce.

Once you've decided which house you'd like to live in, the next step is making the purchase. Traditionally, negotiating a price for a house involves a good deal of bargaining. The home is "listed" at a certain selling price by the seller, meaning the seller would like to receive that price. However, all prices are open to negotiation. Many times the buyer will offer a price below what the home is listed at. The offer can also include conditions or contingencies to be met as part of the contract. For example, you may want appliances or draperies to remain in the home, or your offer may be contingent on being able to close by a certain date.

When the sellers receive an offer from a potential buyer, they can accept the offer, counter the offer, or refuse the offer. The counteroffer is carried between the buyer and the seller by the real estate agent—you may never see the seller face-to-face. In some cases, the haggling can go on for some time until a final price and other conditions are set. However, know that while the negotiating is taking place, another potential buyer may make an offer, and the seller can accept that offer, leaving you flat!

The Contract Once the price is agreed on, an attorney or the real estate agent can draw up a contract to buy the home. Real estate contracts are relatively standard, but make sure your contract has all of the following elements:

- The price, method of payment, buyer and seller, date on which the buyer will take possession, and legal description of the property should all be stated clearly.
- The legal title to the home must be free and clear of all liens and encumbrances. Whether the buyer or the seller pays for the title search should be stated in the contract.
- A house must be certified to be free of termite or radon problems.
- A contingent-on-suitable-funding clause should be included, stating that if you're unable to secure suitable financing (where you specifically state the amount, rate, and terms), the contract will be voided, and you'll receive your deposit back in full.
- If the home will change ownership at some point other than the end of, the year, the contract should state what portion of the utilities, insurance, taxes, and interest on mortgage payments will be paid by the buyer and what portion will be paid by the seller.
- The condition the home will be in at the date of transfer should be stated, and a final walk-through should be provided to assure the buyer that the home is in the contracted condition.
- Any other contingencies that have been agreed on should be included.

Earnest Money
A deposit on the purchase to assure the seller that the buyer is serious about buying the house.

Closing
The time at which the title is transferred and the seller is paid in full for the house. At this time, the buyer takes possession of the house.

Settlement or Closing Statement
A statement listing the funds required at closing, which the real estate broker should furnish to the buyer for review at least 1 business day before closing.

If the contract is accepted, the buyer will give the seller some **earnest money**, which is a deposit on the purchase to assure the seller that the buyer is serious about buying the house.

At **closing**, the title is transferred, the seller is paid in full, and the buyer takes possession of the home. At this point, the buyer must pay the balance of the down payment. For example, if you're buying a home for $150,000 with 20 percent down, at closing you must pay $30,000 less any earnest money you paid when the contract was signed.

In addition to the remaining down payment, you'll have to pay the closing costs with a cashier's or certified check. You don't have to worry about figuring out exactly what you have to pay at closing. The lender will give you a **settlement or closing statement** at least 1 business day before closing. Finally, the legal documents are examined and signed, for which you may want to consult your lawyer, and the keys are passed. You now own a home!

Step 4: Maintain Your Purchase

Once you've purchased a home, you're then in charge of upkeep and maintenance. To say the least, owning a home can take up a good deal of time. In addition, you should always keep an eye out toward making sure that you have financed your home in the least expensive way possible. That leads us to a discussion of refinancing your mortgage.

Refinancing is simply taking out a new mortgage, usually at a lower rate, to pay off your old one. Whenever mortgage interest rates drop, people refinance. No one wants to be paying 12 percent on a mortgage when the going rate is now 8 percent. The typical rule of thumb states that you should refinance when mortgage interest rates fall by 2 percent. However, there's more to refinancing than just interest rates.

When you refinance, you again incur most of the closing costs already discussed, including points, the loan application fee, the termite and radon inspection fees, and so on. The refinancing decision really rides on whether or not the lower rate you could get will compensate for these additional costs in a reasonable amount of time.

MyLab Finance Video

Let's look at an example: You currently have a 15-year-old, 30-year mortgage at 11 percent and are considering refinancing it with a 15-year mortgage at 8 percent. When you bought your home, you took out a $100,000 mortgage with a monthly payment of $952.32. Today, 15 years later, you still have a balance on your mortgage

FIGURE 8.11 Worksheet for Refinancing Analysis

Monthly Benefits from Refinancing	Example	Your Numbers
a. Present monthly mortgage payments	$952.32	
b. Mortgage payments after refinancing	$800.73	
c. Monthly savings, pretax (line a − line b)	$151.59	
d. Lost tax savings (line c × 28% tax rate)	$42.45	
e. Monthly savings on an after-tax basis (line c − line d)	$109.14	
Cost of Refinancing		
f. Total after-tax closing costs, including any prepayment penalty incurred	$2,600	
Number of Months Needed to Break Even		
g. Months needed for interest saved to equal the refinancing costs incurred as a result of taking out a new mortgage loan (line f ÷ line e)	23.8 months	

of $83,789.07. If you refinance this loan over 15 years at 8 percent, your payments will drop to $800.73.

If you estimate that your total after-tax closing costs will be $2,600, it will take you 23.8 months for the savings from the decrease in monthly payments to cover the closing costs incurred as a result of refinancing, as shown in Figure 8.11. Thus, if you expect to continue to live in your home for over 2 years, you should consider refinancing at the lower rate.

BEHAVIORAL INSIGHTS

PRINCIPLE 9

Principle 9: Mind Games, Your Financial Personality, and Your Money While much of this book deals with saving money, much of this chapter looks at spending it—and spending it intelligently, using the smart buying process. Do you think you are a smart buyer? You are at your local mall shopping for a sweater for your dad's birthday. Ever find yourself wishing you had a calculator? How fast can you figure out what 25 percent off of $52.00 is? Would you make your "decision to purchase" faster if the seller just said "$13.00 off these sweaters today"? *Hint:* 25 percent of $52.00 is $13.00!

We all know how important "presentation" is in our daily life. Most of us would be willing to pay a little more for the exact same "eggs over easy with ham and hash browns" when it is served on a china plate with stainless utensils as opposed to being served on a paper plate with a plastic fork! Same breakfast—different presentation. When it comes to smart buying, how a discount is presented can impact sales. Remember that sweater that normally costs $52 and is on sale for $39; it is selling for 25 percent off or $13 off—same thing. But when it is presented to consumers, more people will buy it if they see it on sale for 25 percent off rather than $13 off. On the other hand, if a new HDTV that normally sells for $2,000 is on sale for $1,500, it could be advertised as either 25 percent off or $500 off—but in this case, $500 off would produce more sales. This is referred to as "the Rule of 100," which is a marketing concept that basically says that if a product costs less than $100, a "percentage discount" seems larger than a stated "dollar amount" discount. And it's why you feel better about taking that 25 percent discount on the sweater for dad instead of just $13 off, but you'd want $500 off that TV rather than a 25 percent discount.

When you're spending your own money, it is important to understand the basics so you can look beyond the presentation in order to protect yourself and reach your financial goals. It doesn't matter if you call it "mind games" or "fuzzy math"—either way, if you understand what is going on, you can control your reaction and make an informed decision.

Mental anchoring, which is our tendency to latch onto an idea or fact and use it as a reference point for future decisions, also impacts your spending in ways you may not realize. For example, let's look at buying a house. Your realtor may give you a few examples of the prices of recently sold houses, and those prices will serve as an anchor. The same effect occurs when you look at the realtor.com Web site and you find the highest-priced houses sold listed first. They also serve as a pricing anchor. Keep in mind that the listing price for the house you are looking at may or may not be realistic, but once again it serves as an anchor. If you're making a purchase that you don't often make, anchoring is particularly dangerous. So if you're buying a house, or anything else, do the research, compare costs, and know how anchoring works.

ACTION PLAN

PRINCIPLE 10

Principle 10: Just do it! A home and a car will be two of the largest purchases you'll ever make, and they may be on your list sooner than you think. You may have already purchased your first car and are thinking about a new one and most likely won't purchase a house until you are a bit more settled. But when the time comes, and it will, here are some things to consider.

- **Give serious consideration to a used car.** It will cost less and have a smaller down payment. Moreover, according to Edmunds' Web site, a new car's value declines by between 9 and 11 percent in the first minute of ownership as you leave the lot.
- **If you're considering renting, consider a roommate.** With a roommate, you can cut your housing expenses dramatically. Think of a roommate as a "50 percent off coupon." While your costs may not decline by a full 50 percent, they will go down substantially.
- **Make saving for the down payment on a house one of your first goals.** While you are in the saving mode, check your credit rating—which plays a big role in obtaining financing for a mortgage—allowing yourself some time to get things in order.
- **Keep in mind that a home isn't necessarily a money-making investment.** Make sure your reasons for purchasing reach beyond intending to resell at a profit.
- **When buying a house, beware of the "hidden costs."** Your mortgage payment won't be your only expense. Beyond closing costs, real estate fees, points, insurance, and so on—which might be the obvious costs of buying a home—when you move in you may need/want new furniture to fit the new space, a new paint job, window treatments, landscaping . . . this list can go on and on.
- **Prequalify for your loan so that you'll know approximately how much you can afford.** Don't buy more house than you can afford; in fact, keep below that maximum to give yourself a bit of cushion. You'll need that cushion for those "hidden costs"!
- **Don't forget that, when you're buying a house, you're also "buying" the neighborhood.** Look closely at the neighborhood, schools, any pending zoning issues, and so forth.
- **Make sure you know what you're buying.** If you're considering a home in the secondary market, consider hiring a professional engineer to check out the structure.

Chapter Summaries

Make good buying decisions.

LO1

SUMMARY: The first step in smart buying is to separate your wants from your needs. Once you've determined the alternatives, it's time to compare the different products and make trade-offs involving their quality, features, and price. The key to success in negotiating is knowing as much as possible about the markup on the product. The final step is the postpurchase process, involving maintenance and the resolution of any complaints that might arise. This smart buying process works for just about any purchase decision you make.

Choose a vehicle that suits your needs and budget.

LO2

SUMMARY: While your home may be your largest investment, your automobile is your largest frequent expense. Choose a car that fits both your personal and your financial needs. Once you have decided what is best for you, the next hurdle is getting it for a fair price. The place to start is to find out what the dealer cost or invoice price is. Next, you must make the financing decision. Should you buy or lease? Leasing a car is similar to renting. About 80 percent of all new car leases are closed-end or walk-away leases. With this type of lease, you return the car at the end of the lease and literally walk away from any further responsibilities.

KEY TERMS

Holdback, page 248 In auto sales, an amount of money, generally in the 2 to 3 percent range, that the manufacturer gives the dealer after the sale of an automobile.

Closed-End Lease or Walk-Away Lease, page 250 A vehicle lease in which you return the vehicle at the end of the lease and literally walk away from any further responsibilities. You just need to bring the vehicle back in good condition with normal wear and tear, and the vehicle dealer assumes the responsibility for reselling the vehicle.

Purchase Option, page 250 A vehicle lease option that allows you to buy the vehicle at the end of the lease for either its residual value or a fixed price that is specified in the lease.

Open-End Lease, page 250 A vehicle lease stating that when the lease expires, the current market value of the vehicle will be compared to its residual value, as specified in the lease.

Choose housing that meets your needs.

LO3

SUMMARY: No single type of housing is right for everyone. A single-family house is the traditional choice, and it is the most popular choice for most people because it offers more space, privacy, and owner control. A cooperative, or co-op, is an apartment building or group of apartments owned by a corporation where the residents of the building are the stockholders of the corporation.

KEY TERMS

Cooperative (Co-op), page 254 An apartment building or group of apartments owned by a corporation in which the residents of the building are the stockholders.

Homeowner's Fee, page 255 A monthly fee paid by shareholders to the cooperative corporation for paying property taxes and maintaining the building and grounds.

Condominium (Condo), page 255 A type of apartment building or apartment complex that allows for the individual ownership of the apartment units but joint ownership of the land, common areas, and facilities.

Down Payment, page 256 The amount of money outside of or not covered by mortgage funds that the home buyer puts down on a home at the time of sale.

Closing or Settlement Costs, page 257 Expenses associated with finalizing the transfer of ownership of the house.

Points or Discount Points, page 257 Charges used to raise the effective cost of the mortgage loan, which must be paid in full at the time of the closing.

Loan Origination Fee, page 257 A fee of generally one point, or 1 percent of the loan amount. Its purpose is to compensate the lender for the cost of reviewing and finalizing the loan.

Loan Application Fee, page 257 A fee, generally in the $200 to $300 range, that is meant to defer some of the processing costs associated with the loan.

Appraisal Fee, page 257 A fee for an appraisal of the house, which is generally required before a mortgage loan is approved. Although the cost varies depending on the size and location of the house, it can easily run between $200 and $300.

Title Search, page 257 An investigation of the public land records to determine the legal ownership rights to property or a home.

PITI, page 258 An acronym standing for the total of your monthly principal, interest, taxes, and insurance.

Escrow Account, page 258 A reserve account in which funds are deposited, generally on a monthly basis, and accumulate over time until they are drawn out to pay for property taxes and insurance premiums.

LO4 Decide whether to rent or buy housing.

SUMMARY: There are a number of reasons renting may be preferable to buying. In order to make a logical decision about whether to rent or buy, or about what is truly affordable, you need to have a basic understanding of the costs that come with home ownership. These include one-time or initial costs such as the down payment, points, and closing costs; recurring costs associated with financing, including mortgage payments, property taxes, and insurance; and recurring costs associated with upkeep and maintenance.

LO5 Calculate the costs of buying a home.

SUMMARY: The first step in the housing decision involves preshopping, in which you focus on the rent-versus-buy decision and determine what is affordable. Just as with any other major purchase, the second step involves comparison shopping with an eye on price, product attributes, and the quality of the house or apartment.

Once you decide which house or apartment you'd like to live in, the next step is purchasing the house or, in the case of renting an apartment, signing the lease. Once again, the process is essentially the same as with any other major purchase—negotiate a price and evaluate the financing alternatives. Once you've purchased a home, you're in charge of upkeep and maintenance.

LO6 Get the most out of your mortgage.

SUMMARY: Mortgages can be categorized as conventional or government backed. Conventional mortgages are simply loans from a bank or S&L secured by the property being purchased. With government-backed loans, the bank or S&L still makes the loan, but the government insures the loan. S&Ls and commercial banks are the primary sources of mortgage loans, but they certainly are not the only sources. Mortgage loans are also available from other traditional lenders such as credit unions and mutual savings banks, as well as from specialized lenders such as mortgage bankers and mortgage brokers.

Mortgages also come with fixed or adjustable rates. With a fixed-rate mortgage, the monthly payment does not change, regardless of what happens to interest rates. With an adjustable-rate mortgage (ARM), the interest rate fluctuates up and down with the level of current interest rates, within limits and at specific intervals. If interest rates drop, you may want to refinance your mortgage, which is simply taking out a new mortgage to pay off your old one.

KEY TERMS

Mortgage Banker, page 264 Someone who originates mortgage loans with funds from other investors, such as pension funds and insurance companies, and services the monthly payments.

Mortgage Broker, page 264 A middleman who, for a fee, secures mortgage loans for borrowers but doesn't actually make those mortgage loans. A mortgage broker will find the best loan available for the borrower.

Conventional Mortgage Loan, page 264 A loan from a bank or S&L that is secured by the property being purchased.

Government-Backed Mortgage Loan, page 265 A mortgage loan made by a traditional lender but insured by the government.

Assumable Loan, page 265 A mortgage loan that can be transferred to a new buyer, who simply assumes or takes over the mortgage obligations. Such a mortgage saves the new buyer the costs of obtaining a new mortgage loan.

Prepayment Privilege, page 266 A clause in a mortgage allowing the borrower to make early cash payments that are applied toward the principal.

Adjustable-Rate Mortgage (ARM), page 266 A mortgage in which the interest rate charged fluctuates with the level of current interest rates. The loan fluctuates, or is adjusted, at set intervals (say, every year) and only within set limits.

Initial Rate, page 266 The initial rate charged on an ARM, sometimes called the teaser rate. This rate holds only for a short period, usually between 3 and 24 months, before being adjusted, at which point it generally rises.

Negative Amortization, page 267 A situation in which the monthly payments are less than the interest that's due on the loan. As a result, the unpaid interest is added to the principal, and you end up owing more at the end of the month than you did at the beginning of the month.

Balloon Payment Mortgage, page 268 A mortgage with relatively small monthly payments for several years (generally 5 or 7 years), after which the loan must be paid off in one large balloon payment.

Graduated Payment Mortgage, page 269 A mortgage in which payments are arranged so they steadily rise for a specified period of time, generally 5 to 10 years, and then level off.

Growing Equity Mortgage, page 269 A conventional 30-year mortgage in which prepayment is automatic and planned for. Payments begin at the same level as those for a 30-year fixed-rate mortgage and then rise annually—generally increasing at between 2 and 9 percent per year—allowing the mortgage to be paid off early.

Shared Appreciation Mortgage, page 269 A mortgage in which the borrower receives a below-market interest rate in return for which the lender receives a portion of the future appreciation (generally between 30 and 50 percent) in the value of the home.

Interest-Only Mortgage, page 269 A mortgage with interest-only payments for an initial set period (e.g., for 5 years on a 30-year loan); after this period, the borrower pays interest and principal with payments adjusted upward to reflect full amortization over the remaining years of the loan.

Private Mortgage Insurance, page 273 Insurance that protects the lender in the event that the borrower is unable to make the mortgage payments.

Independent or Exclusive Buyer-Broker, page 274 A real estate agent hired by the prospective home buyer who exclusively represents the home buyer. Such brokers are obligated to get the buyer the best possible deal and, in general, are paid by splitting the commission with the seller's agent.

Real Estate Short Sale, page 274 A sale of property where the proceeds from the sale fall short of the balance owed on the property.

Earnest Money, page 276 A deposit on the purchase to assure the seller that the buyer is serious about buying the house.

Closing, page 276 The time at which the title is transferred and the seller is paid in full for the house. At this time, the buyer takes possession of the house.

Settlement or Closing Statement, page 276 A statement listing the funds required at closing, which the real estate broker should furnish to the buyer for review at least 1 business day before closing.

Problems and Activities

These problems are available in **MyLab Finance**.

1. Determine the total first-year cost of car ownership for Milagros. She has just purchased a vehicle valued for $15,000 with the following costs:

   Auto Loan: Amount—$15,000, Duration—4 years, APR—6.65 percent
   Property Taxes: 2 percent of vehicle value/year
   Sales Taxes: 3 percent of the sales price
   Title and Tags: $40/year
   Maintenance and Usage Costs: $1,500/year
   Insurance: $2,000/year

2. Compute the monthly payment and the total amount spent for a vehicle that costs $20,000 if you finance the entire purchase over 5 years at an annual interest rate of 6 percent. Calculate the payment if you finance the car for only 4 years. Finally, calculate the payment for 3 years. What do you notice about the payment under the different time assumptions?
3. Compute the monthly payments for a vehicle that costs $15,000 if you finance the entire purchase over 4 years at an annual interest rate of 6 percent. Also calculate the loan payments assuming rates of 5 percent and 7 percent. Compare the total amount spent on the vehicle under each assumption.
4. Annie's mortgage statement shows a total payment of $699.12, with $604.60 paid toward principal and interest and $94.52 paid for taxes and insurance. Taxes and insurance for 3 months were collected at closing. Now, after 6 months of payments, she is curious about the total in her escrow account. Calculate the amount for her, and explain the account.
5. Calculate the monthly payments on a 30-year fixed-rate mortgage at 5 percent for $100,000. How much interest is paid over the life of the loan?
6. Calculate how much money a prospective home owner would need for closing costs on a house that costs $100,000. Calculate based on a 20 percent down payment, two discount points on the loan, a one-point origination fee, and $1,400 in other fees.
7. Use your financial calculator to determine the monthly payments for each of the following $100,000 mortgage loans. Assume no prepayments.

   a. 30-year fixed at 5 percent
   b. 15-year fixed at 4 percent
   c. 20-year fixed at 4.5 percent

8. Determine the maximum 30-year fixed-rate mortgage amount for which a couple could qualify if the rate is 4.5 percent. Assume they have other debt payments totaling $500 per month and a combined annual income of $45,500. Monthly escrow payments for real estate taxes and homeowner's insurance are estimated to be $125.

Discussion Case 1

This case is available in **MyLab Finance**.

Samuel and Grace Paganelli want to replace their 2008 Ford F-150 pickup, which Samuel drives for work. They already own two vehicles, but they need to replace Samuel's truck because it has nearly 175,000 miles on the odometer. The replacement must be a vehicle that fits his job as a self-employed electrician.

Samuel knows that he drives a lot on the job and is worried about the high-mileage penalty on many leases, as well as about the fees for excessive wear and tear. However, Grace is more concerned about the depreciation loss on a new truck purchase than about the mileage penalty and would rather lease the new vehicle. She also likes the idea of having a new, safer truck every few years without the hassle of resale. Samuel also does not like the fact that, if they lease, they would not own the vehicle he will use for work. Warranty protection to insure the truck remains in service is very important.

They feel that they can afford to spend $550 per month over 4 years for a new vehicle as long as their other associated expenses such as insurance, gas, and maintenance are not too high. The Paganellis also do not know where to start looking for a vehicle without the hassle of negotiating with dealerships.

Questions

1. Identify seven sources of vehicle purchasing information and the type of information available from each source.
2. From all the information available, what specific information about the different makes and models is the most relevant to Samuel and Grace in making their purchasing decision?
3. What is the highest price they can pay on the new vehicle if they can afford a down payment of $4,000? Assume they finance their purchase for 48 months at 5.5 percent. (*Hint:* This is a present value of an annuity problem.)
4. According to the National Automotive Dealer Association (NADA) guide found at **http://www.nadaguides.com**, are the Paganellis better off to sell their pickup or use it as a trade-in? Consider both price and time in your answer.
5. If they decide to lease, what key factors are important in a good lease?
6. Explain to Grace and Samuel the guidelines of leasing and whether or not it is a smart financial move for them to consider. Would they be better off with a closed-end or an open-end lease? From a purely financial perspective, would you recommend leasing or financing? Complete Worksheet 9 to substantiate your recommendation.
7. If Samuel purchases a "lemon," what alternatives are available to prevent the truck from "short-circuiting" his business?

WORKSHEET 9

Discussion Case 2

This case is available in MyLab Finance.

With a raise from his investment firm, Seyed Abdallah, 31, is inspired to look for a new home. Buying a home will allow Seyed, who is single and in the 25 percent marginal tax bracket, to itemize taxes. He has come to you for help.

Financially, he is fairly secure, but he is also very risk averse. His salary is $63,000 a year, but he does not know how much he should spend on housing. His current housing expenditures include rent of $900 per month and renter's insurance premiums totaling $150 per year. His monthly bills include a $300-per-month lease payment for his 2018 Acura TL and a $280-per-month student loan payment. He also paid a security deposit of 2 months' rent from which he could be earning 4 percent after taxes.

Seyed has researched the recurring costs of home ownership. He has found that the real estate tax rate is $0.91 per $100 of assessed value and homeowner's insurance policies cost approximately $275 per year. He is unsure of the maintenance costs but estimates them at $350 per year.

He likes the idea of owning his own home because as real estate values increase, the value of his home will increase. Local property values have been increasing at 5 percent per year over the last 7 years, and real estate sales commissions equal 6 percent of the purchase price. One of his concerns about buying a home is the immediate cost of the down payment and closing costs. These closing costs, he has found, include a 1 percent origination fee, two discount points on the mortgage, and 3 percent of the home purchase price in various other fees due at closing. He also knows that he will pay a 20 percent down payment up front to qualify for financing. Another concern is the lost investment income on this money, which is currently earning an 4 percent after-tax return.

Questions

1. Write a short description of the four types of housing generally available for Seyed.
2. List several sources of information applicable to any real estate purchase that might be helpful to Seyed in making a decision. Should he consider prequalifying?
3. Use the lending guidelines to determine the maximum dollar amount that he could spend per month on his home payment (PITI).

WORKSHEET 10

4. Calculate Seyed's monthly PITI payment. To calculate principal and interest (PI), assume he has purchased a home for $140,000 and has a $112,000, 30-year, 4.75 percent fixed-rate mortgage. To calculate the local real estate taxes (T), use the real estate tax rate as given in the case, assuming the property has an assessed value of $128,000. Also include Seyed's projected homeowner's insurance (I) cost as given in the case.
5. Complete Worksheet 10 to determine if Seyed should buy or continue renting. To purchase the house considered in Question 4, Seyed would pay $6,000 in closing costs, including $2,500 in discount points. Consider 1- and 7-year time horizons.
6. Seyed is now considering a house that is selling for $180,000. Estimate the dollar amount Seyed should be prepared to pay on the day of closing. Assume an interest rate of 5.25 percent, closing costs of 5 percent of the sale price, and a 20 percent down payment.

WORKSHEET 11

7. Assuming the house in Question 6 is appraised for $180,000 and the information in the case concerning the taxes and insurance holds true, can Seyed afford the home if he finances it for 15 years? 20 years? 30 years? Why or why not? Use Worksheet 11 to guide your answer. (*Hint:* Remember the qualification amount will be the lowest of the three values on the worksheet—not the highest.)
8. Will Seyed need private mortgage insurance? Will he need a gift letter?
9. Given his risk tolerance, what type of mortgage would you recommend to Seyed? Should he consider an interest-only mortgage?

Continuing Case: Cory and Tisha Dumont

Part II: Managing Your Money

Cory and Tisha are back asking for your help, only this time the topics are cash management, credit use, and major purchases. Tempting credit card offers continue to come in the mail. Recall that they have Visa, MasterCard, Discover, and American Express credit cards, as well as several store cards, with a combined average balance of $1,300. Minimum monthly payments equal approximately $50, although they typically pay $100 per month.

Tisha's sister and her husband just bought their first home, making Tisha even more anxious to move from their rented house. Cory wants to wait a while longer before buying a home and has suggested that they should replace their older, high-mileage car. Cory and Tisha realize that funds for another payment are limited, not to mention money for a house payment. Their options are to reduce the payments on their credit cards and to reduce other expenses. At any rate, $300 a month seems to be the maximum amount available for an auto loan, not to mention any likely increase in their auto insurance premium associated with the new vehicle. Help them answer the following questions.

Questions

1. As a result of a recent corporate merger, Tisha is eligible to join a credit union. What are the advantages and disadvantages of doing so instead of remaining with a commercial bank?
2. Should they consider online banking? What are the advantages and disadvantages when compared to traditional banking services?
3. The Dumonts' commercial bank was recently bought by a large, out-of-state bank. Because required minimum balances and bank fees have increased, the Dumonts have considered shopping for a new bank. What factors should they consider?
4. The Dumonts have asked your advice on using a CD, money market mutual fund, or asset management account for their emergency fund. What is the best choice? Why? Is there another type of account they should consider? Why is the balance between liquidity and return so important with an emergency fund?
5. Which provides the higher after-tax yield: the Dumonts' 1 percent bank savings account or a federal and state tax-free money market fund yielding 0.25 percent? The Dumonts are in the 15 percent federal marginal tax bracket.
6. In Chapter 5, it was recommended that you "pay yourself first." Tisha is not sure how to do this but likes the idea of "saving money without having to think about it." Give her some advice about ways to "automate" her savings.
7. Because of his concern over "financial surprises," Cory wants to learn more about identity theft. What practices should he and Tisha follow to protect themselves?
8. The Dumonts' take-home pay (after deductions for taxes and benefits) is approximately $6,045 monthly. Current nonmortgage debt payments equal $911 (i.e., $405 auto, $100 miscellaneous credit, $196 student loan, and $210 furniture). Calculate and interpret their debt limit ratio. Assume they could purchase another auto with a $300 monthly payment. Calculate and interpret their revised debt limit ratio. What advice would you give the Dumonts about purchasing another vehicle?
9. Concerned that they might depend on credit too much, Tisha and Cory have asked you about the typical warning signs of excessive credit use. List five to eight of those signs. What alternatives should they consider if they occasionally can't pay their bills on time?
10. Tisha and Cory are worried that their credit card company might increase their credit card interest rate so much that they will not be able to afford their monthly payments. Explain their rights under the CARD Act of 2009.
11. In anticipation of purchasing a home, Cory and Tisha have been advised to check their credit report. Why? What are the roles of the credit bureau, the credit report, and the FICO score in determining creditworthiness and the cost of credit? How can they get their credit report? What are the Dumonts' alternatives if they find erroneous information in their credit report?
12. What are the "five Cs" of credit? Define and explain each, based on the information provided about the Dumont household.
13. Cory and Tisha are convinced that "good debt" means "cheap debt." Help them identify one or two sources of credit that would be categorized as inexpensive, more expensive, or most expensive. Where would payday loans fit? Why?
14. Discussions over lunch where Tisha works often turn to "making ends meet." One coworker has been to a credit counselor, while another is currently processing a debt consolidation loan application. Are these alternatives helpful for those who can't pay their bills? What two fundamental strategies are imperative for someone recovering from credit overuse?

15. Help Cory and Tisha apply the four steps of the smart buying process to decide whether or not to replace their car. What sources of consumer information might be useful to them?

16. A recent TV advertisement offered a lease option for $259 a month on a car that both Tisha and Cory like. It fits their budget, but they are unsure of the contract obligations. What criteria should they consider to determine if leasing is their best alternative? What cautions would you give them about an open-end lease compared to a closed-end lease?

17. If Cory and Tisha decide to purchase rather than lease another car, what factors must they consider when comparing new- and used-car purchases? What factors should they consider in determining whether to sell their car outright or trade it in toward their next purchase?

18. Cory and Tisha found a used car that costs $12,000. They can finance through their bank for 5.75 percent interest for a maximum of 48 months. The rate for new-car financing is 4.50 percent for 60 months or 4.35 percent for 48 months. If they could find a comparably priced new vehicle, how much would they save per month in interest charges if they financed the vehicle for 48 months?

19. Considering the information in Question 18, how much interest would be saved if the Dumonts financed the used vehicle for 36 months, instead of 48 months, if the rate remains the same?

20. In reviewing the sample auto loan contract, Cory and Tisha questioned the term *secured loan*. They also were unsure of the terms *default*, *repossession*, and *deficiency payment clause*. Explain these terms. What can they do to avoid repossession?

21. In a few years, Tisha and Cory might want to consider a home equity loan to finance a car purchase or to help pay for Chad's or Haley's college costs. What are the advantages and disadvantages of using this credit source as opposed to the typical auto or student loan? Specifically, what are the tax consequences?

22. Last week, the local newspaper mortgage rate column reported that the rate for a 30-year fixed-rate mortgage was 3.88 percent, while the rate for a 7-year balloon payment mortgage was 3.45 percent (payments were calculated on the basis of 30-year amortization). A 1-year ARM was available for 3.25 percent (payments were also calculated on the basis of 30-year amortization). Assuming a loan amount of $120,000, calculate the payment for each mortgage. Aside from the significant differences in the mortgage payment amounts, what other factors should the Dumonts consider when choosing their mortgage? What are the advantages and disadvantages of an interest-only mortgage?

WORKSHEET 11

23. Based on their gross monthly income of $7,000 and monthly debt repayments of $911, what is the maximum mortgage amount for which Cory and Tisha could currently qualify? The monthly real estate tax (T) and homeowner's insurance (I) are estimated at $170 per month. Calculate the mortgage amount using both the 28 percent qualification rule and the 36 percent qualification rule. (*Hint:* Refer to Figure 8.7 or use Worksheet 11.) Use 4 percent as the current rate of interest and assume a 30-year fixed-rate mortgage.

24. How has Cory's student loan affected his creditworthiness in applying for a mortgage? What is the relationship between PITI and consumer credit when calculating the 36 percent qualification rule?

25. Compare the Dumonts' monthly mortgage payment for PITI in Question 23 with their current monthly rent and renter's insurance cost of $1,300. Should Cory and Tisha consider purchasing a house that would require their maximum qualification mortgage loan amount? Defend your answer.

26. Given the maximum mortgage qualification amount determined in Question 23, calculate a 20 percent down payment. If closing costs average 5 percent of the cost of the house, how much will the Dumonts need on the day of closing? How does this compare with the $13,000 in the stock market index mutual fund account for their house down payment?

27. Using the monthly PI payment for the maximum mortgage qualification amount in Question 23, calculate the total cost of the Dumonts' home if the mortgage is not paid off early. How much of this cost is interest?

28. Tisha would like to consider a 15-year mortgage so that the house would be paid for before Haley enters college. Explain how the factors of monthly payment, total interest paid, time value of money, and taxes impact this decision.

29. Briefly explain the concepts of one-time, recurring, and maintenance and operating costs to Cory and Tisha. How should they consider these three categories of costs when shopping for their home?

Appendix

Crunchin' the Numbers—Calculations for Figure 8.6

FIGURE 8A.1 Worksheet for the Rent-Versus-Buy Decision Calculations

ASSUMPTIONS: Buying option: $20,000 down and an $80,000, 30-year mortgage at 8%. Rental option: $900 per month. Time frames: 1 year and 7 years; 28% marginal tax rate; after-tax rate of return = 5%; house appreciates in value at 3% per year; sales commission is 5% of the price of the house; closing costs = $5,000, which includes 2 points.

COST OF RENTING	1 Year	7 Years	Your Numbers
a. Total monthly rent costs (monthly rent $900 × 12 months × no. years)	a. $10,800	a. $75,600	
b. Total renter's insurance (annual renter's insurance $250 × no. years)	+ b. $250	+ b. $1,750	
c. After-tax opportunity cost of interest lost because of having to make a security deposit (security deposit of $1,800 × after-tax rate of return of 5% × no. years)	+ c. $90	+ c. $630	
d. **Total cost of renting (lines a + b + c)**	= d. $11,140	= d. $77,980	
COST OF BUYING			
e. Total mortgage payments (monthly payments $587.01 × 12 months × no. years)	e. $7,044.12	e. $49,308.84	
f. Property taxes on the new house (property taxes of $2,200 × no. years)	+ f. $2,200	+ f. $15,400	
g. Homeowner's insurance (annual homeowner's insurance $600 × no. years)	+ g. $600	+ g. $4,200	
h. Additional operating costs beyond those of renting. Maintenance, repairs, and any additional utilities and heating costs (additional annual operating costs $500 × no. years)	+ h. $500	+ h. $3,500	
i. After-tax opportunity cost of interest lost because of having to make a down payment (down payment of $20,000 × after-tax rate of return of 5% × no. years)	+ i. $1,000	+ i. $7,000	
j. Closing costs, including points (closing costs of $5,000)	+ j. $5,000	+ j. $5,000	
k. Less savings: Total mortgage payments going toward the loan principal*	− k. $668.26	− k. $6,017.84	
l. Less savings: Estimated appreciation in the value of the home less sales commission at the end of the period (current market value of house $100,000 × annual growth in house value of 3% × no. years − sales commission at end of the period of 5% × future value of house)	− l. −($2,150)†	− l. $14,950	
m. **Equals: Total cost of buying a home for those who do not itemize (lines e + f + g + h + i + j − k − l)**	=m. $17,825.86	=m. $63,441.00	
Additional savings to home buyers who itemize			
n. Less savings: Tax savings from the tax deductibility of the interest portion of the mortgage payments (total amount of interest payments made × marginal tax rate of 28%)	− n. $1,785.24	− n. $12,121.48	
o. Less savings: Tax savings from the tax deductibility of the property taxes on the new house (property taxes of $2,200 × marginal tax rate of 28% × no. years)	− o. $616	− o. $4,312	
p. Less savings: Tax savings from the tax deductibility of the points portion of the closing costs (total points paid of $1,600 × marginal tax rate of 28%)	− p. $448	− p. $448	
q. **Total cost of buying a home to home buyers who itemize (line m minus lines n through p)**	= q. $14,976.62	− q. $46,559.52	
Advantage of buying to those who *do not itemize* = Total cost of renting − total cost of buying for those who *do not itemize:* if negative, rent; if positive, buy (line d − line m)	− $6,685.86	− $14,539.00	
Advantage of buying to those who *itemize* = Total cost of renting − total cost of buying for those who *itemize:* if negative, rent; if positive, buy (line d − line q)	− $3,836.62	− $31,420.48	

*The total interest and principal payments can be calculated directly or approximated. To approximate the total annual interest payments, multiply the outstanding size of the loan by the interest rate (in this case, $80,000 × 0.08 = $6,400); then multiply this by the number of years. In the case of the 1-year time horizon, the approximation method yields $6,400 of total interest, while a direct calculation yields $6,375.86. While the approximation method works well for short time horizons, it is less accurate for longer time horizons.

†Note: If you own the home for only 1 year, the value here is negative, meaning the sales commission is greater than the appreciation in home value. Thus, this is an additional cost, not a savings, and we are subtracting a negative–in effect, adding the $2,150 to the cost of buying the house.

PART 3 Protecting Yourself with Insurance

Now that you have an understanding of the financial planning process and managing your money, it's time to turn your attention to protecting yourself with insurance. In putting together your financial plan, insurance is an extremely important topic. After all, the unexpected can happen, and when it does, you want to make sure that your financial plan and the chance to achieve your financial goals don't vanish.

Part 3: Protecting Yourself with Insurance begins with an examination of life and health insurance. You will gain an understanding of the purpose of life insurance and whether you even need it. We will also look at health care and what provisions in a health care plan might be important to you. We will then turn our attention to property and liability insurance, both homeowner's and automobile insurance, and look at how to file an insurance claim.

In Part 3, we will specifically focus on:

Principle 7: Protect Yourself Against Major Catastrophes—Without question, the worst time to find out that you don't have the right amount or right kind of insurance is just after a tragedy occurs. What makes purchasing insurance a problem is that it is extremely difficult to compare policies because of the many subtle differences they contain. Remember, the focus of this book is on planning and control, and while we can't control the unexpected, we can plan in such a way that it does not prevent us from achieving our lifetime goals.

In addition, in Part 3 we will touch on Principle 1: The Best Protection Is Knowledge; Principle 8: Risk and Return Go Hand in Hand; Principle 9: Mind Games, Your Financial Personality, and Your Money; and Principle 10: Just Do It!

CHAPTER 9

Life and Health Insurance

Learning Objectives

LO1	**Understand** the importance of insurance.	The Importance of Insurance
LO2	**Determine** your life insurance needs and design a life insurance program.	Determining Your Life Insurance Needs
LO3	**Describe** the major types of coverage available and the typical provisions that are included.	Major Types of Life Insurance
LO4	**Design** a health-care insurance program and understand what provisions are important to you.	Health Insurance
LO5	**Describe** disability insurance and the choices available to you.	Disability Insurance
LO6	**Explain** the purpose of long-term care insurance and the provisions that might be important to you.	Long-Term Care Insurance

If you were asked who you felt had the greatest need for life insurance, who would you pick—Batman or Fred Flintstone? In a recent survey, 1,000 Americans were asked that question, and the winner, by an almost two-to-one margin, was Batman! Well, as you will learn in this chapter, they got it wrong. There's no question that Batman lives a dangerous life, but he is unmarried and wealthy and, as a result, doesn't need life insurance. How about Fred Flintstone? Well, he's the primary breadwinner for the Flintstones, and if something were to happen to him, life insurance would allow Wilma and Pebbles to maintain their standard of living.

Photo 12/Alamy Stock Photo

How about Walter White, who lived in the TV world of *Breaking Bad*? If you don't know, Walter White, played by Bryan Cranston, led a dull life as a high school chemistry teacher and supplemented his income by working at a car wash. Walter was a family man with a pregnant wife and a high-school-aged son with cerebral palsy. His life became further complicated when he collapsed while at the car wash and when at the hospital was diagnosed with stage-three terminal lung cancer. Having little in the way of savings and desperately wanting to provide for his wife and family, he enlisted a former student, Jesse Pinkman, and went into the drug business as the drug lord "Heisenberg," a move that, as you may know, didn't turn out well. As a high school teacher in New Mexico, Walter probably didn't automatically get a life insurance policy. How much would Walter have paid for a life insurance policy? Judging by his job, it probably wouldn't have been too expensive. Would it have helped? You bet! A good life insurance policy could have taken care of his family, and it would have eliminated any reason for him to become a drug lord.

How about health insurance for Walter? As a high school teacher, Walter probably had reasonable health insurance that would have helped with his many medical bills. One other type of insurance we'll look at in this chapter is disability insurance. While Walter led a dangerous life as a drug lord, disability insurance might have helped, but the job of "drug lord" is not one that would qualify for disability coverage.

No one likes to think about illness or disability, let alone put a lot of effort or money into insuring against it. However, health insurance is an issue none of us can afford to dismiss. Similarly, most of us would prefer to avoid thinking about and planning for our deaths. As a result, when the time is right to get our first life insurance policy, most of us do not seek it out—instead, someone approaches us and convinces us it's important, and then we buy it. Because insurance has a language all its own, it is often difficult to understand all the differences between one policy and another and to know how much to buy.

Life insurance is also an odd thing to purchase—it's not meant to benefit you. Hey, you're dead—you no longer have any needs. When you consider your need for life insurance, you must keep in mind its purpose: to protect your dependents in the event of your death. Life insurance can give you peace of mind by ensuring that your dependents will have the financial resources to pay off your debts and keep their home and that your children will be able to go to college and live comfortably—and as for Walter White, it might have prevented him from his desperate and tragic venture to the dark side of life as a drug lord.

Most college students, as a rule, don't have a need for life insurance—they tend to be single and have no dependents. That doesn't mean they won't buy life insurance, especially if a persuasive salesperson comes to call. It is still vital to have a basic understanding of both life insurance and health insurance. In this chapter, we will examine the types of coverage available and the process of buying insurance. After all, the unexpected can happen—and it can happen to you.

LO1 Understand the importance of insurance.

The Importance of Insurance

PRINCIPLE 7

The need for both life and health insurance arises from **Principle 7: Protect Yourself Against Major Catastrophes.** The key concepts here are *planning* and *control*. After all, this whole book is based on learning to control your financial situation through careful planning. If you plan carefully enough, you can control your finances even after your death. That's pretty powerful.

An insurance policy is a contract with an insurance company that spells out what losses are covered, the cost of the policy, and who receives payments if a loss occurs. Whether or not to take out an insurance policy is a matter of risk–return trade-offs. Are you willing to pay for an insurance policy to cover your risks? To start you on the road to understanding insurance, let's take a look at some of the basic ideas behind it, beginning with the relationship of insurance to risk.

Why Are Health and Life Insurance So Important?

Health insurance provides protection for you and your family against financially devastating medical bills. Life insurance protects your family in case you die. If you haven't planned wisely, your death could be a financial catastrophe for your dependents.

Why Is Health Care So Costly?

Today, health care is costly primarily because there is a lack of incentive to economize. Presently, over 50 percent of Americans receive some government health-care entitlements, such as Medicare or Medicaid, and most Americans have medical insurance. As a result, there simply isn't any incentive for patients, doctors, or hospitals to exercise restraint in medical billing. If you aren't paying out of your own pocket, why should you care what your bills are? And if these bills are certain to be paid, why should doctors or hospitals care how much they charge?

A second reason that health care is so costly is that today's medical care has become extremely sophisticated. For example, it now takes 12 years and costs over $230 million to develop, test, and certify a new drug, and drug companies are passing these costs on to patients. Finally, the cost of litigation from malpractice suits has skyrocketed. It's not uncommon for doctors to pay malpractice insurance premiums of $150,000 or $250,000 per year. These costs, too, are then passed directly on to patients.

What Do These High Costs Mean for You?

First, medical care and medical insurance must become more efficient if we're to continue to be able to afford quality health care. This change may mean that your doctor joins a Health Maintenance Organization (HMO) or that your company's insurance policy no longer covers all your health-care expenses. It also means that many companies will try to cut down on their health-care costs by providing only limited insurance coverage or hiring temporary workers who don't get a full benefits package.

What About Those Who Have No Health Insurance?

This is one of the things the **Patient Protection and Affordable Care Act**, which was signed into law in 2010, tries to address. While this act is under siege in Congress, with many wanting to repeal and replace it or simply repeal it, it did increase the number of Americans who have health insurance by millions.

Patient Protection and Affordable Care Act
Commonly referred to as the *Affordable Care Act* or *ObamaCare*, this major health-care act was signed into law in 2010 and put in place comprehensive health insurance reforms.

Insurance is important. When putting together your personal financial plan, insurance needs to be a top priority. As medical costs go through the roof, so does your risk of having your financial roof cave in due to health-related issues. Without appropriate insurance, one accident or one illness can ruin your whole financial plan.

We will definitely explore the changing world of health insurance, but first let's examine the details of life insurance. You'll find out all you need to know so that your dependents are taken care of in case of your death and so that you can rest easy, knowing that this is the case.

Determining Your Life Insurance Needs

LO2 Determine your life insurance needs and design a life insurance program.

Unless medical science comes up with something mighty impressive in the next few years, we all have to die sometime. Life insurance allows you to eliminate or at least substantially reduce the financial consequences of your death for your dependents.

Do You Need Life Insurance?

Insurance is based on the concept of **risk pooling**, which means that individuals share the financial risks they face. The logic behind risk pooling is drawn from the idea of diversification. Life insurance allows individuals to pool the financial risks associated with death. In effect, everyone pays something into the "pool." When an insured person dies, his or her family receives some of the money from the pot, which offsets the lost income due to death.

Risk Pooling
Sharing the financial consequences associated with risk.

The amount that everyone puts into the pot is called a **premium**, and the size of the premium depends on the probability of when you will die. To determine your chance of death, insurance companies employ **actuaries**, statisticians who specialize in estimating life expectancy based on personal characteristics, such as your age and your general health, as well as lifestyle specifics such as whether or not you exercise. Insurance companies are able to predict with a good deal of accuracy the number of

Premium
A life insurance payment.

Actuaries
Statisticians who specialize in estimating the probability of death based on personal characteristics.

deaths that will occur in a given population of policyholders and charge each policyholder a fair premium. Smokers stand a much higher risk of dying at a younger age than do nonsmokers, for example, so smokers are charged higher premiums.

Face Amount or Face of Policy
The amount of insurance provided by the policy at death.

Insured
The person whose life is insured by the life insurance policy.

Policyholder or Policy Owner
The individual or business that owns the life insurance policy.

Beneficiary
The individual designated to receive the insurance policy's proceeds upon the death of the insured.

The amount of insurance provided by the policy at death is called the **face amount or face of policy**. The **insured** is the person whose life is insured by the life insurance policy. Sometimes the policy is owned (or "held") by an individual, and other times it's held by a business. In either case, the owner is referred to as the **policyholder or policy owner**. The individual designated by the owner of the life insurance policy to receive the insurance policy's proceeds upon the death of the insured is called the **beneficiary**.

How do you know whether you need life insurance? Well, as we said, the purpose of life insurance is to provide for your dependents in the event of your death. If you're single and have no dependents, you generally don't need life insurance. However, you still might want to buy life insurance if you're at a higher risk of contracting a terminal illness, such as cancer or AIDS, or an uninsurable condition that could prevent later purchases of insurance, such as diabetes or heart disease. Although insurance policies don't pay off until you are dead, if you're terminally ill it's possible to receive a reduced settlement, similar to borrowing against your policy, or to sell your insurance policy at a discount before you die. For those with a high risk of serious health problems, a life insurance policy can be viewed as a form of health insurance. But for anyone without a spouse or dependents, life insurance probably doesn't make sense.

If you do have a spouse or dependents, then life insurance can help make up for the wages lost as a result of your death. In addition to replacing lost income, it can cover burial expenses, medical and hospital expenses not covered by your health insurance, outstanding bills and loans, and attorney's fees related to estate settlement. Life insurance can also be used to provide funds for housing and for your children's education and can be used as an estate-planning tool.

In determining whether or not you need life insurance, think back to what we said about the purpose of life insurance at the opening of this chapter—it's meant to benefit not the insured but those left behind. Table 9.1 provides a list of those who might need life insurance.

TABLE 9.1 Should You Buy Life Insurance?

You may not want/need life insurance if:
You're single and don't have any dependents. **You're married, you and your spouse are employed, and you have no children.**
Consider life insurance if:
Your surviving spouse's lifestyle will suffer if you die. **You're married but aren't employed.** **You have young children.** Would your spouse have financial problems with obtaining day care and taking care of the house if you die? **You're retired.** Would your spouse be able to live on your savings, including Social Security and your pension, if you die?
You probably need life insurance if:
You have children. You should have coverage for raising and educating your children until they are financially self-sufficient. **You're married, you're employed but your spouse is not, and you have no children.** You should have insurance to allow your surviving spouse to maintain his or her lifestyle until he or she can become self-sufficient. **You own your own business.** A life insurance policy can allow your family to pay off any business debt if you die. **The value of your estate is over the estate-tax-free-transfer threshold, which was $5.49 million in 2017.** Life insurance can be an effective tool for passing on an estate without incurring taxes.

How Much Life Insurance Do You Need?

Let's say you need life insurance. The question then becomes "*How much* do you need?" The first step is deciding what your priorities and goals are. Do you want to provide enough money for your kids to go to college? Do you want to leave enough money for your wife to buy her own home? Do you want to provide your husband with enough money to live on for the next few years while he takes care of the kids? Different people are going to have different philosophies about providing for their survivors, and none of those philosophies is right or wrong.

After deciding on your goals, the next step, figuring out how much insurance you need, involves some numbers. Start with your net worth because the larger your net worth, the more you have in the way of wealth to support your dependents, and consequently the less life insurance you need. Don't forget to throw in numbers to compensate for inflation and the earnings on possible future investments.

Is the process starting to sound complicated? Luckily, there are two basic approaches you can use to crunch the numbers that will tell you how much life insurance you need: (1) the earnings multiple approach and (2) the needs approach.

Earnings Multiple Approach Some financial planners suggest that you purchase life insurance that covers from 5 to 15 times your annual gross income. The **earnings multiple approach** is used to figure out exactly how much insurance this amounts to. This method doesn't take into account your individual level of savings or your financial well-being.

Earnings Multiple Approach
A method of determining exactly how much life insurance you need by using a multiple of your yearly earnings.

The earnings multiple approach is based on the notion that you want to replace a stream of annual income that's lost due to the death of a breadwinner. That is, you want to replace one stream of annual income with another. What this approach does is tell you how big a lump-sum settlement you will need to replace that stream of annual income.

Actually, a stream of annual income for a set number of years is just like the annuities we looked at in Chapter 3. The earnings multiple approach works the same way present value of annuity problems work. To determine the lump-sum settlement you need, simply multiply your present annual gross income by the appropriate earnings multiple.

Table 9.2 provides an abbreviated table of earnings multiples. To simplify the presentation (and speed the sale), many insurance agents present the earnings multiple

TABLE 9.2 Earnings Multiples for Life Insurance

Number of Years You Want the Lost Earnings Stream Replaced	After-Tax, After-Inflation Return Assumed on the Insurance Settlement		
		4%	5%
3 years	2.83	2.78	2.72
5 years	4.58	4.45	4.33
7 years	6.23	6.00	5.79
10 years	8.53	8.11	7.72
15 years	11.94	11.12	10.38
20 years	14.88	13.59	12.46
25 years	17.41	15.62	14.09
30 years	19.06	17.29	15.37
40 years	23.11	19.79	17.16
50 years	25.73	21.48	18.26

numbers without explaining the logic behind them. You need to keep in mind, then, that the earnings multiple that applies to your situation depends entirely on the number of years you need the lost income stream and the rate of return that you assume you can earn on the insurance settlement in excess of inflation and taxes. The longer you need to replace the income stream, the greater the multiple. The higher the return you believe you can earn on the settlement, the lower the multiple.

Let's examine how this approach might be applied to Leonard and Nancy Cohen. Leonard is the breadwinner, making a cool $80,000 per year. The Cohens currently have two young children, ages 2 and 4, and they don't plan to have any more. The kids won't be self-supporting for another 20 years, and Leonard and Nancy want to make sure they're provided for if something happens to Leonard. Nancy's a good investor and is sure she could get a 5 percent return, after taxes and inflation, on an invested insurance settlement.

How much life insurance do the Cohens need? Rather than simply multiplying Leonard's salary by the earnings multiple, we need to first adjust his salary downward to compensate for the fact that the family's living expenses will drop slightly with Leonard's death. Generally, family living expenses fall by about 30 percent with the loss of an adult family member if there's only one surviving family member. The larger the size of the surviving family, the less the living expenses drop as a percentage of total family expenses. For example, expenses drop by only 26 percent for a surviving family of two and by 22 percent for a surviving family of three, and they continue to drop another 2 percent for each additional surviving family member. To calculate the Cohens' target replacement salary, we adjust Leonard's present salary downward by multiplying it by a factor of $(1 - 0.22)$, or 0.78. The target replacement salary thus becomes $\$80{,}000 \times 0.78 = \$62{,}400$.

Now, we're ready to use the earnings multiples. Remember, we need to measure these amounts in today's dollars. In this case, $n = 20$ years and $i = 5$ percent. Looking in the earnings multiples in Table 9.2, we find an earnings multiple of 12.46. Multiplying Leonard's adjusted salary by this factor, we get $777,504. That is, under the earnings multiple approach, the level of life insurance needed becomes

$$\text{life insurance needs} = \text{income stream to be replaced} \times \left(1 - \frac{\text{percentage of family income}}{\text{spent on deceased's needs}}\right) \times \text{earnings multiple}$$

$$= \$80{,}000 \times (1 - 0.22) \times 12.46$$

$$= \$777{,}504$$

MyLab Finance Video

Calculator Clues

Life Insurance Needs—The Present Value of an Annuity

Let's solve the problem above using a financial calculator. In this example, we're trying to find out how much life insurance we need to generate a 20-year $62,400 annuity, given a discount rate of 5 percent (we expect to earn 5 percent after inflation and taxes). That's the same as solving for the present value of an annuity.

Enter	20	5		62,400	0
	N	I/Y	PV	PMT	FV
Solve for			−777,642		

Aside from a bit of rounding error, this is what we got using the tables. As expected, you get a negative sign on the PV.

Keep in mind, though, that this method isn't very useful unless it considers the effects of taxes and inflation. Also, remember that this method considers only your income replacement needs, not any special need to eliminate debt or save for specific goals. Most important, you've got to remember that your insurance needs are going to change over time. That means that your earnings multiple is going to change over time and that you're going to need to update your insurance coverage from time to time.

Needs Approach The **needs approach** attempts to determine the funds necessary to meet the needs of a family after the death of the primary breadwinner. You can think of the earnings multiple as a "one size fits all" method and the needs approach as a customized method. It is a bit more complicated than the earnings multiplier, but it allows you to account for the fact that your family's needs may be different from the average. Let's look at some of those needs:

Needs Approach
A method of determining how much life insurance you need based on the funds your family will require to maintain their lifestyle after your death.

- **Immediate needs at the time of death:** Sometimes called **cleanup funds**, these include final health costs, burial costs, inheritance taxes, estate taxes, and legal fees.
- **Debt elimination funds:** Funds to cover outstanding debts, including credit card and consumer debt, car loans, and mortgage debt. For example, you may wish to reduce the financial burden on your spouse by paying off half of your outstanding mortgage principal.
- **Immediate transitional funds:** Funds needed to cover expenses such as new job training or a college degree for the surviving spouse and child care during this period. For spouses who are already employed, transitional funds may be used to cover a leave of absence.
- **Dependency expenses:** Funds to cover family expenses incurred while children are in school and dependent on family support. One approach to determining current total household expenses is to use the deceased's income less annual savings as an estimate. Some of this amount may come from the surviving spouse's income, as well as Social Security and the deceased's pension from his or her job.
- **Spousal life income:** Supplemental income for the surviving spouse after the children have left home and are self-supporting but before the surviving spouse retires from whatever job he or she has.
- **Educational expenses for the children.**
- **Retirement income:** Includes any additional income stream that might be needed for the surviving spouse after retirement. It would make up for any shortfall after taking into account Social Security and pension benefits.

Cleanup Funds
Funds needed to cover immediate expenses at the time of your death.

FACTS OF LIFE

According to a recent study, 30 percent of U.S. households have no life insurance coverage—this compares to 22 percent without coverage 10 years ago. While not everyone needs life insurance, the study found that 11 million households with children younger than 18 have no life insurance.

To use the needs approach, you must determine the dollar amount that your family will need in each category. Fortunately, most people have assets or some existing insurance that will partially meet their life insurance needs. To calculate additional life insurance needs, you take the total funds needed and subtract your available assets and insurance.

As you make your calculations, keep in mind that the time value of money is going to come into play if this approach is to have any meaning. For instance, your family will receive the insurance settlement when you die, but some of the uses for that settlement—perhaps funding your children's college education—may be far off in the future. Sometimes insurance salespeople simply add up all the needs, regardless of how far off they are, and use that as a target level for life insurance. What that does is overestimate the amount of insurance you need.

Once you know how much life insurance you need, it's time to figure out what kind of insurance is available.

LO3 Describe the major types of coverage available and the typical provisions that are included.

Term Insurance
A type of insurance that pays the beneficiary a specific amount of money if the policyholder dies while covered by the policy.

Cash-Value Insurance
A type of insurance that has two components: life insurance and a savings plan.

Major Types of Life Insurance

There are two major types of life insurance: term insurance and cash-value insurance. **Term insurance** is pure life insurance. You pay a set premium that's based on the probability of when you'll die. For that premium, you receive a set amount of coverage for a set number of years. Term insurance covers only a very specific period, or "term." If you die during that period, your beneficiary receives your death benefits.

Cash-value insurance is more than simple life insurance. It has two components: life insurance and a savings plan. Some of your premiums go toward life insurance and some go toward savings. With cash-value insurance, when you die, your beneficiary is paid those savings as part of your death benefit. There are an almost infinite number of variations of cash-value insurance, and there are several different categories of term insurance. Table 9.3 summarizes them all, and we now examine them in detail.

Term Insurance and Its Features

As we mentioned, term life insurance is pure life insurance that pays the beneficiary the death benefit of the policy if the insured dies during the coverage period. In effect, term insurance has no face value. Its sole purpose is to provide death benefits to the policyholder's beneficiaries.

The primary advantage of term insurance is its affordability. It's an inexpensive way of protecting your loved ones. The big disadvantage with term insurance is that the cost rises each time your policy is renewed. To counter that complaint, the insurance industry has recently begun to offer 30-year level-term policies. For example, in 2017, a 25-year-old nonsmoking male could lock in an annual rate of about $500 for a policy with a $500,000 death benefit for 30 years from Genworth Financial.

TABLE 9.3 What's What in Life Insurance

Type of Policy	Coverage Period	Annual Premium	Death Benefit	Cash Value
Term Life Insurance	Provides protection for a specified time period—typically, 1 to 30 years.	Least expensive form of life insurance. Low initial premium, with the premium increasing as the insured gets older.	Fixed death benefit.	No cash value.
Whole Life Insurance	Provides permanent protection.	The premium is fixed.	Fixed death benefit.	The cash value is fixed. The investment portion of the policy grows on a tax-deferred basis while the policy is in force.
Universal Life Insurance	Provides permanent protection.	Allows for flexible premium payments so that policyholders can vary the amount and timing of their payments as their financial needs change.	Death benefits are flexible, although proof of insurability may be required if you want to raise them.	The cash value of the policy depends on the level of payments made and the investment results of the insurance company. The investment portion of the policy grows on a tax-deferred basis while the policy is in force.
Variable Life Insurance	Provides permanent protection.	Allows for either fixed or flexible premium.	Death benefits are flexible, reflecting the performance of the mutual funds (subaccounts) in the death benefits account.	The cash value of the policy depends on the performance of the mutual funds (subaccounts) in the cash value account. The policyholder controls the investment risk, choosing the investment strategy for the policy.

FIGURE 9.1 The Rising Cost of Yearly Renewable Term Insurance—Annual Premiums for $100,000 Coverage on a 35-Year-Old Nonsmoking Male

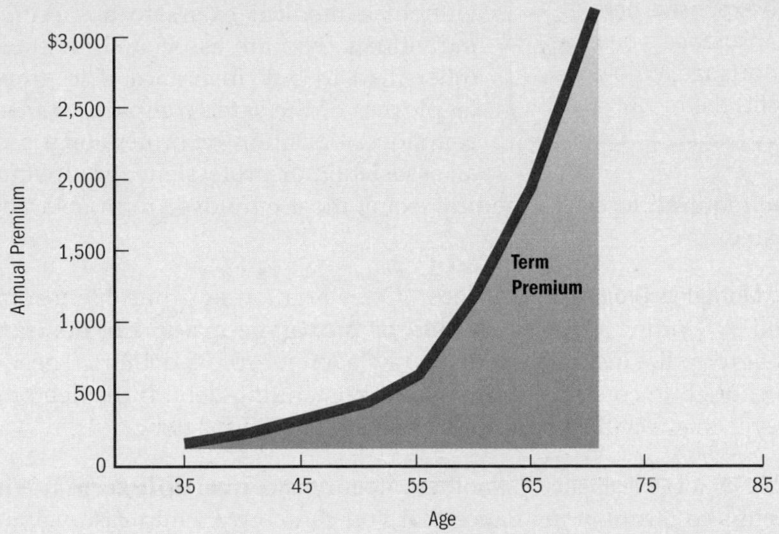

Renewable Term Insurance The "term" of the term life insurance contract can be 1, 5, 10, 20, or 30 years. Coverage terminates at the end of this period unless it's renewed. In general, most term insurance is **renewable term insurance**, which allows it to be continually renewed for an agreed-upon period or up to a specified age, often up to 65, 70, or 75 (and in some cases up to 94), regardless of the insured's health. Even if your health declines after you buy the policy, you're still able to renew your coverage.

Renewable Term Insurance
A type of term insurance that can be renewed for an agreed-on period or up to a specified age (usually 65 or 70), regardless of the insured's health.

The ability to renew term insurance is critical. After all, if you're basing your family's security on a life insurance policy that you suddenly can't renew, you've got a big problem. You shouldn't consider taking on term insurance that isn't renewable. Each time your contract is renewed, the premium is increased to reflect your increased age and the accompanying increase in the chance of mortality. Without proof of insurability (taking and passing another medical exam), most premiums increase dramatically at the end of the term period. Once an individual reaches the age of 55, the premiums increase rather rapidly, as can be seen in Figure 9.1.

Decreasing Term Insurance Each time renewable term insurance is renewed, the premium increases. With **decreasing term insurance**, the premiums remain constant, but the face amount of the policy declines. If you purchase decreasing term insurance, you decide on a premium level, and the face amount—the amount of the death benefit to be paid—declines each year to reflect the increased probability that you'll die during the term of the policy.

Decreasing Term Insurance
Term insurance in which the annual premium remains constant but the face amount of the policy declines each year.

Decreasing term insurance is based on the assumption that your wealth will increase when your children leave home and become self-sufficient and, thus, you will need less insurance. However, just because some individuals' insurance needs decline as they get older doesn't mean yours will. In addition, not all declining term insurance policies decline the same way. Some decline at a constant, steady rate, and others decline at accelerating rates. What's important here is that you choose a policy that's going to cover your future needs completely.

STOP & THINK

If you have a very low interest rate on your home mortgage, you may want your insurance proceeds to go toward paying off some other, more expensive debt. However, with mortgage group life insurance, you have no choice—it goes to pay off your mortgage. Who do you think mortgage insurance benefits the most?

Group Term Insurance This type of insurance refers to the way the insurance is sold rather than to any unusual traits of the policy itself. **Group term insurance** is term insurance provided, usually without a medical exam, to a specific group of individuals who are associated for some purpose other than to buy insurance. The group may be employees of the same company or members of a common association or professional group. If it's an association or professional group, the members might be required to take a medical exam; most employee term insurance doesn't require an exam.

Group Term Insurance
Term insurance provided, usually without a medical exam, to a specific group of individuals, such as company employees, who are associated for some purpose other than to buy insurance.

Credit or Mortgage Group Life Insurance
Group life insurance that's provided by a lender for its debtors.

Convertible Term Life Insurance
Term life insurance that can be converted into cash-value life insurance at the insured's discretion, regardless of his or her medical condition and without a medical exam.

Credit or Mortgage Group Life Insurance One variation of group life insurance that's promoted by lending agencies is **credit or mortgage group life insurance**, which is simply group life insurance provided by a lender for its debtors. The level of coverage is enough to cover the individual's outstanding debt. If the debtor dies while the policy is in effect, the proceeds are used to pay off the debt.

Convertible Term Life Insurance Another category is **convertible term life insurance**, which refers to term life insurance that you can convert into cash-value life insurance (we'll look at this in detail next) at your discretion, regardless of your medical condition and without a medical exam. Many times this conversion feature is offered only during the first years of the policy. The conversion may be accompanied by a corresponding increase in the premium.

Cash-Value Insurance and Its Features

Cash-value insurance is any insurance policy that provides both a death benefit and an opportunity to accumulate cash value. It's a permanent type of insurance—if you make the premium payments, eventually you'll get paid. At some point, you'll have made all the required premium payments (which in the extreme case could last until you're 100), and your cash-value insurance will be completely paid up.

Not all cash-value insurance is the same. In fact, there are many different types. However, there are three *basic* types of cash-value insurance: whole life, universal life, and variable life insurance.

Whole Life Insurance
Cash-value insurance that provides permanent coverage and a death benefit when the insured dies. If the insured turns 100, the policy pays off, even though the insured hasn't died.

Whole Life Insurance and Its Features With **whole life insurance**, a death benefit is provided when the insured dies, turns 100, or reaches the maximum stated age. The face value of the policy will eventually be paid, provided the premiums have been paid. Another distinguishing feature of whole life insurance is that the premiums are known in advance and in many cases are fixed. Although premiums on term insurance tend to be small during your younger years and dizzyingly high during your later years, whole life insurance premiums, because they are constant over your life, fall somewhere in between. Over all, the payments are higher than they are for term insurance because the insurance company is guaranteed to eventually make a payout on the policy.

In the early years of the whole life policy, the insurance company deducts amounts for the commission, sales and administrative expenses, cost of death protection, and some profit from the premiums. What's left of the premiums goes into a savings account and is called the **cash value**. This buildup continues over the initial years of the policy, eventually resulting in a large cash value.

Cash Value
The money that the policyholder is entitled to if the policy is terminated.

As time goes by and you age, the premium, which remains constant, is no longer large enough to cover the death claim. Thus, in the later years the cash value is used to supplement the level premiums and provide the desired level of death coverage.

The cash value of the insurance policy is really your savings. You can borrow against the policy's cash value, or alternatively, you can gain access to the cash value by terminating the policy. Access is gained by exercising your nonforfeiture right. The **nonforfeiture right** gives you the policy's cash value, and in exchange, you give up your right to a death benefit.

Nonforfeiture Right
The right of a policyholder to choose to receive the policy's cash value; in exchange, the policyholder gives up his or her right to a death benefit.

If you don't want cash but instead want insurance, you can use the cash value to purchase paid-up insurance—that is, insurance that doesn't have any additional payments due—or to buy extended term insurance. Many people see the nonforfeiture right as a major advantage to whole life—at least you get something back when you terminate the policy.

There are a number of different premium payment patterns available to whole life policyholders. *Continuous-, level-,* or *straight-premium whole life* requires the policyholder to pay a constant premium until the insured turns 100 or dies. With a *single-premium* or *single-payment whole life* policy, the policyholder makes only one very large initial payment. A hybrid of these two patterns is the *limited-premium whole life* policy, in which large premiums are required for a specified number of years, after which the policy is considered paid up.

FACTS OF LIFE

Every year Taiwan has a Ghost Month, where tradition states that ghosts return to roam the earth—for the believers, this is pretty scary stuff. To ease people's minds, the Taiwan Central Insurance Company sells Ghost Month supplemental insurance that covers only that month. This insurance covers accidents on public transportation, fires, and earthquakes, whether or not the damage was caused by ghosts.

For example, you may pay until you are 65, after which time the policy is paid up. As with all whole life insurance, it then provides insurance protection for your entire life or until you terminate the policy and claim the cash value. The size of the premiums depends, of course, on the number of premiums to be paid and your age. The popularity of the limited-payment plan stems from the fact that the payments will cease when retirement approaches, and at that point, the policy has built up a significant cash value.

As with all else in the life insurance area, there are an almost unlimited number of variations on the whole life theme. One such variation worth noting is *modified whole life*. The premiums begin at a level below comparable whole life policies and gradually rise in steps until the final premiums are above those of comparable whole life policies. There are also *combination whole life* policies, which include elements of whole life and decreasing term insurance. While the face amount of the policy remains constant, the coverage gradually shifts from term to whole life.

What are the primary disadvantages of whole life insurance? First, it doesn't provide nearly the level of death protection that term insurance does for the same price. Second, the yield on the cash value investment portion of the policy generally isn't competitive with yields on alternative investments.

However, whole life insurance does provide for both savings and permanent insurance needs. If you have a need for permanent insurance protection—perhaps you have a child or spouse who'll never be financially independent and for whom you must provide—then you should seriously consider whole life insurance.

Universal Life Insurance and Its Features A **universal life insurance** policy is a type of cash-value insurance combining term insurance with a tax-deferred savings feature in a package in which both the premiums and the benefits are flexible. Premiums can vary between the insurance company's minimum and maximum premium levels as set by the IRS.

Universal Life Insurance
A type of cash-value insurance that's much more flexible than whole life. It allows the policyholder to vary the premium payments and the level of protection.

You start out by paying a premium dictated by the insurance company. After the company subtracts expenses and mortality charges to pay for the life insurance protection, the remainder of the premium plus interest is added to the cash value. You can then increase or decrease premium payments, which will increase or decrease the cash value of the policy. You can also increase or decrease the death benefit.

FIGURE 9.2 Determining the Cash Value on a Universal Life Insurance Policy

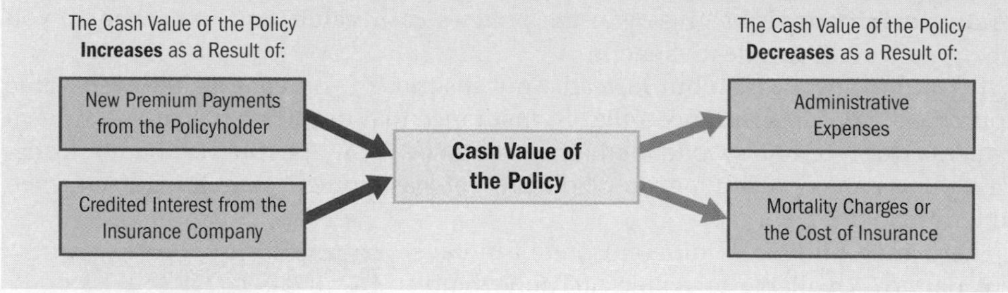

In effect, a universal life policy is much like a term insurance policy, with any additional premium going toward savings.

An important feature of universal life insurance is that the funds are broken down into three separate parts: the mortality charge or term insurance, the cash value or savings, and the administrative expenses. This unbundling is what gives you the flexibility to vary the premium payments. If you skip a payment or don't make one large enough to cover your mortality charge and the administrative expenses, the rest will simply be subtracted from the cash value. If the cash value isn't enough to cover the premium, the policy will lapse!

Although there are limits, if you make a huge payment, the amount greater than that needed to cover the mortality charge and the administrative expenses is credited to your cash value or savings. The relationship that determines the cash value is shown in Figure 9.2.

One of the shortcomings of universal life is that the returns fluctuate dramatically. Moreover, for many policyholders the flexibility to pass on making premium payments is just too tempting, and as a result, many policies simply lapse. Finally, given fluctuating returns and high expense charges, you may not end up with as much in the way of savings as you had anticipated.

The value of universal life is its flexibility. If you have uneven and fluctuating income and need to be able to skip premium payments, this form of insurance might appeal to you. Still, universal life should be approached with caution. Insurance policies should be purchased mainly for their insurance protection. With universal life, the insurance and administrative portions of the policy are very expensive.

Variable Life Insurance
Insurance that provides permanent insurance coverage as whole life does; however, the policyholder, rather than the insurance company, takes on the investment risk.

Variable Life Insurance and Its Features Another category is **variable life insurance**, which is aimed at individuals who want to manage their own investments and are willing to take risks. It's a type of whole life in which the cash value and death benefit are tied to and vary according to the performance of a set of investments chosen by the policyholder. The policyholder, rather than the insurance company, takes on the investment risk—that is, you decide how the cash value or savings portion of your policy is invested. If it does well, you benefit; if it bombs, you lose.

There are two basic forms of variable life: (1) straight variable life, which has fixed premiums, and (2) variable universal life, which has flexible premiums. The array of investment funds from which you choose is quite large, including money market, bond, and stock funds. The returns are

STOP & THINK

Seeing a computer printout that shows with precision exactly what your cash-value life insurance policy will be worth in the future is impressive, but it may be meaningless. As with any other financial analysis, the results are all based on assumptions—if it's "garbage in," it's also "garbage out." Why do you think a salesperson might want to assume very high, unrealistic returns in the future?

earned on a tax-deferred basis just as they are on other cash-value insurance forms. In fact, you can switch between different types of investment funds without suffering any tax consequences.

The cash value of a variable life insurance policy results from fixed premiums minus company expenses and the mortality charges (the cost of the term insurance). There is no guarantee of a minimum cash value, and what happens to the cash value doesn't affect the insurance company. In effect, variable life is similar to buying term insurance and investing money in mutual funds.

Term Versus Cash-Value Life Insurance

With all these different types of insurance, it can be pretty hard to compare policies and figure out what you need. You could spend way too many of your waking hours—and even some of your sleeping hours if you're a vivid dreamer—trying to figure out what's best for you. We suggest starting off slowly. The basic question you need to ask yourself is whether you want term insurance or cash-value insurance.

For most individuals, term insurance is the better alternative. It provides for your life insurance needs at a relatively low cost, which is the real purpose of insurance. It allows for affordable coverage during the years in which you need life insurance most.

With cash-value insurance, the premiums are so high that you may be tempted to carry less insurance than you actually need. The only true advantages of cash-value insurance are tax advantages—the growth of the cash value on a deferred tax basis and the fact that life insurance isn't considered part of your estate. However, these advantages generally don't make cash-value insurance a good investment in a relative sense—other tax-deferred investment plans are better.

Fine-Tuning Your Policy: Contract Clauses, Riders, and Settlement or Payout Options

It's important to know that in the world of insurance there is really no "standard policy." In fact, there are actually hundreds of provisions that you can use to individualize your policy. Be sure that you carefully read this legal document before you sign on the dotted line. We will introduce some common features that appear in almost all insurance contracts.

Contract Clauses Contract clauses are the particular provisions or stipulations that appear in your insurance policy.

Coverage Grace Period
The late-payment period for premiums during which time the policy stays in effect and no interest is charged. If payments still aren't made, the policy can be cancelled after the grace period.

Beneficiary Provision The primary beneficiary is the person designated to receive the death benefits when you die. This beneficiary can be a person, a business, or a trust. You will also name one or more contingent beneficiaries, who will receive the death benefits only if the primary beneficiary dies before the benefits have been distributed.

Coverage Grace Period The **coverage grace period** gives you an extension of generally 30 days in which to make your premium payments without cancelling your policy. During this period, the policy remains in force, and you can make payments without penalty.

FACTS OF LIFE

You can insure specific body parts. Keith Richards, the Rolling Stones guitarist, has insured his hands.

Loan Clause
A clause that provides the right to borrow against the cash value of the policy at a guaranteed interest rate.

Loan Clause Cash-value policies include a **loan clause**, which allows you to borrow against the cash value of the policy. The rate is usually quite favorable, there are no fees or carrying charges, and there is no maturity date on the policy loan. However, if you die with an outstanding policy loan, the death benefit will be reduced by the outstanding amount due. This would probably be contrary to your goals, and there might also be tax penalties associated with policy withdrawals.

Nonforfeiture Clause The nonforfeiture clause defines the choices available to policyholders who miss premium payments, causing the policy to lapse. It protects the cash value of the policy. Options generally include receiving the policy's cash value, exchanging the policy's cash value for a paid-up policy with a reduced face value, and exchanging the policy's face value for a paid-up term policy. While no one should plan on letting a policy lapse, this clause can be very valuable if you should ever "just forget" or be unable to pay your premiums for an extended period.

Policy Reinstatement Clause
A clause that provides the right to restore a policy that has lapsed after the grace period has expired. Generally, reinstatement is provided for within a specified period (usually 3 to 5 years after the policy has expired).

Change of Policy Clause
A clause that gives the policyholder the right to change the form of the policy—for example, from a continuous-premium whole life policy to a limited-premium whole life policy.

Policy Reinstatement Clause The **policy reinstatement clause** deals with the conditions necessary to restore a lapsed policy to its full force and effect, generally within 3 to 5 years after the policy has expired. You must pay all past-due premiums, interest, and policy loans.

Change of Policy Clause The **change of policy clause** allows you to change the form of your policy. For example, you may want to convert your continuous-premium whole life policy to a limited-premium whole life policy so that your premium payments will cease. You might have to pass a physical examination first.

Suicide Clause Virtually all insurance contracts include a suicide clause, which states that the insurance company won't pay off for suicide deaths that occur within the first 2 years of the contract.

Payment Premium Clause This clause defines how you will pay your premiums. Options include annual, semiannual, quarterly, and monthly payments. Annual payments are generally the cheapest.

Incontestability Clause The incontestability clause states that the insurance company cannot dispute the validity of the contract after a specified period of time, usually 2 years. This clause is crucial. It protects your beneficiary against policy cancellations due to error, concealment, or innocent misstatement made by the insured on the original application.

Rider
A special provision that may be added to a policy that either provides extra benefits to the beneficiary or limits the company's liability under certain conditions.

Riders **Riders** are special provisions that may be added to your policy, often at an additional cost, to provide extra benefits or features to a policy in order to meet your specific needs.

Waiver of Premium for Disability Rider This type of rider allows your insurance protection to stay in place by paying your premium if you become disabled before you reach a certain age, usually 65. Because your need for insurance certainly doesn't diminish if you become disabled, this is a pretty good rider to have if it doesn't cost too much. Shop around—you might be able to cover your insurance expenses with a personal disability insurance plan for less.

Accidental Death Benefit Rider or Multiple Indemnity An accidental death benefit rider increases the death benefit—doubling it in the case of "double indemnity" or tripling it in "triple indemnity"—if you die in an accident rather than from natural causes. It is usually an inexpensive rider because of the slim chance that the insurance company will ever have to pay it off.

Guaranteed Insurability Rider A guaranteed insurability rider gives you the right to increase your life insurance protection in the future without a medical exam, regardless of your health. It allows you to purchase additional coverage at specified times, such as after the birth of a child, when you buy a house, or when you increase your business. It is insurance against future uninsurability and is a relatively inexpensive way to ensure that you can get the additional coverage that you might need.

Cost-of-Living Adjustment (COLA) Rider This rider increases your death benefits at the same rate as inflation without forcing you to pass a new medical exam, allowing you to keep up with expected increases in the cost of living.

Living Benefits Rider Some cash-value policies allow for "living benefits" that grant an early payout of a percentage of the anticipated death benefits to the terminally ill insured. It usually requires a doctor's statement saying that you have 6 months to a year to live. These payments are made to the policyholder, not the beneficiary. This rider can often be added to a policy at any time, generally with no extra fee, and can offer peace of mind at a critical time by helping to offset medical costs.

Settlement or Payout Options **Settlement or payout options** are alternative ways a beneficiary can choose to receive the policy benefits upon the death of the insured. It is important to keep in mind any possible tax implications regarding payout. In general, life insurance death benefits are not subject to income taxes.

Settlement or Payout Options
The alternative ways that a beneficiary can choose to receive the policy benefits upon the death of the insured.

Lump-Sum Settlement A lump-sum settlement pays the entire death benefit, tax free, to the beneficiary at one time. It allows the beneficiary to withdraw, use, and/or invest the funds in any way that he or she wishes.

Interest-Only Settlement With an interest-only settlement, instead of receiving the death benefit immediately, it is left on deposit with the insurance company for a specified length of time earning interest that is tied to the market interest rate, with a guaranteed minimum rate.

STOP & THINK

Why do you think medical bills are squeezing more families? While there are a number of reasons, part of the problem is that we all live longer than we did in the past. The life expectancy for a woman born in 1900 was 49; however, for a woman born in 2000, the life expectancy was 80. Medical costs rise as you live longer.

Installment-Payments Settlement The cash value, including both interest and principal, is completely distributed over a fixed period or in fixed payments. When proceeds are taken in installments, the portion of each payment attributable to the basic death benefit is tax free, but the portion attributable to interest earned on the proceeds is taxable. If you choose the fixed-period option, the size of the policy settlement, the number of payment periods, and the interest rate work together to determine the size of the payments.

Instead of choosing a fixed period for the distribution of the settlement, you can actually choose the specific amount of the fixed payments. In this case, the size of the policy settlement, the interest rate credited to the policy settlement, and the desired size of the payments work together to determine the number of periods over which payments will be received.

Calculator Clues

MyLab Finance Video

Calculating an Installment Payment Settlement

You can calculate how much each payment will be, or if you have a certain amount you'd like your beneficiary to receive each year, you can determine the number of payments he or she will get.

(continued)

Calculating the payment size is simply a matter of solving for the payment size (*PMT*), where *PV* is the policy settlement, *I/Y* is the interest rate credited to the policy settlement, and *N* is the number of periods over which the payments are to be made. Let's assume you want your beneficiary to receive annual payments for 20 years, the policy settlement is for $500,000, and the interest credited to the policy settlement is 8 percent. What is the payment's size?

Enter	20	8	500,000		0
	N	I/Y	PV	PMT	FV
Solve for				−50,926.10	

As expected, *PMT* takes on a negative sign, and your beneficiary will receive annual payments of $50,926.10.

To solve for the number of payments, let's now assume you'd like the annual payments to be $75,000. How many annual payments would your beneficiary receive?

Enter		8	−500,000	75,000	0
	N	I/Y	PV	PMT	FV
Solve for	9.9				

You'll notice that we gave the present value, $500,000, a negative sign and the payment, $75,000, a positive sign. Why? Because a calculator looks at cash flows like it's a bank—we deposit our money in the bank (and the sign is negative because the money "leaves our hands"), and later we take our money out of the bank (and the sign is positive because the money "returns to our hands"). As a result, every problem will have positive and negative signs on the cash flows.

Life Annuity Settlement With a life annuity, the beneficiary receives income for life. As you might expect, there are a number of ways this can be paid out, including a straight life annuity that provides the beneficiary a monthly benefit, regardless of how long he or she lives; a certain period annuity that guarantees payments for a certain number of years, with the payments going to a secondary beneficiary if the primary beneficiary dies during that period; a refund annuity that provides the beneficiary with income for life, as well as providing a secondary beneficiary with a death benefit if the primary beneficiary dies; and a joint life and survivorship annuity that provides fixed monthly payments as long as one of two named beneficiaries remains alive.

Buying Life Insurance

Not all insurance *companies* are the same. When you put money in a bank, the government guarantees your account through the Federal Deposit Insurance Corporation. There are no guarantees with life insurance. Although each state has a guarantee association to protect policyholders if an insurance company goes out of business, generally these state funds have no assets. If an insurance company goes under, the other insurance companies doing business in that state are "taxed," and the funds are used to take care of any claims.[1] As you can imagine, delays and confusion are common.

[1] In addition, most states impose a limit on the amount of coverage they'll honor. These limits are generally $100,000 for the cash value and $300,000 for the death benefit of an individual life policy or $300,000 for all claims combined for an individual or family. These limits may be well below your desired coverage level.

It's essential to choose an efficiently run life insurance company that will be around when your policy matures. Fortunately, the selection process is made much easier by a number of insurance rating services, including A. M. Best, Fitch, Moody's, Standard & Poor's, and Weiss, which all rate the ability of insurance companies to pay off claims. Because you'll be charged a small fee for rating information if you call one of the rating agencies, the simplest way to get ratings is to go to your local library.

Selecting an Agent

As you know from **Principle 1: The Best Protection Is Knowledge**, before you deal with an insurance agent, you should know a bit about how insurance sales work. First, keep in mind that most insurance agents make their living through commissions, so they're understandably eager to make a sale. Don't feel obligated to purchase your policy from an agent just because he or she did some research and put together a plan for you—that's the agent's job.

PRINCIPLE 1

Because it's difficult to know all you might like to know about insurance, selecting your agent is extremely important. So how do you find a good agent? Well, it helps to be aware of the agent's professional designation. Is the agent simply licensed to sell insurance, or is he or she a chartered life underwriter (CLU), the most rigorous of all life insurance designations? To obtain this title, a life insurance salesperson must master technical information on insurance and also show mastery in the related areas of finance, accounting, taxation, business law, and economics.

STOP & THINK

It's not unusual for cash-value life insurance policies to have commissions of 80 to 100 percent of the first year's premium. The only way you can find out is to ask. Because this information may help you determine why one policy is being pushed instead of another, the size of the commission is good information to know. Why don't people ask?

To begin the agent search process, make a list of prospects from good companies. This list can come from friends, colleagues, and relatives in addition to recommendations from bankers, accountants, and lawyers who specialize in personal financial planning. Next, interview the agents to find out which ones you feel comfortable with and whether they're full-time insurance agents with some degree of experience. Once you've selected several agents you feel comfortable with, have them give you a quote on your desired insurance plan.

Comparing Costs

Now it's time to compare the costs of the competing policies. There are several comparison methods you can use, the most common of which are the traditional net cost method and the interest-adjusted net cost method, or surrender cost index.

The **traditional net cost (TNC) method** is calculated by summing the premiums over a stated period (usually 10 or 20 years) and subtracting from this the sum of all dividends over that same period. The policy's cash value at the end of the stated period is then subtracted from this amount. The final result is divided by the number of years in the stated period and presented as total net cost per some level of coverage.

Traditional Net Cost (TNC) Method
A method of comparing insurance costs that sums the premiums over a stated period (usually 10 or 20 years) and subtracts from this the sum of all dividends over that same period.

What's important here isn't what's included in the calculations but what's excluded. The traditional net cost method doesn't take into consideration the time value of money. As a result, it's virtually meaningless. If an agent presents it to you as a reasonable means of analyzing the costs of a policy, you might want to consider another insurance agent.

A more widely accepted means of comparing similar but competing policies is the **interest-adjusted net cost (IANC) method**, which is also called the **surrender cost index**. Although this method has its own shortcomings, it does incorporate the time value of money into its calculations and has gained a good deal of acceptance in the insurance industry.

Interest-Adjusted Net Cost (IANC) Method or Surrender Cost Index
A method of comparing insurance costs that incorporates the time value of money into its calculations.

This method is just like the TNC method except that it recognizes the time value of money. However, this method depends on the choice of the appropriate discount rate and the estimate of the dividends and cash value from the policy. The agent's estimates may be high and not realistic. To be safe, take the results of every comparative analysis method with a hefty grain of salt. Note, though, that there are almost as many methods for comparing insurance costs as there are different types of policies, and they all involve making assumptions.

FACTS OF LIFE

You can pay for life insurance annually rather than monthly. For example, according to AccuQuote, a healthy 35-year-old man can get a $250,000, 20-year term policy for just $14.44 per month. The same policy costs $165 if premiums are paid annually versus $173 when you add up the monthly premiums.

Making a Purchase

Once you've decided whether you need life insurance or not and, if so, how much is right for you, the decision becomes term versus cash-value insurance. If you decide on term insurance, consider shopping on the Web. There you can find instant quotes and excellent rates. This is because you can receive instant quotes from over 300 companies, and with that many alternatives, you'll end up with a great rate.

Where do you find this help on the Web? Several instant quote services compile databases of life insurance quotes and provide you with the costs and the companies offering the lowest-cost policies that fit your needs. QuoteSmith has a continually updated database that contains 375 insurance companies. All you have to do is enter some basic information and you'll get a quote.

Does it pay to shop around? You bet it does! Insurance rates vary dramatically from one company to another. In fact, the annual premiums found on the Internet for a 20-year term policy for $500,000 for a 25-year-old male with preferred rates varied from a low of $260 to a high of $1,465. Take a look at these Web quote services:

Insure.com	**http://www.insure.com**
AccuQuote	**http://www.accuquote.com**

Once you decide on a policy, the insurance company will, at its expense, send a nurse or technician to your house to give you a basic physical: He or she will ask questions on your medical history, take blood, and give you an EKG. It's just that simple. To make sure you've gotten the best deal, check at least two of the Web quote services, and give an independent insurance agent a call.

If you've decided on cash-value insurance, things get a bit more complicated. That's because it's almost impossible to compare different policies, all with different features and different assumptions. Still, you can go to the Web to get quotes on different policies.

LO4 Design a health-care insurance program and understand what provisions are important to you.

Health Insurance

Now let's turn our attention to health insurance. Earlier we mentioned the Patient Protection and Affordable Care Act, also referred to as ObamaCare, which was signed into law in 2010—it represents a major shift in health care in America. The purpose of this legislation is to ensure that almost everyone has health insurance. However, it doesn't replace the old system—just as before, there will be health-care options, your insurance will still come from a private insurance company, and that insurance company will still reimburse your doctors for your care.

There are plenty of health-care options available, but most people rely on their employer for health insurance coverage, which is an employee benefit for many workers. If your employer provides you with health insurance benefits, your choices are limited to what it offers. And employer-sponsored health-care coverage usually isn't free. Employees often have to pay for co-payments associated with visits to the doctor, prescriptions, and monthly premiums. In effect, you pay a portion of the premium, and your employer pays the rest. Some employers offer you a variety of choices, but usually if you want additional or better coverage, you will have to make additional payments. Each year you are generally given an opportunity to switch between the different types of coverage that are offered.

If you're not getting insurance through your employer, you can obtain a plan through a health insurance exchange. The exchanges are modeled on the federal employee health program that is available to members of Congress and contain a range of private plans to choose from.

If you're not getting insurance through your employer, you have more options. We live in a world of choices, so, of course, there are several different types of health insurance coverage available. Hey, if you've got 31 choices when buying such a thing as ice cream, you should at least have a few choices when it comes to buying something as important as health insurance. As with buying ice cream, though, it's easy to get carried away with health insurance and want everything you can get. Even though you can obtain insurance to cover just about everything down to a common sneeze (bless you), the purpose of health insurance isn't to cover all the costs of health care—it's to prevent financial ruin. Remember **Principle 5: Stuff Happens, or the Importance of Liquidity**. You're going to have to pay a doctor's bill every now and again, and you'll need to spring for that bottle of Tylenol when you get a headache. Of course, if you've got chronic headaches and go through a bottle of Tylenol every day, you're going to want someone to pick up that cost. Everyone's needs are different, and the key to selecting insurance is to choose only the types of coverage you need. PRINCIPLE 5

2010 Health-Care Reform—Patient Protection and Affordable Care Act

Before we jump in and look at all the different forms of health-care insurance, let's take a look at the health-care reform bill that President Obama signed into law in March 2010, which is commonly called the Affordable Care Act. Again, as you may know, the Affordable Care Act has become a political lighting rod and, as a result, may be modified or repealed and replaced over time. However, if and when any legislative changes to the health care occur, updates, including the personal finance implications, will be provided on the companion website (**http://pearsonhighered.com/keown**).

However, even though the Affordable Care Act makes major changes in health care, your interaction with the U.S. medical system will remain more or less the same—you purchase a policy from a private insurance company, and it reimburses your doctors for care. In addition, while there was much talk of a public health insurance option, there isn't one; instead, you still deal with one of many private insurance companies. In effect, this bill tinkers with the way the current system works rather than scrapping it and replacing it with a new one.

Still, it does some important things that may affect you. Here are a few examples: It prohibits insurance companies from denying coverage to those with preexisting health conditions, allows children to stay on their parents' insurance policy until they turn 26, sets up insurance exchanges to purchase insurance and provides tax credits for insurance purchases to small businesses and to the poor and middle class, and prohibits insurance companies from dropping people who get sick and from setting annual and lifetime limits on what these companies will pay. In addition, for seniors, it works at closing the gap in Medicare prescription drug coverage, known as the "donut hole."

TABLE 9.4 Major Provisions of the Affordable Care Act

Providing New Consumer Protections
• Prohibits insurance companies from denying coverage to children under the age of 19 due to a preexisting condition • Prohibits insurance companies from rescinding coverage due to an error or other technical mistake on a customer's application • Eliminates lifetime dollar limits on essential benefits • Prohibits insurance companies from refusing to sell coverage or renew policies because of an individual's preexisting conditions • Prohibits new plans and existing group plans from imposing annual dollar limits on the amount of coverage an individual may receive • Prohibits dropping or limiting coverage because an individual chooses to participate in a clinical trial
Improving Quality and Lowering Costs
• Provides some small businesses with tax credits to help them provide insurance benefits to their workers • Phases out the Medicare drug "donut hole" coverage gap. • Requires that all new plans cover certain preventive services such as mammograms and colonoscopies without charging a deductible, co-pay, or coinsurance • Provides certain free preventive services, such as annual wellness visits and personalized prevention plans for seniors on Medicare • Provides new funding to state Medicaid programs that choose to cover preventive services for patients at little or no cost • To make coverage affordable, provides tax credits for insurance coverage for people with incomes between 100 percent and 400 percent of the poverty line who are not eligible for other affordable coverage (in 2017, 400 percent of the poverty line was $47,550 for an individual and $97,200 for a family of four), but not everyone qualifies—those eligible for Medicare or other federal insurance don't qualify, nor do those who can get affordable insurance through their work • Establishes health insurance exchanges, so that if your employer doesn't offer insurance, you will be able to buy insurance directly from an exchange where you will be offered a choice of health plans that meet certain benefits and cost standards • Requires most individuals who can afford it to obtain basic health insurance coverage or pay an annual penalty to help offset the costs of caring for uninsured Americans
Increasing Access to Affordable Care
• Ensures children will be allowed to stay on their parents' plan until they turn 26 years old • Increases access to Medicaid by allowing those who earn less than 133 percent of the poverty level to be eligible to enroll in Medicaid • To help fund health care, imposes an excise tax on high-cost employer-provided plans beginning in 2018.
Holding Insurance Companies Accountable
• Requires that at least 85 percent of all premium dollars collected by insurance companies for large employer plans be spent on health-care services and health-care quality improvement

The easiest way to get an understanding this law and its major provisions is to look at the changes it makes as they relate to these different categories. Take a look at Table 9.4, which presents the major provisions in this act.

Basic Health Insurance
A term used to describe most health insurance, which includes a combination of hospital, surgical, and physician expense insurance.

Hospital Insurance
Insurance that covers the costs associated with a hospital stay, including room charges, nursing costs, operating room fees, and drugs supplied by the hospital.

Basic Health Insurance

Most health insurance includes a combination of hospital, surgical, and physician expense insurance sold in a combination called **basic health insurance**. Many policies provide basic health insurance and then allow you to choose from a long list of policy options. Although each additional option provides additional coverage, it also involves an additional premium.

Hospital Insurance **Hospital insurance** is generally part of every insurance plan. It covers the costs associated with a hospital stay, including room charges, nursing costs, operating room fees, and drugs supplied by the hospital. Depending on the policy, hospital insurance may reimburse you for specific charges, give you a set amount of money for each day you are hospitalized, or pay the hospital directly for your expenses.

If you receive a set amount of money per day of hospitalization, you must pay the difference between what is charged and what is paid by the insurance company. Almost all plans, regardless of their type, impose limits on both the daily hospital costs and the number of days covered.

Surgical Insurance **Surgical insurance** covers part or all of the cost of surgery. A surgical policy generally lists the specific operations it covers and either sets a maximum dollar amount for each operation or reimburses the surgeon for what is considered reasonable and customary based on typical charges in that region. You have to pay for any charges above what the policy will cover, and you also might have to pay a deductible. Although surgical insurance may not completely cover surgery charges, it should reduce them to a manageable level.

Surgical Insurance
Insurance that covers the cost of surgery.

Physician Expense Insurance **Physician expense insurance** covers physicians' fees outside of surgery, including office or home visits, lab fees, and x-rays not performed in a hospital.

Physician Expense Insurance
Insurance that covers physicians' fees outside of surgery.

Major Medical Expense Insurance **Major medical expense insurance** is aimed at covering medical costs not covered by basic health insurance. It's meant to offset all the financial effects of a catastrophic illness. Where basic health insurance leaves off, major medical expense insurance takes over.

Major Medical Expense Insurance
Insurance that covers medical costs beyond those covered by basic health insurance.

It generally doesn't provide complete coverage but instead allows for deductibles and coinsurance payments in order to keep costs down. For example, the deductible may require you to pay for the first two office visits beyond what's covered by the basic insurance policy. It may then cover only 80 percent of the costs, leaving you responsible for making up the difference.

FACTS OF LIFE

Twenty-one percent of Americans smoke, and smoking is expensive. The extra lifetime medical cost of smoking is $17,500, and the average hospital bill for lung cancer is $45,500.

Dental and Eye Insurance

As the names imply, dental insurance provides dental coverage, and eye insurance provides coverage for eye examinations, glasses, and contact lenses. Although these are certainly nice to have, don't bother buying them if your employer does not provide them. Dental and eye insurance pay for expenses that are relatively minor and regular—that is, they can be planned for.

Basic Health-Care Choices

There are two basic types of plans available: (1) fee-for-service or traditional indemnity plans and (2) managed health-care or prepaid care plans. Under a **fee-for-service or traditional indemnity plan**, you are reimbursed for all or part of your medical expenditures, and in general, you have a good deal of freedom to choose your doctor and hospital. Under a **managed health-care or prepaid care plan**, most of your expenses are already covered and don't need to be reimbursed, but you're limited to receiving health care from a specified group of participating doctors, hospitals, and clinics.

Fee-for-Service or Traditional Indemnity Plan
An insurance plan that provides reimbursement for all or part of your medical expenditures. In general, it gives you a good deal of freedom to choose your doctor and hospital.

Managed Health-Care or Prepaid Care Plan
An insurance plan that entitles you to the health care provided by a specified group of participating doctors, hospitals, and clinics. These plans are generally offered by health maintenance organizations or variations of them.

Where do we go to get health-care coverage? Well, we basically have two choices: private health care and government-sponsored health care. Let's look at each of these options.

Private Health-Care Plans

There are over 800 private insurance companies whose main business comes from selling health insurance policies to individuals and to employers to be offered as part of a benefits package. These companies offer a variety of traditional fee-for-service and managed health-care plans.

Fee-for-Service or Traditional Indemnity Plans With a fee-for-service plan, the doctor or hospital bills you directly for the cost of services, and the insurance company reimburses you. Although there may be some restrictions on which doctors and hospitals you can use, these plans provide the greatest degree of health provider choice.

Coinsurance or Percentage Participation
An insurance provision that defines the percentage of each claim that the insurance company will pay.

Most fee-for-service plans include a coinsurance provision. A **coinsurance or percentage participation** provision defines the percentage of each claim that the insurance company will pay. For example, if there's 80 percent participation on hospital claims up to $2,000 and 100 percent participation thereafter, then you pay 20 percent of the first $2,000, or $400, of your hospital insurance claim, and the insurance company pays the remainder.

Co-payment or Deductible
The amount of expenses that the insured must pay before the insurance company will pay any insurance benefits.

Most fee-for-service plans also include a co-payment or deductible. A **co-payment or deductible** is the amount of your medical expenses that you must pay before the insurance company will reimburse you on a claim. A deductible can be set up in several different ways. For example, there may be a $10 deductible on all prescriptions. You pay the first $10 of the prescription, and the insurance company covers the rest. There might be an overall deductible of $250 or $500 on all health care. In this case, you pay the first $250 or $500 of any medical care costs you might have, and the insurance company then covers any additional costs.

Overall, fee-for-service plans are very desirable. The big advantage is complete choice of doctors, hospitals, and clinics. Unfortunately, these plans are expensive and involve a good deal of paperwork. While many employers still provide fee-for-service plans for their workers, they are dropping in terms of popularity in favor of the less expensive managed health-care plans.

Managed Health-Care Plans Managed health-care plans are offered by health maintenance organizations and allow members access to needed services from specified doctors and hospitals. Managed health-care plans pay for and provide health-care services. For example, under a managed health-care plan, you may receive all your health services at one location. Under some plans, you may not be guaranteed that you'll see the same doctor each time, just that you'll get the health care you need at low or no cost. However, most managed care plans provide you with a primary care physician of your own choosing (for a slight fee).

Just as with the fee-for-service plans, it's quite common for there to be a co-payment of $20 for a doctor visit and a co-payment of $50 for an emergency room visit. There is also generally a co-payment on prescriptions. The purpose of co-payments is to keep insurance costs down. Not only do they serve as a deductible, forcing the patient to pay the first portion of the health-care bill, but also they serve as a disincentive to seek care.

The big advantage of a managed health-care plan is its efficiency. Because it offers you health care directly, there's considerably less in the way of paperwork and its associated costs. Moreover, because most managed health-care plans involve a number of doctors, the entire facility can provide extended office hours, with each individual doctor responsible for staffing the facility for a limited period. In fact, in many managed health-care facilities, doctors working at that facility also carry on a private practice. There are two basic types of managed health care: (1) health maintenance organizations, or HMOs, and (2) preferred provider organizations, or PPOs.

Managed Health Care: HMOs The most popular form of managed health care is the **health maintenance organization (HMO)**, which is a prepaid insurance plan that entitles members to the services of participating doctors, hospitals, and clinics. Members pay a flat fee for this privilege and then can select a managing physician who is responsible for their care. There may be a co-payment required with each visit to the doctor or each prescription filled. There are three basic types of HMOs: (1) individual practice association plans, (2) group practice plans, and (3) point-of-service plans.

Health Maintenance Organization (HMO)
A prepaid insurance plan that entitles members to the services of participating doctors, hospitals, and clinics.

An **individual practice association plan (IPA)** is an HMO made up of independent doctors. You go to the doctor's office and receive your medical treatment there. In fact, many IPA doctors also maintain a private practice. With a **group practice plan**, doctors are generally employed directly by the HMO and work out of a central, shared facility. You can receive your medical treatment only from these doctors and only at these central facilities. A **point-of-service plan** allows you to seek medical treatment from both affiliated and nonaffiliated doctors. Treatment by HMO-affiliated doctors tends to be free or at least covered at a very low co-payment rate. Co-payments for nonaffiliated doctors tend to be much higher.

Individual Practice Association Plan (IPA)
An HMO made up of independent doctors, in which the patient visits the doctors' regular offices to receive medical treatment.

Group Practice Plan
An insurance plan in which doctors are generally employed directly by an HMO and members of the HMO must receive their medical treatment from these doctors at a central facility.

Point-of-Service Plan
An insurance plan that allows its members to seek medical treatment from both HMO-affiliated doctors and non-HMO-affiliated doctors.

Although there are some individual differences, most HMOs have very broad coverage and include doctor, hospital, laboratory, and emergency costs. Prescription costs are often covered, too. Of course, this coverage also requires co-payments.

Most HMOs are associated with an employer's group coverage. That is, the plans are offered through an employer as a part of the employee benefits package. Still, private individuals can join an HMO—and there are plenty to choose from. There are over 600 HMOs operating in the United States. Because each has its own participating doctors and hospitals, each serves a limited geographic area. In order to use health facilities elsewhere, you usually need a referral.

HMOs provide comprehensive health-care services and emphasize preventive medicine because preventing an illness is an awful lot cheaper than curing it. As a result, many HMOs provide regular physical examinations. In contrast, most fee-for-service plans cover only illness-related health-care claims.

Finally, HMOs are efficient, costing as little as 60 percent of what a comparable fee-for-service insurance plan costs. The preventive care, coupled with minimized paperwork and efficient handling of patients, allows for the cost savings. It's no wonder that employers prefer to offer HMO coverage. If HMOs are cheaper for you, they're also cheaper for your employer, who covers a good deal of your insurance premium each month.

There are, of course, some major drawbacks to HMOs. Service can be too quick or cursory, and waits can be long. If you need a service not provided by your HMO, receiving a referral, especially one outside of the HMO's geographic area, can be a hassle. Many members feel that the lack of choice is far too restricting and that having to choose from a small, fixed list of doctors, or not being able to choose at all, means they are not getting the kind of care they want. They do not like that they're unable to establish a personal relationship with a doctor, and they are also concerned that the available doctors might not be the best or most qualified. More questions about the quality of care stem from some of the incentive systems HMOs use. Doctors often receive bonuses based on the number of patients seen or based on the amount of money saved, leading some to wonder if certain doctors don't cut corners to earn bigger bonuses.

If you're choosing an HMO, take a look at Checklist 9.1 for some guidance.

Preferred Provider Organization (PPO)
An insurance plan under which an employer or insurer negotiates with a group of doctors and hospitals to provide health care for its employees or members at reduced rates.

Managed Health Care: PPOs A **preferred provider organization (PPO)** is a bit like a cross between a traditional fee-for-service plan and an HMO. Under a PPO, an employer or insurer negotiates with a group of doctors and hospitals to provide health care for its employees or members at reduced rates. Doctors and hospitals that

CHECKLIST 9.1 Choosing an HMO

Here are some things to consider when choosing an HMO:

- ☐ Are there many doctors to choose from? Do you select from a list of contract physicians or from the available staff of a group practice? Which doctors are accepting new patients? How hard is it to change doctors if you decide you want someone else?
- ☐ How are referrals to specialists handled?
- ☐ Is it easy to get appointments? How far in advance must routine visits be scheduled? What arrangements does the HMO have for handling emergency care?
- ☐ Does the HMO offer the services you want? What preventive services are provided?
- ☐ What is the service area of the HMO? Where are the facilities located in your community that serve HMO members? How convenient to your home and workplace are the doctors, hospitals, and emergency care centers that make up the HMO network? What happens if you or a family member is out of town and needs medical treatment?
- ☐ What will the HMO plan cost? What is the yearly total for monthly fees? In addition, are there co-payments for office visits, emergency care, prescribed drugs, or other services? How much?

Source: U.S. Department of Health and Human Services, Agency for Health Care Policy and Research and the National Council on Patient Information and Education, Rockville, MD, 2014.

FACTS OF LIFE

Thirty-four percent of Americans are obese. They incur $1,429 per year in additional medical costs versus those of normal weight, and the average hospital bill for a heart attack is $54,400.

agree to the pricing system become members of the PPO. In fact, a doctor or hospital can be a member of a number of different PPOs. To encourage use of member doctors, PPOs generally have an additional, or penalty, co-payment requirement for service from nonmembers. The big advantage of the PPO is that it allows for health care at a discount, with the negotiating power of the insurer or employer determining how great a discount is achieved.

Group Health Insurance
Health insurance that's sold, usually without a medical exam, to a specific group of individuals who are associated for some purpose other than to buy insurance.

Individual Insurance Policy
An insurance policy that is tailor-made for you, reflecting your age, health (as determined by an examination), and chosen deductible size.

Group Versus Individual Health Insurance **Group health insurance** refers to the way the health insurance is sold rather than to the characteristics of the insurance policy. This insurance is provided to a specific group of individuals who are associated for some purpose other than to buy insurance. Usually, this group of individuals works for the same employer or belongs to a common association or professional group.

An **individual insurance policy** is health coverage that you personally purchase for yourself or for your family. With the passage of the Affordable Care Act, there is increased standardization of the benefits that health insurance policies provide, but once again, this legislation has become a political lightening rod and may be modified or even repealed and replaced in the future. However, if and when any legislative changes to the Affordable Care Act occur, updates, including the personal finance implications, will be provided on the companion website (**http://pearsonhighered.com/keown**). Two of the major changes that came with the Affordable Care Act are the requirements that essential health benefits be covered and that enrollment be limited to certain periods.[2] The essential health benefits include

- Ambulatory patient services
- Emergency services

[2] There are some limited exceptions to these rules. For example, some grandfathered health plans don't have to offer all the protections, and there are exceptions as to when you can purchase a new plan.

TABLE 9.5 Appealing Health Insurance Claim Decisions

If your health insurer has denied coverage for medical care you received, you have a right to appeal the claim and ask that the company reverse its decision. You must be your own health-care advocate. Here's what you can do:
Step 1: Review your policy and explanation of benefits. **Step 2:** Contact your insurer and keep detailed records of your contacts (copies of letters, times and dates of conversations, names of the persons you speak with). **Step 3:** Request documentation from your doctor or employer to support your case. **Step 4:** Write a formal complaint letter explaining what care was denied and why you are appealing via the company's internal review process. **Step 5:** If the internal appeal is not granted through Step 4, file a claim with your state's insurance department.
For more information, visit **http://nclnet.org** or **http://statehealthfacts.org**.

Source: U.S. General Services Administration, *Consumer Action Handbook*, 2014, http://www.consumeraction.gov/.

- Hospitalization
- Maternity and newborn care
- Mental health and substance abuse disorder services
- Prescription drugs
- Laboratory services
- Preventive and wellness services
- Pediatric services
- Rehabilitative and habilitative services and devices

These individual policies can be purchased either inside or outside the exchanges or marketplaces and either way must cover the same health benefits. The premium level for individual policies is based on your age, where you live, and the level of coverage you want—that is, do you want 90 percent or just 60 percent of your medical expenses covered? In general, coverage can be purchased only during a relatively short period each year. The purpose of this limited open-enrollment period is to prevent *adverse selection*, where people purchase health insurance only after they know they need it. Of course, if Congress acts to repeal the Affordable Care Act, you have to purchase an individual or group policy. An individual policy will reflect your age, health (as determined by an examination), geographic location, and chosen deductible amount. The big advantage of a group policy is cost. Individual policies tend to be more expensive in most, but not all, cases.

And once you file a health insurance claim, don't give up if your claim is initially denied. Table 9.5 provides a step-by-step approach to appealing your claim.

STOP & THINK

What should you do if you don't qualify for group coverage? You might want to consider joining a group that has coverage. Trade groups and alumni, political, and religious organizations are a few groups to check out. What you save in insurance payments will more than make up for what you pay in the group dues. Where do you think you could get group coverage?

Government-Sponsored Health-Care Plans

Government-sponsored plans fall into two categories: (1) state plans, which provide for work-related accidents and illness under state **workers' compensation laws**, and (2) federal plans, such as Medicare and Medicaid.

Workers' Compensation Laws
State laws that provide payment for work-related accidents and illnesses.

Workers' Compensation Workers' compensation laws date from the early 1900s, when our economy changed from predominantly agricultural to industrial. At that time, workers put in long hours in unsafe conditions, and work-related accidents were all too common. Fueled by the public outcry in response to Upton Sinclair's 1906 book *The Jungle*, states passed a series of laws aimed at providing work-related accident and illness insurance to workers.

Because these are state laws, each state determines the benefit level for workers. Some states provide broad coverage, and others exclude some workers. For example, some states exclude those who work for small businesses. Given the variability in coverage from state to state, you should contact your benefits office to see exactly what coverage you have. For workers without enough workers' compensation coverage or for those with no coverage at all, some private insurance companies offer a type of workers' compensation insurance.

Medicare
A government insurance program enacted in 1968 to provide medical benefits to persons with disabilities and those over 65. It is divided into two parts: Part A, which provides hospital insurance benefits, and Part B, which is supplemental medical insurance.

Medicare The **Medicare** program was enacted in 1968 to provide medical benefits to persons with disabilities and to persons 65 and older who qualify for Social Security benefits. It is a good safety net, but it has gaps. The cost of this insurance is covered by Social Security, with the individual patient paying an annual deductible. The Medicare program is way too complicated for us to explain here—but we'll try anyway. For a complete listing of Medicare benefits, take a look at *Medicare and You*, which is available at any Social Security Administration office and downloadable from the Web at **http://www.medicare.gov**. Table 9.6 provides a look at your Medicare coverage choices. As you can see, there are two main ways to get your Medicare coverage—original Medicare and a Medicare Advantage Plan. While your choice is important, it is not final. That's because you have at least one chance each year to make changes to your Medicare coverage.

The easiest way to understand the coverage provided is to look at the different parts:

- **Medicare Part A—Hospital Insurance:** Part A provides basic hospital insurance benefits. Participation in Part A is compulsory and covers most hospital costs, including operating room costs, nursing care, a semiprivate room, and prescription drugs furnished by the hospital. Part A also helps cover a skilled nursing facility, hospice, and home health care if you meet certain conditions. You or your supplemental insurance company pays set dollar amounts or percentages of the cost depending on services used.
- **Medicare Part B—Supplemental Medical Insurance:** Part B of the Medicare plan is voluntary and provides coverage for doctors' fees and a wide range of medical services and supplies. The medically necessary services of a doctor are covered no matter where you receive them—at home, in the doctor's office, in a clinic, in a nursing home, or in a hospital.

  With Part B, there is a monthly premium, which for most people (individuals earning less than \$85,000 and couples earning less than \$170,000) was \$134 in 2017.
- **Medicare Part C—Medicare Advantage Plans:** Medicare Advantage Plans bring more choices to Medicare by offering a variety of private plans with comprehensive care, combining Medicare health coverage with a drug benefit. In addition, some offer benefits not covered by traditional Medicare, such as vision and dental care and more preventive services.
- **Medicare Part D—Medicare Prescription Drug Coverage:** These plans are available through private companies that work with and are approved by Medicare to provide prescription drug coverage and are available for everyone with Medicare. To get Medicare drug coverage, you must join a Medicare drug plan. You pay a separate premium in addition to your Part B premium.

TABLE 9.6 Medicare Coverage Choices

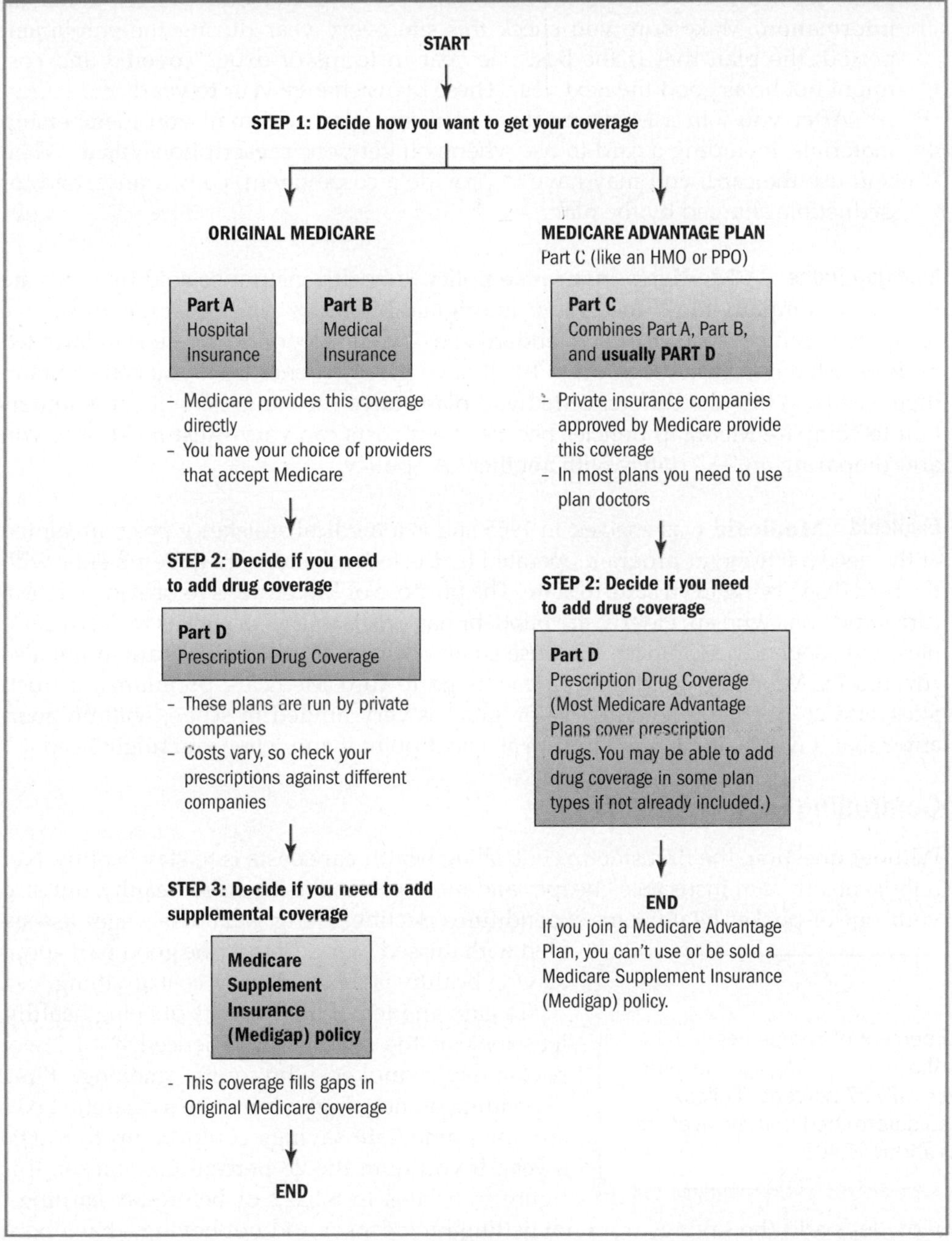

You must enroll in a Medicare drug plan when you are first eligible in order to avoid a late-enrollment penalty. Every year there is a specified time period during which you can switch to a different Medicare drug plan (switch companies) if your plan coverage changes or your specific drug needs change.

Medicare prescription drug plans vary widely in cost and drugs covered. As a result, when you compare plans, you'll want to look closely at

- Coverage—check to see if the plan covers your prescription drugs,
- Cost—check to see how much your prescription drugs cost in each plan, and
- Convenience—make sure the plan's pharmacies include the ones you want to use.

A great Web site is **http://Medicare.gov/part-d/**, which compares available plans according to your specific needs based on your personal prescription drug information. Make sure you check this site every year during the enrollment period; the plan that is the best one year in terms of drugs covered and cost might not be as good the next year. These plans change year to year!

After you join a Medicare drug plan, the plan will mail you membership materials, including a card to use when you get your prescriptions filled. When you use the card, you may have to provide a co-payment, coinsurance, and/or deductible charged by the plan.

Medigap Insurance
Insurance sold by private insurance companies aimed at bridging gaps in Medicare coverage.

Medigap Plans A **Medigap insurance** policy is health insurance sold by a private insurance company to fill the "gaps" in original Medicare plan coverage. Insurance companies can sell you only a "standardized" Medigap policy. These standardized policies (Medigap Plans A through L) all have specific benefits so you can compare them easily. While the different Medigap plans have the same benefits, it is important to compare Medigap policies because their costs can vary—just make sure you are comparing an "A" policy with another "A" policy.

Medicaid
A government medical insurance plan for the needy.

Medicaid **Medicaid** was enacted in 1965 and is a medical assistance program aimed at the needy. It's a joint program operated by the federal and state governments, with the benefits varying from state to state. The purpose of Medicaid is to provide medical care to persons who are elderly, are blind, or have a disability, as well as to needy families with dependent children. Because some of those covered by Medicaid are also covered by Medicare, Medicaid payments go toward Medicare premiums, deductibles, and co-payments. Again, this program is very limited in scope, with no guarantee that it will be in its present form at a later point if and when you might need it.

Controlling Health-Care Costs

Without question, the first step in controlling health-care costs is to stay healthy. Not only is health-care insurance cheaper and more accessible if you're healthy, but also your out-of-pocket health-care expenditures decline, along with lost wages associated with missed work. In fact, the good part about staying healthy is that it doesn't cost anything.

To gain an idea of the benefits of being healthy, let's look at the savings experienced by a "two-pack-a-day" smoker who quits smoking. First, depending on how high your state's cigarette taxes are, the immediate savings could be up to $1,600 a year. If you're in the 28 percent tax bracket, this figure translates to $2,222 of before-tax earnings. Now let's add the savings from not getting lung cancer and not having a baby born with smoking-related illnesses. (Of course, you may have more expenses from living longer than you would if you kept on smoking and died younger.) In addition to staying healthy, you can help control medical costs by using medical reimbursement accounts.

FACTS OF LIFE

A recent study reports that 85 percent of companies with 500 or more employees offer flexible spending accounts for health-care expenses; however, only 27 percent of eligible employees use them. They also determined that the average annual amount contributed is about $1,400.

Flexible Spending Account (FSA)
An employer-sponsored plan that allows each employee to have pretax earnings deposited into a specially designated account for the purpose of paying health-care bills and qualified child care expenses. The employee can withdraw funds from this account to offset unreimbursed medical or dental expenses.

Flexible Spending Accounts A **flexible spending account (FSA)** is a savings plan established by an employer that allows each employee to have pretax earnings deposited into a specially designated account. Employees can withdraw funds from their accounts to pay for unreimbursed medical or dental expenses—for example, co-pays to doctors—or for qualified child care. There's a $2,500 cap set on the maximum an employee can deposit into this account, and employers can allow people to carry up to $500 in their accounts from one year to the next.

An FSA not only provides tax savings on unreimbursed health-care expenditures but also allows pretax dollars to pay for medical expenses that many health-care plans do not cover, such as eyeglasses and orthodontia expenses. In fact, there is a good deal of flexibility with respect to how funds from an FSA can be used.

Health Savings Accounts Health savings accounts (HSAs) are another option to help people pay for medical expenses. Those who may take advantage of HSAs include self-employed persons, small business owners, employees of small to medium-sized businesses that offer only bare-bones health benefits, and persons under age 65 who pay for health care on their own. For 2017, almost anyone *with* a qualified high-deductible health plan (which is a health insurance plan with a minimum deductible of $3,400 if it's self-only coverage or $6,750 if it's family coverage) can also have an HSA. An HSA allows individuals to pay for current health expenses and save for future qualified medical and retiree health expenses on a *tax-free basis*. You can use your HSA funds to pay for expenses before you meet your deductible, as well as for services not covered by your health plan, such as medical expenses after retirement and long-term care expenses. One nice thing about HSAs is that you don't lose HSA funds at the end of the year. Unspent balances remain in your account earning interest until you spend them on medical care.

COBRA and Changing Jobs

Under COBRA, which stands for the Consolidated Omnibus Budget Reconciliation Act, if you work for a company with 20 employees or more, you will be given the opportunity to continue your health insurance coverage for 18 months to 3 years after you leave the company, depending on why you left. To continue your coverage, you must notify your employer of your intent to make payment on your insurance within 60 days of leaving the company.

This law was enacted because individual policies were expensive and often imposed preexisting condition exclusions. However, the Affordable Care Act lessens the importance of COBRA, as it prohibits preexisting condition exclusions and has created state exchanges where coverage to individuals is more affordable. As a result, individuals who lose employer-provided coverage will have the choice of either purchasing their current coverage through COBRA or purchasing new coverage through the exchanges.

What About Choosing Not to Be Insured?

If you can afford health insurance but don't have it, you may have to pay a fee or penalty.[3] And that fee doesn't mean you're covered; you still have to pay for all of your health care. That fee or penalty is sometimes called the "individual responsibility payment" or the "individual mandate." The idea behind it is that when someone without health coverage gets urgent medical care but doesn't pay the bill, everyone else ends up paying the price. The purpose of the fee is to inspire everyone to get health-care coverage.

For 2017, the annual penalty was calculated one of two ways. You had to pay the higher of

- **2.5% of your yearly household income.** The maximum penalty is the national average yearly premium for the Affordable Care Act's bronze plans.
- **$695 per adult and $347.50 per child under 18.** The maximum penalty per family using this method was $2,085.

[3]Some people with limited incomes and a number of other circumstances, including certain hardships and some life events, can get exemptions from the fee.

In future years, the penalty adjusts for inflation. If you're uninsured for just part of the year, 1/12 of the yearly penalty applies to each month you're uninsured. If you're uninsured for less than 3 months, you don't have to make a payment.

FACTS OF LIFE

The most common wellness benefits are smoking cessation classes, health risk assessments, and company gyms. Unfortunately, over 75 percent of workers don't take advantage of these free offers.

What to Look for in a Health Insurance Plan

What should you look for in a health insurance policy? As you might expect, the more you are willing to pay for health insurance, the more coverage you will receive. Let's look at some of the important provisions in health insurance policies.

STOP & THINK

Don't try to save money by buying less health insurance than you actually need—that only defeats the purpose of insurance, which is protection. You should also make sure your policy benefits keep up with inflation and your life circumstances. Review your policy every few years and whenever there's a major change, such as the birth of children, marriage, or divorce. How do you expect your health insurance needs to change in the coming years?

Who's Covered? Health insurance policies can cover individuals, families, or groups. If you have family coverage, you should have an understanding of what happens if you get divorced and whether stepchildren are covered. The point here is that you should understand exactly who's covered under your plan.

Terms of Payment The terms of payment define your financial obligation on a health-care claim, including any deductibles and coinsurance payments.

Deductibles or co-payments identify the amount that you pay on a claim. The higher the deductible, the lower the premium. It's a good idea to take the highest deductible because you get more coverage per dollar that way. The insurance coverage is more efficient, and you accomplish your goal of providing protection against catastrophes.

FACTS OF LIFE

The best insurance is living a healthy, safe life. For young adults, this means driving safely. Auto accidents are the number one killer of teenagers. In fact, across the country teens make up 5 percent of the driving population but account for 14 percent of the country's auto fatalities. Nearly half the deaths of 16- to 19-year-old females occur as a result of automobile accidents. Among boys of the same age, 36 percent of deaths are due to crashes. More than one-quarter of drivers under 21 killed on the roadways have a blood alcohol content of 0.10 or higher. The likelihood of fatal crashes for teenagers is highest between 9 P.M. and 6 A.M.

Exclusions Some policies contain provisions that exclude certain injuries and illnesses. For example, costs associated with certain cosmetic dental procedures and cosmetic surgery are commonly excluded.

Choosing an Insurance Plan

The Health Insurance Marketplace is a new way for you to buy health insurance. To make plans easier to compare, it classifies them in five categories based on how you and the plan can expect to share the costs of care:

- Bronze: Your plan pays 60%. You pay 40%.
- Silver: Your plan pays 70%. You pay 30%.
- Gold: Your plan pays 80%. You pay 20%.
- Platinum: Your plan pays 90%. You pay 10%.
- Catastrophic: Coverage option if you are under 30 or have very low income.

When picking a category and a health insurance plan, there are a number of things you should consider:

- The category you choose affects how much your premium costs each month and what portion of the bill you pay for things like hospital visits or prescription medications, and it also affects your total out-of-pocket costs.
- Plans in all categories offer the same set of 10 essential health benefits, and the categories do not reflect the quality of care the plans provide.
- When choosing your health insurance plan, keep this general rule of thumb in mind: The lower the premium, the higher the out-of-pocket costs when you need care; the higher the premium, the lower the out-of-pocket costs when you need care.
- Think about the health-care needs of your household when considering which marketplace insurance plan to buy. Are you likely to need a lot of care? Or a little?
- Other options like Medicaid and the Children's Health Insurance Program (CHIP) may be available to you. The marketplace also offers catastrophic plans to people under 30 years old and to some people with very low incomes.

Disability Insurance

LO5 Describe disability insurance and the choices available to you.

Disability insurance is related to health insurance, but it's more like earning-power insurance. When a disability occurs, life, along with all its expenses, goes on. What stops is your income. Your house payments continue, your children's educational costs continue, food and utility costs continue, and your medical expenses generally rise—all while your income stops.

Disability Insurance
Health insurance that provides payments to the insured in the event that income is interrupted by illness, sickness, or accident.

Who needs disability insurance? Anyone who relies on income from a job. In fact, for individuals between the ages of 35 and 65, your chance of incurring a disability that would cause you to miss 90 or more days of work is equal to your chance of dying. A 30-year-old has about a 47 percent chance of incurring a 90-day disability before the age of 65. You need disability insurance even if you're single and without dependents. If you have dependents who do rely on your earning power, this insurance is a must. Remember, disability insurance kicks in only if there's a financial catastrophe in the offing. Therefore, it fits in perfectly with our view of necessary insurance.

Given its importance, why are so many people without it? Because of the price. Although that price varies greatly depending on your age, health, and occupation, in addition to the dollar amount of coverage and how long you're disabled before the policy kicks in, it's easy to spend over $1,000 per year on disability insurance.

Your occupation may have the biggest impact on coverage costs. Insurers generally classify customers into one of five risk classes, depending on occupation. A college professor is generally classified as a class 5 risk, and a construction worker is classified as a class 1 risk. These ratings in turn are reflected in the rates charged, with the college professor paying a lower rate than the construction worker because the college professor has a lower probability of becoming disabled.

Sources of Disability Insurance

Many employers provide some level of disability insurance as part of a benefits package. Employers who don't include it in the benefits package may make group disability insurance available at favorable prices. If you're self-employed, you'll have to find a group plan or purchase an individual policy. Most individuals have some degree of coverage from Social Security or workers' compensation.

Although most workers are covered by some form of workers' compensation, these benefits apply only if the disability is work related. The degree of coverage is determined by the individual states, and as a result, there's a good deal of variability from state to state. You shouldn't assume that you're covered or that your coverage is comprehensive.

For those covered by Social Security, disability benefits vary according to the number of years you've been in the Social Security system and your salary. However, if you qualify, your payments won't start until you've been disabled for 5 months, and then you receive benefits only if your disability is expected to last for at least 1 year or until death. Moreover, in order to qualify for benefits, you must not be able to work at any job, not just the job you were trained for.

How Much Disability Coverage Should You Have?

You should have enough disability insurance to maintain your standard of living at an acceptable level if you are no longer able to work. Remember, your investment income won't stop with a disability; it's your income from working that will stop, and it's the portion of your income from working that you rely on to maintain your current standard of living that must be replaced. If you've accumulated some investments and are earning more than you need to live on—that is, saving a good portion of your earnings—you may need to replace only 30 percent of your after-tax income. However, someone with little savings who's living hand-to-mouth may need disability insurance that covers 80 percent of after-tax income.

Most insurance companies don't write disability policies that cover over 67 to 80 percent of a person's after-tax salary. They figure that if too much of your income is covered, you won't have an incentive to go back to work. Notice that the discussion focuses on the replacement of after-tax income. Although the insurance premiums that you pay on disability insurance aren't tax deductible, disability income is generally treated as tax-free income. Figure 9.3 provides a worksheet you can use to estimate how much disability insurance coverage you might want or need.

Disability Features That Make Sense

Disability insurance policies vary more from insurance company to insurance company than do health insurance policies. Therefore, you really need to have an idea of what's desirable in a disability plan. The following sections discuss a few key features to look for.

FIGURE 9.3 Worksheet for Estimating How Much Disability Insurance Coverage You Need

1. Current monthly after-tax job-related income			________
2. Existing disability coverage on an *after-tax basis*			
• Social Security benefits		________	
• Disability insurance from employer	+	________	
• Veterans benefits and other federal and state disability insurance	+	________	
• Other disability coverage in place	+	________	
Total Existing Coverage	=		________
3. Added disability coverage needed to maintain current level of after-tax job-related income in the event of a disability (subtract 2 from 1)			________

Note: We haven't included workers' compensation disability benefits because they accompany only work-related injuries.

Definition of Disability What exactly does your policy consider a disability? In general, most policies define people as having a disability if they can't perform the duties of their "own occupation" or perform the duties of "any occupation for which they are reasonably suited." Unfortunately, deciding the occupations for which you are "reasonably suited" may be difficult. It's wise to stick with a policy that defines you as having a disability if you can't perform your normal job.

An alternative is the combination definition. Under the combination definition, you're covered if you can't perform your "own occupation" for the first 2 years of your disability. Thereafter, you're covered if you can't perform "any occupation for which you're reasonably suited." Defining "disability" in this way promotes retraining during the first 2 years. Policies using this definition tend to be less expensive than those that use only the "own occupation" definition. Given the cost trade-offs, you might want to give serious consideration to policies that use a combination definition.

Residual or Partial Payments When Returning to Work Part-Time Some policies offer partial disability payments that allow you to return to work on a part-time basis and still receive benefits. These payments make up the difference between what you would make if working full-time and your part-time earnings. Partial disability payments are a desirable feature, especially if you are self-employed.

Benefit Duration Disability policies generally provide benefits for a maximum period or until your disability ends (or you reach 65 or 70 years of age). A **short-term disability (STD)** policy generally provides benefits on disabilities lasting from 6 months to 2 years after a short wait of 8 to 30 days. A **long-term disability (LTD)** policy generally provides benefits until you reach the age specified in the contract or for your lifetime. Only a long-term disability policy makes any sense because only a long-term disability policy protects against financial catastrophe.

Short-Term Disability (STD)
An STD policy provides benefits over a given period, generally from 6 months to 2 years.

Long-Term Disability (LTD)
An LTD policy provides benefits until an individual reaches the age specified in the contract, generally 65 or 70, or for the insured's lifetime.

Waiting (or Elimination) Period The **waiting or elimination period** refers to the period after the disability during which no benefits occur. The waiting period is equivalent to a deductible in a health-care insurance policy. Most disability policies have waiting periods that range from 1 to 6 months. Of course, the longer the waiting period, the less expensive the contract. In fact, a contract with a 3-month waiting period might lower costs by almost 30 percent from a contract with a 1-month waiting period.

What disability insurance must protect you against is the loss of income associated with longer-term illnesses. Thus, in light of the cost differences, you should give serious consideration to a 3-month waiting period.

Waiting or Elimination Period
The period after the disability occurs during which no benefits occur.

FACTS OF LIFE

According to the American Council of Life Insurers, by the time you turn 85, you have a 50 percent chance of needing long-term care, and by 2040, when today's college graduates are turning 50, the cost of nursing homes is expected to run about $200,000 a year.

Waiver of Premium In general, it's a good idea to have a **waiver of premium** provision, which waives premium payments if you become disabled. Be sure to look closely at the costs.

Waiver of Premium
A disability insurance provision that allows insurance to stay in force should the policyholder become unable to work because of disability or illness.

Noncancellable You should insist on a policy that's noncancellable. This provision protects you against having your policy cancelled if, for whatever reason, your risk of becoming disabled increases, and it guarantees that the policy is renewable. It also protects against rate increases.

Rehabilitation Coverage A **rehabilitation coverage** provision provides for vocational rehabilitation, allowing you to be retrained for employment. This coverage generally provides for employment-related educational or job-training programs.

Rehabilitation Coverage
A disability insurance provision that provides payments for vocational rehabilitation, allowing the policyholder to be retrained for employment.

LO6 Explain the purpose of long-term care insurance and the provisions that might be important to you.

Long-Term Care Insurance Insurance that's aimed at covering the costs associated with long-term nursing home care, commonly associated with victims of stroke, chronic illness, or Alzheimer's disease or those who can simply no longer manage to live on their own.

Long-Term Care Insurance

Long-term care insurance pays for nursing home expenses, as well as home health care. When first introduced some 25 years ago, it was marketed strictly as "nursing home insurance." Now, it has evolved to meet the needs of individuals who need care but still can stay in their own home. The insurance is meant to cover the costs associated with long-term care for those who have had a stroke or who have a chronic disease or Alzheimer's disease, as well as those who can simply no longer manage to live on their own. In effect, it's another form of disability insurance. Its downside is that it's expensive.

It would seem that long-term health care should either be a part of major medical insurance or be covered under Medicare. It isn't. This is actually a relatively new area of coverage for insurance. It's been partially inspired by our increasing life expectancies and the resultant increase in the chance that you may eventually need some level of care. The interest in long-term health-care coverage has also been inspired by the high cost of such care.

Long-term health-care insurance is meant to protect you against the financial consequences of these costs. These policies are generally set up to provide a daily dollar benefit over the time you require nursing home care, with payments sent directly to the nursing home to cover charges. With most policies, these benefits are not subject to federal taxes. They're often not available to individuals under 40 years of age, with the premiums rising for older policyholders. Unfortunately, many long-term care insurance policies come laden with exceptions and conditions. Moreover, the lack of understanding and uniformity associated with some policies allows them to be sold not as a part of a financial plan but through the use of fear tactics.

If you're going to purchase long-term health-care insurance, make sure you do so while you're healthy and be sure to look for good health and marital discounts. In fact, if you're in good health, you can save up to 10 percent from John Hancock and up to 20 percent from Unum. In addition, most companies offer discounts of 10 to 20 percent for married couples who purchase two policies. As with other types of health-care insurance, it's available only when you don't need it. Be sure to purchase only from high-quality insurance companies that will still be around when you need them. Table 9.7 provides a listing of some of the provisions you might want to

TABLE 9.7 Long-Term Health-Care Provisions

Necessary
Selection of Company Consider only high-quality insurance companies with either an A11 or an A1 rating from A. M. Best. Never consider TV-celebrity-advertised insurance.
Qualifying for Benefits The insured is unable to perform at least two "activities of daily living" (ADLs) without assistance.
Qualifying for Benefits The policy includes coverage for Alzheimer's and Parkinson's diseases.
Qualifying for Benefits A hospital stay is not required for benefits.
Benefit Period The minimum benefit period should be 3 to 6 years.
Inflation Adjustment The policy should give you the option of purchasing inflation coverage.
Noncancellability The policy should not be cancellable.
Desirable, but Not Necessary–Cost-Benefit Trade-Offs
Waiver of Premium While desirable, it may be too expensive to warrant serious consideration.
Type of Care Home care, adult day care, and hospice care for the terminally ill are covered.
Benefit Period Women should consider longer benefit periods.
Cost-Reducing Provision to Consider
Waiting Period Consider a waiting period of 100 days or more–if affordable.
Provisions to Avoid–Not Worth the Cost
Nonforfeiture Clause or Provision This is simply too expensive.

TABLE 9.8 Long-Term Care Insurance

Medical advances have resulted in an increased need for nursing home care and assisted living. Most health insurance plans and Medicare severely limit or exclude long-term care. Here are some questions to ask when considering a separate long-term care insurance policy:
• **What qualifies you for benefits?** Some insurers say you must be unable to perform a specific number of the following activities of daily living: eating, walking, getting from bed to a chair, dressing, bathing, using the restroom, and remaining continent. • **What type of care is covered?** Does the policy cover nursing home care? What about coverage for assisted-living facilities that provide less client care than a nursing home? If you want to stay in your home, will it pay for care provided by visiting nurses and therapists? What about help with food preparation and housecleaning? • **What will the benefit amount be?** Most plans are written to provide a specific dollar benefit per day. The benefit for home care is usually about half the nursing home benefit, but some policies pay the same for both forms of care. Other plans pay only for your actual expenses. • **What is the benefit period?** It is possible to get a policy with lifetime benefits, but this can be very expensive. Other options for coverage are from 1 to 6 years. The average nursing home stay is about 2.44 years. • **Is the benefit adjusted for inflation?** If you buy a policy prior to age 60, you face the risk that a fixed daily benefit will not be enough by the time you need it. • **Is there a waiting period before benefits begin?** A 20- to 100-day period is not unusual.

Source: U.S. General Services Administration, *Consumer Action Handbook*, 2017, http://www.consumeraction.gov/.

include in a long-term health-care policy, while Table 9.8 provides some questions to ask when considering a long-term health-care policy.

Those who have a family history of long-term disabilities, Alzheimer's disease, or Parkinson's disease and those who have savings they want to protect should consider long-term health-care insurance. If you don't have funds to cover nursing home care, Medicaid, which is aimed at the needy, will cover your costs. If you have money but don't have dependents, you probably don't need long-term health-care insurance. If you need nursing home care, pay for it out of your savings. After all, you saved that money to provide for you in retirement.

Most policies require that you be unable to perform at least two "activities of daily living" (ADLs) without assistance. These ADLs include such tasks as walking, dressing, and eating. Some plans also allow cognitive impairment, such as the short-term memory loss suffered by Alzheimer's and Parkinson's disease patients, to be sufficient for benefits. You should consider only policies that include coverage for Alzheimer's and Parkinson's diseases. The following sections discuss some provisions to consider.

Type of Care Policies vary with respect to the coverage of home care. Some policies provide only nursing home care, while others provide for adult day care and hospice care for the terminally ill. In fact, a number of long-term care policies recently have provided for reimbursement for nonlicensed caregivers, including family and friends, rather than requiring that care be provided only by licensed caregivers. It's a good idea to seek a policy with flexible coverage provisions and a home care option.

Benefit Period Benefit periods on long-term health-care insurance can range all the way from 1 year to lifetime. Unfortunately, lifetime coverage provisions tend to be very expensive. Because the average stay in a nursing home is about 2.44 years, you should make sure your coverage has a minimum 3- to 6-year benefit period. In addition, because women tend to spend longer periods in nursing care than men, women should consider a longer benefit period.

Waiting Period Just as with disability insurance, the waiting period on long-term care insurance can be thought of as a deductible—you have to absorb the expense of nursing home care during the waiting period. This waiting period can run anywhere from

0 days up to a full year—but the most common is a waiting period of from 20 to 100 days. As you might expect, the longer the waiting period, the less the cost of the insurance.

For example, at age 65 simply by raising the waiting period from 20 days to 100 days, you can cut the cost of a long-term care policy to just over 10 percent of what it would cost otherwise. That's a pretty hefty savings, but if you do require care, that difference of 80 days in the waiting period would cost you $12,000 the first year and even more as the level of your protection rises with the inflation protection. For that reason, many financial advisors recommend that you go with a 20-day waiting period.

Inflation Adjustment There's no telling what the cost of nursing home care will be when you need it. If nursing home costs increase by 5 percent per year, they will double in only 15 years. Without some inflation protection, your policy may not be of much help when you need it. Make sure to include an inflation protection provision if you buy long-term health-care insurance.

Waiver of Premium A waiver of premium provision allows your insurance to stay in force while you are receiving benefits. This is an area that has undergone a good deal of change recently. Most policies waive premiums once you begin receiving benefits. Recently, many companies have begun to offer dual waiver of premium riders: Both spouses' premiums are waived when either one of them meets the waiver of premium conditions. However, you should be careful in selecting this option because the costs associated with it can vary dramatically from policy to policy.

BEHAVIORAL INSIGHTS

PRINCIPLE 9

Principle 9: Mind Games, Your Financial Personality, and Your Money We've already talked about the behavioral finance concept of anchoring, which refers to the tendency to attach or "anchor" our thoughts to a reference point—even though it may have no logical relevance to the decision at hand. This is definitely a concept you want to keep in mind when talking to someone about "purchasing" life insurance.

Let's review how anchoring works. For example, let's say that you're not from Hawaii but you're asked to guess the population of Hawaii. If you're told that Hawaii has a population smaller or greater than 7 million, your guess will most likely approach the 7 million anchor. However, if you're told that the population of Hawaii is smaller or greater than 1 million, studies have proven that your answer will approach the 1 million mark. That's because the 7 million or 1 million figure is your anchor. By the way, the population of Hawaii is about 1.4 million.

Another example of anchoring, and one you may be familiar with, is the appropriate amount to spend on an engagement ring. Conventional wisdom says that you should spend around 2 months' worth of your salary on a diamond engagement ring. This "standard" of 2 months' worth of salary is an anchor created by the marketing people in the jewelry industry to maximize profits and has nothing to do with the valuation of love. Anchoring is especially dangerous in those areas in which you have little or no experience or knowledge—like the cost of diamonds!

In fact, many people can't afford to put 2 months' worth of salary toward a ring while paying for living expenses. As a result, they borrow money to meet the diamond anchor. And by this point in your study of personal finance, you should know the conflicts that can result from too much debt.

Now, getting back to life insurance, we find that it is an odd product—people don't "buy" life insurance; they are "sold" life insurance. No one wants to think about death, and after all, the goal of life insurance is to provide a certain level of financial security for your family after you die. Life insurance is one of those products that isn't really an exciting thing to buy—but most of us realize that it's something we may need at some point in our life. To get you to purchase more life insurance than you might really need, some unscrupulous agent may use anchoring by suggesting what a "normal level" of coverage might be. For example, an agent might tell you that for people in your age bracket, the common level of coverage is $4 million and it only costs $1,000 per year. What that does is begin the conversation at $4 million of coverage. Once again, let's review: Anchoring is especially dangerous in those areas in which you have little or no experience or knowledge—like the cost of insurance!

Beware of anchoring—it can result in purchases that can lead to financial woes down the line.

ACTION PLAN

PRINCIPLE 10

Principle 10: Just Do It! As your family responsibilities change, so will your need for life insurance. Your primary concern should be a sufficient death benefit to cover your dependents. You'll want health-care insurance, and you'll also want to give disability insurance serious consideration. So here's an action plan that will help you do just that.

- With respect to life insurance, if you have dependents, make sure you have a sufficient death benefit and consider only term insurance.
- With respect to health insurance, you've got to have it—it's even a legal requirement.
- While you've got to have health insurance, try to put yourself in a position of not having to use it. Exercise, eat well, avoid destructive behavior (like smoking), and do your best to stay healthy.
- Stay on your parents' insurance until you turn 26. If you're over 26 and health insurance is not available through your job, look to the Health Insurance Marketplace.
- Once you get a job, look to your employer for health insurance coverage.
- Once you get a job, consider disability insurance.
- Consider a flexible spending or health savings account.

Chapter Summaries

Understand the importance of insurance. LO1

SUMMARY: The purpose of life insurance is to control the financial effect your dependents experience when you die. Life insurance can replace the lost income that results from the death of the wage earner. Insurance is based on the concept of risk pooling. With life insurance, everyone pays a premium, determined by the probability of his or her dying, and no one suffers a big loss.

KEY TERM

Patient Protection and Affordable Care Act, page 293 Commonly referred to as the *Affordable Care Act* or *ObamaCare*, this major health-care act was signed into law in 2010 and put in place comprehensive health insurance reforms.

LO2 Determine your life insurance needs and design a life insurance program.

SUMMARY: The first step in determining how much life insurance you need is to review your net worth. The larger your net worth, the more you have in the way of wealth to support your family, and consequently the less life insurance you need. The earnings multiple approach provides a rough estimate of your needs by using a multiple of your yearly income. An alternative method of determining how much insurance you need is the needs approach.

KEY TERMS

Risk Pooling, page 293 Sharing the financial consequences associated with risk.

Premium, page 293 A life insurance payment.

Actuaries, page 293 Statisticians who specialize in estimating life expectancy based on personal characteristics.

Face Amount or Face of Policy, page 294 The amount of insurance provided by the policy at death.

Insured, page 294 The person whose life is insured by the life insurance policy.

Policyholder or Policy Owner, page 294 The individual or business that owns the life insurance policy.

Beneficiary, page 294 The individual designated to receive the insurance policy's proceeds upon the death of the insured.

Earnings Multiple Approach, page 295 A method of determining exactly how much life insurance you need by using a multiple of your yearly earnings.

Needs Approach, page 297 A method of determining how much life insurance you need based on the funds your family will require to maintain their lifestyle after your death.

Cleanup Funds, page 297 Funds needed to cover immediate expenses at the time of your death.

LO3 Describe the major types of coverage available and the typical provisions that are included.

SUMMARY: There are two very different categories of life insurance—term and cash-value. Term life insurance is pure life insurance that pays the beneficiary the face value of the policy if the insured individual dies during the coverage period. Cash-value insurance is any policy that provides both a death benefit and an opportunity to accumulate cash value.

One way of fine-tuning your insurance policy is through riders. A rider is a special provision that may be added to your policy. In general, life insurance death benefits are income tax free. Thus, if there's a single lump-sum settlement, there are generally no taxes due on the full face value of the contract.

Once you've determined your needs, the first order of business is selecting an insurance company and an agent. The final step is to compare the costs of the competing policies.

KEY TERMS

Term Insurance, page 298 A type of insurance that pays the beneficiary a specific amount of money if the policyholder dies while covered by the policy.

Cash-Value Insurance, page 298 A type of insurance that has two components: life insurance and a savings plan.

Renewable Term Insurance, page 299 A type of term insurance that can be renewed for an agreed-on period or up to a specified age (usually 65 or 70), regardless of the insured's health.

Decreasing Term Insurance, page 299 Term insurance in which the annual premium remains constant but the face amount of the policy declines each year.

Group Term Insurance, page 300 Term insurance provided, usually without a medical exam, to a specific group of individuals, such as company employees, who are associated for some purpose other than to buy insurance.

Credit or Mortgage Group Life Insurance, page 300 Group life insurance that's provided by a lender for its debtors.

Convertible Term Life Insurance, page 300 Term life insurance that can be converted into cash-value life insurance at the insured's discretion, regardless of his or her medical condition and without a medical exam.

Whole Life Insurance, page 300 Cash-value insurance that provides permanent coverage and a death benefit when the insured dies. If the insured turns 100, the policy pays off, even though the insured hasn't died.

Cash Value, page 300 The money that the policyholder is entitled to if the policy is terminated.

Nonforfeiture Right, page 301 The right of a policyholder to choose to receive the policy's cash value; in exchange, the policyholder gives up his or her right to a death benefit.

Universal Life Insurance, page 301 A type of cash-value insurance that's much more flexible than whole life. It allows the policyholder to vary the premium payments and the level of protection.

Variable Life Insurance, page 302 Insurance that provides permanent insurance coverage as whole life does; however, the policyholder, rather than the insurance company, takes on the investment risk.

Coverage Grace Period, page 303 The late-payment period for premiums during which time the policy stays in effect and no interest is charged. If payments still aren't made, the policy can be cancelled after the grace period.

Loan Clause, page 303 A clause that provides the right to borrow against the cash value of the policy at a guaranteed interest rate.

Policy Reinstatement Clause, page 304 A clause that provides the right to restore a policy that has lapsed after the grace period has expired. Generally, reinstatement is provided for within a specified period (usually 3 to 5 years after the policy has expired).

Change of Policy Clause, page 304 A clause that gives the policyholder the right to change the form of the policy—for example, from a continuous-premium whole life policy to a limited-premium whole life policy.

Rider, page 304 A special provision that may be added to a policy that either provides extra benefits to the beneficiary or limits the company's liability under certain conditions.

Settlement or Payout Options, page 305 The alternative ways that a beneficiary can choose to receive the policy benefits upon the death of the insured.

Traditional Net Cost (TNC) Method, page 307 A method of comparing insurance costs that sums the premiums over a stated period (usually 10 or 20 years) and subtracts from this the sum of all dividends over that same period.

Interest-Adjusted Net Cost (IANC) Method or Surrender Cost Index, page 307 A method of comparing insurance costs that incorporates the time value of money into its calculations.

Design a health-care insurance program and understand what provisions are important to you. LO4

SUMMARY: The Affordable Care Act has made major changes in health care, but your interaction with the U.S. medical system will remain more or less the same—you pay for a policy with a private insurance company, and it reimburses your doctors for care. The law is aimed at providing new consumer protections, improving quality and lowering costs, increasing access to affordable care, and holding insurance companies accountable.

Health insurance serves the same purpose as other forms of insurance—to protect you and your dependents from financial catastrophe. Most health insurance includes a combination of hospital, surgical, and physician expense insurance, which is generally sold in a combination called basic health insurance. Major medical expense insurance is aimed at covering medical costs beyond those covered by basic health insurance.

The choices for health insurance providers are traditional fee-for-service plans and managed health care or prepaid care. Many times under a fee-for-service plan, there's a deductible or coinsurance fee. A deductible is the amount the insured must pay before the insurance company will begin paying benefits, and a coinsurance or percentage participation provision defines the percentage of each claim that the insurance company will pay.

KEY TERMS

Basic Health Insurance, page 310 A term used to describe most health insurance, which includes a combination of hospital, surgical, and physician expense insurance.

Hospital Insurance, page 310 Insurance that covers the costs associated with a hospital stay, including room charges, nursing costs, operating room fees, and drugs supplied by the hospital.

Surgical Insurance, page 311 Insurance that covers the cost of surgery.

Physician Expense Insurance, page 311 Insurance that covers physicians' fees outside of surgery.

Major Medical Expense Insurance, page 311 Insurance that covers medical costs beyond those covered by basic health insurance.

Fee-for-Service or Traditional Indemnity Plan, page 311 An insurance plan that provides reimbursement for all or part of your medical expenditures. In general, it gives you a good deal of freedom to choose your doctor and hospital.

Managed Health-Care or Prepaid Care Plan, page 311 An insurance plan that entitles you to the health care provided by a specified group of participating doctors, hospitals, and clinics. These plans are generally offered by health maintenance organizations or variations of them.

Coinsurance or Percentage Participation, page 312 An insurance provision that defines the percentage of each claim that the insurance company will pay.

Co-payment or Deductible, page 312 The amount of expenses that the insured must pay before the insurance company will pay any insurance benefits.

Health Maintenance Organization (HMO), page 313 A prepaid insurance plan that entitles members to the services of participating doctors, hospitals, and clinics.

Individual Practice Association Plan (IPA), page 313 An HMO made up of independent doctors, in which the patient visits the doctors' regular offices to receive medical treatment.

Group Practice Plan, page 313 An insurance plan in which doctors are generally employed directly by an HMO and members of the HMO must receive their medical treatment from these doctors at a central facility.

Point-of-Service Plan, page 313 An insurance plan that allows its members to seek medical treatment from both HMO-affiliated doctors and non-HMO-affiliated doctors.

Preferred Provider Organization (PPO), page 313 An insurance plan under which an employer or insurer negotiates with a group of doctors and hospitals to provide health care for its employees or members at reduced rates.

Group Health Insurance, page 314 Health insurance that's sold, usually without a medical exam, to a specific group of individuals who are associated for some purpose other than to buy insurance.

Individual Insurance Policy, page 314 An insurance policy that is tailor-made for you, reflecting your age, health (as determined by an examination), and chosen deductible size.

Workers' Compensation Laws, page 315 State laws that provide payment for work-related accidents and illnesses.

Medicare, page 316 A government insurance program enacted in 1968 to provide medical benefits to persons with disabilities and those over 65. It is divided into two parts: Part A, which provides hospital insurance benefits, and Part B, which is supplemental medical insurance.

Medigap Insurance, page 318 Insurance sold by private insurance companies aimed at bridging gaps in Medicare coverage.

Medicaid, page 318 A government medical insurance plan for the needy.

Flexible Spending Account (FSA), page 318 An employer-sponsored plan that allows each employee to have pretax earnings deposited into a specially designated account for the purpose of paying health-care bills and qualified child care expenses. The employee can withdraw funds from this account to offset unreimbursed medical or dental expenses.

Describe disability insurance and the choices available to you. LO5

SUMMARY: Disability insurance provides income in the event of a disability. Anyone who relies on income from a job for financial support needs disability insurance. Many employers provide some level of disability insurance as part of their benefits package.

KEY TERMS

Disability Insurance, page 321 Health insurance that provides payments to the insured in the event that income is interrupted by illness, sickness, or accident.

Short-Term Disability (STD), page 323 An STD policy provides benefits over a given period, generally from 6 months to 2 years.

Long-Term Disability (LTD), page 323 An LTD policy provides benefits until an individual reaches the age specified in the contract, generally 65 or 70, or for the insured's lifetime.

Waiting or Elimination Period, page 323 The period after the disability occurs during which no benefits occur.

Waiver of Premium, page 323 A disability insurance provision that allows insurance to stay in force should the policyholder become unable to work because of disability or illness.

Rehabilitation Coverage, page 323 A disability insurance provision that provides payments for vocational rehabilitation, allowing the policyholder to be retrained for employment.

Explain the purpose of long-term care insurance and the provisions that might be important to you. LO6

SUMMARY: Long-term care insurance is another form of disability insurance that covers the cost of long-term nursing home care. Provisions to consider include the type of care, the benefit period, the waiting period, inflation adjustment, and a waiver of premium.

KEY TERM

Long-Term Care Insurance, page 324 Insurance that's aimed at covering the costs associated with long-term nursing home care, commonly associated with victims of stroke, chronic illness, or Alzheimer's disease or those who can simply no longer manage to live on their own.

Problems and Activities

These problems are available in MyLab Finance.

1. What are the major provisions of the Affordable Care Act?

2. Renee has a bad history of family health problems. Her niece, Abilyn, was recently declined coverage because of a congenital heart defect that she was born with 6 months ago. Her brother, Micah, is 24 years old and getting ready to finish college and was told he had to apply for individual coverage through the health insurance exchange system. Renee's grandmother has already used $900,000 worth of insurance benefits over her lifetime. Her insurance company is threatening to stop paying benefits once she reaches $1,000,000 of benefits. Are these actions taken by the insurance companies legal? Why or why not?

3. Joetta Hernandez is a single parent with two children and earns $45,000 a year. Her employer's group life insurance policy will pay 2.5 times her salary. She also has $60,000 saved in a 401(k) plan, $5,000 in mutual funds, and a $3,000 certificate of deposit. She wants to purchase term life insurance for 15 years, until her youngest child is self-supporting. She is not concerned about her outstanding mortgage, as the children would live with her sister in the event of Joetta's death. Assuming she can receive a 3 percent after-tax, after-inflation return on insurance proceeds, use the earnings multiple method to calculate her insurance need. How much more insurance does Joetta need to buy? What other information would you need to know to use the needs approach to calculate Joetta's insurance coverage?

4. Virgil Cronk wants to purchase a life insurance policy that will allow him to increase his future coverage without having to take another medical exam. Virgil's family has a history of cardiac problems. Name at least two policy riders that he should consider adding to his policy.
5. The Baulding family has a basic health insurance plan that pays 80 percent of out-of-hospital expenses after a deductible of $250 per person. If three family members have doctor and prescription drug expenses of $980, $1,840, and $220, respectively, how much will the Baulding family and the insurance company each pay? How could they benefit from a flexible spending account established through Mr. Baulding's employer? What are the advantages and disadvantages of establishing such an account?
6. Latesha Moore has a choice at work between a traditional health insurance plan that pays 80 percent of the cost of doctor visits after a $250 deductible and an HMO that charges a $10 co-payment per visit plus a $20 monthly premium deduction from her paycheck. Latesha anticipates seeing a doctor once a month for her high blood pressure. The cost of each office visit is $50. She normally sees the doctor an average of three times a year for other health concerns. Comment on the difference in costs between the two health-care plans and the advantages and disadvantages of each.
7. Julie Rios has take-home pay of $3,200 per month and a disability insurance policy that replaces 60 percent of earnings after a 90-day (3-month) waiting period. She has accumulated 80 sick days at work. Julie was involved in an auto accident and was out of work for 4 months. How much income did she lose, and how much was replaced by her disability policy? How else could she replace her lost earnings? If after 4 months Julie could return to work only half-time for an additional 3 months due to continuing physical therapy, how might she benefit from a residual benefits clause? How much will she receive in disability benefits for this period?
8. Bobbi Hilton, 62, is considering the purchase of a 5-year long-term care policy. If nursing home costs average $5,000 per month in her area, how much could she have to pay out-of-pocket for 5 years without long-term care insurance? What can Bobbi do to reduce the cost of this coverage?

Discussion Case 1

This case is available in **MyLab Finance**.

Adam and Cassie Porterfield, a healthy couple in their mid-30s, were delighted when Adam landed a new job with a promotion and increased salary. But they were disappointed to learn that he would not be eligible for benefits for 90 days. The company offers a comprehensive package of health insurance, vision insurance, dental insurance, life insurance (1.5 times salary at no premium charge), short- and long-term disability insurance, and long-term care insurance. An employee can choose how to spend the employer-provided premium dollars to purchase any combination of insurance or additional life insurance.

Questions

1. In the mix of premiums the Porterfields can spend, how should Adam and Cassie rank Adam's insurance needs for the seven types of coverage offered? What factors should they consider?
2. Should Adam consider purchasing more life insurance than the company-provided free benefit? What two methods could he use to assess his needs relative to his total life insurance coverage?
3. Name two or three important factors to consider when purchasing disability insurance. Should Adam first consider short-term or long-term disability?
4. Should the Porterfields consider changing their company-provided insurance benefits if they become parents? Defend your answer.

Discussion Case 2

This case is available in **MyLab Finance**.

Wendy and Frank Kampe, 30 and 35, are considering the purchase of life insurance. Wendy doesn't have any coverage, whereas Frank has a $150,000 group policy at work. The Kampes have two young children, ages 3 and 5. Wendy earns $28,000 annually from a part-time, home-based business. Frank's annual salary is $55,000. From their income, they save $7,500 a year. The rest goes for expenses. The couple estimates that the children will be financially dependent, except for college costs, for about another 15 years. Once the children are in college, Wendy assumes their annual expenses will be $60,000.

In preparation for a visit with their insurance agent, the Kampes have estimated the following expenses if Frank were to die:

Immediate needs at death	$25,000
Outstanding debt (including mortgage repayment)	$90,000
Transitional funds for Wendy to expand her business to fully support the family	$15,000
College expenses for their two children	$205,000

They also anticipate, should Frank die, that Wendy will receive $8,000 a year in Social Security survivor's benefits until the youngest child turns 18 and $5,000 annually in pension benefits until Wendy turns 80. Wendy projects her gross annual income to be $40,000 after her business expansion. Once the children are self-supporting, Wendy wants to plan a spousal life income—that is, funds to make up the difference between her income and pension benefits and her expenses for 15 more years, from age 45 to age 60. Lastly, she wants to plan on $30,000 a year in retirement income for another 20 years, from age 60 to age 80. She anticipates receiving a 5 percent after-tax, after-inflation return on their investments.

To date, the Kampes have accumulated a total of $107,000 of assets, not including $45,000 of home equity. Their assets include $10,000 in an emergency fund, $12,000 in IRA funds for Wendy, $35,000 in other investments, and $50,000 in Frank's 401(k) plan through his employer.

Questions

1. What method should the Kampes use to determine how much insurance they need? WORKSHEET 12
2. Should Wendy purchase an insurance policy? Why or why not? If so, what type of policy would you recommend for Wendy?
3. What type of life insurance policy would you recommend that Frank purchase?
4. What will happen to Frank's group life insurance if he leaves his present job?
5. What could happen to the Kampes' children if Frank or Wendy should die without adequate life insurance coverage?
6. Should the Kampes name the children as life insurance beneficiaries?
7. Which life insurance riders might the Kampes select when purchasing a policy?
8. Since they will make a concerted effort to become informed about life insurance, should the Kampes also purchase life insurance on the children rather than waiting until later when they would have to reeducate themselves for life insurance shopping?
9. The Kampes save $7,500 a year for an emergency fund, retirement, and other investments, with the remainder spent to support their lifestyle. How might the concept of mental accounting and **Principle 9: Mind Games, Your Financial Personality, and Your Money** affect their decision to purchase life insurance? PRINCIPLE 9

CHAPTER 10

Property and Liability Insurance

Learning Objectives

LO1	**Understand,** buy, and maintain homeowner's insurance in a cost-effective way.	**Protecting Your Home**
LO2	**Protect** your property effectively while keeping your costs down.	**Your Insurance Needs**
LO3	**Manage** your insurance.	**Making Your Coverage Work**
LO4	**Pick** out the right auto insurance and file a claim.	**Automobile Insurance**

If you've got good stuff, consider insurance, and if you've got serious bling, make sure it's insured. That's the lesson that Kim Kardashian learned in the fall of 2016 after she was robbed at gunpoint in her Paris hotel. Kim was in Paris for Fashion Week, and just after midnight she returned to her luxury hotel suite. About two and a half hours later, two gunmen dressed as policemen stormed into her room, gagged her and tied her up, put her in the bathtub, and escaped with a 20-carat (yes, 20-carat) emerald-cut diamond ring.

When Kim received the diamond ring from her husband, Kanye West, initial reports were that the diamond was worth an estimated $10 million. But when the insurance claim was filed for that diamond ring and the other items stolen, it was revealed that the ring was insured for only $4 million, while the other 13 stolen pieces of jewelry were worth about $1.6 million, bringing the total value of the crime and insurance claim to $5.6 million.

Will Kim and the insurance company fight over the true market or replacement value of the ring? Not at all, because Kim's jewelry is insured under what is called

Ricky Fitchett/ZUMA Wire/Alamy Stock Photo

an "agreed value" policy, which means that the insurance company and Kim had already agreed on what she would receive if there was ever a loss. This is different from a replacement policy, where you receive the actual retail dollar value of the insured item. Regardless of what the diamond ring cost, or what it is worth, Kim and Kanye get the agreed value from the insurance company. This eliminates any squabbling that may have taken place over the market or replacement value of the 20-carat diamond ring because, after all, coming up with the replacement value on something like that might not be an easy thing to do.

People don't like to think about tragedy. Mulling over robberies, fires, floods, and car accidents just isn't much fun. However, unless you're mega rich and can afford a huge loss, you need to prepare for these unlikely, unlucky events. That brings us back to insurance. Let's face it—if you haven't prepared ahead of time by buying insurance, the experience becomes much worse. But you also need to know that just having an insurance policy isn't the end of the story. You actually have to take care of your house, your car, and, if you've got one, your 20-carat diamond ring. If your negligence has caused the problem, you're probably going to be out of luck. So to avoid problems like this, you have to learn what kind of insurance you need and buy it, and you have to maintain your assets.

As you will learn in this chapter, not all insurance policies are created equal, so buyer beware! While you certainly don't want to buy much more insurance than you might actually need, there is the temptation to not buy enough. So let's dig in—and let's learn something from Kim Kardashian. I'll bet you never expected to read that line in a college textbook!

Protecting Your Home

LO1 Understand, buy, and maintain homeowner's insurance in a cost-effective way.

In the United States, the first type of homeowner's insurance was fire insurance, offered in 1735 by a small company in Charleston, South Carolina. It wasn't until 1958 that the first modern "homeowner's" policy was sold.

Before homeowner's insurance, a separate insurance policy was needed for each **peril**; that is, there was an insurance policy to cover fire, one to cover theft, one to cover windstorm damage, and so forth. Homeowner's insurance simplified the process by offering protection against multiple perils in one overarching policy. This new type of policy gave families peace of mind. It also helped them keep better track

Peril
An event or happening, whether natural or man-made, that causes a financial loss.

of their coverage by consolidating what would have previously been numerous different policies, probably with numerous different companies.

Today's homeowner's policies are sold in six basic versions. While you can add extra forms of coverage and individualize your insurance, the standardization makes comparison shopping easy—much easier than shopping for any other type of insurance. Unfortunately, standardization has actually stifled competition a bit. As a result, the homeowner's insurance industry is dominated by the five largest insurers, who insure about half of all homes. Let's take a look at these six standardized policies.

HOs
The six standardized homeowner's insurance policies available to home owners and renters.

Named Perils
A type of insurance that covers a specific set of named perils. If a peril isn't specifically named, it isn't covered.

Open Perils
A type of insurance that covers all perils except those specifically noted as excluded.

Property Insurance
Insurance that protects you against the loss of your property or possessions.

Personal Liability Insurance
Insurance covering all liabilities other than those resulting from the negligent operation of an automobile or those associated with business or professional causes.

Packaged Policies: HOs

Today's six basic homeowner's policies are known as **HOs**, which stands for home owners. Although they're called homeowner's insurance, they cover more than the home. They also provide liability insurance and cover renters. Three of them—HO-1, HO-2, and HO-3—provide basic, broad policies specifically for home owners, with HO-1 and HO-2 offering **named perils** insurance and HO-3 offering **open perils** insurance. Policy HO-4 is actually renter's insurance, HO-6 is for condominium owners, and HO-8 is for older homes.

Table 10.1 summarizes the basic coverage provided under each of these policies. Although each packaged policy provides a different type and level of insurance, all six HOs are divided into two sections. Section I addresses **property insurance**, which protects you against the loss of your property or possessions due to various perils. Section II provides for **personal liability insurance**, which protects you from the financial losses incurred if someone is injured on your property or as a result of your actions.

TABLE 10.1 Comparing Homeowner's Insurance Policies

HO-1 (Basic Form)–Provides such very narrow coverage that it isn't available in most states.

A. Dwelling: Based on structure's replacement value; minimum $15,000
B. Other structures: 10% of insurance on house
C. Personal property: 50% of insurance on house
D. Loss of use: 10% of insurance on house
E. Personal liability: $100,000
F. Medical payments to others: $1,000 per person

Covered Perils:

- Fire or lightning
- Vandalism or malicious mischief
- Riot or civil commotion
- Volcanic eruption
- Smoke
- Explosion
- Glass breakage
- Vehicles
- Windstorm or hail
- Theft
- Aircraft

HO-2 (Broad Form)–A named perils form of insurance. That is, it covers a set of named perils, such as fire, lightning, windstorm, and so on. If a peril isn't specifically named in this policy, it isn't covered. Typically costs 5% to 10% more than HO-1 coverage.

A, B, C, E, and F. Coverage is the same as HO-1.

D. Loss of use: 20% of insurance on house

Covered Perils: Same as HO-1, plus

- Falling objects
- Weight of ice, snow, or sleet
- Accidental discharge of water or steam
- Accidental tearing apart or cracking of heating system, air-conditioning, fire sprinkler, or appliance
- Freezing of plumbing, heating, air-conditioning, fire sprinkler, or appliance
- Accidental damage from electrical current

TABLE 10.1 Comparing Homeowner's Insurance Policies *(continued)*

HO-3 (All-Risk Form)—Covers all direct physical losses to your home. It offers open perils protection, meaning it covers all perils except those specifically excluded. Excluded perils might include flood, earthquake, war, and nuclear accident. Typically costs 10% to 15% more than an HO-1 policy. A. Dwelling: Based on structure's replacement value; minimum $20,000 B, C, D, E, and F. Coverage is the same as HO-2. *Covered Perils: Same perils for personal property as HO-2* • Dwelling and other structures are covered against risk of direct loss to property. All losses are covered except those losses specifically excluded.
HO-4 (Renter's Form)—Aimed at renters or tenants and covers personal belongings but does not include liability insurance. A. Dwelling: Not applicable B. Other structures: Not applicable C. Personal property: Minimum varies by company D. Loss of use: 20% of insurance on personal property E and F. Coverage is the same as HO-1 and HO-2. *Covered Perils: Same perils for personal property as HO-2*
HO-6 (Condominium Form)—Provides personal property and liability insurance for co-op or condominium owners. A. Dwelling: $1,000 minimum on the unit B. Other structures: Included in Coverage A C. Personal property: Minimum varies by company D. Loss of use: 40% of insurance on personal property E and F. Coverage is the same as HO-1 and HO-2. *Covered Perils: Same perils for personal property as HO-2*
HO-8 (Older Homes Form)—Designed for older homes, insuring them for repair costs or actual cash value rather than replacement cost. A. Dwelling: Based on structure's market value B. Other structures: 10% of insurance on house C. Personal property: 50% of insurance on house D. Loss of use: 10% of insurance on house E and F. Coverage is the same as HO-1 and HO-2. *Covered Perils: Same as HO-1*

Section I: Property Coverage Under homeowner's insurance, property is covered for a certain dollar amount. This is the maximum amount the insurance company will pay out for a given claim. If an item is insured for $100,000, the insurance company will pay out claims of up to $100,000. You can see that it would be a good idea to know what you are insuring is worth!

Within Section I of all HO policies except HO-4, there are four basic coverages:

- Coverage A: Dwelling
- Coverage B: Other structures
- Coverage C: Personal property
- Coverage D: Loss of use

Coverage A protects the house and any attachments to it—for example, an attached garage. However, if the land surrounding the house is destroyed by an explosion, this coverage won't pay to repair or restore it.

FACTS OF LIFE

When you apply for homeowner's insurance, don't add the cost of the land. After all, your land will still be there no matter what happens. If you add in the land value, you'll be buying more insurance than you need, and you'll be spending more than is necessary.

Coverage B protects other structures on the premises that aren't attached to the house—for example, your landscaping, a detached garage, or an outhouse. The level of this coverage is limited to 10 percent of the home's coverage. For example, if the home carries $200,000 of insurance, the other structures carry $20,000 of insurance. Still, at $20,000, that's one valuable outhouse! Again, the land isn't covered, and if the additional structure is used for business purposes, it's not covered.

Coverage C protects any personal property that's owned or used by the policyholder, regardless of the location of this property. In other words, if you're on a vacation in Hawaii and someone hits you with a pineapple and steals your suitcase, your personal property is still covered. In addition, the personal property of your guest is covered while that property is in your home. So if your home burns down during a party, any personal property losses incurred by your guests are covered.

The amount of this coverage is equal to 50 percent of the home's coverage. Thus, if the home carries $200,000 of insurance, the personal property insurance is $100,000. Within this coverage, there are limits on some types of losses. For example, there's a $200 limit on money, bank notes, gold, and silver. There's also a $1,000 limit on securities, valuable papers, manuscripts, tickets, and stamps and a $2,500 limit on the theft of silverware, goldware, and pewterware. In addition, certain property is excluded from coverage—for example, animals, birds, and fish. Before buying any policy, be aware of all of its limitations.

Coverage D provides benefits if your home can't be used because of an insured loss. The amount of loss of use coverage is limited to 20 percent of the amount of insurance on the house. Under this coverage, three benefits are provided: additional living expenses, fair rental value, and prohibited use. The additional living expenses benefit reimburses you for the cost of living in a temporary location until your home is repaired. The fair rental value benefit covers any rental losses you might experience. For example, if you rent a room in your home for $300 per month and it's uninhabitable for 2 months because of a fire, you'll receive $600 for the loss of rent. Prohibited use coverage provides living expenses for up to 2 weeks if a civil authority declares your home to be uninhabitable, perhaps because of a gas leak in a neighbor's home.

STOP & THINK

When you consider buying a house, keep in mind how much the insurance will cost. The cost may affect your choice of an older versus a new home because insurance companies may offer discounts of from 8 to 15 percent on a new house. Why do you think this is so?

Section II: Personal Liability Coverage Section II of a homeowner's insurance policy covers personal liability, which protects policyholders and their family members from financial loss if someone is injured on their property or as a result of their actions. It's extremely important because of the protection it provides against potentially catastrophic losses from liability lawsuits. This protection covers all liabilities other than business and professional liabilities and liabilities resulting from the negligent operation of an automobile. The minimum level of liability coverage per accident is $100,000.

Personal liability also covers the medical expenses of anyone injured by the policyholder, his or her family, or an animal they own. These days, when everyone wants to sue everyone else for outrageous settlements, it's good to have your liabilities covered. You never know when a close friend or dear Aunt Edith might slip on your stairs, scrape a shin, and sue you for several million dollars in damages.

This portion of Section II is really a small medical insurance policy. It covers payments up to $1,000 for medical expenses to nonfamily members who are injured in your home. For example, if someone falls down your stairs and breaks a leg, this coverage takes care of up to $1,000 worth of his or her medical expenses.

Supplemental Coverage

Coverage C of Section I of an HO provides protection for your personal property. However, depending on the type and dollar value of your assets or the perils that you face, you might want to consider supplemental coverage. There are dozens of types of supplemental coverage to choose from. Some of the more common types that we will look at in detail next include personal articles floaters, earthquake protection, flood protection, inflation guard, and replacement cost. In general, the additional coverage can be added through an **endorsement**, which is a written attachment to an insurance policy to add or subtract coverage.

Endorsement
A written attachment to an insurance policy to add or subtract coverage.

Personal Articles Floaters **Personal articles floaters** provide extended coverage for all personal property, regardless of where the property is located, for the policyholder and all household residents except children away at school. This coverage is generally sold as an extension to the homeowner's policy on an "all-risk" basis; it covers losses of any kind other than specifically excluded perils, which generally include war, wear and tear, mechanical breakdown, vermin, and nuclear disaster.

Personal Articles Floater
An extension to a homeowner's insurance policy that provides coverage for all personal property, regardless of where it's located. This coverage applies to the policyholder and all household residents except children away at school.

There are a number of variations of the personal articles floater, but they all perform the same task: They provide extended coverage to personal property. Recall that the limit on personal property coverage is set at 50 percent of the dwelling coverage, but within this coverage, there are also limits on some specific types of losses. For example, there's a $2,500 limit on the theft of silverware, goldware, and pewterware, so if the value of your silverware is $25,000, you might want a personal articles floater to cover your silverware to its market value.

Earthquake Coverage Because damage from earthquakes is specifically excluded from coverage in the standardized packaged HO policies, supplemental earthquake coverage is an important addition in high-risk areas. In fact, in California, insurers are required to offer earthquake coverage as an add-on. Of course, not all Californians elect to buy such coverage—only about 20 percent of those affected by the 1989 San Francisco earthquake had earthquake coverage. The rates on this coverage vary depending on the earthquake risk. Rates near the San Andreas fault cost up to $4 per $1,000 of coverage, which means coverage on a $200,000 home would run $800 per year.

Flood Protection Floods are the top natural disaster in the United States. Flood protection includes coverage not only for flood but also for water damage due to hurricanes, mudslides, and unusual erosion along the Great Lakes and the Great Salt Lake. It's also a bit different from other coverage in that it's generally administered and subsidized by the federal government through the Department of Housing and Urban Development (HUD).

To be eligible for flood insurance, your community must comply with HUD requirements, which involve floodplain studies and planning. Once a community receives approval from HUD, you can purchase up to $250,000 of coverage on your dwelling and an additional $100,000 on its contents.

Inflation Guard
An endorsement that automatically updates the level of property coverage based on an index of replacement costs that continually updates the cost of building a home.

Inflation Guard An **inflation guard** endorsement automatically updates your property coverage based on an index of replacement costs that continually updates the cost of building a home. In effect, the coverage—along with the premiums—automatically increases each year.

Actual Cash Value
The replacement value of the property less accumulated depreciation (which is the decline in value over time due to wear and tear).

Personal Property Replacement Cost Coverage Homeowner's insurance is set up to pay the policyholder the **actual cash value** of the loss. Unfortunately, when you're talking about personal property, the actual cash value, which is the replacement cost minus estimated depreciation (wear-and-tear costs), can be well below the cost of actually replacing the asset. For example, if the property could be replaced for $500 and it's been used for half its expected life, it would have an actual cash value of $250. Moreover, under the actual cash value, you're responsible for maintaining detailed records of the date of purchase, purchase price, and estimated depreciation of all your property.

Replacement Cost Coverage
Additional homeowner's coverage that provides for the actual replacement cost of stolen or destroyed property as opposed to the actual cash value.

As an alternative, most homeowner's policies come with optional **replacement cost coverage**, which provides for the actual replacement cost of a stolen or destroyed item as opposed to its actual cash value. Replacement cost coverage can generally be added for an additional 5 to 15 percent over the cost of the homeowner's insurance. Although replacement cost coverage doesn't mean that you no longer have to keep track of your possessions, it does mean that you'll be able to replace them in the event of a loss.

Added Liability Insurance Basic policies generally provide $100,000 of liability coverage. Although this figure may sound like a lot, it's no longer uncommon for court judgments to climb well above this amount. Also, if you've accumulated a relatively sizable net worth, you need increased liability insurance to protect your assets. Fortunately, for a relatively small fee, most insurance companies will allow you to raise your level of liability coverage to $300,000 or $500,000.

Personal Umbrella Policy
A homeowner's policy that provides excess liability insurance with protection generally ranging from $1 million to $10 million against lawsuits and judgments.

Alternatively, you might want to buy a **personal umbrella policy**, which, for a reasonable cost, provides protection ranging from $1 million to $10 million against lawsuits and judgments. An umbrella policy provides excess liability insurance over basic underlying contracts. It doesn't go into effect until you've exhausted your automobile or homeowner's liability coverage.

Its coverage is also quite broad, generally covering most losses. However, it does exclude acts committed with intent to cause injury, activities associated with aircraft and some watercraft, and most business and professional activities. Business owner and professional policies must be purchased separately.

LO2 Protect your property effectively while keeping your costs down.

Your Insurance Needs

How much insurance do you need? Answering this question is easy. In fact, we've already started answering it. Recall that we've discussed both the need for inflation guard coverage to make sure inflation doesn't negate insurance coverage and the need for replacement cost coverage on possessions.

What about replacement cost coverage on your house? This coverage actually provides us with the final answer to our question: You need enough insurance to allow for full replacement of your house in the event of a loss—a total loss.

Coinsurance and the "80 Percent Rule"

Coinsurance Provision
A provision of homeowner's insurance that requires the insured to pay a portion of the claim if he or she purchased an inadequate amount of insurance (in this case, less than 80 percent of the home's full replacement cost).

80 Percent Rule
A homeowner's insurance rule stating that the replacement cost coverage is in effect only if the home is insured for at least 80 percent of its replacement cost. This rule is intended to discourage home owners from insuring for less than the replacement cost of their homes.

Insurance companies have a way of encouraging you to be covered for a total loss. It's called a **coinsurance provision**, and it requires that you pay a portion of your own losses if you don't purchase what they consider an adequate level of insurance. Many companies follow the **80 percent rule** and require you to purchase insurance to cover at least 80 percent of your home's full replacement cost. This 80 percent rule relates to losses on your dwelling only—not those on your personal property.

There are some restrictions to this coverage, though. First, the amount paid is limited to the limits of the policy—that is, a $100,000 insurance policy will pay only up to its $100,000 limit. Second, you usually have to rebuild your home on the same location. Third, if you don't rebuild your home, the insurer is liable only for the actual cash-value loss, which is generally quite a bit less than the replacement cost. Finally, the replacement cost coverage is in effect only if your home is insured for at least 80 percent of its replacement cost.

This 80 percent rule makes insuring your home for less than at least 80 percent of its replacement cost seem unattractive. If your home currently has a replacement value of $100,000 and is insured for $80,000 and a fire causes damages of $50,000, you will be paid the full $50,000 with no deduction for depreciation (wear and tear). However, if the fire destroys your home, you will collect only $80,000, the face value of your policy.

If the 80 percent rule isn't met, you must pay for part of any losses. This is commonly referred to as the coinsurance provision. If your house is insured for less than 80 percent of its replacement value, in the event of a loss you'll receive the greater of the following:

- The actual cash value of the portion of your house that was destroyed (remember that the actual cash value is the replacement cost minus depreciation)

or

- The amount of insurance purchased (80% of replacement cost × the amount of loss)

What does all this mean? It means that it would be a grave mistake not to insure your home for at least 80 percent of its replacement cost. If you satisfy the 80 percent rule and your house is destroyed or damaged, your policy will pay to fully repair or replace your home up to the amount of insurance purchased. If you don't satisfy the 80 percent rule, you probably won't get enough to replace it. You may want more insurance—but certainly not less.

The Bottom Line

Unfortunately, there's no neat, tidy formula to tell you exactly how much homeowner's insurance you need. Determining the amount of coverage you need is a procedure that requires some thought and foresight on your part. Because the amount of assets and possessions you've managed to acquire is always changing, so are your insurance needs. As has been the case for just about every personal finance matter we've examined so far, you need to revisit your insurance needs from time to time, just to make sure those needs are being met. When determining how much homeowner's insurance you need, you should look at Checklist 10.1 for direction.

Keeping Your Costs Down—Insurance Credit Scoring

In recent years, insurance companies have turned to credit scoring models to help them identify customers who are most likely to make claims. In effect, insurers are using credit scoring system data to create a new scale—the **insurance credit score**—based on the same information as your credit score, which we looked at in Chapter 6. That's right—not only do you have a credit score that determines whether you can get credit and what rate you'll be paying when you borrow, but also you have an insurance credit score that helps determine what your home and auto insurance rates will be.

Insurance Credit Score
A credit score, based on the same information as your traditional credit score, that is used in determining what your home and auto insurance rates will be.

How do insurers justify using your credit score to determine what they should charge you for insurance? For whatever reason, there appears to be a link between your credit score and your insurance loss ratio, which is a measure that includes both claim frequency and cost for both homeowner's and auto insurance. This relationship is shown in Figure 10.1. Once this relationship was uncovered in the late 1980s,

CHECKLIST 10.1 How Much Insurance Do You Need?

- ☐ You need enough insurance to cover the replacement cost of your home in the event of a complete loss. This coverage will need to reflect any changes in increased costs due to changing building codes.
- ☐ You should have protection against inflation eroding your coverage.
- ☐ If you're in a flood or earthquake area, you need special protection against these disasters—just think about the devastation of Hurricane Katrina in New Orleans.
- ☐ If you have detached structures or elaborate landscaping, you should determine whether or not they're adequately covered under a standard policy.
- ☐ If you have a home office, you should consider additional coverage. Remember, your homeowner's policy doesn't provide business liability coverage.
- ☐ You need adequate coverage for personal property. For most people, replacement cost property insurance is a good idea.
- ☐ If you have possessions that need special protection—for example, a valuable coin collection or jewelry—you should consider a floater policy.
- ☐ If your assets are much greater than the liability limits on your homeowner's policy, you should consider additional liability coverage.
- ☐ If you're renting, you need adequate insurance for your personal property.

FIGURE 10.1 The Relationship Between Your Credit Score and the Cost of Your Homeowner's Insurance Policy to Your Insurance Company

Individuals with the lowest scores have losses that are 32.4 percent above average; those with the best scores have losses that are 23.3 percent below average.

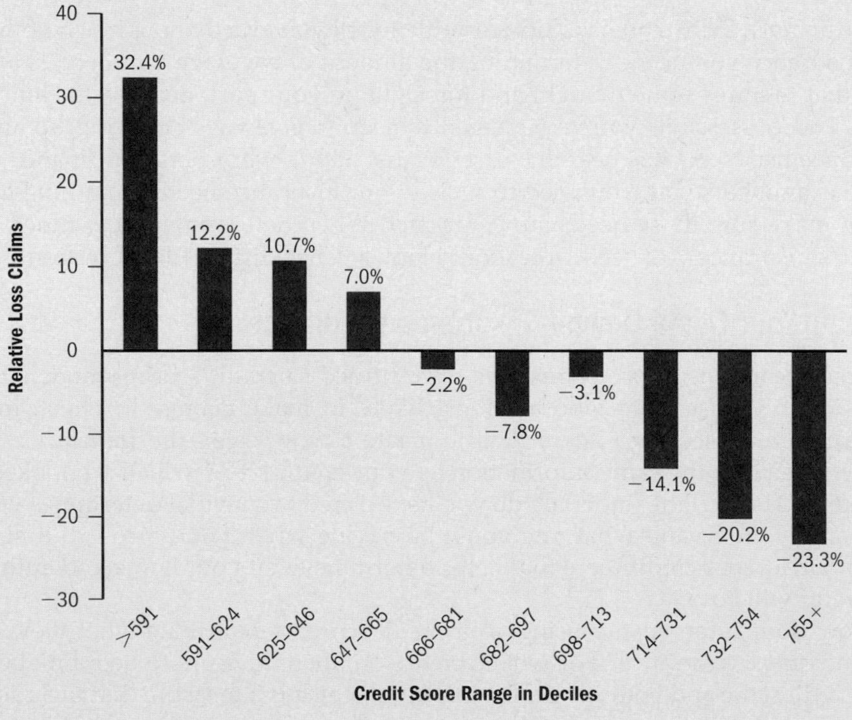

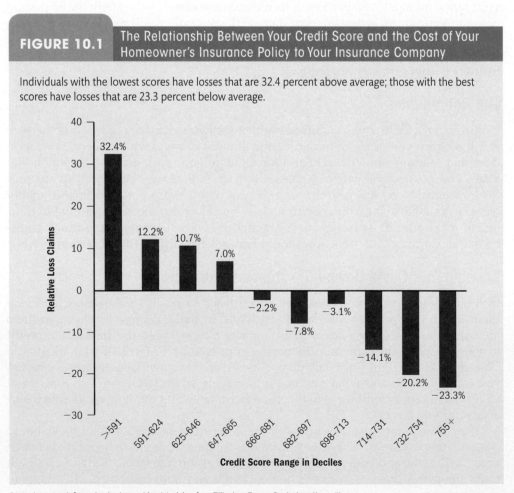

Source: Insurance Information Institute, with original data from Tillinghast Towers-Perrin, http://www.iii.org.

insurance companies jumped on it to set rates. In fact, it is estimated that 85 percent of home insurers use insurance credit scores in setting their homeowner's policy rates, and those with poor credit pay at least twice as much as those with excellent credit scores in almost all states, with those in West Virginia paying 208 percent more and those in Ohio paying 185 percent more.[1] After all, insurance companies try to set rates that reflect the cost of claims. They've done this for years using age and gender; for example, men and teenagers generally pay higher auto insurance rates. Why? Because according to the National Safety Council, men are 69 percent more likely to be driving in fatal automobile accidents than are women. As a result, men pay more for auto insurance. Similarly, drivers aged 16 to 20 are two to three times more likely to have an automobile accident than older drivers, and therefore they pay quite a bit more for their auto insurance.

The bottom line is this: The lower your insurance credit score, the higher your homeowner's insurance rate will be. While there isn't much controversy as to whether there is a relationship between credit standing and insurance claims, no one has yet to come up with a definitive answer as to why this relationship exists. Regardless of the reason, the courts have ruled that it's legal to use credit scoring in setting insurance rates, and the Fair Credit Reporting Act (FCRA) allows for insurance companies to obtain credit reports and use them in setting insurance rates. However, some states have set restrictions as to the use of insurance credit scoring. For example, it is illegal in Hawaii.

Your insurance credit score is calculated in a manner very similar to your normal credit score. Once again, just as Fair Isaac provides information as to how it calculates your credit score, it provides information as to how it calculates your insurance credit score. In this case, the weightings are a little different, with a slightly greater weight given to your payment history and a slightly lesser weight given to the types of credit used.

What does this mean for you? It means that your normal credit score and your insurance credit score are going to be very closely related. As a result, you've got to be very serious about managing your credit score because if it is low, not only will you have a hard time borrowing money and pay more for the money that you do borrow, but also you will be paying more for both your homeowner's and your automobile insurance. To manage your insurance credit score, you'll want to follow the steps outlined in Figure 10.2.

STOP & THINK

Getting insurance quotes online is a good idea. It takes only a minute, and you'll get three to five quotes from insurance companies. But there are a lot more than five insurance companies in your state, and you want as many quotes as you can get. That means you want to visit as many insurance quote sites as possible. What things have you saved money on by buying over the Internet?

Keeping Your Costs Down—Discounts and Savings

What determines the cost of your homeowner's policy? Three basic factors are involved: (1) the location of your home, (2) the type of structure, and (3) your level of coverage and policy type. Location affects coverage because of differences in crime levels and regional perils (such as earthquakes in California and tornadoes in the Midwest). Older and less-sound structures cost more to insure because they're more likely to have problems. In addition, the greater the coverage and the more comprehensive the policy, the more it costs.

[1]Federal Trade Commission, "Credit Scores," http://www.consumer.ftc.gov/articles/0152-how-credit-scores-affect-price-credit-and-insurance, accessed April 22, 2017; Insurance Journal, "How Much Credit Score Effect on Home Insurance Premiums Varies by State," http://www.insurancejournal.com/news/national/2014/08/14/337527.htm, accessed April 22, 2017.

FIGURE 10.2 Improving Your Credit Score

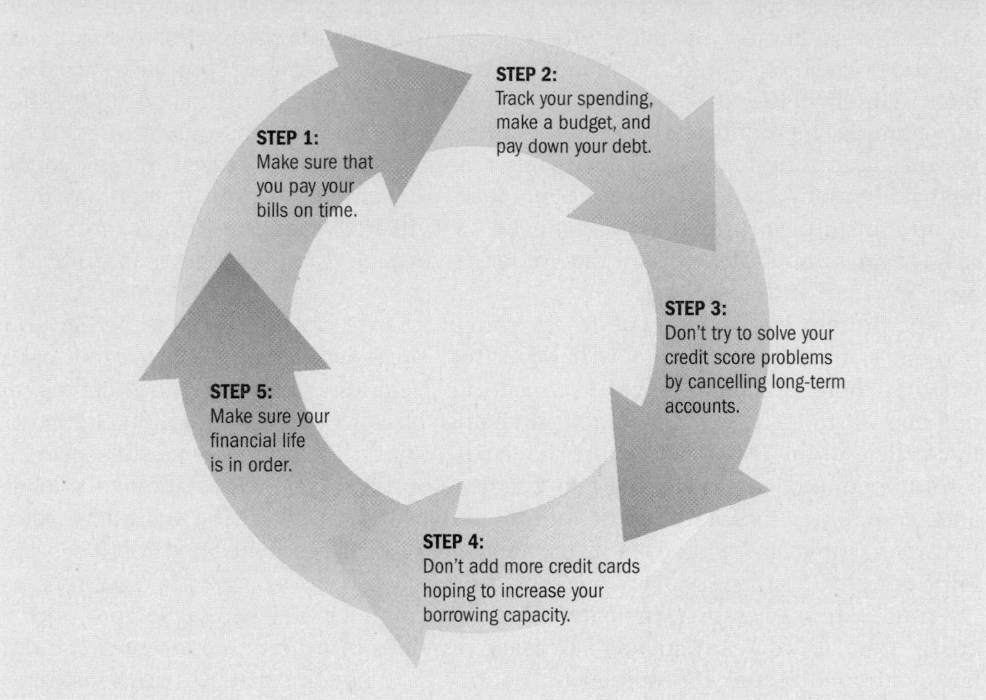
STEP 1:
Make sure that you pay your bills on time.
STEP 2:
Track your spending, make a budget, and pay down your debt.
STEP 3:
Don't try to solve your credit score problems by cancelling long-term accounts.
STEP 4:
Don't add more credit cards hoping to increase your borrowing capacity.
STEP 5:
Make sure your financial life is in order.

Still, there are some ways that you can keep down the cost of homeowner's insurance. Start by selecting a financially sound insurer with low comparative costs. Then take advantage of as many discounts as possible. Here are some potential discounts and savings methods:

Deductible
The amount that you are responsible for paying before insurance coverage kicks in.

- **High-deductible discounts.** The **deductible**, which is the amount you agree to pay before insurance coverage kicks in, can be thought of as coinsurance. The larger the deductible you are willing to accept, the less you pay for insurance coverage. Typically, insurance companies require a $250 deductible and provide discounts if you're willing to accept a higher deductible.

  Keep in mind that the purpose of insurance is not to offset all costs, only catastrophic ones. To keep the cost of homeowner's insurance under control, you'll have to share some of the risks with the insurance company. In other words, you should be responsible for all minor expenses, and the insurance company should cover all large expenses. Give serious consideration to taking as large a deductible as you can afford. Here are some other things to keep in mind that might save you money:

STOP & THINK

Typically, the deductible on a homeowner's policy starts at $250. By increasing your deductible to $500, you could save up to 12 percent; to $1,000, up to 24 percent; to $2,500, up to 30 percent; and to $5,000, up to 37 percent. Why do you think this is the case?

- **Security system/smoke detector discounts.** Many insurance companies offer discounts from 2 to 5 percent if you install security and smoke detector systems. Larger discounts are available if you install in-home sprinkler systems.
- **Multiple policy discounts.** Insurance companies often provide discounts to customers who have more than one policy with them: for example, their automobile *and* homeowner's coverage.

CHECKLIST 10.2 A Checklist for Homeowner's Insurance

- ☐ Determine the amount and type of homeowner's insurance you need.
- ☐ Put together a list of top-quality insurance companies (as listed in *A.M. Best's Key Rating Guide on Property and Casualty Insurers*, also located on their Web site at **http://www.ambest.com**) with a good local reputation.
- ☐ Consult with agents, letting them know what you are looking for. Give consideration to any recommendations or modifications they might suggest.
- ☐ If you already have an auto insurance policy, you'll want to contact that agent or insurer—you may get a discount by purchasing both coverages through one company.
- ☐ In addition to contacting your auto insurance agent, you'll want to make at least three more calls for quotes, including one to a direct writer—an insurance company that uses an 800-number-based sales force, such as Amica (800-242-6422) or, if you have a military connection, USAA (800-531-8100). One call should also be to an insurer with its own sales force, such as State Farm or Allstate, and one call should be to an independent agent, who can quote you a variety of prices.
- ☐ Get several bids on the total package, including all modifications, floaters, and extensions.
- ☐ Conduct an annual review of your homeowner's insurance coverage.

- ◆ **Pay your insurance premiums annually.** If you pay your insurance premiums annually in one lump sum rather than quarterly, or extended over several months, most insurance companies will offer you a discount.
- ◆ **Other discounts.** Some companies offer a discount for homes made with fire-resistant materials, for home owners over the age of 55, and for individuals who've had homeowner's insurance with a single company for an extended number of years.
- ◆ **Consider a direct writer.** A **direct writer** is an insurance company that distributes its products to customers without the use of agents. Companies that don't use agents don't have to pay salaries or commissions, so they can afford to offer lower prices.

Direct Writer
An insurance company that distributes its products directly to customers, without the use of agents.

- ◆ **Shop around.** Compare costs among high-quality insurers. Premiums for similar coverage can vary by as much as 25 percent. Checklist 10.2 reviews the process of shopping for homeowner's insurance.
- ◆ **Double-check your policy.** Make sure the policy you receive is what you ordered. Check the type and level of coverage and any endorsements that you requested. It'll be too late to correct any errors once you file a claim.

Making Your Coverage Work

LO3 Manage your insurance.

By now, you should be able to go out and buy the homeowner's insurance policy that's just right for you. However, is that policy enough to protect you from losing your possessions and assets? Nope. How can your insurance company make good on your policy and pay you for a loss if it doesn't know what possessions you've lost or what they were worth?

For your homeowner's insurance to provide effective protection against loss, you need to establish proof of ownership and value your assets using a detailed inventory of everything you own. If you can't prove that you owned a stereo worth $2,000, your insurance company isn't going to reimburse you for it if it gets stolen.

Fortunately, the inventory process isn't all that difficult. Begin by putting together a list of household items. To aid you in this process, most insurance agents should

CHECKLIST 10.3 What to Do in the Event of a Loss

- ☐ Report your loss immediately. In the case of a burglary or theft, report the incident immediately to the police. If a credit or ATM card has been stolen, you should also notify the issuing company. In addition, you should notify your insurance agent.
- ☐ Make temporary repairs to protect your property. If your house has sustained damage and your insurance agent hasn't had time to inspect it, don't let the damage sit untouched. Board up broken windows and holes in the roof or walls to prevent any further damage and to protect your home against burglary.
- ☐ Make a detailed list of everything lost or damaged. Using your inventory—now you'll be glad you made one—put together a detailed list describing the items that were lost or damaged and their value. Present this list to your insurance agent and the police.
- ☐ Maintain records of the insurance settlement process. Keep records of all your expenses.
- ☐ Confirm the adjuster's estimate. Your insurance company will send an adjuster to evaluate the claim and recommend to the insurance company a dollar amount for the settlement. Before settling, get an estimate from a local contractor as to how much the repairs will cost. Don't agree to anything less than a fair settlement.

FACTS OF LIFE

Why don't renters have renter's insurance? Twenty-six percent said they felt it was too expensive, while 17 percent said they didn't know they needed it, and 8 percent said they had never heard of it. Is it too expensive? According to a recent study, the average cost of renter's insurance is $195 a year.

be able to provide you with an inventory worksheet, or you can get one on the Web by googling "Century 21 home inventory worksheet." It's also a good idea to walk through your home or apartment videotaping and describing the contents. Ideally, your inventory should be as detailed as possible and include the date of purchase, the cost, the model and serial number, and the brand name for each item. Note the original cost and date of purchase of major items whenever possible. In addition, make sure each room is taped from a number of different angles, with all closet doors open. Be sure to videotape the contents of drawers and cabinets. When taping valuables such as jewelry and silverware, take a careful shot of them.

Once you've finished your video or written inventory, you should keep it in a safety-deposit box, with a family member living elsewhere, or with your insurance agent. Why not keep it yourself? Well, if your house burns down, your inventory would burn, too, and all your efforts would quickly go up in smoke.

OK, now you've got a good insurance policy and an inventory of your possessions. Now you're effectively covered, right? Not exactly. To collect on a loss, you must follow a few basic steps outlined in Checklist 10.3.

LO4 Pick out the right auto insurance and file a claim.

Automobile Insurance

At this point, you should be feeling pretty safe at home, thanks to your homeowner's insurance and your newfound knowledge of how to manage it and file claims. You do need to leave home at least every now and again, though. What happens when you get in your car? Are you safe there, too? Not unless you have automobile insurance.

Think about it—there are around 10 million automobile accidents each year in the United States alone. That works out to about one accident for every 15 licensed drivers, which is why most states require by law that all licensed drivers be covered by auto insurance. Let's start our discussion by taking a look at the standardized personal automobile policy.

LOVE & MONEY

In this chapter, we are examining insurance and how to protect your assets. Now let's look at how you can protect your marriage or relationship. Combining money and working as financial partners isn't necessarily something that comes naturally. After all, after you've been on your own for a while, it feels good to be in full control of your money decisions. On top of that, making joint decisions about spending means that you've got to open up and talk about money, and at the beginning, that can be difficult and somewhat unnatural. This is especially true for those who come from families where financial matters were not discussed openly, if at all. In addition, we all have feelings about money and spending that may be rooted in our upbringing and the financial challenges that our parents faced.

Everyone spends some money without their partner's permission, but how often do couples spend money they don't want their partner to *know* about? The answer is probably more often than you might expect. According to a recent *Money* magazine survey, nearly a quarter of married people don't come clean with their spouse about things they've bought. On top of that, about 6 percent have a separate financial account that they don't want their partner to know about. We all know that financial secrets aren't a good idea, so why are they so common? As you might expect, it's to avoid lectures and fights, but if they are uncovered, the fights only become worse. Interestingly, while both men and women secretly spend money, they buy different things:

As you know, trust is important in any relationship, and when it's violated, there may be consequences. That may explain why a recent TD Ameritrade survey revealed that over 1 in 10 respondents said they'd consider breaking up if they found out their partner was keeping a financial secret.

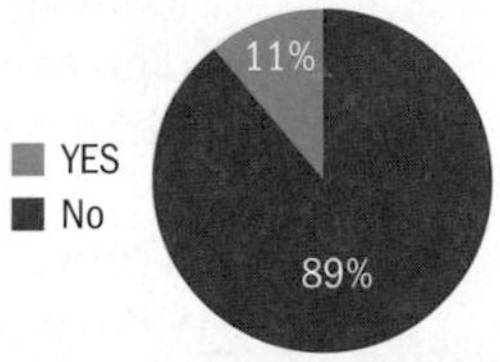

*Would you **consider breaking up** with your partner if you discovered **a financial secret** such as hidden debt or a bad credit score?*

But keep in mind that this is really a hypothetical situation, so it is very difficult to say how you might actually react. While it might not lead to breaking up, it certainly won't help bring you closer together. If you aren't ready to explain why you made the purchase without consulting with your partner, you probably shouldn't be making it.

So what can you do to prevent all this from happening? The answer lies in how you develop your budget. For your partnership to be financially successful, you must sit down together and develop a plan for the money coming in and going out. You develop this together and revisit it at regular intervals. Building a little financial freedom into your budget will go a long way toward a financial life without secrets. That way you don't have to justify your desire for that insulated travel mug with your college emblem on it that has a French press built inside of it. Even if you combine your checking accounts, it makes sense to allow for a little financial freedom. In fact, research has found that couples are happiest when they have some discretionary money in addition to having a joint account for essentials.

Personal Automobile Policy

Fortunately, automobile insurance is relatively standard, with all policies following a similar package format called the **personal automobile policy (PAP)**. Each policy contains both liability and property damage coverage, and each package of insurance includes four basic parts:

Personal Automobile Policy (PAP)
A standardized automobile insurance policy for an individual or family.

- **Part A: Liability coverage.** This coverage provides protection for you if you're legally liable for bodily injury and property damage caused by your automobile. It includes payment for any judgment awarded, court costs, and legal defense fees.
- **Part B: Medical expenses coverage.** This coverage pays medical bills and funeral expenses, with limits per person for you and your passengers.
- **Part C: Uninsured motorist's protection coverage.** This coverage is required in many states and protects you by covering bodily injury (and property damage in a few states) caused by drivers without liability insurance.
- **Part D: Damage to your automobile coverage.** This coverage is also known as collision or comprehensive insurance and provides coverage for collision damage as well as for theft of your auto and for damage from almost any peril other than collision.

Figure 10.3 illustrates the typical policy parts as they relate to liability and property coverage. Now, let's look at each coverage part in greater detail.

PAP Part A: Liability Coverage Part A of a personal automobile policy involves liability coverage, which provides protection from loss resulting from lawsuits that might arise because of an auto accident.

Combined Single-Limit Coverage
Auto insurance liability coverage that combines both bodily injury and property damage liability.

Split-Limit Coverage
Auto insurance liability coverage that allows for separate coverage limits for bodily injury and property damage, split-coverage limits per person, or both.

Liability coverage can be presented as **combined single-limit coverage**, meaning that the coverage applies to a combination of both bodily injury and property damage liability, without a separate limit for each person, or as **split-limit coverage**, which allows for separate coverage limits for bodily injury and property damage, split-coverage limits per person, or both. Figure 10.4 provides an example of how this works.

Considering the enormous sums of money judges are handing out in settlements of lawsuits over automobile accidents, it's important to carry adequate liability insurance. Although most states require minimum levels of coverage, this is generally well below what is needed by most people who are involved in auto accidents. In fact, most professional financial planners recommend that you carry

FIGURE 10.3 Personal Automobile Insurance Coverage

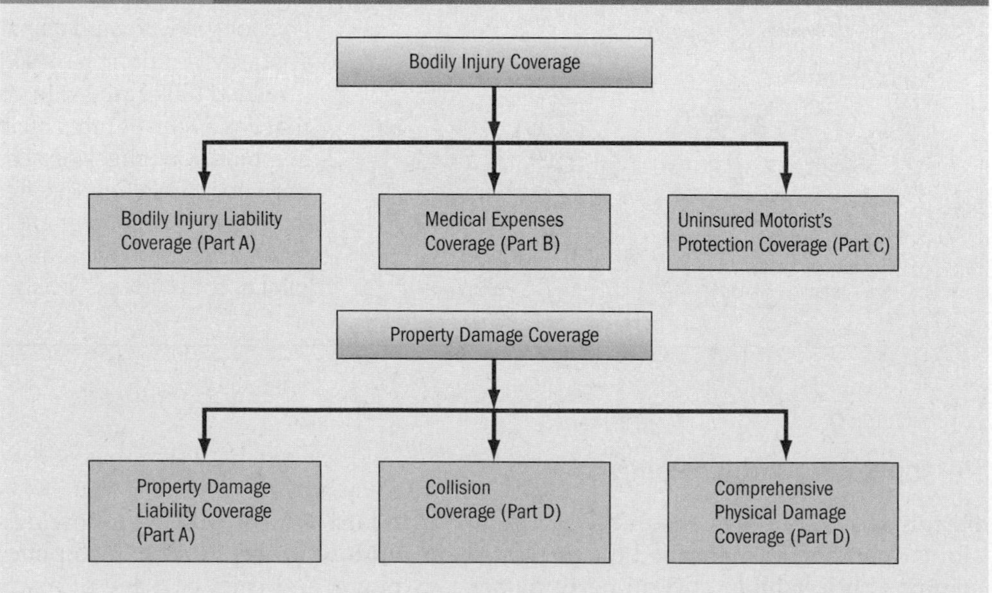

FIGURE 10.4 Reading Automobile Liability Insurance Limits Quoted as Split-Limit Coverage or Combined Single-Limit Coverage

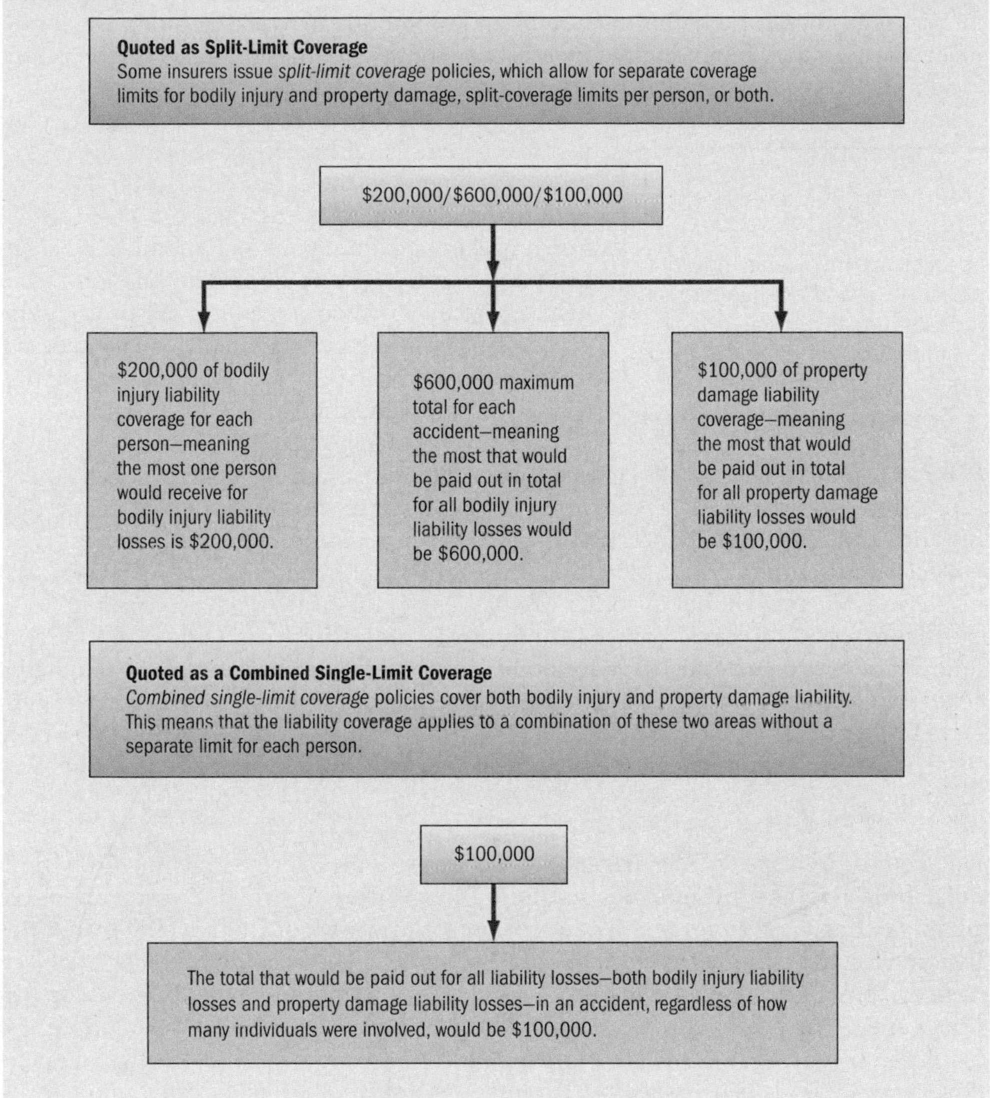
Quoted as Split-Limit Coverage
Some insurers issue *split-limit coverage* policies, which allow for separate coverage limits for bodily injury and property damage, split-coverage limits per person, or both.
$200,000/$600,000/$100,000
$200,000 of bodily injury liability coverage for each person—meaning the most one person would receive for bodily injury liability losses is $200,000.
$600,000 maximum total for each accident—meaning the most that would be paid out in total for all bodily injury liability losses would be $600,000.
$100,000 of property damage liability coverage—meaning the most that would be paid out in total for all property damage liability losses would be $100,000.
Quoted as a Combined Single-Limit Coverage
Combined single-limit coverage policies cover both bodily injury and property damage liability. This means that the liability coverage applies to a combination of these two areas without a separate limit for each person.
$100,000
The total that would be paid out for all liability losses—both bodily injury liability losses and property damage liability losses—in an accident, regardless of how many individuals were involved, would be $100,000.

at least $100,000 of bodily injury liability coverage per person and $300,000 of bodily injury liability coverage for all persons, and if you have sizable assets, you should consider raising this to $250,000 per person and $500,000 per accident—making that change will increase your premiums by about 10 percent. It is also recommended that you carry at least $100,000 of property damage liability coverage. Of course, these are general recommendations, and what you carry should reflect your net worth and annual income—the greater your assets, the more coverage you should carry.

In addition to paying the policy limits for the damages you caused, the insurer agrees under Part A to defend you in any civil cases arising from the accident and to pay all legal costs. These legal costs are paid *in addition* to your policy limits. However, the insurance company won't defend you against any criminal charges brought against you as a result of a charge such as drunk driving.

PAP Part B: Medical Expenses Coverage The medical expenses coverage pays all reasonable medical and funeral expenses incurred within 3 years of an accident by the policyholder, his or her family members, and other persons injured in an accident involving a covered automobile. In fact, it covers the policyholder and his or her family, regardless of whether they're in an automobile or walking along the street, just as long as they're not injured by a vehicle that wasn't designed for use on public roads, such as a snowmobile or farm tractor.

If you're driving a car you don't own, your medical expenses will be covered but not those of other passengers in the car or pedestrians who are injured—the owner of the car is responsible for that insurance. In addition, your PAP medical expenses coverage doesn't specify fault. That is, you're not insured based on who is at fault in an accident. As a result, you receive payment for any medical expenses faster because the insurance company doesn't need to take time to establish fault.

> **FACTS OF LIFE**
>
> Almost anything can cause an accident. According to an MSNBC report, one of the weirdest claims involved a motorist who said a frozen squirrel fell out of a tree and crashed through the windshield. Another involved a motorist who stated, "As I was driving around a bend, one of the doors opened and a frozen kebab flew out, hitting and damaging a passing car."

PAP Part C: Uninsured Motorist's Protection Coverage Coverage for injuries caused by an uninsured motorist, a negligent driver whose insurance company is insolvent, or a hit-and-run driver is provided by **uninsured motorist's protection coverage**. To collect on a claim, not only must the other driver not have available insurance, but also it must be shown that the other driver was at fault.

Uninsured Motorist's Protection Coverage
Coverage against injuries caused by a hit-and-run driver, an uninsured motorist, or a negligent driver whose insurance company is insolvent.

It's important to carry uninsured motorist's protection. You will want the same amount of coverage as you have for bodily injury coverage because up to 15 percent of all drivers don't carry any insurance at all and you never know when one might slam into your car. You can also add *under*insured motorist's coverage to your policy to provide protection against negligent drivers who don't carry adequate liability insurance.

PAP Part D: Damage to Your Automobile Coverage Part D coverage includes both **collision loss** and **other than collision loss**, generally called **comprehensive physical damage coverage**. The collision loss portion of the coverage provides benefits to cover damage resulting from an accident with another vehicle or object. Your automobile is covered if it is in an accident with another automobile or if it hits a telephone pole. Likewise, your car is covered if it is hit in a parking lot or if it is dented by the door of the car parked next to it. Comprehensive physical damage coverage provides benefits to cover damage from fire, theft or larceny, windstorm, falling objects, earthquakes, and similar causes.

Other than Collision Loss or Comprehensive Physical Damage Coverage
The portion of auto insurance coverage that provides benefits to cover noncollision losses. For example, it covers the damage if the car is hit in a parking lot or is dented by the door of the car parked next to it.

Collision Loss
The portion of auto insurance coverage that provides benefits to cover damage resulting from an accident with another vehicle or object.

Collision insurance covers losses, regardless of who caused the accident. You should keep in mind that if the other driver is at fault and has liability insurance, you should be able to recover your losses, regardless of whether or not you have collision coverage. Collision coverage assures that you'll be able to pay for any damage to your car, regardless of who is at fault. Collision coverage *used to* cover damage suffered to rental cars used for business purposes, but many insurers have stopped this practice, so if you commonly rent automobiles for business purposes, you might want to check your coverage.

> **FACTS OF LIFE**
>
> In 2017, one out of four auto collisions involved cell phones, and 21 percent of teen drivers involved in fatal accidents were distracted by their cell phone. The minimum amount of time that texting takes away from your attention to the road is 5 seconds, and in 5 seconds, driving at 55 mph, you are traveling the length of a football field without looking.

The recommended limit on both collision and comprehensive physical damage coverage is equal to the cash value of your automobile. Both coverages generally have deductibles associated with them. Usually, the deductible associated with collision coverage is larger than that for comprehensive physical damage coverage. Also, be aware that premiums decline sharply as deductibles are raised. As a result, you want to choose the highest deductible you can afford to pay out of pocket, and you want to make the deductible at least $500.

For example, one major insurance company charges an annual premium of $488 on comprehensive insurance on a new Ford Focus for a youthful operator based on a deductible of $50. If the deductible is raised to $100, the premium drops to $420. By raising the deductible by $50, you can save $68 in annual premiums. In effect, a premium of $68 is being charged for $50 of additional coverage. If you have less than one accident per year, you're better off with the $100 deductible. If you have more than one accident per year, you should probably pay some attention to improving your driving skills. Table 10.2 provides a summary of the different parts of the PAP.

FACTS OF LIFE

Text messaging makes a crash 23 times more likely, and dialing while driving increases the likelihood of an accident by 2.8 times.

Exclusions The PAP provides broad coverage, but there are a number of standard exclusions. Although there may be others, standard exclusions generally include the following:

- You're not covered in the case of intentional injury or damage.
- You're not covered if you're using a vehicle without the permission of the owner.
- You're not covered if you're using a vehicle with fewer than four wheels.
- You're not covered if you're driving another person's car that is provided for you on a regular basis.

TABLE 10.2 The Personal Automobile Policy (PAP)

Coverage Description	Individuals Covered	Recommended Policy Limits
Part A–Liability Coverage Part A of a PAP involves liability coverage and provides coverage against lawsuits that might arise from negligent ownership or operation of an automobile.	Nonexcluded relatives who live with the insured, regardless of whether the automobile is owned or not.	$100,000 of bodily injury liability coverage per person and $300,000 of bodily injury liability coverage for all persons, and if you have sizable assets, raise this to $250,000 per person and $500,000 per accident. $100,000 of property damage liability coverage.
Part B–Medical Expenses Coverage Your medical expenses coverage includes all reasonable medical and funeral expenses incurred by the policyholder and family members in addition to other persons injured while occupying a covered automobile.	The policyholder and his or her family, regardless of whether they are in an automobile or walking, as long as they are injured by a vehicle that was designed for use on public roads.	A minimum of $50,000 of coverage per person.
Part C–Uninsured Motorist's Protection Coverage Uninsured motorist's protection coverage provides benefits for injuries caused by an uninsured motorist, a negligent driver whose insurance company is insolvent, or a hit-and-run driver.	Insured family members driving a nonowned automobile with permission and anyone driving an insured car with permission.	$250,000 of coverage per person and $500,000 of coverage per accident.
Part D–Damage to Your Automobile Coverage Protection against damage to or theft of your automobile is provided in Part D coverage. This coverage includes both collision loss and other than collision loss, generally called comprehensive physical damage coverage.	Anyone driving an insured automobile with permission.	Actual cash value of your automobile. In addition, you'll want to choose the highest deductible you can afford to pay out of pocket, and you'll want to make the deductible at least $500.

- You're not covered if you own the automobile but don't have it listed on your insurance policy.
- You're not covered if you're carrying passengers for a fee.
- You're not covered while driving in a race or other speed contest.

No-Fault Insurance

No-Fault Insurance
A type of auto insurance in which your insurance company protects you in the case of an accident, regardless of who is at fault.

In an attempt to keep insurance costs down—in particular, those costs associated with settling claims—many states have turned to the concept of **no-fault insurance**. Today, over half of all states have some variation of a no-fault system.

No-fault insurance is based on the idea that your insurance company should pay for your losses, regardless of who's at fault. All the legal expenses associated with attaching blame would then be lifted, and insurance coverage should prove to be less costly.

Under no-fault insurance, if you are in an accident, your insurance company pays for your losses and the losses suffered by your passengers, and the other driver's insurance company pays for his or her losses. Sounds like a good idea, right? Well, no-fault insurance has its problems. The biggest problem is that no-fault insurance imposes limits on medical expenses and other claims. In some states, the limited coverage may not be enough to cover all legitimate medical expenses.

You can still sue for "pain and suffering"—but only if the other driver is at fault.

> **STOP & THINK**
>
> Just having home and auto insurance may not be enough. Too often things happen that are unrelated to your home or car. What if you're riding your bike and you bump into an elderly man who falls and fractures his spine? Also, keep in mind that the liability coverage on your homeowner's insurance generally runs about $100,000 to $300,000, while the liability coverage on your auto insurance often is only $100,000. In a lawsuit today, that's peanuts. Don't take the risk: Consider an **umbrella liability insurance policy or umbrella policy**—they aren't that expensive. An umbrella policy supplements the liability coverage you already have through your home and auto insurance and provides an extra layer of protection. These policies kick in after the liability insurance in your homeowner's and auto policies runs out and provide coverage for claims that are not covered under your homeowner's insurance. What types of claims do you think this type of policy might cover?

Buying Automobile Insurance

Now that you know about the basic types of coverage provided by automobile insurance, you can make an informed choice in buying some. How much will you need to spend? Well, that depends on how good a comparison shopper you are. It also depends on some factors that are pretty much beyond your control. Let's take a look at these factors and then at what you can do to get the best possible deal.

Determinants of the Cost of Automobile Insurance The following are the major determinants of the cost of automobile insurance:

Umbrella Liability Insurance Policy or Umbrella Policy
An insurance policy that supplements liability coverage on a homeowner's and/or automobile insurance policy. This insurance kicks in after the homeowner's and/or automobile policy coverage runs out and provides coverage for claims not covered under homeowner's insurance such as libel, slander, and invasion of privacy.

- **The type of automobile.** The sportier and more high-powered your car is, the more your insurance will cost. In fact, when buying an automobile, the cost of insurance should be factored into the purchase decision.
- **The use of your automobile.** The less you use your car, the less you have to pay in insurance premiums.
- **Your personal characteristics.** Young unmarried males generally pay the most for their insurance because they have a statistically greater chance of having an accident. Age, sex, and marital status all go into determining how much you pay for insurance.
- **Your driving record.** If you've received traffic tickets or had traffic accidents, you'll probably have to pay more for your insurance. Exactly how much your premiums go up depends on the nature of your violations. If you receive a driving-under-the-influence-of-alcohol (DUI) citation, you can expect a hefty increase in your premiums.

- **Where you live.** In general, because of a higher incidence of accidents and theft, insurance is more expensive for those who live in urban areas.
- **Discounts that you qualify for.** A wide variety of discounts are available for cars that have certain safety features and for individuals who have characteristics identified with safe drivers. Table 10.3 lists some of the most common automobile insurance discounts.
- **Your insurance credit score.** Just as with homeowner's insurance, your insurance credit score goes a long way in determining what you pay for auto insurance. In fact, insurance credit scoring is even more common with automobile insurance than it is with homeowner's insurance, with about 92 of the 100 largest personal automobile insurers using some sort of insurance credit scoring. How do insurance companies justify this? They have found that drivers with poorer insurance credit scores incur much higher losses than do those with stronger insurance credit scores. In fact, those whose insurance credit scores are in the lowest 10 percent generated losses that were nearly twice as large for property damage liability claims and more than twice as large for bodily injury liability, collision, and comprehensive claims as those whose scores are in the highest 10 percent. As a result, many insurers use insurance credit scoring to set rates.

STOP & THINK

As you know, there are so many reasons not to get behind the wheel of a car when you've been drinking. One more reason, while perhaps minor relative to the more obvious reasons not to drink and drive, is that your insurance rates (or your parents' rates if you're on their policy) will climb. In the year after getting a DUI, your car insurance premiums will soar on average by 93 percent. And these increased insurance rates will continue for 3 to 5 years. In fact, by the time your DUI is 3 years old, your insurance rates will still be up there, averaging over 63 percent higher than they would be otherwise.

Keeping Your Costs Down There are several general ways you can keep your automobile insurance rates down while ensuring complete coverage. They include the following:

TABLE 10.3 Common Automobile Insurance Discounts
You can reduce your auto insurance premiums significantly by taking advantage of discounts. Listed below are the most common automobile insurance discounts.
Accident Free. Ten percent discounts on most coverage after 3 years without a chargeable accident. After 6 years, the discount rises to 15 percent.
Multiple Automobiles. Fifteen percent discount for insuring more than one car with the same company.
Low Annual Mileage. Fifteen percent discount if you drive fewer than 7,500 miles per year.
Automobile and Homeowner's Together. Five to 15 percent off both policies if with the same company.
Low "Damageability." Ten to 30 percent off collision and comprehensive premiums if the car is statistically less likely to result in an expensive claim because it is cheaper to repair or less appealing to thieves.
Good Student. Up to 25 percent discount for unmarried drivers under 25 who rank in the top 20 percent of their class, have a B average, or are on the honor roll.
Over 50. Ten percent discount off the usual adult rate if you are over 50.
Defensive Driving Course. Five percent discount if you complete a defensive driving course (many times only applies to drivers 55 or older).
Passive Restraints. Up to 40 percent discount on some coverages if you have air bags or automatic seatbelts. Antilock brakes also add a 5 percent discount.
Noncommuter or Carpooler. Fifteen percent discount if you drive less than 30 miles to and from work each day.
Antitheft Devices. Fifteen percent discount depending on where you live and the type of device.

- **Shop comparatively.** Different insurers don't charge identical prices for identical coverage. In fact, rates can vary by as much as 100 percent from carrier to carrier, and that's why you'll want to get a minimum of three different quotes on your automobile insurance. In addition, make sure you get quotes with different-size deductibles from each insurer.
- **Consider only high-quality insurers.** Check out the A.M. Best Web site (**http://www.ambest.com**) to assess the quality of insurers before purchasing insurance, and consider only those earning one of Best's two highest rankings.
- **Take advantage of discounts.** You can lower your premiums considerably by taking available discounts. Those in driver's education courses, persons over 50, graduates of defensive driving courses, students with good grades, and carpool participants all have the potential for discounts.
- **Buy a car that's relatively inexpensive to insure.** When making your purchase decision, factor in the cost of insurance on your new car.
- **Improve your driving record.** You have control over your driving record, and it goes a long way toward determining your premiums.
- **Raise your deductible.** As with homeowner's insurance, raising your deductible can significantly lower your premiums.
- **Keep adequate liability insurance.** With increasing medical and hospital expenses, damage awards have risen dramatically in recent years.

FACTS OF LIFE

To claim or not to claim? InsuranceQuotes and Quadrant Information Services looked at the average impact of filing claims on an auto insurance policy and found that just one car insurance claim will likely cause a hike in your insurance premiums of 44 percent and a second claim in the same year can result in an annual increase in your premiums of 98 percent! To help make the decision, InsuranceQuotes.com has a "How car insurance claims affect rates" calculator (**http://www.insurancequotes.com/calculators/car-insurance-claim-calculator**) that will, based on what it calculates your possible rate increase to be, tell you if you should make the claim or not.

Filing a Claim

There are a number of steps that you should take if you're involved in an automobile accident. It's a good idea to keep a list of these steps in your glove compartment because after an accident you may be too shaken up to recall them. Your "to do" list should include the following actions:

1. Get help for anyone injured. Because it's a felony to leave the scene of an accident, you should have someone call the police and an ambulance.
2. Move your car to a safe place or put up flares to prevent further accidents.
3. Get the names and addresses of any witnesses. Get their license plate numbers if you can't get their names. Also get the names of those in the other car (or cars) involved in the accident.
4. Cooperate with the police.
5. Do you think the other driver may have been driving under the influence? Insist that you both be tested for alcohol.
6. Write down your recollection of what happened. If you have a camera, take pictures of the scene.
7. Don't sign anything, don't admit guilt, and don't comment on how much insurance you have.
8. Get a copy of the police report, and make sure it's accurate.
9. Call your insurance agent as soon as possible.
10. Cooperate with your insurer. Remember, if there is a lawsuit, your insurer will defend you.
11. Keep records of all your expenditures associated with the accident.
12. In the case of a serious accident, meet with a lawyer so that you know what your rights are and what you can do to protect them.

BEHAVIORAL INSIGHTS

PRINCIPLE 9 PRINCIPLE 7 PRINCIPLE 1

Principle 9: Mind Games, Your Financial Personality, and Your Money While the idea of insurance is relatively simple and is based on **Principle 7: Protect Yourself Against Major Catastrophes**, it can be boring and seem like a waste of money. However, it is considered an essential piece of a solid financial plan, and when needed, it could save your financial plan. But buyer beware! Remember **Principle 1: Knowledge Is the Best Protection** because when it comes to insurance, know what you need—there is a lot out there and you don't need it all.

Once you've purchased an insurance policy, why do you consider adding riders? And why aren't those riders built into your policy? The answer deals with a behavioral finance concept called "integrated losses." What this concept tells us is that once you've spent a significant chunk of money, adding a bit more to your bill doesn't really have that much impact on you. So if you're already dealing with a $1,000 annual premium cost, adding another $50 option to "get a little extra something added" isn't really a big deal (at the time)—and it isn't as significant as spending $50 on another (unrelated) item. For example, why are you offered an opportunity to buy insurance that goes beyond the 100,000-mile bumper-to-bumper warranty on that new car you are purchasing right when you are ready to pay for it? The reason is because that's the easiest time and place to sell it—after all, you are sitting in the car dealer's office, getting ready to sign the check or the loan papers for a $30,000 purchase, so an extra thousand or two for some "additional protection" doesn't seem like that much money!

Adding options to an automobile or house purchase is the classic, well-known example. Insurance companies frequently sell riders to home or car insurance policies that are attractive (I believe) only because of this concept. One company has been advertising a "paint spill" rider for its homeowner's policy. (This is apparently designed for do-it-yourselfers who have not yet discovered drop cloths.)

Another behavioral finance concept that finds its way into insurance dealings is "representativeness bias," which results when individuals put too much weight on (bad) things that have recently happened. After you hear about someone experiencing a hurricane, flood, or mudslide, you are more inclined to buy insurance to cover that type of natural disaster. When in the throes of making a substantial purchase—like insurance with payments that last long into the future—it pays to take a step back, do your research, and really look at the likelihood that those events will actually happen to you.

ACTION PLAN

PRINCIPLE 10 PRINCIPLE 7

Principle 10: Just Do It! Once you have a car and some possessions, it's time for some insurance. Your goal should be to put **Principle 7: Protect Yourself Against Major Catastrophes** into action. Here are some things to consider:

- **Renter's insurance—do you need it?** Living in a dorm on campus? Chances are you are covered by your parents' "off-premise coverage." Living off-campus is another story. Do you own any computer equipment? Television? Stereo? DVD player? Textbooks? Bicycle? Kitchen gear? Furniture? Shoes and clothing? If you answered "yes," add up how much it would cost to replace all of these items. CNN estimates renter's insurance to be $184 per year. Now what do you think?

- **Auto insurance—required by law.** Take advantage of available discounts—some include those for having good grades, being a teacher, being a safe driver, having safety features in your car (air bags, antilock brakes, or an alarm), and completing a defensive driving course. Shop around.

PRINCIPLE 7

- **Remember Principle 7: Protect Yourself Against Major Catastrophes.** The purpose of insurance is to protect you from major losses—it isn't a maintenance plan. Have a realistic idea of how much insurance coverage you need. If you need to lower expenses, raise the deductible; don't sabotage your longer-term financial plan by lowering the amount of coverage. A higher deductible can pay off in other ways: It can help you avoid the temptation to file claims for small losses and avoid a history of multiple claims, which could result in your policy being cancelled. If you do this, make sure you have the amount of your higher deductible available in your emergency fund.

Chapter Summaries

LO1 Understand, buy, and maintain homeowner's insurance in a cost-effective way.

SUMMARY: There are six standardized, packaged homeowner's policies, each with a different type and level of insurance, available to home owners and renters. All policies are identified as HOs. Three of them—HO-1, HO-2, and HO-3—are basic, broad policies specifically for home owners. HO-4 is renter's insurance, HO-6 is for condominium owners, and HO-8 is for older homes. Each of these HO policies is divided into sections that provide property insurance (Section I) and liability coverage (Section II).

Because there are some gaps in coverage, many home owners purchase supplemental coverage. Some of the more common types of added coverage include personal articles floaters, earthquake protection, flood protection, inflation guard, and replacement cost.

KEY TERMS

Peril, page 335 An event or happening, whether natural or man-made, that causes a financial loss.

HOs, page 336 The six standardized homeowner's insurance policies available to home owners and renters.

Named Perils, page 336 A type of insurance that covers a specific set of named perils. If a peril isn't specifically named, it isn't covered.

Open Perils, page 336 A type of insurance that covers all perils except those specifically noted as excluded.

Property Insurance, page 336 Insurance that protects you against the loss of your property or possessions.

Personal Liability Insurance, page 336 Insurance covering all liabilities other than those resulting from the negligent operation of an automobile or those associated with business or professional causes.

Endorsement, page 339 A written attachment to an insurance policy to add or subtract coverage.

Personal Articles Floater, page 339 An extension to a homeowner's insurance policy that provides coverage for all personal property, regardless of where it's located. This coverage applies to the policyholder and all household residents except children away at school.

Inflation Guard, page 339 An endorsement that automatically updates the level of property coverage based on an index of replacement costs that continually updates the cost of building a home.

Actual Cash Value, page 339 The replacement value of the property less accumulated depreciation (which is the decline in value over time due to wear and tear).

Replacement Cost Coverage, page 340 Additional homeowner's coverage that provides for the actual replacement cost of stolen or destroyed property as opposed to the actual cash value.

Personal Umbrella Policy, page 340 A homeowner's policy that provides excess liability insurance with protection generally ranging from $1 million to $10 million against lawsuits and judgments.

Protect your property effectively while keeping your costs down. LO2

SUMMARY: You need enough homeowner's insurance to cover the replacement of your home in the event of a complete loss. This coverage needs to reflect any increased costs due to changing building codes. As your assets grow in value, it's important that you continuously review your homeowner's coverage to make sure that it reflects these changes.

How do you keep costs down? There are several ways, including taking a high deductible, installing a security system and smoke detector, having multiple policies with the same company, paying premiums annually, considering a direct writer, and shopping around.

KEY TERMS

Coinsurance Provision, page 340 A provision of homeowner's insurance that requires the insured to pay a portion of the claim if he or she purchased an inadequate amount of insurance (in this case, less than 80 percent of the home's full replacement cost).

80 Percent Rule, page 340 A homeowner's insurance rule stating that the replacement cost coverage is in effect only if the home is insured for at least 80 percent of its replacement cost. This rule is intended to discourage home owners from insuring for less than the replacement cost of their homes.

Insurance Credit Score, page 341 A credit score, based on the same information as your traditional credit score, that is used in determining what your home and auto insurance rates will be.

Deductible, page 344 The amount that you are responsible for paying before insurance coverage kicks in.

Direct Writer, page 345 An insurance company that distributes its products directly to customers, without the use of agents.

Manage your insurance. LO3

SUMMARY: For your homeowner's insurance to provide effective protection, you must be able to verify your loss by establishing proof of ownership and the value of your assets with a detailed asset inventory. In the event of a loss, you should report your loss immediately, make temporary repairs to protect your property, make a detailed list of everything lost or damaged, maintain records of the settlement process, and confirm the adjuster's estimate.

Pick out the right auto insurance and file a claim. LO4

SUMMARY: With automobile insurance, each policy is divided up into parts. There are two primary areas of automobile protection, which are detailed in the first four parts of your policy. First, there's protection against bodily injury, which includes bodily injury liability coverage (Part A), medical expenses coverage (Part B), and uninsured motorist's protection coverage (Part C). Second, there's protection against property damage, which includes property damage liability coverage (Part A), collision coverage (Part D), and comprehensive physical damage coverage (Part D); see Figure 10.3.

The five major determinants of the cost of automobile insurance are (1) the type of automobile and its use; (2) your age, sex, marital status, and driving record characteristics; (3) where you live; (4) the discounts you qualify for; and (5) your insurance credit score.

There are several general ways you can keep your automobile insurance rates down, while ensuring complete coverage. They include being a comparison shopper, considering only high-quality insurers, taking advantage of discounts, improving your driving record, raising your deductible, and keeping adequate liability insurance.

Once you have your auto insurance, you need to be able to file a claim. A list of what to do is given in the section titled "Filing a Claim"—you might want to photocopy that and keep it in the glove compartment of your car.

KEY TERMS

Personal Automobile Policy (PAP), page 347 A standardized automobile insurance policy for an individual or family.

Combined Single-Limit Coverage, page 348 Auto insurance liability coverage that combines both bodily injury and property damage liability.

Split-Limit Coverage, page 348 Auto insurance liability coverage that allows for separate coverage limits for bodily injury and property damage, split-coverage limits per person, or both.

Uninsured Motorist's Protection Coverage, page 350 Coverage against injuries caused by a hit-and-run driver, an uninsured motorist, or a negligent driver whose insurance company is insolvent.

Collision Loss, page 350 The portion of auto insurance coverage that provides benefits to cover damages resulting from an accident with another vehicle or object.

Other than Collision Loss or Comprehensive Physical Damage Coverage, page 350 The portion of auto insurance coverage that provides benefits to cover noncollision losses. For example, it covers the damage if the car is hit in a parking lot or is dented by the door of the car parked next to it.

No-Fault Insurance, page 352 A type of auto insurance in which your insurance company protects you in the case of an accident, regardless of who is at fault.

Umbrella Liability Insurance Policy or Umbrella Policy, page 352 An insurance policy that supplements liability coverage on a homeowner's and/or automobile insurance policy. This insurance kicks in after the homeowner's and/or automobile policy coverage runs out and provides coverage for claims not covered under homeowner's insurance such as libel, slander, and invasion of privacy.

Problems and Activities

These problems are available in MyLab Finance.

1. Jody Solan currently insures her home for 100 percent of its replacement value with an HO-3 policy. For Jody, this works out to $140,000 in dwelling (Part A) coverage. What are the maximum dollar coverage amounts for Parts B, C, and D of her homeowner's policy?
2. Keith and Dena Diem have personal property coverage with a $250 limit on currency, a $1,000 limit on jewelry, and a $2,500 limit on gold, silver, and pewter. They do not have a personal property floater. If $500 in cash, $2,400 of jewelry, and $1,500 of pewterware are stolen from their home, what amount of loss will be covered by their homeowner's policy? If the Diems' deductible is $250, how much will they receive on their claim?

3. How much would a home owner receive with actual cash-value coverage and with replacement cost coverage for a 3-year-old sofa destroyed by a fire? The sofa would cost $1,000 to replace today, whereas it cost $850 3 years ago, and it has an estimated life of 6 years.
4. Carmella Estevez has a homeowner's insurance policy with $100,000 of liability insurance. She is concerned about the risk of lawsuits because her property borders a neighborhood park. What can she do to increase her liability coverage? How much will Carmella's yearly premiums change as a result of increasing her liability coverage?
5. Jerry Carter's home is currently valued, on a replacement cost basis, at $315,000. When he last checked his policy, his home was insured for $235,000, and he did not have an inflation guard endorsement. If he has a $25,500 claim due to a kitchen fire, how much will his homeowner's insurance policy pay? How much will he be paid if his home is totally destroyed? In order to obtain full replacement coverage, how much insurance should Jerry carry on his house?
6. Carmen Viers lost everything to a fire and has spent the last 8 weeks living in a motel room at a cost of $4,500. Her dwelling, which was destroyed as a result of a lighting strike, was insured with an HO-2 policy for $280,000. Prior to the loss, her home was valued at $300,000, her detached garage and pool house were valued at $38,000, and her personal property had an actual cash value of $91,000. To make matters worse, she sustained $10,000 in injuries while trying without success to save her three Greyhound dogs valued at $6,000 each. How much of her total losses and expenses will be reimbursed if she has a $1,000 deductible?
7. Larry Simmons has split-limit 100/300/50 automobile liability insurance. Several months ago Larry was in an accident in which he was found to be at fault. Four passengers were seriously injured in the accident and were awarded $100,000 each because of Larry's negligence. How much of this judgment will Larry's insurance policy cover? What amount will Larry have to pay out of pocket?
8. Bill Buckely has split-limit 25/50/10 automobile liability insurance on his 2012 Subaru. Driving home from work in a snowstorm, he hit a Mercedes, slid into a guardrail, and knocked down a telephone pole. Damages to the Mercedes, the guardrail, and the telephone pole were $8,500, $2,000, and $4,500, respectively. How much will Bill's insurance company pay? How much will Bill be required to pay directly?
9. Jessica Railes is purchasing a condo and is shopping for an HO-6 policy. Her auto insurer quoted her an annual rate of $550. However, if she insures both her condo and her car with the same company, the insurer will give her an additional 8 percent discount on her HO-6 policy and a 10 percent discount on her $1,200 annual auto premium. By how much will this reduce Jessica's premium? In addition to the discount, what are other advantages of purchasing both auto and homeowner's insurance with the same company?
10. The Superior Insurance Company of Maine recently advertised the following discounts for qualified drivers:
    - 10 percent discount for drivers who have not had an accident in the past 7 years
    - 15 percent discount for those with two or more cars; 5 percent discount for insuring both home and car
    - 10 percent discount for those who drive less than 10,000 miles a year
    - 25 percent discount for drivers who are good students (have a B average or above)

- 10 percent discount for drivers aged 50 or older; 5 percent discount for drivers aged 24 to 49
- 5 percent discount for drivers who have taken a defensive driving course
- 15 percent discount for noncommuters (less than 30 miles round-trip)
- 15 percent discount for cars with antitheft devices

Jana, 25 years old, currently pays $1,200 annually for a PAP for her 2011 Chevy Malibu. She uses her car to commute 40 miles round-trip to work and to make biannual cross-country trips to visit relatives. Last year she received a speeding ticket but took a defensive driving course in order to remove the ticket from her record; she has never had an accident. When she purchased her car, she had an alarm installed. Jana is sure that she qualifies for at least one or more discounts. Calculate her new premium if she transfers to the Superior Insurance Company.

Discussion Case 1

This case is available in **MyLab Finance.**

Graham and Eustacia Leyland are planning to buy a $185,000 home near Bethel Corners, New York. The home is in "snow country," about a mile from Lake Ontario, and is situated on the Salmon River, which overflows its banks about every 2 years. They estimate that their personal property is worth $165,000, but they really aren't sure. This includes nearly $30,000 of computer and other electronic equipment, a $15,000 coin collection inherited from Graham's father, and $25,000 in irreplaceable artwork. The Leylands' net worth, including their current $120,000 home, is about $600,000. The Leylands have asked their insurance agent to find them the best coverage, taking advantage of all possible cost-saving measures. They do not want a lot of out-of-pocket expenses if their home or personal property is damaged or lost, and they want their insurance to keep pace with increasing costs.

Questions

1. What type of homeowner's insurance policy is best for the Leylands? Which covered perils would be of greatest interest living in their location?
2. What is the minimum amount of Coverage A that the Leylands should purchase on their new home? What risks do they face if they purchase only the minimum required coverage? How much insurance should they purchase in order to reduce their financial risks?
3. Given the value and nature of their personal property and the restrictive Coverage C limits, what other supplemental coverages would you recommend that the Leylands purchase? Document your recommendations in terms of both the protection offered and the cost of coverage.
4. Given the winter snow and ice common to upstate New York, what recommendations would you make for their Section II coverage?
5. Should the Leylands buy flood insurance? If so, how do they go about purchasing it? If not, explain why.
6. Should the Leylands consider purchasing an umbrella policy? Why or why not?

Discussion Case 2

This case is available in **MyLab Finance.**

Bronwyn Lipper, a 2014 graduate with a degree in biochemistry, has a promising career ahead of her. Already, her employer has offered to pay for graduate school, and in the past

2 years, she has been promoted three times. Three years ago she purchased a townhouse for $210,000 in Laurel, Maryland. Today, her townhouse is valued at over $270,000. More recently, Bronwyn purchased a new Ford Escape hybrid. She appreciates the energy savings and the safety the SUV gives her on her 45-mile round-trip commute into Baltimore. Overall, Bronwyn feels economically secure. She has over $35,000 in savings and growing retirement accounts. On her drive home from work last night, she heard a radio report about a person who lost everything when he caused an auto accident and was underinsured. Bronwyn certainly does not want this to happen to her. Help her consider the following questions and issues.

Questions

1. After reviewing her personal automobile policy, Bronwyn realized that she had $75,000 of single-limit, Part A coverage; $15,000 of Part B coverage; $75,000 of Part C coverage; and "full" Part D coverage. Is Bronwyn adequately insured? Explain your answer.
2. Bronwyn was quoted $1,400 a year for split-limit coverage with the following limits: 75/150/50, assuming a $100 deductible. Are these limits adequate, given Bronwyn's financial situation and potential liability? What would you recommend as a minimum limit for this coverage? What will be the impact of your recommendation on her policy premium?
3. The insurance company that gave her the quote for split-limit coverage also indicated that she could choose a $100, $250, $500, or $1,000 deductible. If Bronwyn wants to reduce her premium costs, what deductible should she choose? Why?
4. If she decides not to boost her liability limits, how will others be compensated for their losses—property, medical, or funeral—if she is involved in a serious accident and found liable for expenses that exceed her policy limits? Would others be compensated by Bronwyn's policy for their injuries if she is not liable? If so, under what part of the policy?
5. Should Bronwyn continue to purchase Part C and Part D coverage? Why or why not?
6. What types of discounts might be available for Bronwyn that will help reduce her annual insurance premium?
7. How does **Principle 5: Stuff Happens, or the Importance of Liquidity** address Bronwyn's concerns about balancing adequate coverage, a reasonably high deductible to reduce the premium, and the need for emergency savings? PRINCIPLE 5
8. Bronwyn has heard about an umbrella policy but is unsure if it is needed. Would you recommend that she purchase such a policy? Explain your answer. Approximately how much will such a policy cost, assuming that she insures her townhouse and car with the same insurance company?
9. If Bronwyn was to get in an accident during her daily commute, why should she never admit guilt, sign anything, or comment on how much insurance she has?

Continuing Case: Cory and Tisha Dumont

Part III: Protecting Yourself with Insurance

Cory and Tisha read a recent newspaper article stating that personal bankruptcy and other financial problems often result from uninsured losses. This made them curious about their own insurance coverage, so they have come back to you for assistance. Because they want to buy a home very soon, they are also interested in homeowner's insurance. They compiled the following information for you to review.

Life Insurance

Type	Cory	Tisha
Group life insurance	2 times gross income	1.50 times gross income
Whole life insurance	None	$50,000
Cash value		$1,800
Annual life insurance premiums	$0; employer paid	$0 for employer provided; $720 for whole life (due next month)
Beneficiary	Tisha	Cory
Contingent beneficiary	Tisha's parents	Tisha's parents

Health Insurance

Tisha's employer provides a comprehensive major medical insurance policy that covers all members of the Dumont family with an 80/20 coinsurance provision. The Dumonts are subject to a $500 annual family deductible. Tisha's employer deducts $267 per month toward the premium; her employer pays the remainder of the premium. Because Tisha's company offered the better coverage, Cory chose to "opt out" of his coverage and receives an "opt out fee" of $100 per month (included in gross income).

Automobile Insurance (Both Cars)

Type	Personal Auto Policy
Coverages	25/50/25 split-limit liability
Uninsured motorist	25/50/25 split-limit liability
Medical expenses	$20,000
Collision	$200 deductible
Comprehensive	$200 deductible
Annual premium car 1	$1,250
Annual premium car 2	$950

Umbrella Liability Insurance

None

Disability Insurance

Tisha: $2,000 per month up to 6 months; premium paid by employer
Cory: None

Homeowner's/Renter's Insurance

HO-4 renter's insurance policy with $25,000 of actual cash-value coverage on personal property and an annual premium of $600

Questions

1. After reviewing the earnings multiple approach and the needs approach, Cory and Tisha opt for the simpler earnings multiple approach to estimate their life insurance needs. As Cory explains, "There are just too many unknowns in that needs approach formula. Years of income to be replaced I can understand. If I die tomorrow, I want to know that Tisha can buy a home and the kids can finish college. Chad is 4 and Haley is 2. With 20 years of my income, they should be able to do that." Tisha agrees, although she cautions that before purchasing insurance she would like to confirm their estimates by completing the needs formula. They agree that they could earn a 5 percent after-tax, after-inflation return on the insurance benefit. Do Tisha and Cory have adequate life insurance? If not, how much should each consider purchasing? (*Hint:* Remember that expenses drop by 22 percent for a surviving family of three. Be sure to consult Table 9.2, "Earnings Multiples for Life Insurance.")
2. All of Cory's life insurance and half of Tisha's are provided through their employers. Is this a good idea?
3. Cory's been on the Internet again, this time to read about universal life and variable life insurance. He has asked your opinion about purchasing one of these policies to provide additional insurance coverage for his family. What would you advise him to do? Defend your answer.
4. The Dumonts have asked you to review their life insurance policies and explain them "in plain English." What standard life insurance policy clauses or optional riders would you consider to be most important to Cory and Tisha?
5. An insurance agent recently suggested purchasing whole life policies for Chad and Haley. Costs would be cheap, and Cory and Tisha could rest assured that the kids would always be insured. Is this a good idea? Defend your answer.
6. Do Tisha and Cory have adequate health insurance? If not, what changes would you suggest and why?
7. Assume Tisha is injured in a car accident and incurs $5,000 of medical bills. What are the options for paying these bills? How would your answer change if the $5,000 of medical bills resulted from an emergency appendectomy? Assuming that no one else in her family has made a claim this year, how much of these bills will her insurance company pay?
8. Next month is the "annual open enrollment period" for health insurance benefits through Tisha's employer. It is the only time of the year when she can make changes to her policy. Tisha is considering switching to a different HMO or PPO plan. What are the advantages and disadvantages of each form of managed care?
9. Tisha is concerned about a possible layoff due to mergers among several accounting firms. What are some health insurance options available to the Dumonts if Tisha is "downsized"? What are the advantages and disadvantages of Cory "opting out" in this situation? Tisha has considered self-employment from a home office. How will this affect their options for family health-care coverage?
10. Both Tisha and Cory are considering the purchase of disability insurance because Cory has none and Tisha's employer-provided policy is very short-term. What policy features would you recommend they include?
11. Do Tisha and Cory have adequate renter's insurance? What recommendation would you make? Why?

12. Evaluate the Dumonts' auto insurance. What recommendations for changes, if any, would you make? Why?

13. How much would the Dumonts' policy pay if Cory or Tisha was at fault for an accident that resulted in $65,000 of bodily injury losses? How would the claim be paid?

14. What policy options could the Dumonts select to reduce the cost of their property and liability insurance?

15. What type of homeowner's policy should the Dumonts select when they purchase their first home, assuming they are very cautious about protecting their financial situation? Also, recall that Cory does not like financial surprises, so they will not be considering an older home or a condominium! Should they consider adding an umbrella policy at this time? Explain your answer.

PART 4

Managing Your Investments

You now have an understanding of the financial planning process, including managing your money and assessing your insurance needs. What's next? It's time to turn your attention to how you make your money grow—that is, how you turn money into wealth—and to do that, you need a basic understanding of investments. This all goes back to Principle 1: The Best Protection Is Knowledge; with an understanding of investments, not only do you have the ability to manage your own investments, but also you are able to protect yourself against bad, or unscrupulous, investment advice. In effect, investment knowledge serves as an insurance policy against this problem.

In Part 4, we will specifically focus on Principles 8 and 9:

Principle 8: Risk and Return Go Hand in Hand—While this principle focuses on the relationship between risk and return, it also introduces the concept of diversification, which allows you to eliminate risk without impacting return. In addition, you will see why you can afford to take on more risk when you have a longer period of time until you need your money.

Principle 9: Mind Games, Your Financial Personality, and Your Money—Unfortunately, we all seem to be programmed for failure. Apparently, many of the financial mistakes we make are built right into our brains. However, by understanding the behavioral biases we all have, we can avoid these mistakes.

In addition, in Part 4 we will touch on these principles:

Principle 1: The Best Protection Is Knowledge

Principle 2: Nothing Happens Without a Plan

Principle 3: The Time Value of Money

Principle 4: Taxes Affect Personal Finance Decisions

Principle 10: Just Do It!

CHAPTER 11 Investment Basics

Learning Objectives

LO1	**Set** your goals and be ready to invest.	**Before You Invest**
LO2	**Manage** risk in your investments.	**A Look at Risk-Return Trade-Offs**
LO3	**Allocate** your assets in the manner that is best for you.	**The Time Dimension of Investing and Asset Allocation**
LO4	**Understand** how difficult it is to beat the market.	**What You Should Know About Efficient Markets**
LO5	**Identify** and describe the primary and secondary securities markets.	**Securities Markets**
LO6	**Trade** securities using a broker.	**How Securities Are Traded**
LO7	**Locate** and use several different sources of investment information to trade securities.	**Sources of Investment Information**

Most parents don't buy stocks on the recommendation of their children, but that's what Mary and Tom Sanchez did. In March 1986, their 13-year-old daughter, Jennifer, a self-proclaimed "computer geek," convinced them to invest $10,000, which was about 15 percent of their total savings, in a stock that was going public at the time—Microsoft. In fact, Jennifer also invested her entire savings—paper route and babysitting money, along with some money from her grandparents—of $750.

Back then, Microsoft was a small firm in Seattle with an unknown future, run by a young, untested computer genius, Bill Gates. In fact, Microsoft was so small and unknown that it was difficult finding a stockbroker who had access to Microsoft stock at its initial price of $21 per share. The Sanchezes did though, and they're glad of it. They even convinced Mary's brother Jim to invest $5,000 in Microsoft. He wasn't fortunate enough to be able to buy in at $21, but he was able to buy the stock later that month at $26. By 2017, the Sanchezes' $10,000 investment had grown to about $8.9 million, and Mary's brother Jim's investment of $5,000 had grown to about $3.6 million. It may well be worth considerably more today. As for Jennifer, her $750 would have been worth about $667,000, but instead it took the form of a new Porsche 911 convertible and some other investments.

Daxiao Productions/Fotolia

About 20 years after her first stock recommendation, in March and April 2003, Jennifer made a second recommendation—it was Apple. She had just purchased her first iPod—it was the third-generation iPod and the first one to feature an all-touch interface and a dock connector. As Jennifer said, "I truly thought the iPod would change the world—and I was right." On Jennifer's recommendation, both she and her parents invested $100,000 each. By 2017, that $100,000 investment had grown to about $13.8 million! Jennifer also hit it big with Netflix, turning an investment of $25,000 in 2005 to over $2.6 million in 2017. And even though she doesn't always make money—for example, she turned an investment of $100,000 in **Pets.com** in 2000 to $0 in just about a year—Jennifer is now known as an "investment wizard" rather than a "computer geek."

Not everyone does as well with investments as the Sanchezes. However, one way to greatly improve your chances for success is to understand the rules of the investment game—in this case, how the securities markets work. Very few people feel comfortable, or should feel comfortable, playing a game without knowing the rules. That's the purpose of this chapter—to introduce you to the rules of the securities markets. We will look at how the investments markets operate and prepare you to go out and make your own investments.

It would be nice if we could all have the same success as the Sanchezes. Unfortunately, that kind of success can't be guaranteed. However, one thing is certain: The first step to becoming wealthy through a great investment is learning how to make that investment.

LO1 Set your goals and be ready to invest.

Before You Invest

In personal financial planning, everything begins and ends with your goals, and investments are no exception. Before developing an investment plan, you must first decide what your goals are and how much you can set aside to meet those goals. Before we look at goal setting and making a plan, however, let's look at the difference between investing and speculating.

Investment
An asset that generates value or a return. For example, stocks pay dividends and bonds pay interest, so these are considered investments.

Income Return
Investment return received directly from the company or organization in which you've invested, usually in the form of dividends or interest payments.

Speculation
Buying an asset whose value depends solely on supply and demand as opposed to being based on the return that it generates. For example, gold coins and baseball cards are worth more in the future only if someone is willing to pay more for them.

Investing Versus Speculating

This chapter is about investing, not about speculating. What's the difference? Well, although they both involve risk, when you buy an **investment**, you put your money in an asset that generates value or a return. For example, part of its return or value may come in the form of an **income return** such as dividends or interest payments. Part may also come from the fact that the investment is creating value or wealth—that is, it is earning money and plowing that money back into the investment so that the investment itself appreciates in value. Real estate pays rent, stocks appreciate in value and oftentimes pay dividends, and bonds pay interest. Even if the stock isn't paying dividends now—such as with the common stock of Alphabet, the parent company of Google—it is creating wealth or value and appreciating in price. It is the *return* that the asset generates now and will generate in the future that determines its value.

Speculation, on the other hand, involves assets that don't generate wealth or a return and entails a much higher level of risk, and in general, you are *hoping* for a very high return. Gold coins and baseball cards, for example, are worth more in the future only if someone is willing to buy them at a higher price than you paid when you bought them. Their value depends *entirely* on supply and demand, and demand for these assets can change quickly. As a result, an asset of this type is considered speculative. Other examples of speculative assets include comic books, autographs, Beanie Babies®, and gems—it's the same as betting on the Super Bowl in hopes that you will make a lot of money quickly.

You can make a pretty penny speculating. The first issue of the *X-Men* comic book appeared in September 1963 and cost 12¢. Fifty-four years later it was worth over $75,000 in near mint condition—that's an appreciation rate of over 28.7 percent per year. But be warned: You can also lose a lot through speculating. Just look at Mark McGwire's 1985 Topps Tiffany baseball card—it sold at a peak price of $10,000, but in 2017, it was down to $50; the same thing happened to Jason Giambi's 1991 Topps rookie card, which peaked at $400 before falling to $7 in 2017. Why did the value of these

STOP & THINK

If an asset doesn't generate a return, its value is determined by supply and demand. Putting money into such an asset is speculating. Gold is a good example. Although recently a number of financial gurus (along with gold sellers trying to push the price of gold up) have been claiming that gold is a good investment, it's simply a form of speculation. While salesmen may make gold sound like a sure bet, it's far from that. In early 1980, the price of an ounce of gold was just over $850. Since 1980, however, the price has bounced a bit, hitting $1,900 in September 2011 before dropping below $1,232 in 2017. While gold did very well in 2010 and early 2011, its average annual return since 1980 is just over 1 percent per year, much less than inflation over that time. The common stock of a typical large company, conversely, increased at an average annual rate of 11.4 percent from the beginning of 1980 to the beginning of 2017. The bottom line is *invest*; don't speculate.

cards drop so much? No one wanted to buy them. It all boils down to supply and demand.

Today's new variation of speculative securities is derivatives. **Derivative securities** are those whose value is derived from the value of other assets—these include options.

Derivative Securities
Securities whose value is derived from the value of other assets.

An **option** gives its owner *the right* to buy or sell an asset—generally common stock. In other words, if the asset is not of value, you don't have to exercise the option. The price at which the option holder can buy or sell the asset is specified along with the maturity or expiration date of the option. There are two basic types of options: a call option, which gives you the option to buy the underlying asset at a set price on or before the option's maturity date, and a put option, which gives you the option to sell the underlying asset at a set price on or before the option's maturity date.

Option
A security that gives its owner the right to buy or sell an asset–generally common stock–at a specified price over a specified period.

With options, you find the buyer and seller are, in a sense, betting against each other. For this reason, the options markets are often referred to as a "zero sum game" less transactions costs. If someone makes money, then someone must lose money; if profits and losses were added up, the total for all options, ignoring trading costs, would equal zero. To say the least, the options markets are quite complicated and risky. In fact, some experts refer to them as legalized institutions for transferring wealth from the unsophisticated to the sophisticated. These derivatives can be extremely dangerous. For the beginning investor, options should be considered speculative in nature. In short, they're not something to rely on to achieve your financial goals.

With *investing*, as opposed to speculating, the value of an asset is determined by what return it earns. Investments have intrinsic value because they produce wealth and income, and although in the short term their price may wander a bit from their intrinsic value, in the long run the price approaches the intrinsic value. Investment is less risky than speculation, and value is based on how much income the investment is producing now, along with what it is expected to produce in the future. Certainly, investment is not as exciting as speculation, but "exciting" is not that great if it means losing your nest egg.

Setting Investment Goals

Most of us have goals or at least dreams—we'd like to buy a house or maybe retire early—but to reach those goals, they must be formalized. That's the point of **Principle 2: Nothing Happens Without a Plan**. When making your plan, you must (1) write your goals down and prioritize them, (2) attach costs to them, (3) figure out when the money for those goals will be needed, and (4) periodically reevaluate your goals.

PRINCIPLE 2

As we said in Chapter 1, when formalizing your goals, it's easiest to think about them in terms of short-term, intermediate-term, and long-term time horizons. Short-term goals are any financial goals that can be accomplished within a 1-year period, such as buying a television or taking a vacation. An intermediate-term goal is one that will take between 1 and 10 years to accomplish—perhaps paying for college for an older child or accumulating enough money for a down payment on a new house. A long-term goal is one for which it will take more than 10 years to accumulate the money—retiring, for example.

In setting these goals, the key is to be realistic, which means your goals should reflect your financial and life situations. The following questions might help you focus on what goals are important to you:

- If I don't accomplish this goal, what are the consequences?
- Am I willing to make the financial sacrifices necessary to meet this goal?
- How much money do I need to accomplish this goal?
- When do I need this money?

STOP & THINK

Is it possible to reach your financial goals? Yes, and it may be easier to reach them than you think because time is on your side. A small change in your spending and investment habits could produce big returns later on. For example, if you're 20 now and you save $15 per month—that works out to about 50 cents per day—at 12 percent, 50 years later your savings will have grown to over $585,000. This may sound like a mighty high return, but keep in mind that over the last 50 years the market has returned about 10 percent, and small company stocks have performed even better over this period. The key is to start early. What could you cut out in order to save $15 per month?

Once you've set your goals, you then have to use your time value of money skills to translate them into action. For example, if you'd like to retire in 40 years with $1,000,000, you have to first consider what you can earn on your savings and then determine how much you need to set aside each year.

Financial Reality Check

Before you put your investment program into place, it's important that you have a grip on your financial affairs. Make sure you're living within your means, have adequate insurance, and keep emergency funds—in effect, put your financial house in order before you consider investing.

Starting Your Investment Program

PRINCIPLE 3

PRINCIPLE 10

The sooner you invest, the more you earn. Keep in mind **Principle 3: The Time Value of Money**. As you know by now, there's no substitute for time when it comes to investments—the earlier you begin planning for the future, the easier it is to achieve your goals. That's why **Principle 10: Just Do It!** is so important. Regardless of your level of income, you can make room for investing.

How do you go about starting an investment program? The first step is to revisit the first two questions you asked when setting up your goals: If I don't accomplish this goal, what are the consequences? Am I willing to make the financial sacrifices necessary to meet this goal? Once you have the commitment, the next step is to come up with the money. Here are some tips to get started.

Pay Yourself First First, set aside your savings, and what's left becomes the amount you can spend. When you pay yourself first, you're acknowledging the fact that your long-term goals are paramount.

Make Investing Automatic Make your saving and investing automatic. If your employer allows automatic withholding, take advantage of it, or have an amount automatically deducted from your checking account and sent to a brokerage firm or mutual fund.

Take Advantage of Uncle Sam and Your Employer If your employer offers matching investments, don't pass them by. Matching investments are about as close to something for nothing as you'll ever get. Also, keep an eye out for investments that are tax favored, such as traditional IRAs and Roth IRAs.

Windfalls If you're ever lucky enough to receive a bit of a windfall—perhaps an inheritance, a salary bonus, a gift, a tax refund, or maybe even something from the lottery—don't fritter it away. Investing some (or all) of it is a speedy way to build your investments.

Make 2 Months a Year Investment Months Some financial advisors suggest that if you're having trouble starting your investment program, pick 2 months per year to cut back on your spending and make those your investment months. If you know that your "life of poverty" is over at the end of the month, it may be easier to stick to your savings plan.

Fitting Taxes into Investing

When we compare investment returns, we want to make our comparison on an after-tax basis—that is, what we pay to Uncle Sam doesn't count. As we examine the different investment alternatives, we'll look more closely at taxes, but several points hold true, regardless of what we invest in.

- The marginal tax rate is the rate you pay on the next dollar of earnings.
- Tax-free investment alternatives should be compared only on an after-tax basis. Of course, the higher your marginal tax bracket, the more attractive tax-free investments become.
- You can make investments on a *tax-deferred* basis, which means that not only does your investment grow free of taxes but also the money you invest is before-tax income and is not taxed until you liquidate your investment.
- When it comes to taxes, capital gains and dividend income are better than ordinary income. Recall from Chapter 4 that in 2017 both the long-term capital gains tax rate and the tax rate on qualified dividends are reduced to 15 percent for taxpayers whose top tax bracket exceeds 15 percent but is below 39.6 percent, and for taxpayers in the 10 and 15 percent tax brackets, these tax rates are reduced to 0 percent. If you're lucky enough to have enough income to land in the 39.6 percent tax bracket, your long-term capital gains will be taxed at 20 percent.

If you were in the 35 percent marginal tax bracket in 2017 and had $50,000 of additional ordinary income, your tax bill would come to ($50,000 × 35 percent) = $17,500. If this $50,000 of additional income came in the form of long-term capital gains, your taxes would be only ($50,000 × 15 percent) = $7,500. Just as valuable as the tax break on capital gains income is the fact that you don't have to claim it—and therefore pay taxes on it until you sell the asset. That is, you can time when you want to claim your capital gains.

Taxes make some investments better than they would otherwise be and others worse—it all goes back to **Principle 4: Taxes Affect Personal Finance Decisions.**

PRINCIPLE 4

Investment Choices

Today, there are really only two basic categories of investments:

- **Lending investments.** Savings accounts and bonds, which are debt instruments issued by corporations and by the government, are examples of lending investments.
- **Ownership investments.** Preferred stocks and common stocks, which represent an ownership position in a corporation, and income-producing real estate are examples of ownership investments.

Let's take a closer look at each of these.

Lending Investments Whenever you put money in a savings account or buy a bond, you're actually lending someone your money. The amount you've lent them is your investment. A savings account pays you interest on the balance you hold in your account. With a bond, your return is generally fixed and known ahead of time. It has a set **maturity date**, at which time the bond is terminated and the money that you lent is returned to you. The face value of the bond, which is the amount you receive when the bond matures, is referred to as the **par value or principal**.

Most bonds issued by corporations trade in units of $1,000, although bonds issued by federal, state, or local governments may trade in units of $5,000 or $10,000.

Maturity Date
The date at which the borrower must repay the loan or borrowed funds.

Par Value or Principal
The stated amount on the face of a bond, which the firm is to repay at the maturity date.

Coupon Interest Rate
The interest to be paid annually on a bond as a percentage of par value, which is specified in the contractual agreement.

Over the life of the bond, you receive semiannual interest payments, which are set when the bond is issued. The **coupon interest rate** refers to the actual rate of interest the bond pays. Most bonds have fixed interest rates, but some have variable or floating rates, meaning that the interest rate changes periodically to reflect current interest rates.[1]

Let's assume, for example, that you've bought a 20-year bond issued by the government, with a par value of $1,000 and an interest rate of 8 percent. You'll receive $80 per year in interest payments (0.08 × $1,000). Then, at maturity, which in this case is in 20 years, you'll be returned the par value, which is $1,000.

With lending investments, you usually know ahead of time exactly what your return will be, which isn't always a good thing. In the bond example, you've locked in an 8 percent return on your bond, but if inflation suddenly climbs to 16 percent, your return won't even keep up with inflation. On the other hand, if inflation drops, your 8 percent may look even better than it did when you purchased the bond.

The biggest potential problem with lending investments arises when the lender experiences financial difficulties and can't pay the interest on the bond or can't pay off the bond at maturity. If the firm that issued the bond goes bankrupt, the bondholders will most likely lose their entire investment. Unfortunately, even though lending investments let you share a lender's financial pain, they don't let you share any of the pleasure. If the lender suddenly makes a ton of money, you don't.

STOP & THINK

The average American spends 29 hours a week watching TV. How many hours a week do you think he or she spends on financial planning and investing?

With lending investments, the best-case scenario is that the issuer pays you all the interest that's owed and at maturity gives you back your principal. Actually, this best-case scenario is much better than it at first seems. If you carefully choose whose bonds you buy or where you open a savings account, there can be much less risk with lending investments than with ownership investments. In addition, the returns can be quite respectable.

Ownership Investments The two major forms of ownership investment are real estate and stocks. Real estate investments include such things as rental apartments and investments in income-producing property, such as shopping malls and office buildings. In each case, you're investing in something that generates a return: rent. Your home could also be considered a real estate investment. In a sense, it generates income because it eliminates rent payments that you would otherwise have to make.

The major disadvantage of real estate investments is that they tend to be quite illiquid. That is, when it comes time to sell off your investment, you may have a hard time getting a fair price for it or even finding someone interested in buying it.

Stock
A fractional ownership in a corporation.

The most popular ownership investment is stocks, but the actual "ownership" isn't of an asset you can hold in your hand or live in. When you purchase 50 shares of General Electric **stock**, you've purchased a small portion of the General Electric Corporation. Although you own only a tiny fraction of GE, buying stock does make you an owner or equity holder, with "equity" being another term for ownership.

Dividend
A payment by a corporation to its shareholders.

What do you get as an owner of GE? Don't count on any free lightbulbs. In the case of common stock ownership, you get a chance to vote for the board of directors, which oversees GE's operations. If GE earns a profit, you'll most likely receive a portion of those profits in the form of **dividends**, which are generally paid out quarterly. In addition, as profits and dividends continue to increase, investors see the stock as more valuable and are willing to pay more to purchase it. Thus, the price goes up, and there's no limit as to how high a stock's price can rise.

---

[1]There are also zero-coupon bonds that make no interest payments to the bondholder. We talk about these in Chapter 14.

In the case of preferred stock, the dividend is generally fixed, with the preferred stockholder receiving an annual dividend as long as the firm has the cash to pay. You can't vote for the board of directors if you own GE preferred stock unless GE has suffered some financial problems and omitted some preferred stock dividends.

Of course, companies must pay the interest to debt holders before they can distribute dividends to stockholders. Thus, if debt such as bonds eats up a company's profits, stockholders get no dividends. Moreover, preferred stockholders take a "preferred" position to common stockholders—that is, they receive their dividends first. Common stockholders receive their dividends from whatever's left over.

The Returns from Investing

When you invest your money, you can receive your return in one of two ways. First, an investment can go up or down in value—in the language of investments, this is referred to as a **capital gain or loss**. Although most people associate capital gains and losses with real estate and common stock, these gains and losses also come with bonds. In fact, most of the time when you buy a bond, you buy it for something other than its par value—that is, what the issuer gives you back when the bond matures. This means that if you hold it to maturity, you'll experience some capital gains or losses.

Capital Gain or Loss
The gain (or loss) on the sale of a capital asset. For example, any return (or loss) from the appreciation (or drop) in value of a share of stock would be considered a capital gain (or loss).

The second component of the return on your investment is the income return. Income return consists of any payments you receive directly from the company or organization in which you've invested. In the case of bonds, your income return is the interest you receive. In the case of common and preferred stocks, your income return comes in the form of dividends. The rate of return can be calculated as follows:

$$\text{rate of return} = \frac{(\text{ending value} - \text{beginning value}) + \text{income return}}{\text{beginning value}}$$

Thus, if a stock climbs from \$45 to \$55 per share over 1 year, while paying \$3 in dividends, its rate of return over that year would be

$$\text{rate of return} = \frac{(\$55 - \$45) + \$3}{\$45} = \frac{\$10 + \$3}{\$45} = \frac{\$13}{\$45} = 28.89\%$$

If you're calculating the rate of return over a number of years, you may want to break this down into the average annual rate of return. You need only multiply the rate of return by $1/N$, where N is the number of years for which the investment is held. Thus, the average annual rate of return can be calculated as follows:

$$\begin{array}{c}\text{average annual}\\ \text{rate of return}\end{array} = \frac{(\text{ending value} - \text{beginning value}) + \text{income return}}{\text{beginning value}} \times \frac{1}{N}$$

If over a 3-year period a stock climbs from \$45 to \$68 per share and pays a total of \$7 in dividends over 3 years, its average annual rate of return would be

$$\begin{array}{c}\text{average annual}\\ \text{rate of return}\end{array} = \frac{(\$68 - \$45) + \$7}{\$45} \times \frac{1}{3} = \frac{\$23 + \$7}{\$45} \times \frac{1}{3}$$

$$= \frac{\$30}{\$45} \times \frac{1}{3} = 0.667 \times 0.333 = 0.222, \text{ or } 22.2\%$$

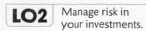

LO2 Manage risk in your investments.

A Look at Risk–Return Trade-Offs

PRINCIPLE 8

From **Principle 8**, you know that risk goes hand in hand with potential return. The more risk you are willing to take on, the greater the potential return—but also the greater the possibility that you will lose money. What does all this mean? It means you must take steps to eliminate risk without affecting potential return.

There's no question that you must accept some risk to meet your long-term financial goals, so you must balance the amount of risk you're willing to take on with the amount of return you need. Before we examine the sources of risk in investments, let's start off by looking at what a real interest rate is and then take a look at the historical levels of risk and return in the investment markets.

Nominal and Real Rates of Return

Nominal (or Quoted) Rate of Return
The rate of return earned on an investment, unadjusted for lost purchasing power.

Real Rate of Return
The current or nominal rate of return minus the inflation rate.

The **nominal (or quoted) rate of return** is the rate of return earned on an investment without any adjustment for inflation. It's the rate that's quoted in the *Wall Street Journal* for specific bonds or the rate your bank advertises for its savings accounts, and it determines how much interest you earn when you lend money to someone. How much have you *really* earned? The **real rate of return**, which is simply the nominal rate of return after you've taken out inflation, tells you how much you've really earned after adjusting for inflation. If you earn 8 percent on an investment while the inflation rate is 3 percent, the nominal rate of return is 8 percent, and the real rate of return is about 5 percent (8% − 3%).

Historical Levels of Risk and Return

Let's look at the historical levels of risk and return for the past 60 years. If you look at these returns graphically, plotting average annual return against risk or variability of returns as your measure of risk, you get the graph in Figure 11.1. As you can

FIGURE 11.1 Risk–Return Relationship

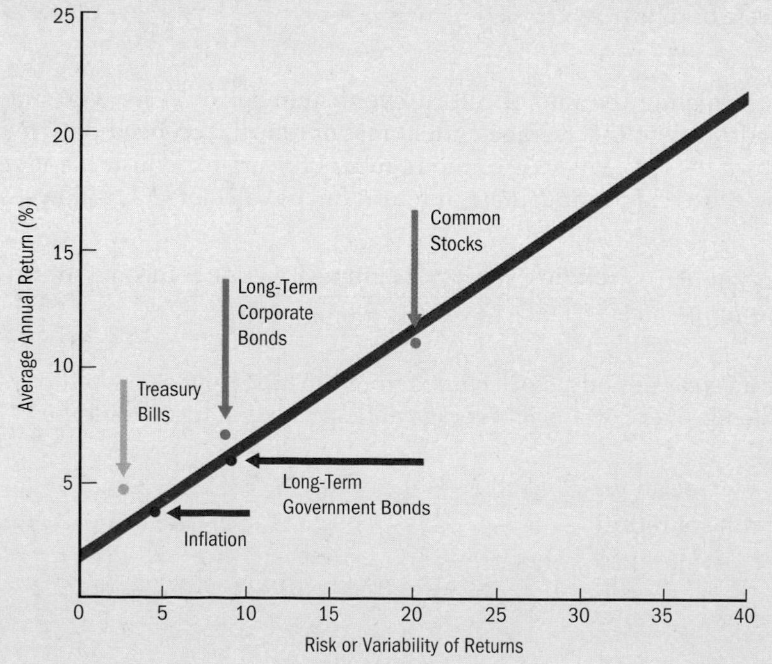

see, it bears a strong resemblance to the risk–return trade-off graph presented in Chapter 1.

PRINCIPLE 9 PRINCIPLE 8

Remember, when we presented the risk–return relationship described in **Principle 8**, we talked about expected return. Here, you see that what was predicted by **Principle 8**, in fact, holds. Investments that produce higher returns have higher levels of risk associated with them.

STOP & THINK

Saving and investing are two things that many people view as unpleasant tasks, but they are also good for you. People often procrastinate when it comes to unpleasant tasks that are good for them—stopping smoking, eliminating credit card debt, dieting, exercising. Procrastination is a behavioral trait we all have—remember **Principle 9: Mind Games, Your Financial Personality, and Your Money**—but when it comes to investing, it can have a huge impact on your financial future. Do you have a tendency to procrastinate? What about the last term paper you wrote or the last time you crammed for an exam?

Sources of Risk in the Risk–Return Trade-Off

The compensation that investors demand for taking on added risk differs for every investment because every investment has a different level of risk. The purpose behind presenting these "sources of risk" is to give you an intuitive understanding of what causes fluctuations in the prices and values of different investments.

Keep in mind that these sources are not mutually exclusive—that is, there's a good deal of overlap between some of them. It's very difficult to look at price fluctuation in an investment and try to attribute it solely to a single source of risk. However, some investments are more vulnerable to one source of risk, while some are more vulnerable to another, so understanding these sources can tell you a lot about many investments.

Interest Rate Risk One source of risk to investors is **interest rate risk**, which finds its roots in changes in interest rates. Regardless of their source, interest rate changes can be bad news for investors. For example, when market interest rates rise, the price of outstanding bonds declines because new bonds with higher interest rates are now available. No one will want to buy your $1,000, 6.5 percent, 10-year bond when $1,000, 8 percent, 10-year bonds are available. The higher the market interest rate climbs, the less your bond will be worth.

Interest Rate Risk
The risk of fluctuations in security prices due to changes in the market interest rate.

Inflation Risk **Inflation risk** reflects the likelihood that rising prices will eat away the purchasing power of your money and that changes in the anticipated level of inflation will result in interest rate changes, which will in turn cause security price fluctuations. Inflation risk is closely linked to interest rate risk, but it is important enough in the valuation and investment processes that it's generally treated as a totally separate source of risk.

Inflation Risk
The risk that rising prices will eat away the purchasing power of your money and that changes in the anticipated level of inflation will result in interest rate changes, which will in turn cause security price fluctuations.

Business Risk Most stocks and bonds are influenced by how well or poorly the company that issued them is performing. **Business risk** deals with fluctuations in investment value that are caused by good or bad management decisions or by how well or poorly the firm's products are doing in the marketplace. Businesses can go bankrupt, and management does make poor decisions. Look at King Digital, maker of Candy Crush. On August 12, 2014, its stock tumbled by almost 21 percent when it announced disappointing profits.

Business Risk
The risk of fluctuations in security prices resulting from good or bad management decisions or how well or poorly the firm's products are doing in the marketplace.

Business risk is different for different companies. Some companies seem to post even profits year in and year out, regardless of what's happening in the economy, while the profit levels of other firms tend to swing wildly.

Financial Risk
The risk associated with a company's use of debt. If a company takes on too much debt and can't meet its obligations, the company may default, or the value of its stock may drop.

Financial Risk **Financial risk** is risk associated with the use of debt by the firm. As a firm takes on more debt, it also takes on interest and principal payments that must be made, regardless of how well the firm does. If the firm can't make the payments, it could go bankrupt. Thus, how the firm raises money affects its level of risk.

Liquidity Risk
Risk associated with the inability to liquidate a security quickly and at a fair market price.

Liquidity Risk **Liquidity risk** deals with the inability to liquidate a security quickly and at a fair market price. For investments that are infrequently traded, it can be hard to find a buyer. Sometimes it's impossible to find a buyer at a fair market price, and you wind up having to sell for less than an asset's worth—sometimes even for a loss.

Buying a piece of your favorite sports team has long been a popular investment for the super-rich, but there's a good deal of liquidity risk in such a venture. Harvey Lighton, owner of 3.1237 percent of the New York Yankees, learned this lesson when he took out a newspaper ad offering a 1 percent stake in the Yankees for $2.95 million. There were no takers. He then considered a plan to take a 2 percent stake in the Yankees and divide it into 20,000 pieces, each representing one-millionth of the team, and sell them for $500 each. That didn't work either. For investors who need money fast, liquidity risk is an important consideration.

Market Risk
Risk associated with overall market movements.

Market Risk **Market risk** is risk associated with overall market movements. There are periods of bull markets—that is, times when all stocks seem to move upward—and periods of bear markets—times when all stocks tend to decline in price. The same tends to be true in the bond markets. This is what happened in the bear market that occurred between the fall of 2007 and spring of 2009 when stocks fell by over 50 percent from their all-time highs, with virtually all stocks dropping in unison. Then in the bull market that followed, stocks rose from their 2009 lows by about 260 percent by spring 2017, with almost all stocks rising.

Political and Regulatory Risk
Risk resulting from unanticipated changes in the tax or legal environment.

Exchange Rate Risk
The risk of fluctuations in security prices due to the variability in earnings resulting from changes in exchange rates.

Political and Regulatory Risk **Political and regulatory risk** results from unanticipated changes in the tax or legal environment that has been imposed by the government. Changes in the capital gains tax rate or in the tax deductibility of interest on municipal bonds and the passage of any new regulatory reform laws affect investment values and are examples of political and regulatory risk.

STOP & THINK

"Most people get interested in stocks when everyone else is. The time to get interested is when no one else is. You can't buy what is popular and do well."—Warren Buffett. What do you think he meant?

Exchange Rate Risk **Exchange rate risk** refers to the variability in earnings resulting from changes in exchange rates. For example, if you invest in a German bond, you first convert your dollars into euros. When you liquidate that investment, you sell your bond for euros and convert those euros into dollars. What you earn on your investment depends on how well the investment performed and what happened to the exchange rate. For the international investor, exchange rate risk is simply another layer of risk.

Call Risk
The risk to bondholders that a bond may be called away from them before maturity.

Calling a Bond
Redeeming a bond before its scheduled maturity. Many bonds are callable.

Call Risk **Call risk** is the risk to callable bondholders that a bond may be called away from them before maturity. **Calling a bond** refers to redeeming the bond early, and many bonds are callable. When a bond is called, the bondholder generally receives the face value of the bond plus 1 year of interest payments.

Diversification

Diversification
The elimination of risk by investing in different assets. It works by allowing the extreme good and bad returns to cancel each other out. The result is that total variability or risk is reduced without affecting expected return.

Diversification is a simple concept: Don't put all your eggs in one basket. **Diversification** works by allowing the extreme good and bad returns to cancel each other out, resulting in a reduction of the total variability or risk without affecting expected return.

It's important to understand the process of diversification. It not only eliminates a lot of risk but also helps us understand what risk is relevant to us as investors. It's also important to understand that diversification reduces risk without affecting the expected return. That's what we saw when we introduced **Principle 8** in Chapter 1. It works by allowing the good and bad returns to cancel each other out. As a result, variability, or risk, is reduced.

PRINCIPLE 8

Diversifying Away Risk As you diversify your investments, much of the risk in the combined holdings of all your investments, which is called your **portfolio**, disappears. This elimination of risk occurs because the stock returns in your portfolio don't always move in the same direction and, as a result, the ups and downs eliminate each other.

Portfolio
A group of investments held by an individual.

To understand how diversification can reduce risk, let's look at a simple example. Suppose you own a sunglasses shop that caters to the tourists on a beautiful Caribbean island and the only product you sell is sunglasses. During the sunny season, you earn 20 percent on sunglasses, but during the rainy season, it's tough to sell sunglasses, and you earn 0 percent.

	Sunglasses
Rainy season	0%
Sunny season	20%

On average, the sunny and rainy seasons each last half the year. As a result, the expected return on your sunglasses shop is 10 percent (half the year you earn 0 percent, and half the year you earn 20 percent). But how long the rainy or sunny season actually lasts in a particular year determines your actual return, and that return has varied from year to year, going from 15 percent when three-fourths of the year was sunny to only 5 percent when three-fourths of the year was rainy. To smooth out sales, you add umbrellas to your product line. Umbrellas produce a 20 percent return in the rainy season and a 0 percent return during the sunny season, giving you an expected return of 10 percent (just as with the sunglasses, half the year you earn 0 percent, and half the year you earn 20 percent).

	Sunglasses	Umbrellas
Rainy season	0%	20%
Sunny season	20%	0%

What's the end result of this diversification? The expected return hasn't changed. It is still 10 percent (half your investment earned 10 percent in sunglasses, and half your investment earned 10 percent in umbrellas), but the annual ups and downs—the variability of the returns—are totally eliminated. The shop will earn a 10 percent rate of return, regardless of how long the sunny and rainy seasons last.

So what can we take away from our foray into diversification? Diversification can reduce risk. However, you should keep in mind that we were able to eliminate *all* the risk because we found two investments that move opposite of each other—and finding two investments that do that is tough. However, since most stocks don't move exactly opposite other stocks and they don't move exactly with other stocks either, as we add more and more stocks to our investment portfolio, the risk in the portfolio declines little by little. As a result, as you increase the number of stocks, the amount of variability in your portfolio declines, as shown in Figure 11.2.

Systematic or Market-Related or Nondiversifiable Risk
That portion of a security's risk or variability that can't be eliminated through investor diversification. This type of variability or risk results from factors that affect all securities.

In the language of investors, we refer to the risk that *can't be eliminated* through diversification as **systematic risk** and the risk that *can be eliminated* through diversification as **unsystematic risk**. In fact, the term *systematic* comes from the fact that this type of risk systematically affects all stocks and, as a result, can't be eliminated through diversification. In effect, all risk can be divided up into two types: systematic and unsystematic. Keep in mind that these are *types* of risk, which are different from the *sources* of risk or variability we examined earlier.

Unsystematic or Firm-Specific or Company-Unique Risk or Diversifiable Risk
Risk or variability that can be eliminated through investor diversification. Unsystematic risk results from factors that are unique to a particular firm.

FIGURE 11.2 The Reduction of Risk as the Number of Stocks in the Portfolio Increases

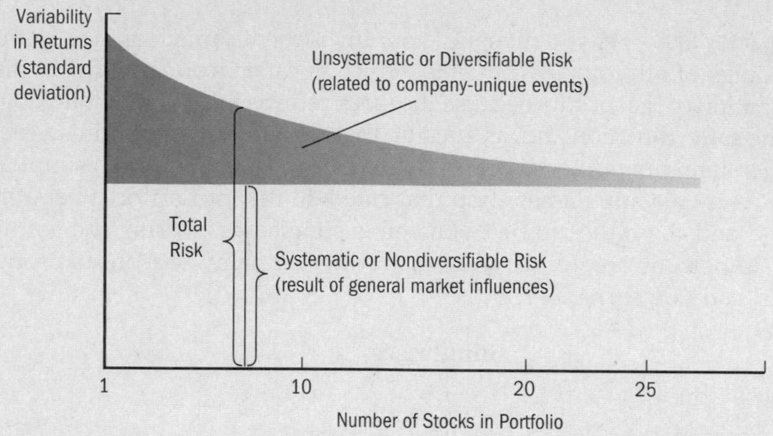

For example, the financial meltdown in the fall of 2008 had a negative effect on the returns of almost all stocks; as a result, that risk could not be diversified away and would be considered a source of systematic risk. On the other hand, unsystematic risk is simply the variability in the returns of an investment that is due to events that are unrelated to the overall market. These returns might be due to the death of the firm's CEO, a product recall, a major fire at a manufacturing plant, or even bad managerial choices. The returns caused by these types of events are not related to the returns of other investments and can be eliminated through diversification. Relating this back to **Principle 8: Risk and Return Go Hand in Hand**, we find that unsystematic risk can be eliminated through diversification. In effect, unsystematic risk doesn't exist for diversified investors. So when diversified investors talk about risk, they are talking about systematic risk.

PRINCIPLE 8

> **STOP & THINK**
>
> In a study out of Washington University, a researcher found that exposure to the opposite sex induces about 8 percent more risk taking in both males and females. Both males and females viewing opposite-sex photos displayed a significant increase in risk tolerance, whereas the control subjects—those not looking at photos of the opposite sex—exhibited no significant change; that's a little more of **Principle 9: Mind Games, Your Financial Personality, and Your Money** at work. What this means is that your tolerance for risk is extremely suggestible. Where have you seen companies use attractive people to their benefit?

Understanding Your Tolerance and Capacity for Risk

Not everyone has the same tolerance for risk. Some individuals are continuously checking their investments' results. Others can take on risk without looking at a financial page in the newspaper for months at a time. Which is better? That's a judgment call.

It doesn't matter whether you freak out at the slightest sign of risk or you act like a complete daredevil. What's important is recognizing your tolerance for risk and acting—and investing—accordingly. One way of developing an understanding of your tolerance for risk is to take one of the many risk-tolerance tests found online, and one of the best is from Rutgers (**http://njaes.rutgers.edu/money/riskquiz/**). But keep in mind that studies have shown your risk tolerance changes as the stock market changes. During times of bull markets, individuals become more risk tolerant and are willing to take on more risk, but during down periods in the stock market, individuals become less risk tolerant and shy away from investing in common stocks.

PRINCIPLE 9

Risk capacity refers to the strength of your safety net. Are you in a strong enough financial state that you will be able to meet your financial goals at their minimum levels? If you are, then you have the capacity to take on additional financial risks. If you aren't, then you have to ask if you have enough safe investments—and a secure prospect of future earnings—to be able to meet your financial goals at their bare-minimum levels. To the extent that you have your basics covered, you are in a good position to take on some financial risk.

The Time Dimension of Investing and Asset Allocation

LO3 Allocate your assets in the manner that is best for you.

PRINCIPLE 8

In Chapter 1, when we introduced **Principle 8: Risk and Return Go Hand in Hand**, we asked: How much risk can you afford to take? The answer was that as the length of the investment horizon increases, you can afford to invest in riskier assets. Thus, whenever someone asks what he or she should invest in, the proper response is a question: What is your investment horizon? This is because the returns on those risky assets—stocks—tend to dominate those of less risky assets—CDs and bonds—as the investment horizon lengthens. So even in the worst-case scenario, you'll probably do quite a bit better with stocks than with the more conservative alternative. It doesn't mean that there isn't any risk to investing in common stock. Clearly, there's still a lot of uncertainty as to how much you'll finally end up with, but if your investment horizon is long, it will probably be a lot more if you invest in some risky assets.

Meeting Your Investment Goals and the Time Dimension of Risk

With any long-term investment, you can be sure that there'll be some bad years and some good years. Over time, these offsetting years result in the dispersion of returns converging toward the average. Consequently, when you invest for a longer period, the exceptionally good and exceptionally bad years usually cancel each other out, and you end up with less variability, as shown in Figure 11.3. This

FIGURE 11.3 Reduction of Risk over Time, 1967–2016

Each bar shows the range of compound annual returns for each asset class over the period 1967–2016.

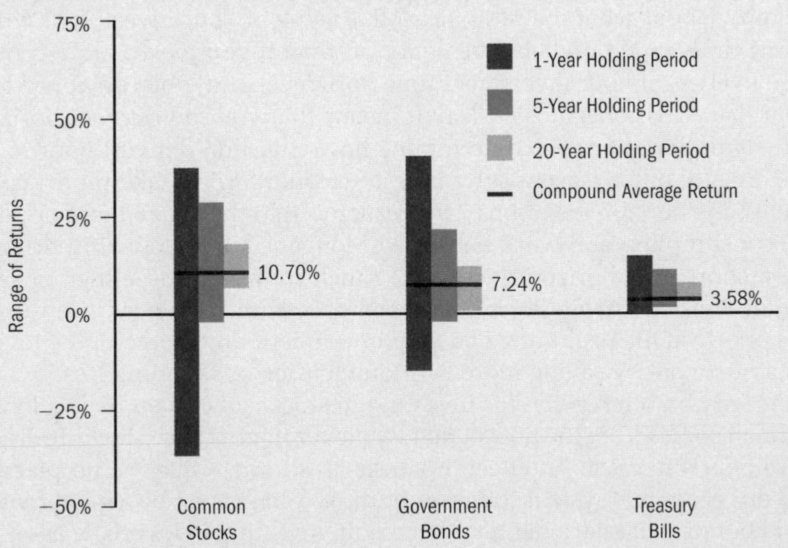

figure shows the range of compound annual returns for stocks, bonds, and cash over 1-, 5-, and 20-year holding periods over the past 50 years. Let's look at the range of returns on common stock. As you can see, the returns of common stock calculated over 1-year periods range from a high of 37.2 percent to a low of −36.6 percent. However, as we increase the length of the holding period to 5-year segments or 20-year segments, the picture changes. Over 5-year periods, the average returns range from 28.6 percent to −2.4 percent, while over 20-year periods they range between 18 percent and 6.5 percent. In effect, over the past 50 years the worst 20-year holding period for stocks still posted a positive 20-year compound annual return of 6.5 percent. Still, there is a lot of risk in stocks, and you are never guaranteed anything—things may change in the future because, let's face it, stocks are risky investments.

So how much risk should you be prepared to assume, or said differently, what kinds of assets should you invest in—stocks or bonds? If you ask a financial planner that question, he or she will most likely answer with several more questions. The first question will deal with your risk tolerance—the less risk tolerant you are, the less risk you should take. The second will deal with your capacity for risk and your financial situation: how secure your job is, how much you have saved, how far along you are toward meeting your goals, and whether you have an emergency fund. The final question will probably deal with when you need the money. The longer it is until you need the money, the more risk you can afford to take.

What can we say about the uncertainty regarding how much your investment will eventually grow? There's no question that as your holding period gets longer, the uncertainty surrounding how much your investment will eventually be worth increases. But that shouldn't stop you from taking risk when you have a longer holding period—for example, when saving for your retirement 45 years off in the future. While there may be less uncertainty surrounding the ultimate dollar value of a 45-year investment in bonds versus common stock, you're probably better off investing in "risky" stocks than "safe" bonds. Why? Because even if stocks perform poorly relative to what they've done historically and bonds perform extremely well relative to what they've done historically, the stock investment will end up larger. That is to say, the investment in bonds will give you less uncertainty about the ultimate value of your investment, but it will also give you a smaller ultimate value. In effect, sometimes it's riskier not to take risks than it is to take them.

What do we know about risk and time? First, if your investment time horizon is long and you invest in something risky such as common stocks, there's still a lot of uncertainty about what the ultimate dollar value of your investment will be. But at the same time, you'll probably be better off than if you took a more conservative approach. In effect, if your investment time horizon is long, you can afford to take on additional risk. This concept is critical: It means that your investment horizon plays an extremely important role in determining how you should invest your savings.

There are still other reasons why investors can afford to take more risk as their investment time horizon lengthens. One reason is that they have more opportunities to adjust consumption and work habits over longer time periods. If they are investing with a short time horizon, there isn't much they can do—either to save more or to spend less—to change their final level of wealth. However, if an investment performs poorly at the beginning of a long investment time horizon, the investor can make an adjustment by saving more, working harder, or spending less.

Another reason often given for investing in stocks when you have a long investment horizon comes from the notion that whatever might cause stocks to crash might also cause bonds to crash. In effect, if stocks crash, there may be no place to hide. That is, if our economic system collapses or the world gets hit by a giant meteor, both stocks and bonds will take a big hit. As a result, investing in less risky assets (bonds) may not really help you if a crash ever comes.

Asset Allocation

PRINCIPLE 8

Asset allocation is an investment term that deals with how your money should be divided among stocks, bonds, and other investments. The logic behind the asset allocation process finds its roots in **Principle 8: Risk and Return Go Hand in Hand**, where we introduced the concept of diversification.

Asset Allocation
An attempt to ensure that the investor's strategy reflects his or her investment time horizon and that the investor is well diversified, generally with assets in several different classes of investments, such as domestic common stocks, international common stocks, and bonds.

First, investors should be well diversified, generally with holdings in several different classes of investments, such as domestic common stocks, international common stocks, and bonds. The objective is to increase your return on those investments while decreasing your risk.

No two investors should allocate in the same way—not all risk is equal. You won't want to do what your Uncle Bill does, nor will you want to follow your neighbor's plan, because you will certainly vary in terms of age, income, family situation, personal financial goals, risk capacity, and tolerance for risk. These factors will lead you in your own direction.

Asset allocation also incorporates the concept of the time dimension of investing. It recognizes that investing in common stocks is more appropriate the longer the investment horizon is, so investors with more time to reach their goals should have a larger proportion of common stocks in their portfolios. The closer you get to retirement, the smaller the proportion of your retirement funds that should be invested in common stocks.

In addition, your capacity for risk and your financial situation impact your asset allocation decision. The less you have saved and the less secure your job is, the less risk you should take when you make your asset allocation decision. Table 11.1 summarizes these important factors.

Asset allocation is the most important task you'll undertake in your investing career. How you go about your asset allocation will have a far greater impact on your return than will choosing each individual stock or bond you hold.

STOP & THINK

When it comes to investment success, probably the biggest enemy you have is something you may have perfected in college: procrastination. While this holds true for all investment decisions, it is particularly damaging when it comes to investing for retirement. Without question, the easiest way to guarantee a worry-free retirement is to start investing early.

TABLE 11.1 Factors Impacting Your Asset Allocation Decision

There isn't a single asset allocation that works for everyone. However, regardless of what asset allocation you use, you should be well diversified with both stocks and bonds. In addition, you should build up an emergency fund before you begin investing for long-term goals. You should consider the following three factors in making your asset allocation decision:
• **Time horizon.** The more time until you need the money, the more risk you can afford to take. The longer time horizon will give you more time to adjust your portfolio, consumption, and working habits if your investments perform poorly during the early years. If your time horizon is more than 10 years, you should emphasize more risky investments such as stocks that carry higher expected returns to achieve your long-term financial goals.
• **Capacity for risk and financial situation.** How much risk can you afford to take? In answering this question, consider these questions: Are you at the point where you feel comfortable that you have enough saved to meet your goals? How secure is your job? Do you have a pension plan at work that will provide a steady income at retirement? How much money do you owe or have you saved? Do you have a big enough emergency fund to allow you to avoid tapping into your long-term investments at an inopportune time such as in the midst of a market downturn? If you have a limited capacity for risk, you should make sure that you have sufficient short-term bonds and cash investments in your portfolio to cover emergencies in case of the unexpected.
• **Risk tolerance.** Different people have different tolerances for risk. Still, to achieve long-term goals, it is probably necessary to take some risks and invest in common stock. If you have a low tolerance for risk, try to learn more about investing—that may make you more comfortable taking the risks you need to take. Nevertheless, you will want to balance your investments in such a way that you can still sleep at night even during times of market volatility. You should also try to develop an investment plan that you are comfortable with and that you can stick with through market ups and downs. And remember, individuals always think they are more risk tolerant when the stock market is soaring.

Asset allocation is not a one-time decision. Adjustments will need to be made as your life circumstances change. As you keep an eye on your portfolio, you may occasionally need to rebalance your mix to keep the percentage of each investment category in line with your current personal financial goals.

Figure 11.4 compares several different asset allocations in terms of their performance over the past 50 years. Remember, as your personal circumstances change—for example, you get married or have a child—your asset allocations will change to reflect these new circumstances. If stocks, for example, rise in value, it is likely that you will find yourself veering away from your target allocations as more money becomes invested in stocks. This is when you'll want to return to Table 11.1 for some direction. In looking at these asset allocations, keep in mind that they do not reflect your emergency fund. Your emergency fund should always be invested in liquid assets and should be large enough to cover 6 to 9 months of expenses.

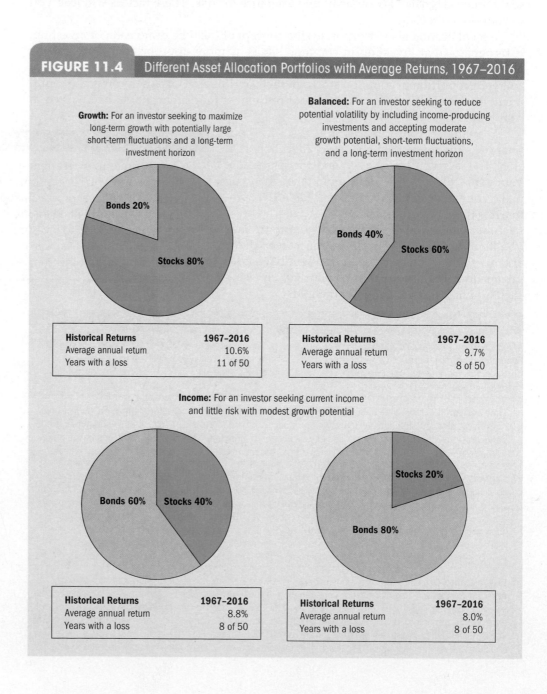

FIGURE 11.4 Different Asset Allocation Portfolios with Average Returns, 1967–2016

Growth: For an investor seeking to maximize long-term growth with potentially large short-term fluctuations and a long-term investment horizon

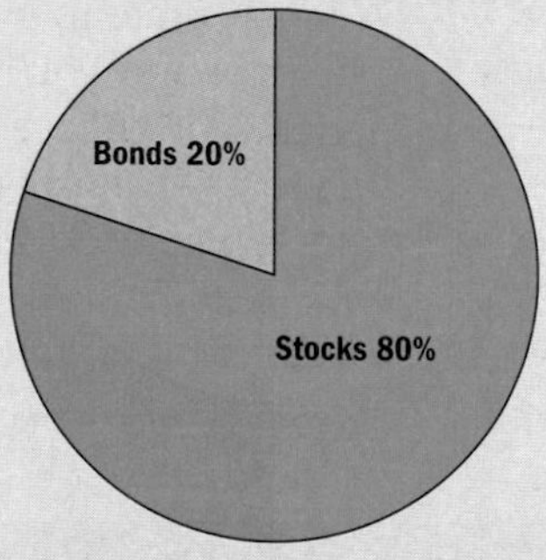

Historical Returns	**1967–2016**
Average annual return	10.6%
Years with a loss	11 of 50

Balanced: For an investor seeking to reduce potential volatility by including income-producing investments and accepting moderate growth potential, short-term fluctuations, and a long-term investment horizon

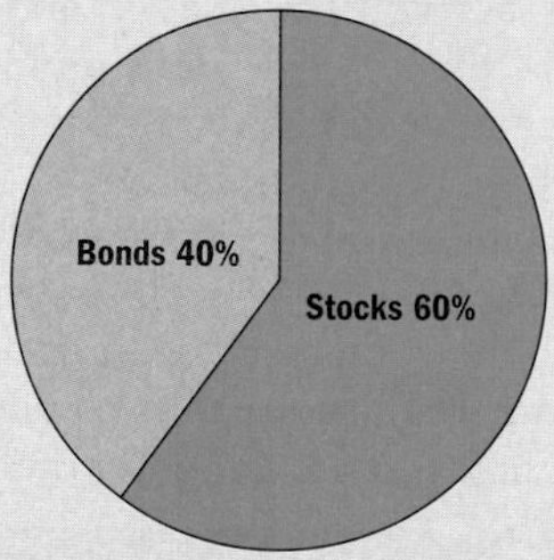

Historical Returns	**1967–2016**
Average annual return	9.7%
Years with a loss	8 of 50

Income: For an investor seeking current income and little risk with modest growth potential

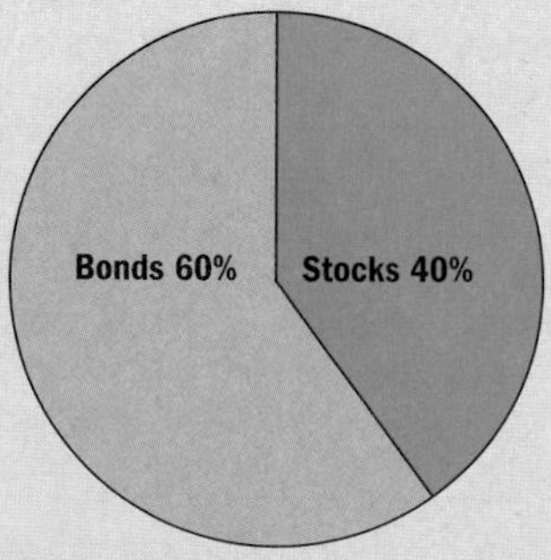

Historical Returns	**1967–2016**
Average annual return	8.8%
Years with a loss	8 of 50

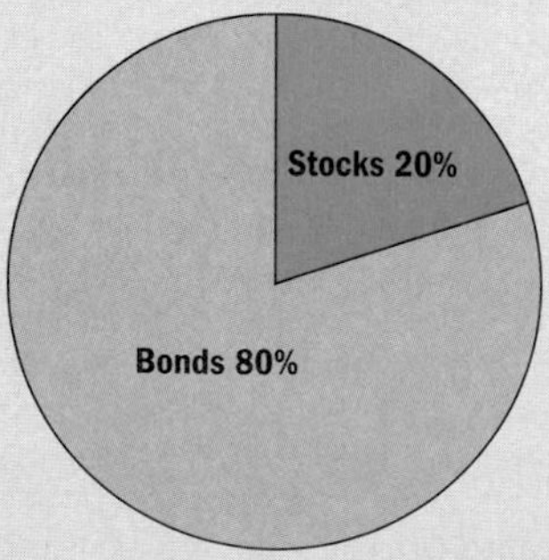

Historical Returns	**1967–2016**
Average annual return	8.0%
Years with a loss	8 of 50

What You Should Know About Efficient Markets

LO4 Understand how difficult it is to beat the market.

Efficient Market
A market in which all relevant information about the stock is reflected in the stock price.

The concept of **efficient markets** concerns the speed at which new information is reflected in prices. The more efficient the market, the faster prices react to new information. If the stock market were a perfectly efficient market, security prices would equal their true value at all times—in other words, you couldn't systematically "beat the market." With efficient markets, you're just as likely to pick winners as losers. So is the stock market an efficient market? Well, if it is truly efficient, then there's no benefit to much of what's done by stock analysts.

There is not a definitive answer to this question. Why not? First of all, there's a question of the degree of efficiency. That is, although security analysis may not help small investors earn abnormal profits, it may have value to large investors. Improving your performance by 0.01 percent may be irrelevant for you, but for a manager with a \$4 billion portfolio, it means an increase in profits of \$400,000 ($0.0001 \times \$4$ billion $= \$400{,}000$). In addition, if someone uncovers a new technique for predicting prices, he or she would be much better off using it rather than publishing it. As a result, we may only see results that indicate that the market is efficient.

However, reports of beating the market don't indicate that the market is inefficient. On average, we would expect, just by chance, that half the investors would outperform the market and half would underperform the market. In general, you usually hear about those who beat the market. Not surprisingly, those who underperform the market tend not to publicize their results. How do mutual funds do against the market? Over the five-year period ending in mid-2015, over 80 percent of mutual funds were laggards—and these are professionals. While we can't provide a definite answer as to whether you can beat the market, we can give you some advice. That advice begins with keeping to your plan and investing for the long term. If you try to time the market, you're just as likely to miss an upswing as you are to avoid a downswing.

STOP & THINK

If a stranger figured out an incredible investment opportunity or a way to beat the market, do you really think he or she would share that secret with you?

Securities Markets

LO5 Identify and describe the primary and secondary securities markets.

Securities—stocks and bonds—are first bought when they are issued by corporations as a means of raising money. After the initial issue, stocks and bonds are traded—bought and sold—among investors. These trades occur in the securities markets. Just as retail goods are bought and sold in markets such as Wal-Mart or Sears, securities are bought and sold in their appropriate markets.

Securities Markets
A term used to describe a place where financial securities or instruments—for example, common stocks and bonds—are traded.

A **securities market** is a place where you can buy or sell securities. These markets can take the form of anything from an actual building on Wall Street in New York City to an electronic hookup linking security dealers all over the world. Securities markets are divided into primary and secondary markets. Let's take a look at what these terms mean.

Primary Markets

Primary Markets
The markets in which newly issued, as opposed to previously issued, securities are traded.

A **primary market** is a market in which new, as opposed to previously issued, securities (i.e., stocks and bonds) are traded. For example, if Nike issues a new batch of stock, this issue is considered a primary market transaction. Actually, there are two different types of offerings in the primary markets: initial public offerings and seasoned new issues.

Initial Public Offering (IPO)
The first time a company's stock is traded publicly.

An **initial public offering (IPO)** is the first time a company's stock is traded publicly. The initial offering of Microsoft stock was an IPO. Initial public offerings draw a good deal of attention in the press because they show how much a company is worth in the public's eye and they are opportunities for substantial financial gains—or losses. For the small investor, it is often difficult to get shares of IPOs. The most promising companies' initial shares tend to be bought up by large investors before smaller investors have a chance to buy in. In effect, there may not be enough stock to go around.

Seasoned New Issue
A stock offering by a company that already has common stock traded in the marketplace.

Investment Banker
The middleman between the firm issuing securities and the buying public. This term describes both the firms that specialize in selling securities to the public and the individuals who work for investment banking firms.

Underwriter
An investment banker who purchases and subsequently resells a new security issue. The issuing company sells its securities directly to the underwriter, who then sells the new issue to the public and assumes the risk of selling it at a satisfactory price.

Prospectus
A legal document that describes a securities issue and is made available to potential investors.

Seasoned new issues, often called seasoned equity offerings, are stock offerings by companies that already have common stock traded in the marketplace. For example, a sale of new shares of stock by Nike would be considered a seasoned new issue.

Stocks and bonds are generally sold in the primary markets with the help of an **investment banker** serving as the **underwriter**. An underwriter is simply a middleman who buys the entire stock or bond issue from the issuing company and then resells it to the general public in individual shares. Morgan Stanley, Goldman Sachs, JP Morgan, Citigroup, and Bank of America/Merrill Lynch all specialize in investment banking. We use the term *investment banker* to refer to both the overall firm and the individuals who work for it.

Single investment banking companies rarely underwrite securities issues by themselves. Usually, one managing investment banking company handles the issue—advising and working with the issuing company on pricing and timing concerns—and then forms a syndicate of other investment banking companies. This syndicate will underwrite the IPO or seasoned new issue. If investors are interested in the offering, they can contact a member of the underwriting syndicate to request a **prospectus**, which describes the issue and the issuing company's financial prospects.

Secondary Markets—Stocks

Secondary Markets
The markets in which previously issued securities are traded.

Securities that have previously been issued and bought are traded in the **secondary markets**. In other words, if you bought 100 shares of stock in an IPO and then wanted to resell them, you'd have to sell the shares in the secondary market. Only issuing companies (and their underwriters) can sell securities in the primary markets. The proceeds from the sale of a share of IBM stock on the secondary market go to the previous owner of the stock, not to IBM. In fact, the only time IBM ever receives money from the sale of one of its securities is when it is sold on the primary market.

Organized Exchange
An exchange that occupies a physical location where trading occurs, such as the New York Stock Exchange.

Over-the-Counter Market
A market in which transactions are conducted over the telephone or via a computer hookup rather than in an organized exchange.

The secondary markets can take the form of either an organized exchange or an over-the-counter market. An **organized exchange** occupies a physical location where trading occurs, such as the New York Stock Exchange. In other words, an organized exchange is actually a building in which stocks are traded. In an **over-the-counter market**, transactions are conducted over the telephone or via a computer hookup. How is it determined where a security will trade? Larger, more frequently traded securities, such as GM, IBM, General Electric, and Disney, are traded on organized exchanges. Those that are less frequently traded, along with many new and high-tech stocks, are relegated to the over-the-counter markets. In either case, the secondary markets make it much easier for sellers to find buyers and vice versa.

The New York Stock Exchange The New York Stock Exchange (NYSE) is the major organized exchange in the United States. If a firm's stock trades on a particular exchange, it is said to be *listed* on that exchange. Securities can be listed on more than one exchange. The NYSE (owned by NYSE Euronext), also called the "Big Board," is the oldest of all the organized exchanges. It began in the spring of 1792 when 24 traders signed the Buttonwood Agreement, a pact named after the tree under which the traders gathered, obligating them to "give preference" to each other in security trading. When winter came, the 24 traders moved to the back room of Wall Street's Tontine Coffee House, leaving other traders out in the cold.

Over-the-Counter Market The over-the-counter (OTC) market is a linkup of dealers, with no listing or membership requirements. For the most part, the OTC market is highly automated. A nationwide computer network allows brokers to see up-to-the-second price quotes on roughly 35,000 securities.

Over-the-counter listings are often made up of companies that are too new or too small to be listed on a major exchange. These companies also often have fewer shares available. As a result, in some cases small amounts of buying or selling may have a significant impact on the price of these companies' stocks.

The largest electronic stock exchange is, which allows dealers to post bid and ask prices for approximately 3,300 OTC stocks, or 15 percent of all shares traded. A **bid price** is the highest price a prospective buyer is willing to pay for a security, and an **ask or offer price** is the lowest price at which a prospective seller is willing to sell the security. The ask or offer price should always be above the bid price.

Bid Price
The highest price someone is willing to pay for a security.

Ask or Offer Price
The lowest price at which someone is willing to sell a security.

The Rise of Electronic Trading When you buy or sell a stock, who do you think you are buying it from or selling it to? The answer most of the time is not a person; it's a computer. Today, over 80 percent of all trades are computer generated. That is, most stock trades come directly from a computer rather than a person. That only makes sense because computers are faster, cheaper, more efficient, and hopefully less error prone than individuals. Today, there are few differences between trading in the OTC market and on the NYSE.

International Markets

International securities markets have been around for centuries. In fact, around 2000 B.C. the Babylonians introduced debt financing, and by 400 B.C., the Greeks had developed a securities market of sorts. Today, many investment advisors recommend that their clients increase their international investments. In fact, since 1980, U.S. foreign holdings have increased more than 100-fold, and foreign equity investments now account for over 10 percent of U.S. investors' holdings. So how do you go about buying a Japanese stock? Here are two of the ways.

First, some foreign shares are traded on exchanges in the United States. For example, over 500 foreign companies are traded on the NYSE. In addition, over 400 are traded on NASDAQ, and about half of these companies are Canadian.

Another way international stocks can be traded is through **American Depository Receipts (ADRs)**. With ADRs, shares of stock aren't traded directly. Instead, the foreign firm's stock is held on deposit in a bank in the foreign firm's country. The foreign bank issues an ADR, which represents direct ownership of one of those stock shares. The ADR then trades internationally just like a normal share of stock. Examples of foreign firms with ADRs include Sony and Toyota.

American Depository Receipt (ADR)
A marketable document (a receipt) that certifies a bank holds shares of a foreign firm's stock that back the receipt. As a result, the ADR trades just like a normal share of stock.

While it is now easier to trade in foreign companies, there are also risks. For example, the Japanese stock market started plummeting in January 1990 and didn't stop until it lost 63 percent of its value by August 1992. From then until 2014, it continued to slowly slide before rising somewhat—missing the great stock market surges that took place in the United States in the late 1990s. By 2017, it still stood at half of its high over the previous 28 years in spite of a mind-boggling return of almost 57 percent in 2013.

Regulation of the Securities Markets

Securities market regulation is aimed at protecting the investor and providing a level playing field so that all investors have a fair chance of making money. There are actually two levels of regulation: general regulation by the Securities and Exchange Commission (SEC, a federal agency) and self-regulation directly by the exchanges (or, in the case of the OTC market, by the Financial Industry Regulatory Authority [FINRA]).

STOP & THINK

What is the purpose of market regulation? It's to give everyone an equal chance of making money in the stock market. The disclosure principle allows all investors to view the same information at the same time and thereby have an equal chance of making trading profits. Giving everyone a fair chance at making money is what guides the majority of the laws governing the securities markets. It doesn't always work. Can you name a Wall Street scandal?

SEC Regulation The great stock market crash of 1929 inspired much of the legislation that governs the securities markets today. In the period following the crash, the Securities Act of 1933 and the Securities Exchange Act of 1934 were enacted. The Securities Exchange Act of 1934 spoke directly to the secondary market and created the Securities and Exchange Commission to enforce the trading laws.

The cornerstone of both pieces of legislation is the disclosure of relevant information relating to the offering of a security. Many other acts and laws have been passed to regulate the securities markets. For example, the Investment Advisers Act of 1940 protects investors against unethical investment advisors and requires advisors to register with the SEC and provide the SEC with semiannual reports. Under the Investor Protection Act of 1970, the Securities Investor Protection Corporation (SIPC) was established to provide up to $500,000 of insurance to cover investors' account balances in the event that their brokerage firm goes bankrupt.

Self-Regulation Much of the day-to-day regulation of the markets is left to the securities industry and is performed by the exchanges and the FINRA. The willingness and zeal with which the exchanges approach self-regulation is inspired by the knowledge that if self-regulation doesn't work, government regulation will be imposed.

After the October 1987 market crash, the NYSE self-regulated like mad and imposed a number of "circuit breakers" to head off or slow potential future market crashes. The idea behind these circuit breakers is that by closing the market in the event of sharp declines, investors will be given a chance to step back and assess the price decline rather than reacting on instinct.

STOP & THINK

Warren Buffett once said, "The stock market is designed to transfer money from the active to the patient." What do you think he meant by that?

Insider Trading and Market Abuses Much of the logic behind regulation of the market stems from the desire we mentioned earlier to level the playing field with respect to the securities markets. The Insider Trading Sanctions Act of 1984 and the Insider Trading and Securities Fraud Enforcement Act of 1988 made it illegal to trade while in the possession of inside information, or "material" nonpublic information held by officers, directors, major stockholders, or anyone with special insider knowledge.

Has insider trading disappeared? Certainly not. In fact, *BusinessWeek*, after analyzing the largest 100 mergers and takeovers of 1994, came to the conclusion that one out of three of those deals was preceded by stock price run-ups or abnormal volume that could not be explained by the publicly available information at the time.

Churning
Excessive trading in a security account that is inappropriate for the customer and serves only to generate commissions.

Another potential abuse involves **churning**, or excessive trading on a client's account, which means the client pays more commissions. Although churning is illegal, it's also practically impossible to prove. Churning can easily take place if the client has relinquished trading control to the broker, but it also takes place on traditional accounts. That's why it's so important to select a broker you can trust.

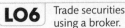

LO6 Trade securities using a broker.

How Securities Are Traded

Let's look now at how to trade securities and examine the different types of trades and trading mechanisms. You'll notice that when we discuss the different trading mechanisms, we refer to all securities as stocks. We're not favoring stocks or saying that these trading mechanisms apply only to stocks. We're just being lazy, and stocks are the most frequently traded of the different securities.

Placing an Order

When you place an order to buy or sell stock, you need to be clear about the size of the order and the length of time the order is to be outstanding.

Round Lot
A group or lot of 100 shares of common stock. Stocks are traded in round lots on the New York Stock Exchange.

Odd Lot
An order involving between 1 and 99 shares of stock.

Order Size Common stock is sold in lots or groups of 100 shares on the NYSE. These lots are referred to as **round lots**. Orders involving between 1 and 99 shares of stock are referred to as **odd lots** and are processed by "odd lot dealers," who buy and sell out of their inventory.

Time Period for Which the Order Will Remain Outstanding When you order a hamburger at Burger King, you want your order filled right away, not in a week. Well, when you order stock, you had better specify when you want your order filled, or you just might have to wait a week and pay more than you bargained for. Ordering alternatives include **day orders**, which expire at the end of the trading day during which they were made; **open orders**, also called **good-till-cancelled (GTC) orders**, which remain effective until filled or cancelled; and **fill-or-kill orders**, which expire if not filled immediately.

FACTS OF LIFE

According to a recent survey by Allianz Life Insurance, 57 percent of women said they wish they had learned more in school about money and finance.

Day Order
A trading order that expires at the end of the trading day during which it was made.

Open or Good-Till-Cancelled (GTC) Order
A trading order that remains effective until filled or cancelled.

Fill-or-Kill Order
A trading order that expires if not filled immediately.

Discretionary Account
An account that gives your broker the power to make trades for you.

You can give your broker the power to make trades for you if you open a **discretionary account**. Because a discretionary account gives your broker power over your money, you should consider it only if you've worked with your broker for years—and only under unusual circumstances. There's no question that problems do occur with discretionary accounts, and the easiest way to avoid these problems is to avoid discretionary accounts.

Types of Orders

Whenever you place an order, you want to make sure that it is carried out in exactly the way you intended. A number of different types of orders act as instructions for how you would like your order to be executed.

Market Order
An order to buy or sell a set number of securities immediately at the best price available.

Market Orders A **market order** is an order to buy or sell a set number of securities immediately at the best price available. These orders can generally be executed within seconds of being placed if they are filled electronically. However, because market prices constantly change, you can't be certain of the price at which the order will be executed.

Limit Order
An order that specifies a security is to be sold only at or above a certain price or bought only at or below a certain price.

Limit Orders A **limit order** specifies that the trade is to be made only at a certain price or better. In other words, if a limit order to sell stock is made, the stock will be sold only at a certain price or above. If a limit order to buy stock is made, the stock will be bought only at a certain price or below. Limit orders allow you to limit your bid or ask price to what you feel is an acceptable level. If the specified price isn't available, your trade isn't made.

Stop or Stop-Loss Order
An order to sell a security if the price drops below a specified level or to buy it if the price climbs above a specified level.

Stop Orders A **stop or stop-loss order** is an order to sell if the price drops *below* a specified level or to buy if the price climbs *above* a specified level. Stop-loss orders are used to protect your profits. They allow you to bail out of the stock if the market starts to tumble or to buy in if the price starts to rise (these are used to protect profit on short selling, which we'll discuss in a moment).

For example, say you purchased stock in Tesoro, the Houston-based refining company, at $10.91 per share, and a year later it was selling at $56.95 per share. Because you never know when Tesoro might have some problems or when the market might fall, you could lock in some of the gains you've already made by using a stop-loss order to sell Tesoro at $50.

You wouldn't use a stop-loss order for the full $56.95 current price because your stock would then be sold immediately while the price remained at $56.95. You also wouldn't use a stop-loss order for an amount very close to $56.95—say, $56 or so—because market prices commonly fluctuate a bit and you wouldn't want your stop-loss order to be executed on a routine fluctuation just before an uncommon rise up to, say, $100 per share.

You want to set the stop-loss order price just right so that you safeguard against only a major fluctuation. Thus, if the price of Tesoro tumbled to $50, your stop-loss order would activate and sell your Tesoro stock at the best price possible, which may end up being less than $50 because there might not be a buyer for the stock at $50. In this way, you can "lock in" some of the paper profits.

Short Selling

MyLab Finance Video

Short Selling
Borrowing stock from your broker and selling it with an obligation to replace the stock later.

Although it's obvious that you can make money in the stock market when stocks rise in price, you can also make money when prices decline. With **short selling**, you're wishing for bad news: The more the stock drops in price, the more money you make. Short selling involves borrowing stock from your broker and selling it. Then if the stock price goes down, you buy it back and return it to your broker. You make a profit by buying it back for less than you sold it.

Beware, however, that if the price of the stock goes up, you have to buy it back at a higher price. You lose! In effect, selling short lets you reverse the order of buying and selling. That is, when you invest in stock, the goal is to buy low and later to sell high. With short selling, the goal is to sell high and later to buy low.

Short selling isn't necessarily free—or even cheap. Because you've borrowed someone's stock and sold it, you not only have to replace it later but also have to repay any dividends that were paid during the period for which the broker was without the stock. Also, to protect the brokerage firm from short sellers who might lose the money, the broker keeps the proceeds from the short sale until the firm gets its stock back. To provide the brokerage firm with a further guarantee that the short seller will be able to repurchase the stock in the future, the short seller must put up some collateral—referred to as a **margin requirement**—during the period of the short sale.

Margin Requirement
The percentage that an investor must have on deposit with a broker when selling short.

Let's suppose you feel strongly that McDonald's stock price is about to fall from its present level of $100 per share and you want to make money off McDonald's misfortune. First, you call your broker and sell 1,000 shares of McDonald's short. The proceeds of $100,000 are credited to your account, although you can't withdraw those funds. Your broker also has a 50 percent margin requirement, which means you must have an additional $50,000 in cash or securities in your account to serve as collateral. Most short sellers keep Treasury bills or notes in their account for this purpose.

STOP & THINK

Warren Buffett once said, "Risk comes from not knowing what you're doing." What do you think he meant by that?

Now, let's assume McDonald's drops to $80 per share and you decide it's time to buy. You tell your broker to purchase 1,000 shares of McDonald's for a total cost of $80,000. Thus, you make $20,000 on your short sale by selling high ($100 per share) and later buying low ($80 per share). Remember, though, that when you sell short, you also have to cover any dividends that occurred during the period the broker was without the stock. Thus, your profits are actually equal to the initial price less the total of the ending price and the dividends, as shown in Figure 11.5.

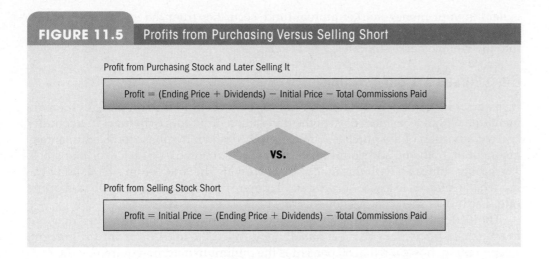

FIGURE 11.5 Profits from Purchasing Versus Selling Short

Profit from Purchasing Stock and Later Selling It

Profit = (Ending Price + Dividends) − Initial Price − Total Commissions Paid

VS.

Profit from Selling Stock Short

Profit = Initial Price − (Ending Price + Dividends) − Total Commissions Paid

Of course, if McDonald's stock price goes up, you will lose money because you will have to buy back the stock at the higher price. Thus, if McDonald's stock goes up to $120 per share, you will lose $20,000 on your short sale, in addition to having to cover any dividends that occurred during the period the stock was sold short. You'll also have to listen to your broker laugh when you give back the more expensive stock. In this case, you have sold low ($100 per share) and later bought high ($120 per share). Given the fact that the long-term trend of the stock market is upward, selling short is extremely risky and isn't something most people should consider.

Dealing with Brokers

The most common way to purchase stock is through a stockbroker, someone who is licensed to buy or sell stocks for others. You can also purchase securities through financial planners, as most are, among other things, stockbrokers.

There are two general categories of brokers: full-service brokers and discount and online brokers. You can deal directly with your broker—that is, over the phone or in person—or you can do your trading online without ever interacting directly with a broker. The differences between these two ways of buying stock center on advice and cost. As we'll see later when we examine the cost of trading, the difference in cost can be substantial.

Brokerage Accounts

Just as a bank account represents money you have on deposit at a bank, a brokerage account represents money or investments you have at a brokerage firm. For most investors, this account includes securities and possibly some cash. It can also include other investments. If there are enough different investments, combining these different accounts into an all-in-one account, called an asset management account, might be best.

When we first introduced the **asset management account** in Chapter 5, we defined it as a comprehensive financial services package offered by a brokerage firm that can include a checking account; a credit card; a money market mutual fund; loans; automatic payment on any fixed debt (such as mortgages); brokerage services (buying and selling stocks or bonds); and a system for the direct payment of interest, dividends, and proceeds from security sales into the money market mutual fund.

Asset Management Account
A comprehensive financial services package offered by a brokerage firm that can include a checking account; credit and debit cards; a money market mutual fund; loans; automatic payment of fixed debt (such as mortgages or other debt); brokerage services (buying and selling stocks or bonds); and a system for the direct payment of interest, dividends, and proceeds from security sales into the money market mutual fund.

The major advantage of such an account is that it automatically coordinates the flow of funds into and out of your money market mutual fund. For example, interest and dividends received from securities owned are automatically "swept" into the money market mutual fund. If you write a check for an amount greater than what is held in your money market mutual fund, securities from the investment portion of your asset management account are automatically sold and the proceeds "swept" into the money market fund to cover the check.

Cash Versus Margin Accounts

Cash Account
A securities trading account in which the investor pays in full for security purchases, with the payment due within 3 business days of the transaction.

Margin Account
A securities trading account in which the investor borrows a portion of the purchase price from the broker.

Margin or Initial Margin
A 50 percent limit set by the Federal Reserve on the minimum percentage of the purchase price of a security that an investor must initially pay.

Investors with **cash accounts** pay in full for their security purchases, with the payment due within 3 business days of the transaction. Investors with **margin accounts** borrow a portion of the purchase price from the broker. In other words, with a margin account, both you and your broker put in $500 to purchase $1,000 worth of stock. The broker comes up with this money by borrowing the funds from a bank and paying what's referred to as the "broker's call money rate," which is generally the prime rate. The broker then charges you this rate plus a 1 to 2 percent service fee.

The Federal Reserve has set a 50 percent limit on the minimum percentage of the purchase price that you must initially pay, called the **margin or initial margin**. Keep in mind, however, that 50 percent is the minimum margin required by the Federal Reserve and that the broker you work with may require more.

The only time purchasing on margin is to the advantage of the investor is when the return on the stocks is greater than the cost of the borrowing. To demonstrate, let's assume that the margin is 50 percent and that you purchase 200 shares of General Electric stock at $50 per share. In this case, the stock will cost a total of $10,000 (200 × $50), and you will pay $5,000 and borrow the remaining $5,000 from your broker.

Total cost: 200 shares at $50 per share	$10,000
Amount borrowed: total cost – margin %	–5,000
Margin: investor's contribution	$5,000

When you purchase securities on margin, they remain in the brokerage firm's name because the shares are used as collateral for the margin loan. What drives investors to make margin purchases is the desire to leverage their profits as those securities go up in price. Let's look at what will happen to your investment if the price of General Electric's stock rises 40 percent to $70 per share.

Total value of 200 shares at $70 per share	$14,000
Margin loan	–5,000
Margin (the net value of your investment)	$ 9,000

Your initial contribution of $5,000 is now worth $9,000, meaning you have made $4,000 on an investment of $5,000—an 80 percent gain on your investment despite a stock price increase of only 40 percent. Actually, your return will be a bit less because you are also paying interest on the portion of the purchase that was financed with borrowed funds, not to mention the commissions you pay when you buy and sell the stock.

Don't get too excited about margin purchases. Although the leverage that margin purchases provide can amplify stock price gains in a positive way, it can also amplify stock price losses in a negative way. Let's assume that the value of the General Electric stock drops to $30 per share.

Total value of 200 shares at $30 per share	$6,000
Margin loan	–5,000
Margin (the net value of your investment)	$ 1,000

Your initial investment of $5,000 is now worth $1,000, meaning you have lost $4,000—an 80 percent loss despite only a 40 percent drop in General Electric's stock price. Thus, the leverage that margin purchases produce is often referred to as a "double-edged sword" because it helps you in the good times and hurts you in the bad times.

> **STOP & THINK**
>
> Keep money in perspective. "I'm just not the acquisitive type. I have three cars, and that's as extravagant as it gets for me. My watch cost me $39 and it keeps good time, so why would I need a more expensive one?" —Denzel Washington, two-time Oscar winner. What do you think of Denzel Washington's attitude?

Margin accounts are set up in such a way that when stock prices fall, only the amount you've put in suffers the loss in value. To protect your broker, a maintenance margin is in place. The **maintenance margin** specifies a minimum percentage margin of collateral that you must maintain—which is often the same as the initial margin. If the margin falls below this percentage, the broker issues a margin call. A **margin call** requires you to replenish the margin account by adding additional cash or securities to bring the margin back up to a minimum level. Alternatively, the broker can sell securities from your margin account to bring the margin percentage up to an acceptable level. Again, you take the loss.

Maintenance Margin
The minimum percentage margin of collateral that you must maintain.

Margin Call
A requirement that you replenish your margin account by adding cash or securities to bring it back to a minimum level.

Joint Accounts

If you and your spouse are buying securities together, there are several alternative forms of joint accounts, each with different estate planning implications. It's important to either thoroughly understand how these joint accounts work or confer with a lawyer before setting up your account.

Two of the most common joint accounts are joint tenancy with the right of survivorship and tenancy-in-common. Under a **joint tenancy account with the right of survivorship**, when one of the individual owners dies, the other receives full ownership of the assets in the account. The assets bypass the lengthy court process called probate, where they are transferred according to the instructions left in the deceased's will. However, even with joint tenancy, the assets may be subject to estate taxes. With a **tenancy-in-common account**, the deceased's portion of the account goes to the heirs of the deceased rather than to the surviving account holder.

Joint Tenancy Account with the Right of Survivorship
A type of joint ownership in which the surviving owner receives full ownership of the assets in the account when the joint owner dies.

Tenancy-in-Common Account
A type of joint ownership in which the deceased's portion of the account goes to the heirs of the deceased rather than to the surviving account holder.

Choosing a Broker

Using a Full-Service Broker Much of your decision as to whether to go with a **discount or online broker** or a **full-service broker** boils down to a choice between service and price—not an uncommon trade-off in many of life's decisions. With a full-service broker, you get the personal service, advice, and hand-holding that you wouldn't get with a discount broker. If that's the only way you feel comfortable, then a full-service broker is your only choice. However, you should keep in mind that your broker is not a securities analyst and most likely does not evaluate the recommendations he or she receives from analysts but instead simply passes them on. In effect, when your broker advises you to buy or sell a security, he or she is acting on an analyst's recommendation, not on firsthand research. This doesn't mean you shouldn't take your broker's advice. Rather, you should take that advice and investigate it.

Discount or Online Broker
A "no-frills" broker who executes trades without giving any advice and thus charges much lower commissions than a full-service broker.

Full-Service Broker or Account Executive
A broker who gives advice and is paid on commission, where that commission is based on the sales volume generated.

This relates back to **Principle 1: The Best Protection Is Knowledge**. As we have said so often throughout this text, you bear all the consequences of bad decisions, so you *must* take responsibility for your own financial affairs. This is also why it's so important to do your homework when selecting a broker.

PRINCIPLE 1

Using a Discount/Online Broker There's one thing you *can* do to increase the performance of your investments and that is to keep the transaction costs—that is, commissions and fees—down to a minimum. Keeping costs down is important, especially if you don't get much for the extra money the commissions and fees represent; remember **Principle 6: Waste Not, Want Not—Smart Spending Matters**. Unfortunately, keeping costs down is difficult with a full-service broker that charges commissions

PRINCIPLE 6

5 to 20 times higher than those charged by a discount broker. Although you might not have an account executive to hold your hand, some discount/online brokers—such as Fidelity, for example—provide an abundance of research reports free of charge and an analysis of your portfolio, along with downloadable tax information, and on top of that, you'll have a greater return on your investments. In fact, some of the discount/online brokers provide services that are very similar to those offered by full-service brokers. However, remember that not all discount/online brokers are the same—services, planning tools, research materials, and costs can vary dramatically from one to another.

When purchasing bonds, there's no advantage to using a discount/online broker. In general, the commissions charged for bonds by full-service and discount/online brokers will pretty much be the same, especially for larger purchases. If you're going to buy bonds through a broker, you might as well use a full-service broker because it doesn't cost more. If you're buying Treasury bonds, there's no reason to go through a broker at all. Treasury bonds can be purchased directly from the Treasury Department or from any of the Federal Reserve Banks, and no commission will be charged.

Making the Decision As with choosing a financial advisor, choosing a broker is a serious decision, one that can have a major impact on your financial future. If you decide on a discount/online broker, look for one with a reputation for honesty and low costs.

PRINCIPLE 1

Remember, your first job is to become knowledgeable (**Principle 1** at work again). You may feel you have to start off with a full-service broker, but as your understanding of the investment process improves, so will your confidence that you can trade through a discount broker. The advantage that full-service brokers have in terms of research tools, retirement planning tools, and portfolio specialists has narrowed dramatically in recent years. So this question remains: Is the added service that full-service brokers provide worth the price?

Online Trading

Online Trading
Making trades on the Internet.

The two basic ways you can execute your trades are dealing directly with a broker and engaging in **online trading**. Although many investors are more comfortable going through a broker, it tends to be less expensive to make the trades yourself online.

PRINCIPLE 1

Because of the fast pace of online trading—that is, the instant access to your account and nearly instantaneous execution of your trades—it is important to protect yourself. As with everything else in investing or personal finance, this all goes back to **Principle 1: The Best Protection Is Knowledge**.

Day Traders
Individuals who trade, generally over the Internet, with a very short time horizon, generally less than 1 day.

While many of these trades are executed by investors with a buy-and-hold philosophy, many are also executed by **day traders**. A day trader is an individual who trades with a very short-term investment horizon. Typically, they station themselves at the computer and look for stocks that are moving up or down in value. Their goal is to ride the momentum of the stock and get out before it changes direction. Day trading is not investing; it is speculating, and to say the least, it is risky. In general, day trading should be avoided. However, if you're lured into trying it, keep a few facts in mind:

- **Be prepared to suffer severe financial losses.** It is typical for day traders to suffer severe financial losses in their first months, and many never make a penny. That means you should never consider day trading with money you can't afford to lose.
- **Don't confuse day trading with investing—they aren't the same.** Day traders aren't interested in value, just in what the stock might do in the next few hours or day.
- **Don't believe claims of easy profits.** People have a tendency to talk more about when they make money but not about when they lose it. In fact, day trading has been called "a trading method for transferring wealth from unsophisticated investors to sophisticated investors."

- **Watch out for "hot tips" and "expert advice" from newsletters and Web sites catering to day traders.** There's no question that someone makes money from these; unfortunately, it isn't the investor. The same is true for those "educational" seminars, classes, and books about day trading—they may not be objective. Many times the seminar speaker, the instructor teaching a class, or the author of a publication about day trading stands to profit if you start day trading.

The bottom line is this: Avoid day trading. It's speculating, not investing.

LOVE & MONEY

In this chapter, we are looking at investment basics, things like asset allocation, securities markets, and how securities are traded. Now, let's take a look at a different type of investment, the "*investment* in relationships." Ninety-five percent of Americans know that 50 percent of all marriages will end in divorce, and those 95 percent of Americans also think that they're part of the 50 percent that won't get divorced. Divorce not only is prevalent but also does major damage to your finances, damage that may take a lifetime to repair. In fact, according to a survey by TD Ameritrade, it takes Americans nearly 5 years on average to rebound financially from a divorce, with ***only 33 percent*** ever recovering fully. So what kind of "investment" can you make that will improve your chances of marital success? The answer is vacations!

According to a recent GoBankingRates survey, 64 percent of happy respondents said they went on a vacation at least once a year. TD Ameritrade also surveyed couples and found similar results: 87 percent of those that traveled together felt that this brought them closer together and made them happier. This was even more dramatic among millennials age 18 through 34: 93 percent felt it made them happier and brought them closer together.

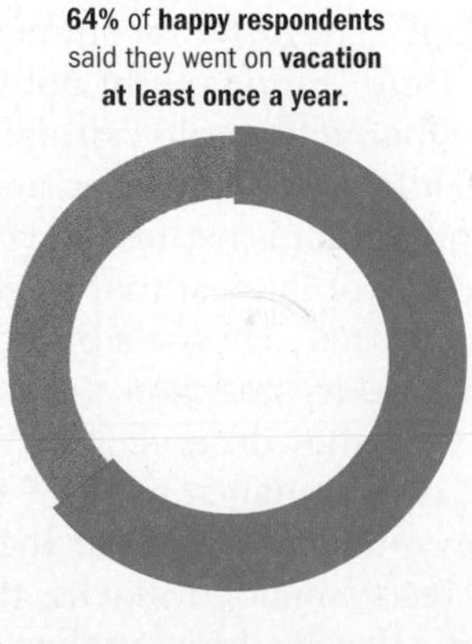

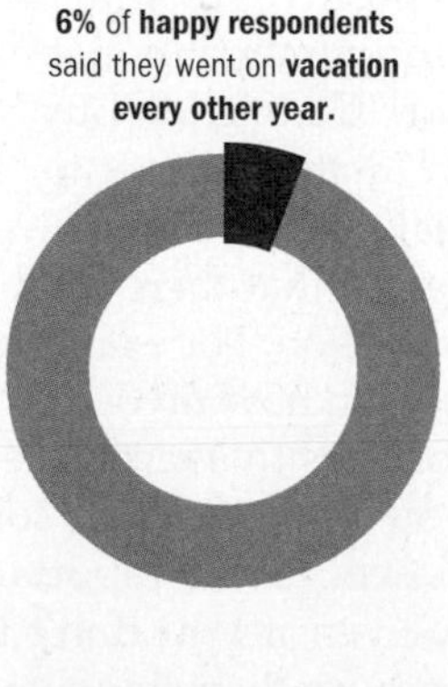

How did they pay for this? The answer is generally through budgeting, saving up specifically for the vacation. That certainly makes sense; it's also a goal that is easy to sacrifice for, since you know it is something you'll enjoy. If it's just a couple, the average amount spent is about $1,220, but for family vacations, that average amount spent is about $1,722. And just as with couples, vacationing as a family makes them feel closer together and happier.

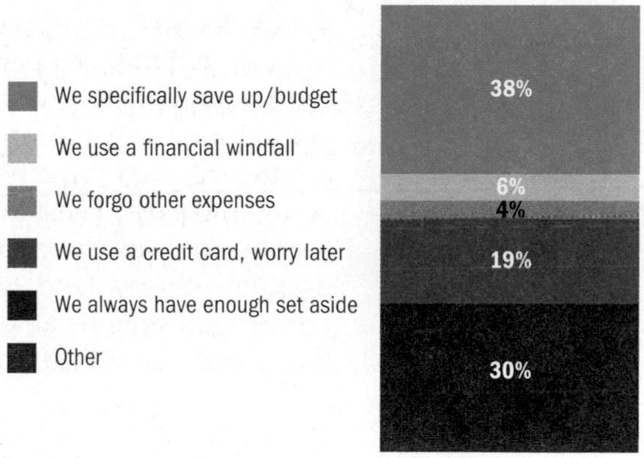

It should come as no surprise that if you really want to go on a vacation, it has to be part of your budget. It is definitely a goal, or an "investment," that you have to save for, and if the above statistics mean anything, it is an important one. If you're having trouble saving up for it, try an app that automates your savings like Qapital, Acorns, Dyme, Mvelopes, or Digit. And even if you decide not to use one of these savings apps, check them out; you might find they have something to offer you. Keep in mind the statistics about the value that this time brings to your life as a couple, and finally keep in mind that one thing that can ruin the glow of your vacation is large credit card bills in the months following if you don't stick to your vacation investment plan!

LO7 Locate and use several different sources of investment information to trade securities.

Sources of Investment Information

Okay, you have set your financial goals, you have developed a plan and a budget to start down your path toward reaching those goals, and you may have even thought about some asset allocation strategies to help get you there. Now that you feel ready to "make some investments," how do you go about choosing the first stock that you will buy? To say the least, there's a wealth of investment information available. And once you're ready to invest, you'll want to gather as much information as you can, read it, and interpret it. Fortunately, you don't have to do your own research. That's already been done for you, and it's available from the companies themselves, from brokerage firms, from the press—magazines, newspapers, and investment advisory services—and, of course, on the Web.

Corporate Sources

Annual reports are a great source of information. Most annual reports are available for free directly from the company itself. When reading an annual report, the first thing to keep in mind is that although the report is factual, those facts are interpreted in as favorable a light as possible. For example, annual reports generally begin with a letter from the president that highlights the year and gives projections for the upcoming year. It does so with real attention to public relations. If the president says, "It was a challenging and troublesome year," he or she may really be trying to say, "We lost a lot of money last year."

When looking at an annual report, examine the trends in sales, profits, and dividends, looking for upward movement in all three. Pay attention to the explanation of how well the firm performed during the year and what management projects for the future. Finally, give close attention to the positives and negatives outlined in the annual report. Are profits up or down? Are new products being introduced? How are the sales on those new products? Are sales climbing or falling? Are new plants being opened or closed?

You look at these items because most of the changes a firm experiences are gradual—things tend to get worse or better over time. By looking at an annual report, you may be able to judge the direction of the changes that are taking place today and that will affect the company's stock price tomorrow.

Brokerage Firm Reports

Most full-service and some discount brokers provide customers access to research reports prepared by the brokerage firm's securities analysts. These reports cover the direction of the economy as a whole and also look directly at individual companies, analyzing the companies' prospects and concluding with recommendations of buy, hold, or sell. "Buy" indicates a positive recommendation, "sell" a negative recommendation, and "hold" a neutral recommendation, but even a "buy" rating might not be a top rating. A "Strong Buy" or "Conviction Buy" may be what you would normally think of as a "buy," and a "buy" may be closer to "Eh" or "Hold." On top of that, analysts may also voice one official opinion in writing and another that is expressed verbally to clients. Also keep in mind that there might be conflicts of interest that might impact the analyst's recommendation. For example, a company may choose a brokerage house for its business based on how favorably the firm rates its stock. As a result, they might receive a much more positive recommendation than they deserve.

The bottom line is that you don't want to solely rely on an analyst's "buy" or "sell" recommendation. However, these reports provide you with valuable logic behind the recommendation. Even if you don't buy the recommended stocks, the reports are of value to read because they show you the logic that leads an analyst to recommend that a stock be bought or sold. If you're interested in a research report on a specific company, simply call up your broker and request it—it's as simple as that.

The Press

To begin with, every investor should read the *Wall Street Journal* or look at it online. It contains essential insights, data, and financial news. There are a number of other excellent personal finance magazines, such as *Money* and *Kiplinger's Personal Finance*. Remember, the more you read, the more you'll understand what investing is all about. And the more you understand, the more comfortable you'll feel making investments.

Investment Advisory Services

Once you're comfortable reading financial trade magazines and the *Wall Street Journal*, there are more in-depth resources of investment news you may want to take a look at. The primary sources of information on the market and on individual stocks are Moody's Investors Service, Standard & Poor's Stock Reports, Morningstar Investment Reports, and the Value Line Investment Survey. They are all available at many libraries. The best way to get started with these resources is to simply head over to your library and ask the librarian what is available in the way of investment advisory services like Value Line or Standard & Poor's.

Internet Sources

There is an incredible amount of corporate information on the Web, including news groups, free software, and discussion groups. For example, corporations' and mutual funds' electronic filings with the SEC can be accessed via its Electronic Data Gathering, Analysis, and Retrieval (EDGAR) project at no charge. Table 11.2 lists several

TABLE 11.2 Great Sources of Investment Information on the Web

Web site	Address and description
Yahoo! Finance	Address: **http://finance.yahoo.com** • This Web site provides news on investments and personal finance, market updates, and a wealth of information on individual stocks, including quotes, historical prices, interactive charts, key statistics, analyst opinions, and financial statements. Without question, it is one of the best Web sites out there, and it's free! Go to it, enter a company's name in the "Quote Lookup" box, and see what you get. Also, click on "Finance Home" and "Personal Finance."
CNNMoney.com	Address: **http://money.cnn.com** • Included on this Web site is up-to-date information on the stock market, including articles and prices, along with business and personal finance news.
Money 101–CNNMoney.com	Address: **http://money.cnn.com/magazines/moneymag/money101/index.html** • This is a small section of the CNNMoney.com Web site, but it has a wealth of information on personal finance. It will introduce you to the basics of investing, making a budget, determining your asset allocation, and many other investment and personal finance topics.
The Motley Fool	Address: **http://www.fool.com** • The Motley Fool provides headline investment news and commentary, along with basic advice on investing and retirement.
EDGAR	Address: **http://www.sec.gov/edgar.shtml** • The Securities and Exchange Commission (the government group that oversees stock trading) provides free electronic access to statements, periodic reports, and other forms that firms are required to file.

excellent sources of information on the Web. Corporate information is also available from investment companies and commercial online services.

Regardless of how small an investor you are, the Internet provides you with the same opportunities as any other investor. Still, you've got to be careful of where you get your information. Remember that there are no controls over who can post information on the Internet. As a result, that market analysis that seems so astute may have been written by a 12-year-old. Also keep in mind that the agency problem abounds on the Internet. Much of what appears is self-serving in nature. It is placed there either by stockbrokers trying to push stocks on their own Web home pages or by companies trying to improve their stock prices. Look out for those get-rich-quick schemes on the Internet. Someone may get rich, but it won't be you.

BEHAVIORAL INSIGHTS

PRINCIPLE 9

Principle 9: Mind Games, Your Financial Personality, and Your Money If you are going to be a successful investor, it helps to have a basic understanding of some of the behavioral quirks that you may be subject to. After all, if you know the tricks your mind may be playing on you, you may be able to avoid them. So let's take a look at some of the common behavioral biases that affect investors.

Overconfidence Investors tend to be overconfident. Simply put, "people think they know more than they do."[2] This overconfidence applies to their abilities, their knowledge, and the future. In effect, most investors think they can beat the market. After all, why try to pick stocks otherwise? In reality, even the most professional of all investors, mutual fund managers, consistently underperform the market.

Overconfidence also leads to trading too often. Of course, there is the chance that those who trade more frequently earn higher returns. To test this, one study examined the trading behavior of 78,000 households, dividing the accounts into five groups based on the level of turnover.[3] The researchers found a net difference of 7 percent between households with the highest and lowest turnover levels, with those that traded more often earning less. Moreover, those who traded more often did worse not only because they experienced higher trading costs but also because they tended to pick stocks that underperformed the market.

STOP & THINK

Do you think overconfidence is a gender thing? Well, it is. Overconfidence afflicts men more than women, and it also leads them to trade too often. Why do you think overconfidence leads to more trades?

Disposition Effect The disposition effect involves the emotions of fearing regret and seeking pride, resulting in selling winners too soon and keeping losers too long.[4] When confronted with the need to sell, investors are more likely to sell one of their winners and hold onto their losers. Why is this so? According to the disposition effect, if they sell a loser, they are admitting that purchasing it was a mistake in the first place. On the other hand, if they sell a winner, they now have results they can feel proud about. The problem is that while they can now claim a winner, they also have to pay taxes. The real problem with the disposition effect is the aversion to recognizing bad deals and cutting losses. This is compounded by investors' overconfidence.

---

[2]Robert J. Shiller, *Irrational Exuberance* (New York: Broadway Books, 2000), 142.

[3]Brad Barber and Terrance Odean, "Trading Is Hazardous to Your Health: The Common Stock Performance of Individual Investors," *Journal of Finance* 55 (2000): 773–806.

[4]Hersh Shefrin and Meir Statman, "The Disposition to Sell Winners Too Early and Ride Losers Too Long: Theory and Evidence," *Journal of Finance* 4 (1984): 777–90.

House Money Effect The house money effect really reflects the way that gamblers act and the way they view their winnings. If a gambler enters a casino with $5,000 and immediately doubles it, winning $5,000, that gambler will act differently with the new $5,000, taking on risks that he or she wouldn't normally undertake. The house money effect asserts that this is how investors acted during the dot-com bubble of the late 1990s. Once they made profits on their initial investment, they took risks they normally wouldn't take with these new earnings, which resulted in strengthening the bubble.

Risk Aversion After Loss Effect Related to the house money effect is the risk aversion effect, where investors who lose money are more reluctant to take risks. This relates to the aftermath of the market downturn of the late 2000s. Once investors lost money in stocks, many of them decided stocks weren't for them and got out of the game completely.

Herd Behavior When investors see stocks moving one way or the other, they have a tendency to join in and follow the crowd.[5] Investors are afraid that others know something about an individual stock or about the market that they don't know or haven't figured out yet. The result is herd behavior. In effect, investors look at behavior and assume that it is based on knowledge. The end result is that they join the crowd and help to push the price in the direction the herd is taking it—a kind of self-fulfilling behavior. Winners are always observed very closely, particularly when a good performance repeats itself a couple of times. New investors are attracted. Finally, no one wants to fight against the massive power of an increasing majority when all investors are running in the same direction.

ACTION PLAN

Principle 10: Just Do It! As soon as you have the money, it's time to begin investing. Just making the move will bring benefits later on in life by breaking down any fears you may have, and as we all know, there's no better way to learn something than by doing it. Along the way, you'll want to take the lessons learned from efficient markets and apply them.

PRINCIPLE 10

- **Systems don't beat the market. It's long-term investing that works.** There simply is no foolproof method for beating the market. Beware of "hot tips" and cold calls from stockbrokers. Remember the lessons of **Principle 1: The Best Protection Is Knowledge**. There's an old saying on Wall Street: "Those that know don't tell, and those that tell don't know." If it sounds too good to be true, it probably is. The good news in all this is that if you can do as well as the market, you have done quite well indeed.

PRINCIPLE 1

- **Keep to the plan.** Don't try to time the market. Keep in mind that stock prices and interest rates go up and go down, but it's almost impossible to buy only when stock prices are low and sell only when they are high. You should invest regularly and view stocks in accordance with your investment horizon.
- **Focus on the asset allocation process.** You should spend your energy on the appropriate asset allocation, given your goals, your plan, and where you are in your financial life cycle. Recognize the time dimension of investing. Your asset allocation strategy should reflect your investment horizon.

---

[5]Shiller, *Irrational Exuberance*, 149–68.

- **Keep the commissions down.** Because it's difficult to beat the market, make sure you don't give away too much of your return in the way of commissions. Be aware of what the commissions are and shop around.
- **Diversify, diversify, diversify.** The benefits of diversification are still unchallenged.
- **If you don't feel comfortable, seek help!** Don't let the fear of investing keep you out of the game. If you feel uncomfortable, seek the help of a qualified financial advisor.

Chapter Summaries

LO1 Set your goals and be ready to invest.

SUMMARY: In personal financial planning, everything begins and ends with your goals. You must first decide what your goals are and how much you can set aside to meet those goals. Once you've done this, you can develop an investment plan.

It's important to know the difference between investments and speculation. Investing involves buying an asset that generates a return. Speculation occurs when an asset's value depends solely on supply and demand. Buying gold coins and baseball cards is considered speculation because they're worth more in the future only if someone is willing to pay more for them.

KEY TERMS

Investment, page 368 An asset that generates value or a return. For example, stocks pay dividends and bonds pay interest, so these are considered investments.

Income Return, page 368 Investment return received directly from the company or organization in which you've invested, usually in the form of dividends or interest payments.

Speculation, page 368 Buying an asset whose value depends solely on supply and demand as opposed to being based on the return that it generates. For example, gold coins and baseball cards are worth more in the future only if someone is willing to pay more for them.

Derivative Securities, page 369 Securities whose value is derived from the value of other assets.

Option, page 369 A security that gives its owner the right to buy or sell an asset—generally common stock—at a specified price over a specified period.

Maturity Date, page 371 The date at which the borrower must repay the loan or borrowed funds.

Par Value or Principal, page 371 The stated amount on the face of a bond, which the firm is to repay at the maturity date.

Coupon Interest Rate, page 372 The interest to be paid annually on a bond as a percentage of par value, which is specified in the contractual agreement.

Stock, page 372 A fractional ownership in a corporation.

Dividend, page 372 A payment by a corporation to its shareholders.

Capital Gain or Loss, page 373 The gain (or loss) on the sale of a capital asset. For example, any return (or loss) from the appreciation (or drop) in value of a share of stock would be considered a capital gain (or loss).

LO2 Manage risk in your investments.

SUMMARY: There are a number of different sources of risk associated with investments, including interest rate risk, inflation risk, business risk, financial risk, liquidity risk, market risk, political and regulatory risk, exchange rate risk, and call risk.

KEY TERMS

Nominal (or Quoted) Rate of Return, page 374 The rate of return earned on an investment, unadjusted for lost purchasing power.

Real Rate of Return, page 374 The current or nominal rate of return minus the inflation rate.

Interest Rate Risk, page 375 The risk of fluctuations in security prices due to changes in the market interest rate.

Inflation Risk, page 375 The risk that rising prices will eat away the purchasing power of your money and that changes in the anticipated level of inflation will result in interest rate changes, which will in turn cause security price fluctuations.

Business Risk, page 375 The risk of fluctuations in security prices resulting from good or bad management decisions or how well or poorly the firm's products are doing in the marketplace.

Financial Risk, page 375 The risk associated with a company's use of debt. If a company takes on too much debt and can't meet its obligations, the company may default, or the value of its stock may drop.

Liquidity Risk, page 376 Risk associated with the inability to liquidate a security quickly and at a fair market price.

Market Risk, page 376 Risk associated with overall market movements.

Political and Regulatory Risk, page 376 Risk resulting from unanticipated changes in the tax or legal environment.

Exchange Rate Risk, page 376 The risk of fluctuations in security prices due to the variability in earnings resulting from changes in exchange rates.

Call Risk, page 376 The risk to bondholders that a bond may be called away from them before maturity.

Calling a Bond, page 376 Redeeming a bond before its scheduled maturity. Many bonds are callable.

Diversification, page 376 The elimination of risk by investing in different assets. It works by allowing the extreme good and bad returns to cancel each other out. The result is that total variability or risk is reduced without affecting expected return.

Portfolio, page 377 A group of investments held by an individual.

Systematic or Market-Related or Nondiversifiable Risk, page 377 That portion of a security's risk or variability that can't be eliminated through investor diversification. This type of variability or risk results from factors that affect all securities.

Unsystematic or Firm-Specific or Company-Unique Risk or Diversifiable Risk, page 377 Risk or variability that can be eliminated through investor diversification. Unsystematic risk results from factors that are unique to a particular firm.

Allocate your assets in the manner that is best for you. LO3

SUMMARY: As your investment horizon lengthens, you can afford to invest more in riskier assets. This is because the returns of risky assets tend to dominate those of less risky assets as the investment horizon lengthens.

Asset allocation attempts to ensure that the investor is well diversified, generally with assets in several different classes of investments, such as domestic common stocks, international common stocks, and bonds. It also incorporates the concept of the time dimension of investing.

KEY TERM

Asset Allocation, page 381 An attempt to ensure that the investor's strategy reflects his or her investment time horizon and that the investor is well diversified, generally with assets in several different classes of investments, such as domestic common stocks, international common stocks, and bonds.

LO4 Understand how difficult it is to beat the market.

SUMMARY: Efficient markets are concerned with the speed at which information is reflected in security prices. The more efficient the market is, the faster prices react to new information. It is very difficult to beat the market, and as a result, you should keep to your plan and invest for the long term.

KEY TERM

Efficient Market, page 383 A market in which all relevant information about the stock is reflected in the stock price.

LO5 Identify and describe the primary and secondary securities markets.

SUMMARY: The primary securities markets are where new securities are sold. A new issue of IBM stock would be considered a primary market transaction. Actually, the primary markets can be divided into two other markets: those for initial public offerings (IPOs) and those for seasoned new issues. An initial public offering is the first time a company's stock is traded publicly. Seasoned new issues are stock offerings by companies that already have common stock traded in the market. Securities that have previously been issued are traded in the secondary markets.

KEY TERMS

Securities Markets, page 383 A term used to describe a place where financial securities or instruments—for example, common stocks and bonds—are traded.

Primary Markets, page 383 The markets in which newly issued, as opposed to previously issued, securities are traded.

Initial Public Offering (IPO), page 384 The first time a company's stock is traded publicly.

Seasoned New Issue, page 384 A stock offering by a company that already has common stock traded in the marketplace.

Investment Banker, page 384 The middleman between the firm issuing securities and the buying public. This term describes both the firms that specialize in selling securities to the public and the individuals who work for investment banking firms.

Underwriter, page 384 An investment banker who purchases and subsequently resells a new security issue. The issuing company sells its securities directly to the underwriter, who then sells the new issue to the public and assumes the risk of selling it at a satisfactory price.

Prospectus, page 384 A legal document that describes a securities issue and is made available to potential investors.

Secondary Markets, page 384 The markets in which previously issued securities are traded.

Organized Exchange, page 384 An exchange that occupies a physical location where trading occurs, such as the New York Stock Exchange.

Over-the-Counter Market, page 384 A market in which transactions are conducted over the telephone or via a computer hookup rather than in an organized exchange.

Bid Price, page 385 The highest price someone is willing to pay for a security.

Ask or Offer Price, page 385 The lowest price at which someone is willing to sell a security.

American Depository Receipt (ADR), page 385 A marketable document (a receipt) that certifies a bank holds shares of a foreign firm's stock that back the receipt. As a result, the ADR trades just like a normal share of stock.

Churning, page 386 Excessive trading in a security account that is inappropriate for the customer and serves only to generate commissions.

LO6 Trade securities using a broker.

SUMMARY: A market order is simply an order to buy or sell a set number of securities immediately at the best price available. A limit order specifies either that a sale is to be made only at or above a certain price or that a purchase is to be made only at or below a certain price. A stop-loss order is an order to sell if the price drops below a specified level or to buy if the price climbs above a specified level.

KEY TERMS

Round Lot, page 387 A group or lot of 100 shares of common stock. Stocks are traded in round lots on the New York Stock Exchange.

Odd Lot, page 387 An order involving between 1 and 99 shares of stock.

Day Order, page 387 A trading order that expires at the end of the trading day during which it was made.

Open or Good-Till-Cancelled (GTC) Order, page 387 A trading order that remains effective until filled or cancelled.

Fill-or-Kill Order, page 387 A trading order that expires if not filled immediately.

Discretionary Account, page 387 An account that gives your broker the power to make trades for you.

Market Order, page 387 An order to buy or sell a set number of securities immediately at the best price available.

Limit Order, page 387 An order that specifies a security is to be sold only at or above a certain price or bought only at or below a certain price.

Stop or Stop-Loss Order, page 387 An order to sell a security if the price drops below a specified level or to buy if the price climbs above a specified level.

Short Selling, page 388 Borrowing stock from your broker and selling it with an obligation to replace the stock later.

Margin Requirement, page 388 The percentage that an investor must have on deposit with a broker when selling short.

Asset Management Account, page 389 A comprehensive financial services package offered by a brokerage firm that can include a checking account; credit and debit cards; a money market mutual fund; loans; automatic payment of fixed debt (such as mortgages or other debt); brokerage services (buying and selling stocks or bonds); and a system for the direct payment of interest, dividends, and proceeds from security sales into the money market mutual fund.

Cash Account, page 390 A securities trading account in which the investor pays in full for security purchases, with the payment due within 3 business days of the transaction.

Margin Account, page 390 A securities trading account in which the investor borrows a portion of the purchase price from the broker.

Margin or Initial Margin, page 390 A 50 percent limit set by the Federal Reserve on the minimum percentage of the purchase price of a security that an investor must initially pay.

Maintenance Margin, page 391 The minimum percentage margin of collateral that you must maintain.

Margin Call, page 391 A requirement that you replenish your margin account by adding cash or securities to bring it back to a minimum level.

Joint Tenancy Account with the Right of Survivorship, page 391 A type of joint ownership in which the surviving owner receives full ownership of the assets in the account when the joint owner dies.

Tenancy-in-Common Account, page 391 A type of joint ownership in which the deceased's portion of the account goes to the heirs of the deceased rather than to the surviving account holder.

Discount or Online Broker, page 391 A "no-frills" broker who executes trades without giving any advice and thus charges much lower commissions than a full-service broker.

Full-Service Broker or Account Executive, page 391 A broker who gives advice and is paid on commission, where that commission is based on the sales volume generated.

Online Trading, page 392 Making trades on the Internet.

Day Traders, page 392 Individuals who trade, generally over the Internet, with a very short time horizon, generally less than 1 day.

LO7 Locate and use several different sources of investment information to trade securities.

SUMMARY: If you're going to make informed investment decisions, you have to seek investment information, read it, and interpret it. Fortunately, you don't have to do your own research. That's already done for you, and it's available from the companies themselves, from brokerage firms, from the press—magazines, newspapers, and investment advisory services—and on the Web. The Web is the first place you'll want to look, with new investment sites being added almost daily. This provides all investors with the same opportunities. Still, because there are no controls on who can post on the Web, you've got to be careful of where you get your information.

Problems and Activities

These problems are available in MyLab Finance.

1. Everyone needs an emergency fund. Assume your best friend asks you to evaluate a list of investments for an emergency savings fund. Comment on the appropriateness of each of the following:
   a. Certificate of deposit
   b. Three-month Treasury bills
   c. Gold and silver coins
   d. Portfolio of energy stocks
   e. Money market mutual fund

2. Jana just found out that she is going to receive an end-of-year bonus of $40,000. She is in the 25 percent marginal tax bracket. Calculate her income tax on this bonus. Now assume that instead of receiving a bonus, Jana receives the $40,000 as a long-term capital gain. What will be her tax? Which form of compensation offers Jana the best after-tax return? Would your calculation be different if the gain was short-term rather than long-term?

3. After reading this chapter, it isn't surprising that you're becoming an investment wizard. With your newfound expertise, you purchase 100 shares of KSU Corporation for $37 per share. Assume the price goes up to $45 per share over the next 12 months and you receive a qualified dividend of $0.50 per share. What would be your total return on your KSU Corporation investment? Assuming you continue to hold the stock, calculate your after-tax return. How is your realized after-tax return different if you sell the stock? In both cases, assume you are in the 25 percent federal marginal tax bracket and 15 percent long-term capital gains and qualified dividends tax bracket and there is no state income tax on investment income.

4. Categorize each of the nine different sources of risk according to the investment class to which it applies. If the risk applies to both stocks and bonds, then categorize it as "both."

5. You just learned that a well-established company will issue a bond with a maturity of 100 years. The bond appears to be a good deal because it yields 8.5 percent. Assuming that the inflation rate stays at 3 percent, what is the bond's real rate of return today? If you are looking for a bond to purchase and hold for several years, will you buy this bond? Explain your answer in terms of future inflation projections and the length of the bond's maturity.

6. Which securities market regulations deal with each of the following?
   a. Requires disclosure of relevant information on initial public offerings and registration with the FTC
   b. Created the Securities and Exchange Commission (SEC)

c. Protects investors against unethical investment advisors by requiring advisors to register with the SEC
d. Established up to $500,000 of insurance to cover investors' account balances in the event that their brokerage firm goes bankrupt
e. Makes it illegal to trade securities while in the possession of inside information

7. Arianna just made a fantastic investment: She purchased 400 shares in Great Gains Corporation for $21.50 per share. Yesterday the stock closed at $56.50 per share. In order to lock in her gains, she has decided to employ a stop-loss order. Assuming she sets the order at $56, what is likely to happen? Why might this not be a wise decision? At what price would you recommend setting the stop-loss order? Why?

8. Harry and Harriett own 1,000 shares of AI Inc. in a brokerage account that is titled "Harry and Harriett, Tenancy-in-Common." Explain how the assets would be handled if Harry passed away. Would this scenario be different if the account was titled "Harry and Harriett, Joint Tenancy with the Right of Survivorship"?

9. Assume you just purchased 250 shares of Home Depot at $40 per share and 50 percent of this was purchased "on the margin." Fill in the blanks to determine your contribution to this transaction:

Total cost	$_____
Amount borrowed	–_____
Contribution	=====

What would happen to your investment if the price of Home Depot stock rose to $50 per share (ignoring any possible dividends)?

Total value	$_____
Loan	–_____
Margin	=====

What was your profit?

What would happen to your investment if the price of Home Depot stock fell to $30 per share (ignoring any possible dividends)?

Total value	$_____
Loan	–_____
Margin	=====

What was your loss?

10. Last year you sold short 400 shares of stock selling at $90 per share. Six months later the stock had fallen to $45 per share, and you bought 400 shares. Over the 6-month period, the company paid out two dividends of $1.50 per share. Your total commission cost for selling and buying the shares came to $125. Determine your profit or loss from this transaction.

11. Match each of the following behaviors with the appropriate bias, as discussed in the chapter.
a. Wanda owns shares in Happy Clam Oil Exploration, but due to recent events, the share price is down 30 percent from when she bought. She doesn't want to sell now because it had previously been up as much as 25 percent.
b. Drew doesn't believe his friends who tell him that he cannot time the market. He has been successful in making profits from his trades this past month and plans to continue his day trading.
c. Yusuf has been watching the gold market go up and up, so he decides that since everyone is buying gold, he needs to do so as well.

Discussion Case 1

This case is available in **MyLab Finance**.

John, age 28, and Emily, age 27, have just had their first child, Lindsey. They have a combined income of $65,000 and rent a two-bedroom apartment. For the past several years, John and Emily have taken financial responsibilities one day at a time, but it has finally dawned on them that they now must start thinking about their financial future. Recently, John has noticed the stock market begin to move higher, and he is convinced that they should be investing in stocks. Emily is more interested in investing in collectibles such as sports memorabilia because she's been reading reports of baseball trading card speculators making huge profits. When asked what their goals are, John replies that he'd like to save for retirement, and Emily mentions her top priority as saving for Lindsey's college expenses. They both agree that they'd like to buy a house and pay off $4,000 in credit card bills. When asked to list their investments, all they can come up with is a savings account worth $950.

Questions

1. What should be John and Emily's first priority before investing or making any investment plans?
2. If John and Emily asked you to prioritize their goals, how would you rank their investment objectives? Now, match some investment alternatives to their objectives.
3. John and Emily are in the 15 percent tax bracket. Using a financial calculator and the investment category compound average returns for stocks, bonds, and Treasury bills given in Figure 11.3, determine the total nominal value (assume inflation is zero) of their portfolio if they invest $2,000 per year for 40 years in common stock. What is the portfolio value if they invest in government bonds? How about Treasury bills?
4. Should John and Emily invest all their money in one investment strategy (stocks or collectibles)? Explain your answer in terms of diversification and the asset allocation process.
5. Given the information in Figures 11.3 and 11.4, explain why anyone would invest in government or corporate bonds.

Discussion Case 2

This case is available in **MyLab Finance.**

Last year Marcelino graduated from high school and received several thousand dollars from an uncle as a graduation gift. Marcelino, now in his first year of college, just heard of a guy in his dorm that invested in an oil exploration company and made a huge profit in a few months. Marcelino likes the idea of making some money fast and is considering investing his graduation gift money in a similar stock. Marcelino's roommate, Luc, just finished a personal finance course and is concerned that Marcelino may be getting himself into trouble. Luc knows that Marcelino likes to shop online, has run up a fairly large credit card bill, and has trouble staying within his monthly budget. In addition, Marcelino really doesn't know much about investing or how people actually "make money investing." Luc has asked you to help him work through the following questions so that he can talk to Marcelino about his investment plans.

Questions

1. Before investing any money, what five things should Marcelino do first?
2. Is Marcelino's strategy of investing in an oil exploration stock to make quick profits investing or speculating? Support your answer.

3. Luc started talking to Marcelino about market efficiency and market timing. Based on what you now know, how likely is it that Marcelino can pick a stock that will "beat the market"?
4. Calculate Marcelino's average annual rate of return if he purchases shares in an Internet stock at $25 per share, holds the shares for 3 years, and sells them for $65. What is his after-tax rate of return if he is in the 25 percent marginal tax bracket?
5. What potentially significant disadvantage does Marcelino face if he sells his stock for $65 per share after only 10 months and incurs a short-term capital gain?
6. What other financial risks does Marcelino face if he invests in an oil exploration stock?
7. By investing in two unrelated domestic stocks rather than in just one stock, would Marcelino increase or decrease his systematic risk exposure? What about his unsystematic risk exposure?
8. Luc has urged Marcelino to invest for the long term using a diversified approach. Marcelino is skeptical. Explain why Luc is probably correct.

Discussion Case 3

This case is available in MyLab Finance.

Hasit and Chandni Kumar are in their early 40s, and until now, they have always kept their savings in the bank. They liked the idea that a deposit in the bank was insured and guaranteed and that, regardless of what happened in the economy or to the bank, they could always get their money. Hasit and Chandni recently talked with a stockbroker about funding their retirement. The stockbroker pointed out that in terms of reaching their retirement goals, a bank account does not pay enough interest. The broker recommended that they invest in a combination of stocks, bonds, mutual funds, and money market accounts. Both are skeptical about the ultimate safety of their investments. Specifically, Hasit is worried about what would happen to their securities and cash if the brokerage firm went bankrupt, and Chandni is concerned that the markets are rigged and that only those with inside information ever make any money. Both are equally concerned that the markets are unregulated gambles and that there is no way to regulate the ethics of brokers. They've come to you for some advice on what to do.

Questions

1. Should Hasit be concerned about the lack of insurance on his brokerage account? Are there any specific securities acts you could cite to back up your answer?
2. Chandni is concerned about insider trading. Do you agree with Chandni's concerns? Why or why not?
3. Provide Hasit and Chandni a list of questions to ask potential brokers to assure the Kumars will receive the best service at the lowest cost.
4. Hasit and Chandni are considering bypassing the broker and going directly online to trade. What cautions would you share with them? What is the difference between online investing and day trading?
5. If an account titling option is available, would you recommend that Hasit and Chandni own their account as tenants-in-common or as joint tenants with right of survivorship? Why? What is the primary difference in the two account titling options?

CHAPTER 12

Investing in Stocks

Learning Objectives

LO1	**Invest** in stocks.	**Why Consider Stocks?**
LO2	**Read** stock quotes online or in the newspaper.	**Stock Indexes and Quotes**
LO3	**Understand** how stocks are valued and what causes them to go up and down in price.	**Valuation of Common Stock**
LO4	**Employ** different investment strategies.	**Stock Investment Strategies**
LO5	**Understand** the risks associated with investing in common stock.	**Risks Associated with Common Stocks**

When you think about Ashton Kutcher, you probably think of Michael Kelso from *That '70s Show*, Walden Schmidt from *Two and a Half Men*, Jesse Montgomery III from *Dude, Where's My Car?* or simply the guy who's married to Mila Kunis. My bet is he's not someone that you think of when it comes to investment prowess, but while he's had a great acting career, he may be an even better stock investor.

Before he became famous, Kutcher worked jobs ranging from doing construction cleanup to skinning and cleaning deer at a meat locker to baling hay, but once he started making money, the first thing he did was invest. He made one of his best investment decisions in 2009 when he invested in Skype, the web-phone service, only to have it purchased by Microsoft two years later and almost tripling his money.

Does Ashton have any advice on what to look for? As a matter of fact, he does: "If you work in a grocery store, pay attention to the items that you can't keep in stock, and the new things that are hitting the shelf. If you are a contractor, investigate the new materials showing up on jobs. Who makes them? Why are they better? You may have a more educated opinion than you are giving yourself credit for. Too often, people speculate on investments based on what's making someone else rich and forget to do a deep index on their own behaviors."[1]

Danny Moloshok/AP Images

You don't have to be a famous actor or a millionaire, although he certainly invested like one. Even without Ashton's investment prowess, it would not have been difficult to make money in the stock market if you had begun investing 60 years ago. For example, if you had invested $100 in the common stock of a typical firm listed on the New York Stock Exchange (NYSE) on the first day of 1957, over the next 60 years it would have grown to $40,096!

Clearly, you can realize serious gains in the stock market, and it doesn't take 60 years. For example, from the end of 2009 through 2016, an investment of $10,000 would have grown to about $22,780! Five years isn't that long to wait to more than double your money, is it? However, as we've said again and again, investing in the stock market is not without risk: During 2008, stocks dropped by about 38 percent and at one point were down by around 50 percent! Investing in the stock market is all about risk and return, about how to eliminate some of that risk, and sometimes about making a fortune.

Why Consider Stocks?

LO1 Invest in stocks.

Just how does investing in stocks generate returns? When you buy common stock, you purchase a small part of the company. When the company does well, you do well and receive a small part of the profits. If the company does poorly, either you receive no return or you lose money.

Returns from shares of stocks come in the form of dividends and capital appreciation. Remember from Chapter 11 that a *dividend* is a company's distribution of profits to its stockholders. It can be in the form of cash or more company stock, but it's always a liquid asset you can use right away. Capital appreciation refers to an increase in the selling price of your shares of stock, perhaps as the company's earning prospects improve. You can't benefit from capital appreciation until you actually sell your stock.

[1]"Ashton Kutcher on His Best Investment (It's Not What You Think)," https://grow.acorns.com/2016/01/ashton-kutcher-on-the-best-investments-you-can-make-in-2016/.

Neither dividends nor capital appreciation is guaranteed with common stocks. Dividends are paid only when the company earns a profit, and even then they are paid only at the company's discretion. For example, Microsoft, which has been consistently profitable, didn't pay dividends for its first 18 years. Capital appreciation takes place only when the company does well, and success is hard to predict. Look, for example, at what happened during the last week of March and the first week of April 2014 to the common stock of King Digital Entertainment, the makers of the game Candy Crush. On March 26, it fell by over 15.6 percent; then, less than a week later, on April 1, it jumped up in price by about 8.6 percent; and then on August 12, it fell by another 21 percent. It kept on that way—unexplainable ups and downs—until November 2015, when Activision Blizzard, Inc., announced it was going to acquire King Digital. It did so in February 2016, and King Digital ceased to exist. Stock prices can jump up and down for many reasons or for what appears to be no reason at all.

So why consider investing in stocks? For these reasons:

- **Over time, common stocks outperform all other investments.** Although stocks aren't guaranteed to give you any return, they *usually* give you a great return. Figure 12.1 compares the returns on various investments over the period 1951–2016. Common stock clearly blows away the alternatives and exceeds the inflation rate by a wide margin.
- **Stocks reduce risk through diversification.** When you include different types of investments that don't move (experience changes in returns) perfectly together over time in your portfolio, you're able to reduce the risk in your portfolio. Stocks move differently than other investments such as bonds, and different stocks move in different ways. Holding stock from different industries can greatly reduce your risk.
- **Stocks are liquid.** You can't be assured of what you'll get when you want to sell your stock, but you won't have difficulty selling it. The secondary markets for common stock are extremely well developed, and as such, you will be able to sell your stock whenever you want with minimum transaction costs.

FIGURE 12.1 Growth of $100 Invested in Different Asset Classes, 1951–2016

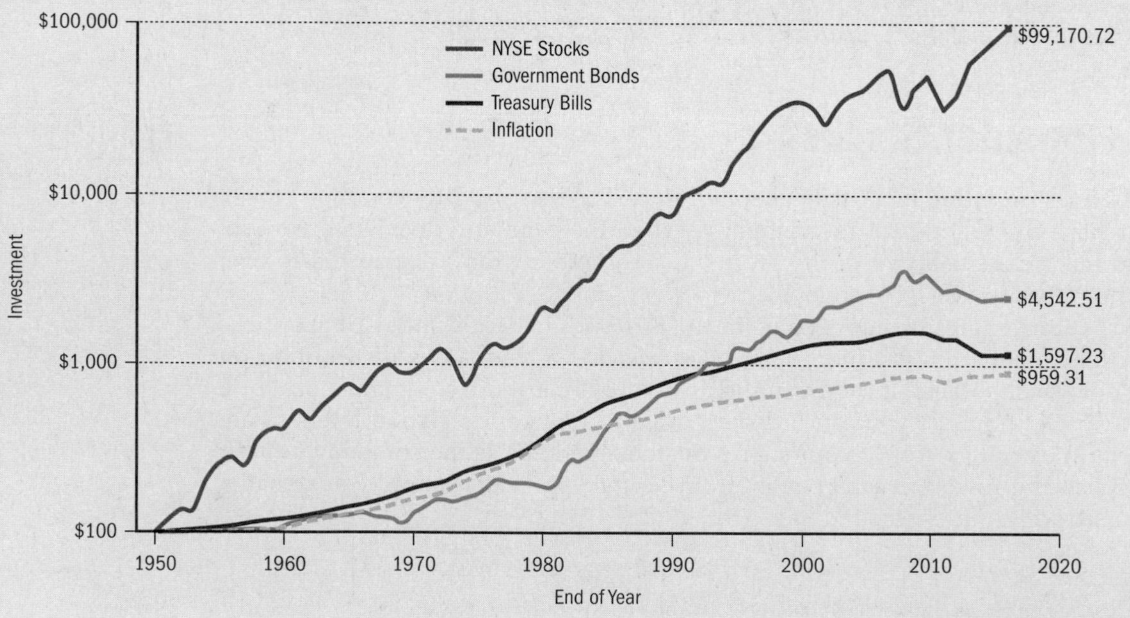

CHECKLIST 12.1 Investment Progress Checklist

- ☐ Is the return on my investment meeting my expectations and goals? Is this investment performing as I was led to believe it would?
- ☐ Is the company making money? How is it doing compared to its competitors?
- ☐ How much money will I get back if I sell my investment today?
- ☐ How much am I paying in commission or fees?
- ☐ Have my goals changed? If so, are my investments still suitable?
- ☐ What criteria will I use to decide when to sell?

- **The growth in your investment is determined by more than just interest rates.** With some investments, the potential for price appreciation is largely a function of interest rates going down. With common stock, you're not a slave to interest rates. Sure, a change in interest rates can and often will affect your stock prices; however, the earning prospects and performance of the firm will also affect stock prices. If you hitch your star to a company that performs well, you can make money even when interest rates jump.

Once you've made the plunge, you'll want to watch over your investment. Checklist 12.1 provides a number of questions to consider as your investment progresses.

Now that you know why stocks make good investments, let's take a look at some stock basics.

The Language of Common Stocks

If you're going to invest in common stocks, you certainly need to know a bit about them and your rights as a common stockholder. Let's look at some specifics.

Limited Liability

Although as a common stockholder you're considered one of the many actual owners of the corporation, your liability in the case of bankruptcy is limited to the amount of your investment. The most you can lose, if the company goes broke, is what you invest.

Claims on Income

As owners of the corporation, common stockholders have the right to any earnings that are left after all debt and other obligations have been paid. The dividend is the typical way to distribute these earnings, but the corporation isn't obligated to pay dividends to its stockholders. Instead, the board of directors decides whether to pay dividends or whether to reinvest the leftover earnings back into the company.

Obviously, common stockholders benefit from the distribution of income in the form of dividends. But they also benefit from the reinvestment of earnings. How? Plowing earnings back into the firm results in an increase in the value of the firm, in its earning power, and in its future dividends. These increases in turn cause the price of the common stock to rise. In effect, leftover earnings are distributed to the common stockholder directly in the form of dividends or indirectly in the form of capital appreciation on the common stock. However, if after paying off debt and other monetary obligations the company has no leftover earnings, the stockholders get zilch.

Although most corporations pay dividends on a quarterly basis, we have noted that common stock dividends aren't automatic. The corporation's board of directors

Declaration Date
The date on which the board of directors announces the size of the dividend, the ex-dividend date, and the payment date.

Ex-dividend Date
The date on which the stock "goes ex," meaning it begins trading in the secondary market "without dividend." In other words, if you buy the stock after its ex-dividend date, you don't get the dividend for that year.

must declare them. On the **declaration date**, the board of directors announces the size of the dividend, which is expressed as the dividend per share, as well as the ex-dividend date and the payment date.

Because companies need to know who actually owns their stock before they can pay a dividend, they set a cutoff date known as the **ex-dividend date**. On the ex-dividend date, the stock begins trading "without dividend"—that is, if you buy it after the ex-dividend date, you don't get the dividend for that year. On the payment date, the corporation sends out dividend checks to stockholders.

Claims on Assets

When a company does well and has a lot of earnings to distribute, common stockholders receive their share only after the company's creditors are paid. What happens when a company does so poorly that it goes bankrupt? Well, common stockholders are stuck waiting in line again. The creditors have the right to sell off the remaining company assets to regain their money. Only after the claims of the creditors have been paid off do stockholders get to sort through the rubble and try to extract the money they invested. Unfortunately, when companies do go bankrupt, the stockholders are usually plain out of luck.

Voting Rights

Common stockholders are entitled to elect the company's board of directors. Usually, one share of stock equals one vote, although some, but not many, companies issue different "classes" of stock with greater or lesser voting power. Common stockholders not only have the right to elect the board but also must approve any changes in the charter, or the rules that govern the corporation.

Proxy
A legal agreement a stockholder signs to allow someone else to vote for him or her at the corporation's annual meeting.

Voting for directors and charter changes occurs at the corporation's annual meeting. Stockholders may attend the meeting and vote in person, but most vote by proxy. A **proxy** is a legal agreement that allows a designated party to vote for a stockholder at the corporation's annual meeting. A proxy vote doesn't mean filling out a voting form and asking your buddy to hand it in for you. Rather, a proxy vote gives your buddy the right to make decisions for you. Usually, the firm's management goes after and gets most of the proxy votes. However, in times of financial distress or when management takeovers are threatened, *proxy fights* occur. Proxy fights are battles for proxy votes between rival groups of shareholders who want to take control of the company or aim it in a new direction.

Stock Splits

Stock Split
Increasing the number of stock shares outstanding by replacing the existing shares of stock with a given number of new shares. For example, in a two-for-one split, for every share of existing stock you hold, you will receive two shares of new stock.

Occasionally, a firm may decide that its stock price is getting too high for the smaller investor to consider purchasing. To keep the price down and thereby encourage more investors to buy, the company "splits the stock." A **stock split** involves substituting more shares for the existing shares of stock. In effect, the number of shares of stock outstanding increases without any increase in the market value of the firm. As a result, each share of stock is worth less.

For example, let's assume you own 100 shares of Coca-Cola common stock and that it's just reached $120 per share. Your investment is worth $12,000. The management of Coca-Cola believes that $120 per share is more than the average small investor can afford and wants the price lowered. Coca-Cola's managers decide to split the stock three for one. Thus, investors receive three shares of "new" Coca-Cola common stock for every share of "old" Coca-Cola common stock that they own. There's no gain in wealth to the stockholder, so each new share of stock is worth

FACTS OF LIFE

Berkshire Hathaway's "A" stock has never split. As a result, in the spring of 2017 one share of its stock was selling at a price of over $266,000 per share.

$40 ($120/3). You now own 300 shares of Coca-Cola stock, which is selling at $40 per share, but your total investment is still worth $12,000.

Stock Repurchases

Sometimes companies buy back their own issued shares of common stock in what's called a **stock repurchase**. This results in fewer shares outstanding, so each remaining stockholder owns a larger proportion of the firm. Stock repurchases are extremely common, with well over 1,000 of these plans announced during most years. For example, in December 2016, Mastercard announced its intent to repurchase up to $4 billion of its stock over the next 5 years.

Stock Repurchase
A company's repurchasing, or buying back, of its own common stock.

Book Value

The book value of a company is calculated by subtracting the value of all the firm's liabilities from the value of all its assets, as given on its balance sheet. To relate book value more easily to the price of the stock, divide the company's book value by the number of shares it has outstanding to get the book value per share.

Book value is a historical number. That is, it reflects the value of the firm's assets when they were purchased, which may be vastly different from their value today. For a firm whose assets were purchased a number of years ago, book value has little or no meaning. Still, this measure of value is often talked about and used in valuing stock.

Earnings per Share

Earnings per share reflects the level of earnings achieved for every share of stock. Because it focuses on the return earned by the common stockholder, it looks at earnings after preferred stock dividends have been paid. Preferred stock dividends are subtracted from net income because, as we will see in the next chapter, they're paid before common stock dividends are paid. Net income less preferred stock dividends is what is available to the common stockholders.

This figure tells investors how much they've earned on each share of stock they own—but not necessarily how much the company will pass along in dividends. This figure is available in the daily stock price listings in most newspapers and can be used to compare the financial performance of different companies. Earnings per share is calculated as follows:

$$\text{earnings per share} = \frac{\text{net income} - \text{preferred stock dividends}}{\text{number of shares of common stock outstanding}}$$

Dividend Yield

The **dividend yield** on a share of common stock is the amount of annual dividends divided by the market price of the stock. The dividend yield tells investors how much in the way of a return they would receive if the stock price and dividend level remained constant. For example, if the price of the stock was $50 and it paid $4 per share in dividends, the dividend yield would be 8 percent ($4/$50 = 8%).

Dividend Yield
The ratio of the annual dividends to the market price of the stock.

Many companies that have tremendous growth possibilities choose to reinvest their earnings rather than paying them out in dividends. As a result, many growth companies simply don't pay dividends. For example, for many years Microsoft didn't pay dividends but instead reinvested its earnings, which has now given it the ability to either pay large dividends or buy back its own stock at hefty prices.

FACTS OF LIFE

Warren Buffett on excessive trading: "We believe that according the name 'investors' to institutions that trade actively is like calling someone who repeatedly engages in one-night stands a 'romantic.'"

TABLE 12.1 Stock Classifications

Classification	Characteristics of the Classification
Blue-Chip Stocks	Common stocks issued by large, nationally known companies with sound financial histories of solid dividend and growth records.
Growth Stocks	Common stocks issued by companies that have exhibited sales and earnings growth well above their industry average. Generally, these are smaller stocks, and many times they are newly formed.
Income Stocks	Common stocks issued by mature firms that pay relatively high dividends, with little increase in earnings.
Speculative Stocks	Common stocks that carry considerably more risk and variability than a typical stock.
Cyclical Stocks	Common stocks issued by companies whose earnings tend to move with the economy.
Defensive Stocks	Common stocks issued by companies whose earnings tend not to be affected by swings in the economy and in some cases actually perform better during downturns.
Large-Cap, Mid-Cap, and Small-Cap Stocks	Classifications of common stock that refer to the size of the issuing firm—more specifically, to the level of the firm's capitalization, or its market value.

Market-to-Book or Price-to-Book Ratio

The market-to-book or price-to-book ratio is a measure of how highly valued the firm is. When interpreting this ratio, remember that book value reflects historical costs and, as such, may not be overly meaningful. This ratio is calculated as follows:

$$\text{market-to-book ratio} = \frac{\text{stock price}}{\text{book value per share}}$$

Most stocks have market-to-book ratios above 1.0, and they commonly range up to about 2.5.

Classification of Stocks

Before we move on and discuss stock indexes and the valuation of stock, let's look at the classification of stocks. Analysts just love to use such terms as *blue-chip*, *speculative*, and *growth* to describe common stocks. These aren't formal classifications, and while they do help you understand how this stock is viewed, they don't necessarily tell you much about the future performance of this stock. Table 12.1 provides a brief description of some of these classifications.

LO2 Read stock quotes online or in the newspaper.

Stock Indexes and Quotes

Stock Market Index
A measure of the performance of a group of stocks that represent the market or a sector of the market.

Every day you hear financial reports on television or the radio in which someone says, "The market was up today as the Dow rose 27 points." Did you ever wonder just what that person was talking about? "The Dow" is a **stock market index** that measures the performance of various stock prices. There are several stock market indexes, and while they won't tell you exactly how each one of your investments performed, they will provide you with a simple way of measuring stock market performance in general. To understand stock listings and stock performance, you need to be familiar with the Dow and other market indexes.

The Dow

The oldest and most widely quoted of the stock indexes or averages is the **Dow Jones Industrial Average (DJIA), or Dow**, started by Charles Dow in 1896. The DJIA's original purpose was to gauge the sense of well-being of the market based on the performance of 12 major companies. The Dow is currently comprised of the prices of 30 large industrial firms, only one of which—General Electric—was in the original group of 12.

Dow Jones Industrial Average (DJIA) or Dow
A commonly used stock index or indicator of how well stocks have done. This index is comprised of the stock prices of 30 large industrial firms.

Because the DJIA is based on the movement of only 30 large, well-established stocks, many investors believe it reflects price movements for large firms rather than for the general market. One odd thing about the DJIA is that it is price weighted—that is, stocks with higher prices per share are given a higher weighting than stocks with lower prices. Still, with these 30 stocks representing over 25 percent of the market value of the NYSE, this index is more representative than one might think at first glance.

However, as we said, the DJIA does weight stocks based on their relative prices, and as a result, when a high-priced stock moves a small amount, it has an inordinately large impact on the index. Even so, the DJIA does a relatively good job of reflecting market movements. In fact, it went from 14,164 on October 9, 2007, down to 6,547 on March 9, 2009, then back up to just under 17,000 by mid-2014, and then up to over 23,000 by the fall of 2017—reflecting the wild movements in stock prices over that time period.

The S&P 500 and Other Indexes

Another well-known stock market index is the **Standard & Poor's 500 Stock Index, or S&P 500**. The S&P 500 is a much broader index than the DJIA because it's based on the movements of 500 stocks—primarily from the NYSE but also including some stocks from the over-the-counter (OTC) market. Because the S&P 500 is a broader index, it probably better represents movements in the overall market than does the Dow.

Standard & Poor's 500 Stock Index or S&P 500
Another commonly used stock index or indicator of how well stocks have done based on the movements of 500 stocks, primarily from the NYSE.

Other indexes include the Russell 1000, which is made up of companies that rank in size from the 1st through 1,000th largest companies; the Russell 2000, which is made up of companies that rank in size from the 1,001st through the 3,000th largest companies; and the Wilshire 5000, which is a very broad-based index made up of all U.S. stocks with readily available price data. In addition, Standard & Poor's calculates six other general indexes. Still, when investors talk about movements in the market, they generally refer to the Dow.

Market Movements

So what do all these indexes tell us? Basically, they tell us whether stock prices in general are rising or falling. A **bear market** is a stock market characterized by falling prices. The term *bear* comes from the fact that bears swipe downward when they attack. A **bull market** is one characterized by rising prices. The term *bull* comes from the fact that bulls fling their horns upward when they attack.

Bear Market
A stock market characterized by falling prices.

Bull Market
A stock market characterized by rising prices.

Reading Stock Quotes Online and in the Newspaper

Figure 12.2 provides a visual summary of how to read NYSE listings. Most online sites (including **http://www.wsj.com**, **http://www.marketwatch.com**, and **http://finance.yahoo.com**) and newspapers include the same basic information for stocks listed on the NYSE, the AMEX, and the OTC market.

By looking at a stock quote online or in the newspaper, investors can see how much the stock's price moved up or down by examining its highest and lowest prices during the previous day, which are listed along with the closing price. Finally,

FIGURE 12.2 How to Read Online Stock Quotes

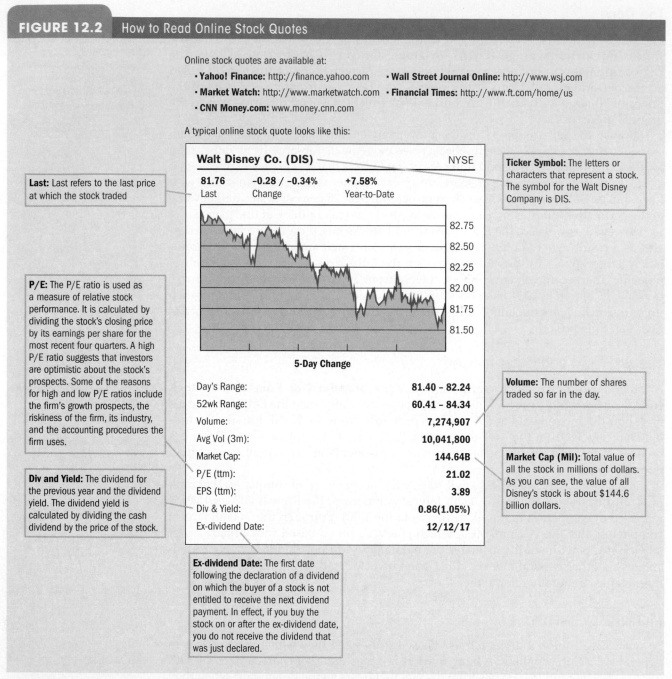

Online stock quotes are available at:

- **Yahoo! Finance:** http://finance.yahoo.com
- **Wall Street Journal Online:** http://www.wsj.com
- **Market Watch:** http://www.marketwatch.com
- **Financial Times:** http://www.ft.com/home/us
- **CNN Money.com:** www.money.cnn.com

A typical online stock quote looks like this:

Walt Disney Co. (DIS) NYSE

81.76	**−0.28 / −0.34%**	**+7.58%**
Last	Change	Year-to-Date

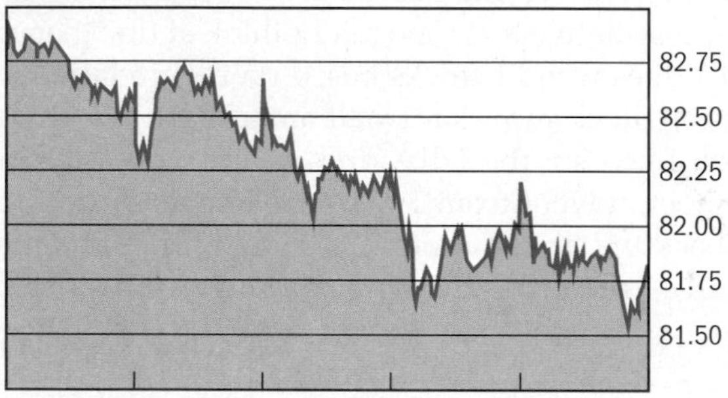

5-Day Change

Day's Range:	**81.40 - 82.24**
52wk Range:	**60.41 - 84.34**
Volume:	**7,274,907**
Avg Vol (3m):	**10,041,800**
Market Cap:	**144.64B**
P/E (ttm):	**21.02**
EPS (ttm):	**3.89**
Div & Yield:	**0.86(1.05%)**
Ex-dividend Date:	**12/12/17**

Last: Last refers to the last price at which the stock traded

Ticker Symbol: The letters or characters that represent a stock. The symbol for the Walt Disney Company is DIS.

P/E: The P/E ratio is used as a measure of relative stock performance. It is calculated by dividing the stock's closing price by its earnings per share for the most recent four quarters. A high P/E ratio suggests that investors are optimistic about the stock's prospects. Some of the reasons for high and low P/E ratios include the firm's growth prospects, the riskiness of the firm, its industry, and the accounting procedures the firm uses.

Volume: The number of shares traded so far in the day.

Market Cap (Mil): Total value of all the stock in millions of dollars. As you can see, the value of all Disney's stock is about $144.6 billion dollars.

Div and Yield: The dividend for the previous year and the dividend yield. The dividend yield is calculated by dividing the cash dividend by the price of the stock.

Ex-dividend Date: The first date following the declaration of a dividend on which the buyer of a stock is not entitled to receive the next dividend payment. In effect, if you buy the stock on or after the ex-dividend date, you do not receive the dividend that was just declared.

Source: Common information taken from http://finance.yahoo.com, http://www.marketwatch.com, http://money.cnn.com, http://www.wsj.com, http://www.ft.com/home/us, and http://investing.money.msn.com/investments/stock-price.

the change from the previous day's closing price is listed, which, along with the stock's high and low over the past 52 weeks, gives you a sense of the direction the stock price is taking.

For example, according to the listing in Figure 12.2, what was the last price Disney sold for? How many shares traded yesterday? What is Disney's ticker symbol? What is the price/earnings ratio for Disney? (The last price Disney sold for was $81.76, and 7,274,907 shares traded during the prior day! Disney's ticker symbol is DIS, and the price/earnings ratio for Disney is 21.02.)

Valuation of Common Stock

LO3 Understand how stocks are valued and what causes them to go up and down in price.

How do you determine the value of any investment? Well, as you can imagine, there are a number of different methods used to determine what an investment is worth. These methods can also help you understand why an investment's price moves one way or the other. Let's take a look at some of the most popular valuation methods.

Fundamental and Technical Analysis Approaches

Two of the basic approaches to security analysis are fundamental analysis and technical analysis. Many analysts use a combination of these two methods. With **fundamental analysis**, the value of a stock is calculated using time value of money tools, where the value of the stock is equal to the present value of its expected future cash flows. In effect, you examine the economy, the industry, and the company to gain insights into the company's future performance. From that analysis, you can determine an appropriate price for the company's stock.

Fundamental Analysis
Determining the value of a share of stock by focusing on such determinants as future earnings and dividends, expected levels of interest rates, and the firm's risk.

The key is that you have to discover something that the market has not yet discovered. If you merely analyze a company and find out it's a really great one, with tremendous prospects for the future, chances are everyone else knows that, and it is already reflected in the stock price. You've got to see something no one else sees or do a more insightful job of analyzing that stock. Sound tough? It is, to say the least. Remember, the competition is made up of professionals who do this for a living. Moreover, you have to do more than just find a stock that's mispriced; before you can make any money, you've got to cover all your costs—trading fees, opportunity cost on your time, and taxes. That's why it's so hard to beat the market.

Technical analysis focuses on supply and demand, using charts and computer programs to identify and project price trends for a stock or for the market as a whole. The logic behind technical analysis is that although economic factors are of great importance in determining stock prices, so are psychological factors, such as *greed* and *fear.*

Technical Analysis
A method of stock analysis that focuses on supply and demand, using charts and computer programs to identify and project price trends for a stock or for the market as a whole.

Technical analysts believe that greed and fear reinforce trends in the market. Greed pushes investors to put their money in the market when the market is rising, and fear has them pull their money out if a downturn appears. In effect, no one wants to be the last aboard a market upturn, and no one wants to be the last out if the market is falling.

Technical analysis takes a number of forms, including the interpretation of charts and graphs and mathematical calculations of trading patterns, all aimed at spotting some trend or direction for stocks. Technical analysts might look into the past for trends or patterns that give some clue as to where investors might be heading. In addition, they might look for price levels where stock prices might get stuck. These price levels are referred to as resistance or support levels.

FACTS OF LIFE

In commenting on technical analysis, Warren Buffett once said, "If past history was all there was to the game, the richest people would be librarians."

Unfortunately, although technical analysis may appeal to the novice investor, it's been found to be of little value. There appear to be distinct trends in past movements of the market, but the problem comes in identifying these trends *before* they surface. Moreover, some of these patterns may have been useful in the past, but without any economic logic behind them, what's to say they'll continue to act as good predictors?

In short, technical analysis should be viewed as something to avoid because it encourages moving in and out of the market, which is dangerous, as opposed to simply buying and holding stocks.

The Price/Earnings Ratio Approach

The **price/earnings (P/E) ratio** is used regularly by security analysts as a measure of a stock's relative value. This price/earnings ratio, or earnings multiplier, is the

Price/Earnings (P/E) Ratio
The price per share divided by the earnings per share. Also called the earnings multiplier.

STOP & THINK

Many analysts and investors use the market's P/E ratio as a measure of whether the market is overpriced or underpriced. In recent years, they've viewed the average market P/E ratio as being in the 10 to 30 range. If the market's P/E ratio is much above this level, the market is overpriced, and if it's much below this level, the market is underpriced. However, keep in mind that anticipated inflation and the health of the economy and future corporate earnings play a major role in determining the market's P/E ratio. Do you think inflation will increase or decrease in the future?

price per share divided by the earnings per share. It's an indication of how much investors are willing to pay for a dollar of the company's earnings. The more positive investors feel about a stock's future prospects, or the less risk they feel the stock has, the higher the stock's P/E ratio.

For example, a stock that is currently selling for $104 with estimated earnings per share of $6.50 has a P/E ratio of 16 ($104/$6.50). If the prospects for this stock improve—perhaps the company introduces a new product that in a few years should greatly increase profits—the stock price might rise to $130, which would result in a new P/E ratio of 20 ($130/$6.50). A stock with a P/E ratio of 20 is referred to as "selling at 20 times earnings." How do we use P/E ratios to value stocks? By deciding whether or not the stock's P/E ratio is too high or too low.

How do you determine an appropriate P/E ratio for a specific stock? First, you determine a justified P/E ratio for the market as a whole by looking at past market P/E ratios, taking into consideration the strength of the economy, interest rates, the deficit, and the inflation rate. This overall market P/E ratio is then adjusted depending on the specific prospects for the individual stock. For example, if the growth potential is above average, the P/E ratio is adjusted upward—but how much higher is the real question. Although determining an appropriate or justified P/E ratio for a given stock is difficult, we can at least point to some of the factors that drive P/E ratios up and down:

- **The higher the firm's earnings growth rate, the higher the firm's P/E ratio.** In effect, the market values a dollar of earnings more if those earnings are expected to grow more in the future. An example of this is Netflix; its earnings skyrocketed, and its stock price rose to eight times its initial price over the five-year period ending March 2017.
- **The higher the investor's required rate of return, the lower the P/E ratio.** What might cause the investor's required rate of return to rise? One thing might be an increase in interest rates—that would mean there are better alternatives available for your money, so your required rate of return would go up. For example, in 1995 declining inflation resulted in a 2 percent drop in interest rates, which in turn saw stocks surge by 37 percent! Also, if the firm becomes riskier, investors will require a higher rate of return, which will lower the P/E ratio and the price of the firm's stock. For example, as Sears's fortunes turned in 2016 and it became riskier as its future became uncertain, its price fell by 44 percent. Thus, if interest rates rise or if the firm becomes more risky, the P/E ratio should fall. Likewise, if interest rates drop or the firm becomes less risky, the P/E ratio should rise.

Figure 12.3 shows the average S&P 500 P/E ratio since 1990, which should give you an idea of a typical P/E ratio. In recent years, the average has been in the 10 to 30 range. The P/E ratio for growth stocks is much higher—generally beginning at 25 to 30 and going on up.

Because this valuation method focuses on such fundamental determinants as future earnings, expected levels of interest rates, and the firm's risk, it's considered to be a type of fundamental analysis.

SWOT Analysis
A framework for analyzing a security in which you look both internally at the firm's Strengths and Weaknesses and externally at the Opportunities and Threats that the firm faces to gain an understanding of what the future holds for that firm and its stock.

SWOT Analysis

SWOT analysis is a framework for analyzing a firm or its common stock. It forces you to look both internally to the firm's Strengths and Weaknesses and externally to

FIGURE 12.3 The Average Price/Earnings Ratio on the S&P 500 Since 1990

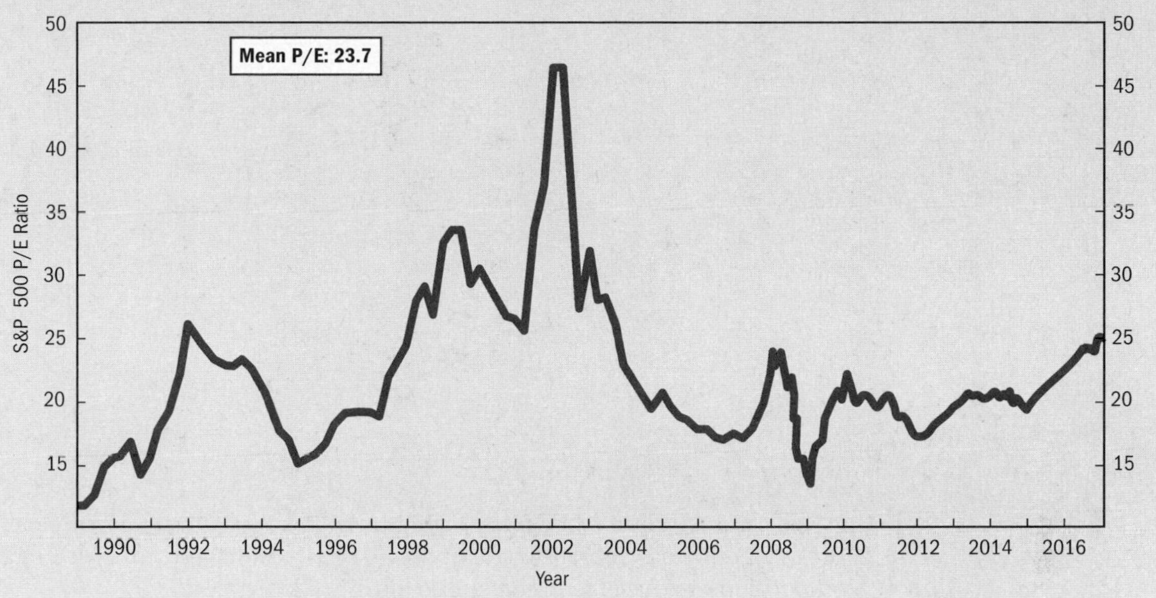

the Opportunities and Threats.[2] What's nice about SWOT analysis is that it allows you to better anticipate changes that might occur in the company. Before you begin your SWOT analysis, you should try to develop an understanding of how the firm makes money. Start by looking at economic factors and structural factors like social trends, changes in technology, and demographic shifts in consumer tastes, and try to understand how these factors might impact the firm in the future. For example, not too many years ago Blockbuster ruled the world in terms of video rentals. But then Netflix moved in with a less expensive and more convenient service, pushing Blockbuster out of the top spot. Netflix then adapted to changing technology by providing online access to movies and television. Finally, Netflix decided to add content.

In addition, try to understand what type of strategy the firm is focusing on in order to be successful. The two primary competitive strategies are low-cost leadership and product differentiation. With respect to low-cost leadership, it may be the firm's low-cost distribution system, low labor costs, or cost reductions due to size and bargaining power—think Wal-Mart. With respect to product differentiation, it may be from strong marketing skills or product engineering—here you can think of Nike athletic shoes, BMW, or Poland Spring water. Now, think about that strategy, and try to answer this question: Can it be sustained?

Finally, it's time to jump into the SWOT analysis to better understand the firm's strategies and whether or not they are sustainable. SWOT analysis focuses on Strengths, Weaknesses, Opportunities, and Threats and is shown graphically in Figure 12.4. It is a good way of breaking a firm down and gaining a better understanding of what the future may hold for it.

The strengths and weaknesses are internal to the company—what it does well and what it struggles with. Strengths represent the firm's competitive advantage—for example, brand loyalty, high-quality products, great customer service, or

---

[2]SWOT analysis draws from Michael E. Porter, *Competitive Strategy* (New York: Free Press, 1980); Michael E. Porter, *Competitive Advantage* (New York: Free Press, 1985); and James English, *Applied Equity Analysis* (New York: McGraw Hill, 2001).

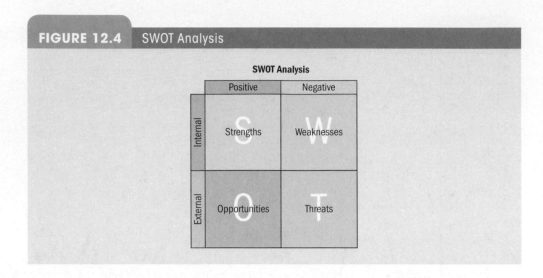

FIGURE 12.4 SWOT Analysis

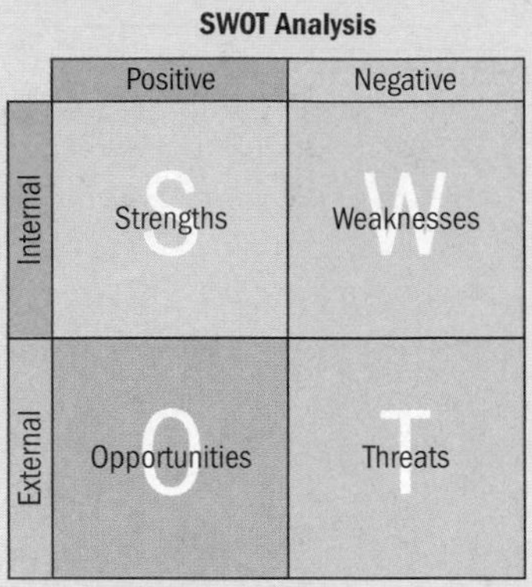

innovative products. In effect, you're trying to understand why the firm does as well as it does. Weaknesses represent the opposite of strengths and involve areas where the competition may be able to make inroads into the firm.

While strengths and weaknesses are internal to the company, opportunities and threats are external and deal with things like competition, changes in technology, government regulation, and international opportunities and threats. Opportunities might come from a growing market, shrinking competition, or the ability to take advantage of new social media for marketing. Threats might come from a slowing economy, increased government regulation, or technological innovation that makes the firm's product obsolete.

By viewing a company from the perspective of its strengths, weaknesses, opportunities, and threats, you can better understand how the firm makes money and whether that will continue into the future and, from that, what the future holds for this firm.

Dollar Cost Averaging
A strategy for purchasing common stock in which the investor purchases a fixed dollar amount of stock at specified intervals—for example, quarterly.

LO4 Employ different investment strategies.

MyLab Finance Video

Stock Investment Strategies

There are several investment strategies you can follow when purchasing stock. As we take a look at a few of them, keep in mind that you can use more than one of these approaches at once. Still, you've got to be alert, especially when your money is on the line. Checklist 12.2 provides a number of things you should look out for.

STOP & THINK

In a "Getting Going" column in the *Wall Street Journal*, Jonathan Clements listed 41 signs that you've become a savvy investor and a smart saver. Sign number two was "You get excited when stock prices fall." Keep in mind that you're trying to reach long-term goals and you should expect the market to rise and fall between now and then. When stock prices are low, you're buying more shares of stock with your investment dollars—after all, the lower stock prices are today, the easier it is to "buy low and sell high." Remember, your goal is not to be rich today but to be rich when you're ready to retire or meet whatever goal you're saving for. Why does this make sense?

Dollar Cost Averaging

Dollar cost averaging is the practice of purchasing a fixed dollar amount of stock at specified intervals. The logic behind dollar cost averaging is that by investing the same dollar amount each period instead of buying in one lump sum, you average out price fluctuations by buying more shares of common stock when the price is lowest and fewer shares when the price is highest.

CHECKLIST 12.2 Be Alert

Look out for:

- ☐ Recommendations from a sales representative based on "inside" or "confidential" information, an "upcoming favorable research report," a "prospective merger or acquisition," or the announcement of a "dynamic new product."
- ☐ Telephone sales pitches; *never* send money to purchase a stock (or other investment) based simply on a telephone sales pitch.
- ☐ Representations of spectacular profit, such as "Your money will double in 6 months." Remember, if it sounds too good to be true, it is!
- ☐ "Guarantees" that you will not lose money on a particular securities transaction or an agreement by the sales representative to share in any losses in your account.
- ☐ An excessive number of transactions in your account. Such activity generates additional commissions for your sales representative but may provide no better investment opportunities for you.
- ☐ A recommendation from your sales representative that you make a dramatic change in your investment strategy, such as moving from low-risk investments to speculative securities or concentrating your investments exclusively in a single product.
- ☐ Pressure to trade the account in a manner that is inconsistent with your investment goals and the risk you want or can afford to take.

Table 12.2 presents an example of dollar cost averaging, where the investor buys $500 worth of stock each quarter for 2 years instead of investing everything all at once. The reason the investor in this example did better with dollar cost averaging is that the market price bounced from $40 to $55, allowing the investor to buy more shares for the same amount of money when prices dipped.

Lucky people buy stocks when the price is low, and unlucky people buy when the price is high. The problem is that no one knows if a given price is going to be a high or a low because you never know what stocks will do in the future. Dollar cost averaging's intent is to even out your luck by letting the highs and lows cancel each other out.

During the bull market of the 1990s, dollar cost averaging came under some criticism as an inefficient way to invest a lump sum in the market. This criticism

TABLE 12.2 Dollar Cost Averaging

	Dollar Cost Averaging, Investing $500 per Quarter					Lump-Sum Investment Buying 80 Shares at $50/Share
Date	Money Invested	Price	Shares Purchased	Total Shares Owned	Market Value	Market Value
Year 1, quarter 1	$500	$50	10.0	10.0	$500	$4,000
Year 1, quarter 2	500	46	10.9	20.9	961	
Year 1, quarter 3	500	40	12.5	33.4	1,336	
Year 1, quarter 4	500	50	10.0	43.4	2,170	
Year 2, quarter 1	500	55	9.1	52.5	2,888	
Year 2, quarter 2	500	45	11.1	63.6	2,862	
Year 2, quarter 3	500	50	10.0	73.6	3,680	
Year 2, quarter 4	500	52	9.6	83.2	4,326	
Total	$4,000	$48.50	83.2	83.2	$4,326	$4,160

centered on the fact that over time, stocks generally tend to rise in price. Therefore, if you have a lump sum of money to invest, it's better to get it into the market as soon as possible to get in on those rising prices. For example, look at the stock market from 1995 through the first half of 1999: It went no place but up. That meant that the sooner investors got their money into the stock market, the more they made. In fact, history shows that over all the 12-month periods from 1926 through 1991, you would have been better off investing a lump sum 64.5 percent of the time. But in recent years, we have watched as stock prices have bounced up and down, and the dollar cost averaging approach has regained much of its lost popularity.

There is no question that dollar cost averaging has merit—let's explore three reasons:

1. If you buy stock over an extended period, it's less likely that all your money will be invested right before a market crash.
2. Dollar cost averaging keeps you from trying to time the market—and that is important! "Timing the market" is an attempt to wait for the lowest possible price before buying. It's virtually impossible to do, although admittedly it's awfully tempting to try. Moreover, when attempting to time the market, an investor can wait and wait for the market to come down and miss a major upturn. That's pretty much what happened from 1995 through the first half of 1999—if you were looking for a low point in the market to invest, you never would have entered the market. And very few investors entered the market in March 2009 after it had dropped by 50 percent in less than a year and a half. At that point, most people simply couldn't afford to lose any more money in the stock market, and it was also a time when doomsayers were predicting another 50 percent drop in the market. People were scared. But look at what happened between March 2009 and 2017—the market climbed, with dividends reinvested, by about 250 percent. In effect, market timing is similar to an antigravity machine— it's a great idea, but making it work is the problem.
3. And most important, dollar cost averaging forces investing discipline. You are investing in stocks regularly, and investing becomes part of your budgeting and planning process.

Buy-and-Hold Strategy

Buy-and-Hold
An investment strategy that involves simply buying stock and holding it for a period of years.

As you might guess, a **buy-and-hold** investment strategy involves buying stock and holding it for a period of years. There are four reasons why such a strategy is worth considering:

1. It avoids attempts at timing the market. By buying and holding the stock, the ups and downs that occur over shorter periods become irrelevant.
2. The buy-and-hold strategy minimizes brokerage fees and other transaction costs. Constant buying and selling really racks up the charges, but buying and holding has only the charge of buying. By keeping these costs down, you retain more of the stock's returns.
3. Holding and not selling the stock postpones any capital gains taxes. The longer you can go without paying taxes, the longer you hold your money, and the longer you have to reinvest and earn returns on your returns.
4. A buy-and-hold strategy means your gains will be taxed as long-term capital gains.

STOP & THINK

If you employ a buy-and-hold strategy while buying stock using the dollar cost averaging method, a downturn in the market isn't necessarily bad. It simply means that when you're buying, you're getting more shares of stocks. Dollar cost averaging is best served by a market that doesn't climb steadily but bounces up and down. Does dollar cost averaging work as well if stocks only move up?

Dividend Reinvestment Plans

If you want to use common stock to accumulate wealth, you must reinvest rather than spending your dividends. Without reinvesting, your accumulation of wealth will be limited to the stock's capital gains. Unfortunately, many dividends may be small enough that you figure you might as well spend them on a pack of Juicy Fruit rather than reinvesting them. Hey, you don't need to pay a brokerage fee to buy Juicy Fruit.

One way to avoid buying too much gum and not enough stock is through a **dividend reinvestment plan (DRIP)**. Under a DRIP, you're allowed to reinvest the dividend in the company's stock automatically without paying any brokerage fees. Most large companies offer such plans, and many stockholders take advantage of them.

Dividend Reinvestment Plan (DRIP)
An investment plan that allows the investor to automatically reinvest stock dividends in the same company's stock without paying any brokerage fees.

As an Investor, What Should You Know?

Before you put your money down and purchase a stock, what should you know about it? There are four basic investment questions that you should feel you can answer before you invest:

- Value: Is this a good price for this stock?
- Quality: Is this firm in a position that will allow it to be profitable into the future?
- Strengths and Weaknesses: What are this firm's strengths and weaknesses, and are they likely to get better or worse?
- Threats and Opportunities: What are this firm's threats and opportunities, and are they likely to get better or worse?

Today, the world of investing is much more competitive than it has ever been. The amount of information and data available on different stocks has increased dramatically. Over the past 15 years, the number of brokerage reports published daily has risen from in the hundreds to in the thousands, while the number of tweets per day is now at 500 million. Clearly, with today's computers, more and more information from the Web, traditional media, and social media sources now finds its way into the pricing of stocks at a pace that could not have been imagined only a few years ago. All of this has resulted in increasingly efficient markets, which have resulted in good investment opportunities that appear and disappear much faster. This has tilted the playing field away from the individual investor and toward the sophisticated professional.

What does this mean for you? It means that it is going to be much more difficult to beat the market by buying individual stocks. It also means that since it is more difficult to beat the market, you should be very aware of the costs of investing. As you will see when we look at mutual funds in Chapter 14, there are opportunities to diversify through low-cost index mutual funds.

STOP & THINK

Nobel Laureate economist Gene Fama, Jr., once commented: "Your money is like soap. The more you handle it, the less you'll have."

Risks Associated with Common Stocks

LO5 Understand the risks associated with investing in common stock.

In Chapter 11, we examined several different sources of risk associated with investing in all securities. Stocks have more risk than other investments, but they also have more potential return. You should already know something about risk and return from **Principle 8: Risk and Return Go Hand in Hand**. Let's take another look at this principle and explore the relationship between stocks and risk to see if we can lower our risk without impacting our return.

PRINCIPLE 8

Another Look at Principle 8: Risk and Return Go Hand in Hand

We can view stocks as being at the upper end of the risk–return line, as shown in Figure 12.5. Watching the DJIA drop by 20 percent during the first 10 days of October 2008 and by 40 percent over the previous year reminds us of the risk associated with common stock. Without those risks, you wouldn't expect the high returns that common stocks provide. Thus, there's a great deal of potential risk if the firm does poorly and a great deal of potential return if the firm does well.

PRINCIPLE 8

Fortunately, as we learned in **Principle 8**, you can eliminate much of the risk associated with common stock simply by diversifying your investments. In this way, when one of your stocks goes bust, another investment soars, making up for the loss. Basically, diversification lets you iron out the ups and downs of investing. You don't experience the great returns, but you don't experience the great losses either.

However, when all stocks move in the same direction, as we saw with the October 2008 market crash, diversification simply among stocks doesn't work as well. But if you had a balanced portfolio of 60 percent stocks and 40 percent bonds, your 12-month loss would have been cut by almost one-half.

Most stocks move up and down when the market as a whole moves up and down. There's an old saying on Wall Street, "A rising tide lifts all boats," meaning that when the stock market goes up, it's good for all stocks, and they all seem to rise in value. But when all stocks move up, some tend to move up more than others, and when the stock market moves down, some stocks fall down farther. To measure the movements of an individual stock relative to the movements of the S&P 500, we use **beta**, which can be found in Value Line and on many investments Web sites. The beta indicates the tendency of a stock to respond to movements in the broad market. The beta for the market is 1.0—that's the benchmark against which specific stock betas are measured. A stock that amplifies the movements in the S&P 500, and as a result is more volatile than the market, would have a beta greater than 1.0, and a stock that mutes the movements in the S&P 500, and as a result is less volatile than the market, would have a beta less than 1.0.

Beta
The measure of how responsive a stock or portfolio is to changes in the market portfolio, such as the S&P 500 Index.

The easiest way to interpret beta is to think of it as a measure of the relative responsiveness of a stock to movements in the market. For example, a stock with a beta of 1.5 would be 50 percent more volatile than the market, while a stock with a beta of 0.5 would be 50 percent less volatile than the market.

FIGURE 12.5 The Risk–Return Relationship

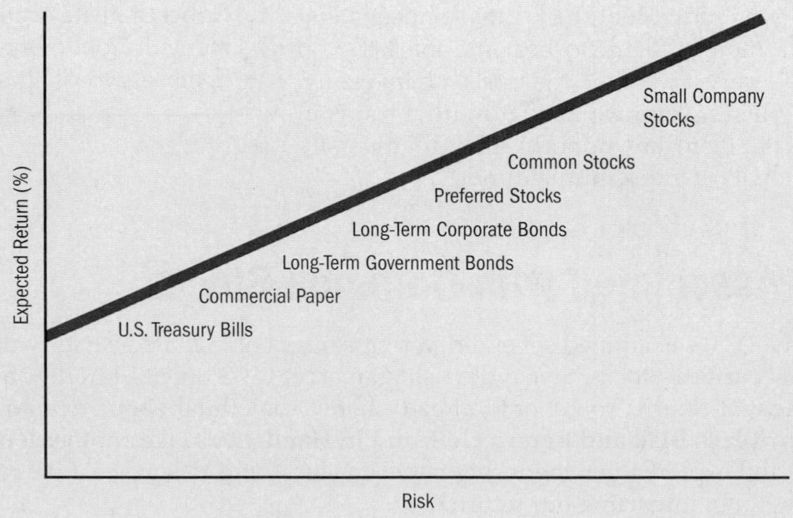

What does all this mean to you as an investor? First, once your stock portfolio is diversified, it tends to move closely with all the other stocks in the marketplace. That is, the returns to a diversified portfolio are more a function of major changes in anticipated inflation, interest rates, or the general economy rather than of events unique to any specific company in the portfolio. Second, it means that the only way to fully diversify is to make sure that you invest in more than one type of investment by including domestic and international stocks along with bonds in your portfolio. Finally, if your portfolio is well diversified, you should keep an eye on its beta.

We know that risk and return go hand in hand, and before you can take on more risk, you need both the risk tolerance and the risk capacity, as we discussed earlier. So wouldn't it be nice if we could also tolerate a little more risk? Well, we can—as long as we're patient. In the short run, market fluctuations are a killer. Nothing is more painful than experiencing a big fat market downturn and then needing your money. However, the longer your investment time horizon is, the more you can afford to invest in riskier assets—that is, stocks.

When you invest in stocks, you're almost certain to experience a bad year or two. Holding on to stock for only a year is very risky because the year you choose to hold it just might be one of those bad years. For example, if you'd chosen to make a 1-year investment in an S&P 500 stock in 2008, you'd have lost about 37 percent, and you'd have been one unhappy camper by year's end. Of course, if you'd made that same investment just 1 year later, you'd have made a hefty return of over 26 percent—more than enough to go out and buy yourself and all of your friends the latest version of the Apple watch.

As you can see, 1-year returns are amazingly variable, making short-term investments in stocks very risky. However, as the length of the investment horizon increases, you can afford to invest in riskier assets. The longer you hold on to stocks, the more likely you are to hit very good years, such as 1995 through 1999 or 2013. Of course, you're also more likely to hit bad years such as 2008, but the very good will cancel out the very bad. Figure 12.6 shows how holding stocks for longer periods

FIGURE 12.6 The Range of Annual Returns on Common Stocks over 50 Years, 1967–2016

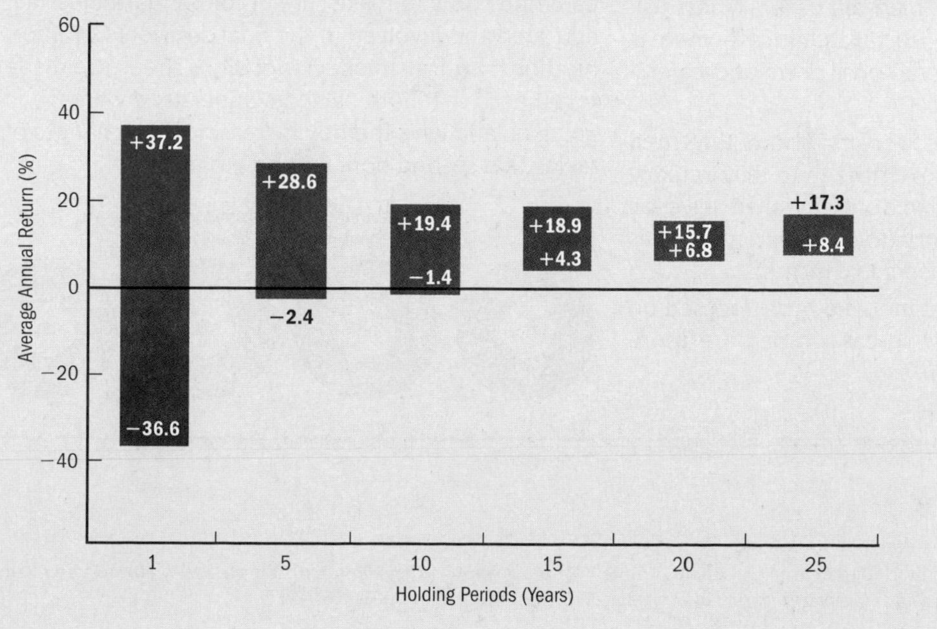

LOVE & MONEY

It was pointed out in the *Wall Street Journal* that newlyweds who gain an understanding of investing, set goals, and have an understanding of their risk tolerance have a good chance not only of affording a second honeymoon but also of wanting to take it with each other.

As you can probably imagine, there has been a good deal of research done on the differences in how women and men invest. One of the earliest studies to find "gender differences" in investing was titled "Boys Will Be Boys: Gender, Overconfidence, and Common Stock Investment."[3] This study found that men traded about 45 percent more than women, a result of overconfidence in their investment skills. The result of this excess trading was to reduce men's net returns by about 2.65 percent per year as opposed to 1.72 percent for women. Interestingly, this difference in turnover and return performance is even more dramatic for single men versus single women, with single men trading 67 percent more than single women.

As your relationship gets serious and you begin to formulate your financial goals, it will most likely become obvious that when it comes to making investment decisions, men and women tend to have their own strengths and weaknesses and their own ways of doing things. This can complicate things as you make investment decisions with respect to what types of assets to invest in and which mutual funds to buy.

What are some of the obstacles that you might have to overcome?

- Risk: Studies show that men are naturally less risk averse—they are willing to take chances—whereas women tend to be more considerate and careful when dealing with money.
- Investment knowledge: Research shows that men often "believe" they know more than they actually do, whereas women often don't give themselves as much credit for what they do know when it comes to dealing with investments and money.
- Goals: Studies show that men are more focused on wealth accumulation, whereas women are more focused on preservation.

Thus, to keep conflicts down and to invest in the best way possible for you as a couple, you'll want to combine your strengths with those of your spouse or partner and make sure that conversations and communication are frequent, which means at a minimum once a month.

There are other differences also. Studies have found that women have higher participation rates in employer-sponsored retirement plans and higher savings rates. Still, women tend to end up with less in the way of retirement savings. Why is this the case? No, it's not because men make better investment decisions; it's because women, for the most part, earn less in their jobs.

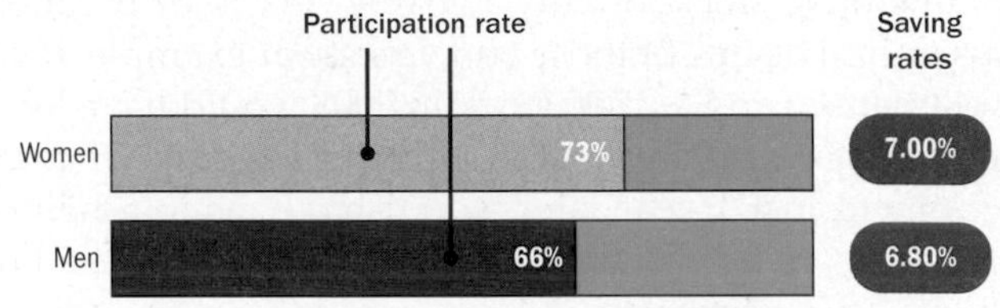

Average Participation and Savings Rate by Gender

Before looking at how best to manage money, you should keep in mind that most people think they are more knowledgeable than their spouse about managing finances, so as you begin to work together with your partner, recognize that your partner may not share your view of your financial skills relative to those of your partner.

So what's the best way to manage your investment portfolio? The answer should come from an open dialogue. If one partner is truly more knowledgeable, that partner can take the lead role, but with that role comes the duty to make sure his or her partner is educated and involved in the final decision. Communication is critical. In effect, decisions should be made together so that both partners understand what is going on and why, thereby increasing their chances of taking that second honeymoon—together.

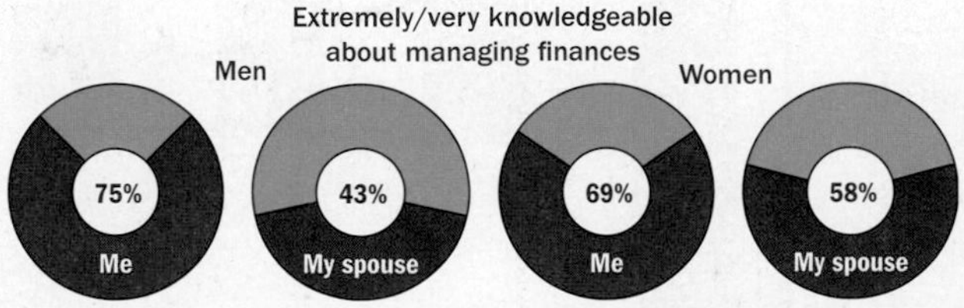

[3] Brad Barber and T. Odean, "Boys Will Be Boys: Gender, Overconfidence, and Common Stock Investment," *Quarterly Journal of Economics* 116, no. 1 (February 2001): 261–292.

reduces the variability of the average annual return on your investment. The truth is that it's hard to beat the long-term return from common stock investments, which is why so many investors favor the buy-and-hold strategy for investing in stocks.

In addition, as an investor you can afford to take on more risk as your investment time horizon increases because you have more opportunities to adjust saving, consumption, and work habits over longer time periods if a risky investment doesn't pan out. If you are investing with a short time horizon, there isn't much you can do to meet your goals.

BEHAVIORAL INSIGHTS

PRINCIPLE 9

Principle 9: Mind Games, Your Financial Personality, and Your Money We all now know that the price of a share of stock should reflect its value, with investors buying stocks that are undervalued and selling stocks that are overvalued until the price reflects the stock's true value. The problem with all this is that "we are human"—we just don't seem to be able to act rationally. There are all kinds of behavioral biases that seem to get in the way of making rational decisions, and the end result is that while we may understand how stocks should be priced, we ignore this and let our emotions take over. Consequently, we can end up making poor decisions, especially when it comes to the timing of when we buy and sell stocks. So let's take a look at several behavioral finance biases that keep many people from making sound decisions when it comes to their money.

The Status Quo Bias People tend to feel comfortable doing what they have done in the past, even if it is not in their best interest. Publishing companies often offer individuals a trial magazine subscription for free. The reason is that it is very likely that once the free trial period has expired, the subscriber will simply continue the subscription—it is almost an inertia that sets in, making it both comfortable and easy to just continue the subscription. How does this apply to investments? Individuals tend not to change their investments around, and they don't rebalance their portfolio—what they have done in the past is what they continue to do. In addition, as individuals earn more money, they many times will not increase their savings but rather will keep their retirement contributions and savings for future goals the same.

Herd Behavior We discussed herd behavior briefly, but given its importance to the stock market, let's take another look at it. There is no question that investors are influenced by what other investors are doing. Back in the 1950s, Solomon Ashe conducted a number of studies in which he asked questions to which the response was clearly false, but because he presented them as if everyone else had said they were true, the subjects answered "true." He referred to this as peer pressure, but it is also part of the herd mentality that we see in investors. When individuals hear that "other investors" are returning to the stock market or investing in a certain stock, they tend to do the same. It doesn't matter that they don't have any idea why they are investing or whether they have the same financial goals—they just follow the herd.

Loss Aversion Whenever you invest, there is the chance that you may lose money, and the pain from losing money is greater than the joy from gaining the same amount. Just think of a coin toss—heads you win, tails you lose. Suppose I approached you and said, "Let's toss a coin, and if you lose, you lose $20." What is the minimum amount you'd have to win in this coin toss in order to agree to do it? If you're like most people, it's somewhere between $30 and $40. That's because of loss aversion—losing money gives more pain than winning gives pleasure.

Let's look at investors' experiences over the past 14 years—a very turbulent time in the investments world with two of the worst bear markets in history. Fortunately, since March 2009, this pattern has turned around with stocks up around 250 percent—but unfortunately, because of their experience in the up-and-down markets before the market turned, individual investors have generally avoided the stock market, investing largely in bonds, and have missed out on this bull market in stocks. Why did investors shun common stock in favor of bonds? One reason is loss aversion—after losing money in the bear markets, the prospect of experiencing the pain of losing money again in stocks prevented them from investing in stocks in spite of the fact that over the long run, stocks have outperformed bonds. Investors turned away from stocks. Not only has loss aversion kept individual investors out of the stock market during the recent bull market, becoming too conservative with their investments, but also it has resulted in their taking profits and selling some of their winners to solidify those gains, while holding on to their losers longer than they should, hoping that they increase again in price.

Let's look at a gambling illustration of this behavioral finance trait. You're in Las Vegas, and you make a bet and lose $500. Will you keep gambling to try to work yourself out of this hole, or will you walk away? Even though you know the odds in Las Vegas are in the house's favor, if you're like most people, you'll try to dig yourself out of this hole by gambling a bit more. But a loss is very painful, and as you continue gambling, you're really trying to eliminate your loss. In effect, that desire to avoid losses is much more important to most people than is the desire to have a gain. So how does this impact your financial behavior? One way is that when investors have made money, they will become conservative, taking profits and selling some of their winners to solidify those gains, but if they have lost money on some of their stocks, they will hold on to their losers longer than they should, hoping that they will increase again in price.

ACTION PLAN

PRINCIPLE 10

Principle 10: Just Do It! Investing in common stock makes enormous sense if you're looking to fund long-term goals. Unfortunately, according to one study by a large brokerage firm, well over half of individual investors lose money or just break even on stock trades. So let's take a look at some things you can do to improve your chances when investing in stocks.

Set Your Goals The first thing to do when it comes to investing is to establish your goals: What do you want? When do you need it? How much money will it take to get you there? That will determine your asset allocation and how much of your savings go into common stocks. And don't forget that you need an emergency fund.

Fill Up Your Roth IRA and Any Employer-Sponsored 401(k) Plan First It only makes sense to take advantage of the tax breaks the government gives you. The place to start is with your Roth IRA and any 401(k) or other tax-advantaged investment plans available to you. If your employer matches your contributions, fund the plan to the max—don't leave "free money" on the table.

Don't Invest Too Heavily in Your Employer Many people purchase large amounts of their employer's stock because they feel that they work for a good company. If the company fails, not only have you lost your job, but also you may have lost a fair amount of your assets. This doesn't mean that you shouldn't take advantage of your company-sponsored stock purchase plan if it's a good one. Keep things in balance.

Avoid Excessive Trading Costs and Taxes The phrase "playing the market" is sadly appropriate for the actions of some people, as they perceive that success in investing lies in moving things around a lot. Don't get caught up in that game. Even if you are lucky enough to make some good choices, trading costs and taxes on short-term gains eat up most of what you make.

Beware of "Systems" and "Hot Tips" There is always someone with a foolproof system for beating the market. We touched on this in the last chapter, but this advice is good enough to repeat: There is no foolproof method for beating the market. Beware of "hot tips" and cold calls from stockbrokers. Keep in mind that "those that know don't tell, and those that tell don't know." If it sounds too good to be true, it probably is.

Asset Allocation and Buy-and-Hold Work If you're saving for a long-term goal, resist the urge to sell when prices fall. After all, if the price of your house fell, would you immediately put it on the market, or would you ride out the price decline? Also, keep an eye on your asset allocation; that will allow you to increase your stock holdings when stock prices decline. That's the process of portfolio rebalancing—keeping your portfolio consistent with your financial goals. By focusing on asset allocation, you'll be able to avoid a downfall common to most small investors: overreacting to news both good and bad, which leads to lower returns.

Chapter Summaries

Invest in stocks. LO1

SUMMARY: Stocks are a solid investment because over time common stocks outperform all other investments, diversification reduces the risk of stocks, stocks are liquid, and the growth in your investment is determined by more than just interest rates.

KEY TERMS

Declaration Date, page 410 The date on which the board of directors announces the size of the dividend, the ex-dividend date, and the payment date.

Ex-dividend Date, page 410 The date on which the stock "goes ex," meaning it begins trading in the secondary market "without dividend." In other words, if you buy the stock after its ex-dividend date, you don't get the dividend for that year.

Proxy, page 410 A legal agreement a stockholder signs to allow someone else to vote for him or her at the corporation's annual meeting.

Stock Split, page 410 Increasing the number of stock shares outstanding by replacing the existing shares of stock with a given number of new shares. For example, in a two-for-one split, for every share of existing stock you hold, you will receive two shares of new stock.

Stock Repurchase, page 411 A company's repurchasing, or buying back, of its own common stock.

Dividend Yield, page 411 The ratio of the annual dividends to the market price of the stock.

Read stock quotes online or in the newspaper. LO2

SUMMARY: The health of the stock market is measured by stock indexes. The oldest and most widely quoted of the stock indexes is the Dow Jones Industrial Average (DJIA), or the Dow. Other useful indexes include the Standard & Poor's 500, the

Russell 1000 and 2000, and the Wilshire 5000. Stocks can be classified according to the traits of the company issuing the stock. Common classifications include blue-chip, growth, income, speculative, cyclical, defensive, and large-, mid-, and small-cap stocks.

KEY TERMS

Stock Market Index, page 412 A measure of the performance of a group of stocks that represent the market or a sector of the market.

Dow Jones Industrial Average (DJIA) or Dow, page 413 A commonly used stock index or indicator of how well stocks have done. This index is comprised of the stock prices of 30 large industrial firms.

Standard & Poor's 500 Stock Index or S&P 500, page 413 Another commonly used stock index or indicator of how well stocks have done based on the movements of 500 stocks, primarily from the NYSE.

Bear Market, page 413 A stock market characterized by falling prices.

Bull Market, page 413 A stock market characterized by rising prices.

LO3 Understand how stocks are valued and what causes them to go up and down in price.

SUMMARY: There are two basic approaches to security analysis—fundamental analysis and technical analysis—although many analysts use a combination of the two. With fundamental analysis, the value of a stock is calculated using time value of money tools, where the value of the stock is the present value of its expected future cash flows using the appropriate required rate of return. Using an alternative approach, a justified price/earnings (P/E) ratio is estimated for each stock. This P/E ratio, or earnings multiplier, is simply the price per share divided by the earnings per share. SWOT analysis is another framework for analyzing a security. It forces you to look both internally to the firm's Strengths and Weaknesses and externally to its Opportunities and Threats.

KEY TERMS

Fundamental Analysis, page 415 Determining the value of a share of stock by focusing on such determinants as future earnings and dividends, expected levels of interest rates, and the firm's risk.

Technical Analysis, page 415 A method of stock analysis that focuses on supply and demand, using charts and computer programs to identify and project price trends for a stock or for the market as a whole.

Price/Earnings (P/E) Ratio, page 415 The price per share divided by the earnings per share. Also called the earnings multiplier.

SWOT Analysis, page 416 A framework for analyzing a security in which you look both internally at the firm's Strengths and Weaknesses and externally at the Opportunities and Threats that the firm faces to gain an understanding of what the future holds for that firm and its stock.

LO4 Employ different investment strategies.

SUMMARY: When purchasing stock, there are several investment strategies you can follow, including dollar cost averaging, buy-and-hold, and dividend reinvestment plans. Dollar cost averaging involves investing over time rather than jumping into the market all at once. Buy-and-hold involves investing and leaving your money invested for a number of years. Dividend reinvestment plans allow you to have your dividends automatically reinvested in the stock.

KEY TERMS

Dollar Cost Averaging, page 418 A strategy for purchasing common stock in which the investor purchases a fixed dollar amount of stock at specified intervals—for example, quarterly.

Buy-and-Hold, page 420 An investment strategy that involves simply buying stock and holding it for a period of years.

Dividend Reinvestment Plan (DRIP), page 421 An investment plan that allows the investor to automatically reinvest stock dividends in the same company's stock without paying any brokerage fees.

Understand the risks associated with investing in common stock. LO5

SUMMARY: Stocks have more risk than other securities; however, you can eliminate much of this risk through diversification. Still, sometimes the stock market drops dramatically, and when that happens, no amount of diversification can help you out. That type of risk, resulting from overall movements in the market, is measured by the beta. The average beta is 1.0, meaning a stock moves up or down about as much as the market does. If a stock has a beta greater than 1.0, it will move up more than the market when the market moves up and will move down more than the market when the market moves down. If a stock's beta is less than 1.0, it will move up less than the market when the market moves up and will move down less than the market when the market moves down.

KEY TERM

Beta, page 422 The measure of how responsive a stock or portfolio is to changes in the market portfolio, such as the S&P 500 Index.

Problems and Activities

These problems are available in MyLab Finance.

1. Assume that you own 200 shares of General Dynamics Corp. (GD), which are selling at $90 per share. In order to make the stock more affordable for the average investor, GD's management has decided to split the stock.

a. How much was your investment worth prior to the split?
b. Assuming GD's management decides to split the stock three-for-one, how many shares would you own after the split?
c. What would the new price per share be immediately after the split?
d. How much would your investment be worth after the three-for-one split?

2. The Gizmo, Inc has just announced year-end results as follows:

Value of company assets	$12,500,000
Value of company liabilities	$6,500,000
Net income	$1,600,000
Common stock dividends	$250,000
Preferred stock dividends	$400,000
Number of shares of common stock outstanding	1,000,000
Closing price of Gizmo Inc.'s stock	$45.00 per share

a. Calculate the book value per share.
b. Calculate the earnings per share.
c. Calculate Gizmo, Inc.'s dividend yield.
d. Calculate the market-to-book ratio.

3. The Smell Fresh Kitty Litter Company has assets of $10 million, liabilities of $4 million, and 2 million shares outstanding. Assuming creditors are paid in full prior to stockholders receiving any money, what is the maximum amount the stockholders would receive in a bankruptcy settlement? What is the amount per share they would receive?

4. Wildcat Corporation recently disclosed the following financial information:

Earnings/revenue	$1,500,000
Assets	$7,000,000
Liabilities	$1,500,000
Shares outstanding	500,000
Market price	$33 per share

Calculate the price-to-book ratio, the price/earnings ratio, and the book value per share for each of the following separate scenarios:

a. Based on current information.
b. Earnings fall to $1,000,000.
c. Liabilities increase to $2,500,000.
d. The company does a three-for-one stock split with no change in market capitalization.
e. The company repurchases 20 percent of the outstanding stock, incurring additional liability to finance the purchase.

5. An investor is considering purchasing one of the following three stocks. Stock X has a market capitalization of $7 billion, pays a relatively high dividend with little increase in earnings, and has a P/E ratio of 11. Stock Y has a market capitalization of $62 billion but does not currently pay a dividend. Stock Y has a P/E ratio of 39. Stock Z, a housing industry company, has a market capitalization of $800 million and a P/E of 18.

a. Classify these stocks according to their market capitalizations.
b. Which of the three would you classify as a growth stock? Why?
c. Which stock would be most appropriate for an aggressive investor?
d. Which stock would be most appropriate for someone seeking a combination of safety and earnings?

6. Use these data to answer the questions that follow.

Company	Beta
Savoy Corp.	0.70
Hokie Industries	1.35
Alison Records	2.05
Expo Enterprises	0.45
S&P 500	1.00

a. If the S&P 500 goes up by 15 percent, how much should the stocks of Savoy, Hokie, Alison, and Expo change in value?
b. If the stock market drops by 10 percent, which one of these stocks should outperform the others? Why?

7. Use the information in the table below to answer the following questions.

52 Weeks						Vol.	Day			Net
Hi	Lo	Stock	Sym	Div	PE	100s	Hi	Lo	Close	Chg
80.65	58.48	Boeing	BA	1.68	16.82	7976	76.71	75.84	76.28	−0.11

a. What is the current dividend yield for Boeing Company based on the stock's recent closing price?

b. What is your estimate of Boeing's earnings for the year based on its recent closing price?

c. Based on the net change, at what price did Boeing close yesterday?

8. Leona is considering starting a tailoring business, Get Stitched Up, to supplement her retirement. She is 60 years old and has been helping family and friends with their sewing and tailoring needs for almost 30 years. She lives in a midsized college town that is known for hosting gorgeous weddings. Leona would be the sole owner and worker in her new business. Conduct a SWOT analysis for Leona to help her determine if she should open Get Stitched Up.

9. Assume an investor made the purchases listed in the table below on the first day of every quarter for a year. Use the information provided to fill in the blanks.

Quarter	Price	Money Invested	Shares Purchased	Total Shares Owned	Market Value
1	$30	$200	________	________	________
2	$50	$200	________	________	________
3	$60	$200	________	________	________
4	$35	$200	________	________	________
Total		$800			

10. Using the calculations from Problem 9, assume that instead of investing $200 every quarter, the investor decided to make a lump-sum $800 purchase on the first day of the year. If at year-end the price of the stock closed at $35 per share, which investment strategy, dollar cost averaging or lump-sum investing, produced the greater return?

Discussion Case 1

This case is available in **MyLab Finance**.

Saddened by the death of her favorite aunt, Shannel (age 35) was extremely surprised to learn that she was named her aunt's only heir. A personal note in the will said "For your own shop." Shannel and her aunt often visited antique shops, and Shannel's dream was to own such a shop as a way to occupy her time in early retirement. She is expecting to receive approximately $50,000 and hopes to invest this money for her future shop, but she knows very little about stocks or investment strategies. After discussing financial planning topics with Shannel, the following issues became clear. First, the $50,000 is all the money she has saved for her goal. Second, Shannel is very cautious financially and is fearful of investing all her money at once because she has heard conflicting reports concerning stock valuation. Use your knowledge of common stock classifications and investment strategies to answer the following questions.

Questions

1. Which type of stock or combination of stocks would be appropriate for Shannel? Develop your answer in terms of Shannel's risk tolerance, time frame, and goals.
2. What role should cyclical and defensive stocks play in Shannel's portfolio?
3. Given Shannel's fear about current stock valuations, what investment strategy would you recommend for her? Why?
4. Provide Shannel with four reasons to consider using a buy-and-hold strategy.
5. What other personal finance factors should Shannel consider before investing in her antique shop?

Discussion Case 2

This case is available in **MyLab Finance**.

Pete and Jessica, on the advice of their next-door neighbor, recently purchased 500 shares of a small-capitalization Internet stock, trading at $80 per share. Their neighbor told them that the stock was a "real money maker" because it recently had a two-for-one stock split and would probably split again soon. Even better, according to the neighbor, the company was expected to earn $1 per share and pay a $0.25 dividend next year. Pete and Jessica have so far been less than impressed with the stock's performance—the stock has underperformed the S&P 500 Index this year. Pete and Jessica have come to you for some independent advice.

Questions

1. Assuming that the stock actually splits two for one, how many shares will Pete and Jessica own? What will be the market value of their stock after the split? How will the split affect the value of their holdings? Was their neighbor correct in thinking that the stock split made the stock a "real money maker"?
2. Using the information provided, calculate the stock's P/E ratio. Would you classify this investment as a growth or value stock?
3. Since Pete, in particular, is worried about the price of the stock, explain to him how and why corporate earnings are so important in the valuation of common stocks.
4. Should Pete and Jessica be using the S&P 500 Index as a benchmark for this stock? Why or why not? What benchmark recommendation would you make?
5. Yesterday they received a cold call from a stockbroker wanting to sell them an initial public offering in a cable television company. Jessica was worried because the broker promised a "no-lose guarantee." Should they invest with this type of broker?
6. Name at least five things Pete and Jessica need to look out for when making stock investments.

CHAPTER 13 Investing in Bonds and Other Alternatives

Learning Objectives

LO1	**Invest** in the bond market.	Why Consider Bonds?
LO2	**Understand** basic bond terminology and compare the various types of bonds.	Basic Bond Terminology and Features
LO3	**Calculate** the value of a bond and understand the factors that cause bond value to change.	Evaluating Bonds
LO4	**Compare** preferred stock to bonds as an investment option.	Preferred Stock—An Alternative to Bonds
LO5	**Understand** the risks associated with investing in real estate.	Investing in Real Estate
LO6	**Know** why you shouldn't *invest* in gold, silver, gems, or collectibles.	Investing—Speculating—in Gold, Silver, Gems, and Collectibles

For Alec Baldwin, the road of life has been exciting, to say the least. He's made headlines, both good and bad, and along the way he's made and lost a lot of money. As one of six children born to a schoolteacher and a football coach, he grew up in a family where "we always worried about money" and family fights centered on financial issues.

His life changed partway through college, when, on a dare from a friend, he auditioned for New York University's drama program, was accepted, and transferred to New York University. He soon landed a role in *The Doctors*, a daytime TV soap opera, and then appeared on the prime-time soap *Knots Landing*. In 1990, after a decade dominated by television work, he was offered the lead role of Jack Ryan in Tom Clancy's *The Hunt for Red October*. When he was given the chance to reprise the Jack Ryan role in the Clancy sequel, *Patriot Games*, it looked like there was no stopping him, but instead of starring in *Patriot Games*, he turned the role down, and the role was given to Harrison Ford—not a good career move.

AF Archive/Alamy Stock Photo

From October 2006 until January 2013, Alec starred in NBC's award-winning comedy series *30 Rock*, playing the role of Jack Donaghy, a slick, humor-challenged, meddling, slightly scary network executive. As far as the critics were concerned, he was perfect, and he won two Emmy Awards, three Golden Globes, and five Screen Actors Guild Awards. In addition, in 2011 he got a star on the Hollywood Walk of Fame.

Throughout his acting career, Alec has taken a lot of chances—for example, turning down that lead role in *Patriot Games* for the lead in the Broadway revival of *A Streetcar Named Desire* and annoying President Trump and many of his supporters with his portrayal of him on *Saturday Night Live*. But when it comes to his financial life, Alec has played it safe by investing a large stash of his money in bonds. He's done well in bonds, but his stock investments haven't always panned out; in fact, he invested quite a bit in telecommunications stocks and lost a ton of money. Alec, in the role of Jack Donaghy, actually poked fun at his investment losses in telecom stocks. In one episode of *30 Rock*, Tracy Jordan (played by Tracy Morgan), the wild and unpredictable movie star, talks to Jack about money:

Tracy: I need a hundred thousand dollars, or I'm gonna lose both my houses.

Jack: Tracy, I don't understand. You've starred in 14 films. You don't have any money saved?

Tracy: No, I lost all of it.

Jack: Really? Who's your money manager?

Tracy: Grizz.

Grizz (one of Tracy's posse): WorldCom, man. WorldCom.

Tracy: (to Grizz) I forgot about that WorldCom mess; why you gotta be so obsessed with telecommunications?

Similar to a lot of investors, Alec chose bonds because they carry less risk than stocks. Other investors are drawn to bonds because of the steady income they provide. But make no mistake: Although bonds are more secure than stocks and offer steady income, it doesn't mean that their returns are necessarily low. In 1995, for example, long-term Treasury bonds went up in value by over 32 percent! In 2008, when the average price of a typical stock dropped by 37 percent, the price of a 10-year Treasury bond climbed 20.1 percent—2008 was definitely a year to be invested in bonds as opposed to stocks. Similarly, while stocks dropped 11.8 percent and 22.0 percent in 2001 and 2002, respectively, bonds grew 5.6 percent and 15.1 percent. But bonds can also fall in value, as happened in 2013, when bond prices dropped by 9.1 percent. However, 2014 was a better year, with bond prices climbing by 10.8 percent. The bottom line here is that bonds are a sound source of income and a good way to diversify your investment portfolio, but as with all investments, a positive return is not guaranteed.

LO1 Invest in the bond market.

Why Consider Bonds?

A bond is a loan; when you buy a bond, you become a lender. The bond issuer—generally a corporation, the federal government and its agencies, a city, or a state—gets the use of your money and in return pays you interest, generally every 6 months, for the life of the bond. At maturity, the issuer pays you the face value of the bond, which may be more or less than what you originally paid for it.

How exactly do bonds fit into your investment portfolio?

- **Bonds reduce risk through diversification.** As you learned earlier, when you put together investments whose returns don't move together over time, you're able to reduce the risk in your portfolio. For example, in the week of April 10–14, 2000, as the dot.com bubble burst, the S&P fell 10.54 percent, and the NASDAQ went down 25.30 percent—and bond prices rose. What happened in 2001 in the days following the terrorist attack on the World Trade Center and the Pentagon? Stock prices fell, while bond prices climbed. And it happened again during the stock crash in the fall of 2008. In the 3 months from September through November 2008, the S&P 500 fell almost 33 percent, while long-term government bonds rose almost 12 percent.
- **Bonds produce steady income.** For those needing some income to achieve their financial goals, bonds are a good choice. For example, you may be retired and desire additional income from your investment portfolio to supplement your pension income. With bonds, provided the issuer doesn't default on its interest payments, you'll receive interest income annually.
- **Bonds can be a safe investment if held to maturity.** Interest on bonds must be paid, or the firm can be forced into bankruptcy. So bond interest payments will be made at all costs—unlike dividend payments on common stocks. As a result, bonds are a relatively safe investment. In addition, bond rating services provide reliable information on the riskiness of bonds. If the bond issuer doesn't default and you hold the bond to maturity, you know exactly what your return will be. In the world of personal finance, it's unusual to find an investment that actually returns exactly what it promises.

Now let's take a look at bond basics.

Basic Bond Terminology and Features

LO2 Understand basic bond terminology and compare the various types of bonds.

Bonds are similar to just about everything else we've seen so far in this book: If you can't talk the talk, you're going to fall flat on your face when you try to walk the walk. This section should help you get fairly conversant in the language of bonds.

Par Value

The **par value** of a bond is its face value, or the amount returned to the bondholder at **maturity**, the date when the bond comes due. For bonds issued by corporations, the par value is generally $1,000. A bond's market price, which is its selling price, is generally expressed as a percentage of the bond's par value. For example, a bond that matures or comes due in 2023 that has a $1,000 par value may be quoted as selling for 95.125. This means that the bond is selling for 95.125 percent of its par value, or $951.25 ($1,000 × 95.125%). At maturity in 2023, the bondholder will receive the par value of $1,000, and the bond will be terminated (but not by Arnold Schwarzenegger).

Par Value
The face value of a bond, or the amount that's returned to the bondholder at maturity. It's also referred to as the bond's denomination.

Maturity
The length of time until the bond issuer returns the par value to the bondholder and terminates the bond.

Coupon Interest Rate

The **coupon interest rate** on a bond indicates what percentage of the par value of the bond will be paid out annually in the form of interest. A bond with an 8 percent coupon interest rate and a $1,000 par value will pay out $80 (8% × $1,000) annually in interest until maturity, generally in semiannual installments, or $40 every 6 months.

Keep in mind that when you purchase a bond and hold it to maturity, your entire return is based on the return of the par value or principal and the payment of interest at the coupon interest rate. The only real risk involved is that the bond issuer won't have the funds to make these payments and will default.

Coupon Interest Rate
The annual rate of interest to be paid out on a bond, calculated as a percentage of the par value.

Indenture

An **indenture** is the legal document that provides the specific terms of the loan agreement, including a description of the bond, the rights of the bondholders, the rights of the issuing firm, and the responsibilities of the bond trustees. A bond trustee, usually a banking institution or trust company, is assigned the task of overseeing the relationship between the bondholder and the issuing firm. A bond indenture may run 100 pages or more in length, with the majority of it devoted to defining protective provisions for the bondholder.

Indenture
A legal agreement between the firm issuing a bond and the bond trustee, who represents the bondholders.

Call Provision

A **call provision** entitles the bond issuer to repurchase, or "call," the bonds from their holders at a stated price prior to maturity. If interest rates go down, the issuer will call the bonds and replace them with lower-cost debt. The terms of the call provision are provided in the indenture and generally set the call provision at approximately the par value plus 1 year's worth of interest.

Call Provision
A bond provision that gives the issuer the right to repurchase, or "call," the bonds from their holders at a stated price prior to maturity.

While a call provision works to the disadvantage of the investor, bonds with call provisions generally pay higher returns as compensation. Still, if you own high-paying long-term bonds and you're counting on receiving those semiannual interest payments for the next 10 years or so, having them called away from you could rain on your parade. To make callable bonds more attractive, the issuer many times includes in the indenture some protection against calls. Generally, that call protection comes in the form of a **deferred call**, meaning that the bond can't be called until a set number of years have passed since the bond was issued. Although not as safe as a noncallable bond, a bond with a deferred call at least provides protection against an immediate call.

Deferred Call
A bond provision stating that the bond can't be called until a set number of years have passed since it was issued.

Sinking Fund

Sinking Fund
A fund in which the bond issuer deposits money to pay off a bond issue.

No one likes to pay off debts all at once, and that goes for bond issuers, too. Most regularly set aside money in a **sinking fund** to pay off the bonds at maturity. With a sinking fund, each year the firm either calls some of the outstanding bonds, using the call provision, or repurchases some of them in the open market. In this way, the issuer spreads out the large payment that would otherwise occur at maturity.

The advantage of a sinking fund for the investor is that the probability that the debt will be successfully paid off at maturity increases, thereby reducing risk. Without a sinking fund, the issuer faces a major payment at maturity. If the issuer is experiencing financial problems when the debt matures, repayment may be jeopardized. The big disadvantage of a sinking fund for investors is that it may result in the bond being called away from them.

Types of Bonds

There's an old joke in the scientific world that says there are four different types of bonds: ionic, covalent, metallic, and James. Well, in the world of finance there are more types of bonds than that (but James is the only one with a license to kill). There are thousands of outstanding bonds floating around the securities markets, and more are probably on the way as you read this. It's a vast understatement to say that these bonds aren't all alike. The easiest way to explain the differences is to break them down into bonds issued by corporations, by the U.S. government and its agencies, and by states and localities and to examine each group separately. As you'll see, each type of bond has unique advantages and disadvantages to the investor.

FACTS OF LIFE

The U.S. bond market is almost twice the size of the combined market value of all U.S. stock markets. Why do you think this is true?

Corporate Bonds

Corporate Bonds
Bonds issued by corporations.

Borrowing money by issuing bonds is a major source of funding for corporations. In fact, **corporate bonds** account for about half of the bonds outstanding. Generally, these bonds are issued in denominations of $1,000 in order to appeal to smaller investors. There are several different types of corporate bonds from which you can choose, with one major difference being whether or not the bond is secured.

Secured Bonds
Bonds that are backed by the pledge of collateral.

Mortgage Bonds
Bonds secured by a lien on real property.

Secured Corporate Debt A **secured bond** is one that's backed by collateral, which, as you remember, is a real asset that can be seized and sold if a debtor doesn't pay off his or her debt. A **mortgage bond** is secured by a lien on real property. Typically, the value of the real property is greater than that of the mortgage bonds issued, providing the investor with a margin of safety in case the market value of the secured property declines.

In the event of bankruptcy, the bond trustees have the power to sell the secured property and use the proceeds to pay the bondholders. If the proceeds from this sale don't cover the bonds, the bondholders fall in line with the other creditors who are owed money.

Debentures
Unsecured long-term bonds.

Unsecured Corporate Debt The term **debenture** applies to any unsecured long-term bond. When bonds are unsecured, the earning ability of the issuing corporation is of great concern to the investor. Debentures are also viewed as being more risky than secured bonds and, as a result, have a higher yield associated with them.

Firms with more than one issue of debentures outstanding often specify a hierarchy by which some debentures are paid back before others if the firm goes bankrupt. The claims of the subordinated debentures—bonds lower down in the hierarchy—are honored only after the claims of secured bonds and unsubordinated debentures have been satisfied. As you might imagine, subordinated debentures are riskier than "normal" or unsubordinated debentures and have a higher return associated with them to compensate for the added risk.

Treasury and Agency Bonds

Without question, the biggest single player—and payer—in the bond market is the U.S. government. Given all the news about our national debt, it should come as no surprise that our government spends more than it takes in. The alternatives to financing an unbalanced budget are to sell some assets (anybody want to buy the Washington Monument?), raise taxes, or borrow more money. The last choice has been found to be the most acceptable approach and has led to the issuance of huge sums of debt by our government. Given the enormous amount of debt financing that goes on, it's not surprising that there are a number of different types of government debt to choose from.

These securities are generally viewed as being risk free, given the government's ability to tax and print more money. When corporations run out of money, they can't just print more, but the government can. Hey, it owns the mints! In addition to no default risk on Treasury bonds, there's no risk that they will be called because the government no longer issues callable bonds.

Because there's no default or call risk associated with government bonds, they generally pay a lower rate of interest than other bonds. In addition, most interest payments received on federal debt are exempt from state and local taxation.[1]

Treasury-issued debt has maturities that range from 3 months to 30 years. When investors speak of Treasury debt with different maturities, they speak of *bills*, *notes*, and *bonds*. The only differences among these are the maturity and the denomination.

If the Treasury debt has a maturity of 3, 6, or 12 months, it's referred to as a Treasury *bill*. If, when issued, it has a maturity of 2, 3, 5, or 10 years, it's referred to as a Treasury *note*. Treasury *bonds* are issued with maturities of 30 years. One advantage of purchasing Treasury securities is that you can do it yourself through a program called Treasury Direct (**http://www.treasurydirect.gov**), thereby avoiding brokerage fees, which range upward from $25 per transaction.

FACTS OF LIFE

In January 2017, the total U.S. federal debt was $19.96 trillion, which works out to about $61,300 per U.S. resident. If you'd like to see how much federal debt there is now, go to the U.S. National Debt Clock at **http://www.usdebtclock.org**.

In addition to the Treasury, a number of other government agencies, such as the Federal National Mortgage Association (FNMA) and the Federal Home Loan Banks (FHLB), issue debt called **agency bonds**. Although these aren't issued directly through the Treasury, they are issued by federal agencies and are authorized by Congress. They're still viewed as being virtually risk free and carry an interest rate slightly higher than that carried on Treasury securities. In general, their minimum denomination is $10,000, with maturities that vary from 1 to 40 years, although the average maturity is approximately 15 years.

Agency Bonds
Bonds issued by U.S. government agencies other than the Treasury.

Pass-Through Certificates Of the agency securities, the most interesting to investors are those issued by the Government National Mortgage Association (GNMA), or "Ginnie Mae," called **pass-through certificates**. A GNMA pass-through certificate represents an interest in a pool of federally insured mortgages. GNMA packages a group of mortgages worth $1 million or more, guarantees those mortgages, and sells "certificates" with minimum denominations of $25,000, called pass-through certificates, to finance the mortgages. In effect, pass-through certificates can put an

Pass-Through Certificates
Certificate that represent a portion of ownership in a pool of federally insured mortgages.

[1]Federal debt issued by the Federal National Mortgage Association (FNMA) is not exempt from state and local taxation because it is has been a publicly traded corporation since 1968.

average homeowner with $25,000 to invest on the other side—the lending side—of a mortgage.

Because all the payments from the mortgages financed by the pass-through certificates (less a processing fee and a GNMA insurance fee) go to the certificate holders, the size of the monthly check the investor receives depends on how fast the mortgages are paid off. In addition, the monthly check represents both principal and interest. At maturity, there's no return of principal as there is with a bond. With the last payment, the pass-through security is completely paid off, just as your home mortgage would be.

Treasury Inflation-Protected Securities (TIPS)
United States Treasury bonds for which the par value changes with the Consumer Price Index to guarantee the investor a real return (i.e., a return that stays above inflation). These bonds have a maturity of 5, 10, or 20 years and a minimum par value of $1,000.

Treasury Inflation-Protected Securities (TIPS) The newest and most exciting Treasury bond for investors is the **Treasury Inflation-Protected Security (TIPS)**. These bonds have a maturity of 5, 10, or 20 years and a minimum par value of $1,000. When there are changes in the Consumer Price Index (the government's measure of the effect of inflation on prices), there's a corresponding change in the par value of the bond.

For example, if there's a 3 percent increase in the Consumer Price Index, the par value of these bonds will go up by 3 percent, from $1,000 to $1,030. That means you get a little more interest each year, and at maturity, you get the new par value. That's because interest payments are then determined using this new par value. So if the par value of the bond rises to $1,030 and the interest rate on the bond is set at 3.8 percent, the bondholder now gets 3.8 percent of $1,030, or $39.14 (3.8% × $1,030) per year, and at maturity, this bond now pays $1,030.

The big headache with respect to these bonds comes in determining taxes. The IRS considers the upward adjustment in the par value of the bonds as interest income, and you have to pay taxes on it during the year the adjustment was made, even though you don't receive this money until the bond matures.

The advantage of these bonds is that investors will be guaranteed a real return—that is, a return above inflation. In addition, the effects of inflation on interest rates will be equalized as the interest payments and the bond's par value rise to reflect inflation. In effect, inflation is no longer an enemy!

U.S. Series EE Bonds The government also issues savings bonds directly aimed at the small investor. United States Series EE bonds are issued by the Treasury with fixed interest rates and denominations so low they can be purchased for as little as $25 each. EE bonds are sold electronically, and they are now sold at face value; that is, you pay $50 for a $50 bond. Series EE bonds are liquid in the sense that they can be cashed in at any time, although cashing them in before they mature may result in a reduced yield. In April 2017, they were paying 0.10 percent interest annually.

I Bonds In addition to Series EE savings bonds, the U.S. Treasury issues I bonds. An I bond is an accrual-type bond, meaning the interest is added to the value of the bond and paid when the bond is cashed in. Like TIPS, these bonds are sold at face value and grow with inflation-indexed earnings for up to 30 years. The return on an I bond is a combination of two separate rates: a fixed rate of return and a semiannual inflation rate. That means you get a fixed rate plus an additional return based on changes in the rate of inflation (as measured by the Consumer Price Index for All Urban Consumers, or CPI-U).

With an I bond, you can invest as little as $50 or as much as $10,000 per year. I bonds also have tax advantages: They allow you to defer federal taxes on earnings for up to 30 years and are exempt from state and local income taxes. In addition, these bonds are very liquid and can be turned into cash any time after 12 months.

Municipal Bonds

Municipal bonds, or "munis," are bonds issued by states, counties, and cities, in addition to other public agencies such as school districts and highway authorities, to fund public projects. There are thousands of different issues of municipal bonds, with about $3.7 trillion in outstanding value. Their popularity stems from the fact that they're tax exempt—interest payments aren't taxed by the federal government or, in general, by the state as long as you live in the state in which the bonds were issued.

Municipal Bonds or "Munis" Bonds issued by states, counties, and cities, as well as other public agencies such as school districts and highway authorities, to fund public projects.

In fact, if you live in a city and buy a municipal bond issued by that city, your income from that bond will be exempt from city, state, and federal taxes. For example, if you live in New York City, which has an income tax, and purchase a municipal bond issued by that city, you'll be exempt from paying taxes on the interest you receive at the federal, state, and city levels. Capital gains from selling municipal bonds before maturity, though, are taxed.

FACTS OF LIFE

The U.S. bond market has been bigger than the U.S. stock market in 24 of the last 25 years, and the municipal bond market makes up about 10 percent of the total U.S. bond market, at a level of just under $4 trillion in 2017.

There are two basic types of municipal bonds: general obligation bonds and revenue bonds. A **general obligation bond** is backed by the full faith and credit—that is, the taxing power—of the issuer and is exempt from all taxes. **Revenue bonds** derive the funds to pay interest and repay the bonds from a designated project or specific tax, can pay only if a sufficient amount of revenue is generated, and are exempt from state and local taxes but not federal taxes. If a revenue bond derives its funding from a toll road and traffic isn't very heavy, the bond might go unpaid.

General Obligation Bonds State or municipal bonds backed by the full faith and credit–that is, the taxing power–of the issuer.

Revenue Bonds State or municipal bonds that have interest and par value paid for with funds from a designated project or specific tax.

Municipal bonds also come with many different maturities. In fact, most municipal bond offerings have **serial maturities**. That is, a portion of the debt comes due, or matures, each year until the issue is exhausted. In effect, it works like a sinking fund. It's important that you choose the maturity date you want so you get the principal back when you need and expect it.

Serial Maturities Bonds, generally municipals, with various maturity dates, usually at set intervals.

Although municipal bonds are issued by a government, they're not risk free. In fact, there have been several cases in which local governments failed to pay on municipal bonds. Cleveland defaulted on some debt in the late 1970s, and then in the mid-1990s, Orange County, California, defaulted on $800 million of its short-term debt. This amount, however, is small compared to Detroit's $19 billion bankruptcy in 2013. The primary revenue source for most general obligation municipal bonds is real estate taxes. If a local government overestimates future tax intakes—say, it thinks more people will move in when instead a bunch of people move out—it gets stuck holding a lot of debt it can't handle.

Remember, unlike the federal government, state and local governments can't print more money when they run short. As you might expect, it's very difficult for an investor to judge the quality of a municipal bond offering. Fortunately, the rating agencies that we will discuss shortly in conjunction with corporate bonds also rate municipal bonds.

One of the disadvantages of municipal bonds is that if you have to sell them before they mature, it can be difficult to find a buyer. This is especially true for many smaller issues for which a secondary market does not exist.

Special Situation Bonds

We've already seen the main classifications of bonds, but before moving on, there are two special types of bonds that deserve mention. They are zero coupon bonds and junk bonds.

Zero Coupon Bonds Bonds that don't pay interest are called **zero coupon bonds**. Instead, these bonds are sold at a deep discount from their face or par value, and at

Zero Coupon Bonds Bonds that don't pay interest and are sold at a deep discount from their par value.

maturity, they return the entire par value. As a result, the entire return is made up of the bond's appreciation in value from its discount purchase price to its price at maturity.

A zero coupon bond can be thought of as something similar to a savings bond, and it appeals to those investors who need a lump sum of money at some future date but don't want to be concerned about reinvesting interest payments. Zero coupon bonds are issued by corporations and municipalities, and there are even mortgage-backed zeros, but without question, the dominant player in this market is the U.S. government. The government's zero coupon bonds are called STRIPS.

The major disadvantage of these bonds is that while you don't receive any income annually, you're taxed as though you do. The IRS considers any annual appreciation in value (or as the IRS calls it, the undistributed interest) as subject to tax. Another disadvantage of zero coupon bonds is that they tend to fluctuate in value with changes in the interest rate more than traditional bonds do. For example, in 1994, the price of 30-year zero coupon Treasury bonds dropped 18.7 percent, and then in 1995, it rose 63.1 percent. Zero coupon bonds aren't a good investment if you may have to sell them before they mature. They are best suited for tax-deferred retirement accounts such as IRAs or Keogh plans, where the tax disadvantage disappears.

Junk Bonds
Very risky, low-rated bonds, also called high-yield bonds. These bonds are rated BB or below.

Junk Bonds **Junk bonds** are low-rated bonds, also called high-yield bonds, which are bonds rated BB or below. (We explain bond ratings in the next section.) Originally, the term applied to bonds issued by firms with sound financial histories that experienced severe financial problems and began suffering from poor credit ratings. Today, the term *junk bond* refers to any bond with a low rating. The major issuers of junk bonds are new firms that haven't yet established a performance record.

Because junk bonds carry a much greater risk of default, they also carry an interest rate 3 to 6 percent above that of AAA-grade long-term bonds. The problem with junk bonds is that they haven't been around long enough for us to really know what will happen in a major recession.

Junk bonds are high-risk investments. Moreover, most junk bonds are callable. That means that if the firm does do well and recovers from its difficulties, then the bond will be called. If the firm doesn't do well, it could default. Neither alternative is a good one. Prudent investors generally avoid junk bonds. Hey, they're not called junk for nothing!

LO3 Calculate the value of a bond and understand the factors that cause bond value to change.

Evaluating Bonds

Not only do you need to know bond terms and what kinds of bonds there are, but also you need to know how to evaluate them. That means understanding what a bond yield and a rating are and knowing how to read a bond quote on the Internet or in the newspaper.

Bond Ratings—A Measure of Riskiness

John Moody first began to rate bonds in 1909. Since that time, two major rating agencies—Moody's and Standard & Poor's—have provided ratings on thousands of corporate, city, and state bonds. These ratings involve a judgment about the future risk potential of a bond—specifically, its default risk, or the chance that the issuer may not be able to meet its obligation to pay interest or repay the principal sometime in the future.

PRINCIPLE 8

The poorer the bond rating, the higher the rate of return demanded by investors. That's exactly what you'd expect, given **Principle 8: Risk and Return Go Hand in Hand**. Generally, these bond ratings run from AAA for the safest bonds to D for

TABLE 13.1 Interpreting Bond Ratings

Bond Ratings Category	Standard & Poor's	Moody's	Description
Prime	AAA	Aaa	Highest quality, extremely strong
Very strong	AA	Aa	Very strong capacity to pay
Strong	A	A	Strong capacity to pay
Medium	BBB	Baa	Changing circumstances could impact the firm's ability to pay
Speculative	BB, B	Ba, B	Has speculative elements
Very speculative	CCC, CC	Caa, Ca	Extremely speculative
Default	C	C	An income bond that doesn't pay interest
Default	D	D	Has not been paying interest or repaying principal

extremely risky bonds. Interestingly, a bond with an A rating is considered only a medium-grade bond rather than a high-grade bond. Table 13.1 provides a description of the different bond ratings.

As an investor, be aware of a bond's rating and its risk. Unfortunately, because bonds are so expensive—selling for around $1,000 each—diversification can be difficult unless you have a great deal of money invested in bonds. Therefore, if you buy bonds, avoid the risky ones. Check their ratings, which are available at most local libraries, or ask your broker.

FACTS OF LIFE

While AAA is the highest corporate bond rating, you might not want to insist on a AAA rating on your bond investments. That's because AAA ratings are relatively rare. Even IBM doesn't have a AAA rating. In fact, only about 2 or so of the Fortune 500 firms are rated AAA. On the other hand, there are plenty of B-rated bonds around; however, although a B may be a good grade in a class, it's only a speculative grade when it comes to bond ratings.

Bond Yield

The bond's yield is simply the return on investment. Note that yield isn't the same as coupon interest rate. The coupon interest rate tells you what interest payments you will receive as a percentage of the bond's par value. The bond's yield tells you what your return is as a percentage of the price of the bond.

There are two ways of measuring yield. The first, called the current yield, looks at the return from interest payments on the bond at the moment. The second, called the yield to maturity, takes into account total return, including interest, and allows for the fact that you may have purchased the bond for either more or less than it returns at maturity.

Current Yield The **current yield** on a bond refers to the ratio of the annual interest payment to the bond's market price. If, for example, you're considering a bond with an 8 percent coupon interest rate, a par value of $1,000, and a market price of $700, it would have a current yield of

Current Yield
The ratio of the annual interest payment to the bond's market price.

$$\text{current yield} = \frac{\text{annual interest payments}}{\text{market price of the bond}}$$

$$= \frac{0.08 \times \$1{,}000}{\$700} = \frac{\$80}{\$700} = 11.4 \text{ percent}$$

Yield to Maturity
The true yield or return that the bondholder receives if a bond is held to maturity. It's the measure of expected return for a bond.

Yield to Maturity The **yield to maturity** is the true yield or return you receive if you hold a bond to maturity. Basically, it's the measure of expected return. In effect, calculating the yield to maturity is the same as solving for the annual interest rate, *i*, as we did in Chapter 3, where we discussed the time value of money. This measure of return considers the annual interest payments you receive, as well as the difference between the bond's current market price and its value at maturity.

Remember, regardless of whether you bought your bond at a price above or below its par value, at maturity you get exactly its par value. If you paid less than $1,000 for your bond, the bond will appreciate over its lifetime, climbing up to $1,000 at maturity. Conversely, if you paid more than $1,000 for your bond, it will slowly drop in value over its lifetime, falling to $1,000 at maturity when it's redeemed.

If you have a financial calculator, solving for the yield to maturity, or *i*, is quite easy. If you don't have a financial calculator, you can use a formula to calculate the approximate yield to maturity (you need a calculator to calculate the actual yield to maturity). With this formula, you first determine the average annual return by adding the annual interest payments to the average amount that the bond increases or decreases in price each year. The annual change in bond price is based on the notion that at maturity the bond will be worth its par value—because it will be redeemed at this price. Therefore, you calculate the amount the bond must increase or decrease to get to its par value and divide this by the number of years left to maturity.

You then divide this average annual return by the average value of the bond—the average of its par value and current market price. Thus, you calculate the *approximate yield to maturity* as follows:

$$\begin{array}{c}\text{approximate}\\ \text{yield to maturity}\end{array} = \frac{\begin{array}{c}\text{annual}\\ \text{interest payments}\end{array} + \dfrac{\text{par value} - \text{current price}}{\text{number of years to maturity}}}{\dfrac{\text{par value} + \text{current price}}{2}}$$

Let's look at an example of a bond that has 10 years left to maturity, a par value of $1,000, a current price of $880, and a coupon interest rate of 10 percent, which it pays annually. Thus, it pays you $100 annually in interest (coupon interest rate × par value = annual interest payment, or 0.10 × $1,000 = $100). Plugging these numbers into the approximate yield to maturity formula, you get

$$\begin{array}{c}\text{approximate}\\ \text{yield to maturity}\end{array} = \frac{\$100 + \dfrac{\$1{,}000 - \$880}{10}}{\dfrac{\$1{,}000 + \$880}{2}}$$

$$= \frac{\$100 + \dfrac{\$120}{10}}{\$1{,}880/2}$$

$$= \$112/\$940 = 11.91 \text{ percent}$$

Calculator Clues

A Bond's Yield to Maturity

Using a financial calculator, let's calculate the yield to maturity on the bond in the previous example. If you don't have a financial calculator, one is available on the MyLab Finance Web site **(http://www.pearson.com/mylab/finance)**. In this example, $N = 10$ because there are 10 years to maturity, $PV = -880$ because you would pay $880 if you purchased this bond, $PMT = 100$ because that is the amount you receive annually in the form of interest (it is equal to the bond's coupon interest rate [10%] times the bond's par value [$1,000]), and $FV = 1{,}000$, which is the bond's par value (the amount you receive at maturity). You'll notice that *PV* took on a negative sign because that is what you would pay for the bond (money "leaves your hands"), while *PMT* and *FV* take on positive signs because that money flows to you (the money "returns to your hands").

Enter	10		−880.00	100	$1,000
	N	I/Y	PV	PMT	FV
Solve for		12.14%			

Thus, the bond's true yield to maturity is 12.14 percent. This result differs by 0.23 percent from the value of 11.91 percent that you got using the approximate yield to maturity formula.

The approximate yield to maturity formula also works for bonds that are selling above their par or maturity value. Let's change the current market price to $1,100 and recalculate the approximate yield to maturity as follows:

$$\text{approximate yield to maturity} = \frac{\$100 + \dfrac{\$1{,}000 - \$1{,}100}{10}}{\dfrac{\$1{,}000 + \$1{,}100}{2}}$$

$$= \frac{\$100 - \dfrac{\$100}{10}}{\$2{,}100/2}$$

$$= \$90/\$1{,}050 = 8.57 \text{ percent}$$

Calculator Clues

A Bond's Yield to Maturity

Let's calculate the yield to maturity on the bond from the previous example using a financial calculator. Again, if you don't have a financial calculator, one is available on the MyLab Finance Web site. In this example, $N = 10$ because there are 10 years to maturity, $PV = -1{,}100$ because you would pay $1,100 if you purchased this bond (remember, when you're solving for I/Y, there must be both positive and negative cash flows), $PMT = 100$ because that is the amount you receive annually in the form of interest (it is equal to the bond's coupon interest rate [10%] times the bond's par value [$1,000]), and $FV = 1{,}000$, which is the bond's par value (the amount you receive at maturity).

Enter	10		−1,100.00	100	$1,000
	N	I/Y	PV	PMT	FV
Solve for		8.48%			

Thus, the bond's yield to maturity is 8.48 percent. You'll notice that there is a small difference of 0.09 percent from what you got using the approximation formula. As you might expect, this is the true answer, and the other is an approximation.

FACTS OF LIFE

Perhaps the most famous bond is James, also known as 007. On an inflation-adjusted basis, *Thunderball* had the highest box office receipts of any James Bond movie.

Equivalent Taxable Yield on Municipal Bonds The appeal of municipal bonds is their tax-exempt status. Thus, in comparing municipal bonds to taxable bonds, the comparison must be between their equivalent taxable yields: That is, what is the yield a taxable bond must offer to match the equivalent taxable yield on the municipal bond? The equivalent taxable yield on a municipal bond is calculated as follows:

$$\text{equivalent taxable yield} = \frac{\text{tax-free yield on the municipal bond}}{(1 - \text{investor's marginal tax bracket})}$$

Keep in mind that the tax bracket referred to includes all taxes avoided by the muni. This bracket could include federal, state, and local taxes. Thus, if the municipal bond yields 7 percent and you are in the 38 percent marginal tax bracket, the equivalent taxable yield on a municipal bond would be

$$\text{equivalent taxable yield} = \frac{0.07}{(1 - 0.38)} = \frac{0.07}{0.62} = 0.1129, \text{ or } 11.29\%$$

The higher your tax bracket, the more attractive municipal bonds are.

Valuation Principles

PRINCIPLE 3

PRINCIPLE 8

The valuation of bonds has its roots in Principles 3 and 8. **Principle 3: The Time Value of Money** allows us to bring the investment returns back to the present, while **Principle 8: Risk and Return Go Hand in Hand** tells us what discount rate to use in bringing those returns back to the present.

From Chapter 12, you already know that the value of any investment is the present value of all the returns that you receive from that investment. This is how you value stocks, and it's also how you value bonds. In effect, we'll bring the future returns or benefits back to the present and add them up. With bonds, the process is quite simple—you find out the values in today's dollars of the interest and principal payments and add them together.

Bond Valuation

When you purchase a bond, you get interest payments for a number of years, and then at maturity, the bond is redeemed, and you receive the par value of the bond back. Thus, *the value of a bond is the present value of the interest payments (this is an annuity) plus the present value of the repayment of the bond's par value at maturity (this is a single cash flow)*. In general, the value of a bond should be approximately the same as its price because that's what you and other investors would be willing to pay for the bond. Therefore, by understanding how bonds are valued, we can also understand what causes bond prices to rise and fall.

Now, let's bring the interest payments and the repayment of the bond's par value at maturity back to the present. The interest payments come in the form of an annuity—that is, you receive the same dollar amount each year. The repayment of the par value comes in the form of a single cash flow.[2] Thus, the value of the bond can be written as

$$\text{value of the bond} = \begin{array}{c}\text{present value of the}\\ \text{interest payments}\\ \text{(an annuity)}\end{array} + \begin{array}{c}\text{present value of repayment}\\ \text{of par at maturity}\\ \text{(a single cash flow)}\end{array}$$

[2]Actually, the calculation of the value of a bond is slightly more complicated because most bonds pay interest semiannually rather than annually. Although accommodating this complication is relatively simple, the principles behind bond valuation don't change. Moreover, the effect on the value of the bond is only slight. Because our presentation is meant to illustrate how the value of a bond is determined in the marketplace and how changes in interest rates are reflected in bond prices, we won't deal with semiannual interest payments.

Rewriting this using the style from Chapter 3, we get

$$\text{value of the bond} = \text{annual interest payments} \times \text{present-value interest factor of an annuity} + \text{par value} \times \text{present-value interest factor of a single cash flow}$$

Let's look at an example. We're considering buying a bond that matures in 20 years with a coupon interest rate of 10 percent and a par value of $1,000. How much should we pay for it? Well, first we need to decide what return we require on that bond. Let's assume that given the current interest rates and risk level of this bond, our required rate of return is also 10 percent per year. To determine the value of the bond, we need only bring the interest payments and repayment of par back to the present using our required rate of return as the discount rate. The annual interest payments we'll receive if we buy this bond are equal to the bond's coupon interest rate of 10 percent times the par value of the bond, which is $1,000. Thus, the annual interest payments are $100. Recall that the *present-value interest factor of an annuity* can be determined using a financial calculator or looked up directly in Appendix D, and the *present-value interest factor* of a single cash flow can also be determined using a financial calculator or looked up directly in Appendix B. The value of the bond can now be calculated as follows (using 10 percent for i and 20 years):

$$\begin{aligned}\text{value of the bond} &= \text{present value of the interest payments} + \text{present value of repayment of par at maturity}\\ &= \$100(\text{present-value interest factor of an annuity})\\ &\quad + \$1{,}000(\text{present-value interest factor of a single cash flow})\\ &= \$100(8.514) + \$1{,}000(0.1486)\\ &= \$851.40 + 148.60\\ &= \$1{,}000\end{aligned}$$

Thus, the value of this bond would be $1,000. If we purchased it for $1,000, we'd be paying exactly its par value. The reason we'd buy at par is that we'd be earning our entire required rate of return from the interest payments—we required a 10 percent return, and we receive a 10 percent return in the form of interest.

Calculator Clues

Value of a Bond When the Required Rate of Return is 10 Percent

Using a financial calculator, let's calculate the value of a bond that matures in 20 years with a coupon interest rate of 10 percent, which is our required rate of return, and a par value of $1,000. In this example, $N = 20$ because there are 20 years to maturity, $I/Y = 10$ because our required rate of return is 10 percent, $PMT = 100$ because that is the amount we receive annually in the form of interest (it is equal to the bond's coupon interest rate [10%] times the bond's par value [$1,000]), and $FV = 1,000$, which is the bond's par value (the amount we receive at maturity).

Enter	20	10		100	$1,000
	N	I/Y	PV	PMT	FV
Solve for			−1,000.00		

Thus, the value of the bond is $1,000. You'll notice that, as expected, we get a negative sign on the *PV*.

Now, let's look at the same bond and assume that the current level of interest rates has gone up and, as a result, so has our required rate of return—to 12 percent. How much should we pay for this bond now? In this case, the only change is in the value of the discount rate or required rate of return. Recalculating the value of the bond (using 12 percent for *i* and 20 years), we find it to be

$$\begin{aligned}\text{value of the bond} &= \text{present value of the interest payments} + \text{present value of repayment of par at maturity}\\ &= \$100(\text{present-value interest factor of an annuity})\\ &\quad + \$1{,}000(\text{present-value interest factor of a single cash flow})\\ &= \$100(7.469) + \$1{,}000(0.104)\\ &= \$746.90 + \$104.00\\ &= \$850.90\end{aligned}$$

Calculator Clues

Value of a Bond When the Required Rate of Return Is 12 Percent

Now, let's recalculate the value of this bond when the required rate of return is 12 percent. The only change is that I/Y now equals 12 percent.

	N	I/Y	PV	PMT	FV
Enter	20	12		100	$1,000
Solve for			−850.61		

This is the same number we got using the tables (other than some rounding error).

> **STOP & THINK**
>
> What do David Bowie and James Brown have in common? They have both issued bonds secured by their past work. David Bowie sold $55 million worth of bonds that were backed by the future earnings on his music. This allowed him to retain ownership of his songs while getting his future royalties both instantly and tax free. Investors got their interest and principal from those same future royalties on Bowie's past recordings–in effect, the sales of "The Rise and Fall of Ziggy Stardust and the Spiders from Mars," along with the rest of Bowie's pre-1990 albums, provided the interest that the "Bowie bondholders" received.

When we raise our required rate of return to 12 percent, the value of the bond falls to $850.90. As a result, we would want to buy this bond *at a discount*—that is, below its par value. We're requiring a 12 percent return on this bond, but its interest rate is only 10 percent. We'd need to receive the remaining return from the appreciation of the bond in value. So we would look to buy it for $850.90 and at maturity receive $1,000 for it.

Let's see what happens to the value of this bond when our required rate of return goes down. Assume that the current level of interest rates has gone down and, as a result, so has our required rate of return—this time to 8 percent. Again, the only change is in the value of the discount rate or required rate of return. Recalculating the value of the bond (using 8 percent as *i* and 20 years), we find it to be

$$\begin{aligned}\text{value of the bond} &= \text{present value of the interest payments} + \text{present value of repayment of par at maturity}\\ &= \$100(\text{present-value interest factor of an annuity})\\ &\quad + \$1{,}000(\text{present-value interest factor of a single cash flow})\end{aligned}$$

$$= \$100(9.818) + \$1{,}000(0.215)$$
$$= \$981.80 + \$215.00$$
$$= \$1{,}196.80$$

Calculator Clues

Value of a Bond When the Required Rate of Return Is 8 Percent

Now, let's recalculate the value of this bond when the required rate of return is 8 percent. The only change is that *I/Y* now equals 8 percent.

Enter	20	8		100	$1,000
	N	I/Y	PV	PMT	FV
Solve for			−1,196.36		

This is the same number we got using the tables (other than some rounding error).

Thus, when the required rate of return drops to 8 percent, the value of the bond climbs to $1,196.80. As a result, we would be willing to buy this bond *at a premium*—that is, above its par value. Again, this makes sense because if the bond pays 10 percent in interest and we require an 8 percent return, we'd be willing to pay more than $1,000 for it.

In reflecting on this example, notice that *when the required rate of return goes up, the value of the bond drops, and when the required rate of return goes down, the value of the bond increases*. What can cause the required rate of return to change?

First, if the firm that issued the bond becomes a riskier investment, the required rate of return should rise. The result of this would be a drop in the value of the bond—that certainly makes intuitive sense. A second factor that can cause you to alter your required rate of return on a bond is a change in general interest rates in the market. When interest rates go up, new bonds are issued with higher interest rates. If you own a bond that pays 8 percent interest and new bonds are available that pay 9 percent interest, no one will want your 8 percent bond unless you lower its price to make it competitive with the 9 percent bonds.

Thus, when interest rates in general rise, the value of an outstanding bond falls. Because the value of this bond falls, so does its price. Alternatively, when interest rates in general fall, the value and price of an outstanding bond rise. As we'll see, this inverse relationship between bond values or prices and interest rates is extremely important.

Why Bonds Fluctuate in Value

If you invest in bonds, it's important to know what makes them move up and down in value—and therefore in price. Let's begin by summarizing the key relationship that underlies bond valuation. *There's an inverse relationship between interest rates and bond values in the secondary market: When interest rates rise, bond values drop, and when interest rates drop, bond values rise.*

As interest rates rise, investors demand a higher return on bonds. If a bond has a fixed coupon interest rate, the only way the bond can increase its return to investors is to drop in value and sell for less. Thus, we have an inverse relationship between interest rates and bond values (and prices).

The importance of this relationship can't be overstated. Bond prices fluctuate dramatically, and this relationship explains much of the fluctuation. For example, in 1999 interest rates went up, and as a result, 10-year Treasury bonds posted average losses

FIGURE 13.1 The Relationship Between Bond Prices and Changes in Interest Rates

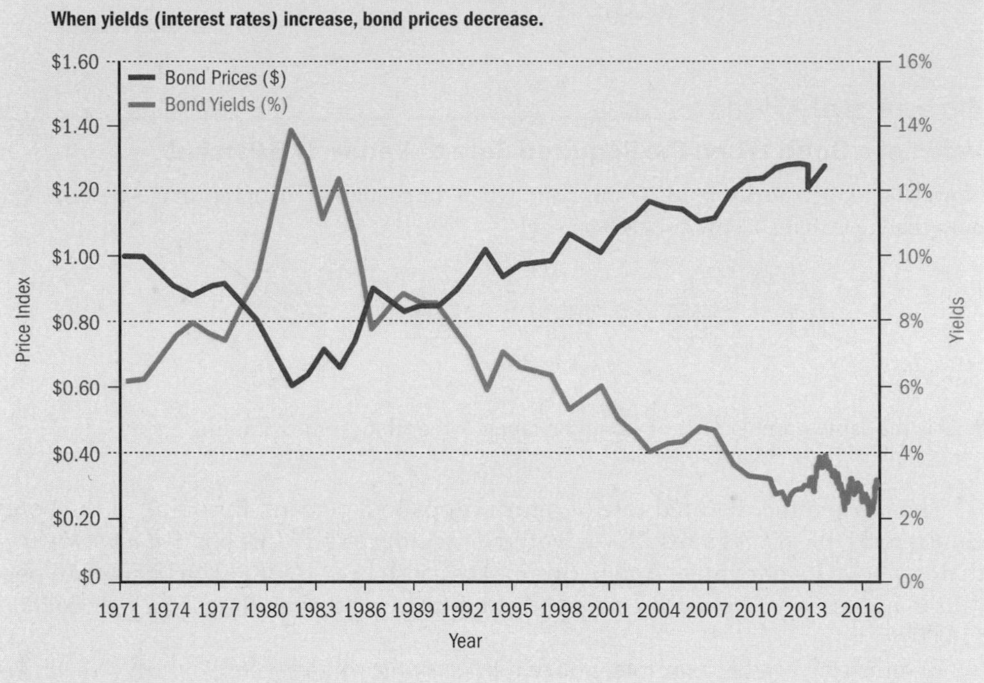

> **STOP & THINK**
>
> Can you use this inverse relationship between interest rates and bond prices to make money? Before you forecast interest rates and invest in bonds, you should realize that beating the market is extremely difficult. To use this inverse relationship between interest rates and bond prices, you not only have to forecast interest rates but also have to outforecast the experts. Knowing which way interest rates are going is not enough if other investors know the same thing: You need to know which way interest rates are going when no one else knows. What's been happening to interest rates lately?

of 8.3 percent. Then in 2000 and in 2002, interest rates fell, and those same bonds returned 16.7 and 15.1 percent, respectively! The same inverse relationship between interest rates and bond prices showed up dramatically in 2008 through 2013. In 2008, interest rates dropped as the economy slid into a recession, and as a result, 30-year Treasury bonds climbed by over 20 percent. Then in 2009, interest rates reversed as investors became concerned about long-term inflation, and as interest rates climbed, 10-year Treasury bonds fell by over 11 percent. Then in 2010 and 2011, interest rates fell again in response to moves by the Federal Reserve, and 10-year Treasury bonds climbed in value by over 8 and 16 percent, respectively. Then in 2013, as interest rates began to climb, 10-year Treasury bonds lost over 9 percent, only to bounce back in 2014 by almost 11 percent. Then in 2015 and 2016, they barely moved. Figure 13.1 shows bond prices and interest rates since the end of 1970 and illustrates the inverse relationship that exists between them.

Not only do bond values change when interest rates change, but also *longer-term bonds fluctuate in price more than shorter-term bonds*. Remember from Chapter 3 that the further in the future a cash flow is, the more its present value will fluctuate as a result of a change in the interest or discount rate. Thus, when interest rates change, longer-term bonds fluctuate in price more than shorter-term bonds. Figure 13.2 looks at bonds with a 5 percent coupon interest rate and various maturities as market interest rates go up and down. It shows that long-term bonds bounce up and down much more dramatically in response to interest rate changes than do short-term bonds.

FIGURE 13.2 The Relationship Between the Length of a Bond's Maturity and the Amount of Price Fluctuation When Interest Rates Change

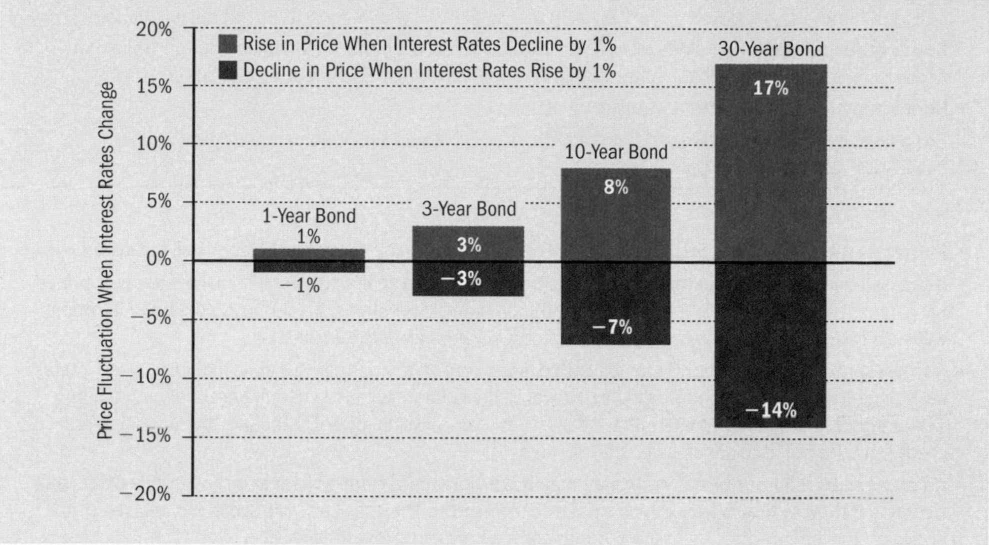

In addition, *as a bond approaches its maturity date, its market value approaches its par or maturity value*. Without question, a bond will sell for its par or maturity value at maturity. We know this because at maturity the bondholder receives the par value from the issuer, and the bond is terminated. As a result, as the bond approaches maturity, the market price of the bond approaches its par value. Figure 13.3 illustrates this point.

Finally, *when interest rates go down, bond prices go up, but the upward price movement on bonds with a call provision is limited by the call price*. In effect, investors won't pay

FIGURE 13.3 The Price Path of a 12 Percent Coupon Bond over Its Life

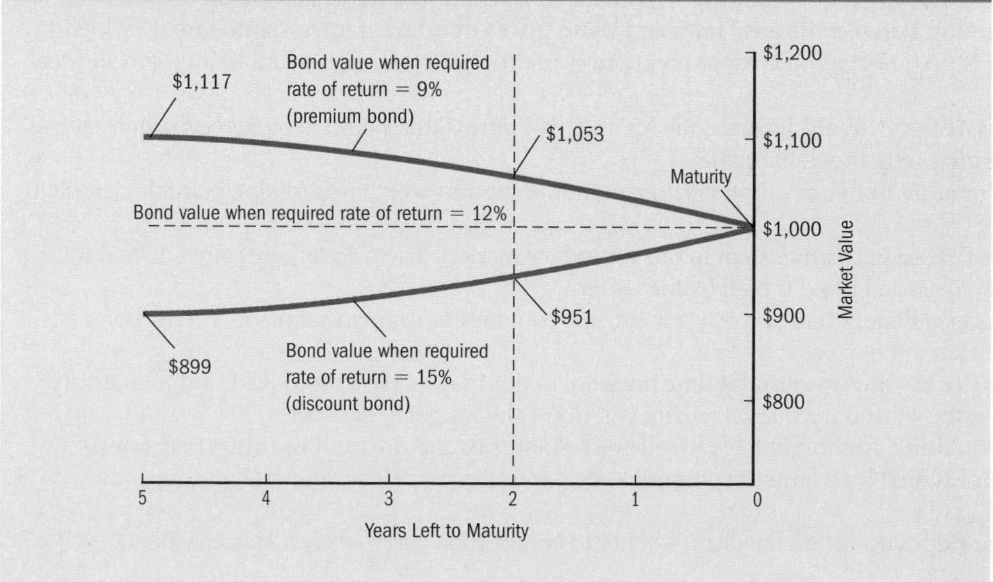

TABLE 13.2 The Pros and Cons of Investing in Bonds

Benefits of Bonds

- **If interest rates drop, bond prices will rise.** If interest rates drop, that inverse relationship between interest rates and bond prices will work in your favor. In that case, you'll want a long-term, noncallable bond.
- **Bonds reduce risk through diversification.** Any time you add a new investment to your portfolio that doesn't move in tandem with the other investments in your portfolio, you reduce your portfolio risk.
- **Bonds produce steady current income.** What more need we say?
- **Bonds can be a safe investment if held to maturity.** If you hold the bond to maturity and it doesn't default, it'll return exactly what it promises.

Dangers of Bonds

- **If interest rates rise, bond prices will fall.** The longer the maturity, the more the bond will fluctuate.
- **If the issuer experiences financial problems, bond values drop.** If an issuer can't make interest or principal payments, the bond will plummet in value. Minor financial problems can also cause the bond to drop in value. Of course, any time the bond rating drops, bond values drop like a stone.
- **If interest rates drop, the bond may be called.** Most corporate bonds are callable. In theory, when interest rates drop, the value of a bond should rise. However, the issuer may decide to refinance the bond offering with bonds that have a lower interest rate. The bonds may be called away, leaving you to reinvest the proceeds from the called bonds at lower interest rates.
- **If you need to sell your bonds early, you may have a problem selling them at a reasonable price, particularly if they're bonds issued by a smaller corporation.** There isn't a strong secondary market for the bonds of smaller corporations. In short, bonds aren't a very liquid investment.
- **Finding a good investment outlet for the interest you receive may be difficult.** If you're using bonds to accumulate wealth, it may be difficult to find a good investment outlet for the interest you receive. Without reinvesting the interest payments, there'll be no accumulation of wealth from investing in bonds unless you're investing in zero or very low coupon bonds.

more than the call price for a bond because they know it could be called away from them for that price at any time. Before moving on, let's make sure you understand the pros and cons of bonds. Table 13.2 lists the benefits and dangers of bonds, while Checklist 13.1 looks at picking a good bond.

CHECKLIST 13.1 Picking a Good Bond

- ☐ **Think about the effect of taxes.** Consider municipals, particularly if you're in a high tax bracket.
- ☐ **Keep the inverse relationship between interest rates and bond prices in mind.** If interest rates are very low, the only way they can go is up (which would cause bond prices to drop), so you might want to invest in shorter-term bonds.
- ☐ **If you're buying a corporate bond, avoid losers.** Look for and avoid firms that might experience major financial problems. All other firms are pretty much the same.
- ☐ **Limit yourself to bonds rated AA or above.** In this way, you minimize any worry regarding a possible default by the issuer.
- ☐ **Buy your bond when it's first issued rather than in the secondary market.** The price is generally fair, and the sales commission on a newly issued bond is paid by the issuer.
- ☐ **Avoid bonds that might get called.** Before you buy a bond, ask your broker or financial planner if the bond is likely to be called. If so, pick another one.
- ☐ **Match your bond's maturity to your investment time horizon.** In this way, you can hold the bond to maturity and avoid having to sell in the secondary market, where you don't always get a fair price.
- ☐ **Stick to large issues.** If you think you might have to sell before maturity and are buying a corporate bond, make sure you buy a bond issued by a large corporation—the secondary market is generally more active for them.
- ☐ **When in doubt, go Treasury!** If you're still unsure, it's better to be safe than sorry—buy a Treasury bond.

What Bond Valuation Relationships Mean to the Investor

You can glean several important points from the discussion of bond valuation relationships. You know that bond prices can fluctuate dramatically and that interest rates drive these changes. In addition, you know that there's an inverse relationship between interest rates and bond prices: When interest rates go up, bond prices go down. Conversely, when interest rates go down, bond prices go up. Given this inverse relationship between interest rates and bond prices:

- If you expect interest rates to go up (and therefore bond prices to fall), you want to mute the inverse relationship by purchasing very short-term bonds. Although there still may be some price fluctuation, it will be minor.
- If you expect interest rates to go down (and therefore bond prices to rise), you want to amplify this relationship as much as possible by purchasing bonds with very long maturities that aren't callable. In this case, the bonds will fluctuate as much as possible, and if interest rates go down, the price of the bonds will rise.

Reading Online Corporate Bond Quotes

Figure 13.4 provides a visual summary of how to read online corporate bond listings. Recall that although corporate bonds generally have a par or face value of $1,000,

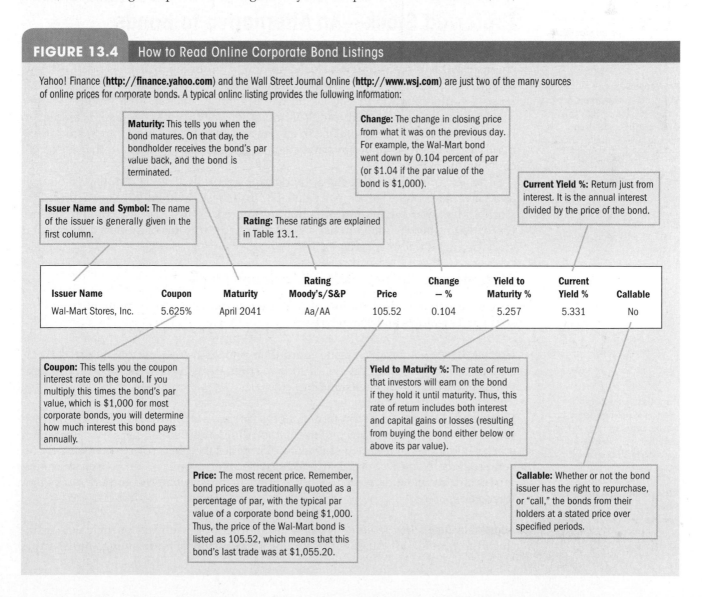

FIGURE 13.4 How to Read Online Corporate Bond Listings

Yahoo! Finance (**http://finance.yahoo.com**) and the Wall Street Journal Online (**http://www.wsj.com**) are just two of the many sources of online prices for corporate bonds. A typical online listing provides the following information:

Maturity: This tells you when the bond matures. On that day, the bondholder receives the bond's par value back, and the bond is terminated.

Change: The change in closing price from what it was on the previous day. For example, the Wal-Mart bond went down by 0.104 percent of par (or $1.04 if the par value of the bond is $1,000).

Current Yield %: Return just from interest. It is the annual interest divided by the price of the bond.

Issuer Name and Symbol: The name of the issuer is generally given in the first column.

Rating: These ratings are explained in Table 13.1.

Issuer Name	Coupon	Maturity	Rating Moody's/S&P	Price	Change – %	Yield to Maturity %	Current Yield %	Callable
Wal-Mart Stores, Inc.	5.625%	April 2041	Aa/AA	105.52	0.104	5.257	5.331	No

Coupon: This tells you the coupon interest rate on the bond. If you multiply this times the bond's par value, which is $1,000 for most corporate bonds, you will determine how much interest this bond pays annually.

Yield to Maturity %: The rate of return that investors will earn on the bond if they hold it until maturity. Thus, this rate of return includes both interest and capital gains or losses (resulting from buying the bond either below or above its par value).

Price: The most recent price. Remember, bond prices are traditionally quoted as a percentage of par, with the typical par value of a corporate bond being $1,000. Thus, the price of the Wal-Mart bond is listed as 105.52, which means that this bond's last trade was at $1,055.20.

Callable: Whether or not the bond issuer has the right to repurchase, or "call," the bonds from their holders at a stated price over specified periods.

FACTS OF LIFE

If you're looking for a safe bond, it's hard to beat a Treasury bond. Sure, they fluctuate when interest rates go up and down just like any other bond, but there is no question about the interest and principal payments being made on time. Treasury bonds issued today are noncallable, won't be downgraded or default, and are liquid. On top of that, you can buy them directly from the Federal Reserve and avoid brokerage commissions.

their selling price is quoted as a percentage of par. Even though a bond may appear to be selling at 101, it's actually selling at 101 percent of its par value, which is $1,000. Thus, a bond listed as selling at 101 is actually selling for $1,010.

What appears in the listing isn't exactly what you'd pay if you purchased the bond. You're also expected to pay for any **accrued interest** on the bond. Remember, interest is generally paid only every 6 months. Thus, if it's been 5 months since interest was last paid, the bond has accrued 5 months' worth of interest. This accrued interest isn't reflected in the listed price of the bond, but you still need to pay the seller for the accrued interest that's already been earned.

Accrued Interest
Interest that has been earned on the bond but has not yet been paid out to the bondholder.

If this bond pays $48 in interest every 6 months, then 5 months' worth of accrued interest would be $\frac{5}{6} \times \$48 = \$40$.

That means that although the bond is listed as selling for $1,010, if you purchase it, you'll pay $\$1{,}010 + \$40 = \$1{,}050$. This sum of both the quoted or stated price and the accrued interest is often referred to as the **invoice price**.

Invoice Price
The sum of both the quoted or stated price of a bond and the bond's accrued interest. It's the price you pay if you buy the bond in the secondary market.

LO4 Compare preferred stock to bonds as an investment option.

Preferred Stock—An Alternative to Bonds

Preferred Stock
Stock that offers no ownership or voting rights and generally pays fixed dividends. The dividends on preferred stock are paid out before dividends on common stock can be issued.

Preferred stock is often referred to as a hybrid security because it has many of the characteristics of both common stock and bonds. From the investor's point of view, preferred stock is probably closer to bonds. On the one hand, preferred stock is similar to common stock in that it has no fixed maturity date and not paying its dividends won't bring on bankruptcy. On the other hand, preferred stock is similar to bonds in that its dividends are of a fixed size and are paid before common stock dividends are paid. A share of preferred stock is also similar to a bond in that it doesn't carry voting rights.

The size of the preferred stock dividend is generally fixed as a dollar amount or as a percentage of the stock's par value. Because these dividends are fixed, preferred stockholders don't share in profits but are limited to their stated annual dividend. Just as with a bond, if the firm has a great year and earns lots of money, the preferred stock dividend doesn't change.

Features and Characteristics of Preferred Stock

To gain a better understanding of preferred stock, let's take a moment to look at some of its features and characteristics.

Multiple Issues A firm can issue more than one series or class of preferred stock, each with a different set dividend. In fact, some firms have well over ten different issues of preferred stock outstanding.

Cumulative Feature
A feature of preferred stock that requires all past unpaid preferred stock dividends to be paid before any common stock dividends can be declared.

Cumulative Feature Most preferred stock carries a **cumulative feature**, which requires that all past unpaid preferred stock dividends be paid before any common stock dividends are declared. This feature provides the preferred stock investor with some degree of protection because otherwise there would be no reason why preferred stock dividends wouldn't be omitted or passed when common stock dividends are passed.

Adjustable-Rate Preferred Stock
Preferred stock on which the quarterly dividends fluctuate with the market interest rate.

Adjustable Rate In the early 1980s, **adjustable-rate preferred stock** was introduced to provide investors with some protection against wide swings in the value of preferred stock that resulted from interest rate swings. With adjustable-rate preferred stock, the amount of the quarterly dividend fluctuates with interest rates under a formula that ties the dividend payment to a market interest rate. As a result, when interest rates rise, the value of the preferred stock doesn't drop; rather, the preferred stock's dividend rises, and the value of the preferred stock stays relatively constant.

Convertibility Some preferred stock is also **convertible preferred stock**, which means that its holder can, at any time, exchange it for a predetermined number of shares of common stock. The trade-off associated with convertible preferred stock is that the convertibility feature may allow the preferred stockholder to participate in the company's capital gains, but the preferred stock has a lower dividend associated with it than regular preferred stock.

Convertible Preferred Stock
Preferred stock that the holder can exchange for a predetermined number of shares of common stock.

Callability Much of the preferred stock outstanding is callable. Just as with bonds, if interest rates drop, there is a good chance that the preferred stock will be called away by the issuing firm.

Valuation of Preferred Stock

When you buy a share of preferred stock, you get a steady stream of dividends that go on forever because preferred stock never matures. Thus, *the value of a share of preferred stock is the present value of the perpetual stream of constant dividends that the preferred stockholder receives.* As such, the value of a share of preferred stock can be written as follows:

$$\text{value of preferred stock} = \text{present value of the perpetual stream of constant dividends}$$

Because preferred stock dividends go on forever, they constitute a perpetuity. (Remember this term from Chapter 3?) The calculation of their present value can be reduced to

$$\text{value of preferred stock} = \frac{\text{annual preferred stock dividend}}{\text{required rate of return}}$$

When interest rates rise (causing your required rate of return to rise), the value of a share of preferred stock declines. Conversely, when interest rates decline (causing your required rate of return to drop), the value of a share of preferred stock rises. This is the primary valuation relationship in valuing preferred stock and, as we just saw, in valuing bonds.

Let's look at an example. If the Gap has an issue of preferred stock outstanding with an annual dividend of \$4 and, given the level of risk on this issue, investors demand a required rate of return of 10 percent, its value would be

$$\text{value of preferred stock} = \frac{\$4}{0.10} = \$40$$

As you can see, if the required rate of return on this preferred stock dropped to 8 percent, its value would climb to \$4/0.08, or \$50. Thus, as market interest rates rise and fall (causing investors' required rates of return to rise and fall), the value of preferred stock moves in an opposite manner.

Risks Associated with Preferred Stock

We've said that preferred stock is a hybrid between bonds and common stock. Unfortunately, when it comes to advantages and disadvantages for the investor, it's also a hybrid, taking disadvantages from both common stock and bonds but advantages from neither. The problems with preferred stock for the individual investor include the following:

- If interest rates rise, the value of the preferred stock drops.
- If interest rates drop, the value of the preferred stock rises, and the preferred stock is called away from the investor (remember, most preferred stock is callable).
- The investor doesn't participate in the capital gains that common stockholders receive.
- The investor doesn't have the safety of bond interest payments because preferred stock dividends can be passed without the risk of bankruptcy.

Given all these drawbacks and very few advantages, you may be wondering who buys preferred stock. The answer is other corporations because corporations receive a tax break on the dividend income from preferred stock.

PRINCIPLE 8

If you do decide to invest in preferred stock, you'll want to pay attention to the preferred stock's rating. Similar to bonds, preferred stocks are rated by Moody's and Standard & Poor's. The majority of preferred stock falls into the medium-grade levels. Just as you'd expect from **Principle 8: Risk and Return Go Hand in Hand**, the lower the preferred stock's rating and therefore the riskier the preferred stock, the higher the expected return.

LO5 Understand the risks associated with investing in real estate.

Investing in Real Estate

Since the end of World War II, real estate investments have created more fortunes than almost any other investment. Unfortunately, in the late 1980s, those same real estate investments destroyed quite a few fortunes. Then, from the late 1990s through the mid-2000s, real estate climbed in value and become a popular investment again. All that changed around 2006, when real estate prices began to drop. Finally, by the beginning of 2017, real estate prices were back to where they were in 2006, but that's before inflation. Adjusting for inflation, they were about 16 percent below their peak. Keep in mind that this is on average, and while some areas are above their historical highs, others still have a long way to go.

Most American households—in fact, about two-thirds—own their own homes, and for them, it's the biggest investment they're likely to make. In fact, as we saw in Chapter 8, housing costs take up over 25 percent of after-tax income. The question now becomes, Do you want to go beyond this personal investment and make an additional investment in real estate? For most people, the answer to this question is "no." Real estate investment requires time, energy, and sophistication that the majority of us just don't have. There are also a lot of risks with real estate investments. For example, the average price of a house in Miami was $380,000 in April 2006, but by 2011, that same house was valued at about $182,000—down about 50 percent! But by 2017, the price had come back to just over $300,000—up considerably but still down over 20 percent from 2006. However, for some people, investing in real estate is an option. So let's discuss what types of investments in real estate you might consider.

Real estate investment can be categorized as direct or indirect. With a direct investment, you directly own the property. This type of investment might include a vacation home, commercial property such as an apartment building, or undeveloped land. With an indirect investment, you're an investor in a group that owns the property and has hired a professional to manage it. Indirect investments include partnerships that buy and manage property, called real estate syndicates, and investment companies that pool the money of many investors and invest in real estate, called real estate investment trusts (REITs).

FACTS OF LIFE

Returns on REITs can vary quite a bit from year to year. According to the Morgan Stanley REIT Index, REITs fell by about 75 percent between March 2007 and March 2009. Then between March 2009 and March 2017, the index rose by over two and a half times, but REITs were still down about 30 percent from their 2007 high.

Direct Investments in Real Estate

Vacation homes are the most popular of all the direct real estate investments. However, only if your vacation home is viewed as your second home can you deduct your mortgage interest and taxes when you compute your income taxes. Since 1987, the investment appeal of vacation homes has suffered because of a change in the tax laws. Now, if you rent your vacation home for more than 14 days per year, which many investors do, it's considered rental property, and your deductions are determined by how the property is managed and by your income. In the best case, your income will cover your expenses, providing you with a home rent free during vacations, but this generally isn't the case. Because of the complexity surrounding the tax benefits of a vacation home, you really need the help of a tax accountant or financial planner to analyze a vacation home before you invest. Even then, it's important to realize that much of your return is likely to depend on future price appreciation. The bottom line is that if you buy a vacation home, buy it for pleasure, not as an investment.

Commercial property, such as apartment buildings, duplexes, and office buildings, is best left to professionals who specialize in the management of such investments. First, it's too active an investment for most individuals, requiring a lot of time and energy. It also takes a good deal of sophistication, since evaluating a price for commercial property is complicated.

Investing in undeveloped land, although popular among very rich and sophisticated investors, is risky, and because the land is undeveloped, it doesn't produce any cash flow. In fact, because you have to pay taxes on the undeveloped land, it produces a cash outflow while you're holding it. The purpose of buying undeveloped land is to hold it until the value rises and then sell it. However, developing the land to the point where it climbs in price can cost a lot of money. Moreover, as we saw in the late 2000s, there's no guarantee that the land will rise in price. As a result, this investment, too, is better left to the experts.

Indirect Investments in Real Estate

Are indirect investments in real estate, where you are part of an investment group that works directly with a professional real estate manager, better suited for the individual investor? Unfortunately, the appeal of real estate syndicates was severely dampened as a result of tax reform in the late 1980s. Moreover, evaluating how attractive an investment a real estate syndicate is can be quite difficult. Therefore, this is another investment alternative that should be left to the experts.

The most attractive real estate alternative for the individual investor is the real estate investment trust (REIT). Because this type of investment is akin to a mutual fund that specializes in real estate investments, we'll hold off discussion until mutual funds are presented in Chapter 14.

Investing in Real Estate: The Bottom Line

The major advantage of investing in real estate is the income the property can generate, coupled with the opportunity for capital gains. Unfortunately, the tax advantages that helped produce real estate fortunes in the past are largely gone or are on

> **STOP & THINK**
>
> "[Gold] gets dug out of the ground in Africa, or someplace. Then we melt it down, dig another hole, bury it again and pay people to stand around guarding it. It has no utility. Anyone watching from Mars would be scratching their head."–Warren Buffet, Harvard, 1998. What do you think he meant by this?

the way out. In addition, direct investments in real estate are very active forms of investing, in which time, energy, and knowledge are all important ingredients.

Another drawback to investing in real estate is illiquidity. That is, if you do have to sell your property holdings, it may take months to find a buyer, and there's no guarantee that you'll get what you feel is a fair price. In addition, overbuilding and the real estate bubble of the late 2000s have in the past resulted—and can in the future result—in a decline of property prices in some areas. The bottom line is that real estate investment is not well suited to the novice investor.

LO6 Know why you shouldn't *invest* in gold, silver, gems, or collectibles.

Investing—Speculating—in Gold, Silver, Gems, and Collectibles

Don't do it! Putting your money in gold, silver, platinum, precious stones, and the like is not investing—it is speculation. When we differentiated between investing and speculating in Chapter 11, we said that with investing, the value of your asset is determined by what return it earns, not merely by whether that asset is a fashionable one to own or not. If an asset doesn't generate a return, its value is determined by supply and demand, and putting money in it is speculating. Should you speculate? Not if your goal is to create a sound personal financial plan.

Gold, silver, platinum, diamonds, rubies, and collectibles are perfect examples of assets whose purchase is speculation rather than investment. Look at gold. In 1980, when the DJIA was below 1,000, gold peaked at around $850 an ounce. Since then, gold has bounced a bit and did very well from 2005 through 2011, hitting a peak of around $1,900 an ounce in September 2011 before dropping to $1,060 at the end of 2015. By 2017, it was only up slightly to $1,200 an ounce. While gold did very well in 2010 and early 2011, its average annual return since 1980 has been less than 1 percent per year. Over that same period, a typical New York Stock Exchange stock increased at an average annual rate of 11.6 percent. Still, on late-night infomercials across the nation, you continue to see hucksters proclaiming gold as "the place for your savings." Don't buy into their sales pitch—it's another form of speculation.

> **STOP & THINK**
>
> Some people make fortunes dealing in collectibles. Look at Mike Gidwitz, for example, an investment advisor from Chicago who is also an avid collector of cultural memorabilia. In 1997, he paid $640,500 for baseball's most famous and valuable card, the T206 Honus Wagner in mint condition. Mike is a very interesting person who also collects and owns over 100 original paintings for the covers of *Mad* magazine. But as Mike says, "I look at baseball cards like gambling–if you can't afford to lose the money then you shouldn't buy them. I don't buy baseball cards for investment, I buy them for the pleasure I get out of them."* That's a good philosophy. By the way, Mike sold that Honus Wagner card in July 2000 for $1.265 million. Interestingly, that same card sold in 2007 for $2.8 million to the owner of the Arizona Diamondbacks. Would you like to see some of Mike's collection? If so, check it out at **http://www.preciouspaper.com**.
>
> *Reprinted with permission from Mike Gidwitz.

Collectibles deserve a bit more discussion because they have entertainment value; a collector often gets joy out of collecting. However, collectibles are not investments because their resale value is speculative. Stamps, coins, comic books, and baseball cards, for example, are worth more in the future only if someone's willing to pay more for them. Their value depends entirely on supply and demand.

Does this mean you should avoid collectibles? Yes, if you're looking at them as an investment. Remember, an investment is quite a bit duller and more certain than speculation, but when you're dealing with your future financial security, dull and certain aren't bad things. Collectibles can be fun, but don't expect them to provide for your financial future. I (the author), for example, collect original art from *Mad* magazine. There's no question that the price of the art may go down, but to me, that's not a concern ("What, me worry?") because these pieces aren't an investment and I really don't intend to sell them!

BEHAVIORAL INSIGHTS

Principle 9: Mind Games, Your Financial Personality, and Your Money Hopefully at this point you understand how different stocks and bonds interact with each other and how you can reduce the level of risk in your portfolio if you diversify among a number of different asset classes—for example, by putting a number of different stocks and bonds in your portfolio.

PRINCIPLE 9

One problem that gets in the way of this is mental accounting. We've talked about it before, and it involves using mental budgets or "buckets of money" to achieve different goals. It has been shown that many investors think of their portfolios as a pyramid of assets, with different layers or mental accounts of assets within the portfolio representing different goals.[3] For example, your investments for your retirement account would represent one of those layers or mental accounts. The problem with this is that individuals then make their investments for each mental account separately and ignore any interaction between the different accounts. Thus, if one of your goals is to provide income for retirement, you might invest in bonds for the income they produce, and if another of your goals is to preserve wealth, again, you might invest this mental account in bonds. Another one of your mental accounts may line up with an investment in common stocks, and these common stocks will produce some income in the form of dividends. The end result is that you may end up with more income than you need and you may be overinvested in bonds because you have viewed each one of the different portfolio layers or mental accounts as a separate goal. Moreover, by viewing your investments as a pyramid of different mental accounts, you end up with a bunch of mini-portfolios that, when put together, don't really achieve your goals as well as you would like.

ACTION PLAN

Principle 10: Just Do It! Bonds and common stocks are two investments that most individuals make. So let's take a look at some things we can do to improve our chances when investing in bonds.

PRINCIPLE 10

- **Set your goals.** As with common stock, the first thing to do when it comes to investing is to establish your goals—this will determine your asset allocation and how much of your savings should go into bonds.
- **Don't discount the value of holding some bonds for diversification.** They may seem boring when the stock market is riding high, but you'll appreciate them when they slow the downward spiral of your portfolio.
- **Understand taxes and bonds.** While the tax-free nature of municipal bonds is great, it isn't of value to everyone. Compute the equivalent taxable yield for your

[3]Hersh Shefrin and Meir Statman, "Behavioral Portfolio Theory," *Journal of Financial and Quantitative Analysis* 35 (June 2000): 127–151.

tax bracket before you choose them. If you are in a low bracket, you may find that you can make enough with taxable alternatives to pay the taxes and still come out ahead. If you are attempting to avoid state income tax, buy municipals issued by your state of residence.

- **Be aware of the potential downside of bonds.** Consider how you would react if interest rates rose and the value of your bonds dropped, and also keep in mind the fact that shorter-term bonds drop less in price when interest rates climb. Let's face it—interest rates are at historical lows right now, and someday they're going to rise.

Chapter Summaries

LO1 Invest in the bond market.

SUMMARY: Why might you consider investing in bonds? There are several reasons. Bonds reduce risk through diversification, produce steady current income, and, if held to maturity, can be a safe investment.

LO2 Understand basic bond terminology and compare the various types of bonds.

SUMMARY: When you invest in a bond and hold it until it matures, your return is based on two things: (1) the semiannual or annual interest payments and (2) the return of the par value or principal. The danger is that the bond issuer will not have the funds to make these payments. There are two measures of return on a bond: current yield and yield to maturity. The current yield on a bond refers to the ratio of the annual interest payment to the bond's market price. The yield to maturity is the true yield or return the bondholder receives if the bond is held to maturity.

Thousands of outstanding bonds have been issued by corporations, the U.S. government and its agencies, states, and localities. There are also a number of special situation bonds, including zero coupon bonds and junk bonds.

KEY TERMS

Par Value, page 437 The face value of a bond, or the amount that's returned to the bondholder at maturity. It's also referred to as the bond's denomination.

Maturity, page 437 The length of time until the bond issuer returns the par value to the bondholder and terminates the bond.

Coupon Interest Rate, page 437 The annual rate of interest to be paid out on a bond, calculated as a percentage of the par value.

Indenture, page 437 A legal agreement between the firm issuing a bond and the bond trustee, who represents the bondholders.

Call Provision, page 437 A bond provision that gives the issuer the right to repurchase, or "call," the bonds from their holders at a stated price prior to maturity.

Deferred Call, page 437 A bond provision stating that the bond can't be called until a set number of years have passed since it was issued.

Sinking Fund, page 438 A fund in which the bond issuer deposits money to pay off a bond issue.

Corporate Bonds, page 438 Bonds issued by corporations.

Secured Bonds, page 438 Bonds that are backed by the pledge of collateral.

Mortgage Bonds, page 438 Bonds secured by a lien on real property.

Debentures, page 438 Unsecured long-term bonds.

Agency Bonds, page 439 Bonds issued by U.S. government agencies other than the Treasury.

Pass-Through Certificates, page 439 Certificates that represent a portion of ownership in a pool of federally insured mortgages.

Treasury Inflation-Protected Securities (TIPS), page 440 United States Treasury bonds for which the par value changes with the Consumer Price Index to guarantee the investor a real return (i.e., a return that stays above inflation). These bonds have a maturity of 5, 10, or 20 years and a minimum par value of $1,000.

Municipal Bonds or "Munis," page 441 Bonds issued by states, counties, and cities, as well as other public agencies such as school districts and highway authorities, to fund public projects.

General Obligation Bonds, page 441 State or municipal bonds backed by the full faith and credit—that is, the taxing power—of the issuer.

Revenue Bonds, page 441 State or municipal bonds that have interest and par value paid for with funds from a designated project or specific tax.

Serial Maturities, page 441 Bonds, generally municipals, with various maturity dates, usually at set intervals.

Zero Coupon Bonds, page 441 Bonds that don't pay interest and are sold at a deep discount from their par value.

Junk Bonds, page 442 Very risky, low-rated bonds, also called high-yield bonds. These bonds are rated BB or below.

Calculate the value of a bond and understand the factors that cause bond value to change. LO3

SUMMARY: The value of a bond is the present value of the stream of interest payments plus the present value of the repayment of the bond's par value at maturity. There is an inverse relationship between the value of a bond and the investor's required rate of return. Thus, when the investor's required rate of return goes up, the value of the bond drops, and when the investor's required rate of return goes down, the value of the bond increases.

KEY TERMS

Current Yield, page 443 The ratio of the annual interest payment to the bond's market price.

Yield to Maturity, page 444 The true yield or return that the bondholder receives if a bond is held to maturity. It's the measure of expected return for a bond.

Accrued Interest, page 454 Interest that has been earned on the bond but has not yet been paid out to the bondholder.

Invoice Price, page 454 The sum of both the quoted or stated price of a bond and the bond's accrued interest. It's the price you pay if you buy the bond in the secondary market.

Compare preferred stock to bonds as an investment option. LO4

SUMMARY: Preferred stock is a security with no fixed maturity date and with dividends that are generally set in amount and don't fluctuate. Just as with bonds, a firm can issue more than one series or class of preferred stock, each with unique characteristics. In addition, most preferred stock carries a cumulative feature, which requires that all past unpaid preferred stock dividends be paid before any common stock dividends are declared.

KEY TERMS

Preferred Stock, page 454 Stock that offers no ownership or voting rights and generally pays fixed dividends. The dividends on preferred stock are paid out before dividends on common stock can be issued.

Cumulative Feature, page 454 A feature of preferred stock that requires all past unpaid preferred stock dividends to be paid before any common stock dividends can be declared.

Adjustable-Rate Preferred Stock, page 454 Preferred stock on which the quarterly dividends fluctuate with the market interest rate.

Convertible Preferred Stock, page 455 Preferred stock that the holder can exchange for a predetermined number of shares of common stock.

LO5 Understand the risks associated with investing in real estate.

SUMMARY: Real estate investments can be categorized as either direct or indirect. With a direct investment, you directly own the property. With an indirect investment, you're an investor in a group that owns the property and has hired a professional to manage it. These are probably investments best left to the professional.

LO6 Know why you shouldn't invest in gold, silver, gems, or collectibles.

SUMMARY: Gold, silver, platinum, diamonds, rubies, and collectibles are perfect examples of assets whose purchase is speculating rather than investing. As such, you should consider purchasing them only if you aren't concerned about what might happen to their price in the future because they aren't an investment.

Problems and Activities

These problems are available in MyLab Finance.

1. Suppose that you are interested in purchasing a bond issued by the VPI Corporation. The bond is quoted in the *Wall Street Journal* as selling for 88.375. How much will you pay for the bond if you purchase it at the quoted price? Assuming you hold the bond until maturity, how much will you receive at that time?

2. A $1,000 Treasury inflation-protected security is currently selling for $940 and carries a coupon interest rate of 4 percent.

a. If you buy this bond, how much will you receive for your first interest payment, assuming no interest adjustment to principal during this time period?

b. If there's a 1 percent increase in inflation, what will be the new par value of the bond?

c. What is your new semiannual interest payment?

d. What will the par value be at maturity, assuming a 2.5 percent annual inflation rate and a 10-year maturity period?

3. How much will a $500 EE savings bond cost when you initially purchase it? Assuming the bond earns 3.6 percent annually, approximately how long will it take for the bond to reach its stated face value?

4. An investor is considering purchasing a bond with a 5.5 percent coupon interest rate, a par value of $1,000, and a market price of $927.50. The bond will mature in 9 years. Based on this information, answer the following questions:

a. What is the bond's current yield?

b. What is the bond's approximate yield to maturity?

c. What is the bond's yield to maturity using a financial calculator?

5. Three friends—Jodie, Natalie, and Neil—have asked you to determine the equivalent taxable yield on a municipal bond. The bond's current yield is 3.75 percent with 5 years left until maturity. Jodie is in the 15 percent marginal tax bracket, Natalie is in the 25 percent bracket, and Neil is in the 35 percent bracket. Calculate the equivalent taxable yield for your three friends. Assuming a similar AAA corporate bond yields 4 percent, which of your friends should purchase the municipal bond?

6. A highly rated corporate bond with 5 years left until maturity was recently quoted as selling for 103.50. The bond's par value is $1,000, and its initial interest rate is 6.5 percent. If this bond pays interest every 6 months and it has been 4 months since interest was last paid, how much will you be required to pay for the bond?

7. An XYZ April 2041 bond with a 5.5 percent coupon interest rate and a par value of $1,000 recently had a price of 95.625. Calculate the following:

a. When will the bond mature?

b. How much will you have to pay to purchase this bond?

c. If you owned the bond, how much would someone have to pay to buy it from you?

d. What is the current yield, assuming a closing price of 95.50?

8. According to Figure 13.3, as a bond approaches maturity, the premium (or discount) reduces to zero. Prove this by calculating the sales price with 7, 5, and 2 years remaining to maturity for the following two bonds. Assume a constant yield to maturity of 8 percent.

a. A 10-year, 10 percent annual coupon bond

b. A 10-year, 6 percent annual coupon bond

9. Using your financial calculator, calculate the value of the following bonds:

Par Value	Interest Rate	Required Rate of Return	Years to Maturity
$1,000	5%	5%	10
$1,000	5%	9%	10
$1,000	5%	4%	10

10. What is the value (today's price) of a preferred stock that pays an annual dividend of $3.50 when the required rate of return is 8.5 percent? What is the value when the required rate of return changes to 6 percent and 11.5 percent?

Discussion Case 1

This case is available in MyLab Finance.

Miguel, a recent college graduate who heard that you know something about investing, wants to ask about investing in bonds. Miguel indicated that, according to his friends, the stock market was too volatile and bonds were a safer place to invest. Miguel admitted that he really doesn't know much about either stocks or bonds but that he hopes to start saving so that he can purchase a house in the next 5 years. Miguel also mentioned that he had heard about preferred stock and real estate as alternatives to bonds. His roommate recommended that he buy a preferred stock that pays a $4.50 annual dividend or purchase farmland outside of his hometown. Answer the following questions in a way that will help Miguel learn investment concepts.

Questions

1. List four advantages and four disadvantages of investing in bonds.
2. If Miguel thinks that interest rates are going to increase, what type and maturity of bond should he purchase? What type and maturity of bond should he avoid? Why?
3. Develop a checklist of rules that Miguel should use when purchasing a bond.
4. To be as safe as possible, what bond maturity should Miguel choose to meet his home purchase goal? What type(s) of risk does this strategy reduce or avoid?
5. Explain to Miguel why he might want to consider investing in preferred stock rather than bonds.
6. What is the fair market value of the preferred stock that Miguel is considering purchasing if his required rate of return is 8 percent?
7. If Miguel really wants to purchase real estate to meet his objective, is a direct or an indirect real estate investment more appropriate for him? Explain your answer in terms of liquidity, diversification, and safety.

Discussion Case 2

This case is available in MyLab Finance.

About 6 months ago, Jinnie inherited a portfolio that included a number of bonds. Jinnie knows very little about investing in general and practically nothing about bonds specifically. She put together the following chart for your review. All Jinnie knows for sure is that she now owns seven bonds, ranging in maturity from 2 to 10 years. The following chart includes each bond, its Standard & Poor's rating, its maturity, and its current yield.

Bond	Standard & Poor's Rating	Years to Maturity	Current Yield
ABC Corp.	AAA	10	4.75%
XYX Industries	AA	3	3.17%
INTL Limited	A	7	6.11%
MED Corp.	BBB	5	4.40%
SPEC, Inc.	B	2	6.67%
LAM Corp.	CCC	3	25.97%
BAD, Inc.	CC	4	10.19%

Questions

1. After a cursory review of the yields, does anything stand out that should cause Jinnie to worry?
2. In terms of bond maturity dates, what should an investor expect? What is happening in this example?
3. In terms of Standard & Poor's ratings, do you think that the differences in yields are reasonable? (Be sure to also consider time remaining to maturity.)
4. Using your responses from Questions 2 and 3, is Jinnie being adequately compensated for the risk she is taking?
5. What is the minimum interest rate differential that Jinnie should expect between an AAA-rated bond and a BBB-rated bond? Is this the case in the example?

6. If interest rates were to increase by 1 percent or 2 percent, which of the bonds would be the least affected? Which one would be the most affected? Why?
7. If Jinnie asked for a recommendation on which bonds to sell and which to buy more of, what would you recommend? If she purchases more of one particular issue, even if it offers the best risk-adjusted return, to what other types of risks could Jinnie be exposed? (*Hint*: Review the types of risks found in Chapter 11.)
8. Since Jinnie does not plan to use these funds for many years, would Series EE savings bonds or Series I bonds offer any advantage as an investment alternative?
9. If another investor were to purchase one XYX Industries bond (par value of $1,000) at a price of $945, how much in annual interest would be earned?
10. Use the information from Question 9 to determine the new investor's approximate yield to maturity for the XYX Industries bond.

CHAPTER 14

Mutual Funds and Exchange Traded Funds: An Easy Way to Diversify

Learning Objectives

LO1	**Weigh** the advantages and disadvantages of investing in mutual funds.	Why Invest in Mutual Funds?
LO2	**Differentiate** among types of mutual funds, ETFs, and investment trusts.	Investment Companies
LO3	**Calculate** mutual fund returns.	Calculating Mutual Fund Costs and Returns
LO4	**Classify** mutual funds according to objectives.	Types and Objectives of Mutual Funds
LO5	**Select** a mutual fund that's right for you.	Buying a Mutual Fund

For Scott Adams, creator of the *Dilbert* comic strip, it's been a winding climb to the financial top. From 1979 to 1995, Adams worked first at Crocker Bank in San Francisco and then at Pacific Bell. It was there, in 1989, that he began drawing Dilbert, a mouthless engineer with a perpetually bent necktie. Adams was earning about $70,000 and working in cubicle 4S700R when he was fired from Pacific Bell in 1995—"budget constraints" was the reason given.

Today, *Dilbert* appears in more than 1,200 newspapers in 29 countries. Adams's *Dilbert* books ride the top of the best-sellers lists, and his speaking fee is $10,000 per engagement (he speaks about 35 times per year). In short, he's doing a lot better than he was at Pacific Bell.

What does Adams do with all his money? He invests it in mutual funds. That might not be what you'd expect from a guy who has often used his cartoon to make fun of mutual funds. In one comic strip, Dilbert was consulting with a financial advisor who was pushing his firm's "churn 'n' burn" family of mutual funds. "We'll turn your worthless equity into valuable brokerage fees in just three days!" the advisor raved.

Ben Margot/AP Images

In another strip, Dogbert, Dilbert's potato-shaped dog and companion, set himself up as a financial consultant and announced, "I'll tell all my clients to invest in the 'Dogbert Deferred Earnings Fund.'"

"Isn't that a conflict of interest?" Dilbert asks.

"Only if I show interest in the client," replies Dogbert.

Scott Adams, similar to so many novice investors, has found mutual funds to be an ideal way of entering and maintaining a presence in the market. There's an awful lot of comfort in letting a professional manager do all the work for you. As more and more investors have taken advantage of this comfort, mutual funds have seen a dramatic surge in popularity.

In fact, there are over 8,000 mutual funds to choose from today—up from a mere 161 in 1960. Mutual funds' total assets have skyrocketed as well—to over $16.3 trillion in 2017. As Table 14.1 shows, over 44 percent of all U.S. households own mutual funds.

TABLE 14.1 Mutual Fund Facts

U.S. Investment Companies' Total Net Assets	$19.2 trillion
Mutual funds	$16.3 trillion
Exchange-traded funds	$2.5 trillion
Closed-end funds	$262 billion
Unit investment trusts	$85 billion
U.S. Ownership of Funds	
Number of households owning funds	55.9 million
Percentage of households owning funds	44.4%
Median number of funds owned	4

Source: Investment Company Institute, *2017 Fact Book*, 57th ed. (Washington, DC: ICI, 2017).

Mutual Fund
An investment fund that raises funds from investors, pools the money, and invests it in stocks, bonds, and other investments. Each investor owns a share of the fund proportionate to the amount of his or her investment.

Mutual funds are not a different category of investments. Instead, they're a way of holding investments such as stocks and bonds. They pool your money with that of other investors and invest it in stocks, bonds, and various short-term securities. Professional managers then tend this investment, working to make it grow. Mutual funds let you diversify even with small investment amounts. In fact, your investment may be $1,000 or even less, and with that investment, you may own a fraction (a very small fraction) of up to 1,000 different stocks.

PRINCIPLE 8

It's this instant diversification that makes mutual funds so popular with many investors. Remember, as **Principle 8: Risk and Return Go Hand in Hand** tells us, diversification lets you reduce or "diversify away" some of your risk without affecting your expected return, and mutual funds give smaller investors the same ability to diversify and reduce risk as big investors with lots of money have. Still, not all mutual funds are created equally—at least from the investor's perspective. This chapter will help you to make good choices when selecting mutual funds and avoid the "churn 'n' burn" family of funds.

LO1 Weigh the advantages and disadvantages of investing in mutual funds.

Why Invest in Mutual Funds?

Investing in mutual funds provides you with a bevy of benefits, especially if you're a small investor. Mutual funds level the investment playing field between large and small investors. Unfortunately, there are also drawbacks to investing in mutual funds. These disadvantages don't outweigh the advantages of mutual funds, particularly for small investors, but it's good to know what they are. After all, forewarned is forearmed. Let's take a look first at the advantages and then examine the disadvantages of investing in mutual funds.

Advantages of Mutual Fund Investing

- **Diversification.** Mutual funds are an inexpensive way to diversify. For the small investor, this is an extremely important benefit. If you have only $10,000 to invest, it is difficult to diversify your holdings without paying commissions. But when you invest in a mutual fund, you're purchasing a small fraction of the mutual fund's already diversified holdings. Table 14.2 provides a description of the sector diversification along with a listing of the ten largest holdings out of the 262 securities held by Vanguard's Windsor II Fund. As you can see, that degree of diversification couldn't be obtained by an individual investor with limited funds.
- **Professional management.** A mutual fund is an inexpensive way to gain access to professional management. Because fund managers control millions and sometimes even billions of dollars in assets and make huge securities transactions, they have access to all the best research from several brokerage houses. As a result, professional managers are in a much better position to evaluate investments, especially alternative investments. For the small or novice investor, having a professional to lead the way may be essential in taking that first step into the market.
- **Minimal transaction costs.** Because mutual funds trade in such large quantities, they pay far less in terms of commissions. For example, if you were trading stocks valued at less than $1,000, the brokerage fees might run up to 50 cents per

TABLE 14.2 A Listing of Sector Diversification and the Ten Largest Holdings of Vanguard's Windsor II Fund, November 30, 2016

	Equity Sector Diversification		
	Windsor II Fund as of 03/31/2017	**Russell 1000 Value Index as of 03/31/2017**	**Ten Largest Holdings as of 03/31/2017 (24.5% of total net assets)**
Consumer Discretionary	10.00%	4.50%	1. Microsoft Corp.
Consumer Staples	10.50%	8.50%	2. Bank of America Corp.
Energy	8.80%	12.20%	3. Pfizer Inc.
Financials	17.30%	26.50%	4. Medtronic plc
Health Care	19.90%	10.80%	5. Citigroup Inc.
Industrials	10.00%	10.20%	6. JPMorgan Chase & Co.
Information Technology	16.90%	10.00%	7. Wells Fargo & Co.
Materials	2.80%	2.90%	8. Oracle Corp.
Real Estate	0.20%	4.60%	9. Phillip Morris International Inc.
Telecommunication Services	3.10%	3.60%	10. Johnson Controls International plc
Utilities	0.50%	6.20%	

Source: Vanguard, Windsor II Fund, https://personal.vanguard.com/us/funds/snapshot?FundId=0073&FundIntExt=INT, accessed May 7, 2017. © The Vanguard Group, Inc., used with permission.

share. For a mutual fund, those fees might be only 2 cents per share because volume traders (investors who make huge numbers of trades) often have the power to negotiate lower fees. Over the long run, these lower transaction costs should translate into higher returns.

- **Liquidity.** Mutual funds are easy to buy and sell—just pick up the phone or go online. Although many securities can be hard to trade, mutual funds never keep your money tied up while you're waiting for a transaction to take place. In effect, mutual funds are liquid enough to provide easy access to your money.
- **Flexibility.** Given that there are over 8,000 different mutual funds to choose from, it should come as no surprise that they cover many objectives and risk levels. As an individual investor, you should be able to spell out your desired objectives and risk level and, from that, find a fund that fits your needs.
- **Service.** Mutual funds provide you with a number of services that just wouldn't be available if you invested individually. For example, they provide bookkeeping services, checking accounts, automatic systems to add to or withdraw from your account, and the ability to buy or sell with a single phone call. With a mutual fund, you can also automatically reinvest your dividends, interest, and capital gains distributions.
- **Avoidance of bad brokers.** With a mutual fund, you avoid the potentially bad advice, high sales commissions, and churning that can come with a bad broker. Remember, a broker's job is trading—brokers don't make money unless you trade. A mutual fund manager's job is to make you money.

Disadvantages of Mutual Fund Investing

- **Lower-than-market performance.** On average, approximately 80 percent of actively managed stock mutual funds (non-index mutual funds) underperform the market (the S&P 500 Index). Of course, since that's only an average, it does tend to vary quite a bit from year to year—but it doesn't say much for the ability of mutual fund managers to beat the market. Why is that so? Simply because they have some expenses to pay—administrative and brokerage costs—whereas "the market" has no transaction costs at all—it's just a measure of how much stocks go up or down. Still, if your goal in investing is to make money, mutual funds do quite well.

- **Costs.** The costs associated with investing in mutual funds can vary dramatically from fund to fund; investigate their costs before investing. Some funds charge a sales fee or load that can run as high as 8.5 percent, in addition to an annual expense ratio that can run up to 3 percent.
- **Risks.** Not all mutual funds are truly safe. In an attempt to beat the competition, many funds have become specialized or segmented. When mutual funds focus on small sectors of the market, such as "health/biotechnology stocks" or "Latin America," they may be diversified within that sector of the market, but they are not diversified across all the different market sectors. As a result, overall they tend not to be very well diversified because the stocks in different sectors tend to move together. As a result, their returns are subject to unsystematic risk.

  Not all mutual funds are well diversified, and as a result, those that are not well diversified may produce widely variable returns in any year. For example, in the 1-year period ending January 31, 2017, the Fidelity Select Natural Gas Fund returned over 53 percent, while over the same period the Fidelity Select Pharmaceuticals Fund lost over 10 percent. A more diversified fund would have been able to smooth out losses with gains in other areas. Remember, diversification is a huge advantage of mutual funds, but choosing a nondiversified, segmented fund turns that advantage into a disadvantage.

STOP & THINK

"There is some evidence that last year's winners tend to repeat next year. But it is very slight. Mostly the effect comes from the fact that really bad funds stay bad. Their expenses are high, and their choices stay haphazard."—Paul Samuelson. What does this statement tell you about how to choose a mutual fund?

- **You Can't Diversify Away a Market Crash.** Many investors view the diversification of mutual funds as eliminating all risk. You should know better. Remember, as **Principle 8: Risk and Return Go Hand in Hand** notes, you can't diversify away a market crash. If there is a market crash, investing in stock mutual funds isn't going to protect you because all stocks will drop together.

PRINCIPLE 8

- **Taxes.** When you invest using a buy-and-hold strategy, you can assure yourself of long-term capital gains, and you don't pay taxes on your capital gains until you sell your stock. Mutual funds, though, tend to trade relatively frequently, and when they sell a security for a profit, you have to pay taxes on your capital gains. Mutual funds don't let you defer your taxes—they make you pay as you go.

Mutual Fund-Amentals

A mutual fund pools money from investors with similar financial goals. When you invest in a mutual fund, you receive shares in that fund. You're really investing in a diversified portfolio that's professionally managed according to set goals or financial objectives—for example, investing only in international stocks or only in high-yield bonds. These investment objectives are clearly stated by the mutual fund and then used by the fund investment advisor in deciding where to invest.

Your shares in the mutual fund give you an ownership claim to a proportion of the mutual fund's portfolio. In effect, individual investors buy mutual fund shares, the mutual fund managers take this money and buy securities, and the mutual fund shareholders then own a portion of this portfolio. This concept is illustrated in Figure 14.1. It's important to note that mutual fund shareholders don't directly own the fund's securities. Rather, they own a proportion of the overall value of the fund itself.

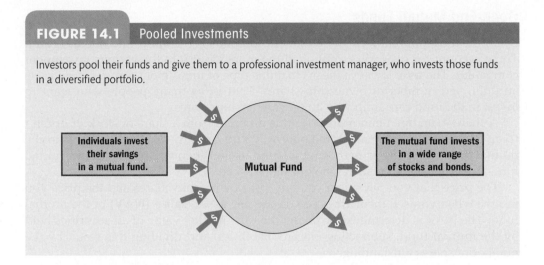

FIGURE 14.1 Pooled Investments

Investors pool their funds and give them to a professional investment manager, who invests those funds in a diversified portfolio.

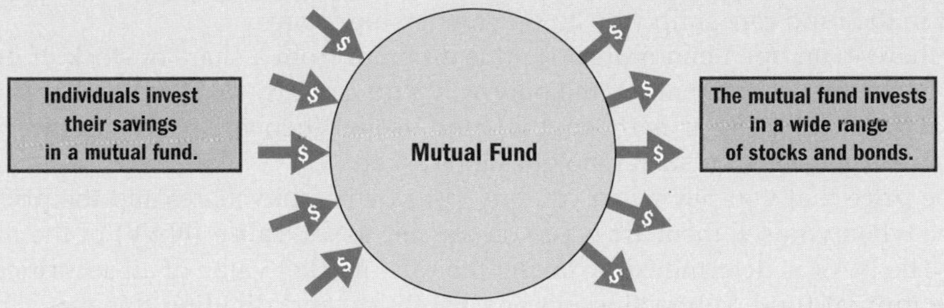

When you own shares in a mutual fund, you make money in three ways:

- First, as the value of all the securities held by the mutual fund increases, the value of each mutual fund share also goes up.
- Second, if a fund receives interest or dividends from its holdings, this income is passed on to shareholders in the form of dividends.
- Third, if the fund sells a security for more than it originally paid for it, the shareholders receive this gain in the form of a capital gains distribution, generally paid annually.

The shareholder, of course, can elect to have these dividends, interest, and capital gains reinvested back into the fund or receive these earnings in the form of a check from the fund. The tax consequence is the same: All distributions, whether paid out or reinvested, are taxable in the year in which they occur.

Before looking at the different types of mutual funds, let's look at how a mutual fund is organized. The fund itself is generally set up as a corporation or trust and is owned by the fund shareholders, who elect a board of directors. The fund is then run by a management company, generally the group that initially organized the fund. Often a management company will run many different mutual funds. In fact, Fidelity and Vanguard, two of the largest management companies, each have a mutual fund for almost every goal.

Each individual fund then hires an investment advisor, generally from the management company, to oversee that particular fund. The advisor supervises the buying and selling of securities. For this service, the advisor is generally paid a percentage of the total value of the fund on an annual basis. This management fee usually runs about one-half of 1 percent, although it can vary considerably from fund to fund. In addition to the management fee, other operating expenses bring the average total cost of operations to about 1 percent of the fund's total assets per year.

Investment Company
A firm that invests the pooled money of a number of investors in return for a fee.

Investment Companies

LO2 Differentiate among types of mutual funds, ETFs, and investment trusts.

Actually, a mutual fund is a special type of **investment company**—that is, a firm that invests the pooled money of a number of investors in return for a fee. In addition to mutual funds, there are a number of other types of investment companies, all of which closely resemble mutual funds.

Open-End Mutual Funds

Open-End Mutual Fund
A mutual fund that has the ability to issue as many shares as investors want. The value of all the investments that the fund holds determines how much each share in the mutual fund is worth.

By far the most popular form of investment company is the **open-end mutual fund**. These account for over 95 percent of all the money put into the various investment companies. The term *open-end* means that this type of investment company can issue an unlimited number of ownership shares. That is, as many people who want to invest in the fund can, simply by buying ownership shares.

A share in an open-end mutual fund is different from a share of stock. It doesn't trade in the secondary market; the only way you can buy ownership shares in the mutual fund is directly from the mutual fund itself. When you want out, the mutual fund will buy back your shares, no questions asked.

Net Asset Value (NAV)
The dollar value of a share in a mutual fund. It's the value of the fund's holdings (minus any debt) divided by the number of shares outstanding.

The price that you pay when you buy your ownership shares and the price you receive when you sell them are based on the **net asset value (NAV)** of the mutual fund. The NAV is determined by taking the total market value of all securities held by the mutual fund, subtracting out any liabilities, and dividing this result by the number of shares outstanding.

$$\text{net asset value (NAV)} = \frac{\text{total market value of all securities} - \text{liabilities}}{\text{total shares outstanding}}$$

For example, if the value of all the fund's holdings is determined to be \$850 million, the liabilities are \$50 million, and there are 40 million shares outstanding, the net asset value would be

$$\text{net asset value (NAV)} = \frac{\$850\text{ million} - \$50\text{ million}}{40\text{ million shares}} = \$20\text{ per share}$$

Closed-End Mutual Fund
A mutual fund that can't issue new shares. These funds raise money only once by issuing a fixed number of shares, and after that, the shares can be traded between investors. The value of each share is determined both by the value of the investments the fund holds and by investor demand for shares in the fund.

In effect, one share, which represents a one-forty-millionth ownership of the fund, can be bought or sold for \$20. Thus, the value of the portfolio that the mutual fund holds determines the value of each share in the mutual fund. Note that the NAV is calculated only once every day, and that happens just after the market close.

Closed-End Mutual Funds

A **closed-end mutual fund** can't issue new shares in response to investor demand. In fact, a closed-end fund has a fixed number of shares. Those shares are initially sold by the investment company at its inception, and after that, they trade between investors at whatever price supply and demand dictate. In effect, a closed-end fund trades more like common stock than a mutual fund.

Just as with common stock, there are a limited number of closed-end fund shares outstanding. When you want to buy (or sell) ownership shares in a closed-end fund that's already in operation, you have to buy them from (or sell them to) another investor in the secondary market. Unlike open-end mutual funds, closed-end funds don't sell directly to you and certainly won't buy back your shares when you want to sell them. Because the price of ownership shares in a closed-end fund is determined by supply and demand for those shares, not by their net asset value, shares in some closed-end funds actually sell above their net asset value, while others sell below it.

FACTS OF LIFE

At the beginning of 2017, bond funds—including both municipal and taxable—made up the largest segment of the \$262 billion closed-end fund market.

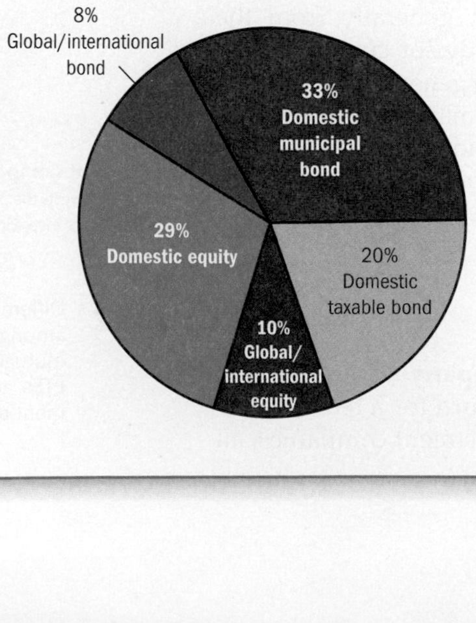

In recent years, closed-end funds have enjoyed a good deal of popularity because they provide investors with a simple way to invest in some markets. For example, the South Korean government holds a relatively tight rein on the common stock of Korean companies. But one easy way to participate in this market is through a closed-end fund such as the Korea Fund; another efficient way is through exchange traded funds, which we will discuss next.

Exchange Traded Funds

Exchange traded funds (ETFs), first issued in 1993, are a hybrid of a mutual fund and an individually traded stock or bond. As the name implies, they are mutual funds that trade on an exchange just as individual securities do and that can be bought and sold throughout the trading day. In effect, whatever you can do with a stock, you can also do with an ETF. You can, for example, sell short or buy them on margin as discussed in Chapter 11. This trading flexibility is the primary advantage that ETFs have over traditional mutual funds. They trade throughout the day, so you can buy and sell them when you want. Table 14.3 lists a number of differences between mutual funds and ETFs.

Exchange Traded Fund (ETF) A hybrid of a mutual fund and an individually traded stock or bond that trades on an exchange just as individual securities do and that can be bought and sold throughout the trading day.

Today, $2.5 trillion is invested in ETFs. Traditionally, ETFs are based on indexes, which means that when you buy an ETF, you're really investing in a bundle of stocks or bonds that make up an index such as the NASDAQ-100 or a sector such as oil services, utilities, or stocks from Japan or Europe. If you're looking to cash in on South Korean, Swedish, or South African companies beyond those that trade on the U.S. exchanges or on small growth companies, where would you go? You'd look for an ETF. And what is nice about them is that they are diversified within a specific sector

TABLE 14.3 Mutual Funds Versus ETFs

	Mutual Funds	ETFs
How They Trade	Prices are determined only once a day—after the market closes—with the price based on the closing price of the fund's holdings. Thus, regardless of when you place your buy or sell order, it will not be processed until after the market closes and will be based on prices at the market's close.	They trade continuously throughout the day, with the price based on supply and demand (investors willing to buy or sell).
Assets (2017)	$16.3 trillion	$2.5 trillion
Trading Costs and Fees	If purchased directly from the fund company, there is no commission. If it is a load fund and purchased through a broker, the commissions can go up to 8.5%, and the asset-weighted average annual expense (mutual fund expenses are weighted by how much money investors have invested in them) for an equity mutual fund is 0.63%. But investors tend to invest in mutual funds with below-average expense ratios, and the simple average expense ratio of equity mutual funds (the simple average for all equity mutual funds) is 1.28%.	A brokerage commission is generally paid when an ETF is bought or sold, and the asset-weighted average annual expense (ETF expenses are weighted by how much money investors have invested in them) for an ETF is only 0.23%. But investors tend to invest in ETFs with below-average expenses, and the simple average expense ratio of EFTs (the simple average for all ETFs) is 0.52%.
Holdings Transparency	They generally report their holdings only on a monthly or quarterly basis.	They generally report the holdings of the ETF daily on the ETF's Web site.

TABLE 14.4 Advantages and Disadvantages of ETFs

Advantages of ETFs

- ETFs trade on an exchange just as individual securities do and can be bought and sold throughout the trading day.
- ETFs can be sold short or bought on margin.
- ETFs allow you to take an instant position in a sector or country that you may not otherwise have access to—for example, biotechnology or Taiwan.
- ETFs have very low annual expenses.
- ETFs are more tax efficient than most mutual funds.

Disadvantages of ETFs

- Because ETFs trade as common stocks do, you pay commissions.
- ETFs don't necessarily trade at their NAVs.
- For investors who trade frequently, ETFs can be more expensive than typical mutual funds. That's because you incur brokerage costs each time you buy or sell ETF shares.

or country. That doesn't mean that they are totally diversified— just that an ETF made up of energy companies will go the way that energy companies as a whole go and not be dominated by one company. Recently, a new variation of ETFs has been introduced, leveraged ETFs, with returns that are a multiple, perhaps two or three times, of the returns on an index. There are also inverse ETFs, which move in an opposite direction to an index; that is, when the index goes up, the ETF goes down.

Because shares in ETFs trade throughout the day just as stocks do, their prices can differ from their NAVs, although in most cases the price differences are quite small. Then, at the end of the trading day, ETFs calculate the value of their holdings to come up with new NAVs for their portfolios, as regular mutual funds do. You can track ETF prices online by name or symbol as you would a share of common stock.

One advantage to ETFs is that they charge lower annual expenses than most mutual funds, ranging all the way down to about 0.05 percent a year. But as with stocks, you pay a commission when you buy or sell. Because you buy them from another investor, you also have the bid-ask spread to deal with. That is, you might be able to buy the ETF at $25.00 but be able to sell it for only $24.85. In short, ETFs may be less expensive than regular mutual funds for those who trade infrequently, but they are more expensive than typical mutual funds for those who trade frequently.

Another advantage to ETFs concerns taxes. With a regular mutual fund, the mutual fund manager must occasionally sell holdings to meet the redemption demands of investors. These sales result in taxable capital gains distributions being paid to shareholders. However, with ETFs, most trading is between shareholders, so the funds don't have to sell stocks to meet redemptions. This fact makes ETFs more tax efficient than most mutual funds.

ETFs have been a huge success because they allow investors who think they know the future direction of a sector, industry, or country to stake out an investment position in that sector, industry, or country. They also allow investors to make their move during the market's trading hours. Table 14.4 lists the advantages and disadvantages of ETFs.

Unit Investment Trusts

Unit Investment Trust
A fixed pool of securities, generally municipal bonds, in which each share represents a proportionate ownership interest in that pool. The bonds are purchased and then held until maturity, at which time the trust is dissolved.

A **unit investment trust** is a fixed pool of securities, generally municipal bonds, with each unit representing a proportionate ownership in that pool. Although very similar to a mutual fund, a unit investment trust is actually an entirely different beast. For example, unit investment trusts aren't managed. Also, instead of actively trading securities (as mutual funds do), unit investment trusts have passive investments.

That is, the trust purchases a fixed amount of bonds and then holds those bonds until maturity, at which time the trust is dissolved. At the beginning of 2017, there were over 5,000 unit investment trusts with a value of $85 billion.

A unit investment trust generally works something like this: First, the investment company announces the formation of the trust and then advertises and sells the ownership shares through brokers. Generally, there's a minimum required investment of around $1,000, from which a sales commission of 3.5 to 4.9 percent is subtracted. The remaining funds are then invested in municipal bonds. The investment company's role is to collect and pass on the interest and principal payments accruing from the bond portfolio to the investors.

The advantage of unit investment trusts comes from the diversification that they offer. Many municipal bonds are relatively risky, and as a result, diversification holds real value. Unfortunately, because most municipal bonds sell with a minimum price of $1,000, many smaller investors simply don't have the funds to allow for sufficient diversification. A unit investment trust solves this problem handily.

Although most investors hold unit investment trusts until maturity, there's a secondary market for some of the larger units. In addition, most brokers stand ready to repurchase and then resell units, although when units are sold to brokers, they generally are sold at a discount. Unit investment trusts are really aimed at the long-term investor. If your time horizon is less than 10 years, avoid unit investment trusts, and stick with mutual funds.

Real Estate Investment Trusts

A **real estate investment trust (REIT)** is similar to a mutual fund in that a professional manager uses the pooled funds of a number of investors to buy and sell a diversified portfolio. In this case, though, all of the holdings in the portfolio deal with real estate. Shares in REITs are traded on the major exchanges, and most REITs have no predetermined life span.

Real Estate Investment Trust (REIT)
An investment vehicle similar to a mutual fund that specializes in real estate investments, such as shopping centers or rental property, or that makes real estate loans.

From the investor's perspective, a REIT looks just like a mutual fund that specializes in real estate rather than securities. There are some technical differences, though. For example, a REIT must collect at least 75 percent of its income from real estate and must distribute at least 95 percent of that income in the form of dividends. In addition, most REITs are actively involved in the management of the real estate that they own.

Note that there are three types of REITs: equity, mortgage, and a hybrid of the two. An equity REIT is one that buys property directly and, in general, also manages that property. When investors buy into an equity REIT, they're hoping that the real estate will appreciate in value. With a mortgage REIT, the investment is limited to mortgages. Investors receive interest payments only, with little chance for capital appreciation. A hybrid REIT invests in both property and mortgages, resulting in some interest and some capital appreciation.

Do REITs make sense? They certainly have some diversification value in that they don't move closely with the general stock market. They're also reasonable alternatives for investors who want to invest in real estate but don't know enough to do it alone. Moreover, although some REITs aren't that liquid, they do tend to be much more liquid than direct investments in real estate.

If you're serious about investing in a REIT, make sure that it's actively traded. (The more heavily traded a security is, the more liquid it is.) However, keep in mind that there are real risks in real estate. As we learned earlier, the real estate market is highly volatile, as the crash in housing prices that began in 2006–2007 demonstrates. As you might have expected, as the housing market plunged in the late 2000s, so did REITs. In fact, the Morgan Stanley REIT Index fell by about 75 percent between March 2007 and March 2009. While it bounced back in the next two years, it still didn't fully recover, and in early 2017, it was still down 8 percent from its 2007 high.

Hedge Funds—Something to Avoid

Hedge Fund
An investment fund that is private, largely unregulated, and very risky and that charges very high fees and allows only wealthy investors to invest.

Hedge funds are investment pools with very few controls—meaning the managers can invest in whatever they want to. That's because they are not regulated by the Securities and Exchange Commission (SEC). They charge very high fees, generally taking "2 and 20"—that is, 2 percent of the assets under management (even when the fund loses money) along with 20 percent of the profits—and some actually take more. For example, the Renaissance Technologies hedge fund takes "5 and 44." On top of that, they won't necessarily give you your money back when you want it, and they generally won't tell you what they're doing with your money. Bernie Madoff ran a hedge fund, and you probably know what happened to it. Because it wasn't truly regulated, Bernie ran it as a Ponzi scheme, where he took money from new investors and used that money to pay the older investors, all the while pocketing most of the money for himself. In the end, around $50 billion was lost, and Bernie ended up behind bars.

Because hedge funds pose so much risk, you can't invest in one unless you are an "accredited investor," which means you have to have a net worth of at least $1 million (not including your house) or your income has to have been at least $200,000 ($300,000 if married) for the past 2 years. Why should you avoid them? Because of their fees, their extreme risk, the fact that you have no idea what they're doing with your money, the inability to get your money back when you want it, and their poor performance. How poor is their performance? Over the 5-year period ending at the beginning of 2017, the average hedge fund returned 37 percent, compared with a return of about 57 percent for the Vanguard Balanced Index Fund, which follows the allocation of 60 percent stocks, 40 percent bonds—and over the same period, the S&P 500 returned about 92 percent. The bottom line is that hedge funds are definitely something you should avoid.

LO3 Calculate mutual fund returns.

Calculating Mutual Fund Costs and Returns

Although some mutual funds have no sales commission, others impose a commission when you buy into the fund or when you liquidate your holdings, some require a hefty annual management fee, and still others pass on marketing expenses to shareholders. To say the least, the costs associated with mutual funds are complicated.

Load Versus No-Load Funds

Load
A sales commission charged on a mutual fund.

Load Fund
A mutual fund on which a load or sales commission is charged.

Mutual funds are classified as either load or no-load funds. As you'll see, the decision between a load versus a no-load mutual fund is an easy one—you want a no-load fund. A **load** is mutual fund "speak" for a sales commission. **Load funds** are actually mutual funds that are sold through brokers, financial advisors, and financial planners, who tack on the sales commissions/loads for themselves. These commissions can be quite large. Typically, they are in the 4 percent to 6 percent range, but they can run all the way up to 8.5 percent. If you decide to buy mutual funds through an advisor or broker, you'll choose from among three different "classes" of funds called Class A, Class B, and Class C shares. These are really the same "pool," or portfolio, of securities but with different fee arrangements.

Back-End Load
A commission that's charged only when the investor liquidates his or her holdings.

- *Class A shares* have a front-end sales load or fee paid when the funds are purchased.
- *Class B shares* have a **back-end load** called a contingent deferred sales load (CDSL), which declines to zero after 5 to 10 years, as well as higher expenses. Thus, with Class B shares, the up-front sales commission is eliminated and

replaced with an annual charge of around 1 percent, in addition to the back-end load, or CDSL, which generally is about 5 percent of your initial investment or the market value of your investments, whichever is smaller. The back-end load then declines annually; you might pay 5 percent if you sell the fund in the first year, 4 percent if you sell the fund in the second year, 3 percent if you sell the fund in the third year, and so forth until the fee just disappears.

- *Class C shares* have you pay both coming and going. Class C shares generally have the highest annual fees; may, although generally don't, have a front-end load; and have a CDSL that may disappear after 2 years or may not disappear at all.

Bear in mind that Classes A, B, and C are all of the same fund; only the fees and expenses change. Many fund families also have other classes of shares, but those are usually for institutional investors or for investments from tax-deferred savings plans such as 401(k) plans.

No-Load Fund
A mutual fund that doesn't charge a commission.

A mutual fund that doesn't charge a commission on your ownership shares is referred to as a **no-load fund**. When you purchase a no-load mutual fund, you generally don't deal with a broker or advisor. Instead, you deal directly with the mutual fund investment company via direct mail or a toll-free telephone number. There's no salesperson to pay and, as a result, no load. If you need advice, simply call one of the no-load families of funds such as Vanguard, and an investment advisor will help you out—and at no cost.

FACTS OF LIFE

Empirical studies suggest that, without question, fees and expenses should be your primary consideration in picking funds. However, according to the Investment Company Institute, only 43 percent of investors make it a consideration when buying a fund.

Keeping costs down is always an excellent idea, which makes no-load funds seem the obvious choice. It's a fact that no-load funds perform just as well as load funds—they just don't have salespeople on commission. Without question, you're better off with a no-load fund.

Management Fees and Expenses

Managing a mutual fund costs money—a lot of it. Funds run up big expenses paying the investment advisor, the custodian, the transfer agent, and the underwriter, in addition to the sales commissions on securities trades, operating expenses, legal fees, and so on. You'd be wise to keep an eye on these expenses. Be sure to check out a fund's **expense ratio**, which compares the fund's expenses to its total assets (expense ratio = expenses/assets). Typically, this ratio ranges from 0.05 to 2 percent, although some funds have expense ratios that run in excess of 4 percent.

Expense Ratio
The ratio of a mutual fund's expenses to its total assets.

You want to be sure to invest in a fund with a nice, low expense ratio. Why? Because the funds themselves don't pay the cost of their expenses—you do. Mutual funds are quick to pass their expenses on to you, with these expenses paid for by selling some of the fund's securities and thereby lowering the net asset value. The trading costs make up a good-sized portion of a typical fund's expenses and are closely related to the fund's **turnover ratio or rate**, which provides a measure of the level of the fund's trading activity. In general, the higher the turnover ratio, the higher the fund's expenses. In addition, the larger the turnover, the greater the short- and/or long-term capital gains taxes. Remember, you pay capital gains taxes only when you sell a stock.

Turnover Ratio or Rate
A measure of the level of a fund's trading activity, indicating what percentage of the fund's investments are turned over during the year.

12b-1 Fees

Because mutual funds must become known in the marketplace, they tend to have some marketing expenses. Marketing expenses, including advertising and

TABLE 14.5 Different Mutual Fund Costs

No-Load Funds:	No sales charge
Load Funds:	Sales charge up to 8%
Class A Shares:	Front-end load
Class B Shares:	Back-end load, also called a contingent deferred sales load, that generally declines to zero after 5 to 10 years, in addition to an annual charge of around 1%
Class C Shares:	Highest annual fees and in some cases a contingent deferred sales load that doesn't disappear
Management Fees:	Fees paid to the fund advisor
Expense Ratio:	The ratio of the fund's expenses to the fund's assets
12b-1 Fees:	Marketing fees passed on to the shareholder, ranging up to 1%

FACTS OF LIFE

Watch out for high fees. Don Philips, president of Morningstar, once said, "If you pay the executives at Sarah Lee more, it doesn't make the cheesecake less good. But with mutual funds, it comes directly out of the batter."

12b-1 Fee
An annual fee, generally ranging from 0.25 to 0.75 percent of a fund's assets, that the mutual fund charges its shareholders for marketing costs.

promotional fees, are passed on to the fund shareholders through **12b-1 fees**. These fees can run up to 1 percent annually, and they don't benefit the shareholders in the least. They serve only to allow the fund manager to pass on some of the fund's expenses. Where do these fees really go? According to a survey by the Investment Company Institute, most of these fees go to brokers and bank trust departments, not for marketing and promotion as initially intended. They do make someone wealthy, but it's not the investor. In fact, studies have found that funds that charge these fees have higher expense ratios but don't exhibit better performance. In effect, a 12b-1 fee is a hidden (you have to read through the fund's literature or ask to find it) and continuous load, as every year you pay out a portion of your investment to cover the fund's marketing costs.

Is there any value to you from the 12b-1 fee? No, no, and no. If your fund earns 10 percent before a 1 percent 12b-1 fee, after the fee it earns only 9 percent. If you invested $10,000 in this fund and left it in for 20 years earning 10 percent, you'd end up with $67,275, but if it was earning 9 percent, you'd end up with only $56,044. The 12b-1 fee just cost you $11,231. There is no advantage to that! After all, the purpose of investing is to make yourself, not your broker, rich.

A summary of the different mutual fund costs is provided in Table 14.5.

Calculating Mutual Fund Returns

Let's now take a look at returns and how you can figure out the return a mutual fund will make for you. The return from investing in a mutual fund can be in the form of distributions of dividends, capital gains, or a change in the NAV of the shares held. To qualify as an investment company and avoid being taxed on the fund's earnings, a fund must distribute a minimum of 97 percent of the interest and dividends earned and at least 90 percent of the capital gains income. (Capital gains result from selling securities for more than you originally paid for those securities.)

Thus, we can calculate the total return from a mutual fund as follows:

$$\text{total return} = \frac{\text{dividends distributed} + \text{capital gains distributed} + \text{ending NAV} - \text{beginning NAV}}{\text{beginning NAV}}$$

For example, let's assume we have a fund with

$$\text{beginning NAV} = \$19.45$$
$$\text{ending NAV} = \$23.59$$
$$\text{dividends distributed} = \$\,0.60$$
$$\text{capital gains distributed} = \$\,0.47$$

We can calculate our return as follows:

$$\text{total return} = \frac{\$0.60 + \$0.47 + (\$23.59 - \$19.45)}{\$19.45}$$
$$= \frac{\$0.60 + \$0.47 + \$4.14}{\$19.45}$$
$$= \frac{\$5.21}{\$19.45} = 26.79\%$$

The return is 26.79 percent.

If you automatically reinvest any distributions, your return is a result of both the increase in the NAV of the shares and the increased number of shares you hold. As you automatically reinvest any distributions, the number of shares that you hold increases. As a result, you can calculate your return by taking the value of your ending holdings minus your initial investment and divide this by the value of your initial investment.

$$\text{total return} = \frac{(\text{number of ending shares} \times \text{ending price}) - (\text{number of beginning shares} \times \text{beginning price})}{\text{number of beginning shares} \times \text{beginning price}}$$

Thus, if you initially purchase 500 shares at an NAV of $19.45 and, as a result of automatically reinvesting any distributions, you end up with 585 shares with an NAV of $23.59, you can calculate your return as follows:

$$\text{total return} = \frac{(585 \times \$23.59) - (500 \times \$19.45)}{500 \times \$19.45}$$
$$= \frac{\$13{,}800.15 - \$9{,}725.00}{\$9{,}725.00}$$
$$= \frac{\$4{,}075.15}{\$9{,}725.00} = 41.90\%$$

The return is 41.9 percent. Keep in mind, though, that these formulas don't take taxes into account.

Calculating a fund's return should help you spot funds that have been consistent winners over time and avoid those that have performed poorly. Once you've found a fund that fits your objectives, keep a close eye on expenses and fees, and try to keep them to a minimum. After that, you might as well go for past winners and avoid losers. There is strong evidence that minimizing fees and expenses can put you on a path toward better returns. There is also evidence that strong performers over the past 3 years remain strong performers for the following 3 years.

STOP & THINK

Look closely at the expenses and fees charged for managing a mutual fund before investing—their impact can be significant. Look, for example, at a mutual fund with an expense ratio of 1.3 percent (the average expense ratio for an actively managed equity fund—that is, a non-index mutual fund—is around 1.25 percent) versus one with an expense ratio of 0.05 percent. If you put $25,000 in both of these funds, each returning 10 percent compounded over the next 25 years, you'd end up with a not so insignificant $64,000 more in the lower-expense fund. In choosing a mutual fund, what would you look for?

LOVE & MONEY

Getting divorced is expensive and painful, and as you will see in Chapter 17, avoiding divorce is one of the 12 keys to financial success. Those who stay married tend to do better financially than those who divorce—and it's not even close. On top of that, they also tend to be happier, so is there anything you can do when making money-related decisions that will help you improve your odds of staying married? As it turns out, it appears that there may be a number of steps you can take, and these steps will not only improve your odds of staying together but also make you a happier couple. But keep in mind, that while these relationships we will discuss may not be causal, they sure are interesting and thought provoking.

First, don't equate an expensive engagement ring with a more lasting commitment. A study by Emory University researchers found that couples were 1.3 times more likely to divorce if their engagement ring cost between $2,000 and $4,000 versus $500 to $2,000.[1] Why might this be the case? One answer could be that spending more on an engagement ring adds to the financial stress that a couple might experience once they are married. On the other hand, you probably don't want to cheap out either. That same study found that those who spent less than $500 on an engagement ring also experienced higher divorce rates.

The same logic and findings also hold for how much you spend on your actual wedding. You might think that spending a lot on a wedding is a sign of commitment and will lead to a longer marriage. The findings show the opposite: The more you spend, the more likely you'll eventually get divorced, and given the fact that The Knot's 2016 Real Wedding Study found that the average cost of a wedding was $32,641, this is a scary finding! Specifically, researchers found that couples that spent $20,000 or more as opposed to $5,000 to $10,000 were almost 50 percent more likely to divorce.[2] We don't know exactly why this takes place, but again it may simply be that the financial burden resulting from an expensive wedding leads to financial stress that eventually contributes to divorce.

While spending on a wedding doesn't seem to help the marriage's longevity, spending on a honeymoon does. It seems that couples who go on a honeymoon lower their chance for divorce by 41 percent relative to those who skip the honeymoon. Perhaps the lesson from this finding is to trim a bit from the wedding and put it toward the honeymoon. Just don't put that honeymoon on your credit card! Remember, you are trying to lower the financial pressure that you are putting on your new life together.

Other relationships are a bit more expected. For example, credit card or other consumer debt has a dramatically negative impact on married life. As newlyweds take on more debt, both their financial unease and their fights over money increase. And research has shown that fights over money are the top predictor of divorce.[3] On the other hand, couples that are able to accumulate assets together reduce their chances of divorce.

The bottom line here is that you've got to be money-smart when you're approaching marriage, and don't just think that spending for the glamour of an over-the-top wedding equals a happy marriage. More important is financial control as you combine two separate lives into a married relationship with common goals and purpose. You both need to confront and resolve financial issues, making sure that you aren't spending money that you don't have for show.

---

[1]Andrew M. Francis and Hugo M. Mialon, "'A Diamond Is Forever' and Other Fairy Tales: The Relationship Between Wedding Expenses and Marriage Duration," September 15, 2014, https://ssrn.com/abstract=2501480.

[2]Ibid.

[3]J. Dew, S. Britt, and S. Huston, "Examining the Relationship Between Financial Issues and Divorce," *Family Relations* 61 (2012): 615–628.

Types and Objectives of Mutual Funds

LO4 Classify mutual funds according to objectives.

To make choosing mutual funds a little easier, funds are categorized according to objective. However, these classifications aren't always completely reliable because fund managers classify their own funds. A fund manager might classify a fund as a stock fund when, in reality, its major holdings are bonds. Hey, you don't have to believe everything you read.

When choosing a mutual fund, first figure out what your objectives are. What do you want a mutual fund to do for you? Once you've figured that out, you have but to look, and chances are one of the many mutual funds will suit your needs perfectly—or at least claim to. Before investing, be sure that a given mutual fund actually lives up to its classification. Look deeper than the title of the fund, and check out what it really holds. And also take a close look at expenses. You want them low because, regardless of the mutual fund's objectives, if the expenses are high, there is a good chance it won't perform as well as you want.

Money Market Mutual Funds

Money market mutual funds invest in Treasury bills, certificates of deposit, and other very short-term investments, usually those with maturities of less than 30 days. Because these investments are of such short maturity, they're generally regarded as practically risk free. Money market securities require significant investments—ranging from $10,000 upward, placing them out of the reach of the common investor. Money market mutual funds, on the other hand, use the pooling principle to make these short-term investments available to the smaller investor.

Money Market Mutual Fund
A mutual fund that invests in Treasury bills, certificates of deposit, commercial paper, and other short-term notes, generally with a maturity of less than 30 days.

You may have even seen money market funds offered at your local bank, and, in fact, many of these funds work much like interest-bearing checking accounts. For a minimum investment of usually $1,000, you tend to get interest rates that are tied to short-term interest rates and are, thus, higher than you can earn on a basic savings account, as well as limited check-writing privileges. One of the limits on this privilege is that you can't write checks for less than $250 to $500. Money market mutual funds have proved immensely popular because they carry no loads, trade at a constant NAV of $1, and have very minimal expense ratios.

The extreme popularity of money market mutual funds has spawned several specialized variations. One is the **tax-exempt money market mutual fund**, which invests only in very short-term municipal debt. The returns on these funds are exempt from federal taxes, making them popular investments among people in higher tax brackets.

Tax-Exempt Money Market Mutual Fund
A money market mutual fund that invests only in very short-term municipal debt.

There are also money market mutual funds that invest solely in U.S. government securities in order to avoid any risk whatsoever. These funds are commonly called **government securities money market mutual funds**. They pay a rate slightly lower than that of traditional money market mutual funds but in theory are safer. However, because of the very short maturities of their holdings and the extreme diversification associated with money market mutual funds, there's virtually no risk in them anyway.

Government Securities Money Market Mutual Fund
A money market mutual fund that invests solely in U.S. government securities in order to avoid any risk whatsoever.

Stock Mutual Funds

Of the different types of mutual funds, **stock funds** or equity funds are by far the most popular, accounting for over half of all mutual funds, as Figure 14.2 shows. But don't think that these funds hold *nothing* but stocks. They do have some limited holdings in cash, bonds, and short-term investments. Nevertheless, their main emphasis is indeed firmly on stock.

Stock Fund
A mutual fund that invests primarily in common stock.

Because the stock market is so varied and wide-ranging, there are many different types of stock funds to choose from. When reading the following discussion of

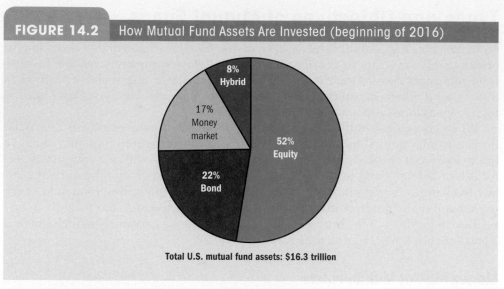

FIGURE 14.2 How Mutual Fund Assets Are Invested (beginning of 2016)

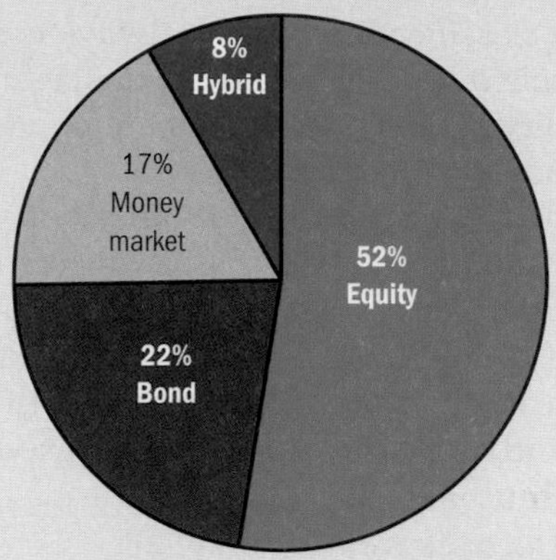

Source: Investment Company Institute, *2017 Fact Book*, 57th ed. (Washington, DC: ICI, 2017).

some of the more popular types of stock funds, think about which ones might be best suited for your investment objectives.

Aggressive Growth Funds An aggressive growth fund is one that tries to maximize capital appreciation while ignoring income. In other words, these funds tend to go for stocks whose prices could rise dramatically, even though these stocks tend to pay very small dividends. Thus, the dividend yield on stocks in funds of this type tends to be quite low. Stocks with high price/earnings (P/E) ratios and those of young companies are perfect for aggressive growth funds. Unfortunately, these stocks not only can gain big but can lose big, too. As a result, the ownership shares of aggressive growth funds tend to experience wider price swings, both up and down, than do the share prices on other funds.

Small Company Growth Funds Small company growth funds are similar to aggressive growth funds except they limit their investments to small companies. The purpose of small company growth funds is to uncover and invest in undiscovered companies with unlimited future growth. Again, these are very risky funds with a good deal of price volatility.

Growth Funds The differences between aggressive growth funds and growth funds are pretty small, but growth funds generally pay more attention to strong firms that pay dividends. Growth funds are still looking for the potential big gainers, but they are less risky than their aggressive growth cousins. Because of the stable dividends, their shares tend to bounce around less in price.

Growth-and-Income Funds This general category of funds tries to invest in a portfolio that will provide the investor with a steady stream of income in addition to having the potential for increasing value. These funds focus on everything from well-established blue-chip companies with strong stable dividends and growth opportunities to stocks with low P/E ratios and above-average dividends. Because of the steady income these funds provide, the shares tend to fluctuate in price less than the market as a whole.

Sector Funds A sector fund is a specialized mutual fund that generally invests at least 65 percent of its assets in securities from a specific industry. For example, there are sector funds dealing with the chemicals, computer, financial services, health/biotechnology, automobile, environmental, utilities, and natural resources industries, to name just a few. Although investing in these funds is much less risky than investing in a single stock, sector funds are riskier than traditional mutual funds because they're less diversified. In fact, the idea behind a sector fund is to *limit* the degree of diversification by limiting investment to a specific industry.

If that industry or part of the world does well, the sector fund does well. If that industry or part of the world has a rough time, so does the sector fund. For example, Russian stocks did very well in 2016, boosted by the election of Donald Trump. As a result, mutual funds that bet against Russian stocks lost—for example, the Direxion Russian Bear 3X dropped by over 97 percent in 2016. On the other hand, mutual funds that bet with the Russian stock market did extremely well in 2016, and as a result, the VnEck Vctrs:Russia SmCp went up by just over 100 percent. So if you're going to invest in a sector or country fund, make sure that you diversify your holdings, perhaps among a number of different mutual funds. Investing in a single sector fund isn't going to provide you with the diversity that makes mutual funds so advantageous.

> **STOP & THINK**
>
> When you see a listing of the best-performing mutual funds, invariably a sector or country fund will appear at the top of the list. However, a sector fund will also appear at the bottom of the list. Their lack of diversity makes sector funds highly volatile and not for the faint of heart. Would you risk putting all your eggs—and dollars—in a single industry? If not, sector funds aren't for you.

Index Funds An index fund is one that tries to track a market index. For example, an S&P 500 index fund buys the stocks that make up the S&P 500. Much of the value of an index fund comes from its low expense ratio, which can be anywhere from 0.10 to 1.35 percent lower than the ratios of other funds. These funds are great for those who don't want to try to "beat the market" and who want the diversification of a mutual fund with costs as low as possible. Also, index funds tend to outperform actively managed funds—that is, those that try to pick winners. This is because actively managed funds incur more expenses. We've already pointed out that it is easy to spot fund characteristics that result in poor performance: high expense ratios and high turnover ratios resulting from more trading. Unfortunately it's tougher to identify mutual funds that outperform the market. The bottom line here is that, on average, index funds tend to beat actively managed funds.

International Funds An international fund concentrates its investments in securities from other countries. In fact, two-thirds of the fund's assets must be invested outside the United States. Some international funds focus on general world regions—the Pacific Basin, Latin America, or other emerging markets. Some focus on specific countries—Japan, Canada, and even places like Peru—in an attempt to capture abnormal growth in their specific area of the world. Other international funds look for companies outside the United States that have the potential for abnormal growth and invest directly in them, regardless of location. One advantage of these funds is that they tend not to move perfectly with the U.S. stock market and, thus, can serve to reduce the variability of returns for all your holdings combined.

Since these funds open you up to political and currency risks not present with domestic stocks, it's important to understand the political and economic climate of all the countries represented in an international fund.

Balanced Mutual Funds

A **balanced mutual fund** is one that holds both common stock and bonds and, in many cases, also preferred stock. The objective of these funds is to earn steady income plus some capital gains. In general, these funds are aimed at those who need steady

Balanced Mutual Fund
A mutual fund that tries to "balance" the objectives of long-term growth, income, and stability. To do this, these funds invest in a mix of common stock and bonds, as well as preferred stock in some cases.

FACTS OF LIFE

Today, almost half of all U.S. households own mutual funds.

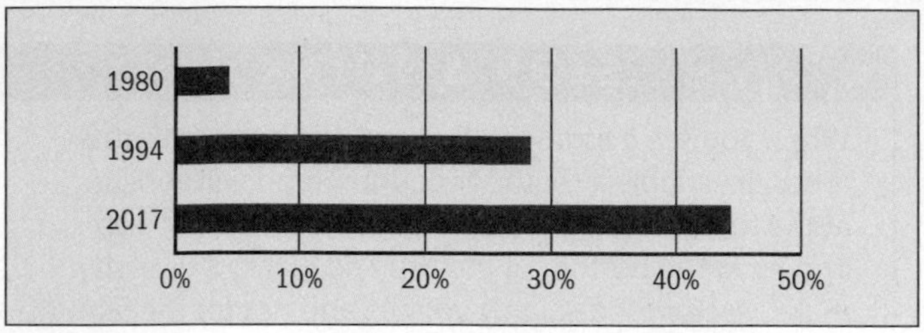

Source: Investment Company Institute, *2017 Fact Book*, 57th ed. (Washington, DC: ICI, 2017).

income to live on, moderate growth in capital, and moderate stability in their investments.

As you might expect, the ratio of bonds to stocks can vary dramatically between balanced funds. Not all balanced funds are equally balanced. In fact, some balanced mutual funds specialize in international securities, hoping to cash in on high returns elsewhere around the world. Still, on the whole, balanced funds tend to be less volatile than stock mutual funds.

Asset Allocation Funds

Asset Allocation Fund
A mutual fund that invests in a mix of stocks, bonds, and money market securities.

An **asset allocation fund** is quite similar to a balanced fund in that it invests in a mix of stocks, bonds, and money market securities. In fact, these funds have been described as balanced funds with an attitude. Asset allocation funds differ from balanced funds in that they move money between stocks and bonds in an attempt to outperform the market. That is, when the fund manager feels stocks are on the rise, a higher proportion of the fund's assets are allocated to stocks.

Asset allocation funds can be viewed as balanced funds that practice market timing. Unfortunately, the track record for market timers is less than impressive. In fact, market-timing attempts are more likely to produce additional transaction costs rather than additional returns. Think carefully before investing in such a fund.

Life Cycle and Target Retirement Funds

Life Cycle Fund
A mutual fund that tries to tailor its holdings to the investor's individual characteristics, such as age and risk tolerance.

Life cycle funds are the newest type of mutual fund to hit the market. They're basically asset allocation funds that try to tailor their holdings to the investor's individual characteristics, such as age and risk tolerance. Life cycle funds go beyond the traditional strategies of growth and income and instead focus on where you are in your financial life cycle. For example, in 2017, Vanguard had four LifeStrategy funds, each one aimed at satisfying the objectives of the four different stages of the financial life cycle we discussed in Chapter 1.

Target Retirement Fund
A mutual fund professionally managed for an investor's stage of retirement planning, with the investments in the fund automatically growing more conservative as the investor's retirement date nears.

With **target retirement funds**, the decision as to how much to invest in stocks, bonds, and money market instruments is made for you, and the only decision you have to make is when you plan to retire. Once you've invested in a target retirement fund, that fund is professionally managed for your stage of retirement planning, with the investments in the fund automatically growing more conservative as your retirement date nears. For example, if you're in your 40s and have 20 years until retirement, you might invest in Vanguard's Target Retirement 2040 Fund. This fund begins with an 87/13 stocks/bonds mix when you have 20 years left to retirement and gradually declines to a 50/50 stocks/bonds mix by the time you retire.

Bond Funds

Bond Fund
A mutual fund that invests primarily in bonds.

Bond funds appeal to investors who want to invest in bonds but don't have enough money to diversify adequately. In general, bond funds emphasize income over growth. Although they tend to be less volatile than stock funds, bond funds fluctuate in value as market interest rates move up and down.

Bond funds have a number of differences from individual bond purchases.

- With an investment of as little as $1,000 you can buy into a diversified bond portfolio. Then you can add to your investment with smaller amounts whenever you wish.
- Bond funds offer more liquidity than individual bonds. As we noted in Chapter 13, one of the disadvantages of investing in bonds is that they can be

difficult to sell before maturity. With a bond fund, you can both buy and sell at whatever the fund's NAV is, and you don't have to worry about getting a bad price when forced to sell an individual bond at the "wrong time."

- With a bond fund, you're getting professional management.
- Similar to an individual bond, a bond fund produces regular income. However, with a bond fund, you can choose to receive a monthly check to help your cash flow, or you can have your money automatically reinvested in the fund to buy more shares in it.
- If you buy bonds directly rather than through a bond fund, you won't have any mutual fund expenses to deal with.
- The bond fund doesn't mature, whereas individual bonds do. When bonds within the bond fund mature, they're replaced with new bonds. As a result, you're never guaranteed to receive a lump-sum payment.

STOP & THINK

The expense ratios on bond mutual funds can vary dramatically. The average expense ratio in 2016 for all bond funds, both index funds and actively managed funds, was 0.54 percent, and this ratio ranged from approximately 0.08 to over 2 percent. Given the fact that long-term government bonds averaged a return of only about 4.44 percent from 2000 to the beginning of 2017, it's extremely important to keep expenses low if you're investing in bond funds. If your expenses are 2 percent and your return is only 4.44 percent, almost half of your return is already gone. What does this tell you about what to look for when choosing a bond mutual fund?

If your objective is income, bonds or a bond fund is a logical choice. Whether to buy a bond or a bond fund will depend on your individual situation and needs. You'll probably look closer at a bond fund if you want to invest small amounts of money, if you need to keep your investments liquid, or if you'll sleep better at night knowing a professional's choosing the securities and keeping them well diversified. Conversely, if you need to know with certainty that in a specific number of years you'll get the principal back, you have a large amount to invest, and you're disciplined enough to reinvest your interest payments, then you might want to stick with individual bonds.

Bond funds can be differentiated both by the type of bonds that they invest in—U.S. government, municipal, or corporate—and by maturity—short term, intermediate term, or long term.

U.S. Government Bond Funds and GNMA Bond Funds A U.S. government bond fund invests in securities issued by the federal government or its agencies. For example, U.S. Treasury bond funds specialize in Treasury securities. There's no default risk associated with these funds. However, they do fluctuate in value as interest rates move up and down.

A number of funds specialize in mortgage-backed securities issued primarily by the Government National Mortgage Association (GNMA), also known as Ginnie Mae. These funds hold pools of individual residential mortgages that have been packaged by GNMA and resold to the bond fund. This type of fund carries interest rate risk in addition to prepayment risk—that is, the risk that as interest rates drop, the mortgages will be refinanced and prepaid. As with other bond funds, a government bond fund is aimed at those who need steady current income.

Municipal Bond Funds The advantage of municipal bond funds is that the interest is generally exempt from federal taxes. The higher your tax rate is, the more value municipal bond funds have for you. Moreover, if you invest in a municipal bond fund that invests only in bonds from your state, the income may also be exempt from state taxes. In fact, if you live in New York City and invest in a fund that limits its investments to municipal bonds issued by New York City, you avoid federal, state, and local income taxes on the interest payments. For investors in higher tax brackets, avoiding taxes is a big deal.

Corporate Bond Funds Unless you haven't been paying any attention at all, you've probably guessed that corporate bond funds invest in various corporate bonds. Some corporate bond funds focus mainly on high-quality, highly rated bonds, but others, usually called high-yield corporate bond funds, focus on the much lower-rated and much riskier junk bonds. As you know from **Principle 8: Risk and Return Go Hand in Hand**, when you take on more risk, as you do when you invest in junk bonds, your expected return is higher.

PRINCIPLE 8

Because corporate bonds have the potential for defaulting, it's essential that you diversify if you're going to invest in them. That's where a corporate bond fund comes in—it does the diversifying for you. Of course, you'll want to carry this diversification a bit further by investing in more than just bonds.

When selecting a corporate bond fund, remember that over one-third of them carry loads in the 4 to 5 percent range. Although the loads are pretty constant, the returns aren't. As interest rates go up, corporate bond fund values go down, along with their NAV. As interest rates drop, corporate bond fund values rise, along with their NAV.

Bond Funds and Their Maturities Different bond funds also specialize in maturities of different lengths, with short-term (1 to 5 years to maturity), intermediate-term (5 to 10 years to maturity), and long-term (10 to 30 years to maturity) funds. We know from the bond valuation relationships presented in Chapter 13 that there's an inverse relationship between interest rates and bond prices. That is, when interest rates rise, bond prices drop, and when interest rates drop, bond prices rise. We also know that when interest rates change, longer-term bonds fluctuate in price more than shorter-term bonds. As a result, the longer the bond fund's maturity, the higher its expected return, but also the greater the fluctuation in its NAV if interest rates change.

Mutual Fund Services

Aside from the fact that you can probably find a mutual fund with objectives that almost perfectly match your investment goals, what's so special about mutual funds? A lot, actually. Diversification is probably the biggest advantage, but convenience may well be a close second. Mutual funds offer the convenience of being able to buy and sell securities at will, with reduced commissions and professional advice.

That's really just the tip of the convenience iceberg, though. Mutual funds offer myriad services for investors—services that make investing easy and even fun. Let's take a look at a few of the more popular services. As we do, think about which services would be most helpful and appealing to you.

Automatic Investment and Withdrawal Plans An automatic investment plan allows you to make regular deposits directly from your bank account. For example, if you want to invest $100 on the fifteenth of each month, an automatic investment plan lets you do so without lifting a finger. Basically, all you need do is check a box on the mutual fund's account registration form and *voilà*—your $100 will find its way from your savings account to your fund account each and every month. An automatic investment plan is a way of dollar cost averaging when investing in a mutual fund. Recall from Chapter 12 that the logic behind dollar cost averaging is that by investing the same dollar amount on a regular basis, you'll be buying more common stock when the price is lowest and less when the price is highest.

The automatic investment plan is also a good way of moving excess funds from a money market account into the stock market. For example, if you have more money than you feel you need invested in a money market account but are worried about transferring it all at once into the stock market, an automatic investment plan will let you move the funds into the market smoothly over a longer period of time.

Conversely, an automatic or systematic withdrawal plan allows you to withdraw a dollar amount or a percentage of your mutual fund account on a monthly basis. For example, if you were retired and wanted to supplement your income, you might elect to have $250 paid out to you automatically on a monthly basis. Many funds require a minimum fund balance of between $5,000 and $10,000 to participate in an automatic withdrawal plan, with a minimum withdrawal of $50 per month.

Automatic Reinvestment of Interest, Dividends, and Capital Gains With a mutual fund, you have your choice of receiving interest, dividends, and capital gains payments or having them reinvested by purchasing more shares in the fund. If you're using the mutual fund as a long-term investment, have the distributions automatically reinvested. Reinvestment in the securities markets produces the same growth effects as compound interest; that is, you'll start earning money on your past earnings.

If you're investing in a bond and income fund, you'll get little or no capital appreciation on your holdings. Instead, most of your return will be from the distribution of interest, which comes to you each year in the form of dividends. If you don't reinvest these distributions, you won't accumulate much wealth. You'll be spending your earnings instead. Over 70 percent of all mutual fund shareholders choose to reinvest their dividends and capital gains.

Wiring and Funds Express Options If you anticipate needing your funds or your returns fast, you can choose a wiring and funds express option. This option allows you to have your returns/money wired directly to your bank account. It also works the other way and allows you to invest money in the fund immediately by wiring money directly to the fund. In this way, you can have your money sent and invested in the fund in the same day. This option is a bit like the automatic investment and withdrawal plan, except the transactions don't happen automatically/monthly.

Online and Phone Switching This option allows you to move money from one fund to another simply by making a phone request or making a request on the fund's Web site. If you want to move some of your money from your domestic stock fund to an international stock fund, you can do it easily and generally cost free with just one phone call or online.

Easy Establishment of Retirement Plans Most mutual funds provide for the easy establishment of IRS-approved tax-deferred retirement accounts, including traditional and Roth IRAs and plans. The fund will provide you with everything you need to establish such a plan and then handle the administrative duties. In addition, most funds have representatives available to answer questions you might have when setting the plan up. Retirement plans are a key part of any sound personal financial plan, and getting someone else to set one up and manage it for you is a huge advantage.

Check Writing Check-writing privileges associated with money market mutual funds can prove to be very handy when you need to use money from your investments directly to make purchases or to take care of an emergency. As we mentioned before, there are minimum levels, generally in the $250 to $500 range, for which the checks can be written.

Bookkeeping and Help with Taxes Some of the larger investment companies provide a "tax cost" service that actually calculates your taxable gains or losses when you sell shares. Because the calculation of taxes associated with buying and selling shares in a mutual fund can be enough to drive you crazy, this is a service well worth having. Unfortunately, it's also a service not offered by all mutual funds.

LO5 Select a mutual fund that's right for you.

Buying a Mutual Fund

Now that you know something about mutual funds, you may well be wondering how you go out and buy one. The process of buying a mutual fund involves determining your investment goals, identifying funds that meet your objectives, and evaluating those funds. Your local library and the Internet hold a wealth of information to help your evaluation. Brush up on your math, though, because much of the evaluation process is going to focus on cost. As you learned earlier, mutual fund expenses can vary dramatically from one fund to another. So when you're picking a mutual fund, keep an eye on the expenses.

Step 1: Determining Your Goals

The first step in buying a mutual fund involves determining exactly what your investment goals and time horizon are. In Chapters 1 and 2, we discussed identifying your goals and putting together an investment plan. We described the budgeting and planning procedure as a five-step process. Investing in mutual funds conforms to Step 4: Implement Your Plan. However, before you make it to Step 4, you must have a clear understanding of why you're investing. Is it to provide additional income to supplement your retirement income, or is it to save for your children's education or for your own retirement 30 years from now? Do you want your investments to be tax deferred? How much risk are you comfortable with? Once you've answered these questions, you're ready to go out and find a fund.

Step 2: Meeting Your Objectives

As we saw earlier, there are quite a few different classifications of mutual funds—money market, stock, balanced, asset allocation, life cycle, and bond funds—and within each of these classifications, there can be quite a few different subtypes; for example, subclassifications under stock mutual funds include growth, sector, and index funds, among others. Your investment objectives are going to lead you to one of those classifications. For example, if you are saving for an emergency fund, you might want to invest in a money market mutual fund because it is safe and the money is easily accessible, but if you are saving for retirement 40 years from now, you might want to invest in a stock index fund. To identify a fund's objectives, the first place to look is on one of the mutual fund screening Web sites listed in Table 14.6. For example, the Wall Street Journal Mutual Fund and ETF Screeners let you begin by picking a broad category and then moving to an expanded list of criteria and categories, while the Morningstar Fund Screener provides fund analysis and classifies funds by objective and management style. One of the advantages of the Yahoo! Finance Mutual Fund Screener is that it's free and lets you begin with a broad category and then immediately filter through that category by relative rank and ratings, making the selection process much simpler. The addresses for all these Web sites are provided in Table 14.6.

In assessing a fund's objective, pay close attention to the expense ratio and to past performance. If it's intended as a long-term investment, how has it done over the past year, 3 years, and 10 years? If it's intended to produce current income, what is it paying out in terms of its current yield?

Step 3: Selecting a Fund

Once you've found some funds with objectives that match your own, it's time to evaluate them. Evaluation means looking closely at past performance and scrutinizing the costs associated with the funds. Although past performance doesn't necessarily predict future results, research has shown that mutual funds that have done

TABLE 14.6 Mutual Fund Information on the Web

Web Site: **Wall Street Journal Mutual Fund and ETF Screeners**
Addresses: **http://online.wsj.com/public/quotes/mutualfund_screener.html**
http://online.wsj.com/public/quotes/etf_screener.html
Features:

- Free.
- Provides the ability to identify funds and ETFs based on expense ratios and on broad categories (Equity, Fixed Income–Taxable, or Fixed Income–Tax Exempt) and then to see an expanded list of criteria (International Mid-Cap Growth, Pacific Region Funds, etc.).
- Provides a simple screening tool. You can select a Lipper score for total return that reflects the funds' historical total return performance relative to peers. You can also screen funds by historical returns, fees and expenses, portfolio characteristics, P/E ratios for equity funds, and average quality ratings for bond funds.

Web Site: **Yahoo! Finance Mutual Fund Screener**
Address: **http://screener.finance.yahoo.com/funds.html**
Features:

- Free.
- Allows for screening by fund type, fund family, rank in category, manager's tenure, Morningstar rating, returns over different periods, initial investment, front loads, expense ratio, and size.

Web Site: **Morningstar Fund Screener**
Address: **http://screen.morningstar.com/FundSelector.html**
Features:

- Free but you need to register.
- Extremely easy to use.
- Provides explanations if you aren't familiar with the terms (simply click on the light bulb next to the term).
- Allows for screening by fund type, manager's tenure, initial investment, cost, expenses, Morningstar rating, returns over different periods, turnover, and size.

Web Site: **Various Brokerage Web sites**
Features:

- If you have an account with an online brokerage, chances are it provides an excellent screening feature.
- You can enter any fund ticker symbol and will be provided with information on risk, performance, ratings, composition, fees, and features.

poorly in the past tend to do poorly in the future, and there is some slight evidence that good performance may carry into the future. Research also shows that funds with lower expenses and lower turnover ratios tend to outperform those with higher expenses. So what do you look for in a mutual fund? Make sure it meets your objectives, has not done poorly in the recent past, and has low expenses. You can also use a fund's past performance to gain further insights into the investment philosophy and style of the fund. Checklist 14.1 and Table 14.6 should help you with your decision.

CHECKLIST 14.1 Buying a Mutual Fund

Before you buy a mutual fund, can you answer these questions?

☐ How has this fund performed over the long run?
☐ What is the fund's expense ratio?
☐ What specific risks are associated with this fund?
☐ What type of securities does the fund hold? How often does the portfolio change?
☐ How does the fund perform compared to other funds of the same type or to an index of the same type of investment?
☐ Have I obtained an independent evaluation of this fund?
☐ How much will the fund charge me when I buy shares? What other ongoing fees are charged?
☐ How tax efficient is this fund?

TABLE 14.7 What's in a Mutual Fund Prospectus?

- **The fund's goal and investment strategy.**
- **The fund manager's past experience.** You'll want to look closely at this. Many times when the mutual fund manager changes, so do the style and performance of the fund.
- **Any investment limitations that the fund may have.** For example, can the mutual fund invest in foreign securities?
- **Any tax considerations of importance to investors.**
- **The redemption and investment process for buying and selling shares in the fund.**
- **Services provided to investors.** For example, does the mutual fund provide 24-hour telephone service?
- **Performance over the past 10 years or since the fund has been in existence.** Most funds generally show this by demonstrating what would have happened if you had put $10,000 in the fund 10 years earlier or when the fund was formed.
- **Fund fees and expenses.** Look closely at the fund's sales and redemption charges. In addition, information on the management fee and fees for marketing expenses, called 12b-1 fees, is included.
- **The fund's annual turnover ratio.** There's also an additional part to the prospectus, which can be obtained separately and contains a listing of the fund's holdings, as well as additional information on the fund management.

Where to Look—Sources of Information You may be thinking "I have a hard time finding my socks. How am I supposed to find all this stuff about mutual funds?" There is plenty of help to be had. Some places you'll want to look include the mutual fund's prospectus, the *Wall Street Journal*, and, most importantly, the Web. You can get the **mutual fund prospectus** simply by calling the mutual fund and asking. Investment companies are required by law to offer a prospectus, and Table 14.7 provides a brief overview of what is provided in a prospectus.

Mutual Fund Prospectus
A description of the mutual fund, including the fund's objectives and risks, its historical performance, its expenses, the manager's history, and other information.

For the most recent returns, you'll want to look online. Figure 14.3 shows how a typical fund listing generally appears on one of the many online finance Web sites (**http://finance.yahoo.com**, **http://www.marketwatch.com**, or **http://www.wsj.com**), along with an explanation of the terminology.

FIGURE 14.3 Typical Online Mutual Fund Quote

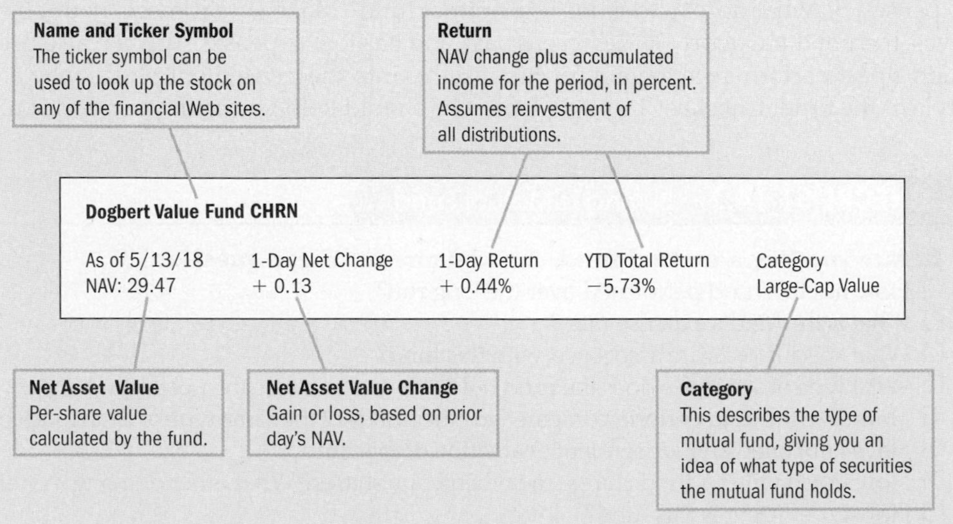

TABLE 14.8 Screening Criteria for Mutual Funds

- **Load Funds**—Avoid both front-load funds and those with contingent deferred sales charges.
- **12b-1 Fees**—Avoid them; there are plenty of good funds that don't charge them.
- **Expenses Ratio**—Keep it under 1.10%. The lower the expense ratio, the more likely the fund will outperform the market in the future.
- **Turnover Ratio**—Focus on funds with low turnover; they are liable for less taxes, and they produce higher returns.
- **Morningstar Rating**—Morningstar's star rating compares historical returns to risk; you want to start out screening for five-star funds.
- **Historical Returns**—Avoid any fund with poor performance over the past 1-year and 3-year periods, and look for funds with strong returns over these periods. But most importantly, avoid losers.
- **Morningstar Risk**—Lower is better; that way, you know the fund hasn't done well just because it made risky bets.
- **Initial Investment**—Make sure you pick a fund that you can invest in. Some funds require a high initial investment.
- **Manager's Tenure**—Avoid a fund if the manager has just left because historical returns mean nothing once the manager leaves.

As mentioned before, there's plenty of mutual fund material available on the Web, with some of the best sources listed in Table 14.6. Perhaps the best thing about Internet sources of information is that they're interactive; that is, you can use them to screen through different criteria easily and find the fund that fits your needs.

Internet Screening to Find the Right Mutual Fund Internet screening involves using an Internet program that searches out funds that meet the criteria that you've selected. That is, you may want a growth stock fund with low expenses that has been one of the top performers for the past 3 years. With a mutual fund Internet screening program, all you have to do is select those criteria and the program will instantly deliver to you the names of the mutual funds that fit. What kind of things should you be screening for? Table 14.8 provides a listing of possible screening criteria.

Step 4: Making the Purchase

After all of your figuring, matching, picking, evaluating, and calculating, you should now know exactly what fund you want. Now, it's time to do some buying. Load funds are generally sold through salespeople—perhaps a broker or a financial advisor. No-load funds, though, tend to be sold directly by the investment company. If you decide to keep costs down and go for a no-load fund, you have two choices. You can deal directly with the investment company that runs the fund, or you can purchase the no-load fund through a "mutual fund supermarket."

Buying Direct The easiest way to buy a mutual fund is to pick up the phone or go on the Internet. Vanguard and Fidelity, the two largest mutual fund families, both have toll-free telephone numbers and Web sites that you can use to set up an account, to move money into and out of your funds, to switch funds, and to request educational material. You can transfer money electronically or send a check to Vanguard or Fidelity through the mail. When you sell your holdings, you can receive a check in the mail or have the proceeds automatically deposited into an account you hold with these companies or into your checking account.

Buying Through a Mutual Fund Supermarket The downside of buying directly from different mutual funds is that if you have money in eight different mutual fund families, you'll have eight different statements to deal with. If you decide you want to move money from one family to another, you're in for a real headache.

Luckily, there are mutual fund supermarkets such as Charles Schwab & Co. and Fidelity, where you can pick mutual funds from different mutual fund families. However, you should also be aware that you might be charged a small transaction fee when you buy a no-load fund through a mutual fund supermarket. You can avoid transaction fees altogether by purchasing these funds directly from their mutual fund families. In addition, many banks sell mutual funds. Unfortunately, investors often don't realize that the federal government doesn't insure mutual funds sold by banks, as it does most bank accounts. Moreover, most mutual funds sold by banks are load funds.

BEHAVIORAL INSIGHTS

PRINCIPLE 9

Principle 9: Mind Games, Your Financial Personality, and Your Money Finding a pattern of action is usually a good way to predict future action—right? The study of behavioral finance tells us that people are always looking for patterns and they put a good amount of faith into the fact that the pattern will continue into the future. Unfortunately, when it comes to mutual funds, sometimes they continue and sometimes they don't because there is no earthly way of discerning if one year's mutual fund performance is meaningful at all—it may simply be a matter of luck. But we do have a behavioral tendency to want to attribute this to a *meaningful* pattern rather than *chance*. For example, if half of all mutual funds "beat" the market and half don't, then you would expect that from sheer chance more than 10 percent of all mutual funds would beat the market for 3 straight years and, likewise, more than 10 percent would lose to the market for 3 straight years—but it's all chance.

So are there any predictors for mutual funds? First, if a mutual fund underperforms the market for some period of time, it is likely to continue to do that. That's where patterns appear to have some predictive power. How about picking winners? That's tough. Just because a mutual fund has outperformed the market in the past does not tell us much about its future. So what does all this tell you? Be careful about reading too much into past patterns—they may just be a result of chance.

Fortunately, there is something you can do that will help you pick winners—it's something that most people ignore for behavioral reasons. What is it? Pay attention to the small numbers. People tend to ignore or assume away the impact of small numbers. When we talked about the time value of money, we saw their impact. For example, while the difference between earning 8 percent versus 7 percent on $10,000 invested for 45 years may not seem like a lot, in fact, it is—it is the difference between $319,000 when invested at 8 percent and only $210,000 when invested at 7 percent. That's more than a 50 percent increase at 8 percent.

Now, how does all this relate to mutual funds? Do you know where we are going with this? The answer is in the mutual fund costs. The number one predictor of mutual fund performance that seems to work the best is looking at the mutual fund's costs—the lower they are, the better the predicted performance. This means you'll want to avoid all load mutual funds and stick to those funds with the lowest expenses. Unfortunately, most investors don't think too much about tacking on 1 percent here or there; after all, 1 percent is a small number. But studies have shown that this is a "big mistake," particularly over time—at least when we're talking about mutual funds.

ACTION PLAN

PRINCIPLE 10

Principle 10: Just Do It! You've got your financial goals down on paper—now it's time to work toward making them happen. Mutual funds are a great way to start. Once you have the minimum saved—which is about $3,000 for most Vanguard mutual funds—it's time to start investing. Here are things you'll want to keep in mind:

- **Your goals.** Set up your investment plan to meet those goals.
- **Put it on autopilot.** The easiest way to save is never to see the money in the first place. Just about every mutual fund allows you to have money automatically pulled from your checking account each month and invested in the mutual fund of your choice. What you're really doing is paying yourself first, and that makes sense.
- **Taxes.** As you invest, keep your tax situation in mind because mutual funds pass along taxable income from their investments in the form of dividends and capital gains—and even if you keep your money invested in your mutual fund, there may be some taxes to pay.
- **Taxes when you move money.** When you move money from one fund to another, even within the same fund family, the IRS looks at this as a sale and a purchase, and you are taxed on any gain from the sale.
- **The losers.** While it's hard to pick winners, it's much easier to pick losers—if a fund has done poorly in the past, chances are it will do poorly in the future. Take the time to check out the past performance of a fund you are interested in.
- **Costs, costs, costs.** Keep your costs down—lower-cost mutual funds tend to do better than higher-cost funds. Read the fine print. Watch for commissions, maintenance, and other fees that eat away at your money!

Chapter Summaries

Weigh the advantages and disadvantages of investing in mutual funds.

LO1

SUMMARY: When you invest in a mutual fund, you're buying a fraction of a very large portfolio. This portfolio may include stocks, bonds, short-term securities, and even cash. Your money is pooled with that of other investors to purchase the fund's holdings. The shareholders then own a proportionate share of the overall portfolio. The value of mutual fund shares goes up and down as the value of the mutual fund's investments goes up and down.

KEY TERM

Mutual Fund, page 468 An investment fund that raises funds from investors, pools the money, and invests it in stocks, bonds, and other investments. Each investor owns a share of the fund proportionate to the amount of his or her investment.

LO2 Differentiate among types of mutual funds, ETFs, and investment trusts.

SUMMARY: Investment companies invest the pooled money in return for a fee. An open-end investment company is actually an open-end mutual fund. It has the ability to issue and redeem shares on a daily basis, and the value of the portfolio that it holds determines the value of each ownership share in the mutual fund. The price paid for an open-end mutual fund share or received when the share is sold is the net asset value (NAV). An ETF is very similar to a mutual fund but trades on an exchange just like common stock and can be traded throughout the day.

A closed-end fund has a fixed number of shares. Those shares are initially sold by the fund at its inception, and after that, they trade between investors at whatever price supply and demand dictate. A unit investment trust is a pool of securities, generally municipal bonds, with each share representing a proportionate ownership in that pool. A real estate investment trust (REIT) is similar to a mutual fund, with the funds going into real estate, real estate loans (mortgages), or a combination of the two.

KEY TERMS

Investment Company, page 471 A firm that invests the pooled money of a number of investors in return for a fee.

Open-End Mutual Fund, page 472 A mutual fund that has the ability to issue as many shares as investors want. The value of all the investments that the fund holds determines how much each share in the mutual fund is worth.

Net Asset Value (NAV), page 472 The dollar value of a share in a mutual fund. It's the value of the fund's holdings (minus any debt) divided by the number of shares outstanding.

Closed-End Mutual Fund, page 472 A mutual fund that can't issue new shares. These funds raise money only once by issuing a fixed number of shares, and after that, the shares can be traded between investors. The value of each share is determined both by the value of the investments the fund holds and by investor demand for shares in the fund.

Exchange Traded Fund (ETF), page 473 A hybrid of a mutual fund and an individually traded stock or bond that trades on an exchange just as individual securities do and that can be bought and sold throughout the trading day.

Unit Investment Trust, page 474 A fixed pool of securities, generally municipal bonds, in which each share represents a proportionate ownership interest in that pool. The bonds are purchased and then held until maturity, at which time the trust is dissolved.

Real Estate Investment Trust (REIT), page 475 An investment vehicle similar to a mutual fund that specializes in real estate investments, such as shopping centers or rental property, or that makes real estate loans.

Hedge Fund, page 476 An investment fund that is private, largely unregulated, and very risky and that charges very high fees and allows only wealthy investors to invest.

LO3 Calculate mutual fund returns.

SUMMARY: Although some mutual funds have no sales commission, others impose a sales commission, and still others require a hefty annual management fee. A load is a sales commission; thus, a load fund is one that charges a sales commission. A mutual fund that doesn't charge a commission is referred to as a no-load fund.

Be very aware of any and all mutual fund expenses, and try to avoid them. The return from investing in a mutual fund can be in the form of dividends, capital gains distributions, or a change in the NAV of the shares held. Capital gains result from selling securities for more than what they were originally bought for.

KEY TERMS

Load, page 476 A sales commission charged on a mutual fund.

Load Fund, page 476 A mutual fund on which a load or sales commission is charged.

Back-End Load, page 476 A commission that's charged only when the investor liquidates his or her holdings.

No-Load Fund, page 477 A mutual fund that doesn't charge a commission.

Expense Ratio, page 477 The ratio of a mutual fund's expenses to its total assets.

Turnover Ratio or Rate, page 477 A measure of the level of a fund's trading activity, indicating what percentage of the fund's investments are turned over during the year.

12b-1 Fee, page 478 An annual fee, generally ranging from 0.25 to 0.75 percent of a fund's assets, that the mutual fund charges its shareholders for marketing costs.

Classify mutual funds according to objectives. LO4

SUMMARY: To allow you to more easily choose from over 8,000 mutual funds available, funds are categorized according to objective.

KEY TERMS

Money Market Mutual Fund, page 481 A mutual fund that invests in Treasury bills, certificates of deposit, commercial paper, and other short-term notes, generally with a maturity of less than 30 days.

Tax-Exempt Money Market Mutual Fund, page 481 A money market mutual fund that invests only in very short-term municipal debt.

Government Securities Money Market Mutual Fund, page 481 A money market mutual fund that invests solely in U.S. government securities in order to avoid any risk whatsoever.

Stock Fund, page 481 A mutual fund that invests primarily in common stock.

Balanced Mutual Fund, page 483 A mutual fund that tries to "balance" the objectives of long-term growth, income, and stability. To do this, these funds invest in a mix of common stock and bonds, as well as preferred stock in some cases.

Asset Allocation Fund, page 484 A mutual fund that invests in a mix of stocks, bonds, and money market securities.

Life Cycle Fund, page 484 A mutual fund that tries to tailor its holdings to the investor's individual characteristics, such as age and risk tolerance.

Target Retirement Fund, page 484 A mutual fund professionally managed for an investor's stage of retirement planning, with the investments in the fund automatically growing more conservative as the investor's retirement date nears.

Bond Fund, page 484 A mutual fund that invests primarily in bonds.

Select a mutual fund that's right for you. LO5

SUMMARY: The process of selecting a mutual fund involves determining your investment goals, identifying funds that meet your objectives, and evaluating those funds. There's a wealth of information and screening tools available online to help you evaluate mutual funds.

KEY TERM

Mutual Fund Prospectus, page 490 A description of the mutual fund, including the fund's objectives and risks, its historical performance, its expenses, the manager's history, and other information.

Problems and Activities

These problems are available in MyLab Finance.

PRINCIPLE 8

1. List and explain the seven advantages associated with owning a mutual fund. Which of these advantages relate to **Principle 8**? How?

2. You must choose between a no-load, open-end mutual fund with an annual expense ratio of 0.85 percent but no transaction cost and an ETF with an annual expense ratio of 0.25 percent and a transaction cost of $20.00.

a. Calculate which is the lower cost alternative to purchase.
b. Calculate which is the lower cost to own over 6 months, if you sell after 7 percent gain.
c. Calculate which is the lower cost to own over 2 years, if you achieve a 10 percent per year gain.
d. Calculate which is the lower cost to own over 2 years, if you experience a 10 percent per year loss.

3. Calculate the NAV for a mutual fund with the following values:

Market value of securities held in the portfolio	= $1.2 billion
Liabilities of the fund	= $37 million
Shares outstanding	= 60 million

4. The following information pertains to the Big Returns Fund:

Cost	Class A	Class B	Class C
Front-end load	5.50	0.00	0.00
Back-end load	0.00	5.00	1.00
		Declining 1% per year	First year only
Management fee	0.90	0.90	0.90
12b-1 fee	0.25	0.50	1.00

For each share class, calculate (a) how much you would pay in initial commissions, (b) how much you would pay in back-end commissions if you sold after 2 years, and (c) how much you would pay in annual expenses over a 2-year holding period. Assume that you purchased $2,500 worth of shares in this fund and that prior to reductions for management and 12b-1 fees the gross fund return was 10 percent each year.

5. Mason is thinking about getting married. What advice would you give him regarding how much to budget for the engagement ring, wedding, and honeymoon? Explain your rationale to him.

6. Match the following types of funds to the securities that would typically be found in each portfolio.

a. Growth funds	(1) Foreign stocks
b. U.S. government bond funds	(2) Moves money from stocks to bonds to maximize return
c. Growth and income funds	(3) Market basket that represents the S&P 500
d. Life cycle funds	(4) Mix of stocks, bonds, and money market securities
e. Sector funds	(5) 65 percent of stocks from the technology industry
f. Index funds	(6) Dividend-paying blue-chip stocks
g. Balanced funds	(7) Tailored to investor characteristics
h. International funds	(8) High-growth and high P/E companies
i. Small company funds	(9) Companies with strong earnings and some dividends
j. Asset allocation funds	(10) Federal agency securities
k. Aggressive growth funds	(11) Companies that probably trade on the OTC market

7. Zap Fund is the mainstay of your portfolio. The investment company just announced its year-end distributions. The long-term capital gain per share is $4.60, and the dividend per share is $2.10. Assuming the NAV increased from $39.10 to $46.21, calculate your total annual return.

8. At the beginning of last year, Thomas purchased 200 shares of the Web.com Fund at an NAV of $26.00 and automatically reinvested all distributions. As a result of reinvesting, Thomas ended the year with 265 shares of the fund with an NAV of $32.20. What was his total return for the year on this investment?

9. Calculate the after-withdrawal future value of $10,000 invested for 5 years in each share class in the table below. In terms of costs, which would be the best investment for someone who knows the fund will be sold at the end of the 5-year period? Assume that each fund's gross (before fees) total return is 12 percent per year.

Cost	Class A	Class B	Class C
Front-end load	5.75	0.00	0.00
Back-end load	0.00	5.00	1.00
		Declining 1% per year	First year only
Management fee	0.55	0.90	1.00
12b-1 fee	0.25	0.50	1.00

10. Melanie is considering purchasing shares in an international bond fund. She has limited her search to one open-end and one closed-end fund. Information on the funds follows:

	Open-End	Closed-End
NAV	$12.00	$24.05
Sales price	No-load	$21.95
Annual expenses	1.45%	1.15%
YTD return	12.00%	12.50%

a. How much would Melanie pay for the open-end fund? How much would she pay for the closed-end fund?
b. Is the closed-end fund selling at a discount or a premium relative to its NAV?
c. Given both funds' similar returns and expense ratios, would you recommend that Melanie purchase the closed-end fund? Why or why not?

11. The reinvestment of capital gains and dividends can make a significant difference in your total return. Consider the following situation to determine the difference reinvestment can make over a 5-year period.

Initial purchase amount	$10,000
Initial purchase date	January 1
Initial purchase price	$19.30 per share
Annual capital gains distribution rate	1.5%
Annual dividend distribution rate	0.6%
Annual price appreciation rate	7.4%

Assume all distributions are made on the last day of the year at the closing NAV. Ignore tax consequences for the scenarios in a and b, below.

a. Calculate the ending investment value plus the total of distributions received assuming no reinvestment.
b. Calculate the ending investment value assuming all distributions are reinvested.
c. Calculate and explain the difference.

Discussion Case 1

This case is available in MyLab Finance.

Rick has usually been just a market watcher and not a market participant; however, he recently received $15,000 for the movie rights to his new book. Rick has never before had the resources to invest and therefore owns no other security investments, but he has followed several alternative energy stocks over the past year. The share prices have fluctuated dramatically, but Rick is definitely interested in this type of stock. He feels that alternative energy technology is the way of the future. When you asked Rick if he was comfortable with the risk associated with such an investment, he indicated that he would be if superior returns could be obtained.

Questions

1. Given the fact that Rick has only $15,000 to invest, explain why he should consider investing in mutual funds rather than individual stocks.

2. In what type(s) of stock mutual fund(s) would you recommend Rick invest? Why?
3. In helping Rick make an investment choice, what factors would you explain to him as most important when choosing a mutual fund?
4. Although most mutual funds will provide Rick with some level of diversification, what type of risk will Rick still be exposed to if he purchases a single mutual fund?
5. To assure Rick of the liquidity and marketability of his investment, would you recommend that he invest in an open-end or a closed-end mutual fund? Why?
6. In terms of costs, would you recommend load or no-load funds to Rick? Why?
7. Develop a model portfolio of three mutual fund types (index, growth, bond, etc.) to help Rick understand the benefits of diversification. Explain your choices. Be sure to consider issues of risk and volatility.

Discussion Case 2

This case is available in **MyLab Finance**.

Mahalia has decided that she needs to invest her savings somewhere other than her online bank account where she is earning only 1.05 percent annually. She has heard that money market mutual funds and short-term bond funds may provide higher yields than bank accounts and offer stability of principal similar to the bank. Mahalia's primary investment goal is to keep her savings (about $15,000 when she last checked) secure and accessible so that she can make a down payment on a house within the next 3 years. She has several questions regarding investing in mutual funds and has come to you for help.

Questions

1. What are the types of mutual funds that would be appropriate in meeting Mahalia's objective?
2. What sources could Mahalia use to obtain specific information and ratings on different funds?
3. When reviewing a fund's prospectus or an analysis provided by Morningstar, for what specific type of information should Mahalia look?
4. When evaluating a fund, how much importance should Mahalia place on a fund's past performance?
5. Given Mahalia's goal and your response to Question 1, how important are loads, fees, and expenses in her search for a good mutual fund?
6. Provide Mahalia with six reasons why she should consider purchasing shares in a bond fund.
7. What type of bond fund would you recommend? Why?
8. In terms of the risk–return trade-off, what length of maturity for a bond fund would be appropriate for Mahalia?

Continuing Case: Cory and Tisha Dumont

Part IV: Managing Your Investments

As Cory and Tisha Dumont have reviewed your answers to their previous questions, they have recognized that their need for financial planning assistance is far greater than they realized. They have taken your advice and consistently reduced expenses. To their great surprise, they have already accumulated $1,500 for an emergency fund. They feel that they are getting a handle on their basic money management skills and are more confident in their insurance knowledge and product selection. Now they want to develop an investment plan.

Recall that Cory and Tisha have $13,000 invested in a stock market index mutual fund for a house down payment. They also have $2,500 in a savings account earning 3 percent interest and an average of $1,800 in their checking account earning 0.75 percent interest. (Their $1,500 in emergency funds is in addition to these savings amounts and has been temporarily deposited in their savings account.) The shares of Great Basin Balanced Mutual Fund, given to Tisha by her father, are worth $2,300. After completing a risk tolerance questionnaire on an investment Web site, Tisha and Cory confirmed that their attitudes toward risk are very different. Tisha is much more comfortable with "gambling" higher risks for higher returns, whereas Cory wants a "safe bet." Help the Dumonts answer the following questions regarding the management of their investments.

Questions

1. Fundamentally, what must Cory and Tisha understand about themselves *and* the risk–return trade-off of investments to achieve their long-term investment goals?
2. To protect their investment plan, what behavioral quirks should Cory and Tisha avoid?
3. Based on the Dumonts' stage in the life cycle, what type of investment asset allocation would be appropriate, assuming they want to establish a retirement savings fund? What types of stocks, mutual funds, or ETFs should they consider for the equity portion of their asset allocation plan? Should they consider international common stocks, international mutual funds, or international ETFs? Why or why not? What types of bonds, bond funds, or bond ETFs would be appropriate for the fixed-income portion of their asset allocation plan? (*Hint:* Be sure to consider the bond maturity, rating, and type of issuer.)
4. Briefly explain the concept of efficient markets for Cory and Tisha. Based on that understanding, explain to Cory and Tisha what the best long-term investment strategy would be for them.
5. Explain to Cory and Tisha the advantages and disadvantages associated with managing an investment portfolio through a full-service brokerage firm versus a discount or online brokerage firm. How will the trade-off between service and price affect their choice of a broker?
6. Explain to the Dumonts how owning a combination of securities can reduce risks as addressed by **Principle 8: Risk and Return Go Hand in Hand.** Why is it important to know, and be able to interpret, the beta of a diversified portfolio?

PRINCIPLE 8

7. The Dumonts, in the 15 percent marginal tax bracket, are concerned about the federal taxes paid on investment earnings. Show the calculations to answer the following questions.
   a. A tax-free money market mutual fund is currently yielding 2.40 percent. Should the Dumonts move their savings or keep their money in the bank earning 3 percent?
   b. If a U.S. Treasury note is currently yielding 8 percent, what is the minimum interest rate that the Dumonts must receive in order to purchase an equivalent municipal bond?
8. Calculate the amount of money the Dumonts will have in their savings account if they add no other funds and keep it invested at 3 percent over the next 25 years. Calculate how much they can accumulate over 25 years if they move the money into a money market mutual fund earning 5 percent. Now, calculate how much they can accumulate over 25 years if they move the money into a diversified stock

mutual fund earning 9 percent. Based on your calculations and the Dumonts' risk tolerance, would you advise them to move their savings into the money market mutual fund? Into the diversified stock mutual fund? What advantages and disadvantages should be considered? (*Hint:* Use your financial calculator or see Chapter 3.)

9. Cory's parents recently gave the Dumonts $40,000 to start education funds for Chad and Haley. A stockbroker has recommended that Cory and Tisha include a 10-year corporate bond for Chad in the portfolio. The bond currently yields 8 percent and sells for $1,000. If interest rates increase 2 percentage points and the bond is sold, how much will the bond sell for at that time? Calculate the bond price if rates fall 1 percentage point. What investing rule does this prove?

10. The same stockbroker who recommended a bond for Chad's college savings also recommended that Haley's college savings portfolio include a preferred stock currently selling for $53 and paying a $5 dividend. If the Dumonts' required rate of return is 10 percent, for how much should the preferred stock sell?

11. Should the Dumonts take the stockbroker's advice on education savings and buy the bond for Chad and the preferred stock for Haley? Defend your answer and provide other investment alternatives that the Dumonts should consider.

12. Explain to Cory and Tisha why mutual funds may be a good alternative for meeting their investment objectives. What specific types of mutual funds would be appropriate for meeting the following investment objectives, given their time horizon and risk tolerance? (*Hint:* Try to develop an asset allocation strategy by suggesting a percentage for each fund type included.)

a. Emergency fund
b. House down payment savings
c. College fund for Chad
d. College fund for Haley
e. Retirement fund for Cory
f. Retirement fund for Tisha

13. Recall that when Tisha turned 21, her father gave her shares in the Great Basin Balanced Mutual Fund. Today, the fund is worth $2,300. Assuming that Tisha will use this fund as a long-term investment (maybe for retirement) and given her risk tolerance and age, does this type of fund match her objective? What investment risk is most important when thinking about investments for a college fund or retirement? Would this be a good fund to use to save for college expenses for Chad and Haley? Defend your answers.

14. Cory and Tisha invested in a stock market index mutual fund to save for their "dream house," which they expect to purchase in 3 to 5 years. Would you recommend that they maintain, increase, or decrease their holdings in this type of fund, given their objective? Explain your answer. What type of fund or other investment would you recommend?

15. What mutual fund services would you recommend that the Dumonts use to save for their goals systematically? Why? How might these services be integrated with a portfolio accumulation strategy?

16. Would you recommend no-load or load funds to the Dumonts? Why? What other factors are important to consider when comparing different mutual funds with the same objective?

17. Should the Dumonts consider using a mutual fund supermarket? What are the advantages and disadvantages of using this investment strategy? Might a bank offer a better option?

18. Given the time horizon of their goals and their knowledge of investment strategies, what are the advantages and disadvantages of considering ETFs for the house, college, or retirement?

19. When Cory and Tisha do purchase a house, should they consider this an investment? Explain your answer in terms of (a) liquidity and (b) how market values for real estate are determined.

20. What sources of investment information can Cory and Tisha use to learn more about potential stock, bond, and mutual fund investments? Recall that Cory likes to use the Internet for research.

PART 5 Life Cycle Issues

Part 5: Life Cycle Issues focuses on financial planning for the future—your retirement years, and beyond, with a look at estate planning. The key word here is planning. Without a plan, nothing will happen, and putting a plan into place requires an understanding of the issues you face and the alternatives available that will take you where you want to go. Moreover, without an understanding of the issues confronting you and the importance of putting a plan into place, it's easy to become complacent and procrastinate.

Part 5 closes by tying the different personal finance topics together to provide you with a step-by-step action plan by looking at ten "Financial Life Events." In addition, it examines a dozen financial and lifestyle decisions that will have a major impact on your financial future and offers a close look at the keys to successful debt management.

In Part 5, we will specifically focus on Principle 10:

Principle 10: Just Do It!—After all, making the commitment to financial planning may be the most difficult step in the financial planning process.

In addition, in Part 5 we will touch on the following principles:

Principle 1: The Best Protection Is Knowledge

Principle 2: Nothing Happens Without a Plan

Principle 3: The Time Value of Money

Principle 4: Taxes Affect Personal Finance Decisions

Principle 5: Stuff Happens, or the Importance of Liquidity

Principle 6: Waste Not, Want Not—Smart Spending Matters

Principle 7: Protect Yourself Against Major Catastrophes

Principle 8: Risk and Return Go Hand in Hand

Principle 9: Mind Games, Your Financial Personality, and Your Money

CHAPTER 15 Retirement Planning

Learning Objectives

LO1	**Understand** the changing nature of retirement planning.	**Social Security and Employer-Funded Pensions**
LO2	**Set up** a retirement plan.	**Plan Now, Retire Later**
LO3	**Understand** how different retirement plans work.	**Retirement Plans in Addition to Social Security and Employer-Funded Pensions**
LO4	**Choose** how your retirement benefits are paid out to you.	**Facing Retirement—The Payout**
LO5	**Put** together a retirement plan and effectively monitor it.	**Putting a Plan Together and Monitoring It**

Most people assume that if you make it big early in life, you'll surely retire to a life of luxury. Not so. Retiring comfortably takes planning. Just look at musical icon Tina Turner.

Turner was born in 1939 to cotton plantation workers in Brownsville, Tennessee, and moved to St. Louis to live with relatives when she was in her teens. It was there she met Ike Turner, her future husband and singing partner. Together they hit the big time, becoming huge stars in the 1970s with hits such as "River Deep, Mountain Wide," and an R&B-style version of Creedence Clearwater Revival's "Proud Mary." Unfortunately, the big time isn't all that Ike hit. After being beaten bloody in July 1976, Tina Turner finally walked out of her 20-year abusive marriage to Ike. When she left, she had no recording contract, no savings, no fancy cars or homes—just 36 cents and a Mobil gas card.

For a while, Turner and her four children lived on food stamps. Although facing poverty, she refused any financial help from Ike when the couple finally divorced in 1978. Instead, she managed to support herself and her family by playing Holiday Inns and other minor clubs. By 1979, she was $500,000 in debt, with no prospects and no one to lend a helping hand. It looked as if Tina Turner had retired to a life of poverty and obscurity.

Frank Augstein/AP Images

Fortunately, along came Roger Davies, a young Australian promoter, who signed on as her manager. With his help, Turner paid off her bills, put together a new backup band, and got a fresh start. Despite record company skepticism, she managed to get a new recording contract, and by 1984, she had a number-one hit with "What's Love Got to Do with It." Today, Turner continues to be a major star. In 2010, at age 70, she rose to the top of the UK charts one more time just after finishing her Tina!: 50th Anniversary Tour, one of the highest-grossing tours of all time; in 2014, at age 74, she became the oldest person to appear on the cover of *Vogue*; and in 2018, *TINA The Musical*, a new musical based on her life, is set to hit the stage in London's West End. While this time around Turner has surely planned for her retirement, let's hope she never stops performing!

You may think you're too young or not wealthy enough to worry about retirement. Think again. Regardless of your age, you need to start planning for retirement. By doing so, you're focusing on a specific financial goal. As you learned in Chapters 1 and 2, you're going to have a lot of financial goals in your life. Retirement, though, is a biggie. After all, how well you do in achieving your retirement goal is probably going to determine how much you enjoy the last 20 or more years of your life.

It's hard to think about retiring when you're young. For most people, today looms larger than tomorrow. That car loan or mortgage you're trying to pay off this year will no doubt seem far more important than your financial situation 30 to 40 years from now. But just think how worried you'll be when you're 65 and you don't have a dime to retire on. Big money in a second career may have worked for Tina Turner, but it's a long shot for most of us. Fortunately, with a sound plan and a little discipline, you can retire to a life of relative ease without ever having to fret or fear.

There used to be a time when retirement planning wasn't necessary—retirement meant taking a pension from your employer and letting Social Security pick up any slack. Not anymore. Thanks to the recent drive to cut spending, employers tend not to pay pensions, and those that still do have reduced them to as little as possible. That leaves a lot of slack for Social Security, and given some of the Social Security reform proposals that have been tossed around, coupled with the government's drive to cut its own spending, there might not be such a thing as Social Security by the time you retire.

Nowadays, you've got to come up with the funds for your retirement all by yourself. Sound scary? Well, it's actually not. We'll explain exactly how to make a good retirement plan. But first we should explain how Social Security and employer-funded pensions work. No, we're not trying to rub it in and show you what you're missing. You simply need to know about past retirement plans before you can dive into the present ones.

LO1 Understand the changing nature of retirement planning.

Social Security and Employer-Funded Pensions

For many senior citizens, Social Security is their primary source of retirement income. For younger workers who won't face retirement for 40 years, the Social Security system may no longer be available or may have changed dramatically. Still, for many of the millions of individuals receiving benefits today, Social Security is the difference between living in poverty and modest comfort. Let's take a look at how the Social Security system currently functions.

Financing Social Security

To begin with, Social Security isn't an investment. When you pay money into Social Security, you're purchasing mandatory insurance that provides for you and your family in the event of death, disability, health problems, or retirement. Moreover, the benefits paid by Social Security aren't intended to allow you to live in comfort after you retire. They're intended to provide a base level of protection.

Whether you want to or not, you fund Social Security during your working years by paying taxes directly to the Social Security system. If you're not self-employed, both you and your employer pay into the system—each pays 7.65 percent of your gross salary up to $127,200 in 2017. This deduction appears on your pay slip as FICA, which stands for the Federal Insurance Contributions Act.

These funds actually go to both Social Security and Medicare (the government's health insurance program for the elderly, which we discussed in Chapter 9). Medicare also keeps on taxing after the Social Security cap has been reached, taking an additional 1.45 percent from both you and your employer.

If your salary was $127,200 in 2017, your FICA contribution would have been $9,730.80. If you were self-employed, you would have had to pay both the employer and the employee portions of FICA, at a rate of 15.3 percent up to the $127,200 limit, so you would have paid a total of $19,451.60. In addition, you would have paid Medicare 2.9 percent on all net earnings above $127,200.

These funds cover the payments currently being made to today's retirees by Social Security, while allowing for a "built-in surplus" for payouts in the future. The Social Security Trust Fund is up to $2.9 trillion so far and is invested in special-issue Treasury bonds. These bonds are housed in a Bureau of the Public Debt safe in Parkersburg, West Virginia; on the bond, a congressional instruction declares, "the United States is pledged to . . . the obligation with respect to both principal and interest." In other words, the FICA taxes being paid by today's workers are providing the money for benefit payments for today's retirees, and any excess collected by the government is lent to itself (by buying Treasury bonds from the government). The money you pay to FICA isn't saved up and invested in an account just for you. Instead, it gets pooled with the money all other current workers are paying to FICA and goes into a current senior citizen's Social Security benefits check.

FACTS OF LIFE

"Isn't this exciting! I earned this. I wiped tables for it, I steamed milk for it, and it's—(opening her paycheck)—not worth it! Who's FICA? Why is he getting my money?" These are the words of Rachel Green on the TV show *Friends*, seeing her first Central Perk paycheck in the episode "The One with George Stephanopoulos."

The plan is that when you retire, the FICA taxes paid by people working at that time, along with the money accumulated in the Social Security Trust Fund, will go into your benefits check. Unfortunately, the proportion of current workers to current Social Security recipients is shrinking rapidly. Whereas 40 years ago there were 16 workers for every Social Security recipient, today the ratio is down to three workers to every recipient. And the problem won't go away. In fact, it will only get worse—in 40 years, the ratio of working contributors to recipients will be down to two-to-one. The bottom line here is that there will be some changes in Social Security by the time it's your turn to collect, and some of these changes—perhaps increasing the retirement age or limiting benefits for the wealthy—may happen in the next few years.

Eligibility

Roughly 95 percent of all Americans are covered by Social Security. The major groups outside the system include police officers and workers continuously employed by the government since 1984, both of whom are covered by alternative retirement systems.

To become eligible for Social Security, all you have to do is pay money into the system. As you do, you receive Social Security credits. In 2017, you earned 1 credit for each $1,300 in earnings, up to a maximum of 4 credits per year. To qualify for benefits, you need 40 credits.

Once you've met this requirement, you become eligible for retirement, disability, and survivor benefits. Earning beyond 40 credits won't increase your benefits. If you die, some of your family members may also be eligible for Social Security benefits, even if they never paid into the system.

Retirement Benefits

The size of your Social Security benefits is determined by (1) your number of years of earnings, (2) your average level of earning during the 35 years you had the highest earnings, and (3) an adjustment for inflation. The formula attempts to provide benefits that would replace 42 percent of your average earnings over your working years, adjusted upward somewhat for those in lower income brackets and downward for those in higher income brackets. Thus, the benefits are slightly weighted

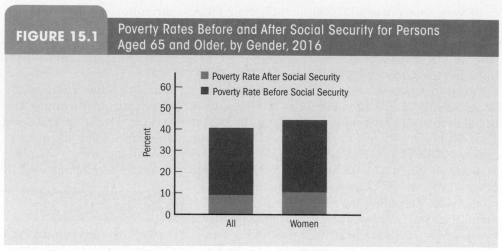

FIGURE 15.1 Poverty Rates Before and After Social Security for Persons Aged 65 and Older, by Gender, 2016

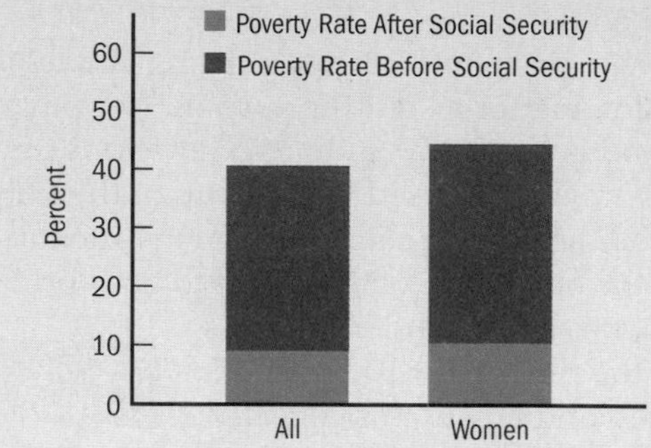

Source: U.S. Census Bureau, Current Population Survey, March 2016.

toward individuals in lower income brackets because they, in general, have less savings to rely on at retirement.

The retirement age to receive full benefits gradually rises until it hits 67 for those born in 1960 or later. Those who retire as early as age 62 can receive reduced benefits. However, those benefits are *permanently* reduced by five-ninths of 1 percent for the first 36 months and five-twelfths of 1 percent for subsequent months before the "full" retirement age. That means people scheduled to receive full benefits at age 67 and who retire at age 62 will receive only 70 percent of their full benefits, and this reduced level of benefits is permanent.

If you delay retirement, you can increase your Social Security benefits. The longer you work, the higher the average earnings base on which your benefits are calculated. In addition, those who delay retirement have a percentage added to their benefits. For example, if you were born in 1943 or later, Social Security adds 8 percent per year to your benefit for each year that you delay signing up for Social Security beyond your full retirement age.

You must notify your Social Security office and file an application 3 months before you want your first check to arrive; the government won't automatically start sending you your Social Security check just because you're officially retired.

How important is Social Security today? Take a look at Figure 15.1. As you can see, many low-income retirees depend on Social Security benefits to get by. The poverty rate for retirees if they did not receive Social Security would be 40.5 percent, with Social Security reducing the poverty rate to less than one in ten. For women, Social Security is particularly important. In fact, 44.3 percent of women 65 years old and older would be living in poverty but for Social Security. Why is Social Security so important to women?

FACTS OF LIFE

According to the 2016 Social Security Trustees Report, the Social Security Trust Fund will be exhausted in 2034, at which point it will be able to pay only about 75 percent of promised benefits.

- Women live longer than men; 60 percent of Social Security beneficiaries are women.
- As Figure 15.1 shows, almost half of all women 65 and older would be poor without Social Security.
- 28 percent of women work part-time, so they are less likely to have workplace retirement benefits.
- Social Security is the only source of income for one of every four unmarried women over 75 years of age.

Disability and Survivor Benefits

Although retirement benefits are the focus of our attention in this chapter, Social Security is actually a mandatory insurance program. Insurance against poverty at retirement is only one portion of its coverage. Social Security also provides disability and survivor benefits.

Disability benefits provide protection for those who experience a physical or mental impairment that is expected to result in death or keep them from doing any substantial work for at least a year. "Substantial work" is generally defined as anything that generates monthly earnings of $500 or more.

Social Security also provides survivor benefits to families when the breadwinner dies. These payments include a small, automatic one-time payment at the time of death to help defray funeral costs, as well as continued monthly payments to the spouse if he or she is over 60, over 50 if disabled, or any age and caring for a child either under 16 or disabled and receiving Social Security benefits. Continued monthly payments are also available to your children if they're under 18 or under 19 but still in elementary or secondary school or if they're disabled. Your parents can also qualify for survivor benefits if you die and they're dependent on you for at least half of their support.

Employer-Funded Pensions

Twenty years ago, a "guaranteed" pension provided by your employer was the norm. You'd work for one company for most or all of your working life, and that company would reward your loyalty and hard work by taking care of you during retirement. In today's job scene, where companies aren't quite so generous and where employees change jobs often, pension plans are rare. However, some companies do still offer pensions, usually referring to them as *defined-benefit plans*.

Defined-Benefit Plans

Under a **defined-benefit plan**, you receive a promised or "defined" payout at retirement. These plans are generally **noncontributory retirement plans**, which means that you don't have to pay anything into them. (With a **contributory retirement plan**, you, and usually your employer, do pay into the plan.) The payout, which you receive as taxable income, is generally based on a formula that takes into account your age at retirement, salary level, and years of service.

Defined-Benefit Plan
A traditional pension plan in which you receive a promised or "defined" pension payout at retirement. The payout is based on a formula that takes into account your age at retirement, salary level, and years of service.

Noncontributory Retirement Plan
A retirement plan in which the employer provides all the funds and the employee need not contribute.

Contributory Retirement Plan
A retirement plan in which the employee, possibly with the help of the employer, provides the funds for the plan.

The formulas can vary dramatically from company to company. Some focus only on salary during the final few years of service, which is better for you, while others use the average salary from all your years of employment as a base to calculate pension benefits. One commonly used formula is to pay out 1.5 percent of the average of your final 3 to 5 years' worth of salary times your number of years of service.

$$\text{annual benefit} = \text{average salary over "final years"} \times \text{years of service} \times 0.015$$

Thus, if you retired after 25 years of service with an average salary of $70,000 over the final years, you'd receive $26,250 ($70,000 × 25 × 0.015 = $26,250), which would be 37.5 percent of your final average salary. In general, the most that employees, even those who've spent their entire careers with the same company, ever receive from a defined-benefit pension is 40 to 45 percent of their before-retirement income.

One nice thing about a defined-benefit plan is that the employer bears the investment risk associated with the plan. That is, regardless of what the stock and bond markets do, you're still promised the same amount. You also have the option of extending pension coverage to your spouse. When you die, your spouse will continue to receive payments.

FACTS OF LIFE

Workers recently surveyed said they used the following methods to determine the amount of savings they will need for retirement.

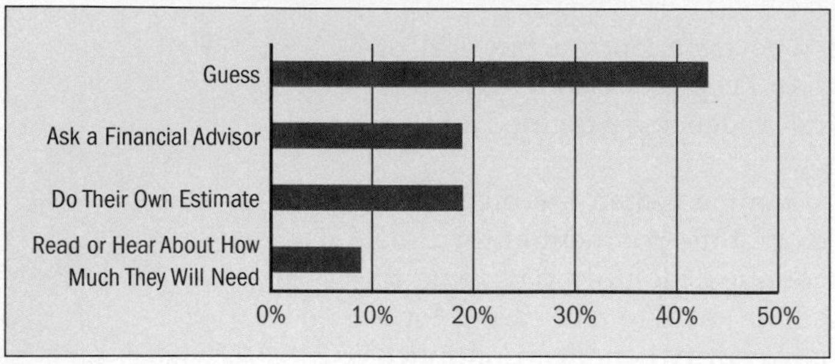

Companies are able to change their pension policies with little notice, and since corporate retirement plans are under pressure to drop traditional pensions, they often do. What has caused this pressure? First, since we live much longer in retirement, that means more pension costs. On top of that, health-care costs have soared in recent years. In addition, low interest rates and a weak stock market have caused pension-funding problems for most corporations. However, the biggest factor pushing corporations to ditch pension funds is competition. While older companies are dumping their pension plans, younger companies just don't offer them to begin with. Look at Microsoft, Wal-Mart, and Southwest Airlines—none of these younger companies offers pension plans.

One additional problem with defined-benefits programs is that they lack **portability**—that is, if you leave the company, your pension doesn't go with you. If you're **vested**, meaning you've worked long enough for the company to have the right to receive pension benefits, you'll eventually get a pension. However, it will likely be small because pensions are generally based on years of service and salary levels. If you're not yet vested and you leave, you can kiss your pension good-bye.

Portability
A pension fund provision that allows employees to retain and transfer any pension benefits already earned to another pension plan if they leave the company.

Vested
To gain the right to the retirement contributions made by your employer in your name. In the case of a pension plan, employees become vested when they've worked for a specified period of time and, thus, gained the right to pension benefits.

Another problem with defined-benefit plans is that few of them—in fact, only one in ten—adjust for inflation once the benefits begin. The benefit level stays constant over your retirement while inflation reduces the spending power of each dollar.

A final problem with defined-benefit plans is that they're not all **funded pension plans**, in which the employer makes regular pension contributions to a trustee who collects and invests the retirement funds. In other words, the employer sets up a separate account to guarantee the payment of pension benefits.

Funded Pension Plan
A pension plan in which the employer makes pension contributions directly to a trustee who holds and invests the employees' retirement funds.

In an **unfunded pension plan**, pension expenses are paid out of current company earnings. These are pay-as-you-go pension plans. Needless to say, a funded plan is much safer than an unfunded plan, which would disappear if the company went under. Fortunately, the law requires employers to notify employees if their pension fund is less than 90 percent funded.

Unfunded Pension Plan
A pension fund in which the benefits are paid out of current earnings on a pay-as-you-go basis.

Cash-Balance Plans: The Latest Twist in Defined-Benefit Plans

In recent years, many large companies, including Eastman Kodak, CBS, Citigroup, and IBM, have switched from traditional defined-benefit plans to **cash-balance plans**. In fact, for firms with fewer than 100 employees, they now make up 29 percent of all defined-benefit plans, up from 2.9 percent in 2001. Cash-balance plans use a different formula for accumulation of benefits, one in which workers are credited with a percentage of their pay each year, plus a predetermined rate of investment earning or interest. Typically, this account earns interest at close to the long-term Treasury bond rate.

Cash-Balance Plan
A retirement plan in which workers are credited with a percentage of their pay, plus a predetermined rate of interest.

With a cash-balance plan, the accounts grow at this set rate regardless of how much is actually earned. In addition, workers don't get to make investment decisions, and they generally get lower returns on their cash balances than they would have been able to earn.

Let's look a bit closer at how these plans work. Under a cash-balance plan, employers contribute a percentage of your salary each year into your account. This generally ranges between 4 and 7 percent. The contribution then grows, generally at the 30-year Treasury bond rate, although some companies allow its growth to be tied to the S&P

500 Index. Then, if you leave the company, you can generally roll the balance into an individual retirement account (explained later in this chapter).

What's the good news? First, your retirement benefits are much easier to track. It is also better for young employees because they start to build up benefits much earlier. In addition, if you leave the company, you can take your cash balance with you. Why have a third of all large companies in the United States converted to cash-balance plans? It's not because these companies are trying to shower their employees with money; it's because they save money with them as a result of reduced future benefits for older workers.

FACTS OF LIFE

One reason it's tougher to save for retirement is that we all live longer than in the past. The average retirement now lasts about 20 years, up from 8 in the 1950s.

Plan Now, Retire Later

LO2 Set up a retirement plan.

PRINCIPLE 2

It's incredibly easy to avoid thinking about retirement. This brings us back to **Principle 2: Nothing Happens Without a Plan**. Saving isn't a natural event—it must be planned. Unfortunately, planning isn't natural either. Although an elaborate, complicated plan might be ideal, you might be better off with a modest, uncomplicated retirement plan. Once the plan becomes part of your financial routine, you can modify and expand it. But a retirement plan can't be postponed; the longer you put it off, the more difficult accomplishing your goals becomes. Figure 15.2 shows the seven steps of the retirement planning process. Let's take a look at each step in depth.

FIGURE 15.2 The Seven Steps to Funding Your Retirement Needs

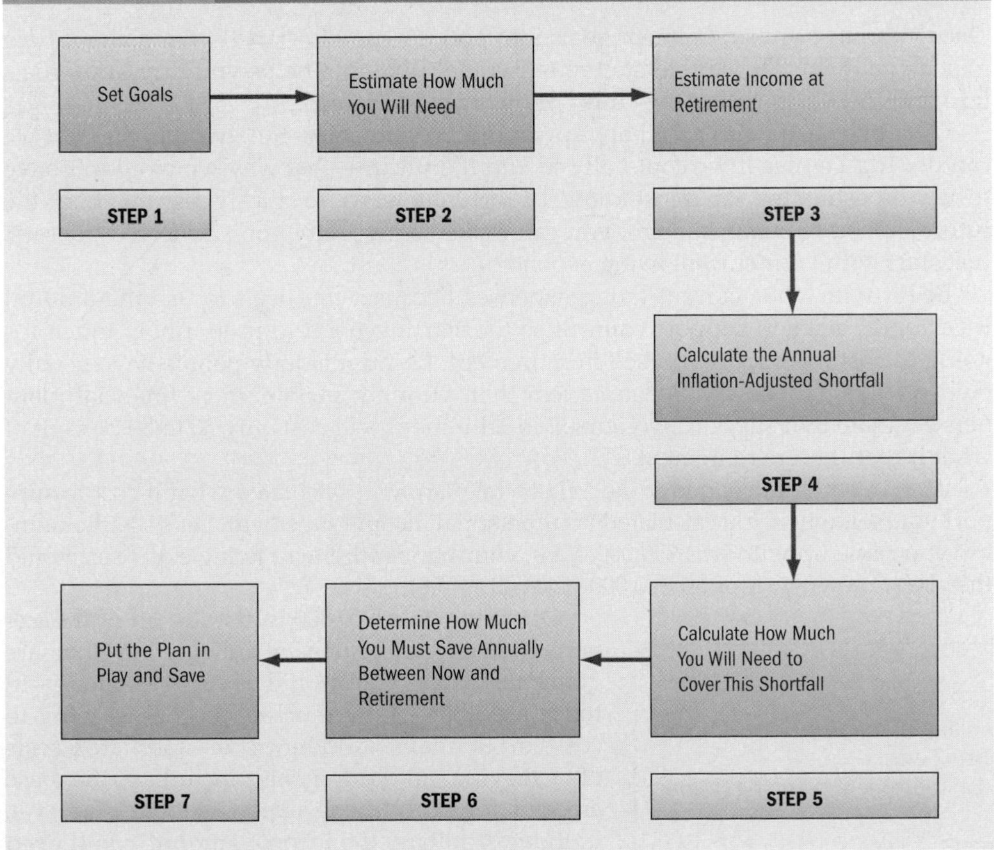

Step 1: Set Goals

The first step in planning for your retirement is figuring out just what you want to do when you retire. Naturally, you want to be able to support yourself and pay any medical bills, but that could cost a little, or it could cost a whole lot. Therefore, you need to start by asking yourself some basic questions: How costly a lifestyle do you want to lead? Do you want to live like a king or more economically, perhaps like a minor duke or nobleman? Do you currently have any medical conditions that you know are going to be costly later in life?

Once you've answered these questions, you can set your first goal as being able to support yourself and pay your medical expenses. Then it's time to think about other goals. Do you want to stay in your current house, or will you want to move to Florida and eat early-bird specials? Do you want to live in a retirement community or your own residence? Do you want to travel? Do you want to be able to buy that Dodge Viper and hit the open road? Do you want to have money set aside for your family? It may be hard to sit down and consider everything you might want to do when you retire, but you'll need to be as exhaustive as possible when setting your goals.

As you learned in Chapter 1, goals aren't entirely useful unless you include the element of time and decide when you hope to achieve them. In the case of retirement, you need to figure out exactly when you'd like to retire. The typical retirement age is 65, but more and more people are putting off retirement until 70 or even later.

The time frame for achieving your goals is more important than you might think. For example, if you want to retire at age 60, you'll need to save up a lot of money to be able to pay for a lengthy retirement. If you really love your job and don't want to retire until you're 70, you won't need to save as much because your period of retirement will likely be shorter and you'll be giving yourself an extra 10 years to prepare for it.

Step 2: Estimate How Much You Will Need

Once you have your retirement goals in place, it's time to start thinking about how to achieve them. The second step of retirement planning helps you turn your goals into dollars by estimating how much money you will need.

Of course, estimates aren't always accurate or reliable—but, hey, it's the best we can do. It'd be nice if we could all see into the future—that way we wouldn't have to rely on estimates. We'd just know. Unfortunately, we're stuck guessing about the future. If you're smart, though, you can make some pretty good educated guesses. Just start with your current living expenses.

Begin with your current living expenses because you need to use the amount it currently takes to support yourself as the starting point to project how much it's going to cost to support yourself in retirement. Because elderly people have usually paid off their house and consume less than younger people, most financial planners estimate that supporting yourself in retirement will cost only 70 to 80 percent of what it costs before retirement.

When you first began to make a financial plan, you calculated what it cost to support yourself when you calculated your personal income statement. Let's say the number you came up with was \$50,000. Well, your basic retirement living expenses would then be somewhere around \$40,000 (\$50,000 × 0.8).

Of course, this \$40,000 is just the tip of the iceberg. Remember, you have other goals that are going to cost money. You'll need to estimate—in today's dollars—how much each goal is going to cost you annually. Adding up the estimated costs of achieving all your goals, including the base amount for your living expenses, will give you, in today's dollars, the income amount you'll need each year to fund your retirement.

FACTS OF LIFE

- Average time spent annually planning for vacations: 4 hours
- Average length of vacation: 1 to 2 weeks
- Average time spent annually on retirement planning: 1 hour or less
- Average time spent in retirement: 19 years

TABLE 15.1 The Average Tax Rate

	Average Tax Rate	
Retirement Income	**Couples Filing Jointly**	**Individuals**
$20,000	7%	10%
30,000	10	14
40,000	12	17
50,000	14	20
60,000	17	22
70,000	19	23
80,000	21	24
90,000	22	25
100,000	23	26
150,000	28	30

Note: To estimate your anticipated average tax rate at retirement, you can use the table above based on current tax rates. Exactly what you pay depends on the number of exemptions, credits, and deductions and on the level of state and sales taxes incurred. If you anticipate a change in future tax rates—for example, a flat tax—use that number.

However, you're not done yet. Don't forget the government. Yes, you need to factor in the effect of taxes. Table 15.1 gives you a rough idea of the average federal and state tax rate you'll pay on your required retirement income. To convert an amount of after-tax retirement income into before-tax income, simply divide the amount of after-tax retirement income you'll need by (1 − your average tax rate), using Table 15.1 to find your average tax rate. For example, if you need $60,000 of after-tax income and you are filing jointly, your tax rate is 17 percent, and you will need $60,000/(1 − 0.17) = $72,289.

Figure 15.3 provides a summary and overview of the calculations involved in funding your retirement needs, while a detailed illustration of these calculations is provided in the appendix to this chapter.

FIGURE 15.3 Funding Your Retirement Needs

A detailed example of the calculations for funding your retirement needs appears in the appendix to this chapter.

Step 1: Set Goals

Step 2: Estimate How Much You Will Need
- Begin with 80% of your present living expenses
- Add in the cost of other goals
- Add in the taxes you'll incur

Step 3: Estimate Income at Retirement
- Income from Social Security
- Any pension benefits
- Any other income

Step 4: Calculate the Annual Inflation-Adjusted Shortfall
- Look at the difference between the totals in Steps 2 and 3
- Adjust for inflation

Step 5: Calculate How Much You Will Need to Cover This Shortfall
- Consider what you'll be earning on your savings after inflation

Step 6: Determine How Much You Must Save Annually Between Now and Retirement
- Determine how much you'll need to save annually to cover the shortfall calculated in Step 5

Step 7: Put the Plan in Play and Save

CHECKLIST 15.1 Questions You Should Be Able to Answer About Your Company's Pension Plan

- ☐ Is this a noncontributory or a contributory plan?
- ☐ What are the pension requirements in terms of age and years of service?
- ☐ Is there an early retirement age, and if so, what are the benefits?
- ☐ What is the full benefits retirement age?
- ☐ How does the vesting process work?
- ☐ If I retire at age 65, how much will I receive in the way of pension payments?
- ☐ If I die, what benefits will my spouse and family receive?
- ☐ What is the present size of my pension credit today?
- ☐ If I am disabled, will I receive pension benefits?
- ☐ Can I withdraw money from my retirement fund before retirement?
- ☐ Can I borrow on my retirement fund, and if so, what are the terms?
- ☐ If my company is taken over or goes bankrupt, what happens to the pension fund?
- ☐ Is the plan funded? If not, what portion of the benefits could the company pay today?
- ☐ What are the choices available to me regarding ways that the pension might be paid out?

Step 3: Estimate Income at Retirement

As you've probably guessed, once you know how much income you're going to need when you retire, the next logical step is to figure out just how much income you're going to have. First, estimate your Social Security benefits. The Social Security Administration mails out annual earnings and benefit statements to all workers age 25 and older (about 125 million) who are not already receiving monthly Social Security benefits. The statement provides estimates of the Social Security retirement, disability, and survivors' benefits you and your family could be eligible to receive now and in the future. (If you didn't save your Social Security statement, call or visit a local Social Security office [1-800-772-1213] or visit the Web site, **http://www.ssa.gov**.) You can also get an estimate of Social Security benefits from the Social Security benefits calculator located at **http://www.ssa.gov/OACT/quickcalc/**. In addition to the Social Security benefits, add any projected pension benefits valued in today's dollars plus any other retirement income available.

To determine how much your pension will pay, stop at your company's employee benefits office. Get a copy of your individual benefit statement, which describes your pension plan and estimates how much your plan is worth today and the level of benefits you'll receive when you retire. There are a number of basic questions included in Checklist 15.1 that you should be able to answer about your company's pension fund.

Step 4: Calculate the Annual Inflation-Adjusted Shortfall

Now it's time to compare the amounts from Steps 2 and 3. For most people, there's a big difference between the retirement income they need and the retirement income they'll have. As pensions are phased out and Social Security becomes less certain, that difference is going to get bigger and bigger.

Step 5: Calculate How Much You Will Need to Cover This Shortfall

By now, you know how much of a projected annual shortfall you have in your retirement funding. That is, you know how much additional money you need to come up with each year to support yourself in retirement. The question then becomes this: How much must you have saved by retirement to fund this annual shortfall?

In determining how much you need to cover this shortfall, you'll want to take into consideration what you can earn on your investments, keeping in mind that each year you'll want a bit more in the way of retirement funds to counteract the effects of inflation.

STOP & THINK

In a survey conducted by Lincoln Financial Group and *Money* magazine, working and retired Americans were asked when their children should start saving for retirement. Their average answer was at age 22. This may sound too soon for most of you, but it's an answer based on experience. The bottom line is that the time to start your retirement savings is now: It will never be easier to reach your goal. Why do you think it's so important to start early?

Step 6: Determine How Much You Must Save Annually Between Now and Retirement

Now you know the total amount you need to save by the time you retire, but don't panic—you're not about to put it all away at once. Instead, you need to put money away little by little, year by year. Let's figure out how much to put away each year.

Once you know how much you need to save, determining how much you need to save annually is pretty easy. You can use the financial calculator on the Web site that accompanies this book to solve for *PMT*, the annual annuity, just as you did in Chapter 3 when you looked at amortized loans. If you'd like a bit of help in determining just what you need to save for retirement, there are several excellent online retirement planning Web sites highlighted in Table 15.2.

Step 7: Put the Plan in Play and Save

OK, you've finally figured out exactly how much you need to save each year to achieve your retirement goals. Now all you need to do is start saving. This last step should be the easiest, right? Wrong. It's actually one of the hardest. There are countless ways to save for retirement, and in order to choose the one that's best for you, you have to know what's available out there.

TABLE 15.2 Online Retirement Planning

Website: T. Rowe Price Retirement Income Calculator
Online Availability: Simply Google "T. Rowe Price Retirement Income Calculator"
Features: • Is free and extremely easy to use. • Allows you to project your monthly retirement income based on different planning scenarios. • Bases results on a Monte Carlo simulation under different market conditions.
Website: Vanguard Retirement Nest Egg Calculator
Online Availability: Simply Google "Vanguard retirement nest egg calculator"
Features: • Is simple and very easy to use; requires only six inputs but is still sophisticated. • Bases results on a Monte Carlo simulation using historical returns.
Website: myPlan by Fidelity
Online Availability: Simply Google "Fidelity Planning & Retirement Center"
Features: • Is free and extremely easy to use. • Uses five easy questions to help you gain a general understanding of how much money you need to retire. • Provides plenty of easy-to-understand guidance and answers to common questions in the Retirement Resource Center.

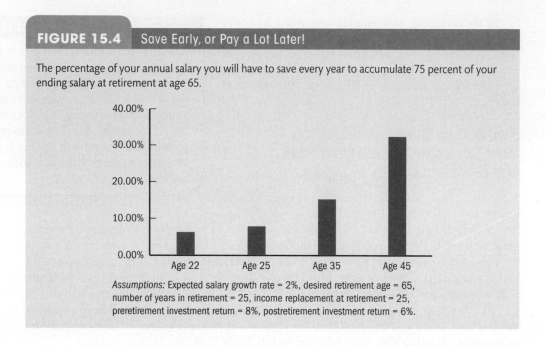

FIGURE 15.4 Save Early, or Pay a Lot Later!

The percentage of your annual salary you will have to save every year to accumulate 75 percent of your ending salary at retirement at age 65.

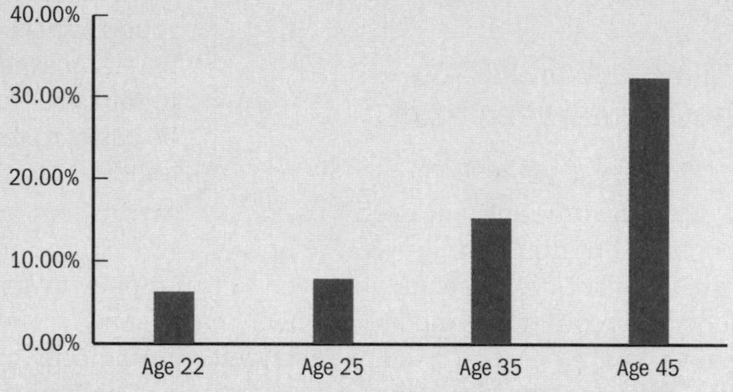

Assumptions: Expected salary growth rate = 2%, desired retirement age = 65, number of years in retirement = 25, income replacement at retirement = 25, preretirement investment return = 8%, postretirement investment return = 6%.

The real key to being successful in saving for your retirement is an appreciation of the power of compounding because with that understanding you know how important it is to start saving for retirement as soon as you get your first paycheck. What's the cost of waiting a few years? It's dramatic, or perhaps overwhelming is the right word. From Figure 15.4, you can see that if you start saving at 22, you'll only need to set aside 6.5 percent of your annual income less any employer match. But if you wait until 25, it climbs to 7.9 percent, and at 35, it climbs to 15.3 percent. If you wait until 45, good luck! You're going to have to set aside 32.3 percent of your income to reach the same goal.

In the next few sections, we will not only walk you through the various types of retirement savings plans but also give you plenty of good advice to get you on your way. Whatever you decide to do, be sure you don't take the "saving" part of the retirement planning process too lightly. Watch out for that last step—it's a doozie!

What Plan Is Best for You?

What's the best way to save for retirement? Well, that really depends on your circumstances. There are so many options available, some of them very job or occupation specific, that it's hard to make general statements about what plans are right for everyone. However, it's safe to say that you should certainly try to use a tax-favored retirement plan.

Most plans are tax deferred and work by allowing investment earnings to go untaxed until you remove these earnings at retirement. In essence, they allow you to put off paying taxes so that you can invest the money that would otherwise have gone to the IRS. In addition, some plans allow for the contributions to be made on either a fully or a partially tax-deductible basis. In retirement planning, **Principle 4: Taxes Affect Personal Finance Decisions** can't be overstressed.

PRINCIPLE 4

There are several advantages to tax-deferred plans. First, because the contributions may not be taxed, you can contribute more. You can contribute funds that would otherwise go to the IRS. Second, because the investment earnings aren't taxed until they're withdrawn at retirement, you can earn money on earnings that also would have otherwise gone to the IRS. In other words, remember the power

FIGURE 15.5 Saving in a Tax-Deferred Retirement Account Versus Saving on a Non-Tax-Deferred Basis

Assume the following: (1) an annual investment of $2,000 of before-tax income in a retirement account where those contributions are fully tax deductible and an annual investment of $2,000 of before-tax income on a non-tax-deferred basis; (2) a 9 percent annual return on these investments, with investment earnings in the tax-deferred account being tax deferred and earnings in the other account being taxed annually; and (3) a marginal state and federal tax rate of 31 percent.

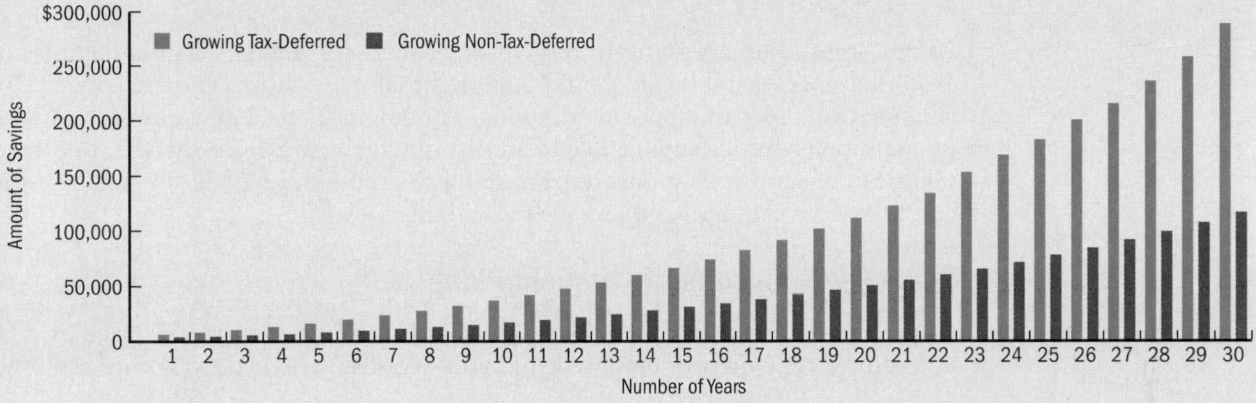

of compounding—you can earn compound interest on money that would normally have gone to the IRS.

Figure 15.5 shows just how dramatic this compounding can be. Let's assume you wish to invest $2,000 of before-tax income on an annual basis in a retirement account. Let's also assume you can earn 9 percent compounded annually on this investment and your marginal state and federal tax rate is 31 percent.

If you invest in a tax-deferred retirement account for which the contributions are fully tax deductible, you start off and end up with more money. You start with more money because, after taxes, you still have your full $2,000 to invest. You end up with more money because you'll be able to compound more of your earnings instead of paying them to the IRS.

Investing in a fully taxable retirement account is a different story. To begin with, you won't be able to invest the entire $2,000 because 31 percent of this amount will go toward your state and federal taxes, leaving you with only $1,380 to invest. In addition, the investment earnings will be taxed annually, at a rate of 31 percent.

Figure 15.5 compares these retirement plans with annual investments of $2,000 of before-tax income for 30 years. After 10 years, you'd have accumulated $33,121 in the tax-deferred account but only $19,511 in the taxable account. After 20 years, the tax-deferred account would have grown to $111,529, whereas the taxable account would be at $55,150. Finally, after 30 years, the tax-deferred account would have grown to $297,150, whereas the taxable account would have accumulated only $120,250.

> **FACTS OF LIFE**
>
> According to a recent survey, over 50 percent of Gen Xers (aged 35 to 54) have less than $10,000 saved for retirement, and over 42 percent of Millennials (aged 18 to 34) have yet to begin saving for retirement. Even scarier is the fact that over 45 percent of Baby Boomers and Seniors (those over 55) have less than $10,000 saved for retirement!

Of course, Uncle Sam does catch up eventually. When you withdraw your retirement funds, the amounts initially invested on a pretax basis and the interest earned on it over the years are taxed, but at least you had the chance to earn plenty of extra interest.

There are major advantages to saving on a tax-deferred basis. It's pure and simple smart investing. Before you look into any other types of retirement investments, check out the ones that are tax favored. There are plenty of these plans currently available. Some are employer sponsored, and others are aimed at the self-employed. Let's take a look.

LO3 Understand how different retirement plans work.

Retirement Plans in Addition to Social Security and Employer-Funded Pensions

For those who aren't going to receive a pension, some type of retirement plan is absolutely necessary. But it should be noted that even those who are covered by a pension can also participate in additional retirement plans. For example, many people with pensions also contribute to an IRA (which we describe shortly). Retirement plans can be employer sponsored, set up for the self-employed or for small-business employees, or set up directly by the individual.

Employer-Sponsored Retirement Plans

Many times your employer will already have a retirement plan in place in which your employer—or your employer and you—contributes directly to your retirement plan.

Defined-Contribution Plan
A pension plan in which you and your employer or your employer alone contributes directly to a retirement account set aside specifically for you. In effect, a defined-contribution plan can be thought of as a savings account for retirement.

Defined-Contributions Plans Under a **defined-contribution plan**, your employer alone or you and your employer together contribute directly to an individual account that is set aside specifically for you. In effect, a defined-contribution plan can be thought of as a personal savings account for retirement. Your eventual payments aren't guaranteed. Instead, what you eventually receive depends on how well your retirement account performs. Many defined-contribution plans allow you to choose how your account is invested.

In recent years, the popularity of such programs has skyrocketed because they involve no risk for the employer. The employer's job involves doing a bit of bookkeeping and making a financial contribution. Employers don't really care what you eventually receive; their responsibility ends with their contribution. In effect, defined-contribution plans pass the responsibility for retirement from employer to employee. They also pass the risk because they aren't insured and payments aren't guaranteed.

Defined-contribution plans generally take one of several basic forms, including profit-sharing plans, money purchase plans, thrift and savings plans, and employee stock ownership plans.

Profit-Sharing Plan
A pension plan in which the company's contributions vary from year to year, depending on the firm's performance. The amount of money contributed to each employee depends on the employee's salary level.

Money Purchase Plan
A pension plan in which the employer contributes a set percentage of employees' salaries to their retirement plans annually.

Thrift and Savings Plan
A pension plan in which the employer matches a percentage of the employees' contributions to their retirement accounts.

Profit-Sharing Plans Under a **profit-sharing plan**, employer contributions can vary from year to year depending on the firm's performance. Although many firms set a minimum and a maximum contribution—for example, between 2 and 12 percent of each employee's salary annually—not all firms do. A contribution is not necessarily guaranteed under this type of plan. If the firm has a poor year, it may pass on making a contribution to the plan.

Money Purchase Plans Under a **money purchase plan**, the employer contributes a set percentage of employees' salaries to their retirement plans annually. For the employer, such a plan offers less flexibility because contributions are required, regardless of how well the firm does. For the employee, these plans are preferable to profit-sharing plans because of the guaranteed contribution.

Thrift and Savings Plans Under a **thrift and savings plan**, the employer matches a percentage of employees' contributions to their retirement accounts.

Employee Stock Ownership Plans Under an **employee stock ownership plan (ESOP)**, the company's contribution is made in the form of company stock. Of all the retirement plans, this is the riskiest because your return at retirement depends on how well the company does. If the company goes bankrupt, you might lose not only your job but also all your retirement benefits. Of course, if the company's stock price soars, you could do extremely well. However, an ESOP doesn't allow for the degree of diversification that you need with your retirement savings. In short, an ESOP isn't something you can safely rely on.

Employee Stock Ownership Plan (ESOP)
A retirement plan in which the retirement funds are invested directly into the company's stock.

401(k) Plans A **401(k) plan** is really a do-it-yourself variation of a profit-sharing/thrift plan. These plans can be set up as part of an employer-sponsored defined-contribution plan, with both the employer and the employee contributing to the plan or with only the employee making a contribution. Over the past 20 years, these plans have exploded in terms of popularity. In fact, about nine out of ten large employers—that is, companies employing over 500 workers—provide 401(k) plans for their workers. Corporations love them because they allow the retirement program to be handed over entirely to the employee.

401(k) Plan
A tax-deferred retirement savings plan in which employees of private corporations may contribute a portion of their wages up to a maximum amount set by law ($18,000 in 2017 and rising in the future with inflation in $500 increments). Employers may contribute a full or partial matching amount and may limit the proportion of the annual salary contributed.

A 401(k) plan is a tax-deferred retirement plan in which both the employee's contributions to the plan and the earnings on those contributions are tax deductible, with all taxes being deferred until retirement withdrawals are made.[1] In essence, a 401(k) is equivalent to the tax-deferred retirement plan presented earlier in Figure 15.5.

The advantages to such an account are twofold. First, you don't pay taxes on money contributed to 401(k) plans, which means you can add money into your retirement account that would have otherwise been paid out as taxes. Second, your earnings on your retirement account are tax deferred. Thus, you can earn a return on money that would otherwise have been paid out in taxes. The end result, as shown in Figure 15.5, is that you can accumulate a much larger retirement nest egg using a 401(k) account than you otherwise could. So you should invest the maximum allowable amount in your 401(k) account. You should do this before you consider any other taxed investment alternatives. Moreover, this should be automatic—that is, your 401(k) should be paid before you receive anything. Only after you have maxed out on your 401(k) contributions should you consider other investments.

Many 401(k) plans are set up as thrift and savings plans, in which the employer matches a percentage of the employee's contribution, with the most common matching program being a 50 percent match on the first 6 percent contributed to the 401(k) plan. There is extremely wide variation on these plans, so you'll want to check on yours. BB&T, for example, has a very generous matching program and matches 100 percent of the first 6 percent of the workers' contributions..

Needless to say, a matching 401(k) program increases participation. In addition, a matching plan is an offer that's too good to refuse. It's free money, and you should take advantage of any matching the company is willing to do.

PRINCIPLE 9

Also, 401(k) plans offer a wide variety of investment options. In fact, over half of all 401(k) plans offer five or more investment choices. These options range from conservative guaranteed investment contracts (GICs) to aggressive stock funds.

How much can you contribute? The limits on contributions to these plans are on the rise. For 2017, the limit on employee contributions to 401(k) and 403(b) plans (and also to SEP-IRA plans, which will be

FACTS OF LIFE

Behavioral finance and **Principle 9: Mind Games, Your Financial Personality, and Your Money** play a major role in how you save for retirement. In fact, Congress acknowledged this when it enacted the Pension Protection Act of 2006, which allows employers to enroll workers automatically in defined-contribution plans.

[1]A *403(b) plan* is essentially the same as a 401(k) plan except that it's aimed at employees of schools and charitable organizations. Although our discussion will focus on 401(k) plans, it also holds true for 403(b) plans.

covered shortly) was set at $18,000, and this limit rises with inflation in $500 increments. Also, taxpayers over 50 are allowed to make additional annual "catch-up" contributions of $6,000, with that limit also indexed for inflation.

Retirement Plans for the Self-Employed and Small-Business Employees

Fully tax-deductible retirement plans for the self-employed or small-business employee—which includes anyone who has his or her own business, works for a small business, or does freelance work on a part-time basis—offer the same basic advantages as employer-sponsored plans available in large corporations. You qualify for such a plan if you do any work for yourself (even if you work full-time for an employer and are covered by another retirement plan there).

It's surprising how many individuals qualify for these plans and either don't realize it or do nothing to take advantage of another tax-deferred retirement tool. Examples of those who are eligible are lawyers, doctors, dentists, carpenters, plumbers, artists, freelance writers, and consultants. Basically, if you're self-employed, either full-time or part-time, or work for an unincorporated business, you can contribute to a Keogh or self-employed retirement plan, a simplified employee pension plan (SEP-IRA), or the newer savings incentive match plan for employees (SIMPLE).

Keogh Plan
A tax-sheltered retirement plan for the self-employed.

Keogh Plans or Self-Employed Retirement Plans **Keogh plans** are similar to corporate pension or profit-sharing plans, and establishing a Keogh plan is relatively easy. These plans can be set up through a bank, mutual fund, or other financial institution.

Keogh plans are all self-directed, meaning you decide what securities to buy and sell and when to do so. As with 401(k) plans, the payment to the plan occurs before you determine your taxes, so any contributions reduce your bill to Uncle Sam. Withdrawals can begin as early as age 59½ and must begin by age 70½. If you need your money early, you'll have to pay a 10 percent penalty, except in cases of serious illness, disability, or death.

Simplified Employee Pension Plan (SEP-IRA)
A tax-sheltered retirement plan (you don't pay taxes on any earnings while they remain in the plan) aimed at small businesses or at the self-employed.

Simplified Employee Pension Plans A **simplified employee pension plan (SEP-IRA)** is similar to a defined-contribution Keogh plan funded by the employer. SEP-IRAs are used primarily by small-business owners with no or very few employees. Each employee sets up his or her own individual retirement account, and the employer makes annual contributions to that account. For 2017, the total deduction limit is 25 percent of the employee's salary or $54,000, whichever is less. This contribution limit is indexed annually for inflation.

In addition, there's flexibility in making contributions. For example, they can be made one year and not the next, and when they are made, they're immediately vested. The advantage of a SEP-IRA program is that it works about the same as a Keogh plan but is easier to set up. In addition, a SEP-IRA doesn't have the reporting requirements of a Keogh.

FACTS OF LIFE

According to a recent TransAmerica survey, one out of four Millennials who have saved for retirement is not sure how his or her retirement savings are invested.

Savings Incentive Match Plan for Employees (SIMPLE)
A tax-sheltered retirement plan aimed at small businesses or the self-employed that provides for some matching funds by the employer to be deposited into the employee's retirement account.

Savings Incentive Match Plans for Employees Small employers can establish a **savings incentive match plan for employees (SIMPLE)**—there are SIMPLE IRAs and SIMPLE 401(k)s. These new plans may be set up by employers with fewer than 100 employees earning $5,000 or more, covering all their employees, including themselves. Employee contributions are excluded from income, and the earnings in the retirement plan are tax deferred. In addition to employee contributions, there are some matching funds provided by the employer—although the employer does have some flexibility in determining how much to contribute.

Why did Congress decide to establish one more type of retirement plan? Because many smaller businesses were put off by complex and expensive alternative plans and, thus, didn't provide retirement plans for their employees. That's where the SIMPLE fits in—because the rules governing it are, as the name implies, simple.

Individual Retirement Arrangements

There are three types of **individual retirement arrangements (IRAs)**, often referred to as *individual retirement accounts*, to choose from: the traditional IRA, the Roth IRA, and the Coverdell Education Savings Account, previously called the Education IRA. Let's look at each of them.

Individual Retirement Arrangement (IRA)
A tax-advantaged retirement account. The contribution may or may not be tax deductible, depending on the individual's income level and whether he or she, or his or her spouse, is covered by a company retirement plan.

Traditional IRAs Traditional IRAs, often called *individual retirement accounts*, are personal savings plans that give you tax advantages for saving for retirement. Contributions to a traditional IRA may be tax deductible—either in whole or in part, depending on the level of your earnings and whether you or your spouse has a company retirement plan. Also, you don't pay any taxes on the money as it grows in your IRA until it is distributed. In addition, the portion of the tax-deductible contribution is not taxed until it is distributed.

The maximum amount you could contribute to an IRA was $5,500 in 2017, and thereafter that limit will be adjusted for inflation in $500 increments, but individuals age 50 and over are permitted to make an additional annual contribution of $1,000.

If both you and your spouse are employed and aren't covered by a company retirement plan, you can each contribute up to the maximum annually to an IRA on a tax-deferred basis. Even if only one of you works outside the home, both of you can contribute to an IRA, provided the "working spouse" has earned income at least equal to the amount you both contribute. If neither of you is an "active participant" in a retirement plan at work or if your joint adjusted gross income is below the IRS cutoff, your IRA contributions are entirely tax deductible.

What's an "active participant"? If you have a defined-benefit retirement plan, you're considered an active participant. In addition, if you have a defined-contribution plan and either you or your employer contributed to it during the year, you're considered an active participant, and there is an income limit after which your IRA contributions are no longer tax deductible. However, if neither you nor your employer contributed to your defined-contribution plan during the year or your income is below the cutoff level, you can make a fully deductible contribution to your IRA.

There's also a provision that allows a nonworking spouse to make a deductible contribution to an IRA even if the working spouse is covered by a qualified retirement plan or his or her income is high. Under this provision, a nonworking spouse can make a fully deductible contribution to an IRA as long as his or her "modified" adjusted gross income (AGI) is below $184,000,[2] even if the other spouse is covered by a qualified retirement plan, where modified AGI is adjusted gross income before subtracting IRA deductions. In addition, a partial deduction is allowed until income hits $194,000. Partial tax deductions are also available for IRA contributions, again depending on income level.

FACTS OF LIFE

According to a recent TransAmerica survey, 86% of Gen Xers are concerned that Social Security will *not* be there for them when they are ready to retire.

For the tax year 2017, if you were covered by a retirement plan at work, the trigger point for full deductibility of IRA contributions was $62,000 of modified AGI for those filing single returns and $99,000 for those filing joint returns. Once modified AGI reached $72,000 for those filing single returns and $119,000 for those filing joint

[2]For the 2017 tax year.

returns, deductibility was totally phased out. But keep in mind, if you were not covered by a retirement plan at work, you could have taken a full deduction up to your contribution limit of $5,500 if you're under 50 years old.

If all contributions to your IRA are tax deductible, then all withdrawals from your IRA will be taxed unless you're just moving your money into another IRA. There are also restrictions on the timing and amount of IRA withdrawals, as follows:

- Distributions before age 59½ are subject to a 10 percent tax penalty with few exceptions.
- After you turn 70½, you must start receiving annual distributions under a life expectancy calculation.
- You can make penalty-free withdrawals provided you (a) are making them to buy your first home, (b) are using them for college expenses, (c) become disabled, (d) need the money to pay medical expenses in excess of 7.5 percent of your AGI, or (e) need the money to pay medical insurance payments if you've been unemployed for at least 12 consecutive weeks. There is, however, a limit of $10,000 on penalty-free withdrawals to buy a first home.

In addition to annual contributions to an IRA, you can roll over a distribution from a qualified employer plan or from another IRA into a new IRA. Why would you ever do this? If you get a new job or if you retire early, you may be faced with that 10 percent early distribution penalty. To get around this penalty, you can instead have your distributions rolled over into a new IRA. If you're going to roll over your distributions into a new IRA, make sure you see a financial advisor or tax accountant ahead of time because there are a number of rollover rules you need to follow to avoid taxes.

What are your investment choices with an IRA? You can go with stocks, bonds, mutual funds, real estate, certificates of deposit (CDs)—almost anything. It's your call because IRAs are self-directed, and you can change your IRA funds from one investment to another at any time without paying taxes. The only things you can't invest in are life insurance and collectibles other than gold or silver U.S. coins. You also can't borrow from your IRA, and you can't use it as collateral for a loan.

FACTS OF LIFE

The average personal savings rate in the United States has declined dramatically in the last four decades:

1970s: 9.6%	1990s: 5.5%	February 2017: 5.6%
1980s: 8.6%	2000s: 2.9%	

Saver's Tax Credit Low- and moderate-income workers are also provided with help in saving for retirement in the form of the saver's tax credit. The saver's credit helps offset part of the first $2,000 ($4,000 if married filing jointly) workers voluntarily contribute to IRAs and to 401(k) plans and similar workplace retirement programs and is available in addition to any other tax savings that apply. The maximum saver's credit is $1,000 for individuals and $2,000 for married couples, with the taxpayer's credit amount based on his or her filing status, adjusted gross income, tax liability, and amount contributed to qualifying retirement programs.

The idea behind this tax credit is to encourage low- and moderate-income workers to save for retirement. There are income limits on this tax credit; for example, a married couple filing a joint return earning more than $62,000 in 2017 was not eligible. Similar to other tax credits, the saver's credit can increase a taxpayer's refund or reduce the tax owed. Needless to say, this is a credit that you want to take advantage of if you qualify.

Roth IRA
An IRA in which contributions are not tax deductible. That is, you make your contribution to this IRA out of after-tax income. But once the money is in there, it grows tax free, and when it is withdrawn, the withdrawals are tax free.

Roth IRAs A **Roth IRA** is a personal savings plan similar to a traditional IRA, but it operates in a somewhat reverse manner. For instance, while contributions to a traditional IRA may be tax deductible, contributions to a Roth IRA are *not* tax deductible. However, while distributions (including earnings) from a traditional IRA are taxed, the distributions (including earnings) from a Roth IRA are distributed on an after-tax basis. One similarity between the traditional IRA and the Roth IRA is that with both, you don't pay any taxes while your money is in the IRA.

The big advantage of the Roth IRA is that you can avoid taxes when you finally withdraw your money. Of course, as with everything else in the tax code, there are some exceptions. First, to avoid taxes, you must keep your money in your Roth IRA for at least 5 years.

Who's eligible to put money into a Roth IRA? A lot of people! The income limits are inflation adjusted and in 2017 didn't begin until $118,000 for single taxpayers and $186,000 for couples (but there is a backdoor around those limits, which we will mention in a moment). Keep in mind that even if you have a 401(k) account, you can also contribute to an IRA. You can have both a traditional IRA and a Roth IRA; however, your total contributions to both are limited to the maximum IRA contribution level, which was $5,500 in 2017 and thereafter will be adjusted for inflation in $500 increments.

Another great feature of the Roth IRA is that, at any time, you can pull out an amount up to your original contribution without getting hit with a tax penalty. Also with the Roth IRA, there is no requirement that distributions begin by age 70½.

In addition to your annual contribution, you can roll money from your existing IRA into your Roth IRA without incurring a 10 percent penalty. For the tax year 2017 and thereafter (unless Congress closes this loophole), you can use this conversion loophole to fund a Roth IRA, regardless of your income level. This is the backdoor method of funding a Roth IRA mentioned earlier that sidesteps the income limits on Roth IRAs. Since anyone can make after-tax contributions to a traditional IRA, regardless of his or her income level, you can put after-tax money in a traditional IRA and then convert it to a Roth IRA, thereby sidestepping the income eligibility requirements attached to the Roth IRA. Remember, when you convert a traditional IRA to a Roth IRA, you have to pay taxes on any pretax contributions as well as any growth in the investment value, but since your contributions to your traditional IRA were made on an after-tax basis, you would pay taxes only on any growth in investment value.

FACTS OF LIFE

If you are 27 right now and contribute $5,500 (remember that was the maximum contribution in 2017, and it will be small in comparison to allowable future contributions) to a Roth IRA and if you earn 9.854 percent on your investments (that's the average return on large company stocks since 1960), when you turn 67, you'll have $2,339,624 and no taxes! Not too shabby, eh? If you started when you were 22, you'd end up with over $3.77 million.

Traditional Versus Roth IRA: Which Is Best for You? Mathematically, you end up with the same amount to spend at retirement if you use a traditional IRA or a Roth IRA and you put the same amount of money into both, provided both are taxed at the same rate. So which one should you choose? If you can afford it, the answer is the Roth IRA. That's because you can take care of taxes ahead of time and end up with more money to *spend* at retirement. In effect, you're putting more money into the Roth IRA because the Roth IRA includes a $5,500 contribution *plus* the taxes you'd pay on that $5,500 contribution.

In terms of after-tax contributions, if you are in the 28 percent tax bracket, a $5,500 contribution to a Roth IRA will cost you $7,639 of before-tax income—$5,500 for the contribution and $2,139 for taxes ($7,639 × 0.28 = $2,139)—that is, to come up with $5,500 of after-tax income, you would first need to pay taxes, and you'd need $7,739 to cover your taxes and leave you with $5,500 to invest in your Roth IRA. If you put $5,500 in a traditional IRA and let it grow at 10 percent for 40 years, you'd end up with $248,926 before you paid any taxes—after taxes, at 28 percent, you'd have $194,162. If you put $5,500 in a Roth IRA, you need a bit more money on the front end (as we just showed, $7,639) because you have to pay taxes, but you'd end up with $248,926 after 40 years and no taxes!

LOVE & MONEY

When it comes to retirement planning, there seems to be a gap between what Millennial couples say and what they understand. According to a new *Money* magazine poll, 79 percent of Millennials say they are in agreement with their partner on saving for retirement. On the other hand, only one in four knew their partner's retirement account balance, and 40 percent of them had no idea their partner planned to retire.

What all this means is that many couples really haven't come to grips with retirement planning, and without question, given how much money must be amassed in order to retire comfortably, retirement planning should be a top priority for everyone. It's tough enough planning for the weekend, but to plan 40 years out is daunting at best. Moreover, given the fact that you may have grown up in a family where saving for retirement—or money in general, for that matter—was not something talked about as a family, you may be entering this discussion with no background at all. Add to this the fact that women live longer and are less likely to have a pension, that you and your partner may be different ages, and you and your partner may have different needs when it comes to retirement. And for example, by different needs, it could be that one partner may be expected to live 10 years longer than the other. The bottom line is that it can get very complicated.

So how do you begin to come up with a retirement plan? Without question, the key is that you must work out this plan together. One challenge to this is the fact that many times one partner thinks he or she is better at retirement planning than the other partner is. That's a bad way to begin the retirement planning conversation. Remember, another key is listening to and respecting the other person, and if you think you're better at retirement planning, many times you don't listen as you should.

Thus, the first step, as with almost everything else in financial planning, is an open conversation. Yes, you need a plan, but before you can hammer out a plan, you need to determine when you want to retire (even if that might be 40 years from now), where you want to live (it's a big world and you need to at least narrow your choices—maybe someplace warm and exotic or near your future grandchildren), and what kind of lifestyle you and your partner expect. From there, the question becomes, Are you saving enough to reach your goals?

You'll want to make sure you're acting as a team when it comes to saving and investing. As you start out in life, it is likely that your tax bracket will be at its lowest level. That means you'll want to first take advantage of any cash matches that your firm might offer on your 401(k) and then contribute to your Roth IRA at the maximum level, if possible. If you're a two-income household, you probably have access to two 401(k) or 403(b) accounts—you'll want to make the maximum contributions there, if possible, but you at least want to contribute enough to get your full company match. If maxing out your contributions simply isn't feasible, every time you get a raise, increase those contributions.

As for what to invest in? Don't be disturbed if you and your partner view risk differently. In fact, a UBS survey found that about half of couples have divergent risk tolerances and that those who were most happy ended up choosing an asset allocation falling somewhere between their risk preferences. All this begins with a dialogue, and once you've got things in motion, check back on your progress often—just to make sure you are on track!

Who Thinks They Are Better at Retirement Planning?

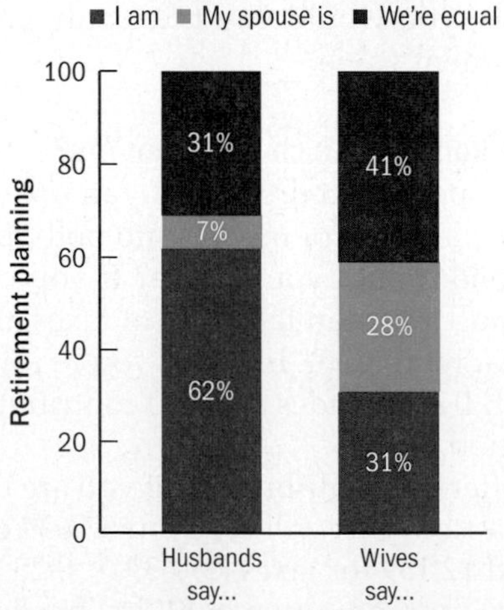

Saving for College: Coverdell Education Savings Accounts Sure, college isn't retirement, but if you don't save properly for your children's college education, you may end up having to postpone retirement after dipping into your retirement savings. Fortunately, there are some tools out there meant to both help and inspire you to save for college. While we looked at them in depth in Chapter 7, a quick refresher is in order. One is the **Coverdell Education Savings Account**, which was previously called the **Education IRA**. This works just like the Roth IRA except with respect to contributions. Again, the earnings are tax free, there is no tax on withdrawals to pay for education, and the definition of a qualified educational expense now includes certain elementary and secondary school expenses.

The other way to save for college is through a 529 plan. A **529 plan** is a tax-advantaged savings plan used only for college and graduate school; it allows you to contribute up to $250,000 to $380,000 (depending on the state-sponsored plan), which can then grow tax free. These plans began in the 1990s because of the rule that doesn't allow the federal government to tax money that's given to a state. The result was that these accounts were tax deferred, a situation that was later made permanent by Congress. Although these plans are sponsored by individual states, they are open to all applicants, regardless of where they live, and can be used at any accredited college or university in the country (including some foreign institutions). Thus, if you are a resident of North Carolina, you can put money in a 529 plan in Michigan, or in any state for that matter, and use the funds in another state. You can also invest directly, or you can invest through a financial advisor (and, of course, pay a commission). In addition, in some states, part or all of your contribution may be tax deductible.

Coverdell Education Savings Account or Education IRA
An IRA that works just like the Roth IRA except with respect to contributions. Contributions are limited to $2,000 annually per child for each child younger than 18, with income limits beginning at $110,000 for single taxpayers and $220,000 for couples. The earnings are tax free, and there is no tax on withdrawals to pay for education.

529 Plan
A tax-advantaged savings plan used only for college and graduate school.

Facing Retirement—The Payout

LO4 Choose how your retirement benefits are paid out to you.

You might think that once you've saved enough for retirement, coming up with a plan for distributing those savings would be simple. Think again. Your distribution or payout decision affects how much you receive, how it's taxed, whether you're protected against inflation, whether you might outlive your retirement funds, and a host of other important concerns. Checklist 15.2 provides a listing of key ages associated with retirement planning.

Some plans have more flexibility than others—for example, traditional (non-Roth) IRAs allow for withdrawals to begin at age 59½, with withdrawals becoming compulsory at age 70½. Still, there are several basic distribution choices, which include receiving your payout as a lump sum, in the form of an annuity for a set number of years or for your lifetime, or as some combination of the two. Although there isn't one best way to receive your retirement distribution, there are a number of important points to keep in mind when making this decision.

- **Taxes:** Make sure you plan ahead before you decide how to receive a payout. Make sure you understand the tax consequences of any decision.
- **Flow:** In deciding how to receive a payout, make sure you look at all your retirement plan payouts together. You may want to take some plan distributions in a lump sum and others as an annuity.
- **Use:** Once you receive your retirement plan payout, make sure you use your understanding of investing, including diversification and the time dimension of risk, when deciding what to do with those funds.

Let's now take a look at some of the specifics behind these distribution options.

CHECKLIST 15.2 A Retirement Checklist for the Ages

- ☐ **Age 50:** At 50, you are eligible to make extra or "catch-up" contributions (beyond what younger individuals can contribute) to your 401(k) or similar retirement plan and to your IRA. For 401(k), 403(b), 457, SIMPLE IRA, and salary reduction SEP plans, the catch-up amount was $5,500 in 2017 and is indexed to inflation in the future. For an IRA, the catch-up amount was $1,000.
- ☐ **Age 55:** If you leave your job or retire and you're between the ages of 55 and 59½, you can begin withdrawals from your 401(k) without paying a 10 percent early withdrawal penalty. However, unless you roll the money over into an IRA or another 401(k), you will have to pay income taxes on your withdrawal.
- ☐ **Age 59½:** Once you reach 59½, regardless of whether you've retired or left your job, the 10 percent penalty on early withdrawals from your 401(k) or your IRA no longer applies. Unless you roll the money over into an IRA or another 401(k), you'll have to pay income tax on it.
- ☐ **Age 62:** At 62, you've finally reached the Social Security early retirement age. At that age, you become eligible to start receiving Social Security. However, the longer you wait (up until age 70), the higher your benefit will be (**http://www.ssa.gov/planners/calculators.htm**). Also, the more money you make at your job, the more you will receive in Social Security benefits.
- ☐ **Age 62 to 70:** The longer you wait to begin receiving Social Security, the larger your benefit will be. The exact size of your benefit depends on your "full retirement age," which is determined by the year you were born (**http://www.ssa.gov/retire2**).
- ☐ **Age 65:** At 65, you qualify for Medicare coverage. You'll want to take it even if you want to postpone Social Security a bit longer (**http://www.medicare.gov**). One thing you want to make sure of is that you have health insurance if you retire before you turn 65 and Medicare kicks in. You don't want to be retired without health care coverage—that's a recipe for financial disaster.
- ☐ **Age 70½:** Once you've reached 70½, you can no longer contribute to your 401(k) or traditional IRA (but you can continue to contribute to a Roth IRA as long as you have earned income). You must also begin withdrawing money in the form of a required minimum distribution (RMD), which is based on a formula that looks at your life expectancy by April 1 of the year following the year you turn 70½. In addition, you have to pay income taxes on these withdrawals unless they're from a Roth IRA.

An Annuity, or Lifetime Payments

An annuity provides you with an annual payout. This payout can go for a set number of years, it can be in the form of lifetime payments for either you or you and your spouse, or it can be in the form of lifetime payments with a minimum number of payments guaranteed. In short, just deciding on an annuity isn't enough—you must also decide among several variations of an annuity.

Single Life Annuity
An annuity in which you receive a set monthly payment for the rest of your life.

A Single Life Annuity Under a **single life annuity**, you receive a set monthly payment for your entire life. Think of this type of annuity as the Energizer® bunny—it just keeps going and going, at least as long as you do. If you die after 1 year, the payments cease. Alternatively, if you live to be 100, so do your payments.

Annuity for Life or a "Certain Period"
A single life annuity that allows you to receive your payments for a fixed period of time. Payments will be made to you for the remainder of your life, but if you die before the end of the time period (generally either 10 or 20 years), payments will continue to be made to your beneficiary until the end of the period.

An Annuity for Life or a "Certain Period" Under an **annuity for life or a "certain period,"** you receive annuity payments for life. However, if you die before the end of the "certain period," which is generally either 10 or 20 years, payments will continue to your beneficiary until the end of that period. Because a minimum number of payments must be made (payments must continue until the end of the certain period), an annuity for life or a "certain period" pays a smaller amount than a single life annuity. In addition, the longer the "certain period," the smaller the monthly amount.

Joint and Survivor Annuity
An annuity that provides payments over the life of both you and your spouse.

A Joint and Survivor Annuity A **joint and survivor annuity** provides payments over the life of both you and your spouse. Under this choice, the two most common options are (1) a 50 percent survivor benefit, which pays your spouse 50 percent of the original annuity after you die, and (2) a 100 percent survivor benefit, which continues benefits to your spouse at the same level after you die. Of course, the larger the survivor benefit, the smaller the size of the annuity. Many firms provide medical benefits to pensioners and their spouses over their entire life when this type of annuity is chosen as the payout method.

Most individuals who are married choose this option. In fact, if you're married and you choose another option, your spouse must sign a waiver giving you permission to accept that alternative payout.

The advantages of an annuity include the fact that it can be set up so that you or you and your spouse will continue to receive benefits, regardless of how long you live, and that some firms continue to pay for medical benefits while an annuity pension payout is being received.

The disadvantages include the fact that there's no inflation protection. Although you know for certain how much you'll receive each month, inflation continuously erodes the spending power of this amount. In addition, such an annuity payout method doesn't allow for flexibility in payout patterns, so if there's a financial emergency, the pattern can't be altered to deal with it. Another important drawback is that under the annuity there is little flexibility to leave money to heirs.

Annuities are usually available with employer-sponsored retirement plans, but insurance companies also sell them. Depending on how attractive your employer's annuity options are, you may be better off taking a lump-sum distribution and purchasing an insurance company annuity on your own. The point here is that you aren't restricted to the annuity options offered by your employer. You should compare them with the other options available from the highest-rated insurance companies before making a decision.

A Lump-Sum Payment

Under a **lump-sum option**, you receive your benefits in one single payment. If you're concerned about inflation protection or if you're concerned about having access to emergency funds, a lump-sum distribution or taking part of your money in a lump sum and putting the rest toward an annuity may be best. If you do take your benefits in a lump sum, you'll be faced with the task of making your money last for your lifetime and for your loved ones after you're gone. That's not all bad—you get to invest the money wherever you choose, and you may end up earning a high return.

Lump-Sum Option
A payout arrangement in which you receive all of your benefits in one single payment.

The big advantage to a lump-sum payout is the flexibility it provides. Unfortunately, you run the risk of making a bad investment and losing the money you so carefully saved. Table 15.3 provides a listing of some of the advantages and disadvantages of an annuity versus a lump-sum payout.

TABLE 15.3 An Annuity or Lifetime Payments Versus a Lump-Sum Payout

Annuity or Lifetime Payments	Lump-Sum Payout
Advantages Payments continue as long as you live. Employer health benefits may continue along with the annuity.	**Advantages** Flexibility to allow for emergency withdrawals. Allows for big-ticket purchases—for example, a retirement home if desired. Potential for inflation protection. Allows for money to be passed on to heirs. Control over how the money is invested.
Disadvantages In general, no inflation protection. No flexibility to make withdrawals in the event of a financial emergency. Doesn't allow for money to be passed on to heirs—payments stop when you die.	**Disadvantages** You could run out of money. You might not have the discipline to keep from spending the money. Complicates the financial planning process because you're responsible for your own retirement funding.

Tax Treatment of Distributions

If you receive your payout in the form of an annuity, those payments will generally be taxed as normal income.

With a lump-sum payout, you pay taxes all at once. An alternative to paying taxes on a lump-sum payout is to have the distribution rolled over into an IRA or qualified plan. This rollover makes a lot of sense if you've taken a new job or retired early and don't need the money now. You avoid paying taxes on the distribution, while the funds continue to grow on a tax-deferred basis.

LO5 Put together a retirement plan and effectively monitor it.

Putting a Plan Together and Monitoring It

For most individuals, there won't be a single source of retirement income: Most people rely on retirement savings from a combination of different plans. What works best for you depends on where you work and what your retirement benefits are. However, the place to start is with the seven steps outlined at the beginning of this chapter. In addition, make sure you invest the maximum allowable amount in tax-sheltered retirement plans because they both reduce your taxes and allow your retirement funds to grow on a tax-deferred basis.

Your investment strategy should reflect your investment time horizon. Early on, you should be willing to take on more risk—going with a strong dose of stocks in your retirement portfolio. As retirement draws near, you should gradually switch over to less risky investments. If you're uncertain about putting together your plan or if you'd like another opinion, don't hesitate to see a professional financial planner. Figure 15.6 illustrates the typical sources of retirement income for a senior family unit (that is, a couple over 65 or an individual over 65 living alone). As you can see, income comes from four primary sources, with Social Security accounting for 33.2 percent, earnings for 32.2 percent, pensions for 20.9 percent, and asset income (primarily stock dividends and interest from bonds) for 9.7 percent. Only 4.0 percent comes from other sources (including public assistance). Social Security is much more important for senior family units with lower incomes. In fact, if you rank senior family units by total income and divide them into five equal groups or quintiles, Social Security provides

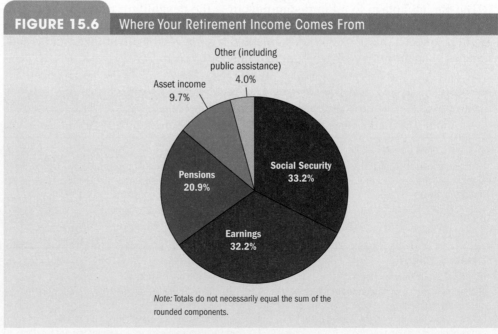

FIGURE 15.6 Where Your Retirement Income Comes From

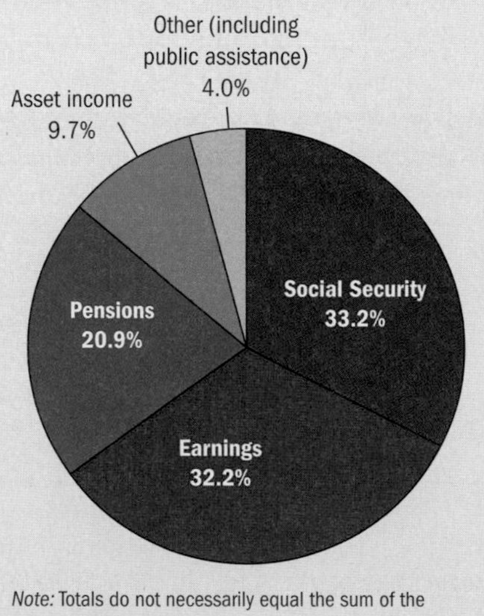

Note: Totals do not necessarily equal the sum of the rounded components.

Source: Social Security Administration, *Income of the Aged Chartbook, 2014*, released April 2016.

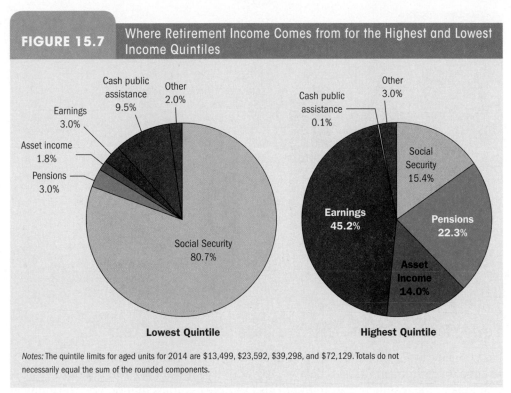

FIGURE 15.7 Where Retirement Income Comes from for the Highest and Lowest Income Quintiles

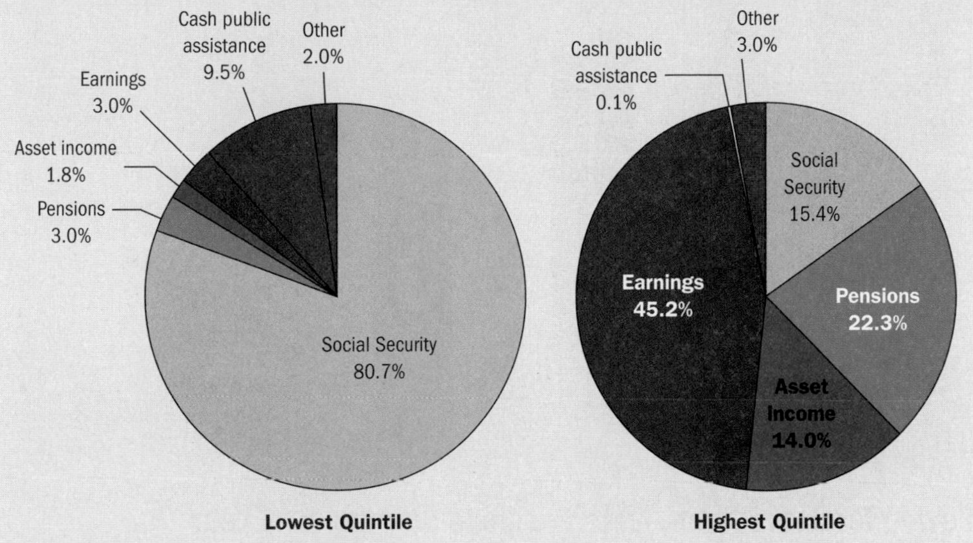

Notes: The quintile limits for aged units for 2014 are $13,499, $23,592, $39,298, and $72,129. Totals do not necessarily equal the sum of the rounded components.

Source: Social Security Administration, *Income of the Aged Chartbook, 2014*, released April 2016.

only 15.4 percent of the income to the highest income quintile but provides a whopping 80.7 percent of the income to the lowest income quintile, as shown in Figure 15.7.

Monitoring your retirement planning, both before and after you retire, is an ongoing process in which adjustments are constantly made for new and unexpected changes in your financial and personal life. Although it's impossible to point out all the complications that might occur, a number of things that should be kept in mind are provided in Checklist 15.3.

CHECKLIST 15.3 Possible Complications

- ☐ Changes in inflation can have a drastic effect on your retirement. Not only do changes in anticipated inflation affect the value of any stocks and bonds that you own, but also they affect the amount of money that you'll need for a comfortable retirement.
- ☐ Once you retire, you may live for a long time. Your investment strategy should include a dose of stocks that reflect your investment time horizon. The strategy of investing in bonds and CDs after retirement, while widely advised, probably doesn't match most retirees' time horizons. Remember, you want to earn enough on your retirement savings to cover inflation and allow your money to grow conservatively—but grow just the same.
- ☐ Monitor your progress, and monitor your company. Don't be afraid to adjust your goals along with what's necessary to meet those goals. Make sure you track the performance of your retirement investments. In addition, monitor your company's health, especially if you participate in an ESOP. If your company's financial future is questionable, try to move your investments into something other than company stock.
- ☐ Don't neglect insurance coverage. There's no quicker way to get in financial trouble than to experience a disaster that should have been covered by insurance but wasn't. Make sure your coverage is both up-to-date and at an adequate level.
- ☐ An investment-planning program may make things easier. There are a number of very good Internet sites provided in Table 15.2 that will help. In addition, AARP, Kiplinger, and CNN Money, along with Fidelity and Vanguard, all have retirement sections on their Web sites.

FIGURE 15.8 At 8 Percent, Skipping Just 1 Year Can Cost You Almost $235,000

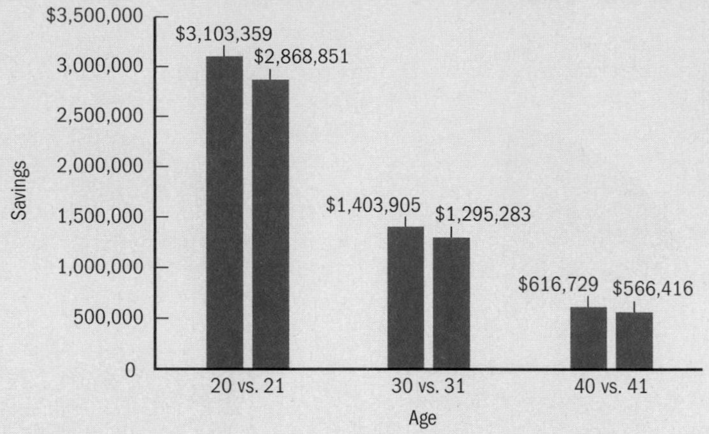

Saving for Retirement—Let's Postpone Starting for 1 Year

As you saw in Figure 15.4, it is extremely important that you not delay beginning to save for retirement. In fact, delaying by only 1 year can cost you almost $235,000. Just look at the results in Figure 15.8. This example assumes that on your birthday at the specified age, you contribute $5,000 to an IRA that earns 8 percent per year and you continue making contributions until age 70. You can see that not only do you end up with more when you begin earlier, but also you lose quite a bit just by postponing your savings by 1 year.

BEHAVIORAL INSIGHTS

PRINCIPLE 9

Principle 9: Mind Games, Your Financial Personality, and Your Money We all know retirement is coming—at least we hope it will someday. The problem is that it's a long way off, and for many, by the time it's close enough to take planning for it seriously, it's too late. What are the ugly facts about retirement planning? About 26 percent of workers have less than $1,000 in savings and investments that could be used for retirement (not counting their primary residence or defined-benefits plan, such as a traditional pension), and 54 percent of workers have saved less than $25,000—and you know that amount won't support you for very long. In fact, only 21 percent of workers are "very confident" they will have enough money put aside to retire comfortably. Since we all know retirement is coming, what's the problem? For most individuals, the problem is behavioral in nature. So let's take a look at some of the behavioral issues that we face as we try to prepare for retirement.

Procrastination and Lack of Self-Control If we know we need to save for retirement, why don't we do it? One reason is that there is comfort in postponing difficult decisions. Many individuals simply don't have the self-control to do something that doesn't pay off in an immediate reward. They know they would like to save money, but they don't have the self-control to follow through. Remember when we talked about temporal myopia in Chapter 5? When they are uncertain about the future (like retirement), they tend to discount it dramatically and fixate on the now. This shouldn't be surprising because individuals seem to exhibit the same behavior when trying to diet, get in shape, quit smoking, and follow through on their New Year's resolutions. It is for this reason that many employers enroll their new employees automatically into a retirement plan.

For those companies that don't have automatic enrollment in a defined-contribution plan, employees must actively change their status quo from "not saving" to "joining and contributing." And we know how the status quo bias strengthens our preference for keeping things the way they are and makes us resistant to change—especially when a change will cost us some money.

Choice Overload and the Complexity of the Decision Studies have shown that as the number of retirement options increases, participation actually decreases. The task of choosing a retirement plan simply becomes overwhelming. This tendency to freeze up when there are too many choices has also been demonstrated in other areas. Take, for example, one well-known study where shoppers in a gourmet food store had to pass by a large selection of speciality jams and jellies. It was found that although they spent more time looking at them, fewer shoppers actually made a purchase. But when a small display with only four choices was presented, almost everyone who stopped to look also bought a jar.

When it comes to retirement planning, the behavioral problems go beyond the problem of too many choices. Individuals are also thrown off by the complexity and importance of the decision—their reaction many times is to simply try to get it over with. In fact, a survey of the University of Southern California faculty and staff found that 58 percent of the respondents took less than 1 hour to determine both their contribution rate and their investment elections. If you think about it, you probably spend a lot more time than that planning for Spring Break.

Inertia in Contributions and Investment Choices or Decision Paralysis Many individuals start out with relatively low contribution levels—which are usually in line with their beginning salary—and never change them as their salary level increases. They also never change their investment choices. For example, if they initially sign up for the retirement plan with a default contribution rate of 2 or 3 percent, they never change this contribution rate. In addition, if they initially put their retirement money in a money market fund, they don't change that either. Today, there are roughly 8,000 publicly traded stock and bond funds, and for many workers, the prospect of choosing among them is paralyzing.

One proposed solution to this problem is the Save More Tomorrow (or SmarT) program.[3] Under this program, plan participants precommit to increasing their retirement saving rates when their salary increases or on a regularly scheduled basis—for example, on their anniversary date with the company. This solution avoids self-control problems by allowing for precommitment, and since workers sign up for the program when they join the company, no future decision is required, so inertia works to their benefit.

When it comes to saving for your retirement, you often hear this argument: "Well, what if I don't live long enough to enjoy retirement?" The simple answer is another question: "What if you do?" Be prepared.

ACTION PLAN

Principle 10: Just Do It! It may seem like a long way off, but now is the time to begin saving for retirement. Here are some tips. PRINCIPLE 10

- **Don't procrastinate.** Remember how the time value of money works: The longer your investment time horizon is, the more your money grows. For example, if you're 22 and plan on retiring at 67, you could begin funding your Roth IRA at

[3] Richard Thaler and Shlomo Benartzi, "Save More Tomorrow: Using Behavioral Economics to Increase Employee Saving," *Journal of Political Economy* 112, no. 1, pt. 2 (2004): S164.

the end of this year. If you make 45 end-of-year annual payments of $5,500 into your Roth IRA and if you earn 9 percent on your investments, you'll have almost $2.9 million at retirement. If you wait until you are 32 and make 35 end-of-year payments, you'll have under $1.2 million at retirement.

- **Your *first move* is to set up and fully fund a Roth IRA.** It's just too good a deal to pass up. You lose a small tax deduction now (doing the Roth IRA), but you'll end up with some serious tax-free money at retirement. As you already know, fees and expenses can take a big bite out of what you eventually have at retirement—avoid them. Vanguard and Fidelity are two low-cost mutual fund families that offer Roth IRAs—stick to them or another mutual fund family with low costs and expenses. Or try an index fund—they generally offer very low expenses along with diversification.
- **If your employer offers a 401(k) or 403(b) plan, make sure you participate.** It's convenient and easy to do—and with many plans, there is a company match. That's free money; you've got to take advantage of it.
- **Keep your hands off it.** Don't view your retirement savings as an emergency fund. If you withdraw money from a qualified retirement account, you can end up paying taxes and penalties.
- **Check out one of the retirement planning Web sites.** Table 15.2 presents several retirement planning Web sites—check them out. Determine which plan is the best plan for you, and then do it!

Chapter Summaries

LO1 Understand the changing nature of retirement planning.

SUMMARY: For many individuals, Social Security is the primary source of retirement income. About 95 percent of all Americans are covered by Social Security. The size of your Social Security benefit is determined by (1) the number of years of earnings, (2) the average level of earning, and (3) an adjustment for inflation.

KEY TERMS

Defined-Benefit Plan, page 509 A traditional pension plan in which you receive a promised or "defined" pension payout at retirement. The payout is based on a formula that takes into account your age at retirement, salary level, and years of service.

Noncontributory Retirement Plan, page 509 A retirement plan in which the employer provides all the funds and the employee need not contribute.

Contributory Retirement Plan, page 509 A retirement plan in which the employee, possibly with the help of the employer, provides the funds for the plan.

Portability, page 510 A pension fund provision that allows employees to retain and transfer any pension benefits already earned to another pension plan if they leave the company.

Vested, page 510 To gain the right to the retirement contributions made by your employer in your name. In the case of a pension plan, employees become vested when they've worked for a specified period of time and, thus, gained the right to pension benefits.

Funded Pension Plan, page 510 A pension plan in which the employer makes pension contributions directly to a trustee who holds and invests the employees' retirement funds.

Unfunded Pension Plan, page 510 A pension fund in which the benefits are paid out of current earnings on a pay-as-you-go basis.

Cash-Balance Plan, page 510 A retirement plan in which workers are credited with a percentage of their pay, plus a predetermined rate of interest.

Set up a retirement plan. LO2

SUMMARY: Funding your retirement needs can be thought of as a seven-step process: Set goals, estimate how much you'll need to meet your goals, estimate your income at retirement, calculate the annual inflation-adjusted shortfall, calculate the funds you need to cover this shortfall, determine how much you must save annually between now and retirement, and put the plan in place and save.

Understand how different retirement plans work. LO3

SUMMARY: One way in which you can earn more on your investments is through tax-deferred retirement plans. Some of these are employer-sponsored plans, whereas others are aimed at the self-employed individual. In either case, the advantages are essentially the same. First, because the contributions may not be taxed, you can contribute more. In essence, you can contribute funds that would otherwise go to the IRS. Second, because the investment earnings aren't taxed, you can earn money on earnings that also would have otherwise gone to the IRS.

A 401(k) plan is really a do-it-yourself tax-deferred retirement plan. Over the past 20 years, 401(k)s have exploded in terms of popularity. A 403(b) plan is essentially the same as a 401(k) plan except that it is aimed at employees of schools and charitable organizations. These are excellent ways to save.

The three basic types of plans for the self-employed are the SEP-IRA, SIMPLE, and Keogh plans. Another method for funding retirement is an individual retirement arrangement (IRA). There are three types of IRAs: traditional IRAs, Roth IRAs, and Coverdell Education Savings Accounts, which were covered in Chapter 7.

KEY TERMS

Defined-Contribution Plan, page 518 A pension plan in which you and your employer or your employer alone contributes directly to a retirement account set aside specifically for you. In effect, a defined-contribution plan can be thought of as a savings account for retirement.

Profit-Sharing Plan, page 518 A pension plan in which the company's contributions vary from year to year, depending on the firm's performance. The amount of money contributed to each employee depends on the employee's salary level.

Money Purchase Plan, page 518 A pension plan in which the employer contributes a set percentage of employees' salaries to their retirement plans annually.

Thrift and Savings Plan, page 518 A pension plan in which the employer matches a percentage of the employees' contributions to their retirement accounts.

Employee Stock Ownership Plan (ESOP), page 519 A retirement plan in which the retirement funds are invested directly in the company's stock.

401(k) Plan, page 519 A tax-deferred retirement savings plan in which employees of private corporations may contribute a portion of their wages up to a maximum amount set by law ($18,000 in 2017 and rising in the future with inflation in $500 increments). Employers may contribute a full or partial matching amount and may limit the proportion of the annual salary contributed.

Keogh Plan, page 520 A tax-sheltered retirement plan for the self-employed.

Simplified Employee Pension Plan (SEP-IRA), page 520 A tax-sheltered retirement plan (you don't pay taxes on any earnings while they remain in the plan) aimed at small businesses or at the self-employed.

Savings Incentive Match Plan for Employees (SIMPLE), page 520 A tax-sheltered retirement plan aimed at small businesses or the self-employed that provides for some matching funds by the employer to be deposited into the employee's retirement account.

Individual Retirement Arrangement (IRA), page 521 A tax-advantaged retirement account. The contribution may or may not be tax deductible, depending on the individual's income level and whether he or she, or his or her spouse, is covered by a company retirement plan.

Roth IRA, page 522 An IRA in which contributions are not tax deductible. That is, you make your contribution to this IRA out of after-tax income. But once the money is in there, it grows tax free, and when it is withdrawn, the withdrawals are tax free.

Coverdell Education Savings Account or Education IRA, page 525 An IRA that works just like the Roth IRA except with respect to contributions. Contributions are limited to $2,000 annually per child for each child younger than 18, with income limits beginning at $110,000 for single taxpayers and $220,000 for couples. The earnings are tax free, and there is no tax on withdrawals to pay for education.

529 Plan, page 525 A tax-advantaged savings plan used only for college and graduate school.

LO4 Choose how your retirement benefits are paid out to you.

SUMMARY: Another important retirement decision is the distribution or payout decision, which affects how much you receive, how it is taxed, whether you are protected against inflation, whether you might outlive your retirement funds, and a host of other important concerns. Your basic distribution choices are to receive your payout as a lump sum, in the form of an annuity or lifetime payments, or as some combination of the two.

KEY TERMS

Single Life Annuity, page 526 An annuity in which you receive a set monthly payment for your entire life.

Annuity for Life or a "Certain Period," page 526 A single life annuity that allows you to receive your payments for a fixed period of time. Payments will be made to you for the remainder of your life, but if you die before the end of the time period (generally either 10 or 20 years), payments will continue to be made to your beneficiary until the end of the period.

Joint and Survivor Annuity, page 526 An annuity that provides payments over the life of both you and your spouse.

Lump-Sum Option, page 527 A payout arrangement in which you receive all your benefits in one single payment.

LO5 Put together a retirement plan and effectively monitor it.

SUMMARY: You must monitor your progress toward your retirement goal, both before and after you retire, constantly allowing for new and unexpected changes that occur in your financial and personal life.

Problems and Activities

These problems are available in MyLab Finance.

1. Jazmin earned $51,250 this year. Calculate her total FICA contribution for the year. How much did her employer pay toward FICA?
2. Grady Zebrowski, age 25, just graduated from college, accepted his first job with a $50,000 salary, and is already looking forward to retirement in 40 years. He assumes a 3 percent inflation rate and plans to live in retirement for 20 years. He does not want to plan on any Social Security benefits. Assume Grady can earn an 8 percent rate of return on his investments prior to retirement and a 5 percent rate of return on his investments postretirement to answer the following questions using your financial calculator.

a. Grady wants to replace 90 percent of his current income. What is his annual need in today's dollars?

b. Using Table 15.1, Grady thinks he might have an average tax rate of 14 percent at retirement if he is married. Adjusting for taxes, how much does Grady really need per year, in today's dollars?

c. Adjusting for inflation, how much does Grady need per year in future dollars when he begins retirement in 40 years? Use the tax-adjusted income from part b.

d. If he needs this amount (from part c) for 20 years, how much does he need in total for retirement?

e. How much does Grady need to save per month to reach his retirement goal, assuming he does not receive any employer match on his retirement savings?

3. Sedki earned $129,750 in 2017. How much did he pay in Social Security taxes? In Medicare taxes? In total FICA taxes? (*Hint:* Don't forget the annual Social Security earnings cap.)

4. Anne-Marie and Yancy calculate their current living expenditures to be $67,000 a year. During retirement, they plan to take one cruise a year that will cost $5,000 in today's dollars. Anne-Marie estimated that their average tax rate in retirement would be 12 percent. Yancy estimated their Social Security income would be about $22,000 and their retirement benefits would be approximately $35,000. Use this information to answer the following questions:

a. How much income, in today's dollars, will Anne-Marie and Yancy need in retirement, assuming 70 percent replacement and an additional $5,000 for the cruise?

b. Assuming the 12 percent income tax estimate during retirement, what is their tax-adjusted need from part a?

c. Calculate their projected annual income shortfall in today's dollars.

d. Determine, in dollars, the future value of the shortfall 30 years from now, assuming an inflation rate of 5 percent.

e. Assuming an 8 percent nominal rate of return and 25 years in retirement, calculate their necessary annual investment to reach their retirement goals.

5. Russell and Charmin have current living expenses of $97,000 a year. Estimate the present value amount of income they will need to maintain their level of living in retirement. Assume an average tax rate of 20 percent and an 80 percent income replacement ratio.

6. Reece is comparing retirement plans with prospective employers. ABC, Inc., offering a salary of $38,000, will match 75 percent of his contributions up to 10 percent of his salary, his maximum contribution. XYZ Company will match 100 percent of his contributions up to 6 percent of his salary, but he can contribute up to 15 percent of his salary. XYZ Company is offering a $35,000 salary. If Reece assumes that he will contribute the maximum amount allowed and keep these first-year retirement funds invested for 30 years with a 9 percent return, how much will each account be worth? How can he use this information when choosing an employer?

7. Peter and Blair recently reviewed their future retirement income and expense projections. They hope to retire in 30 years and anticipate they will need funding for an additional 20 years. They determined that they would have a retirement income of $61,000 in today's dollars but that they would actually need $86,000 in retirement income to meet all of their objectives. Calculate the total amount that Peter and Blair must save if they wish to completely fund their income shortfall, assuming a 3 percent inflation rate and a return of 8 percent.

8. Min-Jun and Min-Suh want to contribute $120,000 to a 529 plan for the benefit of their new grandchild. If done shortly after the birth of the child, with a 7 percent annual return and no other contributions, what will the account be worth when the child is 18 and ready to enter college?

9. Assuming a 7 percent annual return with a Coverdell Education Savings Account, how much would $2,000 annual contributions be worth when the child from the previous question is 18 and ready to enter college?

Discussion Case 1

This case is available in **MyLab Finance**.

Bill (age 42) and Molly (age 39) Hickok, residents of Anchorage, Alaska, recently told you that they have become increasingly worried about their retirement. Bill, a public school teacher, dreams of retiring at 62 so they can travel and visit family. Molly, a self-employed travel consultant, is unsure that their current retirement plan will achieve that goal. She is concerned that the cost of living in Alaska along with their lifestyle have them spending at a level they could not maintain. Although they have a nice income of more than $100,000 per year, they got a late start planning for retirement, which is now just 20 years away. Bill has tried to plan for the future by contributing to his 403(b) plan, but he is only investing 6 percent of his income when he could be investing 10 percent. Use what they told you along with the information below to help them prepare for a prosperous retirement.

Molly's income	$78,000
Bill's income	$42,000
Social Security income at retirement	$2,600/mo
Current annual expenditures	$70,000
Bill's Roth IRA	$20,000
Bill's 403(b) plan	$47,800
Marginal tax bracket	25 percent

Questions

1. Do Bill and Molly qualify for any other tax-advantaged saving vehicles? If so, which ones? To what extent?
2. Since Bill does not receive an employer match, should he invest the maximum amount in his Roth IRA annually or just invest more in his 403(b)? Defend your answer.
3. Assuming Bill and Molly can reduce expenses and invest more, how do their retirement savings limits differ before and after age 50?
4. Calculate the future value income need for their first year in retirement, assuming a 3 percent inflation rate and an 80 percent income replacement.
5. Calculate the projected annual income at retirement that will be generated by their portfolio, assuming an 8 percent nominal rate of return, a 20-year retirement period, and no further contributions.
6. Given their projected Social Security and investment income, how much will Bill and Molly need to invest annually to make up their income shortfall? Into what account(s) would you suggest they make the investments?
7. Bill and Molly don't feel like they have very good self-control with saving beyond the limits they initially set for themselves 10 years ago. What recommendations do you have for them in dealing with annual pay increases at work?

PRINCIPLE 10

8. Given Molly's concerns about their retirement preparation, what changes might they implement based on **Principle 10: Just Do It!** to secure their travel plans?

Discussion Case 2

This case is available in **MyLab Finance**.

Timur and Marguerite recently met with the benefits administrator at Timur's employer to establish his retirement date and to discuss payout options for his pension. Timur just turned 67, while Marguerite, a self-employed artist, will be 62 in 6 months. The benefits administrator was helpful in outlining potential sources of income that they can expect in retirement. Annual estimates are as follows:

Social Security	$12,000
Defined-benefit plan	$18,000 (single life annuity)
Marguerite's work	$7,000
Defined-contribution plan	$10,000 (single life annuity)
Other	$4,000

The defined-contribution payout was calculated based on a 401(k) balance of $250,000 earning approximately 8 percent. The benefits administrator indicated that a 100 percent joint and survivor annuity would decrease yearly benefits by about $3,000 in the defined-benefit plan and $1,500 in the defined-contribution plan.

Questions

1. What are the advantages associated with taking the pension payouts in the form of an annuity? What are the disadvantages?
2. Based on the information provided, which type of annuity would you recommend that Timur and Marguerite choose, given the difference in their ages and earnings?
3. Would you advise them to take the annuity offered in the defined-contribution plan, which guarantees a 4 percent rate of return, or would you recommend the lump-sum payment? Why? What are the disadvantages associated with your recommendation?
4. What recommendations would you make to Timur and Marguerite to help them monitor expenses and safeguard their retirement lifestyle?
5. Timur is anxious to replace work with babysitting his new grandson. He and Marguerite want to establish a 529 account this year. If all of the relatives together can contribute an average of $6,500 per year for the next 18 years and the 529 account earns 7.5 percent, how much will be available for Timur's grandson's college expenses in 18 years?

Appendix

Crunchin' the Numbers—Funding Your Retirement Needs

Step 1: Set Goals

Step 2: Estimate How Much You Will Need

Take a look at Larry and Louise Tate, introduced in Chapter 2. They have calculated their annual living expenditures to be $52,234. To obtain an estimate of their annual living expenses at retirement in today's dollars, they need to multiply this amount by 0.8, which comes to $41,787. They then need to adjust this amount for any additional expenditures to meet their other goals. For example, the Tates may wish to move to a more expensive area of the country, or they may wish to travel more after retirement.

Let's assume that the Tates wish to take two additional vacation trips annually at $2,000 per trip, measured in today's dollars, for an increase in expenses of $4,000 per year. They, thus, need a total of $45,787 for their annual living expenditures at retirement in today's dollars, as calculated on line D of Figure 15A.1. The Tates now must adjust this number for taxes. Using Table 15.1, we see that the average tax rate for retirement income between $40,000 and $50,000 is approximately 12 percent. However, since the Tates intend to retire in a state with a relatively high state income tax, they have decided to use 14 percent rather than 12 percent as their estimated tax rate. The Tates must divide their annual living expenditures by (1 − 0.14), or 0.86, resulting in $53,241. In effect, 14 percent of this $53,241, or $7,454, will go to pay taxes, leaving $45,787 to cover living expenditures.

Step 3: Estimate Income at Retirement

The Tates estimate their Social Security income to be $18,000 and their pension benefits to be $25,000, giving them a total level of retirement income of $43,000 in today's dollars.

Step 4: Calculate the Annual Inflation-Adjusted Shortfall

For the Tates, the before-tax income level they need is $53,241 (line F of Figure 15A.1), whereas their available income is only $43,000 (line J), leaving a shortfall of $10,241 (line K).

Of course, this shortfall is in today's dollars, as are all our calculations so far. To determine what the shortfall will be in retirement dollars 30 years from now, the Tates must project $10,241 into the future. This is a problem involving the future value of a single cash flow.

As you should recall, we need an inflation rate to work a future value problem. Let's assume that the inflation rate over the next 30 years will be 4 percent annually. To move money forward in time 30 years, assuming a 4 percent rate of inflation, multiply it ($10,241) by the *future-value interest factor*, which is 3.243 (as found in Appendix A in the 4% column and 30-year row), yielding an inflation-adjusted shortfall of $33,212.

FIGURE 15A.1 Worksheet for Funding Retirement Needs

	The Tates Example	Your Numbers
Step 1: Set Goals		
Step 2: Estimate How Much You Will Need		
A. Present level of living expenditures on an after-tax basis	$52,234	______
B. Times 0.80 equals: Base retirement expenditure in today's dollars	× 0.80 = $41,787	______
C. Plus or minus: Anticipated increases or decreases in living expenditures after retirement	+ $4,000	______
D. Equals: Annual living expenditures at retirement in today's dollars on an after-tax basis	= $45,787	______
E. Before-tax adjustment factor, based on average tax rate of 14% (If the average tax rate is not known, it can be estimated using Table 15.1, "The Average Tax Rate.") This is used to calculate the before-tax income necessary to cover the annual living expenses in line D. In this case, assume an average tax rate of 14%. Thus, line F, the before-tax income = line D/line E, where line E = (1 − Average Tax Rate)	÷ 0.86	______
F. Equals: The before-tax income necessary to cover the annual living expenses in line D	line D divided by line E = $53,241	______
Step 3: Estimate Income at Retirement		
G. Income from Social Security in today's dollars	$18,000	______
H. Plus: Projected pension benefits in today's dollars	+ $25,000	______
I. Other income in today's dollars	+ $0	______
J. Equals (lines G + H + I): Anticipated retirement income, in today's dollars	= $43,000	______
Step 4: Calculate the Annual Inflation-Adjusted Shortfall		
K. Anticipated shortfall in today's dollars (line F minus line J)	= $10,241	______
L. Inflation adjustment factor, based on anticipated inflation rate of 4% between now and retirement with 30 years to retirement (*FVIF*s are found in Appendix A): $FVIF_{\text{inflation rate \%, no. years to retirement}}$	× 3.243	______
M. Equals: Inflation-adjusted shortfall (line K × line L)	= $33,212	______
Step 5: Calculate How Much You Will Need to Cover This Shortfall (over the number of years you expect to be retired, assuming an inflation-adjusted return of 5% [return (9%) minus the inflation rate (4%)] during your retirement period, with retirement anticipated to last 30 years)		
N. Calculate the funds needed at retirement to cover the inflation-adjusted shortfall over the entire retirement period, assuming that these funds can be invested at 9% and that the inflation rate over this period is 4%. Thus, determining the present value of a 30-year annuity assuming a 5% inflation-adjusted return (*PVIFA*s are found in Appendix D): $PVIFA_{\text{inflation-adjusted return, no. years in retirement}}$	= 15.373	______
O. Equals: Funds needed at retirement to finance the shortfall (line M × line N)	× line M = $510,568	______
Step 6: Determine How Much You Must Save Annually Between Now and Retirement (with 30 years until retirement and a 9% return to cover the shortfall)		
P. Future-value interest factor for an annuity for 30 years, given a 9% expected annual return (*FVIFA*s are found in Appendix C): $FVIFA_{\text{expected rate of return, no. years to retirement}}$	= 136.305	______
Q. Equals: *PMT*, or the amount that must be saved annually for 30 years and invested at 9% in order to accumulate the line O amount at the end of 30 years	line O divided by line P $3,746	______

Calculator Clues

Calculating Step 4: Inflation-Adjusted Shortfall

Calculating the inflation-adjusted shortfall is easy with a financial calculator. Remember, if you don't have a calculator handy, there's one waiting for you on MyLab Finance. In the example above, we want to determine how much the shortfall of $10,241 will be in 30 years, assuming it grows at the 4 percent rate of inflation.

Enter	30	4	10,241	0	
	N	I/Y	PV	PMT	FV
Solve for					−33,216

Due to rounding error, this answer is slightly different from the one calculated using the tables. In addition, as expected, the *FV* takes on a negative sign.

Step 5: Calculate How Much You Will Need to Cover This Shortfall

We know the Tates have an annual shortfall of $33,212 in retirement (future) dollars. They don't want inflation to erode the value of their savings. That means they'll want their retirement savings to grow by 4 percent each year just to cover inflation. In addition, assume they can earn a 9 percent return on their retirement funds. That is to say, whereas the shortfall payout will increase by 4 percent per year to compensate for inflation, they earn 9 percent per year on their investment. In effect, they earn an inflation-adjusted rate of 5 percent (that is, 9% − 4%) per year.[4]

Thus, in determining how much the Tates need to have saved if they wish to withdraw $33,212 per year while earning a 5 percent inflation-adjusted return, you're really determining the present value of an annuity. In this case, it's a 30-year annuity because the Tates want this retirement supplement to continue for 30 years, and it's discounted back to the present at 5 percent. To do this, we multiply the inflation-adjusted shortfall of $33,212 by the *present-value interest factor for an annuity* of 15.373 (found in Appendix D in the 5% column and the 30-year row) and find that $510,568 is the amount that the Tates need to accumulate by retirement.

Calculator Clues

Calculating Step 5: Funds Needed to Cover the Shortfall

Let's try the above problem using a financial calculator. We are solving for the *PV* of a 30-year annuity of $33,212 at 5 percent.

Enter	30	5		33,212	0
	N	I/Y	PV	PMT	FV
Solve for			−510.550		

Again, due to rounding error in the tables, this answer is slightly different from the one we just calculated. In addition, as expected, the *PV* takes on a negative sign.

[4]Actually, the inflation-adjusted or real rate of return would be a bit less because of the cross product or Fisher effect, but for pedagogical purposes, we will ignore it. This relationship was first analyzed by Irving Fisher and shows that $R_{nominal} = r_{real} - I_{nflation} - (r_{real} \times I_{nflation})$. A detailed examination of the Fisher effect is presented in Peter N. Ireland, "Long-Term Interest Rates and Inflation: A Fisherian Approach," *Economic Quarterly* (Federal Reserve Bank of Richmond) 82 (Winter 1996): 22–26.

Step 6: Determine How Much You Must Save Annually Between Now and Retirement

The Tates know they need to accumulate $510,568 by the time they retire in 30 years. To determine how much they need to put away each year to achieve this amount, they need to know how much they can earn on their investments between now and when they retire. Let's assume they can earn 9 percent. This then becomes a simple future value of an annuity problem, solving for *PMT* in the formula, where the *future-value interest factor for an annuity* is found in Appendix C in the 9% column and 30-year row.

$$\begin{aligned} FV &= PMT\ (\textit{Future-Value Interest Factor for an Annuity}) \\ 510{,}568 &= PMT\,(136.305) \\ PMT &= 3{,}746 \end{aligned}$$

Therefore, the Tates must save $3,746 each year for the next 30 years at 9 percent to meet their retirement goals.

Calculator Clues

Calculating Step 6: How Much the Tates Need to Save Annually

Calculating the inflation-adjusted shortfall is easy with a financial calculator. Remember, if you don't have a calculator handy, there's one waiting for you on MyLab Finance. In the example above, we want to determine how much the shortfall of $10,241 will be in 30 years, assuming it grows at the 4 percent rate of inflation.

Enter	30	9	0		510,568
	N	I/Y	PV	PMT	FV
Solve for				−3,746	

You'll notice that *PMT* takes on a negative sign.

Step 7: Put the Plan in Play and Save

CHAPTER 16 Estate Planning: Saving Your Heirs Money and Headaches

Learning Objectives

LO1	**Understand the importance and the process of estate planning and estate taxes.**	**The Estate Planning Process**
LO2	**Draft a will and understand its purpose in estate planning.**	**Wills**
LO3	**Avoid probate.**	**Avoiding Probate**

It seemed like Tony Soprano was always prepared—always planning ahead; after all, who else might have lived by the motto "What use is an unloaded gun?" But James Gandolfini, the actor who portrayed Tony Soprano, might not have been prepared—he certainly wasn't expecting his life to end at the age of 51. There's no question that Tony Soprano was an expert at hiding money from the Feds, but apparently James Gandolfini didn't have that skill.

While he did have a will when he died of a massive heart attack while vacationing in Rome in 2013, a will was not enough, and settling his estate may result in more estate taxes than he had intended. There's no question that he wanted to share his money; in fact, through his will he left 80 percent of his estate to his sisters and his nine-month-old daughter, with the remaining 20 percent going to his wife—but the big beneficiary of his estate may be the IRS. That's because while there will be no taxes on the portion of his estate left to his wife, the rest will be taxed, and as we will see, estate taxes can be pretty high. In fact, it was estimated that his tax bill may go over $30 million, and like many wealthy individuals, his assets weren't very liquid—which means that the family is going to be scrambling around, selling assets to pay off that tax bill.

Since his death, there have been hundreds of blogs and articles commenting on his will—and this didn't need to happen. He could have kept everything private by creating a simple trust for his assets. This is what John Lennon did, and it allowed his affairs to remain private. Unfortunately, the situation following the death of Prince, the musical artist, is far worse. In April 2016, he died without a will, a spouse, children, or surviving parents, setting off a scramble among his sister, his five half-siblings, and someone claiming to be his long lost son—and Minnesota law treats surviving half-siblings the same as full siblings. Only time will tell what will happen to Prince's sprawling financial estate and musical legacy, but one thing is certain. The estate lawyers are going to win big! In fact, the special administrator handling Prince's estate racked up \$2.3 million in bills within the first 3 months of work, while another law firm billed the estate over \$1.8 million. The bottom line here is that a little estate planning is a good idea for everyone.

Home Box Office/Album/Newscom

Pictorial Press Ltd/Alamy Stock Photo

Most people cringe at the thought of estate planning, mostly because it involves death. As a result, many individuals avoid it, ignoring the inevitable or assuming that only the rich need to deal with it. However, there is value in estate planning for practically everyone. Once you're dead, there might not be anyone to provide for your spouse or kids. With estate planning, you're ensuring that you preserve as much of your wealth as possible—no matter how much or how little that may be—for your heirs. It also ensures that the guardianship of your children will fall to whomever you wish. Basically, estate planning finds much of its logic in **Principle 7: Protect Yourself Against Major Catastrophes**—in this case, the catastrophe is your death. You'll also find that much of what happens in estate planning is done

PRINCIPLE 7

PRINCIPLE 4

to keep taxes to a minimum, which brings us back to **Principle 4: Taxes Affect Personal Finance Decisions**. As you'll see, the basic choices available to you with respect to minimizing taxes and passing your estate on to your designated heirs are your will, gifts, and trusts.

You'll also see that estate planning can be an extremely complicated process. Our purpose here isn't to make you an expert in estate planning but to alert you to its benefits and challenges. After studying this chapter, you'll have a better understanding of the concepts, terminology, process, techniques, and tools of estate planning. And you'll be better able to plan for the disposition of whatever you have accumulated.

Estate Planning The process of planning for what happens to your accumulated wealth and your dependents after you die.

Estate planning is planning for what happens to your wealth and your dependents after you die. And regardless of how large your estate is, the basic objectives remain the same: First, you want to make sure that your property is distributed according to your wishes and that you have provided for your dependents. Providing for your dependents will involve, among other things, selecting a guardian for your children if they're under 18. Second, you want to pass on as much of your estate as possible, which means you want to minimize estate and inheritance taxes. Finally, you want to keep settlement costs, including legal and accounting fees, to a minimum. In essence, you'll be developing a strategy to give away and distribute your assets while paying the minimum in taxes and fees. Estate planning may seem a bit gloomy because it forces you to think about your own demise. Fortunately, there's one aspect of estate planning that doesn't deal with your own death—unfortunately, it deals with your incapacitation. Yes, the final objective of estate planning is determining who is to have decision-making authority in the event that you become unable to care for yourself as a result of physical or mental impairment.

With actor James Gandolfini's sudden passing, it's not clear how the actor's estate might be finally settled. Still, the tragic loss of "Tony Soprano" serves as a somber reminder that life can be unpredictable and, in true Soprano spirit, that it's important to protect your family.

LO1 Understand the importance and the process of estate planning and estate taxes.

The Estate Planning Process

Once you recognize these basic objectives of the estate planning process, you'll want to fine-tune them to meet your specific needs and goals. For example, you might want to protect your current spouse from claims on your assets by your ex-spouse. You might also want to induce your kids to go to college by leaving all of your money to them in a fund that they can access only after they graduate. No matter how you choose to fine-tune the basic objectives of estate planning, the financial planning process remains the same for everyone. Let's take a look at that process.

The estate planning process has four steps.

Step 1: Determine the Value of Your Estate

Estate planning starts with determining the value of your assets. After all, you can't determine how to distribute what you own if you don't know what you own. The easiest way to figure out what you've got and what it's worth is by looking at your personal balance sheet (see Chapter 2). It should list all of your assets and their respective values, as well as your net worth.

Your net worth is calculated by determining what you own and subtracting from that what you owe.

$$\text{your estate's net worth} = \text{value of your estate} - \text{level of estate's liabilities}$$

In estate planning, your net worth must be recalculated, based on the following. First, you must keep in mind that when you die, your life insurance will pay off, so it adds to your net worth. In calculating the value of your life insurance, you should use the death benefit as its value rather than its cash or surrender value. In addition, you should include any death benefits associated with an employer-sponsored retirement plan.

> **FACTS OF LIFE**
>
> Most people are surprised to see how much their estate is worth. Once you start adding a home plus furnishings to a couple of automobiles, savings, and investments, things add up. The only way to determine what your estate is worth is to go through the numbers.

It's important to get a sense of your wealth, not only because you need to know what you have to distribute but also because its level will determine how much tax planning you need. For example, in 2017 the first $5.49 million of your estate can be passed on tax free, and in years forward, this amount will be adjusted for inflation. As you can imagine, you will approach estate planning differently if your estate is worth $100,000 than you will if it is worth $20 million.

Step 2: Choose Your Heirs and Decide What They Receive

Once you know just what you have, you can figure out who's going to get it when you go. Most married people will just leave everything to their spouse. However, you may want to consider the relationships you have with various people and the needs of your dependents and potential heirs.

If, for example, you have a child with special needs who requires special schooling, you may want to make sure that need is taken care of first. Or perhaps if some of your children have already completed college, you may want to earmark college funds for those children who haven't yet finished or even started college.

Step 3: Determine the Cash Needs of the Estate

Once you know what you've got and who's going to get it, your estate planning is done, right? Nope. Before your property can be distributed to your heirs, uncovered medical costs, funeral expenses, all legal fees, outstanding debt, and estate and inheritance taxes must be paid. It's a good idea to have enough funds in the form of liquid assets—Treasury bills, stocks, and bonds—to cover your estate tax needs or to provide tax-free income to your heirs from a life insurance policy that will cover your estate taxes. While every estate is different, a general rule of thumb is that funeral and settlement costs generally run at around $15,000 or 4 percent of the estate.

Step 4: Select and Implement Your Estate Planning Techniques

The final step is determining which estate planning tools are most appropriate to achieve your goals. In general, you'll need a combination of several planning techniques. Some of the most commonly used include a will, a durable power of attorney, joint ownership, trusts, life insurance, and gifts.

These tools can be a little tricky to use, and once you've figured out how to use them, implementing your estate plan can be complex. As a result, you should consult a legal specialist in estate planning to help you with the tools and to handle the details of implementing your plan.

But just because you need a professional to help you use them doesn't mean you don't need to understand the tools of estate planning. After all, you need to be able to speak the same language as the professional so you can fully understand his or her advice. Remember **Principle 1: The Best Protection Is Knowledge**. Before we examine and explain all the major tools of estate planning that you need to understand, we need to discuss taxes because the use of most estate planning tools is based on tax consequences.

PRINCIPLE 1

MyLab Finance Video

Understanding and Avoiding Estate Taxes

Estate taxes are a central element to consider in estate planning because of the high tax rate imposed on estates. Earlier we mentioned that in 2017 the first $5.49 million of an estate could be passed on tax free and that this will be indexed upward for inflation every year. However, in the future there may be legislative changes to the tax code occur, and if and when changes are made, updates, including the personal finance implications, will be provided on the companion website (http://pearsonhighered.com/keown).

To understand how estate taxes work, you need to understand the estate tax exemption or unified tax credit. To do this, let's look at the 2017 tax year. If you had died in 2017, instead of charging no taxes at all on the first $5.49 million of your estate, the IRS actually would have charged a hefty 18 percent tax rate on the first $10,000 of your estate and would have kept raising this rate all the way up to 40 percent when the amount hit $5.49 million. To offset the taxes on the first $5.49 million of your estate, the IRS would then have issued an estate tax credit, called a **unified tax credit**, which effectively would have nullified the taxes on the first $5.49 million of your estate. Above this tax-free threshold of $5.49 million, the estate would have paid a tax rate of 40 percent. What does all this really mean? Forty percent of any amount that you would have passed on beyond $5.49 million will have been lost to federal taxes in 2017!

Unified Tax Credit
An estate and gift tax credit that, in 2017, allows the first $5.49 million of an estate and lifetime gifts (beyond the annual gift exclusion) to be passed on tax free.

The Portability Feature—Passing on Credit to the Surviving Spouse One thing you should keep in mind is that the estate tax exemption is portable, which means that when one spouse dies, the unused amount goes to the surviving spouse and can be used at his or her death. So if the husband dies and used $2.49 million of his credit, at his wife's death, she can use her $5.49 million credit in addition to the remaining $3 million of her husband's credit. This portability feature means that since the federal estate tax exemption is $5.49 million per person and the exemption of the first to die is now transferable to the surviving spouse, a husband and wife can now avoid federal estate taxes with combined assets of almost $10.98 million even without good estate planning. In effect, for most people, avoiding federal estate taxes isn't a problem. Since the federal tax exemption is adjusted each year for inflation, how big an estate can be passed on tax free is a moving target. As a result, sometimes we'll refer to this amount as the *estate-tax-free transfer threshold* and not even mention the dollar amount because it changes each year.

Given the high estate tax rates imposed, your personal tax strategy should shift toward estate tax planning once your net worth climbs above the

STOP & THINK

For years, there has been a debate on whether to repeal estate taxes, often referred to as "death taxes," entirely. While this would benefit the wealthy, not all wealthy individuals are in favor of its repeal.

"Without the estate tax, you will in effect have an aristocracy of wealth, which means you pass down the ability to command the resources of the nation based on heredity rather than merit. [Repeal would be like] choosing the 2020 Olympic team by picking the eldest sons of the gold-medal winners in the 2000 Olympics." —Warren Buffett. What do you think?

estate-tax-free transfer threshold. Individuals with a net worth below the estate-tax-free transfer threshold should focus on income tax strategies and on nontax estate planning concerns.

To deal with your estate taxes properly, you need to calculate what these taxes will be. However, before you can calculate these taxes, there are a couple other taxes, gift and generation-skipping taxes, as well as a deduction, that we need to consider.

Gift Taxes Gifts are an excellent way of transferring wealth before you die. They reduce the taxable value of your estate and allow you to help out your heirs while you're still alive—*and the recipient of the gift isn't taxed.* Under the present law, as of 2017, you're permitted to give $14,000 per year tax free to as many different people as you like.

Let's look at a couple with four children, eight grandchildren, and an estate valued at $14 million. Over a 5-year period, the couple could transfer to each of their children and grandchildren a total of $28,000 per year tax free—$14,000 from the husband and $14,000 from the wife—for a total of $140,000 to each child and grandchild. These gifts would reduce the couple's taxable estate from $14 million to $12.32 million and result in significantly lower estate taxes. Remember that the exclusion for annual gifts applies to each spouse. That is, a husband and wife can give up to $28,000 jointly to each of their children or to whomever they wish without paying any taxes.

If you'd like to give more than that, you can. However, the gift tax and the estate tax *work together*, which is why it is referred to as the unified estate and gift tax, with a total lifetime tax-exempt limit (which was $5.49 million in 2017) on gifts over and above the yearly tax-free limit of $14,000 per recipient. Therefore, in 2017 the first $5.49 million of your estate *minus* total lifetime non-tax-exempt gifts (that portion of gifts in excess of $14,000 per year per person) would be transferred tax free. If your lifetime non-tax-exempt gifts totaled $100,000, in 2017 the first $5.39 million rather than the first $5.49 million of your estate would not be taxed. In effect, the lifetime gift tax exemption is linked to the estate tax exemption, which means that if you gift away any amount of your lifetime gift tax exemption (remember, gifts of up to $14,000 per year don't count against this—just the amount over $14,000), then this amount will be subtracted from your estate tax exemption after you die. Also, this $14,000-per-year tax-free gift limit is indexed to inflation in $1,000 increments, and in the future, it will rise to match inflation in $1,000 increments.

Unlimited Marital Deduction The U.S. tax code allows for an unlimited marital deduction for gift and estate tax purposes, which means that there's no limit to the size of transfers between spouses that can be made on a tax-free basis. In other words, when a husband or wife dies, the estate, regardless of size, can be transferred to the survivor totally tax free. Whereas an estate valued at up to the estate-tax-free transfer threshold (which was $5.49 million in 2017) can be transferred tax free to any beneficiary, there's no limit on the value of an estate that can be transferred to a spouse. All federal estate taxes can be avoided through the use of the unlimited marital deduction.

The unlimited marital deduction doesn't apply to spouses who aren't U.S. citizens. The logic behind this law is to prevent non-U.S. spouses from returning to their home countries with an untaxed estate. Once they left the United States, Uncle Sam would never get any more tax dollars from the estate, and the IRS isn't about to let that happen.

The Generation-Skipping Transfer Tax There's an additional tax imposed on gifts and bequests that skip a generation—for example, gifts or bequests that pass assets from a grandparent to a grandchild. The purpose of the **generation-skipping tax** is to wring potentially lost tax dollars from the intervening generation. In effect, the assets are taxed as if they moved from the grandparents to their own children and then from their children to their grandchildren.

Generation-Skipping Tax
A tax on wealth and property transfers to a person two or more generations younger than the donor.

Calculating Estate Taxes

You can view the calculation of estate taxes as a four-step process, as outlined in Figure 16.1. To walk you through this process, we use the example with the 2017 estate-tax-free transfer threshold of $5.49 million presented in Figure 16.2.

FIGURE 16.1 Calculation of Estate Taxes

STEP 1	STEP 2	STEP 3	STEP 4
Calculate Your *Gross Estate*	**Calculate Your *Taxable Estate***	**Calculate Your *Gift-Adjusted Taxable Estate***	**Calculate Your *Estate Taxes***
Your gross estate is the value of all your assets and property. This includes proceeds of life insurance and pension plans, collectibles, and investments, in addition to the value of other assets owned at the time of your death. →	Your taxable estate is equal to your gross estate less funeral and administrative expenses; any debt, liabilities, or mortgages; certain taxes; and any marital or charitable deductions. →	Before calculating your estate taxes, your cumulative taxable lifetime gifts must be added to your taxable estate, as calculated in Step 2. Then the estate-tax-free transfer threshold, which for 2017 is $5.49 million, is subtracted from this amount. →	Estate taxes are then calculated by multiplying your gift-adjusted taxable estate, calculated in Step 3, times the federal estate tax rate, which is 40% for 2017. Keep in mind that there may also be estate taxes imposed by the state.

FIGURE 16.2 Calculation of Estate Taxes for the 2017 Tax Year

	Amount	Total Amount
STEP 1: Calculate Your *Gross Estate*		$6,390,000
A. Value of gross estate		
STEP 2: Calculate Your *Taxable Estate*		
Less:		
Funeral expenses	$10,000	
Estate administrative expenses	40,000	
Debt	0	
Taxes	0	
Marital deduction	0	
Charitable deduction	50,000	
Total		− $100,000
Equals:		
B. Taxable estate		= $6,290,00
STEP 3: Calculate Your *Gift-Adjusted Taxable Estate*		
Plus:		
Cumulative taxable lifetime gifts (in excess of annual tax-free gift allowance per person)		+ $200,000
Less:		
Estate-tax-free transfer threshold		− $5,490,000
Equals:		
Gift-adjusted taxable estate		= $1,000,000
STEP 4: Calculate Your *Estate Taxes*		
Gift-adjusted taxable estate × 0.40		$400,000

The process of calculating your estate taxes starts by calculating the value of your gross estate, which is the value of all your assets and property at the time of your death. Remember to include the death benefits of any insurance policy or retirement plan you have. The example in Figure 16.2 assumes you have a gross estate of $6.39 million.

In Step 2, you calculate your taxable estate by subtracting the funeral and estate administrative expenses, along with any debts and taxes you owe, from the gross estate calculated in Step 1. Keep in mind that in Step 2 you need to subtract any and all liabilities or mortgages existing at the time of death. In addition, you subtract any allowable deductions, such as the unlimited marriage deduction and any charitable deductions you have made. Remember, gifts to charity are tax deductible, and there's no limit on the size of charitable gifts. Our example in Figure 16.2 assumes that your expenses, debt, and income and other taxes owed total $100,000.

To calculate the gift-adjusted taxable estate in Step 3, the Step 2 value must be adjusted for any taxable lifetime gifts that you've made. Remember that the annual gift tax exclusion allows for only one $14,000 (in 2017) gift per year per individual. Let's assume over your life you have given heavily to your children and one of your gifts exceeded the allowable gift tax exclusion by $200,000. Thus, the gift-adjusted taxable estate is $1,000,000, which results in Step 4 in federal taxes of $400,000 ($1,000,000 × 0.40 = $400,000).

How about state death taxes? These depend on which state you live in. Some states have eliminated estate taxes completely, while others don't impose a state tax on estates that fall below the federal estate-tax-free transfer threshold, which was $5.49 million in 2017. As of 2017, 13 states and the District of Columbia imposed some sort of state or inheritance tax, which means higher tax bills—and they can be pretty high, with Washington's estate tax ranging up to 20 percent.

Will
A legal document that describes how you want your property to be transferred to others after your death.

Beneficiary
An individual who is willed your property.

Wills

LO2 Draft a will and understand its purpose in estate planning.

A **will** is a legal document that describes how you want your property to be transferred to others. Within your will, you designate **beneficiaries**, or individuals who are willed your property; an **executor**, sometimes called a **personal representative**, who will be responsible for carrying out the provisions of your will; and a **guardian**, who will care for any of your children under the age of 18 and manage their property. A will is the cornerstone of solid estate planning.

Executor or Personal Representative
An individual who is responsible for carrying out the provisions of your will and managing your property until the estate is passed on to your heirs.

Wills and Probate

Probate is the legal process of distributing an estate's assets. The first step in the probate process is the validation of the will. Once the court is satisfied that the will is valid, the process of distributing the assets begins. First, the probate court appoints the executor, generally selecting the person designated in the will. The executor usually receives a fee ranging from 2 to 5 percent or more of the value of the estate for overseeing the distribution of the estate's assets and managing those assets during the probate process. Once the assets have been distributed and the taxes have been paid, a report is filed with the court, and the estate is closed.

Guardian
An individual who'll care for any children under the age of 18 and manage their property.

Probate
The legal procedure that establishes the validity of a will and then distributes the estate's assets.

The advantage, and really the only purpose, of going through the probate process is to validate the will—to allow for challenges and make sure that this is, in fact, the last will and testament of the deceased. In the case of a challenge to the will, probate allows for the challenge or dispute to be settled. Probate also allows for an orderly distribution of the assets of an individual who dies intestate, or without a valid will.

FACTS OF LIFE

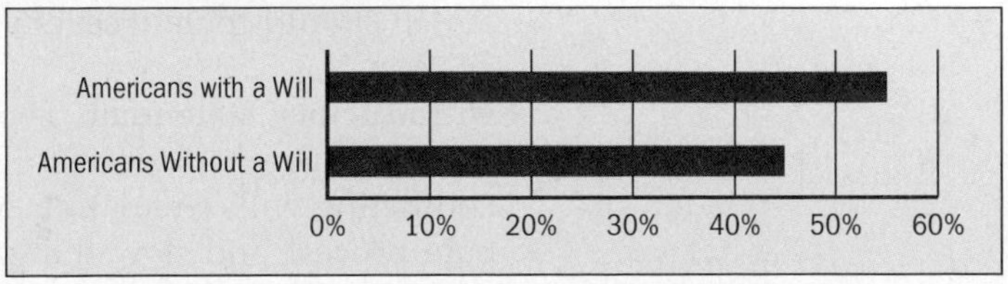

The disadvantages associated with probate center on its cost and speed. There are numerous expenses—legal fees, executor fees, court costs—that make the probate process expensive. In fact, probate can run from 1 to 8 percent of the value of the estate, depending on the laws of the state in which the deceased lived. In addition, the probate process can be quite slow, especially if there are challenges to the will or tax problems.

Wills and Estate Planning

Because all wills must go through the potentially slow and costly probate process, wills aren't the preferred way to pass on your property. However, wills still play an extremely important role in the estate planning process. There are a number of reasons why you need to have a will, including the following:

- If you don't have a will, the court will likely choose a relative as the guardian of your children under the age of 18 and their property. This relative may or may not be someone you would choose; therefore, it is important to specify in your will a guardian for your children.
- In the case of children with special needs, a will may be the most appropriate way of providing for those needs.
- Property that isn't co-owned or included in a trust is transferred according to your wishes as expressed in your will.
- You can make special gifts or bequests through a will. You can even handle the future care of your pets through a will.
- If you don't have a will, the court will appoint an administrator to distribute your assets. Not only might this distribution conflict with your desires, but also the costs of an administrator for your estate will be more than the cost of drawing up a will, leaving less for your heirs.

Writing a Will

Although it's possible to write your own will, it's not a particularly good idea. Handwritten wills, and even oral wills, are accepted in some states, but they're a lot riskier than a formally prepared legal will. You're taking the chance that the probate court might disallow your will on the grounds of some overlooked technicality.

You should have a lawyer either draw up or review your will. Fortunately, a simple will costs only around $250. Of course, the more complicated the will is, the more expensive its preparation will be.

Once your will has been drawn up, you must sign it, and the signing must be witnessed by two or more people. It must then be stored in a safe place and periodically reviewed and updated. The most common storage place is with your lawyer. If you change lawyers, you need to remember to retrieve and relocate your will. An alternative is to store it at home in a safe, fireproof place. Of course, you should make sure that others know exactly where they can find it.

Many people store their wills in safety-deposit boxes. However, after you die, your safety-deposit box may be sealed until it can be examined and inventoried for tax purposes. Thus, storing your will there isn't a particularly good idea. In some states, you can store your will with the clerk of the probate court.

A will should contain several basic features or clauses, including the following:

- **Introductory statement.** The introductory statement identifies whose will it is and revokes any prior wills. Revoking prior wills is important so that there aren't conflicting wills circulating. Multiple wills can really make a mess out of the probate process and slow things down terribly (to the point that your heirs might drop dead from old age before your estate is settled).

- **Payment of debt and taxes clause.** This clause directs the payment of any debts, death and funeral expenses, and taxes.
- **Disposition of property clause.** This clause allows for the distribution of money and property. It states who is to receive what and what happens to the remainder of the estate after all the bequests have been honored.
- **Appointment clause.** This clause names the executor of the estate and the guardian if there are children under 18.
- **Common disaster clause.** This clause identifies which spouse is assumed to have died first in the event that both die simultaneously.
- **Attestation and witness clause.** This clause dates and validates the will with a signing before two or more witnesses.

Approximately one in three wills is challenged. For that reason, it's important that you understand the requirements for a valid will. First, you must be mentally competent when the will is written. Second, you can't be under undue influence of another person. For example, if you're physically threatened or forced to sign the will, it will be invalidated. Finally, the will must conform to the laws of the state.

Updating or Changing a Will—The Codicil

A **codicil** is an attachment to a will that alters or amends a portion of the will. You should periodically review your will to make sure it conforms to your present situation. If your family expands or if you get married or divorced, you should alter your will appropriately. If the changes are substantial, it's best to write a new will and expressly revoke all prior wills. If the changes are minor, they can be effected through a codicil. A codicil should be drawn up by a lawyer, witnessed, and attached to the will.

Codicil
An attachment to a will that alters or amends a portion of the will.

Letter of Last Instructions

A **letter of last instructions** isn't a legally binding document. It's a letter, generally to the surviving spouse, that provides information and directions with respect to the execution of the will. Much of what's contained in the letter of last instructions is information such as the location of the will, legal documents such as birth certificates, Social Security numbers, and tax returns. It also has information as to the location of financial assets, including insurance policies, bank accounts, safety-deposit boxes, stocks, and bonds. Also, this letter indicates everyone who should be notified of your death.

Letter of Last Instructions
A letter, generally to your surviving spouse, that provides information and directions with respect to the execution of the will.

A letter of last instructions often includes a listing of personal property and valuables as well. In addition, you might consider providing a listing of social media sites like Facebook and LinkedIn that you use, along with passwords and instructions on how you would like them handled after your death. Finally, the letter contains funeral and burial instructions, along with your wishes regarding organ donation. The purpose of such a listing is to make dealing with your estate easier on your survivors. Generally, if you have an attorney prepare your will, he or she will also prepare a letter of last instructions. Although it doesn't carry the same legal weight as a will, it's honored in most states.

Selecting an Executor

An executor takes on the dual role of (1) making sure that your wishes are carried out and (2) managing your property until the estate is passed on to your heirs. To say the least, this is both an important and a time-consuming task. You should take care in naming your executor. For smaller estates, it may be a family member, but for larger estates, it should be a lawyer or a bank trust officer with experience as an executor. Generally, executors are paid for their services, but on smaller estates, family members many times accept money only to cover expenses.

Not only does the executor deal with personal matters such as sending copies of the will to all the beneficiaries and publishing death notices, but also he or she is responsible for paying any necessary taxes, paying off the debts of the estate, managing the financial matters of the estate, distributing the assets remaining after bequests have been honored as specified in the will, and reporting a final accounting of the distribution to the court.

Durable Power of Attorney
A document that provides for someone to act on your behalf in the event that you become mentally incapacitated.

Living Will
A directive to a physician that allows you to state your wishes regarding medical treatment in the event of an illness or injury that renders you unable to make decisions regarding life support or other measures to extend your life.

Durable Health-Care Power of Attorney
A document that designates someone to make life-support decisions for you if you lose the capacity to decide.

Other Estate Planning Documents

A **durable power of attorney** provides for someone to act on your behalf in the event that you become mentally incapacitated. In effect, it empowers someone to act as your legal representative. The durable power of attorney is, of course, separate from your will, and it goes into effect while you're alive but unable to act on your own. You can set up the power of attorney so that any degree of legal power is transferred. It should be very specific as to which aspects of your affairs it covers and does not cover, and it should mention specific accounts.

A **living will** allows you to state your wishes regarding medical treatment in the event of a terminal illness or injury. Included with the living will should be a health-care proxy, which designates someone to make health-care decisions should you become unable to make those decisions for yourself. A **durable health-care power of attorney**, or health-care proxy, would allow you to designate a trusted friend to make life-support decisions for you if you lose the capacity to decide.

LO3 Avoid probate.

Avoiding Probate

Unless you really want to tie up the time and money of your heirs, it's a good idea to avoid probate. Think of probate as a necessary evil. It's essential to validate your will and ensure that its provisions are carried out, but it can be a time- and money-consuming hassle. The three simplest ways of avoiding probate are through joint ownership, gifts, and trusts.

Tenancy by the Entirety
A type of ownership limited to married couples. Property held this way can be transferred only if both the husband and the wife agree. In addition, upon the death of one, the property automatically passes directly to the survivor.

Joint Tenancy with the Right of Survivorship
A type of ownership in which two or more individuals share the ownership of assets, usually in a joint account at a bank or a brokerage firm. When one joint owner dies, the ownership passes directly to the surviving owners, bypassing the will.

Tenancy in Common
A type of ownership in which two or more individuals share ownership of assets. When one of the owners dies, that owner's share isn't passed on to the other owners. It becomes part of the deceased owner's estate and is distributed according to the deceased owner's will.

Joint Ownership

When assets are owned jointly, they're transferred to the surviving owner(s) without going through probate. In effect, the surviving owner(s) immediately assumes his or her ownership share of the property. There are three different forms of joint ownership: tenancy by the entirety, joint tenancy, and tenancy in common. **Tenancy by the entirety** ownership exists only between married couples. Property held by a married couple under tenancy by the entirety can be transferred only if both husband and wife agree. In addition, upon the death of one, the property automatically passes directly to the survivor.

Under **joint tenancy with the right of survivorship**, two or more individuals share the ownership of assets, which many times are held in a joint account at a bank or a brokerage firm. When one joint owner dies, the ownership passes directly on to the surviving owner or owners, bypassing the will.

With **tenancy in common**, two or more individuals share ownership of the assets. When one of the owners dies, that owner's share becomes part of his or her estate and is distributed according to his or her will. The other joint owner or owners don't receive the deceased owner's share unless the deceased owner's will states so expressly.

Although joint ownership—particularly tenancy by the entirety and joint tenancy—is probably the simplest way of avoiding probate, it does have some drawbacks. If the relationship between those involved deteriorates, one of the joint owners could use up the asset. For example, if a bank account is jointly owned, one of the joint owners could "take the money and run." This nasty kind of rip-off is illegal, but it's also difficult to stop. As another example, one individual may wish to sell some jointly owned property for a great profit, but another joint owner might block the sale just out of spite. Without cooperation between the parties, joint ownership can seem like a prison. In addition, joint ownership can be dissolved only by mutual agreement or a divorce settlement.

Still, there are situations in which joint ownership is an excellent idea. For example, a jointly owned bank account allows survivors to access funds immediately, which can help pay for funeral expenses. In addition, joint property is valuable in a divorce because it gives both parties some bargaining power, thereby forcing compromises that might not otherwise occur.

FACTS OF LIFE

Less than half of all Americans report assigning a power of attorney for health-care purposes.

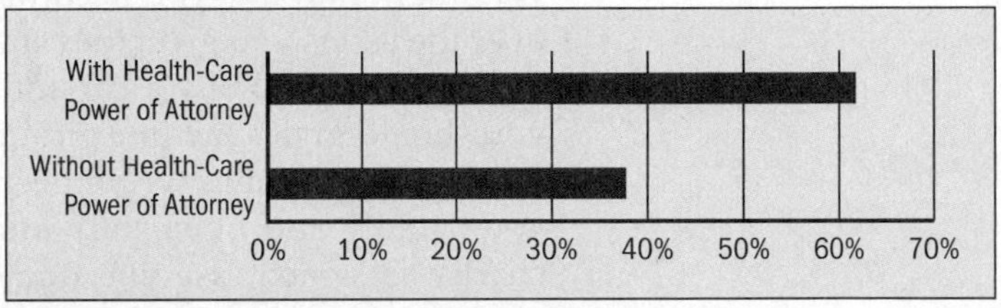

The concept of **community property** represents another form of joint ownership. Community property is any property acquired during a marriage, assuming both husband and wife share equally in the ownership of any assets acquired during the marriage. It doesn't include assets each spouse owned individually before the marriage or gifts and inheritances acquired during marriage that have been kept separate.

Community Property
Property acquired during marriage (depends on state law).

Upon the death of either the husband or the wife, the surviving spouse automatically receives one-half of the community property. The remaining portion of the property is disposed of according to the will or, in the absence of a will, according to state law. Currently, only a few states, located primarily in the West, recognize community property.

Gifts

Not only can you give away $14,000 per year (in 2017) tax free to as many people as you want, but also anything you have given away is no longer yours, so these gifts don't go through probate. Gifts avoid probate, reduce the taxable value of your estate, and allow you to help out your heirs while you're still alive. And the recipient doesn't pay taxes on the gift.

Gifts are also a good way of transferring property that grows in value, such as stocks or real estate. If, for example, you hold onto a stock investment that continues to grow in value, your estate will continue to grow in value, and the more the value of your estate exceeds the estate-tax-free transfer threshold, the more your heirs will lose to estate taxes. If you can afford to part with the stock investment and you know you want to pass it on to someone else anyway, you might consider giving it as a gift.

One major exception to the annual gift exclusion rule deals with life insurance policies, and it's called the "Three Year Rule." If a life insurance policy is given away within 3 years of the owner's death, it is included in the estate for tax purposes. Here's how it works. Let's assume that you gave your daughter a $500,000 policy that had a cash value of $14,000. First, there'd be no gift tax on the gift because its cash value would fall into the $14,000 or less category. Then let's assume that 3 years and 1 day later you die. In this case, the $500,000 insurance policy payout would not be included in your estate for tax purposes. If, however, you die 1 day before 3 years is up since you gave the policy to your daughter, the entire $500,000 would be included in your estate for tax purposes. The bottom line is that if you're intending to give away a life insurance policy, it's much better to do it sooner rather than later.

FACTS OF LIFE

When it comes to estate planning, ignorance is bliss. One in ten American adults who do not have any elements of an estate plan say it's because they don't want to think about dying or becoming incapacitated.

In addition to the $14,000 gift tax exclusion, there is an unlimited gift tax exclusion on payments made for medical or educational expenses. You can make this type of gift to anyone, regardless of whether the person is related to you or not. The only requirement is that you make the payment directly to the school, in the case of education expenses, or to the institution providing the service, in the case of medical expenses. In fact, the unlimited gift tax exclusion for medical expenses can even cover health insurance payments. You can give someone $14,000 and then pay for his or her health insurance, medical, and educational expenses!

The primary disadvantage to gifts is that once you've given your assets away, you might find that you need them. In addition, because you no longer have control over the assets you give, they may be squandered. Wouldn't it just stink to give your son $14,000 to go buy a car and watch him squander it on a full-body tattoo? Still, you should give a lifetime gift-giving program serious consideration.

Up to this point, we've been talking about avoiding probate by giving gifts to your family and other individuals. You can also avoid probate by giving gifts to charity, in which case you don't have to worry about any limits on what you can give tax free—because there aren't any. You can give an unlimited amount of your estate away to federally recognized charities on a tax-free basis. In fact, your charitable gifts are even tax deductible, so you not only reduce your estate taxes by giving to charity but also reduce your yearly income tax. See—it pays to be charitable!

Naming Beneficiaries in Contracts—Life Insurance and Retirement Plans

Insurance contracts and employee retirement plans can be used to transfer wealth while avoiding probate. Insurance policies, either term or cash-value, can be set up so that someone other than the insured owns the policy. For example, a wife could own an insurance policy on the life of her husband, or a child could own an insurance policy on the life of a parent. One of the major advantages of life insurance is that the proceeds don't go through probate.

Many employee retirement plans pay benefits to the spouse upon the death of the employee. These benefits don't go through probate and begin immediately upon the death of the worker. In addition, Social Security benefits go directly to the surviving spouse and dependent children.

Trusts

Trust
A legal entity in which some of your property is held for the benefit of another person.

A **trust** is a legal entity that holds and manages an asset for another person. A trust is created when an individual, called a grantor, transfers property to a trustee, which can be an individual, an investment firm, or a bank, for the benefit of one or more people, the beneficiaries. Virtually any asset—money, securities, life insurance policies, and property—can be put in a trust.

Why do people use trusts? Here are some of the more common reasons:

- **Trusts avoid probate.** Trusts bypass the costly and time-consuming process of probate.
- **Trusts are much more difficult to challenge in court than are wills.** If there are any concerns that a will may be challenged, placing the property in a trust can minimize the problem. Challenges to the will don't affect a trust unless the challenge is that the deceased was incompetent or was under undue influence when the trust was formed.
- **Trusts can reduce estate taxes.** Trusts can be used to shelter assets from estate taxes.
- **Trusts allow for professional management.** If a spouse doesn't have the understanding or desire to manage money effectively, a trust can provide the desired professional management.

- **Trusts provide for confidentiality.** Whereas a will becomes a matter of public record, a trust does not. Thus, if you want privacy, perhaps to keep from offending a relative who doesn't receive all he or she may expect, a trust may be just the thing for you.
- **Trusts can be used to provide for a child with special needs.** A trust can be set up to provide the necessary funds for a child with special needs. A special needs trust can provide funds for children with disabilities of majority age without eliminating government benefit programs such as Medicaid.

FACTS OF LIFE

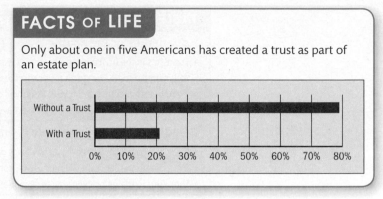

Only about one in five Americans has created a trust as part of an estate plan.

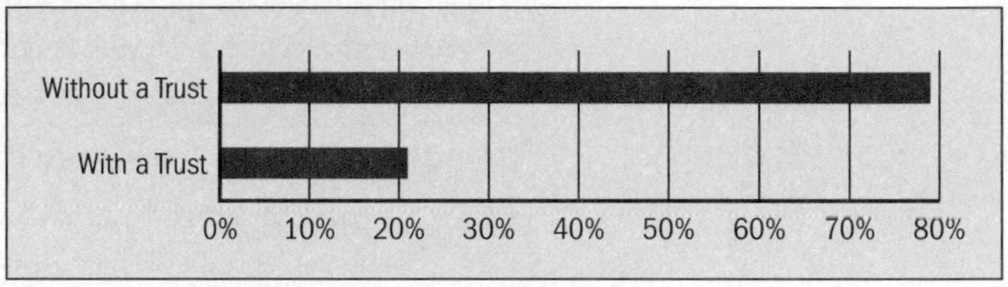

- **Trusts can be used to hold money until a child reaches maturity.** Because most children don't have the maturity or understanding necessary to handle large sums of money, a trust can be used to hold those funds until the children reach a designated age. The funds don't have to be immediately dispersed. Instead, they can be distributed over any period of time that is desired.
- **Trusts can ensure that children from a previous marriage will receive some inheritance.** If you leave your estate to a second spouse, children from your previous marriage may never receive any inheritance. A trust can ensure that they receive what you wish.

Because there are so many different types of trusts, many people find them confusing. However, all trusts can be classified as being either living trusts or testamentary trusts.

Living Trusts

A **living trust** is one in which you place your assets while you're alive. There are two types of living trusts, revocable and irrevocable.

Living Trust
A trust created during your life.

Revocable Living Trusts With a **revocable living trust**, you place the assets into the trust while you're alive, and you can withdraw the funds from the trust later if you wish. It's an alternative way to hold your assets. While your assets—for example, your house—are in a revocable living trust, you have access to them, can receive income from them, and can use them. In addition, you pay taxes on whatever income your assets earn.

Revocable Living Trust
A trust in which you control the assets in the trust and can receive income from the trust without removing assets from the estate.

In other words, there isn't much difference between assets in a revocable living trust and assets owned outright until you die or become incompetent, at which point the trust beneficiary takes control of the assets in the trust. It's important to remember that there are no tax advantages to a revocable living trust—they don't reduce your estate taxes. However, when you die, assets held in a living trust go directly to your beneficiary. Revocable living trusts allow you to avoid the high costs of probate and ensure the privacy that a will does not afford. Table 16.1 summarizes the advantages and disadvantages of revocable living trusts.

Irrevocable Living Trusts An **irrevocable living trust**, as the name suggests, is permanent. It can't be changed or altered once it's been established because you no longer hold title to the assets in the trust. The trust becomes a separate legal entity. It pays taxes on the income and capital gains that its assets produce. This fact takes on major importance when you die because assets in an irrevocable living trust aren't considered part of your estate, and any appreciation of assets would not be subject to estate tax. This type of trust also bypasses probate. Table 16.2 summarizes the advantages and disadvantages of irrevocable living trusts.

Irrevocable Living Trust
A trust in which you relinquish title and control of the assets when they are placed in the trust.

TABLE 16.1 Advantages and Disadvantages of Revocable Living Trusts

Advantages of Revocable Living Trusts
• The assets in the trust avoid probate upon your death. • You maintain the power to alter or cancel the trust. • If you become incompetent, your assets will continue to be professionally managed by the trustee. • You can replace the trustee if you do not have confidence in his or her skills.
Disadvantages of Revocable Living Trusts
• There are no tax advantages—you pay taxes on any income and capital gains on the assets in the trust. • The assets in the revocable living trust are considered part of your estate for estate tax purposes. • The assets in the revocable living trust cannot be used as collateral for a loan.

TABLE 16.2 Advantages and Disadvantages of Irrevocable Living Trusts

Advantages of Irrevocable Living Trusts
• The assets in the trust avoid probate upon your death. • Any price appreciation on an asset in the trust is not considered part of your estate, and no estate taxes are imposed on it when you die. • Income earned on assets in the trust can be directed to the beneficiary, which can result in tax savings if the beneficiary is in a lower tax bracket.
Disadvantages of Irrevocable Living Trusts
• You no longer maintain control over the assets in the trust. • The assets in the trust cannot be used as collateral for a loan. • It may be more expensive to set up than the probate costs you are trying to avoid. • Setting up the trust can involve a lot of paperwork.

The major difference between a revocable and an irrevocable living trust centers on the fact that with a revocable trust, you retain title to and have control of the assets in the trust.

Testamentary Trusts

Testamentary Trust
A trust created by your will, which becomes active after you die.

A **testamentary trust** is one created by a will: It doesn't exist until probate has been completed. There are a number of different purposes for testamentary trusts, including reducing estate taxes, providing professional investment management, and making sure your estate ends up in the right hands. Let's look at some of the more common types of testamentary trusts.

Family Trust
A trust established to transfer assets to your children, while allowing the surviving spouse access to funds in the trust if necessary. Upon the death of the surviving spouse, the remaining funds in the trust are distributed to the children tax free.

Portable Estate Exemption
An exemption that allows a deceased spouse's unused estate tax exclusion to be shifted to the surviving spouse.

Standard Family Trusts (also known as A-B Trusts, Credit-Shelter Trusts, and Unified Credit Trusts) For years, standard **family trusts** were a cornerstone of estate planning for married couples. The primary objective of these trusts for married couples was to ensure that the surviving spouse could use the estate tax exemption of the first spouse to die. Setting up a trust did this for the survivor, thus keeping the value of those assets out of the survivor's taxable estate. In this way, the surviving spouse was able to take advantage not only of his or her own estate tax exemption at death but also the deceased spouse's exemption, thus sheltering twice the amount that would otherwise be possible. However, among other provisions in the 2010 Tax Relief Act was the **portable estate exemption**, which allows a deceased spouse's unused estate tax exclusion to be shifted to the surviving spouse. In effect, the initial spouse to die not only leaves his or her assets to the surviving spouse but also leaves any unused estate tax exemption to be used at the surviving spouse's death. This is in addition to the surviving spouse's own exemption. The only thing you have to do to receive this benefit is to indicate on the estate tax return, Form 706, filed when the first spouse dies, that you would like this feature. Keep in mind that you still have to file this form even if the estate is not otherwise required to file a Form 706. Also, only the last spouse's exemption is portable, so you can't build up a huge exemption by remarrying and outliving a lot of spouses.

For example, assume that the estate tax exemption is $5.49 million, as it was in 2017, and that John and Chrissy are married. If John dies first and has $3 million that he owns solely in his estate, the $3 million will be transferred directly to Chrissy, leaving no taxable estate. Then when Chrissy dies, she will be able to use John's unused estate tax exclusion amount. As a result, Chrissy's estate tax exclusion will now be $7.98 million (her $5.49 million basic exclusion amount plus the $2.49 million unused exclusion from her late husband).

How will all this work out if John's assets are jointly held? If John and Chrissy have all of their assets jointly titled, when John dies his estate will not use any of the $5.49 million estate tax exemption because of the unlimited marital deduction, which allows John's share of the jointly owned assets to be automatically transferred to Chrissy by right of survivorship without incurring any estate taxes. Then when Chrissy dies, the concept of portability of the estate tax exemption comes into play. John's unused $5.49 million estate tax exemption is added to Chrissy's, resulting in a $10.98 million exemption for Chrissy. As just mentioned, for all this to happen, Chrissy must file an IRS Form 706 when John dies.

This portable estate exemption makes one of the primary features of a standard family trust irrelevant. Still, family trusts are a good idea for a number of reasons. First, as we have seen many times, tax laws come and go, and to base an estate plan on a law that may not be there when needed is not a good idea. Remember, this portability feature makes it possible for a married couple to transfer up to $10.98 million free of federal estate tax without having to use a family trust. That said, family trusts provide other benefits, two of which include protecting assets from a lawsuit against the surviving spouse and protecting assets in the event the surviving spouse remarries.

Qualified Terminable Interest Property (Q-TIP) Trust A **qualified terminable interest property (Q-TIP) trust** gives the individual establishing the trust the ability to direct income from the trust to his or her spouse over the spouse's life and then, at the spouse's death, to choose to whom the assets go. The primary reason for using a Q-TIP trust is to keep your estate from ending up in the hands of your spouse's future husband or wife rather than your children after you die. Q-TIP trusts are generally set up so that your spouse receives the income on your estate while he or she is alive, and after your spouse's death, the assets in the trust are passed on to your children.

Qualified Terminable Interest Property (Q-TIP) Trust
A trust that gives the individual establishing the trust the ability to direct income from the trust to his or her spouse over the spouse's life and then, at the spouse's death, to choose to whom the assets go.

Sprinkling Trusts A **sprinkling trust** is a trust that distributes income according to need rather than some preset formula. The trustee is given discretion to determine who needs what among a designated group of beneficiaries and then "sprinkles" the income among them according to need.

Sprinkling Trust
A trust that distributes income according to need rather than some preset formula. The trustee is given discretion to determine who needs what among the designated beneficiaries and then "sprinkles" the income among them according to need.

A Last Word on Estate Planning

The complexities associated with estate planning, coupled with the fact that estate planning is essentially about your death, cause many of us to put off the process. Don't. Now that you have a basic understanding of the process, objectives, and tools of estate planning, approach a professional. By no means should you attempt your own estate planning. Finally, make sure your family knows where your estate planning documents are. Checklist 16.1 will help you organize your affairs.

CHECKLIST 16.1 Estate Planning

Do you and the members of your family know . . .

- ☐ The location of your will, durable power of attorney, and living will (with the name of the attorney who drafted them)?
- ☐ The name of your attorney?
- ☐ Where to find your letter of last instructions, including burial requests and organ donor information?
- ☐ Your Social Security number?
- ☐ The location of your safety-deposit box and the key to it?
- ☐ Where you stored your birth certificate? Your marriage certificate? Any military discharge papers?
- ☐ Where to find your insurance policies (life, health, and property/liability) along with the name of your insurance agent?
- ☐ The whereabouts of deeds and titles to property (both real estate and, for example, automobiles)?
- ☐ The site of your stocks, bonds, and other securities and name of your broker?
- ☐ How to find any business agreements, including any debts owed to you?
- ☐ All checking, savings, and brokerage account numbers, along with the location of those accounts?
- ☐ The name of your accountant?
- ☐ Your last year's income tax return?
- ☐ The names of past employers, along with any pension or retirement benefits information?

You should also . . .

- ☐ Calculate the size of your estate.
- ☐ Estimate how much of your estate would be lost to taxes if you died.
- ☐ Know who the executor of your will is and who your beneficiaries are.
- ☐ Select a guardian for your children if they are under 18.

BEHAVIORAL INSIGHTS

PRINCIPLE 9

Principle 9: Mind Games, Your Financial Personality, and Your Money As you might imagine, when we talk about topics that deal with death, there are several behavioral biases that get in the way of good financial planning. Let's take a look at a few of them.

Optimism or Superman Bias It's wonderful to be optimistic and to estimate your odds of experiencing a good outcome to be higher than average or to believe you are invincible, as those with a superman bias do. Living a long and healthy life is a great goal—if you didn't feel you were going to keep on living, life could be pretty depressing. But this kind of optimism has a downside to it. These biases have a tendency to make you resistant to discussions or decision making regarding estate planning. Emotions and fear often get in the way of rational, logical behavior. So if you feel you're immortal, you might not have a will, a durable power of attorney, and a living will—but when you need them, they are good things to have. Your loved ones will be grateful.

Inertia and Procrastination By now, you probably understand how inertia and procrastination can prevent you from doing things you know you should do—after all, "there is always tomorrow." With respect to estate planning, most people feel very comfortable postponing any decision—and as a result, for many, estate planning never happens at all. It's much better to have a will than to die without one and let a judge in your state make all the decisions.

How do you get by these behavioral biases? The answer is to understand the consequences of your "failure to act" for your loved ones if something unfortunate happens to you.

ACTION PLAN

PRINCIPLE 10

Principle 10: Just Do It! It probably seemed really strange to read about planning for your retirement . . . and then you get to this chapter! No one wants to think about, much less plan for, a time when you might be incapacitated or dead—but you cannot consider yourself fully protected until you have this critical paperwork under control.

- **If you have any assets, a spouse, and/or children, get a will!** If you die without one, your state will "write one for you" based on intestacy laws. Often these laws are directly opposed to your intent. For example, part of your estate may go to your parents when you would have wanted your spouse to inherit everything. And once you have children, you will understand the importance of having a say in who is appointed as the guardian of any minors under your care.
- **Make sure you have a durable power of attorney and a living will.** Give someone who cares for you the right to make decisions for you when and if you are no longer able to. These will cover both legal and health-care decisions. Make sure your doctor and family know you have these documents and where they are kept. You may not want to talk about these, but there might be a time when someone else needs to act on your behalf.
- **Beware of do-it-yourself will packages or computer software.** Although many are good, some leave out very important sections of a viable will or are not valid in your state. Also, such tools may not provide any coaching on how bequests should be worded to avoid confusion at probate. One error could cost your beneficiaries more in probate costs than the attorney's fee to prepare you will correctly the first time.

Chapter Summaries

Understand the importance and the process of estate planning and estate taxes. LO1

SUMMARY: Estate planning involves planning for what happens to your accumulated wealth and your dependents after you die. Estate planning can be viewed as a four-step process: Determine the value of your estate; choose your heirs, determine their needs, and decide what they receive; determine the cash needs of the estate; and select and implement your estate planning techniques.

The purpose of going through the probate process is to validate the will—to allow for challenges and make sure it is, in fact, the last will and testament of the deceased. A will is a legal document that describes how you want your property to be transferred to others.

KEY TERMS

Estate Planning, page 544 The process of planning for what happens to your accumulated wealth and your dependents after you die.

Unified Tax Credit, page 546 An estate and gift tax credit that, in 2017, allows the first $5.49 million of an estate and lifetime gifts (beyond the annual gift exclusion) to be passed on tax free.

Generation-Skipping Tax, page 547 A tax on wealth and property transfers to a person two or more generations younger than the donor.

Draft a will and understand its purpose in estate planning. LO2

SUMMARY: Within your will, you designate beneficiaries or individuals who are willed your property. You also designate an executor who will be responsible for carrying out the provisions of your will. In addition, you can designate a guardian who will care for any children under the age of 18 and manage their property. You should periodically review your will to make sure that it conforms to your present situation.

KEY TERMS

Will, page 549 A legal document that describes how you want your property to be transferred to others after your death.

Beneficiary, page 549 An individual who is willed your property.

Executor or Personal Representative, page 549 An individual who is responsible for carrying out the provisions of your will and managing your property until the estate is passed on to your heirs.

Guardian, page 549 An individual who'll care for any children under the age of 18 and manage their property.

Probate, page 549 The legal procedure that establishes the validity of a will and then distributes the estate's assets.

Codicil, page 551 An attachment to a will that alters or amends a portion of the will.

Letter of Last Instructions, page 551 A letter, generally to your surviving spouse, that provides information and directions with respect to the execution of the will.

Durable Power of Attorney, page 552 A document that provides for someone to act on your behalf in the event that you become mentally incapacitated.

Living Will, page 552 A directive to a physician that allows you to state your wishes regarding medical treatment in the event of an illness or injury that renders you unable to make decisions regarding life support or other measures to extend your life.

Durable Health-Care Power of Attorney, page 552 A document that designates someone to make life-support decisions for you if you lose the capacity to decide.

LO3 Avoid probate.

SUMMARY: Trusts are legal entities that hold money or assets. Some of the more common reasons for trusts are (1) trusts avoid probate, (2) trusts are much more difficult to challenge in court than are wills, (3) trusts can reduce estate taxes, (4) trusts allow for professional management, (5) trusts provide for confidentiality, (6) trusts can be used to provide for a child with special needs, (7) trusts can be used to hold money until a child reaches maturity, and (8) trusts can ensure that children from a previous marriage will receive some inheritance.

With a revocable living trust, you place the assets into the trust while you are alive, and you can withdraw the assets from the trust later if you wish. An irrevocable living trust, as the name suggests, is permanent. A testamentary trust is one that is created by a will. Because these trusts are established by a will, they aren't created until probate has been completed.

KEY TERMS

Tenancy by the Entirety, page 552 A type of ownership limited to married couples. Property held this way can be transferred only if both the husband and the wife agree. In addition, upon the death of one, the property automatically passes directly to the survivor.

Joint Tenancy with the Right of Survivorship, page 552 A type of ownership in which two or more individuals share the ownership of assets, usually in a joint account at a bank or a brokerage firm. When one joint owner dies, the ownership passes directly to the surviving owners, bypassing the will.

Tenancy in Common, page 552 A type of ownership in which two or more individuals share ownership of assets. When one of the owners dies, that owner's share isn't passed on to the other owners. It becomes part of the deceased owner's estate and is distributed according to the deceased owner's will.

Community Property, page 553 Property acquired during marriage (depends on state law).

Trust, page 554 A legal entity in which some of your property is held for the benefit of another person.

Living Trust, page 555 A trust created during your life.

Revocable Living Trust, page 555 A trust in which you control the assets in the trust and can receive income from the trust without removing assets from the estate.

Irrevocable Living Trust, page 555 A trust in which you relinquish title and control of the assets when they are placed in the trust.

Testamentary Trust, page 556 A trust created by your will, which becomes active after you die.

Family Trust, page 556 A trust established to transfer assets to your children, while allowing the surviving spouse access to funds in the trust if necessary. Upon the death of the surviving spouse, the remaining funds in the trust are distributed to the children tax free.

Portable Estate Exemption, page 556 An exemption that allows a deceased spouse's unused estate tax exclusion to be shifted to the surviving spouse.

Qualified Terminable Interest Property (Q-TIP) Trust, page 557 A trust that gives the individual establishing the trust the ability to direct income from the trust to his or her spouse over the spouse's life and then, at the spouse's death, to choose to whom the assets go.

Sprinkling Trust, page 557 A trust that distributes income according to need rather than some preset formula. The trustee is given discretion to determine who needs what among the designated beneficiaries and then "sprinkles" the income among them according to need.

Problems and Activities

These problems are available in **MyLab Finance**.

1. Which of the following estate planning documents—will, codicil, letter of last instructions, living will—do the following individuals/families need? Explain your rationale.
   a. Kayla, a recent college graduate with only a few personal assets, all jointly owned with her parents.
   b. Justin and Edee, a couple in their 30s with two young children. They already have a will that they made when they were first married 10 years ago—before they had their second child.
   c. Mac, a widowed man living with a close personal friend to whom he would like to leave his personal assets upon death.
2. As the first gift from their estate, Lily and Tom Phillips plan to give $20,000 to their son, Raoul, for a down payment on a house.
   a. How much gift tax will be owed by Lily and Tom?
   b. How much income tax will be owed by Raoul?
   c. List three advantages of making this gift.
3. Morgan, a widow, recently passed away. The value of her assets at the time of death was $8,600,000. The cost of her funeral was $18,000, while estate administrative costs totaled $52,000. As stipulated in her will, she left $1,000,000 to charities. Based on this information, answer the following questions:
   a. Determine the value of Morgan's gross estate.
   b. Calculate the value of her taxable estate.
   c. What is her gift-adjusted taxable estate value?
   d. Assuming she died in 2017, how much of her estate would be subject to taxation?
   e. Calculate the estate tax liability.

4. Determine which of the following gifts are subject to gift taxes and to what extent they need to be included in an estate.
    a. Grandparents gave a grandchild $24,000 for the purchase of a new car.
    b. Father gave $35,000 to a son to start a small business.
    c. Parents paid $35,000 to Wellesley College for their daughter's tuition.
    d. Sister paid $47,000 of her brother's qualified medical expenses to Duke Medical Center.
    e. Widow gave $105,000 to charity.
    f. Mother gave her daughter a life insurance policy with a face value of $50,000 and a cash value of $10,000 2 years prior to the mother's death.
5. Upon her grandmother's death, So-hyun received $100,000 to use for college expenses or for starting her family. The money is in a checking account for So-hyun to use as she chooses. How much tax does So-hyun own on the gift from her grandmother?
6. Elsa and Ludvik Hansen have $6.8 million of assets: $2,400,000 in Ludvik's name, $2,400,000 in Elsa's name, and $2 million of jointly owned property. Their jointly owned property is titled using joint tenancy with right of survivorship. Elsa also co-owns a $500,000 beach house with her sister as tenants in common.
    a. What are the advantages or disadvantages of the Hansens' plan to rely on the unlimited marital deduction?
    b. What could the Hansens do to reduce their expected estate tax liability prior to either spouse's death?
    c. Who would receive Elsa's half share in the beach house if she were to die?

Discussion Case 1

This case is available in **MyLab Finance**.

Lee and Marta Howard are in their early 70s. Recently, they have grown concerned about probate and estate taxes. They calculated that this year they will have a combined net worth of $6,100,000. In addition, Lee owns a $500,000 whole life insurance policy on his life. Marta is the beneficiary. They are also considering giving their recently divorced son $100,000 to start a financial counseling practice. He is their only child and he has two children of his own. One, age 25, is disabled, lives in a group home, and receives Medicaid. The other is a freshman in college. Although a bit ashamed to admit as much, the Howards do not have a will and have made no plans for their estate. Their overriding fear is that they will outlive their money.

Questions

1. Should Lee and Marta be concerned about probate? Why or why not?
2. What should Lee and Marta include in a letter of last instructions?
3. Help the Howards understand the differences between revocable and irrevocable living trusts by listing the advantages and disadvantages of both.
4. How might the Howards use trusts to benefit their grandchildren? How might these strategies affect their estate taxes?
5. What options does Lee have for gifting his whole life insurance policy, either to an individual or to a charity? What are the consequences for his estate tax planning?
6. Would you recommend that Lee and Marta write their own will, or should they hire an attorney? Explain your answer.
7. Once they have a completed and signed will, where should they keep it? Where should they definitely not keep the will?

8. Assume that Lee and Marta (a) own all assets jointly, except for the life insurance policy that Lee owns, and (b) decide not to gift or establish trusts. If Lee were to die in 2017 and leave his assets to Marta through a marital transfer, how much of the estate would be subject to taxes if Marta dies later in 2017 (assuming the estate growth is offset by all expenses incurred in 2017)?
9. If after Lee's death Marta decided to (a) give her son the $100,000, (b) establish two $1,000,000 irrevocable trusts for the grandchildren, and (c) give another $500,000 to charity, how much of the estate would be subject to taxes if Marta were to die later in 2017 (assuming the estate growth is offset by all expenses incurred in 2017)?
10. Given the ages of the Howards, should they consider naming their son in a durable power of attorney document? What are the advantages and disadvantages of this?

Discussion Case 2

This case is available in **MyLab Finance**.

Cindy and Ned Lipman were recently married, each for the second time. Both are concerned about leaving assets to the adult children from their previous marriages and are reluctant to combine their individual assets. Together, they have an estate valued at $7.25 million, of which $3,100,000 is in Cindy's name and $3,350,000 is in Ned's name. They live in Cindy's $800,000 home, which she received in her divorce settlement. Cindy and Ned have not revised their wills since their marriage. The wills still name their previous spouses as executor and beneficiary of their respective estates.

Planning for incapacitation is another estate planning concern. Cindy's 86-year-old mother and 84-year-old uncle both have Alzheimer's disease, and she is concerned that it may be hereditary. Ned recently lost his father to a long-term illness and has vowed never to be kept "alive" by medi cal technology, confined to a hospital bed. Cindy, on the other hand, believes all steps should be taken to prolong a person's life.

Questions

1. What type of trust is appropriate for remarried couples such as the Lipmans? How might your answer change if each spouse has sufficient assets to provide for himself or herself independently following the death of the other spouse?
2. Should either of them die in 2017, how much estate tax would Cindy and Ned owe on their respective estates? How does the portable estate exemption affect their potential tax liability?
3. What can Cindy and Ned do to address their concerns about estate planning in the event of incapacitation?
4. Would Cindy and Ned make good health-care proxies for one another? Why or why not?
5. Since Cindy and Ned both have valid wills, are revisions necessary? If so, what changes should be made?

Continuing Case: Cory and Tisha Dumont

Part V: Life Cycle Issues

After finding the Web site deathclock.com, Cory talked Tisha into checking out their life expectancies. The "pessimistic" view projected that Cory would die at age 53. Cory jokingly commented, "Forget the life insurance premiums and saving for retirement, I'm living it up *now*!" The "normal" perspective projected that Cory would live to age 73, whereas Tisha was projected to die at the age of 79. Her reply to Cory, "You may live it up now, but I've got 6 years to live it up without you! And if I inherit all our assets, I could be a wealthy old lady! We need to save and invest even more. I wonder how much fun a wealthy old lady could have." Although Cory and Tisha could joke about their deathclock.com experience, it did raise some important financial issues for them to consider. They don't plan to retire or to transfer their estate anytime soon, but their concerns are clearly a part of the financial planning process.

With your assistance, they have reviewed their spending, credit usage, insurance needs, and investment plans. In short, by developing a financial plan and changing a few spending habits, they are building an estate for the future. They are concerned about financial independence during their "golden years"—however long that might be—and want to make the most of their retirement options. They are also concerned about preserving their estate for the benefit of Chad and Haley, regardless of the timing of their deaths.

Questions

1. Assuming the deathclock.com projection is accurate, Cory is concerned about getting back as much as possible of his Social Security taxes. At what age can he retire and receive full Social Security benefits? If he delays retirement, what percentage increase in his benefits can he expect? What is the earliest age that Cory can retire and receive Social Security? How will early retirement affect his benefits?

2. If Cory or Tisha were to die tomorrow, what kind of Social Security benefits, if any, would the surviving spouse, Chad, and Haley receive? For how long?

3. Both Cory and Tisha are contributing to a "qualified" or tax-favored 401(k) retirement plan at work.

a. What are two unique benefits of such a plan?

b. Why are these benefits and the time value of money particularly important in retirement planning?

c. What must the Dumonts do to be "active participants"?

d. What are "catch-up" provisions? Why and how are they used?

4. Cory and Tisha are interested in other retirement saving strategies. What is the maximum amount they could contribute to an IRA? If they decided to contribute to a traditional IRA, would they receive a full or partial tax deduction? Why? What are the advantages and disadvantages of opening a Roth IRA instead of a traditional IRA? What advantages are common to both plans?

5. Cory's company is planning to convert all employees to a cash-balance retirement plan. Explain this plan, noting advantages and disadvantages for Cory.

6. The Dumonts estimate their current living expenses at approximately $81,000, which they joke could be very comfortable *without the kids* that they won't have during retirement.

a. How much income, before and after taxes, will they need to retire, assuming an average tax rate of 17 percent during retirement?

b. Assume that through a combination of savings, Social Security, and retirement plan distributions, Cory and Tisha are able to receive $45,000 annually in retirement. Determine their retirement income shortfall. Assuming a 4 percent inflation rate and 35 years until retirement, calculate their inflation-adjusted shortfall.

c. If Cory and Tisha can earn a 5 percent inflation-adjusted return, determine how much they must accumulate in savings over the 35 years to fund the annual inflation-adjusted shortfall calculated earlier.

d. How much do the Dumonts need to start saving each year for the next 35 years at 9 percent to meet their savings accumulation goal calculated in item c?

7. If Cory and Tisha invested $2,000 in a tax-free account at the end of every year for 30 years, what would be the future value of the account if they earned 9 percent annually? If, instead, they first paid taxes (marginal tax rate of 15 percent) and then made the investment, how much would the account be worth at the end of 30 years? Based on these calculations, what advice would you give to Cory and Tisha regarding their retirement savings? What principle of saving in an IRS tax-deferred plan does this example demonstrate?

8. Recall that Cory has $2,500 in retirement funds with a former employer. When Cory resigned, the account value was almost $4,000, but only part of it was available to him. Explain how vesting rules explain the difference between the two dollar amounts. What options and tax implications should Cory compare to claim his retirement benefits?
9. Cory has considered using the $2,500 for a surprise vacation for the family, an IRA account, or another mutual fund account to fund a 25-year anniversary trip with Tisha. Could he roll over the distribution from the qualified plan to a traditional IRA invested in a mutual fund (remember, no income taxes have been paid on the contributions) and in 19 years take money out for the trip? What are the tax implications of this plan instead of funding a taxable mutual fund account?
10. Tisha has considered offering accounting services to small businesses. She has obtained a business license and plans to work out of her home. Would she qualify for a small business/self-employed retirement plan? If so, what plan should she consider?
11. Tisha has indicated that she thinks a single life annuity will be her choice when she begins to receive retirement pension benefits. She thinks this is the best payout structure because (a) she has earned the entire benefit, (b) she can control the investment of the funds, and (c) Cory will receive his own pension. Will Tisha automatically be able to choose a single life annuity payout option? Assuming that Cory does not want Tisha to have a single life annuity, what type of joint and survivor annuity will provide the greatest immediate payout and afford Cory a guaranteed income should he outlive Tisha?
12. After retirement, what expected and unexpected changes should the Dumonts monitor to safeguard their future?
13. At this stage of the life cycle, which of the objectives of estate planning are most important to the Dumont household? Preparation of what two estate planning documents would enable them to accomplish these objectives? Where should the documents be kept?
14. Recall that Cory's parents recently gave each of the children a $20,000 gift to be invested for college. How much federal income tax and gift tax are due on this transfer? Will there be any generation-skipping transfer tax due? The senior Dumonts planned to give Chad $30,000 instead of $20,000 but were advised not to. Why?
15. Cory and Tisha want to develop other saving strategies to fund education costs. What are the advantages or disadvantages of opening a Coverdell Education Savings Account or a 529 plan for each of the children? Could they establish both types of accounts?
16. The Dumonts are curious as to why someone would want to avoid probate. Having the court oversee the will and the distribution of assets sounds like a good thing. Explain why avoiding probate may be an important issue in estate planning. What four steps could the Dumonts take to avoid probate?
17. Recently, Cory reluctantly agreed to be named as executor for his older sister Elsa's estate. Does serving as executor include acting as guardian for her child, who is younger than Chad and Haley? What are the duties that Cory would be expected to perform as executor?
18. The Dumonts recently noticed on their bank statement that their accounts are owned jointly with right of survivorship. Provide a simple explanation of this term.
19. The Dumonts have always considered a trust a financial tool of the wealthy. But they do want to learn more about estate planning. Provide a simple explanation of how both living and testamentary trusts, which by definition are quite different, can accomplish the same purpose of reducing estate taxes.
20. Cory's parents have always joked that they plan to cheat the "tax man" by dying broke. Their estate planning strategy involves utilizing the unlimited marital deduction. Explain how relying on the unlimited marital deduction may not always be an effective planning strategy

CHAPTER 17

Financial Life Events—Fitting the Pieces Together

Learning Objectives

LO1	**Understand** the importance of beginning your financial planning early.	**The Ingredients of Success**
LO2	**Recognize** the ten financial life events and strategies to deal with them.	**Financial Life Events**
LO3	**Understand** and manage the keys to financial success.	**The Keys to Success: A Dozen Decisions**
LO4	**Deal** with all kinds of debt in the real world.	**Tying Things Together: Debt and the Real World**

It may seem strange to take personal finance advice from a television sitcom, but Fox's hit comedy *New Girl* is chock-full of examples of things *not to do* regarding your financial life. Most of these financial lessons revolve around the character Nick Miller (played by Jake Johnson), a dropout law student who is tending bar even though he has actually passed the bar exam.

Through Nick's misadventures, we learn about insurance, banking, smart spending, the importance of a good credit score, and staying financially organized. For example, we learn that health insurance is a good thing to have—Nick, of course, doesn't have any and after getting injured in a friendly football game ends up at an OB-GYN, who sees Nick as a favor to Jess (played by Zooey Deschanel). We also learn that it makes more sense to put your money in a bank, which Nick refers to as "a paper bag with fancier walls" than an actual paper bag—which was how Nick received his $8,000 inheritance from his father's estate. Shocked at the inheritance and the amount, his first impulse is to "spend it all." He buys giant tins of popcorn, a huge number of shoes (many of which don't fit him), and a professional photography session because "rich guys always have photos of themselves in their house." It never occurs to him to pay off some of his debt. As for Nick's credit score, which turns out to be an absurdly low score of 250, it's so low that he can't get a cell phone. "I've just never seen a score this low," a worker says. "Did you just wake up from a coma?" And as we know, a low credit score can have all kinds of repercussions. The lesson on being organized financially comes from "Nick's box," where Nick keeps all of his financial documents, including unpaid bills, letters from debt collectors, outstanding parking tickets, titles to vehicles he no longer owns, and who knows what else. Lucky for Nick his girlfriend, Jess, has a good head on her shoulders, is very financially responsible, and is determined to "fix Nick and his bad habits." She gets him to a doctor, secretly takes some of his inheritance and pays off some of his debt, and after discovering "the box" gets him to a bank to open his first bank account.

Justin Stephens/Everett Collection

So let's face it—on TV as well as in real life, good financial habits can and do pay off handsomely. Moreover, when it comes to money, how much you have, how you get it, and what you do with it determine not only whether or not you meet your goals but also how people relate to you. This includes not only your friends but, as we have shown throughout this book in the "Love and Money" features, also your family; as has been pointed out several times, money problems are the number one cause of divorce. The bottom line is that money does matter.

Most of us already know this, but most of us never learn how to truly manage money. But you're ahead of the game: You've been introduced to the basics of financial planning. In this chapter, we recap much of what you've already learned, and we put it together in the form of an action plan. We also look at some of the special problems you may face in the near future—focusing on life events that could throw a monkey wrench into your financial plan. We examine the keys to financial success and ruin. Finally, we talk about getting started—that is, putting your financial plan into action. Following the advice in this chapter sets the stage for a sound financial future.

And your financial future starts now. The challenges you will face may include student loans and credit card debt; budgeting, spending, and saving; and the financial shocks of marriage and children. But it is time to make a choice: You can take control now, or you can put it off and make financial management a heck of a lot tougher in the future. Money does matter, and after all, you don't want to be like Nick Miller—going through life without a wallet and using a sandwich bag to house your license and some money. So let's get started.

LO1 Understand the importance of beginning your financial planning early.

The Ingredients of Success

It is simply impossible to succeed financially unless you

- Evaluate your financial health.
- Plan and budget.
- Manage your cash and credit.
- Control your debt.
- Make knowledgeable consumer decisions.
- Have adequate health, life, property, and liability insurance.
- Understand investing principles.
- Make investment decisions that reflect your goals.
- Plan for retirement.
- Plan for what happens to your accumulated wealth and your dependents after you die.

Everything in personal finance starts with the budgeting and planning process first outlined in Chapter 1. You must periodically review your financial progress and reexamine your financial plan. In other words, personal finance is an ongoing process, with no financial plan being fixed for life. But even though financial plans don't last forever, without them, goals are a mere fantasy.

There isn't a topic covered in this book that is not essential to your personal financial health. As such, you'll want to keep revisiting all these topics to make sure that your financial plan reflects your current financial health and what's going on in your life.

Now let's try to put all this together. First, we will take a look at where you are in the financial life cycle. Then let's look at ten financial life events—events that will change your goals, impact your financial resources, and create new financial obligations for you. Then we will examine 12 decisions that you will be making that will determine whether you succeed financially. Finally, we will end with a call to action—to begin your financial plan today.

The Financial Life Cycle

Let's look at where the typical recent college grad is in the financial life cycle we outlined in Chapter 1. Recent graduates make a lot of financial decisions in their first decade out of college. They may purchase their first car and possibly their first home, they will be establishing credit and paying taxes, and they may even get married and begin families. If you're a recent graduate, you will want to set up an emergency fund, start saving for your goals, and begin putting money into an IRA and a retirement account. In terms of saving, these are an exceedingly important 10 years. The financial decisions you make now will affect the rest of your life.

If the day you turn 19 you start to put away $5,500 on your birthday each year for 8 years in a Roth IRA that earns 10 percent per year (that's about the average annual return on the S&P 500 over the past 50 years) and then nothing thereafter, at age 65 you will have about $2.6 million! If you wait until your 26th birthday to start that Roth IRA and make payments on your birthday for 40 years, you still won't catch up—you end up with only $2.4 million. Moreover, if you wait until your 31st birthday to start that IRA and make 35 payments, you'll end up with $1.4 million! There's simply no substitute for starting early. It's without doubt the simplest strategy: Recognize your financial future starts now and just do it.

Women and Personal Finance

The basic principles of personal finance are the same for men and women, as is the desire for financial security. However, the effort needed to achieve their financial goals does differ: It's much tougher to achieve financial security if you're a woman. Some of the reasons for this are that women generally earn less money, are less likely to have pensions, qualify for less income from Social Security because they generally earn less over their lifetime, and live on average 7 years longer than men—living longer is a real disadvantage when it comes to planning for retirement. As a result, planning for financial independence, in particular during retirement years, is more difficult for women than it is for men.

Financial Life Events

LO2 Recognize the ten financial life events and strategies to deal with them.

In the course of your lifetime, you will experience many events that will change your goals, affect your financial resources, and create new financial obligations or opportunities for you. While the number of these types of life events is almost unlimited, we will focus on ten of the most common.

- Life Event 1: Getting Started
- Life Event 2: Marriage
- Life Event 3: Buying a Home
- Life Event 4: Having a Child
- Life Event 5: Inheritances, Bonuses, or Unexpected Money
- Life Event 6: A Major Illness
- Life Event 7: Caring for an Elderly Parent
- Life Event 8: Retiring
- Life Event 9: Death of a Spouse
- Life Event 10: Divorce

Life Event 1: Getting Started

There is a beginning for everything, even for your financial future. For most of us, getting started begins with graduation from school or with the realization that we have to get our financial life on track. Let's take a look at some of the steps involved in getting started.

Step 1: Manage Your Life One of the first things you'll want to do is eliminate things that may lead to your failure.

- *Delete Any Eyebrow-Raising Photos from Facebook and Other Social Media.* Potential employers will look at Twitter, Instagram, Facebook, and other social media, so any photos of you drinking or having fun on Spring Break must go—really. Perhaps better yet would be not to post anything that might hurt your job-hunting efforts later on—even if it is posted "privately," possible employers may gain access to it.
- *Don't Be Afraid to Invest in Yourself.* In a way, your largest financial asset is your "human capital." You'll most likely have several jobs over your lifetime, so make sure your skill set grows over time.
- *Be Able to Describe What You Do.* When you meet someone and he or she asks what you do, be ready with a tight answer that encourages conversation. After all, you never know when you're going to meet your next employer.

Step 2: Lay the Groundwork Before you can make financial progress and plant the seeds for your future financial success, you need an understanding of investments and personal finance. This course will take you a long way toward that goal, but it will also be important to keep up with all the changes that occur in the financial world by making a habit of reading periodicals such as *Money* and *Kiplinger's Personal Finance* and newspapers such as the *Wall Street Journal.* Laying the groundwork involves more than just gaining an understanding of personal finance; it also involves an assessment of your current finances, a plan for both the expected and the unexpected events of the future, and a realization as to how you view money—your financial personality.

- *Track Expenses and Create a Budget.* Know how much money you make. Know how and where you spend it. For tracking expenses, there is nothing simpler and easier to use than Level Money, and when it comes to online budgeting, **Mint.com** is one of the best online resources. Go back and check out Figure 2.7, which appeared earlier in the book; you'll find a short write-up on all the features of Level Money and **Mint.com**.
- *Control Your Debt.* Eliminate any high-interest debt you have, and control your credit card purchases.

PRINCIPLE 5

- *Establish an Emergency Fund.* Remember **Principle 5: Stuff Happens, or the Importance of Liquidity**.
- *Insure Yourself.* Make sure you have the kind of insurance that you need (i.e., the right health and disability insurance), but consider life insurance only if you really need it.
- *Control Your Credit Score.* A high credit score will have quite a few financial benefits. If you're having trouble controlling your credit score, check back to Chapter 6 for some help.

PRINCIPLE 1

- *Keep Current on Personal Finance.* Remember **Principle 1: The Best Protection Is Knowledge**.

Step 3: Identify Your Goals Nothing happens without a plan. Identifying your goals is the first step in setting up your financial plan.

PRINCIPLE 2

- *Identify and Prioritize Financial Goals.* Remember **Principle 2: Nothing Happens Without a Plan**.
- *Set a Time Frame.* When would you like to reach these goals? In 1 year, 10 years, 40 years?

- *Identify the Costs of Your Goals.* How much in the way of capital will it take to reach these goals?
- *Revisit Your Goals Annually.* Set a time every year—or if you are married, set up an annual meeting with your spouse—to review your financial health. Put together a personal balance sheet and a personal cash flow statement for the past year. This may sound like a good deal of work, but if you're using **Mint.com**, all the work is done for you. Check out the progress you're making toward your goals, make the necessary adjustments, and make sure your retirement goals are part of your discussion.

Step 4: Begin Saving for Your Goals When you have so many years to meet your goals, it may be difficult to realize the need for immediacy, but starting to save today will make it much easier to realize those financial goals later. Not only does **Mint.com** provide you with help in setting up goals, but also it helps in putting together a savings plan to meet those goals. Whether you're saving to buy a home, to live comfortably after retirement, to pay down your student loans, or to pay off your credit cards, **Mint.com** provides a structure to meet those goals. **Mint.com** also gives you updates on your progress toward your goals, which reinforces your saving efforts.

- *Save More than You Think You Can.* Don't let your expenses determine how much you save—decide to save and do it.
- *Make Saving Automatic.* Have money taken directly out of your paycheck and put into savings. Remember **Principle 10: Just Do It!**

PRINCIPLE 10

- *Avoid Expenses Whenever You Can.* Look closely at no-load, low-expense mutual funds when investing in stocks—check out the Vanguard and Fidelity Web sites.
- *Don't Procrastinate.* Don't put off saving because "I'll have more money to invest later"—that can be a recipe for financial ruin. For many, this is the biggest financial challenge you will face.
- *Catch Your Matches.* Take advantage of any matching contributions that your employer offers. If your employer matches 401(k) contributions, max them out.
- *Consider a Roth IRA.* If you anticipate being in a higher tax bracket when you retire, consider a Roth IRA, where the earnings that accumulate are tax exempt.
- *Determine Your Risk Capacity and How Much Risk You Can Tolerate.* Gain a good understanding of your risk capacity and tolerance. Do you have an emergency fund? Can you afford to take risk, and if you can, how comfortable are you if the value of your investments declines? If you're not quite sure of your risk tolerance, check out the excellent risk tolerance quiz located at **http://njaes.rutgers.edu/money/riskquiz/**. When you take this quiz or try to determine your risk tolerance, keep in mind that individuals often are more tolerant of risk when the stock market is climbing and the economy is strong and less tolerant of risk during troubled times in the stock market and economy.
- *Pay Attention to Asset Allocation.* Understand the importance of asset allocation and diversification.
- *Put Together a Strategy.* Base your investment strategy on when you need your money, your risk tolerance, and your asset allocation.
- *Control Your Spending.* Just because you earn it doesn't mean you have to spend it. That probably means you don't want to buy a brand new car that depreciates as soon as you drive it off the lot. Just knowing how much you are spending and how those spending decisions impact the amount of money you'll have at the end of the month helps control spending. Once again, Level Money and **Mint.com** can help you keep on budget.

- *Don't Keep Up with the Joneses.* Academic research has shown that our spending decisions are influenced not just by our needs and wants but also by a drive to keep up with those around us.[1] Researchers found that neighbors of lottery winners appear more likely to buy cars and remodel their houses to show that they can keep up—and in the process, they end up going broke. Don't get caught up in this urge. Either make an effort to avoid this temptation, or pick the right Joneses to live next to.

Step 5: Manage Your Portfolio Once your plan is in place, make sure that it changes to reflect changing goals and the progress made toward those goals. This means monitoring progress and periodically rebalancing investments.

- *Monitor Your Portfolio.* Make it an annual event to review your investment performance and make appropriate adjustments to your savings and investment strategy. When it comes to managing your portfolio, the easiest way to do it is online through your broker's Web site; if you have investments at a number of different financial institutions, you might try **Mint.com**.
- *Stay Current.* Stay abreast of any changes in the tax laws that might impact your investment portfolio.
- *Adjust to Changes.* When necessary, change your investment goals to match changes in your life.

Life Event 2: Marriage

Most married couples plan their wedding down to the smallest detail but spend little time talking about money and planning their financial lives together. That's probably not a great idea, given the fact that money problems are the top reason people get divorced. Managing your money when you're single is tough enough. But when you're married, you have to plan not only for your own expenses but also for those of your partner.

Your partner may bring student loans, credit card debt, a past bankruptcy, or other financial problems to the marriage. And let's face it—you're marrying this person's money, too. On top of all this is the fact that opposites tend to attract. That means if you're a saver, you might end up married to a spender, and if you're a spender, there might be a saver in your future. In either case, if you don't do some financial planning from the beginning, there will also be some arguments in your future.

The place to start your life together is with a discussion about money. The aim is to find out your partner's financial history, habits, and goals. Checklist 17.1 offers guidelines for this very important discussion.

Once you have an understanding of each other's financial personality and views on money, it's time to see how this translates into spending habits. You'll want to track your expenses carefully for a month. When you do this, it's important to keep track of *all* your expenses, including money you spend on books on Amazon and on lattes at Starbucks. This should provide fuel for more discussion as you see

FACTS OF LIFE

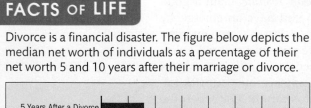

Divorce is a financial disaster. The figure below depicts the median net worth of individuals as a percentage of their net worth 5 and 10 years after their marriage or divorce.

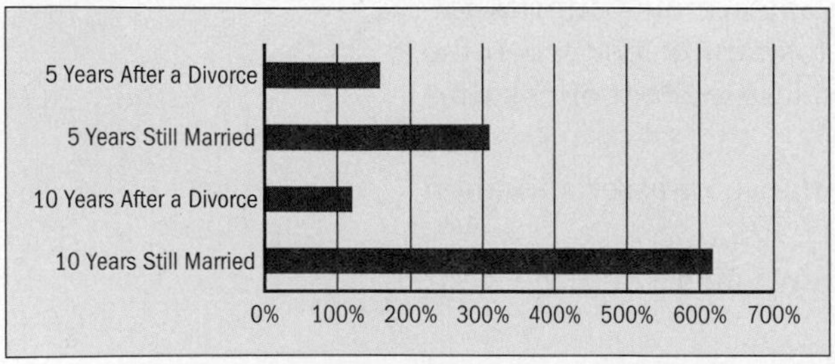

[1]Sumit Agarwal, Vyacheslav Mikhed, and Barry Scholnick, *Does Keeping Up with the Joneses Cause Financial Distress? Evidence from Lottery Winners and Neighboring Bankruptcies*, Working Paper 16-04/R (Philadelphia: The Federal Reserve Bank of Philadelphia, 2016).

CHECKLIST 17.1 Marriage, Money, and Financial Personalities

When talking with your future partner, ask these questions:

- ☐ How did your family handle money? Did they have debt problems? Did they use credit cards?
- ☐ How much income is enough? How do you feel about both spouses working after you have children?
- ☐ How much do you earn? Do you have other sources of income? What do you own?
- ☐ How do you feel about debt? Do you have debt? Do you have other financial commitments—for example, aging parents who may need financial support or children from a previous marriage?
- ☐ Once you're married, will you invest separately? Who will pay for what? Will you have one or two checking accounts?
- ☐ Do you or your partner need life insurance and, if so, how much? How about health insurance? What do your employee benefits include?

how financial views translate into action. You will now have enough background to make a budget. Set out your goals and make plans to attain them using what you've learned in this book. Just as important as setting up a budget is identifying expenses that you can eliminate. Tracking your spending will also let you plan savings, which you'll want to make automatic.

Once you're married, review and revise your plan annually or whenever there is a significant change in your life—for example, the birth of a child. If you can't get your financial plans settled by yourself, be sure to contact a financial planner. A planner will help you set up a plan that works and will guide you through any conflicts you might have. If you're still having problems, you can seek the help of a financial counselor, a financial planner who specializes in counseling couples about money.

Two of the many financial decisions you face when you get married are whether to have joint or separate checking accounts and credit cards. Clearly, one checking account is easiest for most couples, but if you have incompatible money management styles, consider two accounts. That's kind of the financial equivalent of two bathrooms. It makes record keeping more tedious, and you may not get as good a deal on your checking account from the bank, but if your money management styles are dramatically different, it may be the best choice.

With respect to credit cards, you want to control credit card spending and to use your credit card to establish a strong credit history. If you've ever heard stories of a divorced, widowed, or separated stay-at-home spouse unable to get credit, you know how difficult this can be. The way to avoid this potential problem is for each spouse to have his or her own credit card.

When you are first married, it is time to reexamine your goals and begin planning for any children you might expect in the future, as well as for your eventual retirement.

Step 1: Get Organized You now have a new financial partner and new considerations to work with, so the first step is to review and reorganize your finances.

- *Get Talking.* Discuss your approaches to handling money, as it comes in and goes out, and create rules to handle differences.
- *Update All Your Financial Records.* Make sure your driver's license, passport, Social Security identification, bills, and any financial accounts reflect any name and address changes that might have occurred. Consider making your new spouse the beneficiary on your financial accounts—for example, investment accounts, workplace retirement savings accounts, or employer stock plan accounts you might have.

- *Decide What's Common and What's Separate.* Decide whether to keep separate bank accounts, merge everything, or do a bit of each.
- *Gain Control of Your Debt and Your Credit Score.* Life will be much easier if you can work together to gain control of any credit card or other type of debt that one partner may bring to the marriage. Once your debt is under control, your credit score should rise, and it will be much easier to successfully apply for a home mortgage. When dealing with debt that you or your partner brings into the marriage, you should begin with a discussion detailing all the debt each of you may have. Next, determine how to pay it off. Will both spouses chip in, or will each spouse pay down his or her own loans? Also, in order to control debt, you should create a strategy to save for one-time expenses—like a vacation or a new piece of furniture—without incurring debt.
- *Consolidate Your Credit Cards.* Avoid having twice the number of cards needed.
- *Merge Your Finances to Make Good Decisions.* If you don't consolidate your finances, allowing you to see the big picture—that is, your combined income and savings—you won't be able to make good joint decisions. Once again, **Mint.com** is a great tool to tie things together and create a budget that works for the whole family.
- *Set Up a Plan to Pay Household Expenses.* If it's not realistic to merge all finances, one alternative is to create a joint checking account, with each spouse contributing money to pay for household expenses like the mortgage, utilities, and groceries.
- *Set Aside an Area Dedicated to Your Financial Paperwork.* It will be much easier for you to keep track of your finances, pay bills, monitor your budget, and plan for the future if there is a central, dedicated location for dealing with personal finances.

Step 2: Revisit Your Financial Goals A new financial partner means new financial goals. This is a good time to revisit your financial goals, both short- and long-term, and set in place what is necessary to accomplish these goals. It is also a time to make decisions on how to manage your finances. Remember **Principle 2: Nothing Happens Without a Plan**.

PRINCIPLE 2

- *Reexamine Your Financial Goals.* Have you changed your mind or time frame with respect to purchasing a home? Are children now a consideration?
- *Begin Saving for Your Goals.* Even if you don't have children—but are planning to have them—begin saving for their education. Combining your incomes should allow you to save more. This is also the time to get serious about saving for your future. You'll find that your expenses will only grow as you get older, which means you need to start saving now.
- *Make Your Saving Automatic.* Have money automatically deducted from your paycheck.
- *Make Sure You Have an Emergency Fund.* Be prepared for the unexpected. The importance of an emergency fund cannot be overstated when it comes to marriage. Financial emergencies put enormous stress on a marriage. An emergency fund will not only help in the time of need but also provide a level of financial security that is important—you may not be able to avoid the emergency, but you can avoid the stress. Put a plan in place to have 3 to 6 months of living expenses set aside in a savings account or money market account, and make sure to keep it strictly off limits until there's a real emergency.
- *Begin Working Toward Retirement.* Make sure you have begun to save for retirement, and if you are both working, you might want to do it separately.

Step 3: Reexamine Your Insurance and Benefits With a new partner in life, you may want to change your insurance beneficiaries, consider purchasing additional insurance, and make sure your benefits are coordinated.

- ◆ *Review Your Beneficiaries.* Make sure you review all insurance beneficiary designations.
- ◆ *Include All Family Members.* Are all family members covered?
- ◆ *Review Your Insurance.* Review your health insurance coverage. Also, review your homeowner's and auto insurance.
- ◆ *Assess Your Disability Insurance.* If you don't already have it, make sure you obtain adequate disability insurance.
- ◆ *Coordinate Your Benefits.* If you both work, study your benefit options to identify the best and cheapest protection. Then coordinate your benefits; perhaps you can drop a benefit that is covered in your spouse's plan.

Step 4: Reexamine Your Taxes Your tax status and the tax-advantaged benefits and opportunities afforded you by your employer may change as a result of your marriage. However, there may be legislative changes to the tax code occur. If this happens, updates, including the personal finance implications, will be provided on the companion website (**http://pearsonhighered.com/keown**).

- ◆ *Update Your W-4 Forms.* Your W-4 forms should reflect your new tax status as a couple.
- ◆ *Take Advantage of Tax Breaks.* One spouse may receive tax breaks; make sure you shift savings from one spouse to the other to take full advantage of any tax breaks offered by employers.

Step 5: Make a Will You must be concerned about providing for your spouse and possible children in the event of your death.

- ◆ *Make a Will.* Make or update your will to include your spouse and possible children—also, make sure you have a living will.
- ◆ *Review Your Beneficiaries.* Review all beneficiary designations on your retirement accounts.

Step 6: Make It Work Money is a major cause of friction in marriage, and while a good dose of financial planning will help, there are also things you should avoid doing.

- ◆ *Don't Keep Money Secrets.* If you or your spouse overspends, don't hide it from the other half. There is no good outcome from financial secrets.
- ◆ *Don't Let One Partner Take All the Financial Responsibility.* While only one of you may be in charge of paying the bills, that doesn't mean your partner should live in ignorance and spend without consequence.
- ◆ *Avoid Bad Debt.* Think twice before taking out a loan for something that will decline in value over time, like a car, keeping in mind that eventually you could owe more than your purchase is worth.

Life Event 3: Buying a Home

Your home is your biggest investment, so it shouldn't come as a surprise that purchasing it has financial implications. Let's look at some of the things to consider when buying a home.

Step 1: Make Sure the Purchase Fits Your Financial Plan Make sure that your purchase falls within the limits of your financial goals and budget.

- *Keep Track of Your Credit Score.* Many things affect your credit score, including the number of credit cards, your debt level, and any late payments you've made. Knowing your score might affect your purchase decision and the ease of buying your dream home.

Step 2: Consider Tax Implications

- *Take Advantage of the Tax Benefits.* When your major purchase is the renovation of your home, you might consider using a home equity loan, with tax-deductible interest, to fund it. Or use a home equity line to purchase your car or pay tuition; the interest, with some restrictions, will be tax deductible.
- *Build the Tax Benefits into Your Budget.* Include the tax savings, which include your home mortgage interest and real estate tax payments, in your budget.
- *Reexamine Your Investments.* If you invest in municipal bonds and you've moved to a new state, consider moving your investments to municipal bonds issued by your new state to take the full tax advantage.
- *Update Your Employer Records.* Meet with the employee benefits coordinator to update your W-2 with your new address and possible changes in deductions.
- *Know Your State.* If you are moving to a new state, visit its tax Web site. These sites generally provide great information, from the cost of registering your auto to your new income tax rate—check them out. Higher or lower taxes mean less or more money for meeting your goals—either way, don't be surprised.

Step 3: Take Care of the Details

- *Update Your Address.* Provide your credit card companies, bank, and other financial institutions with your new address.
- *Update Your Insurance Policies.* Update your insurance policies to reflect the value of your new home, as well as its contents. Note that your auto insurance rate may be impacted by the location of your new home.

Life Event 4: Having a Child

As we saw in Chapter 1, the cost of raising a child from birth to age 18 runs about $233,610, and the cost is rising. When you add in the cost of a college education and lost wages resulting from child-rearing duties, *U.S. News and World Reports* estimates that for a medium-income family, a child requires an investment in excess of $1.45 million over 22 years. Yikes!

Certainly, there is more to life than money, and you just can't quantify the joys and satisfaction of raising children. But you want to make sure you take the financial pain out of having children by planning ahead.

Step 1: Survey Your Finances Reassess where you are in light of your growing family, and develop a financial plan for both the expected and the unexpected costs of your new child, as well as your short- and long-term goals. Make sure that you and your spouse are in agreement over your spending priorities.

- *Assess Your Current Financial Situation.* Before you begin putting together a new financial plan, you've got to know where you are right now. As you develop your plan, make sure that you have an adequate emergency fund.

LOVE & MONEY

Talking about money is uncomfortable; after all, there's a lot of hidden subtext and meaning that comes with "money." Depending on how you were raised, how financially well off your parents were, how they used money to reward or punish, and many other factors in your upbringing, money can mean almost anything to you—such as power, happiness, or success. But regardless of what it means to you, it most likely comes with a good deal of hidden subtext and meaning. According to a Wells Fargo survey of just over 1,000, nonstudent adults (ages 25–75) who are the primary or joint financial decision makers in the household, discussions about money are something that 44 percent of Americans point to as the most difficult chat to have—even more difficult than talking about death (or politics). Almost as interesting is the fact that half of the women said that they "find it difficult talking with others about personal finances" versus 38 percent of men. In addition, women felt less confident in their investment knowledge, with only 29 percent of women saying that "they know where to invest in today's market," compared to 42 percent of men.

Unfortunately, avoiding this discussion before committing to a permanent relationship can be costly in the long run. While Americans don't want to talk about money, they do worry about it. In fact, according to the American Psychological Association, money is the top source of stress for Americans.[2] Moreover, it's the area of biggest regret for Americans. When asked what they would do differently if they could go back 5 years, survey respondents most frequently chose "saving and spending":

- Saving and spending (49%)
- Taking better care of their physical health, diet, and fitness (42%)
- Pursuing different personal relationships (21%)
- Working more to improve their career (16%)

If you could go *back* 5 years, what would you do differently?

When you fall in love, it's easy to assume that your partner's money views and money personality are the same as yours—but that's not always true. That's why having a conversation about money is so important. It eliminates surprises down the line that might be damaging and allows you to put in place a plan to deal with those differences.

But given the level of difficulty people have in talking about money, a subject that is often considered taboo, when and how do you make that conversation work? Once you realize that you are both serious about making a life together, it's time. Do not wait until you are married! Once you are engaged, it's a conversation whose time has come.

In order to make the conversation work, you both have to realize that everyone dreads a discussion about money—that you aren't alone in this feeling. It's a discussion that takes trust, respect, and openness—and it is definitely not a time for judgment. The importance of openness cannot be overemphasized. If you're having problems opening up and getting the conversation going, it may be time for help from a financial planner. Even if you have to pay for help, in the long run you'll most likely be saving more, possibly including your marriage.

As part of your discussion you'll want to talk about your beliefs about money and your money personality. For example, are you a spender or saver? In this way, you can keep those beliefs from becoming a source of future conflict. This is also the time to let your future partner know what your assets and liabilities are. For example, do you have student loans, credit card debt, or unpaid medical bills? After this reveal, you'll want to discuss how these debts will be paid off: jointly or by the person who incurred them. These may not be easy topics to discuss—but it has to happen!

This would also be a good time to discuss how you will organize your finances—that is, who will be responsible for paying bills and whether all your assets will be pooled. After all, these are questions you're going to have to deal with shortly. Finally, it's a good time to discuss goals. Don't think that just because you're in love your partner shares your goals. Do you want kids? What are your spending priorities? When and how would you like to retire? The nice thing about talking about goals is that it tends to be fun rather than stressful. After all, you're planning your life together.

---

[2]American Psychological Association (2017). *Stress in America: Coping with Change*. Stress in America™ Survey. http://www.apa.org/news/press/releases/stress/2016/coping-with-change.PDF

STOP & THINK

It's generally considered bad taste to look at the decision to have children in economic terms. After all, children are their parents' hope for the future and the continuation of the family's bloodlines. Let's look at Table 17.1, which shows you what you might do with *just some* of the money it takes to raise children if you decide to pass on parenthood. What sacrifices did your parents make to raise you?

- *Reexamine Your Financial Goals.* With a new child, your financial goals, both short- and long-term, may also change. A new short-term goal might be to find a bigger place to live, whereas planning for your child's college tuition might be among your long-term goals.
- *Revise Your Budget.* Revise your budget to reflect the new goals and expenses associated with a new child. You or your spouse might be taking some time off from work or even quitting a job. That should be factored into your budget. Make sure that you continue your contributions toward your retirement.

TABLE 17.1 What You Can Do with Just Some of the Money if You Decide to Pass on Parenthood

	Some of What You Might Spend on Your Child		How You Might Spend That Money on Yourself	
Age	**Expense**	**Cost**	**Expense**	**Cost**
0	Average cost of delivery	$6,400	7-day safari for two in Kenya	$6,400
1	An au pair (live-in nanny)	$30,000	New 2018 MINI John Cooper S	$25,770
3	Montessori preschool	$4,000	Set of Ping G2 golf clubs	$4,000
5	The must-have toy: the (very rare) 1959 Blond Ponytail Barbie	$1,800	Mint copy of Beatles "Butcher Block" cover to *Yesterday and Today* signed by all the Beatles	$1,800
7	After-school program for the gifted	$3,564	2 box-seat season tickets to the Baltimore Orioles	$3,564
8–9	Private school	$19,770	A 2018 Volkswagen Jetta Sportwagen	$24,000
10	Violin and lessons (three times per week)	$4,150	Membership in a health club with personal trainer (three times per week)	$4,150
11	Self-defense lessons (three times per week) after being beaten up when going to violin lessons after school	$3,750	One more year of a personal trainer (three times per week)	$3,750
12	Therapy to improve self-esteem (once a week)	$5,000	Another year of personal training plus a week in Cancun (to show off)	$5,000
13	Must-have clothes from Zara's (to help with self-image)	$5,500	LG 65" Class OLED 2160p Smart 3D 4K Ultra HD TV and home theater with home theater surround sound	$5,500
14	Transportation to and from community sentencing for using fake ID	$299	Apple iPhone 8 in white with 128 GB	$299
15	Bill from Mystic Tattoos	$239	Navy SEALs watch from the Sharper Image catalog	$239
16	Laser tattoo removal	$2,796	Executive massage chair from Sharper Image and 3 nights at the Plaza Hotel	$2,796
16	Increased automobile insurance premiums	$1,345	Orvis 2-day fly-fishing course and basic gear	$1,345
16.5	Increase in auto insurance after two tickets and one accident (including lawyer fees)	$2,250	SoundBase 5.0 home theater system	$2,250
17	SAT prep course	$600	Jimmy Choo handbag for you (or your friend!)	$600
Total (not including college)		**$93,202**	**Total (not including college savings)**	**$93,202**
Now add in 5 years of college for your child or a Mercedes-Benz SL65 at $145,280 for you!				

Step 2: Plan for College As we saw earlier, now is the time to start saving if you plan on funding your child's college education. The sooner you start to save, the easier it will be to reach that goal—this is a perfect example of **Principle 3: The Time Value of Money**. Be sure to revisit the discussion of paying for college in Chapter 7.

PRINCIPLE 3

- *Estimate the Costs.* Fortunately, there are a number of college tuition planning calculators on the Web—for example, the College Cost Calculator (**http://www.offtocollege.com/calculate/**) and the College Savings Calculator (**http://www.dinkytown.net/java/CollegeSavings.html**). Open a 529 plan—and encourage contributions from family and friends—to maximize the benefits offered by the tax-advantaged plan. Keep in mind that you don't necessarily have to use the plan sponsored by your state.
- *Automate Your Savings.* Have savings withdrawn directly from your salary.

Step 3: Reconsider Your Insurance Needs Your insurance coverage needs will change when you have a child. When it comes to providing protection for a child, remember **Principle 7: Protect Yourself Against Major Catastrophes.**

PRINCIPLE 7

- *Review and Update Life, Health, and Disability Insurance Coverage.* For many individuals, the arrival of a child signals a need for life insurance—take a serious look at term life insurance. Is your health and disability insurance adequate?

Step 4: Update Your Wills and Trusts Now is the time to consider estate planning. At a minimum, you'll want to designate a guardian for your children in the event something happens to you and your spouse.

- *Update or Make a Will.* If you don't already have a will, make one now. Designate a guardian to raise your child, and specify how your child will be provided for in the event something happens to you and your spouse.
- *Update Your Retirement Account Beneficiary Designations.* Contact the retirement and benefits department where you work, and update your beneficiary designations.

Step 5: Take Advantage of Tax Savings Along with a child come some tax advantages.

- *Get Your Child a Social Security Number.* Apply for a Social Security number for your child. It's not that you expect your child to work, but you want the tax breaks that a child brings, and the IRS requires both your child's name and his or her Social Security number.
- *Update Your W-4 Form.* Update your W-4 form to reflect the new exemption.
- *Set Up or Update Your Flexible Spending Accounts (FSAs).* If you don't have an FSA, contact your employee benefits department at work, and find out if your employer offers flexible spending accounts—if so, open one. If you already have one, you know there will be additional medical expenses, so adjust your FSA. To keep the after-tax costs down, pay for them through your FSA.

Life Event 5: Inheritances, Bonuses, or Unexpected Money

An unexpected windfall can go a long way toward helping you reach your goals if you make it part of your financial plan.

Step 1: Examine the Priority of Your Goals This windfall affords you the opportunity to achieve goals that might have been out of reach.

Step 2: Reexamine Your Goals Take a look at your goals, and determine which ones are most important. This extra money might mean that the timeline for achieving certain goals has changed. You might be able to move to a larger house, invest in retirement property, or pay off a certain debt now. Once you've done this, it will become easier not to spend your windfall but to save it instead.

Step 3: Consider Estate Planning If your estate is large, you may want control over how your assets are passed on to inheritors—that would be the job of estate planning.

- *Choose How to Transfer of Your Estate.* Through careful estate planning, you will be able to control the transfer of your estate. For example, you might have a child who has special needs, or you might not want your children to have access to their inheritance until they are a certain age.

Step 4: Examine the Tax Implications Depending on how large your windfall is and how you obtain it, there may be tax implications. For example, getting a bonus or winning a prize on a TV show will generate taxes; however, an inheritance won't.

- *Plan for Tax Implications.* If there are tax implications associated with your windfall, make sure they are incorporated into your budget.
- *Consider Estate Taxes.* While estate taxes are at present moving targets, if your estate is now of a size that it might be impacted by them, take steps to minimize them, and if legislative changes to the tax code occur, updates, including the personal finance implications, will be provided on the companion website (**http://pearsonhighered.com/keown**).

Life Event 6: A Major Illness

It can happen to anyone—in fact, most of us know someone who has had to face the news of a major illness. The impact is twofold—first, the devastating news; then the financial impact. If you ever have to face such a tragedy, you'll want to make sure the financial impact is as controlled as possible, thereby allowing you to focus on the healing aspect.

Step 1: Reexamine Your Finances Reexamine your needs and goals in light of the future medical and rehabilitation costs and the changes in your future earning potential.

- *Assess Your Current Financial Situation.* Begin by taking a careful look at where you are now.
- *Use Your Emergency Fund—Maintain Adequate Liquidity.* This is the time to tap into your emergency fund. Make sure you have adequate liquid funds available.
- *Review Financial Goals.* Depending on the prospects and challenges you face, you may need to revise your financial goals to deal with the future.
- *Reexamine Your Investment Strategy.* Your working time horizon may be shortened—for example, you may now expect to work 5 years instead of 15. Since you may be tapping into your retirement savings earlier than expected, you may need to change your asset allocation to reflect your shorter investment time horizon.
- *Revise Your Budget.* Your budget needs to reflect the new expenses you are experiencing and your redefined financial goals.

Step 2: Take Advantage of Tax Breaks With an increase in medical expenses, there may be an accompanying increase in tax deductions. Make sure you take advantage of any tax breaks that might come your way.

- *Understand the Tax Implications.* Fortunately, there are tax deductions associated with medical expenses and co-pays. Get a copy of IRS Publication 502, which outlines what expenses qualify.
- *Explore Flexible Spending Accounts (FSAs).* Contact your employee benefits department at work, and find out if your employer offers flexible spending accounts—if so, open one. Talk to your doctor to get an idea of what the out-of-pocket expenses might be.

Step 3: Consider Alternatives to Finance Your Illness Depending on your diagnosis, you may want to consider tapping into your home equity or cash-value life insurance policy. If coming up with additional funds is a matter of life and death, it's something you've got to do.

> **FACTS OF LIFE**
>
> Costly illnesses trigger about half of all personal bankruptcies, and most of those who go bankrupt because of medical problems have health insurance, according to findings from a Harvard University study.

- *Look into a Reverse Mortgage.* To qualify for a reverse mortgage, you must be at least 62. With a reverse mortgage, you maintain ownership of your home, just as you would with a normal mortgage. You pay your real estate taxes and homeowner's insurance and maintain your home just as before. Of course, you've got to remember that with a reverse mortgage you won't be leaving the house to your kids—instead, it will be left to the bank.
- *Determine How Much You Can Get with a Reverse Mortgage.* To do this, go to the National Reverse Mortgage Lenders Association reverse mortgage calculator: **http://www.reversemortgage.org/About/ReverseMortgageCalculator.aspx.**
- *Life Insurance.* If you are lucky enough to have a cash-value life insurance policy, you might consider taking a cash-value loan, which doesn't have to be paid back. With a cash-value loan, you are borrowing against the cash value of the policy, which is the dollar amount that you would be paid if you cancelled the policy. If the diagnosis be terminal and your policy includes a living benefits clause, you can access part of the policy proceeds to supplement your budget, with the balance of the policy paid to your beneficiary.
- *Disability Insurance.* Depending on your insurance coverage, short- or long-term disability benefits may be available should you be unable to return to work.

Life Event 7: Caring for an Elderly Parent

Complicated emotional and financial issues can arise as you reach out to help elderly parents. Finding the right solutions takes positive and clear thinking and, as with all of the areas we have looked at, works best with a plan.

Step 1: Discuss Health-Care and Estate Planning Concerns

- *Initiate a Dialogue with Your Parents.* While this may be an uncomfortable discussion, it is one that can prevent a great deal of pain later, allowing family members to express their personal needs and wishes.

Step 2: Oversee Your Parents' Financial Affairs Make sure your parents' financial affairs are managed in the same general way you are managing your own. All of these actions are aimed at making sure your parents' interests and desires become part of their financial plans.

- *Organize the Paperwork.* Know where financial documents are kept.
- *Gain an Understanding of Their Goals and Budget.* Discuss financial goals with your parents. Make sure they are receiving all the benefits in terms of pensions and Social Security to which they are entitled.

- *Develop a Budget.* Help your parents put together a budget.
- *Protect Your Parents.* Make sure your parents have their wishes expressed with a health-care proxy. Also make sure they do not give out any financial information to anyone calling on the phone.
- *Durable Power of Attorney.* Try to have your parents look ahead to a time when they may no longer be able to manage their financial affairs.
- *Living Will.* Make sure your parents' wishes are known ahead of time.

Step 3: Discuss Long-Term Health-Care Options Make sure your parents are aware of the options and costs of long-term health care, although this may be prohibitively expensive, depending on their age.

- *Look into Long-Term Health-Care Insurance.* Depending on their total assets, if they have more than $150,000 but less than $450,000 in retirement assets, including their home, they may want to purchase long-term health-care insurance.

Step 4: Consider Estate Planning Depending on the size of your parents' estate, you may want to preserve their estate through estate planning.

- *Discuss Estate Planning.* Discuss any appropriate estate planning options with your parents. A good estate-planning attorney will help them preserve their assets by reducing estate taxes. If the estate is large enough, gifts of money or other assets may be recommended. To avoid future family conflicts, help them and other family members resolve any questions about the gifting of personal property, such as furniture, china, tools, or jewelry.

Life Event 8: Retiring

While it may seem like it will never happen, there will be a time when you retire. Just as with everything else in life, the only way it will happen successfully is if it is planned. Retirement means that you'll be living off any income you continue to receive, your personal savings, your pension (if you have one) or other employer-provided retirement plans, and Social Security (if available).

Step 1: Develop a Retirement Income Plan If you want retirement to be successful, you need to prepare and plan.

- *Prepare Mentally.* Retirement brings on not only the loss of a paycheck but also tremendous lifestyle changes. Your routine, your working identity, and your social relationships will all change as you leave your professional life. Being psychologically prepared for retirement can be just as important as being financially prepared.
- *Prepare Financially.* Make sure you have enough money saved to fund your retirement lifestyle, and continue to monitor your asset allocation and earnings.
- *Plan How You Will Use Your Retirement Savings.* A well-thought-out plan will help you make decisions as to when to tap into different retirement plans—for example, any 401(k)s, 403(b)s, and 457(b)s that you might have, as well as your Roth or traditional IRA. Rules regarding distribution and taxation vary for different accounts, so use the rules to your advantage or seek professional help.

Step 2: Manage Your Income in Retirement Develop a plan for managing your money during retirement. Carefully consider the kind of lifestyle you currently have and the kind of lifestyle you wish to have during your retirement years.

- ◆ *Choose a Withdrawal Strategy.* Establish an appropriate withdrawal strategy to help ensure that your assets last your lifetime—and that you keep taxes to a minimum.
- ◆ *Monitor Your Investments.* Develop an income management strategy to monitor your plan to stay on track for the retirement you envision.
- ◆ *Maintain an Emergency Fund.* Always have an emergency fund—plan for the unexpected.

Step 3: Review Your Insurance Coverage and Your Will The loss or reduction of your retirement income could adversely affect your surviving spouse or family members. Life insurance can provide financial resources they will need during a difficult time.

- ◆ *Look into Employer Retiree Health Care.* Contact your firm's benefits office, and investigate the retiree health-care options.
- ◆ *Learn About Medicare.* Examine Medicare coverage and requirements, and see how this fits in with your employer retiree health-care coverage.
- ◆ *Research Medicare Supplemental Insurance.* Find out what is available in terms of coverage and costs from Medicare supplemental insurance.
- ◆ *Consider Long-Term Health-Care Insurance.* Investigate the costs and benefits of long-term health-care insurance, and make a decision. If you wait too long, the cost of long-term health care will become prohibitive.
- ◆ *Revisit Your Homeowner's Insurance.* Many individuals ignore their homeowner's insurance once it is purchased. Retirement provides a convenient time to revisit your policy and make sure that your coverage is adequate.
- ◆ *Review Your Will.* Regardless of your level of assets, ensure that they will be used to help the people and organizations that are most important to you. Also, make sure you have a living will.

Step 4: Keep Track of Important Retirement Planning Dates Financial milestones abound as you approach retirement. Keep a close watch on these dates:

Financial Milestones

What to Do	Time to Act
Apply for Social Security benefits	• Apply at age 61 years, 9 months to collect at age 62. • Apply at age 66 years, 9 months to collect full benefits at age 67. (For people born between 1937 and 1959, the full retirement age varies from 65 years, 2 months to 67 years.) • Apply at age 69 years, 9 months to collect maximum benefits at age 70.
Apply for Medicare benefits	• If you start receiving Social Security benefits before age 65, you will be enrolled automatically in Medicare. • Otherwise, apply at age 64 years, 9 months, even if you won't be collecting Social Security right away.
Receive distributions from your retirement accounts	• Before age 59½, withdrawals are generally considered premature distributions and may be subject to a 10% penalty. • Between ages 59½ and 70½, you choose whether or not to make withdrawals.
Take mandatory retirement distributions	• By April 1 of the year after you turn 70½, you generally must begin making required minimum distributions (RMDs). (Roth IRAs are not subject to RMD rules.)
Become eligible for a reverse mortgage	• At age 62, you can apply for a reverse mortgage, which lets you turn the equity in your home into a regular stream of income. Note that reverse mortgages are not appropriate for everyone. See your financial consultant for more information.

Life Event 9: Death of a Spouse

The loss of a spouse has substantial financial effects. You need to review your financial plans and the financial plans of your spouse to make sure that the assets are distributed properly.

Step 1: Organize Financial Material Organization is the key.

- *Assemble the Papers.* Collect the papers necessary to file for benefits and finalize the estate, including at least ten certified death certificates, insurance policies, Social Security numbers, military discharge papers, marriage certificate, birth certificates of dependents, the will, and a list of assets.
- *Locate the Will.* If there is a will, locate it. This will represent the first step in distributing the assets.

Step 2: Contact Sources of Survivor Benefits Make sure you receive any benefits to which you are entitled.

- *Contact Insurers.* Contact any insurers who have issued policies to the deceased.
- *Check with Social Security.* Contact your local Social Security office to determine if the deceased was eligible for benefits, and keep in mind that there is both a death benefit and a survivor's benefits from Social Security. Also, contact the regional office of the Department of Veterans Affairs if your spouse was a veteran.
- *Talk to Past Employers.* You may be entitled to employee benefits from the deceased's employer or past employer—these may include a paycheck for vacation or sick pay, pension payments, or proceeds from an employer-issued life insurance policy.

Step 3: If You Are the Executor, Carry Out Your Responsibilities If you are the executor, you are responsible for overseeing the estate and managing it through probate, making sure expenses and taxes are paid, and satisfying any financial obligations that might exist.

- *Look into the Distribution of Assets Without a Will.* If your loved one dies without a will, state laws will dictate how his or her assets will be distributed. Contact an attorney or the probate court in the community for more information.

Step 4: Change Ownership or Title to Assets Make sure that ownership or title to assets is changed.

- *Change Insurance Beneficiaries.* You may have to change beneficiaries on your insurance policies.
- *Re-title Automobiles.* The car titles may need to be changed.
- *Update Titles to Bank Accounts, Stocks, Bonds, and Safety-Deposit Boxes.* To change the title on stocks or bonds, contact your broker (if applicable) or the company, mutual fund, or other financial services company that issued the product.
- *Review Credit Cards.* Notify each credit card company of the death, and ask that the card be listed in your name only or that the account be closed.

Step 5: Review Your Financial and Retirement Needs With the loss of a spouse, your financial needs will change. You'll want to do the following:

- *Determine if Your Benefits Change.* If your spouse is covered by a pension, your future benefits may change as a result of his or her death.
- *Contact the Employer.* You should contact your spouse's employer and find out whether you are due any benefits.

- *Review Your Insurance.* You may no longer need to have the same level of insurance if you do not have dependents.
- *Review Your Medical Insurance.* If your medical insurance was through your spouse, you will need to make sure you continue to be covered. COBRA can provide you with temporary coverage until you get medical insurance on your own.

Life Event 10: Divorce

With over 40 percent of all first marriages ending in divorce, this is a life event that affects many of us. Not only are money problems the major cause of divorce, but also divorce usually leads to reduced income and the burden of expenses that were formerly shared. Moreover, the financial impact of divorce is many times compounded by the cost of the divorce itself. If you have to experience this life event, there are a number of steps you can take to lessen its financial impact.

Step 1: Prepare for Divorce The best way to lessen the financial impact of a divorce is to prepare for it.

- *Pay Down Debt.* Dividing assets is tough enough; try not to have much debt to divide.
- *Keep the Costs Down.* The nastier the divorce, the more the cost—keep things as civil as possible.
- *Remember* ***Principle 1: The Best Protection Is Knowledge.*** Protect yourself—seek help from a financial planner specializing in divorce if you need advice.

PRINCIPLE 1

Step 2: Avoid Credit Damage Many times credit scores go down during a divorce; you'll want to avoid this if possible. Starting over financially is difficult enough without adding to it.

- *Deal with Joint Accounts.* Having the divorce finalized isn't enough to separate accounts that remain open in both names; you'll have to take care of that. You may not feel financially responsible for these accounts, but monitoring them to make sure payments are made will be in your best interest. Consider options for paying the balance on accounts and opening new individual accounts. Recognize that joint accounts will still be reported on your credit history, so getting them closed will protect your future score and access to credit.
- *Explain Late Payments on Your Credit Report.* If late payments occur, add a note to your credit report explaining why they occurred. All three credit bureaus allow you to add a 100-word note at the end of your credit report.
- *Have Your Accounts "Re-aged" to Remove Late Payments.* Once you have your finances under control, contact your creditors to see if they would be willing to "re-age" your accounts, listing your accounts as current and erasing late payments from your file.

FACTS OF LIFE

"Failure is the opportunity to begin again, more intelligently."
—Henry Ford

Step 3: Revisit Your Financial Goals Divorce may alter your financial goals and your ability to reach them.

- *Reevaluate Your Goals.* Take another look at your financial goals, and put together a new plan to reach them.
- *Look into Social Security Benefits Based on Your Ex-spouse's Earnings History.* If your marriage lasted 10 years and you didn't remarry, you may be entitled to Social Security benefits based on your ex-spouse's earnings, even including earnings after the divorce. Make sure you get the benefits to which you're entitled.

Step 4: Reexamine Your Insurance Coverage Make sure you have adequate insurance coverage—health, life, auto, and property insurance.

- *Maintain Health-Care Insurance Coverage.* If you have been covered under your ex-spouse's policy, make sure coverage continues for you and your children. Either get coverage on your own, or keep your coverage under COBRA until you can get permanent health insurance. Keep in mind that there may be changes to the Affordable Care Act (ACA) and that COBRA coverage may not be the best deal now. As of 2017, under the ACA you could not be rejected or charged more because of your health. Also, while your insurance costs depend on your age, insurance companies could not charge you more than three times the premium for younger people, whether you buy coverage on or off the health-care exchanges. However, the rules governing health-care insurance have been moving targets. However, if and when any legislative changes to the health care occur, updates, including the personal finance implications, will be provided on the companion website (**http://pearsonhighered.com/keown**).
- *Check Out Life Insurance to Ensure Alimony or Child Support.* You might want a policy in your ex-spouse's name to cover these costs in case your ex-spouse dies. And don't forget the tax implications of paying or receiving alimony.
- *Review Your Life Insurance Policy.* Carefully review your life insurance policy (i.e., name, beneficiaries, and amounts). There may be changes you should make.

Step 5: Rework Your Budget A new budget should accompany your new lifestyle.

- *Revise Your Budget.* Revise your budget to reflect your new income level and the burden of expenses that were formerly shared.
- *Maintain Retirement Savings.* With divorce, many individuals put retirement savings on the back burner and focus on taking care of more immediate needs—try not to fall into this trap. Retirement is going to come someday, like it or not.
- *Reexamine Your Expenses.* For example, don't keep the house if you can't afford it.
- *Have an Emergency Fund.* When you're on your own, you no longer have a partner to rely on if you run into financial trouble, which makes having an emergency fund even more important.
- *Look into Tax Breaks.* Your loss of income may qualify you for tax breaks to which you weren't previously entitled. Your filing status and standard deduction will change, as may your right to claim your child as an exemption, depending on the divorce decree—so plan accordingly.

LO3 Understand and manage the keys to financial success.

The Keys to Success: A Dozen Decisions

In the process of building wealth, you will face a number of different hurdles and decisions—some of them financial and some of them lifestyle. And here's a scary thought: You'll make some of these decisions without even knowing it! What we'll do now is take a look at 12 keys to success; we'll identify them and try to understand their ramifications.

Number 1: Become Knowledgeable

PRINCIPLE 1

Armed with an understanding of the basics of personal finance, it becomes much easier to avoid financial pitfalls and bad advice—remember **Principle 1: The Best Protection Is Knowledge**. In fact, you'll find your ability to evaluate financial advice and make good financial decisions is invaluable. Unfortunately, managing personal finances is one of the few things people seem willing to do without an understanding of what they're actually doing. Certainly, no one would attempt a heart bypass if they didn't know what they were facing, but when it comes to personal finance and investing, too many people are willing to take a stab at it even though they don't have the slightest idea what they're doing. The results are generally sad: Often that lack of knowledge attracts the unethical and incompetent characters who loiter wherever money is present.

Knowledge will keep you from falling prey to those who are always willing to *help* you with (or help themselves to) your money. In addition, knowledge will spur on your commitment to personal finance. When you understand the concepts of the time value of money and stock valuation, you gain an appreciation for starting your financial plan early in life, and that appreciation leads to action. An understanding of personal finance also gives you the ability to handle those unwanted financial surprises that are all too frequent in life. In short, knowledge will keep you out of financial trouble because, as we all know, it's a lot easier to do things right if you understand what you're doing.

Number 2: Don't Procrastinate

Remember **Principle 9: Mind Games, Your Financial Personality, and Your Money**; the biggest threat to your financial future comes from within. Although bad advice can slow your financial progress, procrastination stops it. Unfortunately, very few things are more natural than procrastination. In fact, you're probably pretty good at it already. Postponing the completion of that term paper really didn't hurt you; after all, as long as you handed it in on time, it didn't matter. As you should know by now, it's not the same with personal finance: There's a big difference in whether you invest $2,000 for retirement now or the day before you retire.

PRINCIPLE 9

Still, it's awfully easy to put off facing your financial future. If you aren't married, you may be keeping your life on hold, waiting for that special person to make financial sacrifices with. Or when you graduate, you may think you deserve a break from "student poverty." Or you may just think there's no sense saving now, when in the future you'll earn a lot more and saving will be a lot easier.

Unfortunately, there's always a reason to put it off. But while you may feel you aren't earning enough money right now, wait until you get married and have kids. How about adding those home mortgage payments into the mix? And just when you think you've made it out of the woods, paying for college will be staring you in the face.

The bottom line is that your financial future starts now. You know enough about the time value of money to realize that procrastination will only make your future work a lot harder. As the Rolling Stones sang, "Time is on my side." With personal finance, there is no truer statement. Remember **Principle 10: Just Do It!**

PRINCIPLE 10

> **FACTS OF LIFE**
>
> If you aren't making the financial progress you want, challenge yourself to understand why.

Number 3: Live Below Your Means

You always hear people saying "We don't spend money on anything extravagant, but we just can't seem to get ahead." The answer to their problem is uncomfortably simple: *You can't save money unless you spend less than you earn.* The problem is that people tend to spend to their level of earning—and in many cases, beyond. Unfortunately, our culture makes that natural. For many people, "you are what you buy." Their self-image comes from the car they drive, the labels on their clothes, and the wine they drink. It seems many people think that if they earn a certain amount of money, they should live and look a certain way. Even worse, shopping has gone from a chore to a hobby for some—and to a lifestyle for others. The result is, regardless of how much you make, it all goes toward the necessities of life—the more you make, the more necessities there are.

How do you get out of this trap? The answer is "you've got to change your attitude toward spending." You've got to be realistic with respect to what you can really afford. This all flows from a basic truth: You can't have it all; you have to make choices. The place to start is to track your spending. Once you see what you're spending, you'll also see what you can cut. For example, that morning *USA Today*, cinnamon scone, and large cappuccino that you pick up on the way to work may cost you $6.75 a day. If there are 22 workdays in a month, say good-bye to $148.50 each month and $1,782.00 over the year. And even worse, before you spent it, there were taxes. If you're in the 25 percent marginal tax bracket, that means you needed to earn $2,376 [that is, $1,782/(1 − 0.25)] to cover your morning fix on the way to work. Cutting out the nonnecessities will allow you to make savings automatic.

Number 4: Realize You Aren't Indestructible

You're young, you're healthy, and the mere fact you can eat dorm food and live means you're indestructible. That doesn't mean your TV might not fail you or your car might not meet an untimely death. So make sure you have an emergency fund.

Now let's look at insurance. If you're single and don't have any dependents, you probably don't need any life insurance. In fact, you can take a look back at Table 9.1 to see whether or not you need any. If you do need it, keep your costs down by shopping for term insurance on the Internet, and when there's a major change in your life, such as the birth of a child, review your coverage. As for health insurance, let's face it—you need it. And let's face it—it's expensive. Hopefully, your job will provide you with adequate coverage. In fact, when you're job hunting, make sure you look very closely at the health-care benefits.

OK, you've got your life and health insurance; are you ready for action? The answer is "no." Consider this fact: If you're under 35, there is a 65 percent chance that an accident or long-term illness will keep you out of work for a minimum of 6 months. Moreover, about half of all mortgage foreclosures come as a result of insufficient disability insurance. That's because while you're down, your bills won't stop, and Social Security won't kick in unless the illness is terminal or you're disabled for at least a year. In fact, Social Security's rules are so restrictive that you might not get any help from it. That means you've got to protect yourself. Where do you start? Check your company's disability coverage. If your company provides it, make sure it's enough. If not, find a personal policy and get covered.

> **STOP & THINK**
>
> If you ever saw the movie *Willie Wonka and the Chocolate Factory* or read the book *Charlie and the Chocolate Factory*, on which the movie is based, you'll remember a little girl named Veruca Salt. She was a nasty piece of work. She constantly demanded things, screaming "*I want it now!*" Her desires and the way she acted were clearly out of control. She didn't make it through the story—but if she had, with that attitude her financial future would not have been very bright. There's no easier way to foil a financial plan than with a lack of control and with impulse buying. Control is crucial. Can you think of any impulse purchases you've made?

Is that it? Heck no! The most important thing you can do is recognize that *you* aren't indestructible. Lead a healthy lifestyle. That means have regular checkups, don't smoke, exercise regularly, eat healthy, keep your stress level down, become a defensive driver, and avoid excessive alcohol consumption. The bottom line is that a healthy lifestyle will save you a good deal of money.

Number 5: Protect Your Stuff (and Look Out for Lawyers)

Having home and auto insurance is something of a no-brainer: You need it, assuming you have a home and a car. Fortunately, there are ways to keep the cost down. The key is to keep your deductibles as high as you can afford to keep them. After that, go for as many discounts as you can. Keep in mind that insurance isn't a maintenance plan; it's protection against major financial disasters.

As you look at your auto insurance policy, take a good look at the level of liability insurance. Considering the level of jury awards given to auto fatalities, you're probably underinsured. If you're driving and someone is injured, you could be facing financial ruin. Remember, the liability coverage on your auto liability insurance generally is only $50,000, while the median jury award for traffic fatalities runs above $500,000.

What happens if you're driving and your cute little dog Pooksie jumps on your lap and you lose control of your car and hit someone? Your insurance company will pay the cost to defend you and Pooksie in court and pay damage awards—but only up to the policy limit. All this means that going for "the minimum I need" may set you up for a financial disaster. You need more than the minimum level of coverage, and one way to afford it is to raise your deductible. That also means you may need a larger emergency fund in the case of an accident. An alternative approach is to give some serious thought to a personal umbrella policy. The bottom line here is to make sure your insurance actually protects you from financial ruin.

Number 6: Embrace the "B" Word (Budget)

When most people think of a budget, they think of a financial straitjacket, something that takes all the spontaneity out of life. After all, your "20-something" years are supposed to be a "live for the moment" time. In reality, a budget is a means to reach your goals. If it makes you feel too much like your folks to think about sticking to a budget, think of it as a "cash flow plan."

Unfortunately, the thought of a budget doesn't excite many people, so the best thing to do is make it as easy on yourself as possible. Probably the easiest way to do this and actually make the budgeting process successful is through the use of an online budgeting tool, and **Mint.com** is one of the best. **Mint.com** calculates your average spending in different categories that you can use to create a budget based on your historical spending patterns. In addition, it shows you how your spending decisions impact how much you have left at the end of the month. You can also get a free app for **Mint.com** that allows you to keep track of your budget in addition to sending you e-mail or text alerts when you go over budget. If you check out Figure 2.7, you'll find a short write-up on all of the features of **Mint.com** and also of Level Money, which is another online "mobile money meter."

What does a budget (or cash flow plan) do for you? It forces you to use restraint, to think about what you spend money on, to live below your means, and (yes) to be frugal. For example, if you've already spent this month's budgeted amount on restaurants, you'll be eating at home the rest of the month, or you'll have to save up money, perhaps from passing on that new Led Zeppelin reunion CD, if you want to eat out. Unfortunately, self-restraint is tough, especially given all those advertisers with their sights on your money bombarding you from TV, the Internet, the radio, newspapers, and magazines.

WORKSHEET 7

Without a budget, your financial future is bleak at best. Stick with a budget and you'll avoid the nightmares financial chaos brings and be able to save.

Before you can put a budget or cash flow plan in place, you've got to find out where your money is going. To do that, you'll want to track your expenses carefully for a month. To help you with this, take a look at Worksheet 7, "The Budget Tracker." You'll also want to go back to Chapter 2 and review the

FACTS OF LIFE

In 2015, the average amount spent on a high school prom was $919 according to a Visa survey. Most disturbing about the finding was that families with total household income below $50,000 a year plan to spend $1,109 on the prom, while families making under $25,000 will spend a total of $1,393 for the prom. Families with income over $50,000 spend the least: on average, $799—which is still a lot of money! Where do high schoolers get this kind of money for prom night? The Visa survey says that parents pay on average 73 percent of the prom costs.

sections titled "Developing a Cash Budget" and "Implementing the Cash Budget." You'll find that when you begin to set up your budget, knowing what expenses you can eliminate will be a great way to start. Also, make sure your savings are automatically deposited in a mutual fund or other investment so you don't have a chance to get to that money.

Number 7: Reinvent and Upgrade Your Skills

There was a time when the first job you took would be your job for life. You'd stick with the same company for 30 or 40 years, collect a gold watch, and retire. Welcome to the new world: the world of downsizing, restructuring, and reorganizing—all words that mean you're gone. In today's world, it doesn't matter that you've been a loyal employee for 20 years, and it doesn't matter that you come in early and leave late. What matters is your skills: Are they needed? What do they bring to the company? Your history with the company is irrelevant; the real question is "What do you add to the company today?" Sounds pretty cold, doesn't it? Well, it is, but that's how the business world works today. Nothing is long-term. If a company needs your skills and talents, you're in good shape. If not, you're out.

The question is "How do you prepare for this kind of job insecurity?" The answer is that you make sure your skills and talents are needed. This means you want skills that are valuable and that can't be acquired with little or no effort. You also want to take some care in picking a career. You want to have a skill businesses are willing to pay for. Maybe that skill is being a Certified Public Accountant, or having a unique computer skill, or having more advanced building construction skills. How do you keep your skill level both valuable and unique? The answer is to continuously reinvent and upgrade your skills through education. The education you're getting right now will prepare you for a job when you graduate, but it won't be enough to keep that job for life. Given the pace of innovation, no one can stand still and expect to survive. Let there be no doubt—education is the best investment you'll ever make.

Number 8: Hide Your Plastic

There probably isn't a more dangerous threat to your financial well-being than credit cards. The real problem is that there's no real problem with credit cards themselves, just with credit card debt. Unfortunately, for most people these two go hand in hand, especially if you're a student with lots of needs but no real income. It would seem that college students would be the last people credit card issuers would want to tap—after all, given their income, they can't be great credit risks.

But that is far from the case. Credit card companies set up tables on campus and bribe students into filling out an application with offers of free Frisbees, calling cards, and other goodies. And it works. In fact, one-fifth of all college students have four or more cards. With credit cards in hand, it simply becomes too easy to spend money—that pizza late at night or those must-have tickets to the Rolling Stones 55th Anniversary Tour. People simply spend more with credit cards—about 30 percent more—than they do with cash. For students, it's particularly tempting to use credit cards. After all, you'll be earning the big bucks in a few years, so paying them off shouldn't be any problem . . . should it? According to a survey, the average undergraduate has credit card debt of just under $1,000.

The only real answer is restraint. Don't use credit cards except for emergencies, and then use them with the utmost restraint. Your goal should be to make it into the next stage of your financial life (that stage where you make money) with as little debt as possible. When you get there, credit cards are great, but make sure you pay off the total balance every month. If not, take the scissors to them.

Number 9: Stocks Are Risky, but Not as Risky as Not Investing in Them

Stocks are risky. If you didn't learn that in Chapter 12, you probably learned it by listening to stories on the nightly news describing the recent wild market gyrations. Should you put your money in these risky investments? If your investment horizon is long, the answer is "yes," but you want to eliminate as much risk as you can through diversification. One easy way to do this is through a stock index mutual fund. If all this talk of investing in stocks gives you heart palpitations, go back to Chapter 11, and take another look at the section called "The Time Dimension of Investing and Asset Allocation." As long as your investment time horizon is long, stocks are prudent.

If the risk of stock price fluctuations is not your biggest fear, what is? It is the fear of not keeping up with inflation and taxes. In effect, it is the fear that you won't earn enough on your investments to meet your goals. Just look at a 3 percent rate of inflation. After 23 years, you'll have lost half your purchasing power, and if the inflation rate is 4 percent, it will take less than 18 years. In fact, as shown in Figure 17.1, over the 60 years from 1957 to the beginning of 2017 the annual rate of inflation has been over 3.7 percent. Given the very low average annual return on Treasury bills of only 4.6 percent, you can see that most of those returns are taken up by inflation. Throw in taxes and things get even worse. What does all this mean? If you don't take some prudent risks, you don't have a chance of meeting your goals.

Number 10: Exploit Tax-Favored Retirement Plans to the Fullest

If you're lucky, you'll have a chance to participate in the best investment (aside from education) around. What is it? It's a tax-deductible contribution to an employer's retirement savings plan with a matching contribution from the employer. Why is it so great? Because your contributions aren't taxed; that means you can contribute money that would have otherwise gone to the IRS. In addition, because the investment earnings aren't taxed until they're withdrawn, you earn money on earnings that the IRS would have collected. While you're doing all this, don't forget to take full advantage of a Roth or traditional IRA.

What should your strategy be? When you get out in the real world, max out on these tax-favored retirement plans. If you aren't sure this is the right approach, go back to Chapter 15 and reread the section titled "What Plan Is Best for You?" If that doesn't convince you, read it again until you are convinced.

FIGURE 17.1 Average Annual Returns Before and After Inflation from 1957 to the Beginning of 2017

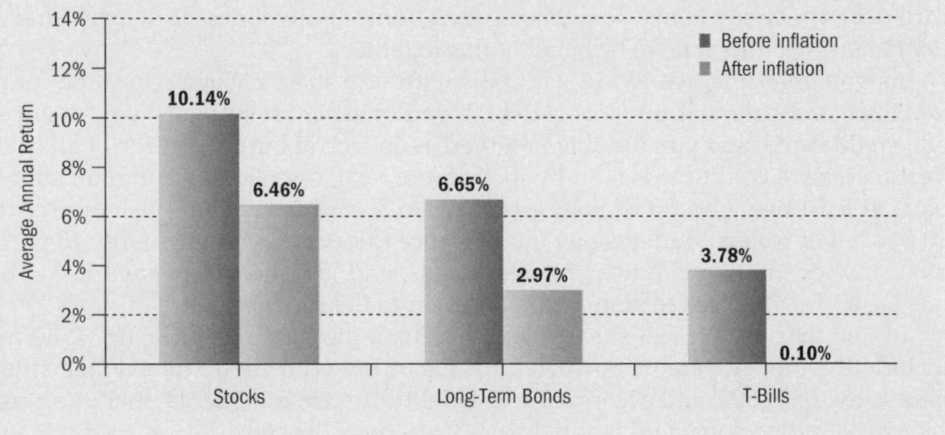

Number 11: Plan for the Number of Children You Want

Children can be wonderful, but they are expensive. At one time, children were money in the bank. When they were young, they worked on the family farm or in the family business, and when you got old, your children were there to take care of you. In short, it was a great deal. Times have changed, to say the least. This doesn't mean you shouldn't have as many children as you want, but you should be aware of the costs involved.

Number 12: Stay Married

Divorce is expensive, really expensive. An amicable divorce runs in excess of $1,000, while an unfriendly one can easily hit $10,000 and up with no limit. But it isn't just the cost of divorce that makes it in your best financial interests to stay married; it's also the fact that married people tend to earn more money and accumulate more wealth than single people living separately or together. The statistics are convincing: Married men earn 26 percent more than unmarried men, and married couples earn 61 percent more than families headed by single men. For divorced women with children, the tale is the saddest: Their income is only about 40 percent of that of a married couple. Clearly, for women with children, divorce opens the doors to poverty.

Why do married couples do better financially? One reason is that the cooperation learned in a successful marriage can translate into a career advantage. In addition, a successful marriage requires money management and budgeting. Unnecessary expenditures are eliminated, and you now have someone to answer to when you spend $1,400 for an autographed picture of the Three Stooges on eBay. On top of all this, being single is expensive. Most people spend a lot of time and money searching for that right person. What does all this mean? You should take real care in picking a spouse and, once you're married, put serious effort into making your marriage work. It also means you shouldn't have children if you aren't married—no two ways about it. Things don't always turn out as planned, but if you don't plan, they never turn out.

FACTS OF LIFE

Divorce is expensive! Just look at the Paul McCartney-Heather Mills divorce. After 5 years of marriage, he paid her $49 million. If you look at this cost on a per day basis, it runs to $26,849 per day, not counting attorney's fees and court costs. That's a mighty expensive divorce.

LO4 Deal with all kinds of debt in the real world.

Tying Things Together: Debt and the Real World

We've talked about debt a number of times in this book. We've talked about credit card debt, consumer loans, home mortgages, home equity loans, auto loans, and student loans. It's now time to bring all of this together.

As you enter the real world, you take with you some college education, unlimited hope and potential, and lots of debt. If you're like most students, you've got several credit cards, and you use them regularly—in fact, about two-thirds of all college freshmen have credit cards, and by their senior year, over 90 percent of all students have at least one. On top of that, according to a *Time* magazine article, fewer than 10 percent of college students pay their balance in full every month. Only 15 percent have any idea how much their interest rate is, and less than 10 percent know their late fee and over-limit fee amounts in addition to their interest rate.

By the time the typical student leaves school, the debt has piled up. When you include the money parents borrowed for his or her education, the average student debt is over $29,000; and according to a Fidelity survey, total debt—including credit card debt and personal and family loans—runs over $35,000.

The Trap of Too Much Debt

Today, debt is being marketed to adults the same way toys are marketed to children—and for many, it's just too hard to resist. Here are some of the results:

- Students and those with little capacity to repay are being given the opportunity to ring up debts at will. Look at Cal Duncan, 24, of Blacksburg, Virginia. He got his first credit card (along with a free Frisbee) as a sophomore at Virginia Tech. "All I needed to get that credit card," Cal recalls, "was my college ID and a pulse." After 4 years at Virginia Tech, Cal graduated with a degree in business and eight credit cards. These cards came with all kinds of free goodies, including phone calling cards, a savings bond, thermos coffee cups for the car, and meals at Burger King and Taco Bell. "It was like I was getting something for nothing. All I had to do was sign my name and I'd get a free gift along with a credit card. And, once I had the cards, it was hard not to use them."

  Most of Cal's charges during his college days came during his senior year. "I figured I'd be earning the big bucks next year, so there was no reason to deprive myself of that pizza, or that night out." That same attitude stayed with Cal during his first year on the job. When reality finally set in, Cal had amassed credit card debt, which, along with his outstanding student loans, more than equaled his annual salary. As Cal says, "It was all too easy. It just didn't seem like I was spending real money. I remember heading to Kroger to buy a box of macaroni and cheese and part way there thinking of all the money I was going to make the next year. I turned around and headed home and on the way I would grab food at Chipotle or call Papa John's Pizza when I got home because they take Visa and MasterCard—why suffer when I was planning on making the big bucks in the future? Never did I imagine that it would be anything but easy to pay it off."
- People are encouraged to borrow more than they should; in fact, borrowing is becoming part of our culture. As long as you make your credit card payments, regardless of how painful those payments are, you'll be tempted by increased borrowing limits, and you'll receive more credit card offers. Now that Cal is in the real world, working to pay off his debts, he still receives "a weekly offer" of a new credit card. It's the youngest group of consumers who are most at risk here. They're the ones who grew up on plastic and seem to have the biggest problem controlling its usage. In fact, according to a recent survey, of those aged 30 and under, almost 60 percent do not pay off their credit card bills every month—for those aged 60 or older, this number falls to less than 15 percent.
- Debt as a percentage of annual disposable income has nearly doubled over the past 40 years. Unfortunately, that's more debt than many of us can accommodate. The result in 2016 was that over 800,000 Americans filed for bankruptcy.

With all this bad debt and low teaser rates, it would seem that banks wouldn't be making any money, but that's not the case. Today, banks make mortgage, credit card, and auto loans; package them; and sell them as collateralized securities. That means that an investor, rather than the bank that issued your credit card, may be holding your credit card debt. What this does is make it easier for banks to make more credit card loans, and if you don't pay, it's not their problem. It's now the problem of the investor that bought the credit card loans from your bank. The result: a never-ending stream of credit card offers, regardless of the borrower's ability to repay.

Successful Debt Management

After hearing all the stories of doom associated with people taking on too much debt, you should keep in mind that debt isn't all bad. In fact, without it, it would be impossible for most people to ever buy a home. The bottom line is that debt and borrowing are pretty complicated, and as a result, you want to understand the six keys to successful debt management.

Key 1: The Obvious: Spend Less than You Earn and Budget Your Money The key to controlling debt is both obvious and simple: Spend less than you earn, and if you can't afford it, don't charge it. This all goes back to living below your means. Of course, that may mean some changes in your lifestyle, but no matter what else you do with your financial plan, its success depends on your ability to spend less than you earn.

This also means that you've got to have an active budget and you've got to stick to it. Of course, the budget has to be flexible enough to work, but it also means you can't borrow to make spending match up with money that comes in. Even more important, it means control; that is, not letting lenders decide where and when you're going to borrow. A budget simply doesn't make sense if it relies on borrowing to pay for day-to-day expenditures. A budget also doesn't make sense if it doesn't have any savings built into it. Let's face it—apart from saving for retirement and your children's education, you're going to run into some emergencies along the way; perhaps medical needs, unemployment, or divorce will force you to dip into your reserves.

Key 2: Know the Costs Perhaps the best deterrent against unnecessary borrowing is knowing the costs. You should know your credit card interest rate, your statement due date, and your credit limit. You should also know that if you don't pay your bill in full each month, you'll be paying interest.

When economists talk about borrowing, they talk about "forgoing future consumption opportunities in lieu of present consumption"—that is, spending money that you haven't yet earned and paying it back with future earnings. In fact, there's an old saying that "spending money you haven't earned yet is like using up years you haven't lived yet." What all this means, of course, is that you won't be able to spend as much in the future—most people understand that, but they don't understand how *much* future consumption they have given up when they put that pizza on their credit card. If you put that pizza on a credit card that charges 18 percent and you don't pay off your balance each month, you bought one expensive pizza. Moreover, as shown in Table 6.5, if you pay off only the minimum, you may be paying interest on that pizza for 32 months! Things are even worse with payday loans, as we saw earlier in Chapter 7. The annual interest rate can get up in the 400 percent range. Just knowing what you're paying may be enough to control that need to spend.

If you do end up borrowing money, make sure you do it from a quality lender. Checklist 17.2 provides some early warning signs on lenders.

CHECKLIST 17.2 Lenders: Early Warning Signs

Avoid Any Lender Who . . .

- ☐ Tells you to falsify information on the loan application—for example, if the lender tells you to say your loan is primarily for business purposes when it's not.
- ☐ Pressures you into applying for a loan or applying for more money than you need.
- ☐ Pressures you into accepting monthly payments you can't make.
- ☐ Fails to provide required loan disclosures or tells you not to read them.
- ☐ Misrepresents the kind of credit you're getting—for example, if the lender calls a one-time loan a line of credit.
- ☐ Promises one set of terms when you apply and gives you another set of terms to sign—with no legitimate explanation for the change.
- ☐ Tells you to sign blank forms and says he or she will fill them in later.
- ☐ Says you can't have copies of documents that you've signed.

Sources: "Putting Your Home on the Line is a Risky Business," Federal Deposit Insurance Corporation. https://www.fdic.gov/consumers/assistance/protection/mortgages/predatory/index.html

Key 3: Understand the Difference Between Good and Bad Debt Not all borrowing is a bad idea. When does borrowing make sense? Whenever the item fulfills one of your goals. It should outlive the financing, and it should provide a return that is greater than the cost. For example, borrowing to finance your education makes sense because you will use that education long after you've paid off your student loans and your education should more than pay for itself in terms of employment opportunities. The same is true for a home mortgage. Your house should be standing long after you've paid off your mortgage. In addition, you'll no longer have to pay rent, and hopefully, your home will appreciate in value. An auto loan may also fit this definition of good debt because your car should still be running when your loan is paid off.

But auto loans aren't always good debt. In order for them to qualify as good debt, you must have a sufficient down payment and make sure the payments are large enough to pay the car off as opposed to rolling unpaid debt from this car to the next one. With 6-year auto loans now available, you may really be "renting" your car because it may not be worth anything by the time it's paid off. If that's the case, try a less expensive car or consider the used car market.

How about that big screen TV and home theater system? They should last longer than the payments. Having a big screen TV and home theater system may be one of your goals, but it won't provide a return greater than the cost. Once that system is in your home, its value is only a fraction of what it was originally. Try to save up to pay for this type of expenditure, and don't let the seller decide how you're going to finance it. What about normal day-to-day operating expenses—food, rent, and clothes? Borrowing to finance these expenses will set you up for future problems that only winning the lottery can solve.

Unfortunately, sometimes there isn't a real choice, such as when an emergency comes up. If that happens, you should know that you are going to have to adjust your lifestyle as soon as possible so you can undo the financial damage that you've done.

Key 4: Make Sure You Can Repay What You Borrow—Set Your Own Standards Just because someone is willing to lend you money is no reason to accept the loan. For example, most mortgage lenders set a limit to the amount that they will lend you based on the ratio of your mortgage payments (along with taxes and insurance plus other debt payments) to your monthly gross income, and it is generally limited to 36 percent or less. What if you find a lender who is willing to lend up to the point where your mortgage payments along with taxes and insurance plus other debt payments reach 40 percent of your gross monthly income? Should you go with that loan and buy a bigger house? The answer is that you have to determine your own borrowing capacity and stick to it. Your mortgage broker may push you towards taking out a larger mortgage so that he or she can collect a larger commission whether or not you can make the payments. You are the one that suffers if you have problems making your debt payments, and let's face it—getting in debt over your head is easy to do if you aren't careful.

One way to avoid such debt is to apply the standards a bank would to yourself. Don't let someone else dictate how much you borrow. Remember, you are the one that has to make the payments. If you think the loan obligates too much of your monthly income, lower the amount that you are borrowing. The problem many people run into is that once they get the home mortgage, they take on even more debt. They buy furniture, appliances, and electronics to fill the house and a car to fill the garage. Also keep an eye on your debt limit ratio and the debt resolution rule that we introduced in Chapter 7.

The bottom line is that, regardless of how you decide to do it, you have to manage your own debt. You have to limit yourself because with all the competition in the lending industry, you may get the opportunity to borrow more than you can afford.

Key 5: Keep Your Credit Score Strong—It Keeps Costs Down and Is a Source of Emergency Money A poor credit score can hurt you in getting a car loan, an apartment, and even a job. That, by itself, should be enough inspiration to keep your credit score strong. However, one thing many people don't realize is that your credit score also determines what rate you're going to pay when you borrow. Those who have the greatest need for low borrowing rates end up paying the highest rates. This holds true for the interest rate on credit cards all the way to the rate on home mortgages. Is the rate differential significant? You bet. In fact, the interest rate on mortgage home loans can be up to 6 percent more for individuals with poor credit ratings—that's about twice as high.

You can also look at your borrowing capacity as an emergency account. If and when an emergency comes, having untapped borrowing capacity will allow you to borrow money when you most need it. A habit of borrowing up to your limit only sets you up for problems in the future. It forces you to keep a larger emergency fund than you would otherwise have to. And because less liquid investments generally have a higher return than do highly liquid investments, you will be able to earn more on your investments with a smaller emergency fund.

The way to avoid these problems is to avoid borrowing up to your full capacity, to pay your bills on time, and to make sure no errors pop up in your credit reports. You'll want to review your credit report every year—remember, you can get them free. If you look back to Table 6.3, you'll find the locations of the major credit bureaus. If you find an error, make sure it gets corrected.

STOP & THINK

In an emergency, the best asset you have is good credit.

Key 6: Don't Live with Bad (and Expensive) Debt In March 2016, the average credit card debt for households carrying credit card debt was $16,048. Unless your credit card debt is paid off every month, it's "bad" debt. It's debt that often is a result of buying without forethought. Because in 2017 the average interest rate on a credit card was around 15.1 percent, that's expensive borrowing.

The strategy many credit card borrowers use is to jump to a teaser rate—a low rate that lasts, in general, for 6 months. After the 6-month period is over, the rate jumps to the postpromotional level, generally somewhere around 15 to 18 percent. The idea is to then jump again. Unfortunately, credit card companies have strategies to counter this ploy. On some cards, a balance cannot be transferred for an entire year, or on the new card, the low rate may apply only to new purchases. One alternative is to try to negotiate down your rate on your current card. A better alternative is to get rid of your bad debt entirely.

If you want to rid yourself of bad debt, the first thing that you must do is eliminate the lifestyle pattern that led to the debt in the first place. You've got to start living below your means. Once you've made the necessary lifestyle adjustments, you've got to attack your debt with dogged determination. First, you've got to pay much more than the minimum. Table 6.5 will give you an idea of how long it will take to eliminate your debt. This is no fun, but the alternative is no hope.

If you're paying 15 percent on your debt and it doesn't look like an end is in sight, you might consider liquidating some investments that pay less than that. For example, if you have money in a savings account that pays 1 percent, you'll be much better off using your savings account to pay off your debt. In fact, you'll save more than the differential of 14 percent (eliminating 15 percent debt payments but losing 1 percent income from your savings account) because you'd have to pay taxes on that 1 percent return from your savings.

If you don't have an investment to liquidate, you might consider borrowing at a lower rate to pay off your 15 percent debt. For example, you might want to get a home equity loan. One advantage of such a loan is that the interest you pay is tax deductible. You could also consider borrowing against your life insurance if it has cash value or borrowing from friends and family. Of course, these are desperate measures, and they can be taken only once. That means you've got to make a serious lifestyle change if you're going to take this path. This should also make clear the crippling effect bad debt can have on your financial future.

BEHAVIORAL INSIGHTS

PRINCIPLE 9

Principle 9: Mind Games, Your Financial Personality, and Your Money **One last bias to avoid: The Prince Charming Bias.** This is the last bias we will discuss, and it's one that seems to impact those who can least afford it. The name, of course, comes from Prince Charming in Cinderella, whose father holds a royal ball and invites all of the maidens in the kingdom in the hope that his son will meet his one true love. We all know the ending—he dances with Cinderella and falls in love, she runs away and he finds her through her discarded glass slipper, and then he saves her from a life of sweeping and servitude and from her wicked stepmother. This behavioral bias is based on the idea that something, regardless of how unlikely, is going to come along and save you from all of your "money problems" and deliver you into a life of wealth. With this bias, you ignore probabilities because you know that somehow something is going to make your dream of a life of riches come true.

So let's take a look at the lottery because that's a perfect example of the Prince Charming bias at work. A recent Mega Millions jackpot brought in $1.5 billion in ticket sales running up to the drawing. Keep in mind that's $4.50 for every man, woman, and child in the United States. Most of that money is spent by the poorest among us, with 54 percent of lottery players earning less than $40,000. Studies show that there is an inverse relationship between education and playing the lottery. What is the chance of picking the winning Mega Millions number—5 balls and the Mega ball? It's 1 in 258,890,850. Not great odds—in fact, you are nine times more likely to die from being crushed by your TV set than win the lottery. And even if you win, where are you? Forty-three percent of lottery winners end up broke within five years. So try to think about your investments rationally, and don't waste money.

Changing Habits Now that you know a bit about behavioral finance and the impact it has on your spending and saving, it's time to make changes that will allow you to meet your financial goals. A habit is something you do without thinking about it—you do it on autopilot. As you might imagine, changing your financial habits isn't easy, but it is doable. If you look on the Internet, you'll see a number of articles that say the magic number is 21—that is, it takes 21 days to break a habit. Unfortunately, like many things on the Internet, this is simply urban legend. It is tougher than that to change a habit, and while there isn't a "magic number" of days needed, researchers at the University of London came up with an estimate of 66 days on average. That said, there is a good deal of variation in the timetable to change a habit, but the good news is that it is possible—it's just that it is not easy.

So where do we begin? If you think about it, most of our "bad financial habits" involve spending money, and we want to turn them around into "good financial habits" to help us save money. Studies show that in order to change a bad habit, you first must identify it and what triggers it. If you are stressed at work (or at home) and just feel a need to procrastinate (take your mind off something), do you shop online? Okay, you know your trigger is stress, so consciously choose a different activity that will not involve spending money—call a friend, take a walk—and then acknowledge that you just made a deliberate step toward the real reward, which is one of your financial goals. Keep this up and eventually, as you work on a new routine or response to the stress trigger, you will develop a new "good financial habit."

Since so many of us have financial habits that we would like to change, it should be no surprise that a number of self-help books have recently come out, including one titled *Making Habits, Breaking Habits: Why We Do Things, Why We Don't, and How to Make Any Change Stick* by Jeremy Dean, a British psychologist. His advice is to make connections between a situation and a resulting action—using an "if . . . then" approach—and to use this as a starting point to change your habits. For example, if you're building up too much credit card debt, you decide that "if I'm buying something that costs less than $50, then I will pay cash."

Dean also advocates something called *mental contrasting*, which involves thinking about the positive aspects of the change you want to make and then thinking about the barriers you face in achieving that goal. If you think about it, it's very similar to looking at the pros and cons of something. But what studies have shown is that this provides motivation for change and commitment. After that, it's perseverance—making it for those 66 days or so until a new habit is formed.

The bottom line is there is a lot of helpful advice out there on changing habits. Find out what works for you. You have been introduced to several behavioral financial biases; keep these biases in mind. If you recognize them, it's much easier to avoid them and ultimately change your behavior in ways that will help you put more money in your pocket.

ACTION PLAN

PRINCIPLE 10

Principle 10: Just Do It! It's now time to put things together and begin to build your financial future. Let's put some of the concepts we've examined in the previous chapters to work. And if all this has made your head spin, this section will give you enough direction to get going.

Now for a quick summary: If you're having second thoughts about starting, just look back a bit in this chapter at the section titled "Number 2: Don't Procrastinate." Starting your plan today may be the most important financial decision you'll ever make.

Begin with *budgeting and planning*. Figure 1.1 gives an outline of this process. Find out where you stand, define your goals, develop a plan, and revise the plan as your life changes. This means putting together a balance sheet, income statement, ratio analysis, record-keeping system, and budget. You'll want to rely heavily on Chapter 2 for this.

You'll also want to pay close attention to *managing your cash*—things like controlling banking fees and ATM charges. It also means making sure you have the necessary emergency funds. Chapter 5 should help here.

If you've got "bad" debt, get rid of it. If you don't have it, avoid it. You might want to review the section on "Tying Things Together: Debt and the Real World" in this chapter, along with the material in Chapters 6 and 7. If you're one of the many with student loans, take a good look at Chapter 7—anything you can do to minimize them will pay great benefits in the future.

Your *safety net*—your life, health, disability, property, and liability insurance—should be in order. Chapters 9 and 10 should help you with this.

It's also time to *start investing*. Try stocks and mutual funds. You'll find that success breeds an enthusiasm for investing (and saving) that simply cannot be explained in a text. You'll want to keep your attention *focused on taxes*—take advantage of any tax-favored plans like IRAs and 401(k)s available to you. You'll want to begin thinking about, and planning for, *retirement*—it simply is never too soon, at least if you want to enjoy retirement. You'll find help with this in Chapters 3, 4, 15, 16, and 17. You don't have to know everything about investing to get started. In fact, right now, if you've gotten this far in this class, you're well ahead of most people when they begin investing.

Still, nothing in this book will be of help to you if you procrastinate. That means follow **Principle 10: Just Do It!**—*and start right here:*

PRINCIPLE 10

- ***When you get down to it, it all comes to living below your means.*** Exercise common sense about your spending, which may mean "learning to live without"—you will not be able to save unless you do. Identifying needs versus wants, prioritizing them, and living below your means are the keys.
- ***You don't have to have everything they have.*** Keeping up with what others have can lead to tremendous debt, low self-esteem, and generally poor financial health. Making informed decisions and focusing on personal goals, rather than trying to buy status and happiness or conforming to the ideal of the hour, are the ingredients of good personal finance.
- ***Make it a habit.*** The only way to succeed financially is to make good money management a habit. As you just saw in the behavioral finance section, changing behavior and habits, while difficult, will pay big dividends over your lifetime—and bad money habits will lead you where you don't want to go. If you develop a habit of using credit as a safety net for overspending, there is no quick fix. Just proclaiming your goals won't make them happen. The continuous positive movement toward them with tried and proven methods results in accomplishment.
- ***Remember Principle 1: The Best Protection Is Knowledge—So Try Doing It Yourself.*** Especially for women, the development of financial autonomy is important. If you are married, knowledge and input from both parties are essential. If you are single, cut the apron strings, and learn to make decisions on your own. Depending on a parent or spouse to handle your finances can result in your being without a resource at the very time you need it most—at the death of a parent or the departure of a spouse.

PRINCIPLE 1

You now know enough to put a financial plan in play, keep more of what you have, and really start your successful path toward *Turning Money into Wealth.*

Chapter Summaries

LO1 Understand the importance of beginning your financial planning early.

SUMMARY: There is no substitute for starting early when it comes to financial planning and saving.

LO2 Recognize the ten financial life events and strategies to deal with them.

SUMMARY: Marriage and children further complicate planning for your financial future. The key to controlling financial problems before you marry is an open and frank discussion about money with your partner. The goal is to find out your partner's financial history, habits, and goals. You can also take the financial pain out of having children by planning ahead of time.

LO3 Understand and manage the keys to financial success.

SUMMARY: As for becoming rich, the one common trait seems to be frugality. Several key decisions in life will determine how your financial future turns out. You'll want to gain an understanding of personal finance; avoid procrastination; live below your means; have adequate life, health, property, and liability insurance; become an active budgeter; keep your skills fresh; avoid credit card debt; take some prudent risks with your long-term investments; max out on tax-favored retirement plans; understand that children are expensive and plan accordingly; and stay married.

LO4 Deal with all kinds of debt in the real world.

SUMMARY: Controlling debt is another financial challenge. One key to doing this is to spend less that you earn and budget your money. You should also know the costs of taking on additional debt. In fact, this may be the best deterrent to unnecessary debt. You should also understand the difference between good and bad debt. Borrowing makes sense whenever the item purchased fulfills one of your goals, outlives the financing, and provides a return greater than the cost. Just because someone is willing to lend you money is no reason to accept the loan. In addition, you should keep a clean credit record, and if you have any bad (and expensive) debt, get rid of it. Begin by eliminating the lifestyle pattern that led to the bad debt in the first place—start living below your means.

Problems and Activities

These problems are available in MyLab Finance.

1. Calculate the future value of an account after you've contributed $1,000 at the end of each year for 40 years, assuming you can earn 9 percent compounded annually and you don't make a withdrawal during the 40-year period. Now calculate the value of the same account if you stop making contributions after 30 years. What does this tell you about the power of time when trying to accumulate wealth?
2. Why is financial planning more important for women than men?

3. Review the ten financial life events, and identify the ones that mention an emergency fund. Why is an emergency fund of 3 to 6 months' worth of expenses recommended for everyone? Why is it particularly important when planning for some financial life events?
4. Why do insurance products play such a critical role when planning for financial life events? Do any of the life events *not* prompt an insurance review? What insurance products do you consider essential for yourself after graduation when you are "getting started"? What coverage might your employer provide? What insurance products will you need to purchase?
5. What are some of the key financial topics that should be discussed toward the beginning of a serious relationship?
6. Why should you continue to upgrade your skills even after graduation? Name a few methods for upgrading and reinventing your skills in your career field. Estimate the costs associated with these strategies. Will you or your employer likely be responsible for the cost of these investments in yourself? Have these issues come up in job interviews?
7. Review the 12 keys to financial success, noting how many mention financial restraint. How can an understanding of living below your means and financial planning give you the freedom to spend while still accomplishing your goals?
8. Explain whether the following consumer goods are classified as good or bad debt. Explain your rationale.

   a. Mortgage
   b. Home equity line of credit to build a new patio
   c. Student loan
   d. Gap credit card to purchase new wardrobe
   e. Car loan for 2018 Dodge Charger with $0 down payment
   f. Car loan for 2018 Ford Focus with $5,000 down payment

Discussion Case 1

This case is available in MyLab Finance.

Your sister Mindy and her boyfriend Doug recently announced plans to be married after graduation in May. Although you are fond of them both and want their relationship to succeed, you are concerned about their financial future. Neither Mindy nor Doug completed a personal finance course while in college. Mindy is a spender who has known few limits on her wants since she was a teenager. Doug, on the other hand, has worked, saved, and invested since he was a teenager to help provide for college costs. He will complete college with approximately $12,600 in student loans. Their income in their first year out of college will total $90,000, due in large part to Doug's choice of major and practical work experience during college. Mindy, who admits having no financial skill or interest, is content to let Doug handle all those matters, since he seems to be good at it and will likely earn more than she does.

Questions

1. The discussion of money issues is the first of a four-step process to help couples successfully manage their finances. The process might be summarized as (a) talk, (b) track, (c) plan and act, and (d) review and revise. Describe the steps and the objective of each.
2. Doug and Mindy, similar to many young couples, are combining two life events: getting started and getting married. Integrate the planning steps and create a new list to ensure that Doug and Mindy don't overlook anything.

3. Explain to Mindy why it is important that she become informed about and involved in her financial future—regardless of how well Doug fulfills the role he hopes to have as husband and provider.
4. Mindy and Doug's ideal is for Mindy to work for a few years and then be a "stay-at-home mom." If she invested $4,000 for 8 consecutive years in a Roth IRA that earned 9 percent annually, how much would she have after 35 years? (*Note:* The first 8 years are an annuity, after which the balance will continue to grow, without deposits, for the remaining 27 years.)
5. Identify three essential actions that Mindy should take to ensure her financial future.
6. Help Mindy and Doug consider the issues of joint or separate checking accounts and credit cards. Why are these important issues to resolve prior to marriage?
7. What financial issues should Mindy and Doug review, and perhaps take action on, prior to the birth of a child?
8. Aside from the obvious pain and emotional turmoil to Mindy, Doug, and their extended family that would be caused by a divorce, why is it financially sound advice to stay married?
9. Doug is anxious to repay his student loan debt quickly, but he also wants to take advantage of the matching contribution on his employer-provided retirement account. Assuming his student loans are bank loans at a rate of 8.25 percent, determine his monthly loan payments over a 5-year term (60 monthly payments), using the time value of money tools you learned in Chapter 3.
10. If Mindy and Doug lose 30 percent of their gross salary to taxes and benefits, determine their debt limit ratio (from Chapter 7) based on the student loan payment. How much additional debt repayment could they add and not exceed the 15 percent safety margin?
11. Advise Doug on the priorities of repaying student loans or other debts, as well as including retirement savings in their budget. Assuming he has a choice of equity and fixed-income investment products, which category would you recommend for his retirement savings? Defend your answers.
12. Why should insurance protection be a critical component of the financial plan developed by Mindy and Doug? What strategies can help keep insurance costs down?
13. Provide at least three tips for Mindy in helping her break her habit of buying a new necklace every time she goes to the mall.

Discussion Case 2

This case is available in **MyLab Finance**.

Jena has been so excited about what she has learned in her personal finance class that she has been telling everyone "You should take this class." Now her dormitory hall monitor has asked her to prepare a talk on "credit and the young professional." She has decided to use a question-and-answer format. Help her answer the following questions.

Questions

1. Why is it easy for college students to get and use credit cards? Aside from the obvious impact of "forgoing future consumption" to repay the debt, how can students' credit practices affect their financial future?
2. What are three debt and credit trends that suggest few people are practicing frugality?
3. What does it mean to determine your own borrowing capacity and stick to it? Why is this strategy necessary when "choosing wealth?"
4. What is the relationship between borrowing capacity and an emergency account? What is the advantage or disadvantage of using less liquid accounts for emergency savings and, in the event of an emergency, immediately relying on credit?

5. What financial ratios are useful in monitoring your borrowing capacity? How are these ratios calculated and interpreted?
6. Review the 12 keys to success. Which strategies could you utilize to avoid bad debt?
7. Jena has decided to use the time value of money tools from Chapter 3 to calculate the size of the monthly payments that a typical undergraduate would need to make to pay off the average credit card debt $1,000 over 1 year (12 monthly payments), assuming an annual interest rate of 17.5 percent. If, instead of having to make that credit card payment, a new college graduate invested that same amount monthly for one year in a mutual fund earning 8 percent on average, how much would he or she have for retirement in 45 years?

APPENDIX

A Compound Sum of $1

n	1%	2%	3%	4%	5%	6%	7%	8%	9%	10%
1	1.010	1.020	1.030	1.040	1.050	1.060	1.070	1.080	1.090	1.100
2	1.020	1.040	1.061	1.082	1.103	1.124	1.145	1.166	1.188	1.210
3	1.030	1.061	1.093	1.125	1.158	1.191	1.225	1.260	1.295	1.331
4	1.041	1.082	1.126	1.170	1.216	1.262	1.311	1.360	1.412	1.464
5	1.051	1.104	1.159	1.217	1.276	1.338	1.403	1.469	1.539	1.611
6	1.062	1.126	1.194	1.265	1.340	1.419	1.501	1.587	1.677	1.772
7	1.072	1.149	1.230	1.316	1.407	1.504	1.606	1.714	1.828	1.949
8	1.083	1.172	1.267	1.369	1.477	1.594	1.718	1.851	1.993	2.144
9	1.094	1.195	1.305	1.423	1.551	1.689	1.838	1.999	2.172	2.358
10	1.105	1.219	1.344	1.480	1.629	1.791	1.967	2.159	2.367	2.594
11	1.116	1.243	1.384	1.539	1.710	1.898	2.105	2.332	2.580	2.853
12	1.127	1.268	1.426	1.601	1.796	2.012	2.252	2.518	2.813	3.138
13	1.138	1.294	1.469	1.665	1.886	2.133	2.410	2.720	3.066	3.452
14	1.149	1.319	1.513	1.732	1.980	2.261	2.579	2.937	3.342	3.797
15	1.161	1.346	1.558	1.801	2.079	2.397	2.759	3.172	3.642	4.177
16	1.173	1.373	1.605	1.873	2.183	2.540	2.952	3.426	3.970	4.595
17	1.184	1.400	1.653	1.948	2.292	2.693	3.159	3.700	4.328	5.054
18	1.196	1.428	1.702	2.026	2.407	2.854	3.380	3.996	4.717	5.560
19	1.208	1.457	1.754	2.107	2.527	3.026	3.617	4.316	5.142	6.116
20	1.220	1.486	1.806	2.191	2.653	3.207	3.870	4.661	5.604	6.727
21	1.232	1.516	1.860	2.279	2.786	3.400	4.141	5.034	6.109	7.400
22	1.245	1.546	1.916	2.370	2.925	3.604	4.430	5.437	6.659	8.140
23	1.257	1.577	1.974	2.465	3.072	3.820	4.741	5.871	7.258	8.954
24	1.270	1.608	2.033	2.563	3.225	4.049	5.072	6.341	7.911	9.850
25	1.282	1.641	2.094	2.666	3.386	4.292	5.427	6.848	8.623	10.835
30	1.348	1.811	2.427	3.243	4.322	5.743	7.612	10.063	13.268	17.449
40	1.489	2.208	3.262	4.801	7.040	10.286	14.974	21.725	31.409	45.259
50	1.645	2.692	4.384	7.107	11.467	18.420	29.457	46.902	74.358	117.391

n	11%	12%	13%	14%	15%	16%	17%	18%	19%	20%
1	1.110	1.120	1.130	1.140	1.150	1.160	1.170	1.180	1.190	1.200
2	1.232	1.254	1.277	1.300	1.323	1.346	1.369	1.392	1.416	1.440
3	1.368	1.405	1.443	1.482	1.521	1.561	1.602	1.643	1.685	1.728
4	1.518	1.574	1.630	1.689	1.749	1.811	1.874	1.939	2.005	2.074
5	1.685	1.762	1.842	1.925	2.011	2.100	2.192	2.288	2.386	2.488
6	1.870	1.974	2.082	2.195	2.313	2.436	2.565	2.700	2.840	2.986
7	2.076	2.211	2.353	2.502	2.660	2.826	3.001	3.185	3.379	3.583
8	2.305	2.476	2.658	2.853	3.059	3.278	3.511	3.759	4.021	4.300
9	2.558	2.773	3.004	3.252	3.518	3.803	4.108	4.435	4.785	5.160
10	2.839	3.106	3.395	3.707	4.046	4.411	4.807	5.234	5.695	6.192
11	3.152	3.479	3.836	4.226	4.652	5.117	5.624	6.176	6.777	7.430
12	3.498	3.896	4.335	4.818	5.350	5.936	6.580	7.288	8.064	8.916
13	3.883	4.363	4.898	5.492	6.153	6.886	7.699	8.599	9.596	10.699
14	4.310	4.887	5.535	6.261	7.076	7.988	9.007	10.147	11.420	12.839
15	4.785	5.474	6.254	7.138	8.137	9.266	10.539	11.974	13.590	15.407
16	5.311	6.130	7.067	8.137	9.358	10.748	12.330	14.129	16.172	18.488
17	5.895	6.866	7.986	9.276	10.761	12.468	14.426	16.672	19.244	22.186
18	6.544	7.690	9.024	10.575	12.375	14.463	16.879	19.673	22.901	26.623
19	7.263	8.613	10.197	12.056	14.232	16.777	19.748	23.214	27.252	31.948
20	8.062	9.646	11.523	13.743	16.367	19.461	23.106	27.393	32.429	38.338
21	8.949	10.804	13.021	15.668	18.822	22.574	27.034	32.324	38.591	46.005
22	9.934	12.100	14.714	17.861	21.645	26.186	31.629	38.142	45.923	55.206
23	11.026	13.552	16.627	20.362	24.891	30.376	37.006	45.008	54.649	66.247
24	12.239	15.179	18.788	23.212	28.625	35.236	43.297	53.109	65.032	79.497
25	13.585	17.000	21.231	26.462	32.919	40.874	50.658	62.669	77.388	95.396
30	22.892	29.960	39.116	50.950	66.212	85.850	111.065	143.371	184.675	237.376
40	65.001	93.051	132.782	188.884	267.864	378.721	533.869	750.378	1051.668	1469.772
50	184.565	289.002	450.736	700.233	1083.657	1670.704	2566.215	3927.357	5988.914	9100.438

n	21%	22%	23%	24%	25%	26%	27%	28%	29%	30%
1	1.210	1.220	1.230	1.240	1.250	1.260	1.270	1.280	1.290	1.300
2	1.464	1.488	1.513	1.538	1.563	1.588	1.613	1.638	1.664	1.690
3	1.772	1.816	1.861	1.907	1.953	2.000	2.048	2.097	2.147	2.197
4	2.144	2.215	2.289	2.364	2.441	2.520	2.601	2.684	2.769	2.856
5	2.594	2.703	2.815	2.932	3.052	3.176	3.304	3.436	3.572	3.713
6	3.138	3.297	3.463	3.635	3.815	4.002	4.196	4.398	4.608	4.827
7	3.797	4.023	4.259	4.508	4.768	5.042	5.329	5.629	5.945	6.275
8	4.595	4.908	5.239	5.590	5.960	6.353	6.768	7.206	7.669	8.157
9	5.560	5.987	6.444	6.931	7.451	8.005	8.595	9.223	9.893	10.604
10	6.727	7.305	7.926	8.594	9.313	10.086	10.915	11.806	12.761	13.786
11	8.140	8.912	9.749	10.657	11.642	12.708	13.862	15.112	16.462	17.922
12	9.850	10.872	11.991	13.215	14.552	16.012	17.605	19.343	21.236	23.298
13	11.918	13.264	14.749	16.386	18.190	20.175	22.359	24.759	27.395	30.288
14	14.421	16.182	18.141	20.319	22.737	25.421	28.396	31.691	35.339	39.374
15	17.449	19.742	22.314	25.196	28.422	32.030	36.062	40.565	45.587	51.186
16	21.114	24.086	27.446	31.243	35.527	40.358	45.799	51.923	58.808	66.542
17	25.548	29.384	33.759	38.741	44.409	50.851	58.165	66.461	75.862	86.504
18	30.913	35.849	41.523	48.039	55.511	64.072	73.870	85.071	97.862	112.455
19	37.404	43.736	51.074	59.568	69.389	80.731	93.815	108.890	126.242	146.192
20	45.259	53.358	62.821	73.864	86.736	101.721	119.145	139.380	162.852	190.050
21	54.764	65.096	77.269	91.592	108.420	128.169	151.314	178.406	210.080	247.065
22	66.264	79.418	95.041	113.574	135.525	161.492	192.168	228.360	271.003	321.184
23	80.180	96.889	116.901	140.831	169.407	203.480	244.054	292.300	349.593	417.539
24	97.017	118.205	143.788	174.631	211.758	256.385	309.948	374.144	450.976	542.801
25	117.391	144.210	176.859	216.542	264.698	323.045	393.634	478.905	581.759	705.641
30	304.482	389.758	497.913	634.820	807.794	1025.927	1300.504	1645.505	2078.219	2619.996
40	2048.400	2847.038	3946.430	5455.913	7523.164	10347.175	14195.439	19426.689	26520.909	36118.865
50	13780.612	20796.561	31279.195	46890.435	70064.923	104358.362	154948.026	229349.862	338442.984	497929.223

n	31%	32%	33%	34%	35%	36%	37%	38%	39%	40%
1	1.310	1.320	1.330	1.340	1.350	1.360	1.370	1.380	1.390	1.400
2	1.716	1.742	1.769	1.796	1.823	1.850	1.877	1.904	1.932	1.960
3	2.248	2.300	2.353	2.406	2.460	2.515	2.571	2.628	2.686	2.744
4	2.945	3.036	3.129	3.224	3.322	3.421	3.523	3.627	3.733	3.842
5	3.858	4.007	4.162	4.320	4.484	4.653	4.826	5.005	5.189	5.378
6	5.054	5.290	5.535	5.789	6.053	6.328	6.612	6.907	7.213	7.530
7	6.621	6.983	7.361	7.758	8.172	8.605	9.058	9.531	10.025	10.541
8	8.673	9.217	9.791	10.395	11.032	11.703	12.410	13.153	13.935	14.758
9	11.362	12.166	13.022	13.930	14.894	15.917	17.001	18.151	19.370	20.661
10	14.884	16.060	17.319	18.666	20.107	21.647	23.292	25.049	26.925	28.925
11	19.498	21.199	23.034	25.012	27.144	29.439	31.910	34.568	37.425	40.496
12	25.542	27.983	30.635	33.516	36.644	40.037	43.717	47.703	52.021	56.694
13	33.460	36.937	40.745	44.912	49.470	54.451	59.892	65.831	72.309	79.371
14	43.833	48.757	54.190	60.182	66.784	74.053	82.052	90.846	100.510	111.120
15	57.421	64.359	72.073	80.644	90.158	100.713	112.411	125.368	139.708	155.568
16	75.221	84.954	95.858	108.063	121.714	136.969	154.003	173.008	194.194	217.795
17	98.540	112.139	127.491	144.804	164.314	186.278	210.984	238.751	269.930	304.913
18	129.087	148.024	169.562	194.038	221.824	253.338	289.048	329.476	375.203	426.879
19	169.104	195.391	225.518	260.011	299.462	344.540	395.996	454.677	521.532	597.630
20	221.527	257.916	299.939	348.414	404.274	468.574	542.514	627.454	724.930	836.683
21	290.200	340.449	398.919	466.875	545.769	637.261	743.245	865.886	1007.653	1171.356
22	380.162	449.393	530.562	625.613	736.789	866.674	1018.245	1194.923	1400.637	1639.898
23	498.012	593.199	705.647	838.321	994.665	1178.677	1394.996	1648.994	1946.885	2295.857
24	652.396	783.023	938.511	1123.350	1342.797	1603.001	1911.145	2275.611	2706.171	3214.200
25	854.638	1033.590	1248.220	1505.289	1812.776	2180.081	2618.268	3140.344	3761.577	4499.880
30	3297.151	4142.075	5194.566	6503.452	8128.550	10143.019	12636.215	15717.106	19518.391	24201.432
40	49074.042	66520.767	89963.354	121392.522	163437.135	219561.574	294321.973	393698.224	525523.341	700037.697

APPENDIX

B Present Value of $1

n	1%	2%	3%	4%	5%	6%	7%	8%	9%	10%
1	0.990	0.980	0.971	0.962	0.952	0.943	0.935	0.926	0.917	0.909
2	0.980	0.961	0.943	0.925	0.907	0.890	0.873	0.857	0.842	0.826
3	0.971	0.942	0.915	0.889	0.864	0.840	0.816	0.794	0.772	0.751
4	0.961	0.924	0.888	0.855	0.823	0.792	0.763	0.735	0.708	0.683
5	0.951	0.906	0.863	0.822	0.784	0.747	0.713	0.681	0.650	0.621
6	0.942	0.888	0.837	0.790	0.746	0.705	0.666	0.630	0.596	0.564
7	0.933	0.871	0.813	0.760	0.711	0.665	0.623	0.583	0.547	0.513
8	0.923	0.853	0.789	0.731	0.677	0.627	0.582	0.540	0.502	0.467
9	0.914	0.837	0.766	0.703	0.645	0.592	0.544	0.500	0.460	0.424
10	0.905	0.820	0.744	0.676	0.614	0.558	0.508	0.463	0.422	0.386
11	0.896	0.804	0.722	0.650	0.585	0.527	0.475	0.429	0.388	0.350
12	0.887	0.788	0.701	0.625	0.557	0.497	0.444	0.397	0.356	0.319
13	0.879	0.773	0.681	0.601	0.530	0.469	0.415	0.368	0.326	0.290
14	0.870	0.758	0.661	0.577	0.505	0.442	0.388	0.340	0.299	0.263
15	0.861	0.743	0.642	0.555	0.481	0.417	0.362	0.315	0.275	0.239
16	0.853	0.728	0.623	0.534	0.458	0.394	0.339	0.292	0.252	0.218
17	0.844	0.714	0.605	0.513	0.436	0.371	0.317	0.270	0.231	0.198
18	0.836	0.700	0.587	0.494	0.416	0.350	0.296	0.250	0.212	0.180
19	0.828	0.686	0.570	0.475	0.396	0.331	0.277	0.232	0.194	0.164
20	0.820	0.673	0.554	0.456	0.377	0.312	0.258	0.215	0.178	0.149
21	0.811	0.660	0.538	0.439	0.359	0.294	0.242	0.199	0.164	0.135
22	0.803	0.647	0.522	0.422	0.342	0.278	0.226	0.184	0.150	0.123
23	0.795	0.634	0.507	0.406	0.326	0.262	0.211	0.170	0.138	0.112
24	0.788	0.622	0.492	0.390	0.310	0.247	0.197	0.158	0.126	0.102
25	0.780	0.610	0.478	0.375	0.295	0.233	0.184	0.146	0.116	0.092
30	0.742	0.552	0.412	0.308	0.231	0.174	0.131	0.099	0.075	0.057
40	0.672	0.453	0.307	0.208	0.142	0.097	0.067	0.046	0.032	0.022
50	0.608	0.372	0.228	0.141	0.087	0.054	0.034	0.021	0.013	0.009

n	11%	12%	13%	14%	15%	16%	17%	18%	19%	20%
1	0.901	0.893	0.885	0.877	0.870	0.862	0.855	0.847	0.840	0.833
2	0.812	0.797	0.783	0.769	0.756	0.743	0.731	0.718	0.706	0.694
3	0.731	0.712	0.693	0.675	0.658	0.641	0.624	0.609	0.593	0.579
4	0.659	0.636	0.613	0.592	0.572	0.552	0.534	0.516	0.499	0.482
5	0.593	0.567	0.543	0.519	0.497	0.476	0.456	0.437	0.419	0.402
6	0.535	0.507	0.480	0.456	0.432	0.410	0.390	0.370	0.352	0.335
7	0.482	0.452	0.425	0.400	0.376	0.354	0.333	0.314	0.296	0.279
8	0.434	0.404	0.376	0.351	0.327	0.305	0.285	0.266	0.249	0.233
9	0.391	0.361	0.333	0.308	0.284	0.263	0.243	0.225	0.209	0.194
10	0.352	0.322	0.295	0.270	0.247	0.227	0.208	0.191	0.176	0.162
11	0.317	0.287	0.261	0.237	0.215	0.195	0.178	0.162	0.148	0.135
12	0.286	0.257	0.231	0.208	0.187	0.168	0.152	0.137	0.124	0.112
13	0.258	0.229	0.204	0.182	0.163	0.145	0.130	0.116	0.104	0.093
14	0.232	0.205	0.181	0.160	0.141	0.125	0.111	0.099	0.088	0.078
15	0.209	0.183	0.160	0.140	0.123	0.108	0.095	0.084	0.074	0.065
16	0.188	0.163	0.141	0.123	0.107	0.093	0.081	0.071	0.062	0.054
17	0.170	0.146	0.125	0.108	0.093	0.080	0.069	0.060	0.052	0.045
18	0.153	0.130	0.111	0.095	0.081	0.069	0.059	0.051	0.044	0.038
19	0.138	0.116	0.098	0.083	0.070	0.060	0.051	0.043	0.037	0.031
20	0.124	0.104	0.087	0.073	0.061	0.051	0.043	0.037	0.031	0.026
21	0.112	0.093	0.077	0.064	0.053	0.044	0.037	0.031	0.026	0.022
22	0.101	0.083	0.068	0.056	0.046	0.038	0.032	0.026	0.022	0.018
23	0.091	0.074	0.060	0.049	0.040	0.033	0.027	0.022	0.018	0.015
24	0.082	0.066	0.053	0.043	0.035	0.028	0.023	0.019	0.015	0.013
25	0.074	0.059	0.047	0.038	0.030	0.024	0.020	0.016	0.013	0.010
30	0.044	0.033	0.026	0.020	0.015	0.012	0.009	0.007	0.005	0.004
40	0.015	0.011	0.008	0.005	0.004	0.003	0.002	0.001	0.001	0.001
50	0.005	0.003	0.002	0.001	0.001	0.001	0.000	0.000	0.000	0.000

n	21%	22%	23%	24%	25%	26%	27%	28%	29%	30%
1	0.826	0.820	0.813	0.806	0.800	0.794	0.787	0.781	0.775	0.769
2	0.683	0.672	0.661	0.650	0.640	0.630	0.620	0.610	0.601	0.592
3	0.564	0.551	0.537	0.524	0.512	0.500	0.488	0.477	0.466	0.455
4	0.467	0.451	0.437	0.423	0.410	0.397	0.384	0.373	0.361	0.350
5	0.386	0.370	0.355	0.341	0.328	0.315	0.303	0.291	0.280	0.269
6	0.319	0.303	0.289	0.275	0.262	0.250	0.238	0.227	0.217	0.207
7	0.263	0.249	0.235	0.222	0.210	0.198	0.188	0.178	0.168	0.159
8	0.218	0.204	0.191	0.179	0.168	0.157	0.148	0.139	0.130	0.123
9	0.180	0.167	0.155	0.144	0.134	0.125	0.116	0.108	0.101	0.094
10	0.149	0.137	0.126	0.116	0.107	0.099	0.092	0.085	0.078	0.073
11	0.123	0.112	0.103	0.094	0.086	0.079	0.072	0.066	0.061	0.056
12	0.102	0.092	0.083	0.076	0.069	0.062	0.057	0.052	0.047	0.043
13	0.084	0.075	0.068	0.061	0.055	0.050	0.045	0.040	0.037	0.033
14	0.069	0.062	0.055	0.049	0.044	0.039	0.035	0.032	0.028	0.025
15	0.057	0.051	0.045	0.040	0.035	0.031	0.028	0.025	0.022	0.020
16	0.047	0.042	0.036	0.032	0.028	0.025	0.022	0.019	0.017	0.015
17	0.039	0.034	0.030	0.026	0.023	0.020	0.017	0.015	0.013	0.012
18	0.032	0.028	0.024	0.021	0.018	0.016	0.014	0.012	0.010	0.009
19	0.027	0.023	0.020	0.017	0.014	0.012	0.011	0.009	0.008	0.007
20	0.022	0.019	0.016	0.014	0.012	0.010	0.008	0.007	0.006	0.005
21	0.018	0.015	0.013	0.011	0.009	0.008	0.007	0.006	0.005	0.004
22	0.015	0.013	0.011	0.009	0.007	0.006	0.005	0.004	0.004	0.003
23	0.012	0.010	0.009	0.007	0.006	0.005	0.004	0.003	0.003	0.002
24	0.010	0.008	0.007	0.006	0.005	0.004	0.003	0.003	0.002	0.002
25	0.009	0.007	0.006	0.005	0.004	0.003	0.003	0.002	0.002	0.001
30	0.003	0.003	0.002	0.002	0.001	0.001	0.001	0.001	0.000	0.000
40	0.000	0.000	0.000	0.000	0.000	0.000	0.000	0.000	0.000	0.000
50	0.000	0.000	0.000	0.000	0.000	0.000	0.000	0.000	0.000	0.000

n	31%	32%	33%	34%	35%	36%	37%	38%	39%	40%
1	0.763	0.758	0.752	0.746	0.741	0.735	0.730	0.725	0.719	0.714
2	0.583	0.574	0.565	0.557	0.549	0.541	0.533	0.525	0.518	0.510
3	0.445	0.435	0.425	0.416	0.406	0.398	0.389	0.381	0.372	0.364
4	0.340	0.329	0.320	0.310	0.301	0.292	0.284	0.276	0.268	0.260
5	0.259	0.250	0.240	0.231	0.223	0.215	0.207	0.200	0.193	0.186
6	0.198	0.189	0.181	0.173	0.165	0.158	0.151	0.145	0.139	0.133
7	0.151	0.143	0.136	0.129	0.122	0.116	0.110	0.105	0.100	0.095
8	0.115	0.108	0.102	0.096	0.091	0.085	0.081	0.076	0.072	0.068
9	0.088	0.082	0.077	0.072	0.067	0.063	0.059	0.055	0.052	0.048
10	0.067	0.062	0.058	0.054	0.050	0.046	0.043	0.040	0.037	0.035
11	0.051	0.047	0.043	0.040	0.037	0.034	0.031	0.029	0.027	0.025
12	0.039	0.036	0.033	0.030	0.027	0.025	0.023	0.021	0.019	0.018
13	0.030	0.027	0.025	0.022	0.020	0.018	0.017	0.015	0.014	0.013
14	0.023	0.021	0.018	0.017	0.015	0.014	0.012	0.011	0.010	0.009
15	0.017	0.016	0.014	0.012	0.011	0.010	0.009	0.008	0.007	0.006
16	0.013	0.012	0.010	0.009	0.008	0.007	0.006	0.006	0.005	0.005
17	0.010	0.009	0.008	0.007	0.006	0.005	0.005	0.004	0.004	0.003
18	0.008	0.007	0.006	0.005	0.005	0.004	0.003	0.003	0.003	0.002
19	0.006	0.005	0.004	0.004	0.003	0.003	0.003	0.002	0.002	0.002
20	0.005	0.004	0.003	0.003	0.002	0.002	0.002	0.002	0.001	0.001
21	0.003	0.003	0.003	0.002	0.002	0.002	0.001	0.001	0.001	0.001
22	0.003	0.002	0.002	0.002	0.001	0.001	0.001	0.001	0.001	0.001
23	0.002	0.002	0.001	0.001	0.001	0.001	0.001	0.001	0.001	0.000
24	0.002	0.001	0.001	0.001	0.001	0.001	0.001	0.000	0.000	0.000
25	0.001	0.001	0.001	0.001	0.001	0.000	0.000	0.000	0.000	0.000
30	0.000	0.000	0.000	0.000	0.000	0.000	0.000	0.000	0.000	0.000
40	0.000	0.000	0.000	0.000	0.000	0.000	0.000	0.000	0.000	0.000

APPENDIX

C Compound Sum of an Annuity of $1 for *n* Periods

n	1%	2%	3%	4%	5%	6%	7%	8%	9%	10%
1	1.000	1.000	1.000	1.000	1.000	1.000	1.000	1.000	1.000	1.000
2	2.010	2.020	2.030	2.040	2.050	2.060	2.070	2.080	2.090	2.100
3	3.030	3.060	3.091	3.122	3.153	3.184	3.215	3.246	3.278	3.310
4	4.060	4.122	4.184	4.246	4.310	4.375	4.440	4.506	4.573	4.641
5	5.101	5.204	5.309	5.416	5.526	5.637	5.751	5.867	5.985	6.105
6	6.152	6.308	6.468	6.633	6.802	6.975	7.153	7.336	7.523	7.716
7	7.214	7.434	7.662	7.898	8.142	8.394	8.654	8.923	9.200	9.487
8	8.286	8.583	8.892	9.214	9.549	9.897	10.260	10.637	11.028	11.436
9	9.369	9.755	10.159	10.583	11.027	11.491	11.978	12.488	13.021	13.579
10	10.462	10.950	11.464	12.006	12.578	13.181	13.816	14.487	15.193	15.937
11	11.567	12.169	12.808	13.486	14.207	14.972	15.784	16.645	17.560	18.531
12	12.683	13.412	14.192	15.026	15.917	16.870	17.888	18.977	20.141	21.384
13	13.809	14.680	15.618	16.627	17.713	18.882	20.141	21.495	22.953	24.523
14	14.947	15.974	17.086	18.292	19.599	21.015	22.550	24.215	26.019	27.975
15	16.097	17.293	18.599	20.024	21.579	23.276	25.129	27.152	29.361	31.772
16	17.258	18.639	20.157	21.825	23.657	25.673	27.888	30.324	33.003	35.950
17	18.430	20.012	21.762	23.698	25.840	28.213	30.840	33.750	36.974	40.545
18	19.615	21.412	23.414	25.645	28.132	30.906	33.999	37.450	41.301	45.599
19	20.811	22.841	25.117	27.671	30.539	33.760	37.379	41.446	46.018	51.159
20	22.019	24.297	26.870	29.778	33.066	36.786	40.995	45.762	51.160	57.275
21	23.239	25.783	28.676	31.969	35.719	39.993	44.865	50.422	56.765	64.002
22	24.472	27.299	30.537	34.248	38.505	43.392	49.006	55.456	62.873	71.403
23	25.716	28.845	32.453	36.618	41.430	46.996	53.436	60.893	69.532	79.543
24	26.973	30.422	34.426	39.083	44.502	50.816	58.177	66.764	76.790	88.497
25	28.243	32.030	36.459	41.646	47.727	54.865	63.249	73.105	84.701	98.347
30	34.785	40.568	47.575	56.085	66.439	79.058	94.461	113.282	136.308	164.494
40	48.886	60.402	75.401	95.026	120.800	154.762	199.635	259.052	337.882	442.593
50	64.463	84.579	112.797	152.667	209.348	290.336	406.529	573.756	815.084	1163.909

n	11%	12%	13%	14%	15%	16%	17%	18%	19%	20%
1	1.000	1.000	1.000	1.000	1.000	1.000	1.000	1.000	1.000	1.000
2	2.110	2.120	2.130	2.140	2.150	2.160	2.170	2.180	2.190	2.200
3	3.342	3.374	3.407	3.440	3.473	3.506	3.539	3.572	3.606	3.640
4	4.710	4.779	4.850	4.921	4.993	5.066	5.141	5.215	5.291	5.368
5	6.228	6.353	6.480	6.610	6.742	6.877	7.014	7.154	7.297	7.442
6	7.913	8.115	8.323	8.536	8.754	8.977	9.207	9.442	9.683	9.930
7	9.783	10.089	10.405	10.730	11.067	11.414	11.772	12.142	12.523	12.916
8	11.859	12.300	12.757	13.233	13.727	14.240	14.773	15.327	15.902	16.499
9	14.164	14.776	15.416	16.085	16.786	17.519	18.285	19.086	19.923	20.799
10	16.722	17.549	18.420	19.337	20.304	21.321	22.393	23.521	24.709	25.959
11	19.561	20.655	21.814	23.045	24.349	25.733	27.200	28.755	30.404	32.150
12	22.713	24.133	25.650	27.271	29.002	30.850	32.824	34.931	37.180	39.581
13	26.212	28.029	29.985	32.089	34.352	36.786	39.404	42.219	45.244	48.497
14	30.095	32.393	34.883	37.581	40.505	43.672	47.103	50.818	54.841	59.196
15	34.405	37.280	40.417	43.842	47.580	51.660	56.110	60.965	66.261	72.035
16	39.190	42.753	46.672	50.980	55.717	60.925	66.649	72.939	79.850	87.442
17	44.501	48.884	53.739	59.118	65.075	71.673	78.979	87.068	96.022	105.931
18	50.396	55.750	61.725	68.394	75.836	84.141	93.406	103.740	115.266	128.117
19	56.939	63.440	70.749	78.969	88.212	98.603	110.285	123.414	138.166	154.740
20	64.203	72.052	80.947	91.025	102.444	115.380	130.033	146.628	165.418	186.688
21	72.265	81.699	92.470	104.768	118.810	134.841	153.139	174.021	197.847	225.026
22	81.214	92.503	105.491	120.436	137.632	157.415	180.172	206.345	236.438	271.031
23	91.148	104.603	120.205	138.297	159.276	183.601	211.801	244.487	282.362	326.237
24	102.174	118.155	136.831	158.659	184.168	213.978	248.808	289.494	337.010	392.484
25	114.413	133.334	155.620	181.871	212.793	249.214	292.105	342.603	402.042	471.981
30	199.021	241.333	293.199	356.787	434.745	530.312	647.439	790.948	966.712	1181.882
40	581.826	767.091	1013.704	1342.025	1779.090	2360.757	3134.522	4163.213	5529.829	7343.858
50	1668.771	2400.018	3459.507	4994.521	7217.716	10435.649	15089.502	21813.094	31515.336	45497.191

n	21%	22%	23%	24%	25%	26%	27%	28%	29%	30%
1	1.000	1.000	1.000	1.000	1.000	1.000	1.000	1.000	1.000	1.000
2	2.210	2.220	2.230	2.240	2.250	2.260	2.270	2.280	2.290	2.300
3	3.674	3.708	3.743	3.778	3.813	3.848	3.883	3.918	3.954	3.990
4	5.446	5.524	5.604	5.684	5.766	5.848	5.931	6.016	6.101	6.187
5	7.589	7.740	7.893	8.048	8.207	8.368	8.533	8.700	8.870	9.043
6	10.183	10.442	10.708	10.980	11.259	11.544	11.837	12.136	12.442	12.756
7	13.321	13.740	14.171	14.615	15.073	15.546	16.032	16.534	17.051	17.583
8	17.119	17.762	18.430	19.123	19.842	20.588	21.361	22.163	22.995	23.858
9	21.714	22.670	23.669	24.712	25.802	26.940	28.129	29.369	30.664	32.015
10	27.274	28.657	30.113	31.643	33.253	34.945	36.723	38.593	40.556	42.619
11	34.001	35.962	38.039	40.238	42.566	45.031	47.639	50.398	53.318	56.405
12	42.142	44.874	47.788	50.895	54.208	57.739	61.501	65.510	69.780	74.327
13	51.991	55.746	59.779	64.110	68.760	73.751	79.107	84.853	91.016	97.625
14	63.909	69.010	74.528	80.496	86.949	93.926	101.465	109.612	118.411	127.913
15	78.330	85.192	92.669	100.815	109.687	119.347	129.861	141.303	153.750	167.286
16	95.780	104.935	114.983	126.011	138.109	151.377	165.924	181.868	199.337	218.472
17	116.894	129.020	142.430	157.253	173.636	191.735	211.723	233.791	258.145	285.014
18	142.441	158.405	176.188	195.994	218.045	242.585	269.888	300.252	334.007	371.518
19	173.354	194.254	217.712	244.033	273.556	306.658	343.758	385.323	431.870	483.973
20	210.758	237.989	268.785	303.601	342.945	387.389	437.573	494.213	558.112	630.165
21	256.018	291.347	331.606	377.465	429.681	489.110	556.717	633.593	720.964	820.215
22	310.781	356.443	408.875	469.056	538.101	617.278	708.031	811.999	931.044	1067.280
23	377.045	435.861	503.917	582.630	673.626	778.771	900.199	1040.358	1202.047	1388.464
24	457.225	532.750	620.817	723.461	843.033	982.251	1144.253	1332.659	1551.640	1806.003
25	554.242	650.955	764.605	898.092	1054.791	1238.636	1454.201	1706.803	2002.616	2348.803
30	1445.151	1767.081	2160.491	2640.916	3227.174	3942.026	4812.977	5873.231	7162.824	8729.985
40	9749.525	12936.535	17154.046	22728.803	30088.655	39792.982	52571.998	69377.460	91447.963	120392.883

n	31%	32%	33%	34%	35%	36%	37%	38%	39%	40%
1	1.000	1.000	1.000	1.000	1.000	1.000	1.000	1.000	1.000	1.000
2	2.310	2.320	2.330	2.340	2.350	2.360	2.370	2.380	2.390	2.400
3	4.026	4.062	4.099	4.136	4.173	4.210	4.247	4.284	4.322	4.360
4	6.274	6.362	6.452	6.542	6.633	6.725	6.818	6.912	7.008	7.104
5	9.219	9.398	9.581	9.766	9.954	10.146	10.341	10.539	10.741	10.946
6	13.077	13.406	13.742	14.086	14.438	14.799	15.167	15.544	15.930	16.324
7	18.131	18.696	19.277	19.876	20.492	21.126	21.779	22.451	23.142	23.853
8	24.752	25.678	26.638	27.633	28.664	29.732	30.837	31.982	33.168	34.395
9	33.425	34.895	36.429	38.029	39.696	41.435	43.247	45.135	47.103	49.153
10	44.786	47.062	49.451	51.958	54.590	57.352	60.248	63.287	66.473	69.814
11	59.670	63.122	66.769	70.624	74.697	78.998	83.540	88.336	93.398	98.739
12	79.168	84.320	89.803	95.637	101.841	108.437	115.450	122.904	130.823	139.235
13	104.710	112.303	120.439	129.153	138.485	148.475	159.167	170.607	182.844	195.929
14	138.170	149.240	161.183	174.065	187.954	202.926	219.059	236.438	255.153	275.300
15	182.003	197.997	215.374	234.247	254.738	276.979	301.111	327.284	355.662	386.420
16	239.423	262.356	287.447	314.891	344.897	377.692	413.522	452.652	495.370	541.988
17	314.645	347.309	383.305	422.954	466.611	514.661	567.524	625.659	689.565	759.784
18	413.185	459.449	510.795	567.758	630.925	700.939	778.509	864.410	959.495	1064.697
19	542.272	607.472	680.358	761.796	852.748	954.277	1067.557	1193.886	1334.698	1491.576
20	711.376	802.863	905.876	1021.807	1152.210	1298.817	1463.553	1648.563	1856.230	2089.206
21	932.903	1060.779	1205.814	1370.221	1556.484	1767.391	2006.067	2276.016	2581.160	2925.889
22	1223.103	1401.229	1604.733	1837.096	2102.253	2404.651	2749.312	3141.902	3588.813	4097.245
23	1603.264	1850.622	2135.295	2462.709	2839.042	3271.326	3767.557	4336.825	4989.450	5737.142
24	2101.276	2443.821	2840.943	3301.030	3833.706	4450.003	5162.554	5985.819	6936.335	8032.999
25	2753.672	3226.844	3779.454	4424.380	5176.504	6053.004	7073.699	8261.430	9642.506	11247.199
30	10632.746	12940.859	15738.077	19124.859	23221.570	28172.276	34149.230	41358.175	50044.592	60501.081

APPENDIX

D Present Value of an Annuity of $1 for *n* Periods

n	1%	2%	3%	4%	5%	6%	7%	8%	9%	10%
1	0.990	0.980	0.971	0.962	0.952	0.943	0.935	0.926	0.917	0.909
2	1.970	1.942	1.913	1.886	1.859	1.833	1.808	1.783	1.759	1.736
3	2.941	2.884	2.829	2.775	2.723	2.673	2.624	2.577	2.531	2.487
4	3.902	3.808	3.717	3.630	3.546	3.465	3.387	3.312	3.240	3.170
5	4.853	4.713	4.580	4.452	4.329	4.212	4.100	3.993	3.890	3.791
6	5.795	5.601	5.417	5.242	5.076	4.917	4.767	4.623	4.486	4.355
7	6.728	6.472	6.230	6.002	5.786	5.582	5.389	5.206	5.033	4.868
8	7.652	7.325	7.020	6.733	6.463	6.210	5.971	5.747	5.535	5.335
9	8.566	8.162	7.786	7.435	7.108	6.802	6.515	6.247	5.995	5.759
10	9.471	8.983	8.530	8.111	7.722	7.360	7.024	6.710	6.418	6.145
11	10.368	9.787	9.253	8.760	8.306	7.887	7.499	7.139	6.805	6.495
12	11.255	10.575	9.954	9.385	8.863	8.384	7.943	7.536	7.161	6.814
13	12.134	11.348	10.635	9.986	9.394	8.853	8.358	7.904	7.487	7.103
14	13.004	12.106	11.296	10.563	9.899	9.295	8.745	8.244	7.786	7.367
15	13.865	12.849	11.938	11.118	10.380	9.712	9.108	8.559	8.061	7.606
16	14.718	13.578	12.561	11.652	10.838	10.106	9.447	8.851	8.313	7.824
17	15.562	14.292	13.166	12.166	11.274	10.477	9.763	9.122	8.544	8.022
18	16.398	14.992	13.754	12.659	11.690	10.828	10.059	9.372	8.756	8.201
19	17.226	15.678	14.324	13.134	12.085	11.158	10.336	9.604	8.950	8.365
20	18.046	16.351	14.877	13.590	12.462	11.470	10.594	9.818	9.129	8.514
21	18.857	17.011	15.415	14.029	12.821	11.764	10.836	10.017	9.292	8.649
22	19.660	17.658	15.937	14.451	13.163	12.042	11.061	10.201	9.442	8.772
23	20.456	18.292	16.444	14.857	13.489	12.303	11.272	10.371	9.580	8.883
24	21.243	18.914	16.936	15.247	13.799	12.550	11.469	10.529	9.707	8.985
25	22.023	19.523	17.413	15.622	14.094	12.783	11.654	10.675	9.823	9.077
30	25.808	22.396	19.600	17.292	15.372	13.765	12.409	11.258	10.274	9.427
40	32.835	27.355	23.115	19.793	17.159	15.046	13.332	11.925	10.757	9.779
50	39.196	31.424	25.730	21.482	18.256	15.762	13.801	12.233	10.962	9.915

n	11%	12%	13%	14%	15%	16%	17%	18%	19%	20%
1	0.901	0.893	0.885	0.877	0.870	0.862	0.855	0.847	0.840	0.833
2	1.713	1.690	1.668	1.647	1.626	1.605	1.585	1.566	1.547	1.528
3	2.444	2.402	2.361	2.322	2.283	2.246	2.210	2.174	2.140	2.106
4	3.102	3.037	2.974	2.914	2.855	2.798	2.743	2.690	2.639	2.589
5	3.696	3.605	3.517	3.433	3.352	3.274	3.199	3.127	3.058	2.991
6	4.231	4.111	3.998	3.889	3.784	3.685	3.589	3.498	3.410	3.326
7	4.712	4.564	4.423	4.288	4.160	4.039	3.922	3.812	3.706	3.605
8	5.146	4.968	4.799	4.639	4.487	4.344	4.207	4.078	3.954	3.837
9	5.537	5.328	5.132	4.946	4.772	4.607	4.451	4.303	4.163	4.031
10	5.889	5.650	5.426	5.216	5.019	4.833	4.659	4.494	4.339	4.192
11	6.207	5.938	5.687	5.453	5.234	5.029	4.836	4.656	4.486	4.327
12	6.492	6.194	5.918	5.660	5.421	5.197	4.988	4.793	4.611	4.439
13	6.750	6.424	6.122	5.842	5.583	5.342	5.118	4.910	4.715	4.533
14	6.982	6.628	6.302	6.002	5.724	5.468	5.229	5.008	4.802	4.611
15	7.191	6.811	6.462	6.142	5.847	5.575	5.324	5.092	4.876	4.675
16	7.379	6.974	6.604	6.265	5.954	5.668	5.405	5.162	4.938	4.730
17	7.549	7.120	6.729	6.373	6.047	5.749	5.475	5.222	4.990	4.775
18	7.702	7.250	6.840	6.467	6.128	5.818	5.534	5.273	5.033	4.812
19	7.839	7.366	6.938	6.550	6.198	5.877	5.584	5.316	5.070	4.843
20	7.963	7.469	7.025	6.623	6.259	5.929	5.628	5.353	5.101	4.870
21	8.075	7.562	7.102	6.687	6.312	5.973	5.665	5.384	5.127	4.891
22	8.176	7.645	7.170	6.743	6.359	6.011	5.696	5.410	5.149	4.909
23	8.266	7.718	7.230	6.792	6.399	6.044	5.723	5.432	5.167	4.925
24	8.348	7.784	7.283	6.835	6.434	6.073	5.746	5.451	5.182	4.937
25	8.422	7.843	7.330	6.873	6.464	6.097	5.766	5.467	5.195	4.948
30	8.694	8.055	7.496	7.003	6.566	6.177	5.829	5.517	5.235	4.979
40	8.951	8.244	7.634	7.105	6.642	6.233	5.871	5.548	5.258	4.997
50	9.042	8.304	7.675	7.133	6.661	6.246	5.880	5.554	5.262	4.999

n	21%	22%	23%	24%	25%	26%	27%	28%	29%	30%
1	0.826	0.820	0.813	0.806	0.800	0.794	0.787	0.781	0.775	0.769
2	1.509	1.492	1.474	1.457	1.440	1.424	1.407	1.392	1.376	1.361
3	2.074	2.042	2.011	1.981	1.952	1.923	1.896	1.868	1.842	1.816
4	2.540	2.494	2.448	2.404	2.362	2.320	2.280	2.241	2.203	2.166
5	2.926	2.864	2.803	2.745	2.689	2.635	2.583	2.532	2.483	2.436
6	3.245	3.167	3.092	3.020	2.951	2.885	2.821	2.759	2.700	2.643
7	3.508	3.416	3.327	3.242	3.161	3.083	3.009	2.937	2.868	2.802
8	3.726	3.619	3.518	3.421	3.329	3.241	3.156	3.076	2.999	2.925
9	3.905	3.786	3.673	3.566	3.463	3.366	3.273	3.184	3.100	3.019
10	4.054	3.923	3.799	3.682	3.571	3.465	3.364	3.269	3.178	3.092
11	4.177	4.035	3.902	3.776	3.656	3.543	3.437	3.335	3.239	3.147
12	4.278	4.127	3.985	3.851	3.725	3.606	3.493	3.387	3.286	3.190
13	4.362	4.203	4.053	3.912	3.780	3.656	3.538	3.427	3.322	3.223
14	4.432	4.265	4.108	3.962	3.824	3.695	3.573	3.459	3.351	3.249
15	4.489	4.315	4.153	4.001	3.859	3.726	3.601	3.483	3.373	3.268
16	4.536	4.357	4.189	4.033	3.887	3.751	3.623	3.503	3.390	3.283
17	4.576	4.391	4.219	4.059	3.910	3.771	3.640	3.518	3.403	3.295
18	4.608	4.419	4.243	4.080	3.928	3.786	3.654	3.529	3.413	3.304
19	4.635	4.442	4.263	4.097	3.942	3.799	3.664	3.539	3.421	3.311
20	4.657	4.460	4.279	4.110	3.954	3.808	3.673	3.546	3.427	3.316
21	4.675	4.476	4.292	4.121	3.963	3.816	3.679	3.551	3.432	3.320
22	4.690	4.488	4.302	4.130	3.970	3.822	3.684	3.556	3.436	3.323
23	4.703	4.499	4.311	4.137	3.976	3.827	3.689	3.559	3.438	3.325
24	4.713	4.507	4.318	4.143	3.981	3.831	3.692	3.562	3.441	3.327
25	4.721	4.514	4.323	4.147	3.985	3.834	3.694	3.564	3.442	3.329
30	4.746	4.534	4.339	4.160	3.995	3.842	3.701	3.569	3.447	3.332
40	4.760	4.544	4.347	4.166	3.999	3.846	3.703	3.571	3.448	3.333
50	4.762	4.545	4.348	4.167	4.000	3.846	3.704	3.571	3.448	3.333

n	31%	32%	33%	34%	35%	36%	37%	38%	39%	40%
1	0.763	0.758	0.752	0.746	0.741	0.735	0.730	0.725	0.719	0.714
2	1.346	1.331	1.317	1.303	1.289	1.276	1.263	1.250	1.237	1.224
3	1.791	1.766	1.742	1.719	1.696	1.673	1.652	1.630	1.609	1.589
4	2.130	2.096	2.062	2.029	1.997	1.966	1.935	1.906	1.877	1.849
5	2.390	2.345	2.302	2.260	2.220	2.181	2.143	2.106	2.070	2.035
6	2.588	2.534	2.483	2.433	2.385	2.339	2.294	2.251	2.209	2.168
7	2.739	2.677	2.619	2.562	2.508	2.455	2.404	2.355	2.308	2.263
8	2.854	2.786	2.721	2.658	2.598	2.540	2.485	2.432	2.380	2.331
9	2.942	2.868	2.798	2.730	2.665	2.603	2.544	2.487	2.432	2.379
10	3.009	2.930	2.855	2.784	2.715	2.649	2.587	2.527	2.469	2.414
11	3.060	2.978	2.899	2.824	2.752	2.683	2.618	2.555	2.496	2.438
12	3.100	3.013	2.931	2.853	2.779	2.708	2.641	2.576	2.515	2.456
13	3.129	3.040	2.956	2.876	2.799	2.727	2.658	2.592	2.529	2.469
14	3.152	3.061	2.974	2.892	2.814	2.740	2.670	2.603	2.539	2.478
15	3.170	3.076	2.988	2.905	2.825	2.750	2.679	2.611	2.546	2.484
16	3.183	3.088	2.999	2.914	2.834	2.757	2.685	2.616	2.551	2.489
17	3.193	3.097	3.007	2.921	2.840	2.763	2.690	2.621	2.555	2.492
18	3.201	3.104	3.012	2.926	2.844	2.767	2.693	2.624	2.557	2.494
19	3.207	3.109	3.017	2.930	2.848	2.770	2.696	2.626	2.559	2.496
20	3.211	3.113	3.020	2.933	2.850	2.772	2.698	2.627	2.561	2.497
21	3.215	3.116	3.023	2.935	2.852	2.773	2.699	2.629	2.562	2.498
22	3.217	3.118	3.025	2.936	2.853	2.775	2.700	2.629	2.562	2.498
23	3.219	3.120	3.026	2.938	2.854	2.775	2.701	2.630	2.563	2.499
24	3.221	3.121	3.027	2.939	2.855	2.776	2.701	2.630	2.563	2.499
25	3.222	3.122	3.028	2.939	2.856	2.777	2.702	2.631	2.563	2.499
30	3.225	3.124	3.030	2.941	2.857	2.778	2.702	2.631	2.564	2.500
40	3.226	3.125	3.030	2.941	2.857	2.778	2.703	2.632	2.564	2.500
50	3.226	3.125	3.030	2.941	2.857	2.778	2.703	2.632	2.564	2.500

APPENDIX

E Monthly Installment Loan Tables ($1,000 loan with interest payments compounded monthly)

Loan Maturity (in months)

Interest	6	12	18	24	30	36	48	60	72	84	96
4.00%	168.62	85.15	57.33	43.42	35.08	29.52	22.58	18.42	15.65	13.67	12.19
4.25%	168.74	85.26	57.44	43.54	35.19	29.64	22.69	18.53	15.76	13.78	12.31
4.50%	168.86	85.38	57.56	43.65	35.31	29.75	22.80	18.64	15.87	13.90	12.42
4.75%	168.98	85.49	57.67	43.76	35.42	29.86	22.92	18.76	15.99	14.02	12.54
5.00%	169.11	85.61	57.78	43.87	35.53	29.97	23.03	18.87	16.10	14.13	12.66
5.25%	169.23	85.72	57.89	43.98	35.64	30.08	23.14	18.99	16.22	14.25	12.78
5.50%	169.35	85.84	58.01	44.10	35.75	30.20	23.26	19.10	16.34	14.37	12.90
5.75%	169.47	85.95	58.12	44.21	35.87	30.31	23.37	19.22	16.46	14.49	13.02
6.00%	169.60	86.07	58.23	44.32	35.98	30.42	23.49	19.33	16.57	14.61	13.14
6.25%	169.72	86.18	58.34	44.43	36.09	30.54	23.60	19.45	16.69	14.73	13.26
6.50%	169.84	86.30	58.46	44.55	36.20	30.65	23.71	19.57	16.81	14.85	13.39
6.75%	169.96	86.41	58.57	44.66	36.32	30.76	23.83	19.68	16.93	14.97	13.51
7.00%	170.09	86.53	58.68	44.77	36.43	30.88	23.95	19.80	17.05	15.09	13.63
7.25%	170.21	86.64	58.80	44.89	36.55	30.99	24.06	19.92	17.17	15.22	13.76
7.50%	170.33	86.76	58.91	45.00	36.66	31.11	24.18	20.04	17.29	15.34	13.88
7.75%	170.45	86.87	59.03	45.11	36.77	31.22	24.30	20.16	17.41	15.46	14.01
8.00%	170.58	86.99	59.14	45.23	36.89	31.34	24.41	20.28	17.53	15.59	14.14
8.25%	170.70	87.10	59.25	45.34	37.00	31.45	24.53	20.40	17.66	15.71	14.26
8.50%	170.82	87.22	59.37	45.46	37.12	31.57	24.65	20.52	17.78	15.84	14.39
8.75%	170.95	87.34	59.48	45.57	37.23	31.68	24.77	20.64	17.90	15.96	14.52
9.00%	171.07	87.45	59.60	45.68	37.35	31.80	24.89	20.76	18.03	16.09	14.65
9.25%	171.19	87.57	59.71	45.80	37.46	31.92	25.00	20.88	18.15	16.22	14.78
9.50%	171.32	87.68	59.83	45.91	37.58	32.03	25.12	21.00	18.27	16.34	14.91
9.75%	171.44	87.80	59.94	46.03	37.70	32.15	25.24	21.12	18.40	16.47	15.04
10.00%	171.56	87.92	60.06	46.14	37.81	32.27	25.36	21.25	18.53	16.60	15.17
10.25%	171.68	88.03	60.17	46.26	37.93	32.38	25.48	21.37	18.65	16.73	15.31
10.50%	171.81	88.15	60.29	46.38	38.04	32.50	25.60	21.49	18.78	16.86	15.44
10.75%	171.93	88.27	60.40	46.49	38.16	32.62	25.72	21.62	18.91	16.99	15.57
11.00%	172.05	88.38	60.52	46.61	38.28	32.74	25.85	21.74	19.03	17.12	15.71
11.25%	172.18	88.50	60.63	46.72	38.40	32.86	25.97	21.87	19.16	17.25	15.84
11.50%	172.30	88.62	60.75	46.84	38.51	32.98	26.09	21.99	19.29	17.39	15.98
11.75%	172.42	88.73	60.87	46.96	38.63	33.10	26.21	22.12	19.42	17.52	16.12
12.00%	172.55	88.85	60.98	47.07	38.75	33.21	26.33	22.24	19.55	17.65	16.25
12.25%	172.67	88.97	61.10	47.19	38.87	33.33	26.46	22.37	19.68	17.79	16.39
12.50%	172.80	89.08	61.21	47.31	38.98	33.45	26.58	22.50	19.81	17.92	16.53
12.75%	172.92	89.20	61.33	47.42	39.10	33.57	26.70	22.63	19.94	18.06	16.67
13.00%	173.04	89.32	61.45	47.54	39.22	33.69	26.83	22.75	20.07	18.19	16.81
13.25%	173.17	89.43	61.56	47.66	39.34	33.81	26.95	22.88	20.21	18.33	16.95
13.50%	173.29	89.55	61.68	47.78	39.46	33.94	27.08	23.01	20.34	18.46	17.09
13.75%	173.41	89.67	61.80	47.89	39.58	34.06	27.20	23.14	20.47	18.60	17.23
14.00%	173.54	89.79	61.92	48.01	39.70	34.18	27.33	23.27	20.61	18.74	17.37
14.25%	173.66	89.90	62.03	48.13	39.82	34.30	27.45	23.40	20.74	18.88	17.51

Loan Maturity
(in months)

Interest	6	12	18	24	30	36	48	60	72	84	96
14.50%	173.79	90.02	62.15	48.25	39.94	34.42	27.58	23.53	20.87	19.02	17.66
14.75%	173.91	90.14	62.27	48.37	40.06	34.54	27.70	23.66	21.01	19.16	17.80
15.00%	174.03	90.26	62.38	48.49	40.18	34.67	27.83	23.79	21.15	19.30	17.95
15.25%	174.16	90.38	62.50	48.61	40.30	34.79	27.96	23.92	21.28	19.44	18.09
15.50%	174.28	90.49	62.62	48.72	40.42	34.91	28.08	24.05	21.42	19.58	18.24
15.75%	174.41	90.61	62.74	48.84	40.54	35.03	28.21	24.19	21.55	19.72	18.38
16.00%	174.53	90.73	62.86	48.96	40.66	35.16	28.34	24.32	21.69	19.86	18.53
16.25%	174.65	90.85	62.97	49.08	40.78	35.28	28.47	24.45	21.83	20.00	18.68
16.50%	174.78	90.97	63.09	49.20	40.91	35.40	28.60	24.58	21.97	20.15	18.82
16.75%	174.90	91.09	63.21	49.32	41.03	35.53	28.73	24.72	22.11	20.29	18.97
17.00%	175.03	91.20	63.33	49.44	41.15	35.65	28.86	24.85	22.25	20.24	19.12
17.25%	175.15	91.32	63.45	49.56	41.27	35.78	28.98	24.99	22.39	20.58	19.27
17.50%	175.28	91.44	63.57	49.68	41.39	35.90	29.11	25.12	22.53	20.73	19.42
17.75%	175.40	91.56	63.69	49.80	41.52	36.03	29.24	25.26	22.67	20.87	19.57
18.00%	175.53	91.68	63.81	49.92	41.64	36.15	29.37	25.39	22.81	21.02	19.72
18.25%	175.65	91.80	63.93	50.04	41.76	36.28	29.51	25.53	22.95	21.16	19.88
18.50%	175.77	91.92	64.04	50.17	41.89	36.40	29.64	25.67	23.09	21.31	20.03
18.75%	175.90	92.04	64.16	50.29	42.01	36.53	29.77	25.80	23.23	21.46	20.18
19.00%	176.02	92.16	64.28	50.41	42.13	36.66	29.90	25.94	23.38	21.61	20.33
19.25%	176.15	92.28	64.40	50.53	42.26	36.78	30.03	26.08	23.52	21.76	20.49
19.50%	176.27	92.40	64.52	50.65	42.38	36.91	30.16	26.22	23.66	21.91	20.64
19.75%	176.40	92.51	64.64	50.77	42.51	37.04	30.30	26.35	23.81	22.06	20.80
20.00%	176.52	92.63	64.76	50.90	42.63	37.16	30.43	26.49	23.95	22.21	20.95
20.25%	176.65	92.75	64.88	51.02	42.75	37.29	30.56	26.63	24.10	22.36	21.11
20.50%	176.77	92.87	65.00	51.14	42.88	37.42	30.70	26.77	24.24	22.51	21.27
20.75%	176.90	92.99	65.12	51.26	43.00	37.55	30.83	26.91	24.39	22.66	21.42
21.00%	177.02	93.11	65.24	51.39	43.13	37.68	30.97	27.05	24.54	22.81	21.58
21.25%	177.15	93.23	65.37	51.51	43.26	37.80	31.10	27.19	24.68	22.96	21.74
21.50%	177.27	93.35	65.49	51.63	43.38	37.93	31.24	27.34	24.83	23.12	21.90
21.75%	177.40	93.47	65.61	51.75	43.51	38.06	31.37	27.48	24.98	23.27	22.06
22.00%	177.52	93.59	65.73	51.88	43.63	38.19	31.51	27.62	25.13	23.43	22.22
22.25%	177.65	93.71	65.85	52.00	43.76	38.32	31.64	27.76	25.27	23.58	22.38
22.50%	177.77	93.84	65.97	52.13	43.89	38.45	31.78	27.90	25.42	23.74	22.54
22.75%	177.90	93.96	66.09	52.25	44.01	38.58	31.91	28.05	25.57	23.89	22.70
23.00%	178.02	94.08	66.21	52.37	44.14	38.71	32.05	28.19	25.72	24.05	22.86
23.25%	178.15	94.20	66.34	52.50	44.27	38.84	32.19	28.33	25.87	24.20	23.02
23.50%	178.27	94.32	66.46	52.62	44.39	38.97	32.33	28.48	26.02	24.36	23.19
23.75%	178.40	94.44	66.58	52.75	44.52	39.10	32.46	28.62	26.18	24.52	23.35
24.00%	178.53	94.56	66.70	52.87	44.65	39.23	32.60	28.77	26.33	24.68	23.51
24.25%	178.65	94.68	66.82	53.00	44.78	39.36	32.74	28.91	26.48	24.83	23.68
24.50%	178.78	94.80	66.95	53.12	44.91	39.50	32.88	29.06	26.63	24.99	23.84
24.75%	178.90	94.92	67.07	53.25	45.03	39.63	33.02	29.20	26.78	25.15	24.01
25.00%	179.03	95.04	67.19	53.37	45.16	39.76	33.16	29.35	26.94	25.31	24.17

Index

Note: **Boldface** *page numbers indicate definitions of key terms.*

A

B

D

E

F

J

K

L

M

T